This is America

Our Reading Heritage

This is America

Harold H. Wagenheim

Matthew Dolkey

Donald G. Kobler

 Holt, Rinehart and Winston, Inc., New York

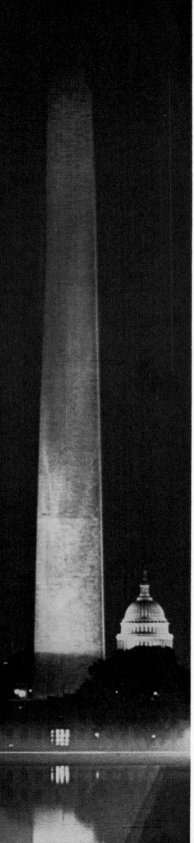

THE EDITORS

Harold H. Wagenheim, Principal, Mabel Dean Bacon Vocational High School, has had a wealth of experience in the teaching of English and in the development of materials for the appreciation of literature. Formerly a junior high and senior high school English teacher in the New York City schools, he was at one time English Department Chairman at Bronx Vocational High School. In addition to editing the Our Reading Heritage Series, Mr. Wagenheim edited *Read Up On Life*. He is a consultant for the Committee on Curriculum Standards and has contributed articles to *High Point* and the *English Journal*.

Matthew Dolkey, Chairman of the English Deparment, Newark State College, Newark, New Jersey, received his doctorate from Teacher's College, Columbia University. Before going into college teaching, Dr. Dolkey taught English at Booker T. Washington Junior High School and Alexander Hamilton Vocational High School, New York.

Donald G. Kobler, Chairman of the English Department, Housatonic Valley Regional High School, Falls Village, Connecticut, taught English in the Bloomfield, New York, schools before he came to Housatonic. He has been interested in the development of a high school program in the humanities and was recently awarded a John Hay fellowship to continue his studies in this field. Mr. Kobler has been an active participant in state committees on reading and curriculum.

The Our Reading Heritage Series

New Trails	Ourselves and Others
Wide Horizons	This Is America
Exploring Life	England and the World

Photographs
Front cover The *Lincoln Memorial,* Washington, D. C. (Jack Zehrt, SHOSTAL)
Back cover "The Gettysburg Address" (FREE LANCE PHOTOGRAPHERS GUILD)

Illustrations
John C. Wonsetler, Leonard Everett Fisher, Mircea Vasiliu, Douglas Gorsline, Sideo Fromboluti, Roger Vernam

ACKNOWLEDGMENTS

Grateful acknowledgment is given for use of the photographs on the following pages: ii–iii Susan McCartney, Photo Researchers; iv Elliott Erwitt, Magnum; vi–vii Ernst Haas, Magnum; ix Thomas Hollyman, Photo Researchers; x–xi Susan McCartney, Photo Researchers; xii–xiii Burt Glinn, Magnum.

We wish to thank the following authors, publishers, and other holders of copyright for permission to use and adapt copyrighted materials:

Agnes Rogers Allen for "Sleeping Outdoors" by Frederick Lewis Allen. Originally published in *Century Magazine*.

Appleton-Century-Crofts, Inc. for "The Flower-fed Buffaloes" from *Going-to-the-Stars* by Vachel Lindsay, copyright, 1926, by D. Appleton & Company. Reprinted by permission of the publishers.

Arthur S. Bourinot for "Paul Bunyan" from *This Green Earth* by Arthur S. Bourinot. Used by permission of the author.

Brandt & Brandt for "the hours rise up" from *Poems 1923–1954* by E. E. Cummings, copyright, 1923, 1951, by E. E. Cummings, published by Harcourt, Brace and Company; for "Mary Lou Wingate" from "John Brown's Body" and "The Devil and Daniel Webster" in *Selected Works of Stephen Vincent Benét*, copyright, 1927, 1928, 1936, by Stephen Vincent Benét, published by Rinehart & Company; for "Recuerdo" from *A Few Figs from Thistles* by Edna St. Vincent Millay, copyright, 1918, 1919, 1922, by Edna St. Vincent Millay, published by Harper & Brothers; and for "You Can't Do That" by John P. Marquand, copyright, 1935, by The Curtis Publishing Company.

The Evening and Sunday Bulletin, Philadelphia, for "High Water" by John Hersey.

Bennett Cerf for "He Made His Country Laugh," copyright, 1947, by Bennett Cerf.

George M. Cohan Corporation for *Pigeons and People* by George M. Cohan, copyright U. S. A. by George M. Cohan, December 27, 1932. Assigned to George M. Cohan Corporation.

Coward-McCann, Inc. for the selection from *Talking Through My Hats* by Lilly Daché and Dorothy Roe Lewis, copyright, 1946, by Lilly Daché and Dorothy Roe Lewis.

Richard E. Danielson for "Corporal Hardy."

Doubleday & Company, Inc. for "fate is unfair" and "takes talent" from *The Lives and Times of Archy and Mehitabel* by Don Marquis, copyright, 1927, by Doubleday & Company, Inc.; and for "The Riverman" from *Blazed Trail Stories* by Stewart Edward White, copyright, 1903, 1908, by Stewart Edward White. All reprinted by permission of Doubleday & Company, Inc.

Constance Garland Doyle and Isabel Garland Lord for "A Day's Pleasure" and "Under the Lion's Paw" from *Main Travelled Roads;* and for "The Mountains Are a Lonely Folk" by Hamlin Garland.

E. P. Dutton & Co., Inc. for "Happiness" by William Lyon Phelps, copyright, 1927, by The Curtis Publishing Company, renewal, 1955, by Dryden L. Phelps, published by E. P. Dutton & Co., Inc.; and for "Daniel Boone" from *I Sing the Pioneer* by Arthur Guiterman, copyright, 1926, by E. P. Dutton & Co., Inc., renewal, 1954, by Mrs. Vida Lindo Guiterman.

Barthold Fles for "Tuputala" by Robert P. Parsons, copyright, 1944 by The Atlantic Monthly Company, Boston 16, Massachusetts.

Samuel French for *Finders-Keepers* by George Kelly, copyright, 1916, by George Kelly (under the title *The Lesson*), copyright, 1943 (in renewal), by George Kelly, copyright, 1923, by Stewart Kidd, copyright, 1951 (in renewal), by George Kelly.

Harcourt, Brace and Company, Inc. for "The Battle of Finney's Ford" from *The Friendly Persuasion* by Jessamyn West, copyright, 1940, 1943, 1944, 1945, by Jessamyn West; for "Locomotive 38, the Ojibway" from *My Name is Aram* by William Saroyan, copyright, 1937, 1938, 1939, 1940, by William Saroyan; for "Washington Monument by Night" from *Slabs of the Sunburnt West* by Carl Sandburg, copyright, 1922, by Harcourt Brace and Company, Inc., renewed, 1950, by Carl Sandburg; for "Stars, Songs, Faces" from *Smoke and Steel* by Carl Sandburg, copyright, 1920, by Harcourt, Brace and Company, Inc., renewed by Carl Sandburg; for "The Free Man . . ." from *The People, Yes* by Carl Sandburg, copyright, 1936, by Harcourt, Brace and Company, Inc.; for "Strange Friend, Friendly Stranger" from *Abraham Lincoln: The Prairie Years and The War Years,* One-Volume Pictorial Review; copyright, 1939, by Harcourt, Brace & World, Inc.; copyright, 1953, 1954, by Carl Sandburg; all reprinted by permission of the publishers; and for "The Trip to Bountiful" © copyright, 1953, 1954, 1956, by Horton Foote. Reprinted from *Harrison, Texas* by Horton Foote by permission of Harcourt, Brace & World, Inc.

Harold Ober Associates, Inc., for "Science Has Spoiled My Supper" by Philip Wylie; copyright © 1954 by The Atlantic Monthly Company. Reprinted by permission of Harold Ober Associates Incorporated.

Harper & Brothers for the use of the name Mark Twain (registered trade mark) for "A Daring Deed" from *Life on the Mississippi* and for "My Watch" and "How I Edited an Agricultural Paper" from *Sketches New and Old* by Mark Twain; for "Go Seeker, . . ." from *You Can't Go Home Again* by Thomas Wolfe, copyright, 1940, by Maxwell Perkins as Executor; for "City Evening" from *The Lady Is Cold* by E. B. White, copyright, 1929, by Harper and Brothers; for "Walden" from *One Man's Meat* by E. B. White, copyright, 1939, by E. B. White; and for "Home Founding" from *Giants in the Earth* by O. E. Rölvaag, copyright, 1927, by Harper & Brothers, copyright, 1955, by Jennie Marie Berdahl Rölvaag.

Rupert Hart-Davis Limited for permission to reprint in Canada: "Letter to an Intending Immigrant" from *One Man's America* by Alistair Cooke, published in Canada by Rupert Hart-Davis Limited under the English title, *Letters from America.*

Zenna Henderson for "Ararat" by Zenna Henderson, copyright, 1952, by Fantasy House, Inc. Originally published in *The Magazine of Fantasy and Science Fiction,* October, 1952.

Hill and Wang, Inc., Publishers, for "Divine Things" from *Jonathan Edwards* edited by Clarence H. Faust and Thomas H. Johnson. Copyright 1935 by Hill and Wang, Inc. Reprinted by permission of Hill and Wang.

Henry Holt and Company, Inc. for "Hannibal," "Good-by and Keep Cold," "The

Gift Outright," "A Leaf Treader," and "Acquainted with the Night" from *Complete Poems of Robert Frost,* copyright, 1930, 1949, by Henry Holt and Company, Inc., copyright, 1936, 1948, by Robert Frost; and for "Chicago" from *Chicago Poems* by Carl Sandburg, copyright, 1916, by Henry Holt and Company, Inc., copyright, 1944, by Carl Sandburg. All reprinted by permission of the publishers.

Houghton Mifflin Company for "A Lady," "Wind and Silver," and "Music" by Amy Lowell; for "Texas" from *What's O'Clock* by Amy Lowell; for "The Hiltons' Holiday" from *Collected Stories* by Sarah Orne Jewett; for "Mliss" by Bret Harte; and for "A Calendar of Great Americans" from *Mere Literature* by Woodrow Wilson. Reprinted by permission of the publisher.

Alfred A. Knopf, Inc. for "Let No Charitable Hope," "Parting Gift," and "Velvet Shoes," from *The Collected Poems of Elinor Wylie,* copyright, 1921, 1923, 1932, by Alfred A. Knopf, Inc.; for "Neighbor Rosicky" from *Obscure Destinies* by Willa Cather, copyright, 1930, 1932, by Willa Cather; for "Spanish Johnny" from *April Twilights and Other Poems* by Willa Cather, copyright, 1923, by Willa Cather; for "A Man Saw a Ball of Gold in the Sky" and "Fable" from *The Collected Poems of Stephen Crane,* copyright, 1930, by Alfred A. Knopf, Inc.; for "Letter to an Intending Immigrant" from *One Man's America* by Alistair Cooke, copyright, 1952, by Alistair Cooke; and for "A Gray Sleeve" from *Twenty Stories* by Stephen Crane, copyright, 1925, by William H. Crane. All reprinted by permission of Alfred A. Knopf, Inc.

Walter Lippmann and New York Herald Tribune, Inc. for "False Gods" by Walter Lippmann, copyright, 1932, by New York Herald Tribune, Inc.

Little, Brown & Company for "Deep Horizons" from *Prairie Guns* by Ernest Haycox, copyright, 1936, by Jill Marie Haycox; for "Look What You Did, Christopher!" from *Many Long Years Ago* by Ogden Nash, copyright, 1933, by Ogden Nash; for "A Word," and "I'll Tell You How the Sun Rose," from *Poems by Emily Dickinson,* edited by Martha Dickinson Bianchi and Alfred Leete Hampson. All reprinted by permission of Little, Brown & Company.

Estate of Charmian K. London for "All Gold Canyon" and "San Francisco Is Gone!" by Jack London.

The Macmillan Company for "Sunset: St. Louis" and "Blue Squills" from *Collected Poems* by Sara Teasdale, copyright, 1937, by The Macmillan Company; for "The Sheaves" from *Sonnets* by Edwin Arlington Robinson, copyright, 1948, by Edwin Arlington Robinson, and reprinted by permission of The Macmillan Company; for "What Is Once Loved" from *Alice All By Herself* by Elizabeth Coatsworth, copyright, 1937, by The Macmillan Company; for "A Farm" from *There Will Be Bread and Love* by Robert P. Tristram Coffin, copyright, 1942, by The Macmillan Company; and for "My Lady Is Compared to a Young Tree" from *Collected Poems* by Vachel Lindsay, copyright, 1920, 1948, by The Macmillan Company.

Ellen C. Masters for "Lucinda Matlock" and "Anne Rutledge" from *Spoon River Anthology* by Edgar Lee Masters, published by The Macmillan Company.

G. & C. Merriam Company and Margaret Caskey for "I Like Words" by Margaret Caskey, from *Word Study,* copyright, 1942, by G. & C. Merriam Company. Reprinted by permission.

Juanita Joaquina Miller for "Charity" by Joaquin Miller.

Portia Washington Pittman for "Birth and Early Childhood" from *The Story of My Life and Work* by Booker T. Washington.

G. P. Putnam's Sons for "This Hero Business" from *Skyward* by Richard E. Byrd, copyright, 1928, by Richard E. Byrd.

Rand McNally and Company for "Lee Says Farewell to a Brave Army" and "Lincoln Dedicates a People" from *By These Words* by Paul M. Angle, copyright, 1954, by Rand McNally and Company, publishers.

Random House, Inc. for "The Big Breach" from *Grandfather Stories* by Samuel Hopkins Adams, copyright, 1953, by Samuel Hopkins Adams, originally appeared in The *New Yorker;* for "Sunday: New Guinea," copyright 1943 by Karl Shapiro. Reprinted from *Poems of a Jew,* by Karl Shapiro, by permission of Random House, Inc. For "2 Soldiers," copyright 1942 by The Curtis Publishing Co., reprinted from *Collected Stories of William Faulkner* by permission of Random House, Inc; for "First Play" from *Act One,* by Moss Hart; © copyright 1959 by Catherine Carlisle Hart and Joseph M. Hyman, Trustees. All reprinted by permission of Random House, Inc.

Rinehart & Company, Inc. for "Nathan Hale" by Nancy Hale, "Walt Whitman" by Mark Van Doren, and "Benjamin Franklin" by Carl Van Doren, all from *There Were Giants in the Land: Twenty-eight Historic Americans as Seen by Twenty-eight Contemporary Americans,* copyright, 1942, by Rinehart & Company, Inc.; and for "Down the Mississippi—Embarkation" from *Selected Poems* by John Gould Fletcher, copyright, 1938, by John Gould Fletcher. All reprinted by permission of Rinehart & Company, Inc., Publishers.

Archibald Rutledge for "Exile."

Mrs. Lew Sarett for "The Sheepherder" from *Slow Smoke* by Lew Sarett, copyright, 1925, by Henry Holt and Company, Inc., copyright, 1953, by Lew Sarett. Reprinted by permission of Mrs. Lew Sarett.

Charles Scribner's Sons for "My Friend Moe" from *Cross Creek* by Marjorie Kinnan Rawlings, copyright, 1942, by Marjorie Kinnan Rawlings; and for "I Have a Rendezvous with Death" from *Poems* by Alan Seeger, copyright, 1916, by Charles Scribner's Sons, 1944, by Elsie Adams Seeger.

Scripps-Howard Newspapers for "A Worm's Eye View" by Ernie Pyle, originally published in *The New York World-Telegram,* May 3 and May 5, 1943. Reprinted by permission.

Jesse Stuart for "My Land Is Fair for Any Eyes to See" from *Man with a Bull-Tongue Plow.*

Simon and Schuster, Inc. for the introductions to "Jack London Sees a City Die" and "A Worm's Eye View" from *A Treasury of Great Reporting* by L. L. Snyder and R. B. Morris, copyright, 1949, by Simon and Schuster, Inc. Reprinted by permission of the publishers.

The Viking Press, Inc. for "Evening Hymn" from *Song in the Meadow* by Elizabeth Madox Roberts, copyright, 1940, by Elizabeth Madox Roberts; for "Eleven o'Clock News Summary" from *Stones from a Glass House* by Phyllis McGinley, originally appeared in *The New Yorker,* copyright, 1945, by Phyllis McGinley; for "Without a Cloak" from *A Short Walk from the Station* by Phyllis McGinley, originally appeared in *The New Yorker,* copyright, 1944, by Phyllis McGinley; and for "The Gift" from *The Red Pony* by John Steinbeck, included in *The Portable Steinbeck,* copyright, 1937, by John Steinbeck. All reprinted by permission of The Viking Press, Inc., New York.

Robert Penn Warren for "Bearded Oaks" from *Selected Poems 1923–1943* by Robert Penn Warren, copyright, 1944, by Robert Penn Warren.

Woman's Day, the A & P Magazine, for "The House on Beacon Hill" by Robert Hillyer, copyright, February, 1953.

CONTENTS

GIANTS IN THE LAND   PART THREE

OUR DAILY BREAD   Part Six

A TIME TO ENJOY   Part Seven

AMERICANS AND THE WORLD   PART EIGHT

A TIME FOR ACTION   PART NINE

LIVING IN AMERICA

The story of America is the story of many people who settled a new land, helped it grow, and fought to keep it free. In LIVING IN AMERICA you will learn to know some of these people, either from their own stories, or from stories about them. Though they lived at different periods, they were guided by the same belief: that each person must do what he believes is right.

Americans have expressed this belief in acts of heroism and in simple kindliness. It has led some men to risk the dangers of new frontiers and others to seek solitude. At times, it has even led them to stand in judgment against their neighbors. It is a strong belief and has helped to shape a strong nation, when it was tempered "with malice toward none; with charity for all." Through the years Americans have had to earn the right to act according to their deepest convictions. How they acted and why, is told in their individual stories and in the story of their country.

LIVING IN AMERICA

Captain John Smith and Pocahontas

JOHN SMITH

Learning to live with the Indians was one of the many challenges the early American settlers faced. Captain John Smith describes being captured by the Indians and rescued from death by Pocahontas.

From: **THE GENERAL HISTORY OF VIRGINIA**

At last they brought him (Captain Smith) to Meronocomoco, where was Powhatan, their Emperor. Here more than two hundred of those grim courtiers stood wondering at him, as he had been a monster; till Powhatan and his train had put themselves in their greatest braveries. Before a fire upon a seat like a bedstead, he sat covered with a great robe, made of raccoon skins, and all the tails hanging by. On either hand did sit a young wench of sixteen or eighteen years, and along on each side the house, two rows of men, and behind them as many women, with all their heads and shoulders painted red; many of their heads bedecked with the white down of birds; but every one with something, and a great chain of white beads about their necks.

At his entrance before the King, all the people gave a great shout. The Queen of Appomatuck was appointed to bring him water to wash his hands, and another brought him a bunch of feathers, instead of a towel, to dry them: having feasted him after their best barbarous manner they could, a long consultation was held; but the conclusion was, two great stones were brought before Powhatan: then as many as could laid hands on him, dragged him to

them, and thereon laid his head, and being ready with their clubs, to beat out his brains, Pocahontas, the King's dearest daughter, when no intreaty could prevail, got his head in her arms, and laid her own upon his to save him from death: whereat the Emperor was contented he should live to make him hatchets, and her bells, beads, and copper; for they thought him as well of all occupations as themselves. For the King himself will make his own robes, shoes, bows, arrows, pots; plant, hunt, or do anything so well as the rest.

The man who wrote this selection

CAPTAIN JOHN SMITH 1580–1631

While still a youth, John Smith left his home in Lincolnshire, England to enter military service. His journeys as a soldier-of-fortune led him through Europe, Asia, and Africa. Smith's military life was filled with adventure. Once he was nearly drowned as a result of a shipwreck. Another time he was captured by the Turks and sold as a slave but managed to escape by killing his guard.

When Smith arrived in Jamestown, he was under arrest for attempted mutiny, although the charges were never proved. In the two years he remained in Jamestown, he rose to a position of leadership, and his skill and resourcefulness saved the colony from almost certain disaster. Smith was particularly successful in establishing friendly relations with the Indians.

He recorded his Virginia adventures and explorations in several books. These volumes also included maps and surveys which proved particularly useful to later colonists. His writing did much to lure reluctant Englishmen to Virginia.

Let's consider . . .

1. What did you learn from this selection about Indian life and customs?

2. Almost every American has heard of the incident involving Pocahontas and John Smith. How do you account for the great popularity of this story?

3. Captain Smith was writing of his personal experiences, but he told his story in the third person. Re-write several sentences replacing the third person words such as *he* and *him* with the first person terms *I* and *me*. What changes are brought about in the tone of the story by shifting from the third to the first person? Which way do you like the story told? Explain why.

The writer's craft . . .

Although Captain Smith entitled the book from which the Pocahontas incident was taken *The General History of Virginia,* he described his experiences in narrative fashion, almost as though writing fiction. Perhaps he was. In an earlier history of Virginia he did not mention the incident involving Pocahontas. Some critics suspect that this entire episode is fictitious, while others declare that it really occurred. All agree that at times Captain Smith embellished the plain facts of history.

1. If the Pocahontas incident did not actually happen, what reasons might Captain Smith have had for inventing it?

2. Examine Captain Smith's narrative technique.

a. What effect did he achieve by first describing the Indians and their chief?

b. At no point in the story did he write about the emotions of the characters. What did the story gain by this omission? What did it lose?

3. Recall a recent event which you either experienced first-hand or read about. Describe the incident in a completely objective way limiting yourself to the plain facts.

Knowing words . . .

Captain John Smith wrote that Pocahontas put his head in her arms when no entreaty would prevail. The word *prevail* as used in this context means to prove effective or have influence. If you prevail upon someone you influence him to act as you wish. Prevail, however, does not refer to the use of physical force.

Two other forms of the word are *prevailing* and *prevalent.* Prevailing means current or of the moment, while prevalent refers to customary or common.

Use each of these words in sentences of your own: *prevail, prevailing,* and *prevalent.*

Housewifery

EDWARD TAYLOR

The colonial poet Edward Taylor used everyday images in his poetry to express his belief in the glory of God. In "Housewifery" he compares Puritan life with the process of making cloth. He begins by referring to the spinning wheel and ends with the cloth itself, made "in holy robes for glory."

Make me O Lord, Thy spinning-wheel complete.
    Thy holy Word my distaff make for me;
Make mine affections Thy swift flyers neat;
    And make my soul Thy holy spool to be;
    My conversation make to be Thy reel,
    And reel the yarn thereon spun of Thy wheel.

Make me Thy loom then; knit therein this twine;
    And make Thy Holy Spirit, Lord, wind quills.
Then weave the web Thyself. The yarn is fine.
    Thine ordinances make my fulling mills.
    Then dye the same in heavenly colors choice,
    All pinked with varnished flowers of paradise.

Then clothe therewith mine understanding will,
    Affections, judgment, conscience, memory,
My words and actions, that their shine may fill
    My ways with glory and Thee glorify.
    Then mine apparel shall display before Ye
    That I am clothed in holy robes for glory.

The man who wrote this poem

EDWARD TAYLOR 1645–1729

Little is known of the life of Edward Taylor. Leaving his home in England while still a young man, he emigrated to Boston and enrolled at Harvard College. Upon graduating he became both minister and physician to the people of Westfield, Massachusetts. During his years at Westfield, Taylor married twice and was the father of thirteen children. His grandson Ezra Stiles once described him in these words: "A man of small stature but firm: of quick passions—yet serious and grave."

Because much of Taylor's poetry expressed his personal devotion to God, he left orders that none of it should be published. After Taylor's death in 1729, Ezra Stiles inherited the poems and placed them in the Yale Library where they remained virtually unknown until 1939. Their discovery and subsequent publication has provided an important addition to the body of colonial literature.

The poet's art . . .

In "Housewifery" Edward Taylor speaks directly to the Lord in a spirit of prayer and asks that he be made worthy of God's glory. To make his poem graphic and concrete, the poet uses images that refer to the process of making cloth: the spinning wheel, the loom, the fulling mills, and finally the actual piece of clothing.

Look again at the first stanza. Here Edward Taylor compares parts of a spinning wheel, such as a distaff, flyers, spool, and reel to various aspects of a spiritual life. For example, Taylor writes: "Thy Holy Worde my distaff make for me." The distaff is the bar that holds the flax or wool in spinning. He implies that just as the distaff holds the basic raw material from which the cloth will eventually be made, so does the *Bible* ("Thy Holy Word") hold the basic truth necessary for the development of his spiritual life. By comparing the distaff to the *Bible,* Taylor suggests that the *Bible* is the source of his life substance. In the second stanza Taylor compares his life to a loom on which the Lord may weave a holy life. Taylor also speaks of the fulling mills which were mills where the cloth was cleaned and thickened. In the third stanza Taylor refers to the actual cloth which has been woven into "holy robes for glory."

1. Explain why it was logical for the poet to develop his images in the following order: the spinning wheel, the loom, and the robes.

2. Why would reference to the making of yarn, cloth, and clothing be an effective device in a poem by a colonial poet?

3. In the last stanza Taylor identifies certain qualities which he asks God to clothe. List these qualities. For what purpose did he want God to clothe them?

4. Check the meaning of the word *housewifery* in the glossary. Now explain the significance of the title.

The Trial of Susanna Martin

COTTON MATHER

The problem of witchcraft was of great concern to the early colonists as well as to the Europeans of the seventeenth century. Anyone who seemed out-of-the-ordinary, or a little bit strange and unusual, might be condemned as a witch. The punishment was death. So many people were suspected that it became necessary to hold special trials in which the accused were questioned about their so-called devilish activities.

Cotton Mather, a Puritan minister, was deeply interested in witchcraft. He was active in the New England trials and kept detailed records of the various cases. In this selection, Mather has described the trial of Susanna Martin. As you will see, it did not take much to prove the guilt of a person "in league with the Devil."

Susanna Martin, pleading not guilty to the indictment of witchcraft brought in against her, there were produced the evidences of many persons very sensibly and grievously bewitched, who all complained of the prisoner at the bar as the person whom they believed the cause of their miseries. And now, as well as in the other trials, there was an extraordinary endeavor by witchcrafts, with cruel and frequent fits, to hinder the poor sufferers from giving in their complaints, which the court was forced with much patience to obtain, by much waiting and watching for it.

There was now also an account given of what passed at her first examination before the magistrates, the cast of her eye then striking the afflicted people to the ground, whether they saw that cast or no. There were these among other passages between the magistrates and the examinate.

Magistrate. Pray, what ails these people?

Martin. I don't know.

Magistrate. But what do you think ails them?

Martin. I don't desire to spend my judgment upon it.

Magistrate. Don't you think they are bewitched?

Martin. No, I do not think they are.

Magistrate. Tell us your thoughts about them, then.

Martin. No, my thoughts are my own, when they are in, but when they are out they are another's. Their master . . .

Magistrate. Their master? Who do you think is their master?

Martin. If they be dealing in the black art, you may know as well as I.

Magistrate. Well, what have you done towards this?

Martin. Nothing at all.

Magistrate. Why, 'tis you or your appearance.

Martin. I cannot help it.

Magistrate. Is it not your master? How comes your appearance to hurt these?

Martin. How do I know? He that appeared in the shape of Samuel, a glorified saint, may appear in any-one's shape.

It was then also noted in her, as in others like her, that if the afflicted went to approach her, they were flung down to the ground. And when she was asked the reason of it, she said, "I cannot tell; it may be the Devil bears me more malice than another."

The court accounted themselves alarmed by these things, to inquire further into the conversation of the prisoner and see what there might occur to render these accusations further credible. Whereupon John Allen of Salisbury testified that he refusing, because of the weakness of his oxen, to cart some staves at the request of this Martin, she was displeased at it and said, *It had been as good that he had, for his oxen should never do him much more service.*

Whereupon this deponent said, "Dost thou threaten me, thou old witch? I'll throw thee into the brook."

Which to avoid, she flew over the bridge and escaped. But as he was going home one of his oxen tired, so that he was forced to unyoke him, that he might get him home. He then put his oxen, with many more, upon Salisbury Beach, where cattle did use to get flesh. In a few days, all the oxen upon the beach were found by their tracks to have run into the mouth of Merrimack River and not returned; but the next day they were found come ashore upon Plum Island. They that sought them used all imaginable gentleness, but they would still run away with a violence that seemed wholly diabolical, till they came near the mouth of Merrimack River, when they ran right into the sea, swimming as far as they could be seen. One of them then swam back again, with a swiftness amazing to the beholders, who stood ready to receive him

and help up his tired carcass. But the beast ran furiously up into the island, and from thence through the marshes up into New-bury Town, and so up into the woods; and there after a while was found near Ames-bury. So that, of fourteen good oxen, there was only this saved. The rest were all cast up, some in one place, and some in another, drowned.

John Atkinson testified that he exchanged a cow with a son of Susanna Martin's, whereat she muttered, and was unwilling he should have it. Going to receive this cow, though he hamstringed her and haltered her, she from a tame creature grew so mad that they could scarce get her along. She broke all the ropes that were fastened unto her, and though she were tied fast unto a tree, yet she made her escape, and gave them such further trouble as they could ascribe to no cause but witchcraft.

Robert Downer testified that this prisoner being some years ago prosecuted at court for a witch, he then said unto her he believed she was a witch. Whereat she being dissatisfied said, *That some she-devil would shortly fetch him away!* Which words were heard by others, as well as himself. The night following, as he lay in his bed, there came in at the window the likeness of a cat, which flew upon him, took fast hold of his throat, lay on him a considerable while, and almost killed him. At length he remembered what Susanna Martin had threatened the day before, and with much striving he cried out, "Avoid, thou she-devil! In the name of God the Father, the Son, and the Holy Ghost, avoid!" Whereupon it left him, leaped on the floor, and flew out at the window.

And there also came in several testimonies that before ever Downer spoke a word of this accident, Susanna Martin and her family had related how this Downer had been handled!

John Kembal testified that Susanna Martin, upon a causeless disgust, had threatened him about a certain cow of his, *That*

she should never do him any more good; and it came to pass accordingly. For soon after the cow was found stark dead on the dry ground, without any distemper to be discerned upon her. Upon which he was followed with a strange death upon more of his cattle, whereof he lost in one spring to the value of thirty pounds.

But the said John Kembal had a further testimony to give in against the prisoner which was truly admirable.

Being desirous to furnish himself with a dog, he applied himself to buy one of this Martin, who had a bitch with whelps in her house. But she not letting him have his choice, he said he would supply himself then at one Blezdel's. Having marked a puppy which he liked at Blezdel's, he met George Martin, the husband of the prisoner, going by, who asked him whether he would not have one of his wife's puppies, and he answered no. The same day one Edmond Eliot, being at Martin's house, heard George Martin relate where this Kembal had been and what he had

said. Whereupon Susanna Martin replied, "If I live, I'll give him puppies enough!"

Within a few days after, this Kembal coming out of the woods, there arose a little black cloud in the northwest, and Kembal immediately felt a force upon him which made him not able to avoid running upon the stumps of trees that were before him, albeit he had a broad plain cartway before him; but though he had his ax also on his shoulder to endanger him in his falls, he could not forbear going out of his way to tumble over them. When he came below the meetinghouse, there appeared unto him a little thing like a puppy, of a darkish color, and it shot backwards and forwards between his legs. He had courage to use all possible endeavors of cutting it with his ax, but he could not hit it. The puppy gave a jump from him and went, as to him it seemed, into the ground. Going a little further, there appeared unto him a black puppy, somewhat bigger than the first, but as black as coal. Its motions were quicker than those of his ax; it flew at his belly and away; then at his throat; so, over his shoulder one way, and then over his shoulder another way. His heart now began to fail him, and he thought the dog would have tore his throat out. But he recovered himself, and called upon God in his distress; and naming the name of JESUS CHRIST, it vanished away at once.

The deponent spoke not one word of these accidents for fear of affrighting his wife. But the next morning Edmond Eliot going into Martin's house, this woman asked him where Kembal was. He replied, At home abed, for ought he knew. She returned, "They say he was frighted last night." Eliot asked, "With what?" She answered, "With puppies." Eliot asked where he heard of it, for he had heard nothing of it. She rejoined, "About the town." Although Kembal had mentioned the matter to no creature living.

Note. This woman was one of the most impudent, scurrilous, wicked creatures in the world; and she did now throughout her whole trial discover herself to be such an one. Yet when she was asked what she had to say for herself, her chief plea was, *That she had led a most virtuous and holy life.*

[Abridged]

The man who wrote this selection

COTTON MATHER   1663–1728

Cotton Mather belonged to one of the most famous families in early New England and grew up in an atmosphere which was both intensely religious and keenly intellectual. His father, Increase Mather, was pastor of the North Church in Boston and, for several years, president of Harvard University. Young Mather was something of a child prodigy, graduating from Harvard when he was only fifteen years old. Three years later he became co-pastor, with his father, at North Church and remained at that post for the rest of his life.

Mather was very learned. He owned one of the largest libraries in the colony, was interested in science, and helped support the new idea of smallpox inoculation against a superstitious public. Yet he devoted himself to preserving the harsh Puritanism of the earliest settlers and was active in the New England witch trials.

An exceptionally productive writer, Mather completed over four hundred works. Few of these are read today except by specialists in American literature or colonial history. They are nevertheless important, as they present a vivid picture of the thoughts and feelings of one period in America's development. One of Mather's works, *Essays to Do Good,* later influenced another great American, Benjamin Franklin.

Let's consider . . .

1. Cotton Mather wrote his description of the trial from the viewpoint of an observer. In the first sentence he spoke of "the evidence of many persons very sensibly and grievously bewitched." Do you think Mather sympathized with these "persons"?

2. Mather included Susanna's replies to the magistrates as part of the evidence used to condemn her. Do you think her replies proved she was guilty? Could she have said anything which would have changed Mather's viewpoint or the opinions of the witnesses and the magistrates?

3. One by one the witnesses testified against Susanna. Did any of them have actual proof of Susanna's "magic"? Each witness had been involved in an argument with Susanna. Do you think this influenced their testimony?

4. See if you can offer a natural explanation of one of the incidents for which Susanna was blamed.

5. This trial took place in 1692. Since then man has learned the reason for many actions which were once considered magical. Even today, however, people sometimes take an unreasonable attitude toward others because of foolish superstitions and prejudices. What are some of these modern superstitions?

The writer's craft . . .

If a modern writer had reported this trial, he would have listed just the facts of the case. He would not have stated his own opinion, even in a note. He would have let the reader determine for himself whether the person on trial was guilty or innocent. Such reporting would be objective because it presented all the facts and let them speak for themselves.

Cotton Mather was not writing such an objective report. In fact, he could hardly be completely objective in describing what he saw and heard because he, too, was caught in the fear and superstition of the time. Therefore, he may have slanted his report somewhat by giving the reader only that information which he considered important. **Slanting** is a term often used to describe that kind of writing which presents a biased point of view.

1. In the opening paragraphs, before the passages between Susanna and the magistrates were presented, what words or phrases can you find which might indicate that Cotton Mather already considered Susanna Martin a witch?

2. From Mather's report you suspect that Susanna was convicted of witchcraft and punished. Judging from the report, do you think she was ever given a fair chance to prove her innocence? Did Mather include any facts in his report to indicate that she might *not* have been a witch?

3. Write a report which would present both sides of the trial. Or you might like to prepare a defense for Susanna, as though you were her lawyer in 1692.

Knowing words . . .

In reading literature written in the early days of America, you will often find unfamiliar words, or familiar words used in an unusual way. Although a word may look strange at first, you can usually discover its meaning from the context.

In each of the following sentences, one word is italicized. Modernize each of these sentences, substituting a present-day word or expression for each word in italics.

1. I don't desire to *spend* my judgment on it.

2. She gave them such further trouble as they could *ascribe* to no other cause but witchcraft.

3. Having *marked* a puppy which he liked at Blezdel's, he met George Martin, the husband of the prisoner, going by, who asked him whether he would not have one of his wife's puppies, and he answered no.

4. He had courage to use all possible *endeavors* of cutting it with his ax, but he could not hit it.

5. She did now throughout her whole trial *discover* herself to be such an one.

Divine Things

JONATHAN EDWARDS

When Jonathan Edwards was seventeen, he had a mystical experience—a feeling of deep union with God and a sudden vision of spiritual truth. With eloquent simplicity he describes his experience.

The sense I had of divine things, would often of a sudden kindle up, as it were, a sweet burning in my heart; an ardor of soul, that I know not how to express.

Not long after I first began to experience these things, I gave an account to my father of some things that had passed in my mind. I was pretty much affected by the discourse we had together; and when the discourse was ended, I walked abroad alone, in a solitary place in my father's pasture, for contemplation. And as I was walking there, and looking up on the sky and clouds, there came into my mind so sweet a sense of the glorious majesty and grace of God, that I know not how to express. I seemed to see them both in a sweet conjunction; majesty and meekness joined together; it was a sweet, and gentle, and holy majesty; and also a majestic meekness; an awful sweetness; a high, and great, and holy gentleness.

After this my sense of divine things gradually increased, and became more and more lively, and had more of that inward sweetness. The appearance of every thing was altered; there seemed to be, as it were, a calm, sweet cast, or appearance of divine glory, in almost every thing; in the sun, moon, and stars; in the clouds, and blue sky; in the grass, flowers, trees; in the water, and all nature.

The man who wrote this story

JONATHAN EDWARDS 1703–1758

Jonathan Edwards possessed one of the finest minds of colonial America. He was born in East Windsor, Connecticut, in 1703, and while still a child began to study Latin. At the age of twelve he wrote a serious, scientific paper on the habits of the flying spider. At thirteen he entered Yale to prepare for the ministry, and although his interest in scientific matters continued, theology and philosophy became increasingly important to him. After graduating with highest honors, he became a tutor at Yale.

Edwards left teaching to become a Presbyterian minister at Northampton, Massachusetts. While serving as pastor he became a leader in the Great Awakening, a revivalist movement in American religious life. During this period he wrote his famous sermon "Sinners in the Hands of An Angry God" which, in an agonizing appeal to the emotions, pictures man held over the fires of hell. Later, however, Edwards deplored the emotional extremes to which the movement led.

In 1750 he was dismissed by his parishioners because of his strict religious doctrines. He then became a missionary to the Indians of Stockbridge, Massachusetts. While at Stockbridge he completed his brilliant defense of Calvinistic beliefs "Freedom of the Will." Shortly before his death he was made president of the college of New Jersey, which has since become Princeton University.

Let's consider . . .

1. After Jonathan Edwards had talked with his father, he walked alone in the fields. Describe how he felt toward nature and toward God.

2. Why do people often require solitude to do their best thinking?

3. Nature was obviously important to Edwards. Think of another American writer who was interested in nature. Describe the similarities and differences between each writer's attitude toward nature.

The writer's craft . . .

Edwards wrote: "The sense I had of divine things, would often of a sudden kindle up, as it were, a sweet burning in my heart . . . ." By graphically comparing his feelings to the sudden blazing of a fire, Edwards was able to communicate the peculiar quality of his emotions. Such a comparison is called a *metaphor*: an implied comparison between two unlike objects having at least one thing in common. What qualities might Edwards' religious feelings and a sudden flame have in common?

Edwards created a particularly vivid metaphor by describing the burning in his heart as being sweet. While everyone is familiar with the separate qualities of burning and sweetness, the two terms are seldom used in relation to one another. By combining them Edwards suggests that his feelings had the intensity of fire, but a sensation of sweet delight.

Writers use metaphors in both prose and poetry because this figure of speech has the power to make abstractions, such as emotions and ideas, vivid and clear. A vague abstraction may take on specific personal meaning for the reader if he can identify it with a familiar, concrete object.

1. Think of an emotional experience in your life. Try to recall the exact quality of your feeling. By means of a metaphor, compare your emotion with a specific concrete object with which it has one thing in common, so that others will be able to share your feeling.

2. Now write a short essay in which you describe the incident which evoked your emotional response. When describing your feelings be sure to use the metaphor that you wrote in exercise one.

Nathan Hale

NANCY HALE

One of Nathan Hale's brothers was the author's great-great-grandfather. In this selection Nancy Hale writes of her ancestor, "a young American who'd gone to war, who'd lived for twenty-one ordinary enough years before—in the day's work—he died for his country."

"The boy was only a couple of years out of New Haven when he joined up. He'd hardly got started. He'd been teaching school, you know, up at East Haddam and then down in New London, and it looked as if he was shaping up into a fine teacher. He'd made a lot of friends everywhere he went, and the girls always liked him. They say he was a good-looking boy.

"Then the war came. Things had looked bad to us Americans for a long time, but when the first gun was fired on that April day it seemed to light a sudden strong fire in everyone's heart. It seemed to call out—'Americans!' The boy's brothers, John and Joseph, volunteered first off. It was a patriotic family—the father'd been a Deputy in the old Connecticut Assembly. The boy himself had signed up with the school for a year. He wasn't the kind to let people down, but he did write and ask to be released from his contract two weeks early. He joined up in July, as a Lieutenant in Webb's Seventh Connecticut.

"Well, you know how things went after that. The boy was in camp up near Boston all winter. It wasn't an exciting siege. But there was a lot to do getting the men to re-enlist. Most of their terms of enlistment ran out in December. The General

was worried about it. Our boy offered the men in his company his own pay for a month if they'd stay that much longer. Anyway the siege was maintained.

"He got a leave in the winter and went home. Maybe that was when he got engaged. Alicia Adams. A lovely girl; they would have made a handsome couple. When Spring came the enemy evacuated Boston and our army went down to New York, where real trouble was threatening. The boy'd been made a captain by that time. He was twenty-one years old.

"Our Long Island campaign was just this side of disastrous. Morale was none too good, afterwards. I don't suppose the General was in a worse spot in the whole war than he was for those three weeks right after the Battle of Long Island. There we lay, facing the enemy across the East River, and no way of knowing what they had up their sleeve. Surprise was what we feared. The answer to that was companies of rangers, to scout around and find out what was up. Knowlton's Rangers was organized, and our boy switched over to it. He wanted action, you see.

"But the rangers weren't enough. The General wanted to know two things: when the enemy was planning to attack, and

where. Nobody could tell him. The General let it be known that he'd welcome volunteers to spy.

"Now, people didn't take kindly to the word 'spy' around these parts. It didn't mean excitement or glamour or any of those things. It meant something degrading. It was a job they gave to bums, who didn't care. But the General said he wanted a spy. Well, our boy volunteered. His friends tried to talk him out of it. They spoke of the indignity; they also told him he'd make a terrible spy—frank, open boy like him.

"But his idea was, the job was necessary. That was the great thing. Its being necessary seemed to him to make it honorable. He was sent through the enemy lines dressed up like a Dutch schoolmaster.

"He didn't make such a bad spy, after all. He got what he went after, and hid the drawings in his shoes. He was on his way back, crossing their lines, when they caught him. They found the information on him. He admitted he was over there to spy. You know what a spy gets. They hanged him in the morning. He wrote some letters to the family at home, but they were destroyed before his eyes, they say. But in his last moment, they let him say what he wanted to. And later one of their officers told one of our officers what he'd said.

"There he was, with the noose around his neck. He hadn't got much done. He'd got caught on the first big job of his life. He wasn't going to marry Alicia Adams, nor to have any children, nor to do any more teaching, nor to finish fighting this war. He stood there in the morning air, and he spoke and said who he was, his commission and all. And then he added, 'I only regret that I have but one life to lose for my country.'"

You could tell the story like that, simply, because it is a simple story, and when you'd finished you'd have told about all there is to tell about Nathan Hale. There isn't even a contemporary picture of him. Most of the friends to whom he wrote didn't keep his letters. He was just a young American who'd gone to war, who'd lived for twenty-one ordinary enough years before—in the day's work—he died for his country.

One of his brothers, Enoch, was my great-great-grandfather.

When I was a child there was a small bronze statue, about four feet high, that stood in the corner of the living room at home. It was just about my height, but it wasn't another child. It was a young man, with his wrists tied behind him and his ankles bound. I passed it several times a day, every day of my childhood. Sometimes I used to touch the bronze face. It was a small-scale replica of the Nathan Hale statue at Yale.

I must have been told his story, because I always knew it. But my father never went on about it, if you know what I mean. There his story was; for what it might mean to you. Some of my other ancestors were the kind of characters that have a whole legend of anecdotes surrounding them, pointed, stirring, or uproarious. But the young man with his hands bound had died at twenty-one, a patriot, as stark and all alone and anecdoteless as young men of twenty-one must be.

Once I was set upon the knees of an old gentleman whose grandmother had been Alicia Adams. She had married and had children, and lived to be eighty-eight, a pretty, sparkling old lady. And when she died she said, "Where is Nathan?" But about the young man himself there were no family reminiscences, no odd little jokes, no tales beyond the short, plain story of his life and death. He had had no time to do anything memorable but die.

Nevertheless . . . It was my job as a child to fill the kitchen scuttle with coal from the cellar. I was not a brave child, and to me the long corners of the cellar seemed menacing and full of queer, moving shadows—wolves? robbers? I cannot remember when I first started taking the thought of Nathan Hale down cellar with me, for a shield and buckler. I thought, "If he could be hanged, I can go down cellar." The thing was, he was no impossible hero; he was a member of the family, and he was young too. He was a hero you could take along with you into the cellar of a New England farmhouse. You felt he'd be likely to say, "Aren't any wolves or robbers back there that I can see."

Well, I am grown up now and I know very little more about Nathan Hale than I did then. There are, of course, a mass of details about his short life. A devoted scholar named George Dudley Seymour has spent years in collecting all that can be collected about him. There's a wartime diary. They know his friends. He played football and checkers at camp. He drank wine at Brown's Tavern and cider at Stone's. But when you add all these little things you only affirm the peculiar simplicity of the story.

Hale is a symbol of all the young American men who fight and who die for us. Partly he is a symbol because he was the first of our heroes in the first of our own wars. He was the first to show the world what Americans are made of. The reason they destroyed his letters home at the time of his death was, they said, so that "the rebels should not know they have a man who can die so firmly." He showed them.

He is no Washington or Jefferson although he ranks with the heroes. Washington was a great general and Jefferson was a genius. All of our nation's heroes are great men who are great by their minds and by their deeds and by their careers. All except Hale. His special gift to his country, and to us who love that country, was the manner of his death.

He is the young American. He is the patron of all the young Americans who have grown up as he did in quiet self-respecting families; who have gone to college and done well, and had fun too; and who have started out along their life's careers, well spoke of, promising; and then broken off to join their country's forces in time of war without an instant's hesitation; knowing what must be done and who must do it. He was no different than they. He was an American boy. Everything that can be said of them can be said of him. In the letters of his friends written about him after his death, certain words keep cropping up. They sound oddly familiar. "Promising . . . patriotic . . . generous . . . modest . . . high-spirited . . . devoted . . ." His friends fitted the words to Hale. They fit Americans.

Nothing was more American in Hale than his taking on the duties that led to his death. It was a dirty job, spying. Nobody wanted it. He took it. There's something about that, taking on a dirty job that's got to be done, that rings a bell. It's an American custom of American heroes. He wasn't a remarkably articulate boy. His letters are nothing special. He just jotted things in his diary. But he became the spokesman for young American fighting men who have to die for their country. He chanced to say the thing they think; the thing they mean, when there's not even a split second to think. He stood there at Turtle Bay on Manhattan Island. Don't think he declaimed. He wasn't that kind. He had those few moments, and he was thinking about all the different things that were ending for him. He said and I think it was more like a remark:

"I only regret . . ."

The woman who wrote this biography

NANCY HALE 1908–

Nancy Hale is a prolific writer. Her short stories are published in leading magazines, and many of them have been reprinted in anthologies.

Miss Hale comes from a distinguished family of artists and writers. Her grandfather, Edward Everett Hale, wrote *The Man Without a Country;* her great aunt, Lucretia Hale, wrote *The Peterkin Papers,* a masterpiece of comedy. Her father, Philip Hale, was a painter.

Miss Hale served as an editor on *Vogue* and *Vanity Fair,* fashion magazines, and as a reporter for *The New York Times.* She has written four novels, but she is best known for her short stories. The best of these stories are published in *Between the Dark and the Daylight* (1943) and *The Empress's Ring* (1955). Many of her stories are set either in Boston, where Miss Hale was born and raised, or in Virginia, where she now lives.

Let's consider . . .

1. Why were Nathan Hale and his brothers among the first to volunteer?

2. What was Nathan Hale's reason for becoming a spy?

3. State in one sentence three important facts you learned about Nathan Hale's life after he left Yale. (Remember that parallel thoughts require parallel construction.)

4. Why did Nathan Hale's story seem so simple? Why is its simplicity important to the way you feel about this young man?

5. Write a **précis** of the last two paragraphs: a condensed statement of the main ideas in your own words. These paragraphs contain about 300 words. Try to limit your précis to about seventy-five words, but do not omit any of the information which your reader would need in his understanding of Nathan Hale.

6. Do you think the last two paragraphs added to the value of this selection? Explain.

The writer's craft . . .

The struggle for independence had a marked influence on American writing. Soldiers, statesmen, farmers—Americans from all walks of life used their pens and their voices to serve the cause of liberty. Like Thomas Paine, they wrote rousing pamphlets to provoke indifferent colonists to fight for freedom. Like Patrick Henry, they gave fiery speeches to forge one nation out of the thirteen colonies. And they used all the beauty and power of the English language to frame these ideals into such national documents as the Declaration of Independence.

The literature of the Revolution is a patriotic literature. Men fought and died because they believed in freedom. Their literature reflects their belief.

Nathan Hale believed in freedom. Nancy Hale wrote, "His special gift to his country, and to us who love that country, was the manner of his death." In dying, Nathan Hale gave to Americans a sentence which will live as long as our national literature remains alive. "I only regret that I have but one life to lose for my country."

1. Explain why Nathan Hale's last words have such a dramatic quality.

2. Think of other famous statements you have heard. Try to explain why these statements have such lasting appeal.

Knowing words . . .

In speaking of Nathan Hale's last words, Nancy Hale wrote, "Don't think he *declaimed* . . . it was more like a *remark*." Both *declaim* and *remark* are words which mean "say," yet each describes a different manner in which an utterance could be made.

To *declaim* is to speak in a stately or even pompous manner. To *remark* is simply to mention in a casual way the thoughts that are in one's mind.

By writing that Nathan Hale *remarked* rather than *declaimed*, Nancy Hale pointed up the simple dignity with which she believed Nathan Hale spoke his dying words.

1. Decide which of the famous sayings listed below were probably declaimed and which were probably remarked.

"When in the course of human events . . ."

"You can fool some of the people all of the time, and all of the people some of the time. But you can't fool all of the people all of the time."

"Give me liberty, or give me death."

"I cannot tell a lie."

"The only thing to fear is fear itself."

2. Think of other famous statements. Decide whether they were declaimed or remarked.

Hannibal

Was there ever a cause too lost,
Ever a cause that was lost too long,
Or that showed with the lapse of time too vain
For the generous tears of youth and song?
                                    Robert Frost

Walden

Excerpts

HENRY DAVID THOREAU

Thoreau felt that "Our life is frittered away by detail." To get away from that detail, he determined to go to the woods and live as simply as he could. By this experience Thoreau hoped to learn the true meaning of life and freedom.

Why I Went to the Woods

I went to the woods because I wished to live deliberately, to front only the essential facts of life, and see if I could not learn what it had to teach, and not, when I came to die, discover that I had not lived. I did not wish to live what was not life, living is so dear; nor did I wish to practice resignation, unless it was quite necessary. I wanted to live deep and suck out all the marrow of life, to live so sturdily and Spartan-like [1] as to put to rout all that was not life, to cut a broad swath and shave close, to drive life into a corner, and reduce it to its lowest terms, and, if it proved to be mean, why then to get the whole and genuine meanness of it, and publish its meanness to the world; or if it were sublime, to know it by experience, and be able to give a true account of it in my next excursion.[2] For most men, it appears to me, are in a strange uncertainty about it, whether it is of the devil or of God, and have *somewhat hastily* concluded that it is the chief end of man here to "glorify God and enjoy Him forever." [3]

Still we live meanly, like ants; though the fable tells us that we were long ago changed into men; like pygmies we fight with cranes,[4] it is error upon error, and clout upon clout, and our best virtue has for its occasion a superfluous and evitable wretchedness. Our life is frittered away by detail. An honest man has hardly need to count more than his ten fingers or in extreme cases he may add his ten toes, and lump the rest.

Simplicity, simplicity, simplicity! I say, let your affairs be as two or three, and not a hundred or a thousand; instead of a million count half a dozen, and keep your accounts on your thumbnail. In the midst of this chopping sea of civilized life, such are the clouds and storms and quicksands and thousand-and-one items to be allowed for, that a man has to live, if he would not founder and go to the bottom and not make his port at all, by dead reckoning,[5]

and he must be a great calculator indeed who succeeds. Simplify, simplify. Instead of three meals a day, if it be necessary eat but one; instead of a hundred dishes, five; and reduce other things in proportion. Our life is like a German Confederacy, made up of petty states, with its boundary forever fluctuating, so that even a German cannot tell you how it is bounded at any moment. The nation itself, with all its so-called internal improvements, which, by the way, are all external and superficial, is just such an unwieldy and overgrown establishment, cluttered with furniture and tripped up by its own traps, ruined by luxury and heedless expense, by want of calculation and a worthy aim, as the million households in the land; and the only cure for it as for them is in a rigid economy, a stern and more than Spartan simplicity of life and elevation of purpose. It lives too fast. Men think that it is essential that the *Nation* have commerce, and export ice, and talk through a telegraph, and ride thirty miles an hour, without a doubt, whether *they* do or not; but whether we should live like baboons or like men, is a little uncertain. If we do not get out sleepers, and forge rails, and devote days and nights to the work, but go to tinkering upon our *lives* to improve *them*, who will build railroads? And if railroads are not built, how shall we get to heaven in season? But if we stay at home and mind our business, who will want railroads? We do not ride on the railroad; it rides upon us.

My House by Walden Pond

The exact cost of my house, paying the usual price for such materials as I used, but not counting the work, all of which was done by myself, was as follows; and I give the details because very few are able to tell exactly what their houses cost, and fewer still, if any, the separate cost of the various materials which compose them: —

---

[1] *Spartan-like,* like the people of the Greek city, Sparta, who were noted for their severe, rigorous way of living

[2] *my next excursion,* my future life

[3] *"glorify God and enjoy Him forever,"* Thoreau's quotation of the response in the Presbyterian Catechism to the question, "What is the chief end of man?"

[4] *like pygmies we fight with cranes,* a reference to the ancient belief that the pygmies of Africa battled with cranes

[5] *dead reckoning,* way of navigating a ship without observing sun and stars; hence, navigation by guesswork

Boards .... $	8.03½
mostly shanty boards	
Refuse shingles for roof and sides ..	4.00
Laths	1.25
Two second-hand windows with glass	2.43
One thousand old brick	4.00
Two casks of lime	2.40
That was high.	
Hair	.31
More than I needed.	
Mantel-tree iron [1]	.15
Nails	3.90
Hinges and screws	.14
Latch	.10
Chalk	.01
Transportation	1.40
I carried a good part on my back.	
In all .... $	28.12½

These are all the materials excepting the timber, stones, and sand, which I claimed by squatter's right. I have also a small woodshed adjoining, made chiefly of the stuff which was left after building the house.

I intend to build me a house which will surpass any on the main street in Concord in grandeur and luxury, as soon as it pleases me as much and will cost me no more than my present one.

I thus found that the student who wishes for a shelter can obtain one for a lifetime at an expense not greater than the rent which he now pays annually. If I seem to boast more than is becoming, my excuse is that I brag for humanity rather than for myself; and my shortcomings and inconsistencies do not affect the truth of my statement. Notwithstanding much cant and hypocrisy,—chaff which I find it difficult to separate from my wheat, but for which I am as sorry as any man,—I will breathe freely and stretch myself in this respect, it is such a relief to both the moral and physical system; and I am resolved that I will not through humility become the devil's attorney. I will endeavor to speak a good word for the truth. At Cambridge College [2] the mere rent of a student's room,

which is only a little larger than my own, is thirty dollars each year, though the corporation [3] had the advantage of building thirty-two side by side and under one roof, and the occupant suffers the inconvenience of many and noisy neighbors, and perhaps a residence in the fourth story. . . . Of the present economical and social arrangements I was more independent than any farmer in Concord, for I was not anchored to a house or farm, but could follow the bent of my genius, which is a very crooked one, every moment. . . .

By surveying, carpentry, and day-labor of various other kinds in the village in the meanwhile, for I have as many trades as fingers, I had earned $13.34. The expense of food for eight months, namely, from July 4 to March 1, the time when these estimates were made, though I lived there more than two years,—not counting potatoes, a little green corn, and some peas, which I had raised, nor considering the value of what was on hand at the last date, was

Rice .... $	1.73½	
Molasses	1.73	
(Cheapest form of the saccharine.)		
Rye meal	1.04¾	
Indian meal	.99¾	
(Cheaper than rye.)		
Pork	.22	All experiments which failed.
Flour	.88	
(Cost more than Indian meal, both money and trouble.)		
Sugar	.80	
Lard	.65	
Apples	.25	
Dried apples	.22	
Sweet potatoes	.10	
One pumpkin	.06	
One watermelon	.02	
Salt	.03	

Yes, I did eat $8.74, all told; but I should not thus unblushingly publish my guilt, if I did not know that most of my readers were equally guilty with myself, and their deeds would look no better in print. The

---

[1] *mantel-tree iron*, a part of a fireplace
[2] *Cambridge College*, Harvard University

[3] *corporation*, governing board of the college

next year I sometimes caught a mess of fish for my dinner, and once I went so far as to slaughter a woodchuck which ravaged my beanfield,—effect his transmigration, as a Tartar would say [4]—and devour him, partly for experiment's sake; but though it afforded me a momentary enjoyment, notwithstanding a musky flavor, I saw that the longest use would not make that a good practice, however it might seem to have your woodchucks ready dressed by the village butcher.

Clothing and some incidental expenses within the same dates,
though little can be inferred from
this item, amounted to $8.40¾
Oil and some household utensils . . . 2.00

So that all the pecuniary outgoes, ex-
cepting for washing and mending, which for the most part were done out of the house, and their bills have not yet been received,—and these are all and more than all the ways by which money necessarily goes out in this part of the world,—were

House $28.12½
Farm, one year 14.72½
Food, eight months 8.74
Clothing, etc., eight months 8.40¾
Oil, etc., eight months 2.00
In all $61.99¾

I address myself now to those of my readers who have a living to get. And to meet this I have

For farm produce sold $23.44
Earned by day-labor 13.34
In all $36.78

which subtracted from the sum of the out-goes leaves a balance of $25.21¾ on the one side,—this being very nearly the means with which I started, and the measure of expenses to be incurred,—and on the other,

---

[4] *effect his transmigration, as a Tartar would say,* by killing and eating the woodchuck, cause its soul to move to another body. The transmigra-tion of souls is a belief that the soul of a person, after death, moves to another body. This belief was held by the Tartars, various primitive Mon-golian and Turkish tribes.

besides the leisure and independence and health thus secured, a comfortable house for me as long as I choose to occupy it.

These statistics, however accidental and therefore uninstructive they may appear, as they have a certain completeness, have a certain value also. Nothing was given me of which I have not rendered some ac-count. It appears from the above estimate, that my food alone cost me in money about twenty-seven cents a week. It was for nearly two years after this, rye and Indian meal, without yeast, potatoes, rice, a very little salt pork, molasses, and salt, and my drink, water. It was fit that I should live on rice, mainly, who loved so well the philosophy of India. To meet the objec-tions of some inveterate cavilers, I may as well state that if I dined out occasionally, as I always had done, and I trust shall have opportunities to do again, it was frequently to the detriment of my domestic arrange-ments. But the dining out, being, as I have stated, a constant element, does not in the least affect a comparative statement like this.

I learned from my two years' experience that it would cost incredibly little trouble to obtain one's necessary food, even in this latitude; that a man may use as simple a diet as the animals, and yet retain health and strength. I have made a satisfactory dinner, satisfactory on several accounts, simply off a dish of purslane (*Portulaca oleracea*) which I gathered in my cornfield, boiled and salted. I give the Latin on ac-count of the savoriness of the trivial name. And pray what more can a reasonable man desire, in peaceful times, in ordinary noons, than a sufficient number of ears of green sweet-corn boiled, with the addition of salt? Even the little variety that I used was a yielding to the demands of appetite, and not of health. Yet men have come to such a pass that they frequently starve, not for want of necessaries, but for want of lux-uries; and I know a good woman who thinks that her son lost his life because he took to drinking water only. . . .

Solitude

I find it wholesome to be alone the greater part of the time. To be in company, even with the best, is soon wearisome and dissipating. I love to be alone. I never found the companion that was so companionable as solitude. We are for the most part more lonely when we go abroad among men than when we stay in our chambers. A man thinking or working is always alone, let him be where he will. Solitude is not measured by the miles of space that intervene between a man and his fellows. The really diligent student in one of the crowded hives of Cambridge College is as solitary as a dervish in the desert. The farmer can work alone in the field or the woods all day, hoeing or chopping, and not feel lonesome, because he is employed; but when he comes home at night he cannot sit down in a room alone, at the mercy of his thoughts, but must be where he can "see the folks," and recreate, and, as he thinks, remunerate himself for his day's solitude; and hence he wonders how the student can sit alone in the house, is still at work in *his* field, and chopping in *his* woods, as the farmer in his, and in turn seeks the same recreation and society that the latter does, though it may be a more condensed form of it.

Society is commonly too cheap. We meet at very short intervals, not having had time to acquire any new value for each other. We meet at meals three times a day, and give each other a new taste of that old musty cheese that we are. We have had to agree on a certain set of rules, called etiquette and politeness, to make this frequent meeting tolerable and that we need not come to open war. We meet at the post-office, and at the sociable, and about the fireside every night; we live thick and are in each other's way, and stumble over one another, and I think that we thus lose some respect for one another. Certainly less frequency would suffice for all important and hearty communications. Consider the girls in a factory,—never alone, hardly in their dreams. It would be better if there were but one inhabitant to a square mile, as where I live. The value of a man is not in his skin, that we should touch him.

I have heard of a man lost in the woods and dying of famine and exhaustion at the foot of a tree, whose loneliness was relieved by the grotesque visions with which, owing to bodily weakness, his diseased imagination surrounded him, and which he believed to be real. So also, owing to bodily and mental health and strength, we may be continually cheered by a like but more normal and natural society, and come to know that we are never alone.

I have a great deal of company in my house; especially in the morning, when nobody calls. Let me suggest a few comparisons, that some one may convey an idea of my situation. I am no more lonely that the loon in the pond that laughs so loud, or than Walden Pond itself. What company has that lonely lake, I pray? And yet it has not the blue devils, but the blue angels in it, in the azure tint of its waters. The sun is alone, except in thick weather, when there sometimes appear to be two, but one is a mock sun. God is alone,— but the devil, he is far from being alone; he sees a great deal of company; he is legion. I am no more lonely than a single mullein or dandelion in a pasture, or a bean leaf, or sorrel, or a horse-fly, or a bumblebee. I am no more lonely than the Mill Brook, or a weathercock, or the North Star, or the South Wind, or an April shower, or a January thaw, or the first spider in a new house.

The Pond

Sometimes, having had a surfeit of human society and gossip, and worn out all my village friends, I rambled still farther westward than I habitually dwell, into yet more unfrequented parts of the town, "to fresh woods and pastures new," or, while the sun was setting, made my supper of huckleberries and blueberries on Fair Haven Hill, and laid up a store for several days. The fruits do not yield their true flavor to the purchaser of them, nor to him who raises them for the market. There is but one way to obtain it, yet few take that way. If you would know the flavor of huckleberries, ask the cow-boy or the partridge. It is a vulgar error to suppose that you have tasted huckleberries who never plucked them. A huckleberry never reaches Boston; they have not been known there since they grew on her three hills. The ambrosial and essential part of the fruit is lost with the bloom which is rubbed off in the market cart, and they become mere provender. As long as Eternal Justice reigns, not one innocent huckleberry can be transported thither from the country's hills.

Occasionally, after my hoeing was done for the day, I joined some impatient companion who had been fishing on the pond since morning, as silent and motionless as a duck or a floating leaf, and, after practising various kinds of philosophy, had concluded commonly, by the time I arrived, that he belonged to the ancient sect of Coenobites. There was one older man, an excellent fisher and skilled in all kinds of woodcraft, who was pleased to look upon my house as a building erected for the convenience of fishermen; and I was equally pleased when he sat in my doorway to arrange his lines. Once in a while we sat together on the pond, he at one end of the boat, and I at the other; but not many words passed between us, for he had grown deaf in his later years, but he occasionally hummed a psalm, which harmonized well enough with my philosophy. Our intercourse was thus altogether one of unbroken harmony, far more pleasing to remember than if it had been carried on by speech. When, as was commonly the case, I had none to commune with, I used to raise the echoes by striking with a paddle on the side of my boat, filling the surrounding woods with circling and dilating sound, stirring them up as the keeper of a menagerie his wild beasts, until I elicited a growl from every wooded vale and hillside.

In warm evenings I frequently sat in the boat playing the flute, and saw the perch, which I seem to have charmed, hovering around me, and the moon travelling over the ribbed bottom, which was strewed with the wrecks of the forest. Formerly I had come to this pond adventurously, from time to time, in dark summer nights, with a companion, and, making a fire close to the water's edge, which we thought attracted the fishes, we caught pouts with a bunch of worms strung on a thread, and when we had done, far in the night, threw the burning brands high into the air like skyrockets, which, coming down into the pond, were quenched with a loud hissing, and we were suddenly groping in total darkness. Through this, whistling a tune, we took our way to the haunts of men again. But now I had made my home by the shore.

Sometimes, after staying in a village parlor till the family had all retired, I have returned to the woods, and, partly with a view to the next day's dinner, spent the hours of midnight fishing from a boat by moonlight, serenaded by owls and foxes, and hearing, from time to time, the creaking note of some unknown bird close at hand. These experiences were very memorable and valuable to me,—anchored in forty feet of water, and twenty or thirty rods from the shore, surrounded sometimes by thousands of small perch and shiners, dimpling the surface with their tails in the moonlight, and communicating by a long flaxen line with mysterious nocturnal fishes which had their dwelling forty feet below, or sometimes dragging sixty feet of line about the pond as I drifted in the gentle night breeze, now and then feeling a slight vibration along it, indicative of some life prowling about its extremity, of dull uncertain blundering purpose there, and slow to make up its mind. At length you slowly raise, pulling hand over hand, some horned pout squeaking and squirming to the upper air. It was very queer, especially in dark nights, when your thought had wandered to vast and cosmogonal themes in other spheres, to feel this faint jerk, which came to interrupt your dreams and link you to Nature again. It seemed as if I might next cast my line upward into the air, as well as downward into this element, which was scarcely more dense. Thus I caught two fishes as it were with one hook.

Why I Left the Woods

I left the woods for as good a reason as I went there. Perhaps it seemed to me that I had several more lives to live, and could not spare any more time for that one. It is remarkable how easily and insensibly we fall into a particular route, and make a beaten track for ourselves. I had not lived there a week before my feet wore a path from my door to the pondside; and though it is five or six years since I trod it, it is still quite distinct. It is true, I fear, that others may have fallen into it, and so helped to keep it open. The surface of the earth is soft and impressible by the feet of men; and so with the paths which the mind travels. How worn and dusty, then, must be the highways of the world, how deep the ruts of tradition and conformity! I did not wish to take a cabin passage, but rather to go before the mast and on the deck of the world, for there I could best see the moonlight amid the mountains. I do not wish to go below now.

I learned this, at least, by my experiment: that if one advances confidently in the direction of his dreams, and endeavors to live the life which he has imagined, he will meet with a success unexpected in common hours. He will put some things behind, will pass an invisible boundary; new, universal, and more liberal laws will begin to establish themselves around and within him; or the old laws be expanded, and interpreted in his favor in a more liberal sense, and he will live with the license of a higher order of beings. In proportion as he simplifies his life, the laws of the universe will appear less complex, and solitude will not be solitude, nor poverty poverty, nor weakness weakness. If you have built castles in the air, your work need not be lost; that is where they should be. Now put the foundation under them.

The man who wrote this selection

HENRY DAVID THOREAU   1817–1862

More than any other New England writer of the nineteenth century, Thoreau knew nature at first hand and demonstrated in his life and writings a belief in Ralph Waldo Emerson's principle of self-reliance: that the primary obligation of the individual is to perfect his own life. It is not surprising, then, that Thoreau felt the need for independence, that his aim was always to "adventure on life," and that he "went to the woods" because he "wished to live deliberately." Two years later he left Walden, not because of a sense of failure or disappointment, but because he "had several more lives to live and could not spare any more time for that one."

In order to be always free to "adventure," Thoreau never tied himself down to one profession or vocation. Rather, he earned his food, lodgings, and clothing by performing various odd jobs at which he was adept: carpentering, fence building, berry picking, and surveying. He did not accumulate possessions, believing that a man was free only so long as he could move everything he owned in a knapsack. As he grew older, he became more and more absorbed in observing and describing the world of nature, not only in the Concord woods but throughout New England. These excursions furnished material for much writing, some of it appearing in magazines during his life time.

In his lectures, as well as in *Walden,* Thoreau spoke out loudly and boldly against the mechanization of American life. He sincerely believed that there was no improvement in man merely because his machines allowed him to produce more goods with less effort. Material progress meant little to him; it was only "an improved means to an unimproved end." In a way, Thoreau marked a turning point in the American way of life. As a result of the industrial revolution and the advancing machine age, the primitive and frontier life of the early settlers was being replaced by a life of comparative ease which Thoreau believed would soon rob men of their self-reliance and their right to think for themselves. Today Thoreau's lessons in simplicity and economy have a special appeal to those who rebel at the complexity and expense of modern life.

Let's consider . . .

Why I Went to the Woods

1. What were Thoreau's reasons for going to the woods?

2. Thoreau spoke of "reducing life to its lowest terms." What did he mean?

3. In what way did Thoreau intend to make an intimate acquaintance with life?

4. Thoreau believed "our life is frittered away by detail and our nation . . . ruined by luxury and needless expense." Debate this statement pro and con.

5. Most people probably think of progress in a different way than did Thoreau. Explain what Thoreau probably conceived to be progress. What does the average person think of as progress?

My House by Walden Pond

6. Suppose you decided to repeat Thoreau's experiment today. Estimate as nearly as you can how much you would need of the various items on his food list (except those no longer on sale) and how much they would cost. How great a difference is there between your food costs and Thoreau's? Compare your estimated costs with your classmates. Are they very different or about the same?

7. By living in the woods, Thoreau found "leisure and independence and health." Do you think these gains would balance the material comforts he gave up for nearly two years? Explain why.

Solitude

8. What were Thoreau's reasons for saying that he found it wholesome to be alone the greater part of the time?

9. Do you disagree with Thoreau's statement? "A man thinking or working is always alone, let him be where he will." Give reasons for your reaction, based upon experience.

10. What effective use can you make of solitude? How has Thoreau helped you to appreciate the values of solitude?

11. How did Thoreau account for etiquette and politeness? Can you think of more positive reasons which might explain the desire to be well-mannered?

My Pond

12. Describe some of the pleasures which Thoreau derived from his pond.

13. What were the two fishes that Thoreau caught with a single hook?

Why I Left the Woods

14. Why did Thoreau leave the woods? Why are the comparisons he uses particularly meaningful in light of his reason?

15. Describe Thoreau's attitude toward dreams and castles in the air. Explain why you think that his attitude is sound or unsound.

16. Thoreau was a great individualist with a strong determination to live according to his own convictions. What were some of these convictions? Are these convictions applicable to modern American life? Give several reasons to support your answer.

17. Some people regard Thoreau as a confirmed pessimist; others admire him as the great optimist of his period. With which of these opinions do you agree? Why?

The writer's craft . . .

During the middle of the nineteenth century, there appeared in New England a group of authors who were largely responsible for developing a truly American literature. This group included such distinguished writers as Ralph Waldo Emerson, John Greenleaf Whittier, Nathaniel Hawthorne and Henry David Thoreau.

Thoreau was a vigorous champion of individualism. He wanted to enjoy a life of simplicity and freedom, and he thought that he could best do so by living close to nature. He did not believe Americans were living wisely or courageously. They were putting too much emphasis on industry and material progress, and too little on the simple but basic values of life.

To discover what a simple life actually had to offer, Thoreau lived alone in the woods for about two years. His book *Walden* not only recounts his experiment but also contains many brief, pungent comments which express his individual philosophy of life.

1. Find several of his remarks which you think contain a world of meaning in just a few words. Then in your own words explain what Thoreau's remarks mean to you.

2. You have probably found that it is more difficult to put an idea into a brief statement which is packed with meaning than to express it in several pages. Look again at Thoreau's writing. Then try your hand at writing one or two crisp, brief statements which sum up your philosophy of life.

The Big Breach

SAMUEL HOPKINS ADAMS

Grandfather could be something of a problem, but his grandchildren knew how to handle him. If they could just lead him into remembering his adventures along the Erie Canal, he would forget their sins and launch into one of his famous stories. This is one of the many his grandson Samuel remembered.

By dint of subjecting ourselves to grinding penury over a period of months, my cousin, Sireno, and I became joint owners of a Flaubert .22 rifle. The weapon and a cartridge box of "shorts" cost, as I remember, four dollars at Hamilton & Matthews, Rochester's leading hardware store in the 1880's. Though the rifle was of limited range and uncertain accuracy, it was the pride of our lives.

On a brisk September Saturday we two rose early and tramped out to the Wide Waters, a place where the Erie Canal broadened out across half a mile of flats. After several hours of stalking, Reno killed a muskrat. This feat made our day. It was accomplished just before we and the other Adams grandchildren were due at the South Union Street cottage for our weekly duty call.

We debated, on the way, as to what we should do with our muskrat. Only too vividly we remembered a previous hunt when we had triumphantly brought in the day's bag, consisting of a brown thrasher. On that painful occasion, Grandfather had denounced us as midsummer murderers and hedgerow hoodlums. He might, we feared, feel the same about our present prey.

"I'll hide it in my shirt-front," Reno said. "It'll be O.K. there."

The other cousins, Jenny, John, and Charlie, were already in the house when we arrived. Grandfather sat beside the stove, sipping his favorite temperance tonic, Hop Bitters (alcoholic content forty per cent) while his callers politely nibbled our step-grandmother's caraway cookies. On the marble-top stand at the old gentleman's elbow lay an open copy of *Sartor Resartus*. We faced the imminent prospect of having our minds improved by the reading of Mr. Thomas Carlyle, the leading oracle of the day.

Setting down his glass, Grandfather accidentally knocked the book to the floor. Reno, being nearest, stooped to pick it up. A shirt-button gave. He grabbed for his waistline too late; the furry corpse rolled out.

Grandfather adjusted his hexagonal spectacles and regarded it.

"*What*," he demanded, "is this?"

"It's a muskrat, sir," the hunter replied.

"And how comes it here?"

"We shot it at the Wide Waters," Reno said.

(I considered that "we" a cowardly shirking of responsibility.)

"Canalside, eh?" the old gentleman asked in a tone of surprising amiability.

"Yes, sir. He was just crawling into his hole."

"In my heyday on the Grand Western Canal," said Grandfather, giving the Erie its early popular name, "a musquash taken within five furlongs of the waterway fetched a bonus of one dollar and keep the pelt, which might bring in fifteen cents additional."

"Oh, my!" Jenny sighed. "Only fifteen cents. I could have had a muskrat-skin coat."

"Not in my house," Grandfather snapped. "I still harbor a just ambition against the slithery, slinking, burrowing, undermining creatures, dead or alive. Pathmaster's penance, we canallers used to call them."

"What's pathmaster, Grandpa?" Charlie inquired.

A pathmaster, Grandfather explained, was the guardian angel and unchallenged autocrat of path, berm [1] and water for the fifteen miles of the canal he patrolled and was responsible for the safety of man, beast and boat thereon.

"But no more," he added with that touch of sentiment which he reserved for his beloved Erie Canal alone. "The last pathmaster has sounded his last alarum on his silver whistle."

"What was the silver whistle for?" Charlie asked.

"To summon help at need, to be sure. . . . And so, when I heard the shrill call sounding through the darkness and the rain one night, I knew there was danger afoot."

There was a musing tone in Grandfather's voice that held promise of a reprieve from Mr. Carlyle if we could only hold the old gentleman to the path of reminiscence.

John said quickly, "Who was it that whistled, sir?"

"Tom Culver," was the reply. "No bet-ter canaller could be found between Hudson's River and the Long Level."

"What year was it?" John asked persuasively.

It was 1829 or 1830, Grandfather thought. Anyway, it was the year of the five-day August rains when every tributary stream roared over its banks and Erie Water rose a foot an hour.

Grandfather had been to Clyde on a trade in marsh-eels for pickling and barrelling and, that night of rain, was riding his sorrel mare westward along the pike toward Lyons where he would find lodging. From out the blackness on his left came a feeble whistle. He reined in.

"What's that?" he shouted.

A gasping voice answered, "Pathmaster's summons. Lend a hand, whoever you be."

Under the rules, regulations and penalties of the Honorables, the Canal Commissioners of the State of New York, a pathmaster could commandeer help, and the order must be obeyed.

Detaching his saddle lantern, Grandfather dismounted and approached the canal on the berm side. The embankment was spouting like a leaky colander, for it was riddled with musquash holes which had been forced clear through by the pressure of the water. To his expert eye, it was a hopeless case. He climbed the slope and swept his light downward.

Flat on his belly below, Tom Culver was floundering from place to place, feebly striving to plug an irregular circle of widening holes. His progress was that of a broken-backed animal. His arms would flail upward, grasp and wrench away a branch of an alder or a willow, stuff it into a hole, and tamp it down with such rubble as he could scrape up. Grandfather called to him to give over.

"You'll do no good there," he shouted. "She's going to breach." [2]

"You're a liar!" the pathmaster yelled. "What do you know about canal berm? Get down here and do some work."

---

[1] *berm*, the bank of a canal opposite the towpath

[2] *breach*, break, as in a dike

"I was plugging breach when you were mumbling pipsissiway suckets in your cradle, Tom Culver," Grandfather retorted, and held up his light.

"It's Squire Adams," Culver exclaimed. "You think she'll breach?"

"I know she'll breach. Get up and get out of there."

"I can't. My leg's broke and my ribs is stove in."

Grandfather went down and took him under the armpits and dragged him to refuge under Farmer Stitt's occupation bridge which the Commission had kindly built for the farmer to join the two sections of his land, separated by the canal.

"You used to be an Erie man yourself, Squire," he said between groans. "You know the saying, 'Once a canaller, always a canaller.' You're an older man than me, but I'm pathmaster here. Will you take my orders?"

"Yes, sir," Grandfather said.

"Get to your horse and raise the countryside."

"And leave you here with your broken bones?" Grandfather objected.

Tom Culver cursed him in full canal terms. "If she breaches now and we don't check her, she'll be the Falls of the Genesee, come morning," he said. "Here! Take my badge and whistle. You're Deputy Pathmaster of this section with full authority. Now get 'em out."

Grandfather paused, then said to us, "You might think it would be difficult to harry decent folk from their beds for a thankless task in the wind and rain of a black night, it being then close on to ten o'clock."

"Yes, sir," John assented.

"As it doubtless would be," the old gentleman continued, "in this thin-blooded age, when loyalty is a dull spark and patriotism the echo of Independence Day rhetoric. But to the York Stater of a hardier time the Grand Western Canal was the pride and glory of the nation, vaunted as the eighth wonder of the world.

We had wrought it with our hands and filled it with our sweat. We stood ready to fight and die for it. Our fervor was stimulated by the orators who rhapsodized it and the poets who sang of it in deathless numbers through the pages of the New York *Evening Post*."

"I wrote a commencement song about the Erie Canal," Jenny put in. "Fatty Cook, our principal, wouldn't pass it. He said I couldn't rhyme 'Erie' with 'We love you dearly.' Can't I, Grandpa?"

"Not with my approval," the old gentleman said, "however commendable the sentiment," and he resumed his account.

Remounting his mare, he said, he headed for Lyons. On the outskirts of the town he saw a light in Ephraim Rowbottom's tavern, Pride of the West, and pulled up. The innkeeper was sitting belatedly over his accounts.

"What fetches you out this foul night, Squire?" he cried.

"Erie's breached," said Grandfather. "Who's on your books?"

Ephraim consulted his day ledger. "Gents, sixteen; ladies, five," he said.

The new deputy stepped to the stair foot. "All good men and true, up and out!" he shouted. "Erie's breaching at Stitt's Crossing."

The stairwell was immediately lined with nightcaps. There was a sharp exchange of questions and answers. A quick poll was taken. Thirteen men agreed to go. The other three were too old.

"Report to Tom Culver at the occupation bridge," the official bade the volunteers.

With the thirteen from abovestairs he had made a good start. He went out into the night, and in a few rods riding was in the flourishing town of Lyons. Here he was confident of aid.

Being an active member of the Wayne County Horse-thief Society, a fraternal group ostensibly dedicated to stamping out horse-stealing, he knew where to find cooperation. He had but to locate the Honorary Chief Constable, whom he found playing draw poker at the Eagle House.

Within ten minutes, peaceful Lyons was a pandemonium. Churchbells pealed. Rifles and pistols cracked. A coachee paraded Main Street, blaring on his horn, and the 1812 carronade on the green wakened everybody for miles around with one tremendous BOOM! The air rang with rallying cries.

"Breached!" "She's breached!" "Erie's dreening out at Stitt's Crossing!" "All out to staunch the break!"

At the Eagle, Grandfather picked up the news for which he had been hoping. The hurry-up boat was moored in Harris's Basin, two miles west.

"Was it called 'hurry-up' because it went fast?" Charlie asked.

"Ten furious miles an hour with a bone in its teeth," Grandfather answered.

Every section of Erie, he explained, had its own patrol-and-repair boat. It was commanded by a section superintendent, manned by a picked crew of former canal builders—toughened experts, every one—and equipped with planks, girders, joists, ropes, chains, picks, spades, mauls, mattocks and other gear. Horses chosen for speed drew it.

Grandfather got back into the saddle and rode to Harris's Basin. No light showed aboard the hurry-up boat, but in a shack on the wharf a small betty-lamp burned low. Grandfather pounded on the door and shouted, "Breached!"

Everyone seemed to wake at once. Voices called in the dimness. Feet pattered. A man who had been sleeping in his clothes opened the door.

"I'm Superintendent Glenn," he said. "We've been expecting trouble. Where?"

"Stitt's Crossing."

"That's Tom Culver's section."

"Tom's hurt. I'm acting deputy."

The superintendent cupped his hands to his mouth. "Horses! Ready aboard in three minutes. Check your kits. Go with us?" This last to Grandfather.

"No. I've got to get more workers. You'll need 'em."

As he swung back into the saddle, he saw the crew swarming aboard the thirty-foot needleboat, and three impatient horses bent on to the towrope.

"Cast off!" snapped the Super and the boat was whisked away.

Easing his mount, for the pace had been hard, the deputy trotted back through Lyons and took to the towpath. From that vantage point he could spy out some of the side-road homesteads from which he might stir up aid.

Most of the roused inmates responded with alacrity. The Erie had brought a new and wonderful prosperity to their farms, for which they were grateful. If Clinton's Ditch was in danger, they would put in their best licks to save it. House after house gave up its volunteers.

As Grandfather was about to head back to Stitt's, cattle, huddled in the corner of a field, brought to his mind the realization that draft animals might be needed. A narrow trail led him to a darkened log house. Leaning from his saddle, he rapped smartly on the door.

A window opened, disclosing a gaunt figure of a man in a butternut nightshift and peaked headgear. A musket was leveled at the caller's midriff.

"It's loaded," the figure said.

"Put it down," said Grandfather. "I'm Deputy Pathmaster Adams. The canal's breaching."

"Let 'er breach," the man said. "It ain't my canawl." And he quoted a ribald jingle derisive of Governor Clinton.

Grandfather recognized the type. The man was a hater of the great Governor and his life-work, the Erie; a makebate, a dawplucker, a malcontent politicaster. Nevertheless he had two strong, workmanlike arms.

"We need your help," Grandfather told him.

"You don't git it."

"Not for pay?"

"That's different, Mister. How much?"

"Shilling an hour."

"You've hired you a hand."

"Got any critters?"

"Yoke of oxen."

"Six shillings for the night's work."

"Keno! You can have 'em."

"Got any boys?"

"Nope. Got a wife. She's old but she's hale. Four bits for her."

"Fetch her along," Grandfather said.

He wheeled the mare, feeling well satisfied with his evening's rounds. Counting Lyons, he figured, there should be a good hundred workers on hand to aid the hurry-up crew, who should be at the place by this time. He would report back there and surrender his brief authority to the Super.

At Stitt's Crossing, fires threw a red glare upon the low, dribbling clouds. As Grandfather broke through the brush into the open, a scene of wild confusion met his eyes. There were at least one hundred and fifty people scurrying about. More were arriving every moment, on foot, on horseback or muleback, or in home-made flats, poled on the lessening water. Nobody seemed to be in charge. Grandfather caught at the shoulder of a man who was dragging a spile toward the berm.

"Where's Tom Culver?" he demanded.

"In the barn yonder," the man answered. "Dead by this time, for all I know."

"Why isn't the hurry-up boat here?"

"Mudlarked two miles west, I hear."

"Who's running things?"

"Not knowin', can't say. Tail onto the end of this spile [3] if you want to help."

One spile was not going to do any good against the current that was pouring through the five-yard breach. Nor were the haphazard efforts of the unorganized crowd, so far as Grandfather could see. Lines of men were pushing wheelbarrows and dumping soil which was immediately washed into the cornfield below.

Others were busy with mauls and sledges, trying to put up a retaining wall. As fast as the piles were driven, the flood plucked them out and whirled them away. An unpleasant sound, as if a soft-mouthed giant were smacking his lips, reached Grandfather's ears. A shoulder of berm as big as a springhouse let go and slithered

---

[3] *spile*, heavy stake or beam

down, carrying with it several struggling volunteers, who floundered to safety as best they might. Of repair work on such a large scale, he had had no experience. But he remembered a saying of his father, the canal contractor: "For a big breach, big timber."

The wood in sight of where Grandfather stood was no better than toothpicks. He ran up on the occupation bridge and blew his whistle.

"Woodsmen and sawyers report here," he shouted.

A number of men came on the run. Here was someone who could tell them what to do. He sent them to Farmer Stitt's timber lot, an eighth of a mile east, with orders to fell and trim two-to-three-foot softwoods and float them in the water. The current would carry them to the breach.

One of the woodcutters protested that rolling logs of that size up the slope of the berm would be impossible. Grandfather blew his whistle again and called for ox teams. The canal-hater's oxen and another yoke plodded up, dragging their chains. They got their orders to snake the timber out and float it as fast as it was cut. Grandfather figured that the logs should begin to come down within half an hour.

"What were you going to do with the logs when you got them, sir?" John asked.

The old gentleman smiled. "That is what I kept asking myself every time another chunk of soil flaked loose from the berm. My only plan was to do the best I could and pray that it was right."

He was forming up a gang of polemen to handle the timber on its arrival, he went on, when the wind carried a bugle-note to his ears. ("Sweetest sound ever I heard in my life," he interpolated.) The hurry-up boat came foaming through the water, the hoggee whaling his tandem with an ox-quirt borrowed for the occasion. The boat had been pried loose of the mudbank and was making its best ten miles an hour.

Grandfather ran down to meet the Super who made a flying leap from the prow and stood, staring in dismay at the cataract that roared through the widening breach.

"Good Lord of mercies!" he groaned in Grandfather's ear. "Every keel between here and Montezuma Marsh will be mudlarked by sunup. If only we had timber."

"Timber coming down!" Grandfather assured him, and pointed.

As if in answer to prayer, the current whirled down toward them two fine tree boles, a hemlock and a sycamore. Recovering quickly from his amazement, the Super yelled, "Poles!"

His crew swarmed over the gunnels of the boat and took each his proper place. Grandfather's worries were lifted from his overburdened shoulders as the experts with their peaveys checked the speeding timber and prodded it into place. Exultantly he watched two more great logs come dashing down, then a group of half a dozen. Those woodsmen were doing a job. Grandfather got a pole for himself and fell to work.

At this point the old gentleman commanded pad and pencil and drew intricate designs to show us the wonders of engineering improvised by the hurry-up men to improvise a dam and save the berm. John may have understood. He assumed a knowing expression and put several appropriate questions; but the whole matter was beyond my comprehension. I was content with the conclusion, which was that when the sun broke through the clouds at dawn, the flood was under control.

The fires went out. The people went home. Farmer Stitt threatened to sue the Canal Commission for damage to ten acres of corn. Superintendent Glenn shook hands with Grandfather and offered him a permanent job. Grandfather curled up on the occupation bridge and went to sleep, still a Deputy Pathmaster on guard over his section.

"Did Tom Culver die?" Jenny asked.

"Not he," the old gentleman replied. "He lost his leg and his job. A one-legged pathmaster would not measure up to the standards of the Honorables, the Canal Commissioners of the State of New York."

Jenny, flushing with indignation, declared her conviction that the Honorable Canal Commissioners were old meanies.

"Do not misprize that body of just and patriotic men," the old gentleman rebuked her mildly. "They not only paid for Tom's

peg leg, but also voted him a pension of five dollars a month *in perpetuum*.[4] Upon this, eked out with what he could earn trapping musquashes at a dollar bonus, he lived handsomely to the ripe age of forty-five. The Grand Western Canal," Grandfather added with pride, "looked after its own."

---

[4] *in perpetuum*, forever

The man who wrote this story

SAMUEL HOPKINS ADAMS 1871–

Whether Samuel Hopkins Adams is writing an article, a short story, or a novel, he is, first and foremost, essentially a reporter—a man relating facts and events. Today, he is considered one of America's great reporters.

Mr. Adams began his career with the *New York Sun,* where he served for nine years. He spent five more years with *McClure Magazine* and then became a free-lance writer. One of his free-lance articles, a criticism of the patent-medicine business, strongly influenced the adoption of the Pure Food and Drug Act. His short stories have always been popular, many of them being made into outstanding motion pictures.

In 1940 Mr. Adams turned his abilities as a reporter to the re-creation of history, particularly to that period between 1800 and 1850. Whether he is writing about a national figure—as in his biography of Warren G. Harding—or about life in a mill town, he skillfully combines historical fact with narrative for good reading.

The setting for many of his most popular books is upstate New York and the Erie Canal country where he was born and raised. These books include *Canal Town* (1940), *Banner by the Wayside* (1947), *Sunrise to Sunset* (1950), and *Grandfather Stories* (1955), the book from which this selection was taken.

Let's consider . . .

1. Why did the Adams children worry about the dead muskrat? What did they expect would happen?

2. Why was John so quick to encourage Grandfather to tell one of his Erie Canal stories?

3. Why did Tom Culver need help? Why was Grandfather obligated to help him? Why might he have resented taking orders from Tom?

4. How did the "York Staters" feel about the Canal? What was Grandfather's opinion of the present generation?

5. Where did Grandfather find his first recruits? What happened at Lyons?

6. Grandfather said the hurry-up boat could make "ten furious miles an hour *with a bone in its teeth.*" What did he mean? What provided the power for moving the boat?

7. Why were most of the farmers along the Canal so willing to help? Which farmer wasn't? Why?

8. What plan did Grandfather work out for plugging the breach in the Canal?

9. What delayed the hurry-up boat? What did its crew do when they arrived?

10. At the end of the story, Grandfather came back to Tom Culver and his fate. Do you really think the Grand River Canal had "looked after its own"? Today, five dollars would hardly buy a week's groceries. Why might this sum have seemed adequate, if not generous, a hundred years ago?

The writer's craft . . .

Samuel Hopkins Adams wrote "The Big Breach" in an unusual and interesting way. He began with a story about himself and his cousins and their weekly visit to Grandfather. He even built up quite a little suspense over what Grandfather would do about the muskrat. But that story just provided the setting for the main story: the one Grandfather told about the big flood. Every once in a while, Mr. Adams would slip back into the first story to let the children make comments or ask questions to which Grandfather always had a reply before the main story continued.

In this way, the author played a dual role. Part of the time he was one of the children visiting Grandfather and listening to his story. Part of the time he was the storyteller relating to you, the reader, the story which he heard that day of the visit. Only a very skillful writer could keep two stories going at the same time and shift back and forth between them so naturally that you never lost your interest either in the children or in Grandfather's tale of adventure.

1. In a few sentences, tell the plot of the story about the cousins. The **plot** is what happens, the planned sequence of events. Remember that, at points, this story comes *into* Grandfather's story.

2. Now tell the plot of Grandfather's story: how he helped to stop the breach during the flood.

3. You learned to know Grandfather by seeing him through the eyes of his grandson Samuel. How did this understanding add to your appreciation of Grandfather as the leading character in the main story? Did he act as you expected he would? Do you think he made himself appear more of a hero than he really was?

4. Mr. Adams told Grandfather's story as he remembered it, just as you might tell the story of a book you had read or a movie you had seen. Yet he made you feel as though you were right there with Grandfather. Try to explain how the author achieved this effect. How much of the effect was due to the author's inclusion of **dialogue:** conversations between the characters in the story? Was the dialogue **consistent;** that is, was it the kind of conversation you would expect from those characters? Explain why.

Knowing words . . .

Grandfather was never at a loss for words to describe the dramatic, whether it was the enthusiastic turnout of recruits at Lyons or the frantic efforts to plug the breach. Sometimes his language was a little old fashioned, but it served its purpose.

Look up any of the words in the following paragraph which you might have difficulty explaining. Then discuss the dramatic effect which these few lines create.

"Within ten minutes, peaceful Lyons was a pandemonium. Churchbells pealed. Rifles and pistols cracked. A coachee paraded Main Street, blaring on his horn, and the 1812 carronade on the green awakened everybody for miles around with one tremendous BOOM! The air rang with rallying cries."

The Battle of Finney's Ford

JESSAMYN WEST

As a Quaker, Joshua was brought up to hate fighting. That is why his decision to take up arms in the War Between the States required unusual courage. "Good-bye, Joshua," his mother said. "I hope thee won't have to kill." With these parting words, the boy rode off to war.

Except for the name of Morgan the morning of the eleventh opened up like any other in July: clear, with promise of heat to come. Overhead arched the great cloudless sky of summer, tranquil above reports, the rumors, the whisperings, the fears. And above the true evidence. The evidence brought in by the eye witnesses; by the boy who had hid himself and horse in the thicket while Morgan's outriders galloped past; by the girl who had waded along the branch and was not seen; the stories of the burnings, the shootings, the looting.

The mind knew Morgan's name had altered the day, yet the untutored eye could find no difference, either in it or the horizon which framed it. Eliza, standing in the doorway of the summer kitchen, breakfast bell in hand, searched every crevice of the landscape, but in so far as she could see there was no shred of alteration in it. The cows, milked early, stood in the shade along the banks of the south branch; heat waves already rippled above the well-tasseled corn; the windmill turned round three or four times with considerable speed, then stopped, as if forever.

Eliza lifted her breakfast bell to ring, then let arm and soundless bell drop to her side. She felt a profound reluctance to disturb in any way the morning quiet.

She had a conviction unreasoning, but deep, that the sound of her bell might be all that was needed to shatter tranquillity, call up from out of the wood lot, or across the river side, John Morgan himself.

Jess looked down at his wife. "Thee want me to ring it?" he asked.

"No," Eliza said. "I'll ring it. The boys need to be called up for their breakfasts." But she did not raise her arm nor sound the bell. "All's so quiet," she said. "It gives me the feeling I'd oughtn't disturb it. As if ringing the bell might be the beginning . . . as if hearing it, John Morgan might ride up and say, 'Has thee any horses . . . any silver . . . any blankets?'"

"He don't ask, from what I hear," Jess said. "He takes."

"Ride up and take," Eliza said, as if digesting the fact. "Well, that's a happenchance. Flood or fire could do the same. One bolt of lightning's enough if it's the Lord's will. Talking's not my concern. It's what the boys would do."

"The boys?" Jess asked.

"Joshua," his wife answered.

Jess nodded.

"If hearing the name alone's enough . . ." Eliza began, "if the very sound of it's strong enough . . ."

"Yes," Jess said, nodding again.

Morgan's name had been heard in the southern counties before July, but it was in July that it began to be heard above everything else: above the rustle of the growing corn, the clack of mills, the plop of the big bass in the deep pools. Women churning stopped their dashers to listen, children stayed away from the wood lots, men worked quietly behind their horses, foregoing all talk lest their words muffle the approach of Morgan's scouts.

But it was the young men who listened most intently, the skin tightening across their cheek bones. Not with apprehension or fear so much as with wonder. What would they do? If the hoof beats along the wood's trace were made by John Morgan's men? If the press-gang said, "Unhitch your horses, bub, bring out your hams and bacon, show us where the old man keeps his silver." Would they unhitch, the young men wondered . . . hand

over Prince and Dolly, walk up through the fine dust of the field-path, lay the meat and silver on the outstretched hands? Would they? The young men did not know. They had no way of knowing.

Since childhood they had dreamed of resistance, but the foes they had resisted were mythical: the vanished Indian, the unseen highwayman, the long-gone river pirate, figures who fled easily, whose bullets ricocheted from resolute hearts. Morgan's men were not mythical, they did not flee, their bullets pierced even the most steadfast hearts. The young men at dusk on the river road, where the banks were shoulder high and fox-grapes, thick as curtains, hung between the shadowy trees, did not look back, nor hasten. But they listened. And wondered. And hearing nothing, were not reassured. Silence also was ominous.

Eliza once again lifted the breakfast bell. "Thee think I should ring it?" she asked.

"Ring it," Jess told her. "I got no mind to meet John Morgan on an empty stomach."

Breakfast was almost over when Joshua came in. He noted with astonishment the nearly empty gravy bowl, the meat platter with its single egg, the plates crusted with jam and biscuit crumbs. It was a wonder to him that people had been able on such a morning to sit down to the table, put gravy onto biscuits, spear slices of ham and then opening and shutting their mouths, chew such things with relish. Such eating, such self-concern, seemed, when their neighbors were dying, calloused and unspiritual.

It was not only that these men were their neighbors nor that their deaths were in a sense for them, since they had died defending beliefs Joshua and his family held dear: it was the whole matter of death to which Joshua was not yet reconciled. Nor was he reconciled to the apathy of his elders in the face of death, their indifference and mild acceptance. They said

Amen and God's will be done. This he could have borne, had he been convinced that they really suffered, that God's name and the Amen had not come easy. Old people, and for Joshua all who were somewhat advanced beyond his own eighteen years were old, did suffer when they lost a member of their own households. This, Joshua was ready to admit.

But Josh sorrowed over death as an abstract fact: he resented it for unknown men and women. He went without meals because of an item in *The Banner News* about a woman dead in a millpond in another county; because of a man dragged to death behind his team. He made himself forgo all one fall—in so far as he was able —any sight of the frosty, autumnal constellations in which he delighted because of a conversation of his mother's which he had overheard. After a long sickness stretching through more than a year (his mother had told a visitor) a young woman, whose name was Lydia, had said, "I know I must die, but I wish I could live long enough to see Orion outside my window once more." This girl (unknown to him) named Lydia had died, his mother said, in early August, long before Orion had come near her window. All that fall Joshua had kept his eyes off the evening sky, saying stubbornly, "I won't take anything she can't have. I won't look since she can't."

For the most part Josh kept these feelings to himself, for when they burst out, as they occasionally did, what his mother and father had to say about them angered him.

"Thee should rejoice, son," Eliza had once said when he had spoken sorrowfully of the death of a young boy who had gone through the ice and drowned. "Thee should rejoice. Young Quincy's in heaven, spared all this world's misery."

"Quincy didn't think this world was a miserable place," Joshua, who had known the boy, said.

"He'll find heaven a better place, Josh," his mother had insisted.

"He's cheated," Josh had flashed out. "He's cheated."

"Thee's not to question the Lord, Joshua," his mother said.

Ordinarily he was able to hear his father speak about death with more tolerance than his mother. His father was not so sure as his mother. Joshua saw that possibilities his mother had never laid an eye on opened their long avenues of chance to his father's sight. But his father had a kind of calm, a tolerant pliability which sometimes set Joshua's teeth on edge. Old people, Josh thought, get so eroded by time and events that they are as slippery as a handful of wettened stones at a branch bottom. Rolling and tumbling against each other, slippery as soap, not a single rough, jagged spot left with which to hold on—or resist, or strike out.

"Thee'll find a lot of things worse than death, Josh," his father had said to him one day—more as if reading his mind than answering anything Josh had spoken.

Joshua had answered his father sharply. "Death was a curse, wasn't it? A curse put on man for his disobedience?"

"Well, yes," Jess had said. "In a way thee can . . ."

But Joshua had not waited for qualifications. "What's worse than the Lord's curse? If the Lord put a curse on thee, thee'd be wrong to find anything worse, wouldn't thee?"

This logic seemed inescapable to Joshua, but his father, with his usual suppleness, escaped it. "The Lord's curses," he said mildly, "can usually be borne. There are some few man devises for himself that bite deeper."

Joshua never spoke of these things to his brother, Laban, but Labe once asked him, incuriously, Josh thought, and in his usual sleepy way, "Is thee afraid to die, Josh?"

Josh had not known what to answer. He was opposed to dying . . . was he afraid of it? He didn't know. He remembered being frightened, years ago, by sounds at night which he couldn't account for, being so frightened that the thumping of his heart had stirred the bed covers like a hand. Then he had been able to calm himself by thinking: What's the worst that can happen to me? Nothing but this: the burglar will creep nearer and nearer, finally give me one hard clunk on the head and I'll be killed. This had always calmed him, had seemed so insignificant a thing that he would cease listening and fearing and sleep.

That was imagined death, though, and imagined danger; the sounds he heard, perhaps mice in back of the studding or nails snapping in a heavy frost. If the death were real death—the sounds of danger real sounds? The click of the breech-lock in the musket before firing, a man's sucked-in-breath as he pressed the trigger? He didn't know.

"I don't know, Labe," he said. But like the other young men he wondered.

Now Josh stood with hands tightly clenched over the rounded top of the chair in which his brother, Little Jess, sat. He knew, in his self-conscious way, that his family was looking at him, and he made a strong effort to control his feelings. He was particularly aware of Labe's calm, cool gaze, and he supposed that Labe, in what he thought of as Labe's belittling way, was enumerating his own physical shortcomings (Labe who was muscular, smooth-jointed, supple): Built like a beanpole, black hair like a wig, high, burning cheek bones, a lopsided mouth that trembles when he's in earnest.

"What kept thee, son?" his father asked.

"I went over to Whiteys'," Josh said.

"Sit, sit, Josh," his mother bade, bustling up from her place. "I'll cook thee fresh eggs."

"I couldn't swallow an egg," said Josh.

"What do they hear at the Whiteys'?" asked his father.

"Morgan's heading this way—he's following the railroad up from Vienna. He's making for Vernon. He'll be here today or tomorrow."

"Vernon," said his mother. She put the two eggs she had in her hand back in the egg crock. Vernon was home. Josh had as well've said the Maple Grove Nursery. Or the south forty.

"How they know so much over at Whiteys'?" his father asked. "Morgan didn't cross the Ohio till evening of fourth day. Morgan's lost out there in the woods . . . got guerrillas trained to stay out of sight. Yet people'll sit at their breakfast tables and say just where John Morgan is. Tell you whether he's shaved yet this morning . . . and where he'll be this time tomorrow."

Josh felt, many times, like a stone beneath the cold waves of his father's detached unconcern. As if in spite of all he knew, and burningly believed, he would in time be worn down, effaced by all that ceaseless, quiet questioning.

"People at breakfast tables . . ." he began angrily, then stopped. "Ben Whitey was in Harrison County when Morgan crossed over. He's been riding ahead of him for three days."

"Did thee talk to Ben?" asked his father.

"Yes."

"What did he say?"

This shift of approach, this willingness to learn, cutting from beneath his feet ground for reasonable anger, angered Josh anew.

"Nothing about whether Morgan'd shaved yet, or not, this morning."

"Son," said his father, "sit thyself down and tell us. Get up, Little Jess. Give thy brother thy chair."

Little Jess went around the table to Eliza's chair and hung over his mother's shoulder, awaiting Josh's word. Josh himself, without intending to do so, sat suddenly in the chair that was pushed out for him—and also without conscious intent, began to chew hurriedly on a cold biscuit. His mother made a gesture toward passing him butter and jam, but Jess shook his head and said, "Well, Josh?"

Josh spoke rapidly, his voice a little muffled by dry biscuit crumbs. "Ben Whitey passed a dozen of Morgan's outriders last night camped down this side of Blocher. Not more'n twenty miles from Vernon. They're following the railroad. They'll raid Vernon."

"Raid Vernon," said his mother. "What does that mean?" It was a word whose meaning on the page of any book she knew perfectly well. But "Raid Vernon"—the town where she sold her eggs, the church town, the county fair town, with its white-washed brick houses, its quiet, dusty streets, its snowball bushes dangling their white blossoms over the unpainted picket fences—what did that mean? "Raid Vernon," she said once again as if the words themselves might somehow suddenly focus, as a stereopticon glass [1] did when given just the proper shove, to show a landscape, lifelike in its dimensions, distances—and ruin.

Josh knew what the word meant. Ben Whitey had told him. "Raid means," he said, "burn, kill, take what you want."

"Are Morgan's men killing people?" Eliza asked.

For a second the world his mother saw flickered before Josh's eyes: a world of such loving companionableness that the word war had no other meaning for her than murder; where deliberate killing was unthinkable as though in her own household son should turn on son; but it flickered for a second only, then disappeared, leaving him angry again.

"Doesn't thee know there's a war?" Josh asked with intensity. "Doesn't thee know what a war is?"

"Thy mother knows there's a war, Josh," his father reminded him, "but she don't know what a war is. Let alone what a war in Vernon'd be like. She's more used to think of caring for people than killing them."

<hr />

[1] *stereopticon glass,* a device through which an observer views two pictures of the same object taken at slightly different angles, producing the effect of depth

"John Morgan thinks of killing them," Josh said. "He shot a boy through the legs who didn't run fast enough. He shot an old man in the back. I don't know how many's dead in Harrison County. Ben Whitey said he could smell the smoke of Morgan's burnings the whole way up. He said he didn't think there was a mill left standing in Harrison County. He said the country's scoured of horses—and anything else in any house a trooper wanted and could carry across his saddle-bow."

Eliza leaned across the table. "The earth," she said, "and the fullness thereof is the Lord's. What's Morgan's men but a ruckus of boys with their pants in their boots? Trying to get something they've never had a taste of before? We've got more'n we need here. High time we're called on to share it with someone. If John Morgan's men came here," Eliza said—and Josh saw his mother's eyes turn toward the door of the summer kitchen as if she saw there a dusty, slouch-hatted trooper, "I'd offer them the best I had on hand. No man's my enemy," she said.

Josh stood up, crumbling in one hand the biscuit he had been quickly munching. "Some men are my enemies," he said. "Any man's my enemy who kills innocent men and makes slaves. They're my mortal enemies."

Josh felt his sister Mattie's hand, long-fingered—and cold for so warm a morning—touch, then feel its way into his clenched fist, and he gave way to its insistent downward pressure and sat again. "I will share with my friends," he said. "If thee gives all thee's got to a thief, thy friends will have to go hungry—there's not enough to go round. What's good about that?" he asked.

No one answered his question, but Jess said evenly, "Tales like these are always a part of war times."

Tales were lies. Josh picked up a case-knife and tried to ease off some of his feelings in clenching it. "Ben Whitey don't lie . . . some he saw with his own eyes

. . . some was told him. He saw the fires . . . he heard the people whose horses were stolen. He saw an outrider with a bird-cage and bird looped to his saddle. They said he'd been carrying that bird all the way from Maukport."

Josh was interrupted by his mother. She had started up, taken two steps toward the kitchen window where Ebony, the starling, hung in his cage. There, after the two steps, she stopped, stood stock still in her tracks, as if just then aware of what she'd been doing. "This is thy chance," Josh told himself, "to keep thy mouth shut, not shove a contradiction down thy mother's own throat." But he could not do it. He wrapped his hand round the cutting edge of the case-knife, but there was not enough pain in its blunt edge to divert him.

"I thought thee said," Josh told his mother, his mouth trembling with scorn for himself, "that this was our chance to share? Thee's got a good chance now to share Ebony. Thee's had that bird a long time and every single man riding with Morgan's never had him once in his life time."

Eliza turned back facing the table and her family. Josh gazed at his mother's neat, dark head, saw her black eyes move for a moment toward the head of the table where his father sat, then turn resolutely toward himself. "I was thinking he might be mistreated," she said. "I've grown over-fond of the particular."

"Mistreated," Josh shouted, ignoring her admission. "Thee can worry about a bird's being mistreated while men are being shot. Thee'd try to save it and not turn thy hand to help the men. No man's thy enemy . . . unless he tries to take thy bird. Every man's enemy is my enemy. I'd do as much any day for a man as a bird."

Jess and Labe both started at once to speak, but Eliza held up her hand, as if she were in meeting. "I was wrong, Josh-ua," she said. "I'd give Ebony to any man who'd care for him."

"Care for him," Josh again shouted.

"Thee was right the first time. Thee think that bird Ben Whitey saw's alive now? Its neck's been wrung long ago. If it was a big bird it's been boiled and eat. Ebony'd end up in no time on a forked stick over a fire."

Joshua leaned across the table toward his mother, gesturing with the case-knife, making Ebony the whole issue of war and peace, of life and death; talking to Eliza, but for his whole family . . . for Labe . . . to hear and contradict. "Thee has re-sponsibilities. Thee can't just take birds and make them tame. Slit their tongues and fatten them so's they can't fly. Then let anybody grab them. And cook them. Thee don't have any right to be good and generous to such a price. A price thee don't pay. Old Ebony's got to pay that price. And that old man. And the boy shot in the legs. And the Harrison County Militia. And the Vernon Militia. I'd rather die," Josh said.

There was a long silence about the breakfast table. Eliza reseated herself. Little Jess looked from face to face with nervousness. He was embarrassed when grown-ups showed emotion. He thought it did not suit their faces. He saw it break the smooth surface of authority and knowl-edgeability with which they were accus-tomed to front him. And without that where were they? And where was he? Lost, not a thing to fall back on, flounder-ing from notion to notion.

Mattie gazed at Ebony, jauntily cracking sunflower seeds in his wooden cage. She saw there both her mother's bird, who was first of all God's bird, and now was no man's bird, but belonged to all, and she saw Joshua's bird, the defenseless pet who would be plucked like a chicken and eaten unless they were willing to fight and die for him. And because she oscillated between the two ways of seeing Ebony, she suffered: when she was generous and peaceful, as was her mother, she thought herself a coward, and when she was, like Joshua, ready to fight (she supposed) she felt herself a renegade, an outcast from faith and scriptures.

Only Labe sat quietly at the table, his calm face touched neither by sorrow nor eagerness. One way only opened before him, and except that he believed this to be a matter between his mother and brother, and presently his father, he would have spoken, and said better words, he thought, for loving all men than his mother had said. And he would have gotten that bird from out the center of the conversation, where its feathers, its litter, its long periods of sulky quiet muffled and strangled the thing they should be really speaking of.

In the long silence . . . while there was no talk, sounds of great clarity filled the room. All, except Little Jess, harkened to them as if they were omens; as if each, properly apprehended, might carry some kind of a revelation: the slow grating start of the windmill easing into rhythmic clicking as the wind freshened; two distant notes as old Bess the bell-cow reached forward toward uncropped grass; the prolonged, sweet morning trill of a warbler, who, uncaged and undesired either by raiders or raided, flew, singing, near the windows, then flipped out of sight.

Jess, from his place at the head of the table, looked down toward his eldest son. He bent upon him a face of so much love and regard—and good humor, too, as if behind this talk of war there were still a few reasons to laugh—that Josh thought he might be unable to bear his father's gaze, would have to lay his arms across the table and bury his face in them, and so hidden, say, "Yes, pa," or "No, pa," to whatever his father had to say. But as his father continued to gaze, quizzically and lovingly, Josh knew that he had left behind him forever the happy time of freedom from decision and sat very straight, back teeth clamped together, lips trembling, waiting his father's word.

"Thee knows, Josh," his father said, "dying's only half of it. Any of us here, I hope"—and Jess included Little Jess and Mattie in the nod of his head—"is ready to die for what he believes. If it's asked of us and can be turned to good account. I'm not for dying, willy-nilly, thee understands," Jess said, his big nose wrinkling at the bridge. "It's an awful final thing, and more often than not nobody's much discommoded by it, except thyself, but there are times when it's the only answer a man can give to certain questions. Then I'm for it. But thee's not been asked such a question, now, Josh. Thee can go out on the pike, and if thee can find John Morgan, die there in front of him by his own hand if thee can manage it, and nothing'll be decided. He'll move right on, take Ebony, if he's a mind to, though I give John Morgan credit for being a smarter man than that and thee'll be back there on the pike just as dead and just as forgotten as if thee'd tied a stone round thy neck and jumped off Clifty Falls. No, Josh, dying won't turn the trick. What thee'll be asked to do now—is kill."

The word hung in the air. A fly circled the table, loudly and slowly, and still the sound of the word was there . . . louder than the ugly humming. It hung in the air like an open wound. Kill. In the Quaker household the word was bare and stark. Bare as in Cain and Abel's time with none of the panoply of wars and regiments and campaigns to clothe it. Kill. Kill a man. Kill thy brother. Josh regarded the word. He explored it, his hand tightening again about the knife.

"I know that," he said. "I am ready to fight." But that wouldn't do. He could not pretend that he was ready for the necessary act so long as he flinched away—from even the word. "I will kill these men if I have to."

"No, Josh," Eliza said.

Josh was glad to be relieved of the need of facing his father and regarding death abstractly. He turned to his mother. "Yes," he said. "I will. I'm going to meet Ben Whitey at eight. Soon as he's had two hours' rest. The Governor's made a proclamation. Every man's to join the Home Guard and help defend his town. We're going right down to Vernon and join. Morgan'll be there any time. I'd ought to've gone a week ago."

"Joshua, Joshua," cried his mother. "Thee knows what thee's turning thy back on? On thy church. On thy God. Thy great-grandfather came here with William Penn to establish ways of peace. And he did," Eliza declared passionately. "With savage Indians. Men of blood. Now thee proves thyself to be worse than the Indians. They kept the peace."

Josh felt better. The picture of himself as bloodier than a savage Indian was so fantastic it hid for the time such savagery and bloodthirstiness as he did possess— and hid too, what Josh felt to be, perhaps even worse, his lack of these qualities. "The Indians," he said, "weren't dealing with John Morgan."

Jess spoke. First that bird, now William Penn and the Indians. The human mind could move, if it moved at all, only from symbol to symbol and these so chosen that sharp and even final issues were padded enough to make them more tolerable. "Josh," he said, "those who take the sword shall perish by it."

They were back to dying: only a nicer word. "I am ready to perish," said Josh.

But Jess wouldn't let them stay there. " 'Thou shalt not kill,' " said Jess.

There it was. "But He said, 'Render unto Caesar the things that are Caesar's,' " Josh said desperately. "I live here—in Jennings County. My town is Vernon. The Governor said to defend it. My body is my country's."

"Thy soul, son, is God's."

"God won't want it," Josh said, "if I don't do what I think's my duty." He was standing again, half crying, a horrible way for a man to be starting to war. "Thee can live with God now, maybe. I can't. I don't want to die . . . and I don't even know if I could kill anyone if I tried. But I got to try," he said, "as long as people around me

have to. I'm no better'n they are. I can't be separated from them."

He left the table and ran toward the kitchen stairway. "I'm going," he said. "I'm meeting Ben Whitey at eight."

As he went up the stairs he heard his father say, "No, Eliza, no."

In his room Josh said, "Packing to go to war," but it didn't mean much. He scarcely believed it; though the pain that started at the bottom of his throat and seemed to run the whole length of his chest told him this was no ordinary departure. There wasn't much packing to do. Extra socks, Ben Whitey said. Spare hand-kerchiefs—good in case of a wound. Stout shoes—he had them on. A heavy coat— no telling how long they'd be in the field; they might have to chase Morgan the length of the state. Musket—his musket was always oiled, cleaned, ready; shot—he didn't know whether he had enough or not. He didn't know how many . . . He didn't know how good he'd be at . . . Knife —yes. Cup—he'd get that downstairs, and the tin plate. Two blankets to roll round all the stuff, saddle old Snorty—Morgan'd have to be a pretty slow runner if old Snorty was ever to catch up with him.

He was finished. Getting ready for war was a short horse and soon curried, it seemed. There was nothing to do now but go. He'd keep that a short horse, too, but it'd be a horse of a different color. Josh marveled at himself. Cracking jokes, for that was what it was even though there was no one to hear. Ten minutes ago he'd been crying, his mouth full of death, duty and the scriptures, and here he was dry-eyed, a pain in his chest, to be sure, but somewhat outside the whole matter, far enough apart, anyway, to say it was like this or that. It was very peculiar—but the pain itself lay like a bar between him and what had gone before. There was the pain, wide, heavy, real, and he needn't, in-deed he couldn't cross over it to explore its causes.

He looked about the room—his and Labe's—neat, orderly, the bed covers tossed back to air, the way his mother had taught them, clothes on pegs, chest drawers closed. He felt as if he wanted to say a prayer of some kind . . . God, take care of this room, or something like that, but he thought perhaps he'd better not. He wasn't sure God was with him in this move, in spite of what he had said downstairs, and there was no use involving Him in something He wouldn't approve. He'd picked up his bed-roll to go when Mattie came in. He would rather have seen almost anyone else.

As far as Josh could tell Mattie acted parts from morning to night: very delicate and fainty at one hour like she's too fine-haired to live on a farm, the next loud and yelling as if she had Comanche blood and a quarter section wasn't big enough to give her scope. She'd help him with a piece of work, doing more than her share, one time —the next sit half a day on a tree-stump, breathing, Josh supposed, but giving no sign of it.

"Oh, Joshua," said Mattie.

Josh held onto his bed-roll. Mattie'd been crying and Josh wasn't sure who he was seeing: sister Mattie or actress Mattie. A little of both, maybe, but when she threw her arms around his neck he thought he knew which one was clasping him most warmly.

"Oh, Joshua," said Mattie again.

"I've got to go, Matt," Josh said. "I'm late now."

Mattie took her arms down. "Josh," she said, "I want thee to take this." She had a little New Testament in her hand and she reached up and slipped it gently into Josh's shirt pocket. "There," she said. "Over thy heart it will guard thee from all harm." Then in her natural voice she added, "I read about two soldiers who'd've been shot through the heart except for their Bibles." Then sister Mattie was hidden away again, lost behind inclined head and folded hands.

Josh couldn't help laughing, so long and loud he was surprised.

"What's so funny?" Mattie asked. "Thee setting up to be an atheist?"

"No," Josh said, "I ain't. I'll take it, and read it, too, maybe." He put the little book in his hip pocket.

"Thee going to sit on it?" Mattie asked.

Josh shouldered his bed-roll again and went to the door. "It's the one sure foundation," he said.

"Why, Josh Birdwell," said Mattie. She had come upstairs expecting a pious and tearful farewell, and here was Josh laughing and joking, and not very reverently, either. Outside the door Josh turned back to reassure his sister. "Thee don't sit on thy hip pockets," he said. "Thee sits between them."

Mattie said feebly, "Good-bye, Josh."

The rest of the good-byes, Josh figured, had been said, in as far as they could be said, downstairs about the breakfast table. He went quietly out the front door and to the barn without seeing anyone. Not until he had saddled and tied his bed-roll to the saddle and led old Snorty out into the sunny barnyard did he see his mother and Little Jess standing at the bottom of the lane waiting for him. Seeing them, he was glad they were there.

Eliza's face was very serious but she wasn't crying. She held up a package to Josh. "Here's food, Josh. You'll have to eat. I didn't know what was best. This's mostly meat and cold biscuits."

Thinking of food Josh remembered the forgotten tin cup and plate.

"Run fetch them, Little Jess," Eliza said. "Be lively," she called after him. "Josh mustn't be late."

Josh let old Snorty's reins hang and laid his arms about his mother's shoulders, hugging her tight.

"Good-bye, Joshua," his mother said, and then not a word about his coming home safe, only, "I hope thee doesn't have to kill anyone." Joshua shut his eyes for a minute. "If thee has to die that's thy own business and thee won't anyway unless it's the Lord's will—but, oh, son," Eliza said, "I hope thee don't have to kill."

Josh opened his eyes and smiled. That was just the right thing to say . . . the words he would've chosen for her. He patted his mother's shoulder. Sticking by her principles and not getting over-fond of the particular—even when it was her own son. Josh bent and kissed her. He could not have borne it if she had broken down, put his safety first.

"Good-bye," Josh said. "Don't thee worry. I'll be shaking too hard to hit or get hit." He kissed his mother and got into the saddle. Eliza made a gesture toward him of love and farewell and walked resolutely back up the lane.

Little Jess trotted along the pike beside Josh for a way. Before turning homewards he held onto the stirrup for a minute and whispered fiercely up to his brother, "Thee shoot one for me, Josh." Josh then, looking down into Little Jess' drawn face and lips thinned with whispering, saw that no man acted to himself.

Josh was to meet Ben Whitey at the Milford cut-off, but even now, riding alone, he supposed he was a soldier and he tried to carry himself, through the warm morning and down the dusty road, like a Home Guardsman: scanning the horizon for signs of smoke or dust, keeping an eye out for single horsemen. There was no telling; if outriders of Morgan's were only twenty miles away last night, they could easily be in this neighborhood now.

In spite of his conviction that his intentions made him a militia-man, sworn to hunt down and stop or kill John Morgan, Josh would fall into looking at the farmland with a country man's eyes: sizing up a field of wheat unaccountably left standing, or noting how the apples were shaping up in an orchard. To offset this he stopped and loaded his gun. If he were to meet or sight a raider it would be his duty to shoot. He tried to think how it would be to come

upon a man, emerging from the woods, say, or around a sharp turn, not speak, not pause to pass the time of day, but instantly with raised musket fire and hope to blow the stranger's head off. The idea made Josh sweat. My God, Josh thought or prayed—he didn't know which—I hope it's no boy or old man. I hope it's some hard, old slave-driving bugger. Thinking of this hard old slave-driving bugger Josh remembered that he might be a man handy with firearms himself, and he settled deeper into the saddle and listened more intently.

The pain he had felt in his chest after breakfast was gone: in its place he now had in his middle a curious, dry, empty, swollen feeling. As if he carried something inside him, hollow, but beyond his size and growing bigger.

Ben Whitey was waiting for him at the Milford cut-off, impatient, fuming. "You're half an hour late," he yelled.

"I know it," Josh said. "We'll make up for it now," but they were only fairly started when Ben, looking back down the pike, said, "Looks like Labe on Rome Beauty. He joining too?"

"No," Josh said, "he's got convictions the other way."

"Well, you forgot something then," Ben Whitey said, "and your ma's sending it you." He rode on while Josh turned back to meet Labe.

Labe came up at a long trot, the only kind Rome Beauty had, dismounted and said, "Get on. Father said for thee to take Rome."

Josh sat atop old Snorty, unmoving, unbelieving.

"Get down," said Labe. "If thee's going to fight Morgan, fight him. Don't set there like a bump on a log."

"Father's against my going," said Josh.

"He's against it, but that didn't stop thee. Now get on. He says as far as he knows, Rome's no Quaker. From all he can tell thee and Rome think about alike. Get on."

Josh got off Snorty, transferred his bed-roll to Rome's saddle and stood in the dusty road beside his brother. He was taller than Labe but Labe's shoulders and stance made him feel small.

"Tell Father—" he began, but Labe interrupted him.

"Father said to tell thee most killing's caused by fear . . . . Rome's being under thee ought to help a little. He don't send thee Rome because his mind's changed about anything."

"Labe," Josh asked, "thee don't think about going?"

"No," said Labe, "I don't."

"I got to," said Josh. "Otherwise I'd always think maybe it was because . . ."

"Get on," said Labe, giving him no time to finish.

Astride the big red horse Josh rode after Ben Whitey, but before he overtook him he finished his sentence. "I am afraid," he said.

"You got a fine mount now," Ben Whitey told him when he drew alongside. "If you can just keep his nose headed the right direction you ought to make out."

"Never thee fear," Josh began . . . but he shut his mouth at that point. "Thee don't know," he told himself.

They rode into Vernon together; a roan, and a claybank, two rawboned farm boys: Ben Whitey, a born fighter, and Josh who was trying to do his duty. They entered Vernon and saw it the way a man who thinks he has been dreaming wakes and sees the landscape of his dream lying all about him, the disaster real, hard and unmelting as sunlight—and dreaming the only means of escape. Deep in the country, on the farms they had believed—and not believed. To come here with loaded guns had been an act of faith and now their faith was justified. Morgan was true; he existed; he was killing and looting; he would be here at any hour. There were tens of mouths to tell them.

The town blazed under the July sun; it throbbed with the heat of the season—and the heat of fear and excitement and wonder and resolution. At first Josh thought it was alive as he had seen it for an August fair or Fourth of July celebration. And there was something of a holiday spirit in the plunging, headlong activity. As if fifty years of seeing the Muscatatuck rise and fall, the crops ripen and be harvested, the summer rains harden and whiten into winter's snow and hail, were enough for Vernon, as if tired now of this placid punkin-butter existence, they would turn to something with sharper flavor.

That was the surface: the movement, the shouts, the numbers of horses in the street, the vehicles, the laughter even. That was what Josh saw when he saw everything at once and heard everything at once. A medley in which all the sounds, blending, were a holiday roar; all the sights, the excess movements of celebration when steps reach higher and higher into the air, bows go lower and lower toward earth and smiles strain at the limitations of a single face.

When he saw the sights, one by one, there was no holiday in them. There were spring wagons full of women, children and bedding headed for back country farms and supposedly greater safety.

"No sense in that," Ben Whitey said. "That way a couple of outriders can pick up the best any household has to offer without being put to the bother of ripping up the feather ticks and taking the insides out of clocks."

But in spite of what Ben Whitey thought, they were there: spring wagons, democrats, gigs, buckboards, all filled with women, children and valuables, and headed for back country and the hills. There were men throwing shovelfuls of earth out of deep holes, preparing to bury silver, money, keepsakes: whatever they and their wives cherished and thought a raider might fancy. There were boys barricading doors, boarding up windows, reinforcing bolts. There was a man who had turned his house into a store and was now busy ripping down his sign and trying to make his store look like a house again. There was an old fellow atop the gable of his house, peering off to the south through a long spy-glass. The voices, too, when Josh listened were not celebrating anything; they rasped; they started even, then broke; a man began yelling, looked around, ended whispering.

"Let's get out of this," Ben Whitey said. "Let's find the Home Guard."

They pulled up beside a one-legged man calmly taking his ease on a street corner.

"Where's Morgan?" yelled Ben Whitey.

"Don't know for sure. Reports are thicker'n toads after a rain, but he's near. Hear tell the old boy slept in Lexington last night."

"We're here to join the Home Guard," said Ben.

" 'Bout a week late," said the one-legged man, sucking on a cold pipe.

"We know that," Ben told him, "but we come up as fast as we could. We're here now. We got prime mounts and we'll give good accounts of ourselves. Where's the commander?"

"Not sittin' around recruiting."

Ben Whitey put his heel in his horse's flank. "Come on back," yelled the one-legged man. More quietly he said, "You johnnies rile me, though. Every drumstick of a boy comes in here from back country, brasher'n a parched pea, and ready to spit in old Johnnie Morgan's eye. It'll take more spit'n you got, bub, or I miss my guess. Morgan's clear grit, ginger to the backbone and no more fear in him than a rifle."

"Which side you on?" Ben asked.

"Our side. I'm for whipping Morgan but you ain't gonna do it by . . ."

"Save thy breath to cool thy broth," Josh said. "Where's the Home Guard?"

"Well, God kiss me," said the peg-legger. He took his pipe from his mouth and elevated his weather-beaten chops as if awaiting the salutation. "A Quaker sure's the Lord made Moses. What's thee planning to do, sonny? Pray for the boys?"

"Come on," said Ben and the two rode on down the street.

"How we going to get any place with men like that?" Josh asked.

"They ain't all like that," said Ben.

From across a picket fence an old man beckoned to them. "Want to mix in it?" he asked.

"That's what we're here for. Where's the Home Guard?"

"Everywhere," said the old man. He picked up the end of his long beard and used it to point with. "Spread thin, but mostly to the south. Morgan could circle us—but reports are he's hitting us solid from the south. Coming up the railroad from Vienna. They got companies posted at every ford, road and bridge south of town."

"Where you figger we could do the most good?"

"The bridge below the Forks. I been thinking about this for two days. I figger John Morgan being the man he is will come straight in, cross the bridge and bust into town from there. If you want to get in some telling licks, that's the place I'd head for."

"That's the place we want," Ben said.

The Muscatatuck where it is bridged below the Forks flows between banks of considerable height. Here the Home Guard Commander had massed as many men as could be spared from the other approaches to Vernon. Of these, the majority and among them the men Colonel Williams considered most steady and level headed were stationed on the west bank of the stream ready to fall upon the raiders should the smaller force which was holding the approaches to the bridge be overpowered. The Colonel hoped to stop by show of force, if possible, if not, by force itself any thrust the raiders might make before they reached the bridge. Failing this the guard on the west bank would have a fine chance to pick off the men as they debouched [2]

------

[2] *debouched*, emerged; marched out

from the bridge and headed toward town.

That was the plan. The captain in command of the river could use as many men as he could get and when Ben and Josh showed up, well mounted, he sent them at once to join the company beyond the bridge.

"They're headed this way," the captain told them. "Some of them," he said, pointing, "are sitting right there on top of that hill. Them, we fooled. Our men marched across the cliff road and then out of sight of Morgan—if he's there—a half dozen times over. Musta looked like quite an army to him. But there's likely others and they may be here soon. If we don't stop them nothing will. Once they're past us, it will be Maukport and Salem and Lexington all over again. Keep your guns handy. Dismount and rest your horses, but stay by them and keep them quiet. I'm glad you're here. I need you."

Overhead the July sun had weight as well as heat. It lay across Josh's shoulders like a burning timber. Though Ben was on one side of him, and big Gum Anson, a beefy farmer, was on the other, still Josh felt bereft of shelter, unshielded and alone —a naked target.

For a long time he scanned the road before him with rigid and unrelaxing vigilance. There was not much to be seen: the dusty road, the lush growth of summer, dock, volunteer oats, some daisies, a small field of shoulder high corn, and beyond these a thicket and the road curving out of sight around it. Above earth and river and the river's rank growth were the heat waves, the massive clouds of noon skies, the burning sun. Josh, who felt as if the whole duty of seeing and apprising rested with him, inspected every leaf and shadow. When a sudden movement of air fluttered the leaves of the elders up the road and rasped through the corn he lifted his gun, then put it down shamefacedly. He could feel the sweat trickle down the sides of his chest, then drop to his middle and soak in around his belt.

"Have some cherries," said Gum. "You can't keep that up all afternoon." He held out a big bag. The cherries were cool and firm and Josh took a handful.

"When Nance brought these out this morning," Gum said, "I'd've thrown 'em down except to please her. Goin' off to fight Morgan with a bag of cherries tied to my saddle like a doggone picnicker." He munched away and spat pits. "Looks like they might be the handiest article I brought."

"Wait'll Morgan gets here, Gum," somebody yelled. "It's gonna take more'n cherry-stones to stop that old shite-poke."

"I got more'n cherry-stones," Gum called back and the men around him laughed.

Josh shifted in his saddle and looked around. He was amazed at the sound of laughter, amazed that men waiting to kill or be killed should laugh and joke. He scanned the faces of those who were laughing: old fellows, middle-aged farmers, boys younger than himself. Sweating, chewing tobacco, some lolling in their saddles. Most, dismounted. Some in uniform, others not. Mounted on farm plugs. Mounted on fast animals he had seen at county fairs. Every kind of firearm. One man with a bayonet even. The sight of that lifted Josh up in his saddle again. Did the raiders carry bayonets? His sweating which he had not noticed for a while had started up once more.

"Have some more cherries?" asked Gum.

Josh took another handful. "Thanks," he said. "I was awful dry. And hungry, too. I can't remember when I had anything to eat last."

"Go kinda slow on them cherries, then. They don't set too good on'n empty stomach."

"They're setting good on mine," Josh said, chewing and spitting, but keeping his eyes up-road.

"Take it easy," advised Gum. "You'll be petered out before Johnnie gets here. They's scouts up ahead. They'll let us know if anything's twitchin'."

Josh felt a fool not to have thought of that before rearing up till his backbone was petrified, and staring till his eyes popped, acting like he was scout, trooper, captain, everything; the other men were relaxed, guns dangling or laid across their bed-rolls; some smoking; a man behind him was having a nip of something that didn't smell like switchel.

"Old Morgan'll never come this way," one bearded farmer was saying. "That boy's shiftier than a creased buck. He ain't never goin' to fight his way in the front door when the back door's open."

"Back door ain't so all-fired open's you might think."

"Open or shut—what's it to Morgan? With five thousand men you go in where it pleasures you and don't wait for the welcome mat to be put out."

"Five thousand," somebody yelled. "What we doing here? Why ain't we making a good hickory [3] for Indianapolis?"

"Indianapolis, boy? You better stay clear of there. Morton's waitin' for you there with a writ."

"Five thousand or ten thousand," said a quiet voice, "I'm going to stay right here. I'm going to give Morgan the butt-end of my mind if nothing else before he busts over that bridge and into my store."

"Me too. Only I'm goin' to talk with lead. My folks live down in Harrison County."

"Did you hear about old man Yardell?"

"Ya—shot in the back."

"Not doin' a thing—just come to his door to see what the ruckus was about."

"Did you hear about 'em down at Versailles? Had the cannon loaded, ready to let go smack dab in the middle of the rebs."

"What happened?"

"Cannoneer dropped his coal and before they could get another the rebs took the gun."

"Oughta court-martial the feller who done that."

" 'Fore the afternoon's over, Grogan,

[3] *making a good hickory,* making a run

you'll likely change your tune as to that."

The afternoon wore on. To the funky smell of the river and of lush river growth was added that of sweating men and horses. Josh eased Rome's girth and hoisted his blankets so a little air could flow under them. Back in the saddle he felt light-headed and detached. Gum had been right about the cherries; they weren't setting right. He felt kind of sick but happy. He'd got here, he was all right, he was where he belonged. By twisting about he could see a curve of the Muscatatuck where it flowed in shallow ripples across a sandbar, then darkened as the channel deepened near the bridge. It was three or four o'clock. The sun went through the water and onto the sandbar, then flashed, pulsing with the movement of the water in his temples. He could see the silvery glint of the little minnows, like bullets; a dragon-fly ran its darning needle in-and-out—in-and-out of the flowing water. It was July . . . a summer afternoon . . . the cool water . . . the hot sun . . . the darting . . . the silver bullets.

Josh's neck stiffened, his head snapped up, his hand closed round the stock of his gun. A horseman was pounding up the road.

"It's one of our scouts," said Ben Whitey.

The rider, a little fellow in uniform on a lathered black, pulled up beside the captain. Josh couldn't hear what he was saying, but after a minute the captain turned and told them, his voice quiet but with an edge to it that let them know that this was it, the time had come.

"Boys," he said, "they're closing in. They're up the road a couple of miles. Less of 'em than we figured. I expect them to charge. There's just two things to remember: first, stand steady. Second, don't fire till I give the word." He stood in his stirrups and pounded the words home. "Don't fire till I give the word. If you fire before you can make your shots good, it's all over. They'll ride you down. Hold it.

Your guns carry just as far as theirs, and you're better shots. Those men've been in the saddle for weeks now, and it's telling on them. Shoot low so's if you miss a man you get a horse. But don't miss."

The scout went on past them at a gallop and Josh could hear the black's hooves ring out on the bridge planking, then quiet as he hit the dust of the road on the west bank where the men in hiding were waiting the news. The captain himself wheeled round to await the attack with his men.

Josh reached for his gun. Waves of something, he didn't know what, were hitting his chest. It's like riding through the woods and being hit by branches that leave thee in the saddle, but so belabored thy chest aches, he thought. Other waves, or perhaps the same ones, pounded against his ears, broke in deafening crashes as if he were deep under water, buffeted by currents that could break bones, could rip a man out of his flesh and let him run, liquid, away. Then, in the midst of the pain and crashing, Josh thought, It's thy heart beating. Nothing but thy heart.

Gum said, "Fix those lines, boy." And again, "Get those reins fixed. If your horse jerks his head he'll spoil your aim."

Josh saw that Gum was right. He got his hand out of the reins and rubbed it

along Rome's neck. "Good boy," he said. "Good old Rome. Thee'll be all right." He knew he was encouraging himself. Rome didn't need cheering—he stood solid as a meeting house, only his big head moving up and down a little.

They were all waiting. Ben Whitey was cussing, a long line of words as if he was dreaming, or singing, in a kind of funny way. But they were mostly quiet—listening. Something came down, or perhaps it came up, out of the earth, something very thin and fine, like a spun web, and held them all together. Josh could feel it. Anybody could break away from it, if he liked, but while they headed the same way, waited the same thing, it held them. You could lean against it like steel. Josh felt its support . . . the waves beat against him, but he leaned against the fabric and it held him.

It held him until he heard the first sounds: a rebel yell from up the road, beyond the elder thicket—then another. Josh never knew a man could make a sound like that. It was a screech such as

an animal might make—only it was in a man's voice, a voice that could say "Farewell" or "Rain tomorrow" . . . and that made it worse. It sounded crazy . . . it sounded as if the tongue that gave it could lap blood. It broke the web that held them together, it left Josh alone.

He could hear far away the thud of hooves and the waves that had beat against his ears before began now to say words: Rome's fast, Rome's mighty fast. Run for it, run for it. The minute they turn the curve, run for it.

He looked around, he picked out the likely path. "Sure wish I had a cherry-stone to suck on," said Gum Anson. "Sure am parched."

Gum's words drowned out the others. The hoof beats came nearer. What's the worst can happen to thee? Josh asked himself. Get a bullet in thy gizzard. Get killed. Nothing else. . . . It was all right. He settled down to wait.

"Hold it, hold it," the captain was calling. "Wait for the word. Hold it. Hold it."

From around the bend, very slowly, came a single man, carrying a white flag. A few paces behind him were perhaps twenty or thirty mounted men.

"It's a trick, it's a trick," the Home Guardsmen were yelling. "Watch it, captain. It's funny business."

"Don't shoot," shouted the colonel who had ridden up. "Don't fire on a white flag. But watch 'em. Keep 'em covered."

He rode forward a couple of paces. "Are you surrendering?" he called.

The man with the white flag called back, "No. No surrender. We want to parley."

"Come on in," said the colonel. "You," he yelled. "You with the white flag. The rest of you stay back."

"Trying to get up inside our range and ride us down," said Gum.

The flag-bearer came up alongside the Home Guard colonel and saluted.

"Keep your guns on those men," the colonel called back, then lowered his own. Josh couldn't hear his words, but could see that the raider was talking fast and earnestly.

"Could be your brother," said Gum.

It was so. The rebel doing the talking was tow haired and young, a gaunt brown-faced boy, very broad shouldered and supple in the saddle. Josh's gun, which had been leveled on him, wavered, but he brought it to bear, once again.

The Guardsmen were getting restless. "Tell him to make up his mind. Surrender and talk—or shut his mouth and fight."

"What's he doin'? Preachin'?"

"Lectioneering for Jeff Davis."

"Shut him up, colonel. Shut him up."

"We'll make him talk outa the other corner of his mouth."

"You the one shot old man Yardell?"

The colonel turned his back on the raiders and rode up to his own men. "Don't take your guns off them," he told them. "He says we're surrounded. He says they've cut in back of us—that they've got five thousand men circled around Vernon and it's suicide to resist. He says every bridge and ford can be rushed. He says surrender and save bloodshed. He says if we surrender nobody'll be harmed. Provisions and fresh mounts taken only. What do you say?"

The storekeeper who had wanted to give Morgan the butt-end of his mind rose now in his stirrups and delivered a piece of it. "He's lying. Men don't start talking until they're past fighting."

"If he had five thousand men they'd be in Vernon now. Bloodshed, so long's it's your blood, ain't nothin' to a reb."

"Horses and provisions, eh? Who appointed us quartermaster corps to the Confederate Army?"

Ben Whitey gave the final answer. He yelled. His yell wasn't practiced like the rebel screech; it hadn't the long falsetto midnight quaver which could raise the hackles and slide between the bones like cold steel, but it was very strong and it

lifted toward the end with a raw, un-
sheathed resonance of its own. It seemed
what they had waited for—it seemed the
only answer to give. It drained away the
uncertainty, the distrust, the fear of the
long wait. Above the quiet river it rose in
great volume and flowed in a roiled and
mounting current across the summer fields.
Josh's musket quivered with the violence
of his own shouting.

The colonel regarded his men quizzically, then shrugged his shoulders as if to
say to the raiders, What can I do with such
fire-eaters? and rode back to the rebel
leader. There was another conference
shorter than the first one, after which the
raiders turned, cantered back down the
road up which they had just ridden.

"They give us two hours," the colonel
said, "to get our women and children out
of town. After which, they attack."

At eight that evening they were still
waiting, drawn up, ready. The new moon
had set and the night was very dark and
warm, filled with soft summer stars which
seemed to escape from set star shapes and
let light shimmer fluidly—and it almost
seemed, moistly—across the sky. Some
time later the captain with a militia-man
came up to the group Josh was in.

"Count off here," he said. "I'm sending
twenty of you men to Finney's Ford. The
rebs could come through there as well as
here if they knew the crick. There's a
company there now—but no use having
any if you don't have enough." He turned
to the militia-man. "Let some of your men
sleep," he said, "but keep a heavy guard
posted."

Josh rode with the twenty men slowly
and quietly through the night, back across
the bridge and to a bank above the river
where any party attempting to use the ford
could be fired on while in the water. He
rode among strangers. Gum and Ben
Whitey had been left behind, and he
thought, as he had been thinking all day,
Now it begins.

In the darkness the company at the ford
seemed very large; the men dismounted,
speaking in muffled voices, their horses
tethered and resting behind them.

"The crick takes a turn here," the new
men were told. "Twenty feet down to the
bottom here, so keep your eyes peeled. I'm
going to let you men have a couple of
hours' sleep, then you can relieve some of
us. Get out of your saddles and get some
rest—but don't rest so hard you can't hear
a raider crossin' that branch."

Josh dismounted and felt his way along
the bank in the layered darkness. He felt
rather than saw the stream below him,
smelled it, really, he believed, though he
could hear the occasional lap of a little
eddy against a stone, and see here and
there a prick of light reflected from a star.
He ate cold biscuit with dried beef, gave
Rome a biscuit, then stretched out on his
blankets, somewhat withdrawn from the
main body of the militia and near the bank
of the stream. Rome stood behind him
snuffing at the scent of the strange men
and horses about him, mouthing the already cropped-over grass in search of a
neglected tuft.

War, Josh thought, seemed a hard thing
to come at. The dying and killing he had
declared himself ready for at the breakfast
table, and which he had imagined he
would meet face to face as soon as he'd
gotten out onto the road, seemed always to
lurk round another corner. He had forti-
fied himself for so many encounters with
either or both that there were now almost
no breastworks he could fling up, or arma-
ments he could assemble. His supply of
anticipation was about used up. War appeared to consist not of the dramatic and
immediate sacrifice, either of his body in
dying, or his spirit in killing, as he had
foreseen it at the breakfast table, but of an
infinite series of waitings and postpone-
ments.

This is it, he had said, and it was only
Ben Whitey waiting at the cut-off. This
is it, and it was Vernon as much like

Fourth of July as war. This surely is it, he had said, and it was the wind in the elder clump. This, this: a man with a white flag. And now in the dark night to defend the vulnerable ford—and this was not it either, but simply lying at ease on his blankets, his cherry-addled stomach settled with good beef and biscuit, Rome munching by his side and the Milky Way banding the sky familiarly. Except for the gun under his hand it could be any summer night, lying outside for a time to cool off before bed time. And if John Morgan himself, lantern in hand, should bend over him, prod him with his toe and say, "This is it, bub," he didn't know whether he'd believe him or not. Maybe John Morgan was waiting and hunting, too, no more an authority on *its* arrival than he. Getting ready for war might be a short horse and soon curried, but war itself was a horse liable to stretch, so far as he could see, from July to eternity . . . head at Maple Grove and hocks in Beulah Land.

Josh closed his eyes to sleep; but beneath his lids there flowed not only the remembered sights of the day, the faces, attitudes, gestures he had seen and noted, but the multitudinous sights that there had been in daylight no time to name, or space within the crowded mind to delineate. Now in darkness, behind shut lids, they lived again. He saw the L-shaped rip in the pants of the raider who had carried the white flag, and beneath the rip, the long, improperly healed wound which reddened the man's calf from knee to ankle. He saw now, what he had missed then, the downward motion of the raider's hand toward his gun when Ben Whitey's yell lunged unexpectedly toward him. He saw now, trying to sleep, the controlled drop of a spider, delicately spinning, from the spire of an unblooming head of goldenrod to the yellowed grass beneath it. He heard Gum Anson's answer to someone who asked him, "What you doing here, Gum?" "I'm a farmer," said Gum, "and you can't farm unless you keep the varmints down." He

heard another voice—the storekeeper's, he thought—say, "I'm a man of peace—but there ain't any peace when your neighbors are being killed. And if it's a question of good blood, or bad, on my hands, by God, I choose bad."

At last he slept—and continued to see and hear . . . a raider was trying to take Ebony . . . he had ridden his horse inside the summer kitchen, and overturned the table, trampled the crockery and was snatching at Ebony, who above the sounds of confusion was screaming, "Wake up, wake up."

Josh woke up. He found himself in the center of a great, bubbling cauldron of noise: men shouting, screaming advice, cursing; horses neighing; and in the creek below the splash and clatter of men and animals crossing the ford. There was a spattering of shots. Someone was calling over and over, "Mount, mount, mount."

Josh stepped cautiously, felt for Rome in the dark, said his name, doubled his hands hoping to feel them close upon horse flesh, harkened to the billowing roll of sound. Then suddenly the sound fanned out, burst inside his head, roared against the bones of his skull and breaking through bone and tissue, trickled out by way of mouth and nose; it fluttered a few last times against his ear drums, then left him in quiet.

It was daylight before he was sure what had happened: he had gone over the cliff, through the branches of a willow which grew almost parallel with the stream, and now lay within hand's reach of the creek itself. At first he had tried to call out, but the sound of his own voice had detonated like gun fire inside his head and he was afraid that his skull, which he reckoned was broken, might fall apart with the effort. He was half-conscious, and wholly sick, but between bouts of retching he thought: This is it. I've come to it at last. This is war. It's falling over a cliff, cracking my skull and puking.

It was just after sunup when Labe found him. He had about given up when he heard sounds from beneath the willow.

"Josh," he cried, "thee's alive, thee's all right."

"No, I'm not," said Josh morosely.

"Oh, Josh," Labe said again, and knelt beside him, "thee's all right."

"I wish thee'd stop saying that," Josh told him. "It makes me feel sicker. I'm not all right. My head's split, I think."

Labe looked at it. "It does kind of look that way," he said, "but if thee's not died yet I reckon thee's not going to."

Josh moaned.

"Why didn't thee call out—get some help?" Labe asked.

"At first," Josh said, "because I didn't know anything. Then when I did, if I even opened my mouth to whisper, my whole head like to fell off. Then I got so's I could talk—but if I did, I puked. I still do," he said, and did. "I wish thee'd go away," he told Labe finally, "and leave me alone. I was beginning to get a little easy." He lay back for a while, then painfully lifted himself on one elbow. "Did we get Morgan?"

"They didn't come this way."

"Didn't come this way?" asked Josh. "I heard them. They crossed the crick last night."

"That wasn't Morgan," Labe said. "That was some cotton-headed farmers over'n the south bank who took a freak to drive their stock across so's the rebs wouldn't get 'em."

"I thought it was Morgan," Josh said. "I was fooled."

"Thee had plenty of company," Labe said. "They's all fooled."

"Where's Morgan now?"

"Dupont they say. He gave Vernon the go-by."

Josh lay back again. "We stood them off," he said proudly. "We kept Morgan out of Vernon."

There was nothing Labe could say to that. Presently he asked, "If I get some help does thee think thee could move,

Josh? They're worried about thee at home."

"How'd thee come to find me?" Josh asked.

"Rome came home without thee."

"I'd just as lief stay here," Josh said bitterly. "Go to war and fall off a cliff."

"Thee needn't let that fash [4] you," Labe said. "More did than didn't."

With the help of Guardsmen who were still lingering about the ford, discussing the night's events, Labe got Josh, unwilling and protesting, up the bank and into Rome's saddle. Labe rode behind and let Josh lean against him, and thus supported Josh was able to travel.

"Am I bleeding?" Josh asked weakly after they'd covered a mile or so. A thin trickle of blood was coming across his shoulder and down his shirt front.

"No," Labe said, "that's me."

"Thee?" asked Josh, for whom the events of the past twenty-four hours were still uncertain. "Thee wasn't fighting, was thee?"

"Well, I was a little," Labe admitted.

"In the Guard?" Josh asked.

"No," Labe said, "just kind of privately."

"Why?"

"Well," said Labe, "when I's hunting thee a man sung a song."

"I wouldn't fight anybody about any song," Josh said.

Labe didn't say anything.

"I purely hate fighting," Josh said. "Don't thee, Labe?"

"Not so much," Labe answered.

"I hate it," Josh said. "That's why I got to."

"And I got not to," Labe said, "because I like it."

Josh wanted to be with them, so they carried the sofa out of the sitting-room into the summer kitchen, and he lay on it, a cool wet towel wrapped round his head. He felt as if his skull had been peeled away and his brain left so exposed that even the changed cadence of a voice could

---

[4] *fash*, vex

strike it like a blow. He pushed the towel a little way off his eyes. Labe was in a chair, head back, wet cloth across his nose, and broken hand in a bucket of hot water. They were both awaiting a doctor if one could be found who was not busy. His mother was changing cloths and minding breakfast, stepping very light so's not to jar his head. His father was at the table where he'd been the morning before. There was a mingling of looks on his face.

"Well," Jess said, "I never had a First Day morning like this before and never hope to again. Though I reckon everybody's done what had to be done. Josh anyway. I'm not so sure about Labe."

Labe lifted the cloth which covered mouth as well as nose. "Mine was kind of an accident," he admitted.

Jess turned toward his eldest son. Their eyes met and Jess nodded. "Well," he said again, "no reason why we can't eat, is there, Eliza? Have a sup of hot coffee and some biscuit and gravy?"

Josh groaned.

"I can't chew," Labe muttered.

Jess seemed to be feeling better and better. "I ain't been doing any fighting," he said, "in the militia or on the side. I got a good appetite. If you boys, don't mind, and thy mother'll set it forth, I'll have a bite. So far's I can remember there wasn't much eating done here yesterday. Eliza," he asked, "won't thee sit and eat?"

"Thee go ahead, Jess," Eliza said. "I'm busy with the boys just now."

"Mattie?"

"No," Mattie said delicately, ". . . all this blood and broken bones . . ."

"Little Jess?"

"Thee don't need to wait for me," said Little Jess.

"Well, then," Jess said heartily, "let us eat. But before we eat let's return thanks. This is First Day morning and we've much to be thankful for."

Josh listened to his father's words . . .

they were a part of his happiness. When he had first come to, found himself lying at the edge of the crick, he had thought he would hate coming home, admit he'd been hurt, not by gun or saber, but falling over a bank onto his head. Now it didn't matter. Yesterday morning and his talk of dying and killing seemed almost a lifetime away . . . the past twenty-four hours a prolonged campaign from which he had emerged, a veteran, with mind much cleared as to what mattered and what did not.

Next time . . . he wouldn't talk so big . . . about fighting . . . and dying. But that didn't matter either, now. What mattered was that he had stood there . . . he had been afraid, but he had stood at the bridge. He had thought of running . . . but he hadn't done it . . . he had stood in the front line, not knowing but that Morgan himself might tear down upon them . . . he had stood at the crick's edge in the darkness and confusion and had been hunting gun and horse when he had fallen.

And there were the things he had learned . . . that talk beforehand is no good . . . that in darkness on a twenty-foot cliff it is best not to hurry . . . that death, when you moved toward it, seemed to retreat . . . that it was only when you turned your back on it . . . and ran . . . that it pursued.

With these thoughts the words of his father's grace mingled very well . . . "Eternal Father . . . blessed Son . . . life everlasting. . . . "

He had thought his father was still praying, his tone was still so prayerful. But the words had changed. Josh once more cautiously pushed the towel away from his eyes. Jess was looking about the sunlit kitchen now, inspecting his family. "All here," he said, "right side up and forked end down." But then, maybe he was still praying, for he said next, "Amen, amen." Either way it was all right with Josh.

The woman who wrote this story

JESSAMYN WEST

It would be hard to classify Jessamyn West's books as either novels or collections of short stories. They are composed of closely-connected episodes, usually centering around a Quaker family, but having no over-all plot to bind them together. The characters and the setting in each episode are the same, yet the individual episodes are independent of each other.

Miss West's stories reflect her Quaker background not only in their content but also in their style. Her writing reflects an economy of expression and lightness of touch which is characteristic of the Quaker way of life. Gentleness is another quality of Miss West's style which derives from her Quaker upbringing. The kindly, quiet, "Battle of Finney's Ford" is perhaps the most violent of her stories. It was included as one of the related episodes in *The Friendly Persuasion,* published in 1945.

Miss West is also the author of two other episodic novels, an opera libretto, and a number of short poems.

Let's consider . . .

1. Early in the story you were told that "Joshua sorrowed over death as an abstract fact." He believed that his elders were indifferent to death except when it occurred in their own households. In what way was this belief responsible for Josh's determination to "join up" and defend Vernon against Morgan's raiders?

2. "A Quaker sure's the Lord made Moses." With these words, the one-legged man greeted Josh. How did you first know the Birdwells were Quakers?

3. Go back over the story and make a list of all the principles, beliefs, and practices of this Quaker family. The girls could list those which were revealed through Eliza's actions and comments. The boys could list those revealed by Jess. Which of these principles, beliefs, and practices were a part of the Quaker way of life?

4. How did Josh explain to his family his determination "to go right down to Vernon and join"? How did his father take the news? How did his mother react?

5. In what ways was Josh's father good for him? Do you think Eliza was intolerant? Explain.

6. How did "Ebony" get into the controversy about fighting Morgan's men? What were the "two ways of seeing Ebony" that made Mattie suffer? When did she regard herself as a coward? When as a renegade?

7. Describe Josh's preparations and his departure. Do you think they were natural? Compare them with the way a friend or relative of yours got ready to leave for service with the Armed Forces.

8. Describe Vernon on that July morning when Josh arrived to join the Home Guards.

9. How did the Home Guards feel about Morgan as they stood massed at the bridge below the forks?

10. Describe Josh's feelings when he heard the first rebel yell.

11. Give an account of the white flag episode. How did the behavior of these "homespun" soldiers resemble the behavior of the American boys in World War II or the Korean Conflict?

12. Why didn't the Home Guard fight Morgan's raiders?

13. Do you think the Battle of Finney's Ford was really a battle? Explain. What was Josh's part in it?

14. Before the conclusion of this story, you saw the Birdwell family again united. Now you might consider the evidence for your impression of these Quaker people. You know Josh's real reason for "joining up," and Labe's real reason for keeping out. You see again the genuine concern of the father and mother for their boys. You know what Josh learned from his experience. You see the workings of a firm faith.

What is your reaction to the Quaker beliefs and way of life? What have you learned from the Birdwells that would make you more understanding of others?

The writer's craft . . .

If someone were to ask you what this story was about, you would probably answer, "People." Of course, there was action —even a certain amount of suspense, as you would expect in a war story. The real focus of the story, however, was on the Birdwell family, and especially on Josh.

When an outside threat in the form of Morgan's Raiders upset the quiet harmony of the family, each member reacted in a different way. From their reactions, you learned to know Jess, Eliza, Josh, Mattie and Labe as distinct individuals. Miss West was primarily concerned with exploring their different reactions and providing each character with adequate reasons for his or her particular reactions. Moreover, both the reasons and the reactions had to be consistent with what the author had told you about each character: with his beliefs, values, personality, and way of looking at life. In this way, Miss West provided adequate motivation for her story.

As the story progressed, you soon became aware of *why* each character acted as he did. For example, when you first met Josh you were given certain insights into his personality. You learned his views on death in general, as well as his uncertain feelings about the possibility of his own death. The conversation at the breakfast table revealed additional reasons which accounted for his decision to defend Vernon, even if it meant death for himself or other soldiers.

1. When Josh realized that his mother did not understand his point of view, he brought Ebony into the conversation. In what way did his mother's pet bird serve to explain his reasons for defending Vernon with force?

2. Describe Josh's feelings and thoughts as he rode to meet Ben. Were his reactions to the experience of going to war consistent with his personality as Miss West had developed it? Discuss.

3. How did Josh react to his "accident"? Were his reactions consistent with what you knew about him? Discuss.

4. At the end of the story Miss West summarized what Josh learned from his short twenty-four-hour experience. Were his conclusions consistent with (1) his beliefs, (2) his previous actions, (3) what had happened to him, and (4) his relationship with his family? Before you can answer this question, you will need to think back carefully over (1) the way Josh reacted in each situation calling for a decision or an action; and (2) the reasons which determined each of his decisions or actions. Either write out your answer or present it orally—perhaps as a panel discussion.

5. Select one of the following characters. On one side of your paper list specific situations in which that character (1) had to make a decision, or (2) had to act. Opposite each situation, describe briefly how that person reacted and give the reason that determined that decision or action.

Eliza   Mattie
Labe   Jess

Knowing words . . .

Each of the following sentences has one word in italics. When you are sure of the meaning of the italicized word, use it in a sentence of your own.

1. But his father had a kind of calm, a tolerant *pliability* which sometimes set Joshua's teeth on edge.

2. He was particularly aware of Labe's calm, cool gaze, and he supposed that Labe, in what he thought of as Labe's belittling way, was *enumerating* his own physical short-comings.

3. She *oscillated* between the two ways of seeing Ebony.

4. She felt herself a *renegade*, an outcast from faith and scriptures.

5. Failing this, the guard on the west bank would have a fine chance to pick off the men as they *debouched* from the bridge and headed toward town.

6. Josh felt *bereft* of shelter, unshielded and alone—a naked target.

7. "Josh," he cried, "thee's alive, thee's all right." "No, I'm not," said Josh *morosely*.

8. Above the quiet river it rose in great volume and flowed in a *roiled* and mounting current across the summer fields.

As Toilsome I Wander'd Virginia's Woods

As toilsome I wander'd Virginia's woods,
To the music of rustling leaves kick'd by my feet
   (for 'twas autumn),
I mark'd at the foot of a tree the grave of a soldier;
Mortally wounded he and buried on the retreat
   (easily all could I understand),
The halt of a mid-day hour, when up! no time to lose
   —yet this sign left,
On a tablet scrawl'd and nail'd on the tree by the grave:
Bold, cautious, true, and my loving comrade.

Long, long I muse, then on my way go wandering,
Many a changeful season to follow, and many a scene of life,
Yet at times through changeful season and scene,
   abrupt, alone, or in the crowded street,
Comes before me the unknown soldier's grave,
   comes the inscription rude in Virginia's woods,
Bold, cautious, true, and my loving comrade.

Walt Whitman

Deep Horizons

ERNEST HAYCOX

As the frontier pushed westward, circuit riding preachers like Matt Hobart moved with it. Matt was a proud, strong man who could withstand the hardships and fierce cold of the Nebraska prairie. But he could not bear to have his family face an empty, desolate Christmas.

A long wind whirled out of the prairie's dark and empty distance, shouldering heavily against the sod house. When Matt Hobart came in he was quick to close the door, but a momentary gust of that bitter December weather rushed through the room and the flame of the oil lamp on the table wavered and licked a sooty smudge up its chimney.

Matt stood a moment by the door, his lips pressed thin and all his face raw and pinched. Going forward to him, Eileen knew that he was dead beat—there was that betraying blackness in his eyes. She said, "Theo, put a chair by the stove," and reached up and unwrapped Matt's muffler, silently enraged because he had no overcoat and could afford none. "You sit down, Matt."

Theo turned a chair to the fire and stood beside it, watching her father but not speaking. At seven she was a slender little girl, with deep auburn hair and a strange faith that steadied her childlike eagerness and made her undeniably Eileen Hobart's daughter. When Matt dropped into the chair Theo bent and kissed the back of his neck and stood behind him, straight and still. Jackie came from a dark corner of the room then and stationed himself by the stove. He put his arms behind him and rocked on his heels. Pretending not to see his father he looked slyly from the corner of his eyes, ready to chuckle. He was six, already taller than Theo.

Looking on, Eileen saw this scene with comprehending relief. Matt smiled and pointed his finger at Jackie and the boy let out a quick laugh. There was an affection in this room that softened the threat of the wind outside and lessened her own worry. She went to the stove and dished up the meal. "What you need is something hot, Matt. Come to the table."

It hurt her to see how slowly he got up from the chair, this man so usually full of vitality. He went to the basin and washed without soap and poured the water into a stand-by pail, for water was too scarce to waste this dry winter. They all sat up to the table and Matt said grace in a quick, hopeful manner. He was more cheerful, with the warmth of the room banishing the misery in his eyes. He had that power to throw off discouragement, that resilience of spirit which could shake aside this prairie poverty. It caused Eileen to wonder, as she had wondered so often before, at the strangeness of his choice of the ministry. He wasn't a bookish man, he wasn't a meek one. There was a turbulence and a temper in him that even now, after five years of the cloth, colored all his acts; a fighting energy he so frequently had to

59

grit his teeth against. His shoulders were big and his knuckles solid.

He was watching her; he was looking at her plate, which held almost nothing. She said, "I've lost my appetite from staying indoors so much."

She knew he didn't believe it. His glance went over the table and saw what there was, and the color of his eyes changed again. She understood he wouldn't mention it in front of the children, yet she was afraid—and changed the subject.

"You didn't see anything of the yearling?"

"I lost its tracks at the bottoms. The ground's frozen."

"Somebody stealed it?" said Jackie.

"It was taken," said Matt Hobart.

"It was the wind last night," said Eileen. "We couldn't have heard anyone in the barn." She lowered her eyes. Her voice trembled, not from despair but from suppressed anger. "To us. Why should anyone do that to us?"

He said, "Eileen," and the gentleness of his talk lifted her head. He was smiling. There wasn't much comfort left in him, but such as he had left he was giving to her.

Jackie said mysteriously: "Know what the next day after tomorrow is?"

Theo nodded her head and was quite scornful. "Anybody does. It's Christmas."

"Christmas!" exclaimed Jackie, and laughed hugely.

Matt pushed back his chair; he got up and said quickly, quietly: "It is time for lessons." Eileen had one long look at his features and pulled her eyes away and set about clearing the table, Theo helping her. Matt Hobart brought a book from the window ledge, but he was thinking of another thing, for he crossed the room to the small offset pantry and looked in. He wheeled abruptly back to the table where the children were waiting for him. He opened the book and gave it to Theo. "You will read tonight about a Christmas of long ago when George Washington's soldiers were

camped at Valley Forge. Listen carefully to this story, Jackie. Pronounce your words, Theo, so as not to slide them together."

Eileen poised her hands over the warm dishwater, comforted by that scene. Matt's body was loose in the chair and his head dropped a little forward as he listened to Theo's careful words rise and fall. Jackie stood still, rooted by the weight of his father's arm on his small shoulder. They were all grave and attentive. The lamplight softened the pressures around Matt's face and Eileen saw that he too was being comforted.

Matt said: "Your voice, Theo, should pause but not drop when you reach a comma."

Outside a man said, "Hello, hello," and knocked and immediately shouldered his way into the room and closed the door. A blue military coat completely covered him and his hatbrim shut out all features save the bright narrow strip of his eyes.

Matt got up. He said, "How are you, Tom? Take off your things." The children obediently turned and faced this newcomer.

"I ain't got the time," said the newcomer. He looked curiously around. "I passed Jim Grisim's house. He's dyin' and wants to see you. It's a terrible night to go out."

Eileen looked at Matt with a sudden unspoken protest. His shoulders dropped—and rose. She saw his face change; she saw the grinding weariness return. But he put down his book. "Certainly. Right now."

The man broke in: "I'd like to take you, but I'm late and my old woman'll be full of worry. There's a hard freeze comin'." He turned toward the door. Matt Hobart's talk caught him with one hand turning the knob.

"I lost my bull calf last night. Have you seen any strays along the road?"

"Why, no."

"A blooded calf, worth seventy-five dollars."

"Brindle and white. I remember it."
The man's eyes narrowed. "Lot of tough
customers are traveling through the country these days. But I got five miles to go."
He went out in haste, anxious to be away
before Matt laid any claim of service on
him. They heard him swearing at his
horses; and then the swearing died down-
wind. Eileen found Matt's eyes watching
her with a patient, resigned understanding. "Tom's got a long way to drive," he
said. "Every keg must stand on its own bottom."

She said, with a cruelty she could not
help: "Then let Jim Grisim stand on his!"
He wasn't shocked. He only shook his
head. "That's one trip men hate to start
on alone. Maybe I can say something
that'll make it a little easier for him." He
was putting on his muffler and his wool
gloves, but he stared at the door and the
whine of the gusty wind made him imper-
ceptibly flinch. He picked up a lantern
and lighted it. Eileen said, "Wait." She
went into the bedroom and got a blanket
and brought it back, covering Matt with
it and pinning it at his neck. When he
opened the door she came behind.

"Go back in the house, Eileen."

"Go on—go on!"

The wind ran smotheringly against her
face; it swirled her skirts and drove point-
edly into her skin, like the prick of needles.
She caught hold of his arm and struggled
on beside him, toward the narrow sod barn;
inside it she took the lantern and held it
over her head, trembling, while he harnessed the horse. The pale light sparkled
against the frostiness of that freezing air.
The Guernsey cow grunted plaintively in
her stanchion. Matt said:

"So we're down to a sack of potatoes
and a half side of bacon. Why haven't you
told me?"

She said: "I didn't marry you for a
kitchen husband, Matt. That's my business—and we'll make out. Have you seen
the deacon about your salary?"

"I'll be riding his way tomorrow."

He came forward, leading the horse, and
stood before her a moment—a tall, formless shape against the cold shadows. He
wanted to say something to her, but his
mouth pinched together and he didn't say
it. He went out and backed the horse into
the shafts of the buggy and hooked up. He
called out, "Go back to the house before
you're chilled," and drove straight into the
windy, buffeting blackness.

Eileen bent her head and ran for the
house. The sky was very black, with all
the stars laying a glittering, remote brilliance against it. The windows were glaz-
ing over and the yellow light coming
through them was diffused and soft. Three
miles in the south the nearest neighbor's
house threw off a minute gleam; elsewhere
the prairie lay formless and empty and
wild. She closed the door and extinguished
the lantern. Her hands were cold and
numb and the fire of the stove seemed to
have no power in it. Both children sat up
to the table, heads bent together above the
book.

"It's bedtime," said Eileen.

The thought of Christmas disciplined
them enormously; its secrets and anticipa-
tions colored all that their eyes saw and
put laughter in them. They were soon
undressed, warming themselves at the fire.
Jackie lifted his sly glance and chuckled
and trotted toward the bedroom; but Theo
walked soberly, lips soft from her dreams.
Standing by the stove, Eileen saw them
kneel at the bed, one on each side. Jackie
never prayed aloud. He laced his fingers
together and kept his attention on Theo,
who dutifully asked God to care for her
people. Her voice fell to a whispering and
rose definitely again. "Skates for Jackie
and a dolly for me—a wax doll with clothes
and a lace cap. Amen."

"Amen," said Jackie, and made a long
jump into the warm side of the bed. Theo
exclaimed: "You had that side last night.
It's mine tonight!" But Jackie pulled the
blankets over his head, chuckling beneath
them. Theo pounded him with her fists

and walked around and crept in the other side. She said, "You little scoundrel." But she got in and sat bolt upright and her face held a glow of hope that was very real. "It will really be here Christmas morning."

Eileen said, "Good night," and turned her back to them.

They were asleep when Matt got home two hours later. His hands were too stiff to undo the pinned blanket. Eileen had to take it off. The wind had raked up small flakes of skin on his cheek and all his features were wooden with cold and the punishment of the night was in his eyes. Eileen thought, in bitter rage, "Not even a dog deserves to be treated this way," and touched him on the shoulder. He went over to the stove and stood there, rubbing his arms slowly. He said:

"Theo still wants that doll she's talked about?"

"I think she's forgotten it, Matt."

"No. She wouldn't forget. I had depended a lot on that bull calf. It was worth seventy-five dollars."

She said: "It doesn't matter. We're warm."

He sat down, his big shoulders bent over, his black head bowed at the stove. He didn't speak again.

At seven in the morning a lowering, grisly light stained the windows. The wind still blew, its thin and bitter fingers searching through the chinks of the sod house. Eileen wrapped two sandwiches of bread and wild-plum butter and stuffed them in his pockets; and secured her shawl around his shoulders. The blanket he would not use. He stood at the door a moment, a ragged and harassed light in his eyes, and she knew then his spirit was shamed from knowing that he could not give them the things they needed. He only said: "I'm going toward the south. It will probably be quite late before I get back." He bent and kissed her faintly, with something warm gone out of him, with something proud missing; and closed the door quickly behind.

He drove eastward along a road that was only two straggling wheel lines across the prairie. The wind came up from the south, hard and severely cold. All his features were soon raw, and from time to time he had to scrub warmth into them with his mittened hand; the breath of his horse made an evanescent fog against the air. Far off in the southeast Dike Tyler's windmill reared up against a dull and mealy light, but elsewhere the prairie ran its lonely and undulating way into the deep horizons without a visible break. Life in this new Nebraska country hid itself in sod huts below the sky line, in sheltered ravines and creek bottoms. They were so painfully poor, the people of his district; so poor and so discouraged by the misfortunes of another tinder-dry grasshopper year. At the bridge across Irene Creek he turned due south, aiming for Dike Tyler's place. Elyria, only settlement in this country, was twenty-five miles in the east.

He passed a pond whose foot-deep water was hard frozen, which made him think of the skates Jackie desired and of the store doll Theo wouldn't get. She was Eileen's girl altogether—patient and full of dreams; and it was brutal to sit on this chilly buggy seat and visualize Theo's small and clear face struggle against disappointment on Christmas morning. She seldom asked for anything. He could accept whatever happened to him, but the old fury rose and would not be quenched at the thought of poverty striking through his front door at Eileen and the children.

The reflection of this was cut deeply across his face when he drove into Dike Tyler's road. He drove around to the lee side of the house and stopped beside Tyler, who swung an ax deeply into a chopping block and lifted wet, bearded cheeks. Dike Tyler looked at him. He said:

"Man, you shouldn't be out in this with no overcoat. You're comin' down with the grippe." But he saw the shawl pinned around Matt Hobart's shoulders and knew why. He said: "I been meanin' to drive over and tell you about your salary. I'll admit fifteen dollars a month isn't much, particularly when it ain't paid for three months in row. But the fact is, parson, this district hasn't got the money. Nobody's got any money. You know—the drought and the grasshoppers."

Through Matt's thundering disappointment crept one small feeling of relief. He had not been put to the necessity of asking about that money. He had pride, too much of it for a Methodist minister in a Nebraska circuit in 1878. There were some emotions in him, stubborn and unruly, that only years of punishment would take out. How long would it take to wear down that intractable grain of his free years? He bowed his head a little. He said, through his chapped, motionless lips: "That's all right, Dike. You haven't seen a brindle and white yearling calf?"

"Yours? No."

"Jim Grisim's pretty low. Go see him if you can."

He turned back to the jiggling wheel tracks and followed them, up and down the slow swell of the prairie. The day was darker than it had been, with the smell of cold growing stronger and the frost haze closing slowly down along the horizon. The wind drummed a constant tone against his ears. His feet were very heavy. He dropped off the buggy then and walked beside it a quarter mile and got back in, and later dropped off again. He stopped a few minutes at Len Hoogeman's place and had a cup of tea, surrounded by Hoogeman's seven tow-headed girl children. There was a blanket partitioning off one corner of the sod hut, and behind it he heard a woman groaning. That would be Hoogeman's oldest girl having a baby. When he left the hut Hoogeman came up from the sod barn with half a sack of cabbages which he dumped into the buggy. He smiled. He said: "Merry Christmas, parson. This is a devil of a country. I don't see how any of us live—but we seem to."

Matt Hobart went on down the road, walking beside the buggy until the sensation of weight began to reach the bottom of his feet. Four miles from Hoogeman's the wagon tracks dropped to the bottom of a coulee,[1] where a freshly planted post held a board arrow that said, "S. A. Slade, 1 m." It would be a new family in the district, Matt thought, and turned his buggy west into the coulee.

He was below the sweep of the wind and for a while the roar left his ears. Ahead of him an antelope trotted into view with a bouncing step, saw him, and shot up the side of the coulee in flat surges. Around the next bend Matt came upon a house built back into the lip of the coulee, nothing facing the day but a front wall and a door. A stack sticking horizontally from the wall emitted a spiral of smoke. There was a canvas-topped prairie wagon standing in front of the place and two thin horses standing motionless on their picket ropes. A dog came around the wagon and walked forward, growling. Suddenly, directly behind the wagon, Matt Hobart saw his brindle-and-white bull calf.

Matt let himself down from the buggy. The door of the dugout came faintly open and a man's face looked through in thin profile, suspiciously. Afterward he came out, crossing the coulee with a slow, rolling gait. He was bald and broad, with an undershot chin that pushed his lower lip over the upper. He cocked his head a little and waited.

Matt Hobart said evenly: "My name's Hobart. I'm the minister in this circuit."

"Sure," said the man, and waited.

There wasn't anything in his profession, Matt understood, that would help him. He had to go back to his earlier days for support, when he had known and handled men like this. His voice turned smooth. "You've done me a service. I see you've caught up my calf which strayed off two nights ago."

The man's eyes were almost lost behind

---

[1] *coulee*, deep ravine

the quick constriction of his lids. He said
swiftly: "Your mistake. I brought that
calf from Ioway."

"That's odd," murmured Matt. "Let me
have a closer look at him."

But the man grunted out a peremptory
order: "Never mind. You take my word.
It's good enough, ain't it? Harry, come out
here."

The door opened again and a younger
man, straight as a lath, moved across the
ground. He stood behind the bald man,
with his long arms hanging loosely down,
his eyes severely attentive. Matt Hobart
said firmly: "Nevertheless, I'll have a
look," and stepped one pace forward. The
bald one raised an arm; he pushed Hobart
back. His teeth were brightly exposed by
the quick twist of his lips. "Get on your
way, parson. We ain't particularly religious. That's so, ain't it, Harry?"

Matt Hobart looked down at his feet,
breath drawing strongly in and out. He
steadied himself on his legs and felt warm

for the first time that bitter day. A faint
memory of Bishop Dover's soft words came
to him: "Militancy for the church, my son.
But for your personal self, humbleness always." The very tone of the bishop's voice
sounded like a bell in his memory; and
then, like the echoes of a bell, it died out
utterly and left him lonely. He lifted his
face. The bald man took one instant half
step backward and lifted both heavy arms
in front of him, his body squatting. The
younger man wheeled on the run, back to
the house. He snatched up a broken ax
handle; he turned and circled around Matt
Hobart with a sliding, exaggerated step.
The bald man's eyes were wide and round.
A deep grunt jerked out of him as he
sprang toward Matt.

The cow, Eileen saw, was giving less
and less milk. It could not be helped of
course—for there wasn't enough feed—but
it was like the shutting down of a last
hope. Milk meant so much to the children.

She went out of the sod barn with the bucket, her head turned away from the slice of the wind, and hurried back to the house. She stood a moment in the room, reluctant to face that bitter blast again, her eyes on the children. They were in the bedroom, going through the pantomimed gestures of some secret game of their own. Theo's face was soft and sober and dreaming. She would be thinking, Eileen knew, of tomorrow morning, which was Christmas morning. The child lived on hope. Eileen caught up the water pail and went to the well. The windlass payed out the rope almost to the end, and there was a definite banging on the bottom. The long burning summer and the freezing winter winds had dried most of the moisture from the earth. This was the beginning of real poverty.

She went back into the house and threw herself into a quick, furious activity. She swept the room and changed it and found things to keep her hands busy. "I mustn't," she told herself, "let myself have time to think."

At noon they sat down to bread and mush and milk. Jackie said: "But we had this for breakfast."

"Jackie," warned Theo. "You know what tomorrow is?"

Jackie smiled over his mush bowl: "Christmas!"

Theo said, "Then you better be careful," and looked mysteriously at her mother.

After the dishes were washed, Eileen looked into her narrow cupboard. She asked herself with a sort of angry insistence: "How can I cook potatoes a new way?" Onions and potatoes, with a little bacon grease. But Jackie couldn't eat onions. She held her mind rigidly to these little calculations, afraid to let it go free. All across the prairie other women were staring at their pantries with the same dark anxiety. The grasshopper year had stripped this country clean. A picture of the land filled her mind then, completely and tragically: of men crouched on wagon seats and dumbly enduring the slash of the wind—of women standing mutely before empty pantries, waiting.

Waiting was hardest. She was surprised to find she had sat down before the table. Her body was bent and taut and the fingers of one hand tapped the table's plain top with the dead insistence of dripping water. She pulled her hand away and put her teeth together. She felt herself letting go. She drew a long breath and asked herself obstinately: "How can I fix potatoes a new way?"

A man's voice shot through the wall of the sod hut. He said, "Whoa." Afterward, and before she had quite risen, his fist struck the door with a single peremptory warning. He came in, then, not waiting for invitation, and shut the door. An overcoat covered him from ankles to ears and in the dull light of the room his face was a blur beneath the shadow of his hat. Presently his head came up and she saw his eyes strike around the room, touch the silent children, and come back to her with a measuring interest. He had long, black and narrow cheeks; he had a week's growth of rust-red whiskers.

He came on to the stove, stripping off his gloves and unbuttoning the overcoat. When he threw it open she saw the gun sagging against his right hip. Eileen put her hands back to the table, supporting herself. She didn't protest; she knew this kind of a man.

He said in a curt voice, "Get me something to eat," and walked to the window, bending his long body to look through it. Eileen went obediently into the pantry; she brought out a loaf of bread and a jar of jelly and a pitcher of milk. She found a knife and a cup for him—and stood back by the stove, out of his way. The children were posted against the bedroom wall, speechless. Theo's face was round and without fear, but Jackie showed his scowling dislike. The man whirled, as though struck by the silence, and his hand dropped definitely toward his belt, and then fell aside. He shrugged his shoulders. "I guess," he said, "I'm a little jumpy." But he saw the food and wasn't pleased. "That's chicken mash, ma'am. I need something to eat."

She said, quietly: "I have nothing else."

He went around her to the pantry and looked in. He turned. He said irritably: "Whose house is this?"

"Matt Hobart's."

His lips turned at the corners disagreeably. "Who'd expect a parson's family to be livin' like miserable squatters on the side of a hill? If the Lord ain't providin' you food then your man had better get a job rustlin' something for his family." He went to the table and cut himself a piece of bread; he laid jelly on the slice and ate it with wicked hunger.

The room was very still; his eyes came over to her and were appraising and approving. "You're young and good-lookin'. Why don't you get out of this miserable country?"

She didn't answer. He stared at her. "You don't like it, do you?" He lifted his arm at the window, at the sullen square of earth and sky showing through it. "You don't like that?"

She pulled up her head. It was an effort to meet his eyes. He said, almost brutally: "Answer me!"

"Yes," she said. "I like it."

"That?" he said. "Look at it! It's a place for wild animals, not for men! A miserable country that burns hide off people in the summer and crucifies 'em in winter. There ain't any water; there ain't any trees. The grasshoppers eat up the crops and the wind blows the ground away and the heat cuts everything but weeds down to the roots. A man breaks his neck at it and tears out his heart waitin'—and then he's got to live like an animal in a hole, with his wife and kids starvin' to death, too poor to buy seed or move back East! Look at it!"

His mouth was thin; it was cruel. He buttoned up his coat and got into his mittens. He looked at the children again. He looked at the scowling Jackie, and back to Eileen. There was a sudden haste in him. "Your husband's a fool, ma'am. If people are crazy enough to live here they ain't worth savin'. Tell him to get out of it." He opened the door, and turned, struck by a last savage thought. "If there's a God, why does he let things like this happen, and why does he make men like me run? I don't believe in your religion!" The door slammed and the echo of his horse pounded off into the west.

Eileen went to the window, watching him disappear into a far roll of the prairie. The room was filled with cold air and her knees trembled. She moved back and sat abruptly down in a chair. She felt very weak.

Jackie said, "I don't like him."

Eileen looked at the children. "Don't tell your father about this. It would only worry him."

She thought, "How shall I fix those potatoes?" But she couldn't discipline her feelings any more. The man had said she was young and good-looking; he had stared at her with approval. She got up then and went to a small wall mirror; her face came back to her, oval and orderly, with a stained darkness in her eyes that wouldn't come out. She was twenty-eight, and this was her lot. Back in Ohio now her people would be making mincemeat pies and the long, cheerful house would have the smell of spices and fir throughout it and people would be laughing and on the road the cutters would pass by, bells jingling against a frosty dusk.

The rebellion rose, wild and uncontrolled. She said, under her breath, "I have let go," and had no power to hold in her bitter emotions. This was their lot, without grace, without hope. She was twenty-eight and in time would be as the other women on the prairie, old and quiet and homely. In time Matt would be as the others were, abraded down to a patience that had in it nothing of his old spirit. Her children were growing up without re-sources, without gentility, with less educa-tion than she had been given. In this empty wildness they had nothing. They could not even hope for Christmas Day.

Theo came softly across the floor. Her hand, warm and firm, rested on Eileen's knee. She said, in a strange voice: "Mother, what?"

Eileen got up. She said: "Your father would want you to be reading, Theo," and turned away. It was a long day—would it never end? She said, "I must do something —I must do something," and looked into her pantry and fell furiously to making up a pan of bread dough. Afterwards she went out and split some wood from the pile ricked against the house. She drew another pail of water, and in the thinning light fed and milked the cow. It was al-most immediately full dark, with a lonely night pressing against them and an ac-centuated wind wailing and sliding along the house. She trimmed the lamp. There was no new way to fix the potatoes. She boiled them, fried a few strips of bacon and set out the milk and bread. She said: "Your father will be late. I'll eat when he comes."

They were always hungry children, but they were remembering Christmas morn-ing and weren't hungry now. Jackie's thoughts rose out of him in soft chuckles; and all Theo's features were caught in a far thinking. Eileen turned away and put her eyes to the dark window; and remained thus until they had finished eating. Theo cleared the table and wanted to wash the dishes. But Eileen did that. When bed-time came she lifted the lamp and carried it to the bedroom, and held it aloft while they prayed. Jackie said then: "You can have the warm side, Theo," and crawled beneath the covers. Eileen murmured, "Good night," and wheeled away. She heard them whispering in suppressed ea-gerness, the fullness of their deep hope too strong to contain. Theo's voice lifted out of the bedroom, round and certain.

"Mother, I have decided to use the shoe box for the new doll's bed."

Eileen put the lamp on the table and went back into the bedroom. She stood over them. Their eyes watched her with a sudden grave intentness. It was hard for her to speak. The words stopped in her mouth; she had to push them out:

"You must not expect too much. You must not cry if nothing comes to us. We are so far away, Theo, and there are so many people in the world who need things. If we are missed this year you must think that others who needed gifts worse got them."

They weren't believing her. They were listening only. She couldn't break through that hope—that trust in eventual justice. She said, in one breath, "Good night," and bent to kiss them and moved away. She sat down in a chair, her hands on the table, empty and motionless. She thought: "Why should the world be so hard?" and listened to the incessant pound of the wind. Thin drafts reached in through the win-dow and door cracks and turned the room cold. She got up, filled the stove, and sat down again. Waiting was always hard-est. She looked at her hands and found the light cruel to them. She was twenty-eight, yet the softness was gone from her skin. It didn't matter. But what had happened to her courage?

It was after eight when she heard Matt drive up to the door, and she knew in-stantly something was wrong. It was al-ways his custom to go first to the barn, out of kindness to the horse. But he had stopped by the door. She knew she had a duty here, which was to rise and go to the door and be there, smiling, when he came in. Yet she sat still, full of dread, and didn't move until after a long and drag-ging interval he came through and closed the door behind him with a heavy, dead roll of his shoulders. She sprang up then. She said, startled and fearing, "Matt!"

There were great bruises on his face, and his lips were swollen and crushed, and blood had frozen in small crystals in his nose. A long welt ran out of his hair, down across temple and jawbone. She walked toward him and put a hand to his wind-bitten skin. "Matt?"

"I found the calf," he said. "It was worth sixty-five dollars in Elyria. Jim Kelly of the Star Cross ranch bought it. That's what made me late. Are the children asleep?"

He went to the table and she noticed for the first time he was carrying a broad bundle under his arm. He put it on the table and took off his gloves, and fumbled at the string on the package with unresponsive fingers. He got impatient and broke the string—and rolled back the paper. Tired as he was, he was smiling crookedly out of his scarred mouth. There was a wax doll and a pair of skates lying on top of a piece of material. He put the toys aside and lifted the material. When it unrolled she saw it to be a dress, a fashionable silk dress of a mulberry color, such as she had seen in a magazine. He said, uncertainly, "This is Christmas, Eileen."

She swayed against him, suddenly crying without reserve, terribly and quietly. He pulled the dress from between them and held it in one hand, supporting her with the other. She said: "Why did you do it? We need food so badly." The stiff, icy coldness of his clothes stung her face.

"Henry Elser will be out with his wagon tomorrow, with food enough," he said. He was silent a moment. "But we needed these things worse than food, Eileen."

She wasn't able to look at him. Her answer was like a cry. "But I have nothing to give you!"

He put the dress carefully on the table; he pulled up her head. They clung to each other, two people remembering how merciless the years had been—and could yet be. There wasn't any security, and courage was hard to hold. But they clung to each other and the bitterness went from Matt Hobart's eyes. He bent down and kissed her. His voice steadied her. "Hard times will come again for us, Eileen. Often enough, I suppose. Nothing is as easy as we thought it would be. But there is something inside these four walls nothing can destroy."

The man who wrote this story

ERNEST HAYCOX   1899–1950

Raised in the rugged timber sections of Oregon and Washington, Ernest Haycox spent a hard but adventurous youth following his father from one logging camp to another. When the time came for him to attend high school, he worked his way as a bellhop. After World War I, he also managed to attend college.

Mr. Haycox wrote over three hundred short stories and twenty-four novels, most of them about the region he knew: the Northwest. The strongly regional setting which he gave to most of his fiction earned him the unofficial title, "dean of western storytellers."

In the last years of his life, Mr. Haycox planned a series of novels which would tell of the early settling and growth of the Northwest. These novels were to be different from any he had written before. Unfortunately he died before he could finish the series. Just *The Adventures* and *The Earthbreakers* have been published.

Let's consider . . .

1. What did you learn from the description of the Hobarts' home that suggested they were a poor family?

2. During the dinner, Eileen said, "I've lost my appetite from staying indoors too much." What was the real reason for her almost empty plate?

3. Why did Matt decide to visit Jim Grisim in spite of the bad weather and Eileen's protest?

4. How did Matt and Eileen accept their hard life? Whom did they blame?

5. How did Matt act when he first saw his missing calf? Why did he try to avoid a fight with the bald man and Harry? What "soft words" did he remember?

6. What problems did Eileen face in preparing meals for her family? How did she spend her day alone with the children?

7. What kind of person was the stranger who came to the Hobarts demanding food? What was his opinion about life in the prairie? How did his speech affect Eileen?

8. Why was Christmas a hard time for the Hobarts? How did the children make it even more difficult?

9. Matt and Eileen Hobart faced different kinds of challenges. What were they? Which challenge do you think required greater amount of courage? Give several reasons to support your answer.

10. Do you admire these pioneers for remaining to struggle with hostile Nature and hostile men? Or do you think they should have gone back East to comparative comfort? What does this country owe to them? Give good reasons for your answers.

11. Consider the structure of the story: the total make-up or arrangement of episodes. What is the purpose of the whole episode of the yearling?

12. What can you say in favor of reading a sad story now and then? Is this story without hope? Why or why not?

The writer's craft . . .

A. In every short story there are characters, a plot, and a setting. The **characters** are the people in the story. You learn to know them by their speech, by their actions, and by what the author tells you about them. They must seem real and believable. One of the responsibilities of an author is to make his characters **consistent:** their speech and actions must follow a pattern. Ernest Haycox created consistent characters in Matt and Eileen. They tried to overcome their difficulties with courage. They were self-sacrificing, humble, and brave. They were concerned with the happiness of their children. This was the pattern of behavior which the author set for them.

Even the minor characters in a story should be consistent. What information were you given about each of the following characters: Tom, Dike Tyler, the man who stole the calf, and the stranger? Explain why their speech and actions were consistent with what you expected. If any of them did not seem consistent, explain why.

B. You will remember that the plot of a story describes what happens. In "Deep Horizons" the plot might be summarized in a few sentences: Matt Hobart, a minister, is trying to make a happy life for his family in the Nebraska prairie. They are very poor and often do not have enough to eat. The children are looking forward to Christmas, but unless Matt can find who stole his calf and get it back, he will have to disappoint them. Matt is forced into a fight against his will but he wins out and is able to buy Christmas gifts for his family.

Every novel, short story, theater play, or movie has a plot. Select a movie you have seen or a book you have read. Very briefly summarize what happened. Be sure to include the important events in the order in which they occurred.

C. The action of every story is placed in a particular setting. The **setting** of a story is its background of time and place.

1. What is the setting of "Deep Horizons"?

2. How did the author make you aware of the severe cold and bad weather? Why do you think he emphasized the season of the year? Would the story have lost some of its dramatic effect if the action had occurred in spring or summer? Why or why not?

Locomotive 38, the Ojibway

WILLIAM SAROYAN

Americans do not need a war or other national emergency to do the "right thing." They often act unselfishly just to make others feel good.

One day a man came to town on a donkey and began loafing around in the public library where I used to spend most of my time in those days. He was a tall young Indian of the Ojibway tribe. He told me his name was Locomotive 38. Everybody in town believed he had escaped from an asylum.

Six days after he arrived in town his animal was struck by the Tulare Street trolley and seriously injured. The following day the animal passed away, most likely of internal injuries, on the corner of Mariposa and Fulton streets. The animal sank to the pavement, fell on the Indian's leg, groaned and died. When the Indian got his leg free he got up and limped into the drugstore on the corner and made a long-distance telephone call. He telephoned his brother in Oklahoma. The call cost him a lot of money, which he dropped into the slot as requested by the operator as if he were in the habit of making such calls every day.

I was in the drugstore at the time, eating a Royal Banana Special, with crushed walnuts.

When he came out of the telephone booth he saw me sitting at the soda fountain eating this fancy dish.

Hello, Willie, he said.

He knew my name wasn't Willie—he just liked to call me that.

He limped to the front of the store where the gum was, and bought three packages of Juicy Fruit. Then he limped back to me and said, What's that you're eating, Willie? It looks good.

This is what they call a Royal Banana Special, I said.

The Indian got up on the stool next to me.

Give me the same, he said to the soda fountain girl.

That's too bad about your animal, I said.

There's no place for an animal in this world, he said. What kind of an automobile should I buy?

Are you going to buy an automobile? I said.

I've been thinking about it for several minutes now, he said.

I didn't think you had any money, I said. I thought you were poor.

That's the impression people get, he said. Another impression they get is that I'm crazy.

I didn't get the impression that you were crazy, I said, but I didn't get the impression that you were rich, either.

Well, I am, the Indian said.

I wish I was rich, I said.

What for? he said.

Well, I said, I've been wanting to go fishing at Mendota for three years in a row now. I need some equipment and some kind of an automobile to get out there in.

Can you drive an automobile? the Indian said.

I can drive anything, I said.

Have you ever driven an automobile? he said.

Not yet, I said. So far I haven't had any automobile to drive, and it's against my family religion to steal an automobile.

Do you mean to tell me you believe you could get into an automobile and start driving? he said.

That's right, I said.

Remember what I was telling you on the steps of the public library the other evening? he said.

You mean about the machine age? I said.

Yes, he said.

I remember, I said.

All right, he said. Indians are born with an instinct for riding, rowing, hunting, fishing, and swimming. Americans are born with an instinct for fooling around with machines.

I'm no American, I said.

I know, the Indian said. You're an Armenian. I remember. I asked you and you told me. You're an Armenian born in America. You're fourteen years old and already you know you'll be able to drive an automobile the minute you get into one. You're a typical American, although your complexion, like my own, is dark.

Driving a car is no trick, I said. There's nothing to it. It's easier than riding a donkey.

All right, the Indian said. Just as you say. If I go up the street and buy an automobile, will you drive for me?

Of course, I said.

How much in wages would you want? he said.

You mean you want to give me wages for driving an automobile? I said.

Of course, the Ojibway said.

Well, I said, that's very nice of you, but I don't want any money for driving an automobile.

Some of the journeys may be long ones, he said.

The longer the better, I said.

Are you restless? he said.

I was born in this little old town, I said.

Don't you like it? he said.

I like mountains and streams and mountain lakes, I said.

Have you ever been in the mountains? he said.

Not yet, I said, but I'm going to reach them some day.

I see, he said. What kind of an automobile do you think I ought to buy?

How about a Ford roadster? I said.

Is that the best automobile? he said.

Do you want the *best*? I said.

Shouldn't I have the best? he said.

I don't know, I said. The best costs a lot of money.

What is the best? he said.

Well, I said, some people think the Cadillac is the best. Others like the Packard. They're both pretty good. I wouldn't know which is best. The Packard is beautiful to see going down the highway, but so is the Cadillac. I've watched a lot of them fine cars going down the highway.

How much is a Packard? he said.

Around three thousand dollars, I said. Maybe a little more.

Can we get one right away? he said.

I got down off the stool. He sounded crazy, but I knew he wasn't.

Listen, Mr. Locomotive, I said, do you really want to buy a Packard right away?

You know my animal passed away a few minutes ago, he said.

I saw it happen, I said. They'll probably be arresting you any minute now for leaving the animal in the street.

They won't arrest me, he said.

They will if there's a law against leaving a dead donkey in the street, I said.

No, they won't, he said.

Why not? I said.

Well, he said, they won't after I show them a few papers I carry around with me all the time. The people of this country have a lot of respect for money, and I've got a lot of money.

I guess he is crazy after all, I thought.

Where'd you get all this money? I said.

I own some land in Oklahoma, he said. About fifty thousand acres.

Is it worth money? I said.

No, he said. All but about twenty acres of it is worthless. I've got some oil wells on them twenty acres. My brother and I.

How did you Ojibways ever get down to Oklahoma? I said. I always thought the Ojibways lived up north, up around the Great Lakes.

That's right, the Indian said. We used to live up around the Great Lakes but my grandfather was a pioneer. He moved west when everybody else did.

Oh, I said. Well, I guess they won't bother you about the dead donkey at that.

They won't bother me about anything, he said. It won't be because I've got money. It'll be because they think I'm crazy. Nobody in this town but you knows I've got money. Do you know where we can get one of them automobiles right away?

The Packard agency is up on Broadway, two blocks beyond the public library, I said.

All right, he said. If you're sure you won't mind driving for me, let's go get one of them. Something bright in color, he said. Red, if they've got red. Where would you like to drive to first?

Would you care to go fishing at Mendota? I said.

I'll take the ride, he said. I'll watch you fish. Where can we get some equipment for you?

Right around the corner at Homan's, I said.

We went around the corner to Homan's and the Indian bought twenty-seven dollars' worth of fishing equipment for me. Then we went up to the Packard agency on Broadway. They didn't have a red Packard, but there was a beautiful green one. It was light green, the color of new grass. This was back there in 1922. The car was a beautiful sports touring model.

Do you think you could drive this great big car? the Indian said.

I *know* I can drive it, I said.

The police found us in the Packard agency and wanted to arrest the Indian for leaving the dead donkey in the street. He showed them the papers he had told me about and the police apologized and went away. They said they'd removed the animal and were sorry they'd troubled him about it.

I'll take this car, he said.

He turned to the manager of the Packard agency, Jim Lewis, who used to run for Mayor every time election time came around.

I'll take this car, he said.

I'll draw up the papers immediately, Jim said.

What papers? the Indian said. I'm going to pay for it now.

You mean you want to pay three thousand two hundred seventeen dollars and sixty-five cents *cash*? Jim said.

Yes, the Indian said. It's ready to drive, isn't it?

Of course, Jim said. I'll have the boys go over it with a cloth to take off any dust on it. I'll have them check the motor too, and fill the gasoline tank. It won't take more than ten minutes. If you'll step into the office I'll close the transaction immediately.

Jim and the Indian stepped into Jim's office.

About three minutes later Jim came over to me, a man shaken to the roots.

Aram, he said, who is this guy? I thought he was a nut. I had Johnny telephone the Pacific-Southwest and they said his bank account is being transferred from somewhere in Oklahoma. They said his account is something over a million dollars. I thought he was a nut. Do you know him?

He told me his name is Locomotive 38, I said. That's no name.

That's a translation of his Indian name, Jim said. We've got his full name on the contract. Do you know him?

I've talked to him every day since he came to town on that donkey that died this morning, I said, but I never thought he had any money.

He says you're going to drive for him, Jim said. Are you sure you're the man to drive a great big car like this, son?

Wait a minute now, Mr. Lewis, I said. Don't try to push me out of this chance of a lifetime. I can drive this big Packard as well as anybody else in town.

I'm not trying to push you out of anything, Jim said. I just don't want you to drive out of here and run over six or seven innocent people and maybe smash the car. Get into the car and I'll give you a few pointers. Do you know anything about the gearshift?

I don't know anything about anything yet, I said, but I'll soon find out.

All right, Jim said. Just let me help you.

I got into the car and sat down behind the wheel. Jim got in beside me.

From now on, son, he said, I want you to regard me as a friend who will give you the shirt off his back. I want to thank you for bringing me this fine Indian gentleman.

He told me he wanted the best car on the market, I said. You know I've always been crazy about driving a Packard. Now how do I do it?

Well, Jim said, let's see.

He looked down at my feet.

Great Scott, son, he said, your feet don't reach the pedals.

Never mind that, I said. You just explain the gearshift.

Jim explained everything while the boys wiped the dust off the car and went over the motor and filled the gasoline tank. When the Indian came out and got into the car, in the back where I insisted he should sit, I had the motor going.

He says he knows how to drive, the Indian said to Jim Lewis. By instinct, he said. I believe him, too.

You needn't worry about Aram here, Jim said. He can drive all right. Clear the way there, boys, he shouted. Let him have all the room necessary.

I turned the big car around slowly, shifted, and shot out of the agency at about fifty miles an hour, with Jim Lewis running after the car and shouting, Take it easy, son. Don't open up until you get out on the highway. The speed limit in town is twenty-five miles an hour.

The Indian wasn't at all excited, even though I was throwing him around a good deal.

I wasn't doing it on purpose, though. It was simply that I wasn't very familiar with the manner in which the automobile worked.

You're an excellent driver, Willie, he said. It's like I said. You're an American and you were born with an instinct for mechanical contraptions like this.

We'll be in Mendota in an hour, I said. You'll see some great fishing out there.

How far is Mendota? the Indian said.

About ninety miles, I said.

Ninety miles is too far to go in an hour, the Indian said. Take two hours. We're passing a lot of interesting scenery I'd like to look at a little more closely.

All right, I said, but I sure am anxious to get out there and fish.

Well, all right then, the Indian said. Go as fast as you like this time, but some time I'll expect you to drive a little more slowly, so I can see some of the scenery. I'm missing everything. I don't even get a chance to read the signs.

I'll travel slowly *now* if you want me to, I said.

No, he insisted. Let her go. Let her go as fast as she'll go.

Well, we got out to Mendota in an hour and seventeen minutes. I would have made better time except for the long stretch of dirt road.

I drove the car right up to the riverbank. The Indian asked if I knew how to get the top down, so he could sit in the open and watch me fish. I didn't know how to get the top down, but I got it down. It took me twenty minutes to do it.

I fished for about three hours, fell into the river twice, and finally landed a small one.

You don't know the first thing about fishing, the Indian said.

What am I doing wrong? I said.

Everything, he said. Have you ever fished before?

No, I said.

I didn't think so, he said.

What am I doing wrong? I said.

Well, he said, nothing in particular, only you're fishing at about the same rate of speed that you drive an automobile.

Is that wrong? I said.

It's not exactly wrong, he said, except that it'll keep you from getting anything to speak of, and you'll go on falling into the river.

I'm not falling, I said. They're pulling me in. They've got an awful pull. This grass is mighty slippery, too. There ain't nothing around here to grab hold of.

I reeled in one more little one and then I asked if he'd like to go home. He said he would if I wanted to, too, so I put away the fishing equipment and the two fish and got in the car and started driving back to town.

I drove that big Packard for this Ojibway Indian, Locomotive 38, as long as he stayed in town, which was all summer. He stayed at the hotel all the time. I tried to get him to learn to drive, but he said it was out of the question. I drove that Packard all over the San Joaquín Valley that summer, with the Indian in the back, chewing eight or nine sticks of gum. He told me to drive anywhere I cared to go, so it was either to some place where I could fish, or some place where I could hunt. He claimed I didn't know anything about fishing or hunting, but he was glad to see me trying. As long as I knew him he never laughed, except once. That was the time I shot at a jack rabbit with a twelve-gauge shotgun that had a terrible kick, and killed a crow. He tried to tell me all the time that that was my average. To shoot at a jack rabbit and kill a crow. You're an American, he said. Look at the way you took to this big automobile.

One day in November that year his brother came to town from Oklahoma, and

the next day when I went down to the hotel to get him, they told me he'd gone back to Oklahoma with his brother.

Where's the Packard? I said.

They took the Packard, the hotel clerk said.

Who drove? I said.

The Indian, the clerk said.

They're both Indians, I said. Which of the brothers drove the car?

The one who lived at this hotel, the clerk said.

Are you sure? I said.

Well, I only saw him get into the car out front and drive away, the clerk said. That's all.

Do you mean to tell me he knew how to shift gears? I said.

It *looked* as if he did, the clerk said. He looked like an expert driver to me.

Thanks, I said.

On the way home I figured he'd just wanted me to *believe* he couldn't drive, so *I* could drive all the time and feel good. He was just a young man who'd come to town on a donkey, bored to death or something, who'd taken advantage of the chance to be entertained by a small-town kid who was bored to death, too. That's the only way I could figure it out without accepting the general theory that he was crazy.

The man who wrote this story

WILLIAM SAROYAN 1908–

William Saroyan has made his own background, an Armenian colony in Fresno, California, the material for many of his stories and books. Saroyan found that these people had a special humor and bravery, even when facing the most severe trials.

Saroyan wanted to be a writer from the time he was thirteen. Unlike most American authors, he was not to have much formal education. He dropped out of school in the eighth grade to go to work, but he educated himself by reading during every spare moment. He was twenty-five when his first story was printed, and he soon found himself successful both as an author and a playwright.

Saroyan's stories and novels have a special atmosphere of their own. They are not like most stories; they do not follow the usual rules about plot and character. They are more like sketches than stories. Yet Saroyan's subtle skill and sensitivity to people have made these stories popular and enduring. *The Assyrian and Other Stories* (1949) is a popular collection of his stories.

Let's consider . . .

1. What information were you given about the Ojibway's appearance? About Aram's appearance?

2. Indians are often spoken of as simple people with simple tastes. What did you find in this story that would support or contradict such an opinion?

3. When a story is told in dialogue, many details are left to the reader's imagination. What do you imagine the Indian told his brother when he made the long-distance telephone call?

4. "Mr. Locomotive" had a great deal of confidence in certain papers. What do you think these papers were?

5. Why didn't the Indian teach "Willie" how to fish and hunt?

6. At the end of the story, Aram gave *his* explanation of the Ojibway's summer escapades. What is *your* explanation?

The writer's craft . . .

1. Each author has a **style:** the words he chooses and the way he arranges them. William Saroyan's style is simple and free-flowing. Still he achieved an effect which

could hardly be improved by an elaborate structure and vocabulary. In your opinion, what is the most pleasing quality of Saroyan's style?

2. In the first four paragraphs, Saroyan gave you the **exposition** of the story: the background information and situation from which the story developed. From then on, he told the story almost entirely in dialogue, except for a few necessary statements of explanation. What are the advantages of using so much direct conversation to tell a story? What are the disadvantages?

3. You have probably been told, when writing conversation in a story of your own, to use other expressions besides "he said." Saroyan repeated "he said" and "I said" throughout the story. Why do you suppose he did this? What effect did this repetition have on you?

4. It was part of Saroyan's style to use very few punctuation marks. Copy several lines of dialogue from the story and punctuate them. How is the effect of the story changed by punctuation? Explain.

5. The author tells this story from the **first-person point of view:** as the "I" in the story would tell it. Why did the author's choice of this point of view make the story seem more believable? What tone did it give the story?

fate is unfair

in many places here and
there
i think that fate
is quite unfair
yon centipede upon
the floor
can boast of
tootsies by the score
consider my
distressing fix
my feet are limited
to six
did i a hundred
feet possess
would all that glorious
footfulness
enable me
to stagger less
when i am
overcome by heat

or if i had
a hundred feet
would i
careering oer the floor
stagger
proportionately more
well i suppose
the mind serene
will not tell
destiny its mean
the truly
philosophic mind
will use
such feet as it can find
and follow calmly
fast or slow
the feet it has
where eer they go

　　　　archy
　　　Don Marquis

2 Soldiers

WILLIAM FAULKNER

Pete's little brother did not really understand what war was all about.
Neither did he understand that he couldn't take matters into his own
hands. When Pete enlisted in the army, the eight-year-old boy felt he
should go along. It wasn't easy to convince him that his place was home
on the farm, looking after "Maw" and Pete's ten acres.

Me and Pete would go down to Old
Man Killegrew's and listen to his radio.
We would wait until after supper, after
dark, and we would stand outside Old
Man Killegrew's parlor window, and we
could hear it because Old Man Killegrew's
wife was deaf, and so he run the radio as
loud as it would run, and so me and Pete
could hear it plain as Old Man Killegrew's
wife could, I reckon, even standing outside with the window closed.

And that night I said, "What? Japanese?
What's a pearl harbor?" and Pete said,
"Hush."

And so we stood there, it was cold, listening to the fellow in the radio talking,
only I couldn't make no heads nor tails
out of it. Then the fellow said that would
be all for a while, and me and Pete walked
back up the road to home, and Pete told
me what it was. Because he was nigh
twenty and he had done finished the Consolidated [1] last June and he knowed a
heap: about them Japanese dropping
bombs on Pearl Harbor and that Pearl
Harbor was across the water.

"Across what water?" I said. "Across
that Government reservoy up at Oxford?" [2]

"Naw," Pete said. "Across the big water.
The Pacific Ocean."

We went home. Maw and pap was already asleep and me and Pete laid in bed,
and I still couldn't understand where it
was, and Pete told me again—the Pacific
Ocean.

"What's the matter with you?" Pete said.
"You're going on nine years old. You
been in school now ever since September.
Ain't you learned nothing yet?"

"I reckon we ain't got as fer as the Pacific Ocean yet," I said.

We was still sowing the vetch [3] then
that ought to been all finished by the fifteenth of November, because pap was still
behind, just like he had been ever since
me and Pete had knowed him. And we
had firewood to git in, too, but every night
me and Pete would go down to Old Man
Killegrew's and stand outside his parlor
window in the cold and listen to his radio;
then we would come back home and lay
in bed and Pete would tell me what it was.
That is, he would tell me for a while.
Then he wouldn't tell me. It was like
he didn't want to talk about it no more.
He would tell me to shut up because he

[1] *Consolidated,* consolidated school
[2] *Oxford,* a town in northern Mississippi
[3] *vetch,* plant used as food for certain farm animals

wanted to go to sleep, but he never wanted to go to sleep.

He would lay there, a heap stiller than if he was asleep, and it would be something, I could feel it coming out of him, like he was mad at me, or like he was worried about something, and it wasn't that neither, because he never had nothing to worry about. He never got behind like pap, let alone stayed behind. Pap give him ten acres when he graduated from the Consolidated, and me and Pete both reckoned pap was durn glad to get shut of at least ten acres, less to have to worry about himself; and Pete had them ten acres all sowed to vetch and busted out and bedded for the winter, and so it wasn't that. But it was something. And still we would go down to Old Man Killegrew's every night and listen to his radio, and they was at it in the Philippines now, but General MacArthur was holding um. Then we would come back home and lay in the bed, and Pete wouldn't tell me nothing or talk at all. He would just lay there still as an ambush and when I would touch him, his side or his leg would feel hard and still as iron, until after a while and I would go to sleep.

Then one night—it was the first time he had said nothing to me except to jump on me about not chopping enough wood at the wood tree where he was cutting—he said, "I got to go."

"Go where?" I said.

"To that war," Pete said.

"Before we even finish gettin' in the firewood?"

"Firewood, heck," Pete said.

"All right," I said. "When we going to start?"

But he wasn't even listening. He laid there, hard and still as iron in the dark. "I got to go," he said. "I jest ain't going to put up with no folks treating the Unity States that way."

"Yes," I said. "Firewood or no firewood, I reckon we got to go."

This time he heard me. He laid still again, but it was a different kind of still.

"You?" he said. "To a war?"

"You'll whup the big uns and I'll whup the little uns," I said.

Then he told me I couldn't go. At first I thought he just never wanted me tagging after him, like he wouldn't leave me go with him when he went sparking them girls of Tull's. Then he told me the Army wouldn't leave me go because I was too little, and then I knowed he really meant it and that I couldn't go nohow noways. And somehow I hadn't believed until then that he was going himself, but now I knowed he was and that he wasn't going to leave me go with him a-tall.

"I'll chop the wood and tote the water for you-all then!" I said. "You got to have wood and water!"

Anyway, he was listening to me now. He wasn't like iron now.

He turned onto his side and put his hand on my chest because it was me that was laying straight and hard on my back now.

"No," he said. "You got to stay here and help pap."

"Help him what?" I said. "He ain't never caught up nohow. He can't get no further behind. He can sholy take care of this little shirttail of a farm while me and you are whupping them Japanese. I got to go too. If you got to go, then so have I."

"No," Pete said. "Hush now. Hush." And he meant it, and I knowed he did. Only I made sho from his own mouth. I quit.

"So I just can't go then," I said.

"No," Pete said. "You just can't go. You're too little, in the first place, and in the second place—"

"All right," I said. "Then shut up and leave me to go to sleep."

So he hushed then and laid back. And I laid there like I was already asleep, and pretty soon he was asleep and I knowed it was the wanting to go to the war that had worried him and kept him awake, and now that he had decided to go, he wasn't worried any more.

The next morning he told maw and pap. Maw was all right. She cried.

"No," she said, crying, "I don't want him to go. I would rather go myself in his place, if I could. I don't want to save the country. Them Japanese could take it all and keep it, so long as they left me and my family and my children alone. But I remember my brother Marsh in that other war. He had to go to that one when he wasn't but nineteen and our mother couldn't understand it then any more than I can now. But she told Marsh if he had to go, he had to go. And so, if Pete's got to go to this one, he's got to go to it. Jest don't ask me to understand why."

But pap was the one. He was the feller. "To the war?" he said. "Why I don't see a bit of use in that. You ain't old enough for the draft, and the country ain't being invaded. Our President in Washington, D. C., is watching the conditions and he will notify us. Besides, in that other war your ma just mentioned, I was drafted and sent clean to Texas and was held there nigh eight months until they finally quit fighting. It seems to me that that, along with your Uncle Marsh who received a actual wound on the battlefields of France, is enough for me and mine to have to do to protect the country, at least in my lifetime. Besides, what'll I do for help on the farm with you gone? It seems to me I'll get mighty far behind."

"You been behind as long as I can remember," Pete said. "Anyway I'm going. I got to."

"Of course he's got to go," I said. "Them Japanese—"

"You hush your mouth!" maw said, crying. "Nobody's talking to you! Go and get Ma a armful of wood! That's what you can do!"

So I got the wood. And all the next day, while me and Pete and pap was getting in as much wood as we could in that time because Pete said how pap's idea of plenty of wood was one more stick laying against the wall that maw ain't put on the fire yet,

maw was getting Pete ready to go. She washed and mended his clothes and cooked him a shoe box of vittles. And that night me and Pete laid in the bed and listened to her packing his grip and crying, until after a while Pete got up in his nightshirt and went back there, and I could hear them talking, until at last maw said, "You ought to go, and so I want you to go. But I don't understand it, and I won't never, and so don't expect me to." And Pete come back and got into bed again and laid again still and hard as iron on his back, and then he said, and he wasn't talking to me, he wasn't talking to nobody: "I got to go. I just got to."

"Sho you got to," I said. "Them Japanese—" He turned over hard, he kind of surged over onto his side, looking at me in the dark.

"Anyway, you're all right," he said. "I expected to have more trouble with you than with all the rest of them put together."

"I reckon I can't help it neither," I said. "But maybe it will run a few years longer and I can get there. Maybe someday I will jest walk in on you."

"I hope not," Pete said. "Folks don't go to wars for fun. A man don't leave his maw crying just for fun."

"Then why are you going?" I said.

"I got to," he said. "I just got to. Now you go on to sleep. I got to ketch that early bus in the morning."

"All right," I said, "I hear tell Memphis is a big place. How will you find where the Army's at?"

"I'll ask somebody where to go to join it," Pete said. "Go on to sleep now."

"Is that what you'll ask for? Where to join the Army?" I said.

"Yes," Pete said. He turned onto his back again. "Shut up and go to sleep."

We went to sleep. The next morning we et breakfast by lamplight because the bus would pass at six o'clock. Maw wasn't crying now. She just looked grim and busy, putting breakfast on the table while we et it. Then she finished packing Pete's grip, except he never wanted to take no grip to the war, but maw said decent folks never went nowhere, not even to a war, without change of clothes and something to tote them in. She put in the shoe box of fried chicken and biscuits and she put the Bible in, too, and then it was time to go. We didn't know until then that maw wasn't going to the bus. She jest brought Pete's cap and overcoat, and still she didn't cry no more, she jest stood with her hands on Pete's shoulders and she didn't move, but somehow, and just holding Pete's shoulders, she looked as hard and fierce as when Pete had turned toward me in the bed last night and tole me that anyway I was all right.

"They could take the country and keep the country, as long as they never bothered me and mine," she said. Then she said, "Don't never forget who you are. You ain't rich and the rest of the world outside of Frenchman's Bend never heard of you. But your blood is good as any blood anywhere, and don't you never forget it."

Then she kissed him, and then we was out of the house, with pap toting Pete's grip whether Pete wanted him to or not. There wasn't no dawn even yet, not even after we had stood on the highway by the mailbox, awhile. Then we seen the lights of the bus coming and I was watching the bus until it come up and Pete flagged it, and then, sho enough, there was daylight —it had started while I wasn't watching. And now me and Pete expected pap to say something else foolish, like he done before, about how Uncle Marsh getting wounded in France and that trip to Texas pap had taken in 1918 ought to be enough to save the Unity States in 1942, but he never. He done all right too. He jest said, "Good-by, son. Always remember what your ma told you and write her whenever you find the time." Then he shaken Pete's hand, and Pete looked at me a minute and put his hand on my head and rubbed my head durn nigh hard enough to wring my

neck off and jumped into the bus, and the feller wound the door shut and the bus begun to hum; then it was moving, humming and grinding and whining louder and louder; it was going fast, with two little red lights behind it that never seemed to get no littler, but jest seemed to be running together until pretty soon they would touch and jest be one light. But they never did, and then the bus was gone, and even like it was, I could have pretty nigh busted out crying, nigh to nine years old and all.

Me and pap went back to the house. All that day we worked at the wood tree, and so I never had no good chance until about middle of the afternoon. Then I taken my slingshot and I would have liked to took all my bird eggs, too, because Pete had give me his collection and he holp me with mine, and he would like to git the box out and look at them as good as I would, even if he was nigh twenty years old. But the box was too big to tote a long ways and have to worry with, so I just taken the shikepoke egg,[4] because it was the best un, and wropped it up good into a matchbox and hid it and the slingshot under the corner of the barn. Then we et supper and went to bed, and I thought then how if I would 'a' had to stayed in that room and that bed like that even for one more night, I jest couldn't 'a' stood it. Then I could hear pap snoring, but I never heard no sound from maw, whether she was asleep or not, and I don't reckon she was. So I taken my shoes and drapped them out the window, and then I clumb out like I used to watch Pete do when he was still jest seventeen and pap wouldn't leave him out, and I put on my shoes and went to the barn and got the slingshot and the shikepoke egg and went to the highway.

It wasn't cold, it was jest durn confounded dark, and that highway stretched on in front of me like, without nobody using it, it had stretched out half again as fer just like a man does when he lays down, so that for a time it looked like full

---

[4] *shikepoke egg,* heron's egg

sun was going to ketch me before I had finished them twenty-two miles to Jefferson. But it didn't. Daybreak was jest starting when I walked up the hill into town. I could smell breakfast cooking in the cabins and I wished I had thought to brought me a cold biscuit, but that was too late now. And Pete had told me Memphis was a piece beyond Jefferson, but I never knowed it was no eighty miles. So I stood there on that empty square, with daylight coming and coming and the street lights still burning and that Law [5] looking down at me, and me still eighty miles from Memphis, and it had took me all night to walk jest twenty-two miles, and so, by the time I got to Memphis at that rate, Pete would 'a' done already started for Pearl Harbor.

"Where do you come from?" the Law said. And I told him again. "I got to git to Memphis. My brother's there."

"You mean you ain't got any folks around here?" the Law said. "Nobody but

that brother? What are you doing way off down here and your brother in Memphis?"

And I told him again, "I got to git to Memphis. I ain't got no time to waste talking about it and I ain't got time to walk it. I got to git there today."

"Come on here," the Law said.

We went down another street. And there was the bus, jest like when Pete got into it yestiddy morning, except there wasn't no lights on it now and it was empty. There was a regular bus dee-po like a railroad dee-po, with a ticket counter and a feller behind it, and the Law said, "Set down over there," and I set down on the bench, and the Law said, "I want to use your telephone," and he talked into the telephone a minute and put it down and said to the feller behind the ticket counter, "Keep your eye on him. I'll be back as soon as Mrs. Habersham can arrange to get herself up and dressed." He went out. I got up and went to the ticket counter.

"I want to go to Memphis," I said.

"You bet," the feller said. "You set

5 *Law,* policeman

down on the bench now. Mr. Foote will be back in a minute."

"I don't know no Mr. Foote," I said. "I want to ride that bus to Memphis."

"You got some money?" he said. "It'll cost seventy-two cents."

I taken out the matchbox and unwropped the shikepoke egg. "I'll swap you this for a ticket to Memphis," I said.

"What's that?" he said.

"It's a shikepoke egg," I said. "You never seen one before. It's worth a dollar. I'll take seventy-two cents fer it."

"No," he said, "the fellers that own that bus insist on a cash basis. If I started swapping tickets for bird eggs and livestock and such, they would fire me. You go and set down on the bench now, like Mr. Foote—"

I started for the door, but he caught me, he put one hand on the ticket counter and jumped over it and caught up with me and reached his hand out to ketch my shirt.

"You put a hand on me and I'll cut it off," I said.

I tried to dodge him and run at the door, but he could move quicker than any grown man I ever see, quick as Pete almost. He cut me off and stood with his back against the door and one foot raised a little, and there wasn't no other way to get out. "Get back on that bench and stay there," he said.

And there wasn't no other way out. And he stood against the door. So I went back to the bench. And then it seemed like to me that dee-po was full of folks. There was that Law again, and there was two ladies in fur coats and their faces already painted. But they still looked like they had got up in a hurry and they still never liked it, a old one and a young one, looking down at me.

"He hasn't got an overcoat!" the old one said. "How in the world did he ever get down here by himself?"

"I ask you," the Law said. "I couldn't get nothing out of him except his brother is in Memphis and he wants to get back up there."

"That's right," I said. "I got to git to Memphis today."

"Of course you must," the old one said. "Are you sure you can find your brother when you get to Memphis?"

"I reckon I can," I said. "I ain't got but one and I have knowed him all my life. I reckon I will know him again when I see him."

The old one looked at me. "Somehow he doesn't look like he lives in Memphis," she said.

"He probably don't," the Law said. "You can't tell though. He might live anywhere, overhalls or not. This day and time they get scattered overnight from hope to breakfast; boys and girls, too, almost before they can walk good. He might have been in Missouri or Texas either yestiddy, for all we know. But he don't seem to have any doubt his brother is in Memphis. All I know to do is send him up there and leave him look."

"Yes," the old one said.

The young one set down on the bench by me and opened a hand satchel and taken out a artermatic writing pen and some papers.

"Now, honey," the old one said, "we're going to see that you find your brother, but we must have a case history for our files first. We want to know your name and your brother's name and where you were born and when your parents died."

"I don't need no case history neither," I said. "All I want is to git to Memphis. I got to git there today."

"You see?" the Law said. He said it almost like he enjoyed it. "That's what I told you."

"You're lucky, at that, Mrs. Habersham," the bus feller said. "I don't think he's got a gun on him, but he can open that knife fast enough to suit any man."

But the old one just stood there looking at me.

"Well," she said. "Well. I really don't know what to do."

"I do," the bus feller said. "I'm going to

give him a ticket out of my own pocket, as a measure of protecting the company against riot and bloodshed. And when Mr. Foote tells the city board about it, it will be a civic matter and they will give me a medal too. Hey, Mr. Foote?"

But nobody paid him no mind. The old one still stood looking down at me. She said, "Well," again. Then she taken a dollar from her purse and give it to the bus feller. "I suppose he will travel on a child's ticket, won't he?"

"Wellum," the bus feller said, "I just don't know what the regulations would be. Likely I will be fired for not crating him and marking the crate Poison. But I'll risk it."

Then they were gone. Then the Law come back with a sandwich and give it to me.

"You're sure you can find that brother?" he said.

"I ain't yet convinced why not," I said. "If I don't see Pete first, he'll see me. He knows me too."

Then the Law went out for good, too, and I et the sandwich. Then more folks come in and bought tickets, and then the bus feller said it was time to go, and I got into the bus just like Pete done, and we were gone.

I seen all the towns. I seen all of them. When the bus got to going good, I found out I was jest about wore out for sleep. But there was too much I hadn't never saw before. We run out of Jefferson and run past fields and woods, then we would run into another town and out of that un and past fields and woods again, and then into another town with stores and gins [6] and water tanks, and we run along by the railroad for a spell and I seen the signal arm move, and then some more towns, and I was jest about plumb wore out for sleep, but I couldn't resk it. Then Memphis begun. It seemed like, to me, it went on for miles. We would pass a patch of stores

and I would think that was sholy it and the bus would even stop. But it wouldn't be Memphis yet and we would go on again past water tanks and smokestacks on top of the mills, and if they was gins and sawmills, I never knowed there was that many and I never seen any that big, and where they got enough cotton and logs to run um I don't know.

Then I seen Memphis. I knowed I was right this time. It was standing up into the air. It looked like about a dozen whole towns bigger than Jefferson was set up on one edge in a field, standing up into the air higher than ara [7] hill in all Yoknapatawpha County. Then we was in it, with the bus stopping every few feet, it seemed like to me, and cars rushing past on both sides of it and the streets crowded with folks from ever'where in town that day, until I didn't see how there could 'a' been nobody left in Mis'sippi a-tall to even sell me a bus ticket, let alone write out no case histories. Then the bus stopped. It was another bus dee-po, a heap bigger than the one in Jefferson. And I said, "All right. Where do folks join the Army?"

"What?" the bus feller said.

And I said it again, "Where do folks join the Army?"

"Oh," he said. Then he told me how to get there. I was afraid at first I wouldn't ketch on how to do in a town as big as Memphis. But I caught on all right. I never had to ask but twice more. Then I was there, and I was durn glad to git out of all them rushing cars and shoving folks and all that racket for a spell, and I thought, it won't be long now, and I thought how if there was any kind of a crowd there that had done already joined the Army, too, Pete would likely see me before I seen him. And so I walked into the room. And Pete wasn't there.

He wasn't even there. There was a soldier with a big arrerhead on his sleeve, writing, and two fellers standing in front of him, and there was some more folks

---

[6] *gins,* cotton gins; machines for picking seeds out of cotton

[7] *ara,* any

there, I reckon. It seems to me I remember some more folks there.

I went to the table where the soldier was writing, and I said, "Where's Pete?" and he looked up and I said, "My brother. Pete Grier. Where is he?"

"What?" the soldier said. "Who?"

And I told him again. "He joined the Army yestiddy. He's going to Pearl Harbor. So am I. I want to ketch him. Where you all got him?" Now they were all looking at me, but I never paid them no mind. "Come on," I said. "Where is he?"

The soldier had quit writing. He had both hands spraddled out on the table. "Oh," he said. "You're going, too, hah?"

"Yes," I said. "They got to have wood and water. I can chop it and tote it. Come on. Where's Pete?"

The soldier stood up. "Who let you in here?" he said. "Go on. Beat it."

"Durn that," I said. "You tell me where Pete—"

I be dog if he couldn't move faster than the bus feller even. He never come over the table, he come around it, he was on me almost before I knowed it, so that I jest had time to jump back and whup out my pocketknife and snap it open. He hollared and jumped back and grabbed one hand with the other and stood there cussing and hollering.

One of the other fellers grabbed me from behind, and I hit at him, but I couldn't reach him.

Then both of the fellers had me from behind, and then another soldier come out of a door at the back. He had on a belt with a britching strop over one shoulder.

"What's this?" he said.

"That little guy tried to knife me!" the first soldier hollared. Both them fellers was holding me, two against one, and the soldier with the backing strop said, "Here, here. Put your knife up, feller. None of us are armed. A man don't knife-fight folks that are bare-handed." I could begin to hear him then. He sounded jest like

Pete talked to me. "Let him go," he said. They let me go. "Now what's all the trouble about?" And I told him. "I see," he said. "And you come up to see if he was all right before he left."

"No," I said. "I came to—"

But he had already turned to the first soldier.

"Have you got him?" he said. The first soldier went back to the table and looked at some papers.

"Here he is," he said. "He enlisted yestiddy. He's in a detachment leaving this morning for Little Rock." He had a watch stropped on his arm. He looked at it. "The train leaves in about fifty minutes. If I know country boys, they're probably all down there at the station right now."

"Get him up here," the one with the backing strop said. "Phone the station. Tell the porter to get him a cab. And you come with me," he said.

It was another office behind that un, with jest a table and some chairs. We set there while the soldier smoked, and it wasn't long; I knowed Pete's feet soon as I heard them. Then the first soldier opened the door and Pete come in. He never had no soldier clothes on. He looked just like he did when he got on the bus yestiddy morning, except it seemed to me like it was at least a week, so much had happened, and I had done had to do so much traveling. He come in and there he was, looking at me like he hadn't never left home, except that here we was in Memphis, on the way to Pearl Harbor.

"What in durnation are you doing here?" he said.

And I told him, "You got to have wood and water to cook with. I can chop it and tote it for you-all."

"No," Pete said. "You're going back home."

"No, Pete," I said. "I got to go too. I got to. It hurts my heart, Pete."

"No," Pete said. He looked at the soldier. "I jest don't know what could have happened to him, lootenant," he said. "He never drawed a knife on anybody before in his life."

He looked at me. "What did you do it for?"

"I don't know," I said. "I jest had to. I jest had to git here. I jest had to find you."

"Well, don't you never do it again, you hear?" Pete said. "You put that knife in your pocket and you keep it there. If I ever again hear of you drawing it on anybody, I'm coming back from wherever I am at and whup the fire out of you. You hear me?"

"I would pure cut a throat if it would bring you back to stay," I said. "Pete," I said. "Pete."

"No," Pete said. Now his voice wasn't hard and quick no more, it was almost quiet, and I knowed now I wouldn't never change him. "You must go home. You must look after maw, and I am depending on you to look after my ten acres. I want you to go back home. Today. Do you hear?"

"I hear," I said.

"Can he get back home by himself?" the soldier said.

"He come up here by himself," Pete said.

"I can get back, I reckon," I said. "I don't live in but one place. I don't reckon it's moved."

Pete taken a dollar out of his pocket and give it to me. "That'll buy your bus ticket right to our mailbox," he said. "I want you to mind the lootenant. He'll send you to the bus. And you go back home and you take care of maw and look after my ten acres and keep that durn knife in your pocket. You hear me?"

"Yes, Pete," I said.

"All right," Pete said. "Now I got to go." He put his hand on my head again. But this time he never wrung my neck. He just laid his hand on my head a minute. And then I be dog if he didn't lean down and kiss me, and I heard his feet and then the door, and I never looked up and that was all, me setting there, rubbing

the place where Pete kissed me and the soldier throwed back in his chair, looking out the window and coughing. He reached into his pocket and handed something to me without looking around. It was a piece of chewing gum.

"Much obliged," I said. "Well, I reckon I might as well start back. I got a right fer piece to go."

"Wait," the soldier said. Then he telephoned again and I said again I better start back, and he said again, "Wait. Remember what Pete told you."

So we waited, and then another lady come in, old, too, in a fur coat, too, but she smelled all right, she never had no artermatic writing pen nor no case history neither. She come in and the soldier got up, and she looked around quick until she saw me, and come and put her hand on my shoulder light and quick and easy as maw herself might 'a' done it.

"Come on," she said. "Let's go home to dinner."

"Nome," I said. "I got to ketch the bus to Jefferson."

"I know. There's plenty of time. We'll go home and eat dinner first."

She had a car. And now we was right down in the middle of all them other cars. We was almost under the busses, and all them crowds of people on the street close enough to where I could have talked to them if I had knowed who they was. After a while she stopped the car. "Here we are," she said, and I looked at it, and if all that was her house, she sho had a big family. But all of it wasn't. We crossed a hall with trees growing in it and went into a little room without nothing in it but a man dressed up in a uniform a heap shinier than them soldiers had, and the man shut the door, and then I hollered, "Look out!" and grabbed, but it was all right; that whole little room jest went right on up and stopped and the door opened and we was in another hall, and the lady unlocked a door and we went in, and there was another soldier, an old feller, with a britching strop, too, and a silver-colored bird on each shoulder.

"Here we are," the lady said. "This is Colonel McKellogg. Now, what would you like for dinner?"

"I reckon I'll jest have some ham and eggs and coffee," I said.

She had done started to pick up the telephone. She stopped. "Coffee?" she said. "When did you start drinking coffee?"

"I don't know," I said. "I reckon it was before I could remember."

"You're about eight, aren't you?" she said.

"Nome," I said. "I'm eight and ten months. Going on eleven months."

She telephoned then. Then we set there and I told them how Pete had jest left that morning for Pearl Harbor and I had aimed to go with him, but I would have to go back home to take care of maw and look after Pete's ten acres, and she said how they had a little boy about my size, too, in a school in the East. Then a man, another one, in a short kind of shirttail coat, rolled a kind of wheelbarrer in. It had my ham and eggs and a glass of milk and a piece of pie, too, and I thought I was hungry. But when I taken the first bite I found out I couldn't swallow it, and I got up quick.

"I got to go," I said.

"Wait," she said.

"I got to go," I said.

"Just a minute," she said. "I've already telephoned for the car. It won't be but a minute now. Can't you drink the milk even? Or maybe some of your coffee?"

"Nome," I said. "I ain't hungry. I'll eat when I git home." Then the telephone rung. She never even answered it.

"There," she said. "There's the car." And we went back down in that 'ere little moving room with the dressed-up man. This time it was a big car with a soldier driving it. I got into the front with him. She give the soldier a dollar. "He might get hungry," she said. "Try to find a decent place for him."

"O.K., Mrs. McKellogg," the soldier said.

Then we was gone again. And now I could see Memphis good, bright in the sunshine, while we was swinging around it. And the first thing I knowed, we was back on the same highway the bus run on this morning—the patches of stores and them big gins and sawmills, and Memphis running on for miles, it seemed like to me, before it begun to give out. Then we was running again between the fields and woods, running fast now, and except for that soldier, it was like I hadn't never been to Memphis a-tall. We was going fast now. At this rate, before I knowed it we would be home again, and I thought about me riding up to Frenchman's Bend in this here big car with a soldier running it, and all of a sudden I begun to cry. I never knowed I was fixing to, and I couldn't stop it. I set there by that soldier, crying. We was going fast.

The man who wrote this story

WILLIAM FAULKNER 1897–

At the end of World War I, the part of the country which still seemed to stand apart as a region was the South. Yet it had few voices. Its authors either were not writing about their own region or were writing about a South that had never existed except in romantic imaginations.

The sudden awakening of the South to its literary and industrial possibilities caused its authors to explore their own region for literary material. Among these authors were Thomas Wolfe and William Faulkner. The Southern awakening was similar in its regional importance to the

New England awakening of Emerson, Thoreau, and Hawthorne during the nineteenth century.

After finishing his service with the Canadian Air Force, Faulkner returned to his home in Mississippi. His first novel, *Soldier's Pay,* expressed his disillusionment on returning home from the war. Since then Faulkner has been writing many novels and short stories. Most of his stories are about people who live in a mythical county in Mississippi. They are not actual reflections of life; rather, they express Faulkner's ideas of the conflicts and problems which man must face. Faulkner traces the rise of the poor whites, the strength and permanence of the negroes, and the gradual decay and downfall of the old aristocracy.

Faulkner's writings are often not easy to read, and "2 Soldiers" must be considered an exception to the kind of stories he usually writes. More often he writes about confused characters in a complicated environment.

The amazing strength and depth of Faulkner's writings won him the Nobel Prize for Literature in 1950. In his acceptance speech, he revealed the fundamental idea behind his writings—a belief in man's ability to "endure" and "prevail."

Let's consider . . .

1. At first Pete explained to his little brother what they heard on the radio. Why do you think he later stopped talking about it?

2. When Pete finally decided to enlist, all he said was "I got to go." Explain as clearly as you can how he probably felt and why it was so hard for him to explain his reasons to his little brother.

3. Why could Pete's "maw" accept his going even though she said, "Jest don't expect me to understand why"? Why do you think she didn't go to the bus when Pete left?

4. You know from the comments of the little brother that "pap's" objections to Pete's going weren't entirely respected. Explain why. What did "pap" do that made the little boy remark, "He done all right too"?

5. Why did the little brother question Pete about where he would go to enlist? Why did he disobey Pete's orders about staying home? Why did he decide to take the shikepoke egg to Memphis?

6. In each incident that occurred as the little boy was making his way to Memphis, he somehow managed to persuade everyone of the importance of his trip. Describe what happened and how he reacted to each new experience.

7. By the time Pete's little brother arrived at the recruiting station, he was tired and a little confused by so many people. He didn't understand the attitude of the soldier at the desk, and he certainly didn't intend to be brushed off after he had come that far. He was a rather desperate little boy acting in a way that Pete might understand but would never approve. How do you explain the boy's striking out at the soldier? In what way was the soldier partly responsible? Contrast the soldier's behavior with the lieutenant's. What did the lieutenant say that reminded the boy of Pete?

8. When Pete returned to the recruiting station to see his little brother, did his behavior surprise you? Explain your answer.

9. Why do you think the little brother couldn't eat any supper at Colonel Mc-Kellogg's? Why did he suddenly break down and cry on the way home?

The writer's craft . . .

1. The effectiveness of this story depended upon the author's skill in creating the character of the little brother. Without him there would have been no story. Not only was he the central character around which most of the action and interest revolved; he was also the narrator who re-

vealed everything that was known about the other characters and what went on in the story. Most authors find it difficult to make a young boy a believable and consistent character. Mr. Faulkner not only had to make the little brother believable; he also had to make sure that what the little brother observed and reported as he told the story was also believable because it was consistent with the little brother's character.

You probably felt that this was a fairly simple story and that the little brother was a fairly simple character. But his reactions to the other characters and to the situations in the story reveal him as being sympathetic, shrewd, stubborn, impressed, defiant, subdued, and just plain "little boy."

Select passages or incidents from the story in which each of these qualities is revealed.

2. Because the little brother told the story, his language was a very important part of his characterization. He used such expressions as "I reckon" and "I hear tell" that were common to the part of the country in which he lived. He also used many expressions which would not be considered good English and which he had probably learned from the children in his community. Before he finished school, he would probably change his way of speaking, as Pete had.

Why was the little brother's language important, both in what it added to his characterization and in your reaction to the story?

My Land Is Fair for Any Eyes to See

My land is fair for any eyes to see—
Now look, my friends—look to the east and west!
You see the purple hills far in the west—
Hills lined with pine and gum and black-oak tree—
Now to the east you see the fertile valley!
This land is mine, I sing of it to you—
My land beneath the skies of white and blue.

This land is mine, for I am part of it.
I am the land, for it is part of me—
We are akin and thus our kinship be!
It would make me a brother to the tree!
And far as eyes can see this land is mine.
Not for one foot of it I have a deed—
To own this land I do not need a deed—
They all belong to me—gum, oak, and pine.

Jesse Stuart

First Play

MOSS HART

How does an author write his first play? What ideas and motives prompt his first attempt? In this excerpt from his autobiography Moss Hart reveals how and why an overworked office boy was prompted to take pen in hand, and the startling events behind his discovery!

It was a Sunday afternoon and I remember it well. The moment was not accompanied by any such sensible thought as, "Why, I could write a better play than any of these myself." I was simply bored to distraction by the trash I had been thumbing through all day, and without thinking too much about it, I simply sat down at a battered typewriter that I had rescued from the ash-heap of a Brooklyn relative's largesse and wrote on a piece of paper, "Act One. Scene One." By twelve o'clock that night Act One was completed and the next morning I took it into the office with me. Some demon of mischief was already at work, however, for on the title page I did not put my own name, but instead strung together the first three names of some of the boys of the block and listed as the author of the play "Robert Arnold Conrad." Candor compels me to reveal that the title was *The Beloved Bandit,* a secret I have arranged to keep rather well through the years. But I do not believed the demands of candor decree that I reveal any more of the play than that.

The next morning I handed the act to Mr. Pitou, and with a proper edge of the casual in my voice said, "I read an act of a play last night that I think is very good. You ought to read it."

"Who wrote it?" asked Mr. Pitou.

"A fellow named Robert Arnold Conrad," I replied. "He's a friend of mine."

"All right, I'll read it this evening. Put it in my briefcase," he said. And that was that.

I do not believe I gave it even a passing thought during the rest of that day or evening. I'm certain to this day that I meant it to be no more than a mild joke between us to enliven the drudgery we were going through in the search for the new vehicle. But I was utterly unprepared for what happened the following morning when Mr. Pitou entered the office. With his hat still on his head, he slapped the act down on the desk, turned to me triumphantly and said, "We found it. Don't have to look any further. This is it. If the second and third acts hold up anything like as well, we're home. When can I get the second act?"

"Tomorrow morning," I replied, too stunned to know what I was saying.

"Great," said Mr. Pitou. "Take a letter to Mr. Conrad—will you be seeing him tonight?"

"I guess so," I replied, truthfully enough I suppose.

"Well, if you don't," said Mr. Pitou, still under the spell of being out of the woods at last, "mail it special delivery so that he gets it first thing in the morning. I want to point out a few things he ought to do in the second act."

Still stunned, I sat down at the typewriter and solemnly took the long letter to Robert Arnold Conrad that Mr. Pitou poured forth. Why I did not tell Mr. Pitou the truth then and there escapes me even now. Perhaps I was too startled by his completely unexpected enthusiasm to puncture the bubble so quickly, or it may be I was suddenly titillated by the idea of carrying the joke through to the end; but whatever it was that possessed me to keep silent in those first few minutes set in motion a chain of events that I was powerless afterward to stop. By the time he signed the letter and handed it over to me, I knew I was doomed to go on.

That night I went home and wrote Act II. It took me until almost five o'clock in the morning to do it, but unbelievable as it may sound, I finished it that night. Bleary-eyed, I handed it to Mr. Pitou the next morning. He promptly turned off the

telephone and read it at once. This time his enthusiasm was even greater.

"Mouse," he said, "telephone your friend and ask him to come and see me this afternoon, or give me his number—I'd like to speak to him myself."

Panic-stricken, I managed to blurt out, "Oh, he's very seldom in his office, Mr. Pitou. He's in court most of the day. He's a lawyer." Quick thinking and an unholy gift of invention seem to spring to the aid of all liars at moments like these.

"Well, ask him to come in and see me tomorrow," said Mr. Pitou after a moment. "And when do you think he'll have the third act finished? Did he say anything to you about it?"

"No, he didn't," I replied a little haltingly, "but I guess he could have it for you by tomorrow."

"Fine, fine," said Mr. Pitou. "He writes fast, just what we need right now. Better take a letter and give it to him tonight in case you can't get him on the phone."

And there poured forth under my panic-frozen fingers another four-page single-spaced letter from Mr. Pitou. Glassy-eyed,

I watched him sign it, and in a moment of sweet clarity the thought flashed through my mind: "You've got to tell him now." But before I could screw up sufficient courage to speak, Mr. Pitou spoke instead.

"You know, Mouse," he said, a satisfied smile on his lips, "I don't often go around giving myself pats on the back, but I think my letter helped Mr. Conrad. I wish I had kept a copy of it. As a matter of fact, I wish you'd make a copy of this one right now. I'd like to take it home and show it to Mrs. Pitou tonight. I've been telling the family how you discovered this young fellow just in the nick of time."

That did it, of course. To confess to Mr. Pitou that he had been writing these wonderful letters to his office boy was bad enough; but to make him out an utter fool in the eyes of his family was something I could not face. Any kind of delay would give me time to think—something was bound to happen to make that terrible moment of confession a little less awful than it seemed to me just then.

That night I went home and tackled the third act. Alas, third acts are notoriously tough even for hardened veterans, and Robert Arnold Conrad, a tired and sorry spectacle by this time, did not finish the act that night. The next day another and still longer letter was tolled off to Mr. Conrad—longer, I believe, because Mr. Pitou was daily growing more proud of his new-found prowess as a teacher of playwriting, the while I sat there miserably taking it all down. During the day there was again the same insistence on Mr. Pitou's part of wanting to see Mr. Conrad or at least talk to him on the telephone, and I fended this off as best I could by muttering, "He's on a case—in court—he'll be finished in a couple of days." I was almost too tired to care. All I wanted was to finish the third act, tell Mr. Pitou the truth, and have it over with. All I cared about now was not losing my wonderful job as a consequence of this miserable joke. I silently prayed

for a propitious moment for telling him. If only I could get that act finished quickly, so that there need be no more letters, each one of which, of course, could only make him feel more foolish as he remembered sitting there and dictating them to me, all might not be lost.

That night I went to sleep after dinner and slept until midnight. Then I got up, sat down at the typewriter, and did not get up until I had typed "The curtain falls." It was eight o'clock in the morning. Now that it was done and I could tell Mr. Pitou at last, I felt strangely awake and refreshed. I could hardly wait to get down to the office and face him with the truth at last. When I walked in at nine o'clock Mr. Pitou was already there. I was surprised to see him there so early, for he usually arrived at the office between ten and ten thirty and he looked immensely pleased with himself into the bargain. Not another letter! I thought. I must tell him immediately. He spoke while I was still in the doorway.

"Got that third act?" he said. I nodded and handed it to him.

"Mr. Pitou," I began—but I got no further than that.

"Get your friend on the phone right away," he interrupted. "I showed these two acts to Mrs. Henry B. Harris last night, and you know what? She says this play is too good for the road—she wants to co-produce it with me and do it on Broadway. I'm going to bring the company back to New York, rehearse the play here, open in Rochester, play Chicago for four weeks, and then we'll bring it in. It will be my first New York production, so get your friend on the phone right away and tell him to come up here and sign the contract —I'm going downstairs to the booking office to book the time."

I stared numbly after him as he passed me in the doorway. After a moment, I sat down in a chair and tried hard to think, but I could not think; I could only keep looking around the office as though I were seeing it for the last time. I was still sitting there transfixed in the chair when Mr. Pitou returned from the booking office.

"What time is Mr. Conrad coming in?" he asked. "The theatres are all set. What time is he coming in?"

"Two o'clock," I replied, promptly and automatically, as though somebody else were using my voice.

"Fine," said Mr. Pitou, "let's get going— we've got a lot to do before lunch and I want to read that third act before he gets here."

The enormity of what I had done settled over me like a suit of mail. It is bad enough to make a man look foolish within the confines of his family, but quite another thing to make him a figure of ridicule outside, for I had no doubt that he had told Mrs. Harris the whole story and had showed her his letters to Robert Arnold Conrad as well. I stared so hard at Mr. Pitou that he finally became aware of it and said, "What is it? Were you going to say something?" I shook my head. There are certain moments when the process of thinking is frozen, when the ability to act, speak or move is completely and totally paralyzed. I could no more have told Mr. Pitou the truth right then, or even have given him the correct time had he asked me to, if my life had depended on it. I took down the telegrams, went through the morning's mail, and did the various other office chores without speaking and actually without quite knowing what I was doing.

When Mr. Pitou went out for lunch, taking the third act with him, I again sat down in the chair and stared unseeingly around the office. I was still sitting there when Mr. Pitou returned from lunch a little before two o'clock.

"It's just right," he said as he closed the door behind him. "He certainly read my letter carefully." He looked at his watch. "You said he was coming in at two o'clock, didn't you?" I nodded. "I'm kind of anxious to meet him now," he said, as he picked up the *Railway Guide* and settled back to wait.

I sat silently in the chair and watched the moments drag by. Finally he put the *Railway Guide* back on the desk and looked at his watch unbelievingly. "Why, it's three o'clock," he said. "Where is he?"

This time I had to speak—tell the last lie to fend off approaching doom if only for a little while longer. "He must have been held up in court, Mr. Pitou. Sometimes they don't recess until four o'clock," I said, pulling out a legal term.

For the first time Mr. Pitou looked hard at me. He had, of course, no suspicion of the truth, but he sensed something was wrong. He rose from the desk and reached for his hat and coat. "Get your coat, Mouse," he said, "we'll go down to his office and wait for him, if we have to wait there all day. I'm bringing a company back from Omaha and I've got Rochester and Chicago booked. I've got to have those contracts signed. What's the matter with him, anyway? Come on, let's go." This last was added rather sharply, for I still sat there immobilized.

Somehow I put on my hat and coat and followed him to the elevator. I knew that I must tell him before we reached the lobby; I realized the terrible moment had come at last—for if we got to the street and he asked me for the address of the office where Robert Arnold Conrad worked, what in the world would I say? The moment had arrived—there could be no more delay. I was trapped and I knew it. We got into the elevator and it started down. I made my revelation between the eighth and fifth floors as the elevator shot downward, and I remember every word I spoke, for the two short declarative sentences I managed to get out had an enviable economy and a dramatic brevity that I was not able to appreciate fully until long afterward.

"Mr. Pitou," I began, "I have a confession to make."

Mr. Pitou turned and looked at me a little wonderingly, as well he might have, for my voice had gone at least two octaves higher and seemed even to my own ears to be coming through an echo chamber some great distance away. I swallowed and got the rest of it out.

"Mr. Pitou," I said, "I am Robert Arnold Conrad."

The elevator doors opened and we both stepped out into the lobby. In silence we walked the length of the lobby and out into 42nd Street. Only then did Mr. Pitou give any indication that he had heard me.

"Mouse," he said at last, "I don't know whether you know it or not, but when an author writes his first play he doesn't get the regular royalties."

I could hardly believe my ears. "You mean—it's all right, Mr. Pitou?" I faltered.

"Certainly it's all right," he replied, "as long as you understand that a new author doesn't get the regular royalties. We'll have to make out new contracts. I guess I'd better go over and see Mrs. Harris and tell her the good news."

He patted me on the shoulder paternally, smiled down at me, and started off briskly toward 44th Street. I stood stock still for a moment, and my first emotion, if such it may be called, was one of hunger. Suddenly I seemed to be literally starving. I could not remember having eaten anything at all for the last three days. I walked to the Nedick's orange-juice stand on the corner and ate one frankfurter after another, until all my money except the subway fare I needed to get home ran out. I must have eaten at least ten frankfurters, for the counterman finally said, "You'll be sick, buddy—better knock off."

He was right. I just managed to get back to the office and into the bathroom in time. My debut as a playwright was a portent for the future: I have been sick in the men's room every opening night of a play of mine in theatres all over the country.

The man who wrote this autobiography

MOSS HART 1904–1961

Even before selling his first play to Augustus Pitou, Moss Hart was fascinated by the theatre. As a high school student in New York City he wrote dramatic sketches and attended the theatre as often as possible. After graduating from high school, he became social director at various resorts in the Catskill Mountains where he produced and directed plays for many summers.

Moss Hart has collaborated with both Irving Berlin and George S. Kaufman in a number of successful plays, and in 1937 the Kaufman and Hart play *You Can't Take it With You* was awarded the Pulitzer Prize. During World War II Hart wrote *Winged Victory,* a play depicting the achievements of the American Air Force. In addition to writing, Hart has brilliantly directed such plays as *My Fair Lady* and *Camelot.*

Let's consider . . .

1. How did Moss Hart explain his failure to inform Mr. Pitou immediately of the playwright's true identity? How else might you account for his reluctance?

2. Why did it become increasingly difficult for him to tell Mr. Pitou the truth?

3. On the basis of your own experiences, explain why you agree or disagree with Hart when he wrote: "There are certain moments when the process of thinking is frozen, when the ability to act, speak or move is completely and totally paralyzed."

4. Moss Hart used his dramatic imagination to keep the truth from Mr. Pitou. List some of the things that he made up. Why would a fertile imagination be a useful resource to a budding playwright?

5. Hart described his confession as having "an enviable economy and a dramatic brevity." Explain why these terms were particularly well-suited to describe his confession.

The writer's craft . . .

In an autobiography, the author recounts and evaluates the story of his own life. Few people are able to see themselves either as they are or as other people see them. Yet self-appraisal is one of the author's major responsibilities if he is going to tell his story honestly and without prejudice. What motives have been largely responsible for the kind of life he chose to lead? His primary motive may have been to acquire wealth, to achieve social, political, or professional recognition, or to make a worthwhile contribution to society or to his country. Very likely, however, as different crises have arisen in his life, his actions and decisions have been governed by a variety of motives, both generous and selfish.

The better he understands himself, the better he can interpret the forces which have influenced what he became and what he accomplished. He can help you see what part his environment, family, and early childhood played in shaping his life. He can help you know the people and experience the events in his life in terms of what they meant to him at the time and also in later life. He can, and should, reveal not only what he thinks—his beliefs, attitudes, and prejudices—but also how he feels about the experiences which have helped to shape his character or determine the course of his life.

1. How would you describe Moss Hart's attitude toward his early attempt at playwriting? Give several reasons to support your answer.

2. What did "First Play" reveal to you about Moss Hart's character and personality as (1) a young person growing up and (2) a mature man recalling an episode from his youth? Refer to specific incidents in "First Play" to support your answer.

Appraising, and interpreting—these are major tasks, and much of the success of the autobiography depends upon them. However, the author has still another task to perform: to create an interesting and well-written story. This task requires many of the skills which novelists use to good advantage. For one thing, the author must be able to characterize the people who have been important in his life. In addition to telling you about them, he must recreate what they said and did.

3. What was Hart's attitude toward Mr. Pitou? How did Mr. Pitou evaluate himself? What is your opinion of him? Refer to passages in the selection to justify your opinion.

4. What could Hart learn from Mr. Pitou? What might he want to avoid in his own drive toward success?

Look What You Did, Christopher!

OGDEN NASH

In fourteen hundred and ninety-two,
Somebody sailed the ocean blue.
Somebody borrowed the fare in Spain
For a business trip on the bounding main,
And to prove to people, by actual test,
You could get to the East by traveling West.
Somebody said, Sail on! Sail on!
And studied China and China's lingo,
And cried from the bow, There's China now!
And promptly bumped into San Domingo.
Somebody murmured, Oh dear, oh dear!
I've discovered the Western Hemisphere.

And that, you may think, my friends, was that.
But it wasn't. Not by a fireman's hat.
Well enough wasn't left alone,
And Columbus was only a cornerstone.
There came the Spaniards,
There came the Greeks,
There came the Pilgrims in leather breeks.[1]
There came the Dutch,
And the Poles and Swedes,
The Persians, too,
And perhaps the Medes,
The Letts, the Lapps and the Lithuanians,
Regal Russians, and ripe Roumanians.
There came the French
And there came the Finns,
And the Japanese
With their formal grins.
The Tartars came,
And the Terrible Turks—
In a word, humanity shot the works.
And the country that should have been Cathay
Decided to be
The U. S. A.

[1] *breeks,* breeches

95

And that, you may think, my friends, was that.
But it wasn't. Not by a fireman's hat.
Christopher C. was the cornerstone,
And well enough wasn't left alone.
For those who followed
When he was through,
They burned to discover something, too.
Somebody, bored with rural scenery,
Went to work and invented machinery,
While a couple of other mental giants
Got together
And thought up Science.
Platinum blondes
(They were once peroxide),
Peruvian bonds
And carbon monoxide,
Tax evaders
And Vitamin A,
Vice Crusaders,
And tattletale gray—
These, with many another phobia,
We owe to that famous Twelfth of Octobia.
O misery, misery, mumble and moan!
Someone invented the telephone,
And interrupted a nation's slumbers,
Ringing wrong but similar numbers.
Someone devised the silver screen
And the intimate Hollywood magazine,
And life is a Hades
Of clicking cameras,
And foreign ladies
Behaving amorous.
Gags have erased
Amusing dialog,
As gas replaced
The crackling firelog.
All that glitters is sold as gold,

And our daily diet grows odder and odder,
And breakfast foods are dusty and cold—
It's a wise child
That knows its fodder.
Someone invented the automobile,
And good Americans took the wheel
To view American rivers and rills
And justly famous forests and hills—
But somebody equally enterprising
Had invented billboard advertising.
You linger at home
In dark despair,
And wistfully try the electric air.
You hope against hope for a quizz imperial,
And what do they give you?
A doctor serial.
Oh, Columbus was only a cornerstone,
And well enough wasn't left alone,
For the Inquisition [2] was less tyrannical
Than the iron rules of an age mechanical,
Which, because of an error in '92,
Are clamped like corsets on me and you,
While Children of Nature we'd be today
If San Domingo
Had been Cathay.

And that, you may think, my friends, is that.
But it isn't—not by a fireman's hat.
The American people,
With grins jocose,
Always survive the fatal dose.
And though our systems are slightly wobbly,
We'll fool the doctor this time, probly.

---

[2] *Inquisition,* systematic prosecution and punishment of heretics: in particular, the Inquisition of Spain
during the fifteenth and sixteenth centuries, which was marked by extreme severity

The man who wrote this poem

OGDEN NASH 1902–

One of the cleverest of modern humorous poets, Ogden Nash has capitalized on his talent for rhyming words like "Cinderella-ry" with "celery" or "minimum" with "cinnamum." His unusual views on some of the ridiculous aspects of society, expressed in poems like "To a Small Boy Standing on My Shoes While I Am Wearing Them" and "Don't Grin, Or You'll Have to Bear It," are an important part of his humor.

Privately educated in Newport, Rhode Island, Ogden Nash spent a brief year at Harvard before going to work for a publisher. After the success of his first two volumes of light verse, he withdrew from publishing to keep up with the demand for his poetry. Nash is probably the most popular poet living in America today; his name and his poetry are so tied together that any poetry of the same type is described as "Ogden Nashery."

The poet's art . . .

1. Invent another title or a sub-title for this poem. It will probably be less amusing than Ogden Nash's, but try for a good one.

2. Humor often depends on the unexpected and, at first glance, the inappropriate. Nash achieved part of his humor through **satire**: a light criticism in the form of ridicule which is not bitter, but amusing. Point out several places in this poem where you think he was being satirical; for example, when he ridiculed modern "conveniences."

3. Which lines did you find especially entertaining? What was there about them that made you smile?

4. Nash intended to amuse his readers with the way he used **rhyme**: the agreement of final sounds of end words in matching lines of poetry. Sometimes these rhymes were intentionally imperfect or false, as when he rhymed *phobia* and *Octobia*. Other times, as in *odder* and *fodder*, he created a rhyme and also introduced a **pun**: a play on words. Some of his rhymes were based on colloquial pronunciation, as in *wobbly* and *probly*. Whatever rhyme scheme Nash used, he was using it intentionally. Which rhymes in this poem did you find humorous? Can you explain why?

5. Select at least three instances of Nash's knowledge of history. He made light of this knowledge, but it was there.

6. List five things Christopher did for which Nash reproached him. Remember that humorists exaggerate.

7. **Alliteration** is a device used by serious poets to enrich their writings. It is the repetition of the initial sound of two or more words which occur close together. Nash used alliteration with *humorous* effect because it is unexpected in light verse. Note this line: "O misery, misery, mumble and moan!" Find another example of alliteration in this poem and read it aloud to the class.

NOW THINK BACK

1. Living in America from colonial days to the present time has called for sacrifice, courage, self-reliance, and hard work. Which of the people you have been reading about had to make an important sacrifice? Which showed great courage? Which were most self-reliant? How many of them succeeded because of hard work? As you answer these questions, you will probably name the same people several times.

2. In LIVING IN AMERICA you have seen pioneers in New England, in Ohio, and on the prairies. In your opinion, which section of the country offered the greatest challenge to these hardy Americans? Explain what the challenge was and how it was met.

3. Which of the experiences of pioneer life in America would you have found rewarding? Name several and explain why you would have liked to share in them.

4. Both "The Battle of Finney's Ford" and "2 Soldiers" deal with a young man's need to act in defense of his country. For Josh, the enemy was nearby; for Pete, he was far away in Japan, yet the feelings of these two boys were very similar. Compare their reasons for deciding to go to war. For which of these was the decision more difficult? Explain why. Compare the attitudes taken by each boy's parents.

5. Both men and women figure in this unit. Which stand out more clearly in your mind, the individual men or the individual women? Support your answer with specific references to the selections. Most characters are remembered because the author used concrete details, natural-sounding dialogue, and dramatic situations to make them seem real. Read several short passages aloud which you feel best portray your favorite character, man or woman.

6. You will recall that Thoreau's advice to his fellow-Americans was "Simplicity. Simplicity. Simplicity." Explain why you think each of the following people must have shared appreciation of the simple life:

    The Birdwell family
    Nathan Hale
    Locomotive 38, the Ojibway

7. Of all the selections in LIVING IN AMERICA, which one do you expect to remember the longest? If you had to explain why, would you say it was the characters, the setting, or the situation? Was the story sad or happy in tone? In a short paragraph, name the one story that impressed you the most and tell why.

Things to do . . .

1. LIVING IN AMERICA provides opportunity for investigation in several fields. If you are especially interested in science, you may want to read those chapters in *Walden* which record Thoreau's careful observations of the plant and animal life around Walden Pond. Select several of the most interesting passages and read them aloud to the class.

If history is your favorite subject, consult an encyclopedia and find out all that is known about Squanto, his life among the white settlers, his aid in their planting, and his death on Cape Cod. Write a description of him as Mrs. Carver, the governor's wife, might have written it in a letter to England.

You may also be interested in Massasoit and his son Philip, who waged a bloody war on the New England colonists, known in history as King Philip's War. Read in the library about his raids and massacres. Choose one of the more dramatic incidents and write it up as a modern news article. Give it a good headline and a brisk, newspaper style.

2. Prepare a bulletin board to illustrate LIVING IN AMERICA. Use pictures which represent the various periods covered by the selections you have read. Also use original drawings by class members which illustrate scenes or characters from the selections. Bring your "picture story" of life in America up to date by adding characters and scenes of your own period.

3. Any study of American life should help you to recognize qualities that are characteristically American. As a class, make a list of those qualities which are revealed in the selections you have read in this part. To this list add other qualities which you think are also characteristically American. As you discuss these qualities, point out which ones are common to all freedom-loving people the world over. Are any of these qualities solely American? If your answer is *yes*, explain why.

More to read . . .

A Lantern in her Hand by BESS STREETER ALDRICH.
   D. Appleton-Century Company, 1929.
The Red Badge of Courage by STEPHEN CRANE.
   D. Appleton-Century Company, 1925.
The Edge of Time by LOULA GRACE ERDMAN.
   Dodd, Mead & Company, 1950.
Seasoned Timber by DOROTHY CANFIELD FISHER.
   Harcourt, Brace and Company, 1939.
Stories From Seventeen by BRYNA IVENS.
   J. B. Lippincott Company, 1955.
Laughing Boy by OLIVER LAFARGE.
   Houghton Mifflin Company, 1929.
Martin Eden by JACK LONDON.
   New American Library of World Literature, Inc., 1908.
The Cut of her Jib by CLARA NICKERSON.
   Coward-McCann, Inc., 1954.

The Human Comedy by WILLIAM SAROYAN.
   Harcourt, Brace and Company, 1943.
Kit Carson by STANLEY VESTAL.
   Houghton Mifflin Company, 1928.
The Virginia Exiles by ELIZABETH GRAY VINING.
   J. B. Lippincott Company, 1955.
The Age of Innocence by EDITH WHARTON.
   Modern Library, Inc., 1920.

*   *   *

"Winterset" by MAXWELL ANDERSON, in *Eleven Verse Plays*.
   Harcourt, Brace and Company, 1940.
Our Town by THORNTON WILDER.
   Coward-McCann, Inc., 1938.

*   *   *

The Epic of America by JAMES TRUSLOW ADAMS.
   Little, Brown and Company, 1931.
Twenty Years at Hull House by JANE ADDAMS.
   The Macmillan Company, 1910.
The Big Change by FREDERICK LEWIS ALLEN.
   Harper & Brothers, 1952.
Profile of America by EMILY DAVIE. Foreword by Charles Lindbergh. Introduction by Louis Bromfield.
   Thomas Y. Crowell Company, 1954.
We Grew Up in America by ALICE I. HAZELTINE.
   Abingdon-Cokesbury Press, 1954.
On Our Way by ROBERT PATTERSON, MILDRED MEBEL, and LAWRENCE HILL.
   Holiday House, 1952.
We The American People by MARGUERITE STEWART.
   John Day Company, 1951.
The Way Our People Lived by W. E. WOODWARD.
   E. P. Dutton & Co., 1944.

FROM ATLANTIC TO PACIFIC

"Where do they come from?" "What are they like?" If you listen, sometimes you can guess. You say, "They sound like Middle Westerners, Southerners, New Englanders." You think, "They are different from me, not so much in *what* they do as in *how* they do it. Perhaps it is *where* they live—the region they call home—that makes the difference. If I had grown up there, I would have been like them."

Some of the best writers in America have discovered in these regional differences a wealth of tradition, interesting customs, and a kind of speech, dress, and manners which gives to each region its local color. From Atlantic to Pacific they have found love, adventure, and rich humor in the daily life of ordinary people. And the stories they tell are dramatic. Each is rooted deep in a region and in a way of life that is truly American.

Literature that is truly regional penetrates beneath the surface of local color—the clothes, speech, and manners associated with a particular locality. Local color is the flavor of a region, but by itself it is too narrow and limited. Regional literature provides an interpretation of life that is characteristic of a region and illuminates those qualities of human experience which are universal. It speaks to all men, even though the language and setting are characteristic of a given time and place.

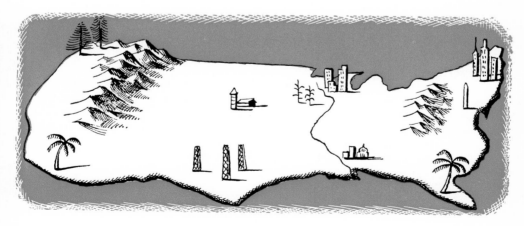

FROM ATLANTIC TO PACIFIC

"Go, Seeker, . . ."

THOMAS WOLFE

If you were seeking the promise of America, where would you go? Thomas Wolfe would send you throughout the land, from north to south, from east to west. In every region you would see the promise coming true.

Go, seeker, if you will, throughout the land and you will find us burning in the night.

There where the hackles of the Rocky Mountains blaze in the blank and naked radiance of the moon, go make your resting stool upon the highest peak. Can you not see us now? The continental wall juts sheer and flat, its huge black shadow on the plain, and the plain sweeps out against the East, two thousand miles away. The great snake that you see there is the Mississippi River.

Behold the gem-strung towns and cities of the good green East, flung like stardust through the field of night. That spreading constellation to the north is called Chicago, and that giant wink that blazes in the moon is the pendant lake that it is built upon. Beyond, close-set and dense as a clenched fist, are all the jeweled cities of the eastern seaboard. There's Boston, ringed with the bracelet of its shining little towns, and all the lights that sparkle on the rocky indentations of New England. Here, southward and a little to the west, and yet still coasted to the sea, is our intensest ray, the splintered firmament of the towered island of Manhattan. Round about here, sown thick as grain, is the glitter of a hundred towns and cities. The long chain of lights there is the necklace of Long Island and the Jersey shore.

Southward and inland, by a foot or two, behold the duller glare of Philadelphia. Southward further still, the twin constellations—Baltimore and Washington. Westward, but still within the borders of the good, green East, that nighttime glow and smolder of hell fire is Pittsburgh. Here, St. Louis, hot and humid in the corn-field belly of the land, and bedded on the mid-length coil and fringes of the snake. There at the snake's mouth, southward six hundred miles or so, you see the jeweled crescent of old New Orleans. Here, west and south again, you see the gemmy glitter of the cities on the Texas border.

Turn now, seeker, on your resting stool atop the Rocky Mountains, and look another thousand miles or so across moon-blazing fiend-worlds of the Painted Desert and beyond Sierras' ridge. That magic congeries [1] of lights there to the west, ringed like a studded belt around the magic setting of its lovely harbor, is the fabled town of San Francisco. Below it, Los Angeles and all the cities of the California shore. A thousand miles to north and west, the sparkling towns of Oregon and Washington.

Observe the whole of it, survey it as you might survey a field. Make it your garden,

---

[1] *congeries,* collection of several bodies or particles in a single mass

seeker, or your backyard patch. Be at ease in it. It's your oyster—yours to open if you will. Don't be frightened, it's not so big now, when your footstool is the Rocky Mountains. Reach out and dip a hatful of cold water from Lake Michigan. Drink it —we've tried it—you'll not find it bad. Take your shoes off and work your toes down in the river oozes of the Mississippi bottom—it's very refreshing on a hot night in the summertime. Help yourself to a bunch of Concord grapes up there in northern New York State—they're getting good now. Or raid that watermelon patch down there in Georgia. Or, if you like, you can try the Rockyfords here at your elbow, in Colorado. Just make yourself at home, refresh yourself, get the feel of things, adjust your sights, and get the scale. It's your pasture now, and it's not so big— only three thousand miles from east to west, only two thousand miles from north to south—but all between, where ten thousand points of light prick out the cities, towns, and villages, there, seeker, you will find us burning in the night.

So, then, to every man his chance—to every man, regardless of his birth, his shining, golden opportunity—to every man the right to live, to work, to be himself, and to become whatever thing his manhood and his vision can combine to make him— this, seeker, is the promise of America.

The man who wrote this selection

THOMAS WOLFE   1900–1938

Thomas Wolfe was a Southern writer who, like William Faulkner, turned to his own section of the country for literary material. Unlike Faulkner, however, Thomas Wolfe wrote more about himself, his own feelings and experiences, than about the region in which he lived. There was such a close likeness between his major characters and himself that his novels are largely autobiographical.

Wolfe had something of Walt Whitman's great energy and love for his country. He was an enormous man physically, with an immense appetite, and few Americans so delighted in describing foods. Nothing seemed impossible to him; he was determined to read every book in the New York Public Library.

He wrote almost constantly, but only a few novels have been published from his piles of manuscript. One part of a later novel was originally over twice as long as the completed novel itself. Probably his work would never have been published if his editor, Maxwell Perkins, had not helped Wolfe to cut away the excess material and reduce the manuscript to publishable size.

While Wolfe was a student at the University of North Carolina, he completed several plays. Upon graduation he went to Harvard in order to study more about play writing, but after he left school he turned to short stories and novels. The rest of his short life was spent teaching, traveling, and writing.

Let's consider . . .

1. Get an outline map of the United States or draw one yourself. Then follow Thomas Wolfe's directions, marking the "gem-strung towns and cities," the mountains, rivers, and plains as they move up and down, across and back, over the thousands of miles. They will help you to feel at home in your country, to adjust your sights, and to get the scale of your vast land.

2. What feelings did the author inspire in you for your country? Why did he tell you to make it "your garden" or your "backyard patch"?

3. How did Wolfe help you to feel that this land is *yours,* all of it?

4. What is the "promise of America"?

The writer's craft . . .

1. Thomas Wolfe's vivid expression of ideas and feelings has sometimes been called "extravagant rhetoric." Point out several expressions which you consider unusually vivid.

2. Wolfe was noted for the extreme exuberance of spirit which he expressed in lyric prose. (The word *lyric* is usually applied to poetry because it pertains to the spontaneous, glowing expression of feeling usually found in poetry.) Find all the instances in this prose selection which reflected Wolfe's exuberant spirits.

3. The lyric quality of Thomas Wolfe's writing was heightened by his use of **metaphor:** an implied comparison between two objects which are not completely alike but have at least one thing in common. Wolfe wrote, "Behold the gem-strung towns and cities of the good green East . . ." "Beyond . . . are all the jeweled cities of the eastern seaboard." Anyone who has flown over a large city at night, or seen night aerial photographs of a large city, can see how the many blazing lights resemble *gems* and *jewels.* After establishing this comparison between city lights and jewels, Wolfe continued to build his comparison with other metaphors:

"There's Boston, ringed with the *bracelet* of its shining little towns."

"The long chain of lights there is the *necklace* of Long Island."

"You see the *jeweled crescent* of New Orleans."

Find other examples of metaphor in "Go, Seeker" which you liked and read them aloud to the class. Also try to write one or two metaphors of your own. Select a familiar idea or scene that will lend itself to such a comparison.

4. Read the first four lines aloud until you get the feeling of their rhythm. Note the way they might quite naturally be broken into shorter lines of **free verse:** poetry that has rhythm but does not follow a set pattern. Now set these four lines into eight lines of free verse. Follow the punctuation given in the prose but remember to capitalize the first word in each line of your poem. Read your poetic version of these opening prose lines aloud to the class.

Good-by and Keep Cold

ROBERT FROST

As you begin your journey into the regions of America, pause first on the Atlantic seaboard. You will hear the New England poet, Robert Frost, speaking gently to a young orchard.

This saying good-by on the edge of the dark
And the cold to an orchard so young in the bark
Reminds me of all that can happen to harm
An orchard away at the end of the farm
All winter, cut off by a hill from the house.
I don't want it girdled by rabbit and mouse,
I don't want it dreamily nibbled for browse
By deer, and I don't want it budded by grouse.
(If certain it wouldn't be idle to call
I'd summon grouse, rabbit, and deer to the wall
And warn them away with a stick for a gun.)
I don't want it stirred by the heat of the sun.
(We made it secure against being, I hope,
By setting it out on a northerly slope.)
No orchard's the worse for the wintriest storm;
But one thing about it, it mustn't get warm.
'How often already you've had to be told,
Keep cold, young orchard. Good-by and keep cold.
Dread fifty above more than fifty below.'
I have to be gone for a season or so.
My business awhile is with different trees,
Less carefully nurtured, less fruitful than these,
And such as is done to their wood with an ax—
Maples and birches and tamaracks.
I wish I could promise to lie in the night
And think of an orchard's arboreal plight
When slowly (and nobody comes with a light)
Its heart sinks lower under the sod.
But something has to be left to God.

Gorsline

The man who wrote this poem

ROBERT FROST 1875–

One of the most respected American poets living today is Robert Frost. As his name might suggest, he is from an old New England family, though he was born in San Francisco. Most of his life has been spent in that part of New England "North of Boston."

Frost worked long and hard to become a poet. His first poems were written when he was fifteen, but it was many years before he received any recognition. He regularly sent poems to magazines like *The Atlantic Monthly* and *Harper's,* and just as regularly the poems were returned.

Finally, Frost decided that if he were ever to be a poet, he must give poetry a real chance. Therefore, he sold his farm, packed his bags, and with his wife and children went to England. It is characteristic of Frost that instead of staying in London, he lived in the country. His poems were well received in England, and when he returned to America a few years later, he was already internationally known as a poet.

In his poems Frost expresses the sureness and down-to-earth quality of the New England farmer. Nothing is wasted. He speaks of what he knows well. This gives his writing an honesty and integrity that has made his name important in American poetry.

The poet's art . . .

A. As you bite into an apple, you probably never think of all the care that has gone into its growth and ripening. Many things can happen to a young orchard. What harm from animals did Robert Frost fear? What greater harm was threatened by the winter season? What might happen if the weather became too warm? How could a farmer prevent this harm to his orchard?

Although Robert Frost was born in San Francisco, his roots were deep in New England. What evidence was there in the poem that he knew New England?

As the poet left the orchard, he said, "My business awhile is with different *trees.*" Use your imagination and tell what you think he would do during the winter. Remember that poets imply more than they actually say. Why do you think he would not lie awake thinking of the orchard?

B. Robert Frost's poetry is usually written in an easy, conversational style. In "Good-by and Keep Cold" he used simple language to suggest the quality of conversation.

1. In what other ways did he capture the flavor of everyday speech?

2. At first glance, you might think the rhyme in the poem would detract from its conversational quality. **Rhyme** is the repetition of similar or identical sounds in the end words of matching lines: *dark—bark; harm—farm.* The lines which carry this pattern of rhyme are called **matching lines.** Of course, people do not converse in rhyme. However, you will hear the conversational flow of the words in "Good-by and Keep Cold," if you put your attention first on the *meaning* rather than on the rhyme. Notice how frequently the thought in one line is completed in the following line. Read again the opening two lines but do not pause after the word *dark.* The thought continues to the word *cold.* Your next logical pause is after the word *winter.* Read the entire poem aloud. Pause just long enough at the end of each line to hear the rhyme. Make your longer pauses where you want to show divisions of thought within the poem.

Snowbound

A WINTER IDYL

JOHN GREENLEAF WHITTIER

The sun that brief December day
Rose cheerless over hills of gray,
And, darkly circled, gave at noon
A sadder light than waning moon.
Slow tracing down the thickening sky
Its mute and ominous prophecy,
A portent seeming less than threat,
It sank from sight before it set.

A chill no coat, however stout,
Of homespun stuff could quite shut out,
A hard, dull bitterness of cold,
That checked, mid-vein, the circling race
Of life-blood in the sharpened face,
The coming of the snow-storm told.
The wind blew east; we heard the roar
Of Ocean on his wintry shore,
And felt the strong pulse throbbing there
Beat with low rhythm our island air.

Meanwhile we did our nightly chores,—
Brought in the wood from out of doors,
Littered the stalls, and from the mows
Raked down the herd's-grass for the cows:
Heard the horse whinnying for his corn;
And, sharply clashing horn on horn,
Impatient down the stanchion rows
The cattle shake their walnut bows;
While, peering from his early perch
Upon the scaffold's pole of birch,
The cock his crested helmet bent
And down his querulous challenge sent.

Unwarmed by any sunset light
The gray day darkened into night,
A night made hoary with the swarm,
And whirl-dance of the blinding storm,
As zigzag wavering to and fro
Crossed and recrossed the wingèd snow:
And ere the early bedtime came
The white drift piled the window-frame,
And through the glass the clothes-line posts
Looked in like tall and sheeted ghosts.

So all night long the storm roared on:
The morning broke without a sun;
In tiny spherule traced with lines
Of Nature's geometric signs,
In starry flake, and pellicle [1]
All day the hoary meteor fell;
And, when the second morning shone,
We looked upon a world unknown,
On nothing we could call our own.
Around the glistening wonder bent
The blue walls of the firmament,
No cloud above, no earth below,—
A universe of sky and snow!
The old familiar sights of ours
Took marvelous shapes; strange domes and
    towers
Rose up where sty or corn-crib stood,
Or garden wall, or belt of wood;
A smooth white mound the brush-pile
    showed,

[1] *pellicle,* a thin flake

A fenceless drift what once was road;
The bridle-post an old man sat
With loose-flung coat and high cocked hat;
The well-curb had a Chinese roof;
And even the long sweep,[2] high aloof,
In its slant splendor, seemed to tell
Of Pisa's leaning miracle.[3]

A prompt, decisive man, no breath
Our father wasted: "Boys, a path!"
Well pleased, (for when did farmer boy
Count such a summons less than joy?)
Our buskins [4] on our feet we drew;
With mittened hands, and caps drawn low,
To guard our necks and ears from snow,
We cut the solid whitness through.
And, where the drift was deepest, made
A tunnel walled and overlaid
With dazzling crystal: we had read
Of rare Aladdin's wondrous cave,
And to our own his name we gave,
With many a wish the luck were ours
To test his lamp's supernal powers.
We reached the barn with merry din,
And roused the prisoned brutes within.

The old horse thrust his long head out,
And grave with wonder gazed about;
The cock his lusty greeting said,
And forth his speckled harem led;
The oxen lashed their tails, and hooked,
And mild reproach of hunger looked;
The hornéd patriarch of the sheep,
Like Egypt's Amun [5] roused from sleep,
Shook his sage head with gesture mute,
And emphasized with stamp of foot.

All day the gusty north-wind bore
The loosening drift its breath before;
Low circling round its southern zone,
The sun through dazzling snow-mist shone.
No church bell lent its Christian tone
To the savage air, no social smoke
Curled over woods of snow-hung oak.
A solitude made more intense
By dreary-voicèd elements,
The shrieking of the mindless wind,
The moaning tree boughs swaying blind,
And on the glass the unmeaning beat
Of ghostly fingertips of sleet.
Beyond the circle of our hearth
No welcome sound of toil or mirth
Unbound the spell, and testified

---

[2] *sweep*, pole used to lift a bucket from a well
[3] *Pisa's leaning miracle*, the leaning tower located
   in the Italian city of Pisa
[4] *buskins*, overshoes

[5] *Amun*, an Egyptian god usually shown as having the head of a ram

Of human life and thought outside.
We minded that the sharpest ear
The buried brooklet could not hear,
The music of whose liquid lip
Had been to us companionship,
And, in our lonely life, had grown
To have an almost human tone.

As night drew on, and, from the crest
Of wooded knolls that ridged the west,
The sun, a snow-blown traveler, sank
From sight beneath the smothering bank,
We piled with care our nightly stack
Of wood against the chimney-back,—
The oaken log, green, huge, and thick,
And on its top the stout backstick;
The knotty forestick laid apart,
And filled between with curious art
The ragged brush; then, hovering near,
We watched the first red blaze appear,
Heard the sharp crackle, caught the gleam
On whitewashed wall and sagging beam,
Until the old, rude-furnished room
Burst, flower-like, into rosy bloom;
While radiant with a mimic flame
Outside the sparkling drift became,
And through the bare-boughed lilac tree
Our own warm hearth seemed blazing free.
The crane and pendent trammels showed,
The Turk's heads on the andirons glowed;
While childish fancy, prompt to tell
The meaning of the miracle,
Whispered the old rhyme: *"Under the
    tree,*
When fire outdoors burns merrily,
There the witches are making tea."

Shut in from all the world without,
We sat the clean-winged hearth [6] about,
Content to let the north-wind roar
In baffled rage at pane and door,
While the red logs before us beat
The frost line back with tropic heat;
And ever, when a louder blast
Shook beam and rafter as it passed,
The merrier up its roaring draught
The great throat of the chimney laughed;

The house-dog on his paws outspread
Laid to the fire his drowsy head,
The cat's dark silhouette on the wall
A couchant [7] tiger's seemed to fall;
And, for the winter fireside meet,
Between the andirons' straddling feet,
The mug of cider simmered slow,
The apples sputtered in a row,
And, close at hand, the basket stood
With nuts from brown October's wood.

We sped the time with stories old,
Wrought puzzles out, and riddles told,
Or stammered from our schoolbook lore
"The Chief of Gambia's golden shore." [8]
How often since, when all the land
Was clay in Slavery's shaping hand,
As if a far-blown trumpet stirred
The languorous sin-sick air, I heard:
"Does not the voice of reason cry,
    Claim the first right which Nature gave,
From the red scourge of bondage fly,
    Nor deign to live a burdened slave!" [9]

Our father rode again his ride
On Memphremagog's [10] wooden side;
Sat down again to moose and samp [11]
In trapper's hut and Indian camp;
Lived o'er the old idyllic ease
Beneath St. François' [12] hemlock trees;
Again for him the moonlight shone
On Norman cap and bodiced zone; [13]
Again he heard the violin play
Which led the village dance away.
And mingled in its merry whirl
The grandam and the laughing girl.
Or, nearer home, our steps he led

---

[6] *clean-winged hearth,* the hearth swept clean with
a turkey wing

[7] *couchant,* crouching
[8] *"The Chief of Gambia's golden shore,"* a line
from "The African Chief," a poem in one of
Whittier's school books
[9] lines from "The African Chief"
[10] *Memphremagog,* a lake located between Vermont and the province of Quebec
[11] *samp,* porridge
[12] *St. François,* a Canadian river in the province of
Quebec
[13] *Norman cap and bodiced zone,* a reference to
French-Canadian girls

Where Salisbury's [14] level marshes spread
    Mile-wide as flies the laden bee;
Where merry mowers, hale and strong,
Swept, scythe on scythe, their swaths along
    The low green prairies of the sea.
We shared the fishing off Boar's Head, [15]
    And round the rocky Isles of Shoals
    The hake-broil [16] on the drift-wood coals;
The chowder on the sand-beach made,
Dipped by the hungry, steaming hot,
With spoons of clam-shell from the pot.
We heard the tales of witchcraft old,
And dream and sign and marvel told
To sleepy listeners as they lay
Stretched idly on the salted hay,
Adrift along the winding shores,
    When favoring breezes deigned to blow
    The square sail of the gundelow, [17]
And idle lay the useless oars.

Our mother, while she turned her wheel
Or run the new-knit stocking-heel,
Told how the Indian hordes came down
At midnight on Cocheco town, [18]
And how her own great-uncle bore
His cruel scalp-mark to fourscore.
Recalling, in her fitting phrase,
So rich and picturesque and free,
(The common unrhymed poetry
Of simple life and country ways,)
The story of her early days,—
She made us welcome to her home;
Old hearths grew wide to give us room;
We stole with her a frightened look
At the gray wizard's conjuring-book,
The fame whereof went far and wide
Through all the simple country-side;
We heard the hawks at twilight play,
The boat-horn on Piscataqua, [19]
The loon's weird laughter far away;
We fished her little trout-brook, knew
What flowers in wood and meadow grew,

What sunny hillsides autumn-brown
She climbed to shake the ripe nuts down,
Saw where in sheltered cove and bay
The ducks' black squadron anchored lay,
And heard the wild geese calling loud
Beneath the gray November cloud.

Our uncle, innocent of books,
Was rich in lore of fields and brooks,
The ancient teachers never dumb
Of Nature's unhoused lyceum.
He read the clouds as prophecies,
And foul or fair could well divine,
In moons and tides and weather wise,
By many an occult hint and sign,
Holding the cunning-warded keys
To all the woodcraft mysteries;
Himself to Nature's heart so near
That all her voices in his ear
Of beast or bird had meanings clear,
Like Apollonius [20] of old,
Who knew the tales the sparrows told,
Or Hermes [21] who interpreted

---

[14] *Salisbury,* a town in Massachusetts
[15] *Boar's Head,* a high bluff on the coast of New
    Hampshire, opposite the Isles of Shoals
[16] *hake-broil,* broil of a fish similar to cod
[17] *gundelow,* a flat-bottomed boat
[18] *Cocheco town,* Dover, New Hampshire
[19] *Piscataqua,* a river near Dover, New Hampshire

[20] *Apollonius,* an ancient Greek philosopher
[21] *Hermes,* ancient Greek god of science, inven-
    tion, and eloquence who wrote many books
    about astrology, ritual, and mysticism

What the sage cranes of Nilus [22] said;
A simple, guileless, childlike man,
Content to live where life began;
Strong only on his native grounds,
The little world of sights and sounds
Whose girdle was the parish bounds,
Whereof his fondly partial pride
The common features magnified,
As Surrey hills to mountains grew
In White [23] of Selborne's loving view,—
He told how teal and loon he shot,
And how the eagle's eggs he got,
The feats on pond and river done,
The prodigies of rod and gun;
Till, warming with the tales he told,
Forgotten was the outside cold,
The bitter wind unheeded blew,
From ripening corn the pigeons flew,
The partridge drummed i' the wood, the
      mink
Went fishing down the river brink.
In fields with bean or clover gay,
The woodchuck, like a hermit gray,
Peered from the doorway of his cell;
The muskrat plied the mason's trade,
And tier by tier his mud walls laid;
And from the shagbark overhead
The grizzled squirrel dropped his shell.

Next, the dear aunt, whose smile of cheer
And voice in dreams I see and hear,—
The sweetest woman ever Fate
Perverse denied a household mate,
Who, lonely, homeless, not the less
Found peace in love's unselfishness,
And welcome wheresoe'er she went,
A calm and gracious element,
Whose presence seemed the sweet income
And womanly atmosphere of home,—
Called up her girlhood memories,
The huskings and the apple-bees,
The sleigh-rides and the summer sails,
Weaving through all the poor details
And homespun warp of circumstance

A golden woof-thread of romance.
For well she kept her genial mood
And simple faith of maidenhood;
Before her still a cloudland lay,
The mirage loomed across her way;
The morning dew, that dries so soon
With others, glistened at her noon;
Through years of toil and soil and care,
From glossy tress to thin gray hair,
All unprofaned she held apart
The virgin fancies of the heart.
Be shame to him of woman born
Who hath for such but thought of scorn.

There, too, our elder sister plied
Her evening task the stand beside;
A full, rich nature, free to trust,
Truthful, and almost sternly just,
Impulsive, earnest, prompt to act,
And make her generous thought a fact,
Keeping with many a light disguise
The secret of self-sacrifice.
O heart sore tried! thou hast the best
That Heaven itself could give thee,—rest,
Rest from all bitter thoughts and things!
    How many a poor one's blessing went
    With thee beneath the low green tent
Whose curtain never outward swings!

As one who held herself a part
Of all she saw, and let her heart
    Against the household bosom lean,
Upon the motley-braided mat
Our youngest and our dearest sat,
Lifting her large, sweet, asking eyes,
    Now bathed in the unfading green
And holy peace of Paradise.
Oh, looking from some heavenly hill,
    Or from the shade of saintly palms,
    Or silver reach of river calms,
Do those large eyes behold me still?
With me one little year ago:—
The chill weight of the winter snow
    For months upon her grave has lain;
And now, when summer south winds blow
    And brier and harebell bloom again,
I tread the pleasant paths we trod,
I see the violet-sprinkled sod
Whereon she leaned, too frail and weak

---

[22] *cranes of Nilus,* ancient Egyptian wise men
[23] *White,* Gilbert White, English naturalist and
    preacher. He wrote a detailed account of the
    natural history of Selborne, in Surrey, England.

The hillside flowers she loved to seek,
Yet following me where'er I went
With dark eyes full of love's content.
The birds are glad; the brier rose fills
The air with sweetness; all the hills
Stretch green to June's unclouded sky;
But still I wait with ear and eye
For something gone which should be nigh,
A loss in all familiar things,
In flower that blooms, and bird that sings.
And yet, dear heart! remembering thee,
  Am I not richer than of old?
Safe in thy immortality,
    What change can reach the wealth I
      hold?
    What chance can mar the pearl and gold
Thy love hath left in trust with me?
And while in life's late afternoon,
  Where cool and long the shadows grow,
I walk to meet the night that soon
    Shall shape and shadow overflow,
I cannot feel that thou art far,
Since near at need the angels are;
And when the sunset gates unbar,
    Shall I not see thee waiting stand,
And, white against the evening star,
    The welcome of thy beckoning hand?

Brisk wielder of the birch and rule,
The master of the district school
Held at the fire his favored place;
Its warm glow lit a laughing face
Fresh-hued and fair, where scarce appeared
The uncertain prophecy of beard.
He teased the mitten-blinded cat,
Played cross-pins on my uncle's hat,
Sang songs, and told us what befalls
In classic Dartmouth's college halls.
Born the wild Northern hills among,
From whence his yeoman father wrung
By patient toil subsistence scant,
Not competence and yet not want,
He early gained the power to pay
His cheerful, self-reliant way;
Could doff at ease his scholar's gown
To peddle wares from town to town;
Or through the long vacation's reach
In lonely lowlands districts teach,
Where all the droll experience found

At stranger hearths in boarding round,
The moonlit skater's keen delight,
The sleigh-drive through the frosty night,
The rustic party, with its rough
Accompaniment of blind-man's-buff,
And whirling plate, the forfeits paid,
His winter task a pastime made.
Happy the snow-locked homes wherein
He tuned his merry violin,
Or played the athlete in the barn,
Or held the good dame's winding-yarn,
Or mirth-provoking versions told
Of classic legends rare and old,
Wherein the scenes of Greece and Rome
Had all the commonplace of home,
And little seemed at best the odds
'Twixt Yankee pedlers and old gods;
Where Pindus-born Araxes [24] took
The guise of any grist-mill brook,
And dread Olympus [25] at his will
Became a huckleberry hill.

---

[24] *Pindus-born Araxes,* a sacred river of Greece
    which has its source in the Pindus Mountains
[25] *Olympus,* a mountain in Greece said to be the
    home of the Greek gods

A careless boy that night he seemed;
  But at his desk he had the look
And air of one who wisely schemed,
  And hostage from the future took
  In trainèd thought and lore of book.
Large-brained, clear-eyed, of such as he
Shall Freedom's young apostles be,
Who, following in War's bloody trail,
Shall every lingering wrong assail;
All chains from limb and spirit strike,
Uplift the black and white alike;
Scatter before their swift advance
The darkness and the ignorance,
The pride, the lust, the squalid sloth,
Which   nurtured   Treason's   monstrous
    growth,
Made murder pastime, and the hell
Of prison torture possible;
The cruel lie of caste refute,
Old forms remold, and substitute
For Slavery's lash the freeman's will,
For blind routine, wise-handed skill;
A schoolhouse plant on every hill,
Stretching in radiate nerve-lines thence
The quick wires of intelligence;
Till North and South together brought
Shall own the same electric thought,
In peace a common flag salute,
And, side by side in labor's free
And unresentful rivalry,
Harvest the fields wherein they fought.

At last the great logs, crumbling low,
Sent out a dull and duller glow,
The bull's-eye watch that hung in view,
Ticking its weary circuit through,
Pointed with mutely warning sign
Its black hand to the hour of nine.
That sign the pleasant circle broke:
My uncle ceased his pipe to smoke,
Knocked from its bowl the refuse gray,
And laid it tenderly away,
Then roused himself to safely cover
The dull red brands with ashes over.
And while, with care, our mother laid
The work aside, her steps she stayed
One moment, seeking to express
Her grateful sense of happiness
For food and shelter, warmth and health,

And love's contentment more than wealth,
With simple wishes (not the weak,
Vain prayers which no fulfillment seek,
But such as warm the generous heart,
O'erprompt to do with Heaven its part)
That none might lack, that bitter night,
For bread and clothing, warmth and light.

Within our beds awhile we heard
The wind that round the gables roared,
With now and then a ruder shock,
Which made our very bedsteads rock.
We heard the loosened clapboards tost,
The board-nails snapping in the frost;
And on us, through the unplastered wall,
Felt the light sifted snow-flakes fall.
But sleep stole on, as sleep will do
When hearts are light and life is new;
Faint and more faint the murmurs grew,
Till in the summer-land of dreams
They softened to the sound of streams,
Low stir of leaves, and dip of oars,
And lapsing waves on quiet shores.

Next morn we wakened with the shout
Of merry voices high and clear;
And saw the teamsters drawing near
To break the drifted highways out.
Down the long hillside treading slow
We saw the half-buried oxen go,
Shaking the snow from heads uptossed,
Their straining nostrils white with frost.
Before our door the straggling train
Drew up, an added team to gain.
The elders threshed their hands a-cold,
  Passed, with the cider-mug, their jokes
  From lip to lip; the younger folks
Down the loose snow-banks, wrestling,
    rolled,
Then toiled again the cavalcade
  O'er windy hill, through clogged ravine,
  And woodland paths that wound be-
    tween
Low drooping pine-boughs winter-weighed.
From every barn a team afoot,
At every house a new recruit,
Where, drawn by Nature's subtlest law,
Haply the watchful young men saw
Sweet doorway pictures of the curls

And curious eyes of merry girls,
Lifting their hands in mock defense
Against the snow-balls' compliments,
And reading in each missive tost
The charm with Eden never lost.

We heard once more the sleigh-bells'
    sound;
    And, following where the teamsters led,
The wise old Doctor went his round,
Just pausing at our door to say
In the brief autocratic way
Of one who, prompt at Duty's call,
Was free to urge her claim on all,
    That some poor neighbor sick abed
At night our mother's aid would need.
For, one in generous thought and deed,
    What mattered in the sufferer's sight
    The Quaker matron's inward light,
The Doctor's mail of Calvin's creed? [26]
All hearts confess the saints elect
    Who, twain in faith, in love agree,
And melt not in an acid sect
    The Christian pearl of charity!

So days went on: a week had passed
Since the great world was heard from last.
The Almanac we studied o'er,
Read and reread our little store
Of books and pamphlets, scarce a score;
One harmless novel, mostly hid
From younger eyes, a book forbid,
And poetry, (or good or bad,
A single book was all we had,)
Where Ellwood's [27] meek, drab-skirted
    Muse,[28]

A stranger to the heathen Nine,[29]
    Sang, with a somewhat nasal whine,
The wars of David and the Jews.
At last the floundering carrier bore
The village paper to our door.
Lo! broadening outward as we read,
To warmer zones the horizon spread;
In panoramic length unrolled
We saw the marvel that it told.
Before us passed the painted Creeks,[30]
    And daft McGregor [31] on his raids
    In Costa Rica's everglades.
And up Taygetos [32] winding slow
Rode Ypsilanti's [33] Mainote [34] Greeks,
A Turk's head at each saddlebow!
Welcome to us its week-old news,
Its corner for the rustic Muse,
    Its monthly gauge of snow and rain,
Its record, mingling in a breath
The wedding bell and dirge of death;
Jest, anecdote, and lovelorn tale,
The latest culprit sent to jail;
Its hue and cry of stolen and lost,
Its vendue [35] sales and goods at cost,
    And traffic calling loud for gain.
We felt the stir of all and street,
The pulse of life that round us beat;
The chill embargo of the snow
Was melted in the genial glow;
Wide swung again our ice-locked door,
And all the world was ours once more!

[Abridged]

---

[26] *the Doctor's mail of Calvin's creed,* the doctor's
   faith as a follower of John Calvin, a religious
   reformer
[27] *Ellwood,* Thomas Ellwood, a Quaker who wrote
   a poem about King David
[28] *Muse,* goddess or power who inspires poets
[29] *the heathen Nine,* the nine Greek muses
[30] *Creeks,* Creek Indians
[31] *McGregor,* a Scottish adventurer who tried to
   establish a colony in Costa Rica
[32] *Taygetos,* a Greek mountain range
[33] *Ypsilanti,* a Greek patriot who fought the
   Turks
[34] *Mainote,* a warlike Greek tribe
[35] *vendue,* public auction

The man who wrote this poem

JOHN GREENLEAF WHITTIER
1807–1892

Most of you have heard the old story about the poet-to-be and his stern father. The father says that poetry will not earn the boy's bread; the boy had better give up his dreams and go into business. This could have been the story of Whittier's early life.

The elder Whittier was a Quaker who could not imagine why his son should bother with what seemed to him a form of nonsense. Whittier's sisters encouraged him, however, and while he was still a boy, his poetry was being published in the local papers.

Except for one book of poems and prose about the legends of New England, Whittier wrote little of importance until he joined the Abolitionists, the anti-slavery movement which was slowly gaining power. At the time Whittier became its official voice, this movement was unpopular even in New England. He wrote so many propaganda poems against slavery that James Russell Lowell commented in *The Fable for Critics* that Whittier had

"A fervor of mind that knows no separation
'Twixt simple excitement and pure inspiration—"

After the War Between the States had put an end to the issue of slavery, Whittier devoted himself to democracy, to politics (he is one of the founders of the Republican party), and to pure poetry. It was then that he wrote his best works, including "Snowbound," a description of a New England winter.

The poet's art . . .

1. Whittier was nearly sixty years old when he recorded these recollections of being snowbound in his boyhood home. That was many years ago, in 1866, when a typical New England winter had a quite different effect on people's lives. Today there are centrally heated houses, good roads, all kinds of snow-clearing apparatus, telephones, radio, and television. If you live in the city, tell what features of the three-day storm seemed strangest to you. If you live in the country, tell what tasks would be easier for you now in a heavy snowstorm.

2. Which features of being snowbound at Haverhill would you have enjoyed most? Which features would you have disliked? Give details.

3. New Englanders are noted for their industry. Give five instances of real industry in the Whittier family, even in this week of comparative inactivity.

4. In what ways did the boy Whittier enjoy himself during the storm?

5. In this poem you became acquainted with the whole household. Each member had some quality of character which distinguished him or her from the others. Write a well-constructed sentence in which your portray him or her as an individual.

6. Choose two members of the family whom you especially liked. Explain your choice by telling what sort of people they were.

7. In which portraits did Whittier display a mild and kindly sort of humor?

8. How would you know that Whittier was an Abolitionist?

9. Any poem that tells a story may be called a narrative poem. When such a poem pictures the simple pleasures of rural life, it is called an **idyl.** Select several passages from "Snowbound" which justify Whittier's calling this narrative poem an idyl.

10. As a rule, Quakers are quiet, kindly people. What examples of graciousness did you note in the Whittier family? Read the lines which give evidence of their religious tolerance.

11. There were few books in this household. Why was it, therefore, an advantage

to Whittier as a boy to have the school-master boarding at his home? Be definite in your answer.

12. The village newspaper was slow in arriving at the Whittiers' snowbound door, but when it finally came, the family were as eager to read certain sections as you are today. Read over the news items and features which this paper carried. Tell which ones you would find in your own morning paper. Tell what special features were not included and which *you* would miss if these were not included today.

13. This early New England family did not have the conveniences and distractions of the average modern family. Do you think they were as happy? Support your answer.

The Snow-storm

Announced by all the trumpets of the sky,
Arrives the snow, and, driving o'er the fields,
Seems nowhere to alight: the whited air
Hides hills and woods, the river, and the heaven,
And veils the farm-house at the garden's end.
The sled and traveller stopped, the courier's feet
Delayed, all friends shut out, the housemates sit
Around the radiant fireplace, enclosed
In a tumultuous privacy of storm.

Come see the north wind's masonry.
Out of an unseen quarry evermore
Furnished with tile, the fierce artificer
Curves his white bastions with projected roof
Round every windward stake, or tree, or door.
Speeding, the myriad-handed, his wild work
So fanciful, so savage, nought cares he
For number or proportion. Mockingly,
On coop or kennel he hangs Parian [1] wreaths;
A swan-like form invests the hidden thorn;
Fills up the farmer's lane from wall to wall,
Maugre [2] the farmer's sighs; and, at the gate,
A tapering turret overtops the work:
And when his hours are numbered, and the world
Is all his own, retiring, as he were not,
Leaves, when the sun appears, astonished Art
To mimic in slow structures, stone by stone,
Built in an age, the mad wind's night-work,
The frolic architecture of the snow.

Ralph Waldo Emerson

---

[1] *Parian,* a dazzling white marble much used in ancient Greece
[2] *Maugre,* in spite of [*Archaic*]

The House on Beacon Hill

ROBERT HILLYER

The Bowen sisters lived together quietly in their Boston home on Beacon
Hill. Their Sunday afternoon teas were never dull, especially when they
talked about Sarah and her psychic powers.

When I was a young instructor in Harvard College, I often found relaxation with a group of older acquaintances in Boston, who might be described as *nouveaux pauvres*.[1] Some of these newly poor still maintained old houses gone shabby; some had moved into apartments, with as many of their heirlooms as they could crowd into the more limited space. Some might have been considered eccentric. There was, for example, Mrs. Grandeville-Wickford, who, attired in faded velvet and nodding ostrich plumes, attended all the teas at the art galleries. She would go the rounds carrying an old reticule, which she filled, not surreptitiously, with sandwiches and cakes enough to provide supper for herself and her nine cats. There was Mrs. Dumaine, whose current financial state could be gauged by noting whether the rented piano was being hoisted up to the windows of her apartment or descending to be taken away. And there were the Bowen sisters, Abby and Helena, impoverished descendants of sea captains, whose house on West Cedar Street was crammed with treasures that would have made them rich again could they have been persuaded to part with a few.

Their house was one of my favorites.

[1] *nouveaux pauvres,* newly poor [French]

They were a lovable pair of noble spinsters, and they had a stock of weird tales sufficient to transport me to the world of shadows through many a Sunday afternoon, far from the bleak reality of a freshman English class at nine the next morning.

Abby believed every story she told. No one could doubt the conviction in her earnest hazel eyes. She would sit demurely, hands folded in her lap, the candlelight gleaming on her coronet of braided gray hair, and relate prodigies that seemed plausible at the time. She looked like a Puritan spinster ready to face anything, even the modern world.

Abby's sister, Helena, was a silent partner, seldom speaking except when called upon for corroboration. At such times she briefly registered agreement, then immediately effaced herself again.

The two sisters kept up the house at the foot of Beacon Hill, where their family, of whom they were the last, had lived for four generations. They employed, according to Abby, an excellent old servant named Sarah. Sarah always seemed to have taken the afternoon off when company arrived; but she must have been a highly efficient woman, for the mahogany and brass in the old house shone, and the nutcakes and brownies at teatime were of a quality unequaled in the everyday world. Furthermore, Sarah was clairvoyant.

Her specialty was the recovery of lost articles. Abby told me, for example, about a woman visiting the Bowens who lost a sapphire ring. Sarah was called in. Closing her eyes, she immediately saw in her inner vision a Chinese lacquer box decorated with golden dragons and silver chrysanthemums. At this point the visitor interrupted with a cry of relief and amazement, recalling that she had left her ring at home in the very box so accurately described. There were many other instances of Sarah's extra-sensory skill, some, perhaps, even more striking.

"I have known Sarah to fail only once," Abby told me. "And that time, I am sorry to say, was the most important of all."

"What was it?" I asked.

Abby and her sister looked at each other and, surprisingly, giggled.

"She failed to recover a man," Abby answered. "Helena's young man."

"His name was George Wales," Helena announced unexpectedly. "He was tall and had dark, curly hair and a beautiful cleft chin." Then, as she grew shy again, her voice trailed off. "I was very fond of him."

"We both were," said Abby briskly. "But Helena was much handsomer than I was. George Wales had just come to the point where we knew he was going to propose to Helena. Then—he disappeared. He walked out the front door of this very house and was never seen again."

"September thirtieth, it was," Helena said. "Wednesday, September thirtieth, back in—"

"Never mind the year, Helena dear. It was a long time ago, and we were all young—even Sarah. Mama and Papa were alive, and they were comparatively young, too; though I didn't think so at the time. We knew that George Wales was going to propose to Helena on Thursday. 'Good-by, all,' he called before he closed the door. 'I'll see you tomorrow. And be prepared

for a shock, Helena.' He laughed and was gone. Gone forever. He just vanished into thin air. I have a theory about that."

I asked what it was, but Abby shook her head. "How does Sarah come into it?" I inquired.

Helena came to life again. "Sarah saw him in her vision. She saw him return to this house with a ledger under his arm. But for once she was wrong. He never did come back—in the flesh, at any time. He was Sarah's one failure."

Perhaps to change the subject, Abby told a story concerning a man on Cape Cod. Abby and Helena were taking snapshots of Colonial doorways in the back lanes of Harwichport. Sarah, laden with provisions, met them just as they stopped before an abandoned cottage set back from the lane. The front yard was overgrown with tall grass. The house was unpainted and sagging. The doorway, however, ruinous as it was, showed exceptional beauty of design.

"And the dear old gentleman taking his nap in the sun," said Sarah.

As she spoke, Abby and Helena became aware of him. Seated in a cane chair, he was dozing on the little porch. His chin rested on his hands, which were clasped over a knotted stick. Because his face was in shadow and his clothes blended with the weathered shingles, he had not been noticeable at first glance.

"Do you suppose he would mind our taking a picture?" asked Abby.

"Let's speak to him and get his permission," said her sister. "That would be more polite."

"Oh, I wouldn't do that," Sarah said. "Why wake the poor old gentleman?"

The sisters agreed that Sarah's advice showed great tact and common sense. Abby remarked that if he stayed as he was, he would add much to the interest of the snapshot.

So they took a picture without waking the old man, and when they returned to Boston, they had it developed with some

fifty others. It was by far the best of the
lot and took a prize in a contest sponsored
by the Boston *Transcript*. The sisters titled
it "The Old Man"; but no one knew why,
because there was no old man in the picture. Abby showed it to me, and I can
attest that no one was visible on the porch.

"We never dreamed it was merely an
etheric body—what people commonly call
a ghost," said Abby. "Imagine the shock!
But rather an interesting one. We both
think the old gentleman came back to the
abandoned house in answer to Sarah's psychic powers."

I was not to learn the extent of Sarah's
psychic powers until my first formal dinner with the Bowens. High tea on Sundays had been the usual extent of their
hospitality, so I was surprised and flattered
one day to receive from Abby a brief note
in fine Spencerian script, inviting me to
dinner the following Tuesday at seven.

I donned my dinner coat for the occasion
and was pleased to find I had done the
right thing. My hostesses wore dinner
dresses whose elegance was archaic but unmistakable, and their jewelry—Abby's wide

bracelets of gold and jet cameo, and Helena's set of amethyst earrings, necklace,
and brooch—was beyond price. Their
manner was shyer and more ceremonious
than usual. The second-floor parlor and
the dining room were lighted by scores of
candles; not one electric light bulb cut the
soft radiance that glimmered on damask
and old silver.

I realized immediately that I was the
only guest.

Abby served the dinner herself, but so
unobtrusively that conversation flowed on
unbroken as she tiptoed back and forth to
the pantry. I was disappointed, for I
longed to cast eyes on Sarah. Helena ate
daintily and in silence, acknowledging
every glance with a smile and a nod. The
dinner was wonderful; the clear turtle
soup, the lamb chops, the chocolate soufflé
were beyond praise, and I was agog to
speak of Sarah, but refrained each time for
fear of sounding like people in restaurants
who send their compliments to the cook.
Perhaps, being young, I was overcareful
about politeness.

At last, when we were settled in the
parlor with our tiny allotments of coffee in

rose-and-gold porcelain cups, Abby, as though she had read my curiosity said, "I hope you agree with us that Sarah does very well."

"Very well!" I exclaimed. "Why, I haven't had a dinner like this in—oh, I don't believe I ever have. It was beyond perfection."

" 'Simple but perfect, ma'am'—those were Sarah's very words," Abby said, smiling. "You see, when Sarah passed over to the other plane of existence some years ago—"

I looked up, startled.

"The month of August it was, in—" Helena began.

"Never mind the year, Helena dearest. It was some time ago."

"Abby had never cooked in her life," said Helena.

"No, I never had. We were quite at a loss. I tried, of course, by following a cookbook; but the results were frightful. Helena and I became panic-stricken. What should we do? We tried eating out, but the restaurant food was so expensive and indigestible. Unpalatable, too, after Sarah's cooking."

"I can well believe that," I declared fervently.

"So I determined to try again. It was late one rainy November afternoon—how I remember it! I was crying, literally crying, the tears running down my face, as I stood in the kitchen with that wretched cookbook in my hand. Suddenly I heard a chuckle. It was unmistakably Sarah's; there was no other sound quite like it, a sort of under-laughter, you might say, throaty and warm. Then my whole personality was seized by a power from beyond our plane of existence. Without conscious thought, I cut up the chicken, got out the pans—well, a young man wouldn't be interested in the culinary details. But Sarah prepared the entire dinner that night— through me. Even the dessert."

"I'll never forget it," said Helena. "It was one of Sarah's finest—curried chicken with rice, eggplant, and the most succulent pumpkin pie."

"Helena has an exceptionally wonderful memory," said Abby. "I had forgotten the eggplant. It was delicious—now, wasn't it, Helena?"

Helena clasped her hands and nodded her agreement.

"From that day to this," Abby concluded, "Sarah has cooked for us through me. I am never the slightest bit tired. I just yield up my personality to hers, and turn out such meals as we all enjoyed tonight. We always say, 'Thank you, Sarah,' and I know she hears." Abby closed her eyes and sat in silence for a moment. "And this is the strangest part," she went on presently. "Sarah takes Thursday and Sunday afternoons off just as in the old days. On Saturdays she makes a batch of nutcakes and brownies for our Sunday teas. Thursdays we have canned soup and scrambled eggs. I can cook that much. I always feel Sarah's amusement on Friday mornings, and she gives us a specially fine dinner Friday evening to make up for our horrid repast on Thursday."

The candles seemed to blur before my eyes. I had a momentary and somewhat chilling conviction that Sarah was about to appear and refill my coffee cup. But Abby did that—or was it Sarah reminding Abby to do it?

When I said good-night, I asked Abby to thank Sarah for me and tell her how superb her dinner was, especially to a young instructor who normally frequented cafeterias.

"Oh, Sarah knows already," Abby said with a charming smile. "I could feel her pleasure at your appreciation. It isn't as if she were very far away. And I know she would want you to come to dinner again."

I did go again several times during the next two years I was in Boston, and each time I went away with the feeling that I had shared in some magic that redeemed and transfigured an otherwise prosaic world.

The man who wrote this story

ROBERT HILLYER   1895–

Many writers of the twentieth century have tried new forms or developed startling new themes, but Robert Hillyer has been content to follow the traditional pattern. At times he has been criticized for his complete separation from present-day life, but he does not care to write about his own time. He is concerned only with the old and established poetic themes. While critics have not always praised Hillyer's choice of themes, they are generally agreed on the technical excellence of his writing. In 1934 Hillyer was awarded a Pulitzer Prize for his *Collected Poems*.

During World War I, Hillyer was a volunteer ambulance driver for the French army. After he returned to civilian life, he became a professor of English at Harvard University and has since continued to write and teach. Though he is primarily known as a poet, he has written several short stories.

Let's consider . . .

1. Robert Hillyer spoke of the "newly poor" among his Boston acquaintances. What were some of the signs which indicated that until recently they had been "well-to-do"?

2. What significant differences did you discover in the two sisters?

3. Why did Hillyer never see Sarah when he called?

4. Abby spoke of Sarah's "psychic powers." List all the incidents in the story which show this clairvoyance. Describe in detail the incident that you found most amusing.

5. What did Hillyer learn about Sarah and Abby the night he came to dinner?

6. Why do you suppose Hillyer "had a momentary and somewhat chilling conviction" that Sarah was about to fill his cup?

7. Each time the author visited the sisters, he felt that he "shared in some magic that redeemed and transfigured an otherwise prosaic world." How did he make the reader believe, temporarily at least, that the magic was real?

The writer's craft . . .

In stories involving supernatural events, the author must convince the reader, temporarily at least, that the events *might* have occurred. He must make the story seem **plausible:** having the appearance of truth or reason. Otherwise it becomes so fantastic that it loses its force and seems like a rather silly yarn. Robert Hillyer's story seemed plausible, at least while you were reading it, because he carefully prepared you for what might *not* seem plausible.

His first task was to establish the "eccentric" Bowen sisters as somewhat unusual characters but unquestionably honest and sincere. Their life with Sarah seemed so completely natural to them that they assumed everyone else would accept it as perfectly natural, too. Therefore, how could you, the reader, doubt their story unless you also doubted their honesty?

Furthermore, Hillyer told the entire story sympathetically. Although he did not attempt to explain their occult powers, nowhere did he scoff at their supernatural beliefs or hint that perhaps the sisters may have been deceiving themselves. Instead he presented their story as unusual but completely delightful.

1. Examine this story closely to see how the author made each new incident seem plausible. Discuss (1) the way he developed each character, (2) the tone of the story, and (3) the way he presented the incidents. Why did he first prepare you with stories *about* Sarah before he introduced her as an unseen but very evident character?

2. Do you think the author made the story seem more plausible by telling it in

the first person? Why do you find it easier to believe a first-hand report than a second- or third-hand report?

3. If, as you were reading the story, you were not convinced of its plausibility, explain why.

Knowing words . . .

Robert Hillyer described his older Boston acquaintances as being *nouveaux pauvres*. In doing this he took the liberty of improvising on the French expression *nouveaux riches* frequently used in the English language with its meaning of "newly rich." This play on a much-used expression called more attention to the financial status of the people he was writing about than if he had merely said they had recently lost their fortunes.

Here are four other foreign expressions which are commonly used in the English language. Find each of them in your dictionary. Write down the definition, including the name of the country from which each expression was borrowed. Then use each expression in a sentence of your own. Remember that you always underline foreign words.

bon voyage hasta mañana
maître d'hôtel Gesundheit
à la carte

A Lady

You are beautiful and faded
Like an old opera tune
Played upon a harpsichord;
Or like the sun-flooded silks
Of an eighteenth-century boudoir.
In your eyes
Smolder the fallen roses of outlived minutes,
And the perfume of your soul
Is vague and suffusing,
With the pungence of sealed spice jars.
Your half tones delight me,
And I grow mad with gazing
At your blent colors.
My vigor is a new-minted penny,
Which I cast at your feet.
Gather it up from the dust,
That its sparkle may amuse you.
       Amy Lowell

City Evening

E. B. WHITE

The light that burned me up by day
Decides a little while to stay,
And writes a long and golden scrawl
In tree-leaf shadows on my wall.
The bulbous sun has spilled his fire,
Impaled upon a Jersey spire;
And hard day-objects of the street
Grow soft, in the long light, and sweet.
Noon's hot fortissimo still clings,
Muted in many murmurings;
And with the lingering light o'erspread
My thoughts are all new garmented.
Far down the block in yellow ease
Behind a row of gold-tipped trees
The "L," like some old dream, goes by
Betwixt the Avenue and sky.

The man who wrote this poem

E. B. WHITE 1899–

The name of E. B. White is closely associated with New York and with several of New York's best-written magazines. For many years he wrote the *New Yorker* column, "The Talk of the Town," which was a perfect outlet for his original and amusing comments about the city and its people. A long essay, *Here Is New York,* analyzes the "personality" of the great city.

In recent years, Mr. White has fled the city to put down roots in New England soil. For five years he wrote a monthly record of life on his Maine farm for *Harper's Magazine,* under the title "One Man's Meat." These essays were later published (1944) in a book which bears the same title.

Mr. White is the author of two delightful books which are enjoyed by children and grown-ups alike, *Stuart Little* and *Charlotte's Web.* His most recent work is *The Second Tree from the Corner,* a collection of poems and essays.

The poet's art . . .

1. Few writers know New York as well as E. B. White. In this poem, he described the way he felt about it at a particular season and time of day. How did you know what season it was? What effect did the time of day have on the appearance of the city?

2. Poets often intensify their pictures by the use of **contrast:** the bringing together of ideas and images to show how they differ. Pick out several lines in this poem which show a contrast between the city at noon and at sunset. Read these lines aloud.

3. When a poet assigns human qualities to nature or to inanimate objects, he is using **personification.** Find two uses of personification in this poem. Why do they add force to the poem?

4. Poetry does not have to rhyme, but many readers find that rhyme increases their enjoyment of a poem. Sounds in poetry are a source of pleasure. Sometimes a sound is repeated at the end of matching lines, as in *fire* and *spire,* to form a **rhyme.** Or it may be repeated within a line, as in "lingering light," and "Muted in many murmurings." This is called **alliteration.** The sounds of the words add to the musical quality of the poem.

Select several lines from "City Evening" in which the repetition of sounds heightens your enjoyment.

5. What effect did the "lingering light" have on the poet himself?

6. Most people did not see any beauty in a New York "L" (elevated train). How did the "L" affect White?

7. Do you like this poem? Explain your feelings about it.

"the hours rise up"

e. e. cummings

the hours rise up putting off stars and it is
dawn
into the street of the sky light walks scattering poems

on earth a candle is
extinguished   the city
wakes
with a song upon her
mouth having death in her eyes

and it is dawn
the world
goes forth to murder dreams . . .

i see in the street where strong
men are digging bread
and i see the brutal faces of
people contented hideous hopeless cruel happy

and it is day,

in the mirror
i see a frail
man
dreaming
dreams
dreams in the mirror

Vasiliu

and it
is dusk   on earth

a candle is lighted
and it is dark.
the people are in their houses
the frail man is in his bed
the city

sleeps with death upon her mouth having a song in her eyes
the hours descend,
putting on stars . . .

in the street of the sky night walks scattering poems

The man who wrote this poem

E. E. CUMMINGS 1894–

The early life of Edward Estlin Cummings was spent in Cambridge, Massachusetts. Cummings' father was a professor at Harvard University, so it was natural for Cummings to earn his degree there.

In 1917, Cummings enlisted in the ambulance corps and was sent to France. Asked by a French official if he hated the Germans, Cummings replied No; he loved the French—and joined his best friend in a concentration camp. The prison in which he stayed for three months was later the subject of *The Enormous Room.* This was Cummings' first book, and it is still one of the most powerful American novels written about World War I.

When Cummings' first volume of poetry, *Tulips and Chimneys,* appeared in 1923, it attracted much attention. The lack of capitalization and punctuation astounded many readers. The spelling was often erratic, and the words did not always follow in normal order. Lines like "and eddieandbill come" shocked some readers. Sometimes the very appearance of a poem in type was striking because of its unusual spacing and short lines.

Although these devices were resented by some readers who liked more conventional forms, they proved effective. Cummings is an excellent craftsman who really understands the effect he wants to create. Probably the best summary of Cummings' poetic philosophy was expressed in the first line of the poem "315": "you shall above all things be glad and young."

The poet's art . . .

The poet can often bring a fresh understanding to common, everyday occurrences because he is able to see them more clearly in the mind's eye. For example, in "the hours rise up" E. E. Cummings looked at the coming of day in a great city. What he saw filled his mind with impressions which he translated into images—word images in the language and visual images in the patterning of the lines. If these images evoked in you, the reader, a similar impression, then you, too, were seeing the commonplace in a fresh and unusual way.

1. Look again at the opening stanza. Notice how the poet achieved freshness by his use of personification. He said, "the hours *rise up*" and "light *walks, scattering* poems." Dawn and light are portrayed as

living and capable of action. Note also the unexpected use of the word *poems,* not for its **denotative meaning** (what it identifies), but for its **connotative meaning**—what it suggests or implies. What did the image "scattering poems" suggest to you? Also discuss the connotative meanings of these images:

> putting off stars (line 1)
> murder dreams (line 11)
> the hours descend (line 31)

2. Sometimes Cummings captured the sharpness and emotion of an impression by placing together certain words which do not usually appear together. For example, he spoke of men "digging bread." He named both the act and the end product secured as a result of the act. Thus he condensed a chain of impressions into two words and increased the emotional response of the reader. Explain what you think he meant and what series of impressions this image created for you.

In the last line of stanza four, he used the same device but with a different effect: "people contented hideous hopeless cruel happy." What effect did he create by combining words with very different meanings? How adequately do they describe the kinds of people you would see in a large city? Would you add other words?

3. His use of contrast also gave the poem a fresh quality. Note this stanza:

> "the city
> wakes
> with a song upon her
> mouth having death in her eyes"

Your response to these words may be an impression or feeling rather than a concrete thought. Be sure to notice that when the city wakes it is with a song upon her mouth and death in her eyes. When the city sleeps, it is with death upon her mouth and a song in her eyes. These lines are open to many possible interpretations. One is that the sounds of an awakening city are like a song which is silent, like death, at night. How would you interpret the "song in the city's eyes"?

4. Notice, too the uneven length of the lines. The rather long opening line is followed by a single-word line. Thus, the poet gives to the word *dawn* far greater emphasis than if he had added it to the end of the first line. Why did Cummings wish to call attention to this word? Find other examples in which the length of a line has added to the effect of the poem.

5. Cummings used no capital letters and very little punctuation. How did these omissions help you see the poem with fresh eyes?

My Friend Moe

MARJORIE KINNAN RAWLINGS

Far from the noise and confusion of cities, Marjorie Kinnan Rawlings found Cross Creek, a quiet region of rural Florida. She also found Moe— or perhaps he found her. At least he told the villagers, "Me and her is buddies, see?"

Sometimes there are friendships that have no apparent reason for existence, between people set apart by every circumstance of life, yet so firm in their foundations that they survive conditions that would separate friends of more apparent suitability. My friendship with Moe was one of these. Moe said and believed that we were friends because we needed each other.

In the village he said once, "Me and her is buddies, see? If her gate falls down, I go and fix it. If I git in a tight for money she helps me if she's got it, and if she ain't got it, she gits it for me. We stick together. You got to stick to the bridge that carries you across."

If he had never fixed a gate for me, waving aside any offer of pay, leaving a profitable carpenter's job to do it—for I certainly could not be bothered with the neighbors' stock coming in, could I?—if I had never scratched up a dollar for him, Moe and I would have been friends. Beyond our admiration of something in each other that might pass for courage, beyond our mutual helpfulness, there was a warm tenderness that made us like just to sit down together on the back steps and talk about the world as we saw it, while three or four of his boys squatted patiently on their heels waiting for us to be finished.

Sometimes he would wave his arm at them and boom in his deep voice, "You scapers go on and eat oranges now. Me and her ain't half done talkin'."

He introduced himself on my first Christmas Day at the Creek. He came out with a man named Whitey and it was a formal Christmas call. I was bustling about cooking Christmas dinner, some of the family were there, and Moe and Whitey sat on the back steps and visited with the men. It was long past the country noon dinner hour and I grew uneasy as the turkey browned and the squash and potatoes were done and the hard sauce finished for the plum pudding. I took my outdoor shower and dressed. I delayed, pushing the gravy to the back of the wood range. Moe and Whitey sat on. The turkey was beginning to dry out and the sauce had stood too long on the oyster cocktails in the ice-box.

In desperation, I said, "Dinner is ready. Won't you men join us?"

According to my bringing up, that was the signal for uninvited guests to be on their way. I found that in rural Florida, to refuse an invitation to a meal, if one is there at the time it is ready or nearly so, is to insult hospitality so grievously that the damage can seldom be repaired. Moe and Whitey had of course had their dinner, but to my horror Moe said, "Thank you, Ma'am," led Whitey to the pump stand to wash up and came in. The family dinner was ruined for me. The intruders were as unhappy as I, but applied themselves with lowered heads and high-lifted elbows to their plates. Whitey was plainly only a follower and I stole a look at Moe. He was a great burly man with long arms and thick shoulders, slightly hunched from years of labor. His head was massive and beyond a full fine forehead the receding hair was shaggy and leonine. There was the look there of a man who might have been a statesman. He had one of the most beautiful speaking voices that I have ever heard. It had the deep resonance of a bass fiddle.

He plowed his way through the many-coursed dinner without comment. When I served the plum pudding that had taken so long to make and decorate, he looked briefly at the blanched almonds and sugared fruits on the top and scraped them to one side, as I should scrape unexpected insects. The dinner had been one of my best, and it seemed to me from the rough worn clothes and the backwoods speech that it must surely have been a little out of the ordinary for these men. My vanity about my cooking is known and pandered to, and it seemed incredible to me that uninvited guests like these should not only pay me no compliments, but should have put down the choice dishes like so much hay.

I said, "You men have just eaten a typical Yankee Christmas dinner. Now tell me, what is the usual Cracker Christmas dinner?"

Moe lifted his big head and looked at me gravely.

"Whatever we can git, Ma'am," he said. "Whatever we can git."

I should have given the dinner and all my work over it, not to have asked that question.

I heard later that in the village Moe described the meal dish by dish. He spoke even of the edible decorations on the plum pudding that he rejected.

"A meal like that," I was told he said, "a feller don't know what's cold-out rations and what's fancy fixin's. When I seed her face, I knowed I'd ought to of run the risk and et everything."

I do not remember when we became friends. The occasion is bound to have been one when he did me some kindness. It seems to me that it was the hot Sunday morning when he passed by with his boys from a night's frog-hunting and found me in hell. I shall always associate my conception of hell with hot Sunday summer mornings at the Creek.

I was without household help at the time and I slept late without hearing a sound on the place to disturb me. The lowing of the cow finally penetrated my sleep and I awoke in a humid heat to an uneasy sense that all was not well. I dressed and went out to the stillness of a desert island.

The cow was old Laura, weather-beaten, gray and gaunt, and the only cow I have known with a more evil nature than hers is her daughter Dora. Laura was busily and angrily engaged in tearing down the pasture fence. An early daughter, then a calf, little Atrocia, a repulsive creature whom I later traded for a week's hoeing, was jumping back and forth through the hole in the fence that Laura had begun. The young bull had broken through the fence by the road, and at the sight of me began bellowing and pawing the earth. The chickens, unfed and protesting, got under my feet and tripped me as I made my way through the sandspurs to the pasture gate. It had been fastened with an intricate African arrangement of chains, and by the time I had them loosened and the gate swung wide, Laura had knocked down two more fence posts and was making her way loftily to the barn. She then decided to be coy, and food being what I supposed she wanted, refused to go into the pen where it waited. She gambolled like a heifer through the grove, her bony hips heaving, little Atrocia at her heels in delight at the sudden friskiness of her aged parent. I was obliged to give up getting her into the pen. I lugged the feed trough out into the open by the barn and brought a bucket of water, for the lake was low beside the pasture and the stock must be watered by hand. I went into the barn for feed. A new sack had to be opened and I bruised my fingers working at the chain-stitch binding. I took a bucket of the feed and emptied it into the trough. Laura was in front of the house eating blue plumbago blossoms and asparagus fern. I climbed up the rickety ladder to the hayloft to pitch down hay, for the bull must have some of this too. A chicken snake and two rats ran across my feet as I lifted a forkful. A leather-winged bat, disturbed from its slumbers in the rafters, swooped out of the loft, brushing my hair. A setting hen under the hay flew into my face and floated to earth, squawking and shrilling. I pitched down the hay and descended the ladder. The next to the last rung broke under me and I slid to the ground and walked limping to the feed trough. Laura had come, eaten all the feed, and was now over by the tenant house. Being full, she had no intention of standing for milking. She had a greedy nature and I lured her back to the trough with another bucket of feed. The calf was only two months old, though weaned, and Laura's bag in mid-morning was full and tight. I had never milked in my life. I had never expected to milk in my life. I should not have tried it now, but I was certain Laura would burst if she were not somehow relieved.

I knelt down beside her, put the milk bucket under her, and tightened my fingers around two of the udders. Nothing happened. With her mouth dripping feed, Laura turned her head over her shoulder and looked at me, as though to say, "What on earth are you doing?" In annoyance, she moved a foot to the side. I moved too. I began again. I constricted desperately,

trying to recall the motion I had seen the milkers use. The knack suddenly came to me, and I saw the first thin streams of milk drop into the bucket as though I had brought up pearls from the sea. By this time the second bucket of feed was gone, Laura walked off, and I was obliged to go for a third bucket and lure her back again. She was indifferent, but she had become also a little lethargic, and I got her back to the trough. This time, because she ate so slowly, I got a quart of milk. A sense of proud competence filled me. I was dripping with perspiration and the flies hummed around us. When they stung me, I went frantically on with my milking. When they stung Laura, she switched her long tail across my face. Now she stood immobile, ruminating placidly. With no provocation at all, because the stinging flies were on me, she lifted a hind foot and kicked the bucket of milk into my lap. I looked at her bag. It seemed as full as ever. I went back to the milking. Humanitarian motives had left me, but I did not want a good milch cow to swell up and die. I got another pint, and Laura lifted a hind leg and kicked me square in the middle. There was only one thing left to do. I kicked her in the middle, said to her, "You may burst for all of me," and she stalked off into the coffee-weed. I tottered to the pen to close the gate. It was at this moment that Moe and his boys drew up by the fence and hailed me.

His big voice boomed out, "What you doin' with a milk bucket?"

I leaned weakly on the fence to answer him.

"My man didn't show up and I tried to milk the cow."

"Where is she?"

He was already putting his long legs out of the old car. His boys tumbled out behind him.

"Over there in the coffee-weed. I hope she pops wide open."

I must have begun to know him as a friend, for he did not laugh. He gave di-

rections to the boys and they scattered to the points of the compass. Two of them drove back the cow. Two made a noose of a rope from the barn. All together they held her tied tight to an orange tree while Moe rested on his heels and milked and stripped her.

"What else you got around here ain't done?"

The chickens had not been fed and water for all the animals had not been pumped. They did that.

He was always indignant when he found me doing work that he considered too difficult or too heavy, and called his boys in a swarm to take over. They were silent, unsmiling youngsters, undersized and pale. They went to school passively, and since they showed no interest in education, Moe was trying to train them in his own profession of carpentering, and was teaching them frog-hunting on the side.

"Them scapers is the best frog hunters

in the county," he said. "No fear o' them or their mammy starvin' when I'm done for, long as they can haul in a hundred pounds o' frogs of a night."

The boys smiled then, wanly. The irresponsible night hunting was to their taste. I am sure the carpentering was not, though they did accurate enough work under Moe's critical eye. Moe's true love was an orange grove, and he would have liked to raise oranges for a living. His father, and his grandfather before him, had been superintendent for the Fairbanks grove, one of the oldest Florida groves, of which my choice seven acres in Big Hammock is a part. Moe had lived on the grove as a boy. One day I heard his voice giving orders at the gate. The boys were bringing in a bedstead. It was handmade, spool turned, of pine, put together with wooden pegs. It had the grace of all good handmade things.

"This mought seem like pure trash to

you," Moe said, and the boys set the bed down in front of me. "But if you want it, it's yours. It was made for Major Fairbanks, and before he died he give it to my daddy. It's been out in the barn for fifty years. You want it?"

The bed had real value as Floridiana. There are almost no native Florida antiques. Major Fairbanks was not only a famous early grove owner, but the founder and first president of the Florida Historical Society and the author of *Fairbanks' History of Florida* and the *History and Antiquities of St. Augustine*, both now collectors' items.

I said, "It's beautiful, Moe, but it's valuable. You should keep it."

"We got no use fer it," he said contemptuously, not of the bed, but of his household's way of life, which grieved him. "The way I got to figgerin', a thing belongs to be used and used right, and you livin' nice, and havin' a piece o' the Major's old grove, why, you're the one to have it. Been layin' up all these years waitin' for the right person."

The bed is now my own, and it is promised when I am done with it to the Historical Society.

I did not understand it at the time, but as I look back on our friendship, I believe that Moe lived vicariously in my grove and in my "livin' nice." He was intrigued with every detail of my housekeeping. He put in a new kitchen floor for me, saying of the old one through which 'Geechee had scrubbed a hole, "Why, Ma'am, they was places you could of throwed a dog through it." As he worked, he noticed a row of glass jars of huckleberries that I had canned. His grave face brightened.

"Now that's the way to live," he said. "All the good things we got here in Florida, blueberries and blackberries and beans and cow-peas, all them things had ought to be canned and put up on a clean cupboard shelf with white paper on it. That's the way my Ma did. She lived fine, not the way you live, but just as good when it

comes to cannin' things and keepin' things clean." His face darkened. "I've tried and I've done tried to get my wife to do that-a-way but it just ain't no use. One time I bought two dozen glass jars and I went out by myself and I picked about a bushel o' blackberries and I went to the store and bought a twenty-five pound sack o' sugar and I takened it home, and I said, 'Wife, here's a bait o' blackberries to put up for us for jam and jelly for the winter.'" He hesitated, his loyalty pricking him.

"She probably didn't have time to do it," I suggested.

"She had time. She let the blackberries spoil, and the antses got in the sugar, and I found the jars throwed out in the back yard."

I had light on the matter when I met his mother, who came to visit in the village. Moe brought her out and left her with me for the day. She was of the admirable Florida pioneer type, plump, immaculate, wise and kindly. We talked of her life on the Fairbanks grove and we talked of Moe.

"It like to killed me when he married," she said. "Moe did love bein' to home and havin' things nice. I said to him, 'Son, don't you marry that girl. She ain't your kind and she'll not make you the home you want.' He looked kind o' sorrowful, and he said, real slow, 'I know, Ma. But I love the little old thing.'"

Moe followed the fortunes of my grove as closely as if it had been his own. When I planted ten acres of Valencias [1] across the road where the dingy pecan trees had been cut down and the vacant space had stared at me, he rejoiced with me. We were sure that the new ten acres would make the needed difference between profit and loss. I had put my last hundreds of dollars in the planting and was obliged to watch my simple grocery supplies in consequence. I went to the Everglades in the winter on a hunting trip with Dessie and the Chanceys. The weather in late November was warm

[1] *Valencias*, a kind of orange which ripens in the summer

when we left Tampa. Cold weather set in the second day at camp. Even so far south, we were obliged to have a roaring camp fire night and morning, and the pond water in which we bathed struck us with icy power. We wore sweaters under our hunting clothes and were hard put to it, as we stood motionless on our deer and turkey stands, not to stamp our feet and clap our hands to keep our circulation moving against the cold. The hunt and the companions were so delightful that I did not think to associate the cold with any menace to my new young grove.

When I returned to the Creek, I found that a disastrous freeze had come in to north and central Florida. Old groves showed much damage, fruit was nipped, and many young groves had been frozen to the ground. I looked across the road to my small frail Valencia trees. A miracle had happened. They had been mounded with earth almost to their tops and below the frozen tips they were safe. No one could have done this but Moe. That evening I drove in to his house to see him.

"Bet you was surprised," he chuckled. "The cold begun comin' in that afternoon and it got wuss and wusser. I drove out to the Creek to tell you somethin' had ought to be done. You wasn't there and Martha said you was off huntin' in the south and likely didn't know it was freezin' up here. Dogged if I aimed to let them trees freeze behind your back. I got my boys together, and Ivey Sykes, and Whitey, and a couple more, and I borried all the spades and shovels in Island Grove, and we went out and we worked all night 'til sunrise. The wust cold come in about day and by that time we had the job done."

Such things that Moe did for me could never be paid for.

He tried me out a little later. He came out one evening with the boys and sat stiffly on the veranda.

He burst out, "I got to have forty dollars. How about it?" He looked me in the eye with something like belligerence.

I said, "As long as I've got it, it's yours."

The loan caught me very short. I wrote out the check and as I handed it to the man, I sensed in him a feeling of triumph. He returned the money a week later. I happened to know that he had not worked that week. He was only making certain that he could count on me. After that, he borrowed only when he was in dire straits. Sometimes I myself had to borrow the money when half of his immense family was sick, but my credit was better than his. If he could not pay me back in cash, he paid in work worth twice what he owed me.

One summer I decided to make a hurried trip to New York to consult with my editor. I put my car in storage and bought my ticket for New York. My grove man would drive me in the truck to the train at the village stop. The morning that I was to leave, Moe drove out to see me. His face was gray.

He said, "I'm in trouble. Mary's dyin'. Seems like I'm turned to stone. I cain't think. I cain't figger out what to do."

Mary was one of the youngest of his brood of twelve, a shy child with a certain brightness of face the others did not possess.

I said, "I'll come," and drove the farm truck behind him to his house.

The child lay like a crumpled rag doll on her small bed, her blue eyelids closed, her breathing hoarse and labored. The mother sat nearby in a slovenly incompetence. Moe had taken Mary to the doctor two days before, and while there was a chance, he had said, that her illness might pass into pneumonia, there was an equal chance, with proper nursing, of no danger at all. The pneumonia had developed rapidly and literally nothing had been done. Moe had been ill and unable to work and his funds were exhausted. His wife thought the illness was unimportant. The child was plainly in a critical condition.

A heavy downpour of rain had set in, the roof of the farm truck leaked like a sieve, I was dressed for my trip and had only two hours before train time. But my own plans were trivial before Moe's trouble. I drove to Ocala in the rain, arranged for a doctor and a nurse, drew money out of the bank for Moe, and went back to tell him that help was on the way. The doctor and nurse had arrived ahead of me and were working over the sick child. Moe looked at my soaked clothes. He dropped down on the porch of his house and tears ran down the deep furrows of his face.

He said, "I hadn't ought to of let you do this. I reckon you can't figger why I'd take on so over one young un, and me with a whole houseful of 'em."

He wiped away his tears unashamed with the back of his big hand.

"Mary's different," he said. "All them other young uns, and their Ma, they don't pay me a bit o' mind. When I come home, times they don't even pass the time o' day with me, lessen to ask maybe did I bring home meat for supper. They don't none of 'em care do I come or go. But Mary sets by the road and waits for me. She comes runnin' and I carry her in on my shoulder. She calls me 'Bubber.' "

The tears ran like rain.

"I don't know how I'll live if she dies," he said. "I just couldn't make out without Mary."

I took my train for New York, but I had almost forgotten why I was going. I could not get Moe out of my mind. All day, far up into Georgia, the rain fell, and they were Moe's tears, falling for Mary, the only one who cared whether he came or went. All night, the wheels of the train repeated, "Moe and Mary! Moe and Mary!" It seemed to me that I should be obliged to get off the train and go back to them.

I had a brief interview with my editor and hurried home. Mary was safe. She smiled shyly when Moe took me to her bed. The nurse had the sickroom in order and Moe was in his best bib and tucker. His face was luminous.

"I shore went to pieces," he apologized.

"When I think o' you comin', all dressed in your best clothes and soppin' wet from helpin' me, I'm ashamed. But them things gits made up somehow. I'll git a chance to do somethin' for you sometime. Tell you what I'll do. I'll take you alligator-huntin'. You ain't never been and I'll bet you could write a fine story about it if you saw it yourself."

Moe continued to keep an eye on my grove and on tottering fences, leaking roofs and broken plumbing. He tried to keep his own garden, single-handed, and he brought me always the first of his crop; lettuce, squash, watermelons. He brought up the matter of the 'gator hunt every time he came, but somehow we never got together on it.

"How about that 'gator hunt tonight?" he would say and I would have some engagement that prevented it.

He could not have been much past fifty in age, but he began to break like a man much older. There were increasing periods when he could not do his carpentering and when he could not go frog-hunting with his boys. The last summer of his life he was very ill. He asked if the boys might help with my summer grove pruning. I was glad of the extra labor. At the time Moe owed me twenty-five dollars and since I knew it fretted him, I asked if he wanted the boys' pay applied on the debt. He hesitated.

"No, jest pay 'em right out," he said. "That other's somethin' between you and me."

There was no hope for him. Years of improper food and overwork, of anxiety over the future of his family, above all, I think, despair at not living as he longed to have them live, had eaten at his big burly frame and great gentle mind. He knew that he was going. He sent the boys out for me one day. He sat propped in a chair, his face gaunt, his hair tousled above the broad forehead.

"I ain't goin' to make it," he said and his

voice was as deep and rich as ever. "I ain't never taken you on that 'gator hunt like I promised, and I hate that."

A few days later I stopped by his place, drawn by an uneasy instinct. Moe was still propped in his chair. As I stood in the doorway, his breath made a strangling sound in his throat and the big head dropped forward on his chest and did not lift again. The family stood stonily. Only Mary huddled behind his chair with a desperate small face. Only she and I have missed him, finding the world less generous for his going.

The woman who wrote this selection

MARJORIE KINNAN RAWLINGS
1896–1953

After completing her education, Marjorie Kinnan Rawlings went to work on a newspaper. For many years she wrote articles, poems, and columns for newspapers across the nation. In 1928 she gave up newspaper writing to grow oranges in Florida.

Before long she was writing again, but this time it was stories about her new surroundings. At first she could not get them published, but after one was finally sold, her stories were in demand. She wrote slowly and carefully about her home in the orange grove.

The Yearling, a delightful novel about a young backwoods Floridian, was her greatest success. It won a Pulitzer Prize, was a best seller, and was later made into a popular movie.

Let's consider . . .

1. As Mrs. Rawlings wrote about Moe, she revealed a great deal about herself. What did you learn about her that would explain why she and Moe became friends?

2. The author was living at Cross Creek, in the backwoods of Florida, when she made Moe's acquaintance. What part did the setting play in their friendship?

3. Why did Moe and Whitey accept Mrs. Rawlings' invitation to stay for Christmas dinner?

4. When did Moe first come to Mrs. Rawlings' rescue? Describe this incident and others which followed.

5. Moe took great pride in people "livin' nice." What did you learn about his own way of living, both from what he said and from what his mother told Mrs. Rawlings?

6. How did Moe save the orange grove?

7. When Mary was sick, what did Mrs. Rawlings do for Moe which proved her true friendship?

8. After reading this account of an unusual friendship, how do you feel about the suitability of making close friends with people of wholly different backgrounds: economic, educational, religious? Perhaps your teacher will let you have a panel discussion on this question.

The writer's craft . . .

Characterization is the way in which a writer brings his characters to life. One of the most difficult tasks that all writers face is to find ways to create believable characters. Certainly Moe was believable, but *how* did Mrs. Rawlings make him seem believable? One reason for her success was that she let you see him in action. She did not presume to interpret what he was thinking or feeling; rather, she let you see Moe through her eyes and let you hear what he said.

1. Why would this portrait of Moe have been less effective if Mrs. Rawlings had merely talked about Moe?

2. List the incidents which told you the most about Moe as a person. Then explain what quality of his character was revealed by each of these incidents.

3. Mrs. Rawlings was careful not to over-dramatize either Moe and what he did, or the unusual nature of their friendship. Part of the charm of her writing—as well as its appropriateness to the region about which she was writing—was due to her use of **understatement:** representing something less strongly than the truth will admit. What understanding of the people and region did you get from Mrs. Rawlings' way of telling her story?

4. Create a word-portrait of someone you know. Reveal only those qualities which are evident from what that person says and does. Include the following:

   a. The person's appearance

   b. His manner of speaking (actual dialogue)

   c. Several incidents which reveal how that person acts and feels

Knowing words . . .

In speaking of the bed that Moe gave to her, Marjorie Kinnan Rawlings wrote "The bed had real value as Floridiana." *Floridiana* is a term applied to such things as documents, facts, art, craftsmanship, products, etc., which relate to the history or geography of Florida. The bed was considered a piece of *Floridiana* because it had originally been made for a person who played an important part in the state's history.

The suffix *-ana* or *-iana* is sometimes added to a proper name, usually of a person or place, to form a noun. In this way it is possible to identify items, facts, or pieces of information as related to that person or place. The term *Americana* is frequently used to identify things which are particularly representative of America. List three or four things (items, facts, or pieces of information) which you would identify as Americana.

Let No Charitable Hope

Now let no charitable hope
Confuse my mind with images
Of eagle and of antelope:
I am in nature none of these.

I was, being human, born alone;
I am, being woman, hard beset;
I live by squeezing from a stone
The little nourishment I get.

In masks outrageous and austere
The years go by in single file;
But none has merited my fear,
And none has quite escaped my smile.

Elinor Wylie

Exile

ARCHIBALD RUTLEDGE

So we were married, and I brought her home.
But, after a little while, she could not bear
The country that I loved. The big dark pines,
That kept on looming loftier in the dusk,
Gave her, she said, the shudders. The old owls,
The oaks' dim oracles, made her afraid.
The sounds and silences I understood
Were to her heart mysterious. I saw
Her longing for the city and its ways.
Yet she was very gallant for a time.
But once she said, "If we stay here, I know
The gray moss will be growing on us both.
It takes a savage to love the wilderness;
And you can't love it here as you love me."

So, from the old plantation, cityward
We came, leaving the hollies and the oaks behind
To sentinel the home that we had left;
Leaving the wild birds singing on the boughs
Of blossoming myrtles—how I envied them!
We left the Negroes in the cotton, singing;
The river flowing limpid by our doors;
The sibilant whisper of the growing corn;
The hounds to hunt without my hearing them;
The jasmine and the woodbine, that would toss
Saffron and carmine showers, stayed in air;
The wild azalea flaming in the woods—
We unbeholding. And I left my gun,
Forever standing lonely in the hall.

About me now the city towers; the cries
Of many voices sound, but make no song
For me, a woodsman lost in Babylon.[1]
And yet above me still the pine trees soar,
And still I hear the music of their harps.
I cannot see for all that I have seen:
The shadowy deer, furtively stealing forth
To roam the dewy country of the dark;
The old wild gobbler, that all night has slept
In starlight, in the shrouded cypress crest,
Sail to the ground at sunrise in the wilds.
And sometimes, when the wind is in the south,
I'm sure I smell the jasmine in the swamp,
And hear the mallards clamoring in the marsh.

---

[1] *Babylon,* any great luxurious city

The man who wrote this poem

ARCHIBALD RUTLEDGE 1883–

Mr. Rutledge summarizes his early childhood in these words: "I was born on a plantation that has been with my people since 1686. I lived a wild free boyhood. The study of nature was a passion with me (and still is)." He also comments that after he was graduated from Union College, he "tried to teach English for thirty-three years."

All of Archibald Rutledge's fifty-nine published books show his sincere love of nature and the way of life he has known on the plantation. Both of these are reflected in "Exile."

Mr. Rutledge is the official poet laureate of South Carolina and spends most of his time on his plantation. He frequently contributes articles, stories, and poems to popular magazines.

The poet's art . . .

A. This is a poem with tragic implications. It tells the story of a man and his wife who really loved each other but disagreed on one fundamental issue: where they wanted to live. This story is told in blank verse, a poetic form that is age old. It has been used in English poetry ever since Thomas Wyatt and the Earl of Surrey brought it from Italy to England during the Renaissance in the sixteenth century. This form lends itself to the telling of all kinds of narratives—simple stories or fast-moving tales: to oratory that moves to tears or scorn; to the gentle wooing of a Romeo. Shakespeare used it, as did also Tennyson and Robert Frost. Yet in each age, poets have used this blank verse form to achieve somewhat different effects.

Its rhythm is what makes it so flexible. Try reading some of the lines of this poem aloud. Your voice will naturally stress certain syllables more heavily than others. These stresses fall into a pattern called **meter.** Notice in this poem that a light stress immediately precedes a heavier one, and that five of these heavier stresses occur in each line. A regular pattern of five alternating light and heavy stresses is called **iambic pentameter.** When verse of this pattern is unrhymed, it is called **blank verse.** Sometimes a line has an extra unstressed syllable; sometimes two stressed syllables follow each other. This variation prevents monotony.

Compare several lines of blank verse by

Shakespeare, Tennyson, and Frost. You will see that the blank verse of the older poets sounds more formal than the blank verse of modern poets.

B. Notice the number of **run-on lines** in this poem: lines in which the thought is carried over from one line to the next. If you were to pause at the end of the line, you would break the thought. In blank verse you do not have to pause for end rhyme. Now, read the poem aloud. Try to bring out the intense emotions of each character, as well as the story that is being told. Notice how sensitive the husband was to his wife's feelings, and how keen his memories were of the old plantation he loved so well.

1. Point out three examples of run-on lines. As you read them aloud to the class, carry those lines over to the end of the thought.

2. Find two lines in which the poet varied the iambic pattern.

3. Read the lines which best show the wife's strong feelings about "the wilderness."

4. Read the lines which tell what part of the country the couple left behind.

5. Read the lines which best show the husband's sad homesickness.

Bearded Oaks

The oaks, how subtle and marine,
Bearded, and all the layered light
Above them swims; and thus the scene,
Recessed, awaits the positive night.

So, waiting, we in the grass now lie
Beneath the languorous tread of light:
The grasses, kelp-like, satisfy
The nameless motions of the air.

Upon the floor of light, and time,
Unmurmuring, of polyp made,
We rest; we are, as light withdraws,
Twin atolls on a shelf of shade.

Ages to our construction went,
Dim architecture, hour by hour;
And violence, forgot now, lent
The present stillness all its power.

The storm of noon above us rolled,
Of light the fury, furious gold,
The long drag troubling us, the depth:
Dark is unrocking, unrippling, still.

Passion and slaughter, ruth, decay
Descend, minutely whispering, down,
Silted down swaying streams, to lay
Foundation for our voicelessness.

All our debate is voiceless here,
As all our rage, the rage of stone;
If hope is hopeless, then fearless fear,
And history is thus undone.

Our feet once wrought the hollow street
With echo when the lamps were dead
At windows, once our headlight glare
Disturbed the doe that, leaping, fled.

I do not love you less that now
The caged heart makes iron stroke,
Or less that all that light once gave
The graduate dark should now revoke.

We live in time so little time
And we learn all so painfully,
That we may spare this hour's term
To practice for eternity.

Robert Penn Warren

Sunset: St. Louis

SARA TEASDALE

Hushed in the smoky haze of summer sunset
When I came home again from far-off places,
How many times I saw my western city
Dream by her river.

Then for an hour the water wore a mantle
Of tawny gold and mauve and misted turquoise
Under the tall and darkened arches bearing
Gray, high-flung bridges.

Against the sunset, water towers and steeples
Flickered with fire up the slope to westward,
And old warehouses poured their purple shadows
Across the levee.

High over them the black train swept with thunder
Cleaving the city, leaving far beneath it
Wharf-boats moored beside the old side-wheelers [1]
Resting in the twilight.

[1] *side-wheelers,* steamboats with a paddle wheel on each side

The woman who wrote this poem

SARA TEASDALE   1884–1933

Sara Teasdale was a born poet. Her poetic ability was given to her by nature. One critic said her poetry was "the unmistakable voice of a woman born to sing." Another called her a "lyric poet by outright gift."

Her poetic sensitiveness was obvious at an early age. She was too frail and delicate to attend public school and was educated at home and in private schools. This delicacy kept her in ill health for the rest of her life. However, her sickness did not prevent her from writing eight volumes of poetry.

Miss Teasdale had a particularly unhappy life. She had very few friends, her marriage was unsuccessful, and she did not think that her work was appreciated. Today she is regarded as one of America's best lyric poets.

The poet's art . . .

1. In this quiet poem, Sara Teasdale tried to communicate the beauty of St. Louis at sunset. Which lines best expressed that beauty for you?

2. The poet spoke of seeing "my western city Dream by her river." What do you call such a figure of speech?

3. Often poets choose words that have rich overtones which evoke certain responses in the reader. Miss Teasdale wrote, "When I came home again from far-off places." The word *home* has many warm connotations. What feelings and impressions does the word *home* create for you? From this poem, what do you think it meant to Miss Teasdale? Find other words or phrases with connotative meanings.

4. In "Sunset: St. Louis" the first three lines of each stanza are of similar length, but the last line is considerably shorter. Read the poem aloud and notice how these short lines create a rhythm.

Evening Hymn

The day is done;
The lamps are lit;
Woods-ward the birds are flown.
Shadows draw close,—
Peace be unto this house.

The cloth is fair;
The food is set.
God's night draw near.
Quiet and love and peace
Be to this, our rest, our place.
Elizabeth Madox Roberts

Chicago

CARL SANDBURG

Hog Butcher for the World,
Toolmaker, Stacker of Wheat,
Player with Railroads and the Nation's Freight Handler;
Stormy, husky, brawling,
City of the Big Shoulders:

They tell me you are wicked and I believe them, for I have seen your painted
    women under the gas lamps luring the farmboys.
And they tell me you are crooked and I answer: Yes, it is true I have seen the gun-
    man kill and go free to kill again.
And they tell me you are brutal and my reply is: On the faces of women and
    children I have seen the marks of wanton hunger.
And having answered so I turn once more to those who sneer at this my city, and I
    give them back the sneer and say to them:
Come and show me another city with lifted head singing so proud to be alive and
    coarse and strong and cunning.
Flinging magnetic curses amid the toil of piling job on job, here is a tall bold slug-
    ger set vivid against the little soft cities;
Fierce as a dog with tongue lapping for action, cunning as a savage pitted against
    the wilderness,
       Bareheaded,
       Shoveling,
       Wrecking,
       Planning,
       Building, breaking, rebuilding,
Under the smoke, dust all over his mouth, laughing with white teeth,
Under the terrible burden of destiny laughing as a young man laughs,
Laughing even as an ignorant fighter laughs who has never lost a battle,
Bragging and laughing that under his wrist is the pulse, and under his ribs the
    heart of the people,
              Laughing!
Laughing the stormy, husky, brawling laughter of Youth, half-naked, sweating,
    proud to be Hog Butcher, Toolmaker, Stacker of Wheat, Player with Rail-
    roads, and Freight Handler to the Nation.

The man who wrote this poem

CARL SANDBURG 1878–

The son of an immigrant railroad shop-worker, Carl Sandburg received little formal education. By the time he was seventeen, he had worked at a variety of jobs, from porter in a barbershop to scene-shifter in a theater. Amy Lowell commented on his experience, "Nothing could have been better. The poet was learning modern life through its constructive sources."

In 1915 Sandburg's *Chicago Poems* appeared. These poems were studied closely by other poets because they celebrated things that were new to poetry. Sandburg saw beauty in industrial life—a beauty that other poets had not seen. A moonlit brickyard was more beautiful to him than an elaborate garden. The language of daily life was the voice of his poetry.

Sandburg's experiences as a worker have made him a poet of the people. He uses everyday people as the subject of many of his poems and discovers beauty in the ordinary.

Sandburg frequently makes tours throughout the country with his guitar, singing to audiences in a deep and resonant voice. As you might suspect, he learns his songs from the people he meets in his travels.

The poet's art . . .

1. "Chicago" is written in **free verse:** poetry in which the rhythm, length of stanza, and line are irregular. This does not mean that free verse lacks rhythm. Rather, it means that the rhythm does not follow a set pattern. By using free verse poets attempt to keep poetry from becoming rigid and mechanical. The rhythm of "Chicago," for example, is almost as "free" as everyday speech. Sometimes it moves swiftly with a bold step. Sometimes it is as deliberate as a man thinking out loud. Study this poem carefully to discover how the rhythm varies to keep time with Sandburg's thoughts and feelings. Try to bring out the change in rhythm which reflects the poet's mood as you read aloud the lines which show the following:

    a. The wickedness and cruelty of the city

    b. The poet's defense against those who sneer

    c. The poet's appreciation of the laughter and pride of the people

2. Note that there were only twenty-five words in the opening lines of this poem. What large picture of Chicago did the poet paint in these few lines?

3. Sandburg at once admitted the "wickedness" of Chicago, but he was quick to turn with pride to "my city." Tell in your own words what there was about the "bold slugger" that made the poet proud and appreciative.

4. Usually people refer to a city as "she." What is *masculine* in the poet's picture of Chicago?

5. Do you prefer the rhythm of free verse or are you loyal to the stricter, metrical forms usually associated with poetry? Explain your choice.

6. One school of poets—the Imagist poets—believed in the use of everyday language, in the use of the exact word, and in freedom of choice of subject matter. Which of these characteristics did Sandburg's "Chicago" illustrate? Support your answer by quoting specific lines from the poem.

Neighbor Rosicky

WILLA CATHER

As a young man, Anton Rosicky had to decide what kind of life would satisfy the emptiness he felt in the big city. All he asked was to "see the sun rise and set and to plant things and watch them grow." The life he found on a Nebraska farm was not easy; but it was "complete and beautiful."

I

When Doctor Burleigh told Neighbor Rosicky he had a bad heart, Rosicky protested.

"So? No, I guess my heart was always pretty good. I got a little asthma, maybe. Just a awful short breath when I was pitchin' hay last summer, dat's all."

"Well now, Rosicky, if you know more about it than I do, what did you come to me for? It's your heart that makes you short of breath, I tell you. You're sixty-five years old, and you've always worked hard, and your heart's tired. You've got to be careful from now on, and you can't do heavy work any more. You've got five boys at home to do it for you."

The old farmer looked up at the doctor with a gleam of amusement in his queer triangular-shaped eyes. His eyes were large and lively, but the lids were caught up in the middle in a curious way, so that they formed a triangle. He did not look like a sick man. His brown face was creased but not wrinkled, he had a ruddy color in his smooth-shaven cheeks and in his lips, under his long brown mustache. His hair was thin and ragged around his ears, but very little gray. His forehead, naturally high and crossed by deep parallel lines, now ran all the way up to his pointed crown. Rosicky's face had the habit of looking interested—suggested a contented disposition and a reflective quality that was gay rather than grave. This gave him a certain detachment, the easy manner of an onlooker and observer.

"Well, I guess you ain't got no pills fur a bad heart, Doctor Ed. I guess the only thing is fur me to git me a new one."

Doctor Burleigh swung round in his desk chair and frowned at the old farmer. "I think if I were you I'd take a little care of the old one, Rosicky."

Rosicky shrugged. "Maybe I don't know how. I expect you mean fur me not to drink my coffee no more."

"I wouldn't, in your place. But you'll do as you choose about that. I've never yet been able to separate a Bohemian from his coffee or his pipe. I've quit trying. But the sure thing is you've got to cut out farm work. You can feed the stock and do chores about the barn, but you can't do anything in the fields that makes you short of breath."

"How about shelling corn?"

"Of course not!"

Rosicky considered with puckered brows.

"I can't make my heart go no longer'n it wants to, can I, Doctor Ed?"

"I think it's good for five or six years yet, maybe more, if you'll take the strain off it. Sit around the house and help Mary.

If I had a good wife like yours, I'd want to stay around the house."

His patient chuckled. "It ain't no place fur a man. I don't like no old man hanging round the kitchen too much. An' my wife, she's a awful hard worker her own self."

"That's it; you can help her a little. My Lord, Rosicky, you are one of the few men I know who has a family he can get some comfort out of; happy dispositions, never quarrel among themselves, and they treat you right. I want to see you live a few years and enjoy them."

"Oh, they're good kids, all right," Rosicky assented.

The doctor wrote him a prescription and asked him how his oldest son, Rudolph, who had married in the spring, was getting on. Rudolph had struck out for himself, on rented land. "And how's Polly? I was afraid Mary mightn't like an American daughter-in-law, but it seems to be working out all right."

"Yes, she's a fine girl. Dat widder woman bring her daughters up very nice. Polly got lots of spunk, an' she got some style, too. Da's nice, for young folks to have some style." Rosicky inclined his head gallantly. His voice and his twinkly smile were an affectionate compliment to his daughter-in-law.

"It looks like a storm, and you'd better be getting home before it comes. In town in the car?" Doctor Burleigh rose.

"No, I'm in de wagon. When you got five boys, you ain't got much chance to ride round in de Ford. I ain't much for cars, noway."

"Well, it's a good road out to your place; but I don't want you bumping around in a wagon much. And never again on a hay-rake, remember!"

Rosicky placed the doctor's fee delicately behind the desk telephone, looking the other way, as if this were an absent-minded gesture. He put on his plush cap and his corduroy jacket with a sheepskin collar, and went out.

The doctor picked up his stethoscope and frowned at it as if he were seriously annoyed with the instrument. He wished it had been telling tales about some other man's heart, some old man who didn't look the doctor in the eye so knowingly, or hold out such a warm brown hand when he said good-by. Doctor Burleigh had been a poor boy in the country before he went away to medical school; he had known Rosicky almost ever since he could remember, and he had a deep affection for Mrs. Rosicky.

Only last winter he had had such a good breakfast at Rosicky's, and that when he needed it. He had been out all night on a long, hard confinement case at Tom Marshall's—a big rich farm where there was plenty of stock and plenty of feed and a great deal of expensive farm machinery of the newest model, and no comfort whatever. The woman had too many children and too much work, and she was no manager. When the baby was born at last, and handed over to the assisting neighbor woman, and the mother was properly attended to, Burleigh refused any breakfast in that slovenly house, and drove his buggy —the snow was too deep for a car—eight miles to Anton Rosicky's place. He didn't know another farmhouse where a man could get such a warm welcome, and such good strong coffee with rich cream. No wonder the old chap didn't want to give up his coffee!

He had driven in just when the boys had come back from the barn and were washing up for breakfast. The long table, covered with a bright oilcloth, was set out with dishes waiting for them, and the warm kitchen was full of the smell of coffee and hot biscuit and sausage. Five big handsome boys, running from twenty to twelve, all with what Burleigh called natural good manners—they hadn't a bit of the painful self-consciousness he himself had to struggle with when he was a lad. One ran to put his horse away, another helped him off with his fur coat and hung it up, and

Josephine, the youngest child and the only daughter, quickly set another place under her mother's direction.

With Mary, to feed creatures was the natural expression of affection—her chickens, the calves, her big hungry boys. It was a rare pleasure to feed a young man whom she seldom saw and of whom she was as proud as if he belonged to her. Some country housekeepers would have stopped to spread a white cloth over the oilcloth, to change the thick cups and plates for their best china, and the wooden-handled knives for plated ones. But not Mary.

"You must take us as you find us, Doctor Ed. I'd be glad to put out my good things for you if you was expected, but I'm glad to get you any way at all."

He knew she was glad—she threw back her head and spoke out as if she were announcing him to the whole prairie. Rosicky hadn't said anything at all; he merely smiled his twinkling smile, put some more coal on the fire, and went into his own room to pour the doctor a little drink in a medicine glass. When they were all seated, he watched his wife's face from his end of the table and spoke to her in Czech. Then, with the instinct of politeness which seldom failed him, he turned to the doctor and said slyly, "I was just tellin' her not to ask you no questions about Mrs. Marshall till you eat some breakfast. My wife, she's terrible fur to ask questions."

The boys laughed, and so did Mary. She watched the Doctor devour her biscuit and sausage, too much excited to eat anything herself. She drank her coffee and sat taking in everything about her visitor. She had known him when he was a poor country boy, and was boastfully proud of his success, always saying, "What do people go to Omaha for, to see a doctor, when we got the best one in the state right here?" If Mary liked people at all, she felt physical pleasure in the sight of them, personal exultation in any good fortune that came to

them. Burleigh didn't know many women like that, but he knew she was like that.

When his hunger was satisfied, he did, of course, have to tell them about Mrs. Marshall, and he noticed what a friendly interest the boys took in the matter.

Rudolph, the oldest one (he was still living at home then), said, "The last time I was over there, she was lifting them big heavy milk cans, and I knew she oughtn't to be doing it."

"Yes, Rudolph told me about that when he come home, and I said it wasn't right," Mary put in warmly. "It was all right for me to do them things up to the last, for I was terrible strong, but that woman's weakly. And do you think she'll be able to nurse it, Ed?" She sometimes forgot to give him the title she was so proud of. "And to think of your being up all night and then not able to get a decent breakfast! I don't know what's the matter with such people."

"Why, Mother," said one of the boys, "if Doctor Ed had got breakfast there, we wouldn't have him here. So you ought to be glad."

"He knows I'm glad to have him, John, any time. But I'm sorry for that poor woman, how bad she'll feel the doctor had to go away in the cold without his breakfast."

"I wish I'd been in practice when these were getting born." The doctor looked down the row of close-clipped heads. "I missed some good breakfasts by not being."

The boys began to laugh at their mother because she flushed so red, but she stood her ground and threw up her head. "I don't care, you wouldn't have got away from this house without breakfast. No doctor ever did. I'd have had something ready fixed that Anton could warm up for you."

The boys laughed harder than ever, and exclaimed at her: "I'll bet you would!" "She would, that!"

"Father, did you get breakfast for the doctor when we were born?"

"Yes, and he used to bring me my breakfast, too, mighty nice. I was always awful hungry!" Mary admitted with a guilty laugh.

While the boys were getting the doctor's horse, he went to the window to examine the house plants. "What do you do to your geraniums to keep them blooming all winter, Mary? I never pass this house that from the road I don't see your windows full of flowers."

She snapped off a dark red one, and a ruffled new green leaf, and put them in his buttonhole. "There, that looks better. You look too solemn for a young man, Ed. Why don't you git married? I'm worried about you. Settin' at breakfast, I looked at you real hard, and I seen you've got some gray hairs already."

"Oh, yes! They're coming. Maybe they'd come faster if I married."

"Don't talk so. You'll ruin your health eating at the hotel. I could send your wife a nice loaf of nut bread, if you only had one. I don't like to see a young man getting gray. I'll tell you something, Ed; you make some strong black tea and keep it handy in a bowl, and every morning just brush it into your hair, an' it'll keep the gray from showin' much. That's the way I do!"

Sometimes the Doctor heard the gossipers in the drugstore wondering why Rosicky didn't get on faster. He was industrious, and so were his boys, but they were rather free and easy, weren't pushers, and they didn't always show good judgment. They were comfortable, they were out of debt, but they didn't get much ahead. Maybe, Doctor Burleigh reflected, people as generous and warmhearted and affectionate as the Rosickys never got ahead much; maybe you couldn't enjoy your life and put it into the bank, too.

II

When Rosicky left Doctor Burleigh's office he went into the farm-implement store to light his pipe and put on his glasses and read over the list Mary had given him. Then he went into the general-merchandise place next door and stood about until the pretty girl with the plucked eyebrows, who always waited on him, was free. Those eyebrows, two thin India-ink strokes, amused him, because he remembered how they used to be. Rosicky always prolonged his shopping by a little joking; the girl knew the old fellow admired her, and she liked to chaff with him.

"Seems to me about every other week you buy ticking, Mr. Rosicky, and always the best quality," she remarked as she measured off the heavy bolt with red stripes.

"You see, my wife is always makin' goose-fedder pillows, an' de thin stuff don't hold in dem little down fedders."

"You must have lots of pillows at your house."

"Sure. She makes quilts of dem, too. We sleeps easy. Now she's makin' a fedder quilt for my son's wife. You know Polly, that married my Rudolph. How much my bill, Miss Pearl?"

"Eight eighty-five."

"Chust make it nine, and put in some candy for de women."

"As usual. I never did see a man buy so much candy for his wife. First thing you know, she'll be getting too fat."

"I'd like dat. I ain't much fur all dem slim women like what de style is now."

"That's one for me, I suppose, Mr. Bohunk!" Pearl sniffed and elevated her India-ink strokes.

When Rosicky went out to his wagon, it was beginning to snow—the first snow of the season, and he was glad to see it. He rattled out of town and along the highway through a wonderfully rich stretch of country, the finest farms in the country. He admired this High Prairie, as it was called, and always liked to drive through it. His own place lay in a rougher territory, where there was some clay in the soil and it was not so productive. When he bought his land, he hadn't the money to buy on High

Prairie; so he told his boys, when they grumbled, that if their land hadn't some clay in it, they wouldn't own it at all. All the same, he enjoyed looking at these fine farms, as he enjoyed looking at a prize bull.

After he had gone eight miles, he came to the graveyard, which lay just at the edge of his own hay land. There he stopped his horses and sat still on his wagon seat, looking about at the snowfall. Over yonder on the hill he could see his own house, crouching low, with the clump of orchard behind and the windmill before, and all down the gentle hill slope the rows of pale gold cornstalks stood out against the white field. The snow was falling over the cornfield and the pasture and the hay land, steadily, with very little wind—a nice dry snow. The graveyard had only a light wire fence about it and was all overgrown with long red grass. The fine snow, settling into this red grass and upon the few little evergreens and the headstones, looked very pretty.

It was a nice graveyard, Rosicky reflected, sort of snug and homelike, not cramped or mournful—a big sweep all round it. A man could lie down in the long grass and see the complete arch of the sky over him, hear the wagons go by; in summer the mowing machine rattled right up to the wire fence. And it was so near home. Over there across the cornstalks his own roof and windmill looked so good to him that he promised himself to mind the doctor and take care of himself. He was awful fond of his place, he admitted. He wasn't anxious to leave it. And it was a comfort to think that he would never have to go farther than the

edge of his own hayfield. The snow, falling over his barnyard and the graveyard, seemed to draw things together like. And they were all old neighbors in the graveyard, most of them friends; there was nothing to feel awkward or embarrassed about. Embarrassment was the most disagreeable feeling Rosicky knew. He didn't often have it—only with certain people whom he didn't understand at all.

Well, it was a nice snowstorm; a fine sight to see the snow falling so quietly and graciously over so much open country. On his cap and shoulders, on the horses' backs and manes, light, delicate, mysterious it fell; and with it a dry cool fragrance was released into the air. It meant rest for vegetation and men and beasts, for the ground itself; a season of long nights for sleep, leisurely breakfasts, peace by the fire. This and much more went through Rosicky's mind, but he merely told himself that winter was coming, clucked to his horses, and drove on.

When he reached home, John, the youngest boy, ran out to put away his team for him, and he met Mary coming up from the outside cellar with her apron full of carrots. They went into the house together. On the table, covered with oilcloth figured with clusters of blue grapes, a place was set, and he smelled hot coffeecake of some kind. Anton never lunched in town; he thought that extravagant, and anyhow he didn't like the food. So Mary always had something ready for him when he got home.

After he was settled in his chair, stirring his coffee in a big cup, Mary took out of the oven a pan of kolache stuffed with apricots, examined them anxiously to see whether they had got too dry, put them beside his plate, and then sat down opposite him.

Rosicky asked her in Czech if she wasn't going to have any coffee.

She replied in English, as being somehow the right language for transacting business, "Now what did Doctor Ed say, Anton? You tell me just what."

"He said I was to tell you some compliments, but I forgot 'em." Rosicky's eyes twinkled.

"About you, I mean. What did he say about your asthma?"

"He says I ain't got no asthma." Rosicky took one of the little rolls in his broad brown fingers. The thickened nail of his right thumb told the story of his past.

"Well, what is the matter? And don't try to put me off."

"He don't say nothing much, only I'm a little older, and my heart ain't so good like it used to be."

Mary started and brushed her hair back from her temples with both hands as if she were a little out of her mind. From the way she glared, she might have been in a rage with him.

"He says there's something the matter with your heart? Doctor Ed says so?"

"Now don't yell at me like I was a hog in the garden, Mary. You know I always did like to hear a woman talk soft. He didn't say anything de matter wid my heart, only it ain't so young like it used to be, an' he tell me not to pitch hay or run de corn sheller."

Mary wanted to jump up, but she sat

still. She admired the way he never under any circumstances raised his voice or spoke roughly. He was city-bred, and she was country-bred; she often said she wanted her boys to have their papa's nice ways.

"You never have no pain there, do you? It's your breathing and your stomach that's been wrong. I wouldn't believe nobody but Doctor Ed about it. I guess I'll go see him myself. Didn't he give you no advice?"

"Chust to take it easy like, an' stay round de house dis winter. I guess you got some carpenter work for me to do. I kin make some new shelves for you, and I want dis long time to build a closet in de boys' room and make dem two little fellers keep dere clo'es hung up."

Rosicky drank his coffee from time to time, while he considered. His mustache was of the soft long variety and came down over his mouth like the teeth of a buggy rake over a bundle of hay. Each time he put down his cup, he ran his blue handkerchief over his lips. When he took a drink of water, he managed very neatly with the back of his hand.

Mary sat watching him intently, trying to find any change in his face. It is hard to see anyone who has become like your own body to you. Yes, his hair had got thin, and his high forehead had deep lines running from left to right. But his neck, always clean shaved except in the busiest seasons, was not loose or baggy. It was burned a dark reddish-brown, and there were deep creases in it, but it looked firm and full of blood. His cheeks had a good color. On either side of his mouth there was a halfmoon down the length of his cheek, not wrinkles, but two lines that had come there from his habitual expression. He was shorter and broader than when she married him; his back had grown broad and curved, a good deal like the shell of an old turtle, and his arms and legs were short.

He was fifteen years older than Mary, but she had hardly ever thought about it before. He was her man, and the kind of man she liked. She was rough, and he was gentle—city-bred, as she always said. They had been shipmates on a rough voyage, and had stood by each other in trying times. Life had gone well with them because, at bottom, they had the same ideas about life. They agreed, without discussion, as to what was most important and what was secondary. They didn't often exchange opinions, even in Czech—it was as if they had thought the same thought together. A good deal had to be sacrificed and thrown overboard in a hard life like theirs, and they had never disagreed as to the things that could go. It had been a hard life, and a soft life, too. There wasn't anything brutal in the short, broad-backed man with the three-cornered eyes and the forehead that went on to the top of his skull. He was a city man, a gentle man, and though he had married a rough farm girl, he had never touched her without gentleness.

They had been at one accord not to hurry through life, not to be always skimping and saving. They saw their neighbors buy more land and feed more stock than they did, without discontent. Once when the creamery agent came to the Rosickys to persuade them to sell him their cream, he told them how much money the Fasslers, their nearest neighbors, had made on their cream last year.

"Yes," said Mary, "and look at them Fassler children! Pale, pinched little things, they look like skimmed milk. I'd rather put some color into my children's faces than put money into the bank."

The agent shrugged and turned to Anton.

"I guess we'll do like she says," said Rosicky.

III

Mary very soon got into town to see Doctor Ed, and then she had a talk with her boys and set a guard over Rosicky. Even John, the youngest, had his father on his mind. If Rosicky went to throw hay down from the loft, one of the boys ran up the ladder and took the fork from him. He sometimes complained that though he was getting to be an old man, he wasn't an old woman yet.

That winter he stayed in the house in the afternoons and carpentered, or sat in the chair between the window full of plants and the wooden bench where the two pails of drinking water stood. This spot was called "Father's corner," though it was not a corner at all. He had a shelf there, where he kept his Bohemian papers and his pipes and tobacco, and his shears and needles and thread and tailor's thimble. Having been a tailor in his youth, he couldn't bear to see a woman patching at his clothes, or at the boys'. He liked tailoring, and always patched all the overalls and jackets and work shirts. Occasionally he made over a pair of pants one of the older boys had outgrown, for the little fellow.

While he sewed, he let his mind run back over his life. He had a good deal to remember, really; life in three countries. The only part of his youth he didn't like to remember was the two years he had spent in London, in Cheapside, working for a German tailor who was wretchedly poor. Those days, when he was nearly always hungry, when his clothes were dropping off him for dirt, and the sound of a strange language kept him in continual bewilderment, had left a sore spot in his mind that wouldn't bear touching.

He was twenty when he landed at Castle Garden in New York, and he had a protector who got him work in a tailor shop in Vesey Street, down near the Washington Market. He looked upon that part of his life as very happy. He became a good workman, he was industrious, and his wages were increased from time to time. He minded his own business and envied nobody's good fortune. He went to night school and learned to read English. He often did overtime work and was well paid for it, but somehow he never saved anything. He couldn't refuse a loan to a friend, and he was self-indulgent. He liked a good dinner, and a little went for beer, a little for tobacco; a good deal went to the girls. He often stood through an opera on Saturday nights; he could get standing room for a dollar. Those were the great days of opera in New York, and it gave a fellow something to think about for the rest of the week. Rosicky had a quick ear, and a childish love of all the stage splendor; the scenery, the costumes, the ballet. He usually went with a chum, and after the performance they had beer and maybe some oysters somewhere. It was a fine life; for the first five years or so it satisfied him completely. He was never hungry or cold or dirty, and everything amused him: a fire, a dogfight, a parade, a storm, a ferry ride. He thought New York the finest, richest, friendliest city in the world.

Moreover, he had what he called a happy home life. Very near the tailor shop was a small furniture factory, where an old Austrian, Loeffler, employed a few skilled men and made unusual furniture, most of it to order, for the rich German housewives uptown. The top floor of Loeffler's five-story factory was a loft, where he kept his choice lumber and stored the odd pieces of furniture left on his hands. One of the young workmen he employed was a Czech, and he and Rosicky became fast friends. They persuaded Loeffler to let them have a sleeping room in one corner of the loft. They bought good beds and bedding and had their pick of the furniture kept up there. The loft was low-pitched, but light and airy, full of windows, and good-smelling by reason of the fine lumber put up there to season. Old Loeffler used to go down to the docks and buy wood from South America and the East from the sea captains. The young men were as foolish about their house as a bridal pair. Zichec, the young cabinetmaker, devised every sort of convenience, and Rosicky kept their clothes in order. At night and on Sundays, when the quiver of machinery underneath was still, it was the quietest place in the

world, and on summer nights all the sea winds blew in. Zichec often practiced on his flute in the evening. They were both fond of music and went to the opera together. Rosicky thought he wanted to live like that forever.

But as the years passed, all alike, he began to get a little restless. When spring came round, he would begin to feel fretted, and he got to drinking. He was likely to drink too much of a Saturday night. On Sunday he was languid and heavy, getting over his spree. On Monday he plunged into work again. So he never had time to figure out what ailed him, though he knew something did. When the grass turned green in Park Place, and the lilac hedge at the back of Trinity churchyard put out its blossoms, he was tormented by a longing to run away. That was why he drank too much; to get a temporary illusion of freedom and wide horizons.

Rosicky, the old Rosicky, could remember as if it were yesterday the day when the young Rosicky found out what was the matter with him. It was on a Fourth of July afternoon, and he was sitting in Park Place in the sun. The lower part of New York was empty. Wall Street, Liberty Street, Broadway, all empty. So much stone and asphalt with nothing going on, so many empty windows. The emptiness was intense, like the stillness in a great factory when the machinery stops and the belts and bands cease running. It was too great a change, it took all the strength out of one. Those blank buildings, without the stream of life pouring through them, were like empty jails. It struck young Rosicky that this was the trouble with big cities; they built you in from the earth itself, cemented you away from any contact with the ground. You lived in an unnatural world, like the fish in an aquarium, who were probably much more comfortable than they ever were in the sea.

On that very day he began to think seriously about the articles he had read in the Bohemian papers, describing prosperous

Czech farming communities in the West. He believed he would like to go out there as a farm hand; it was hardly possible that he could ever have land of his own. His people had always been workmen; his father and grandfather had worked in shops. His mother's parents had lived in the country, but they rented their farm and had a hard time to get along. Nobody in his family had ever owned any land—that belonged to a different station of life altogether. Anton's mother died when he was little, and he was sent into the country to her parents. He stayed with them until he was twelve, and formed those ties with the earth and the farm animals and growing things which are never made at all unless they are made early. After his grandfather died, he went back to live with his father and stepmother, but she was very hard on him, and his father helped him to get passage to London.

After that Fourth of July day in Park Place, the desire to return to the country never left him. To work on another man's farm would be all he asked; to see the sun rise and set and to plant things and watch them grow. He was a very simple man. He was like a tree that has not many roots, but one taproot that goes down deep. He subscribed for a Bohemian paper printed in Chicago, then for one printed in Omaha. His mind got farther and farther west. He began to save a little money to buy his liberty. When he was thirty-five, there was a great meeting in New York of Bohemian athletic societies, and Rosicky left the tailor shop and went home with the Omaha delegates to try his fortune in another part of the world.

IV

Perhaps the fact that his own youth was well over before he began to have a family was one reason why Rosicky was so fond of his boys. He had almost a grandfather's indulgence for them. He had never had to worry about any of them—except, just now, a little about Rudolph.

On Saturday night the boys always piled into the Ford, took little Josephine, and went to town to the moving-picture show. One Saturday morning they were talking at the breakfast table about starting early that evening, so that they would have an hour or so to see the Christmas things in the stores before the show began. Rosicky looked down the table.

"I hope you boys ain't disappointed, but I want you to let me have de car tonight. Maybe some of you can go in with de neighbors."

Their faces fell. They worked hard all week, and they were still like children. A new jackknife or a box of candy pleased the older ones as much as the little fellow.

"If you and Mother are going to town," Frank said, "maybe you could take a couple of us along with you, anyway."

"No, I want to take de car down to Rudolph's, and let him an' Polly go in to de show. She don't git into town enough, an' I'm afraid she's gettin' lonesome, an' he can't afford no car yet."

That settled it. The boys were a good deal dashed. Their father took another piece of apple cake and went on: "Maybe next Saturday night de two little fellers can go along wid dem."

"Oh, is Rudolph going to have the car every Saturday night?"

Rosicky did not reply at once; then he began to speak seriously: "Listen, boys; Polly ain't lookin' so good. I don't like to see nobody lookin' sad. It comes hard fur a town girl to be a farmer's wife. I don't want no trouble to start in Rudolph's family. When it starts, it ain't so easy to stop. An American girl don't git used to our ways all at once. I like to tell Polly she and Rudolph can have the car every Saturday night till after New Year's, if it's all right with you boys."

"Sure it's all right, Papa," Mary cut in.

"And it's good you thought about that. Town girls is used to more than country girls. I lay awake nights, scared she'll make Rudolph discontented with the farm."

The boys put as good a face on it as they could. They surely looked forward to their Saturday nights in town. That evening Rosicky drove the car the half mile down to Rudolph's new, bare little house.

Polly was in a short-sleeved gingham dress, clearing away the supper dishes. She was a trim, slim little thing, with blue eyes and shingled yellow hair, and her eyebrows were reduced to a mere brush stroke like Miss Pearl's.

"Good evening, Mr. Rosicky. Rudolph's at the barn, I guess." She never called him father, or Mary mother. She was sensitive about having married a foreigner. She never in the world would have done it if Rudolph hadn't been such a handsome, persuasive fellow and such a gallant lover. He had graduated in her class in the high school in town, and their friendship began in the ninth grade.

Rosicky went in, though he wasn't exactly asked. "My boys ain't goin' to town tonight, an' I brought de car over fur you two to go in to de picture show."

Polly, carrying dishes to the sink, looked over her shoulder at him. "Thank you. But I'm late with my work tonight, and pretty tired. Maybe Rudolph would like to go in with you."

"Oh, I don't go to de shows! I'm too old-fashioned. You won't feel so tired after you ride in de air a ways. It's a nice clear night, an' it ain't cold. You go an' fix yourself up, Polly, an' I'll wash de dishes an' leave everything nice fur you."

Polly blushed and tossed her bob. "I couldn't let you do that, Mr. Rosicky. I wouldn't think of it."

Rosicky said nothing. He found a bib apron on a nail behind the kitchen door. He slipped it over his head and then took Polly by her two elbows and pushed her gently toward the door of her own room. "I washed up de kitchen many times for my wife, when de babies was sick or somethin'. You go an' make yourself look nice."

I like you to look prettier'n any of dem town girls when you go in. De young folks must have some fun, an' I'm goin' to look out fur you, Polly."

That kind, reassuring grip on her elbows, the old man's funny bright eyes, made Polly want to drop her head on his shoulder for a second. She restrained herself, but she lingered in his grasp at the door of her room, murmuring tearfully: "You always lived in the city when you were young, didn't you? Don't you ever get lonesome out here?"

As she turned round to him, her hand fell naturally into his, and he stood holding it and smiling into her face with his peculiar, knowing, indulgent smile without a shadow of reproach in it. "Dem big cities is all right fur de rich but dey is terrible hard fur de poor."

"I don't know. Sometimes I think I'd like to take a chance. You lived in New York, didn't you?"

"An' London. Da's bigger still. I learned my trade dere. Here's Rudolph comin', you better hurry."

"Will you tell me about London some time?"

"Maybe. Only I ain't no talker, Polly. Run an' dress yourself up."

The bedroom door closed behind her, and Rudolph came in from the outside, looking anxious. He had seen the car and was sorry any of his family should come just then. Supper hadn't been a very pleasant occasion. Halting in the doorway, he saw his father in a kitchen apron, carrying dishes to the sink. He flushed crimson and something flashed in his eye. Rosicky held up a warning finger.

"I brought de car over fur you an' Polly to go to de picture show, an' I made her let me finish here so you won't be late. You go put on a clean shirt, quick!"

"But don't the boys want the car, Father?"

"No tonight dey don't." Rosicky fumbled under his apron and found his pants pocket. He took out a silver dollar and said in a hurried whisper: "You go an' buy dat girl some ice cream an' candy tonight, like you was courtin'. She's awful good friends wid me."

Rudolph was very short of cash, but he took the money as if it hurt him. There had been a crop failure all over the county. He had more than once been sorry he'd married this year.

In a few minutes the young people came out, looking clean and a little stiff. Rosicky hurried them off, and then he took his own time with the dishes. He scoured the pots and pans and put away the milk and swept the kitchen. He put some coal in the stove and shut off the draughts, so the place would be warm for them when they got home late at night. Then he sat down and had a pipe and listened to the clock tick.

Generally speaking, marrying an American girl was certainly a risk. A Czech should marry a Czech. It was lucky that Polly was the daughter of a poor widow woman; Rudolph was proud, and if she had a prosperous family to throw up at him, they could never make it go. Polly was one of four sisters, and they all worked; one was bookkeeper in the bank, one taught music, and Polly and her younger sister had been clerks, like Miss Pearl. All four of them were musical, had pretty voices, and sang in the Methodist choir, which the eldest sister directed.

Polly missed the sociability of a store position. She missed the choir, and the company of her sisters. She didn't dislike housework, but she disliked so much of it. Rosicky was a little anxious about this pair. He was afraid Polly would grow so discontented that Rudy would quit the farm and take a factory job in Omaha. He had worked for a winter up there, two years ago, to get money to marry on. He had done very well, and they would always take him back at the stockyards. But to Rosicky that meant the end of everything for his son. To be a landless man was to be a wage earner, a slave all your life; to have nothing; to be nothing.

Rosicky thought he would come over and do a little carpentering for Polly after the New Year. He guessed she needed jollying. Rudolph was a serious sort of chap, serious in love and serious about his work.

Rosicky shook out his pipe and walked home across the fields. Ahead of him the lamplight shone from his kitchen windows. Suppose he were still in a tailor shop on Vesey Street, with a bunch of pale, narrow-chested sons working on machines, all coming home tired and sullen to eat supper in a kitchen that was a parlor also; with another crowded, angry family quarreling just across the dumbwaiter[1] shaft, and squeaking pulleys at the windows where dirty washings hung on dirty lines above a court full of old brooms and mops and ash cans. . . .

He stopped by the windmill to look up at the frosty winter stars and drew a long breath before he went inside. That kitchen with the shining windows was dear to him; but the sleeping fields and bright stars and the noble darkness were dearer still.

V

On the day before Christmas the weather set in very cold; no snow, but a bitter, biting wind that whistled and sang over the flat land and lashed one's face like fine wires. There was baking going on in the Rosicky kitchen all day, and Rosicky sat inside, making over a coat that Albert had outgrown into an overcoat for John. Mary had a big red geranium in bloom for Christmas, and a row of Jerusalem cherry trees, full of berries. It was the first year she had ever grown these; Doctor Ed brought her the seeds from Omaha when he went to some medical convention. They reminded Rosicky of plants he had seen in England; and all afternoon, as he stitched, he sat thinking about those two years in London, which his mind usually shrank from even after all this while.

---

[1] *dumbwaiter*, a lift, generally used in tenements for transporting garbage to the basement

He was a lad of eighteen when he dropped down into London, with no money and no connections except the address of a cousin who was supposed to be working at a confectioner's. When he went to the pastry shop, however, he found that the cousin had gone to America. Anton tramped the streets for several days, sleeping in doorways and on the Embankment,[2] until he was in utter despair. He knew no English, and the sound of the strange language all about him confused him. By chance he met a poor German tailor who had learned his trade in Vienna, and could speak a little Czech. This tailor, Lifschnitz, kept a repair shop in a Cheapside basement, underneath a cobbler. He didn't much need an apprentice, but he was sorry for the boy and took him in for no wages but his keep and what he could pick up. The pickings were supposed to be coppers given you when you took work home to a customer. But most of the customers called for their clothes themselves, and the coppers that came Anton's way were very few. He had, however, a place to sleep. The tailor's family lived upstairs in three rooms; a kitchen, a bedroom, where Lifschnitz and his wife and five children slept, and a living room. Two corners of this living room were curtained off for lodgers; in one Rosicky slept on an old horsehair sofa, with a feather quilt to wrap himself in. The other corner was rented to a wretched, dirty boy, who was studying the violin. He actually practiced there. Rosicky was dirty, too. There was no way to be anything else. Mrs. Lifschnitz got the water she cooked and washed with from a pump in a brick court, four flights down. There were bugs in the place, and multitudes of fleas, though the poor woman did the best she could. Rosicky knew she often went empty to give another potato or a spoonful of dripping to the two hungry, sad-eyed boys who lodged with her. He used to think he would never

[2] *Embankment,* the banks of the Thames River in London

get out of there, never get a clean shirt to his back again. What would he do, he wondered, when his clothes actually dropped to pieces and the worn cloth wouldn't hold patches any longer?

It was still early when the old farmer put aside his sewing and his recollections. The sky had been a dark gray all day, with not a gleam of sun, and the light failed at four o'clock. He went to shave and change his shirt while the turkey was roasting. Rudolph and Polly were coming over for supper.

After supper they sat round in the kitchen, and the younger boys were saying how sorry they were it hadn't snowed. Everybody was sorry. They wanted a deep snow that would lie long and keep the wheat warm, and leave the ground soaked when it melted.

"Yes, sir!" Rudolph broke out fiercely; "if we have another dry year like last year, there's going to be hard times in this country."

Rosicky filled his pipe. "You boys don't know what hard times is. You don't owe nobody, you got plenty to eat an' keep warm, an' plenty water to keep clean. When you got them, you can't have it very hard."

Rudolph frowned, opened and shut his big right hand, and dropped it clenched upon his knee. "I've got to have a good deal more than that, Father, or I'll quit this farming gamble. I can always make good wages railroading, or at the packing house, and be sure of my money."

"Maybe so," his father answered dryly.

Mary, who had just come in from the pantry and was wiping her hands on the roller towel, thought Rudy and his father were getting too serious. She brought her darning basket and sat down in the middle of the group.

"I ain't much afraid of hard times, Rudy," she said heartily. "We've had a plenty, but we've always come through. Your father wouldn't never take nothing very hard, not even hard times. I got a mind to tell you a story on him. Maybe you boys can't hardly remember the year we had that terrible hot wind, that burned everything up on the Fourth of July? All the corn an' the gardens. An' that was in the days when we didn't have alfalfa yet— I guess it wasn't invented.

"Well, that very day your father was out cultivatin' corn, and I was here in the kitchen makin' plum preserves. We had bushels of plums that year. I noticed it was terrible hot, but it's always hot in the kitchen when you're preservin', an' I was too busy with my plums to mind. Anton come in from the field about three o'clock, an' I asked him what was the matter.

" 'Nothin',' he says, 'but it's pretty hot, an' I think I won't work no more today.' He stood round for a few minutes, an' then he says: 'Ain't you near through? I want you should git up a nice supper for us tonight. It's Fourth of July.'

"I told him to git along, that I was right in the middle of preservin', but the plums would taste good on hot biscuit. 'I'm goin' to have fried chicken, too,' he says, and he went off an' killed a couple. You three oldest boys was little fellers, playin' around outside, real hot an' sweaty, an' your father took you to the horse tank down by the windmill an' took off your clothes an' put you in. Them two box elder trees was little then, but they made shade over the tank. Then he took off all his own clothes, an' got in with you. While he was playin' in the water with you, the Methodist preacher drove into our place to say how all the neighbors was goin' to meet at the schoolhouse that night, to pray for rain. He drove right to the windmill, of course, and there was your father and you three with no clothes on. I was in the kitchen door, an' I had to laugh, for the preacher acted like he ain't never seen a naked man before. He surely was embarrassed, an' your father couldn't git to his clothes; they was all hangin' up on the windmill to let the sweat dry out of 'em. So he laid in the

tank where he was, an' put one of you boys on top of him to cover him up a little, an' talked to the preacher.

"When you got through playin' in the water, he put clean clothes on you and a clean shirt on himself, an' by that time I'd begun to get supper. He says: 'It's too hot in here to eat comfortable. Let's have a picnic in the orchard. We'll eat our supper behind the mulberry hedge, under them linden trees.'

"So he carried our supper down, an' a bottle of my wild-grape wine, an' everything tasted good, I can tell you. The wind got cooler as the sun was goin' down, and it turned out pleasant, only I noticed how the leaves was curled up on the linden trees. That made me think, an' I asked your father if that hot wind all day hadn't been terrible hard on the gardens an' the corn.

" 'Corn,' he says, 'there ain't no corn.'

" 'What you talkin' about?' I said. 'Ain't we got forty acres?'

" 'We ain't got an ear,' he says, 'nor nobody else ain't got none. All the corn in this country was cooked by three o'clock today, like you'd roasted it in an oven.'

" 'You mean you won't get no crop at all?' I asked him. I couldn't believe it, after he'd worked so hard.

" 'No crop this year,' he says. 'That's why we're havin' a picnic. We might as well enjoy what we got.'

"An' that's how your father behaved, when all the neighbors was so discouraged they couldn't look you in the face. An' we enjoyed ourselves that year, poor as we was, an' our neighbors wasn't a bit better off for bein' miserable. Some of 'em grieved till they got poor digestions and couldn't relish what they did have."

The younger boys said they thought their father had the best of it. But Rudolph was thinking that, all the same, the neighbors had managed to get ahead more, in the fifteen years since that time. There must be something wrong about his father's way of doing things. He wished he knew what was going on in the back of Polly's mind. He knew she liked his father, but he knew, too, that she was afraid of something. When his mother sent over coffee-cake or prune tarts or a loaf of fresh bread, Polly seemed to regard them with a certain suspicion. When she observed to him that his brothers had nice manners, her tone implied that it was remarkable they should have. With his mother she was stiff and on her guard. Mary's hearty frankness and gusts of good humor irritated her. Polly was afraid of being unusual or conspicuous in any way, of being "ordinary," as she said!

When Mary had finished her story, Rosicky laid aside his pipe.

"You boys like me to tell you about some of dem hard times I been through in London?" Warmly encouraged, he sat rubbing his forehead along the deep creases. It was bothersome to tell a long story in English (he nearly always talked to the boys in Czech), but he wanted Polly to hear this one.

"Well, you know about dat tailor shop I worked in in London? I had one Christmas dere I ain't never forgot. Times was awful bad before Christmas; de boss ain't got much work, an' have it awful hard to pay his rent. It ain't so much fun, bein' poor in a big city like London, I'll say! All de windows is full of good t'ings to eat an' all de pushcarts in de streets is full, an' you smell 'em all de time, an' you ain't got no money—not a darn bit. I didn't mind de cold so much, though I didn't have no overcoat, chust a short jacket I'd outgrowed so it wouldn't meet on me, an' my hands was chapped raw. But I always had a good appetite, like you all know, an' de sight of dem pork pies in the windows was awful fur me!

"Day before Christmas was terrible foggy dat year, an' dat fog gits into your bones and makes you all damp like. Mrs. Lifschnitz didn't give us nothin' but a little bread an' drippin' for supper, because she was savin' to try for to give us a good din-

ner on Christmas Day. After supper de boss say I can go an' enjoy myself, so I went into de streets to listen to de Christmas singers. Dey sing old songs an' make very nice music, an' I run round after dem a good ways, till I got awful hungry. I t'ink maybe if I go home, I can sleep till morning an' forgit my belly.

"I went into my corner real quiet, and roll up in my fedder quilt. But I ain't got my head down till I smell somet'ing good. Seem like it git stronger an' stronger, an' I can't git to sleep noway. I can't understand dat smell. Dere was a gas light in a hall across de court, dat always shine in at my window a little. I got up and look around. I got a little wooden box in my corner fur a stool, 'cause I ain't got no chair. I picks up dat box, and under it dere is a roast goose on a platter! I can't believe my eyes. I carry it to de window where de light comes in, an' touch it and smell it to find out, an' den I taste it to be sure. I say, I will eat chust one little bite of dat goose, so I can go to sleep, and tomorrow I won't eat none at all. But I tell you, boys, when I stop, one half of dat goose was gone!"

The narrator bowed his head, and the boys shouted. But little Josephine slipped behind his chair and kissed him on the neck beneath his ear.

"Poor little Papa, I don't want him to be hungry!"

"Da's long ago, child. I ain't never been hungry since I had your mudder to cook fur me."

"Go on and tell us the rest, please," said Polly.

"Well, when I come to realize what I done, of course, I felt terrible. I felt better in de stomach, but very bad in de heart. I set on my bed wid dat platter on my knees, an' it all come to me; how hard dat poor woman save to buy dat goose, and how she get some neighbor to cook it dat got more fire, an' how she put it in my corner to keep it away from dem hungry children. Dey was a old carpet hung up to shut my corner off, an' de children wasn't

allowed to go in dere. An' I know she put
it in my corner because she trust me more'n
she did de violin boy. I can't stand it to
face her after I spoil de Christmas. So I
put on my shoes and go out into de city. I
tell myself I better throw myself in de
river; but I guess I ain't dat kind of a boy.

"It was after twelve o'clock, an' terrible
cold, an' I start out to walk about London
all night. I walk along de river awhile,
but dey was lots of drunks all along; men,
and women too. I chust move along to
keep away from de police. I git onto de
Strand, an' den over to New Oxford Street,
where dere was a big German restaurant
on de ground floor, wid big windows all
fixed up fine, an' I could see de people
havin' parties inside. While I was lookin'
in, two men and two ladies come out,
laughin' and talkin' and feelin' happy
about all dey been eatin' an' drinkin', and
dey was speakin' Czech—not like de Aus-
trians, but like de homefolks talk it.

"I guess I went crazy, an' I done what I
ain't never done before nor since. I went
right up to dem gay people an' begun to
beg dem: 'Fellow countrymen, for God's
sake give me money enough to buy a
goose!'

"Dey laugh, of course, but de ladies
speak awful kind to me, an' dey take me
back into de restaurant and give me hot
coffee and cakes, an' make me tell all about
how I happened to come to London, an'
what I was doin' dere. Dey take my name
and where I work down on paper, an' both
of dem ladies give me ten shillings.

"De big market at Covent Garden ain't
very far away, an' by dat time it was open.
I go dere an' buy a big goose an' some pork
pies, an' potatoes and onions, an' cakes an'
oranges fur de children—all I could carry!
When I git home, everybody is still asleep.
I pile all I bought on de kitchen table, an'
go in an' lay down on my bed, an' I ain't
waken up till I hear dat woman scream
when she come out into her kitchen. My
goodness, but she was surprise! She laugh
an' cry at de same time, an' hug me and

waken all de children. She ain't stop fur
no breakfast; she git de Christmas dinner
ready dat morning, and we all sit down an'
eat all we can hold. I ain't never seen dat
violin boy have all he can hold before.

"Two three days after dat, de two men
come to hunt me up, an' dey ask my boss,
and he give me a good report an' tell dem
I was a steady boy all right. One of dem
Bohemians was very smart an' run a Bohemian newspaper in New York, an' de
odder was a rich man, in de importing
business, an' dey been traveling togedder.
Dey told me how t'ings was easier in New
York, an' offered to pay my passage when
dey was goin' home soon on a boat. My
boss say to me: 'You go. You ain't got no
chance here, an' I like to see you git ahead,
fur you always been a good boy to my
woman, and fur dat fine Christmas dinner
you give us all.' An' da's how I got to New
York."

That night when Rudolph and Polly,

arm in arm, were running home across the
fields with the bitter wind at their backs,
his heart leaped for joy when she said she
thought they might have his family come
over for supper on New Year's Eve. "Let's
get up a nice supper, and not let your
mother help at all; make her be company
for once."

"That would be lovely of you, Polly,"
he said humbly. He was a very simple,
modest boy, and he, too, felt vaguely that
Polly and her sisters were more experienced and wordly than his people.

VI

The winter turned out badly for farmers.
It was bitterly cold, and after the first light
snows before Christmas there was no snow
at all—and no rain. March was as bitter
as February. On those days when the wind
fairly punished the country, Rosicky sat by
his window. In the fall he and the boys
had put in a big wheat planting, and now
the seed had frozen in the ground. All that
land would have to be plowed up and
planted over again, planted in corn. It had
happened before, but he was younger then,
and he never worried about what had to
be. He was sure of himself and of Mary;
he knew they could bear what they had to
bear, that they would always pull through
somehow. But he was not so sure about
the young ones, and he felt troubled because Rudolph and Polly were having such
a hard start.

Sitting beside his flowering window
while the panes rattled and the wind blew
in under the door, Rosicky gave himself to
reflection as he had not done since those
Sundays in the loft of the furniture factory in New York, long ago. Then he was
trying to find what he wanted in life for
himself; now he was trying to find what
he wanted for his boys, and why it was
he so hungered to feel sure they would be
here, working this very land, after he was
gone.

They would have to work hard on the
farm, and probably they would never do

much more than make a living. But if he
could think of them as staying here on the
land, he wouldn't have to fear any great
unkindness for them. Hardships, certainly;
it was a hardship to have the wheat freeze
in the ground when seed was so high; and
to have to sell your stock because you had
no feed. But there would be other years
when everything came along right, and you
caught up. And what you had was your
own. You didn't have to choose between
bosses and strikers, and go wrong either
way. You didn't have to do with dishonest
and cruel people. They were the only
things in his experience he had found ter-
rifying and horrible; the look in the eyes
of a dishonest and crafty man, of a schem-
ing and rapacious woman.

In the country, if you had a mean neighbor, you could keep off his land and make
him keep off yours. But in the city, all the
foulness and misery and brutality of your
neighbors was part of your life. The worst
things he had come upon in his journey
through the world were human—depraved
and poisonous specimens of man. To this
day he could recall certain terrible faces
in the London streets. There were mean
people everywhere, to be sure, even in their
own country town here. But they weren't
tempered, hardened, sharpened, like the
treacherous people in cities who live by
grinding or cheating or poisoning their fellow men. He had helped to bury two of
his fellow workmen in the tailoring trade,
and he was distrustful of the organized industries that see one out of the world in
big cities. Here, if you were sick, you had
Doctor Ed to look after you; and if you
died, fat Mr. Haycock, the kindest man in
the world, buried you.

It seemed to Rosicky that for good, honest boys like his, the worst they could do on
the farm was better than the best they
would be likely to do in the city. If he'd
had a mean boy, now, one who was
crooked and sharp and tried to put anything over on his brothers, then town
would be the place for him. But he had

no such boy. As for Rudolph, the discontented one, he would give the shirt off his back to anyone who touched his heart. What Rosicky really hoped for his boys was that they could get through the world without ever knowing much about the cruelty of human beings. "Their mother and me ain't prepared them for that," he sometimes said to himself.

These thoughts brought him back to a grateful consideration of his own case. What an escape he had had, to be sure! He, too, in his time, had had to take money for repair work from the hand of a hungry child who let it go so wistfully; because it was money due his boss. And now, in all these years, he had never had to take a cent from anyone in bitter need—never had to look at the face of the woman become like a wolf's from struggle and famine. When he thought of these things, Rosicky would put on his cap and jacket and slip down to the barn and give his work horses a little extra oats, letting them eat it out of his hand in their slobbery fashion. It was his way of expressing what he felt, and made him chuckle with pleasure.

The spring came warm, with blue skies —but dry, dry as a bone. The boys began plowing up the wheat fields to plant them over in corn. Rosicky would stand at the fence corner and watch them, and the earth was so dry it blew up in clouds of brown dust that hid the horses and the sulky plow and the driver. It was a bad outlook.

The big alfalfa field that lay between the home place and Rudolph's came up green, but Rosicky was worried because during that open windy winter a great many Russian thistle plants had blown in there and lodged. He kept asking the boys to rake them out; he was afraid their seed would root and "take the alfalfa." Rudolph said that was nonsense. The boys were working so hard planting corn, their father felt he couldn't insist about the thistles, but he set great store by that big

alfalfa field. It was a feed you could depend on—and there was some deeper reason, vague, but strong. The peculiar green of that clover woke early memories in old Rosicky, went back to something in his childhood in the old world. When he was a little boy, he had played in fields of that strong blue-green color.

One morning, when Rudolph had gone to town in the car, leaving a work team idle in his barn, Rosicky went over to his son's place, put the horses to the buggy rake, and set about quietly raking up those thistles. He behaved with guilty caution, and rather enjoyed stealing a march on Doctor Ed, who was just then taking his first vacation in seven years of practice and was attending a clinic in Chicago. Rosicky got the thistles raked up, but did not stop to burn them. That would take some time, and his breath was pretty short, so he thought he had better get the horses back to the barn.

He got them into the barn and to their stalls, but the pain had come on so sharp in his chest that he didn't try to take the harness off. He started for the house, bending lower with every step. The cramp in his chest was shutting him up like a jackknife. When he reached the windmill, he swayed and caught at the ladder. He say Polly coming down the hill, running with the swiftness of a slim greyhound. In a flash she had her shoulder under his armpit.

"Lean on me, Father, hard! Don't be afraid. We can get to the house all right."

Somehow they did, though Rosicky became blind with pain; he could keep on his legs, but he couldn't steer his course. The next thing he was conscious of was lying on Polly's bed, and Polly bending over him wringing out bath towels in hot water and putting them on his chest. She stopped only to throw coal into the stove, and she kept the teakettle and the black pot going. She put these hot applications on him for nearly an hour, she told him afterward, and all that time he was drawn

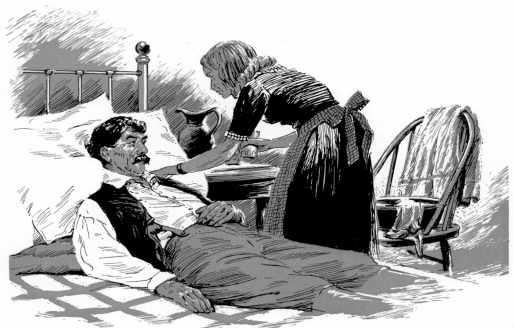

up stiff and blue, with the sweat pouring off him.

As the pain gradually loosed its grip, the stiffness went out of his jaws, the black circles around his eyes disappeared, and a little of his natural color came back. When his daughter-in-law buttoned his shirt over his chest at last, he sighed.

"Da's fine, de way I feel now, Polly. It was a awful bad spell, an' I was so sorry it all come on you like it did."

Polly was flushed and excited. "Is the pain really gone? Can I leave you long enough to telephone over to your place?"

Rosicky's eyelids fluttered. "Don't telephone, Polly. It ain't no use to scare my wife. It's nice and quiet here, an' if I ain't too much trouble to you, just let me lay still till I feel like myself. I ain't got no pain now. It's nice here."

Polly bent over him and wiped the moisture from his face. "Oh, I'm so glad it's over!" she broke out impulsively. "It just broke my heart to see you suffer so, Father."

Rosicky motioned her to sit down on the chair where the teakettle had been, and looked up at her with that lively affectionate gleam in his eyes. "You was awful good to me, I won't never forgit dat. I hate it to be sick on you like dis. Down at de barn I say to myself, dat young girl ain't had much experience in sickness, I don't want to scare her, an' maybe she's got a baby comin' or somet'ing."

Polly took his hand. He was looking at her so intently and affectionately and confidingly; his eyes seemed to caress her face, to regard it with pleasure. She frowned with her funny streaks of eyebrows, and then smiled back at him.

"I guess maybe there is something of that kind going to happen. But I haven't told anyone yet, not my mother or Rudolph. You'll be the first to know."

His hand pressed hers. She noticed that it was warm again. The twinkle in his yellow-brown eyes seemed to come nearer.

"I like mighty well to see dat little child, Polly," was all he said. Then he closed his eyes and lay half smiling. But Polly sat still, thinking hard. She had a sudden feeling that nobody in the world, not her mother, not Rudolph, or anyone, really loved her as much as old Rosicky did. It perplexed her. She sat frowning and trying to puzzle it out. It was as if Rosicky had a special gift for loving people, something that was like an ear for music or an eye for color. It was quiet, unobtrusive; it was merely there. You saw it in his eyes —perhaps that was why they were merry. You felt it in his hands, too. After he dropped off to sleep, she sat holding his warm, broad, flexible brown hand. She had never seen another in the least like it. She wondered if it wasn't a kind of gypsy hand, it was so alive and quick and light in its communications—very strange in a farmer. Nearly all the farmers she knew had huge lumps of fists, like mauls, or they were knotty and bony and uncomfortable looking, with stiff fingers. But Rosicky's was like quicksilver, flexible, muscular, about the color of a pale cigar, with deep, deep creases across the palm. It wasn't nervous, it wasn't a stupid lump; it was a warm, brown, human hand, with some cleverness in it, a great deal of generosity, and something else which Polly could only call "gypsylike"—something nimble and lively and sure, in the way that animals are.

Polly remembered that hour long afterward; it had been like an awakening to her. It seemed to her that she had never learned so much about life from anything as from old Rosicky's hand. It brought her to herself; it communicated some direct and untranslatable message.

When she heard Rudolph coming in the car, she ran out to meet him.

"Oh, Rudy, your father's been awful sick! He raked up those thistles he's been worrying about, and afterward he could hardly get to the house. He suffered so I was afraid he was going to die."

Rudolph jumped to the ground. "Where is he now?"

"On the bed. He's asleep. I was terribly scared, because, you know, I'm so fond of your father." She slipped her arm through his and they went into the house. That afternoon they took Rosicky home and put him to bed, though he protested that he was quite well again.

The next morning he got up and dressed and sat down to breakfast with his family. He told Mary that his coffee tasted better than usual to him, and he warned the boys not to bear any tales to Doctor Ed when he got home. After breakfast he sat down by his window to do some patching and asked Mary to thread several needles for him before she went to feed her chickens—her eyes were better than his, and her hands steadier. He lit his pipe and took up John's overalls. Mary had been watching him anxiously all morning, and as she went out of the door with her bucket of scraps, she saw that he was smiling. He was thinking, indeed, about Polly, and how he might never have known what a tender heart she had if he hadn't got sick over there. Girls nowadays didn't wear their heart on their sleeve. But now he knew Polly would make a fine woman after the foolishness wore off. Either a woman had that sweetness at her heart or she hadn't. You couldn't always tell by the look of them; but if they had that, everything came out right in the end.

After he had taken a few stitches, the cramp began in his chest, like yesterday. He put his pipe cautiously down on the window sill and bent over to ease the pull. No use—he had better try to get to his bed if he could. He rose and groped his way across the familiar floor, which was rising and falling like the deck of a ship. At the door he fell. When Mary came in, she found him lying there, and the moment she touched him she knew that he was gone.

Doctor Ed was away when Rosicky died, and for the first few weeks after he got home he was hard-driven. Every day he said to himself that he must get out to see that family that had lost their father. One soft, warm moonlight night in early summer he started for the farm. His mind was on other things, and not until his road ran by the graveyard did he realize that Rosicky wasn't over there on the hill where the red lamplight shone, but here, in the moonlight. He stopped his car, shut off the engine, and sat there for awhile.

A sudden hush had fallen on his soul. Everything here seemed strangely moving and significant, though signifying what, he did not know. Close by the wire fence stood Rosicky's mowing machine, where one of the boys had been cutting hay that afternoon; his own work horses had been going up and down there. The new-cut hay perfumed all the night air. The moonlight silvered the long, billowy grass that grew over the graves and hid the fence; the few little evergreens stood out black in it, like shadows in a pool. The sky was very blue and soft, the stars rather faint because the moon was full.

For the first time it struck Doctor Ed that this was really a beautiful graveyard. He thought of city cemeteries; acres of shrubbery and heavy stone, so arranged and lonely and unlike anything in the living world. Cities of the dead, indeed; cities of the forgotten, of the "put away." But this was open and free, this little square of long grass which the wind forever stirred. Nothing but the sky overhead, and the many-colored fields running on until they met that sky. The horses worked here in summer; the neighbors passed on their way to town; and over yonder, in the cornfield, Rosicky's own cattle would be eating fodder as winter came on. Nothing could be more undeathlike than this place; nothing could be more right for a man who had helped to do the work of great cities and had always longed for the open country and had got to it at last. Rosicky's life seemed to him complete and beautiful.

The woman who wrote this story

WILLA CATHER   1879–1947

When the Cather family moved from Virginia to Nebraska, Willa Cather was only eight years old. She found the plains exciting, filled with a new and different life. She also found Americans who had come from Norway, Denmark, Sweden, and Bohemia. Willa Cather was fascinated by these settlers, and the stories they told her would, as she said, ". . . go round and round in my head at night."

It was a time when immigrants were flooding into America. Many of them migrated to the West and settled there, trying to make a life from the soil. It was a hard life, and sometimes these newcomers were misunderstood by other Americans who were not used to their ideas and traditions. Willa Cather was to explain these immigrants to the rest of America in stories like "Neighbor Rosicky."

After completing college in Nebraska, Miss Cather returned to the East to work for several newspapers and magazines. In 1912 she left a job with a famous woman's magazine in order to have more time for her own writing. She completed many novels and short stories which earned her a high place among American authors. Her style has often been praised as one of the best in American literature.

Let's consider . . .

1. In this story you came to know a man well and from many points of view. Each incident strengthened your impression of his character. The scene in the doctor's office was your introduction to Rosicky. What did the discussion there tell you about him?

2. The doctor's recollections of having breakfast at Rosicky's home brought out the "natural good manners" of the family.

How were these shown? How did this scene add to your knowledge of Rosicky?

3. The gossipers in the drugstore wondered why Rosicky "didn't get on faster." Why didn't he? How did he feel about his neighbors' more obvious "success"? How do you know that his wife, Mary, felt the same way?

4. Doctor Burleigh reflected that perhaps "people as generous and warm-hearted and affectionate" as the Rosickys "never get ahead much." Think about this statement in connection with people you know. Do you agree or disagree with it? Explain your conclusion by giving examples.

5. Gradually, you learned of Rosicky's past life. To Mary, Anton was "gentle—city-bred." Describe his experiences in London. How might they have made him anything but a gentle man?

6. At one time the young Rosicky considered New York "the finest, richest, *friendliest* city in the world." What made him change his mind?

7. Rosicky could understand Polly's loneliness because of his own early experiences. Why did Polly feel she was an outsider? What did Rosicky fear might happen if she became too lonely?

8. At the Christmas Day gathering the Rosicky family discussed the hard times they had known. Mary told of the day the corn crop was burned by the heat, and Rosicky told about the roast goose. What had Rosicky learned from his London experience which made him more philosophical than his neighbors about the loss of the corn crop? Why was Rudolph's attitude toward "hard times" different from his father's?

9. The relationship between Rosicky and his daughter-in-law Polly is a little story in itself. Trace the steps by which Polly came to know and love Rosicky.

10. The passage at the beginning of section VI gave you Rosicky's reflections on the differences between city and country life. Write a paragraph summarizing these reflections. Then explain in a few words why you do or do not agree with Rosicky. Base your opinion on your own experiences.

11. What brought on the heart attack which resulted in Rosicky's death? Why did it seem natural for him to disregard the doctor's orders in this case? Do you think Rosicky ever could have been truly happy in the way of life recommended by Doctor Burleigh?

12. Early in the story, Rosicky stopped at the graveyard at the edge of his land; in the final paragraphs, Dr. Burleigh also stopped there. Reread these passages. How do they help you realize that Rosicky's death was not wholly sad?

The writer's craft . . .

"Neighbor Rosicky" is an excellent example of a penetrating character study. You came to know Anton Rosicky by seeing him from the point of view of several people, by sharing his memories of the past, and by watching him react to his particular environment.

A. Willa Cather characterized Rosicky from the point of view of different people. You learned to know him from his relationship with (1) his wife, (2) his sons (especially Rudolph), (3) Polly, and (4) Dr. Burleigh. Divide into four groups. Each group will discuss one of these relationships and report to the class what it learned about Rosicky.

B. In order to give you insight into Rosicky's past, Willa Cather wrote section III in the form of a **flashback:** a device by which the author interrupts the story to present events which occurred at a previous time. She wrote, "While he sewed he let his mind run back over his life." What experiences did he recall? How did these memories help you to understand him?

C. The setting also helped you know Rosicky. The **setting** includes the geographical location, the period in time, and the social and emotional environment in which a story takes place. Like the characters and the plot, the setting is always a part of the whole story. However, when a writer uses the setting as a means of developing character, it gains added significance.

1. What problems did Rosicky face which grew out of the setting?

2. What were Rosicky's feelings toward the Nebraska farmland?

3. How did his feeling toward the landscape help you to understand him as a person?

4. How did the setting reflect Rosicky's "complete and beautiful life"?

Knowing words . . .

In "Neighbor Rosicky" the author used several words and expressions which are common to rural life. Explain the meaning of each of the italicized words in the following sentences. Then make up a new sentence of your own for each italicized word.

1. You can feed the *stock* and do *chores* about the barn, but you can't do anything in the fields that makes you short of breath.

2. And never again on a *hay-rake,* remember!

3. Then he went into the *general-merchandise* place next door and stood about until the pretty girl with the plucked eyebrows, who always waited on him, was free.

4. Your father took you to the *horse tank* down by the windmill and took off your clothes and put you in.

5. All that land would have to be *plowed up* and planted over again, planted in corn.

The Sheaves

Where long the shadows of the wind had rolled,
Green wheat was yielding to the change assigned,
And as by some vast magic undivined
The world was turning slowly into gold.
Like nothing that was ever bought or sold
It waited there, the body and the mind;
And with a mighty meaning of a kind
That tells the more the more it is not told.

So in a land where all days are not fair,
Fair days went on till on another day
A thousand golden sheaves were lying there,
Shining and still, but not for long to stay—
As if a thousand girls with golden hair
Might rise from where they slept and go away.
                            Edwin Arlington Robinson

The Flower-fed Buffaloes

VACHEL LINDSAY

The flower-fed buffaloes of the spring
In the days of long ago
Ranged where the locomotives sing
And the prairie flowers lie low:—
The tossing, blooming, perfumed grass
Is swept away by the wheat,
Wheels and wheels and wheels spin by
In the spring that still is sweet.
But the flower-fed buffaloes of the spring
Left us, long ago.
They gore no more, they bellow no more,
They trundle around the hills no more:—
With the Blackfeet, lying low,
With the Pawnees, lying low,
Lying low.

The man who wrote this poem

VACHEL LINDSAY   1879–1931

During the summers, when he was free from his various winter lecture jobs, Vachel Lindsay often made long tramps through the country. He toured the South and once walked from Illinois to New Mexico. He earned his food and lodging by reciting his poetry to farmers and townspeople.

Lindsay's mother had wanted her son to be an artist. Therefore, Lindsay left his home in Springfield, Illinois, to study art in Chicago and New York. When his drawings did not attract much attention, he turned to writing poetry. He believed that poetry should remain close to the people and so made his poems as simple as folk songs. Almost all of his poems contain a simple, strong rhythm, and are most effective when chanted or sung.

The poet's art . . .

"The Flower-fed Buffaloes" has only a faint echo of the exuberant, galloping, noisy rhythms of Lindsay's longer poems: "General William Booth Enters Into Heaven," "The Santa Fe Trail," and "The Congo." There is just a suggestion of the chant here, effected by the repetition of open vowels and the soft sound of *l: long ago, locomotives, blooming, bellow, lying low, lying low.* These sounds have a rather sad, nostalgic effect, even on a reader who has never seen a prairie or a buffalo.

1. Read the lines which you like best simply for their sound.

2. The rhyme scheme—the pattern of the rhyme—is varied and interesting, quite suitable for the theme. How many different rhymes are there?

3. What has happened to the prairies since the flower-fed buffaloes have left?

Spanish Johnny

WILLA CATHER

The old West, the old time,
  The old wind singing through
The red, red grass a thousand miles—
  And, Spanish Johnny, you!
He'd sit beside the water ditch
  When all his herd was in,
And never mind a child, but sing
  To his mandolin.

The big stars, the blue night,
  The moon-enchanted lane;
The olive man who never spoke,
  But sang the songs of Spain.
His speech with men was wicked talk—
  To hear it was a sin;
But those were golden things he said
  To his mandolin.

The gold song, the gold stars,
  The world so golden then;
And the hand so tender to a child
  Had killed so many men.
He died a hard death long ago
  Before the Road came in—
The night before he swung, he sang
  To his mandolin.

The poet's art . . .

Willa Cather's novels are much better known than her poetry, though her few poems show the same perfection of style, of lucid diction, and studied structure as her prose. This little folk song grew out of her intimate knowledge of the Southwest and its people as surely as did her more ambitious but just as beautifully simple novel *Death Comes for the Archbishop*. Note the eight-line stanzas, with two rhymes in each, and a short repeated line at the end.

1. Willa Cather felt an obligation to say exactly what she wished to convey. Pick out the colors she mentioned and comment on their fitness.

2. Each stanza contributed to your impression of Johnny. Explain in your own words what you learned from each of them.

3. How did the poet use contrast in this poem to show the opposite sides of Johnny's character?

Texas

AMY LOWELL

I went a-riding, a-riding,
Over a great long plain.
And the plain went a-sliding, a-sliding
Away from my bridle rein.

Fields of cotton, and fields of wheat,
Thunder-blue gentians by a wire fence,
Standing cypress, red and tense,
Holding its flower rigid like a gun,
Dressed for parade by the running wheat,
By the little bouncing cotton. Terribly sweet
The cardinals sing in the live-oak trees,
And the long plain breeze,
The prairie breeze,
Blows across from swell to swell
With a ginger smell.
Just ahead, where the road curves round,
A long-eared rabbit makes a bound
Into a wheat field, into a cotton field,
His track glitters after him and goes still again
Over to the left of my bridle rein.

But over to the right is a glare—glare—glare—
Of sharp glass windows.
A narrow square of brick jerks thickly up
    above the cotton plants,
A raucous mercantile thing flaring the sun
    from thirty-six windows,
Brazenly declaring itself to the lovely fields.
Tramcars run like worms about the feet of
    this thing,
The coffins of cotton bales feed it,
The threshed wheat is its golden blood.
But here it has no feet,
It has only the steep ironic grin of its thirty-six
    windows,
Only its basilisk eyes counting the fields,
Doing sums of how many buildings to a city,
    all day and all night.

Once they went a-riding, a-riding,
Over the great long plain.
Cowboys singing to their dogie steers,
Cowboys perched on forty-dollar saddles,
Riding to the North, six months to get there,
Six months to reach Wyoming.
"Hold up, paint horse, herd the little dogies,
Over the lone prairie."
Bones of dead steers,
Bones of cowboys,
Under the wheat, maybe.

The skyscraper sings another way,
A tune of steel, of wheels, of gold.
And the ginger breeze blows, blows all day
Tanged with flowers and mold.
And the Texas sky whirls down, whirls down,
Taking long looks at the fussy town.
An old sky and a long plain
Beyond, beyond, my bridle rein.

The woman who wrote this poem

AMY LOWELL   1874–1925

Amy Lowell was a member of one of New England's most distinguished families. One of her brothers was a famous astronomer, another was president of Har-vard University, and her grandfather, James Russell Lowell, had been a well-known poet. Amy Lowell was determined to live up to her family's great reputation. For a time she wanted to be an actress, but her appearance was against her. Therefore she decided to become a poet. Probably her happiest moment was when a critic wrote that her poetry was superior to her grandfather's.

Miss Lowell, who once described herself as a born businesswoman, did not suddenly become a poet. She wrote and studied for ten years before her first small volume of poems appeared. When this volume went almost unnoticed, she decided to bring poetry more into the public eye. Though she wrote some beautiful and delicate poems, Amy Lowell was not so much a poet as a supporter and an organizer. She helped many new poets, Carl Sandburg for one, to get an audience. Whenever a new idea about writing poetry appeared, she was one of the first to give it encouragement and support.

The poet's art . . .

Around 1914 a group of poets who called themselves "imagists" revolted against the kind of poetry being written at that time. The **Imagists** believed that poets should use the language of everyday speech, but always employ the *exact* word; they should have complete freedom in their choice of subjects; and they should create sharp images. Amy Lowell has been identified with the Imagists because she used precise, sharp, and strikingly-fresh images. "Thunder-blue gentians," and "ginger-breeze" are two images in this poem.

1. Select several images from this poem which you consider "strikingly fresh."

2. The use of color is characteristic of Amy Lowell's poetry. What three colors are definitely used? What others are suggested in this poem?

3. Some poems tell a story; others present an experience. Miss Lowell told you not only what she saw as she "went a-riding" but how she felt about it. How did she feel about the "great long plain"? Point out the particular sights, sounds, and smells which caught her attention.

4. How did the poet feel about the "narrow square of brick" which had broken the peace of the "lovely fields"? Why didn't this "raucous mercantile thing" have feet?

5. If you were planning a mural to illustrate Amy Lowell's "Texas," with which part of the poem would you begin? With which part would you end? How would you portray the first four lines?

Wind and Silver

Greatly shining,
The Autumn moon floats in the thin sky;
And the fish-ponds shake their backs and flash their dragon scales
As she passes over them.

Amy Lowell

Mliss

BRET HARTE

Mliss was a wild, and sometimes violent, young girl who grew up in a California mining town. Everyone said she was different except the master. He knew she was really like everybody else. Mliss just needed someone to love.

Chapter I

Just where the Sierra Nevada begins to subside in gentler undulations, and the rivers grow less rapid and yellow, on the side of a great red mountain, stands "Smith's Pocket." Seen from the red road at sunset, in the red light and the red dust, its white houses look like the outcropping of quartz on the mountain-side. The red stage, topped with red-shirted passengers, is lost to view half-a-dozen times in the tortuous descent, turning up unexpectedly in out-of-the-way places, and vanishing altogether within a hundred yards of the town. It is probably owing to this sudden twist in the road that the advent of a stranger at Smith's Pocket is usually attended with a peculiar circumstance. Dismounting from the vehicle at the stage-office, the too confident traveller is apt to walk straight out of town under the impression that it lies in quite another direction. It is related that one of the tunnel-men, two miles from town, met one of these self-reliant passengers with a carpet-bag, umbrella, *Harper's Magazine,* and other evidences of "Civilisation and Refinement," plodding along over the road he had just ridden, vainly endeavouring to find the settlement of Smith's Pocket.

An observant traveller might have found

some compensation for his disappointment in the weird aspect of that vicinity. There were huge fissures on the hill-side, and displacements of the red soil, resembling more the chaos of some primary elemental upheaval than the work of man; while, half-way down, a long flume [1] straddled its narrow body and disproportionate legs over the chasm, like an enormous fossil of some forgotten antediluvian. At every step smaller ditches crossed the road, hiding in their sallow depths unlovely streams that crept away to a clandestine union with the great yellow torrent below, and here and there were the ruins of some cabin, with the chimney alone left intact and the hearthstone open to the skies.

The settlement of Smith's Pocket owed its origin to the finding of a "pocket" on its site by a veritable Smith. Five thousand dollars were taken out of it in one half-hour by Smith. Three thousand dollars were expended by Smith and others in erecting a flume and in tunnelling. And then Smith's Pocket was found to be only a pocket, and subject, like other pockets, to depletion. Although Smith pierced the bowels of the great red mountain, that five thousand dollars was the first and last re-

[1] *flume,* an inclined chute, generally made of wood, to carry water

turn of his labour. The mountain grew reticent of its golden secrets, and the flume steadily ebbed away the remainder of Smith's fortune. Then Smith went into quartz-mining; then into quartz-milling; then into hydraulics and ditching; and then by easy degrees into saloon-keeping. But the settlement of Smith's Pocket, like that of most discoveries, was happily not dependent on the fortune of its pioneer, and other parties projected tunnels and found pockets. So Smith's Pocket became a settlement, with its two fancy stores, its two hotels, its one express-office, and its two first families. Occasionally its one long straggling street was overawed by the assumption of the latest San Francisco fashions, imported per express, exclusively to the first families; making outraged Nature, in the ragged outline of her furrowed surface, look still more homely, and putting personal insult on that greater portion of the population to whom the Sabbath, with a change of linen, brought merely the necessity of cleanliness, without the luxury of adornment. Then there was a Methodist Church, and hard by a Monte Bank, and a little beyond, on the mountain-side, a graveyard; and then a little school-house.

"The Master," as he was known to his little flock, sat alone one night in the school-house, with some open copy-books before him, carefully making those bold and full characters which are supposed to combine the extremes of chirographical and moral excellence, and had got as far as "Riches are deceitful," and was elaborating the noun with an insincerity of flourish that was quite in the spirit of his text, when he heard a gentle tapping. The woodpeckers had been busy about the roof during the day, and the noise did not disturb his work. But the opening of the door, and the tapping continuing from the inside, caused him to look up. He was slightly startled by the figure of a young girl, dirty and shabbily clad. Still, her great black eyes, her coarse, uncombed, lustreless black hair falling over her sunburned face, her red arms and feet streaked with the red soil, were all familiar to him. It was Melissa Smith—Smith's motherless child.

"What can she want here?" thought the

master. Everybody knew "Mliss," as she was called, throughout the length and height of Red Mountain. Everybody knew her as an incorrigible girl. Her fierce, ungovernable disposition, her mad freaks and lawless character, were in their way as proverbial as the story of her father's weaknesses, and as philosophically accepted by the townsfolk. She wrangled with and fought the school-boys with keener invective and quite as powerful arm. She followed the trails with a woodman's craft, and the master had met her before, miles away, shoeless, stockingless, and bareheaded on the mountain road. The miners' camps along the stream supplied her with subsistence during these voluntary pilgrimages, in freely offered alms. Not but that a larger protection had been previously extended to Mliss. The Rev. Joshua McSnagley, "stated" preacher, had placed her in the hotel as servant, by way of preliminary refinement, and had introduced her to his scholars at Sunday school. But she threw plates occasionally at the landlord, and quickly retorted to the cheap witticisms of the guests, and created in the Sabbath school a sensation that was so inimical to the orthodox dullness and placidity of that institution, that with a decent regard for the starched frocks and unblemished morals of the two pink-and-white-faced children of the first families, the reverend gentleman had her ignominiously expelled. Such were the antecedents and such the character of Mliss, as she stood before the master. It was shown in the ragged dress, the unkempt hair and bleeding feet, and asked his pity. It flashed from her black, fearless eyes, and commanded his respect.

"I come here to-night," she said rapidly and boldly, keeping her hard glance on his, "because I knew you was alone. I wouldn't come here when them gals was here. I hate 'em, and they hates me. That's why. You keep school, don't you? I want to be teached!"

If to the shabbiness of her apparel and uncomeliness of her tangled hair and dirty face she had added the humility of tears, the master would have extended to her the usual moiety of pity, and nothing more. But with the natural, though illogical instincts of his species, her boldness awakened in him something of that respect which all original natures pay unconsciously to one another in any grade. And he gazed at her the more fixedly as she went on still rapidly, her hand on that door-latch and her eyes on his:—

"My name's Mliss—Mliss Smith! You can bet your life on that. My father's Old Smith—Old Bummer Smith—that's what's the matter with him. Mliss Smith—and I'm coming to school!"

"Well?" said the master.

Accustomed to be thwarted and opposed, often wantonly and cruelly, for no other purpose than to excite the violent impulses of her nature, the master's phlegm evidently took her by surprise. She stopped; she began to twist a lock of her hair between her fingers; and the rigid line of upper lip drawn over the wicked little teeth, relaxed and quivered slightly. Then her eyes dropped, and something like a blush struggled up to her cheek, and tried to assert itself through the splashes of redder soil and the sunburn of years. Suddenly she threw herself forward, calling on God to strike her dead, and fell, quite weak and helpless, with her face on the master's desk, crying and sobbing as if her heart would break.

The master lifted her gently, and waited for the paroxysm to pass. When, with face still averted, she was repeating between her sobs the *mea culpa*[2] of childish penitence —that "she'd be good, she didn't mean to," *etc.*—it came to him to ask her why she had left Sabbath school.

Why had she left the Sabbath school?— why? Oh yes. What did he (McSnagley) want to tell her she was wicked for? What did he tell her that God hated her for? If God hated her, what did she want to go to

---

[2] *mea culpa*, admission of guilt; literally "my guilt" [*Latin*]

Sabbath school for? *She* didn't want to be "beholden" to anybody who hated her.

Had she told McSnagley this?

Yes, she had.

The master laughed. It was a hearty laugh, and echoed so oddly in the little school-house, and seemed so inconsistent and discordant with the sighing of the pines without, that he shortly corrected himself with a sigh. The sigh was quite as sincere in its own way, however, and after a moment of serious silence he asked about her father.

Her father? What father? Whose father? What had he ever done for her? Why did the girls hate her? Come now! what made the folks say, "Old Bummer Smith's Mliss!" when she passed? Yes; oh yes. She wished he was dead—she was dead—everybody was dead; and her sobs broke forth anew.

The master then, leaning over her, told her as well as he could what you or I might have said after hearing such unnatural theories from childish lips; only bearing in mind, perhaps better than you or I, the unnatural facts of her ragged dress, her bleeding feet, and the omnipresent shadow of her father. Then, raising her to her feet, he wrapped his shawl around her, and, bidding her come early in the morning, he walked with her down the road. There he bade her "goodnight." The moon shone brightly on the narrow path before them. He stood and watched the bent little figure as it staggered down the road, and waited until it had passed the little graveyard and reached the curve of the hill, where it turned and stood for a moment, a mere atom of suffering outlined against the far-off patient stars. Then he went back to his work. But the lines of the copy-book thereafter faded into long parallels of never-ending road, over which childish figures seemed to pass sobbing and crying into the night. Then, the little school-house seeming lonelier than before, he shut the door and went home.

The next morning Mliss came to school.

Her face had been washed, and her coarse black hair bore evidence of recent struggles with the comb, in which both had evidently suffered. The old defiant look shone occasionally in her eyes, but her manner was tamer and more subdued. Then began a series of little trials and self-sacrifices, in which master and pupil bore an equal part, and which increased the confidence and sympathy between them. Although obedient under the master's eye, at times during recess, if thwarted or stung by a fancied slight, Mliss would rage in ungovernable fury, and many a palpitating young savage, finding himself matched with his own weapons of torment, would seek the master with torn jacket and scratched face, and complaints of the dreadful Mliss. There was a serious division among the townspeople on the subject, some threatening to withdraw their children from such evil companionship, and others as warmly upholding the course of the master in his work of reclamation. Meanwhile, with a steady persistence that seemed quite astonishing to him, on looking back afterward, the master drew Mliss gradually out of the shadow of her past life, as though it were but her natural progress down the narrow path on which he had set her feet the moonlit night of their first meeting. Remembering the experience of the evangelical McSnagley, he carefully avoided that Rock of Ages on which that unskilful pilot had shipwrecked her young faith. But if, in the course of her reading, she chanced to stumble upon those few words which have lifted such as she above the level of the older, the wiser, and the more prudent —if she learned something of a faith that is symbolised by suffering, and the old light softened in her eyes, it did not take the shape of a lesson. A few of the plainer people had made up a little sum by which the ragged Mliss was enabled to assume the garments of respect and civilization; and often a rough shake of the hand, and words of homely commendation from a red-shirted and burly figure, sent a glow to the cheek of the young master, and set him to thinking if it was altogether deserved.

Three months had passed from the time of their first meeting, and the master was sitting late one evening over the moral and sententious copies, when there came a tap at the door, and again Mliss stood before him. She was neatly clad and clean-faced, and there was nothing, perhaps, but the long black hair and bright black eyes to remind him of his former apparition. "Are you busy?" she asked. "Can you come with me?"—and on his signifying his readiness, in her old wilful way she said, "Come, then, quick!"

They passed out of the door together, and into the dark road. As they entered the town, the master asked her whither she was going. She replied, "To see my father."

It was the first time he had heard her call him by that filial title, or, indeed, anything more than "Old Smith" or the "Old Man." It was the first time in three months that she had spoken of him at all, and the master knew she had kept resolutely aloof from him since her great change. Satisfied, from her manner, that it was fruitless to question her purpose, he passively followed. In out-of-the-way places, the master, preceded by Mliss, came and went. In the reeking smoke and blasphemous outcries of low dens, the child, holding the master's hand, stood and anxiously gazed, seemingly unconscious of all, in the one absorbing nature of her pursuit. Some of the revellers, recognising Mliss, called to the child to sing and dance for them, and would have forced liquor upon her but for the interference of the master. Others, recognising him mutely, made way for them to pass. So an hour slipped by. Then the child whispered in his ear that there was a cabin on the other side of the creek crossed by the long flume, where she thought he still might be. Thither they crossed—a toilsome half-hour's walk—but in vain. They were returning by the ditch at the abutment [3] of the flume, gazing at

[3] *abutment,* a support at the end of the flume

the lights of the town on the opposite bank, when suddenly, sharply, a quick report rang out on the clear night air. The echoes caught it, and carried it round and round Red Mountain, and set the dogs to barking all along the streams. Lights seemed to dance and move quickly on the outskirts of the town for a few moments, the stream rippled quite audibly beside them, a few stones loosened themselves from the hill-side and splashed into the stream, a heavy wind seemed to surge the branches of the funereal pines, and then the silence seemed to fall thicker, heavier, and deadlier. The master turned towards Mliss with an unconscious gesture of protection, but the child had gone. Oppressed by a strange fear, he ran quickly down the trail to the river's bed, and, jumping from boulder to boulder, reached the base of Red Mountain and the outskirts of the village. Midway of the crossing, he looked up and held his breath in awe. For high above him on the narrow flume, he saw the fluttering little figure of his late companion, crossing swiftly in the darkness.

He climbed the bank, and, guided by a few lights, moving about a central point on the mountain, soon found himself breathless among a crowd of awe-stricken and sorrowful men. Out from among them the child appeared, and, taking the master's hand, led him silently before what seemed a ragged hole in the mountain. Her face was quite white, but her excited manner gone, and her look that of one to whom some long-expected event had at last happened—an expression that, to the master in his bewilderment, seemed almost like relief. The walls of the cavern were partly propped by decaying timbers. The child pointed to what appeared to be some ragged, cast-off clothes, left in the hole by the late occupant. The master approached nearer with his flaming dip, and bent over them.

It was Smith, already cold, with a pistol in his hand and a bullet in his heart, lying beside his empty "pocket."

CHAPTER II

The opinion which McSnagley expressed in reference to a "change of heart" supposed to be experienced by Mliss was more forcibly described in the gulches and tunnels. It was thought there that Mliss had "struck a good lead." So when there was a new grave added to the little enclosure, and, at the expense of the master, a little board and inscription put above it, the *Red Mountain Banner* came out quite handsomely, and did the fair thing to the memory of one of "our oldest Pioneers," alluding gracefully to that "bane of noble intellects," and otherwise genteelly shelving our dear brother with the past. "He leaves an only child to mourn his loss," says the *Banner,* "who is now an exemplary scholar, thanks to the efforts of the Rev. Mr. McSnagley." The Rev. McSnagley, in fact, made a strong point of Mliss's conversion, and, indirectly attributing to the unfortunate child the suicide of her father, made affecting allusions in Sunday school to the beneficial effects of the "silent tomb," and in this cheerful contemplation drove most of the children into speechless horror, and caused the pink-and-white scions of the first families to howl dismally, and refuse to be comforted.

The long dry summer came. As each fierce day burned itself out in little whiffs of pearl grey smoke on the mountain summits, and the up-springing breeze scattered its red embers over the landscape, the green wave which in early spring upheaved above Smith's grave grew sere, and dry, and hard. In those days the master, strolling in the little churchyard of a Sabbath afternoon, was sometimes surprised to find a few wild flowers plucked from the damp pine-forests scattered there, and oftener rude wreaths hung upon the little pine cross. Most of these wreaths were formed of a sweet-scented grass, which the children loved to keep in their desks, intertwined with the plumes of the buckeye, the syringa, and the wood-anemone; and here and there the master noticed the dark blue cowl of the monk's-hood or deadly aconite. There was something in the odd association of this noxious plant with these memorials which occasioned a painful sensation to the master, deeper than his aesthetic sense. One day, during a long walk, in crossing a wooded ridge he came upon Mliss in the heart of the forest, perched upon a prostrate pine, on a fantastic throne formed by the hanging plumes of lifeless branches, her lap full of grasses and pine-burrs, and crooning to herself one of the negro melodies of her younger life. Recognising him at a distance, she made room for him on her elevated throne, and with a grave assumption of hospitality and patronage that would have been ridiculous had it not been so terribly earnest, she fed him with pine-nuts and crab-apples. The master took that opportunity to point out to her the noxious and deadly qualities of the monk's-hood, whose dark blossoms he saw in her lap, and extorted from her a promise not to meddle with it as long as she remained his pupil. This done—as the master had tested her integrity before—he rested satisfied, and the strange feeling which had overcome him on seeing them died away.

Of the homes that were offered Mliss when her conversion became known, the master preferred that of Mrs. Morpher, a womanly and kind-hearted specimen of Southwestern efflorescence, known in her maidenhood as the "Per-rairie Rose." Being one of those who contend resolutely against their own natures, Mrs. Morpher, by a long series of self-sacrifices and struggles, had at last subjugated her naturally careless disposition to principles of "order," which she considered, in common with Mr. Pope, as "Heaven's first law." But she could not entirely govern the orbits of her satellites, however regular her own movements, and even her own "Jeemes" sometimes collided with her. Again her old nature asserted itself in her children. Lycurgus dipped into the cupboard "between meals," and Aristides came home from school without shoes, leaving those important articles on the threshold for the delight of a barefooted walk down the ditches. Octavia and Cassandra were "keerless" of their clothes. So with but one exception, however much the "Prairie Rose" might have trimmed and pruned and trained her own matured luxuriance, the little shoots came up defiantly wild and straggling. That one exception was Clytemnestra Morpher, aged fifteen. She was the realisation of her mother's dream—neat, orderly, and dull.

It was an amiable weakness of Mrs. Morpher to imagine that "Clytie" was a consolation and model for Mliss. Following this fallacy, Mrs. Morpher threw Clytie at the head of Mliss when she was "bad," and set her up before the child for adoration in her penitential moments. It was not, therefore, surprising to the master to hear that Clytie was coming to school, obviously as a favour to the master, and as an example for Mliss and others. For "Clytie" was quite a young lady. The youth of Smith's Pocket sighed for her in April and languished in May. Enamoured swains haunted the school-house at the hour of dismissal. A few were jealous of the master.

Perhaps it was this latter circumstance that opened the master's eyes to another. He could not help noticing that Clytie was romantic; that in school she required a great deal of attention; that her pens were uniformly bad and wanted fixing; that she usually accompanied the request with a certain expectation in her eye that was somewhat disproportionate to the quality of service she verbally required; that she sometimes allowed the curves of a round, plump white arm to rest on his when he was writing her copies; that she always blushed and flung back her blonde curls when she did so. I don't remember whether I have stated that the master was a young man—it's of little consequence, however; he had been severely educated in the school in which Clytie was taking her first lesson, and, on the whole, with-

stood the flexible curves and factitious glance like the fine young Spartan[4] that he was. He generally avoided Clytie; but one evening, when she returned to the schoolhouse after something she had forgotten, and did not find it until the master walked home with her, I hear that he endeavoured to make himself particularly agreeable—partly from the fact, I imagine, that his conduct was adding gall and bitterness to the already overcharged hearts of Clytemnestra's admirers.

The morning after this affecting episode Mliss did not come to school. Noon came, but not Mliss. Questioning Clytie on the subject, it appeared that they had left for school together, but the willful Mliss had taken another road. The afternoon brought her not. In the evening he called on Mrs. Morpher, whose motherly heart was really alarmed. Mr. Morpher had spent all day in search of her, without discovering a trace that might lead to her discovery. Aristides was summoned as a probable accomplice, but that equitable infant succeeded in impressing the household with his innocence. Mrs. Morpher entertained a vivid impression that the child would yet be found drowned in a ditch, or, what was almost as terrible, muddied and soiled beyond the redemption of soap and water. Sick at heart, the master returned to the school-house. As he lit his lamp and seated himself at his desk, he found a note lying before him addressed to himself in Mliss's handwriting. It seemed to be written on a leaf torn from some old memorandum book, and, to prevent sacrilegious trifling, had been sealed with six broken wafers. Opening it almost tenderly, the master read as follows:—

RESPECTED SIR,

When you read this, I am run away. Never to come back. *Never*, NEVER, NEVER. You can give my beeds to Mary

---

[4] *Spartan,* citizen of the Greek city, Sparta, whose people were noted for their fortitude and discipline

Jennings, and my Amerika's Pride [a highly coloured lithograph from a tobacco-box] to Sally Flanders. But don't you give anything to Clytie Morpher. Don't you dare to. Do you know what my opinion is of her, it is this, she is perfekly disgustin. This is all and no more at present from

Yours respectfully,
MELISSA SMITH

The master sat pondering on this strange epistle till the moon lifted its bright face above the distant hills, and illuminated the trail that led to the school-house, beaten quite hard with the coming and going of little feet. Then, more satisfied in mind, he tore the missive into fragments, and scattered them along the road.

At sunrise the next morning he was picking his way through the palm-like fern and thick underbrush of the pine-forest, starting the hare from its form, and awakening a querulous protest from a few dissipated crows, who had evidently been making a night of it, and so came to the wooded ridge where he had once found Mliss. There he found the prostrate pine and tasselled branches, but the throne was vacant. As he drew nearer, what might have been some frightened animal started through the crackling limbs. It ran up the tossed arms of the fallen monarch, and sheltered itself in some friendly foliage. The master, reaching the old seat, found the nest still warm; looking up in the intertwining branches, he met the black eyes of the errant Mliss. They gazed at each other without speaking. She was first to break the silence.

"What do you want?" she asked, curtly.

The master had decided on a course of action.

"I want some crab-apples," he said, humbly.

"Sha'n't have 'em! go away. Why don't you get 'em of Clytemnerestera?" (It seemed to be a relief to Mliss to express her contempt in additional syllables to that classical young woman's already long-drawn title.) "O, you wicked thing!"

"I am hungry, Lissy. I have eaten nothing since dinner yesterday. I am famished!" and the young man, in a state of remarkable exhaustion, leaned against a tree.

Melissa's heart was touched. In the bitter days of her gipsy life she had known the sensation he so artfully simulated. Overcome by his heart-broken tone, but not entirely divested of suspicion, she said—

"Dig under the tree near the roots, and you'll find lots; but mind you don't tell;" for Mliss had *her* hoards as well as the rats and squirrels.

But the master, of course, was unable to find them, the effects of hunger probably blinding his senses. Mliss grew uneasy. At length she peered at him through the leaves in an elfish way, and questioned:—

"If I come down and give you some, you'll promise you won't touch me?"

The master promised.

"Hope you'll die if you do!"

The master accepted instant dissolution as a forfeit. Mliss slid down the tree. For a few moments nothing transpired but the munching of the pine-nuts.

"Do you feel better?" she asked, with some solicitude. The master confessed to a recuperated feeling, and then, gravely thanking her, proceeded to retrace his steps. As he expected, he had not gone far before she called him. He turned. She was standing there quite white, with tears in her widely-opened orbs. The master felt that the right moment had come. Going up to her, he took both her hands, and, looking in her tearful eyes, said gravely, "Lissy, do you remember the first evening you came to see me?"

Lissy remembered.

"You asked me if you might come to school, for you wanted to learn something and be better, and I said—"

"Come," responded the child, promptly.

"What would *you* say if the master now came to you and said that he was lonely without his little scholar, and that he

wanted her to come and teach him to be better?"

The child hung her head for a few moments in silence. The master waited patiently. Tempted by the quiet, a hare ran close to the couple, and, raising her bright eyes and velvet fore-paws, sat and gazed at them. A squirrel ran half-way down the furrowed bark of the fallen tree, and there stopped.

"We are waiting, Lissy," said the master, in a whisper, and the child smiled. Stirred by a passing breeze, the tree-tops rocked, and a long pencil of light stole through their interlaced boughs full on the doubting face and irresolute little figure. Suddenly she took the master's hand in her quick way. What she said was scarcely audible, but the master, putting the black hair from her forehead, kissed her; and so, hand in hand, they passed out of the damp aisles and forest odours into the open sunlit road.

Chapter III

Somewhat less spiteful toward other scholars, Mliss still retained an offensive attitude in regard to Clytemnestra. Per-

haps the jealous element was not entirely lulled in her passionate little breast.

The master, in his first estimate of the child's character, could not conceive that she had ever possessed a doll. But the master, like many other professed readers of character, was safer in *a posteriori* [5] than *a priori* [6] reasoning. Mliss had a doll, but then it was emphatically Mliss's doll—a smaller copy of herself. Its unhappy existence had been a secret discovered accidentally by Mrs. Morpher. It had been the old-time companion of Mliss's wanderings, and bore evident marks of suffering. Its original complexion was long since washed away by the weather and annointed by the slime of ditches. It looked very much as Mliss had in days past. Its one gown of faded stuff was dirty and ragged, as hers had been. Mliss had never been known to apply to it any childish term of endearment. She never exhibited it in the presence of other children. It was put severely to bed in a hollow tree near the school-

---

[5] *a posteriori,* based on experience or observation of fact

[6] *a priori,* not based on observed facts or experience

house, and only allowed exercise during Mliss's rambles. Fulfilling a stern duty to her doll, as she would to herself, it knew no luxuries.

Now Mrs. Morpher, obeying a commendable impulse, bought another doll and gave it to Mliss. The child received it gravely and curiously. The master, on looking at it one day, fancied he saw a slight resemblance in its round red cheeks and mild blue eyes to Clytemnestra. It became evident before long that Mliss had also noticed the same resemblance. Accordingly she hammered its waxen head on the rocks when she was alone, and sometimes dragged it with a string round its neck to and from school. At other times, setting it up on her desk she made a pin-cushion of its patient and inoffensive body. Whether this was done in revenge of what she considered a second figurative obtrusion of Clytie's excellencies upon her, or whether she had an intuitive appreciation of the rites of certain other heathens, and, indulging in that "fetish" ceremony,[7] imagined that the original of her wax model would pine away and finally die, is a metaphysical question I shall not now consider.

In spite of these moral vagaries, the master could not help noticing in her different tasks the working of a quick, restless, and vigorous perception. She knew neither the hesitancy nor the doubts of childhood. Her answers in class were always slightly dashed with audacity. Of course she was not infallible. But her courage and daring in passing beyond her own depth and that of the floundering little swimmers around her, in their minds outweighed all errors of judgment. Children are not better than grown people in this respect, I fancy; and whenever the little red hand flashed above her desk, there was a wondering silence, and even the master was sometimes oppressed with a doubt of his own experience and judgment.

[7] "fetish" ceremony, a ceremony in which an inanimate object represents a spirit

Nevertheless, certain attributes which at first amused and entertained his fancy began to afflict him with grave doubts. He could not but see that Mliss was revengeful, irreverent, and willful. That there was but one better quality which pertained to her semi-savage disposition—the faculty of physical fortitude and self-sacrifice; and another, though not always an attribute of the noble savage—Truth. Mliss was both fearless and sincere; perhaps in such a character the adjectives were synonymous.

The master had been doing some hard thinking on this subject, and had arrived at that conclusion quite common to all who think sincerely, that he was generally the slave of his own prejudices, when he determined to call on the Rev. McSnagley for advice. This decision was somewhat humiliating to his pride, as he and McSnagley were not friends. But he thought of Mliss and the evening of their first meeting; and perhaps, with a pardonable superstition that it was not chance alone that had guided her willful feet to the schoolhouse, and perhaps with a complacent consciousness of the rare magnanimity of the act, he choked back his dislike and went to McSnagley.

The reverend gentleman was glad to see him. Moreover, he observed that the master was looking "peartish," and hoped he had got over the "neuralgy" and "rheumatiz." He himself had been troubled with a dumb "ager" since last conference. But he had learned to "rastle and pray."

Pausing a moment to enable the master to write his certain method of curing the dumb "ager" upon the book and volume of his brain, Mr. McSnagley proceeded to inquire after Sister Morpher. "She is an adornment to Christewanity, and has a likely growin' young family," added Mr. McSnagley; "and there's that mannerly young gal—so well behaved—Miss Clytie." In fact, Clytie's perfections seemed to affect him to such an extent that he dwelt for several minutes upon them. The master was doubly embarrassed.

In the first place, there was an enforced contrast with poor Mliss in all this praise of Clytie. Secondly, there was something unpleasantly confidential in his tone of speaking of Mrs. Morpher's earliest born. So that the master, after a few futile efforts to say something natural, found it convenient to recall another engagement, and left without asking the information required, but in his after-reflections somewhat unjustly giving the Rev. Mr. McSnagley the full benefit of having refused it.

Perhaps this rebuff placed the master and pupil once more in the close communion of old. The child seemed to notice the change in the master's manner, which had of late been constrained, and in one of their long post-prandial [8] walks she stopped suddenly, and, mounting a stump, looked full in his face with big, searching eyes.

"You ain't mad?" said she, with an interrogative shake of the black braids.

"No."

"Nor bothered?"

"No."

"Nor hungry?" (Hunger was to Mliss a sickness that might attack a person at any moment.)

"No."

"Nor thinking of her?"

"Of whom, Lissy?"

"That white girl." (This was the latest epithet invented by Mliss, who was a very dark brunette, to express Clytemnestra.)

"No."

"Upon your word?" (A substitute for "Hope you'll die!" proposed by the master.)

"Yes."

"And sacred honour?"

"Yes."

Then Mliss gave him a fierce little kiss, and, hopping down, fluttered off. For two or three days after that she condescended to appear more like other children, and be, as she expressed it, "good."

Two years had passed since the master's

---
[8] *post-prandial*, after-dinner

advent at Smith's Pocket, and as his salary was not large, and the prospects of Smith's Pocket eventually becoming the capital of the State not entirely definite, he contemplated a change. He had informed the school trustees privately of his intentions, but educated young men of unblemished moral character being scarce at that time, he consented to continue his school term through the winter to early spring. None else knew of his intention except his one friend, a Dr. Duchesne, a young Creole physician, known to the people of Wingdam as "Duchesny." He never mentioned it to Mrs. Morpher, Clytie, or any of his scholars. His reticence was partly the result of a constitutional indisposition to fuss, partly a desire to be spared the questions and surmises of vulgar curiosity, and partly that he never really believed he was going to do anything before it was done.

He did not like to think of Mliss. It was a selfish instinct, perhaps, which made him try to fancy his feeling for the child was foolish, romantic, and unpractical. He even tried to imagine that she would do better under the control of an older and sterner teacher. Then she was nearly eleven, and in a few years, by the rules of Red Mountain, would be a woman. He had done his duty. After Smith's death he addressed letters to Smith's relatives, and received one answer from a sister of Melissa's mother. Thanking the master, she stated her intention of leaving the Atlantic States for California with her husband in a few months. This was a slight superstructure for the airy castle which the master pictured for Mliss's home, but it was easy to fancy that some loving, sympathetic woman, with the claims of kindred, might better guide her wayward nature. Yet, when the master had read the letter, Mliss listened to it carelessly, received it submissively, and afterwards cut figures out of it with her scissors, supposed to represent Clytemnestra, labelled "the white girl," to prevent mistakes, and impaled them upon the outer walls of the school-house.

When the summer was about spent, and the last harvest had been gathered in the valleys, the master bethought him of gathering in a few ripened shoots of the young idea, and of having his Harvest-Home, or Examination. So the savants and professionals of Smith's Pocket were gathered to witness that time-honoured custom of placing timid children in a constrained position, and bullying them as in a witness-box. As usual in such cases, the most audacious and self-possessed were the lucky recipients of the honours. The reader will imagine that in the present instance Mliss and Clytie were pre-eminent, and divided public attention: Mliss with her clearness of material perception and self-reliance, Clytie with her placid self-esteem and saint-like correctness of deportment. The other little ones were timid and blundering. Mliss's readiness and brilliancy, of course, captivated the greatest number and provoked the greatest applause. Mliss's antecedents had unconsciously awakened the strongest sympathies of a class whose athletic forms were ranged against the walls, or whose

handsome bearded faces looked in at the windows. But Mliss's popularity was overthrown by an unexpected circumstance.

McSnagley had invited himself, and had been going through the pleasing entertainment of frightening the more timid pupils by the vaguest and most ambiguous questions, delivered in an impressive funereal tone; and Mliss had soared into Astronomy, and was tracking the course of our spotted ball through space, and keeping time with the music of the spheres, and defining the tethered orbits of the planets, when McSnagley impressively arose.

"Meelissy! Ye were speaking of the revolutions of this yere yearth, and the move*ments* of the sun, and I think ye said it had been a-doing of it since the creashun, eh?"

Mliss nodded a scornful affirmative.

"Well, war that the truth?" said McSnagley, folding his arms.

"Yes," said Mliss, shutting up her little red lips tightly.

The handsome outlines at the windows peered farther in the school-room, and a saintly Raphael-like [9] face, with blonde

[9] *Raphael-like,* resembling faces painted by Raphael

LEONARD EVERETT FISHER

beard and soft blue eyes, belonging to the biggest scamp in the diggings, turned towards the child and whispered, "Stick to it, Mliss!"

The reverend gentleman heaved a deep sigh, and cast a compassionate glance at the master, then at the children, and then rested his look on Clytie. There was a momentary silence. Clytie's round cheeks were very pink and soft. Clytie's big eyes were very bright and blue. Clytie's low-necked white book-muslin rested softly on Clytie's white, plump shoulders. Clytie looked at the master, and the master nodded. Then Clytie spoke softly—

"Joshua commanded the sun to stand still, and it obeyed him!" There was a low hum of applause in the school-room, a triumphant expression on McSnagley's face, a grave shadow on the master's, and a comical look of disappointment reflected from the windows. Mliss skimmed rapidly over her Astronomy, and then shut the book with a loud snap. A groan burst from McSnagley, an expression of astonishment from the school-room, a yell from the windows, as Mliss brought her red fist down on the desk, with the emphatic declaration:—

"I don't believe it!"

CHAPTER IV

The long wet season had drawn near its close. Signs of spring were visible in the swelling buds and rushing torrents. The pine-forests exhaled the fresher spicery. The azaleas were already budding, the ceanothus getting ready its lilac livery for spring. On the green upland which climbed Red Mountain at its southern aspect, the long spike of the monk's-hood shot up from its broad-leaved stool, and once more shook its dark blue bells. Again the billow above Smith's grave was soft and green, its crest just tossed with the foam of daisies and buttercups. The little grave-yard had gathered a few new dwellers in the past year, and the mounds were placed two by two by the little paling, until they reached Smith's grave, and there there was but one. General superstition had shunned it, and the plot beside Smith was vacant.

There had been several placards posted about the town, intimating that, at a certain period, a celebrated dramatic company would perform, for a few days, a series of "side-splitting" and "screaming farces;" that, alternating pleasantly with this, there would be some melodrama, and a grand divertissement, which would include singing, dancing, etc. These announcements occasioned a great fluttering among the little folk, and were the theme of much excitement and great speculation among the master's scholars. The master had promised Mliss, to whom this sort of thing was sacred and rare, that she should go, and on that momentous evening the master and Mliss "assisted."

The performance was the prevalent style of heavy mediocrity; the melodrama was not bad enough to laugh at, nor good enough to excite. But the master, turning wearily to the child, was astonished, and felt something like self-accusation, in noticing the peculiar effect upon her excitable nature. The red blood flushed in her cheeks at each stroke of her panting little heart. Her small, passionate lips were slightly parted, to give vent to her hurried breath. Her widely opened lids threw up and arched her black eyebrows. She did not laugh at the dismal comicalities of the funny man, for Mliss seldom laughed. Nor was she discreetly affected to the delicate extremes of the corner of a white handkerchief, as was the tender-hearted "Clytie" who was talking with her "feller," and ogling the master at the same moment. But when the performance was over, and the green curtain fell on the little stage, Mliss drew a long deep breath, and turned to the master's grave face with a half-apologetic smile and wearied gesture. Then she said, "Now take me home!" and dropped the lids of her black eyes, as if to dwell once more in fancy on the mimic stage.

On their way to Mrs. Morpher's, the master thought proper to ridicule the whole performance. Now, he shouldn't wonder if Mliss thought that the young lady who acted so beautifully was really in earnest, and in love with the gentleman who wore such fine clothes. Well, if she were in love with him, it was a very unfortunate thing! "Why?" said Mliss, with an upward sweep of the drooping lid. "Oh! well he couldn't support his wife at his present salary, and pay so much a week for his fine clothes, and then they wouldn't receive as much wages if they were married; but I think the husband of the pretty young countess takes the tickets at the door, or pulls up the curtain, or snuffs the candles, or does something equally refined and elegant. As to the young man with nice clothes, which are really nice now, and must cost at least two and a half or three dollars, not to speak of that mantle of red drugget,[10] which I happen to know the price of, for I bought some of it for my room once—as to this young man, Lissy, he is a pretty good fellow, and I don't think people ought to take advantage and give him black eyes, and throw him in the mud. Do you? I am sure he might owe me two dollars and a half a long time before I would throw it up in his face, as the fellow did the other night at Wingdam."

Mliss had taken his hand in both of hers, and was trying to look in his eyes, which the young man kept as resolutely averted. Mliss had a faint idea of irony, indulging herself sometimes in a species of sardonic humour, which was equally visible in her actions and her speech. But the young man continued in this strain until they had reached Mrs. Morpher's and he had deposited Mliss in her maternal charge. Waiving the invitation of Mrs. Morpher to refreshment and rest, he excused himself and went home.

For two or three days after the advent of the dramatic company Mliss was late at

10 *mantle of red drugget,* a red cloak woven wholly or partly of wool

school, and the master's usual Friday afternoon ramble was for once omitted, owing to the absence of his trustworthy guide. As he was putting away his books and preparing to leave the school-house, a small voice piped at his side, "Please, sir?" The master turned, and there stood Aristides Morpher.

"Well, my little man," said the master, impatiently, "what is it? quick!"

"Please, sir, me and 'Kerg' thinks that Mliss is going to run away agin."

"What's that, sir?" said the master, with that unjust testiness with which we always receive disagreeable news.

"Why, sir, she don't stay home any more, and 'Kerg' and me see her talking with one of those actor fellers, and she's with him now; and please, sir, yesterday she told 'Kerg' and me she could make a speech as well as Miss Cellerstina Montmoressy, and she spouted right off by heart;" and the little fellow paused in a collapsed condition.

"What actor?" asked the master.

"Him as wears the shiny hat. And hair. And gold pin. And gold chain," said the just Aristides, putting periods for commas to eke out his breath.

The master put on his gloves and hat, feeling an unpleasant tightness in his chest and thorax, and walked out in the road. Aristides trotted along by his side, endeavouring to keep pace with his short legs to the master's strides, when the master stopped suddenly, and Aristides bumped up against him. "Where were they talking?" asked the master, as if continuing the conversation.

"At the Arcade," said Aristides.

When they reached the main street the master paused. "Run down home," said he to the boy. "If Mliss is there, come to the Arcade and tell me. If she isn't there, stay home; run!" And off trotted the short-legged Aristides.

The Arcade was just across the way—a long, rambling building, containing a billiard-room and restaurant. As the young man crossed the plaza he noticed that two

or three of the passersby turned and looked after him. He looked at his clothes, took out his handkerchief and wiped his face, before he entered. It contained the usual number of loungers, who stared at him as he entered. One of them looked at him so fixedly, and with such a strange expression, that the master stopped and looked again, and then saw it was only his own reflection in a large mirror. This made the master think that perhaps he was a little excited, and so he took up a copy of the *Red Mountain Banner* from one of the tables, and tried to recover his composure by reading the column of advertisements.

He then walked through the restaurant into the billiard-room. The child was not there. In the latter apartment a person was standing by one of the tables with a broad-brimmed glazed hat on his head. The master recognized him as the agent of the dramatic company; he had taken a dislike to him at their first meeting, from the peculiar fashion of wearing his beard and hair. Satisfied that the object of his search

was not there, he turned to the man with a glazed hat. He had noticed the master, but tried that common trick of unconsciousness in which vulgar natures always fail. Balancing a billiard-cue in his hand, he pretended to play with a ball in the centre of the table. The master stood opposite to him until he raised his eyes; when their glances met, the master walked up to him.

He had intended to avoid a scene or quarrel, but when he began to speak, something kept rising in his throat and retarded his utterance, and his own voice frightened him, it sounded so distant, low, and resonant. "I understand," he began, "that Melissa Smith, an orphan, and one of my scholars, has talked with you about adopting your profession. Is that so?"

The man with the glazed hat leaned over the table, and made an imaginary shot, that sent the ball spinning round the cushions, then walking round the table, he recovered the ball, and placed it upon the spot. This duty discharged, getting ready for another shot, he said—

"S'pose she has?"

The master choked up again, but squeezing the cushion of the table in his gloved hand, he went on—

"If you are a gentleman, I have only to tell you that I am her guardian, and responsible for her career. You know as well as I do the kind of life you offer her. As you may learn of any one here, I have already brought her out of an existence worse than death. I am trying to do so again. Let us talk like men. She has neither father, mother, sister, nor brother. Are you seeking to give her an equivalent for these?"

The man with the glazed hat examined the point of his cue and then looked around for somebody to enjoy the joke with him.

"I know that she is a strange, willful girl," continued the master, "but she is better than she was. I believe that I have some influence over her still. I beg and hope, therefore, that you will take no further steps in this matter, but as a man, as a gentleman, leave her to me. I am willing—" But here something rose again in the master's throat, and the sentence remained unfinished.

The man with the glazed hat, mistaking the master's silence, raised his head with a coarse, brutal laugh, and said in a loud voice—

"Want her yourself, do you?"

The insult was more in the tone than the words, more in the glance than tone, and more in the man's instinctive nature than all these. The best appreciable rhetoric to this kind of animal is a blow. The master felt this, and, with his pent-up nervous energy finding expression in the one act, he struck the brute full in his grinning face. The blow sent the glazed hat one way and the cue another, and tore the glove and skin from the master's hand from knuckle to joint. It opened up the corners of the fellow's mouth, and spoilt the peculiar shape of his beard for some time to come.

There was a shout, an imprecation, a scuffle, and the trampling of many feet. Then the crowd parted right and left, and two sharp quick reports followed each other in rapid succession. Then they closed again about his opponent, and the master was standing alone. He remembered picking bits of burning wadding from his coatsleeve with his left hand. Someone was holding his other hand. Looking at it, he saw it was still bleeding from the blow.

The man who was holding his hand was Mr. Morpher. He hurried the master to the door, but the master held back, and tried to tell him as well as he could with his parched throat about "Mliss."

"It's all right, my boy," said Mr. Morpher. "She's home!" And they passed out into the street together. As they walked along Mr. Morpher said that Mliss had come running into the house a few moments before, and had dragged him out, saying that somebody was trying to kill the master at the Arcade. Wishing to be alone, the master promised Mr. Morpher that he would not seek the agent again that night, and parted from him, taking the road toward the school-house. He was surprised in nearing it to find the door open— still more surprised to find Mliss sitting there.

The master's nature, as I have hinted before, had, like most sensitive organizations, a selfish basis. The brutal taunt thrown out by his late adversary still rankled in his heart. It was possible, he thought, that such a construction might be put upon his affection for the child. And he had been a participant in a fight with a common boor, and risked his life to prove what? What had he proved? Nothing. What would the people say? What would his friends say? What would McSnagley say?

In his self-accusation the last person he should have wished to meet was Mliss. He entered the door, and, going up to his desk, told the child, in a few cold words, that he was busy, and wished to be alone. As she rose, he took her vacant seat, and, sitting down, buried his head in his hands. When he looked up again she was still standing there. She was looking at his face with an anxious expression.

"Did you kill him?" she asked.

"No!" said the master.

"If you'd asked me, I'd told you I was off with the play-actors. Why was I off with the play-actors? Because you wouldn't tell me you was going away. I knew it. I heard you tell the Doctor so. I wasn't a goin' to stay here alone with those Morphers. I'd rather die first."

With a dramatic gesture which was perfectly consistent with her character, she drew from her bosom a few limp green leaves, and, holding them out at arm's-length, said in her quick vivid way, and in the queer pronunciation of her old life, which she fell into when unduly excited—

"That's the poison plant you said would kill me. I'll go with the play-actors, or I'll eat this and die here. I don't care which. I won't stay here, where they hate and despise me! Neither would you let me, if you didn't hate and despise me too!"

The passionate little breast heaved, and two big tears peeped over the edge of Mliss's eyelids, but she whisked them away with the corner of her apron as if they had been wasps.

"If you lock me up in jail," said Mliss, fiercely, "to keep me from the play-actors, I'll poison myself. You said a mouthful of that root would kill me, and I always carry it here," and she struck her breast with her clenched fist.

The master thought of the vacant plot beside Smith's grave, and of the passionate little figure before him. Seizing her hands in his, and looking full into her truthful eyes, he said—

"Lissy, will you go with me?"

The child put her arms around his neck, and said joyfully, "Yes."

"But now—to-night?"

"To-night."

And hand in hand they passed into the road—the narrow road that had once brought her weary feet to the master's door, and which it seemed she should not tread again alone. The stars glittered brightly above them. For good or ill, the lesson had been learned, and behind them the school of Red Mountain closed upon them for ever.

[Abridged]

The man who wrote this novelette

BRET HARTE   1838–1902

Many writers are associated with a certain American region or with a movement in American literature. Bret Harte has become associated with the early West and the famous California Gold Rush.

Bret Harte was a New Yorker, but his family moved to California when he was still in his teens. There he observed life in the boom towns which sprang up around the gold-mining areas, collecting the raw material for his later stories.

Later, as editor of the *Overland Monthly,* a California literary magazine, Harte wrote about this life in such stories as "The Luck of Roaring Camp" and "The Outcasts of Poker Flat." These stories won him great popularity, and when he returned to the East, *The Atlantic Monthly* was willing to offer him ten thousand dollars for anything he could write in a year.

His popularity rapidly faded, however. Having left the West, Harte seemed to lose his knack of portraying western life accurately in his stories. Perhaps easterners expected him to look like one of the characters in his stories—a rough, burly miner. But Harte was a gentleman: in fact he was considered a "dandy."

He spent the last years of his life in Europe, where he held various political posts. He had to work hard to support his extravagant family and died without ever returning to the United States.

Let's consider . . .

1. Bret Harte took pains at the beginning of his story to acquaint you with Smith's Pocket. Why might a stranger think he had missed it? Why did the town look like some "elemental upheaval"? Where did it get its name?

2. What was the author's chief purpose in giving you a brief but vivid account of Smith? What part did Smith play in the story?

3. Mliss made a dramatic entrance into the story. (Whatever is dramatic in literature has an element of the unexpected about it and in some way affects the emotions, either of one of the characters, of the reader, or of both.) Describe her entrance, emphasizing the dramatic features of it.

4. Each of the four chapters in the novelette threw new light on the character of Mliss and made you better acquainted with her. Write a statement about each chapter which will indicate what additional understanding you gained about Mliss. Make your statements informative rather than striking.

5. After the burial of Smith, Mliss was offered several homes. The school master preferred Mrs. Morpher's. Would you have liked to live there? Why or why not? What do the children's names tell you about their mother?

6. What purpose did Clytie serve in the story? What was at the bottom of Mliss's dislike and resentment of her?

7. Did you ever feel sorry for Mliss? Why or why not?

8. The master was quite different from most teachers you have known. (This story was printed in 1860.) In what way did he surprise you the most? For what did you admire him the most? Why was Mliss so attached to him?

9. This story has many dramatic moments. Which one affected you the most? Describe what happened.

10. One critic said of Mliss, "She was as unconventional as a coyote, and when crossed she was as fiercely alive." Prove the truth of that statement by referring to several incidents in the story.

The writer's craft . . .

A. Bret Harte was one of the earliest writers to give the Far West its rightful place in American literature. He merged the background of the region with the plot and characterizations to give his stories a strong local color. In what ways did Smith's Pocket have a specific regional atmosphere which set it apart from other cities?

In stories with strong local color, the setting is usually important. How vital was the setting in "Mliss"? Could the story have taken place in other regions of the United States? Give several reasons.

B. "Mliss" is a **novelette:** a type of fiction which stands midway between the short story and the full-length novel. It differs from the short story in being longer and less restricted, both in content and development. The short story usually creates a single impression of situation, event, or character. The novelette attempts a fuller interpretation of life and, therefore, may create several impressions. It also allows for a fuller development of several characters and a more detailed treatment of the setting. However, because the novelette is not a full-length book, the plot must remain relatively simple.

If Bret Harte had written "Mliss" as a short story, he might have used only one of the several incidents now included in the novelette. Harte preferred to widen the scope of his story so that he could present a fuller view of life in Smith's Pocket. If he had included a greater number of incidents and characters, he could have expanded "Mliss" into a full-length novel.

1. Select one or two situations from "Mliss" which you think might have been developed into a good short story.

2. Choose a situation from "Mliss" which you could expand into a short story of your own. Write a synopsis of your plot; a condensed statement of the situation and events as you would use them in your story.

3. Suppose that you are writing a novel based on "Mliss." What additional incidents might you include? Suppose that you are going to carry the story along by adding another chapter. Write a summary of the events you would include, being sure to keep them consistent with the pattern of events and the characterizations already established.

Knowing words . . .

Bret Harte's language reflects the manner of speaking and writing in the middle nineteenth century. Many of the words and expressions he used in "Mliss" might be changed in modern use. The sentences listed below were taken from the selection. Each contains one or more words printed in italics. Rewrite the sentences, substituting one of the more familiar synonyms from the following list.

teacher's	dull	fit
blocked	calmness	spent
	unfeelingly	

1. Five thousand dollars were *expended* by Smith and others in erecting a flume and in tunneling.

2. Still, her great black eyes, her coarse, uncombed, *lustreless* black hair falling over her sun-burned face, her red arms and feet streaked with the red soil, were all familiar to him.

3. Accustomed to be *thwarted* and opposed, often *wantonly* and cruelly, for no other purpose than to excite the violent impulses of her nature, the *master's phlegm* evidently took her by surprise.

4. The master lifted her gently, and waited for the *paroxysm* to pass.

The Mountains Are a Lonely Folk

The mountains they are silent folk,
    They stand afar—alone,
And the clouds that kiss their brows at night
    Hear neither sigh nor groan.
Each bears him in his ordered place
    As soldiers do, and bold and high
They fold their forests round their feet
    And bolster up the sky.

Hamlin Garland

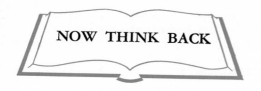

NOW THINK BACK

1. In FROM ATLANTIC TO PACIFIC, you sampled the "wealth of tradition, interesting customs, and a kind of speech, dress, and manners which gives to each region its local color." Think back over the selections in this part. Which section of the country (previously unfamiliar to you) do you now feel you understand best? Name two distinguishing features of this region and tell why they impressed you.

2. Probably you are partial to your own locality, but if you had to leave your present home, to what other place portrayed in this part would you like to move?

3. You have learned about the regions of America through poetry, short stories, and a novelette. In your opinion, which type of literature best conveyed the *feeling* of a region? Select your favorite selection of this type. Explain why you felt it helped you understand a region or a place which represented a region.

4. Which character in the part do you feel was affected most by the environment in which he or she lived? Give several reasons for your choice.

5. Many of the selections in this part were vivid accounts of adventures. Which adventure best revealed the qualities of character of the person or persons concerned? How were these qualities brought out by the situation or the events?

6. Several poems dealt with great cities. Point out the differences in each poet's attitude toward the city. What qualities did each see in the city he described? Which qualities do you think are common to all cities?

7. Unusual friendships grow up in different sections of the country. Which of the friendships described in Part Two seemed most amazing? Defend your choice.

Things to do . . .

1. Take the map you made for "Go, Seeker." Study it in the light of other selections in this part. Tell the class where these selections would lead you to seek "the promise of America."

2. Since the Rosicky family first settled in the great Middle West plains, this region has changed a great deal. Consult library sources for recent information about this region. What qualities of character in these early pioneers helped to bring about the development of this region?

3. Make separate lists of men and women you learned to know in this part. List those who stand out clearly. Which writers were particularly successful in portraying men? Which were particularly successful in portraying women? Be ready to defend your opinions.

4. In the library look up Amy Lowell's poem "London: 2 A.M." Compare and contrast this poem with "City Evening" and "Chicago."

5. Perhaps you know something about a region not included in this part and would like to interest others in it. Use the library to find a story or poem about this region which you could share with the class. From your own knowledge, explain why the selection gives, or does not give, a good picture of the region.

More to read . . .

Canal Town by SAMUEL HOPKINS ADAMS. Random House, Inc., 1947.

Golden Tales of New England by MAY LAMBERTON BECKER. Dodd, Mead & Company, 1931.

Grandissimes by GEORGE WASHINGTON CABLE. Charles Scribner's Sons, 1908.

The Adventures of Huckleberry Finn by SAMUEL LANGHORNE CLEMENS (MARK TWAIN *pseud.*). Harper & Brothers, 1923.

Cimarron by EDNA FERBER.
  Doubleday & Company, 1930.
Uncle Remus by JOEL CHANDLER HARRIS.
  Appleton-Century-Crofts, Inc., 1880.
Selected Stories of Bret Harte by BRET
  HARTE.
  Caxton Printers, Ltd., 1946.
The House of the Seven Gables by NA-
  THANIEL HAWTHORNE.
  Dodd, Mead & Company, 1950.
The Bayous of Louisiana by HARNETT T.
  KANE.
  William Morrow & Company, Inc.,
  1943.
Gone With the Wind by MARGARET
  MITCHELL.
  The Macmillan Company, 1936.
The Yearling by MARJORIE KINNAN RAWL-
  INGS.
  Charles Scribner's Sons, 1939.
Trees of Heaven by JESSE STUART.
  E. P. Dutton & Co., Inc., 1940.
The Grandmothers by GLENWAY WESCOTT.
  Harper & Brothers, 1927.
Ethan Frome by EDITH WHARTON.
  Charles Scribner's Sons, 1938.

*   *   *

Sidewalks of America by B. A. BOTKIN.
  Bobbs-Merrill Company, Inc., 1955.
Stars Fell on Alabama by CARL CARMER.
  Doubleday & Company, Inc., 1952.
A Goodly Heritage by MARY ELLEN CHASE.
  Henry Holt and Company, Inc., 1932.
Maine Ballads by ROBERT P. TRISTRAM COF-
  FIN.
  The Macmillan Company, 1938.
Quare Woman by LUCY FURMAN.
  Little, Brown and Company, 1923.
A Walker in the City by ALFRED KAZIN.
  Harcourt, Brace and Company, 1951.
American Regionalism by HOWARD W.
  ODUM and HARRY E. MOORE.
  Henry Holt and Company, Inc., 1932.
*American Skylines: The Growth and Form
  of our Cities and Towns* by CHRISTO-
  PHER TUNNARD.
  Houghton Mifflin Company, 1955.

*   *   *

Carolina Folk Plays by FREDERICK KOCH.
  Introduction by Paul Green.
  Henry Holt and Company, 1941.
The Late George Apley by JOHN P. MAR-
  QUAND and GEORGE S. KAUFMAN.
  Dramatists Play Service, Inc., 1946.

GIANTS IN THE LAND

When Commander Byrd returned from his flight across the North Pole in 1926, he could not believe that he had suddenly become a national hero. At first, he just accepted the unexpected fame. Then he began to wonder what it meant to be a hero in America. Why had his flight so captured the imagination of the American people? What did they see in him which somehow rewarded them with such deep feelings of pride and satisfaction?

He could answer these questions only after he had traveled across the country and talked with hundreds of Americans. By listening, he learned that he had come to symbolize the ambitions of youth as well as the dreams of men. People saw in him the spirit of America.

Like Commander Byrd, all American heroes represent this spirit. They possess the human qualities which the people most admire. Look carefully at the men and women whom Americans have taken to their hearts, beginning with the present and moving back into the past. You will see that your country's heroes symbolize America at her very best.

GIANTS IN THE LAND

A Calendar of Great Americans

WOODROW WILSON

In this thoughtful essay, Woodrow Wilson presents his views on great Americans. As you read, notice the clear, precise way in which he analyzes the qualities which have made certain Americans great.

Before a calendar of great Americans can be made out, a valid canon of Americanism must first be established. Not every great man born and bred in America was a great "American." Some of the notable men born among us were simply great Englishmen; others had in all the habits of their thought and life the strong flavor of a peculiar region, and were great New Englanders or great Southerners; others, masters in the fields of science or of pure thought, showed nothing either distinctively national or characteristically provincial, and were simply great men; while a few displayed odd cross-strains of blood or breeding. The great Englishmen bred in America, like Hamilton and Madison; the great provincials, like John Adams and Calhoun; the authors of such thought as might have been native to any clime, like Asa Gray [1] and Emerson; and the men of mixed breed, like Jefferson and Benton,[2] must be excluded from our present list. We must pick out men who have created or exemplified a distinctively American standard and type of greatness.

To make such a selection is not to create an artificial standard of greatness, or to claim that greatness is in any case hallowed or exalted merely because it is American. It is simply to recognize a peculiar stamp of character, a special make-up of mind and faculties, as the specific product of our national life, not displacing or eclipsing talents of a different kind, but supplementing them, and so adding to the world's variety. There is an American type of man, and those who have exhibited this type with a certain unmistakable distinction and perfection have been great "Americans." It has required the utmost variety of character and energy to establish a great nation, with a polity at once free and firm, upon this continent, and no sound type of manliness could have been dispensed with in the effort. We could no more have done without our great Englishmen, to keep the past steadily in mind and make every change conservative of principle, than we could have done without the men whose whole impulse was forward, whose whole genius was for origination, natural masters of the art of subduing a wilderness . . . .

It is by the frank consideration of concrete cases that we may construct our canons of Americanism. The American spirit is something more than the old, the immemorial Saxon spirit of liberty from which it sprung. It has been bred by the conditions attending the great task which we have all the century been carrying forward: the

[1] *Asa Gray* (1810–1888), American botanist
[2] *Thomas Holt Benton* (1782–1858), United States Senator from Missouri

195

task, at once material and ideal, of subduing a wilderness and covering all the wide stretches of a vast continent with a single free and stable polity. It is, accordingly, above all things a hopeful and confident spirit. It is progressive, optimistically progressive, and ambitious of objects of national scope and advantage. It is unpedantic, unprovincial, unspeculative, unfastidious; regardful of law, but as using it, not as being used by it or dominated by any formalism whatever; in a sense unrefined, because full of rude force; but prompted by large and generous motives, and often as tolerant as it is resolute. No one man, unless it be Lincoln, has ever proved big or various enough to embody this active and full-hearted spirit in all its qualities; and the men who have been too narrow or too speculative or too pedantic to represent it have, nevertheless, added to the strong and stirring variety of our national life, making it fuller and richer in motive and energy; but its several aspects are none the less noteworthy as they separately appear in different men.

One of the first men to exhibit this American spirit with an unmistakable touch of greatness and distinction was Benjamin Franklin. It was characteristic of America that this self-made man should become a philosopher, a founder of philosophical societies, an authoritative man of science; that his philosophy of life should be so homely and so practical in its maxims, and uttered with so shrewd a wit; that one region should be his birthplace and another his home; that he should favor effective political union among the colonies from the first, and should play a sage and active part in the establishment of national independence and the planning of a national organization; and that he should represent his countrymen in diplomacy abroad. They could have had no spokesman who represented more sides of their character. Franklin was a sort of multiple American. He was versatile without lacking solidity; he

was a practical statesman without ceasing to be a sagacious philosopher. He came of the people, and was democratic; but he had raised himself out of the general mass of unnamed men, and so stood for the democratic law, not of equality, but of self-selection in endeavor. One can feel sure that Franklin would have succeeded in any part of the national life that it might have fallen to his lot to take part in. He will stand the final and characteristic test of Americanism; he would unquestionably have made a successful frontiersman, capable at once of wielding the ax and of administering justice from the fallen trunk.

Washington hardly seems an American, as most of his biographers depict him. He is too colorless, too cold, too prudent. He seems more like a wise and dispassionate Mr. Allworthy, advising a nation as he would a parish, than like a man building states and marshaling a nation in a wilderness. But the real Washington was as thoroughly an American as Jackson or Lincoln. What we take for lack of passion in him was but the reserve and self-mastery natural to a man of his class and breeding in Virginia. He was no parlor politician, either. He had seen the frontier, and far beyond it where the French forts lay. He knew the rough life of the country as few other men could. His thoughts did not live at Mount Vernon. He knew difficulty as intimately and faced it always with as quiet a mastery as William the Silent.[3] This calm, straightforward, high-spirited man, making charts of the western country, noting the natural land and water routes into the heart of the continent, marking how the French power lay, conceiving the policy which should dispossess it and the engineering achievement which should make the utmost resources of the land our own; counseling Braddock how to enter the forest, but not deserting him because he would not take advice; planning step by

[3] *William the Silent,* a sixteenth century Dutch patriot and hero

step, by patient correspondence with influential men everywhere, the meetings, conferences, common resolves which were finally to bring the great constitutional convention together; planning, too, always for the country as well as Virginia; and presiding at last over the establishment and organization of the government of the Union: he certainly—the most suitable instrument of the national life at every moment of crisis—is a great American. These noble words which he uttered amidst the first doubtings of the Constitutional Convention might serve as a motto for the best efforts of liberty wherever free men strive: "Let us raise a standard to which the wise and honest can repair; the event is in the hand of God."

In Henry Clay we have an American of a most authentic pattern. There was no man of his generation who represented more of America than he did. The singular, almost irresistible attraction he had for men of every class and every temperament came, not from the arts of the politician, but from the instant sympathy established between him and every fellow countryman of his. He does not seem to have exercised the same fascination upon foreigners. They felt toward him as some New Englanders did: he seemed to them plausible merely, too indiscriminately open and cordial to be sincere,—a bit of a charlatan. No man who really takes the trouble to understand Henry Clay, or who has quick enough parts to sympathize with him, can deem him false. It is the odd combination of two different elements in him that makes him seem irregular and inconstant. His nature was of the West, blown through with quick winds of ardor and aggression, a bit reckless and defiant; but his art was of the East, ready with soft and placating phrases, reminiscent of old and reverenced ideals, thoughtful of compromise and accommodation. He had all the address of the trained and sophisticated politician, bred in an old and sensitive society; but his purposes ran free of cautious restraints, and his real ideals were those of the somewhat bumptious Americanism which was pushing the frontier forward in the West, which believed itself capable of doing anything it might put its hand to, despised conventional restraints, and followed a vague but resplendent "manifest destiny" with lusty hurrahs. His purposes were sincere, even if often crude and uninstructed; it was only because the subtle arts of politics seemed inconsistent with the direct dash and bold spirit of the man that they sat upon him like an insincerity. He thoroughly, and by mere unconscious sympathy represented the double America of his day, made up of a West which hurried and gave bold strokes, and of an East which held back, fearing the pace, thoughtful and mindful of the instructive past. The one part had to be served without offending the other: and that was Clay's mediatorial function.

Andrew Jackson was altogether of the West. Of his sincerity nobody has ever had any real doubt; and his Americanism is now at any rate equally unimpeachable. He was like Clay, with the social imagination of the orator and the art and sophistication of the Eastern politician left out. He came into our national politics like a cyclone from off the Western prairies. Americans of the present day perceptibly shudder at the very recollection of Jackson. He seems to them a great Vandal, playing fast and loose alike with institutions and with tested and established policy, debauching politics like a modern spoilsman. But whether we would accept him as a type of ourselves or not, the men of his own day accepted him with enthusiasm. He did not need to be explained to them. They crowded to his standard like men free at last, after long and tedious restraint, to make their own choice, follow their own man. There can be no mistaking the spontaneity of the thoroughgoing support he received. He was the new type of energy and self-confidence bred by life outside the States that had been colonies. It was a terrible energy, threatening sheer destruction to many a carefully wrought arrangement handed on to us from the past; it was a perilous self-confidence, founded in sheer strength rather than in wisdom. The government did not pass through the throes of that signal awakening of the new national spirit without serious rack and damage. But it was no disease. It was only an incautious, abounding, madcap strength which proved so dangerous in its readiness for every rash endeavor. It was necessary that the West should be let into the play: it was even necessary that she should assert her right to the leading role. It was done without good taste, but that does not condemn it. We have, no doubt, refined and schooled the hoyden influences of that crude time, and they are vastly safer now than then, when they first came bounding in; but they mightily stirred and enriched our blood from the first. Now that we have thoroughly suffered this Jackson change and it is over, we are ready to recognize it as quite as radically American as anything in all our history.

Lincoln, nevertheless, rather than Jackson, was the supreme American of our history. In Clay, East and West were mixed without being fused or harmonized: he seems like two men. In Jackson there was not even a mixture; he was all of a piece, and altogether unacceptable to some parts of the country—a frontier statesman. But in Lincoln the elements were combined and harmonized. The most singular thing about the wonderful career of the man is the way in which he steadily grew into a national stature. He began an amorphous, unlicked cub, bred in the rudest of human lairs; but, as he grew, everything formed, informed, transformed him. The process was slow but unbroken. He was not fit to be President until he actually became President. He was fit then because, learn-ing everything as he went, he had found out how much there was to learn, and had still an infinite capacity for learning. The quiet voices of sentiment and murmurs of resolution that went whispering through the land, his ear always caught, when others could hear nothing but their own words. He never ceased to be a common man: that was his source of strength. But he was a common man with genius, a genius for things American, for insight into the common thought, for mastery of the fundamental things of politics that inhere in human nature and cast hardly more than their shadows on constitutions; for the practical niceties of affairs; for judging men and assessing arguments. Jackson had no social imagination: no unfamiliar community made any impression on him. His whole fiber stiffened young, and nothing afterward could modify or even deeply affect it. But Lincoln was always a-making; he would have died unfinished if the terrible storms of the war had not stung him to learn in those four years what no other twenty could have taught him. And, as he stands there in his complete manhood, at the most perilous helm in Christendom, what a marvelous composite figure he is! The whole country is summed up in him: the rude Western strength, tempered with shrewdness and a broad and human wit; the Eastern conservatism, regardful of law and devoted to fixed standards of duty. He even understood the South, as no other Northern man of his generation did. He respected, because he comprehended, though he could not hold, its view of the Constitution; he appreciated the inexorable compulsions of its past in respect of slavery; he would have secured it once more, and speedily if possible, in its right to self-government, when the fight was fought out. To the Eastern politicians he seemed like an accident; but to history he must seem like a providence.

Grant was Lincoln's suitable instrument, a great American general, the appropriate product of West Point. A Western man, he had no thought of commonwealths politically separate, and was instinctively for the Union; a man of the common people, he deemed himself always an instrument, never a master, and did his work, though ruthlessly, without malice; a sturdy, hard-willed, taciturn man, a sort of Lincoln the Silent in thought and spirit. He does not appeal to the imagination very deeply; there is a sort of common greatness about him, great gifts combined singularly with a great mediocrity; but such peculiarities seem to make him all the more American—national in spirit, thoroughgoing in method, masterful in purpose.

And yet it is no contradiction to say that Robert E. Lee also was a great American. He fought on the opposite side, but he fought in the same spirit, and for a principle which is in a sense scarcely less American than the principle of Union. He represented the idea of the inherent—the essential—separateness of self-government. This was not the principle of secession; that principle involved the separate right of the several self-governing units of the federal system to judge of national questions independently, and as a check upon the federal government—to adjudge the very objects of the Union. Lee did not believe in secession, but he did believe in the local rootage of all government. This is at the bottom, no doubt, an English idea; but it has had a characteristic American development. It is the reverse side of the shield which bears upon its obverse the devices of the Union, a side too much overlooked and obscured since the war. It conceives the individual State a community united by the most intimate associations, the first home and foster mother of every man born into the citizenship of the nation. Lee considered himself a member of one of these great families; he could not conceive of the nation apart from the State; above all, he could not live in the nation divorced from his neighbors. His own community should

decide his political destiny and duty.

This was also the spirit of Patrick Henry and of Sam Houston—men much alike in the cardinal principle of their natures. Patrick Henry resisted the formation of the Union only because he feared to disturb the local rootage of self-government, to disperse power so widely that neighbors could not control it. It was not a disloyal or a separatist spirit, but only a jealous spirit of liberty. Sam Houston, too, deemed the character a community should give itself so great a matter that the community, once made, ought itself to judge of the national associations most conducive to its liberty and progress. Without liberty of this intensive character there could have been no vital national liberty; and Sam Houston, Patrick Henry, and Robert E. Lee are none the less great Americans because they represented only one cardinal principle of the national life. Self-government has its intrinsic antinomies as well as its harmonies.

Among men of letters Lowell is doubtless most typically American, though Curtis [4] must find an eligible place in the list. Lowell was self-conscious, though the truest greatness is not; he was a trifle too "smart," besides, and there is no "smartness" in great literature. But both the self-consciousness and the smartness must be admitted to be American; and Lowell was so versatile, so urbane, of so large a spirit, and so admirable in the scope of his sympathies that he must certainly go on the calendar.

There need be no fear that we shall be obliged to stop with Lowell in literature, or with any of the men who have been named in the field of achievement. We shall not in the future have to take one type of Americanism at a time. The frontier is gone: it has reached the Pacific. The country grows rapidly homogeneous. With the same pace it grows various, and multiform

---

[4] *George William Curtis* (1824–1892), an American writer and critic who was concerned with reform movements

in all its life. The man of the simple or local type cannot any longer deal in the great manner with any national problem. The great men of our future must be of the composite type of greatness: sound-hearted, hopeful, confident of the validity of liberty, tenacious of the deeper principles of American institutions, but with the old rashness

schooled and sobered, and instinct tempered by instruction. They must be wise with an adult, not with an adolescent wisdom. Some day we shall be of one mind, our ideals fixed, our purposes harmonized, our nationality complete and consentaneous: then will come our great literature and our greatest men.

The man who wrote this essay

WOODROW WILSON 1856–1924

Before becoming the twenty-eighth President of the United States, Woodrow Wilson spent most of his time as a distinguished member of the academic world. He was a professor of history and government at Princeton and later became the president of the University. After leaving Princeton, he was elected the governor of New Jersey and from here he moved on to the White House. During his first term in office he was instrumental in getting Congress to pass banking reforms as well as laws to control business monopolies. At the outbreak of World War I, Wilson advised the nation to remain neutral, but after German submarines began attacking United States ships, he instructed Congress to declare war on Germany.

When the war ended President Wilson worked diligently to develop the League of Nations, an international organization dedicated to the preservation of peace. The Senate, however, refused to recognize the League and the United States did not become a member. Wilson died a disappointed man not too long after he ended his second term in office.

Let's consider . . .

1. What were Wilson's reasons for saying that all great men born and bred in America were not necessarily great Americans? Explain why you agree or disagree.

2. What was the great task which, according to Wilson, bred the American spirit?

3. How did Wilson describe this American spirit?

4. What characteristics did Franklin possess which enabled Wilson to call him "a sort of multiple American"?

5. Contrast Wilson's descriptions of Washington and Clay.

6. What was Andrew Jackson's great contribution to the American spirit? How important is this quality today? Discuss.

7. Why did Wilson believe that Lincoln was the supreme American? Explain why you agree or disagree.

8. What concept did Robert E. Lee represent? Discuss the significance of this concept in present day American life.

9. What qualities must the great men in America's future possess?

10. Paraphrase Wilson's final sentence. Explain why you agree or disagree with the idea expressed in this concluding sentence.

The writer's craft . . .

1. Good style in writing is always appropriate to the subject matter and the intention of the writer. Analyze Woodrow Wilson's style in "A Calendar of Great Americans."

a. Describe the vocabulary in this essay. Did Wilson's choice of words add to or detract from your interest. Explain.

b. What tone did his fairly long sentences produce. Explain how this tone helped you to understand his attitude toward these great Americans.

c. Occasionally Wilson used imagery, such as, "He came into our national life like a cyclone from off the Western prairies." Find several other images. What did these figures of speech add to the style of essay?

d. Would you say that Wilson's style was appropriate to his subject matter and intention? Explain.

2. Follow Woodrow Wilson's technique of referring to specific men and women who embody the American spirit, and write your own "Calendar of Great Americans."

a. From your list of great Americans select the names of several men or women who exemplify America at its best. After each name write a brief statement explaining why you believe that person is rightfully called a great American.

b. Identify the similarities that exist among this group. Then write a paragraph in which you sum up the qualities that these great Americans possess.

c. You are now ready to write your "Calendar of Great Americans." You may wish to follow this pattern:

Introduction: A description of the qualities of great Americans

Body: Reference to specific Americans and an explanation of why each is considered great

Conclusion: A statement predicting the kind of great man America will need in the future

Knowing words . . .

At one point in his essay, Wilson described the American spirit by using a series of words which began with the prefix *un* meaning "not." He wrote, "It is *unpedantic, unprovincial, unspeculative, unfastidious* . . ."

1. Explain the meaning of each italicized word.

2. Are these accurate terms to describe the American spirit? Discuss.

3. Use each word in a sentence of your own.

4. Now write a sentence for each word, omitting the prefix.

This Hero Business

RICHARD E. BYRD

The "torrent of attention" heaped upon Commander Byrd pleased him,
but it also secretly worried him. He had a discovery to make, and what he
found out was almost as exciting as "the sensation of circling the Pole."

Before the "Chantier" had steamed many
miles toward home, I began to realize that
we had stirred up something by flying to
the Pole. First there were radios of congratulation and good wishes. Then radios
of inquiry. And finally, radios that literally
ordered me to do things I had never even
dreamed of doing, couldn't do even if I
wanted—such as to make a speech at three
different banquets, to be held in three different cities on one and the same night. I
felt rather stunned about it; but, of course,
greatly appreciative.

It was all more of a surprise than people could realize. To go back for a moment: When I broke my leg at Annapolis
I was only trying to best the other fellow.
When I crowded into aviation during the
war I was only satisfying my great desire
to fly and at the same time doing what any
patriotic American would do to help his
country. When I took charge of the navigational preparations of the Navy's trans-
atlantic flight in 1919, I believed I was con-
tributing to my service and to the art of
flying. I felt pretty much the same about
my Greenland work and during my preparations to fly to the North Pole.

Now I discovered that the success of our
flight from Spitzbergen [1] touched some re-
sponsive public chord which loosed a torrent of attention upon me and my expedi-

tion. I was much pleased, of course. But I
was also astonished, and secretly worried.
My fear was that personal fame might
overlay the good I had hoped to do for
aviation.

I wondered exactly what it all meant.
What I ultimately found out about being
a hero gave me almost as much of a kick
as did the sensation of circling the Pole.

We arrived at New York on the morning of June 22, 1926. We were met by
the mayor's official tug, the "Macom," on
board which were several official welcom-
ing committees, a delegation of senators
and representatives from Congress, a regi-
ment of newspaper reporters, and enough
photographers to man a battleship.

For half an hour I was tossed about like
a leaf in a storm. Then a friend cornered
me. I could see he was laboring under
high tension. He spoke feverishly:

"We arrive at the Battery at noon. You
will be presented with a medal and the
keys to the city at twelve-fifteen. You will
make two speeches in reply. At lunch you
will make another speech. At four-thirty-
two we leave for Washington. On arrival
you will be met by a committee of welcome. Twenty minutes later President
Coolidge will present you with a gold
medal. You will make a speech—"

"But I'm not a speechmaker," I protested.

My friend seemed to grind his teeth.
"Makes not the slightest difference," he

---

[1] *Spitzbergen,* a group of islands in the Arctic
Ocean

snapped. "You are now a national hero. You—"

I felt myself whirled bodily about. "Look up, Commander. Stick an eye on that airplane up there," yelled some one.

Involuntarily I glanced skyward. Twenty cameras clicked.

A heavy man jostled against me. "I want you to meet the president of the—" He didn't finish. I found myself grasping the hand of an important-looking individual.

"You are a national hero," he declared. "I am pleased—"

"Be sure you speak of leaving this port in the mayor's speech," broke a hoarse whisper in one ear. My feverish friend again.

Before I could answer, the broad-shouldered chairman of the reception committee elbowed his way in.

"Excuse me, Commander, but these fellows want a picture of you and your mother." Ten more cameras infiltrated through the crowd. I began to feel like a promising halfback who has to carry the ball at every down. Things began to be going more rapidly. Between the erupting fireboats, the airplanes, and the yacht escorts I felt a stiff neck coming on. The whistles were deafening.

All of this was entirely unexpected. I felt bewildered. But most grateful that the nation should do all this for us. Of course, I didn't take it all to myself. Far from it. There was Bennett by my side who deserved equally with me and perhaps more. Then there were our half-hundred shipmates who had unselfishly put every ounce of their strength and energy into the job. Then my thought dwelt on the dozen or so other men who had formed necessary links in our success.

The scene at the Battery resembled a riot. A parade was formed. As we passed up Broadway the air grew thick with a blizzard of paper streamers and confetti. The sidewalks were packed with people. Traffic stopped.

The City Hall was surrounded by a dense mass of humanity. A cordon of mounted police kept open just enough space to let our party pass. We wound up into the ceremonial chambers. The auditorium was jammed to its doors. The oratory began. . . .

And so on all that day, ending with President Coolidge's presentation in Washington that night. And all the next day. And the next, and the next. The high point came in Richmond, Virginia, my native state. Thousands turned out the night we arrived. There were glare-lights, speeches, and brass bands; a swirling friendly multitude.

What did it mean? I asked myself the question; but could find no answer. I asked my friends. But all they would reply was the same refrain in one form or another, "Don't you know you are a national hero now?"

Of course I realized that an adventure like our polar flight aroused great public interest. I knew before I left that there would be a certain amount of risk in crossing the polar ice, just as there is in any flight over an unknown terrain. I had a notion that such a stunt is great stuff for the publicity people.

But my idea of a national hero was somebody like George Washington or John J. Pershing. They had held the safety of our country in their hands. They had suffered the agony of long campaigns. They had led armies to victory against a public enemy.

We hadn't done anything so valiant.

"But what is a national hero, and why?" I asked a newspaper friend of mine.

"Oh, some one who's worth two columns and a front-page streamer, fireboats, and a basket of medals," came the cynical reply.

But I wasn't satisfied; not when I thought of the thousands of American citizens who had grasped my hand since my return; and of the tens of thousands of jubilant letters and telegrams that had reached me.

No, there was something more, something deeper.

The first inkling of the great discovery came in Washington just before I faced the President and a large audience of distinguished diplomats. I had never spoken before so august an assemblage. To rehearse some of the thoughts that crowded my mind, I managed to sneak away for a few moments in the stage wings of the giant auditorium where the ceremony was being held. I stood in a little bare alcove glancing over my notes. Suddenly a door behind me opened, then softly closed. I turned. Facing me stood a little white-haired lady in black bonnet and gown. Despite the age in her face, her eyes were brown and bright. They looked into mine unblinking.

"You are Commander Byrd?" she asked.

"Yes, madam."

She came a step forward in a sudden wistful eagerness. "And you reached the North Pole?"

"There seems to be no doubt of it."

Her lips parted as if to speak again. But before she could utter a word an abrupt change came over her. She gave a quick sigh. Her mouth trembled. She thrust out one hand as if to touch me. Her eyes dimmed and filled. Then she cried out:

"Oh, I'm so glad!" Before I could stop her she was gone.

I heard a step behind me. "All right, Byrd." The same irritating whiplash of necessity that fame brings. "The President is arriving. You will have to go on the stage at once."

I went on the stage. But the mystery of the little lady in black clung to me. I espied her in the audience. I managed to inquire about her during a lull in the ponderous proceedings of the evening.

"Poor thing," whispered my informant. "She's had a tough break in life. Lost her husband twenty years ago. Brought up two fine boys on what she could make herself. Lost both of them in the World War. Now she's all alone."

In a flash of understanding I knew something of the answer to my question: What is a national hero?

I was a hero to that sad little mother, but not in a way the word is usually used. No doubt she admired us for having succeeded. Probably the story of it all gave her daily newspaper a fresh flavor. Possibly she speculated over what it felt like to fly. But those weren't the things that made her seek me out and face me firsthand with her gladness.

What that mother saw in me was the living memory of her husband and sons. They had been splendid men. I later learned that they had been adventurous and so were the kind who would have liked to have flown to the North Pole. They were fine, keen, courageous men. And if they were all that to the passing acquaintance who retailed their virtues to me, what demigods must they have been to that little white-haired lady.

To her I was the living flesh she so longed to touch. I, she knew, was son and husband. Now she would sit out there among a great throng and listen while the President of the United States extolled Bennett and me, even as she might have sat and listened had Fate been equally generous to her.

It may sound incredible, but in that moment I got the philosophy of the thing. I had been human in my home-coming. The grand public welcome had moved me, though I had felt humble and more or less undeserving of such recognition. I had had to pinch myself every now and then to see if it were all true. I had felt like a man who had unexpectedly reached a mountaintop and finds a gorgeous panorama spread before his eyes. I had wanted to throw my hat in the air and shout, "Gosh, but this is great!"

Now, in a trice, another man's mother had wiped away my smug acceptance of unexpected fame.

My memory sprang back to Annapolis days. I recalled the first time I marched down the town street as color bearer. The

band was playing. As I passed, men uncovered, ladies applauded, children waved
their hands. I was stirred by this show of
admiration. Pride filled me. I seemed
walking on the air. I felt brave, superior,
triumphant. Then with a thump, came
the truth. People weren't saluting and
cheering me. They were saluting the Stars
and Stripes which I carried.

Exactly that was happening now. The
cheers and the handclasps, the waving hats
and flags, the music and the speeches,
weren't really meant for me any more now
than that boyhood morning in Annapolis
when I marched at the head of the procession holding aloft the flag of my country.
The banner I carried now wasn't so visible,
nor easily painted. It didn't in its symbolism depict the stormy history of a people.
It never would stir a nation to righteous indignation against an invader. It couldn't
be nailed to the mast of a sinking ship.

No, my banner was none of these. In
our success people saw success that might
have been their own. In Bennett and me
mothers saw their sons, wives their husbands, sisters their brothers. In us, men
saw what they too might have done had
they had the chance. In us, youth saw
ambition realized.

In us America for the moment drama-
tized that superb world-conquering fire
which is American spirit. For the moment
we seemed to have caught up the banner
of American progress. For the moment we
appeared to typify to them the spirit of
America.

It was great to think that, even for these
precious moments, we were destined to
carry the banner.

Was I proud? Of course. But humble,
grateful. There were a half-hundred members of our expedition who deserved
equally with me to carry that banner.

Now that my eyes were opened I began
to look about for more manifestations of
this discovery of mine. I went to the Middle West to lecture. In a small town off
the beaten track I stopped for a one-night

stay. A leading citizen drove me about just
before sunset.

"We are very proud of our parkways,"
he said. "They are all built by personal
contribution. Those who can't give money
contribute their services. By the way, the
engineer of our steamroller told me the
other day he hoped I'd introduce him to
you when you came here."

"Why not see him now?" I suggested.
The thought of the people building their
home town's boulevards by pure community spirit appealed to my imagination.

We drove to a frame bungalow near the
edge of the town. Two urchins hung on
the gates of an untidy yard. A tired-looking
woman with a kindly smile met us at the
door. Two more urchins clung to her skirt.

"Come right in. Jim's just back from
the factory. He'll be out soon's he's
changed his shirt."

Jim came in wiping his hands. He was
tall and lean. His whole face lit up when
his townsman introduced me.

"Commander Byrd speaks at eight," said
my escort. "Don't forget." Jim nodded, his
eyes fixed on my face. His wife must have
felt the strain of the situation; her husband's sudden inarticulate silence.

She made a few irrelevant remarks, then
suddenly turned to him: "Jim, tell Commander Byrd about your invention."

Jim flushed. He began to talk, haltingly
at first, about a scheme for vertical flight,
a sort of helicopter. He had a small workshop out in the woodshed. He was building a model of his device.

"You ought to get some one to back you,"
I told him. "If the idea is practicable the
right sort of engineering assistance will put
it through in no time."

"But that isn't it." Jim put up his hands
as if to shape the thought he could not accurately convey in words.

His wife broke in with, "I told him that
very thing."

Jim's fingers groped. He said:
"It isn't a question of money. It's somebody to look ahead and see what we're com-

ing to." The words were tumbling out now. "All they think of is profits. One man turned me down because he said it wouldn't pay dividends this year.

"Another said he'd pay me a big lump sum if I'd give him what I'd worked out so far. They're both wrong.

"I want to move slowly. The Wrights did when they started. They could have sold out early, to an amusement company. We wouldn't have been flying today if they had."

The wife was angry now. "Don't go on like that," she said.

But Jim could not be stopped. I didn't want to stop him. He poured out his whole story, a lifetime of struggle and hard work. Yet he could not sacrifice his idea for quick gain.

We had to break away before he finished. As we drove back my friend the leading citizen said: "I have known him for years. That is the first time he has ever loosened up. You see what it is, of course. He thinks you would do the same as he is doing if you were in his boots. I believe your visit helped him."

That gave me my second cue to appreciation of my discovery, and again I felt humble and grateful. Listening became one of the best things I did. What a paradox it was too! I had always looked on the returned explorer as a sort of traveling oracle. True, people seemed to like my films of the flight and politely followed my yarn of how we reached the Pole and returned. There were speeches of introduction before hand, and handshaking afterward. But these were routine. The interesting moments I looked forward to were when some one got me off in a corner and told his story.

These stories were superior to mine. Mine was hemmed in by realities like time and distance, whereas the others were usually bounded only by the elastic horizon of human imagination.

It would take a dozen thick volumes to record all my experiences that confirm that discovery I had made in Washington. My mail alone in the months since my return contains a thousand stories of human happiness, hope, and heartbreak.

"Why don't you get out a form letter thanking these people who write you?" suggested an efficient friend of mine.

Coincidence played into my hands. I handed him two letters I had just opened. "Read these and you will understand."

He read aloud:

Dear Captain Byrd: You never heard of me, and will probably never see me. I keep house for my two brothers. Our mother and father are dead. It may sound silly to tell you such things, but all last winter we have had a hard time. One of my brothers lost his job. The other had an abscess on his back and couldn't work for several months. Then we began reading about your plans and later about your fine trip to the North Pole. I have to work so much there is no chance to get about. We have lived your adventures with you. It has been fun and I want to thank you and wish you luck on your next flight.

Then he read the other letter which was typical of thousands I had received from boys and girls:

My dear Commander: I like you. I like your trip to the North Pole. I have made a model of the "Josephine Ford." [2] Will you please put your name on a piece of paper so that I can paste it on my little airplane. I hope you get across the Atlantic all right. I know you will. I will be reading about you.

My friend tossed the letters back. "Sounds like testimonials for a patent medicine," he said skeptically.

"It might," said I, "if there were only these two. But there are hundreds. Many talk like that when I meet them. The adventures have a real meaning to many people and to all the great youngsters."

"Well you're a national hero, aren't you? Isn't that what does it?"

---

[2] *"Josephine Ford,"* plane in which Byrd first flew over the North Pole

I looked him in the eye. "I'm really only carrying the banner for a little while," said I.

He looked at me as if I had suddenly lost my mind. "The what?"

A tumult in the street below our window put an end to our talk. We looked out. I knew what was happening.

In the sunshine flags twinkled. Black ribbons of humanity lined the avenue. At upper windows were crowding faces. Extra traffic men pranced to and fro. Long gay streamers of confetti floated down from the skyscrapers. A band flashed into view. The quick march it played was the music of victory. Uniformed ranks swung rhythmically behind the band. Then came a column of automobiles.

In the leading car, framed with flowers, stood a sturdy youthful figure, arms outstretched to the cheering multitude. It was Gertrude Ederle.[3]

I leaned far out. I wanted to shout a message, to deliver something I had been holding.

I wanted to shout: "Here is the banner!" and cast that invisible something into the outstretched hands of the girl in the leading car.

But I did not need to. The lusty throats of ten thousand Americans were shouting my message. And the banner was already in the hands of its next fortunate bearer.

That's what this hero business means.

[3] *Gertrude Ederle,* the first woman to swim the English Channel

---

The man who wrote this selection

RICHARD E. BYRD   1888–

Like many national figures, Richard E. Byrd has devoted years of his life to serving his country. Trained at the United States Naval Academy, he began his career with the Navy, but after a short period of service, he was released because of a physical injury. He returned to the Navy after the outbreak of World War I, finished his training at Pensacola as a pilot, and commanded two naval bases in Canada throughout the war. In 1925 he headed the naval unit which took part in an expedition to Greenland. This training in Arctic survival soon led to other opportunities to visit the Polar regions. In 1926 he flew over the North Pole; in 1928 he established Little America, his base in Antarctica.

Admiral Byrd has made many expeditions to the North and South Poles since his first explorations, and he is now considered the major authority on life in polar regions. Like another of America's great flying heroes, Charles Lindbergh, Admiral Byrd is remarkably modest. Yet he has won a great number of citations and medals and received the highest military recognition for his services, the Congressional Medal of Honor. In *Skyward,* the book from which this selection was taken, and in many other exciting and well-written books, he has described his adventures.

Let's consider . . .

1. When Commander Byrd started home from the North Pole, he never expected his homecoming to be such a stunning experience. Think over his progress through New York and on to Washington. What were the steps in his gradual realization that he was a national hero? Why had none of his earlier experiences prepared him for this tremendous welcome?

2. Which features of the first day of his homecoming do you feel were most bewildering? Which would you consider most trying? Which would you consider most heartwarming?

3. All through this account you were given evidence of Byrd's humility and

appreciation of others. What examples of these characteristics impressed you most?

4. Byrd knew he was a "national hero," but when he asked, "What does it mean?" no one could give him a satisfactory answer. What experience gave him his first real inkling of the meaning?

5. From this experience, Byrd formed a concept of the hero in America. Tell as clearly and briefly as you can what that concept was. What did his "invisible banner" symbolize?

6. Listening became one of the best things Byrd did. What did he add to his *own* definition of a national hero after hearing the story of the engineer in the midwestern town?

7. Through all the events honoring him as a hero-returned-home, Byrd showed very *human* characteristics. Choose three incidents from this selection which impressed you because they revealed Byrd as a warm, natural person. Tell how they made you feel toward him.

8. Why didn't Byrd send form letters thanking the people who wrote to him?

9. Byrd closed this autobiographical account by describing the welcome given to another "national hero." Why is this a fitting close for "This Hero Business"?

The writer's craft . . .

Whenever an author tells the story of his own life, he is writing an **autobiography.** This selection told only part of that story, but it communicated the sincerity and modesty of a true hero.

A good piece of writing is always carefully planned so that each part is related to the whole. These various parts must then move in an ordered sequence, each adding something essential to what has gone before. "This Hero Business" may be divided into three general parts: (1) Byrd's discovery that he had become a hero, (2) his talks with people who helped him understand why he had become a hero, and

(3) his new understanding of the meaning of heroes. Each of these parts contributed to Byrd's analysis of heroes.

In each of these parts Byrd used concrete incidents. Find as many of these as you can. Explain why they added to your reading enjoyment.

Using "This Hero Business" as a model, re-tell an experience in which you learned something you hadn't known before. Begin with a generalization. Add several first-hand incidents which illuminate your generalization. Then explain what you learned from your experience. Don't forget that Byrd's use of actual dialogue heightened the dramatic effect of his writing. Be sure to include some dialogue in your composition.

Knowing words . . .

A. If you are not sure of the meaning of the italicized words in the following sentences, check with your dictionary. Then answer the questions in part B.

1. A *cordon* of mounted police kept open just enough space to let our party pass.

2. Now she would sit out there among a great throng and listen while the President of the United States *extolled* Bennett and me . . .

3. Now that my eyes were opened I began to look about for more *manifestations* of this discovery of mine.

4. What a *paradox* it was too!

B.1. Why was a *cordon* of mounted police needed at the City Hall? What function did it serve?

2. In what words do you think the President of the United States might have *extolled* Commander Byrd and Bennett?

3. Tell about one other *manifestation* of Commander Byrd's discovery that he and Bennett "appeared to typify . . . the spirit of America."

4. Why was it a *paradox* that listening became one of the best things Byrd did?

Walt Whitman

MARK VAN DOREN

"No man ever loved his land at closer range, or ever said so more eloquently."

A great poet once loved America with such passion that the whole of it was constantly before his eyes. And what he could not see of it he heard; and what he could not hear of it he touched. Walt Whitman's delight in his country was so enormous and so simple that he could not bear the thought of its absence from him. This is why his poems are so full of the names of things: of rivers, of states, of cities and tools and occupations. He is always itemizing his love, calling it by its myriad titles, bringing it home to his senses so that it shall not escape him and grow cool. No man ever loved his land at closer range, or ever said so more eloquently.

All of it was about him all the time. He possessed in supreme degree the power of pausing and listening to the great life beyond oneself. At this moment, now, his poems seem to say, while I, Walt Whitman, sit in my Brooklyn boardinghouse or stand at the prow of a ferry which is puffing toward Manhattan, a woodsman in Michigan is lifting his ax; an engineer along the Mohawk is peering at his gauges; a slave in the rice fields is bending over his sack; clerks are hurrying to their offices in St. Louis; an officer is barking commands at his soldiers on the Indian frontier; Indians are slipping their fishing canoes into the northwestern waters; a man is bringing meat home in brown paper; a baby is going to sleep in its mother's arms; lovers

are strolling; an old woman is dying in an Allegheny cabin; factories are smoking, whistles are getting ready to blow, the rivers are rushing through their valleys, the fish are quiet in their pools, an eagle is measuring the Rocky Mountains with its wing, and the philosopher is frowning at his desk. Walt Whitman himself was by trade a newspaperman in Brooklyn and New York, nor was he particularly successful at his trade. But his calling was wider. It was the breathing and beautiful earth, whose manifold realities he slowly fashioned into an original kind of poetry to celebrate. *Leaves of Grass* in its various editions, from the first in 1855 to the last which he saw through the press in 1891–1892, is the testament of his love; and it is a book through which Americans have continued to feel, hear, see, touch, and smell their country, and to find it good.

Leaves of Grass enriches our landscape and deepens its tone. In a sense it has created the world in which Americans are aware of being alive. And this world is primarily human. Sensitive as Whitman was to the genius of place, he was still more sensitive to the species of man. The bodies of young men bathing, the runner leaning forward, the miner with his sooty cap, the ox tamer, the tiller of tobacco fields, the bookkeeper, the oarsman, the statesman—all these and more he must keep with him as the companions of his thought. It is almost as if he were jealous of their absence, as if he felt a fierce determination to hold them here. They literally intoxicate him, as the land does, with their nearness and yet their strangeness. For the things and persons Whitman describes are fabulous at the same time that they are familiar. This is America. It is, however, an extraordinary America, a land of superdimensions, a place *Leaves of Grass* brings us back to after an ideal journey elsewhere. It is the same, but better. It is our own, and more. It is perfectly itself.

But the Civil War came to Whitman's America, and it was his "mighty privilege" to live through that terrible time. Terrible as the experience was to him, he did not miss its grandeur. "In my judgment," he wrote after it was over, in the autobiographical work called *Specimen Days*, "it will remain as the most encouraging spectacle in any age, old or new, to political progress and democracy. . . . It is the best

lesson of the century." The awakening of the general will, the prosecution of a huge social task, and then the peaceful surrender of animosities once they could serve no further purpose: these things moved him not only to his best poems, culminating in 1865 with his hymn for Lincoln, "When Lilacs Last in the Door-Yard Bloom'd," but to his best efforts as a man.

Whitman's part in the Civil War was not as soldier but as nurse. Hearing in 1862 that his brother George had been wounded in Virginia, he hastened there from Brooklyn and found him at Falmouth, where for the first time he saw great numbers of maimed men in the field. He had written newspaper articles about a New York hospital, but this was different and it was worse. The sight determined the rest of his life. He went as soon as he could to Washington and began the hospital rounds which kept him busy until 1865 and which, he believed, cost him his health; for he attributed his later paralysis to infection from the fever and gangrene he was never far away from through three years. His *Memoranda* dealing with these days spare the reader no ghastly detail of pain and death, nor did Whitman ever minimize the horrors he witnessed. But the story is chiefly of one who went among the hurt and the dying with a cheerful voice and a friendly hand; who brought comfort also in the form of oranges, jellies, sweet cookies, books and magazines to read, pipes and tobacco, and above all paper on which letters could be written home. When the soldier was too weak to write, Whitman did it for him; or from a collection he had raised in the cities of New England he gave small sums of money to men whose dignity this would restore.

"During those three years in hospital, camp, or field," he writes, "I made over six hundred visits or tours, and went, as I estimate, counting all, among from eighty thousand to a hundred thousand of the wounded and sick. These visits varied from an hour or two to all day or night;

for with dear or critical cases I generally watched all night. . . . Those three years I consider the greatest privilege and satisfaction, and of course the most profound lesson, of my life." The Civil War, in other words, was not lost on the author of *Leaves of Grass*. If his bodily strength declined thereafter, his art gained in purity and strength; and though he continued to make America the subject of his poems, the emphasis changed. He described less and interpreted more. He ceased to accept everything at its present value; indeed, both in prose and in verse he underlined the limitations of postwar America. For it was now the ideal, or future, America that occupied his imagination.

And since he was rigorously ideal he could be unhesitatingly critical. His *Democratic Vistas* (1871) contains some of the most penetrating strictures [1] ever passed upon American morals and manners. He could speak thus because he had no doubt of his basic principle, and because he was that most valuable kind of democrat, the kind who insists at all times upon speaking the truth. Democracy is never served by those who flatter it. Its best lovers know its faults and ask in a firm voice that they be corrected. So with Whitman, whose later poems are far different from his first ones. They are mellower and wiser, and put less stress upon the uniqueness of America, not to say its isolation. The fu-

[1] *strictures,* negative criticisms

ture of the country includes for him now an intellectual and spiritual free trade with the rest of the world, both past and present: with the ripest ancient cultures, which once he had repudiated, and with the best that was being thought and said in contemporary Europe. Walt Whitman's love of America had become mature.

Early or late, however, his poems have a wonderful power to brighten as with dew the features of our land. Whether he is cataloguing facts or revealing their import, whether he is shouting loudly or singing well, he is seldom without this power, which no one has had in like degree. "Night of south winds! night of the large few stars!" "I am he that walks with the tender and growing night." "I loaf and invite my soul." "I am large—I contain multitudes." "Give me the splendid silent sun." "Affection shall solve the problems of Freedom yet; those who love each other shall become invincible." He could make such phrases as those, and they signify another power, another genius. Nor does the word "America" appear anywhere among them. For the final truth about Whitman is that he loved mankind even more than he loved America, the world even more than his continent. This is why his feeling for home can be so sure and strong. The world begins at home and comes around to it again. So with Walt Whitman, whose muse returned to her first love, America, without illusion and without loss.

The man who wrote this biography

MARK VAN DOREN 1894–

The Van Doren family supplied three literary figures in a single generation: Irita Taylor Van Doren, literary critic; Carl Van Doren, specialist in American prose; and Mark Van Doren, poet and critic.

Like his late brother, Mark Van Doren attended the University of Illinois and later

received his doctorate from Columbia where he has been teaching since 1920. However, he was always able to do more, and so he relieved his brother as literary editor of *The Nation*.

Mark Van Doren has written and edited many books. Some are poetry anthologies like *American Poets;* some are works of literary criticism like *John Dryden* and *Nathaniel Hawthorne*. Besides these works which are more or less professional studies, he has written several volumes of original verse. His *Collected Poems* was awarded a Pulitzer Prize in 1940—the same year his brother won the prize for the best biography.

Let's consider . . .

1. Mark Van Doren's enthusiasm for Whitman was almost as great as Whitman's enthusiasm for his country. Select one paragraph in which you think the author's enthusiasm is most apparent. Read it aloud and comment on the impression it makes on you.

2. Van Doren told you concretely how Whitman expressed his love for his native land in his early poems. What did the poet write about that showed how close he was to *all* of America?

3. Naturally, Whitman took part in the War Between the States. To him it was a "mighty privilege" to live through that terrible time. How did Whitman's part make him keenly aware of the horror of it?

4. How did his experiences in the war affect his feeling for his country?

5. Why do you think the war would naturally move Whitman "to his best poems" and "to his best efforts as a man"?

6. In what ways did his writing change after the war? What were some of the differences between his later work and *Leaves of Grass*?

7. As Whitman became more critical of America, he began to express very definite ideas about democracy. What were they?

8. What did his ideal for the future of America include? Has this ideal been realized in America today?

The writer's craft . . .

American writers have always served this country in times of crisis. During World War II, when the democratic way of life was facing a severe challenge, the United States Treasury Department asked twenty-eight writers to pay tribute to American heroes of the past. The group who sponsored this project believed that the faith and hope of the American people would be strengthened by knowing the eloquent stories of earlier patriots.

Mark Van Doren chose to write about Walt Whitman. In this essay he did not limit himself to an analysis of Whitman's poetry. Rather, he interpreted Whitman's genius as a poet in terms of his genius as a man. He found in Whitman's writing a testament of the poet's deep love for his country as well as his deep love for all men.

This tribute could best be described as a **critical essay:** a fairly short piece of writing in which the author presents a point of view about a person, idea, or work —singly or together.

1. Where in this essay did Van Doren illustrate Whitman's love for America?

2. Point out those passages which illustrated Whitman's love for all men.

3. What parts of this essay helped you better to understand American ideals?

Knowing words . . .

Mark Van Doren wrote that Whitman was "always itemizing his love, calling it by its *myriad* titles . . ."

The word myriad comes from the Greek word meaning "ten thousand." In ancient Greece, the number *ten thousand* was so great as to be almost unimaginable. Therefore, the Greeks used it to refer to *innumerable amounts*.

Even in their system of counting, ten thousand was a major point in the scale. Where we designate twenty thousand, thirty thousand, forty thousand—the Greeks would say, "two *ten thousands*," "three *ten thousands*," "four *ten thousands*."

The word *myriad*, as used in the English language, does not refer particularly to ten thousand but is used in a figurative manner to indicate a group of things too numerous to be counted.

Mr. Van Doren also wrote: "For the things and persons Whitman describes are *fabulous* at the same time that they are familiar." The word *fabulous* is too often

used incorrectly to describe anything that is out of the ordinary, as a "fabulous movie" or a "fabulous meal." Look up *fabulous* in the dictionary. Choose the definition or synonym which you feel comes closest to expressing Van Doren's meaning as he used the word.

One's-Self I Sing

One's-self I sing, a simple separate person,
Yet utter the word Democratic, the word En-Masse.

Of physiology from top to toe I sing,
Not physiognomy alone nor brain alone is worthy for the Muse,
   I say the Form complete is worthier far,
The Female equally with the Male I sing.

Of Life immense in passion, pulse, and power,
Cheerful, for freest action form'd under the laws divine,
The Modern Man I sing.

Walt Whitman

When I Heard the Learn'd Astronomer

When I heard the learn'd astonomer,
When the proofs, the figures, were ranged in columns before me,
When I was shown the charts and diagrams, to add, divide,
   and measure them,
When I sitting heard the astronomer where he lectured
   with much applause in the lecture-room,
How soon unaccountable I became tired and sick,
Till rising and gliding out I wander'd off by myself,
In the mystical moist night-air, and from time to time,
Look'd up in perfect silence at the stars.

Walt Whitman

Give Me the Splendid Silent Sun

WALT WHITMAN

Give me the splendid silent sun with all his beams full-dazzling,
Give me juicy autumnal fruit ripe and red from the orchard,
Give me a field where the unmow'd grass grows,
Give me an arbor, give me the trellis'd grape,
Give me fresh corn and wheat, give me serene-moving
    animals teaching content,
Give me nights perfectly quiet as on high plateaus west
    of the Mississippi, and I looking up at the stars,
Give me odorous at sunrise a garden of beautiful flowers
    where I can walk undisturb'd,
Give me for marriage a sweet-breath'd woman of whom
    I should never tire,
Give me a perfect child, give me away aside from the noise
    of the world a rural domestic life,
Give me to warble spontaneous songs recluse by myself,
    for my own ears only,
Give me solitude, give me Nature, give me again O Nature
    your primal sanities!

These demanding to have them, (tired with ceaseless
    excitement, and rack'd by the war-strife,)
These to procure incessantly asking, rising in cries from my heart,
While yet incessantly asking still I adhere to my city,
Day upon day and year upon year O city, walking your streets,
Where you hold me enchain'd a certain time refusing
    to give me up,
Yet giving to make me glutted, enrich'd of soul, you give me
    forever faces;
(O I see what I sought to escape, confronting, reversing my cries,
I see my own soul trampling down what it ask'd for.)

Keep your splendid silent sun,
Keep your woods O Nature, and the quiet places by the woods,
Keep your fields of clover and timothy, and your cornfields
    and orchards,
Keep the blossoming buckwheat fields where the Ninth-
    month bees hum;

Vasiliv

Give me faces and streets—give me these phantoms incessant
    and endless along the trottoirs![1]
Give me interminable eyes—give me women—give me
    comrades and lovers by the thousand!
Let me see new ones every day—let me hold new ones
    by the hand every day!
Give me such shows—give me the streets of Manhattan!
Give me Broadway, with the soldiers marching—give me
    the sound of the trumpets and drums!
(The soldiers in companies or regiments—some starting away,
    flush'd and reckless,
Some, their time up, returning with thinn'd ranks, young,
    yet very old, worn, marching, noticing nothing;)
Give me the shores and wharves heavy-fringed with black ships!
O such for me! O an intense life, full to repletion and varied!
The life of the theatre, bar-room, huge hotel, for me!
The saloon of the steamer! the crowded excursion for me!
    the torchlight procession!
The dense brigade bound for the war, with high piled
    military wagons following;
People, endless, streaming, with strong voices, passions, pageants,
Manhattan streets with their powerful throbs, with beating drums
    as now,
The endless and noisy chorus, the rustle and clank of muskets,
    (even the sight of the wounded,)
Manhattan crowds, with their turbulent musical chorus!
Manhattan faces and eyes forever for me.

[1] *trottoirs,* sidewalks [*French*]

The poet's art . . .

Whitman was the poet of the commonplace, of the average man, of the beauty and the ugliness of life. Because he presented life as he saw it, he was one of America's early **realists.** He excluded nothing in his scope which the sun does not exclude, and he wrote of all things with tremendous exuberance and intensity of spirit. It was this vitality of spirit which permeated his sweeping lines and made him a pioneer in the free-verse movement. It was as if he were freeing poetry of the old shackles of form and speaking out in bold rhythms about common things with a new and ecstatic sense of democracy. "The commonplace I sing," he wrote, but he wrote also of "The splendid silent sun," "A noiseless patient spider," "When lilacs last in the dooryard bloomed," and "the song of the hermit thrush and the tallying song of my soul." His influence on later American—and English—poets can scarcely be estimated.

1. This poem reflected two loves of the poet's heart: his love of Nature and solitude, contrasted with his stronger love for the "faces and streets" of the city. His enthusiasm for all phases of Nature was brought out through sense-images, close at hand and immediate. Mention the gifts of nature which appealed to the poet through his senses: sight, hearing, taste, smell. Perhaps you can even find one or two which appealed to the sense of touch.

2. With all his impulse for quiet and solitude, Whitman felt "enchained" by the city and "enriched of soul." What did Manhattan (one of the boroughs of New York City) offer him that he could not resist? Select the features for which you feel he showed the greatest enthusiasm.

3. In one word, tell what chained him to the city.

4. Read aloud six lines (not consecutive) where you feel that Whitman's exuberant spirit was responsible for the broad sweep of the rhythm.

5. Select two details which earlier poets might have considered too common for poetry.

Mary Lou Wingate

STEPHEN VINCENT BENÉT

Sometimes the story of one person is the story of many people. It may also be the story of a time and a place. Mary Lou Wingate's story speaks for all Southern women who with "tiny hands . . . made courage from terror" during a trying period in American history.

There were three stout pillars that held up all
The weight and tradition of Wingate Hall.
One was Cudjo and one was you
And the third was the mistress, Mary Lou.
Mary Lou Wingate, as slightly made
And as hard to break as a rapier-blade.
Bristol's daughter and Wingate's bride,
Never well since the last child died
But staring at pain with courteous eyes.
When the pain outwits it, the body dies,
Meanwhile the body bears the pain.
She loved her hands and they made her vain,
The tiny hands of her generation
That gathered the reins of the whole plantation;
The velvet sheathing the steel demurely
In the trained, light grip that holds so surely.

She was at work by candlelight,
She was at work in the dead of the night,
Smoothing out troubles and healing schisms
And doctoring phthisics and rheumatisms,
Guiding the cooking and watching the baking,
The sewing, the soap-and-candle-making,
The brewing, the darning, the lady-daughters,
The births and deaths in the negro-quarters,
Seeing that Suke had some new, strong shoes
And Joe got a week in the calaboose,
While Dicey's Jacob escaped a whipping
And the jellybag dripped with its proper dripping,
And the shirts and estrangements were neatly mended,
And all of the tasks that never ended.

Her manner was gracious but hardly fervent
And she seldom raised her voice to a servant.
She was often mistaken, not often blind,
And she knew the whole duty of womankind,
To take the burden and have the power
And seem like the well-protected flower,
To manage a dozen industries
With a casual gesture in scraps of ease,
To hate the sin and to love the sinner
And to see that the gentlemen got their dinner
Ready and plenty and piping-hot
Whether you wanted to eat or not.
And always, always, to have the charm
That makes the gentlemen take your arm
But never the bright, unseemly spell
That makes strange gentlemen love too well,
Once you were married and settled down
With a suitable gentleman of your own.
And when that happened, and you had bred
The requisite children, living and dead,
To pity the fool and comfort the weak
And always let the gentlemen speak,
To succor your love from deep-struck roots
When gentlemen went to bed in their boots,
And manage a gentleman's whole plantation
In the manner befitting your female station.

This was the creed that her mother taught her
And the creed that she taught to every daughter.
She knew her Bible—and how to flirt
With a swansdown fan and a brocade skirt.
For she trusted in God but she liked formalities
And the world and Heaven were both realities.
—In Heaven, of course, we should all be equal,
But, until we came to that golden sequel,
Gentility must keep to gentility
Where God and breeding had made things stable,
While the rest of the cosmos deserved civility
But dined in its boots at the second-table.

This view may be reckoned a trifle narrow,
But it had the driving force of an arrow,
And it helped Mary Lou to stand up straight,
For she was gentle, but she could hate
And she hated the North with the hate of Jael [1]

---

[1] *Jael,* Biblical heroine who slew the enemy of her
people by means of a tent nail

When the dry hot hands went seeking the nail,
The terrible hate of women's ire,
The smoky, the long-consuming fire.
The Yankees were devils, and she could pray,
For devils, no doubt, upon Judgment Day,
But now in the world, she would hate them still
And send the gentlemen out to kill.

The gentlemen killed and the gentlemen died,
But she was the South's incarnate pride
That mended the broken gentlemen
And sent them out to the war again,
That kept the house with the men away
And baked the bricks where there was no clay,
Made courage from terror and bread from bran
And propped the South on a swansdown fan
Through four long years of ruin and stress,
The pride—and the deadly bitterness.

The man who wrote this poem

STEPHEN VINCENT BENÉT 1898–1943

Like his elder sister and brother, Laura and William Rose Benét, Stephen Vincent became a poet. After receiving his master's degree from Yale, Benét went to Paris to study and write.

He continued writing poems, but he soon found that he had to write stories and novels in order to earn his living. Although he was primarily a poet, he wrote some of the best modern American short stories. As in his poems, he turned to American history and folklore for his subject matter. He wrote such well-known stories as "The Devil and Daniel Webster" and "Johnny Pye and the Fool-Killer."

A Guggenheim fellowship enabled Benét to finish his most ambitious poem, *John Brown's Body,* an American epic about the War Between the States, which was awarded a Pulitzer Prize in 1929. Benét left unfinished another American epic about the settling of the West. This was published after his death as *Western Star.*

The poet's art . . .

1. The first stanza of this poem gave a *general* picture of Mary Lou Wingate and an idea of her character. A **stanza** is a group of lines that follow a pattern and mark a division in the poem. Describe the picture in the first stanza.

2. From her mother Mary Lou learned how to manage "her gentlemen" and her plantation. How did she do it? How did she keep the men good-natured?

3. Mary Lou recommended a good practice which any girl might follow "once [she was] married and settled down." What was it?

4. Mary Lou was intriguing, partly because she was surprising and full of contrasts. What were some of the contrasts? Read a few of the lines which give them.

5. Many of the Southern ladies were aristocrats: members of a privileged upper class. How did Mary Lou's attitudes and opinions prove she was an aristocrat?

6. How did she feel toward the North?

7. The "velvet" and "steel" in Mary Lou Wingate "propped the South" during four years of war. How was this done?

Ode

HENRY TIMROD

Sung at the occasion of decorating the graves of the Confederate dead, at
Magnolia Cemetery, Charleston, S. C., 1867

Sleep sweetly in your humble graves,
  Sleep, martyrs of a fallen cause;
Though yet no marble column craves
  The pilgrim here to pause.

In seeds of laurel in the earth
  The blossom of your fame is blown,
And somewhere, waiting for its birth,
  The shaft is in the stone!

Meanwhile, behalf the tardy years
  Which keep in trust your storied [1] tombs,
Behold! your sisters bring their tears,
  And these memorial blooms.

Small tributes! but your shades will smile
  More proudly on these wreaths today,
Than when some cannon-molded pile
  Shall overlook this bay.

Stoop, angels, hither from the skies!
  There is no holier spot of ground
Than where defeated valor lies,
  By mourning beauty crowned!

---

[1] *storied,* recorded in stories

The man who wrote this poem

HENRY TIMROD   1828–1867

When Henry Timrod was born in Charleston, South Carolina, that city was the center of Southern culture. He was educated at one of the best schools in the city and later studied at the University of Georgia until his poor health and his family's lack of funds forced him to leave.

Although Timrod began to have his poetry published when he was twenty years old, it wasn't until the War Between the States that he was first widely recognized. The war helped bring out the best of Timrod's talent, and his war poems were extremely popular throughout the Confederacy. Some of his best were written to celebrate special occasions and events.

When South Carolina was invaded by the Northern Army, Timrod lost all of his possessions. After the war he found it almost impossible to get steady work. His death, caused by tuberculosis, was hastened by lack of food.

The poet's art . . .

In 1868, General Logan established the practice of decorating the graves of *all* soldiers who had died in the War Between the States. Even before that, the South was decorating the graves of Confederate soldiers in the spring.

This ode, sung before Charleston had had time to recover from the devastation of war, shows the high regard in which "defeated valor" was held, even though no "shaft" as yet craved "the pilgrim here to pause." Later a memorial was erected.

1. The real emotion expressed in the ode is emphasized by the strong beat of the verse. Read several lines aloud and show which syllables receive the heavy stress. Where did the poet break the rhythm for dramatic effect? What rhyme scheme did he use?

2. Which stanza do you think expresses the greatest sadness?

3. The **ode** always deals with a serious theme and, therefore, is a dignified, hymn-like poem written to honor or commemorate someone or something worthy of esteem. As you read the ode aloud, pick out the stanza which you feel is most dignified in sound and thought.

Sonnet

Most men know love but as a part of life;
They hide it in some corner of the breast,
Even from themselves; and only when they rest
In the brief pauses of that daily strife,
Wherewith the world might else be not so rife,
They draw it forth (as one draws forth a toy
To soothe some ardent, kiss-exacting boy)
And hold it up to sister, child, or wife.

Ah me! why may not love and life be one?
Why walk we thus alone, when by our side,
Love, like a visible God, might be our guide?
How would the marts grow noble! and the street,
Worn like a dungeon-floor by weary feet,
Seem then a golden court-way of the Sun!

Henry Timrod

Lee Says Farewell to a Brave Army

PAUL M. ANGLE

Both Robert E. Lee and Abraham Lincoln lamented the human suffering brought about by the War Between the States. It was their compassion for the least of their brothers which has made Americans particularly proud of these two men.

For the first time in four years the guns were silent. Along the line of the Army of Northern Virginia gaunt veterans lounged beside stacked arms and unshotted cannon; cavalry horses, their ribs pitifully plain, munched the spring grass. It was good to know that there would be no more killing, but an army takes no pleasure in defeat. Still, when the commanding general came in sight, riding slowly to his own lines from the farmhouse where he had just signed articles of surrender, the troops instinc-tively shouted their welcome. Then, sud-denly realizing that the end had come, they fell silent. Hats came off, and tears rolled down weather-beaten faces. Men in tat-tered uniforms pressed forward to take Lee's hand, or even to touch the white horse he had ridden through victory and defeat. Controlling himself, the General spoke a few words.

"Men, we have fought through the war together; I have done my best for you; my heart is too full to say more."

The next day he issued his last order.

Lee's Farewell to the Army of Northern Virginia
April 10, 1865

After four years of arduous service, marked by unsurpassed courage and for-titude, the Army of Northern Virginia has been compelled to yield to overwhelming numbers and resources. I need not tell the survivors of so many hard-fought battles, who have remained steadfast to the last, that I have consented to this result from no distrust of them; but, feeling that valor and devotion could accomplish nothing that could compensate for the loss that would have attended the continuation of the con-test, I have determined to avoid the use-less sacrifice of those whose past services have endeared them to their countrymen. By the terms of the agreement, officers and men can return to their homes and remain there until exchanged. You will take with you the satisfaction that proceeds from the consciousness of duty faithfully performed;

and I earnestly pray that a merciful God will extend to you His blessing and protection. With an increasing admiration of your constancy and devotion to your country, and a grateful remembrance of your kind and generous consideration of myself, I bid you an affectionate farewell.

Let's consider . . .

1. Paul Angle's introduction to "Lee's Farewell" is very simple, and yet he makes you feel the extreme **pathos** of the scene: the power which it had to evoke a feeling of pity or sympathetic sadness. Pick out the words and phrases which aroused your sympathy. Note especially such phrases as "unshotted cannon" and "ribs pitifully plain." Explain what they mean to you and how they help you recreate that tragic morning.

2. What signs of affection did the troops show their commander?

3. Lee had just come from the farmhouse where he had signed articles of surrender. He praised the army's "courage and fortitude" and said he had no "distrust" of his men. Why, then, did he surrender?

4. "Lee's Farewell" was a very *moving* statement, and yet it lacked some of the dramatic quality of Lincoln's Gettysburg Address. As you compare the two documents, see if you can explain what qualities made each of them memorable.

Lincoln Dedicates a People

PAUL M. ANGLE

The invitation came so tardily that it was almost a slight. The commission which had undertaken to establish a cemetery for the burial of those who had died at Gettysburg had been planning dedicatory ceremonies for weeks before its members asked the President to speak. Even then they invited him only to set apart the grounds by "a few appropriate remarks" after Edward Everett, orator of the day, had concluded.

If Lincoln felt any resentment at the commission's lack of consideration, characteristically he kept his feeling to himself. Fully aware of the solemnity of the occasion, he made his preparations well in advance. At least ten days before November 19, the date finally settled upon for the dedication, he had committed to paper what he intended to say. Nor would he take any chance on arriving late. When the Secretary of War proposed that the presidential party travel from Washington to Gettysburg on the day of the ceremonies, Lincoln interposed a veto. "I do not like this arrangement," he commented. "I do not wish to so go that by the slightest accident we fail entirely, and, at the best, the whole to be a mere breathless running of the gauntlet." [1] So the special train carrying the President and his party left Washington on the eighteenth and reached its destination on the afternoon of the same day.

_____
[1] *gauntlet,* a running course

At noon on the nineteenth—a day warmed by a wan sun—a ragged procession formed and started for the cemetery. There were troops, a band, and dignitaries —with the President, in a long coat and tall silk hat, an ungainly figure astride a horse. After a long prayer and dedicatory ode, Edward Everett took the stand and for two hours delivered a polished oration. Then Lincoln rose, a sheet of paper in one hand. Before the jaded crowd could come to full attention, he had finished. "The music wailed," wrote young John Hay, the President's secretary, "and we went home through crowded and cheering streets."

With no more fanfare than this were immortal words spoken and heard.

The Gettysburg Address
November 19, 1863

Fourscore and seven years ago our fathers brought forth on this continent, a new nation, conceived in liberty, and dedicated to the proposition that all men are created equal.

Now we are engaged in a great civil war, testing whether that nation, or any nation so conceived and so dedicated, can long endure. We are met on a great battlefield of that war. We have come to dedicate a portion of that field, as a final resting-place for those who here gave their lives that that nation might live. It is altogether fitting and proper that we should do this.

But, in a larger sense, we cannot dedicate—we cannot consecrate—we cannot hallow—this ground. The brave men, living and dead, who struggled here, have consecrated it, far above our poor power to add or detract. The world will little note, nor long remember what we say here, but it can never forget what they did here.

It is for us the living, rather, to be dedicated here to the unfinished work which they who fought here have thus far so nobly advanced. It is rather for us to be here dedicated to the great task remaining before us—that from these honored dead we take increased devotion to that cause for which they gave the last full measure of devotion—that we here highly resolve that these dead shall not have died in vain —that this nation, under God, shall have a new birth of freedom—and that government of the people, by the people, for the people, shall not perish from the earth.

The man who edited these selections

PAUL M. ANGLE 1900–

It takes a very special talent to make history readable and exciting without sacrificing accuracy and truth. Because Mr. Angle has that talent, he is a popular author as well as a reputable historian.

Mr. Angle has made American history his field of study. Lincoln, especially, has attracted his attention. He has written three books about Lincoln and collaborated with Carl Sandburg (also an ardent biographer of Lincoln) on a fourth.

A professional historian, Mr. Angle has held official positions with the Abraham Lincoln Association, the Illinois State Historical Society, and the Chicago History Society. He has also served as a consultant in history for the U. S. Air Force.

Let's consider . . .

1. Lincoln had been invited "tardily" to make "a few appropriate remarks" at Gettysburg. Edward Everett was to be the orator of the day. The **irony** of the situation was that the outcome was contrary to what had been expected. What was the great *irony* at Gettysburg?

2. Lincoln's *preparations* for the Gettysburg address were characteristic of him. Give at least three characteristics which were revealed in Mr. Angle's introduction.

3. You have undoubtedly read this address many times. Perhaps you have learned it by heart and have heard it delivered by others. Why do you think these few words have lived in people's hearts and minds although the words of the "orator of the day" are forgotten? Make a list of your reasons.

The writer's craft . . .

All writing—whether it is prose or poetry—has **rhythm:** a movement created by the stresses or accents in the words and phrases. As you read prose or poetry aloud, you naturally follow the rhythm which the writer intended.

A characteristic of all fine prose is its **cadence:** the rhythmical flow of the language. "The Gettysburg Address" is an outstanding example of beautiful prose cadence which you will feel if you read the "Address" aloud. First read it quietly to yourself, then take turns reading it aloud to the class. Be sure your voice reflects the simple dignity and rhythm of the language.

You can develop a rhythmical flow in your own use of language if you listen to the "sound" of your own writing. After you have completed a theme or a letter to a friend, always read it aloud. If it does not have a pleasant cadence, it probably needs further revision and polishing.

Strange Friend and Friendly Stranger

CARL SANDBURG

The life of Abraham Lincoln has become an American legend. By skillful use of colorful analogies, Carl Sandburg sketches a Lincoln portrait that will help you to understand why.

Lincoln was 51 years old. With each year since he had become a grown man, his name and ways, and stories about him, had been spreading among plain people and their children. So tall and so bony, with so peculiar a slouch and so easy a saunter, so sad and so haunted-looking, so quizzical and comic, as if hiding a lantern that lighted and went out and that he lighted again—he was the Strange Friend and the Friendly Stranger. Like something out of a picture book for children—he was. His form of slumping arches and his face of gaunt sockets were a shape a Great Artist had scrawled from careless clay.

He looked like an original plan for an extra-long horse or a lean tawny buffalo, that a Changer had suddenly whisked into a man-shape. Or he met the eye as a clumsy, mystical giant that had walked out of a Chinese or Russian fairy story, or a bogy who had stumbled out of an ancient Saxon myth with a handkerchief full of presents he wanted to divide among all the children in the world.

He didn't wear clothes. Rather, clothes hung upon him as if on a rack to dry, or on a loose ladder up a windswept chimney. His clothes, to keep the chill or the sun off, seemed to whisper, "He put us on when he was thinking about something else."

He dressed any which way at times, in broadcloth, a silk hat, a silk choker, and a flaming red silk handkerchief, so that one court clerk said Lincoln was "fashionably dressed, as neatly attired as any lawyer at court, except Ward Lamon." Or again, people said Lincoln looked like a huge skeleton with skin over the bones, and clothes covering the skin.

The stovepipe hat he wore sort of whistled softly: "I am not a hat at all; I am the little garret roof where he tucks in little thoughts he writes on pieces of paper." The hat, size seven and one-eighth, had a brim one and three-quarters inches wide. The inside band in which the more important letters and notes were tucked, measured two and three-quarters inches. The cylinder of the stovepipe was 22 inches in circumference. The hat was lined with heavy silk and, measured inside, exactly six inches deep. And people tried to guess what was going on under that hat. Written in pencil on the imitation satin paper that formed part of the lining was the signature "A. Lincoln, Springfield, Ill." so that any forgetful person who might take the hat by mistake would know where to bring it back. Also the hatmaker, "George Hall, Springfield, Ill.," had printed his name in the hat so that Lincoln would know where to get another one just like it.

The umbrella with the name "Abraham Lincoln" stitched in, faded and drab from many rains and regular travels, looked sleepy and murmuring. "Sometime we shall have all the sleep we want; we shall turn the law office over to the spiders and the cobwebs; and we shall quit politics for keeps."

There could have been times when children and dreamers looked at Abraham Lincoln and lazily drew their eyelids half shut and let their hearts roam about him—and they half-believed him to be a tall horse chestnut tree or a rangy horse or a big wagon or a log barn full of new-mown hay— something else or more than a man, a lawyer, a Republican candidate with principles, a prominent citizen—something spreading, elusive, and mysterious—the Strange Friend and the Friendly Stranger.

In Springfield and other places, something out of the ordinary seemed to connect with Abraham Lincoln's past, his birth, a mystery of where he came from. The wedding certificate of his father and mother was not known to be on record. Whispers floated of his origin as "low-flung," of circumstances so misty and strange that political friends wished they could be cleared up and made respectable. The wedding license of Thomas Lincoln and Nancy Hanks had been moved to a new county courthouse—where no one had thought to search.

The year of the big debates a boy had called out, "There goes old Mr. Lincoln," and Lincoln hearing it, remarked to a friend, "They commenced it when I was

scarcely thirty years old." Often when people called him "Old Abe" they meant he had the texture and quaint friendliness of old handmade Bibles, old calfskin law books, weather-beaten oak and walnut planks, or wagon axles always willing in storm or stars.

A neighbor boy, Fred Dubois, joined with a gang who tied a string to knock off Lincoln's hat. "Letters and papers fell out of the hat and scattered over the sidewalk," said Dubois. "He stooped to pick them up and us boys climbed all over him." As a young man he played marbles with boys; as an older man he spun tops with his own boys, Tad and Willie.

When William Plato of Kane County came to his office with the little girl, Ella, he stood Ella on a chair and told her, "And you're not as tall as I am, even now." A girl skipping along a sidewalk stumbled on a brick and fell backward, just as Lincoln came along. He caught her, lifted her up in his arms, put her gently down and asked, "What is your name?" "Mary Tuft." "Well, Mary, when you reach home tell your mother you have rested in Abraham's bosom."

Let's consider . . .

1. Select a passage from "Strange Friend and Friendly Stranger" which provides particular insight into Lincoln's character. Give your interpretation of what the passage reveals about his values, attitudes, or thinking.

2. By referring to several passages in the selection, explain why the phrase "Strange Friend and Friendly Stranger" provides a good description of Lincoln.

3. Tell the class of some incident in Lincoln's life with which you are familiar but which did not appear in "Strange Friend and Friendly Stranger."

The writer's craft . . .

The reputable biographer presents his factual data accurately, but he also has a keen eye for those incidents and descriptive phrases which will make his subject "come alive" for the reader. In writing the biography of Lincoln, Carl Sandburg let his readers see the human side of this national hero. A popular hero, like Lincoln, often becomes a legendary figure. Sometimes, the legend becomes so strong that it overshadows the man. As a result, the public forgets that its hero is made of flesh and blood just like everyone else.

In writing his biography, Sandburg characterized Lincoln so that readers would know him as a warm, human person. One way he accomplished this was to use striking images to describe Lincoln.

1. Find several unusual comparisons that helped you to understand the kind of person Lincoln was. Explain each comparison.

2. Sandburg also paid particular attention to Lincoln's way of dressing. Find several passages that describe Lincoln's clothing. How do these descriptions color your attitude toward him?

3. Write a short biographical sketch of someone you know. To suggest the "flavor" of your subject's personality try using several comparisons. You might also include (a) at least one incident so that your readers may see your subject in action and (b) dialogue so that they may hear how your subject speaks.

Paul Bunyan

ARTHUR S. BOURINOT

He came,
striding
over the mountain,
the moon slung on his back,
like a pack,
a great pine
stuck on his shoulder
swayed as he walked,
as he talked
to his blue ox
Babe;
a huge, looming shadow
of a man,
clad
in a mackinaw coat,
his logger's shirt
open at the throat
and the great mane of hair
matching,
meeting
the locks of night,
the smoke from his cauldron pipe
a cloud on the moon
and his laugh
rolled through the mountains
like thunder
on a summer night
while the lightning of his smile
split the heavens
asunder.
His blue ox, Babe,
pawed the ground

till the earth
trembled
and shook
and a high cliff
toppled and fell;
and Babe's bellow
was fellow
to the echo
of Bunyan's laughter;
and then
with one step
he was in the next valley
dragging the moon after,
the stars
tangled,
spangled
in the branches of the great pine.
And as he left,
he whistled in the dark
like a far off train
blowing for a crossing
and plainly heard
were the plodding grunts
of Babe, the blue ox,
trying
to keep pace
from hill to hill,
and then, the sounds,
fading,
dying,
were lost
in the churn of night,—
and all was still.

The man who wrote this poem

ARTHUR S. BOURINOT 1893–

Mr. Bourinot is a Canadian author and poet who has written twenty-four volumes of poetry and several prose works. He was recently editor of the *Canadian Poetry Magazine*. His work is often published in Canadian and English periodicals. Unfortunately, his poems are relatively unknown in the United States.

Mr. Bourinot's poetry is distinguished by exceptional pictures of the country in and around his province in the Laurentians. His descriptions of life in the forest and the simple life of the Canadian backwoodsman have often been praised by Canadian critics.

Mr. Bourinot's poetry lends itself well to music, and a number of his poems now have musical accompaniment. One of these is "Paul Bunyan," which has been frequently broadcast over Canadian radio stations.

When two countries are as close together as Canada and the United States, not only in geography but also in understanding of each other, it is not surprising that they should share a folk "hero."

The poet's art . . .

A. Paul Bunyan, one of America's major folk heroes, actually had his origin in the tall tales of Canadian lumber camps. When the Paul Bunyan legend moved westward into the United States, the American lumbermen soon adopted the champion as their own.

1. Explain why Paul Bunyan is a composite of the "ideal" lumberman.

2. Why does a folk hero always reflect something of the people who created him?

3. Who are the folk heroes in your region of the country? In what way do they reflect the ideas, struggles, and ambitions of early settlers in your part of the land?

B. This poem has been called a **legend:** a story handed down from earlier times and popularly accepted as historical. "Paul Bunyan" is a poetic version of a folk legend by a modern poet.

1. Count the rhymes in this poem. There are not many, and yet these few, as well as the rhythm of the lines, make you conscious that you are reading poetry. As you read the poem aloud, try to capture the rhythm. Then as briefly as you can, write this legend in prose. Read your version aloud. What does the verse form do for the legend? What is the effect of the short lines?

2. "Cauldron pipe" is **graphic:** picture-forming. Look up *cauldron* and explain the picture it created in the poem.

3. Have you ever seen a butter-churn? Have you ever seen a boat's wheel churning the water? What does "churn of night" mean to you? Why do you like or dislike this figure of speech?

4. Arthur S. Bourinot wrote,

> "and his laugh
> rolled through the mountains
> like thunder"

In comparing Paul Bunyan's laugh with thunder, the poet used a **simile:** a figure of speech in which a comparison is made between two objects which have at least one thing in common. Similes are usually introduced by the words *like* or *as*. What did Bunyan's laugh and thunder have in common? Find other similes in "Paul Bunyan." Explain why they make the description more effective.

5. You can make your own writing graphic by using similes. Try making up several of your own about Paul Bunyan.

The Devil and Daniel Webster

STEPHEN VINCENT BENÉT

Daniel Webster was never a man to turn his back on a difficult task. When his old New Hampshire neighbor, Jabez Stone, asked him to argue a law case with the Devil himself, Webster gladly accepted the challenge.

It's a story they tell in the border country, where Massachusetts joins Vermont and New Hampshire.

Yes, Dan'l Webster's dead—or, at least, they buried him. But every time there's a thunderstorm around Marshfield, they say you can hear his rolling voice in the hollows of the sky. And they say that if you go to his grave and speak loud and clear, "Dan'l Webster—Dan'l Webster!" the ground'll begin to shiver and the trees begin to shake. And after a while you'll hear a deep voice saying, "Neighbor, how stands the Union?" Then you better answer the Union stands as she stood, rock bottomed and copper sheathed, one and indivisible, or he's liable to rear right out of the ground. At least, that's what I was told when I was a youngster.

You see, for a while, he was the biggest man in the country. He never got to be President, but he was the biggest man. There were thousands that trusted in him right next to God Almighty, and they told stories about him and all the things that belonged to him that were like the stories of patriarchs and such. They said, when he stood up to speak, stars and stripes came right out in the sky, and once he spoke against a river and made it sink into the ground. They said, when he walked the woods with his fishing rod, Killall, the trout would jump out of the streams right

into his pockets, for they knew it was no use putting up a fight against him; and, when he argued a case, he could turn on the harps of the blessed and the shaking of the earth underground. That was the kind of man he was, and his big farm up at Marshfield was suitable to him. The chickens he raised were all white meat down through the drumsticks, the cows were tended like children, and the big ram he called Goliath had horns with a curl like a morning-glory vine and could butt through an iron door. But Dan'l wasn't one of your gentlemen farmers; he knew all the ways of the land, and he'd be up by candlelight to see that the chores got done. A man with a mouth like a mastiff, a brow like a mountain and eyes like burning anthracite—that was Dan'l Webster in his prime. And the biggest case he argued never got written down in the books, for he argued it against the devil, nip and tuck and no holds barred. And this is the way I used to hear it told.

There was a man named Jabez Stone, lived at Cross Corners, New Hampshire. He wasn't a bad man to start with, but he was an unlucky man. If he planted corn, he got borers; if he planted potatoes, he got blight. He had good-enough land, but it didn't prosper him; he had a decent wife and children, but the more children he had, the less there was to feed them. If stones cropped up in his neighbor's field, boulders boiled up in his; if he had a horse with spavins, he'd trade it for one with the staggers and give something extra. There's some folks bound to be like that, apparently. But one day Jabez Stone got sick of the whole business.

He'd been plowing that morning and he'd just broke the plowshare on a rock that he could have sworn hadn't been there yesterday. And, as he stood looking at the plowshare, the off horse began to cough— that ropy kind of cough that means sickness and horse doctors. There were two children down with the measles, his wife was ailing, and he had a whitlow [1] on his thumb. It was about the last straw for Jabez Stone. "I vow," he said, and he looked around him kind of desperate, "I vow it's enough to make a man want to sell his soul to the devil! And I would, too, for two cents!"

Then he felt a kind of queerness come over him at having said what he'd said; though, naturally, being a New Hampshireman, he wouldn't take it back. But, all the same, when it got to be evening and, as far as he could see, no notice had been taken, he felt relieved in his mind, for he was a religious man. But notice is always taken, sooner or later, just like the Good Book says. And, sure enough, next day, about suppertime, a soft-spoken, dark-dressed stranger drove up in a handsome buggy and asked for Jabez Stone.

Well, Jabez told his family it was a lawyer, come to see him about a legacy. But he knew who it was. He didn't like the looks of the stranger, nor the way he smiled with his teeth. They were white teeth, and plentiful—some say they were filed to a point, but I wouldn't vouch for that. And he didn't like it when the dog took one look at the stranger and ran away howling, with his tail between his legs. But having passed the word, more or less, he stuck to it, and they went out behind the barn and made their bargain. Jabez

Stone had to prick his finger to sign, and the stranger lent him a silver pin. The wound healed clean, but it left a little white scar.

After that, all of a sudden, things began to pick up and prosper for Jabez Stone. His cows got fat and his horses sleek, his crops were the envy of the neighborhood, and lightning might strike all over the valley, but it wouldn't strike his barn. Pretty soon he was one of the prosperous people of the county; they asked him to stand for selectman, [2] and he stood for it; there began to be talk of running him for state senate. All in all, you might say the Stone family was as happy and contented as cats in a dairy. And so they were, except for Jabez Stone.

He'd been contented enough the first few years. It's a great thing when bad luck turns; it drives most other things out of your head. True, every now and then, especially in rainy weather, the little white scar on his finger would give him a twinge. And once a year, punctual as clockwork, the stranger with the handsome buggy would come driving by. But the sixth year the stranger lighted, and, after that, his peace was over for Jabez Stone.

The stranger came up through the lower field, switching his boots with a cane— they were handsome black boots, but Jabez Stone never liked the look of them, particularly the toes. And, after he'd passed the time of day, he said, "Well, Mr. Stone, you're a hummer! It's a very pretty property you've got here, Mr. Stone."

"Well, some might favor it and others might not," said Jabez Stone, for he was a New Hampshireman.

"Oh, no need to decry your industry!" said the stranger, very easy, showing his teeth in a smile. "After all, we know what's been done, and it's been according to contract and specifications. So when— ahem—the mortgage falls due next year, you shouldn't have any regrets."

"Speaking of that mortgage, mister," said

---

[1] *whitlow*, an inflamation

[2] *selectman,* a New England town officer

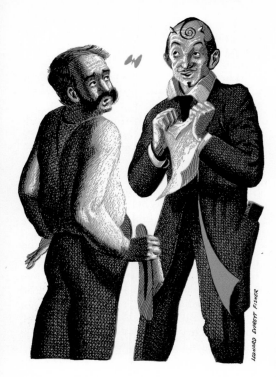

like a moth, but it wasn't a moth. And as Jabez Stone stared at it, it seemed to speak to him in a small sort of piping voice, terrible small and thin, but terrible human. "Neighbor Stone!" it squeaked. "Neighbor Stone! Help me! For God's sake, help me!"

But before Jabez Stone could stir hand or foot, the stranger whipped out a big bandanna handkerchief, caught the creature in it, just like a butterfly, and started tying up the ends of the bandanna.

"Sorry for the interruption," he said. "As I was saying—"

But Jabez Stone was shaking all over like a scared horse.

"That's Miser Stevens' voice!" he said in a croak. "And you've got him in your handkerchief!"

The stranger looked a little embarrassed.

"Yes, I really should have transferred him to the collecting box," he said with a simper, "but there were some rather unusual specimens there and I don't want them crowded. Well, well, these little contretemps [3] will occur."

"I don't know what you mean by contertan," said Jabez Stone. "But that was Miser Stevens' voice! And he ain't dead! You can't tell me he is! He was just as spry and mean as a woodchuck Tuesday!"

"In the midst of life . . ." said the stranger, kind of pious. "Listen!" Then a bell began to toll in the valley and Jabez Stone listened, with the sweat running down his face. For he knew it was tolled for Miser Stevens and that he was dead.

"These long-standing accounts," said the stranger with a sigh; "one really hates to close them. But business is business."

He still had the bandanna in his hand, and Jabez Stone felt sick as he saw the cloth struggle and flutter.

"Are they all as small as that?" he asked hoarsely.

"Small?" said the stranger. "Oh, I see what you mean. Why, they vary." He measured Jabez Stone with his eyes, and

Jabez Stone, and he looked around for help to the earth and the sky, "I'm beginning to have one or two doubts about it."

"Doubts?" said the stranger not quite so pleasantly.

"Why, yes," said Jabez Stone. "This being the U. S. A. and me always having been a religious man." He cleared his throat and got bolder. "Yes, sir," he said, "I'm beginning to have considerable doubts as to that mortgage holding in court."

"There's courts and courts," said the stranger, clicking his teeth. "Still, we might as well have a look at the original document." And he hauled out a big black pocketbook, full of papers. "Sherwin, Slater, Stevens, Stone," he muttered. " 'I, Jabez Stone, for a term of seven years—' Oh, it's quite in order, I think."

But Jabez Stone wasn't listening, for he saw something else flutter out of the black pocketbook. It was something that looked

---

[3] *contretemps,* embarrassing accidents

his teeth showed. "Don't worry, Mr. Stone," he said. "You'll go with a very good grade. I wouldn't trust you outside the collecting box. Now, a man like Dan'l Webster, of course—well, we'd have to build a special box for him, and even at that, I imagine the wing spread would astonish you. He'd certainly be a prize. I wish we could see our way clear to him. But, in your case, as I was saying—"

"Put that handkerchief away!" said Jabez Stone, and he began to beg and to pray. But the best he could get at the end was a three years' extension, with conditions.

But till you make a bargain like that, you've got no idea of how fast four years can run. By the last months of those years Jabez Stone's known all over the state and there's talk of running him for governor— and it's dust and ashes in his mouth. For every day, when he gets up, he thinks, "There's one more night gone," and every night, when he lies down, he thinks of the black pocketbook and the soul of Miser Stevens, and it makes him sick at heart. Till, finally, he can't bear it any longer, and, in the last days of the last year, he hitches up his horse and drives off to seek Dan'l Webster. For Dan'l was born in New Hampshire, only a few miles from Cross Corners, and it's well known that he has a particular soft spot for old neighbors.

It was early in the morning when he got to Marshfield, but Dan'l was up already, talking Latin to the farm hands and wrestling with the ram, Goliath, and trying out a new trotter and working up speeches to make against John C. Calhoun. But when he heard a New Hampshireman had come to see him, he dropped everything else he was doing, for that was Dan'l's way. He gave Jabez Stone a breakfast that five men couldn't eat, went into the living history of every man and woman in Cross Corners, and finally asked him how he could serve him.

Jabez Stone allowed that it was a kind of mortgage case.

"Well, I haven't pleaded a mortgage case in a long time, and I don't generally plead now, except before the Supreme Court," said Dan'l, "but if I can, I'll help you."

"Then I've got hope for the first time in ten years," said Jabez Stone and told him the details.

Dan'l walked up and down as he listened, hands behind his back, now and then asking a question, now and then plunging his eyes to the floor, as if they'd bore through it like gimlets. When Jabez Stone had finished, Dan'l puffed out his cheeks and blew. Then he turned to Jabez Stone and a smile broke over his face like the sunrise over Monadnock.[4]

"You've certainly given yourself the devil's own row to hoe, Neighbor Stone," he said, "but I'll take your case."

"You'll take it?" said Jabez Stone, hardly daring to believe.

"Yes," said Dan'l Webster. "I've got about seventy-five other things to do and the Missouri Compromise to straighten out, but I'll take your case. For if two New Hampshiremen aren't a match for the devil, we might as well give the country back to the Indians."

Then he shook Jabez Stone by the hand and said, "Did you come down here in a hurry?"

"Well, I admit I made time," said Jabez Stone.

"You'll go back faster," said Dan'l Webster, and he told 'em to hitch up Constitution and Constellation to the carriage. They were matched grays with one white forefoot, and they stepped like greased lightning.

Well, I won't describe how excited and pleased the whole Stone family was to have the great Dan'l Webster for a guest, when they finally got there. Jabez Stone had lost his hat on the way, blown off when they overtook a wind, but he didn't take much account of that. But after supper he sent the family off to bed, for he had most par-

---

[4] *Monadnock*, an isolated mountain peak in New Hampshire

ticular business with Mr. Webster. Mrs.
Stone wanted him to sit in the front parlor, but Dan'l Webster knew front parlors
and said he preferred the kitchen. So it
was there they sat, waiting for the stranger,
with a jug on the table between them and
a bright fire on the hearth—the stranger
being scheduled to show up on the stroke
of midnight, according to specification.

Well, most men wouldn't have asked
for better company than Dan'l Webster
and a jug. But with every tick of the clock
Jabez Stone got sadder and sadder. His
eyes roved round, and though he sampled
the jug you could see he couldn't taste it.
Finally, on the stroke of 11:30 he reached
over and grabbed Dan'l Webster by the arm.

"Mr. Webster, Mr. Webster!" he said,
and his voice was shaking with fear and a
desperate courage. "For God's sake, Mr.
Webster, harness your horses and get away
from this place while you can!"

"You've brought me a long way, neighbor, to tell me you don't like my company,"
said Dan'l Webster, quite peaceable, pulling at the jug.

"Miserable wretch that I am!" groaned
Jabez Stone. "I've brought you a devilish
way, and now I see my folly. Let him take
me if he wills. I don't hanker after it, I
must say, but I can stand it. But you're the
Union's stay and New Hampshire's pride!
He musn't get you, Mr. Webster! He
mustn't get you!"

Dan'l Webster looked at the distracted
man, all gray and shaking in the firelight,
and laid a hand on his shoulder.

"I'm obliged to you, Neighbor Stone,"
he said gently. "It's kindly thought of.
But there's a jug on the table and a case
in hand. And I never left a jug or a case
half finished in my life."

And just at that moment there was a
sharp rap on the door.

"Ah," said Dan'l Webster very coolly, "I
thought your clock was a trifle slow, Neighbor Stone." He stepped to the door and
opened it. "Come in!" he said.

The stranger came in—very dark and

tall he looked in the firelight. He was
carrying a box under his arm—a black
japanned box with little air holes in the lid.
At the sight of the box Jabez Stone gave a
low cry and shrank into the corner of the
room.

"Mr. Webster, I presume," said the
stranger, very polite, but with his eyes
glowing like a fox's deep in the woods.

"Attorney of record for Jabez Stone,"
said Dan'l Webster, but his eyes were glowing too. "Might I ask your name?"

"I've gone by a good many," said the
stranger carelessly. "Perhaps Scratch will
do for the evening. I'm often called that in
these regions."

Then he sat down at the table and
poured himself a drink from the jug. The
liquor was cold in the jug, but it came
steaming into the glass.

"And now," said the stranger, smiling
and showing his teeth, "I shall call upon
you, as a law-abiding citizen, to assist me
in taking possession of my property."

Well, with that the argument began—
and it went hot and heavy. At first Jabez
Stone had a flicker of hope, but when he
saw Dan'l Webster being forced back at
point after point, he just sat scrunched in
his corner, with his eyes on that japanned
box. For there wasn't any doubt as to the
deed or the signature—that was the worst
of it. Dan'l Webster twisted and turned
and thumped his fist on the table, but he
couldn't get away from that. He offered
to compromise the case; the stranger
wouldn't hear of it. He pointed out the
property had increased in value, and state
senators ought to be worth more; the
stranger stuck to the letter of the law. He
was a great lawyer, Dan'l Webster, but
we know who's the King of Lawyers, as
the Good Book tells us, and it seemed as if,
for the first time, Dan'l Webster had met
his match.

Finally, the stranger yawned a little.
"Your spirited efforts on behalf of your
client do you credit, Mr. Webster," he
said, "but if you have no more arguments

to adduce, I'm rather pressed for time . . ." and Jabez Stone shuddered.

Dan'l Webster's brow looked dark as a thundercloud.

"Pressed or not, you shall not have this man!" he thundered. "Mr. Stone is an American citizen, and no American citizen may be forced into the service of a foreign prince. We fought England for that in '12 and we'll fight all hell for it again!"

"Foreign?" said the stranger. "And who calls me a foreigner?"

"Well, I never yet heard of the dev—of your claiming American citizenship," said Dan'l Webster with surprise.

"And who with better right?" said the stranger with one of his terrible smiles. "When the first wrong was done to the first Indian, I was there. When the first slaver put out for the Congo, I stood on her deck. Am I not in your books and stories and beliefs, from the first settlements on? Am I not spoken of still in every church in New England? 'Tis true the North claims me for a Southerner and the South for a Northerner, but I am neither. I am merely an honest American like

LEONARD EVERETT FISHER

yourself—and of the best descent—for, to tell the truth, Mr. Webster, though I don't like to boast of it, my name is older in this country than yours."

"Aha!" said Dan'l Webster with the veins standing out in his forehead. "Then I stand on the Constitution! I demand a trial for my client!"

"The case is hardly one for an ordinary court," said the stranger, his eyes flickering. "And, indeed, the lateness of the hour—"

"Let it be any court you choose, so it is an American judge and an American jury!" said Dan'l Webster in his pride. "Let it be the quick or the dead; I'll abide the issue!"

"You have said it," said the stranger, and pointed his finger at the door. And with that, and all of a sudden, there was a rushing of wind outside and a noise of footsteps. They came, clear and distinct,

through the night. And yet they were not like the footsteps of living men.

"In God's name, who comes by so late?" cried Jabez Stone in an ague of fear.

"The jury Mr. Webster demands," said the stranger, sipping at his boiling glass. "You must pardon the rough appearance of one or two; they will have come a long way."

And with that the fire burned blue and the door blew open and twelve men entered, one by one.

If Jabez Stone had been sick with terror before, he was blind with terror now. For there was Walter Butler, the loyalist, who spread fire and horror through the Mohawk Valley in the times of the Revolution; and there was Simon Girty, the renegade, who saw white men burned at the stake and whooped with the Indians to see them burn. His eyes were green, like a catamount's, and the stains on his hunting shirt did not come from the blood of the deer. King Philip was there, wild and proud as he had been in life, with the great gash in his head that gave him his death wound, and cruel Governor Dale, who broke men on the wheel. There was Morton of Merry Mount, who so vexed the Plymouth Colony, with his flushed, loose, handsome face and his hate of the godly. There was Teach, the bloody pirate, with his black beard curling on his breast. The Reverend John Smeet, with his strangler's hands and his Geneva gown, walked as daintily as he had to the gallows. The red print of the rope was still around his neck, but he carried a perfumed handkerchief in one hand. One and all, they came into the room with the fires of hell still upon them, and the stranger named their names and their deeds as they came, till the tale of twelve was told. Yet the stranger had told the truth—they had all played a part in America.

"Are you satisfied with the jury, Mr. Webster?" said the stranger mockingly, when they had taken their places.

The sweat stood upon Dan'l Webster's brow, but his voice was clear.

"Quite satisfied," he said. "Though I miss General Arnold from the company."

"Benedict Arnold is engaged upon other business," said the stranger with a glower. "Ah, you asked for a justice, I believe."

He pointed his finger once more, and a tall man, soberly clad in Puritan garb, with the burning gaze of the fanatic, stalked into the room and took his judge's place.

"Justice Hathorne is a jurist of experience," said the stranger. "He presided at certain witch trials once held in Salem. There were others who repented of the business later, but not he."

"Repent of such notable wonders and undertakings?" said the stern old justice. "Nay, hang them—hang them all!" And he muttered to himself in a way that struck ice into the soul of Jabez Stone.

Then the trial began, and, as you might expect, it didn't look anyways good for the defense. And Jabez Stone didn't make much of a witness in his own behalf. He took one look at Simon Girty and screeched, and they had to put him back in his corner in a kind of swoon.

It didn't halt the trial though; the trial went on, as trials do. Dan'l Webster had faced some hard juries and hanging judges in his time, but this was the hardest he'd ever faced, and he knew it. They sat there with a kind of glitter in their eyes, and the stranger's smooth voice went on and on. Every time he'd raise an objection, it'd be "Objection sustained," but whenever Dan'l objected, it'd be "Objection denied." Well, you couldn't expect fair play from a fellow like this Mr. Scratch.

It got to Dan'l in the end, and he began to heat, like iron in the forge. When he got up to speak he was going to flay that stranger with every trick known to the law, and the judge and jury too. He didn't care if it was contempt of court or what would happen to him for it. He didn't care any more what happened to Jabez Stone. He just got madder and madder, thinking of what he'd say. And yet, curiously enough, the more he thought about

it, the less he was able to arrange his speech in his mind.

Till, finally, it was time for him to get on his feet, and he did so, all ready to bust out with lightnings and denunciations. But before he started he looked over the judge and jury for a moment, such being his custom. And he noticed the glitter in their eyes was twice as strong as before, and they all leaned forward. Like hounds just before they get the fox, they looked, and the blue mist of evil in the room thickened as he watched them. Then he saw what he'd been about to do, and he wiped his forehead, as a man might who's just escaped falling into a pit in the dark.

For it was him they'd come for, not only Jabez Stone. He read it in the glitter of their eyes and in the way the stranger hid his mouth with one hand. And if he fought them with their own weapons, he'd fall into their power; he knew that, though he couldn't have told you how. It was his own anger and horror that burned in their eyes; and he'd have to wipe that out or the case was lost. He stood there for a moment,

his black eyes burning like anthracite.[5] And then he began to speak.

He started off in a low voice, though you could hear every word. They say he could call on the harps of the blessed when he chose. And this was just as simple and easy as a man could talk. But he didn't start out by condemning or reviling. He was talking about the things that make a country a country and a man a man.

And he began with the simple things that everybody's known and felt—the freshness of a fine morning when you're young, and the taste of food when you're hungry, and the new day that's every day when you're a child. He took them up and he turned them in his hands. They were good things for any man. But without freedom they sickened. And when he talked of those enslaved, and the sorrows of slavery, his voice got like a big bell. He talked of the early days of America and the men who had made those days. It wasn't a spread-eagle speech, but he made you see it. He admitted all the wrong that had ever been

[5] *anthracite.* hard coal

done. But he showed how, out of the wrong and the right, the suffering and the starvations, something new had come. And everybody had played a part in it, even the traitors.

Then he turned to Jabez Stone and showed him as he was—an ordinary man who'd had hard luck and wanted to change it. And, because he'd wanted to change it, now he was going to be punished for all eternity. And yet there was good in Jabez Stone, and he showed that good. He was hard and mean, in some ways, but he was a man. There was sadness in being a man, but it was a proud thing too. And he showed what the pride of it was till you couldn't help feeling it. Yes, even in hell, if a man was a man, you'd know it. And he wasn't pleading for any one person any more, though his voice rang like an organ. He was telling the story and the failures and the endless journey of mankind. They got tricked and trapped and bamboozled, but it was a great journey. And no demon that was ever foaled could know the inwardness of it—it took a man to do that.

The fire began to die on the hearth and the wind before morning to blow. The light was getting gray in the room when Dan'l Webster finished. And his words came back at the end to New Hampshire ground, and the one spot of land that each man loves and clings to. He painted a picture of that, and to each one of that jury he spoke of things long forgotten. For his voice could search the heart, and that was his gift and his strength. And to one his voice was like the forest and its secrecy, and to another like the sea and the storms of the sea; and one heard the cry of his lost nation in it, and another saw a little harmless scene he hadn't remembered for years. But each saw something. And when Dan'l Webster finished he didn't know whether or not he'd saved Jabez Stone. But he knew he'd done a miracle. For the glitter was gone from the eyes of judge and jury, and, for the moment, they were men again, and knew they were men.

"The defense rests," said Dan'l Webster, and stood there like a mountain. His ears were still ringing with his speech, and he didn't hear anything else till he heard Judge Hathorne say, "The jury will consider its verdict."

Walter Butler rose in his place and his face had a dark, gay pride on it.

"The jury has considered its verdict," he said and looked the stranger full in the eye. "We find for the defendant, Jabez Stone."

With that, the smile left the stranger's face, but Walter Butler did not flinch.

"Perhaps 'tis not strictly in accordance with the evidence," he said, "but even the damned may salute the eloquence of Mr. Webster."

With that, the long crow of a rooster split the gray morning sky, and judge and jury were gone from the room like a puff of smoke and as if they had never been there. The stranger returned to Dan'l Webster, smiling wryly.

"Major Butler was always a bold man," he said. "I had not thought him quite so bold. Nevertheless, my congratulations, as between two gentlemen."

"I'll have that paper first, if you please," said Dan'l Webster, and he took it and tore it into four pieces. It was queerly warm to the touch. "And now," he said, "I'll have you!" and his hand came down like a bear on the stranger's arm. For he knew that once you bested anybody like Mr. Scratch in fair fight, his power on you was gone. And he could see that Mr. Scratch knew it too.

The stranger twisted and wriggled, but he couldn't get out of that grip. "Come, come, Mr. Webster," he said, smiling palely. "This sort of thing is ridic—ouch! —is ridiculous. If you're worried about the costs of the case, naturally, I'd be glad to pay—"

"And so you shall!" said Dan'l Webster, shaking him till his teeth rattled. "For you'll sit right down at that table and draw up a document, promising never to bother Jabez Stone nor his heirs or assigns nor any other New Hampshireman till doomsday! For any hades we want to raise in this state, we can raise ourselves, without assistance from strangers."

"Ouch!" said the stranger. "Ouch! Well, they never did run very big to the barrel, but—ouch!—I agree!"

So he sat down and drew up the document. But Dan'l Webster kept his hand on his coat collar all the time.

"And now may I go?" said the stranger, quite humble, when Dan'l'd seen the document's in proper and legal form.

"Go?" said Dan'l, giving him another shake. "I'm still trying to figure out what I'll do with you. For you've settled the costs of the case, but you haven't settled with me. I think I'll take you back to Marshfield," he said, kind of reflective. "I've got a ram there named Goliath that can butt through an iron door. I'd kind of like to turn you loose in his field and see what he'd do."

Well, with that the stranger began to beg and to plead. And he begged and he pled so humble that finally Dan'l, who was naturally kindhearted, agreed to let him go. The stranger seemed terrible grateful for that and said, just to show they were friends, he'd tell Dan'l's fortune before leaving. So Dan'l agreed to that, though he didn't take much stock in fortune-tellers ordinarily. But, naturally, the stranger was a little different.

Well, he pried and peered at the lines in Dan'l's hands. And he told him one thing and another that was quite remarkable. But they were all in the past.

"Yes, all that's true, and it happened," said Dan'l Webster. "But what's to come in the future?"

The stranger grinned, kind of happily, and shook his head.

"The future's not as you think it," he said. "It's dark. You have a great ambition, Mr. Webster."

"I have," said Dan'l firmly, for everybody knew he wanted to be President.

"It seems almost within your grasp," said the stranger, "but you will not attain it. Lesser men will be made President and you will be passed over."

"And, if I am, I'll still be Daniel Webster," said Dan'l. "Say on."

"You have two strong sons," said the stranger, shaking his head. "You look to found a line. But each will die in war and neither reach greatness."

"Live or die, they are still my sons," said Dan'l Webster. "Say on."

"You have made great speeches," said the stranger. "You will make more."

"Ah," said Dan'l Webster.

"But the last great speech you make will turn many of your own against you," said the stranger. "They will call you Ichabod; they will call you by other names. Even in New England some will say you have turned your coat and sold your country, and their voices will be loud against you till you die."

"So it is an honest speech, it does not matter what men say," said Dan'l Webster. Then he looked at the stranger and their glances locked.

"One question," he said. "I have fought for the Union all my life. Will I see that fight won against those who would tear it apart?"

"Not while you live," said the stranger grimly, "but it will be won. And after you are dead, there are thousands who will fight for your cause, because of words that you spoke."

"Why, then, you long-barreled, slab-chested, lantern-jawed, fortune-telling note shaver," said Dan'l Webster with a great roar of laughter, "be off with you to your own place before I put my mark on you! For, by the thirteen original colonies, I'd go to the Pit itself to save the Union!"

And with that he drew back his foot for a kick that would have stunned a horse. It was only the tip of his shoe that caught the stranger, but he went flying out of the door with his collecting box under his arm.

"And now," said Dan'l Webster, seeing Jabez Stone beginning to rouse from his swoon, "let's see what's left in the jug, for it's dry work talking all night. I hope there's pie for breakfast, Neighbor Stone."

But they say that whenever the devil comes near Marshfield, even now, he gives it a wide berth. And he hasn't been seen in the state of New Hampshire from that day to this.

I'm not talking about Massachusetts or Vermont.

Let's consider . . .

1. Benét kept pointing out characteristics of "New Hampshiremen." Which of these characteristics did Dan'l Webster exhibit?

2. Describe the dramatic meeting between Dan'l Webster and Scratch.

3. At the beginning of the argument between them, Scratch had the advantage every time. How did he prove his rights to American citizenship? What was humorous in this part of the argument?

4. Webster finally took his "stand on the Constitution" and demanded a trial for his client. How was the court set up? What words of Webster's were responsible for the set-up? Why could he expect little fair play in such a court?

5. When it came Dan'l Webster's turn to face the jury, what realization came over him?

6. Why did Webster begin his speech by referring to the "simple things" in life?

7. Just how had his speech "done a miracle"? What did he say that, for a moment, turned the judge and jury into men? What was the result?

8. Throughout the story, Benét showed that he knew American history. Mention a few historical facts which he brought into the story.

9. At the end of the story, what did the fortune-telling episode do for the reader? What provoked Webster to say to the devil, "on your way before I put my mark on you"?

10. Webster's victory was complete. What amusing bit at the end of the story showed how very complete it was?

The writer's craft . . .

Daniel Webster was not a legendary hero like Paul Bunyan, but in this fantastic story certain feats were attributed to him that made him seem almost as fabulous. However, when you were reading this story, you accepted many of those characters and events as **realistic** because the author had made them seem true-to-life. You do not find this same quality in tales about legendary heroes.

One reason "The Devil and Daniel Webster" seemed very real was that its roots were deep in New Hampshire soil. However, in order to appreciate the supernatural in the story, you had to let your imagination take you outside the everyday New England world. At the very beginning, Benét forewarned you of the supernatural events which were to come.

1. Look again at the second paragraph of the story. How did it lead you to expect certain unusual events?

2. Once you had accepted the possibility of the supernatural, the events and characters seemed quite realistic. Explain why each of the following seemed real though unlikely:

   a. The way Benét introduced Daniel Webster in order to lead up to his encounter with the devil
   b. The hard-luck story of Jabez Stone's farming
   c. The appearance and manner of the devil on his first entrance
   d. The parallel growth of Jabez Stone's prosperity and uneasiness
   e. Jabez Stone's trip to see Daniel Webster and his return

Knowing words . . .

Benét wrote that the stories about Daniel Webster were "like the stories of patriarchs and such." In the Old Testament the patriarchs were the great men, or leaders. *Patriarch* stems from the Latin word *pater* meaning "father" and the Greek word *archos* meaning "leader." Hence, a *patriarch*, or "father-leader," is the ruling head of a family or tribe.

Many English words are based on the Latin root *pater*, as you will see in the following sentences. Explain how each of these words is connected with the idea of "father." If you are not sure of any of these words, consult your dictionary. Then rewrite each sentence, substituting a word or phrase of your own for the word based on *pater*.

1. The principal spoke to the boy in a stern but *paternal* manner.
2. The soldier showed unusual courage because of his earnest *patriotism*.
3. As the *pater-familias*, the young man found he had many new responsibilities.
4. The nobleman lived recklessly, and went through his *patrimony* in a short time.
5. Many ancient societies were based on *patriarchy*.

The Gift Outright

The land was ours before we were the land's.
She was our land more than a hundred years
Before we were her people. She was ours
In Massachusetts, in Virginia,
But we were England's, still colonials,
Possessing what we still were unpossessed by,
Possessed by what we now no more possessed.
Something we were withholding made us weak
Until we found it was ourselves
We were withholding from our land of living,
And forthwith found salvation in surrender.
Such as we were we gave ourselves outright
(The deed of gift was many deeds of war)
To the land vaguely realizing westward,
But still unstoried, artless, unenhanced,
Such as she was, such as she would become.

Robert Frost

Daniel Boone

ARTHUR GUITERMAN

Daniel Boone at twenty-one
Came with his tomahawk, knife and gun
Home from the French and Indian War
To North Carolina and the Yadkin [1] shore.
He married his maid with a golden band,
Builded his house and cleared his land;
But the deep woods claimed their son again
And he turned his face from the homes of
  men.
Over the Blue Ridge, dark and lone,
The Mountains of Iron, the Hills of Stone,
Braving the Shawnee's [2] jealous wrath,
He made his way on the Warrior's Path.
Alone he trod the shadowed trails;
But he was lord of a thousand vales
As he roved Kentucky, far and near,
Hunting the buffalo, elk, and deer.
What joy to see, what joy to win
So fair a land for his kith and kin,
Of streams unstained and woods unhewn!
"Elbowroom!" laughed Daniel Boone.

On the Wilderness Road that his axmen
  made
The settlers flocked to the first stockade;
The deerskin shirts and the coonskin caps
Filed through the glens and the mountain
  gaps;
And hearts were high in the fateful spring
When the land said "Nay!" to the stub-
  born king.
While the men of the East of farms and
  town
Strove with the troops of the British
  Crown,

Daniel Boone from a surge of hate
Guarded a nation's westward gate.
Down on the fort in a wave of flame
The Shawnee horde and the Mingo [3]
  came,
And the stout logs shook in a storm of lead;
But Boone stood firm and the savage fled.
Peace! And the settlers flocked anew,
The farm lands spread, the town lands
  grew;
But Daniel Boone was ill at ease
When he saw the smoke in the forest trees.
"There'll be no game in the country soon.
Elbowroom!" cried Daniel Boone.

Straight as a pine at sixty-five—
Time enough for a man to thrive—
He launched his bateau [4] on Ohio's [5] breast
And his heart was glad as he oared it west;
There were kindly folk and his own true
  blood
Where great Missouri rolls his flood;
New woods, new streams and room to
  spare,
And Daniel Boone found comfort there.
Yet far he ranged toward the sunset still,
Where the Kansas runs and the Smoky
  Hill,
And the prairies toss, by the south wind
  blown;
And he killed his bear on the Yellowstone.
But ever he dreamed of new domains
With vaster woods and wider plains;
Ever he dreamed of a world-to-be

---

[1] Yadkin, a river in North Carolina
[2] Shawnee, an Indian tribe
[3] Mingo, Iroquois, an Indian tribe
[4] bateau, a light, flat-bottomed boat
[5] Ohio, the Ohio river

244

Where there are no bounds and the soul
is free.
At four-score-five, still stout and hale,
He heard a call to a farther trail;
So he turned his face where the stars are
strewn;
"Elbowroom!" sighed Daniel Boone.

Down the Milky Way in its banks of blue
Far he has paddled his white canoe
To the splendid quest of the tameless
soul—
He has reached the goal where there is no
goal.
Now he rides and rides an endless trail
On the Hippogriff [6] of the flaming tail
Or the Horse of the Stars with the golden
mane,

[6] *Hippogriff,* legendary creature having the head
and wings of an eagle and the body of a horse

As he rode the first of the blue-grass strain.
The joy that lies in the Search he seeks
On breathless hills with crystal peaks;
He makes his camp on heights untrod,
The steps of the shrine, alone with God.
Through the woods of the vast, on the
plains of Space
He hunts the pride of the Mammoth race
And the Dinosaur of the triple horn,
The Manticore [7] and the Unicorn, [8]
As once by the broad Missouri's flow
He followed the elk and the buffalo.
East of the Sun and west of the Moon,
"Elbowroom!" laughs Daniel Boone.

[7] *Manticore,* legendary monster having the body
of a lion, the head of a man with horns, and the
tail of a scorpion

[8] *Unicorn,* a legendary animal with the body of a
horse and a single long horn protruding from
its forehead

The man who wrote this poem

ARTHUR GUITERMAN 1871–1943

The poems of Arthur Guiterman have
touched on almost every phase of American life. Joyce Kilmer once called him
"the most American of poets."

Throughout his childhood and education in New York City, he showed an interest in a wide range of activities. Later,
some of these experiences provided subject
matter for his verses.

He would be remembered as the author
of the lyrics for the opera, *Man Without
a Country,* even if he had never written
anything else. However, his many poems
established him as an able author of both
light and serious verse.

Some of Arthur Guiterman's poems are
like songs in praise of the American way
of life. Others are word-pictures of the
American scene—whether it be the prairies
or the cities. Still others are word-portraits
of great Americans, like *Daniel Boone.*

The poet's art . . .

1. Daniel Boone's slogan was "Elbowroom!" What *first* made him feel the need
for more room and urged him to go farther West? What were the stops he made
on his way? What urged him on each
time?

2. Even at eighty-five he was "stout and
hale." What was the call he then heard
"to a farther trail"? (From here on you
will have to watch for metaphors and interpret them.)

3. In the last stanza Arthur Guiterman
continued the idea of Daniel Boone's pushing on "East of the Sun and west of the
Moon." What were some of his adventures
there? How did he link his new experiences with his earlier feats? Do you like
the idea of the mythical and prehistoric
creatures being close to Boone's "camp on
heights untrod, The steps of the shrine,
alone with God"?

4. How is Daniel Boone typically American?

Washington Monument by Night

CARL SANDBURG

1

The stone goes straight.
A lean swimmer dives into night sky,
Into half-moon mist.

2

Two trees are coal black.
This is a great white ghost between.
It is cool to look at.
Strong men, strong women, come here.

3

Eight years is a long time
To be fighting all the time.

4

The republic is a dream.
Nothing happens unless first a dream.

5

The wind bit hard at Valley Forge one Christmas.
Soldiers tied rags on their feet.
Red footprints wrote on the snow . . .
. . . and stone shoots into stars here
. . . into half-moon mist tonight.

6

Tongues wrangled dark at a man.
He buttoned his overcoat and stood alone.
In a snowstorm, red hollyberries, thoughts,
    he stood alone.

7

Women said: He is lonely
. . . fighting . . . fighting . . . eight years . . .

8

The name of an iron man goes over the world.
It takes a long time to forget an iron man.

9

. . . .
. . . .

The poet's art . . .

1. In this poem Sandburg was something of an **imagist:** a creator of images or clear pictures. What images did he use to picture the monument shooting into the sky? Which one do you prefer? Why?

2. As the poet gazed on Washington Monument, what reflections on "an iron man" came to his mind? What scenes did he recall?

3. Explain the line "nothing happens unless first a dream." What was Washington's "dream"?

4. Do you like the image "an iron man"? Do you agree that "It takes a long time to forget an iron man"? Explain.

5. What do *you* suppose Sandburg meant to convey by the ninth stanza, which contains no words? Why wouldn't he want to end his poem with "It takes a long time to forget an iron man"?

Stars, Songs, Faces

Gather the stars if you wish it so.
Gather the songs and keep them.
Gather the faces of women.
Gather for keeping years and years.
    And then . . .
Loosen your hands, let go and say good-by,
    Let the stars and songs go.
    Let the faces and years go.
    Loosen your hands and say good-by.
                        Carl Sandburg

Benjamin Franklin

CARL VAN DOREN

Although the nation's earliest great hero was a man of many talents, most Americans think of him first and foremost as a warm, delightful friend.

Any great American is one of America's national resources, and to cherish his memory is to make continuing use of his greatness. Even though his example may from time to time seem to have grown dim, it is still there, ready to be drawn upon like forests and mines and wells, farms and rivers and the ocean. In dark days he can be trusted to be a light out of the past, if he is remembered for what he really was and still remains.

Let us remember some of the things too many of us have forgotten about Benjamin Franklin, the earliest great American.

When Washington was only twenty-one, Adams eighteen, Jefferson ten, Madison two, and Hamilton not yet born, Franklin in 1753 was already a scientist of world-wide renown. His discoveries in electricity had laid the foundations of that science. His experiments with lightning, and his invention of the lightning rod, had begun to make him thought of, by the people everywhere, as a kind of wizard. Had he not hit upon a secret which enabled him to catch and tame a terrible force which mankind had superstitiously dreaded for thousands of years? Here was another hero of the human race.

But Franklin was no wizard hid in a cave. He was also a humorist and wit. He had created the character of Poor Richard the year Washington was born, and had ever since gone on annually turning the world's proverbs into Poor Richard's sayings, with a new American point and flavor. Probably no man since Solomon has given so many proverbs the form in which they are most familiarly known as Franklin gave.

Scientist and humorist, Franklin was

also the leader among the men who were changing Philadelphia from a little provincial town into the most important city in the American colonies and one of the important cities in the British Empire. In 1753 he became postmaster general for North America and the next year drew up his plan for a union of the colonies which was to be, as it turned out, a forecast of the United States.

Franklin at first had no thought of independence. He desired only to unite the colonies in local affairs within the larger frame of imperial government. His vision for the future included both sides of the Atlantic. If America depended on Great Britain, so did Great Britain depend on America. Together they might, he wrote a little later, set up "the greatest political structure human wisdom ever yet erected."

For eighteen years before 1775 Franklin spent most of his time in London as agent of various colonies and, in effect, ambassador from America. Firmly holding out for justice to his native country, he was also faithful to his imperial vision. Justice to America, he knew, was in the long run a necessity for the whole empire. What he proposed was substantially what was long afterward to be the basic principle of the British Commonwealth of Nations. But the reactionary George III and his obedient ministers were not prophets. Franklin's plans were disregarded, and he was insultingly dismissed from office.

During his voyage home the battles of Lexington and Concord took place and the colonies flared into rebellion. This was something Franklin had feared and had done his best to prevent. He might, like most former crown officers in America, have sided with the king. He might have stubbornly persisted in his plans for reconciliation. He might, at seventy, have withdrawn from the conflict and returned to the scientific studies which had made him famous. Instead, he took his seat in the Continental Congress, the oldest man in it, and thereafter gave his massive energies to the defense of America and to American independence.

The only member of the Congress who had a large European reputation, Franklin was sent to Paris to try to win France as an ally. There his triumph was due perhaps less to what he did than to what he was. For to the French, as to all the rest of Europe outside of England, he was not merely a shrewd diplomat working against many odds. He was a great sage, wise and good and smiling, who spoke for the new nation of Americans because he was so completely one of them while being a citizen of the world. If America could produce a great philosopher it was not, as it was represented by its enemies, a noisy rabble in a wilderness.

Franklin with his outward ease and grace, Washington with his unmistakable gravity and fortitude in America: these were, without question, the two masters of the Revolution, each with the qualities supremely needed in his place. What they had in common was the deep stamina which for eight years kept them from giving up a cause that often looked hopeless. Probably every day of the war Washington wished he were back on his farm, Franklin that he were back at his experiments. Each of them for the sake of his country had turned away from what he liked and valued most in private life. But there they stood, throughout the long struggle, like the towers or temples of an unshakable faith.

When Franklin at eighty left Paris for America he looked forward to a philosopher's retirement. But almost at once he was elected president (governor) of Pennsylvania, and he was inevitably a delegate to the federal convention which formed the Constitution of the United States. His temperate wisdom kept the convention from breaking up into antagonistic parties. The finished Constitution was not altogether what he wished it to be, but without him there might have been no constitution at all.

Too old and feeble to be considered for first president, Franklin lived only long enough to see the first few months of the new government he had done so much to bring into existence and to shape. Then, like Moses on Pisgah,[1] he looked into the Promised Land which his people were to enter and enjoy. In one of his last letters he summed up what amounts to his blessing on this government and every good government.

"God grant that not only the love of liberty but a thorough knowledge of the rights of man may pervade all the nations of the earth, so that a philosopher may set his foot anywhere on its surface and say: 'This is my country.' "

What survives from Franklin's life and work a century and a half after his death? There are, of course, the bequests to Boston and Philadelphia which have grown into the most munificent money gifts ever made by a philosopher. There are the library, the hospital, the fire insurance company, the scientific society, the academy (eventually the university) which he helped found in Philadelphia. His autobiography has been more widely read than any other and has been translated into every language that has a printing press. The stove he invented bears his name, and the lightning rod is forever associated with it. He organized the United States postal service and instituted the dead-letter office.

Things not so well known are that he was the first notable American athlete, published the first foreign-language newspaper

---

[1] *Pisgah,* a mountain range in ancient Palestine. Moses viewed the promised land from its summit, Mount Nebo.

in America, planned the first American magazine, made the original observations out of which the weather bureau developed, drew and printed the first American cartoon, invented a draft for fireplaces and was a pioneer in the science of ventilation, was the first scholar to study the Gulf Stream, saw the first men go up in a free balloon and was first to prophesy that war might be made from the air, and received the first letter carried through the air, by balloon from London to Paris. The oldest of the great Americans of the Revolution, he saw furthest into the future.

Among great American statesmen Franklin is the only one who has a great name in science, the only one who wrote a book that belongs to world literature, the only one who was equally at home in America, England, and France: at once intensely native and perfectly cosmopolitan.

Far from sinking out of sight as time passes, Franklin steadily emerges, like a mountain which seemed no higher than others when we were close to them but which as we move away rises above them all. And yet there is nothing overpowering in Franklin's eminence. The more we learn about him, and the more we wonder at him, the more also we take a comfortable delight in his serenity and good humor and candor and charm. We are proud to belong to the nation that produced him. We honor his talents and achievements. But we feel that the man was more than his works, and that while his works have spread out into the broad stream of American life, the man has somehow managed to outlast them all, still himself, still a delightful friend as well as a mighty hero.

The man who wrote this biography

CARL VAN DOREN   1885–1950

Carl Van Doren devoted his life to scholarship and literature. After his graduation

as an honor student from the University of Illinois, he went to Columbia University in order to earn his doctorate and begin teaching.

From 1911 until 1930, Mr. Van Doren was an instructor at Columbia but still managed to find time to carry out his many plans. As literary editor of *The Nation,* he had an important influence on writers in the 1920's. He helped to introduce and to develop many of America's young authors. With several friends, he also formed the Literary Guild of America, a book club which introduced good reading to a wide public. He was its editor for many years.

In addition to his teaching and editorial work, Carl Van Doren published many critical articles, compiled several excellent prose anthologies, created novels, and wrote literary surveys. His biography of Benjamin Franklin, from which this selection was taken, was awarded a Pulitzer Prize in 1940.

Let's consider . . .

A. Carl Van Doren's account of Benjamin Franklin is simple, clear, and concrete. You ought to find it easy, therefore, to outline under the following topics the information he has given you. Perhaps your teacher will assign different topics to different groups. Use all the sub-topics you need to prove each topic statement. Use the standard method you have learned for numbering and lettering an outline.

1. Franklin was the earliest *great* American.

2. Franklin was a humorist and a wit.

3. Before the Revolution Franklin worked for justice for the colonies with no thought of an independent America.

4. After war broke out, Franklin worked for American independence at home and in France.

5. Franklin and Washington complemented each other.

6. Franklin saved the Constitution.

B. In this selection, Van Doren told you many things which he said "too many of us have forgotten."

1. What did you learn that surprised you most? Why ought you to remember these facts about Franklin?

2. Franklin could claim more "firsts" than most men. Which one of his many "firsts" seems most remarkable to you? Why is it especially worthy of notice?

3. If you agree with Van Doren's first sentence, certainly you consider Franklin one of America's "national resources." Choose three of his accomplishments and tell why you think they make him emerge as a towering giant *in this century.*

4. Franklin was always a foresighted philosopher and statesman. Consider "his blessing on this government." Discuss its appropriateness as an aim for all nations as they strive to live together in peace.

The writer's craft . . .

Mark Van Doren's essay on Walt Whitman was similar in spirit to Carl Van Doren's essay on Benjamin Franklin in that each essay paid tribute to an American hero of the past. However, each author had a somewhat different purpose in writing his essay. Mark Van Doren's purpose was to present Whitman as a human being rather than as a famous literary figure. He gave the essay a rather informal tone so that his reader would come to know Whitman, the man, as well as Whitman, the poet.

Carl Van Doren's essay on Benjamin Franklin was somewhat more formal and impersonal. He did not attempt to communicate Franklin's warmth as a person. This you will find expressed by Franklin himself in the two selections which follow. Carl Van Doren's purpose was to place a man in history, not to reveal him as a personality. To do this, he enumerated and commented on Franklin's contributions to America, particularly noting those which survive a century and a half after his death.

The chief difference between the two essays is that one emphasized a man's personality and the other emphasized a man's contribution to his country. Explain why each treatment was best suited to the purpose which each author had in mind.

Preface to Poor Richard

BENJAMIN FRANKLIN

Almanacs were extremely popular in colonial America because they contained such items as a calendar, recipes, weather forecasts, jokes, wise sayings, and bits of general information. The colonists found them useful as well as a source of entertainment.

Every year from 1732 until 1758 Franklin published *Poor Richard's Almanack,* for which he gathered such items. Sometimes he changed them to fit the Colonial way of life. From his preface to the *Almanack* and from a few of Poor Richard's sayings you see the wise and "folksy" quality of this American who identified himself with the people of his country and, in his own way, was a kind of hero.

Courteous Readers,

Your kind and charitable Assistance last Year, in purchasing so large an Impression [1] of my Almanacks, has made my Circumstances much more easy in the World, and requires my grateful Acknowledgment. My Wife has been enabled to get a Pot of her own, and is no longer oblig'd to borrow one from a Neighbour; nor have we ever since been without something of our own to put in it. She has also got a pair of Shoes, two new Shifts, [2] and a new warm Petticoat; and for my part, I have bought a second-hand Coat, so good, that I am now not asham'd to go to Town or be seen there. These Things have render'd her Temper so much more pacifick than it us'd to be, that I may say, I have slept more, and more quietly within this last Year, than in the three foregoing Years put together. Accept my hearty Thanks therefor, and my sincere Wishes for your Health and Prosperity.

---

[1] *Impression,* printing
[2] *Shifts,* chemises

*　　*　　*

Sayings of Poor Richard

"He does not possess wealth; it possesses him."

"Nothing but money is sweeter than honey."

"Eat to live, and not live to eat."

"He that is rich need not live sparingly, and he that can live sparingly need not be rich."

"Fish and visitors smell in three days."

"The worst wheel of the cart makes the most noise."

"God helps them that help themselves."

"There never was a good war or a bad peace."

"A truly great man will neither trample on a worm nor sneak to an emperor."

"Glass, china, and reputation are easily cracked and never well mended."

"If a man empties his purse into his head, no man can take it away from him. An investment in knowledge always pays the best interest."

Let's consider . . .

1. Note the capitalization of nouns in this eighteenth-century preface. Can you give any explanation for this practice?

2. Frank acknowledgment of indebtedness to subscribers is not always made in books or periodicals. What effect do you think this preface to *Poor Richard's Almanack* would have on the readers and their relationship with its editor? What evidence do you find here of frankness and humility?

3. A terse saying which expresses a general truth is called an **aphorism.** Which of Poor Richard's sayings could be called aphorisms? Which do you think express a general truth for Americans today?

Knowing words . . .

In his preface to *Poor Richard*, in 1734, Franklin wrote that his wife's temper had been rendered more *pacifick* than it used to be. *Pacifick* is the old spelling of *pacific*, a word meaning "peaceful" or "calm." The root of this word, *pac*, is derived from the Latin word meaning "peace."

1. Judging from the name given to the ocean bordering the western coast of the United States, how do you suppose this body of water impressed the people who gave it its name?

2. Explain the meaning of each of the following words. Then write a sentence using each word.

pacify   pacifist   pacifism

The Whistle

BENJAMIN FRANKLIN

Before the days of telephones and rapid transportation, letters took the place of friendly visits. In this letter to Madame Brillon, Franklin "visits" with her about the way people can draw more good from life and suffer less evil.

Passy,[1] November 10, 1779

To Madame Brillon:

I received my dear friend's two letters, one for Wednesday and one for Saturday. This is again Wednesday. I do not deserve one for to-day, because I have not answered the former. But, indolent as I am, and averse to writing, the fear of having no more of your pleasing epistles, if I do not contribute to the correspondence, obliges me to take up my pen; and as Mr. B. has kindly sent me word, that he sets out to-morrow to see you, instead of spending this Wednesday evening as I have done its namesakes, in your delightful company, I sit down to spend it in thinking of you, in writing to you, and in reading over and over again your letters.

I am charmed with your description of Paradise, and with your plan of living there; and I approve much of your conclusion, that, in the mean time, we should draw all the good we can from this world. In my opinion, we might all draw more good from it than we do, and suffer less evil, if we would take care not to give too much for *whistles*. For to me it seems, that most of the unhappy people we meet with, are become so by neglect of that caution.

You ask what I mean? You love stories, and will excuse my telling one of myself. When I was a child of seven years old, my friends, on a holiday, filled my pocket with coppers. I went directly to a shop where they sold toys for children; and, being charmed with the sound of a *whistle*, that I met by the way in the hands of another boy, I voluntarily offered and gave all my money for one. I then came home, and went whistling all over the house, much pleased with my *whistle*, but disturbing all the family. My brothers, and sisters, and cousins, understanding the bargain I had made, told me I had given four times as much for it as it was worth; put me in mind what good things I might have bought with the rest of the money; and laughed at me so much for my folly, that I cried with vexation; and the reflection gave me more chagrin than the *whistle* gave me pleasure.

This however was afterwards of use to me, the impression continuing on my mind; so that often, when I was tempted to buy some unnecessary thing, I said to myself, *Don't give too much for the whistle*; and I saved my money.

As I grew up, came into the world, and observed the actions of men, I thought I met with many, very many, who *gave too much for the whistle*.

[1] *Passy*, a section of Paris, France

When I saw one too ambitious of court favour, sacrificing his time in attendance on levees, his repose, his liberty, his virtue, and perhaps his friends, to attain it, I have said to myself, *This man gives too much for his whistle.*

When I saw another fond of popularity, constantly employing himself in political bustles, neglecting his own affairs, and ruining them by that neglect, *He pays, indeed,* said I, *too much for his whistle.*

If I knew a miser, who gave up every kind of comfortable living, all the pleasure of doing good to others, all the esteem of his fellow-citizens, and the joys of benevolent friendship, for the sake of accumulating wealth, *Poor man,* said I, *you pay too much for your whistle.*

When I met with a man of pleasure, sacrificing every laudable improvement of the mind, or of his fortune, to mere corporeal[2] sensations, and ruining his health in their pursuit, *Mistaken man,* said I, *you are providing pain for yourself, instead of pleasure; you give too much for your whistle.*

If I see one fond of appearance, or fine clothes, fine houses, fine furniture, fine equipages,[3] all above his fortune, for which he contracts debts, and ends his career in a prison, *Alas!* say I, *he has paid dear, very dear, for his whistle.*

When I see a beautiful, sweet-tempered girl married to an ill-natured brute of a husband, *What a pity,* say I, *that she should pay so much for a whistle!*

In short, I conceive that great part of the miseries of mankind are brought upon them by the false estimates they have made of the value of things, and by their *giving too much for their whistles.*

Yet I ought to have charity for these unhappy people, when I consider, that, with all this wisdom of which I am boasting, there are certain things in the world so tempting, for example, the apples of King John, which happily are not to be bought; for if they were put to sale by auction, I might very easily be led to ruin myself in the purchase, and find that I had once more given too much for the *whistle.*

Adieu, my dear friend, and believe me ever yours very sincerely and with unalterable affection,

B. Franklin.

[2] *corporeal,* bodily or physical
[3] *equipages,* elegantly equipped carriages

Let's consider . . .

1. Letter writing in the eighteenth century was a delightful pastime, usually for the class of society with considerable leisure. The style was formal, as were the manners of the period. **Style** is the distinctive manner in which an author uses language: his choice of words and their arrangement to express a special tone, attitude, or manner. Examine the style of this letter. Point out words and phrases which (1) give the letter its formal tone, and (2) identify the writer as belonging to

an earlier period in which life was quite different from what it is today.

2. As you learned from Van Doren's biography, Franklin was a philosopher. State briefly and clearly what lesson in values he learned from his purchase of a whistle.

3. How did he impress that lesson on you? What effect did he achieve by his constant reference to the whistle?

4. Read again the specific examples of "paying too much for a whistle." Now recall one instance in your own life when you also paid too much for something you wanted. Explain how this experience taught you a lesson in values. If you never had such an experience, tell the class about one you have heard about or read in a book.

The writer's craft . . .

So that you may know more about the human side of your national heroes, many of their letters have been collected and published. Certainly there is no more enjoyable way to understand a great man than to read his letters to his family and intimate friends. From them you not only catch the flavor of his personality; you also find clues which explain why he was an understanding person.

1. What did Franklin's letter to Madame Brillon reveal about his personality?

2. Did his letter offer clues which explain why he became a national hero?

3. Although the story about the whistle added to the charm of the letter, Franklin's purpose in using this story was serious. In your own words explain the **theme** of the whistle story: the point or basic idea he was trying to convey. Would you have enjoyed the letter more or less if he had merely written *about* the idea instead of presenting it by means of a story? Give several reasons to support your answer.

Knowing words . . .

In his letter to Madame Brillon, Franklin wrote of the "joys of *benevolent* friendship." The word *benevolent* stems from the Latin words *bene* meaning "well," and *volens* meaning "wishing." Franklin might therefore have written of the "joys of *well-wishing* friendship." Many English words with which you are familiar have the root *bene*, implying either "well" or "good."

1. Write a definition for each of the following words which have *bene* as a root. Be sure to include either the word "well" or the word "good" in your definition.

  benefit   benign
  benefactor   beneficiary
      beneficial

2. Use each of these words in a sentence of your own.

What Is Once Loved

What is once loved
You will find
Is always yours
From that day.
Take it home
In your mind
And nothing ever
Can take it away.
  Elizabeth Coatsworth

NOW THINK BACK

1. The strength of a democracy depends upon its "giants." They are its leaders in many fields; in government, industry, science, and the arts. Review the "giants" presented in the selections you have just read. With what fields were they associated? What contributions did they make to their country? In your discussion, compare these heroes—both men and women—with outstanding people in the news today who might also be considered "giants" in their own fields.

2. What are some of the qualities of character which all of these "giants" have in common?

3. Paul Bunyan is a legendary figure, a folk hero, whom Americans have endowed with certain qualities they admire. Richard E. Byrd is a real person and a national hero. Americans have taken him to their hearts because of what he represents. As you discuss these two figures, see if you can point out the differences in character between a folk hero and a national hero.

4. Which hero in this part do you consider the greatest asset to his country? Be able to support your answer with specific references to the selection about him or her.

5. There is a saying that "imitation is the sincerest form of flattery." Which of these heroes would you sincerely like to imitate? Give reasons for your choice.

6. Lincoln defined American democracy. Whitman recognized its faults and urged correction. Franklin helped to formulate the Constitution which provided for the preservation and growth of American democracy. Explain how each of these "giants" contributed to *your idea* of democracy.

7. Mary Lou Wingate, a fictional character, and Robert E. Lee, a real person, represent those qualities of true dignity and courage which distinguish many Southerners, today and in the past. Explain why the qualities of character represented by these two would endear them to their countrymen. Try to give explicit reasons.

Things to do . . .

1. Plan a quiz program on the national heroes included in this part. Phrase your questions to bring out important information, not easy-to-miss details.

2. Arrange a speaking contest for the class. Divide into groups, each group to study one of the heroes in this unit. From this study, you should learn to know the hero so well you could impersonate him. On a day assigned, select one member of the group to make a speech to the class on a subject which would be of interest to that hero. Others in the group will help to prepare the material for the speech, and if so decided, to provide the make-up and costume which are needed for impersonation. Each of the speeches must reflect the interests and point of view of the hero impersonated. As nearly as possible, the speech should imitate the style of speaking which this hero would probably use.

3. If you liked "Mary Lou Wingate," read *John Brown's Body,* the book from which this excerpt was taken. This book presents a moving and human picture of the War Between the States and is richly rewarding.

4. All these "giants" had interesting faces. Prepare an exhibition of as many of their portraits or photographs as you can find. If your school library has a picture file, look there first. If not, begin a letter-writing project and see how many you can collect. Write to magazines like *Life* and *Look,* to large insurance companies, to nearby museums which have loan collections, and to commercial supply houses.

Sometimes local movie houses can secure "stills" for you. Make this a group project. The *Reader's Guide to Periodical Literature* will prove a valuable reference.

More to read . . .

The Conqueror by GERTRUDE ATHERTON.
  J. B. Lippincott Company, 1939.
Pecos Bill by J. C. BOWMAN.
  Albert Whitman and Company, 1937.
Paul Bunyan by JAMES STEVENS.
  Alfred A. Knopf, Inc., 1947.

*   *   *

The Living Jefferson by JAMES TRUSLOW ADAMS.
  Charles Scribner's Sons, 1936.
Master of the Wilderness: Daniel Boone by JOHN BAKELESS.
  William Morrow & Company, Inc., 1939.
Lee the American by GAMALIEL BRADFORD.
  Houghton Mifflin Company, 1912.
Call Me Lucky by BING CROSBY as told to PETE MARTIN.
  Simon and Schuster, Inc., 1953.
The President of the United States by ERNEST BARKSDALE FINCHER.
  Abelard-Schuman Company, 1955.

Paul Revere and the World He Lived In by ESTHER FORBES.
  Houghton Mifflin Company, 1942.
Americans in Action by MAX HERZBERG and LEON MONES.
  Appleton-Century-Crofts, Inc., 1937.
American Heroes and Hero Worship by GERALD JOHNSON.
  Harper & Brothers, 1943.
The Spirit of St. Louis by CHARLES LINDBERGH.
  Charles Scribner's Sons, 1953.
Theodore Roosevelt's Letters to his Children by THEODORE ROOSEVELT. Edited by J. B. BISHOP.
  Charles Scribner's Sons, 1919.
Abraham Lincoln: The Prairie Years and The War Years by CARL SANDBURG.
  Harcourt, Brace and Company, 1954.
Alexander Hamilton by NATHAN SCHACHNER.
  McGraw-Hill Book Company, Inc., 1952.
Bob Mathias: Champion of Champions by JIM SCOTT.
  Prentice-Hall, Inc., 1952.
Abe Lincoln in Illinois by ROBERT E. SHERWOOD.
  Charles Scribner's Sons, 1938.
Benjamin Franklin by CARL VAN DOREN.
  The Viking Press, 1938.

AMERICANS SPEAK OUT

From the beginning, Americans have never hesitated to voice their opinions. They have expressed themselves on all topics—great and small, serious and amusing. When the colonists realized that they could not receive fair treatment from King George, they spoke out boldly in the "Declaration of Independence." When Oliver Wendell Holmes learned that the *Constitution*, a famous Navy warship, was to be scuttled, he wrote a stirring poem that aroused the public and saved the ship. And when the ordinary American citizen speaks out, the people listen. He may have a story which must be told or a protest which must be made.

Here is a cross-section of Americans speaking out of their hearts. The tones of their voices are keyed to the mood and tenor of their subjects. But no matter how much the tones may differ, each voice is part of the American tradition of saying what must be said.

AMERICANS SPEAK OUT

The Declaration of Independence

This document set in motion a way of life that allowed Americans to speak out.

When in the Course of human events, it becomes necessary for one people to dissolve the political bands which have connected them with another, and to assume among the powers of the earth, the separate and equal station to which the Laws of Nature and of Nature's God entitle them, a decent respect to the opinions of mankind requires that they should declare the causes which impel them to the separation.

We hold these truths to be self-evident, that all men are created equal, that they are endowed by their Creator with certain unalienable Rights, that among these are Life, Liberty, and the pursuit of Happiness. That to secure these rights, Governments are instituted among Men, deriving their just powers from the consent of the governed, That whenever any Form of Government becomes destructive of these ends, it is the Right of the People to alter or to abolish it, and to institute new Government, laying its foundation on such principles and organizing its powers in such form as to them shall seem most likely to effect their Safety and Happiness. Prudence, indeed, will dictate that Governments long established should not be changed for light and transient causes; and accordingly all experience hath shown, that mankind are more disposed to suffer, while evils are sufferable, than to right themselves by abolishing the forms to which they are accustomed. But when a long train of abuses and usurpations,[1] pursuing invariably the same Object evinces

Flags from left to right, top row: Bunker Hill Flag—1775, Betsy Ross Flag—1777, Gadsen Flag—1775; bottom row: Washington's Cruisers Flag—1775, Naval Ensign—1775, Liberty Tree Flag—1776.

[1] *usurpations,* unauthorized acts infringing on another's rights

a design to reduce them under absolute Despotism, it is their right, it is their duty, to throw off such Government, and to provide new Guards for their future security. —Such has been the patient sufferance of these Colonies; and such is now the necessity which constrains them to alter their former Systems of Government. The history of the present King of Great Britain is a history of repeated injuries and usurpations, all having in direct object the establishment of an absolute Tyranny over these States. To prove this, let Facts be submitted to a candid world.

He has refused his Assent to Laws, the most wholesome and necessary for the public good.

He has forbidden his Governors to pass Laws of immediate and pressing importance, unless suspended in their operation till his Assent should be obtained; and when so suspended, he has utterly neglected to attend to them.

He has refused to pass other Laws for the accommodation of large districts of people, unless those people would relinquish the right of Representation in the Legislature, a right inestimable to them and formidable to tyrants only.

He has called together legislative bodies at places unusual, uncomfortable, and distant from the depository of their public Records, for the sole purpose of fatiguing them into compliance with his measures.

He has dissolved Representative Houses repeatedly, for opposing with manly firmness his invasions on the rights of the people.

He has refused for a long time, after such dissolutions, to cause others to be elected; whereby the Legislative powers, incapable of Annihilation, have returned to the People at large for their exercise; the State remaining in the meantime exposed to all the dangers of invasion from without and convulsions within.

He has endeavored to prevent the population of these States; for that purpose obstructing the Laws for Naturalization of Foreigners; refusing to pass others to encourage their migration hither, and raising the conditions of new Appropriations of Lands.

He has obstructed the Administration of Justice, by refusing his Assent to Laws for establishing Judiciary powers.

He has made Judges dependent on his Will alone, for the tenure of their offices, and the amount and payment of their salaries.

He has erected a multitude of New Offices, and sent hither swarms of Officers to harass our people, and eat out their substance.

He has kept among us, in times of peace, Standing Armies without the Consent of our legislature.

He has affected to render the Military independent of and superior to the Civil power.

He has combined with others to subject us to a jurisdiction foreign to our constitution, and unacknowledged by our laws; giving his Assent to their Acts of pretended Legislation: For quartering large bodies of armed troops among us: For protecting them, by a mock Trial, from punishment for any Murders which they should commit on the Inhabitants of these States: For cutting off our Trade with all parts of the world: For imposing Taxes on us without our Consent: For depriving us in many cases, of the benefits of Trial by Jury: For transporting us beyond Seas to be tried for pretended offenses: For abolishing the free System of English Laws in a neighboring Province, establishing therein an Arbitrary government, and enlarging its Boundaries so as to render it at once an example and fit instrument for introducing the same absolute rule into these Colonies. For taking away our Charters, abolishing our most valuable Laws, and altering fundamentally the Forms of our Governments: For suspending our own Legislatures, and declaring themselves invested with power to legislate for us in all cases whatsoever.

He has abdicated Government here, by

declaring us out of his Protection and waging War against us.

He has plundered our seas, ravaged our Coasts, burnt our towns, and destroyed the lives of our people.

He is at this time transporting large Armies of foreign Mercenaries to compleate the works of death, desolation and tyranny, already begun with circumstances of Cruelty & perfidy scarcely paralleled in the most barbarous ages, and totally unworthy the Head of a civilized nation.

He has constrained our fellow Citizens taken Captive on the high Seas to bear Arms against their Country, to become the executioners of their friends and Brethren, or to fall themselves by their Hands.

He has excited domestic insurrections amongst us, and has endeavored to bring on the inhabitants of our frontiers, the merciless Indian Savages, whose known rule of warfare, is an undistinguished destruction of all ages, sexes, and conditions.

In every stage of these Oppressions We have Petitioned for Redress in the most humble terms: Our repeated Petitions have been answered only by repeated injury. A Prince, whose character is thus marked by every act which may define a Tyrant, is unfit to be the ruler of a free people.

Nor have We been wanting in attention to our British brethren. We have warned them from time to time of attempts by their legislature to extend an unwarrantable jurisdiction over us. We have reminded them of the circumstances of our emigration and settlement here. We have appealed to their native justice and magnanimity, and we have conjured [2] them by the ties of our common kindred to disavow these usurpations, which would inevitably interrupt our connections and correspondence. They too have been deaf to the voice of justice and of consanguinity.[3] We must, therefore, acquiesce in the necessity, which denounces our Separation, and hold them, as we hold the rest of mankind, Enemies in War, in Peace Friends.

WE, THEREFORE, the Representatives of the UNITED STATES OF AMERICA, in General Congress, Assembled, appealing to the Supreme Judge of the world for the rectitude [4] of our intentions, do, in the Name, and by Authority of the good People of these Colonies, solemnly publish and declare, That these United Colonies are, and of Right ought to be FREE AND INDEPENDENT STATES; that they are Absolved from all Allegiance to the British Crown, and that all political connection between them and the State of Great Britain, is and ought to be totally dissolved; and that as Free and Independent States, they have full Power to levy War, conclude Peace, contract Alliances, establish Commerce, and to do all other Acts and Things which Independent States may of right do. And for the support of this Declaration, with a firm reliance on the protection of divine Providence, we mutually pledge to each other our Lives, our Fortunes, and our sacred Honor.

---

[2] *conjured,* appealed to
[3] *consanguinity,* blood relationship, descent from a common ancestor
[4] *rectitude,* moral integrity, righteousness

Let's consider . . .

The Declaration of Independence stands not only as a revered documentation of American beliefs and ideas, but also as a great literary classic. Its statement is direct, its language exact, and its logic carefully developed.

A. An analysis of the first two paragraphs of this document will help you to see how its logic is developed.

1. The first paragraph served as an introduction. It set forth the reason for issuing this declaration. What did the people of America find it necessary to do? What did this action require them to declare?

2. The second paragraph set forth the case for America, very much as a lawyer might do for a client.

    a. What truths do Americans believe?

    b. Why are governments instituted?

    c. What is the right of the people if any form of government fails in its obligations?

    d. Why was it necessary for the colonies to alter their former system of government?

B. The remainder of the "Declaration" could be divided into three parts:

1. A listing of the acts of tyranny by the King of England

2. A review of the efforts of the colonists to secure justice

3. A statement of the intention of the colonists to create a separate nation of free and independent States

Use these headings as you work out your analysis of the three parts. Under each heading, list the points which supported the colonists' case for independence.

The writer's craft . . .

A. The Declaration of Independence is a **document:** a legal or official paper furnishing information or evidence. It represents the thinking of some of America's great statesmen, who formed a committee to produce this document. Thomas Jefferson was a member of the committee and was largely responsible for putting it into written form.

B. **Elegance** is a term used to describe the quality of directness, clarity, and conciseness in a piece of writing. It applies not only to the author's choice of words but also to his arrangement of those words in a clear, closely-knit structure. The Declaration of Independence is distinguished for its flawless elegance, a quality which establishes it as great literature.

Choose one or two sentences from this document which you feel illustrate this quality of elegance. Show also how this quality adds strength to the argument Jefferson was presenting.

Knowing words . . .

A. Some of the words in the Declaration of Independence are probably not a part of your everyday speaking vocabulary. However, in order to grasp the spirit of this national document, you must understand what these words mean. Study the italicized words in the sentences below. First try to find the meaning of each word from its context; then see if your definition is the same as that given in the glossary at the back of this book.

1. The history of the present King of Great Britain is a history of repeated injuries and *usurpations* . . .

2. In every stage of these Oppressions We have Petitioned for *Redress* in the most humble terms.

3. We have warned them from time to time of attempts by their legislature to extend an *unwarrantable jurisdiction* over us.

4. We have appealed to their native justice and *magnanimity* . . .

5. We must, therefore, *acquiesce* in the necessity which denounces our Separation . . .

B. Each of the italicized words in Exercise A carries a strong feeling. Each reflects the attitude of the colonists toward the injustices imposed upon them. Explain what feeling or attitude each of these words reflects.

Corporal Hardy

RICHARD E. DANIELSON

Mr. Hardy had never before told anyone about Chancellorsville, but he felt the story had to be told—at least once—if only to a small boy.

In those days, during the haying season, it was my duty to keep the men in the fields supplied with sufficient cooling drink to enable them to support the heat and burden of the day. According to our established practice, this cooling drink consisted of cold water from the spring, flavored, for some obscure New England reason, with molasses, and it had to be freshly renewed every hour. We had plenty of ice in the icehouse, but there was a stubborn tradition that ice water was "bad" for men working in hayfields under the hot sun.

So every hour I carried down a brown jug containing the innocent mixture of "molasses 'n' water" to the hands, each one of whom would pause in his work, throw the jug over his upper arm, drink deeply thereof, wipe the sweat off his forehead, say "Thanks, Bub," and go on making hay. I was only ten years old, but it was no hardship to carry the jug, and it was fun to see their Adam's apples working as they drank.

This was routine practice on our Connecticut farm. Mostly the farm hands— "hired men," we called them—came back to the house at noon and ate in the kitchen, after washing up at the pump outside. But in haymaking season each man sought a patch of shade, and his meal was carried to him there, to be eaten in the fields. I suppose the men's overheated bodies cooled off in the wisps of breeze drifting across the scorching "mowings" more effectively and comfortably than would have been possible in a hot summer kitchen. I am sure that my father did everything he could to make their lot as comfortable and healthy as possible. He worked with them, under the same conditions, setting them an example of careful, efficient labor. He differed from his men only in the fact that he was always cleanly shaved, that he gave orders and directions, and that he wore a silk shirt even in the hayfields. Nobody objected in the least to this token, for he was "the owner," and he had been to college, and everyone admitted that he was fair and square.

On such occasions, when the men were given their "dinners" out of doors, I always carried his victuals to Mr. Hardy, because I liked to sit with him while he ate and listen to his stories. I think he enjoyed talking, in his racy Connecticut vernacular, to such a fascinated audience of one. He was a Civil War veteran, like my father, who, however, had been too young to enlist until the last year of the war and had seen almost no active service. But Mr. Hardy was a soldier. Congress had give him a medal—of honor—and all men regarded him with respect.

As I look back and remember his stories, I think he must have been the most modest man I have ever known. Certainly he

we rated people by their comparative "success." But he worked stoutly and asked no favors of anyone. It was generally conceded that Mr. Hardy, if a failure, was nevertheless a good man.

I remember the last day I served him. I brought him his dinner in a basket—cold meat 'n' potatoes, 'n' bread 'n' butter, 'n' cold coffee, 'n' pie. He was seated in the shade of an oak tree, leaning against a stack of hay. I put the food down beside him and sat down, hugging my knees and rocking back and forth. It was pleasant there, with the smell of the hay and the drone of the bees, and the good, warm feeling of the earth.

Mr. Hardy lay back against the haymow. "Thanks, Jackie," he said. "I don't seem to be hungry today. It's hot and this tree don't give much shade. Why, dammit, it's like that mean little oak tree down to Chancellorsville."

I said, "Oh, Mr. Hardy, you've told me about Antietam and the Wilderness, but

never thought of himself as a hero. He would accept no pension. "I'm able-bodied. I can work, can't I?" But, alas, he was not really able-bodied. He had been grievously wounded several times, and in 1895, when I fetched and carried for him and sat at his feet, it was pitiful to see his valiant efforts to fork hay on the wagon or do the other farming tasks which require muscular strength. He was thin and bent, but his face was brown and clean and his blue eyes bright and indomitable.

My father employed Mr. Hardy whenever there was work to give him, and treated him—I did not, at that time, know why—differently from the other hired men. He was poor, he lived alone, he was unsuccessful, and in New England then you've never told me about Chancellorsville. What was it like?"

He said slowly, "I ain't never told nobody about Chancellorsville, and I don't aim to tell nobody—grown-up, that is. But I'd kind of like to tell somebody that don't know nothing—like you—about it, for the first and last time. You'll forget it, and it would kind of ease my mind."

Mr. Hardy hoisted himself a little higher on the haymow and made a pretense of eating some bread and meat.

"Chancellorsville," he said, "was a bad battle, an awful bad battle. We didn't fight good and they was too many of them and I lost my captain."

"Who was he?" I asked.

"Why," he said, incredulously, "you oughta know that! He was Captain William Armstrong, commandin' Company B, 39th Connecticut. 'N' his twin brother, Ezra, was lootenant. He was younger by an hour or so, and they was identical twins. They never was two men as much alike—in looks, that is, for they was quite unlike inside. The lootenant was always stompin' around an' shoutin' an' wavin' his arms, an' the captain, he was always quiet an' soft-spoken an' brave an' gentle. He was a good man—he was an awful good man. I guess he was the best man I ever knowed."

He paused and took a sip of his cold coffee. Then he said, "Why, when we come to leave town to go in the cars to Hartford and then to Washington, their father—he was old Judge Armstrong, who lived in that big place up on Armstrong Hill—the Judge come up to me and says, 'Nathan, you look after my boys,' he said. 'They're younger than you be. You kind of keep an eye on them, for my sake,' he says. 'They is good boys,' he says. 'I will, Judge,' I says. 'I'll do my best.' An' he says to me, 'I know you will, Nathan Hardy.'"

"But tell me, Mr. Hardy," I broke in, for I was not interested in the Armstrong twins, "what happened at Chancellorsville?"

"It was a bad battle, as I said. Them Rebs come charging out of the woods, hollerin' and yellin' and helligolarrupin', and they was too many of them. The lootenant, he kept stomping up and down, shouting, 'Never give ground, boys! Stay where you are! Take careful aim! Never retreat!' Those was his words. I will never forget them, because he meant them. But my captain—I was next to him—says, 'They're too many; we can't stop 'em. Tell the men to retreat slowly, firing as often as they can reload.' Just then it hit him right in the chest. Thunk! was the noise it made; just like thet—thunk! I caught him as he fell, and the blood began to come out of his mouth. He tried to speak, but he was vomiting blood dreadful, so all he could do was to make faces, and his lips said, 'Tell Elizabeth . . .' and then he died. I put him down and noticed we was under a mean little oak tree on the edge of our trenches.

"Then they was around us, hairy men with bayonets, stabbin' and shootin' and yellin', and we soldiers had kind of drifted together in groups and the lootenant was shouting, 'Don't retreat, men!' and he got hit right in the knee and fell down; and so I picked him up and put him across my shoulder and started for the rear. He kep' hittin' me in the face and swearing, 'You damn coward! You left my brother there and you're making me retreat!' I says to him, 'Ezra, be reasonable; I'm takin' you to an ambulance. You ain't fit to fight, and as soon as I can I'm going back to bury William. They ain't goin' to shovel him into no trench,' I said. So he stopped hitting at me.

"I was strong then, and I must a carried him a mile or a mile and a few rods when we come to some stretcher men near a house, and I said, 'You take this officer to the nearest surgeon. They got to saw his leg off.' And they said, 'We ain't carryin' no wounded. We're a burial detail.' I said, pulling my pistol out, 'You will be if you don't carry this man. I'm kind of tuckered, but I ain't too tuckered to shoot.' So two of them carried him, and I went along with my pistol till we come to a place where surgeons was carving men up and I handed over the lootenant. He come to as I did so, and said, 'You scoundrel, you made me retreat. I'll never forgive you!' I said, 'Ezra, they're going to saw your leg off and you'll never fight again, but I'll bury William if it's the last thing I do.' He says, 'Is that a promise?' And I says, 'That's a promise. But it ain't a promise to you—it's one I made to your pa.'

"So I stayed with him and helped hold him while they sawed his leg off. They havin' run out of chloroform, it took four of us to hold him. And when it was over he was unconscious, and they put him in a car with some others and took him away. So I went back to the house where the burial men were loafing. It was pretty ruined, but I found a shingle that was almos' clean and I wrote on it, in the light of a fire, 'cause it was dark then:—

Capt. William Armstrong
Commanding Co. B., 39 Connecticut
He was an awful good man

"Then I borrowed a spade from this burial party. We had an argument about it, but I persuaded them with my pistol and I started off toward the Rebel lines. I hadn't gone very far when I come to a place which was thick with men moanin' and screamin' and lots that wasn't sayin' nothing at all. I didn't want to walk on them an' I couldn't help them, having nothing on me but a shingle and a spade and a pistol, an' I decided I couldn't find the captain in the dark anyhow, so I set down and tried to sleep, for I was tuckered. I threw away my pistol. I set there the rest of the night waitin' for the dawn. It was a long time comin'.' "

"When it come gray, I started out with my shingle and my spade and I went along till I was challenged by the Rebel pickets and sentries. I answered, 'Union burial de-

tail. I'm comin' for to bury my captain.' They begun shootin' at me and I don't know as I blame them. I was comin' out of the mist and they couldn't see that I was alone an' wasn't armed. So they shot real hard, and one bullet struck me in the left thigh and I fell down. Fortunately I had a belt, and I sat up and took it off and strapped it real tight over my wound, and my britches was tight at the waist so they didn't come down, and I got up and went on.

"They stopped shootin' and a man with a bayonet got up and said, 'Yank, you're my pris'ner.' And I said, 'I know I be, but I ain't your pris'ner till I bury my captain.' And I held up my shingle and spade. He said, 'Where's he lie?' And I said, 'About quarter mile from here and maybe a few rods, under a mean little oak tree; and,' I says, 'you take me there and I'll bury him and then I'm your pris'ner. They ain't goin' to stuff my captain into no ditch,' I says. He says, 'You may be crazy, Yank, or you may be a spy. You come with me an' I'll turn you over to the captain.'

" 'Your captain alive?' I asks.

" 'I reckon so,' he says.

" 'Mine's dead,' I says, 'and I aim for to bury him.'

"So he tuk me away with his bayonet in my back and the blood was squilchin' in my boot, but I got along to where his captain was and the captain asked questions, and the Rebel soldier, he tol' all he knew, an' the captain says, 'Where's he lie?' An' I says, 'By a mean little oak, where our lines was yesterday mornin'.'

"An' the captain says, 'That ain't far away. I'll send a detail to bury him.' I says, 'Ain't nobody goin' to bury the captain but me,' I says. 'After that, I'll be your pris'ner.'

"They was a young man dressed up all pretty with gold braid on his uniform, and he laughed kind of loud and he says, 'Saves us the trouble of buryin' him!' an' the captain turns on him, real stern, and says, 'Lootenant, this is a brave soldier,' he says,

'who come back under fire and was wounded to bury his company commander and give himself up as pris'ner. I will not have him insulted or laughed at,' he says. Then he turns to me an' says, 'What is your name an' rank?'

" 'Corporal Nathan Hardy, Co. B, 39th Connecticut,' I says.

"An' he says, 'Corporal, you and I an' these men,' turnin' around to the five or six Rebs who was listenin', 'will go together to find your captain.'

"So we went and I found him, underneath that mean little oak tree, and he looked dreadful. His eyes was open and they was an awful lot of blood on his shirt where his coat was open, and he was lyin' all sprangled out an' undignified. An' the first thing I done was to straighten him out. I spit on my sleeve and wiped the blood off his mouth the best I could. An' I closed his eyes an' buttoned his coat an' crossed his arms. They was kind of stiff, but I done it, an' I brushed him off and layed him out regular.

"Then I started diggin', and it would have been easy if it hadn't been for my leg and all the blood in my boot. Six foot four

or thereabouts it was, and three foot deep —not as deep as I wanted, but I couldn't dig no deeper, I was so tuckered. But it was an honest grave, for I was real handy with a spade in them days. Then I stood up and said, 'Will two o' you Rebs hand the captain to me?' Which they done, and I laid him in the grave. An' as I stood lookin' down at him lyin' there, I says to myself, 'Ain't nobody goin' to shovel no dirt on the captain's face—nobody, nobody, nobody at all, not even me!' So I took my coat off and laid it over him, coverin' up his face best I could. I didn't want to go to no Rebel prison in my shirt, but I wouldn't have no one shovel dirt on the captain.

"Then the two Rebs pulled me out of the grave, real gentle and considerate. An' then I noticed they was a Rebel general there settin' on a blood horse.[1] How long he bin there I don't know. He looked at me and see I was wounded and peaked, and he says, stern an' hard, 'Captain, what's the meanin' of this? This man's wounded and weak,' he says. 'Do you force wounded men to bury the dead?'

"The captain went over to him and began talkin' to him low and earnest, seemed like, all the time I was fillin' in the grave. An' when I had patted the mound even, so it looked good, and had stuck the shingle in the new earth at the head of the grave, I come over to where the general was, limpin' and leanin' on my spade, an' I saluted,—couldn't help it; I kind of forgot he was a Rebel,—an' I says, 'General, I'm your pris'ner. I buried my captain. I ain't a great hand at askin' favors, an' your captain and these Rebs has been real good to me. But I wanta ask one more. I was raised Episcopal, which was unusual in our town, and so was the captain. I'd kind of like to say a prayer before I surrender. . . .' "

Here Mr. Hardy seemed to doze for a little. "Where was I?" he asked, rousing after a few minutes.

"You had just gone up to the general and asked if you could say a prayer before you surrendered."

"Yes, yes, so it was. The general said, 'Corporal Hardy, I am an Episcopalian too, and you shall say your prayer.'

"So he dismounted and took off his hat, and he and I kneeled down by the grave, and it was awful hard for me to kneel. And when we was there kneelin' I looked up for a minute and all them Rebs was standin' with their caps off and their heads bowed, nice and decent, just like Northern people. An' then I had a dreadful time, for to save my life I couldn't remember a prayer, not a line, not a word. I had heard the burial service often enough and too often, what with Pa and Ma an' all kinds of relatives, but my brains was all watery an' thin, seemed like, an' I couldn't

[1] *blood horse,* thoroughbred

remember nothin' at all. I don't know how long 'twas till something come driftin' into my mind. It wa'n't from the burial service; 'twas somethin' we used to chant in Evenin' Prayer. So I says it, loud as I could, for I was gettin' awful feeble.

" 'Lord,' I says, 'now lettest Thou Thy servant depart in peace, according to Thy Word. . . .' An' I couldn't remember or say any more. The general he helped me to my feet, spade an' all, an' I looked him in the face and, by creepers, they was tears in his beard. Soon as I could speak I says, 'General, you've been real good to me and I thank you. An' now I'm your pris'ner, wherever you want to send me.'

"An' he says, 'Corporal Hardy, you will never be a pris'ner of our people as long as I live and command this corps.'

"An' I broke in, awful scared he had misunderstood, and I says, 'General, you don't think I was prayin' for *me* to go in peace! I'm your pris'ner; I'm not askin' for no favors. I was thinkin' of the captain— and me too, perhaps, but not that way. I can go anywhere now. I—'

"He cut me short. 'Corporal Hardy,' he says, 'I know to Whom you was prayin' and why, an' I haven't misunderstood you at all. Captain,' he says, 'I want a detail of six men an' a stretcher and a flag of truce to take this brave soldier an'—an' Christian gentleman back to the Union lines; an' I want this message, which I have dictated and signed, delivered to the commanding officer to be forwarded through channels to the Secretary of War or the President. Those people can hardly decline this courtesy, under the circumstances. . . . Wait, Carter, I wish to add a few lines.' So he put the paper against his saddle and he wrote for some time.

"Then, kind of in a dream, I heard the Rebel captain say, 'Sir, if the General permits, I would like to lead this detail to the Union lines and ask to be blindfolded and deliver your message to the Division Commander.'

"An' the General says, 'Captain, I am

very glad you made that request, and I commend your behavior. It is only fittin' that the officer escortin' Corporal Hardy with my message should be of field rank, and I shall put in my order for your promotion. You are a pretty good soldier, yourself,' he says—only he didn't say it that way.

"All this time I was kind of waverin' around, but I heard most all they said; and because I was feeble from losing blood an' the battle an' buryin' the captain an' a kind of feverish feelin', things begun to spin around, and I started walkin' this way and that way with my spade, tryin' to stand up, knowin' I couldn't much longer. I heard someone yell, 'Catch him!' An' the next thing I knowed I was in a bed of straw and they was probin' for the bullet in my leg. Then I don't remember nothin' till I woke up in a bed, a clean bed, with a nice-lookin' woman leanin' over me, wipin' my head with a cold, wet towel. I says, 'Where am I?'

"An' she says, 'You're in the hospital of the Sanitary Commission in Washington. An' oh, Corporal Hardy,' she says, 'I'm so glad you're conscious, for to-day the President is comin' to give you the Medal of Honor.' An' I says, 'Listen, sister, I gotta get out of here. I don't care for no President or no medal—I gotta bury the captain. He's lyin' down there under a mean little oak. Gimme my clothes,' I says; 'I want a spade and a shingle.' An' she says, 'Corporal, you buried your captain an' buried him fine. That's why the President is comin' to see you. Now you just drink this and go to sleep for a while, and I'll wake you when the President comes.'

"So I drank it and kind of slept, and when I woke up there was Old Abe, the ugliest man I ever see, leanin' over and pinnin' something to my nightshirt, an' he says, 'Corporal Hardy, even the enemy call you a brave soldier and a good man. Congress has voted you this medal. God bless you,' he says."

＊

Mr. Hardy yawned and closed his eyes, and leaned against the haymow. He had told the tale he had to tell—once, to one person.

"But, Mr. Hardy," I said, "what happened to the lieutenant, and who was Elizabeth?" I wanted the story all tied up in ribbons.

"Who?" he said. "The lootenant? Oh, Ezra come back and married Elizabeth and they went to live in Massachusetts. Seems he went aroun' sayin' he couldn't live in no town where people pointed at him and thought he had run away leavin' his dead brother. Naturally no one done so or thought so. But, for all his stompin' and shoutin', he was sensitive, an' he bore me a grudge for takin' him away. I don't see as how I could a done different. I'd promised the old Judge I'd look after his boys an' I've allus aimed to keep my promises."

Just then my father came up to us. It was unlike Mr. Hardy to sit in the shade while other men had started to work again, and Father looked worried. "How are you feeling, Nathan?" he asked.

"Why, John, I'm plumb tuckered out, and that's a fact. I don't know as I can do much more work to-day. Seems like I never did fare good under these mean little oak trees," and he glanced sharply at me with an expression that was almost a wink. We shared a secret.

Father looked startled, as if he thought Mr. Hardy's wits were wandering.

"I tell you what, Nathan," he said, "you've had all the sun you need. I'll send the wagon and they'll take you up to the house, where you can be cool and rest for a while." And, for once in his life, Mr. Hardy made no protest over having "favors" done for him. Father took me aside. "Jackie," he said, "you run up to the house and tell your mother to make the bed in the spare room ready, and then you go to the village and tell Dr. Fordyce he's wanted. I don't like Nathan's looks."

Before I started running I glanced at Mr. Hardy, and I saw what Father meant. He was pale and flushed in the wrong places, though I hadn't noticed it at all when he was telling me about Chancellorsville.

So Mr. Hardy was put to bed in the spare room, and given such care and aid as we knew how to give. For several days he lay quietly enough, and, as I look back on it after all these years, I think that the weight and burden of his long, valiant struggle must suddenly have proved too great. He couldn't go on forever. Mr. Hardy was tuckered out.

Then for some time he alternated between unconsciousness and a mild delirium. He kept mumbling phrases: "Take that quid out o' your mouth. 'Tain't soldierly!" . . . "Ain't nobody goin' to bury the captain but me." I knew what lots of his bewildered sayings meant, but there were many which were obscure. I sat with him every day for an hour or so when the rest of the household were busy, and I had instructions to call my elders if Mr. Hardy needed help or became conscious.

One day he opened his eyes and said, "Here I am and I'm real easy in my mind— but I can't just remember what I said." I went out and called my parents, who told me to stay outside. But I listened and I heard Mr. Hardy say, "Call the boy in. He knows what I want said and I can't remember. He's young and 'twon't hurt him and he'll forget." So Mother beckoned me to come in and I said, "What can I do, Mr. Hardy?"

"You can say what I said for the captain when I knelt down with the general."

So I knelt down, and, having the parrot-like memory of childhood, I said, "You knelt down and so did the general, and then you couldn't remember any of the words of the burial service, but you did remember something that was sung in the evening, and you said, 'Lord, now lettest Thou Thy servant depart in peace, according to Thy Word. . . .'" And I began to cry.

"That's right," he said very faintly, "that's right; that's it. Yes Captain . . ."

My mother gathered me up and took me out and held me very close, rocking back and forth with me while I wept out how I loved Mr. Hardy and what a good man he was.

And that was why I was sent to my aunt and cousins at New London, where I could swim and fish and forget about battles and wounds and Mr. Hardy. But I didn't forget.

The man who wrote this story

RICHARD ELY DANIELSON 1885–

R. E. Danielson began his editorial career in 1924 as editor of the Boston *Independent*. Three years later he left the newspaper field to become editor of *The Sportsman* magazine. After ten years he joined the staff of *The Atlantic Monthly*, and became president and associate editor of that publication in 1940.

Mr. Danielson was born in Brooklyn, Connecticut and was educated at William Penn Charter School and at Yale University. He graduated from Yale in 1907 and took a Master of Arts degree in 1910.

When World War I broke out in Europe, Mr. Danielson volunteered as a Red Cross ambulance driver in France. After America entered the war, he was commissioned in the U. S. Army and rose to the rank of captain. During World War II he served as a staff officer at army headquarters in Washington, D. C.

He is the author of *Martha Doyle and other Sporting Memories* (1938) and several short stories.

Let's consider . . .

1. Even though most short stories are read chiefly for pleasure, they often provide

the reader with useful information. What did you learn from this story about farm life in Connecticut as it was some fifty years ago?

2. The War Between the States was one of the bloodiest in history. The casualties were high and the suffering was terrible. What evidence of this fact did you find in "Corporal Hardy"? What indispensables in modern warfare would have lessened the suffering?

3. Even the Rebels called Corporal Hardy "a brave soldier and a good man." What do you consider (1) his bravest moment and (2) his finest trait of character?

4. What sort of man was Jackie's father?

5. An old soldier's memories of a battle are not always exciting. Explain why this story seemed dramatic and moving.

6. Too often the participants in a war speak out only for their side. They overlook the fact that among "the enemy" there are people equally humane and devoted to a cause in which they believe. Corporal Hardy was a Northerner, and yet he spoke out for the Confederate side at Chancellorsville. What did he say? What personal obligation did he have to fulfill which made him speak out, even to a Confederate general?

The writer's craft . . .

All writers of fiction must decide how their stories can best be told: the **point of view** they are going to use in the telling. Richard Ely Danielson decided that "Corporal Hardy" should be told from the point of view of an adult who recalls an experience which he had as a boy.

Very often the story itself determines the way it can best be told. You might ask, "Why did Mr. Danielson choose this way to tell 'Corporal Hardy'? Why didn't he tell the story from the point of view of the little boy?" By making the narrator a grown man, the author was able to describe Mr. Hardy more fully than if he had

made the narrator a small boy. For example, early in the story the narrator said, "As I *look back* and remember his stories, I think he [Mr. Hardy] must have been the most modest man I have ever known." The observation about "the most modest man" would never have been made by a small boy. Find other comments about Mr. Hardy that could have been made only by an adult narrator. However, when Mr. Hardy is actually telling his story, the author allows his readers to share the full dramatic effect which this story had on him as a young boy.

1. The author used **reminiscence**—the recalling of a past experience—in telling the story. How did it help to make the ending particularly moving?

2. Did Mr. Danielson's method of writing this story add to your enjoyment in reading it? Give reasons for your answer.

Knowing words . . .

Richard Ely Danielson wrote that Mr. Hardy spoke in a "racy, Connecticut vernacular." The word **vernacular** means "common, everyday language." It is the living language as spoken by the people, even though it is sometimes not what is called Standard English. Here are several examples of Mr. Hardy's use of the vernacular of the time and of the part of the country in which he lived.

"I'm kind of tuckered, but I ain't too tuckered to shoot."

"A man with a bayonet got up and said, 'Yank, you're my pris'ner.' And I said, 'I know I be, but I ain't your pris'ner till I bury my captain.'"

"And when I woke up there was Old Abe, the ugliest man I ever see, leanin' over and pinnin' something to my night-shirt."

1. Give several examples of the vernacular of your own time and region.

2. Now make up two sentences using the word *vernacular*.

Birth and Early Childhood

BOOKER T. WASHINGTON

Each man during his lifetime hears words that have a special meaning for him. Booker T. Washington, the noted Negro educator, never forgot the words his mother spoke on the day they were freed.

I will not trouble those who read these lines with any lengthy historical research concerning my ancestry, for I know nothing of my ancestry beyond my mother. My mother was a slave on a plantation near Hale's Ford, in Franklin County, Virginia, and she was, as I now remember it, the cook for her owners as well as for a large part of the slaves on the plantation. The first time that I got a knowledge of the fact that my mother and I were slaves, was by being awakened by my mother early one morning, while sleeping in a bed of rags, on the clay floor of our little cabin. She was kneeling over me, fervently praying as was her custom to do, that some day she and her children might be free. The name of my mother was Jane. She, to me, will always remain the noblest embodiment of womanhood with which I have come in contact. She was wholly ignorant, as far as books were concerned, and, I presume, never had a book in her hands for two minutes at a time. But the lessons in virtue and thrift which she instilled into me during the short period of my life that she lived will never leave me. Some people blame the Negro for not being more honest, as judged by the Anglo-Saxon's standard of honesty; but I can recall many times

when, after all was dark and still, in the late hours of the night, when her children had been without sufficient food during the day, my mother would awaken us, and we would find that she had gotten from somewhere something in the way of eggs or chickens and cooked the food during the night for us. These eggs and chickens were gotten without my master's permission or knowledge. Perhaps, by some code of ethics, this would be classed as stealing, but deep down in my heart I can never decide that my mother, under such circumstances, was guilty of theft. Had she acted thus as a free woman she would have been a thief, but not so, in my opinion, as a slave. After our freedom no one was stricter than my mother in teaching and observing the highest rules of integrity.

As nearly as I can get at the facts, I was born in the year 1858 or 1859. At the time I came into the world no careful registry of births of people of my complexion was kept. My birthplace was near Hale's Ford, in Franklin County, Virginia. It was about as near to Nowhere as any locality gets to be, so far as I can learn. Hale's Ford, I think, was a town with one house and a postoffice, and my birthplace was on a large plantation several miles distant from it.

I remember very distinctly the appearance of the cabin in which I was born and lived until freedom came. It was a small log cabin about 12 x 16 feet, and without windows. There was no floor except one of dirt. There was a large opening in the center of the floor, where sweet potatoes were kept for my master's family during the winter. In this cabin my mother did the cooking, the greater part of the time, for my master's family. Our bed, or "pallet," as we called it, was made every night on the dirt floor. Our bed clothing consisted of a few rags gathered here and there.

One thing I remember more vividly than any other in connection with the days when I was a slave was my dress, or, rather, my lack of dress.

The years when the war was in progress between the States were especially trying to the slaves, so far as clothing was concerned. The Southern white people found it extremely hard to get clothing for themselves during that war, and, of course, the slaves underwent no little suffering in this respect. The only garment that I remember receiving from my owners during the war was a "tow shirt." When I did not wear this shirt I was positively without any garment. In Virginia, the tow shirt was quite an institution during slavery. This shirt was made of the refuse flax that grew in that part of Virginia, and it was a veritable instrument of torture. It was stiff and coarse. Until it had been worn for about six weeks it made one feel as if a thousand needle points were pricking his flesh. I suppose I was about six years old when I was given one of these shirts to wear. After repeated trials the torture was more than my childish flesh could endure and I gave it up in despair. To this day the sight of a new shirt revives the recollection of the tortures of my first new shirt. In the midst of my despair, in connection with this garment, my brother John, who was about two years older than I, did me a kindness which I shall never forget. He volunteered to wear my new shirt for me until it was "broken in." After he had worn it for several weeks I ventured to wear it myself, but not without pain.

Soon after my shirt experience, when the winter had grown quite cold, I received my first pair of shoes. These shoes had wooden bottoms, and the tops consisted of a coarse kind of leather. I have never felt so proud since of a pair of shoes.

As soon as I was old enough I performed what, to me, was important service, in holding the horses, and riding behind the white women of the household on their long horseback rides, which were very common in those days. At one time, while holding the horses and assisting quite a party of visiting ladies to mount their horses, I remember that, just before the visitors rode away, a tempting plate of ginger cakes was brought out and handed around to the visitors. This, I think, was the first time that I had ever seen ginger cakes, and a very deep impression was made upon my childish mind. I remember I said to myself that if I ever could get to the point where I could eat ginger cakes as I saw those ladies eating them, the height of my ambition would be reached.

When I grew to be still larger and stronger the duty of going to the mill was intrusted to me; that is, a large sack containing three or four bushels of corn was thrown across the back of a horse and I would ride away to the mill, which was often three or four miles distant, wait at the mill until the corn was turned into meal, and then bring it home. More than once, while performing this service, the corn or meal got unevenly balanced on the back of the horse and fell off into the road, carrying me with it. This left me in a very awkward and unfortunate position. I, of course, was unable, with my small strength, to lift the corn or meal upon the horse's back, and therefore would have to wait, often for hours, until someone happened to be passing along the road strong enough to replace the burden for me.

My owner's name was Jones Burroughs, and I am quite sure he was above the average in the treatment of his slaves. That is, except in a few cases, they were not cruelly whipped. Although I was born a slave, I was too young to experience much of its hardships. The thing in connection with slavery that has left the deepest impression on me was the instance of seeing a grown man, my uncle, tied to a tree early one morning, stripped naked, and someone whipping him with a cowhide. As each blow touched his back the cry, "Pray, master! Pray, master!" came from his lips, and made an impression upon my boyish heart that I shall carry with me to my grave.

When I was still quite a child, I could hear the slaves in our "quarter" whispering in subdued tones that something unusual —the war—was about to take place, and that it meant their freedom. These whispered conferences continued, especially at night, until the war actually began.

While there was not a single slave on our plantation that could read a line, in some way we were kept informed of the progress of the war almost as accurately as the most intelligent person. The "grapevine" telegraph was in constant use. When Lee surrendered all of the plantation people knew it, although all of them acted as if they were in ignorance of the fact that anything unusual had taken place.

Early one morning, just after the close of the war, word was sent around to the slave cabins that all the slaves must go to the "big house," the master's house; and in company with my mother and a large number of other slaves, including my sister Amanda and brother John, I went to the "big house," and stood by the side of my mother, and listened to the reading of some papers and a little speech made by the man who read the papers. This was the first public address I had ever heard, and I need not add that it was the most effective one to which it has ever been my privilege to listen. After the reading of the paper, and the speech, my mother leaned over and whispered, "Now, my children, we are free."

The man who wrote this autobiography

BOOKER T. WASHINGTON   1856–1915

Although he had been born a slave and his family had known slavery most of their lives, Booker T. Washington was only a child when the War Between the States ended and the negroes were set free. Almost immediately, he secured his first job tending a salt furnace in a little Virginia town.

Perhaps Mr. Washington had been influenced by his own experiences as a slave and by his mother's stories of slave life. He was determined to make something of himself and to help his people. He traveled five hundred miles to attend college at the Hampton Normal and Agricultural Institute. By working as a janitor there, he was able to complete the course. After graduation Mr. Washington taught at several schools before moving to Alabama to set up Tuskegee Institute.

At first the Institute had only thirty students, a few shacks for classrooms and dormitories, and one teacher—Mr. Washington. Under his guidance students helped to construct additional buildings, and many new teachers joined the Institute. By the time of Mr. Washington's death, Tuskegee Institute had become one of the best negro schools in America.

The contribution which Booker T. Washington made to his country as a great educator and teacher was recognized by all Americans. He received honorary degrees from both Harvard and Dartmouth. He wrote a number of books, including his autobiography, *Up from Slavery*.

Let's consider . . .

1. In this account of his early years as a slave, Booker T. Washington was frank and honest, but not bitter. He was neither too humble nor too proud. Some men who, in later years, had attained the same honor and position might have chosen to conceal certain facts about their childhood. Why do you think Booker T. Washington was so frank about his own childhood?

2. Name several instances in this account which you think might easily have made Mr. Washington bitter.

3. In what did he take justifiable pride?

4. "Had she acted thus as a free woman, she would have been a thief." In this statement Booker T. Washington indicated that there was one code for free men and another for slaves. The institution of slavery has existed since the beginning of recorded time and in almost every corner of the world. You are likely to think of it only in relation to a section of the United States during a certain period in American history. Do you think this double code still exists? Discuss.

5. Naturally, Booker T. Washington had poignant memories of his early years. Which incident seemed to you most pathetic? Which treatment of the little boy seemed most cruel?

6. In what part of this account did you feel the author had been most understanding of those who made life hard for him?

7. From this account you learned something of slave life on a large plantation just before and during the War Between the States. What interested you the most?

The writer's craft . . .

A. "Now, my children, we are free." These words made a strong impression on Booker T. Washington, as they must also have made on you as you read them. From the very beginning of the selection, the author prepared you for this ending. Look again at the opening paragraph. There he spoke of his mother's praying that someday she and her children might be free. Then, as he shared with you his deep love and affection for his mother, you came to know her as a real person.

1. Why did this quoted line make a dramatic ending for the selection?

2. Write a brief character sketch of Booker T. Washington's mother.

B. An autobiography is likely to be more personal and introspective (self-searching) than a biography. In an autobiography, the person is writing about himself and can, therefore, describe exactly what he thought and felt at a certain time and place.

1. In what passages did Booker T. Washington describe his emotional reactions? How did his description of his feelings help you to understand him better?

2. If this selection had been written as a biography instead of an autobiography, how would these passages have been different? What would the writer have had to leave out? What might he have added?

Knowing words . . .

Booker T. Washington wrote that his mother would "always remain the noblest *embodiment* of womanhood." The word *embodiment* here means "the representation in concrete form of an abstract quality or idea." Thus, he meant that his mother represented the noblest qualities in all womanhood. Abstract ideas, such as womanhood, truth, or beauty, are always difficult to communicate, but when they are embodied—represented by something concrete—they become easier to understand.

Choose two abstract qualities like love, faith, fair play, or cooperation. Also choose a person, object, or group which you feel is the embodiment of each of these qualities. Then write two statements like Booker T. Washington's; for example, "For many refugees, the Statue of Liberty is the embodiment of a new hope."

Stanzas on Freedom

JAMES RUSSELL LOWELL

This poem, and the four which follow, were inspired by love of country and of freedom. They deal with ideas and ideals for which Americans have lived and died. All of the authors of these poems belonged to the nineteenth century and used the conventional verse forms popular in their time. Much of what they had to say is still extremely pertinent in present-day America.

Men! whose boast it is that ye
Come of fathers brave and free,
If there breathe on earth a slave,
Are ye truly free and brave?
If ye do not feel the chain,
When it works a brother's pain,
Are ye not base slaves indeed,
Slaves unworthy to be freed?

Women! who shall one day bear
Sons to breathe New England air,
If ye hear, without a blush,
Deeds to make the roused blood rush
Like red lava through your veins,
For your sisters now in chains,—
Answer! are ye fit to be
Mothers of the brave and free?

Is true Freedom but to break
Fetters for our own dear sake,
And, with leathern hearts, forget
That we owe mankind a debt?
No! true freedom is to share
All the chains our brothers wear,
And, with heart and hand, to be
Earnest to make others free!

They are slaves who fear to speak
For the fallen and the weak;
They are slaves who will not choose
Hatred, scoffing, and abuse,
Rather than in silence shrink
From the truth they needs must think;
They are slaves who dare not be
In the right with two or three.

The man who wrote this poem

JAMES RUSSELL LOWELL 1819–1891

For over three generations the Lowell family has been famous in education, science, and art. Perhaps the Lowell who is best known and has established the widest reputation is James Russell.

Like Irving, Lowell was educated for the law. After receiving his degree, he opened an office in Boston, but found that he had more free time than paying clients. He used this time to read and write poetry. A series of lectures on nineteenth-century poets won him a position at Harvard. In fact, he succeeded Longfellow as professor of modern languages. Like Longfellow, he was a good teacher, and his students never forgot his charm and energetic intelligence. In a society that boasted of such gentlemen as Emerson and Longfellow, Lowell was considered the most "perfect gentleman."

Lowell felt more and more restricted by his teaching position and eventually gave it up to go into publishing. He was the first editor of *The Atlantic Monthly* and later edited the *North American Review*. Lowell held very definite opinions about literature and "gentility" and set a standard for future editors that has not been surpassed.

Most of Lowell's poetry appeared before the War Between the States and was popular during his own time. It is less popular today, partly because the problems with which he was concerned—slavery, for one—are no longer of vital interest to modern readers. Like the good editor he was, Lowell knew exactly where his poetry was weakest. In his *A Fable for Critics*, he wrote of himself,

> "The top of the hill he will ne'er
> come nigh reaching
> Till he learns the distinction 'twixt
> singing and preaching."

The poet's art . . .

1. The first two stanzas are addressed to men and women respectively. According to Lowell, when do men deserve *not* to be free? When are women unfit to be mothers "of the brave and free"?

2. What difference was pointed out in the third stanza between selfish and unselfish freedom?

3. Explain the meaning of the last two lines. Show how it has a present-day application to social, business, or political life.

4. This poem illustrates poetic style and techniques which you have already studied. Point out examples of the following:

> the rhymed couplet
> the run-on line
> the alternating of stressed and
> unstressed syllables

Note that there are only four beats in these lines and eight lines to a stanza.

Concord Hymn

Sung at the completion of the Battle Monument, July 4, 1837

RALPH WALDO EMERSON

By the rude bridge that arched the flood,
　Their flag to April's breeze unfurled,
Here once the embattled farmers stood
　And fired the shot heard round the world.

The foe long since in silence slept;
　Alike the conqueror silent sleeps;
And Time the ruined bridge has swept
　Down the dark stream which seaward creeps.

On this green bank, by this soft stream,
    We set to-day a votive stone;
That memory may their deed redeem,
    When, like our sires, our sons are gone.

Spirit, that made those heroes dare
    To die, and leave their children free,
Bid Time and Nature gently spare
    The shaft we raise to them and thee.

The man who wrote this poem

RALPH WALDO EMERSON   1803–1882

The central figure in New England thought of the nineteenth century was Ralph Waldo Emerson. There were other New Englanders living then who were better writers—like Hawthorne and Thoreau—but no other New Englander had as much influence as Emerson on the thought of his own generation and generations to come.

Emerson's ancestors had been ministers since long before the Revolutionary War. After his father's death in 1811, the family was left almost without funds. Emerson was able to work his way through college, however, and after a short period as a teacher and then as a minister, he became a professional lecturer. Many of these lectures were published.

The turning point in his life came after his visit to Europe in 1832. In England he met the men he most wanted to see—famous men in English literature like Carlyle, Coleridge, and Wordsworth. When he returned to America, his philosophy was clear in his mind. With great optimism, he saw life and man as good. Evil, to him, was only a temporary difficulty on the road to becoming good. Individualism, "Trust thyself," and "This is the best of all possible worlds"—these were the essence of Emerson's ideals.

He spent most of his life explaining these ideals in essays, lectures, and poems. His friends were the first to be influenced, then almost every important writer in New England. Longfellow, Lowell, Thoreau, and Hawthorne each reflected something of Emerson's thought.

The poet's art . . .

1. Writers less precise than Emerson used to ask him for the *right* word to describe something with which they were both familiar. He seldom failed them. Look up *rude, creeps,* and *votive.* Explain the exact meaning which each contributes to this poem.

2. What had happened to the bridge? What purpose would the votive stone serve?

3. What is the meaning of the last line of the first stanza? What inspired "the embattled farmers"?

4. This hymn has the same rhythm pattern as Timrod's "Ode": four stresses to a line. From your response to this form, why do you think it was appropriate for both poems?

5. The earlier poets often used **inversion:** a practice of placing the verb before the subject or after the object, thus changing the normal order of an English sentence to suit the beat of the line or to provide rhyme. Point out lines which illustrate the poet's use of inversion.

The Building of the Ship

(Last stanza)

HENRY WADSWORTH LONGFELLOW

Thou, too, sail on, O Ship of State!
Sail on, O Union, strong and great!
Humanity with all its fears,
With all the hopes of future years,
Is hanging breathless on thy fate!
We know what Master laid thy keel,
What Workmen wrought thy ribs of steel,
Who made each mast, and sail, and rope,
What anvils rang, what hammers beat,
In what a forge and what a heat
Were shaped the anchors of thy hope!
Fear not each sudden sound and shock,
'Tis of the wave and not the rock;
'Tis but the flapping of the sail,
And not a rent made by the gale!
In spite of rock and tempest's roar,
In spite of false lights on the shore,
Sail on, nor fear to breast the sea!
Our hearts, our hopes, are all with thee,
Our hearts, our hopes, our prayers, our tears,
Our faith triumphant o'er our fears,
Are all with thee,—are all with thee!

The man who wrote this poem

HENRY WADSWORTH LONGFELLOW
1807–1882

Back in the 1860's, if you had asked any well-read man who was America's greatest poet, his answer would probably have been, "Longfellow." No other poet in America ever enjoyed such a popular success, both in his own country and abroad.

As a young man seeking a career, Long-fellow wanted desperately to be a successful writer. However, he was not quite sure of his talent and so went into teaching soon after his graduation from college. Longfellow was a great success as a professor. He had a marvelous knack for picking up languages and knew French, Italian, German, Portuguese, and Spanish very well. Eventually he held a special post at Harvard as a teacher of modern languages.

As more and more of his poems appeared, it became obvious to the critics that this man was writing not so much about America as it really was but as he wanted to see it. In his treatment of American life, he was a true romantic. It has been said, and truly, that most of Longfellow's poetry could just as well have been written by an Englishman. In fact, he often used European sources for his information. However, since he was not concerned with presenting a realistic picture of America, where he secured his information was unimportant. Like Irving, he dedicated himself to creating a national folk-literature. He achieved his goal in such well-known poems as *Evangeline, The Song of Hiawatha,* and *The Courtship of Miles Standish.*

The poet's art . . .

1. "The Building of the Ship" is a sustained metaphor. This last stanza is a form of personification called **apostrophe:** a form of address to an inanimate object as though it were animate. The poet addressed the Ship of State as though it were human and it could hear and understand. What does the ship stand for? Who laid the keel and wrought the ribs, the masts, sails, ropes, and anchor? All these words are used metaphorically.

2. What other words, used figuratively, told of danger to the ship with the passing of time?

3. What did Longfellow believe would keep the ship sailing on in spite of rocks and storm?

4. Longfellow followed the traditional verse form of the latter half of the nineteenth century. What rhyme scheme did he use? What variations of this rhyme scheme can you find?

5. In World War II, Franklin D. Roosevelt quoted lines from this poem to Winston Churchill. What parts of the last stanza do *you* find applicable to present-day situations? Explain.

Old Ironsides

(September 14, 1830)

OLIVER WENDELL HOLMES

Ay, tear her tattered ensign down!
  Long has it waved on high,
And many an eye has danced to see
  That banner in the sky;
Beneath it rung the battle shout,
  And burst the cannon's roar;—
The meteor of the ocean air
  Shall sweep the clouds no more.

Her deck, once red with heroes' blood,
  Where knelt the vanquished foe,
When winds were hurrying o'er the flood,
  And waves were white below,
No more shall feel the victor's tread,
  Or know the conquered knee;—
The harpies of the shore shall pluck
  The eagle of the sea!

Oh, better that her shattered hulk
Should sink beneath the wave;
Her thunders shook the mighty deep,
And there should be her grave;
Nail to the mast her holy flag,
Set every threadbare sail,
And give her to the god of storms,
The lightning and the gale!

The man who wrote this poem

OLIVER WENDELL HOLMES 1809–1894

The oustanding characteristic of Oliver Wendell Holmes' writing is its quality of graciousness. It is amusing and polished, rather than preachy and profound. It is Dr. Holmes' charming talk transferred to the printed page.

Oliver Wendell Holmes was born into an upper-class Boston family and was educated in the best private schools. For sixty-odd years of his life he wrote poetry, both serious and humorous, not as a profession, but as a kind of avocation. When he was nearly fifty he began to write whimsical essays for *The Atlantic Monthly*, a new magazine edited by his friend James Russell Lowell. The first series of these essays was called *The Autocrat of the Breakfast Table*, which, in book form, is still read with great pleasure.

Dr. Holmes was a medical scholar by profession. He studied medicine at Harvard and in Paris, and, from 1847 to 1882, was a noted professor of anatomy and physiology at Harvard Medical School. One of his projects was the study of the relation between heredity and moral responsibility.

When Dr. Holmes learned that the *Constitution*, frigate of the War of 1812, was being scrapped, he wrote "Old Ironsides" in protest. This poem saved the ship and made him famous.

The poet's art . . .

"Old Ironsides" was a name given to the *Constitution*, a 44-gun frigate of the U. S. Navy, which under Commodore Isaac Hull forced the surrender of the British frigate *Guerrière* in the War of 1812. In 1830 an order went out to dismantle and scuttle the old ship. This poem aroused such patriotic indignation that the order was withdrawn. Three years later the ship was rebuilt and again made sea-worthy. In 1925 Congress authorized a second rebuilding, this time financed by public subscription. School children all over the country contributed most generously. In 1931 the reconditioned ship—called the most famous ship in the Navy—made a tour of the principal seaports in the United States. It was returned to the Charlestown Navy Yard in Boston in 1934 to become a national shrine. Thousands of tourists visit it annually.

1. Who were the "harpies of the shore"? What was the "eagle of the sea"? Explain the meaning of these lines in the poem.

2. Which lines of the poem do you think raised the greatest indignation? Read them aloud in the proper spirit.

3. Which lines do you consider the most patriotic?

4. This poem is unlike a ballad in having eight-line stanzas instead of four-line. It is like a ballad in rhythm pattern and rhyme scheme. In what other way does this poem resemble a ballad?

The Arsenal at Springfield

HENRY WADSWORTH LONGFELLOW

This is the Arsenal. From floor to ceiling,
   Like a huge organ, rise the burnished arms;
But from their silent pipes no anthem pealing
   Startles the villages with strange alarms.

Ah! what a sound will rise, how wild and dreary,
   When the death-angel touches those swift keys!
What loud lament and dismal Miserere [1]
   Will mingle with their awful symphonies!

I hear even now the infinite fierce chorus,
   The cries of agony, the endless groan,
Which, through the ages that have gone before us,
   In long reverberations reach our own.

On helm and harness rings the Saxon [2] hammer,
   Through Cimbric [3] forest roars the Norseman's [4] song,
And loud, amid the universal clamor,
   O'er distant deserts sounds the Tartar [5] gong.

I hear the Florentine,[6] who from his palace
   Wheels out his battle-bell with dreadful din,
And Aztec [7] priests upon their teocallis [8]
   Beat the wild war-drums made of serpent's skin;

The tumult of each sacked and burning village;
   The shout that every prayer for mercy drowns;

---

[1] *Miserere,* hymn of penitence begging for mercy
[2] *Saxon,* referring to the Saxons, an early warlike people who conquered and settled what is now England
[3] *Cimbric,* referring to the Cimbri, a savage Scandinavian tribe destroyed by the Romans in 101 B.C.
[4] *Norseman,* a member of an ancient Scandinavian people noted for their fierceness
[5] *Tartar,* referring to the Tartars (or Tatars), a horde of Mongols and Turks who overran Asia and Eastern Europe in the 13th century
[6] *Florentine,* a citizen of the Italian city, Florence. In medieval times the soldiers of Florence actually wheeled a large bell into battle.
[7] *Aztec,* referring to the Aztecs, an early Indian people who were the rulers of Mexico until they were conquered with much slaughter by the Spanish
[8] *teocallis,* flat-topped pyramids used by the Aztecs for worship

The soldiers' revels in the midst of pillage;
    The wail of famine in beleaguered towns;

The bursting shell, the gateway wrenched asunder,
    The rattling musketry, the clashing blade;
And ever and anon, in tones of thunder,
    The diapason [9] of the cannonade.[10]

Is it, O man, with such discordant noises,
    With such accursed instruments as these,
Thou drownest Nature's sweet and kindly voices,
    And jarrest the celestial harmonies?

Were half the power that fills the world with terror,
    Were half the wealth bestowed on camps and courts,
Given to redeem the human mind from error,
    There were no need of arsenals or forts:

The warrior's name would be a name abhorrèd!
    And every nation, that should lift again
Its hand against a brother, on its forehead
    Would wear forevermore the curse of Cain! [11]

Down the dark future, through long generations,
    The echoing sounds grow fainter and then cease;
And like a bell, with solemn, sweet vibrations,
    I hear once more the voice of Christ say, "Peace!"

Peace! and no longer from its brazen portals
    The blast of War's great organ shakes the skies!
But beautiful as songs of the immortals,
    The holy melodies of love arise.

---

[9] *diapason,* powerful tone
[10] *cannonade,* discharging of the cannon
[11] *Cain,* the first son of Adam and Eve. As a curse from God, Cain was branded on the forehead for killing his brother Abel.

The poet's art . . .

1. Stanza 1 describes the Arsenal. What warning note was sounded in Stanza 2?

2. In the next five stanzas what reverberations from the past came to the poet, as he gazed upon the Arsenal?

3. Why were instruments of war accursed?

4. What better purpose should man's power and wealth serve?

5. How do the thoughts voiced in Stanzas 8, 9, and 10 agree with modern ideas and practice?

6. Longfellow's prophecy in the last two stanzas held for many years after his death. How has his dream of "peace" been shattered in the twentieth century? What do the most modern "arsenals" contain today?

7. Point out the two rhymes in each stanza.

Compensation

RALPH WALDO EMERSON

Not only do generals and statesmen speak out; men of letters also have thoughts to express. In "Compensation," Emerson presents the idea that there is a balance which operates in all spheres of life. "For everything you have missed, you have gained something else; and for everything you gain you lose something." As you read "Compensation," decide whether or not you can accept Emerson's point of view.

Polarity,[1] or action and reaction, we meet in every part of nature; in darkness and light; in heat and cold; in the ebb and flow of waters; in male and female; . . .

The same dualism [2] underlies the nature and condition of man. Every excess causes a defect; every defect an excess. Every sweet hath its sour; every evil its good. . . . For every grain of wit there is a grain of folly. For everything you have missed, you have gained something else; and for everything you gain, you lose something. If riches increase, they are increased that use them. If the gatherer gathers too much, Nature takes out of the man what she puts into his chest; swells the estate, but kills the owner. Nature hates monopolies and exceptions. The waves of the sea do not more speedily seek a level from their loftiest tossing than the varieties of condition tend to equalize themselves. There is always some levelling circumstance that puts down the overbearing, the strong, the rich, the fortunate, substantially on the same ground with all others. Is a man too strong and fierce for society and by temper and position a bad citizen,—a morose ruffian, with a dash of the pirate in him?—Nature sends him a troop of pretty sons and daughters who are getting along in the dame's classes at the village school, and love and fear for them smoothes his grim scowl to courtesy. Thus she contrives to intenerate [3] the granite and felspar, takes the boar out and puts the lamb in and keeps her balance true.

The farmer imagines power and place are fine things. But the President has paid dear for his White House. It has commonly cost him all his peace, and the best of his manly attributes. To preserve for a short time so conspicuous an appearance before the world, he is content to eat dust before the real masters who stand erect behind the throne. . . .

All things are double, one against another.—Tit for tat; an eye for an eye; a tooth for a tooth; blood for blood; measure for measure; love for love.—Give, and it shall be given you.—He that watereth shall be watered himself.—What will you have? quoth God; pay for it and take it.—Nothing venture, nothing have.—Thou shalt

---

[1] *polarity,* the quality of possessing two contrary or opposite powers
[2] *dualism,* the state of being dual or composed of two parts

[3] *intenerate,* soften

be paid exactly for what thou hast done, no more, no less.—Who doth not work shall not eat. . . .

A man cannot speak but he judges himself. With his will or against his will he draws his portrait to the eye of his companions by every word. Every opinion reacts on him who utters it. . . . it is a harpoon hurled at the whale, unwinding, as it flies, a coil of cord in the boat, and, if the harpoon is not good, or not well thrown, it will go nigh to cut the steersman in twain or to sink the boat.

You cannot do wrong without suffering wrong. . . .

All infractions of love and equity in our social relations are speedily punished. They are punished by fear. Whilst I stand in simple relations to my fellow-man, I have no displeasure in meeting him. . . . But as soon as there is any departure from simplicity and attempt at halfness, or good for me that is not good for him, my neighbor feels the wrong; he shrinks from me as far as I have shrunk from him; his eyes no longer seek mine; there is war between us; there is hate in him and fear in me.

A wise man will extend this lesson to all parts of life, and know that it is the part of prudence to face every claimant and pay every just demand on your time, your talents, or your heart. Always pay; for first or last you must pay your entire debt. Persons and events may stand for a time between you and justice, but it is only a postponement. You must pay at last your own debt. If you are wise you will dread a prosperity which only loads you with more. Benefit is the end of nature. But for every benefit which you receive, a tax is levied. He is great who confers the most benefits. He is base,—and that is the one base thing in the universe,—to receive favors and render none. In the order of nature we cannot render benefits to those from whom we receive them, or only seldom. But the benefit we receive must be rendered again, line for line, deed for deed, cent for cent, to somebody. Beware of too much good staying in your hand. It will fast corrupt and worm worms.[4] Pay it away quickly in some sort.

Labor is watched over by the same pitiless laws. Cheapest, say the prudent, is the dearest[5] labor. What we buy in a broom, a mat, a wagon, a knife, is some application of good sense to a common want. It is best to pay in your land a skilful gardener, or to buy good sense applied to gardening; in your sailor, good sense applied to navigation; in the house, good sense applied to cooking, sewing, serving; in your agent, good sense applied to accounts and affairs. So do you multiply your presence, or spread yourself throughout your estate. But because of the dual constitution of things, in labor as in life there can be no cheating. The thief steals from himself. The swindler swindles himself. For the real price of labor is knowledge and virtue, whereof wealth and credit are signs. These signs, like paper money, may be counterfeited or stolen, but that which they represent, namely, knowledge and virtue, cannot be counterfeited or stolen. These ends of labor cannot be answered but by real exertions of the mind, and in obedience to pure motives. The cheat, the defaulter, the gambler, cannot extort the knowledge of material and moral nature which his honest care and pains yield to the operative. The law of nature is, Do the thing, and you shall have the power; but they who do not the thing have not the power. . . .

Our strength grows out of our weakness. The indignation which arms itself with secret forces does not awaken until we are pricked and stung and sorely assailed. A great man is always willing to be little. Whilst he sits on the cushion of advantages, he goes to sleep. When he is pushed, tormented, defeated, he has a chance to learn something; he has been put on his wits, on his manhood; he has gained

---

[4] *worm worms,* develop worms, as maggots develop in spoiled meat
[5] *dearest,* most expensive

facts; learns his ignorance; is cured of the insanity of conceit; has got moderation and real skill. The wise man throws himself on the side of his assailants. It is more his interest than it is theirs to find his weak point. The wound cicatrizes [6] and falls off from him like a dead skin, and when they would triumph, lo! he has passed on invulnerable. Blame is safer than praise. I hate to be defended in a newspaper. As long as all that is said is said against me,

[6] *cicatrizes,* heals to form a scar

I feel a certain assurance of success. But as soon as honeyed words of praise are spoken for me I feel as one that lies unprotected before his enemies. In general, every evil to which we do not succumb is a benefactor. As the Sandwich Islander [7] believes that the strength and valor of the enemy he kills passes into himself, so we gain the strength of the temptation we resist.

[7] *Sandwich Islander,* a Hawaiian, from the former name of the Hawaiian Islands

Let's consider . . .

1. *Poor Richard's Almanack* was full of wise and witty sayings which have been quoted so often that they have become familiar household expressions. "Compensation" also contains many apt words of wisdom, perhaps not so quotable, but certainly applicable to what you do or need to do *now* while you are building your own philosophy of life. For example, take these two:

"A man cannot speak but he judges himself;"

"The thief steals from himself."
Explain each of these statements. Then illustrate its truth with some incident from your own experience.

2. Find at least five other such challenging sentences and show how they are as applicable to life today as they were in Emerson's time.

3. Read again what Emerson said about the price a President pays for his White House. You may or may not agree. Discuss this paragraph.

4. Now give, as simply as you can, your definition of *compensation.* Depend on Emerson, not on Webster.

5. It has been said that young Americans need the warnings, the truths, of this essay more today than when Emerson wrote them. What great truth, here explained, do all young people need to keep in mind?

Why do modern young people forget it easily?

6. How did Emerson impress upon you that "our strength grows out of our weakness"? Do you think he exaggerated his point in the last paragraph? What part of it has special meaning for you?

The writer's craft . . .

A. Because essays are such a flexible type of literature, they are difficult to define. The simplest definition of an **essay** would be "a fairly short literary composition on a particular subject." Nearly any idea or topic can serve as the subject matter of the writer's thoughts or opinions. How the writer handles his subject depends upon its nature and upon the writer's feelings about it—his mood. He may treat the subject humorously, seriously, critically, or reverently. He may limit himself to a few paragraphs or extend his ideas into book length. Most essays, however, are not more than a half dozen book-pages in length.

Essays are generally classified as either formal or informal. "Compensation" is a **formal essay** because it has the following characteristics:

    a. The basic purpose is serious

    b. The language is graceful and polished

    c. The tone is impersonal

d. The treatment of subject matter is dignified

e. The argument or opinion expressed is developed in a logical manner

B. An example of the logic common to formal essays is found in Emerson's use of **antithesis:** a figure of speech in which contrasting ideas and concepts are balanced within a given sentence or paragraph. Emerson wrote,

"Our strength grows out of our weakness."
"A great man is always willing to be little."

The contrast of such opposite ideas as *strength* and *weakness, great* and *little* not only make the sentences provocative but also bring an idea into focus.

1. Find several other examples of antithesis in "Compensation."

2. Write two sentences of your own in which you make use of antithesis.

Knowing words . . .

You know that a word may have many meanings, depending on its place in the sentence and on the context in which it appears. The word may also have a different meaning if you add a meaningful element. When this element is added to the beginning of a word, it is called a **prefix.** The prefixes *in-* and *un-*, for example, are added to many words to give the meaning of "not": *incurable,* not curable, or *unbearable,* not bearable.

Emerson used the word *invulnerable.* "The wound cicatrizes and falls off from him like dead skin, and when they would triumph, lo! he has passed on *invulnerable.*" One of the meanings of the word *vulnerable* is "susceptible to being hurt." Thus *invulnerable* means "not susceptible to being hurt."

1. List ten words which illustrate the addition of either of the prefixes *in-* or *un-* to a word. Select five of these prefixed words and use each of them in a sentence.

2. When a word begins with *m, l,* or *r,* the prefix *in-* changes to *im-, il-,* or *ir-,* to match the following consonant: *immovable, illegible, irresponsible.* List three words of your own which show these prefix changes before the consonants *m, l,* and *r.*

A Man Saw a Ball of Gold in the Sky

A man saw a ball of gold in the sky;
He climbed for it,
And eventually he achieved it—
It was clay.

Now this is the strange part:
When the man went to the earth
And looked again,
Lo, there was the ball of gold.
Now this is the strange part:
It was a ball of gold.
Ay, by the heavens, it was a ball of gold.

Stephen Crane

Compensation

RALPH WALDO EMERSON

I

The wings of Time are black and white,
Pied [1] with morning and with night.
Mountain tall and ocean deep
Trembling balance duly keep.
In changing moon and tidal wave
Glows the feud of Want and Have.
Gauge of more and less through space,
Electric star or pencil plays,
The lonely Earth amid the balls
That hurry through the eternal halls,
A makeweight flying to the void,
Supplemental asteroid,
Or compensatory spark,
Shoots across the neutral Dark.

[1] *pied,* having two or more colors in patches

II

Man's the elm, and Wealth the vine;
Stanch and strong the tendrils twine:
Though the frail ringlets thee deceive,
None from its stock that vine can reave.
Fear not, then, thou child infirm,
There's no god dare wrong a worm;
Laurel crowns cleave to deserts,
And power to him who power exerts.
Hast not thy share? On winged feet,
Lo! it rushes thee to meet;
And all that Nature made thy own,
Floating in air or pent in stone,
Will rive the hills, and swim the sea,
And, like thy shadow, follow thee.

The poet's art . . .

1. "Compensation" was written around a central idea. Explain this idea in your own words and be able to point out specific lines in the poem in which it is developed.

2. Emerson chose to write "Compensation" in **rhymed couplet** form: a pair of lines in which the last accented syllables are rhymed. Often the rhymed couplet is a complete statement of a thought or idea. Point to several couplets which express complete thoughts or ideas.

3. Rhyme is classified according to (1) the positions in which the rhyming syllables occur and (2) the number of syllables which rhyme. In "Compensation" the rhyme occurs in the last syllable of matching lines and is called **end rhyme.**

4. When the rhyme occurs in two consecutive syllables at the end of matching lines—as in *burning* and *learning*—the rhyme is called a **double rhyme.** When the rhyme occurs in three consecutive syllables—as in de*mocracy* and plu*tocracy*—it is called **triple rhyme.**

Write three pairs of words which, if they occurred at the ends of matching lines would illustrate the following kinds of rhyme:

      end rhyme   double rhyme
           triple rhyme

Walden

E. B. WHITE

Thoreau went to live at Walden Pond because he believed that most men lead lives of quiet desperation. About a hundred years later, E. B. White made a visit to this historic spot. In this imaginary letter to Thoreau, Mr. White makes a number of penetrating comparisons between what Walden Pond meant to Thoreau and what it now means to summer visitors.

Miss Nims, take a letter to Henry David Thoreau. Dear Henry: I thought of you the other afternoon as I was approaching Concord doing fifty on Route 62. That is a high speed at which to hold a philosopher in one's mind, but in this century we are a nimble bunch.

On one of the lawns in the outskirts of the village a woman was cutting the grass with a motorized lawn mower. What made me think of you was that the machine had rather got away from her, although she was game enough, and in the brief glimpse I had of the scene it appeared to me that the lawn was mowing the lady. She kept a tight grip on the handles, which throbbed

291

violently with every explosion of the one-cylinder motor, and as she sheered around bushes and lurched along at a reluctant trot behind her impetuous servant, she looked like a puppy who had grabbed something that was too much for him. Concord hasn't changed much, Henry; the farm implements and the animals still have the upper hand.

I may as well admit that I was journeying to Concord with the deliberate intention of visiting your woods; for although I have never knelt at the grave of a philosopher nor placed wreaths on moldy poets, and have often gone a mile out of my way to avoid some place of historical interest, I have always wanted to see Walden Pond. The account which you left of your sojourn there is, you will be amused to learn, a document of increasing pertinence; each year it seems to gain a little headway, as the world loses ground. We may all be transcendental yet, whether we like it or not. As our common complexities increase, any tale of individual simplicity (and yours is the best written and the cockiest) acquires a new fascination; as our goods accumulate, but not our well-being, your report of an existence without material adornment takes on a certain awkward credibility.

My purpose in going to Walden Pond, like yours, was not to live cheaply or to live dearly there, but to transact some private business with the fewest obstacles. Approaching Concord, doing forty, doing forty-five, doing fifty, the steering wheel held snug in my palms, the highway held grimly in my vision, the crown of the road now serving me (on the righthand curves), now defeating me (on the lefthand curves), I began to rouse myself from the stupefaction which a day's motor journey induces. It was a delicious evening, Henry, when the whole body is one sense, and imbibes delight through every pore, if I may coin a phrase. Fields were richly brown where the harrow, drawn by the stripped Ford, had lately sunk its teeth; pastures

were green; and overhead the sky had that same everlasting great look which you will find on page 144 of the Oxford pocket edition.[1] I could feel the road entering me, through tire, wheel, spring, and cushion; shall I not have intelligence with earth too? Am I not partly leaves and vegetable mold myself?—a man of infinite horse-power, yet partly leaves.

Stay with me on 62 and it will take you into Concord. As I say, it was a delicious evening. The snake had come forth to die in a bloody S on the highway, the wheel upon its head, its bowels flat now and exposed. The turtle had come up too to cross the road and die in the attempt, its hard shell smashed under the rubber blow, it's intestinal yearning (for the other side of the road) forever squashed. There was a sign by the wayside which announced that the road had a "cotton surface." You wouldn't know what that is, but neither, for that matter, did I. There is a cryptic ingredient in many of our modern improvements—we are awed and pleased without knowing quite what we are enjoying. It is something to be traveling on a road with a cotton surface.

The civilization round Concord today is an odd distillation of city, village, farm, and manor. The houses, yards, fields look not quite suburban, not quite rural. Under the bronze beech and the blue spruce of the departed baron grazes the milch goat of the heirs. Under the porte-cochère stands the reconditioned station wagon; under the grape arbor sit the puppies for sale. (But why do men degenerate ever? What makes families run out?)

It was June and everywhere June was publishing her immemorial stanza; in the lilacs, in the syringa, in the freshly edged paths and the sweetness of moist beloved gardens, and the little wire wickets that preserve the tulips' front. Farmers were already moving the fruits of their toil into their yards, arranging the rhubarb, the as-

[1] *Oxford pocket edition*, an edition of Thoreau's *Walden*

paragus, the strictly fresh eggs on the painted stands under the little shed roofs with the patent shingles. And though it was almost a hundred years since you had taken your ax and started cutting out your home on Walden Pond, I was interested to observe that the philosophical spirit was still alive in Massachusetts: in the center of a vacant lot some boys were assembling the framework of the rude shelter, their whole mind and skill concentrated in the rather inauspicious helter-skeleton of studs and rafters. They too were escaping from town, to live naturally, in a rich blend of savagery and philosophy.

That evening, after supper at the inn, I strolled out into the twilight to dream my shapeless transcendental dreams and see that the car was locked up for the night (first open the right front door, then reach over, straining, and pull up the handles of the left rear and the left front till you hear the click, then the handle of the right rear, then shut the right front but open it again, remembering that the key is still in the ignition switch, remove the key, shut the right front again with a bang, push the tiny keyhole cover to one side, insert key, turn, and withdraw). It is what we all do, Henry. It is called locking the car. It is said to confuse thieves and keep them from making off with the laprobe. Four doors to lock behind one robe. The driver himself never uses a laprobe, the free movement of his legs being vital to the operation of the vehicle; so that when he locks the car it is a pure and unselfish act. I have in my life gained very little essential heat from laprobes, yet I have ever been at pains to lock them up.

The evening was full of sounds, some of which would have stirred your memory. The robins still love the elms of New England villages at sundown. There is enough of the thrush in them to make song inevitable at the end of the day, and enough of the tramp to make them hang round the dwellings of men. A robin, like many another American, dearly loves a white house

with green blinds. Concord is still full of them.

Your fellow-townsmen were stirring abroad—not many afoot, most of them in their cars; and the sound which they made in Concord at evening was a rustling and a whispering. The sound lacks steadfastness and is wholly unlike that of a train. A train, as you know who lived so near the Fitchburg line, whistles once or twice sadly and is gone, trailing a memory in smoke, soothing to ear and mind. Automobiles, skirting a village green, are like flies that have gained the inner ear—they buzz, cease, pause, start, shift, stop, halt, brake, and the whole effect is a nervous polytone curiously disturbing.

As I wandered along, the toc toc of ping pong balls drifted from an attic window. In front of the Reuben Brown house a Buick was drawn up. At the wheel, motionless, his hat upon his head, a man sat, listening to Amos and Andy on the radio (it is a drama of many scenes and without an end). The deep voice of Andrew Brown, emerging from the car, although it originated more than two hundred miles away, was unstrained by distance. When you used to sit on the shore of your pond on Sunday morning, listening to the church bells of Acton and Concord, you were aware of the excellent filter of the intervening atmosphere. Science has attended to that, and sound now maintains its intensity without regard for distance. Properly sponsored, it goes on forever.

A fire engine, out for a trial spin, roared past Emerson's house, hot with readiness for public duty. Over the barn roofs the martins dipped and chittered. A swarthy daughter of an asparagus grower, in culottes, shirt, and bandanna, pedalled past on her bicycle. It was indeed a delicious evening, and I returned to the inn (I believe it was your house once) to rock with the old ladies on the concrete veranda.

Next morning early I started afoot for Walden, out Main Street and down Thoreau, past the depot and the Minuteman

Chevrolet Company. The morning was fresh, and in a bean field along the way I flushed an agriculturalist, quietly studying his beans. Thoreau Street soon joined Number 126, an artery of the State. We number our highways nowadays, our speed being so great we can remember little of their quality or character and are lucky to remember their number. (Men have an indistinct notion that if they keep up this activity long enough all will at length ride somewhere, in next to no time.) Your pond is on 126.

I knew I must be nearing your woodland retreat when the Golden Pheasant lunchroom came into view—Sealtest ice cream, toasted sandwiches, hot frankfurters, waffles, tonics, and lunches. Were I the proprietor, I should add rice, Indian meal, and molasses—just for old time's sake. The Pheasant, incidentally, is for sale: a chance for some nature lover who wishes to set himself up beside a pond in the Concord atmosphere and live deliberately, fronting only the essential facts of life on Number 126. Beyond the Pheasant was a place called Walden Breezes, an oasis whose porch pillars were made of old green shutters sawed into lengths. On the porch was a distorting mirror, to give the traveler a comical image of himself, who had miraculously learned to gaze in an ordinary glass without smiling. Behind the Breezes, in a sun-parched clearing, dwelt your philosophical descendants in their trailers, each trailer the size of your hut, but all grouped together for the sake of congeniality. Trailer people leave the city, as you did, to discover solitude and in any weather, at any hour of the day or night, to improve the nick of time; but they soon collect in villages and get bogged deeper in the mud than ever. The camp behind Walden Breezes was just rousing itself to the morning. The ground was packed hard under the heel, and the sun came through the clearing to bake the soil and enlarge the wry smell of cramped housekeeping. Cushman's bakery truck had stopped to deliver

an early basket of rolls. A camp dog, seeing me in the road, barked petulantly. A man emerged from one of the trailers and set forth with a bucket to draw water from some forest tap.

Leaving the highway I turned off into the woods toward the pond, which was apparent through the foliage. The floor of the forest was strewn with dried old oak leaves and *Transcripts*. From beneath the flattened popcorn wrapper (*granum explosum*) peeped the frail violet. I followed a footpath and descended to the water's edge. The pond lay clear and blue in the morning light, as you have seen it so many times. In the shallows a man's waterlogged shirt undulated gently. A few flies came out to greet me and convoy me to your cove, past the No Bathing signs on which the fellows and the girls had scrawled their names. I felt strangely excited suddenly to be snooping around your premises, tiptoeing along watchfully, as though not to tread by mistake upon the intervening century. Before I got to the cove I heard something which seemed to me quite wonderful: I heard your frog, a full clear *troonk*, guiding me, still hoarse and solemn, bridging the years as the robins had bridged them in the sweetness of the village evening. But he soon quit, and I came on a couple of young boys throwing stones at him.

Your front yard is marked by a bronze tablet set in a stone. Four small granite posts, a few feet away, show where the house was. On top of the tablet was a pair of faded blue bathing trunks with a white stripe. Back of it is a pile of stones, a sort of cairn, left by your visitors as a tribute I suppose. It is a rather ugly little heap of stones, Henry. In fact the hillside itself seems faded, browbeaten; a few tall skinny pines, bare of lower limbs, a smattering of young maples in suitable green, some birches and oaks, and a number of trees felled by the last big wind. It was from the bole of one of these fallen pines, torn up by the roots, that I extracted the stone which I added to the cairn—a sentimental act in which I was interrupted by a small terrier from a nearby picnic group, who confronted me and wanted to know about the stone.

I sat down for a while on one of the posts of your house to listen to the bluebottles and the dragonflies. The invaded glade sprawled shabby and mean at my feet, but the flies were tuned to the old vibration. There were the remains of a fire in your ru:ns, but I doubt that it was yours; also two beer bottles trodden into the soil and become part of earth. A young oak had taken root in your house, and two or three ferns, unrolling like the ticklers at a banquet. The only other furnishings were a DuBarry pattern sheet, a page torn from a picture magazine, and some crusts in wax paper.

Before I quit I walked clear round the pond and found the place where you used to sit on the northeast side to get the sun in the fall, and the beach where you got sand for scrubbing your floor. On the eastern side of the pond, where the highway borders it, the State has built dressing rooms for swimmers, a float with diving towers, drinking fountains of porcelain, and rowboats for hire. The pond is in fact a State Preserve, and carries a twenty-dollar fine for picking wild flowers, a decree signed in all solemnity by your fellow-citizens Walter C. Wardwell, Erson B. Barlow, and Nathaniel I. Bowditch. There was a smell of creosote where they had been building a wide wooden stairway to the road and the parking area. Swimmers and boaters were arriving; bodies plunged vigorously into the water and emerged wet and beautiful in the bright air. As I left, a boatload of town boys were splashing about in mid-pond, kidding and fooling, the young fellows singing at the tops of their lungs in a wild chorus:

Amer-ica, Amer-ica, God shed his grace on
    thee,
And crown thy good with brotherhood
From sea to shi-ning sea!

I walked back to town along the railroad, following your custom. The rails were expanding noisily in the hot sun, and on the slope of the roadbed the wild grape and the blackberry sent up their creepers to the track.

The expense of my brief sojourn in Concord was:

Canvas shoes	$1.95	
Baseball bat	.25	Gifts to take
Left-handed		back to a boy
fielder's glove ..	1.25	
Hotel and meals ..	4.25	
In all	$7.70	

As you see, this amount was almost what you spent for food for eight months. I cannot defend the shoes or the expenditure for shelter and food: they reveal a meanness and grossness in my nature which you would find contemptible. The baseball equipment, however, is the kind of impediment with which you were never on even terms. You must remember that the house where you practiced the sort of economy which I respect was haunted only by mice and squirrels. You never had to cope with a shortstop.

Let's consider . . .

1. Glance back at "Walden" on page 32 to refresh your memory of Thoreau.
2. E. B. White, a New Yorker of long standing who has written in intimate detail of his own city, shows here that he is also a keen observer of rural landscape. Point out instances in which he recorded impressions which many local residents might have ignored.
3. After reading this selection, why do you think E. B. White wanted particularly to visit Thoreau's Walden?

4. What are some of the changes which Thoreau would have regretted, but which White saw as mildly ridiculous?

5. Reread the paragraph beginning "My purpose in going to Walden Pond. . . ." What evidence do you find that White was familiar with Thoreau's *Walden?* Perhaps you can find other references in the essay which show this acquaintance—even if *you* are familiar with only the selection on page 32.

6. White did not entirely approve of the "progress" he noted in Concord, particularly its motorization. Read aloud some of the passages in which he poked fun, gently, at what he saw in the old town.

7. Thousands visit Walden Pond every year to look for the spot where Thoreau built his hut and to view the surroundings he knew so thoroughly. Suppose you were to leave Route 126 alone and on foot. What would you look for to identify the place? What would you find that would have driven Thoreau back to town long before the end of his two years?

8. Do you enjoy visiting historical or literary shrines? Why or why not?

The writer's craft . . .

Although the author pretended to be writing a letter, his comments took the form of an **informal essay:** a fairly short composition in which the author expresses his ideas on some topic. This essay, like most informal essays, has the quality of a good conversation: the ideas are provocative and the comments are lively and personal. White's frequent use of the pronouns *I* and *my* gave his essay a personal tone. He might have been casually talking to you about his trip to Concord. After reading it, you are not only familiar with Walden but with E. B. White as well.

In addition to being written in a personal style, informal essays are designed to hold your interest. In "Walden" E. B. White aroused your curiosity with his be-

ginning. A letter to Thoreau—what will it contain? Why write to Thoreau? To answer these questions you had to read what E. B. White had to say. Very soon you came to his commentary on the "progress" he observed in Concord. In order to hold your interest he first described *concrete incidents* which he observed along the way; then he commented on them. For example, he described a woman cutting grass with a motorized lawn mower; then he commented that farm implements still have the upper hand.

1. Find several other concrete incidents which E. B. White described. Then explain what conclusions he drew from them.

2. How did casting this essay in the form of an imaginary letter add to its personal tone?

3. In what way did the informal essay "Walden" differ from the formal essay "Compensation"? Make a list of characteristics of the *informal essay* similar to the list for the *formal essay* given on page 296.

4. Compose your own essay. Write it in the form of an imaginary letter to someone who lived in the past. Select an idea which you want to present to your reader, and then choose specific incidents to illustrate and support that idea. To these add your comments on the way in which living conditions have either changed in recent years or remained the same.

Knowing words . . .

E. B. White commented that he was riding on a road with a "cotton surface." He admitted that he didn't know what that meant, and added, "There is a *cryptic* ingredient in many of our modern improvements—we are awed and pleased without knowing quite what we are enjoying." The word *cryptic* comes from a Greek word meaning "to hide;" hence it means "hidden" or "mysterious." The ingredient which gave the road its "cotton surface" was a mystery to E. B. White.

Explain the meaning of each of the following words which have the same root as the word *cryptic*. If you cannot determine the meaning, consult your dictionary. Notice also the meaning of the suffixes (the elements added to the end of a word): *-grapher*, *-gram*, and *-nym*. You have seen these suffixes many times in words like *photographer, telegram,* and *synonym*. Explain what these suffixes add to the meaning of each of the words in this list.

crypt   cryptogram
cryptographer   cryptonym

A Leaf Treader

I have been treading on leaves all day until I am autumn-tired.
God knows all the color and form of leaves I have trodden on and mired.
Perhaps I have put forth too much strength and been too fierce from fear.
I have safely trodden underfoot the leaves of another year.

All summer long they were overhead, more lifted up than I.
To come to their final place in earth they had to pass me by.
All summer long I thought I heard them threatening under their breath.
And when they came it seemed with a will to carry me with them to death.

They spoke to the fugitive in my heart as if it were leaf to leaf.
They tapped at my eyelids and touched my lips with an invitation to grief.
But it was no reason I had to go because they had to go.
Now up my knee to keep on top of another year of snow.

Robert Frost

Lucinda Matlock

EDGAR LEE MASTERS

I went to dances at Chandlerville,
And played snap-out at Winchester.
One time we changed partners,
Driving home in the moonlight of middle June,
And then I found Davis.
We were married and lived together for seventy years,
Enjoying, working, raising the twelve children,
Eight of whom we lost
Ere I had reached the age of sixty.
I spun, I wove, I kept the house, I nursed the sick,
I made the garden, and for holiday
Rambled over the fields where sang the larks,
And by Spoon River gathering many a shell,
And many a flower and medicinal weed—
Shouting to the wooded hills, singing to the green valleys.
At ninety-six I had lived enough, that is all,
And passed to a sweet repose.
What is this I hear of sorrow and weariness,
Anger, discontent, and drooping hopes?
Degenerate sons and daughters,
Life is too strong for you—
It takes life to love Life.

The man who wrote this poem

EDGAR LEE MASTERS 1869–1947

Edgar Lee Masters, a lawyer from Chicago, began writing as a hobby. In 1915 he published a volume of free verse entitled *The Spoon River Anthology*. It was actually a collection of short poetic biographies about the former residents of a make-believe small town in Illinois. Mr. Masters presented these residents as though they had arisen from the Spoon River graveyard and were telling what life had meant for them.

The Spoon River Anthology was a tremendous success. Few authors have built a reputation on a single book, but Edgar Lee Masters' fame rests almost entirely on this one volume. He wrote many books afterwards, but none of his later works ever caught the public fancy.

This book was very important for its time. The American public was evidently ready for a book that would speak honestly about small-town life rather than present it as a special stronghold of goodness and charm. Masters' poems showed that in small towns, as in cities, there was drabness and stupidity. A village was neither all good nor all bad.

Within a few years after the publication of *The Spoon River Anthology*, several novels appeared—one of them Sinclair Lewis' *Main Street*—that revealed even more clearly that life in a small town was not the romantic idyll it had seemed to writers of the nineteenth century.

The poet's art . . .

1. From the information in this poem, at what time do you think Lucinda Matlock lived?
2. She spoke her message from the grave to "degenerate sons and daughters." Whom did she mean?
3. What in her life gave her the right to speak to them and say, "Life is too strong for you"?
4. Which poet represented in this part do you think would agree with the statement, "It takes life to love Life"? Explain what this expression means and tell why you think that poet would agree.

Anne Rutledge

Out of me unworthy and unknown
The vibrations of deathless music;
"With malice toward none, with charity for all."
Out of me the forgiveness of millions toward millions,
And the beneficent face of a nation
Shining with justice and truth.
I am Anne Rutledge who sleep beneath these weeds,
Beloved in life of Abraham Lincoln,
Wedded to him, not through union,
But through separation,
Bloom forever, O Republic,
From the dust of my bosom!

Edgar Lee Masters

*False Gods**

WALTER LIPPMANN

When America "speaks out," you must not expect to hear praise alone. You must look for constructive criticisms, too. Newspaper columnists often provide this criticism, hoping to stimulate thought and prevent smugness.

From what source come these unmanly fears that prevail among us? These dark forebodings? This despairing impotence? What is it that has shaken the nerves of so many? It is the doubt whether there exists among the people that trust in each other which is the first condition of intelligent leadership. That is the root of the matter. The particular projects which we debate so angrily are not so important. The fate of the nation does not hang upon any of them. But upon the power of the people to remain united for purposes which they respect, upon their capacity to have faith in themselves and in their objectives, much depends. It is not the facts of the crisis which we have to fear. They can be endured and dealt with. It is demoralization alone that is dangerous.

A demoralized people is one in which the individual has become isolated and is the prey of his own suspicions. He trusts nobody and nothing, not even himself. He believes nothing, except the worst of everybody and everything. He sees only confusion in himself and conspiracies in other men. That is panic. That is disintegration. That is what comes when in some sudden emergency of their lives men find themselves unsupported by clear convictions that transcend their immediate and personal desires.

The last ten years have been a time of exceptionally drastic change in the underlying convictions of western men. For reasons which it is not easy to state briefly, or even clearly to discern, it seems as if in this decade the change in life brought about by science and machinery and the modern city, by democracy and by popular education, had struck with full impact and with cumulative force against the social conventions and the ideals of the mass of men.

That a period of profound spiritual bewilderment had to ensue was inevitable. But this bewilderment has been greatly aggravated in the United States by what I believe may truthfully be called the moral apathy of those in high places. At the beginning of the decade the national government was attacked by brutal and conspicuous corruption. No clear word about it was spoken by those in high places. On the contrary, they sat silent, hoping that the people would forget, calculating that the evil would be overlooked. Is it surprising that public spirit weakened when it was demonstrated from the highest places

* From the *New York Herald Tribune*, May 20, 1932

that the corruption of government was not something anyone ought to care deeply about?

During this decade the country has been making the experiment of outlawing an ancient and general human appetite. Those in high places have known quite well how badly the experiment was working, what stupendous lawlessness and corruption the prohibition law [1] was producing. Yet in all this time no candid word, no straightforward utterance, no honest inquiry about this matter has come from any high place. The problem has been muffled in hypocrisy, in miserable ambiguities, and in equivocation, to a point where any open, public debate of the matter has become impossible.

During this same decade those in high places have steadfastly preached to the people that it was their destiny to have two-car garages and eight-tube radio sets. That was the ideal they held out before the people, to be acquisitive, to seek feverishly to become richer and richer, to prostrate themselves before the Golden Calf. [2] To read today the rhapsodies which issued from the highest places during the last decade is to find the main reason why now, when the nation must call upon all its resources in integrity and magnanimity and public spirit, a clear devotion to the national interest is not surely available.

For if you teach a people for ten years that the character of its government is not greatly important, that political success is for those who equivocate and evade, and if you tell them that acquisitiveness is the ideal, that things are what matter, that Mammon [3] is God, then you must not be astonished at the confusion in Washington, or the nonchalance of James J. Walker, [4] or the vermin who in a hundred different ways exploited the tragedy of the Lindbergh baby. You cannot set up false gods to confuse the people and not pay the penalty.

Those in high places are more than the administrators of government bureaus. They are more than the writers of laws. They are the custodians of a nation's ideals, of the beliefs it cherishes, of its permanent hopes, of the faith which makes a nation out of a mere aggregation of individuals. They are unfaithful to that trust when by word or example they promote a spirit that is complacent, evasive, and acquisitive.

It is not only against the material consequences of this decade of drift and hallucination, but against the essence of its spirit, that the best and bravest among us are today in revolt. They are looking for new leaders, for men who are truthful and resolute and eloquent in the conviction that the American destiny is to be free and magnanimous, rather than complacent and acquisitive; they are looking for leaders who will talk to the people not about two-car garages and a bonus, but about their duty, and about the sacrifices they must make, and about the discipline they must impose upon themselves, and about their responsibility to the world and to posterity, about all those things which make a people self-respecting, serene, and confident. May they not look in vain!

---

[1] *prohibition law,* a law prohibiting the sale and manufacture of alcoholic beverages. In 1919 the Eighteenth Amendment to the Constitution, forbidding the manufacture and sale of liquor, went into effect. It was repealed in 1933 by the Twenty-first Amendment.

[2] *Golden Calf,* a golden idol which was set up by Aaron, the brother of Moses, while the Israelites waited for Moses to come down from Mount Sinai. To bow before the Golden Calf has come to mean to worship material riches.

[3] *Mammon,* a personification of avarice and riches. This term has come to stand for material wealth.

[4] *James J. Walker,* Mayor of New York City 1925–1933, noted for his happy-go-lucky nonchalance

The man who wrote this feature article

WALTER LIPPMANN 1889–

Walter Lippmann is called "the man with the searchlight mind." He has written twenty books in the field of political philosophy.

He studied at Harvard University and, during his senior year, was assistant to the great philosopher, George Santayana. Even before he was graduated in 1910, Lippmann had written a book on philosophy.

Mr. Lippmann began writing about politics when he joined the editorial staff of *New Republic* magazine in 1914. Five years later he began writing editorials for a New York newspaper, the *World*. In five years more, he was chief editorial writer; in another five years, he was editor. The *World* failed in 1931 and Mr. Lippmann became a special writer for another New York newspaper, the New York *Herald Tribune,* a position he holds today.

Fourteen colleges and universities have awarded him honorary degrees for his illuminating essays on politics and government.

Let's consider . . .

1. In your own words, explain what Lippmann meant by the term "false gods"?
2. The author described the years between 1922 and 1932 as "a time of exceptionally drastic change in the convictions of western men." What did he feel had brought about this change?
3. Why did Lippmann feel that the demoralization of the people was so dangerous? What happened to the individual?
4. What ideal was held out before the people by "those in high places"? Do you think that same ideal is being held out today?
5. Lippmann mentioned certain "false gods" which those in high places exalted

and taught the people to worship. What were they?
6. Whom did he blame for the disintegration and demoralization he found so common and fearsome?
7. This article may have seemed pessimistic, but toward the end there was a ray of hope. The "best and bravest" in that decade were looking for new leaders. What destiny would these leaders see for America? What ideal would they hold out before the people?
8. Do you think that Americans today are "united for purposes which they respect"? Do they show "faith in themselves and in their objectives"? Give thoughtful answers to these questions. Do not make blanket statements which you cannot support.

The writer's craft . . .

A. Closely related to the informal essay is the newspaper **feature article:** a prose commentary on an event or topic of current public interest. "False Gods" originally appeared many years ago in the New York *Herald Tribune,* a daily newspaper, but its well written and provocative message is equally significant today. Some of Mr. Lippmann's commentaries have become a part of American literature.

1. Select several of the comments in this feature article and explain why they appeal to you.
2. Bring a current newspaper feature article to class which you think is particularly well written and which has a message that might extend beyond the present moment.

B. Walter Lippmann began with several **rhetorical questions.** These are questions which no one is expected to answer. They are asked merely for their dramatic effect. Often the person asking such questions proceeds to answer them himself.

They are a good device for arousing the reader's curiosity. Look again at the opening questions. Why did they arouse your curiosity?

1. Do you think that having several questions clustered together strengthens or weakens the provocative quality of the opening? Give several reasons for your answer.

2. Rhetorical questions are often used in advertising. Give several examples. Do you think rhetorical questions have been overworked in this field? How do you react when you are confronted with a great many such questions?

Knowing words . . .

Walter Lippmann used words with precision. Find the exact meaning of each of the italicized words in the following sentences. Discuss in class how they added to the forcefulness of his statements and how they helped to set the tone of the article. What do they show about the author's attitude toward "false gods" which confuse the people?

1. It is *demoralization* alone that is dangerous.

2. The problem has been muffled in *hypocrisy,* in miserable *ambiguities,* and in *equivocation,* to a point where any open, public debate of the matter has become impossible.

3. They are unfaithful to that trust when by word or example they promote a spirit that is *complacent, evasive,* and *acquisitive.*

4. It is not only against the material consequences of this decade of drift and *hallucination,* but against the essence of its spirit, that the best and bravest among us are today in revolt.

Eldorado

Gaily bedight,
A gallant knight,
In sunshine and in shadow,
Had journeyed long,
Singing a song,
In search of Eldorado.[1]

But he grew old—
This knight so bold—
And o'er his heart a shadow
Fell as he found
No spot of ground
That looked like Eldorado.

And, as his strength
Failed him at length,
He met a pilgrim shadow—
'Shadow,' said he,
'Where can it be—
This land of Eldorado?'

'Over the Mountains
Of the Moon,
Down the Valley of the Shadow,
Ride, boldly ride,'
The shade replied,—
'If you seek for Eldorado!'

Edgar Allan Poe

---

[1] *Eldorado,* a legendary city of gold

Eleven o'Clock News Summary

PHYLLIS McGINLEY

Fold up the papers now. It is hushed, it is late;
Now the quick day unwinds.
Yawning, empty the ashtrays into the grate.
Close the Venetian blinds.
Then turn, by custom, the dial a wave length lower.
This is the hour (directly upon the hour)
Briefly to hear
With half-attentive and habitual ear
Important news bulletins.
                                    Our armies are valiant.
They have taken another ridge,
Another town, a fort, a strip, a salient.
They have held a bridge
(With heavy casualties). Our planes today,
According to a recent communique,
Struck (though the loss was high) at a vital border.
Remember to leave a note for the dairy order
And to set the thermostat at sixty-two.
We have captured an island at merely a moderate cost.
One of our submarines is overdue
And must be presumed lost.

In forests, in muddy fields, while winter fades,
Our troops are smashing through the Barricades,
They Push, they Storm, they Forge Ahead, they die
And lie on litters or unburied lie.
Static is bad tonight.
There—twiddle the knob a little to the right.

Here in the nation
Obedient curfews sound their midnight wails.
This is America's leading independent station.

Read the paper tomorrow for further details—
Details of death on the beaches, in the heat, in the cold,
Of death in gliders, in tanks, at a city's gate,
Death of young men who fancied they might grow old
But could not wait
(Being given, of course, no choice).

Well, snap the switch, turn off the announcer's voice,
Plump up the pillows on the green divan,
For day unwinds like a thread
And it is time now for a punctual man,
Drowsy, a little absent, warmed and fed,
To dim the light, turn down the blanketed bed,
And sleep, if he can.

The woman who wrote this poem

PHYLLIS McGINLEY   1905–

Phyllis McGinley's light satiric verse has appeared in every type of periodical. Occasionally she writes a serious poem, but she is best known for her light verse and has been praised for "her expert satire." Miss McGinley likes to think of her poetry as "sticking pins into the smugger aspects of the social scene."

Her best-known volumes of poetry are *One More Manhattan* (1937), *Stones from a Glass House* (1946), *A Short Walk from the Station* (1951), and *Love Letters* (1954).

Miss McGinley was born in Oregon, raised in Colorado, educated in Utah, and now lives in New York. In between schoolteaching, free-lance writing, advertising, editing, and mothering two children, she has also found time for writing poetry.

The poet's art . . .

1. Some parts of this poem were printed in italics; some parts were not. With this change in type, the poet called your attention to the difference in the parts. Look at the parts in italics. To whom was the poet speaking—to herself or to all radio listeners? What purpose did these comments serve?

2. Now look at the parts in regular type. How did the tone change in these parts? What were the poet's feelings about the news broadcast? What words gave you a clue?

3. The simple, natural language in this poem made it seem almost like a conversation in your own living room. What things did the poet mention which are typical of most American homes? How did she make her comments about this one broadcast seem applicable to all wars fought in recent years?

4. Most poems create in their readers a **mood:** a state, feeling, or frame of mind. It might be excitement, pleasure, sadness, thoughtfulness. What mood did this poem create for you? Perhaps it was a mixture of several moods. Try to explain how you felt after your reading.

5. What the poet had to say could have been expressed in an essay. Select from the poem those expressions or figures of speech which you feel made the poetic form a more impressive statement of the idea. If you would prefer the prose form, explain why.

Without a Cloak

PHYLLIS McGINLEY

Hate has a fashionable cut.
   It is the garment man agrees on,
Snug, colorful, the proper weight
   For comfort in an icy season.

And it is weatherproof, they say—
   Becoming, also, to the spirit.
I fetched Hate homeward yesterday,
   But there it hangs. I cannot wear it.

It is a dress that suits me ill,
   However much the mode sustains me.
At once too ample and too small,
   It trips, bewilders, and confines me.

And in my blood do fevers flow,
   Corruptive, where the fabric presses,
Till I must pluck it off as though
   It were the burning shirt of Nessus.[1]

Proud walk the people folded warm
   In Hate. They need not pray for spring.
But threadbare do I face the storm
   Or hug my hearthstone, shivering.

---

[1] *Nessus,* the centaur which Hercules shot with a poisoned arrow. Hercules was then enticed into wearing Nessus' blood-stained shirt, which poisoned his flesh. Suffering horrible agony because he was unable to remove the magic shirt, Hercules killed himself.

The poet's art . . .

1. This poem was built around a **metaphor:** an implied comparison in which two things are identified with each other. Hate was identified as a cloak. Through this poetic device, Miss McGinley could say briefly what you have heard at greater length in school assemblies, in church, and over the air. Point out all the points of resemblance given in the poem between Hate and a cloak.

2. What are the differences in the way people wear this garment?

3. What did the cloak do to the speaker in the poem?

4. Phyllis McGinley was not preaching a sermon in this poem, but she did present a lesson for those who wished to learn it. What is that lesson?

Science Has Spoiled My Supper

PHILIP WYLIE

Some Americans have begun to speak out against the effects of mass production on modern life. "What has happened to quality," they ask?

I am a fan for Science. My education is scientific and I have, in one field, contributed a monograph [1] to a scientific journal. Science, to my mind, is applied honesty, the one reliable means we have to find out truth. That is why, when error, is committed in the name of Science, I feel the way a man would if his favorite uncle had taken to drink.

Over the years, I have come to feel that way about what science has done to food. I agree that America can set as good a table as any nation in the world. I agree that our food is nutritious and that the diet of most of us is well-balanced. What America eats is handsomely packaged; it is usually clean and pure; it is excellently preserved. The only trouble with it is this: year by year it grows less good to eat. It appeals increasingly to the eye. But who eats with his eyes? Almost everything used to taste better when I was a kid. For quite a long time I thought that observation was merely another index of advancing age. But some years ago I married a girl whose mother is an expert cook of the kind called "old-fashioned." This gifted woman's daughter (my wife) was taught her mother's venerable skills. The mother lives in the country and still plants an old-fashioned garden. She still buys dairy products from the

neighbors and, in so far as possible, she uses the same materials her mother and grandmother did—to prepare meals that are superior. They are just as good, in this Year of Grace, as I recall them from my

---

[1] *monograph,* a written account of a single thing or class.

courtship. After eating for a while at the table of my mother-in-law, it is sad to go back to eating with my friends—even the alleged "good cooks" among them. And it is a gruesome experience to have meals at the best big-city restaurants.

Take cheese, for instance. Here and there, in big cities, small stores and delicatessens specialize in cheese. At such places, one can buy at least some of the first-rate cheeses that we used to eat—such as those we had with pie and in macaroni. The latter were sharp but not too sharp. They were a little crumbly. We called them American cheeses, or even rat cheese; actually they were Cheddars. Long ago, this cheese began to be supplanted by a material called "cheese foods." Some cheese foods and "processed" cheese are fairly edible; but not one comes within miles of the old kinds—for flavor.

A grocer used to be very fussy about his cheese. Cheddar was made and sold by hundreds of little factories. Representatives of the factories had particular customers, and cheese was prepared by hand to suit the grocers, who knew precisely what their patrons wanted in rat cheese, pie cheese, American and other cheeses. Some liked them sharper; some liked them yellower; some liked anise seeds in cheese, or caraway.

What happened? Science—or what is called science—stepped in. The old-fashioned cheeses didn't ship well enough. They crumbled, became moldy, dried out. "Scientific" tests disclosed that a great majority of the people will buy a less-good-tasting cheese if that's all they can get. "Scientific marketing" then took effect. Its motto is "Give the people the least quality they'll stand for." In food, as in many other things, the "scientific marketers" regard quality as secondary so long as they can sell most persons anyhow; what they are after is "durability" or "shippability."

It is not possible to make the very best cheese in vast quantities at a low average cost. "Scientific sampling" got in its statistically nasty work. It was found that the largest number of people will buy something that is bland and rather tasteless. Those who prefer a product of a pronounced and individualistic flavor have a variety of preferences. Nobody is altogether pleased by bland foodstuff, in other words; but nobody is very violently put off. The result is that a "reason" has been found for turning out zillions of packages of something that will "do" for nearly all and isn't even imagined to be superlatively good by a single soul!

Economics entered. It is possible to turn out in quantity a bland, impersonal, practically imperishable substance more or less resembling, say, cheese—at lower cost than cheese. Chain groceries shut out the independent stores and "standardization" became a principal means of cutting costs.

Imitations also came into the cheese business. There are American duplications of most of the celebrated European cheeses, mass-produced and cheaper by far than the imports. They would cause European food-lovers to gag or guffaw—but generally the imitations are all that's available in the supermarkets. People buy them and eat them.

Perhaps you don't like cheese—so the fact that decent cheese is hardly ever served in America any more, or used in cooking, doesn't matter to you. Well, take bread. There has been (and still is) something of a hullabaloo about bread. In fact, in the last few years, a few big bakeries have taken to making a fairly good imitation of real bread. It costs much more than what is nowadays called bread, but it is edible. Most persons, however, now eat as "bread" a substance so full of chemicals and so barren of cereals that it approaches a synthetic.

Most bakers are interested mainly in how a loaf of bread looks. They are concerned with how little stuff they can put in it—to get how much money. They are deeply interested in using chemicals that will keep bread from molding, make it seem "fresh" for the longest possible time, and so render it marketable and shippable. They have been at this monkeyshine for a generation. Today a loaf of "bread" looks deceptively real; but it is made from heaven knows what and it resembles, as food, a solidified bubble bath. Some months ago I bought a loaf of the stuff and, experimentally, began pressing it together, like an accordion. With a little effort, I squeezed the whole loaf to a length of about one inch.

Yesterday, at the home of my mother-in-law, I ate with country-churned butter and home-canned wild strawberry jam several slices of actual bread, the same thing we used to have every day at home. People who have eaten actual bread will know what I mean. They will know that the material commonly called bread is not even related to real bread, except in name.

For years, I couldn't figure out what had happened to vegetables. I knew, of course, that most vegetables, to be enjoyed in their full deliciousness, must be picked fresh and cooked at once. I knew that vegetables cannot be overcooked and remain even edible, in the best sense. They cannot stand on the stove. That set of facts makes it impossible, of course, for any American restaurant—or, indeed, any city-dweller separated from supply by more than a few hours—to have decent fresh vegetables. The Parisians manage by getting their vegetables picked at dawn and rushed in farmers' carts to market, where no middleman or marketman delays produce on its way to the pot.

Our vegetables, however, come to us through a long chain of command. There are merchants of several sorts—wholesalers before the retailers, commission men, and so on—with the result that what were once edible products become, in transit, mere wilted leaves and withered tubers.

Homes and restaurants do what they can

with this stuff—which my mother-in-law would discard on the spot. I have long thought that the famed blindfold test for cigarettes should be applied to city vegetables. For I am sure that if you pureed them and ate them blindfolded, you couldn't tell the beans from the peas, the turnips from the squash, the Brussels from the broccoli.

It is only lately that I have found how much science has to do with this reduction of noble victuals to pottage. Here the science of genetics [2] is involved. Agronomists [3] and the like have taken to breeding all sorts of vegetables and fruits—changing their original nature. This sounds wonderful and often is insane. For the scientists have not as a rule taken any interest whatsoever in the taste of the things they've tampered with!

What they've done is to develop "improved" strains of things for every purpose but eating. They work out, say, peas that will ripen all at once. The farmer can then harvest his peas and thresh them and be done with them. It is extremely profitable because it is efficient. What matter if such peas taste like boiled paper wads?

Geneticists have gone crazy over such "opportunities." They've developed string beans that are straight instead of curved, and all one length. This makes them easier to pack in cans, even if, when eating them, you can't tell them from tender string. Ripening time and identity of size and shape are, nowadays, more important in carrots than the fact that they taste like carrots. Personally, I don't care if they hybridize [4] onions till they are as big as your head and come up through the snow; but, in doing so, they are producing onions that only vaguely and feebly remind you of onions. We are getting some varieties, in fact, that have less flavor than the water off last week's leeks. Yet, if people don't eat on-

[2] *genetics,* study of heredity
[3] *agronomists,* scientists who study crops
[4] *hybridize,* cross breed

ions because they taste like onions, what in the name of Luther Burbank do they eat them for?

The women's magazines are about one third dedicated to clothes, one third to mild comment on romance, and the other third to recipes and pictures of handsome salads, desserts, and main courses. "Institutes" exist to experiment and tell housewives how to cook attractive meals and how to turn leftovers into works of art. The food thus pictured looks like famous paintings of still life. The only trouble is it's tasteless. It leaves appetite unquenched and merely serves to stave off famine.

I wonder if this blandness of our diet doesn't explain why so many of us are overweight and even dangerously so. When things had flavor, we knew what we were eating all the while—and it satisfied us. A teaspoonful of my mother-in-law's wild strawberry jam will not just provide a gastronome's [5] ecstasy: it will entirely satisfy your jam desire. But, of the average tinned or glass-packed strawberry jam, you need half a cupful to get the idea of what you're eating. A slice of my mother-in-law's apple pie will satiate you far better than a whole bakery pie.

That thought is worthy of investigation —of genuine scientific investigation. It is merely a hypothesis, so far, and my own. But people—and their ancestors—have been eating according to flavor for upwards of a billion years. The need to satisfy the sense of taste may be innate and important. When food is merely a pretty cascade of viands, with the texture of boiled cardboard and the flavor of library paste, it may be the instinct of *genus homo* to go on eating in the unconscious hope of finally satisfying the ageless craving of the frustrated taste buds. In the days when good-tasting food was the rule in the American home, obesity wasn't such a national curse.

How can you feel you've eaten if you

---

[5] *gastronome,* lover of fine foods

haven't tasted, and fully enjoyed tasting? Why (since science is ever so ready to answer the beck and call of mankind) don't people who want to reduce merely give up eating and get the nourishment they must have in measured doses shot into their arms at hospitals? One ready answer to that question suggests that my theory of overeating is sound: people like to taste! In eating, they try to satisfy that like.

The scientific war against deliciousness has been stepped up enormously in the last decade. Some infernal genius found a way to make biscuit batter keep. Housewives began to buy this premixed stuff. It saved work, of course. But any normally intelligent person can learn, in a short period, how to prepare superb baking powder biscuits. I can make better biscuits, myself, than can be made from patent batters. Yet soon after this fiasco became an American staple, it was discovered that a half-baked substitute for all sorts of breads, pastries, rolls, and the like could be mass-manufactured, frozen—and sold for polishing off in the home oven. None of these two-stage creations is as good as even a fair sample of the thing it imitates. A man of taste, who had eaten one of my wife's cinnamon buns, might use the premixed sort to throw at starlings—but not to eat! Cake mixes, too, come ready-prepared—like cement and not much better-tasting compared with true cake.

It is, however, "deep-freezing" that has really rung down the curtain on American cookery. Nothing is improved by the process. I have yet to taste a deep-frozen victual that measures up, in flavor, to the fresh, unfrosted original. And most foods, cooked or uncooked, are destroyed in the deep freeze for all people of sense and sensibility. Vegetables with crisp and crackling texture emerge as mush, slippery and stringy as hair nets simmered in Vaseline. The essential oils that make peas peas—and cabbage cabbage—must undergo fission and fusion in freezers. Anyhow, they vanish. Some meats turn to leather. Others to wood pulp. Everything, pretty much, tastes like the mosses of tundra, dug up in midwinter. Even the appearance changes, oftentimes. Handsome comestibles [6] you put down in the summer come out looking very much like the corpses of woolly mammoths recovered from the last Ice Age.

Of course, all this scientific "food handling" tends to save money. It certainly preserves food longer. It reduces work at home. But these facts, and especially the last, imply that the first purpose of living is to avoid work—at home, anyhow.

Without thinking, we are making an important confession about ourselves as a nation. We are abandoning quality—even, to some extent, the quality of people. The "best" is becoming too good for us. We are suckling ourselves on machine-made mediocrity. It is bad for our souls, our minds, and our digestion. It is the way our wiser and calmer forebears fed, not people, but hogs: as much as possible and as fast as possible, with no standard of quality.

The Germans say, *"Mann ist was er isst* —Man is what he eats."* If this be true, the

people of the U. S. A. are well on their way to becoming a faceless mob of mediocrities, of robots. And if we apply to other attributes the criteria we apply these days to appetite, that is what would happen! We would not want bright children any more; we'd merely want them to look bright—and get through school fast. We wouldn't be interested in beautiful women —just a good paint job. And we'd be opposed to the most precious quality of man: his individuality, his differentness from the mob.

There are some people—sociologists and psychologists among them—who say that is exactly what we Americans are doing, are becoming. Mass man, they say, is on the increase. Conformity, standardization, similarity—all on a cheap and vulgar level —are replacing the great American ideas of colorful liberty and dignified individualism. If this is so, the process may well begin, like most human behavior, in the home—in those homes where a good meal has been replaced by something-to-eat-in-a-hurry. By something not very good to eat, prepared by a mother without very much to do, for a family that doesn't feel it amounts to much anyhow.

I call, here, for rebellion.

---

[6] *comestibles,* edibles

The man who wrote this essay

PHILIP WYLIE 1902–

You should not be too surprised if you found yourself disagreeing sharply with some of Philip Wylie's comments in "Science Has Spoiled My Supper." He frequently stirs up controversy by his outspoken criticism of contemporary habits and customs. However, Wylie is not always a social critic. Many of his stories and essays, particularly those about fishing, are written in a quiet, relaxed style.

Philip Wylie's career as a writer has taken him into a variety of fields. In addition to serving on the staff of the *New Yorker* Magazine, he has worked both as an editor and a newspaper columnist. During one period of his life he wrote motion picture scenarios in Hollywood. Although many of his short stories have been published in the country's leading magazines, he is perhaps best known for his book of social commentary *Generation of Vipers.*

Let's consider . . .

1. How did Philip Wylie define science? Explain why you think his definition is adequate or inadequate.

2. Summarize Wylie's comments on the changes that have been made in the manufacturing of cheese. How did he account for these changes?

3. What reasons were given to explain overweight? Can you think of others?

4. What were Wylie's objections to frozen foods? Are his objections valid? Explain.

5. What important confession are Americans making about themselves as a result of their new eating habits?

6. According to Wylie, what is the most precious quality of man? Explain why you agree or disagree.

7. What has science done to improve food? Do you think that Wylie should mention the good, as well as the bad, effects of science on food? Explain.

8. Wylie disapproves of new techniques of handling and processing food. Are there other so-called improvements in modern living which you think are inferior to the more old-fashioned way of doing things? If so, mention several.

The writer's craft . . .

In this informal essay Philip Wylie used a casual style of writing to make a serious comment on contemporary American civilization. The style was witty and amusing, yet not quite acid. At the end of the essay, however, the reader was clearly aware that Wylie's purpose in writing was not merely to amuse, but to provoke Americans to do some serious thinking about their society.

1. Identify those characteristics of style which give the writing its informal tone. Explain how each characteristic which you mention contributes to the informal tone.

2. Select two of Wylie's comments which you found particularly amusing.

3. What are the advantages of writing in a light, casual style while making a serious observation? What are the disadvantages?

4. Note the persuasive technique that Philip Wylie used in developing his point of view. In the first paragraph he stated that he was devoted to science. What effect did he achieve by opening with a declaration of his belief in science? In the second paragraph, however, he pointed out that science had spoiled American food. He continued in his third paragraph by offering a concrete illustration of what science had done to a specific food, in this case, cheese.

Continue this analysis showing the way Wylie built his case against the influence of science on food. Be sure to mention the implications for American society that Wylie drew at the conclusion of his essay.

5. Select an aspect of modern society that you believe could be improved, such as popular music, styles in clothes, sports, television programs, or motion pictures. Write an essay on your topic using Wylie's technique of combining an informal style with a serious message. Use your analysis of Wylie's essay as a guide to writing your own.

Finders-Keepers

GEORGE KELLY

Many Americans speak out in defense of truth and justice in the privacy of their own homes. Few men believed more strongly than Eugene Aldrid that people should be honest "for the sake of being so"; and few men suffered a greater loss because they spoke out in defense of their belief.

Plays are written to be seen and heard. They need an audience. If you were sitting in a theater watching a performance of *Finders-Keepers* you would see the stage setting, hear the actors' voices, and watch their actions. You would not see those other people who also had a part in producing this play: the director, the costume and stage designers, the electricians, and many other technicians. They, too, helped to make the performance dramatic and effective.

Reading a play requires full use of your imagination. You must try to "see" the setting and the action, and must project yourself into each character's part. You have only the characters' lines and a few stage directions from which to create an entire production. However, if you will use your imagination, you will find that play-reading can be a rewarding and completely engrossing experience.

CHARACTERS

EUGENE ALDRID   MRS. ALDRID, his wife   MRS. HAMPTON, a neighbor

The action of the play takes place in the living room of EUGENE ALDRID'S *home, which is located in an outlying suburb of the city of Philadelphia, Pennsylvania. The time is about five o'clock of a late September afternoon.[1] All curtains are of quiet cretonne, and there are sheaves of autumn leaves about. The garden, through the window at the back, is bright with scarlet sage.*

SCENE—*After a second's stillness a door closes out at the right, and immediately* MRS. ALDRID *enters through the archway, carrying several parcels, which she hastens to deposit on the center table; then she straightens up and draws a deep breath. She is a trim blonde, in her late twenties, wearing a tailored coat suit of fawn-colored serge, a toque of champagne silk, and a waist of very pale pink silk. Her slippers and stockings are of the lighter shades of brown, and she wears a quite long string of freakish black-and-yellow beads. Before she has had time to take the second breath, the bronze clock on the mantelpiece, at the left, strikes five. She glances at it.*

MRS. ALDRID: Heavens! five o'clock!

(*She hurriedly removes her coat and hat, lays them on the sofa in front of the mantelpiece, and, with a glance at herself in the mirror over the mantelpiece, vanishes through the door at the left.*)

Then there is a slight pause; and EUGENE ALDRID *enters through the archway from the right, carrying a roll of blueprints in one hand and the evening paper in the other. He is a tall and thin, very intelligent-looking man of perhaps thirty-three, wearing a dark-blue, double-breasted business suit, dark shoes, and a dark tie. He sets the roll of blueprints down on the center table, and then* MRS. ALDRID *speaks to him from the room out at the left.*)

MRS. ALDRID: Is that you? Gene?

ALDRID (*Looking toward the left and then starting over toward his desk at the right*): Yes.

_____
[1] In the early 1900's

MRS. ALDRID: You must have been right behind me.

ALDRID (*Laying the newspaper on his desk*): Did you just get in?

MRS. ALDRID (*Coming into the room from the left, adjusting a bungalow apron*): This minute—I've been in town shopping; I had no idea it was so late.

ALDRID (*Picking up a telegram from his desk and opening it*): It's after five.

MRS. ALDRID: I know it is; and there isn't a thing ready. You'll have to wait a while for your dinner.

ALDRID (*With an exaggerated sigh of resignation*): Ah—ho! (*He reads the telegram.*)

MRS. ALDRID: Did you come out on the four-fifty-three?

ALDRID (*Without looking up*): Yes; you weren't on it, were you?

MRS. ALDRID: No, I'd intended coming out on the train, but—something happened that made me change my mind.

ALDRID (*Looking straight ahead, thinking and tapping the telegram, which he has finished reading, against his hand*): Spaulding. (*Turning suddenly to* MRS. ALDRID:) What? Why—what happened?

MRS. ALDRID (*Assuming an air of great confidence*): Wait till I tell you! (*She steps to the back of the room and looks keenly out into the hallway, to assure herself that no one is within hearing, then comes down to the left of her husband, who watches her curiously.*) You know, I went into town this afternoon to get some georgette crepe for that new blouse of mine.

ALDRID: Yes.

MRS. ALDRID: Well, as I went into the Market Street entrance of Blum's—you know, there's a glove counter right inside the Market Street door. (ALDRID *nods.*) Well, I went over to ask the saleslady where I could get the crepe; and as I leaned over to ask her, I stepped on something; it felt like a bracelet or something—rather soft—and yet it was metallic.

ALDRID: Yes.

MRS. ALDRID: Well, I didn't pay any attention to it at first—I thought it might be a joke or something—you know, they're always doing that sort of thing in those department stores.

ALDRID: Yes, I know.

MRS. ALDRID: But as I started away from the counter, I just glanced down at the floor; and what do you suppose it was?

ALDRID: What?

MRS. ALDRID: A purse—one of those little gold mesh purses.

ALDRID: Anything in it?

MRS. ALDRID: Well now, wait till I tell you. I didn't open it right away—I was afraid someone might be looking; so I waited till I got up to the writing room before I opened it; and what do you suppose was in it?

ALDRID: What?

MRS. ALDRID: Four—hundred—dollars.

ALDRID (After a slight pause): Four hundred dollars?

MRS. ALDRID: Hum-hum.

ALDRID (Incredulously): Where is it?

MRS. ALDRID: In my pocketbook.

ALDRID: Well, are you sure it's real money?

MRS. ALDRID: Of course it is; I'll show it to you in a minute. You know, I could scarcely believe my eyes at first; because, you know, I've never found anything in all my life; and then to suddenly pick up eight fifty-dollar bills. Positively, Gene, I don't know how I ever got home.

ALDRID: Were they all fifties?

MRS. ALDRID: Hum-hum; and brand-new ones at that; they look as though they'd just been taken out of a bank.

ALDRID (Turning suddenly and leaning on the chair in front of his desk, then looking at her): Can you imagine losing that!

MRS. ALDRID: Losing it? Can you imagine finding it? I thought I was seeing things. (She starts toward the door at the left.)

ALDRID: Did you say anything about it?

MRS. ALDRID (Stopping and turning to him): How do you mean?

ALDRID: At the "Lost and Found"?

MRS. ALDRID: No, of course I didn't; what do you think I am?

ALDRID: You might have gotten in touch with the owner.

MRS. ALDRID (Smiling indulgently): Positively, Gene, you talk like a boy from the country.

ALDRID: Why so?

MRS. ALDRID (With a touch of impatience, and coming to the left of the center table): Because you do! Don't you know that if I were to turn that amount of money into a "Lost and Found" desk, I'd stand just about as much chance of ever seeing it again as I would of seeing the North Pole?

ALDRID: Well, you wouldn't expect ever to see it again if it were returned to the owner.

MRS. ALDRID: And how would I know that it had been returned to the owner?

ALDRID: Oh, everybody isn't dishonest! (He glances through the telegram again.)

MRS. ALDRID: Well, you let people get their hands on four hundred dollars—you'll find out how many of them are honest! Turn that amount of money over to one of those "Lost and Found" clerks—he'd soon find an owner for it, believe me! (She starts for the door at the left.)

ALDRID (Crushing the telegram in his hand): What are you going to do with it?

(She stops at the door and looks back at him. He gracefully tosses the telegram overhand into the wastepaper basket below his desk.)

MRS. ALDRID: I'm going to keep it!

ALDRID: Ho!

MRS. ALDRID (Surprised that he should ask such a question): What do you suppose I'm going to do with it—throw it away? It's as good in my pocket as it is in anybody else's! (He turns and looks at her in a way that disconcerts her slightly, but as he withdraws his eyes in turning to his desk, she regains herself and comes a step or two farther into the room.) I can get awnings for this whole house for that —and a Victrola, too!

ALDRID (Coming over to the center table for his blueprints, after looking for them on his desk): You'd better not count your chickens before they're hatched.

MRS. ALDRID (After looking at him for a second): What do you mean?

ALDRID (Picking up the roll of blueprints from the table and speaking rather abstractedly): Why, there'll very likely be an ad for it in one of the morning papers.

MRS. ALDRID: Well, what if there is?

ALDRID (Looking at the blueprints): Nothing—only you'd simply have to return it, that's all.

MRS. ALDRID (After thinking for a second, and with an expression of sullen calculation): I don't see why I should.

ALDRID (He raises his eyes from the blueprints and looks at her quizzically): You don't see why you should return lost property to the person who lost it?

MRS. ALDRID: That depends.

ALDRID (In a level tone): Upon what?

MRS. ALDRID (Looking straight ahead): Whether or not I was sure he'd lost it.

ALDRID: Couldn't you make sure?

MRS. ALDRID (After turning and looking at him): How?

ALDRID: Identification.

MRS. ALDRID: Not in this case.

ALDRID: Why not?

MRS. ALDRID: Because there isn't a solitary thing about it, Gene, by which it could possibly be identified: not a card or a paper of any kind!

ALDRID: How about the purse?

MRS. ALDRID: There are a million exactly like it: a plain, gold mesh bag. (Indicating the desk at the right:) I've had one in that top drawer there for the past year.

ALDRID: Couldn't the money be described?

MRS. ALDRID: That wouldn't be any identification.

ALDRID: Why not?

MRS. ALDRID: Why, because money is simply money—unless it's marked; and this isn't, because I've examined it very carefully.

ALDRID (Resting one end of the roll of blueprints on the table and leaning his elbow on the other end): So you don't see any possible way by which this money could be returned to its owner?

MRS. ALDRID: Not unless I took his word for it; (Turning and looking at him:) and, really, I don't see why I should do that.

ALDRID (Evenly): What are you trying to do, make yourself believe it belongs to you?

MRS. ALDRID (Turning her head away): I found it.

ALDRID: And somebody else lost it.

MRS. ALDRID: I suppose so.

ALDRID: Possibly some poor man or woman.

MRS. ALDRID (With a little toss of her head): Now, don't get sentimental, please!

ALDRID (With a touch of impatience, and taking a couple of steps in front of the table toward her): That isn't sentiment at all!

MRS. ALDRID (Turning to him sharply and speaking incisively): No very poor man or woman has any eight fifty-dollar bills to lose. (She turns away and secures a hairpin at the back of her head; he looks at her steadily.) And no matter who lost it, it'll be a very good lesson to him to be a little more careful in the future.

ALDRID: I see. Well, why should he pay you four hundred dollars for that lesson?

MRS. ALDRID: Nobody's paying me any four hundred dollars.

ALDRID: You've often lost things yourself, haven't you?

MRS. ALDRID (Turning to him quickly): Yes, and I never got them back, either!

ALDRID: Whose fault was that?

MRS. ALDRID (Turning away again): I don't know whose fault it was.

ALDRID: Well, try and think.

MRS. ALDRID: Unless the people who

found them weren't honest enough to return them. (*The door out at the right closes.*) Who's that? (*She starts for the archway at the right, tossing her apron onto the sofa as she goes.*)

ALDRID (*Turning and crossing to his desk*): Somebody at the door.

MRS. ALDRID (*In a lowered tone*): Don't say anything about this. (*She reaches the archway.*) Oh, it's you, Mrs. Hampton!

(ALDRID *half glances toward the archway, then picks up the evening paper and flips it open.*)

MRS. HAMPTON (*In the hallway*): Yes, it's me.

MRS. ALDRID (*Rather effusively*): Come right in! (*She extends her arm and hand and leads* MRS. HAMPTON *into the room.*)

(MRS. HAMPTON *is a dark woman, with a pale but lovely face, and a certain Madonna quality about her generally. She is of the same build as* MRS. ALDRID, *and apparently of the same age. She wears a coat suit of good black, a white silk waist, with a little string of purple beads at her throat, and a medium-sized hat of very dark, purple-colored straw, trimmed with an ornament of itself. Her slippers and stockings are black.*)

MRS. HAMPTON: Good evening.

MRS. ALDRID: Good evening, dear, how are you?

ALDRID: Good evening, Mrs. Hampton.

MRS. HAMPTON: Oh, good evening, Mr. Aldrid, I didn't see you. I hope you'll both excuse me for coming in without ringing.

ALDRID (*Tossing his paper onto the desk*): Don't mention it.

MRS. ALDRID (*Standing back of the center table*): Saved me the trouble of answering the door; it's the girl's day out.

MRS. HAMPTON: Well, I *do* hope I haven't intruded.

MRS. ALDRID: You haven't at all, dear, really; I've just gotten in from town.

MRS. HAMPTON: I've been in the city, too; I came out on the four-fifty-three.

ALDRID (*Placing a chair, which he has taken from above his desk, about midway between the center table and the archway*): Won't you take a chair, Mrs. Hampton?

MRS. HAMPTON: No, thank you, Mr. Aldrid. I can't stay a moment.

ALDRID: I'm sorry. (*He moves down to his desk again and picks up the paper.*)

MRS. ALDRID: Why not?

MRS. HAMPTON (*Obviously troubled about something*): Oh, I'm too upset.

MRS. ALDRID: Are you ill, dear?

MRS. HAMPTON: No—but—I'd like to ask your advice about something.

MRS. ALDRID: Well, do sit down for a minute.

(MRS. HAMPTON *hesitates, then sits.* MRS. ALDRID *takes a chair from the back, and placing it above the center table and slightly to the left of it, sits also.* ALDRID *stands at the lower corner of his desk, reading the paper. There is a slight pause.*)

MRS. ALDRID: What is it?

MRS. HAMPTON (*Speaking directly to* MRS. ALDRID): I've lost some money.

(ALDRID *lifts his eyes over the top of his paper and looks straight out;* MRS. ALDRID *looks straight into* MRS. HAMPTON'S *eyes for a second, then rises quietly, still holding her eyes, and moves to the center table.*)

MRS. ALDRID: Much?

MRS. HAMPTON: Quite a bit, yes.

ALDRID (*Without turning*): Where did you lose it, Mrs. Hampton?

MRS. HAMPTON (*Turning to him*): I haven't an idea; (MRS. ALDRID *has been looking intently at her, but at this she shifts her eyes to* ALDRID *with a shade of relief.*) but I think it was in town.

(ALDRID *turns and glances at his wife, but she shifts her eyes back again to* MRS. HAMPTON.)

ALDRID: How much was it?

MRS. HAMPTON: Why—

MRS. ALDRID (*Quickly*): I suppose you don't know the exact amount, do you, dear?

MRS. HAMPTON (*Turning to her*): Four hundred dollars. (ALDRID *looks at*

his wife, but she's looking blankly at MRS. HAMPTON.) Isn't that dreadful! Of course, I know it would only be an item to some people—but, to me! I feel terrible about it! (*She breaks down and cries.*)

(ALDRID *turns and looks at her; then tossing his paper on to the desk and thrusting his hands into his trousers pockets, he turns and strolls toward the back of the room, looking significantly at his wife.*)

MRS. ALDRID (*Advancing and placing her hands on* MRS. HAMPTON'S *arms*): Now, don't cry, Mrs. Hampton; it isn't that bad.

MRS. HAMPTON: Oh, I think it's *dreadful* to lose all that money!

MRS. ALDRID: I know it is, dear; I don't wonder you feel bad.

MRS. HAMPTON: Eight fifty-dollar bills!

(MRS. ALDRID *is frozen into stillness.* ALDRID *steps forward eagerly from the archway, where he has been standing.*)

ALDRID: Eight fifties?

MRS. HAMPTON: Yes.

ALDRID (*Straightening up and looking at his wife with an ingenuous smile*): Eight fifties.

MRS. HAMPTON: And brand-new ones, too! It's awful! (*She begins crying again.*)

ALDRID (*To his wife, voicelessly, and indicating* MRS. HAMPTON *with a nod*): Why don't you tell her?

(MRS. ALDRID *lifts her chin and looks at him icily, whereupon he indicates* MRS. HAMPTON *again, with an austere point of his finger.*)

Mrs. Aldrid (*Choosing the better part of valor, and leaning over the back of* Mrs. Hampton's *chair*): Come now, Mrs. Hampton, you may not have lost it at all!

(Aldrid, *who has been watching his wife narrowly, breaks slowly, and goes to his desk, where he espies a large scribbled note fastened to the desk light, to attract his attention. Detaching this, he sits on the lower corner of his desk and reads it.*)

Mrs. Hampton (*Tearfully*): Oh, but I have, Mrs. Aldrid!

Mrs. Aldrid: I know, my dear, but, you know, sometimes we think we've lost a thing, and we find out later that we haven't lost it at all.

Mrs. Hampton: But I've looked everywhere, and it's lost, I tell you!

Mrs. Aldrid: But you may find it again, honey.

Mrs. Hampton: Oh, I don't think so!

Mrs. Aldrid: Or someone else may find it.

Mrs. Hampton: But that wouldn't do me any good.

Mrs. Aldrid: It would if the person who found it were honest.

Mrs. Hampton: I'm afraid very few people are honest, if it costs them four hundred dollars.

(Aldrid *finishes reading the note and sits looking out, thinking.*)

Mrs. Aldrid: Well now, it may be one of those very few who has found it.

Mrs. Hampton: I don't expect ever to get it again.

Aldrid: Nonsense, Mrs. Hampton!

Mrs. Hampton: I don't.

Aldrid: Nonesense! Now, you wait and see.

(*There is a pause.* Mrs. Hampton *touches her handkerchief to her eyes.*)

Mrs. Aldrid (*Looking away off*): Of course, you'll have to advertise.

(*There is a second before* Aldrid *grasps what she has said; then he turns his head sharply and looks at her; but she is still looking away off.*)

Mrs. Hampton: Yes, that's what I wanted to see Mr. Aldrid about. (*She turns to him.*) Which would be the best paper for me to advertise in?

(*He sits looking at his wife until she turns and meets his eyes; then he abstractedly extends his arm and hand in a gesture of interrogation, to which she responds by a sudden and taut pressing of her closed hand against her breast. He rises, to divert the attention of* Mrs. Hampton, *and after leaning for a second upon the back of his desk chair, starts slowly across the room in front of the center table. As he passes* Mrs. Hampton, *she rises also.*)

Mrs. Hampton: Now, don't let me worry you, Mr. Aldrid!

Aldrid (*Abstractedly*): No, no, it isn't that—I was just—wondering—

Mrs. Hampton (*Turning to* Mrs. Aldrid): If I'd thought it would bother you folks, I shouldn't have told you at all.

Mrs. Aldrid: That's perfectly all right, dear.

Mrs. Hampton: But I was so troubled when I got home, I simply *couldn't* stay in the house! I just *had* to come out and tell someone! And, my dear, I don't know how I'm *ever* going to tell Frank when he comes home tonight; because he said to me this morning, when I told him I was going to town—he said, "Can I *trust* you to deposit this money for me?" And I said, "What do you think I am, a thief?" "Well," he said, "you're always *losing* things!" "Well," I said, "there's no danger of my losing four hundred dollars." "Well," he said, "I hope not, or we'll get a guardian for you!" (*Starting to cry again:*) And then I go straight into the city and lose it! (*She cries a little;* Mrs. Aldrid *stands watching her; and* Aldrid, *who is leaning on his elbow on the mantelpiece over at the left, watches* Mrs. Aldrid.) And, mind you, to make *sure* that nothing would happen to it, I didn't even put it with my other money!

Mrs. Aldrid (*Eagerly, but without moving*): Where *did* you put it?

MRS. HAMPTON: In one of those little gold mesh purses.

(ALDRID *accidentally tears the note paper which he still has in his hand.*)

ALDRID: Mrs. Hampton.

MRS. HAMPTON: Yes?

ALDRID: Where did you first *miss* this money?

MRS. HAMPTON: When I was going up the steps into the bank.

ALDRID: Which bank?

MRS. HAMPTON: The Franklin National.

MRS. ALDRID: Where's that?

ALDRID: Broad and Chestnut. Where had you been before that?

MRS. HAMPTON: Why, when I came out of the station—after I got off the train—

ALDRID: Yes?

MRS. HAMPTON: I went over to Wanamaker's—to get some gloves. (ALDRID *looks at her keenly.*)

MRS. ALDRID: Wanamaker's?

MRS. HAMPTON (*Turning to her*): Yes. (MRS. ALDRID *gives a significant look at* ALDRID, *but he is looking at* MRS. HAMPTON.) But they didn't have my size in what I wanted at Wanamaker's, so I crossed over to Blum's.

ALDRID: Blum's glove counter?

MRS. HAMPTON: Yes.

(ALDRID *glances at his wife, but she is coughing into her handkerchief. He moves rather thoughtfully to the left of the center table, and picking up a book, stands it on its end on the table and leans upon it.* MRS. HAMPTON *is standing on the opposite side of the table, and* MRS. ALDRID *has moved quietly down to a point in front of* ALDRID's *desk.*)

ALDRID: You hadn't missed this money up to that time?

MRS. HAMPTON: No, and I'm quite sure I *had* it up to that time; because I hadn't opened my pocketbook from the time I left the house; and the money was *in* the big pocketbook.

ALDRID: I see; and you went directly from there to the bank?

MRS. HAMPTON: Yes, directly.

ALDRID: Then you think it was somewhere between Blum's glove counter and the bank steps that you lost it?

MRS. HAMPTON: It must have been; I imagine I must have pulled it out without knowing it, when I was paying for the gloves at Blum's.

ALDRID: Very likely.

MRS. HAMPTON: Or else, possibly, someone opened my pocketbook and took out the little purse (*Turning to* MRS. ALDRID) when I wasn't looking. (*She begins to cry again, as she turns back to* MR. ALDRID.) You know they do that, Mr. Aldrid.

ALDRID (*Abstractedly*): Yes, I know they do.

MRS. ALDRID (*Standing at the right, quietly toying with her beads and looking straight ahead with a calculating expression*): There wasn't a card or a paper of any kind in the purse, was there?

MRS. HAMPTON (*Turning to her*): No, there wasn't a thing in it but the money.

MRS. ALDRID: That's too bad. (ALDRID *watches her narrowly.*) No initials on it?

MRS. HAMPTON: No, I've always been going to have my initials put on it, but—oh, I don't know—I never seemed to get around to it.

MRS. ALDRID: That makes it bad.

MRS. HAMPTON (*With the threat of a few more tears*): Dear me, I wish I had, now.

MRS. ALDRID (*Turning to her suddenly with a kind of forced sincerity*): Yes, because if someone finds it and answers your advertisement, he'll naturally expect you to be able to identify it—definitely; that is, before you could reasonably expect him to return it to you, I mean.

MRS. HAMPTON: Yes, I suppose he would; but, then, I could describe the purse and the money.

MRS. ALDRID (*With a tolerant smile*): I know, my dear; but there may be a million purses exactly like it—

MRS. HAMPTON: That's true, too.

MRS. ALDRID: And, as far as the money

is concerned, why—money is simply money, unless it's marked; and this isn't, (*Checking herself:*) as you say—

MRS. HAMPTON: No, it isn't.

MRS. ALDRID: So that, really, a person would be more or less obliged to take your word for it, wouldn't he?

MRS. HAMPTON: I'm afraid he would.

MRS. ALDRID: And that's rather a lot for us to expect of people, isn't it, dear?

MRS. HAMPTON: Too much, I'm afraid.

MRS. ALDRID: Especially when there's four hundred dollars in the bargain. (*She gives a little mirthless, self-conscious laugh and settles the lace on* MRS. HAMPTON's *lapel.* ALDRID, *who has been watching her steadily, turns his head away slowly, and his eyes wander about the floor.*)

MRS. HAMPTON (*Turning to the chair from which she arose*): You're right, it is rather a poor prospect. (*She sits down.*)

MRS. ALDRID: Oh, well—

MRS. HAMPTON: Unless someone who is really honest finds it.

MRS. ALDRID (*Looking curiously at one of the beads in her necklace*): Of course, the only thing you *can* do is to advertise.

MRS. HAMPTON (*Rising*): Yes, I must right away. (*Moving to the right of the center table:*) Which paper do you think it would be best for me to advertise in, Mr. Aldrid? (*He doesn't hear her.*) Mr. Aldrid?

ALDRID (*Turning to her suddenly*): I beg your pardon, Mrs. Hampton, what did—

MRS. ALDRID: She wants to know which paper you think it would be best for her to advertise in?

ALDRID (*Directly to his wife*): None of them—(*to* MRS. HAMPTON, *with a change of tone*) until she hears from me.

MRS. ALDRID (*Quickly, and laying her hands on* MRS. HAMPTON's *shoulder and arm*): He means he'll look up the circulations later, dear.

(ALDRID *looks at her for a rather long pause; she avoids his eyes; then, as* MRS. HAMPTON *turns and looks at him, he speaks.*)

ALDRID: I'll telephone you after dinner, Mrs. Hampton. (*He starts toward the back of the room.*)

MRS. HAMPTON: Well, that's very charming of you, Mr. Aldrid.

ALDRID: Don't mention it. (*He passes out through the window into the garden; then stops abruptly, makes a taut, general movement of desperate irresolution, turns, and steps back in through the window again, where, gripping the draperies in his hands, he stands watching his wife with an expression of stony suspicion.*)

MRS. HAMPTON (*To* MRS. ALDRID): And I really feel that I owe you both a genuine apology for bothering you with my troubles. (*Starting for the archway at the right.*)

MRS. ALDRID (*Turning and following her*): That's what neighbors are for, dear.

MRS. HAMPTON: Good-by, Mr. Aldrid.

ALDRID (*Coming a step or two out of the window alcove*): Good-by, Mrs. Hampton.

MRS. HAMPTON: I'll be waiting to hear from you.

ALDRID: Right away, I'll call you.

MRS. HAMPTON (*Turning at the archway*): And be sure and ask for *me* when you telephone, won't you?

ALDRID: Yes, I shall.

MRS. HAMPTON: Thank you very much.

ALDRID: You're very welcome.

MRS. HAMPTON (*Going out into the hallway at the right, followed by* MRS. ALDRID, *who has been standing at the back of the room, just to the left of the archway*): I don't want Frank to know anything about this, if possible.

MRS. ALDRID: No, there's no need of annoying him.

MRS. HAMPTON: I suppose he'll have to be told soon enough.

(ALDRID, *standing at the back of the room, watches his wife out into the hallway; then he turns sharply, and comes forward several steps in a panic of indecision. Suddenly the impulse to recall* MRS.

HAMPTON *whirls him round into a literal spring in the direction of the hallway, but at this point the definite closing of the front door arrests him, and he stands taut and still for a second, gripping the back of the chair which* MRS. ALDRID *occupied earlier in the action of the play. Then he shifts his position; and gripping the chair with the other hand, leans upon it and waits for his wife to come back from the door. Presently she darts into view between the archway portieres and stands re-garding him with an expression of amused calculation. But he doesn't see her; so after a glance over her shoulder into the hallway, she speaks.*)

MRS. ALDRID: Did you see that?

ALDRID (*In a repressed, ominous tone*): What?

MRS. ALDRID (*With a nod toward the hallway*): She must have heard.

ALDRID: Have you told anybody?

MRS. ALDRID (*Coming a little farther into the room*): No!

ALDRID: I suppose the walls have ears?

MRS. ALDRID: Not necessarily.

ALDRID (*Turning to her sharply and searching her with a look*): Then how would she know?

MRS. ALDRID: She must have heard me —there in the hallway!

ALDRID (*Mercilessly*): When?

MRS. ALDRID (*Becoming slightly disconcerted under his gaze*): A few minutes ago—when I was telling you I'd found a purse.

ALDRID (*After a fractional pause, and tilting his head a bit on one side to look at her more quizzically*): How would she overhear you—she wasn't in the hallway.

MRS. ALDRID: *Wasn't* she!

ALDRID (*Whipping the chair upon which he is leaning out of the way and coming forward in a trembling rage*): You know very well she wasn't! (*She crosses the back of the room toward the left, watching him. He stops in the middle of the room, and forward, and continues speaking, but without looking at her.*) What are you trying to do, kid yourself or me? (*He goes toward his desk at the right, and she comes forward at the left.*)

MRS. ALDRID (*Picking up her apron from the sofa*): I suppose you didn't take notice of the fact that she came in without ringing, did you?

ALDRID: Well, what of it, what of it, what of it?

MRS. ALDRID (*Taking his tone*): Nothing! Only just think it over while I'm getting your dinner! (*She starts toward the door at the left.*)

ALDRID (*Leaning on the back of his desk chair*): You needn't get me any dinner.

(*She stops and looks back at him.*)

MRS. ALDRID: Why not?

ALDRID: Because I don't want any.

MRS. ALDRID: Don't you want anything at all?

ALDRID (*Turning sharply and looking at her*): Yes! (*Starting across toward the back of the center table and indicating the departed* MRS. HAMPTON *with a wide gesture.*) I want to know whether or not you intend to return that woman's property?

MRS. ALDRID: *Her* property.

ALDRID (*Enraged, and lifting his voice*): You heard me!

MRS. ALDRID (*Lifting her hand to silence him*): Sh—sh!

ALDRID (*Disregarding her gesture*): I want an answer, yes or no!

MRS. ALDRID (*Flinging her apron back onto the sofa and stepping up very close to him*): What's the matter with you, Gene; are you blind?

ALDRID (*Stonily*): Not now; but I'm beginning to think I *have* been—*terribly* blind.

MRS. ALDRID (*Turning away from him and taking a couple of steps to the left*): Well, I'm glad something has happened to open your eyes. (*She feigns to be occupied with her right cuff.*)

(ALDRID *crosses to her rigidly and, seizing her by the arm, turns her sharply to him and looks knowingly into her eyes.*)

ALDRID (*After a pause*): If my eyes are not opened after this, it isn't your fault. (*She attempts to move, but he pins her to his side with another quick grip. She shows a trace of fright.*) I want to know whether or not you intend to return that money?

MRS. ALDRID (*With a mingling of fright and conciliation*): When I find the owner, yes!

ALDRID (*Breaking from her in a wrath and going toward the back of the room*): Ah! more hedging!

(*Speaking together—*)

ALDRID (*Turning at the back of the room and coming forward again*): How I hate that attitude!

MRS. ALDRID (*Holding her right upper arm as though he had hurt her*): I'd like to hand over four hundred dollars to every Tom, Dick, and Harry that says he lost it. You must think I'm a—

ALDRID (*Whirling fiercely upon her as he passes in front of the center table*): Please! (*She is instantly silenced.*) Don't drive me out of the house! (*He goes blindly up toward the hallway.*)

MRS. ALDRID (*Regaining herself and half crying*): What do you think I am—some schoolgirl!

ALDRID (*Stopping abruptly just inside the archway*): No! (*Turning to her:*) I think you're a thief!

MRS. ALDRID (*Freezing with resentment*): Do you, really?

ALDRID: More contemptible than the out-and-outer, for he at least doesn't try to justify himself.

MRS. ALDRID: And I'm not trying to justify *my*self either.

ALDRID: You couldn't. There *is* no justification for your attitude.

MRS. ALDRID: There doesn't need to be any.

ALDRID: And there isn't—among honest people!

MRS. ALDRID (*Sarcastically*): So you don't consider me honest?

ALDRID (*Moving a little nearer to her*): You're like a million other people in this world—honest as long as you don't *lose* anything by it; but as soon as you see where the principle of honesty is going to *cost* you a dollar, you begin to *hedge*—just as you've been doing in this!

MRS. ALDRID: I've been doing nothing of the kind!

ALDRID (*Bitterly*): You've been *tinkering* with honesty.

MRS. ALDRID (*Advancing a step or two toward him*): I never took a cent in my life that didn't belong to me!

ALDRID: There are rafts of people can say that. But they wouldn't walk back a block to return ten cents overchange that some clerk has given them. (*She sniffs contemptuously and turns away.*) Pat themselves on the back—as I've heard you do—when the conductor on the trolley doesn't ask them for their carfare! (*He swings down toward his desk.*)

MRS. ALDRID: The trolley companies have enough!

ALDRID: There you are! (*Turning to her:*) That's the psychology of a thief! (*He goes up to the French window at the back of the room and, after glancing out to see that no one has heard them, closes it.*)

MRS. ALDRID (*Ready to cry with madness*): Have I ever stolen anything from you? (*Evidently he doesn't hear her and starts back down toward the right of the center table. She advances a bit toward him*): Have I?

ALDRID (*Stepping on a line with her and looking at her witheringly*): Now, don't start that, please. (*He continues on down to the right of the center table and stands leaning upon it.*)

MRS. ALDRID (*Stepping to the left of the center table and striking her fist upon it*): Answer me! Have I ever stolen anything from you?

(*There is a slight pause; then he sits down on the edge of the table—very wearily—as though weighted with the conviction of having married an inferior woman.*)

ALDRID (*With a complete change of tone*): Listen to me! (*He takes his left hand in his right and looks at the back of it with a kind of vacant curiosity; then he drops his clasped hands on to his leg and looks up and out and away off.*) A man's home, in the majority of cases, is founded upon his belief in the *honesty* of his wife; you've stolen that from me tonight.

MRS. ALDRID: What?

ALDRID: That belief—that I had in you, as an *honest* woman. (*With an impatient toss of her head she crosses over in front of the table to the desk and straightens the desk pad, then stands with her back to him, with one hand resting on the back of the desk chair and the other on her hip.*) You know, there's a line in a book somewhere that says:

"What a little thing makes the world go
      wrong!
  A word too short, or a smile too long;

Then comes the mist and the blinding
    rain,
    And life is never the same again."
Your—(*He feels for the word.*) attitude—
in this affair tonight is that mist and blinding rain: it has shown me that my wife is
not *strictly* honest—for the sake of being
so; and honesty is such a passion with me
that, as far as you are concerned, life will
never be the same again, because I could
never—absolutely *trust* you again. (*He
rises slowly and moves around in front of
the table.*) Never. (*He continues to the
window at the back, then stops and turns
to her.*) I'm very sorry we found that out
—(*He steps into the window alcove and
quietly pushes the window open; then,
after glancing out, he leans against the side
of the window alcove and says half to himself and half to her:*) I'm sorrier—than if
I had lost a million dollars.

(*There is a rather long stillness; then
Mrs. Aldrid, who has been finding it difficult to encompass the situation, abandons
the effort and crosses the room toward the
door at the left.*)
Mrs. Aldrid (*As she turns and starts
across the room*): Well, Gene, if you
hadn't been so *strictly honest* all your life,
we might have *had* a million dollars now.
Aldrid (*Picking her up*): Very true;
but we'd have gotten it the way you are
getting that four hundred.
Mrs. Aldrid (*About to leave the room
and with a return to her former manner*):
And the way I'm going to hold on to it,
incidentally. (*She starts to go out at the
left.*)
Aldrid (*In a sudden rage and seizing
the telephone at his right*): All right! Listen to this! Wait! (*She stops and turns
to him.*) I want you to hear this! (*He

works the telephone hook violently.)
Give me Wayne one—three seven—D.—
Wayne. Please? (*She recognizes the
number, evidently, and takes a couple of
frantic steps toward him; but he meets her
startled expression with a look of quiet
defiance; so she stops dead and turns away,
waiting.*) Hello! Hello? (*He lowers the
telephone again and there is another
pause; then suddenly he is answered.*)
Hello!—Mrs. Hampton?—Is this Mrs.
Hampton?—Mr. Aldrid. (Mrs. ALDRID
turns, and their eyes meet.) I have some
very good news for you.

Mrs. ALDRID (*Advancing in a panic*):
If you tell her I found that money, I'll
deny it!

ALDRID (*Into the telephone and bitterly*): Your money has been found!

Mrs. ALDRID (*Raising her arms and
hands helplessly and turning to the center
table*): Oh, you silly fool!

ALDRID (*Into the telephone*): I found
it.

Mrs. ALDRID (*Looking frantically
among her parcels on the center table*):
Well, if you did, you'll pay it!

ALDRID (*Into the telephone and half
smiling*): I wanted to give you a lesson.

Mrs. ALDRID: For I'm very sure I
won't! (*Glancing under the center table.*)
Where's my pocketbook? (*She hurries
over to the desk and looks.*)

ALDRID (*Into the telephone*): I know,
but I imagine you must be rather careless
to drop that much money.

Mrs. ALDRID (*Hurrying back to the
table and becoming more excited every
minute*): Where's my pocketbook?

ALDRID (*Into the telephone*): All right,
Mrs. Hampton, come ahead—it's here for
you. (*He hangs up, sets down the telephone.*)

Mrs. ALDRID (*Turning to him excitedly*): Listen! Have you seen anything of
my pocketbook?

ALDRID: No.

Mrs. ALDRID (*Looking among her parcels again breathlessly*): I can't find it!

ALDRID: Where'd you have it?

Mrs. ALDRID: Right here among these
parcels!

ALDRID (*Disinterestedly*): I haven't
seen anything of it. (*He comes down to
his desk.*)

Mrs. ALDRID: I wonder if I've lost that!
(*She looks again for a second, then stops
dead and taps the table as though she has
suddenly come to a conclusion.*) I wonder
if *she* could have taken that—

ALDRID (*Turning to her*): Who?

Mrs. ALDRID: Mrs. Hampton.

ALDRID: I'll ask her that—when she
comes over.

Mrs. ALDRID: Don't you dare!

ALDRID (*Bitterly*): Hum-hum. (*He
shakes his head from side to side.*)

Mrs. ALDRID: Well, it's gone!

ALDRID: Maybe you left it in the trolley
car.

Mrs. ALDRID: Oh, wouldn't that be awful! And that four hundred dollars is in
it! (ALDRID *gives a short, dry sound of
amusement and, thrusting his hands into
his trousers pockets, starts across the room
toward the left.*) I don't see anything to
laugh at! (*He throws his head back and
makes another little sound of intensely
derisive laughter.*) And twenty-six dollars
of my own! (*He laughs again.*) What's
the matter with me!

ALDRID (*Turning in front of the sofa*):
Maybe you dropped it out there in the
hallway.

Mrs. ALDRID: Call up the Rapid
Transit "Lost and Found," and see if a
lady's pocketbook has been turned in. I'll
look out here. (*She vanishes into the hallway at the right.* ALDRID *stands still for a
second, then picks up the telephone.*)

ALDRID (*Into the telephone*): Information, please. (*To* Mrs. ALDRID:) Do you
see anything of it?

Mrs. ALDRID (*In the hallway*): Not a
sign!

ALDRID: Why don't you light that light?
(*He stands looking into the hallway until
a light is turned on; then into the tele-*

phone:) Hello? Information? What is the number of the Rapid Transit "Lost and Found"? Yes. Kensington one three—hundred? Will you ask the operator to ring it, please? If you please? (*He lowers the telephone and* MRS. ALDRID *appears at the entrance to the hallway, searching frantically.* ALDRID *laughs dryly.*)

MRS. ALDRID (*Glancing up*): Funny, isn't it! (*She disappears again into the hallway, and immediately there is the sound of a chair being knocked over, as though she had flung it aside in her anger.* ALDRID *looks sharply toward the hallway, then shakes his head slowly and conclusively.*)

ALDRID (*Shifting his attitude and sighing rather wearily*): Ha, ho-ho— (*Into the telephone:*) Hello? Information? (*He glances toward the hallway.*) Oh, this is "Lost and Found"? I'd like to know whether or not a lady's pocketbook has been turned in there this evening?

MRS. ALDRID (*Rushing in from the hallway*): Oh, it isn't out there! What do they say?

(*He silences her with a gesture, then, after a slight pause, speaks suddenly into the telephone again.*)

ALDRID: This minute?

MRS. ALDRID: It *has* been turned in?

ALDRID (*To her*): Yes.

MRS. ALDRID (*Turning and sinking onto the chair at her hand*): Oh, thank God!

ALDRID (*Into the telephone*): No, my wife did.

MRS. ALDRID (*Turning to him*): A regular, lady's black leather pocketbook!

ALDRID (*Into the telephone*): Well, can you wait a minute, please? (*To* MRS. ALDRID:) They want to know whether or not you can identify this?

MRS. ALDRID (*Impatiently*): Oh, certainly I can! It's a regular, lady's black leather pocketbook, with my initials E. A. on the outside.

ALDRID: Yes.

MRS. ALDRID (*Illustrating with her hands*): There's a small, gold mesh purse inside, with four hundred dollars in it; and in the side pocket there are twenty-six dollars. Then there's—

ALDRID (*To* MRS. ALDRID): Wait a minute. (*Into the telephone:*) Hello!

MRS. ALDRID: A gold mesh purse, with—

ALDRID (*To* MRS. ALDRID): Wait a minute. (*Into the telephone:*) A lady's black leather pocketbook with the initials E. A. on the outside. There's a gold—E. A. No, no, no, no! E.—Yes.—Well, that's right. Why—(*He looks at his wife.*)

MRS. ALDRID: A gold mesh purse—

ALDRID: (*Into the telephone*): A gold mesh purse, with four hundred dollars in it; and in the side pocket there are twenty-six dollars—of her own. (MRS. ALDRID *looks at him suddenly.*)

MRS. ALDRID: Five fives and a one.

ALDRID (*Into the telephone*): In bills, yes. (*He looks at her, and she nods confirmation.*) Five fives and a one. One minute. (*To his wife:*) What else?—quick!

MRS. ALDRID (*Becoming very nervous*): Why, there's a silver vanity case—

ALDRID: Yes.

MRS. ALDRID: And a gold bracelet—with the clasp broken—(*He makes a movement of interruption, but she continues*) and a tax receipt, and a—

(ALDRID *and* MRS. ALDRID, *speaking together—*)

ALDRID (*To* MRS. ALDRID): Wait a minute, now, till I get that! (*Into the telephone:*) Hello?

MRS. ALDRID: Sample of georgette crepe, and a face veil, and a handkerchief, and two packages of hairpins, and—

ALDRID (*To* MRS. ALDRID): I can't remember all those! (*She stops and relaxes; then he speaks into the telephone:*) Hello! There's a silver vanity case and a bracelet—

MRS. ALDRID: Broken!

ALDRID (*Into the telephone*): Broken!—A broken bracelet. (*With a touch of annoyance.*) The bracelet is broken. Yes.

And there's a— (*He stops gradually and listens attentively—his eyes wandering to his wife's.*) I see.

Mrs. Aldrid (*Rising slowly and apprehensively*): What is it?

Aldrid (*Silencing her with a deft gesture and continuing into the telephone*): Why, yes, that *is* rather funny.

Mrs. Aldrid (*Impatiently*): What does he say?

Aldrid (*Into the telephone*): How about tomorrow afternoon? No, no, I'll call for it myself. Well, if you will, please? Tha—nk you very much. Thanks. (*He sets the telephone down.*)

Mrs. Aldrid: Is everything all right?

Aldrid: Yes.

Mrs. Aldrid (*Sighing with relief and leaning upon the center table*): Oh!—can you imagine if I'd lost that!

Aldrid (*Coming down thoughtfully toward his desk*): Everything but the money.

Mrs. Aldrid (*Turning and looking at him*): What'd you say?

Aldrid (*Without meeting her eye*): He says that evidently the person who found your pocketbook took all the money out of it before turning it in.

Mrs. Aldrid (*Aghast*): What!

Aldrid (*Indifferently and turning to his desk*): That's what he says.

Mrs. Aldrid (*Morally and physically indignant*): Can you imagine anyone being that contemptible!

Aldrid (*Turning and going up to the archway*): Please, don't make me laugh—I'm not in the mood.

Mrs. Aldrid: You won't laugh when you have to pay that woman four hundred dollars out of your own pocket!

Aldrid (*Turning to her sharply*): I'd have had to do that anyway—there didn't seem to be very much chance of getting it away from you!

Mrs. Aldrid: Well, you're not going to give her four hundred dollars of your *own* money?

Aldrid: That'll do! And when she comes here, don't make it necessary for me to tell her who *found* her money. Now be wise. (*He looks out the hallway, starts slightly, and then steps quickly toward his desk.*) Where is that gold mesh purse of yours?

Mrs. Aldrid: There in that drawer—what are you going to do?

Aldrid (*Speaking directly to her in a level tone*): I'm going to give you a lesson in honesty. Where is it? (*He opens the middle drawer of his desk.*)

Mrs. Aldrid: Right where you're looking; what do you want it for?

Aldrid (*Whipping a little gold mesh purse out of the drawer*): Never mind! Is this it?

Mrs. Aldrid: Yes. What are you going to do?

(*He slams the drawer shut, and simultaneously there is a sharp ring at the front door. He lays his hand on Mrs. Aldred's arm, and they stand still for a second.*)

Aldrid: There she is. (*Then turning and urging Mrs. Aldrid across in front of the center table toward the door at the left:*) Go up to my money box and get me eight fifty-dollar bills—the newest you can find—and hurry! (*He starts back toward the archway.*)

Mrs. Aldrid (*Recovering herself*): I'll do nothing of the kind!

Aldrid (*Whirling upon her and indicating the left door with an imperative gesture*): Quick! Now, you've lost enough tonight, I think!

Mrs. Aldrid (*Turns and goes to the left door, then stops again defiantly*): I will not!

Aldrid: Very well, then; I shall be obliged to tell this woman the particulars.

Mrs. Aldrid (*Bitterly*): Oh, I'll get them! But I never knew, Gene, that you were such a fool! (*She starts to leave the room.*)

Aldrid: Wait! (*She stops and looks at him.*) Wait a minute. (*He starts across toward her, passing back of the center table.*) I'll get them myself.

MRS. ALDRID: Why can't *I* get them?
ALDRID (*Looking at her steadily as he passes above her and out the door*): Because I'd rather get them myself.
(*She stands very still, realizing the implication, until the doorbell has rung three* times; then with a rather slow, general gesture of sullenness and defeat, she moves up and across toward the archway to answer the door.*)

THE CURTAIN DESCENDS SLOWLY

The man who wrote this play

GEORGE KELLY 1887–

One of the best ways to learn how to write a play is to act in one. George Kelly first went on the stage when he was twenty-four. That was not unusual in his family, for his older brother, Walter Kelly, was a well-known vaudeville star.

For five years George Kelly played juvenile roles before going into vaudeville. In those days, when there were comparatively few movie theaters, vaudeville was a very popular form of entertainment. While "on the road" as a star vaudeville performer, Kelly wrote his first play, *Finders-Keepers.* It was a concise one-act play meant to be played before vaudeville audiences. It had to move quickly; there could be no dull spots. Even in this first play, Kelly showed his remarkable playwriting talent.

After the success of *Finders-Keepers,* Kelly left vaudeville to become a full-time playwright. During the 1920's, he wrote a series of hit plays. His first full-length play, *The Torchbearers,* had a long run in New York. Following that were *The Show-off* and *Craig's Wife,* which was awarded a Pulitzer Prize in 1925.

Let's consider . . .

1. This play presents a common problem of honesty. The husband spoke out for complete integrity; the wife compromised with her conscience. Instantly there was a clash of wills, which is the essence of drama. State the problem as briefly as you can. Describe what had happened to Mrs. Aldrid before the opening of the play. What courses of action were open to her?

2. Mrs. Aldrid felt that her husband was a fool to make such a point of honesty in a matter which she preferred to consider "a very good lesson" to the loser. How would *you* consider this matter?

3. Mr. Aldrid assumed at first that his wife had reported her finding of the purse to the store authorities. What excuses did she give for not doing so?

4. During Mrs. Hampton's visit, what did Mr. Aldrid learn about his wife's character by her behavior? How did he feel?

5. When Mrs. Hampton mentioned the gold mesh purse, Mr. Aldrid questioned her closely about her loss. What did he hope to achieve?

6. Why do you think Mr. Aldrid delayed telling Mrs. Hampton that her purse had been found? Why was he indecisive in his actions?

7. What accusation did Mrs. Aldrid make against Mrs. Hampton after she left? How did Mr. Aldrid react?

8. What did Mr. Aldrid mean by the remark, "I'm beginning to think I *have* been—*terribly* blind"?

9. Why did Mr. Aldrid think his wife's kind of thievery more contemptible than criminal thievery? What examples did he give to illustrate what he meant by "tinkering with honesty"?

10. What did Mr. Aldrid accuse his wife of stealing from him?

11. At what point in the play did Mrs. Aldrid show that she had one standard of morality for herself and a different one for others?

12. Why did Mrs. Aldrid believe her husband would change his mind when he had to pay the four hundred dollars out of his own money?

13. Why did Mr. Aldrid decide to get the money from the money box himself?

14. Several times during the play Mrs. Aldrid gave evidence that she *knew* she was doing wrong. Point out as many instances of her guilty conscience as you can find.

15. If you were watching this play on the stage, you would learn much about the Aldrids by their actions. With only the script to follow, you had to depend mostly upon the dialogue to understand the changing relationship between husband and wife. Suppose their problem had been presented in a short story. How would the author have handled it differently? What method of writing would he have used in addition to dialogue? Which literary type do you think provides the most dramatic vehicle for this problem: the short story or the play? Explain your answer.

16. A play often presents a series of small crises which arouse and hold the interest of the audience and also build toward the outcome. Which crises in this play would create the greatest tension in the audience? Why?

17. At the end of the play Mr. Aldrid paid four hundred dollars and kept his integrity; Mrs. Aldrid had long since sold hers for the same price. What would that sale cost her as time went on?

18. Suppose you gave a saleswoman a dollar bill to pay for a sixty-five cent purchase, and she gave you forty cents in change. Would you feel bound to return the nickel? Would your attitude be the same with regard to any sum, however large? Discuss the problem.

19. A student once remarked after reading *Finders-Keepers,* "Mr. and Mrs. Aldrid may separate, but Mrs. Aldrid will have to live with herself for the rest of her life. She'll have a hard time!" Give your rea-

sons for agreeing or disagreeing with this verdict.

20. This play has a very simple theme and only three characters, yet it was played on the stage continuously for three years. How do you account for its popular appeal?

The writer's craft . . .

A play always involves some kind of **conflict:** a situation in which there are two or more opposing forces. It may be a clash of wills—as in this play, a struggle of man against his environment, or even a struggle within the man himself. It is this conflict which is the basis of drama and the reason why theater-goers sit on the edges of their seats. In a tightly knit play like *Finders-Keepers,* the conflict is introduced in one of the early events which, arranged in sequence, make up the plot. As this plot develops, certain complications arise which bring the conflict to a climax. At the end of the play, this conflict is satisfactorily resolved, sometimes happily, sometimes unhappily. Each episode or incident is linked with the one which precedes it and the one which follows. Thus, the playwright holds your interest from the beginning of the play to the end.

The plot of a play can generally be divided into several sections. The **exposition** is the opening section of the play. It provides the necessary background information and performs the following functions: it introduces some of the characters and explains their relationship to one another; it describes incidents which have taken place prior to the time the play begins. (This is sometimes called the **antecedent action.**) The exposition provides the setting, and establishes the mood (emotional tone or atmosphere) of the play. In *Finders-Keepers* the exposition continues to the point where Mr. Aldrid tells his wife that she might have gone to the department store's Lost and Found department to report her discovery of the mesh purse.

List everything that you learned about the characters, the setting, the antecedent action, and the mood of this play up to this point.

The section following the exposition is the **initial incident:** the action or dialogue that introduces the conflict. In *Finders-Keepers,* the initial incident is introduced with these lines:

MR. ALDRID: What are you going to do with it?

MRS. ALDRID: I'm going to keep it.

The incidents which follow the initial incident are called the **rising action.** They make up the third section of the plot and serve to add complications to the conflict and to develop its intensity. The highest point of dramatic intensity is called the **climax** and is usually the turning point in the play. Following the climax is the **falling action** or **denouement:** the resolving of the conflict. The denouement leads logically to the ending, which may be either happy or unhappy depending upon the nature of the conflict, the personalities of the characters, and the kinds of complications.

1. List the incidents which you think were part of the rising action. What complications did they add to the conflict?

2. At which point did the climax occur? Explain why this moment in the play was the turning point.

3. What events took place in the denouement or falling action? Explain how the denouement held your interest even though the climax had been reached.

4. Did the denouement lead logically to the ending? Did the ending seem to emerge logically from the earlier sections of the play? Discuss.

Knowing words . . .

One of the interesting characteristics of the English language is the way in which two or more words combine in a sort of pattern. Some patterns are formed by combining two nouns; the first noun identifying the second, explaining its purpose, or naming its source. In *Finders-Keepers* you found such combinations as *saleslady, pocket book, bungalow apron, evening paper, and window alcove.* Sometimes they are written as separate words, sometimes hyphenated, sometimes compounded as a single word.

List ten common words or expressions which are combinations of two nouns. Try to include at least one example of each of these combinations: (1) separate words, (2) hyphenated words, and (3) compound words.

A Word

A word is dead
When it is said,
Some say.
I say it just
Begins to live
That day.
Emily Dickinson

NOW THINK BACK

1. In this part, poets, soldiers, philosophers, an educator, and a columnist voiced their opinions. Select three of these Americans whose message made a special impression on you. Comment in detail on their messages.

2. Select the writer in this part whom you consider the most critical. Comment on his criticism. Was it deserved? Was it given in a kindly, bitter, or humorous vein? What did he say that made you stop to think? Explain.

3. Consider the poets in this part. Explain why poetry was a more effective medium for their message than prose would have been. Do you think that any of these messages could have been conveyed equally well in prose? Explain your answer.

4. E. B. White recognized the "false gods" of *progress* in "Walden." How does the tone of his criticism differ from the tone of Walter Lippmann's criticism?

5. Not all the Americans who spoke out freely in these selections were famous people. Some of them would have been known only in their own communities, yet what they had to say was important. Try to formulate at least three evident truths, or maxims, which Americans must observe today if they are to preserve their "inalienable right to life, liberty, and the pursuit of happiness."

Things to do . . .

1. Write an editorial for your school paper in which you "speak out" on some prevalent practice in your school. You may commend such a practice or condemn it, but your statement should be sincere and forceful. Keep in mind the readers you hope to reach. Use rhetorical questions if you wish.

2. If you enjoyed Phyllis McGinley's poems, look up "Casualty List," another poem in which she spoke out during World War II. Not all casualties of war occurred in the battle waged on land and sea, and in the air.

3. Write a letter to Booker T. Washington, *or* Corporal Hardy, *or* Lucinda Matlock about a modern incident, law, practice, or portion of the country which you feel would be of special interest to him or to her. Choose the style of writing for your letter that would be most appropriate in addressing the person of your choice.

More to read . . .

By These Words by PAUL M. ANGLE.
Rand McNally & Company, 1954.
We Came to America by FRANCES CAVANAH.
Macrae Smith Company, Publishers, 1954.
The Complete Writings of Ralph Waldo Emerson by RALPH WALDO EMERSON.
William H. Wise and Company, Inc., 1929.
The Measure of Man by JOSEPH WOOD KRUTCH.
Bobbs-Merrill Company, 1954.
Gift from the Sea by ANNE MORROW LINDBERGH.
Pantheon Books, 1955.
And Keep Your Powder Dry by MARGARET MEAD.
William Morrow and Company, Inc., 1942.
This I Believe edited by EDWARD R. MURROW.
Simon and Schuster, Inc., 1952.
The Second Tree from the Corner by E. B. WHITE.
Harper & Brothers, 1954.
Both Your Houses by MAXWELL ANDERSON.
Samuel French, Inc., 1933.

TALES WELL TOLD

Storytelling has universal appeal. Whenever friends are gathered together, the conversation often drifts into the telling of stories. There is quite a difference, however, between the casual stories exchanged among friends and the carefully written stories planned by authors to gain a particular effect.

A well-written short story is always a source of enjoyment, but it usually does more than entertain you. Indirectly, it makes a comment on a particular aspect of human experience. That experience may be a serious problem in human relations, or it may be nothing more than an amusing incident in someone's life. No matter what the experience may be, a story that is well written should give you fresh insights into your own life, as well as into the lives of others.

In TALES WELL TOLD you will read stories by major American writers. Here you will meet new and interesting people. You will see them in action. By sharing in their experiences, you will become a more mature individual.

TALES WELL TOLD

The Legend of Sleepy Hollow

WASHINGTON IRVING

The short story in America had its beginning in the tales of Washington Irving. Later writers developed and perfected the short story as a literary type, but few of them surpassed Irving as the delightful creator of charming and well-told tales.

FOUND AMONG THE PAPERS OF THE
LATE DIEDRICH KNICKERBOCKER

A pleasing land of drowsy head it was,
Of dreams that wave before the half-shut
eye;
And of gay castles in the clouds that pass,
For ever flushing round a summer sky.
CASTLE OF INDOLENCE

In the bosom of one of those spacious coves which indent the eastern shore of the Hudson, at the broad expansion of the river denominated by the ancient Dutch navigators the Tappan Zee, and where they always prudently shortened sail, and implored the protection of St. Nicholas when they crossed, there lies a small market-town or rural port, which by some is called Greensburgh, but which is more generally and properly known by the name of Tarry Town. This name was given, we are told, in former days, by the good housewives of the adjacent country, from the inveterate propensity of their husbands to linger about the village tavern on market days. Be that as it may, I do not vouch for the fact, but merely advert to it, for the sake of being precise and authentic. Not far from this village, perhaps about two miles, there is a little valley, or rather lap of land, among high hills, which is one of the quietest places in the whole world. A small brook glides through it, with just murmur enough to lull one to repose; and the occasional whistle of a quail, or tapping of a woodpecker, is almost the only sound that ever breaks in upon the uniform tranquility.

I recollect that, when a stripling, my first exploit in squirrel-shooting was in a grove of tall walnut-trees that shades one side of the valley. I had wandered into it at noon time, when all nature is peculiarly quiet, and was startled by the roar of my own gun, as it broke the Sabbath stillness around, and was prolonged and reverberated by the angry echoes. If ever I should wish for a retreat, whither I might steal from the world and its distractions, and dream quietly away the remnant of a troubled life, I know of none more promising than this little valley.

From the listless repose of the place, and the peculiar character of its inhabitants, who are descendants from the original Dutch settlers, this sequestered glen has long been known by the name of SLEEPY HOLLOW, and its rustic lads are called the Sleepy Hollow Boys throughout all the neighboring country. A drowsy, dreamy influence seems to hang over the land, and to pervade the very atmosphere. Some say that the place was bewitched by a high German doctor, during the early days of the settlement; others, that an old Indian chief, the prophet or wizard of his tribe, held his powwows there before the country was discovered by Master Hendrick Hudson. Certain it is, the place still continues under the sway of some witching power, that holds a spell over the minds of the good people, causing them to walk in a continual reverie. They are given to all kinds of marvellous beliefs; are subject to trances and visions; and frequently see strange sights, and hear music and voices in the air. The whole neighborhood abounds with local tales, haunted spots, and twilight superstitions, stars shoot and meteors glare oftener across the valley than in any other part of the country, and the nightmare, with her whole nine fold, seems to make it the favorite scene of her gambols.

The dominant spirit, however, that haunts this enchanted region, and seems to be commander-in-chief of all the powers of the air, is the apparition of a figure on horseback without a head. It is said by some to be the ghost of a Hessian trooper,[1] whose head had been carried away by a canon-ball, in some nameless battle during the revolutionary war; and who is ever and anon seen by the country folk, hurrying along in the gloom of night, as if on the wings of the wind. His haunts are not confined to the valley, but extend at times to the adjacent roads, and especially to the vicinity of a church at no great distance. Indeed, certain of the most authentic historians of those parts, who have been careful in collecting and collating the floating facts concerning this spectre, allege that the body of the trooper, having been buried in the church-yard, the ghost rides forth to the scene of battle in nightly quest of his head; and that the rushing speed

with which he sometimes passes along the Hollow, like a midnight blast, is owing to his being belated, and in a hurry to get back to the church-yard before daybreak.

Such is the general purport of this legendary superstition, which has furnished materials for many a wild story in that region of shadows; and the spectre is known, at all the country firesides, by the name of the Headless Horseman of Sleepy Hollow.

It is remarkable that the visionary propensity[2] I have mentioned is not confined to the native inhabitants of the valley, but is unconsciously imbibed by every one who resides there for a time. However wide awake they may have been before they entered that sleepy region, they are sure, in a little time, to inhale the witching influence of the air, and begin to grow imaginative—to dream dreams, and see apparitions.

I mention this peaceful spot with all possible laud; for it is in such little retired Dutch valleys, found here and there embosomed in the great State of New-York, that population, manners, and customs, remain fixed; while the great torrent of migration and improvement, which is making such incessant changes in other parts of this restless country, sweeps by them unobserved. They are like those little nooks of still water which border a rapid stream; where we may see the straw and bubble riding quietly at anchor, or slowly revolving in their mimic harbor, undisturbed by the rush of the passing current. Though many years have elapsed since I trod the drowsy shades of Sleepy Hollow, yet I question whether I should not still find the same trees and the same families vegetating in its sheltered bosom.

In this by-place of nature, there abode, in a remote period of American history, that is to say, some thirty years since, a worthy wight of the name of Ichabod Crane; who sojourned, or, as he expressed

---

[1] *Hessian trooper,* a German mercenary soldier hired by the British during the Revolution

[2] *visionary propensity,* ability to see the supernatural

it, "tarried," in Sleepy Hollow, for the purpose of instructing the children of the vicinity. He was a native of Connecticut;
a State which supplies the Union with
pioneers for the mind as well as for the
forest, and sends forth yearly its legions of
frontier woodsmen and country schoolmasters. The cognomen [3] of Crane was not
inapplicable to his person. He was tall,
but exceedingly lank, with narrow shoulders, long arms and legs, hands that dan-
gled a mile out of his sleeves, feet that
might have served for shovels, and his
whole frame most loosely hung together.
His head was small, and flat at top, with
huge ears, large green glassy eyes, and a
long snipe nose, so that it looked like a
weather-cock, perched upon his spindle
neck, to tell which way the wind blew.
To see him striding along the profile of a
hill on a windy day, with his clothes bag-
ging and fluttering about him, one might
have mistaken him for the genuis of famine descending upon the earth, or some
scarecrow eloped from a cornfield.

His school-house was a low building of
one large room, rudely constructed of logs;
the windows partly glazed, and partly
patched with leaves of old copy-books. It
was most ingeniously secured at vacant
hours, by a withe twisted in the handle of
the door, and stakes set against the window shutters; so that, though a thief might
get in with perfect ease, he would find
some embarrassment in getting out; an idea
most probably borrowed by the architect,
Yost Van Houten, from the mystery of an
eel-pot.[4] The school-house stood in a rather
lonely but pleasant situation, just at the
foot of a woody hill, with a brook running
close by, and a formidable birch tree growing at one end of it. From hence the low
murmur of his pupils' voices, conning over
their lessons, might be heard in a drowsy
summer's day, like the hum of a bee-hive;
interrupted now and then by the authoritative voice of the master, in the tone of

[3] *cognomen,* family name, last name
[4] *eel-pot,* a trap for catching eels

menace or command; or, peradventure, by
the appalling sound of the birch, as he
urged some tardy loiterer along the flowery
path of knowledge. Truth to say, he was
a conscientious man, and ever bore in mind
the golden maxim, "Spare the rod and spoil
the child."—Ichabod Crane's scholars certainly were not spoiled.

I would not have it imagined, however,
that he was one of those cruel potentates
of the school, who joy in the smart of their
subjects; on the contrary, he administered
justice with discrimination rather than
severity; taking the burthen off the backs
of the weak, and laying it on those of the
strong. Your mere puny stripling, that
winced at the least flourish of the rod, was
passed by with indulgence; but the claims
of justice were satisfied by inflicting a
double portion on some little, tough,
wrong-headed, broad-skirted Dutch urchin,
who sulked and swelled and grew dogged
and sullen beneath the birch. All this
he called "doing his duty by their parents;"
and he never inflicted a chastisement
without following it by the assurance,
so consolatory to the smarting urchin, that
"he would remember it, and thank him for
it the longest day he had to live."

When school hours were over, he was
even the companion and playmate of the
larger boys; and on holiday afternoons
would convoy some of the smaller ones
home, who happened to have pretty sisters,
or good housewives for mothers, noted
for the comforts of the cupboard. Indeed
it behooved him to keep on good terms
with his pupils. The revenue arising from
his school was small, and would have been
scarcely sufficient to furnish him with
daily bread, for he was a huge feeder, and
though lank, had the dilating powers of
an anaconda; but to help out his mainte-
nance, he was, according to country custom
in those parts, boarded and lodged at the
houses of the farmers, whose children he
instructed. With these he lived succes-
sively a week at a time; thus going the
rounds of the neighborhood, with all his
worldly effects tied up in a cotton handkerchief.

That all this might not be too onerous
on the purses of his rustic patrons, who are
apt to consider the costs of schooling a
grievous burden, and schoolmasters as mere
drones, he had various ways of rendering
himself both useful and agreeable. He assisted the farmers occasionally in the
lighter labors of their farms; helped to
make hay; mended the fences; took the
horses to water; drove the cows from pasture; and cut wood for the winter fire. He
laid aside, too, all the dominant dignity
and absolute sway with which he lorded
it in his little empire, the school, and became wonderfully gentle and ingratiating.
He found favor in the eyes of the mothers,
by petting the children, particularly the
youngest; and like the lion bold, which
whilom [5] so magnanimously the lamb did
hold, he would sit with a child on one
knee, and rock a cradle with his foot for
whole hours together.

In addition to his other vocations, he
was the singing-master of the neighborhood, and picked up many bright shillings
by instructing the young folks in psalmody.
It was a matter of no little vanity to him,
on Sundays, to take his station in front of
the church gallery, with a band of chosen
singers; where, in his own mind, he completely carried away the palm from the
parson. Certain it is, his voice resounded
far above all the rest of the congregation;
and there are peculiar quavers still to be
heard in that church, and which may even
be heard half a mile off, quite to the opposite side of the mill-pond, on a still Sunday morning, which are said to be legiti-
mately descended from the nose of Ichabod
Crane. Thus, by divers little make-shifts
in that ingenious way which is commonly
denominated "by hook and by crook," the
worthy pedagogue got on tolerably enough,
and was thought, by all who understood
nothing of the labor of headwork, to have
a wonderfully easy life of it.

[5] *whilom,* at one time; formerly

The schoolmaster is generally a man of some importance in the female circle of a rural neighborhood; being considered a kind of idle gentlemanlike personage, of vastly superior taste and accomplishments to the rough country swains, and, indeed, inferior in learning only to the parson. His appearance, therefore, is apt to occasion some little stir at the tea-table of a farmhouse, and the addition of a supernumerary dish of cakes or sweetmeats, or, peradventure, the parade of a silver tea-pot. Our man of letters, therefore, was peculiarly happy in the smiles of all the country damsels. How he would figure among them in the churchyard, between services on Sundays! gathering grapes for them from the wild vines that over-run the surrounding trees; reciting for their amusement all the epitaphs on the tombstones; or sauntering, with a whole bevy of them, along the banks of the adjacent mill-pond; while the more bashful country bumpkins hung sheepishly back, envying his superior elegance and address.

From his half itinerant life, also, he was a kind of travelling gazette, carrying the whole budget of local gossip from house to house; so that his appearance was always greeted with satisfaction. He was, moreover, esteemed by the women as a man of great erudition, for he had read several books quite through, and was a perfect master of Cotton Mather's history of New-England Witchcraft, in which, by the way, he most firmly and potently believed.

He was, in fact, an odd mixture of small shrewdness and simple crudelity. His appetite for the marvellous, and his powers of digesting it, were equally extraordinary; and both had been increased by his residence in this spell-bound region. No tale was too gross or monstrous for his capacious swallow. It was often his delight, after his school was dismissed in the afternoon, to stretch himself on the rich bed of clover, bordering the little brook that whimpered by his school-house, and there con over old Mather's direful tales, until the gathering dusk of the evening made the printed page a mere mist before his eyes. Then, as he wended his way, by swamp and stream and awful woodland, to the farmhouse where he happened to be quartered, every sound of nature, at that witching hour, fluttered his excited imagination: the moan of the whip-poor-will from the hill-side; the boding cry of the tree-toad, that harbinger of storm; the dreary hooting of the screech-owl, or the sudden rustling in the thicket of birds frightened from their roost. The fire-flies, too, which sparkled most vividly in the darkest places, now and then startled him, as one of uncommon brightness would stream across his path; and if, by chance, a huge blockhead of a beetle came winging his blundering flight against him, the poor varlet was ready to give up the ghost, with the idea that he was struck with a witch's token. His only resource on such occasions, either to drown thought, or drive away evil spirits, was to sing psalm tunes;—and the good people of Sleepy Hollow, as they sat by their doors of an evening, were often filled with awe, at hearing his nasal melody, "in linked sweetness long drawn out," [6] floating from the distant hill, or along the dusky road.

Another of his sources of fearful pleasure was, to pass long winter evenings with the old Dutch wives, as they sat spinning by the fire, with a row of apples roasting and spluttering along the hearth, and listen to their marvellous tales of ghosts and goblins, and haunted fields, and haunted brooks, and haunted bridges, and haunted houses, and particularly of the headless horseman, or galloping Hessian of the Hollow, as they sometimes called him. He would delight them equally by his anecdotes of witchcraft, and of the direful omens and portentous sights and sounds in the air, which prevailed in the earlier times of Connecticut; and would frighten them wofully with speculations upon comets and shooting stars; and with the alarming

_____
[6] *"in linked . . . drawn out,"* a line from John Milton's poem "L'Allegro"

fact that the world did absolutely turn round, and that they were half the time topsy-turvy!

But if there was a pleasure in all this, while snugly cuddling in the chimney corner of a chamber that was all of a ruddy glow from the crackling wood fire, and where, of course, no spectre dared to show his face, it was dearly purchased by the terrors of his subsequent walk homewards. What fearful shapes and shadows beset his path amidst the dim and ghastly glare of a snowy night!—With what wistful look did he eye every trembling ray of light streaming across the waste fields from some distant window!—How often was he appalled by some shrub covered with snow, which, like a sheeted spectre, beset his very path!—How often did he shrink with curdling awe at the sound of his own steps on the frosty crust beneath his feet; and dread to look over his shoulder, lest he should behold some uncouth being tramping close behind him!—and how often was he thrown into complete dismay by some rushing blast, howling among the trees, in the idea that it was the Galloping Hessian on one of his nightly scourings!

All these, however, were mere terrors of the night, phantoms of the mind that walk in darkness; and though he had seen many spectres in his time, and been more than once beset by Satan in divers shapes, in his lonely perambulations, yet daylight put an end to all these evils; and he would have passed a pleasant life of it, in despite of the devil and all his works, if his path had not been crossed by a being that causes more perplexity to mortal man than ghosts, goblins, and the whole race of witches put together, and that was—a woman.

Among the musical disciples who assembled, one evening in each week, to receive his instructions in psalmody, was Katrina Van Tassel, the daughter and only child of a substantial Dutch farmer. She was a blooming lass of fresh eighteen; plump as a partridge; ripe and melting and rosy cheeked as one of her father's peaches, and universally famed, not merely for her beauty, but her vast expectations. She was withal a little of a coquette, as might be perceived even in her dress, which was a mixture of ancient and modern fashions, as most suited to set off her charms. She wore the ornaments of pure yellow gold, which her great-great-grandmother had brought over from Saardam; the tempting stomacher [7] of the olden time; and withal a provokingly short petticoat, to display the prettiest foot and ankle in the country round.

Ichabod Crane had a soft and foolish heart towards the sex; and it is not to be wondered at, that so tempting a morsel soon found favor in his eyes; more especially after he had visited her in her paternal mansion. Old Baltus Van Tassel was a perfect picture of a thriving, contented, liberal-hearted farmer. He seldom, it is true, sent either his eyes or his thoughts beyond the boundaries of his own farm; but within those every thing was snug, happy, and well-conditioned. He was satisfied with his wealth, but not proud of it; and piqued himself upon the hearty abundance, rather than the style in which he lived. His stronghold was situated on the banks of the Hudson, in one of those green, sheltered, fertile nooks, in which the Dutch farmers are so fond of nestling. A great elm-tree spread its broad branches over it; at the foot of which bubbled up a spring of the softest and sweetest water, in a little well, formed of a barrel; and then stole sparkling away through the grass, to a neighboring brook, that bubbled along among alders and dwarf willows. Hard by the farmhouse was a vast barn, that might have served for a church; every window and crevice of which seemed bursting forth with the treasures of the farm; the flail was busily resounding within it from morning to night; swallows and martins skimmed twittering about the eaves; and

[7] *stomacher,* an article of dress, worn by the women of Irving's time, to cover the stomach and chest

rows of pigeons, some with one eye turned up, as if watching the weather, some with their heads under their wings, or buried in their bosoms, and others swelling, and cooing, and bowing about their dames, were enjoying the sunshine on the roof. Sleek unwieldy porkers were grunting in the repose and abundance of their pens; whence sallied forth, now and then, troops of sucking pigs, as if to snuff the air. A stately squadron of snowy geese were riding in an adjoining pond, convoying whole fleets of ducks; regiments of turkeys were gobbling through the farmyard, and guinea fowls fretting about it, like ill-tempered housewives, with their peevish discontented cry. Before the barn door strutted the gallant cock, that pattern of a husband, a warrior, and a fine gentleman, clapping his burnished wings, and crowing in the pride and gladness of his heart—sometimes tearing up the earth with his feet, and then generously calling his ever-hungry family of wives and children to enjoy the rich morsel which he had discovered.

The pedagogue's mouth watered, as he looked upon this sumptuous promise of luxurious winter fare. In his devouring mind's eye, he pictured to himself every roasting-pig running about with a pudding in his belly, and an apple in his mouth; the pigeons were snugly put to bed in a comfortable pie, and tucked in with a coverlet of crust; the geese were swimming in their own gravy; and the ducks paring cosily in dishes, like snug married couples, with a decent competency of onion sauce. In the porkers he saw carved out the future sleek side of bacon, and juicy relishing ham; not a turkey but he beheld daintily trussed up, with its gizzard under its wing, and, peradventure, a necklace of savory sausages; and even bright chanticleer himself lay sprawling on his back, in a side-dish, with uplifted claws, as if craving that quarter which his chivalrous spirit disdained to ask while living.

As the enraptured Ichabod fancied all this and as he rolled his great green eyes over the fat meadow-lands, the rich fields of wheat, of rye, of buckwheat, and Indian corn, and the orchards burthened with ruddy fruit, which surrounded the warm tenement of Van Tassel, his heart yearned after the damsel who was to inherit these domains, and his imagination expanded with the idea, how they might be readily turned into cash, and the money invested in immense tracts of wild land, and shingle palaces in the wilderness. Nay, his busy fancy already realized his hopes, and presented to him the blooming Katrina, with a whole family of children, mounted on the top of a wagon loaded with household trumpery, with pots and kettles dangling beneath; and he beheld himself bestriding a pacing mare, with a colt at her heels, setting out for Kentucky, Tennessee, or the Lord knows where.

When he entered the house the conquest of his heart was complete. It was one of those spacious farmhouses, with high-ridged, but lowly-sloping roofs, built in the style handed down from the first Dutch settlers; the low projecting eaves forming a piazza [8] along the front, capable of being closed up in bad weather. Under this were hung flails, harness, various utensils of husbandry, and nets for fishing in the neighboring river. Benches were built along the sides for summer use; and a great spinning-wheel at one end, and a churn at the other, showed the various uses to which this important porch might be devoted. From this piazza the wondering Ichabod entered the hall, which formed the centre of the mansion and the place of usual residence. Here, rows of resplendent pewter, ranged on a long dresser, dazzled his eyes. In one corner stood a huge bag of wool ready to be spun; in another a quantity of linsey-woolsey [9] just from the loom; ears of Indian corn, and strings of dried apples and peaches, hung in gay festoons along the walls,

---

[8] *piazza,* large veranda or porch
[9] *linsey-woolsey,* a coarse fabric woven from linen and wool

mingled with the gaud of red peppers; and a door left ajar gave him a peep into the best parlor, where the claw-footed chairs, and dark mahogany tables, shone like mirrors; and irons, with their accompanying shovel and tongs, glistened from their cover of asparagus tops; mock-oranges and conch-shells decorated the mantelpiece; strings of various colored birds' eggs were suspended above it: a great ostrich egg was hung from the centre of the room, and a corner cupboard, knowingly left open, displayed immense treasures of old silver and well-mended china.

From the moment Ichabod laid his eyes upon these regions of delight, the peace of his mind was at an end, and his only study was how to gain the affections of the peerless daughter of Van Tassel. In this enterprise, however, he had more real difficulties than generally fell to the lot of a knight-errant of yore, who seldom had any thing but giants, enchanters, fiery dragons, and such like easily-conquered adversaries, to contend with; and had to make his way merely through gates of iron and brass, and walls of adamant, to the castle keep, where the lady of his heart was confined; all which he achieved as easily as a man would carve his way to the centre of a Christmas pie; and then the lady gave him her hand as a matter of course. Ichabod, on the contrary, had to win his way to the heart of a country coquette, beset with a labyrinth of whims and caprices, which were for ever presenting new difficulties and impediments; and he had to encounter a host of fearful adversaries of real flesh and blood, the numerous rustic admirers, who beset every portal to her heart; keeping a watchful and angry eye upon each other, but ready to fly out in the common cause against any new competitor.

Among these the most formidable was a burly, roaring, roystering blade, of the name of Abraham, or according to the Dutch abbreviation, Brom Van Brunt, the hero of the country round, which rang with his feats of strength and hardihood.

He was broad-shouldered and double-jointed, with short curly black hair, and a bluff, but not unpleasant countenance, having a mingled air of fun and arrogance. From his Herculean frame and great powers of limb, he had received the nickname of BROM BONES, by which he was universally known. He was famed for great knowledge and skill in horsemanship, being as dexterous on horseback as a Tartar. He was foremost at all races and cockfights; and, with the ascendency which bodily strength acquires in rustic life, was the umpire in all disputes, setting his hat on one side, and giving his decisions with an air and tone admitting of no gainsay or appeal. He was always ready for either a fight or a frolic; but had more mischief than ill-will in his composition; and, with all his overbearing roughness, there was a strong dash of waggish good humor at bottom. He had three or four boon companions, who regarded him as their model, and at the head of whom he scoured the country, attending every scene of feud or merriment for miles round. In cold weather he was distinguished by a fur cap, surmounted with a flaunting fox's tail; and when the folks at a country gathering descried this well-known crest at a distance, whisking about among a squad of hard riders, they always stood by for a squall. Sometimes his crew would be heard dashing along past the farmhouses at midnight, with whoop and halloo, like a troop of Don Cossacks; and the old dames, startled out of their sleep, would listen for a moment till the hurry-scurry had clattered by, and then exclaim, "Ay, there goes Brom Bones and his gang!" The neighbors looked upon him with a mixture of awe, admiration, and good-will; and when any madcap prank, or rustic brawl, occurred in the vicinity, always shook their heads, and warranted Brom Bones was at the bottom of it.

This rantipole [10] hero had for some time singled out the blooming Katrina for the

10 *rantipole,* wild, unruly

object of his uncouth gallantries, and though his amorous toyings were something like the gentle caresses and endearments of a bear, yet it was whispered that she did not altogether discourage his hopes. Certain it is, his advances were signals for rival candidates to retire, who felt no inclination to cross a lion in his amours; insomuch, that when his horse was seen tied to Van Tassel's paling, on a Sunday night, a sure sign that his master was courting, or, as it is termed, "sparking," within all other suitors passed by in despair, and carried the war into other quarters.

Such was the formidable rival with whom Ichabod Crane had to contend, and, considering all things, a stouter man than he would have shrunk from the competition, and a wiser man would have despaired. He had, however, a happy mixture of pliability and perseverance in his nature; he was in form and spirit like a supplejack [11]—yielding, but tough; though he bent, he never broke; and though he bowed beneath the slightest pressure, yet, the moment it was away—jerk! he was erect, and carried his head as high as ever.

To have taken the field openly against his rival would have been madness; for he was not a man to be thwarted in his amours, any more than that stormy lover, Achilles.[12] Ichabod, therefore, made his advances in a quiet and gently-insinuating manner. Under cover of his character of singing-master, he made frequent visits at the farmhouse; not that he had anything to apprehend from the meddlesome interference of parents, which is so often a stumbling-block in the path of lovers. Balt Van Tassel was an easy indulgent soul; he loved his daughter better even than his pipe, and, like a reasonable man and an excellent father, let her have her way in every thing. His notable little wife, too, had enough to do to attend to her housekeeping and man-

age her poultry; for, as she sagely observed, ducks and geese are foolish things, and must be looked after, but girls can take care of themselves. Thus while the busy dame bustled about the house, or plied her spinning-wheel at one end of the piazza, honest Balt would sit smoking his evening pipe at the other, watching the achievements of a little wooden warrior, who, armed with a sword in each hand, was most valiantly fighting the wind on the pinnacle of the barn. In the mean time, Ichabod would carry on his suit with the daughter by the side of the spring under the great elm, or sauntering along in the twilight, that hour so favorable to the lover's eloquence.

I profess not to know how women's hearts are wooed and won. To me they have always been matters of riddle and admiration. Some seem to have but one vulnerable point, or door of access; while others have a thousand avenues, and may be captured in a thousand different ways. It is a great triumph of skill to gain the former, but a still greater proof of generalship to maintain possession of the latter, for the man must battle for his fortress at every door and window. He who wins a thousand common hearts is therefore entitled to some renown; but he who keeps undisputed sway over the heart of a coquette, is indeed a hero. Certain it is, this was not the case with the redoubtable Brom Bones; and from the moment Ichabod Crane made his advances, the interests of the former evidently declined; his horse was no longer seen tied at the palings on Sunday nights, and a deadly feud gradually arose between him and the preceptor of Sleepy Hollow.

Brom, who had a degree of rough chivalry in his nature, would fain have carried matters to open warfare, and have settled their pretensions to the lady, according to the mode of those most concise and simple reasoners, the knights-errant of yore—by single combat; but Ichabod was too conscious of the superior might of his adver-

[11] *supplejack,* a strong flexible cane or walking stick
[12] *Achilles,* a hero in Homer's *Iliad* who quarreled with his warrior leader over a captive girl

sary to enter the lists against him: he had overheard a boast of Bones, that he would "double the schoolmaster up, and lay him on a shelf of his own school-house;" and he was too wary to give him an opportunity. There was something extremely provoking in this obstinately pacific system; it left Brom no alternative but to draw upon the funds of rustic waggery in his disposition, and to play off boorish practical jokes upon his rival. Ichabod became the object of whimsical persecution to Bones, and his gang of rough riders. They harried his hitherto peaceful domains; smoked out his singing school, by stopping up the chimney; broke into the school-house at night, in spite of its formidable fastenings of withe and window stakes, and turned every thing topsy-turvy: so that the poor schoolmaster began to think all the witches in the country held their meetings there. But what was still more annoying, Brom took all opportunities of turning him into ridicule in presence of his mistress, and had a scoundrel dog whom he taught to whine in the most ludicrous manner, and introduced as a rival of Ichabod's to instruct her in psalmody.

In this way matters went on for some time, without producing any material effect on the relative situation of the contending powers. On a fine autumnal afternoon, Ichabod, in pensive mood, sat enthroned on a lofty stool whence he usually watched all the concerns of his little literary realm. In his hand he swayed a ferule,[13] that sceptre of despotic power; the birch of justice reposed on three nails, behind the throne, a constant terror to evil doers; while on the desk before him might be seen sundry contraband articles and prohibited weapons, detected upon the persons of idle urchins; such as half-munched apples, pop-guns, whirligigs, fly-cages, and whole legions of rampant little paper game-cocks. Apparently there had been some appalling act of justice recently inflicted, for his

scholars were all busily intent upon their books, or slyly whispering behind them with one eye kept upon the master; and a kind of buzzing stillness reigned throughout the school-room. It was suddenly interrupted by the appearance of a messenger, in tow-cloth jacket and trowsers, a round-crowned fragment of a hat, like the cap of Mercury,[14] and mounted on the back of a ragged, wild, half-broken colt, which he managed with a rope by way of halter. He came clattering up to the school door with an invitation to Ichabod to attend a merry-making or "quilting frolic," to be held that evening at Mynheer Van Tassel's; and having delivered his message with that air of importance, and effort at fine language, which a servant is apt to display on petty embassies of the kind, he dashed over the brook, and was seen scampering away up the hollow, full of the importance and hurry of his mission.

All was now bustle and hubbub in the late quiet school-room. The scholars were hurried through their lessons, without stopping at trifles; those who were nimble skipped over half with impunity, and those who were tardy, had a smart application now and then in the rear, to quicken their speed, or help them over a tall word. Books were flung aside without being put away on the shelves, inkstands were overturned, benches thrown down, and the whole school was turned loose an hour before the usual time; bursting forth like a legion of young imps, yelping and racketing about the green, in joy at their early emancipation.

The gallant Ichabod now spent at least an extra half hour at his toilet, brushing and furbishing up his best, and indeed only suit of rusty black, and arranging his looks by a bit of broken looking-glass, that hung up in the school-house. That he might make his appearance before his mistress in the true style of a cavalier, he bor-

[13] *ferule,* a birch rod used for administering mild punishment

[14] *Mercury,* a Roman god renowned for his swiftness of foot. He frequently served as messenger for the gods.

rowed a horse from the farmer with whom he was domiciliated, a choleric old Dutchman, of the name of Hans Van Ripper, and thus gallantly mounted, issued forth, like a knight-errant in quest of adventures. But it is meet I should, in the true spirit of romantic story, give some account of the looks and equipments of my hero and his steed. The animal he bestrode was a broken-down plough-horse, that had outlived almost every thing but his viciousness. He was gaunt and shagged, with a ewe neck and a head like a hammer; his rusty mane and tail were tangled and knotted with burrs; one eye had lost its pupil, and was glaring and spectral; but the other had the gleam of a genuine devil in it. Still he must have had fire and mettle in his day, if we may judge from the name he bore of Gunpowder. He had, in fact, been a favorite steed of his master's, the choleric Van Ripper, who was a furious rider, and had infused, very probably, some of his own spirit into the animal; for, old and broken-down as he looked, there was more of the lurking devil in him than in any young filly in the country.

Ichabod was a suitable figure for such a steed. He rode with short stirrups, which brought his knees nearly up to the pommel of the saddle; his sharp elbows stuck out like grasshopper's; he carried his whip perpendicularly in his hand, like a sceptre, and, as his horse jogged on, the motion of his arms was not unlike the flapping of a pair of wings. A small wool hat rested on the top of his nose, for so his scanty strip of forehead might be called; and the skirts of his black coat fluttered out almost to the horse's tail. Such was the appearance of Ichabod and his steed, as they shambled out of the gate of Hans Van Ripper, and it was altogether such an apparition as is seldom to be met with in broad daylight.

It was, as I have said, a fine autumnal day, the sky was clear and serene, and nature wore that rich and golden livery which we always associate with the idea of abundance. The forests had put on their sober brown and yellow, while some trees of the tenderer kind had been nipped by the frosts into brilliant dyes of orange, purple, and scarlet. Streaming files of wild ducks began to make their appearance high in the air; the bark of the squirrel might be heard from the groves of beech and hickory nuts, and the pensive whistle of the quail at intervals from the neighboring stubble-field.

The small birds were taking their farewell banquets. In the fulness of their revelry, they fluttered, chirping and frolicking, from bush to bush, and tree to tree, capricious from the very profusion and variety around them. There was the honest cock-robin, the favorite game of stripling sportsmen, with its loud querulous note; and the twittering blackbirds flying in sable clouds; and the golden-winged woodpecker, with his crimson crest, his broad black gorget and splendid plumage; and the cedar bird, with its red-tipt wings and yellow-tipt tail and its little monteiro cap of feathers; and the blue jay, that noisy coxcomb, in his gay light-blue coat and white under-clothes; screaming and chattering, nodding and bobbing and bowing, and pretending to be on good terms with every songster of the grove.

As Ichabod jobbed slowly on his way, his eye, ever open to every symptom of culinary abundance, ranged with delight over the treasures of jolly autumn. On all sides he beheld vast store of apples; some hanging in oppressive opulence on the trees; some gathered into baskets and barrels for the market; others heaped up in rich piles for the cider-press. Farther on he beheld great fields of Indian corn, with its golden ears peeping from their leafy coverts, and holding out the promise of cakes and hasty pudding; and the yellow pumpkins lying beneath them, turning up their fair round bellies to the sun, and giving ample prospects of the most luxurious of pies; and anon he passed the fragrant buckwheat fields, breathing the odor of the bee-hive, and as he beheld them, soft anticipation stole over his mind of dainty slapjacks, well buttered, and garnished with honey or treacle, by the delicate little dimpled hand of Katrina Van Tassel.

Thus feeding his mind with many sweet thoughts and "sugar suppositions," he journeyed along the sides of a range of hills which look out upon some of the goodliest scenes of the mighty Hudson. The sun gradually wheeled his broad disk down into the west. The wide bosom of the Tappan Zee lay motionless and glassy, excepting that here and there a gentle undulation waved and prolonged the blue shadow of the distant mountain. A few amber clouds floated in the sky, without a breath of air to move them. The horizon was of a fine golden tint, changing gradually into a pure apple green, and from that into the deep blue of the mid-heaven. A slanting ray lingered on the woody crests of the precipices that overhung some parts of the river, giving greater depth to the dark-gray and purple of their rocky sides. A sloop was loitering in the distance, dropping slowly down with the tide, her sail hanging uselessly against the mast; and as the reflection of the sky gleamed along the still water, it seemed as if the vessel was suspended in the air.

It was toward evening that Ichabod arrived at the castle of the Heer Van Tassel, which he found thronged with the pride and flower of the adjacent country. Old farmers, a spare leathern-faced race, in homespun coats and breeches, blue stockings, huge shoes, and magnificent pewter buckles. Their brisk withered little dames, in close crimped caps, long-waisted shortgowns, homespun petticoats, with scissors and pincushions, and gay calico pockets hanging on the outside. Buxom lasses, almost as antiquated as their mothers, excepting where a straw hat, a fine ribbon or perhaps a white frock, gave symptoms of city innovation. The sons, in short square-skirted coats with rows of stupendous brass buttons, and their hair generally queued in the fashion of the times, especially if they could procure an eel-skin for the purpose, it being esteemed, throughout the country, as a potent nourisher and strengthener of the hair.

Brom Bones, however, was the hero of the scene, having come to the gathering on his favorite steed Daredevil, a creature, like himself, full of mettle and mischief, and which no one but himself could manage. He was, in fact, noted for preferring vicious animals, given to all kinds of tricks, which kept the rider in constant risk of his neck, for he held a tractable wellbroken horse as unworthy of a lad of spirit.

Fain would I pause to dwell upon the world of charms that burst upon the enraptured gaze of my hero, as he entered the state parlor of Van Tassel's mansion. Not those of the bevy of buxom lasses with their luxurious display of red and white; but the ample charms of a genuine Dutch country tea-table, in the sumptuous time of autumn. Such heaped-up platters of cakes of various and almost indescribable kinds, known only to experienced Dutch housewives! There was the doughty doughnut, the tenderer olykoek,[15] and the crisp and crumbling cruller; sweet cakes and short cakes, ginger cakes and honey cakes, and the whole family of cakes. And then there were apple pies and peach pies and pumpkin pies; besides slices of ham and smoked beef; and moreover delectable dishes of preserved plums, and peaches, and pears, and quinces; not to mention broiled shad and roasted chickens; together with bowls of milk and cream, all mingled higgledy-piggledy, pretty much as I have enumerated them, with the motherly teapot sending up its clouds of vapor from the midst—Heaven bless the mark! I want breath and time to discuss this banquet as it deserves, and am too eager to get on with my story. Happily, Ichabod Crane was not in so great a hurry as his historian, but did ample justice to every dainty.

[15] *olykoek,* a kind of doughnut or cruller

He was a kind and thankful creature, whose heart dilated in proportion as his skin was filled with good cheer; and whose spirits rose with eating as some men's do with drink. He could not help, too, rolling his large eyes round him as he ate, and chuckling with the possibility that he might one day be lord of all this scene of almost unimaginable luxury and splendor. Then, he thought, how soon he'd turn his back upon the old school-house; snap his fingers in the face of Hans Van Ripper, and every other niggardly patron, and kick any itinerant pedagogue out of doors that should dare to call him comrade!

Old Baltus Van Tassel moved about among his guests with a face dilated with content and good humor, round and jolly as the harvest moon. His hospitable attentions were brief, but expressive, being confined to a shake of the hand, a slap on the shoulder, a loud laugh, and a pressing invitation to "fall to, and help themselves."

And now the sound of the music from the common room or hall, summoned to the dance. The musician was an old gray-headed Negro, who had been the itinerant orchestra of the neighborhood for more than half a century. His instrument was as old and battered as himself. The greater part of the time he scraped on two or three strings, accompanying every movement of the bow with a motion of the head; bowing almost to the ground and stamping with his foot whenever a fresh couple were to start.

Ichabod prided himself upon his dancing as much as upon his vocal powers. Not a limb, not a fibre about him was idle; and to have seen his loosely hung frame in full motion, and clattering about the room, you would have thought Saint Vitus himself, that blessed patron of the dance, was figuring before you in person. He was the admiration of all the Negroes; who having gathered, of all ages and sizes, from the farm and the neighborhood, stood forming a pyramid of shining black faces at every door and window, gazing with delight at the scene, rolling their white eye-balls, and showing grinning rows of ivory from ear to ear. How could the flogger of urchins be otherwise than animated and joyous? The lady of his heart was his partner in the dance; and smiling graciously in reply to all his amorous oglings; while Brom Bones, sorely smitten with love and jealousy, sat brooding by himself in one corner.

When the dance was at an end, Ichabod was attracted to a knot of the sager folks, who, with old Van Tassel, sat smoking at one end of the piazza, gossiping over former times, and drawing out long stories about the war.

This neighborhood, at the time of which I am speaking, was one of those highly-favored places which abound with chronicle and great men. The British and American line had run near it during the war; it had, therefore, been the scene of marauding, and infested with refugees, cowboys, and all kinds of border chivalry. Just sufficient time had elapsed to enable each story-teller to dress up his tale with a little becoming fiction, and, in the indistinctness of his recollection, to make himself the hero of every exploit.

There was the story of Doffue Martling, a large blue-bearded Dutchman, who had nearly taken a British frigate with an old iron nine-pounder from a mud breastwork, only that his gun burst at the sixth discharge. And there was an old gentleman who shall be nameless, being too rich a mynheer [16] to be lightly mentioned, who, in the battle of Whiteplains, being an excellent master of defence, parried a musket ball with a small sword, insomuch that he absolutely felt it whiz round the blade, and glance off at the hilt: in proof of which, he was ready at any time to show the sword with the hilt a little bent. There were several more that had been equally great in the field, not one of whom but was persuaded that he had a considerable hand in bringing the war to a happy termination.

But all these were nothing to the tales of ghosts and apparitions that succeeded. The neighborhood is rich in legendary

treasures of the kind. Local tales and superstitions thrive best in these sheltered long-settled retreats; but are trampled under foot by the shifting throng that forms the population of most of our country places. Besides, there is no encouragement for ghosts in most of our villages, for they have scarcely had time to finish their first nap, and turn themselves in their graves, before their surviving friends have travelled away from the neighborhood; so that when they turn out at night to walk their rounds, they have no acquaintance left to call upon. This is perhaps the reason why we so seldom hear of ghosts except in our long-established Dutch communities.

The immediate cause, however, of the prevalence of supernatural stories in these parts, was doubtless owing to the vicinity of Sleepy Hollow. There was a contagion in the very air that blew from that haunted region; it breathed forth an atmosphere of dreams and fancies infecting all the land. Several of the Sleepy Hollow people were present at Van Tassel's, and, as usual, were doling out their wild and wonderful legends. Many dismal tales were told about funeral trains, and mourning cries and wailings heard and seen about the great tree where the unfortunate Major André [17] was taken, and which stood in the neighborhood. Some mention was made also of the woman in white, that haunted the dark glen at Raven Rock, and was often heard to shriek on winter nights before a storm, having perished there in the snow. The chief part of the stories, however, turned upon the favorite spectre of Sleepy Hollow, the headless horseman, who had been heard several times of late, patrolling the country; and it was said, tethered his horse nightly among the graves in the churchyard.

The sequestered situation of this church seems always to have made it a favorite haunt of troubled spirits. It stands on a

[16] *mynheer*, the Dutch term of honor and respect corresponding to "sir"

[17] *Major André,* an officer in the Revolutionary War, captured by Washington's troops and hanged as a British spy

knoll, surrounded by locust-trees and lofty elms, from among which its decent, white-washed walls shine modestly forth, like Christian purity beaming through the shades of retirement. A gentle slope descends from it to a silver sheet of water, bordered by high trees, between which, peeps may be caught at the blue hills of the Hudson. To look upon its grass-grown yard, where the sunbeams seem to sleep so quietly, one would think that there at least the dead might rest in peace. On one side of the church extends a wide woody dell, along which raves a large brook among broken rocks and trunks of fallen trees. Over a deep black part of the stream, not far from the church, was formerly thrown a wooden bridge; the road that led to it, and the bridge itself, were thickly shaded by overhanging trees, which cast a gloom about it, even in the daytime; but occasioned a fearful darkness at night. This was one of the favorite haunts of the headless horseman; and the place where he was most frequently encountered. The tale was told of old Brouwer, a most heretical disbeliever in ghosts, how he met the horseman returning from his foray into Sleepy Hollow, and was obliged to get up behind him; how they galloped over bush and brake, over hill and swamp, until they reached the bridge; when the horseman suddenly turned into a skeleton, threw old Brouwer into the brook, and sprang away over the tree-tops with a clap of thunder.

This story was immediately matched by a thrice marvellous adventure of Brom Bones, who made light of the galloping Hessian as an arrant jockey. He affirmed that, on returning one night from the neighboring village of Sing Sing, he had been overtaken by this midnight trooper; that he had offered to race with him for a bowl of punch, and should have won it too, for Daredevil beat the goblin horse all hollow, but, just as they came to the church bridge, the Hessian bolted, and vanished in a flash of fire.

All these tales, told in that drowsy undertone with which men talk in the dark, the countenances of the listeners only now and then receiving a casual gleam from the glare of a pipe, sank deep in the mind of Ichabod. He repaid them in kind with large extracts from his invaluable author, Cotton Mather, and added many marvellous events that had taken place in his native State of Connecticut, and fearful sights which he had seen in his nightly walks about Sleepy Hollow.

The revel now gradually broke up. The old farmers gathered together their families in their wagons, and were heard for some time rattling along the hollow roads, and over the distant hills. Some of the damsels mounted on pillions [18] behind their favorite swains, and their light-hearted laughter, mingling with the clatter of hoofs, echoed along the silent woodlands, sounding fainter and fainter until they gradually died away—and the late scene of noise and frolic was all silent and deserted. Ichabod only lingered behind, according to the custom of country lovers, to have a tête-à-tête with the heiress, fully convinced that he was now on the high road to success. What passed at this interview I will not pretend to say, for in fact I do not know. Something, however, I fear me, must have gone wrong, for he certainly sallied forth, after no very great interval, with an air quite desolate and chop-fallen.—Oh these women! these women! Could that girl have been playing off any of her coquettish tricks?—Was her encouragement of the poor pedagogue all a mere sham to secure her conquest of his rival?—Heaven only knows, not I!—Let it suffice to say, Ichabod stole forth with the air of one who had been sacking a hen-roost, rather than a fair lady's heart. Without looking to the right or left to notice the scene of rural wealth, on which he had so often gloated, he went straight to the stable, and with several hearty cuffs and kicks, roused his steed

[18] *pillions,* cushioned seats attached behind a saddle

most uncourteously from the comfortable quarters in which he was soundly sleeping, dreaming of mountains of corn and oats, and whole valleys of timothy and clover.

It was the very witching time of night that Ichabod, heavy-hearted and crest-fallen, pursued his travel homewards, along the sides of the lofty hills which rise above Tarry Town, and which he had traversed so cheerily in the afternoon. The hour was as dismal as himself. Far below him, the Tappan Zee spread its dusky and indistinct waste of waters, with here and there the tall mast of a sloop, riding quietly at anchor under the land. In the dead hush of midnight, he could even hear the barking of the watch dog from the opposite shore of the Hudson; but it was so vague and faint as only to give an idea of his distance from this faithful companion of man. Now and then, too, the long-drawn crowing of a cock, accidentally awakened, would sound far, far off, from some farm-house away among the hills,—but it was like a dreaming sound in his ear. No signs of life occurred near him, but occasionally the melancholy chirp of a cricket, or per-haps the guttural twang of a bull-frog, from a neighboring marsh, as if sleeping uncom-fortably, and turning suddenly in his bed.

All the stories of ghosts and goblins that he had heard in the afternoon, now came crowding upon his recollection. The night grew darker and darker; the stars seemed to sink deeper in the sky, and driving clouds occasionally hid them from his sight. He had never felt so lonely and dismal. He was, moreover, approaching the very place where many of the scenes of the ghost stories had been laid. In the centre of the road stood an enormous tulip-tree, which towered like a giant above all the other trees of the neighborhood, and formed a kind of landmark. Its limbs were gnarled, and fantastic, large enough to form trunks for ordinary trees, twisting down almost to the earth, and rising again into the air. It was connected with the tragical story of the unfortunate André,

who had been taken prisoner hard by; and was universally known by the name of Major André's tree. The common people regarded it with a mixture of respect and superstition, partly out of sympathy for the fate of its ill-starred namesake, and partly from the tales of strange sights and doleful lamentations told concerning it.

As Ichabod approached this fearful tree, he began to whistle; he thought his whistle was answered—it was but a blast sweep-ing sharply through the dry branches. As he approached a little nearer, he thought he saw something white, hanging in the midst of the tree—he paused and ceased whistling; but on looking more narrowly, perceived that it was a place where the tree had been scathed by lightning, and the white wood laid bare. Suddenly he heard a groan—his teeth chattered and his knees smote against the saddle: it was but the rubbing of one huge bough upon an-other, as they were swayed about by the breeze. He passed the tree in safety, but new perils lay before him.

About two hundred yards from the tree a small brook crossed the road, and ran into a marshy and thickly-wooded glen, known by the name of Wiley's swamp. A few rough logs, laid side by side, served for a bridge over this stream. On that side of the road where the brook entered the wood, a group of oaks and chestnuts, matted thick with wild grapevines, threw a cavernous gloom over it. To pass this bridge was the severest trial. It was at this identical spot that the unfortunate André was captured, and under the covert of those chestnuts and vines were the sturdy yeomen concealed who surprised him. This has ever since been considered a haunted stream, and fearful are the feel-ings of the schoolboy who has to pass it alone after dark.

As he approached the stream, his heart began to thump; he summoned up, how-ever, all his resolution, gave his horse half a score of kicks in the ribs, and attempted to dash briskly across the bridge; but instead of starting forward, the perverse old animal made a lateral movement, and ran broadside against the fence. Ichabod, whose fears increased with the delay, jerked the reins on the other side, and kicked lustily with the contrary foot: [19] it was all in vain; his steed started, it is true, but it was only to plunge to the opposite side of the road into a thicket of brambles and alder bushes. The schoolmaster now bestowed both whip and heel upon the starveling ribs of old Gunpowder, who dashed forward, snuffling and snorting, but came to a stand just by the bridge, with a suddenness that had nearly sent his rider sprawling over his head. Just at this moment a plashy tramp by the side of the bridge caught the sensitive ear of Ichabod. In the dark shadow of the grove, on the margin of the brook, he beheld something huge, misshapen, black and towering. It stirred not, but seemed gathered up in the gloom, like some gigantic monster ready to spring upon the traveller.

The hair of the affrighted pedagogue rose upon his head with terror. What was to be done? To turn and fly was now too late; and besides, what chance was there of escaping ghost or goblin, if such it was, which could ride upon the wings of the wind? Summoning up, therefore, a show of courage, he demanded in stammering accents—"Who are you?" He received no reply. He repeated his demand in a still more agitated voice. Still there was no answer. Once more he cudgelled the sides of the inflexible Gunpowder, and shutting his eyes, broke forth with involuntary fervor into a psalm tune. Just then the shadowy object of alarm put itself in motion, and, with a scramble and a bound, stood at once in the middle of the road. Though the night was dark and dismal, yet the form of the unknown might now in some degree be ascertained. He appeared to be a horseman of large dimensions, and mounted on a black horse of powerful frame. He made no offer of

molestation or sociability, but kept aloof on one side of the road, jogging along on the blind side of old Gunpowder, who had now got over his fright and waywardness.

Ichabod, who had no relish for this strange midnight companion, and bethought himself of the adventure of Brom Bones with the Galloping Hessian, now quickened his steed, in hopes of leaving him behind. The stranger, however, quickened his horse to an equal pace. Ichabod pulled up, and fell into a walk, thinking to lag behind—the other did the same. His heart began to sink within him; he endeavored to resume his psalm tune, but his parched tongue clove to the roof of his mouth, and he could not utter a stave. There was something in the moody and dogged silence of this pertinacious companion that was mysterious and appalling. It was soon fearfully accounted for. On mounting a rising ground, which brought the figure of his fellow-traveller in relief against the sky, gigantic in height, and muffled in a cloak, Ichabod was horror-struck, on perceiving that he was headless! —but his horror was still more increased, on observing that the head, which should have rested on his shoulders, was carried before him on the pommel of the saddle: his terror rose to desperation; he rained a shower of kicks and blows upon Gunpowder, hoping, by a sudden movement, to give his companion the slip—but the spectre started full jump with him. Away then they dashed, through thick and thin; stones flying, and sparks flashing at every bound. Ichabod's flimsy garments fluttered in the air, as he stretched his long lank body away over his horse's head, in the eagerness of his flight.

They had now reached the road which turns off to Sleepy Hollow; but Gunpowder, who seemed possessed with a demon, instead of keeping up it, made an opposite turn, and plunged headlong down hill to the left. This road leads through a sandy hollow, shaded by trees for about a quarter of a mile, where it crosses the bridge

---

[19] *contrary foot,* opposite foot

Leonard Everett Fisher

famous in goblin story, and just beyond swells the green knoll on which stands the whitewashed church.

As yet the panic of the steed had given his unskilful rider an apparent advantage in the chase; but just as he had got half way through the hollow, the girths of the saddle gave way, and he felt it slipping from under him. He seized it by the pommel, and endeavored to hold it firm, but in vain; and had just time to save himself by clasping old Gunpowder round the neck, when the saddle fell to the earth, and he heard it trampled under foot by his pursuer. For a moment the terror of Hans Van Ripper's wrath passed across his mind—for it was his Sunday saddle; but this was no time for petty fears; the goblin was hard on his haunches; and (unskilful rider that he was!) he had much ado to maintain his seat; sometimes slipping on one side, sometimes on another, and sometimes jolted on the high ridge of his horse's backbone, with a violence that he verily feared would cleave him asunder.

An opening in the trees now cheered him with the hopes that the church bridge was at hand. The wavering reflection of a silver star in the bosom of the brook told him that he was not mistaken. He saw the walls of the church dimly glaring under the trees beyond. He recollected the place where Brom Bone's ghostly competitor had disappeared. "If I can but reach that bridge," thought Ichabod, "I am safe." Just then he heard the black steed panting and blowing close behind him; he even fancied that he felt his hot breath. Another convulsive kick in the ribs, and old Gunpowder sprang upon the bridge; he thundered over the resounding planks; he gained the opposite side; and now Ichabod cast a look behind to see if his pursuer should vanish, according to rule, in a flash of fire and brimstone. Just then he saw the goblin rising in his stirrups, and in the very act of hurling his head at him. Ichabod endeavored to dodge the horrible missile, but too late. It encountered his cranium with a tremendous crash—he was tumbled headlong into the dust, and Gunpowder, the black steed, and the goblin rider, passed by like a whirlwind.

The next morning the old horse was found without his saddle, and with the bridle under his feet, soberly cropping the grass at his master's gate. Ichabod did not make his appearance at breakfast—dinner-

hour came, but no Ichabod. The boys assembled at the school-house, and strolled idly about the banks of the brook; but no schoolmaster. Hans Van Ripper now began to feel some uneasiness about the fate of poor Ichabod, and his saddle. An inquiry was set on foot, and after diligent investigation they came upon his traces. In one part of the road leading to the church was found the saddle trampled in the dirt; the tracks of horses' hoofs deeply dented in the road, and evidently at furious speed, were traced to the bridge, beyond which, on the bank of a broad part of the brook, where the water ran deep and black, was found the hat of the unfortunate Ichabod, and close beside it a shattered pumpkin.

The brook was searched, but the body of the schoolmaster was not to be discovered. Hans Van Ripper, as executor of his estate, examined the bundle which contained all his wordly effects. They consisted of two shirts and a half; two stocks for the neck; a pair or two of worsted stockings; an old pair of corduroy small-clothes; a rusty razor; a book of psalm tunes, full of dogs' ears; and a broken pitchpipe. As to the books and furniture of the school-house,

they belonged to the community, excepting Cotton Mather's History of Witchcraft, a New England Almanac, and a book of dreams and fortune-telling; in which last was a sheet of foolscap much scribbled and blotted in several fruitless attempts to make a copy of verses in honor of the heiress of Van Tassel. These magic books and the poetic scrawl were forthwith consigned to the flames by Hans Van Ripper; who from that time forward determined to send his children no more to school; observing, that he never knew any good come of this same reading and writing. Whatever money the schoolmaster possessed, and he had received his quarter's pay but a day or two before, he must have had about his person at the time of his disappearance.

The mysterious event caused much speculation at the church on the following Sunday. Knots of gazers and gossips were collected in the churchyard, at the bridge, and at the spot where the hat and pumpkin had been found. The stories of Brouwer, of Bones, and a whole budget of others, were called to mind; and when they had diligently considered them all, and compared them with the symptoms of the present case, they shook their heads, and came to the conclusion that Ichabod had been carried off by the galloping Hessian. As he was a bachelor, and in nobody's debt, nobody troubled his head any more about him. The school was removed to a different quarter of the hollow, and another pedagogue reigned in his stead.

It is true, an old farmer, who had been down to New-York on a visit several years after, and from whom this account of the ghostly adventure was received, brought home the intelligence that Ichabod Crane was still alive; that he had left the neighborhood, partly through fear of the goblin and Hans Van Ripper, and partly in mortification at having been suddenly dismissed by the heiress; that he had changed his quarters to a distant part of the country; had kept school and studied law at the same time, had been admitted to the bar, turned politician, electioneered, written for the newspapers, and finally had been made a justice of the Ten Pound Court. Brom Bones too, who, shortly after his rival's disappearance, conducted the blooming Katrina in triumph to the altar, was observed to look exceedingly knowing whenever the story of Ichabod was related, and always burst into a hearty laugh at the mention of the pumpkin; which led some to suspect that he knew more about the matter than he chose to tell.

The old country wives, however, who are the best judges of these matters, maintain to this day that Ichabod was spirited away by supernatural means; and it is a favorite story often told about the neighborhood round the winter evening fire. The bridge became more than ever an object of superstitious awe, and that may be the reason why the road has been altered of late years, so as to approach the church by the border of the millpond. The schoolhouse being deserted, soon fell to decay, and was reported to be haunted by the ghost of the unfortunate pedagogue; and the plough boy, loitering homeward of a still summer evening, has often fancied his voice at a distance, chanting a melancholy psalm tune among the tranquil solitudes of Sleepy Hollow.

POSTSCRIPT, FOUND IN THE HANDWRITING OF MR. KNICKERBOCKER

The preceding Tale is given, almost in the precise words in which I heard it related at a Corporation meeting of the ancient city of Manhattoes, at which were present many of its sagest and most illustrious burghers. The narrator was a pleasant, shabby, gentlemanly old fellow, in pepper-and-salt clothes, with a sadly humorous face; and one whom I strongly suspected of being poor,—he made such efforts to be entertaining. When his story was concluded, there was much laughter and approbation, particularly from two or three deputy aldermen, who had been asleep the greater part of the time. There was, however, one tall, dry-looking old gentleman, with beetling eyebrows, who maintained a grave and rather severe face throughout; now and then folding his arms, inclining his head, and looking down upon the floor, as if turning a doubt over in his mind. He was one of your wary men, who never laugh, but upon good grounds—when they have reason and the law on their side. When the mirth of the rest of the company had subsided, and silence was restored, he leaned one arm on the elbow of his chair, and sticking the other akimbo, demanded, with a slight, but exceedingly sage motion of the head, and contraction of the brow, what was the moral of the story, and what it went to prove?

The story-teller, who was just putting a glass of wine to his lips, as a refreshment after his toils, paused for a moment, looked at his inquirer with an air of infinite deference, and lowering the glass slowly to the table, observed, that the story was intended most logically to prove:—

"That there is no situation in life but has its advantages and pleasures—provided we will but take a joke as we find it:

"That, therefore, he that runs races with

goblin troopers is likely to have rough riding of it.

"Ergo, for a country schoolmaster to be refused the hand of a Dutch heiress, is a certain step to high preferment, in the state."

The cautious old gentleman knit his brows tenfold closer after this explanation, being sorely puzzled by the ratiocination of the syllogism; while, methought, the one in pepper-and-salt eyed him with something of a triumphant leer. At length he observed, that all this was very well, but still he thought the story a little on the extravagant—there were one or two points on which he had his doubts.

"Faith, sir," replied the story-teller, "as to that matter, I don't believe one-half of it myself."

D. K. 1818–1820

The man who wrote this story

WASHINGTON IRVING   1783–1859

When the English critic, Sydney Smith, asked in 1820, "Who reads an American book?" the answer would have been "Almost no one." Very few authors from the United States were recognized in Europe. Franklin and Jefferson were known, of course, but as statesmen rather than writers.

Washington Irving, the first American author to achieve popularity in both England and the United States, was also one of America's first professional writers. He was born in New York City, then a comparatively small town of 20,000 people. As soon as he could read, he seized upon romantic stories of adventure and travel. Whenever he could escape from his family, he would slip away to the nearby countryside and discover for himself old stories told by the New York settlers. In later life he explored the folk literature of Europe as he had explored the folk tales of New York State. He was to bring many of these European tales back to America.

Irving was a very charming man and welcome in many countries. Some of this charm is reflected in his stories. He developed a pleasant, easy style that was a delight to read. The materials for his stories were drawn from many sources, both in Europe and America. Even when he was rewriting European folk tales, he gave them an American flavor. Some of these tales, like "The Legend of Sleepy Hollow," he transplanted to the New York countryside, stocking them with the traditions and people of that region.

Let's consider . . .

This legend is almost as well known in Europe as it is in this country. Boys and girls studying English in the schools of France read it in their textbooks. To appreciate this legend fully, you may need to read parts of it again. Particularly, you won't want to miss Washington Irving's sly humor.

1. Ichabod made frequent visits to the Van Tassel home. What attractions drew him there?

2. Ichabod's salary as a schoolmaster was extremely meager. What living arrangements were made to supplement his salary? How would you like it if the same practice were still followed in your community today? How do you think your teachers would enjoy it?

3. How did these doughty Dutch regard a schoolmaster? Do you think public opinion about teachers has changed today? Discuss.

4. Irving gave you a good idea of the life and customs of early Dutch settlers in a New York village. Which features impressed you most? Which ones amused you most?

5. Describe the Van Tassel party, paying particular attention to the refreshments. Is the attitude toward food the same today? Bring out the differences in your discussion.

6. "The whole neighborhood," said Irving, "abounds with local tales, haunted spots, and twilight superstitions." By referring to at least three places in the story, show how Irving prepared you for the outcome of the *plot* of this legend: Ichabod's encounter with the galloping Hessian.

7. What evidence can you give that there was a very real explanation, not supernatural at all, for what happened to Ichabod and drove him away from Sleepy Hollow?

8. Read aloud what you consider the best paragraph in the whole story. Tell why you chose it.

9. Do you consider the ending of the story satisfactory? Would you have preferred that the story close earlier? Explain your answer.

The writer's craft . . .

Probably the oldest literary form used by storytellers is the **tale:** a rambling, discursive prose narrative which lacks the tight unity that is characteristic of the short story. This definition does not imply that tales are carelessly written. Washington Irving, for example, wrote his tales with definite aims in view. He once expressed these aims in the following words: "For my part, I consider a story merely as a frame on which to stretch my materials. It is the play of thought, and sentiment, and language; the weaving in of characters, lightly yet expressively delineated; the familiar and faithful exhibition of scenes in common life; and the half-concealed vein of humor that is often playing through the whole,—these are among what I aim at . . ." Thus the story in Irving's tales did little more than provide a framework for the following:

The play of thought, sentiment, and language
  Carefully drawn characters
  Half-concealed humor
  Familiar scenes in common life

1. Certainly in "The Legend of Sleepy Hollow" the story itself was of no great consequence. In a few brief sentences, summarize what happened.

2. Now think about "The Legend of Sleepy Hollow" in terms of Irving's first aim: to provide for "the play of thought, sentiment, and language." Each author has a distinct **style:** his manner of choosing, ordering, and arranging words to create a desired effect. Irving's style has a charm and polish which gives his stories a particular tone or atmosphere. Look again at his leisurely beginning. Notice how his easy flow of language set the tone for the entire tale. What thoughts or sentiments (feelings) did Irving express in this opening? Select other passages in this tale in which he paused in the telling of the story to allow for the "play of thought, sentiment, and language."

3. Irving also aimed at "the weaving in of characters, lightly yet expressively delineated." Few of you will ever forget the character of Ichabod Crane. How did Irving create this wonderful personality? To answer this question you will need to piece together what you are told about him (1) as a schoolmaster, (2) as a singing master, (3) as a guest at the Van Tassel home, and (4) as a person when he was alone. Jot down characteristics of his personality which emerged in each of these situations. Now state in a sentence or two the kind of person you think he was.

4. As you think about Ichabod Crane's personality, you undoubtedly are aware of Irving's next aim: to reveal "the half-concealed vein of humor that is often playing through the whole." The humorous aspects were brought out by means of a light touch deftly applied, so that when Ichabod finally met the headless horseman, you were fully prepared to appreciate the ab-

surd situation. Explain why the incident was funny. Select two other incidents or descriptions which appealed to your sense of humor. How did the language add to the humorous effect? Compare your choices with those selected by others in your class. You will be surprised at the number of humorous parts.

5. Irving also aimed at "the familiar and faithful exhibition of scenes of common life." He took great pains to make the locality seem real—as in his picture of Sleepy Hollow. What details made this place seem real? How did the "familiar scenes" provide a suitable background for the events which took place?

6. While it is true that Irving treated his characters and setting in a way that made them seem "real," his writing had other qualities. The particular way in which any writer looks at the world and the people in it will determine what kinds of material he selects, and it will also color his treatment of these materials. If he sees beauty in the wild, remote parts of the world, if he enjoys giving free rein to his imagination, or if he finds the past somehow more satisfying than the present, he will probably not write about the humdrum, everyday world around him. On the other hand, if he believes that life should be presented as it really is, without imaginative touches, he will *not* select exotic (foreign or strikingly different) people and places as materials for his stories. In literature the first of these two ways of viewing life is called **romantic;** the second way is called **realistic.** Remember that in literature the term *romantic* does not refer to love stories, although they too may be treated in a romantic manner. Because Washington Irving wrote about the picturesque and the unusual, and because he turned to the folklore of the past rather than to the reality of the present for the

materials of his tales, he is called a romantic writer. However, because he made the setting seem "real," and because he treated his characters as true-to-life people, his writing has certain qualities of realism. Literature is seldom purely romantic or purely realistic; it is usually a blending of both. The result is a picture of life, both as the writer sees it and as he hopes it is.

Knowing words . . .

A. Irving wrote that the ghost "rides forth to the scene of battle in nightly *quest* of his head." The word *quest* comes originally from a form of the Latin verb *quaerere,* meaning "to seek" or "to ask." Irving used the word *quest* to mean "a search."

The following words come from the same root as *quest,* but they are related more to the root meaning of "asking" than of "seeking." Explain the meaning of each of the following words, showing clearly how it is related to its root meaning.

question	inquest
request	query
questionnaire	

B. Irving wrote of "cruel *potentates* of the school, who joy in the smart of their subjects." A *potentate* is a ruler or monarch wielding great power. This word comes indirectly from the Latin word *potens* meaning "having power."

Explain how the following italicized words suggest this idea of power. Be sure you know what these words mean.

1. The illness was so severe that the doctor prescribed a *potent* drug.
2. The *potential* speed of the rocket has not yet been fully developed.
3. The man had unsuspected *potentialities* in many fields.
4. He realized the *potency* of the drug.

The Birthmark

NATHANIEL HAWTHORNE

After Washington Irving, the next major American writer who turned to short fiction was Nathaniel Hawthorne. Instead of moving leisurely from one incident to another in the development of his tales, Hawthorne focused his attention primarily on a single dramatic episode. This gave his stories a greater unity than Irving had achieved.

The situations which Hawthorne wrote about were usually concerned with some aspect of human conduct. In "The Birthmark" you will read the fascinating story of a young man's desperate attempt to correct the one imperfection which he could not accept.

In the latter part of the last century there lived a man of science—an eminent [1] proficient in every branch of natural philosophy—who not long before our story opens had made experience of a spiritual affinity more attractive than any chemical one. He had left his laboratory to the care of an assistant, cleared his fine countenance from the furnace-smoke, washed the stain of acids from his fingers, and persuaded a beautiful woman to become his wife. In those days, when the comparatively recent discovery of electricity, and other kindred mysteries of nature, seemed to open paths into the region of miracle, it was not unusual for the love of science to rival the love of woman in its depth and absorbing energy. The higher intellect, the imagination, the spirit, and even the heart, might all find their congenial aliment in pursuits which, as some of their ardent votaries believed, would ascend from one step of powerful intelligence to another until the philosopher should lay his hand on the secret of creative force, and perhaps make new worlds for himself. We know not whether Aylmer possessed this degree of faith in man's ultimate control over nature. He had devoted himself, however, too unreservedly to scientific studies ever to be weaned from them by any second passion. His love for his young wife might prove the stronger of the two, but it could only be by intertwining itself with his love of science and uniting the strength of the latter to its own.

Such an union accordingly took place, and was attended with truly remarkable consequences, and a deeply impressive moral. One day, very soon after their marriage, Aylmer sat gazing at his wife with a trouble in his countenance that grew stronger, until he spoke.

"Georgiana," said he, "has it never occurred to you that the mark upon your cheek might be removed?"

---

[1] *an eminent,* a person well-known as an authority in his field

"No, indeed," said she, smiling; but, perceiving the seriousness of his manner, she blushed deeply. "To tell you the truth, it has been so often called a charm that I was simple enough to imagine it might be so."

"Ah! upon another face perhaps it might," replied her husband, "but never on yours. No, dearest Georgiana; you came so nearly perfect from the hand of Nature that this slightest possible defect—which we hesitate whether to term a defect or a beauty—shocks me as being the visible mark of earthly imperfection."

"Shocks you, my husband!" cried Georgiana, deeply hurt, at first reddening with momentary anger, but then bursting into tears. "Then why did you take me from my mother's side? You cannot love what shocks you."

To explain this conversation it must be mentioned that in the center of Georgiana's left cheek there was a singular mark deeply interwoven, as it were, with the texture and substance of her face. In the usual state of her complexion—a healthy though delicate bloom—the mark wore a tint of deeper crimson which imperfectly defined its shape amid the surrounding rosiness. When she blushed, it gradually became more indistinct, and finally vanished amid the triumphant rush of blood that bathed the whole cheek with its brilliant glow. But if any shifting emotion caused her to turn pale, there was the mark again, a crimson stain upon the snow, in what Aylmer sometimes deemed an almost fearful distinctness. Its shape bore not a little similarity to the human hand, though of the smallest pigmy size. Georgiana's lovers were wont to say that some fairy at her birth-hour had laid her tiny hand upon the infant's cheek, and left this impress there in token of the magic endowments that were to give her such sway over all hearts. Many a desperate swain would have risked life for the privilege of pressing his lips to the mysterious hand. It must not be conceived, however, that the impression wrought by this fairy sign-manual

varied exceedingly according to the difference of temperament in the beholders. Some fastidious persons—but they were exclusively of her own sex—affirmed that the bloody hand, as they chose to call it, quite destroyed the effect of Georgiana's beauty, and rendered her countenance even hideous. But it would be as reasonable to say that one of those small blue stains which sometimes occur in the purest statuary marble would convert the Eve of Powers to a monster. Masculine observers, if the birthmark did not heighten their admiration, contented themselves with wishing it away that the world might possess one living specimen of ideal loveliness without the semblance of a flaw.

After his marriage—for he thought little or nothing of the matter before—Aylmer discovered that this was the case with himself. Had she been less beautiful—if Envy's self could have found aught else to sneer at—he might have felt his affection heightened by the prettiness of this mimic hand, now vaguely portrayed, now lost, now stealing forth again, and glimmering to and fro with every pulse of emotion that throbbed within her heart. But, seeing her otherwise so perfect, he found this one defect grew more and more intolerable with every moment of their united lives. It was the fatal flaw of humanity which Nature in one shape or another stamps ineffaceably on all her productions, either to imply that they are temporary and finite, or that their perfection must be wrought by toil and pain. The crimson hand expressed the ineludible grip in which mortality clutches the highest and purest of earthly mold, degrading them into kindred with the lowest, and even with the very brutes, like whom their visible frames return to dust. In this manner, selecting it as the symbol of his wife's liability to sin, sorrow, decay and death, Aylmer's somber imagination was not long in rendering the birthmark a frightful object, causing him more trouble and horror than ever Georgiana's beauty, whether of soul or sense, had given him delight.

At all the seasons which should have been their happiest, he invariably, and without intending it—nay, in spite of a purpose to the contrary—reverted to this one disastrous topic. Trifling as it at first appeared, it so connected itself with innumerable trains of thought and moods of feeling that it became the central point of all. With the morning twilight Aylmer opened his eyes upon his wife's face and recognized the symbol of imperfection; and when they sat together at the evening hearth, his eyes wandered stealthily to her cheek, and beheld, flickering with the blaze of the wood-fire, the spectral hand that wrote mortality where he would fain

have worshiped. Georgiana soon learned to shudder at his gaze. It needed but a glance, with the peculiar expression that his face often wore, to change the roses of her cheek into a deathlike paleness, amid which the crimson hand was brought strongly out like a bas-relief of ruby on the whitest marble.

Late one night, when the lights were growing dim, so as hardly to betray the stain on the poor wife's cheek, she herself for the first time voluntarily took up the subject.

"Do you remember, my dear Aylmer," said she, with a feeble attempt at a smile —"have you any recollection of a dream last night about this odious hand?"

"None—none whatever," replied Aylmer, starting; but then he added in a dry, cold tone, affected for the sake of concealing the real depth of his emotion, "I might well dream of it, for before I fell asleep it had taken a pretty firm hold of my fancy."

"And you did dream of it," continued Georgiana, hastily; for she dreaded lest a gush of tears should interrupt what she had to say—"a terrible dream. I wonder that you can forget it. Is it possible to forget this one expression?—'It is in her heart now: we must have it out.' Reflect, my husband; for by all means I would have you recall that dream."

The mind is in a sad state when Sleep the all-involving cannot confine her specters within the dim region of her sway, but suffers them to break forth, affrighting this actual life with secrets that perchance belong to a deeper one. Aylmer now remembered his dream. He had fancied himself with his servant Aminadab, attempting an operation for the removal of the birthmark. But the deeper went the knife, the deeper sank the hand, until at length its tiny grasp appeared to have caught hold of Georgiana's heart, whence, however, her husband was inexorably resolved to cut or wrench it away.

When the dream had shaped itself perfectly in his memory, Aylmer sat in his wife's presence with a guilty feeling. Truth often finds its way to the mind close-muffled in robes of sleep, and then speaks with uncompromising directness of matters in regard to which we practice an unconscious self-deception during our waking moments. Until now he had not been aware of the tyrannizing influence acquired by one idea over his mind, and of the lengths which he might find in his heart to go for the sake of giving himself peace.

"Aylmer," resumed Georgiana, solemnly, "I know not what may be the cost to both of us to rid me of this fatal birthmark. Perhaps its removal may cause cureless deformity. Or, it may be, the stain goes as deep as life itself. Again, do we know that there is a possibility, on any terms, of unclasping the firm grip of this little hand which was laid upon me before I came into the world?"

"Dearest Georgiana, I have spent much thought upon the subject," hastily interrupted Aylmer; "I am convinced of the perfect practicability of its removal."

"If there be the remotest possibility of it," continued Georgiana, "let the attempt be made, at whatever risk. Danger is nothing to me, for life, while this hateful mark makes me the object of your horror and disgust—life is a burden which I would fling down with joy. Either remove this dreadful hand or take my wretched life. You have deep science; all the world bears witness of it. You have achieved great wonders; cannot you remove this little, little mark which I cover with the tips of two small fingers? Is this beyond your power, for the sake of your own peace and to save your poor wife from madness?"

"Noblest, dearest, tenderest wife!" cried Aylmer, rapturously. "Doubt not my power. I have already given this matter the deepest thought—thought which might almost have enlightened me to create a being less perfect than yourself.

Georgiana, you have led me deeper than ever into the heart of Science. I feel myself fully competent to render this dear cheek as faultless as its fellow, and then, most beloved, what will be my triumph when I shall have corrected what Nature left imperfect in her fairest work! Even Pygmalion,[2] when his sculptured woman assumed life, felt not greater ecstasy than mine will be."

"It is resolved, then," said Georgiana, faintly smiling. "And, Aylmer, spare me not, though you should find the birthmark take refuge in my heart at last."

Her husband tenderly kissed her cheek —her right cheek, not that which bore the impress of the crimson hand.

The next day Aylmer apprised his wife of a plan that he had formed whereby he might have opportunity for the intense thought and constant watchfulness which the proposed operation would require, while Georgiana, likewise, would enjoy the perfect repose essential to its success. They were to seclude themselves in the extensive apartments occupied by Aylmer as a laboratory, and where during his toilsome youth he had made discoveries in the elemental powers of nature that had roused the admiration of all the learned societies in Europe. Seated calmly in this laboratory, the pale philosopher had investigated the secrets of the highest cloud-region and of the profoundest minds; he had satisfied himself of the causes that kindled and kept alive the fires of the volcano, and had explained the mystery of fountains and how it is that they gush forth, some so bright and pure and others with such rich medicinal virtues, from the dark bosom of the earth. Here, too, at an earlier period, he had studied the wonders of the human frame, and attempted to fathom the very process by which Nature assimilates all her precious influences from earth and air and from the spiritual world to create and foster man,

---

[2] *Pygmalion,* a legendary sculptor who fell in love with a statue he had created. The statue came to life in answer to his prayers.

her masterpiece. The latter pursuit, however, Aylmer had long laid aside in unwilling recognition of the truth against which all seekers sooner or later stumble—that our great creative mother, while she amuses us with apparently working in the broadest sunshine, is yet severely careful to keep her own secrets, and in spite of her pretended openness shows us nothing but results. She permits us, indeed, to mar, but seldom to mend, and, like a jealous patentee,[3] on no account to make. Now, however, Aylmer resumed these half-forgotten investigations—not, of course, with such hopes or wishes as first suggested them, but because they involved much physiological truth and lay in the path of his proposed scheme for the treatment of Georgiana.

As he led her over the threshold of the laboratory Georgiana was cold and tremulous. Aylmer looked cheerfully into her face with intent to reassure her, but was so startled with the intense glow of the birthmark upon the whiteness of her cheek that he could not restrain a strong convulsive shudder. His wife fainted.

"Aminadab! Aminadab!" shouted Aylmer stamping violently on the floor.

Forthwith there issued from an inner apartment a man of low stature but bulky frame, with shaggy hair hanging about his visage, which was grimed with the vapors of the furnace. This personage had been Aylmer's under-worker during his whole scientific career, and was admirably fitted for that office by his great mechanical readiness and the skill with which, while incapable of comprehending a single principle, he executed all the practical details of his master's experiments. With his vast strength, his shaggy hair, his smoky aspect, and the indescribable earthiness that encrusted him, he seemed to represent man's physical nature, while Aylmer's slender figure and pale intellectual face were no less apt a type of the spiritual element.

"Throw open the door of the boudoir,

Aminadab," said Aylmer, "and burn a pastille."[4]

"Yes, master," answered Aminadab, looking intently at the lifeless form of Georgiana; and then he muttered to himself, "If she were my wife, I'd never part with that birthmark."

When Georgiana recovered consciousness, she found herself breathing an atmosphere of penetrating fragrance the gentle potency of which had recalled her from her deathlike faintness. The scene around her looked like enchantment. Aylmer had converted those smoky, dingy, somber rooms where he had spent his brightest years in recondite pursuits into a series of beautiful apartments not unfit to be the secluded abode of a lovely woman. The walls were hung with gorgeous curtains which imparted the combination of grandeur and grace that no other species of adornment can achieve, and as they fell from the ceiling to the floor their rich and ponderous folds, concealing all angles and straight lines, appeared to shut in the scene from infinite space. For aught Georgiana knew, it might be a pavilion among the clouds. And Aylmer, excluding the sunshine, which would have interfered with his chemical processes, had supplied its place with perfumed lamps emitting flames of various hue, but all uniting in a soft, empurpled radiance. He now knelt by his wife's side, watching her earnestly, but without alarm, for he was confident in his science, and felt that he could draw a magic circle round her within which no evil might intrude.

"Where am I? Ah! I remember," said Georgiana faintly; and she placed her hand over her cheek to hide the terrible mark from her husband's eyes.

"Fear not, dearest," exclaimed he. "Do not shrink from me. Believe me, Georgiana, I even rejoice in this single imperfection, since it will be such a rapture to remove it."

---

[3] *patentee,* an inventor; one who has had his invention patented

[4] *pastille,* a roll or cone of aromatic substances, burned as a perfume or disinfectant

"Oh, spare me!" sadly replied his wife. "Pray, do not look at it again. I never can forget that convulsive shudder."

In order to soothe Georgiana, and, as it were, to release her mind from the burden of actual things, Aylmer now put in practice some of the light and playful secrets which science had taught him among its profounder lore. Airy figures, absolutely bodiless ideas and forms of unsubstantial beauty came and danced before her, imprinting their momentary footsteps on beams of light. Though she had some indistinct idea of the method of these optical phenomena, still the illusion was almost perfect enough to warrant the belief that her husband possessed sway over the spiritual world. Then again, when she felt a wish to look forth from her seclusion immediately, as if her thoughts were answered, the procession of external existence flitted across a screen. The scenery and the figures of actual life were perfectly represented, but with that bewitching yet indescribable difference which always makes a picture, an image, or a shadow, so much more attractive than the original. When wearied of this, Aylmer bade her cast her eyes upon a vessel containing a quantity of earth. She did so, with little interest at first, but was soon startled to perceive the germ of a plant shooting upward from the soil. Then came the slender stalk; the leaves gradually unfolded themselves, and amid them was a perfect and lovely flower.

"It is magical," cried Georgiana; "I dare not touch it."

"Nay, pluck it," answered Aylmer— "pluck it and inhale its brief perfume while you may. The flower will wither in a few moments, and leave nothing save its brown seed-vessels; but thence may be perpetuated a race as ephemeral as itself."

But Georgiana had no sooner touched the flower than the whole plant suffered a blight, its leaves turning coal-black, as if by the agency of fire.

"There was too powerful a stimulus," said Aylmer thoughtfully.

To make up for this abortive experiment, he proposed to take her portrait by a scientific process of his own invention. It was to be effected by rays of light striking upon a polished plate of metal. Georgiana assented, but on looking at the result was affrighted to find the features of the portrait blurred and indefinable, while the minute figure of a hand appeared where the cheek should have been. Aylmer snatched the metallic plate and threw it into a jar of corrosive acid.

Soon, however, he forgot these mortifying failures. In the intervals of study and chemical experiment he came to her flushed and exhausted, but seemed invigorated by her presence, and spoke in glowing language of the resources of his art. He gave a history of the long dynasty of the alchemists, who spent so many ages in quest of the universal solvent by which the golden principle might be elicited from all things vile and base. Aylmer appeared to believe that by the plainest scientific logic it was altogether within the limits of possibility to discover this long-sought medium; but, he added, a philosopher who should go deep enough to acquire the power would attain too lofty a wisdom to stoop to the exercise of it. Not less singular were his opinions in regard to the Elixir Vitae.[5] He more than intimated that it was at his option to concoct a liquid that should prolong life for years—perhaps interminably—but that it would produce a discord in nature which all the world, and chiefly the quaffer of the immortal nostrum, would find the cause to curse.

"Aylmer, are you in earnest?" asked Georgiana, looking at him with amazement and fear. "It is terrible to possess such power, or even to dream of possessing it."

"Oh, do not tremble, my love," said her husband; "I would not wrong either you or myself by working such inharmonious

[5] *Elixir Vitae,* a preparation of alchemy made for prolonging life [*Latin*]

effects upon our lives. But I would have you consider how trifling, in comparison, is the skill requisite to remove this little hand."

At the mention of the birthmark, Georgiana, as usual, shrank as if a red-hot iron had touched her cheek.

Again Aylmer applied himself to his labors. She could hear his voice in the distant furnace-room giving directions to Aminadab, whose harsh, uncouth, misshapen tones were audible in response more like the grunt or growl of a brute than human speech. After hours of absence Aylmer reappeared, and proposed that she should now examine his cabinet of chemical products and natural treasures of the earth. Among the former he showed her a small vial in which, he remarked, was contained a gentle yet most powerful fragrance capable of impregnating all the breezes that blow across a kingdom. They were of inestimable value, the contents of that little vial; and as he said so he threw some of the perfume into the air and filled the room with piercing and invigorating delight.

"And what is this?" asked Georgiana, pointing to a small crystal globe containing a gold colored liquid. "It is so beautiful to the eye that I could imagine it the Elixir of Life."

"In one sense it is," replied Aylmer—"or, rather, the Elixir of Immortality. It is the most precious poison that ever was concocted in this world. By its aid I could apportion the lifetime of any mortal at whom you might point your finger. The strength of the dose would determine whether he were to linger out years or drop dead in the midst of a breath. No king on his guarded throne could keep his life, if I, in my private station, should deem that the welfare of millions justified me in depriving him of it."

"Why do you keep such a terrific drug?" inquired Georgiana, in horror.

"Do not mistrust me, dearest," said her husband, smiling; "its virtuous potency is yet greater than its harmful one. But see! here is a powerful cosmetic. With a few drops of this in a vase of water freckles may be washed away as easily as the hands are cleansed. A stronger infusion would take the blood out of the cheek and leave the rosiest beauty a pale ghost."

"Is it with this lotion that you intend to bathe my cheek?" asked Georgiana, anxiously.

"Oh no!" hastily replied her husband; "this is merely superficial. Your case demands a remedy that shall go deeper."

In his interviews with Georgiana, Aylmer generally made minute inquiries as to her sensations, and whether the confinement of the rooms and the temperature of the atmosphere agreed with her. These questions had such a particular drift that Georgiana began to conjecture that she was already subjected to certain physical influences, either breathed in with the fragrant air or taken with her food. She fancied, likewise—but it might be altogether fancy—that there was a stirring up of her system, a strange indefinite sensation creeping through her veins and tingling, half painfully, half pleasurably, at her heart. Still, whenever she dared to look into the mirror, there she beheld herself pale as a white rose and with the crimson birthmark stamped upon her cheek. Not even Aylmer now hated it so much as she.

To dispel the tedium of the hours which her husband found it necessary to devote to the processes of combination and analysis, Georgiana turned over the volumes of his scientific library. In many dark old tomes she met with chapters full of romance and poetry. They were the works of the philosophers of the Middle Ages, such as Albertus Magnus,[6] Cornelius Agrippa,[7] Paracelsus,[8] and the famous friar who created

---

[6] *Albertus Magnus,* a German (Swabian) saint who lived during the 12th and 13th centuries and concerned himself with science

[7] *Cornelius Agrippa,* a German philosopher and student of alchemy and magic (1486–1535)

[8] *Paracelsus,* Philippus Aureolus Paracelsus, Swiss alchemist and physician (1493–1541)

the prophetic Brazen Head.[9] All these antique naturalists stood in advance of their centuries, yet were imbued with some of their credulity, and therefore were believed, and perhaps imagined themselves, to have acquired from the investigation of nature a power above nature, and from physics a sway over the spiritual world. Hardly less curious and imaginative were the early volumes of the *Transactions* of the Royal Society,[10] in which the members, knowing little of the limits of natural possibility, were continually recording wonders or proposing methods whereby wonders might be wrought.

But to Georgiana the most engrossing volume was a large folio from her husband's own hand in which he had recorded every experiment of his scientific career, with its original aim, the methods adopted for its development and its final success or failure, with the circumstances to which either event was attributable. The book, in truth, was both the history and emblem of his ardent, ambitious, imaginative, yet practical and laborious, life. He handled physical details as if there were nothing beyond them, yet spiritualized them all, and redeemed himself from materialism by his strong and eager aspiration toward the infinite. In his grasp the veriest clod of earth assumed a soul. Georgiana, as she read, reverenced Aylmer, and loved him more profoundly than ever, but with less entire dependence on his judgment than heretofore. Much as he had accomplished, she could not but observe that his most splendid successes were almost invariably failures, if compared with the ideal at which he aimed. His brightest diamonds were the merest pebbles, and felt to be so by himself, in comparison with the inesti-

mable gems which lay hidden beyond his reach. The volume rich with achievements that had won renown for its author was yet as melancholy a record as ever mortal hand had penned. It was the sad confession and continued exemplification of the shortcomings of the composite man, the spirit burdened with clay and working in matter, and of the despair that assails the higher nature at finding itself so miserably thwarted by the earthly part. Perhaps every man of genius, in whatever sphere, might recognize the image of his own experience in Aylmer's journal.

So deeply did these reflections affect Georgiana that she laid her face upon the open volume and burst into tears. In this situation she was found by her husband.

"It is dangerous to read in a sorcerer's books," said he, with a smile, though his countenance was uneasy and displeased. "Georgiana, there are pages in that volume which I can scarcely glance over and keep my senses. Take heed lest it prove as detrimental to you."

"It has made me worship you more than ever," said she.

"Ah! wait for this one success," rejoined he, "then worship me if you will. I shall deem myself hardly unworthy of it. But come! I have sought you for the luxury of your voice; sing to me, dearest."

So she poured out the liquid music of her voice to quench the thirst of his spirit. He then took his leave with a boyish exuberance of gayety, assuring her that her seclusion would endure but a little longer, and that the result was already certain. Scarcely had he departed, when Georgiana felt irresistibly impelled to follow him. She had forgotten to inform Aylmer of a symptom which for two or three hours past had begun to excite her attention. It was a sensation in the fatal birthmark—not painful, but which induced a restlessness throughout her system. Hastening after her husband, she intruded for the first time into the laboratory.

The first thing that struck her eye was

---

[9] *famous friar who created the prophetic Brazen Head,* Roger Bacon (c. 1214–1294) an English philosopher, alchemist, and scientist. According to legend he made a bronze head which could tell present, past, and future.

[10] *Royal Society,* Royal Society of London for the Advancement of Science, formed by the British government to assist scientific study.

the furnace, that hot and feverish worker, with the intense glow of its fire, which by the quantities of soot clustered above it seemed to have been burning for ages. There was a distilling apparatus in full operation. Around the room were retorts, tubes, cylinders, crucibles, and other apparatus of chemical research. An electrical machine stood ready for immediate use. The atmosphere felt oppressively close, and was tainted with gaseous odors which had been tormented forth by the processes of Science. The severe and homely simplicity of the apartment, with its naked walls and brick pavement, looked strange, accustomed as Georgiana had become to the fantastic elegance of her boudoir. But what chiefly—indeed, almost solely—drew her attention was the aspect of Aylmer himself.

He was pale as death, anxious and absorbed, and hung over the furnace as if it depended upon his utmost watchfulness whether the liquid which it was distilling should be the draught of immortal happiness or misery. How different from the sanguine and joyous mien that he had assumed for Georgiana's encouragement!

"Carefully now, Aminadab! Carefully, thou human machine! Carefully, thou man of clay!" muttered Aylmer, more to himself than his assistant. "Now, if there be a thought too much or too little, it is all over."

"Hoh! hoh!" mumbled Aminadab. "Look, master, look!"

Aylmer raised his eyes hastily, and at first reddened, then grew paler than ever, on beholding Georgiana. He rushed toward her and seized her arm with a grip that left the print of his fingers upon it.

"Why do you come hither? Have you no trust in your husband?" cried he impetuously. "Would you throw the blight of that fatal birthmark over my labors? It is not well done. Go, prying woman, go!"

"Nay, Aylmer," said Georgiana; with a firmness of which she possessed no stinted endowment, "it is not you that have a right to complain. You mistrust your wife. You have concealed the anxiety with which you watch the development of this experiment. Think not so unworthily of me, my husband. Tell me all the risk we run, and fear not that I shall shrink, for my share in it is far less than your own!"

"No, no, Georgiana!" said Aylmer, impatiently; "it must not be."

"I submit," replied she, calmly. "And, Aylmer, I shall quaff whatever draught you bring me, but it will be on the same principle that would induce me to take a dose of poison if offered by your hand."

"My noble wife!" said Aylmer, deeply moved; "I knew not the height and depth of your nature until now. Nothing shall be concealed. Know, then, that this crimson hand, superficial as it seems, has clutched its grasp into your being with a strength of which I had no previous conception. I have already administered agents powerful enough to do aught except to change your entire physical system. Only one thing remains to be tried; if that fails us, we are ruined!"

"Why did you hesitate to tell me this?" asked she.

"Because, Georgiana," said Aylmer, in a low voice, "there is danger."

"'Danger!' There is but one danger—that this horrible stigma shall be left upon my cheek," cried Georgiana. "Remove it, remove it, whatever be the cost, or we shall both go mad."

"Heaven knows your words are too true," said Aylmer sadly. "And now, dearest, return to your boudoir. In a little while all will be tested."

He conducted her back, and took leave of her with a solemn tenderness which spoke far more than his words how much was now at stake.

After his departure Georgiana became wrapped in musings. She considered the character of Aylmer, and did it completer justice than at any previous moment. Her heart exulted while it trembled at his honorable love, so pure and lofty that it would

accept nothing less than perfection, nor miserably make itself contented with an earthlier nature than he had dreamed of. She felt how much more precious was such a sentiment than that meaner [11] kind which would have borne with the imperfection for her sake, and have been guilty of treason to holy love by degrading its perfect idea to the level of the actual. And with her whole spirit she prayed that for a single moment she might satisfy his highest and

deepest conception. Longer than one moment, she well knew, it could not be, for his spirit was ever on the march, ever ascending, and each instant required something that was beyond the scope of the instant before.

The sound of her husband's footsteps aroused her. He bore a crystal goblet containing a liquor colorless as water, but bright enough to be the draught of immortality. Aylmer was pale, but it seemed rather the consequence of a highly-wrought

[11] *meaner*, inferior

state of mind and tension of spirit than of fear or doubt.

"The concoction of the draught has been perfect," said he in answer to Georgiana's look. "Unless all my science have deceived me, it cannot fail."

"Save on your account, my dearest Aylmer," observed his wife, "I might wish to put off this birthmark of mortality by relinquishing mortality itself, in preference to any other mode. Life is but a sad procession to those who have attained precisely the degree of moral advancement at which I stand. Were I weaker and blinder, it might be happiness; were I stronger, it might be endured hopefully; but, being what I find myself, methinks I am of all mortals the most fit to die."

"You are fit for heaven without tasting death," replied her husband. "But why do you speak of dying? The draught cannot fail. Behold its effect upon this plant."

On the window-seat there stood a geranium diseased with yellow blotches, which had overspread all its leaves. Aylmer poured a small quantity of the liquid upon the soil in which it grew. In a little time, when the roots of the plant had taken up the moisture, the unsightly blotches began to be extinguished in a living verdure.

"There needed no proof," said Georgiana, quietly. "Give me the goblet; I joyfully stake all upon your word."

"Drink, then, thou lofty creature!" exclaimed Aylmer, with fervid admiration. "There is no taint of imperfection on thy spirit. Thy sensible frame, too, shall soon be all perfect."

She quaffed the liquid, and returned the goblet to his hand.

"It is grateful," said she, with a placid smile. "Methinks it is like water from a heavenly fountain, for it contains I know not what of unobtrusive fragrance and deliciousness. It allays a feverish thirst that had parched me for many days. Now, dearest, let me sleep. My earthly senses are closing over my spirit like the leaves around the heart of a rose at sunset."

She spoke the last words with a gentle reluctance, as if it required almost more energy than she could command to pronounce the faint and lingering syllables. Scarcely had they loitered through her lips ere she was lost in slumber. Aylmer sat by her side, watching her aspect with the emotions proper to a man the whole value of whose existence was involved in the process now to be tested. Mingled with this mood, however, was the philosophic investigation characteristic of the man of science. Not the minutest symptoms escaped him. A heightened flush of the cheek, a slight irregularity of breath, a quiver of the eyelid, a hardly perceptible tremor through the frame,—such were the details which as the moments passed he wrote down in his folio volume. Intense thought had set its stamp upon every previous page of that volume, but the thoughts of years were all concentrated upon the last.

While thus employed he failed not to gaze often at the fatal hand, and not without a shudder. Yet once, by a strange and unaccountable impulse, he pressed it with his lips. His spirit recoiled, however, in the very act, and Georgiana, out of the midst of her deep sleep, moved uneasily and murmured, as if in remonstrance. Again Aylmer resumed his watch. Nor was it without avail. The crimson hand, which at first had been strongly visible upon the marble paleness of Georgiana's cheek, now grew more faintly outlined. She remained not less pale than ever, but the birthmark with every breath that came and went lost somewhat of its former distinctness. Its presence had been awful; its departure was more awful still. Watch the stain of the rainbow fading out of the sky, you will know how that mysterious symbol passed away.

"By Heaven, it is well-nigh gone!" said Aylmer to himself, in almost irrepressible ecstasy. "I can scarcely trace it now. Success! Success! And now it is like the faintest rose-color; the slightest flush of blood across her cheek would overcome it. But she is so pale!"

He drew aside the window-curtain and suffered the light of natural day to fall into the room and rest upon her cheek. At the same time he heard a gross, hoarse chuckle which he had long known as his servant Aminadab's expression of delight.

"Ah, clod! Ah, earthly mass!" cried Aylmer, laughing in a sort of frenzy. "You have served me well! Matter and spirit—earth and heaven—have both done their part in this. Laugh, thing of the senses! You have earned the right to laugh."

These exclamations broke Georgiana's sleep. She slowly unclosed her eyes and gazed into the mirror which her husband had arranged for that purpose. A faint smile flitted over her lips when she recognized how barely perceptible was now that crimson hand which had once blazed forth with such disastrous brilliancy as to scare away all their happiness. But then her eyes sought Aylmer's face with a trouble and anxiety that he could by no means account for.

"My poor Aylmer!" murmured she.

"Poor? Nay—richest, happiest, most favored!" exclaimed he. "My peerless bride, it is successful. You are perfect!"

"My poor Aylmer!" she repeated with a more than human tenderness. "You have aimed loftily; you have done nobly. Do not repent that with so high and pure a feeling you have rejected the best the earth could offer. Aylmer, dearest Aylmer, I am dying."

Alas, it was too true! The fatal hand had grappled with the mystery of life, and was the bond by which an angelic spirit kept itself in union with a mortal frame. As the last crimson tint of the birthmark—that sole token of human imperfection—faded from her cheek, the parting breath of the now perfect woman passed into the atmosphere, and her soul, lingering a moment near her husband, took its heavenward flight. Then a hoarse, chuckling laugh was heard again. Thus ever does the gross fatality of earth exult in its invariable triumph over the immortal essence which in this dim sphere of half development demands the completeness of a higher state. Yet, had Aylmer reached a profounder wisdom, he need not thus have flung away the happiness which would have woven his mortal life of the selfsame texture with the celestial. The momentary circumstance was too strong for him: he failed to look beyond the shadowy scope of time, and, living once for all in eternity, to find the perfect future in the present.

The man who wrote this story

NATHANIEL HAWTHORNE   1804–1864

The three most important authors of nineteenth-century New England are generally agreed to be Emerson, Thoreau, and Nathaniel Hawthorne. Hawthorne was quite different from his two famous contemporaries. For one thing, he wrote fiction. While Emerson and Thoreau found joy and satisfaction in nature and in the positive aspects of life, Hawthorne was concerned with what might be called life's "gloomy" side. He expressed in his writings a Puritan sense of sin and damnation which, by his time, had almost become old-fashioned.

Part of Hawthorne's character is explained by his childhood environment. His ancestors had lived in the little seaport of Salem, Massachusetts, for nearly two hundred years. By 1830 the town was old, and weatherbeaten ships rotted at the piers. When Hawthorne was four, his father, a sea captain, died, and Mrs. Hawthorne set herself apart from the rest of the world. She took her meals alone and rarely saw her children. After Hawthorne was graduated from college, he also secluded himself, and for twelve years he seemed to have lived alone.

He was forty-six when his novel, *The Scarlet Letter,* appeared. It was almost immediately accepted by the public as a "classic," and was characteristic of much of Hawthorne's work in that it dealt with the early Colonial period in American history.

Hawthorne was concerned not so much with reality as with morality. Many of his stories have meanings on several levels. They can be enjoyed for just their surface interest, but they also illustrate deeper moral ideas merging and conflicting.

Let's consider . . .

1. What was Aylmer's one consuming passion?

2. Why was Aylmer shocked by the birthmark? How did Georgiana react to his remarks?

3. Georgiana's other admirers were not offended by the birthmark. In what ways were they different from Aylmer?

4. What did Aylmer dream about the birthmark? What did his wife hear him say that upset her?

5. Why was Georgiana willing to take any risk to be rid of the birthmark?

6. What was Aylmer's reaction to her suggestion that he had the power to remove it? What plan did he propose?

7. How had Aminadab served Aylmer in the past? What part of man's nature did he represent? How did he feel about the proposed experiment?

8. Why did Aylmer's attitude toward the birthmark change after he had moved Georgiana to his laboratory apartment?

9. How did Aylmer entertain his wife before he began the fateful experiment? Were his displays of magic always successful? How did he react when they failed? How did Georgiana feel about his possessing such great scientific power?

10. Why do you think Aylmer continued to show Georgiana evidences of his power? Did they reassure her or add to her fear of what he might be planning? Explain.

11. What did Georgiana discover about Aylmer's success in achieving the ideal? How did this discovery affect her?

12. What did Georgiana find when she followed Aylmer into the laboratory? Explain the scene which took place between them. What did she learn?

13. Why do you think Georgiana welcomed the draught? How did it affect her?

14. Do you think Aminadab's laugh showed his pleasure in the success, or was it a cruel laugh because he knew what was going to happen?

15. Why was Aylmer's scientific success such a complete failure for himself as well as for Georgiana?

16. Analyze your feelings toward Georgiana by considering the following questions and the reasons for your answers. Then give your estimate of her.

    a. Does she irritate you at any point?

    b. Do you sympathize with her?

    c. Do you have any personal feeling for her whatsoever?

    d. Do you resent what Aylmer is preparing to do to her?

    e. Do you believe in Aylmer's love for her?

    f. What are your feelings when she says, "Aylmer, dearest Aylmer, I am dying"?

17. At the end you heard again "a hoarse, chuckling laugh." Why was Aminadab introduced again at this point?

18. In some ways this story is similar to a modern science fiction story. How does it differ from science fiction stories you have read?

The writer's craft . . .

A. In "The Birthmark" Hawthorne developed a theme which illustrated a truth about human behavior. A **theme** is the underlying thought or idea upon which a story is based. When the author spells out his theme in an obvious way, his story becomes preachy and loses its effectiveness as a source of enjoyment. The skillful writer weaves his theme into the structure of the story so that it blends with the other ingredients: the plot, action, characters, and setting. The reader grasps the meaning of the story without being *told*.

1. Hawthorne developed his theme in "The Birthmark" by means of a single dramatic situation. Write a synopsis (brief statement) of the **plot**: the series of incidents or events which led to the high point or climax of the story.

2. Now write a brief character sketch of the two main characters.

3. Using your analysis of the plot and the two main characters in Exercises 1 and 2, you should have no difficulty in discovering the theme. Write this theme in a carefully phrased sentence.

4. Do you think that Hawthorne made his theme too obvious or was it unobtrusively woven into the story? Explain.

B. Hawthorne's special attention to theme often influenced his portrayal of the characters. At times they *represent* an idea, a concept (such as Good or Evil), or a particular type of individual, rather than real people. For example, Hawthorne portrayed Aylmer not merely as a man of science but as the personification of intellect without soul. What do the other characters, Georgiana and Aminadab, represent more truly than a beautiful woman and a laboratory assistant?

Knowing words . . .

A. Nathaniel Hawthorne wrote that Nature stamps all of her productions with a flaw, possibly "to imply that they are temporary and *finite*."

The word *finite* means "having limits or boundaries." It comes from the Latin root *fin*, meaning "end."

1. Explain how each of the following words carries along the meaning of its root, *fin*:

finish   finale
infinite   definite

Use each of these words in sentences of your own.

B. Hawthorne's work contains many words which are appropriate to his formal, precise style. Look up each of the italicized words in the following sentences and explain its meaning as used here.

1. "The *concoction* of the draught has been perfect," said he in answer to Georgiana's look.

2. In a little time, when the roots of the plant had taken up the moisture, the unsightly blotch began to be extinguished in a living *verdure*.

3. How different from the *sanguine* and joyous *mien* that he had assumed for Georgiana's encouragement!

4. To *dispel* the *tedium* of the hours which her husband found it necessary to devote to the processes of combination and analysis, Georgiana turned over the volumes of his scientific library.

The Tell-tale Heart

EDGAR ALLAN POE

Edgar Allan Poe was not so much interested in illustrating a theme as in creating a mood: an emotional tone or atmosphere. First, he would decide upon a mood he wished his readers to experience; then he would devise a plot that created this mood.

For a mood to be most effective, it must be unbroken. Poe found that the short story, which could be read at a single sitting, was the ideal form for sustaining the effect he wanted his tales to have upon the reader. In "The Tell-tale Heart" you will see how skillfully he has created and sustained a mood of suspense and horror.

True!—nervous—very, very dreadfully nervous I had been and am; but why *will* you say that I am mad? The disease had sharpened my senses—not destroyed—not dulled them. Above all was the sense of hearing acute. I heard all things in the heaven and in the earth. I heard many things in hell. How, then, am I mad? Hearken! and observe how healthily—how calmly I can tell you the whole story.

It is impossible to say how first the idea entered my brain; but once conceived, it haunted me day and night. Object there was none. Passion there was none. I loved the old man. He had never wronged me. He had never given me insult. For his gold I had no desire. I think it was his eye! yes, it was this! He had the eye of a vulture—a pale blue eye, with a film over it. Whenever it fell upon me, my blood ran cold; and so by degrees—very gradually—I made up my mind to take the life of the old man, and thus rid myself of the eye forever.

Now this is the point. You fancy me mad. Madmen know nothing. But you should have seen *me*. You should have seen how wisely I proceeded—with what caution—with what foresight—with what dissimulation I went to work! I was never kinder to the old man than during the whole week before I killed him. And every night, about midnight, I turned the latch of his door and opened it—oh so gently! And then, when I had made an opening sufficient for my head, I put in a dark lantern, all closed, closed, so that no light shone out, and then I thrust in my head. Oh, you would have laughed to see how cunningly I thrust it in! I moved it slowly—very, very slowly, so that I might not disturb the old man's sleep. It took me an hour to place my whole head within the opening so far that I could see him as he lay upon his bed. Ha!—would a madman have been so wise as this? And then, when my head was well in the room, I undid the lantern cautiously—oh, so cautiously—cautiously (for the hinges creaked)—I undid it just so much that a single thin ray fell upon the vulture eye. And this I did for seven long nights—every night just at midnight—but I found the eye always closed; and so it was impossible to do the work; for it was not the old man who vexed me, but his Evil Eye. And every morning, when the day broke, I went boldly into the chamber, and spoke courageously to him, calling him by name in a hearty tone, and inquiring how he had passed the night. So you see he would have been a very profound old man, indeed, to suspect that every night, just at twelve, I looked in upon him while he slept.

Upon the eighth night I was more than usually cautious in opening the door. A watch's minute hand moves more quickly than did mine. Never before that night, had I *felt* the extent of my own powers —of my sagacity. I could scarcely contain my feelings of triumph. To think that there I was, opening the door, little by little, and he not even to dream of my secret deeds or thoughts. I fairly chuckled at the idea; and perhaps he heard me; for he moved on the bed suddenly, as if startled. Now you may think that I drew back—but no. His room was as black as pitch with the thick darkness (for the shutters were close fastened, through fear of robbers), and so I knew that he could not see the opening of the door, and I kept pushing it on steadily, steadily.

I had my head in, and was about to open the lantern, when my thumb slipped upon the tin fastening, and the old man sprang up in bed, crying out—"Who's there?"

I kept quite still and said nothing. For a whole hour I did not move a muscle, and in the mean time I did not hear him lie down. He was still sitting up in the bed listening;—just as I have done, night after night, hearkening to the death watches in the wall.

Presently I heard a slight groan, and I knew it was the groan of mortal terror. It was not a groan of pain or of grief—oh, no!—it was the low stifled sound that arises from the bottom of the soul when over-charged with awe. I knew the sound well. Many a night, just at midnight, when all the world slept, it has welled up from my own bosom, deepening, with its dreadful echo, the terrors that distracted me. I say I knew it well. I knew what the old man felt, and pitied him, although I chuckled at heart. I knew that he had been lying awake ever since the first slight noise, when he had turned in the bed. His fears had been ever since growing upon him. He had been trying to fancy them cause-

less, but could not. He had been saying to himself—"It is nothing but the wind in the chimney—it is only a mouse crossing the floor," or "it is merely a cricket which has made a single chirp." Yes, he had been trying to comfort himself with these suppositions: but he had found all in vain. *All in vain;* because Death, in approaching him had stalked with his black shadow before him, and enveloped the victim. And it was the mournful influence of the unperceived shadow that caused him to feel—although he neither saw nor heard—to *feel* the presence of my head within the room.

When I had waited a long time, very patiently, without hearing him lie down, I resolved to open a little—a very, very little crevice in the lantern. So I opened it—you cannot imagine how stealthily, stealthily—until, at length a single dim ray, like the thread of the spider, shot from out the crevice and fell full upon the vulture eye.

It was open—wide, wide open—and I grew furious as I gazed upon it. I saw it with perfect distinctness—all a dull blue, with a hideous veil over it that chilled the very marrow in my bones; but I could see nothing else of the old man's face or person: for I had directed the ray as if by instinct, precisely upon the damned spot.

And have I not told you that what you mistake for madness is but over acuteness of the senses?—now, I say, there came to my ears a low, dull, quick sound, such as a watch makes when enveloped in cotton. I knew *that* sound well, too. It was the beating of the old man's heart. It increased my fury, as the beating of a drum stimulates the soldier into courage.

But even yet I refrained and kept still. I scarcely breathed. I held the lantern motionless. I tried how steadily I could maintain the ray upon the eye. Meantime the hellish tattoo of the heart increased. It grew quicker and quicker, and louder and louder every instant. The old man's terror *must* have been extreme! It grew louder, I say, louder every moment!—do you mark

me well? I have told you that I am nervous: so I am. And now at the dead hour of the night, amid the dreadful silence of that old house, so strange a noise as this excited me to uncontrollable terror. Yet, for some minutes longer I refrained and stood still. But the beating grew louder, louder! I thought the heart must burst. And now a new anxiety seized me—the sound would be heard by a neighbour! The old man's hour had come! With a loud yell, I threw open the lantern and leaped into the room. He shrieked once—once only. In an instant I dragged him to the floor, and pulled the heavy bed over him. I then smiled gaily, to find the deed so far done. But, for many minutes, the heart beat on with a muffled sound. This, however, did not vex me; it would not be heard through the wall. At length it ceased. The old man was dead. I removed the bed and examined the corpse. Yes, he was stone, stone dead. I placed my hand upon the heart and held it there many minutes. There was no pulsation. He was stone dead. His eye would trouble me no more.

If still you think me mad, you will think so no longer when I describe the wise precautions I took for the concealment of the body. The night waned, and I worked hastily, but in silence. First of all I dismembered the corpse. I cut off the head and the arms and the legs.

I then took up three planks from the flooring of the chamber, and deposited all between the scantlings. I then replaced the boards so cleverly, so cunningly, that no human eye—not even *his*—could have detected any thing wrong. There was nothing to wash out—no stain of any kind —no blood-spot whatever. I had been too wary for that. A tub had caught all—ha! ha!

When I had made an end of these labours, it was four o'clock—still dark as midnight. As the bell sounded the hour, there came a knocking at the street door. I went down to open it with a light heart, —for what had I *now* to fear? There entered three men, who introduced themselves, with perfect suavity, as officers of the police. A shriek had been heard by a neighbour during the night; suspicion of foul play had been aroused; information had been lodged at the police office, and they (the officers) had been deputed to search the premises.

I smiled,—for *what* had I to fear? I bade the gentlemen welcome. The shriek, I said, was my own in a dream. The old man, I mentioned, was absent in the country. I took my visitors all over the house. I bade them search—search *well*. I led them, at length, to *his* chamber. I showed them his treasures, secure, undisturbed. In the enthusiasm of my confidence, I brought chairs into the room, and desired them *here* to rest from their fatigues, while I myself, in the wild audacity of my perfect triumph, placed my own seat upon the very spot beneath which reposed the corpse of the victim.

The officers were satisfied. My *manner* had convinced them. I was singularly at ease. They sat, and while I answered cheerily, they chatted of familiar things. But, erelong, I felt myself getting pale and wished them gone. My head ached, and I fancied a ringing in my ears: but still they sat and still chatted. The ringing became more distinct:—it continued and became more distinct: I talked more freely to get rid of the feeling: but it continued and gained definiteness—until, at length, I found that the noise was *not* within my ears.

No doubt I now grew *very* pale;—but I talked more fluently, and with a heightened voice. Yet the sound increased—and what could I do? It was *a low, dull, quick sound —much such a sound as a watch makes when enveloped in cotton.* I gasped for breath—and yet the officers heard it not. I talked more quickly—more vehemently; but the noise steadily increased. I arose and argued about trifles, in a high key and with violent gesticulations; but the noise steadily increased. Why *would* they not be gone? I paced the floor to and fro with heavy strides, as if excited to fury by the observations of the men—but the noise steadily increased. What *could* I do? I foamed—I raved—I swore! I swung the chair upon which I had been sitting, and grated it upon the boards, but the noise arose over all and continually increased. It grew louder—louder—*louder!* And still the men chatted pleasantly, and smiled. Was it possible they heard not? No, no! They heard!—they suspected!—they *knew!* —they were making a mockery of my horror!—this I thought, and this I think. But any thing was better than this agony! Any thing was more tolerable than this derision! I could bear those hypocritical smiles no longer! I felt that I must scream or die! and now—again!—hark! louder! louder! louder! *louder!*

"Villains!" I shrieked, "dissemble no more! I admit the deed!—tear up the planks! here, here!—it is the beating of his hideous heart!"

The man who wrote this story

EDGAR ALLAN POE   1809-1849

Unlike the New England writers of his time, Poe was interested not so much in what his writings would say to people as in the effect they would have. He was more interested in literary form than in ideas. Poe was not successful during his life.

His poetry was generally ignored, and his stories, though considered interesting by a few readers, were not widely popular. He was often on the verge of starvation but managed to earn his living by editing magazines. He worked in Richmond, Philadelphia, and New York for various publications, bringing to each of them his remarkable talent and skill as an author and critic.

After his death, Poe became more and more important as a writer. Strangely enough, he was first recognized by French writers. By the end of the nineteenth century, his poems and criticism became the basis for a poetic movement in France which, in turn, affected American literature. However, the full force of this movement was not evident in American literature until the last twenty years.

Poe was an excellent technician with words (Emerson once called him "the jingle-man") and a masterful creator of moods of suspense and terror. He is now recognized as one of America's most important writers.

Let's consider . . .

1. Poe intended that his stories should "attract the reader instantly." Tell in what ways he did or did not succeed.

2. In all of his works, Poe aimed at a "single effect." That is why most of his stories are comparatively short. What single effect did he achieve in "The Tell-tale Heart"?

3. There were really only two characters here: the narrator and the old man. Did either of them seem real or alive? Explain your feelings about them. How did you feel about the officers at the end of the story?

4. How did you expect the story to end? How did Poe sustain the suspense?

5. Tales of mystery, horror, and the grotesque were common here and in Germany about the time this story was published (1843). Compare and contrast this story with any of the modern mysteries you have read, heard on the radio, or seen on television or in the movies. How are these modern thrillers like "The Tell-tale Heart"? How are they different? In your opinion, how successfully do modern writers—of both stories and scripts—capture your interest immediately and create a single effect?

The writer's craft . . .

The basic elements of a short story are the setting, the characters, the plot, the mood, and the style. Although a writer may stress one or two of these elements in any given story, he can hardly avoid using all of them. For example, he may concentrate primarily on the plot, but the working out of the plot would require one or more characters and would create some kind of mood. Or if his first concern was the setting, its purpose would be to provide a background for the characters and the plot. The setting would also color the mood of the story.

1. In "The Tell-tale Heart" Poe emphasized the element of mood: the emotional tone or atmosphere. Describe this mood. Was it suspense, terror, horror, or a combination of these?

2. How did the author present the characters? What do you know about them? How would you describe the narrator (the madman) if you had to identify him?

3. How important was the setting to the creation of the mood? What details were you given about it? Try to describe it.

4. State the plot in a sentence or two. Discuss its importance in establishing the mood.

5. Poe chose to tell his story from the first-person point of view. In that way he could reveal the thoughts and emotions of the leading character. Explain why these thoughts and emotions were of major importance in creating the mood and suspense.

6. When you examined Irving's style, you noted the leisurely flow of the long sentences and the somewhat "flowery" choice of words. Now look at Poe's style. Notice the very short sentences, particularly in the scene with the police officers. Notice the constant use of verbs expressing action or emotion. Point out specific lines in the story which show how Poe intensified the mood by his choice and arrangement of words.

A Day's Pleasure

HAMLIN GARLAND

Hamlin Garland, and certain other writers of the last century, held the opinion that American literature was not truthfully reflecting actual life. They felt that too much emphasis was being placed on the unusual or the "ideal," and too little on the commonplace and "real." These writers were called realists because they wanted literature to be an objective record of actual life.

In "A Day's Pleasure" you will find a realistic account of life on a midwestern farm during the last part of the nineteenth century.

When Markham came in from shovelling his last wagonload of corn into the crib he found that his wife had put the children to bed, and was kneading a batch of dough with the dogged action of a tired and sullen woman.

He slipped his soggy boots off his feet, and having laid a piece of wood on the top of the stove, put his heels on it comfortably. His chair squeaked as he leaned back on its hinder legs, but he paid no attention; he was used to it, exactly as he was used to his wife's lameness and ceaseless toil.

"That closes up my corn," he said after a silence. "I guess I'll go to town tomorrow to git my horses shod."

"I guess I'll git ready and go along," said his wife, in a sorry attempt to be firm and confident of tone.

"What do you want to go to town fer?" he grumbled.

"What does anybody want to go to town fer?" she burst out, facing him. "I ain't been out o' this house fer six months, while you go an' go!"

"Oh, it ain't six months. You went down that day I got the mower."

"When was that? The tenth of July, and you know it."

"Well, mebbe 'twas. I didn't think it was so long ago. I ain't no objection to your goin', only I'm goin' to take a load of wheat."

"Well, jest leave off a sack, an' that'll balance me an' the baby," she said spiritedly.

"All right," he replied good-naturedly, seeing she was roused. "Only that wheat ought to be put up tonight if you're goin'. You won't have any time to hold sacks for me in the morning with them young ones to get off to school."

"Well, let's go do it then," she said, sullenly resolute.

"I hate to go out agin; but I s'pose we'd better."

He yawned dismally and began pulling his boots on again, stamping his swollen feet into them with grunts of pain. She put on his coat and one of the boy's caps, and they went out to the granary. The night was cold and clear.

"Don't look so much like snow as it did last night," said Sam. "It may turn warm."

Laying out the sacks in the light of the

lantern, they sorted out those which were whole, and Sam climbed into the bin with a tin pail in his hand, and the work began.

He was a sturdy fellow, and he worked desperately fast; the shining tin pail dived deep into the cold wheat and dragged heavily on the woman's tired hands as it came to the mouth of the sack, and she trembled with fatigue, but held on and dragged the sacks away when filled, and brought others, till at last Sam climbed out, puffing and wheezing, to tie them up.

"I guess I'll load 'em in the morning," he said. "You needn't wait fer me. I'll tie 'em up alone."

"Oh, I don't mind," she replied, feeling a little touched by his unexpectedly easy acquiescence to her request. When they went back to the house the moon had risen.

It had scarcely set when they were wakened by the crowing roosters. The man rolled stiffly out of bed and began rattling at the stove in the dark, cold kitchen.

His wife arose lamer and stiffer than usual, and began twisting her thin hair into a knot.

Sam did not stop to wash, but went out to the barn. The woman, however, hastily soused her face into the hard limestone water at the sink, and put the kettle on. Then she called the children. She knew it was early, and they would need several callings. She pushed breakfast forward, running over in her mind the things she must have: two spools of thread, six yards of cotton flannel, a can of coffee, and mittens for Kitty. These she must have— there were oceans of things she needed.

The children soon came scudding down out of the darkness of the upstairs to dress tumultuously at the kitchen stove. They humped and shivered, holding up their bare feet from the cold floor, like chickens in new fallen snow. They were irritable, and snarled and snapped and struck like cats and dogs. Mrs. Markham stood it for a while with mere commands to "hush up," but at last her patience gave out, and

she charged down on the struggling mob and cuffed them right and left.

They ate their breakfast by lamplight, and when Sam went back to his work around the barnyard it was scarcely dawn. The children, left alone with their mother, began to tease her to let them go to town also.

"No, sir—nobody goes but the baby. Your father's goin' to take a load of wheat."

She was weak with the worry of it all when she had sent the older children away to school and the kitchen work was finished. She went into the cold bedroom off the little sitting room and put on her best dress. It had never been a good fit, and now she was getting so thin it hung in wrinkled folds everywhere about the shoulders and waist. She lay down on the bed a moment to ease that dull pain in her back. She had a moment's distaste for going out at all. The thought of sleep was more alluring. Then she thought of the long, long day, and the sickening sameness of her life swept over her again, and she rose and prepared the baby for the journey.

It was but little after sunrise when Sam drove out into the road and started for Belleplaine. His wife sat perched upon the wheat sacks behind him holding the baby in her lap, a cotton quilt under her, and a cotton horse blanket over her knees.

Sam was disposed to be very good-natured, and he talked back at her occasionally, though she could only understand him when he turned his face toward her. The baby stared out at the passing fence posts, and wiggled his hands out of his mittens at every opportunity. He was merry at least.

It grew warmer as they went on, and a strong south wind arose. The dust settled upon the woman's shawl and hat. Her hair loosened and blew unkemptly about her face. The road which led across the high, level prairie was quite smooth and dry, but still it jolted her, and the pain in her back increased. She had nothing to lean against, and the weight of the child grew greater,

till she was forced to place him on the sacks beside her, though she could not loose her hold for a moment.

The town drew in sight—a cluster of small frame houses and stores on the dry prairie beside a railway station. There were no trees yet which could be called shade trees. The pitilessly severe light of the sun flooded everything. A few teams were hitched about, and in the lee of the stores a few men could be seen seated comfortably, their broad hat-rims flopping up and down, their faces brown as leather.

Markham put his wife out at one of the grocery stores, and drove off down toward the elevators to sell his wheat.

The grocer greeted Mrs. Markham in a perfunctorily kind manner, and offered her a chair, which she took gratefully. She sat for a quarter of an hour almost without moving, leaning against the back of the high chair. At last the child began to get restless and troublesome, and she spent half an hour helping him amuse himself around the nail-kegs.

At length she rose and went out on the walk, carrying the baby. She went into the dry-goods store and took a seat on one of the little revolving stools. A woman was buying some woollen goods for a dress. It was worth twenty-seven cents a yard the clerk said, but he would knock off two cents if she took ten yards. It looked warm, and Mrs. Markham wished she could afford it for Mary.

A pretty young girl came in and laughed and chatted with the clerk, and bought a pair of gloves. She was the daughter of the grocer. Her happiness made the wife and mother sad. When Sam came back she asked him for some money.

"What you want to do with it?" he asked.

"I want to spend it," she said.

She was not to be trifled with, so he gave her a dollar.

"I need a dollar more."

"Well, I've got to go take up that note at the bank."

"Well, the children's got to have some new underclo'es," she said.

He handed her a two-dollar bill and then went out to pay his note.

She bought her cotton flannel and mittens and thread, and then sat leaning against the counter. It was noon, and she was hungry. She went out to the wagon, got the lunch she had brought, and took it into the grocery to eat it—where she could get a drink of water.

The grocer gave the baby a stick of candy and handed the mother an apple.

"It'll kind o' go down with your dough-nuts," he said.

After eating her lunch she got up and went out. She felt ashamed to sit there any longer. She entered another dry-goods store, but when the clerk came toward her saying, "Anything today, Mrs.—?" she an-swered, "No, I guess not," and turned away with foolish face.

She walked up and down the street, desolately homeless. She did not know what to do with herself. She knew no one except the grocer. She grew bitter as she saw a couple of ladies pass, holding their demitrains [1] in the latest city fashion. An-other woman went by pushing a baby car-riage, in which sat a child just about as big as her own. It was bouncing itself up and down on the long slender springs, and laughing and shouting. Its clean round face glowed from its pretty fringed hood. She looked down at the dusty clothes and grimy face of her own little one, and walked on savagely.

She went into the drug store where the soda fountain was, but it made her thirsty to sit there and she went out on the street again. She heard Sam laugh, and saw him in a group of men over by the blacksmith shop. He was having a good time and had forgotten her.

Her back ached so intolerably that she concluded to go in and rest once more in the grocer's chair. The baby was growing cross and fretful. She bought five cents worth of candy to take home to the chil-dren, and gave baby a little piece to keep him quiet. She wished Sam would come. It must be getting late. The grocer said it was not much after one. Time seemed ter-ribly long. She felt that she ought to do something while she was in town. She ran over her purchases—yes, that was all she had planned to buy. She fell to figuring on the things she needed. It was terrible. It ran away up into twenty or thirty dollars at the least. Sam, as well as she, needed

underwear for the cold weather, but they would have to wear the old ones, even if they were thin and ragged. She would not need a dress, she thought bitterly, because she never went anywhere. She rose and went out on the street once more, and wandered up and down, looking at every-thing in the hope of enjoying something.

A man from Boone Creek backed a load of apples up to the sidewalk, and as he stood waiting for the grocer he noticed Mrs. Markham and the baby, and gave the baby an apple. This was a pleasure. He had such a hearty way about him. He on his part saw an ordinary farmer's wife, with dusty dress, unkempt hair, and tired face. He did not know exactly why she appealed to him, but he tried to cheer her up.

The grocer was familiar with these be-draggled and weary wives. He was accus-tomed to see them sit for hours in his big wooden chair, and nurse tired and fretful children. Their forlorn, aimless, pathetic wandering up and down the street was a daily occurrence, and had never possessed any special meaning to him.

---

[1] *demitrains,* short trains on ladies' dresses of the late nineteenth century

In a cottage around the corner from the grocery store two men and a woman were finishing a dainty luncheon. The woman was dressed in cool, white garments, and she seemed to make the day one of perfect comfort.

The home of the Honorable Mr. Hall was by no means the costliest in the town, but his wife made it the most attractive. He was one of the leading lawyers of the county, and a man of culture and progressive views. He was entertaining a friend who had lectured the night before in the Congregational church.

They were by no means in serious discussion. The talk was rather frivolous. Hall had the ability to caricature men with a few gestures and attitudes, and was giving to his Eastern friend some descriptions of the old-fashioned western lawyers he had met in his practice. He was very amusing, and his guest laughed heartily for a time.

But suddenly Hall became aware that Otis was not listening. Then he perceived that he was peering out of the window at some one, and that on his face a look of bitter sadness was falling.

Hall stopped. "What do you see, Otis?"

Otis replied, "I see a forlorn, weary woman."

Mrs. Hall rose and went to the window. Mrs. Markham was walking by the house, her baby in her arms. Savage anger and weeping were in her eyes and on her lips, and there was hopeless tragedy in her shambling walk and weak back.

In the silence Otis went on: "I saw the poor, dejected creature twice this morning. I couldn't forget her."

"Who is she?" asked Mrs. Hall, very softly.

"Her name is Markham; she's Sam Markham's wife," said Hall.

The young wife led the way into the sitting room, and the men took seats and lit their cigars. Hall was meditating a diversion when Otis resumed suddenly:

"That woman came to town today to get a change, to have a little play-spell, and she's wandering around like a starved and weary cat. I wonder if there is a woman in this town with sympathy enough and courage enough to go out and help that woman? The saloon-keepers, the politicians, and the grocers make it pleasant for the man—so pleasant that he forgets his wife. But the wife is left without a word."

Mrs. Hall's work dropped, and on her pretty face was a look of pain. The man's harsh words had wounded her—and wakened her. She took up her hat and hurried out on the walk. The men looked at each other, and then the husband said:

"It's going to be a little sultry for the men around these diggings. Suppose we go out for a walk."

Delia Markham felt a hand on her arm as she stood at the corner.

"You look tired, Mrs. Markham; won't you come in a little while? I'm Mrs. Hall."

Mrs. Markham turned with a scowl on her face and a biting word on her tongue, but something in the sweet, round little face of the other woman silenced her, and her brow smoothed out.

"Thank you kindly, but it's most time to go home. I'm looking fer Mr. Markham now."

"Oh, come in a little while, the baby is cross and tired out; please do."

Mrs. Markham yielded to the friendly voice, and together the two women reached the gate just as two men hurriedly turned the other corner.

"Let me relieve you," said Mrs. Hall.

The mother hesitated, "He's so dusty."

"Oh, that won't matter. Oh, what a big fellow he is! I haven't any of my own," said Mrs. Hall, and a look passed like an electric spark between the two women, and Delia was her willing guest from that moment.

They went into the little sitting room, so dainty and lovely to the farmer's wife, and as she sank into an easy-chair she was faint and drowsy with the pleasure of it. She submitted to being brushed. She gave the baby into the hands of the Swedish girl, who washed its face and hands and sang it to sleep, while its mother sipped some tea. Through it all she lay back in her easy-chair, not speaking a word, while the ache passed out of her back, and her hot, swollen head ceased to throb.

But she saw everything—the piano, the pictures, the curtains, the wallpaper, the little tea stand. They were almost as pleasing to her as the food and fragrant tea. Such housekeeping as this she had never seen. Her mother had worn her kitchen floor thin as brown paper in keeping a speckless house, and she had been in houses that were larger and costlier, but something of the charm of her hostess was in the arrangement of vases, chairs, or pictures. It was tasteful.

Mrs. Hall did not ask about her affairs. She talked to her about the sturdy little baby, and about the things upon which Delia's eyes dwelt. If she seemed interested in a vase, she was told what it was and where it was made. She was shown all the pictures and books. Mrs. Hall seemed to read her visitor's mind. She kept as far from the farm and her guest's affairs as possible, and at last she opened the piano and sang to her—not slow-moving hymns, but catchy love songs full of sentiment, and then played some simple melodies, knowing that Mrs. Markham's eyes were studying her hands, her rings, and the flash of her fingers on the keys—seeing more than she heard—and through

it all Mrs. Hall conveyed the impression that she, too, was having a good time.

The rattle of the wagon outside roused them both. Sam was at the gate for her. Mrs. Markham rose hastily. "Oh, it's almost sundown!" she gasped in astonishment as she looked out of the window.

"Oh, that won't kill anybody," replied her hostess, "Don't hurry. Carrie, take the baby out to the wagon for Mrs. Markham while I help her with her things."

"Oh, I've had such a good time," Mrs. Markham said as they went down the little walk.

"So have I," replied Mrs. Hall. She took the baby a moment as her guest climbed in. "O, you big, fat fellow!" she cried as she gave him a squeeze. "You must bring your wife in oftener, Mr. Markham," she said, as she handed the baby up.

Sam was staring with amazement.

"Thank you, I will," he finally managed to say.

"Good-night," said Mrs. Markham.

"Good-night, dear," called Mrs. Hall, and the wagon began to rattle off.

The tenderness and sympathy in her voice brought the tears to Delia's eyes, not hot, bitter tears, but tears that cooled her eyes and cleared her mind.

The wind had gone down, and the red sunlight fell mistily over the world of corn and stubble. The crickets were still chirping and the feeding cattle were drifting toward the farm-yards. The day had been made beautiful by human sympathy.

The man who wrote this story

HAMLIN GARLAND   1860–1940

Hamlin Garland won an important position in American literature by simply describing life on a Middle West farm as honestly as he knew it. This was not an easy task. When Garland began to write,

it was very difficult for an author to find a publisher if he wrote about the more "common" aspects of life. Work, especially hard manual labor, was looked upon as "common."

In stories and books, Garland told of the toil, the emptiness, and the heartbreak of a poor Midwest farmer and his family. Critics cried out against this "destructiveness."

All Garland had done was to tell the truth as he saw it, but many people were not yet ready for that truth. They believed literature must be genteel; it was something to be enjoyed in the privacy of one's library after a cup of tea. It was not supposed to offend in any way. Garland rebelled against this false confinement, and his rebellion was successful.

Today, Hamlin Garland is often looked upon as rather conservative, yet he helped to make possible the freedom of expression that one finds in modern literature.

Let's consider . . .

1. Hamlin Garland's stories about the prairie farmers and their wives in the 1870's are as *photographically true* as he could make them. He was the "camera" recording life as he saw it. From this story select three pictures which impressed you because they left no doubt in your mind of their *truth*. What did you find disheartening in them?

2. What part of the farmer's life, as it was pictured here, would you consider the hardest? What part would be the hardest for his wife?

3. On the day Mrs. Markham went to town, it was a *man* who suggested the action which made the day a pleasure for her. What did he realize that had gone unnoticed by others? From your own experience, or from your reading, cite other examples of a man's sensitiveness to a stranger's needs.

4. What was it that Delia Markham needed most that day? In what ways was her need satisfied?

5. Do you feel that this day's pleasure would make Mrs. Markham's daily routine harder or easier to endure? Defend your opinion.

6. In his autobiography, Garland described his early life on a Dakota farm.

When he told about his parents, he seemed to show more sympathy for his mother than for his father. If you were asked to judge from this story only, would you say that men or women had the more difficult struggle? Support your answer by specific references to incidents in the story.

The writer's craft . . .

Realism in literature is the objective portrayal of life as the author sees it. It attempts a selective but truthful record of human experience. The realistic writer does not glamorize life by seeing only the good, nor does he distort it by seeing only the bad. He interprets life as objectively as he can. In selecting people to write about, he does not turn to the great heroic figures of the past. Rather, he finds a wealth of material for his stories in the everyday lives of contemporary people.

1. Explain why "A Day's Pleasure" is a realistic story.

2. The dialogue in realistic fiction has the quality of seeming natural and true to life. Select examples of dialogue in "A Day's Pleasure" which are realistic.

3. In the author's handling of the setting, the characters, the incidents—even the climax of the story—it was almost as though he were saying to the reader, "This is how it was." Now examine the style in which this story was written. Notice the author's choice of words and their arrangement. Notice also the sentence structure: simple sentences and compound sentences which keep the meaning direct and clear. Explain how this style set the tone for the story and why it was effective.

4. If this story had been written from a romantic point of view, which incidents would have been omitted? What kinds of details might have been added by a romantic writer in his portrayal of character or in his choice of incidents?

The Cop and the Anthem

O. HENRY

So long as the nights were warm and the days remained sunny and bright, Soapy wasn't too concerned about having no home and very little money. New York was a big city and he could always get by. But when the leaves began to fall and wild geese honked high, Soapy began to stir uneasily on his favorite park bench.

When O. Henry was writing about New York and characters like Soapy he was at his best. More than any other author of his period, he popularized the short story by adapting it to a wider audience than it had ever known before. Today only a few of his many stories are still read, but they are important because they illustrate O. Henry's method of handling plot and his crisp, journalistic style.

On his bench in Madison Square Soapy moved uneasily. When wild geese honk high of nights, and when women without sealskin coats grow kind to their husbands, and when Soapy moves uneasily on his bench in the park, you may know that winter is near at hand.

A dead leaf fell in Soapy's lap. That was Jack Frost's card. Jack is kind to the regular denizens of Madison Square, and gives fair warning of his annual call. At the corners of four streets he hands his pasteboard to the North Wind, footman of the mansion of All Outdoors, so that the inhabitants thereof may make ready.

Soapy's mind became cognizant of the fact that the time had come for him to resolve himself into a singular Committee of Ways and Means to provide against the coming rigor. And therefore he moved uneasily on his bench.

The hibernatorial ambitions of Soapy were not of the highest. In them were no considerations of Mediterranean cruises, of soporific Southern skies or drifting in the Vesuvian Bay.[1] Three months on the Island was what his soul craved. Three months of assured board and bed and congenial company, safe from Boreas [2] and bluecoats, seemed to Soapy the essence of things desirable.

For years the hospitable Blackwell's [3] had been his winter quarters. Just as his more fortunate fellow New Yorkers had bought their tickets to Palm Beach and the Riviera each winter, so Soapy had made his humble arrangements for his annual hegira [4] to the Island. And now the time was come. On the previous night three Sabbath newspapers, distributed beneath his coat, about his ankles and over his lap, had failed to

---

[1] *Vesuvian Bay*, the bay of Naples, near the volcano Vesuvius

[2] *Boreas*, a personification of the north wind, from Greek mythology

[3] *Blackwell's*, Blackwell's Island, formerly the site of the city prison for New York

[4] *hegira*, a flight, from the flight of Mohammed from Mecca

repulse the cold as he slept on his bench near the spurting fountain in the ancient square. So the Island loomed big and timely in Soapy's mind. He scorned the provisions made in the name of charity for the city's dependents. In Soapy's opinion the Law was more benign than Philanthropy. There was an endless round of institutions, municipal and eleemosynary,[5] on which he might set out and receive lodging and food accordant with the simple life. But to one of Soapy's proud spirit the gifts of charity are encumbered. If not in coin you must pay in humiliation of spirit for every benefit received at the hands of philanthropy. As Caesar had his Brutus, every bed of charity must have its toll of a bath, every loaf of bread its compensation of a private and personal inquisition. Wherefore it is better to be a guest of the law, which, though conducted by rules, does not meddle unduly with a gentleman's private affairs.

Soapy, having decided to go to the Island, at once set about accomplishing his desire. There were many easy ways of doing this. The pleasantest was to dine luxuriously at some expensive restaurant; and then, after declaring insolvency, be handed over quietly and without uproar to a policeman. An accommodating magistrate would do the rest.

Soapy left his bench and strolled out of the square and across the level sea of asphalt, where Broadway and Fifth Avenue flow together. Up Broadway he turned, and halted at a glittering café, where are gathered together nightly the choicest products of the grape, the silkworm, and the protoplasm.

Soapy had confidence in himself from the lowest button of his vest upward. He was shaven, and his coat was decent and his neat black, ready-tied four-in-hand had been presented to him by a lady missionary on Thanksgiving Day. If he could reach a table in the restaurant unsuspected, success would be his. The portion of him that would show above the table would raise no doubt in the waiter's mind. A roasted mallard duck, thought Soapy, would be about the thing—with a bottle of Chablis,[6] and then Camembert,[7] a demitasse, and a cigar. One dollar for the cigar would be enough. The total would not be so high as to call forth any supreme manifestation of revenge from the café management; and yet the meat would leave him filled and happy for the journey to his winter refuge.

But as Soapy set foot inside the restaurant door the head waiter's eye fell upon his frayed trousers and decadent shoes. Strong and ready hands turned him about and conveyed him in silence and haste to the sidewalk and averted the ignoble fate of the menaced mallard.

Soapy turned off Broadway. It seemed that his route to the coveted Island was not to be an epicurean one. Some other way of entering limbo must be thought of.

At a corner of Sixth Avenue electric lights and cunningly displayed wares behind plate glass made a shop window conspicuous. Soapy took a cobblestone and dashed it through the glass. People came running around the corner, a policeman in the lead. Soapy stood still, with his hands in his pockets, and smiled at the sight of brass buttons.

"Where's the man that done that?" inquired the officer, excitedly.

"Don't you figure out that I might have had something to do with it?" said Soapy, not without sarcasm, but friendly, as one greets good fortune.

The policeman's mind refused to accept Soapy even as a clue. Men who smash windows do not remain to parley with the law's minions. They take to their heels. The policeman saw a man halfway down the block running to catch a car. With drawn club he joined in the pursuit. Soapy, with disgust in his heart, loafed along, twice unsuccessful.

On the opposite side of the street was a

---

[6] *Chablis,* a white Burgundy wine
[7] *Camembert,* a rich, soft cheese

[5] *eleemosynary,* pertaining to charity

restaurant of no great pretensions. It catered to large appetites and modest purses. Its crockery and atmosphere were thick; its soup and napery thin. Into this place Soapy took his accusive shoes and telltale trousers without challenge. At a table he sat and consumed beefsteak, flapjacks, doughnuts, and pie. And then to the waiter he betrayed the fact that the minutest coin and himself were strangers.

"Now, get busy and call a cop," said Soapy. "And don't keep a gentleman waiting."

"No cop for youse," said the waiter, with a voice like butter cakes and an eye like the cherry in a Manhattan cocktail. "Hey, Con!"

Neatly upon his left ear on the callous pavement two waiters pitched Soapy. He arose joint by joint, as a carpenter's rule opens, and beat the dust from his clothes. Arrest seemed but a rosy dream. The Island seemed very far away. A policeman who stood before a drugstore two doors away laughed and walked down the street.

Five blocks Soapy travelled before his courage permitted him to woo capture again. This time the opportunity presented what he fatuously termed to himself a "cinch." A young woman of a modest and pleasing guise was standing before

a show window gazing with sprightly interest at its display of shaving mugs and inkstands, and two yards from the window a large policeman of severe demeanor leaned against a water plug.

It was Soapy's design to assume the role of the despicable and execrated "masher." The refined and elegant appearance of his victim and the contiguity of the conscientious cop encouraged him to believe that he would soon feel the pleasant official clutch upon his arm that would insure his winter quarters on the right little, tight little isle.

Soapy straightened the lady missionary's ready-made tie, dragged his shrinking cuffs into the open, set his hat at a killing cant, and sidled toward the young woman. He made eyes at her, was taken with sudden coughs and "hems," smiled, smirked, and went brazenly through the impudent and contemptible litany of the "masher." With half an eye Soapy saw that the policeman was watching him fixedly. The young woman moved away a few steps, and again bestowed her absorbed attention upon the shaving mugs. Soapy followed, boldly stepping to her side, raised his hat, and said:

"Ah there, Bedelia! don't you want to come and play in my yard?"

The policeman was still looking. The persecuted young woman had but to beckon a finger and Soapy would be practically en route for his insular haven. Already he imagined he could feel the cozy warmth of the station house. The young woman faced him and, stretching out a hand, caught Soapy's coat sleeve.

"Sure, Mike," she said, joyfully, "if you'll blow me to a pail of suds. I'd have spoke to you sooner, but the cop was watching."

With the young woman playing the clinging ivy to his oak Soapy walked past the policeman overcome with gloom. He seemed doomed to liberty.

At the next corner he shook off his companion and ran. He halted in the district where by night are found the lightest streets, hearts, vows, and librettos. Women in furs and men in greatcoats moved gaily in the wintry air. A sudden fear seized Soapy that some dreadful enchantment had rendered him immune to arrest. The thought brought a little of panic upon it, and when he came upon another policeman lounging grandly in front of a transplendent theatre he caught at the immediate straw of "disorderly conduct."

On the sidewalk Soapy began to yell drunken gibberish at the top of his harsh voice. He danced, howled, raved, and otherwise disturbed the welkin.[8]

The policeman twirled his club, turned his back to Soapy, and remarked to a citizen.

" 'Tis one of them Yale lads celebratin' the goose egg they give to the Hartford College. Noisy; but no harm. We've instructions to lave them be."

Disconsolate, Soapy ceased his unavailing racket. Would never a policeman lay hands on him? In his fancy the Island seemed an unattainable Arcadia. He buttoned his thin coat against the chilling wind. In a cigar store he saw a well-dressed man lighting a cigar at a swinging light. His silk umbrella he had set by the door on entering. Soapy stepped inside, secured the umbrella, and sauntered off with it slowly. The man at the cigar light followed hastily.

"My umbrella," he said sternly.

"Oh, is it?" sneered Soapy, adding insult to petit larceny.[9] "Well, why don't you call a policeman? I took it. Your umbrella! Why don't you call a cop? There stands one on the corner."

The umbrella owner slowed his steps. Soapy did likewise, with a presentiment that luck would again run against him. The policeman looked at the two curiously.

"Of course," said the umbrella man— "that is—well, you know how these mis-takes occur—I—if it's your umbrella I hope you'll excuse me—I picked it up this morning in a restaurant—if you recognize it as yours, why—I hope you'll—"

"Of course it's mine," said Soapy, viciously.

The ex-umbrella man retreated. The policeman hurried to assist a tall blonde in an opera cloak across the street in front of a street car that was approaching two blocks away.

Soapy walked eastward through a street damaged by improvements. He hurled the umbrella wrathfully into an excavation. He muttered against the men who wear helmets and carry clubs. Because he wanted to fall into their clutches, they seemed to regard him as a king who could do no wrong.

---

[8] *welkin,* the sky

[9] *petit larceny,* theft of articles of small value; as distinguished from *grand larceny*

At length Soapy reached one of the avenues to the east where the glitter and turmoil was but faint. He set his face down this toward Madison Square, for the homing instinct survives even when the home is a park bench.

But on an unusually quiet corner Soapy came to a standstill. Here was an old church, quaint and rambling and gabled. Through one violet-stained window a soft light glowed, where, no doubt, the organist loitered over the keys, making sure of his mastery of the coming Sabbath anthem. For there drifted out to Soapy's ears sweet music that caught and held him transfixed against the convolutions of the iron fence.

The moon was above, lustrous and serene; vehicles and pedestrians were few; sparrows twittered sleepily in the eaves—for a little while the scene might have been a country churchyard. And the anthem that the organist played cemented Soapy to the iron fence, for he had known it well in the days when his life contained such things as mothers and roses and ambitions and friends and immaculate thoughts and collars.

The conjunction of Soapy's receptive state of mind and the influences about the old church wrought a sudden and wonderful change in his soul. He viewed with swift horror the pit into which he had tumbled, the degraded days, unworthy desires, dead hopes, wrecked faculties, and base motives that made up his existence.

And also in a moment his heart responded thrillingly to this novel mood. An instantaneous and strong impulse moved him to battle with his desperate fate. He would pull himself out of the mire; he would make a man of himself again; he would conquer the evil that had taken possession of him. There was time; he was comparatively young yet; he would resurrect his old eager ambitions and pursue them without faltering. Those solemn but sweet organ notes had set up a revolution in him. Tomorrow he would go into the roaring downtown district and find work. A fur importer had once offered him a place as driver. He would find him tomorrow and ask for the position. He would be somebody in the world. He would—

Soapy felt a hand laid on his arm. He looked quickly around into the broad face of a policeman.

"What are you doin' here?" asked the officer.

"Nothin'," said Soapy.

"Then come along," said the policeman.

"Three months on the Island," said the Magistrate in the Police Court the next morning.

The man who wrote this story

O. HENRY
(William Sydney Porter) 1862–1910

One of America's most popular authors got his start in prison. O. Henry, the pen name that William Porter adopted while in prison, had a personal life that was as interesting and exciting as any of his stories. He had worked in a slip-shod bank in Austin, Texas. After the bank was investigated by the government, it was found that some money was missing. Porter was called to trial for embezzlement, but he caught a train to New Orleans. For a year he toured South America with a pair of American bandits, but he returned to Texas when he learned that his wife was ill. He was arrested after her death and served three years in a Federal prison. (It is still a much argued question whether O. Henry was actually guilty.)

While in prison, O. Henry found plenty of free time to write. His stories proved so successful that by the time he left prison editors were vying for him to come to New York. He soon settled in that city, and made it the scene for some of his best stories.

O. Henry contributed one special trick to the art of short story writing that is still frequently imitated. This is the "O. Henry" or "surprise" ending, a sudden twist or turn of events at the end of a story which catches the reader unawares.

Let's consider . . .

1. "Three months on the Island was what Soapy's soul craved." Why did he wish to go to Blackwell's Island? How do you explain his inability to be comfortable anywhere else in winter?

2. Why did Soapy consider the law as being more kindly than charity?

3. Once Soapy had decided to spend the winter on the Island, he planned systematically to tangle with the law. Explain how each of his attempts to get arrested failed.

4. Even men like Soapy have better instincts which are sometimes awakened by poignant memories. What change came over him when the anthem reminded him of better days?

5. In what ways were Soapy's final arrest and sentence particularly ironical? (A situation is **ironical** if it comes out just the opposite from what was intended.)

6. If you tried as hard as Soapy to get arrested, you would probably succeed. How did O. Henry make Soapy's failures seem plausible?

7. Do you expect to remember Soapy for a long time? Why or why not?

The writer's craft . . .

In most of his stories, O. Henry was more interested in evolving a clever plot than in creating believable characters. In fact, the characters are frequently overshadowed by the incidents and events which he has planned so carefully in order to achieve his famous **surprise ending:** a turn of events quite unexpected on the basis of what has gone before.

1. Look back again at "The Cop and the Anthem." List the incidents and events which led to the surprise ending. What did each of these reveal about the character of Soapy? How, and why, did he seem "overshadowed"? Would you have felt more concerned over his welfare if the author had given you a deeper understanding of Soapy as a person?

2. What was the "surprise" at the end of the story? Was it believable? Give several reasons to support your answer.

3. Try your hand at writing a story with a surprise ending. Be sure to save the surprise until the very end. Here are a few suggested titles:

The Unexpected Guest Empty Pockets
A Blind Date   Mistaken Identity

Knowing words . . .

In each of the following sentences, one word is printed in italics. When you are sure of the meaning of the italicized word, use it in a sentence of your own.

1. Jack is kind to the regular *denizens* of Madison Square, and gives fair warning of his annual call.

2. Soapy's mind became *cognizant* of the fact that the time had come.

3. The *hibernatorial* ambitions of Soapy were not of the highest.

4. The pleasantest was to dine luxuriously at some expensive restaurant; and then, after declaring *insolvency,* be handed over quietly and without uproar to a policeman.

5. The total would not be so high as to call forth any supreme *manifestations* of revenge from the cafe management.

6. It seemed that his route to the coveted Island was not to be an *epicurean* one.

7. Men who smash windows do not remain to *parley* with the law's minions.

8. *Disconsolate,* Soapy ceased his unavailing racket.

All Gold Canyon

JACK LONDON

Writers of short stories have unlimited scope in their selection of materials, but few of them have surpassed Jack London in his vivid description of nature and in his creation of characters of unusual strength and courage.

It was the green heart of the canyon, where the walls swerved back from the rigid plan and relieved their harshness of line by making a little sheltered nook and filling it to the brim with sweetness and roundness and softness. Here all things rested. Even the narrow stream ceased its turbulent down-rush long enough to form a quiet pool. Knee-deep in the water, with drooping head and half-shut eyes, drowsed a red-coated, many-antlered buck.

On one side, beginning at the very lip of the pool, was a tiny meadow, a cool, resilient surface of green that extended to the base of the frowning wall. Beyond the pool a gentle slope of earth ran up and up to meet the opposing wall. Fine grass covered the slope—grass that was spangled with flowers, with here and there patches of color, orange and purple and golden. Below, the canyon was shut in. There was no view. The walls leaned together abruptly and the canyon ended in a chaos of rocks, moss-covered and hidden by a green screen of vines and creepers and boughs of trees. Up the canyon rose far hills and peaks, the big foothills, pine-covered and remote. And far beyond, like clouds upon the border of the sky, towered minarets[1] of white, where the Sierra's eternal snows flashed austerely the blazes of the sun.

There was no dust in the canyon. The leaves and flowers were clean and virginal. The grass was young velvet. Over the pool three cottonwoods sent their snowy fluffs fluttering down the quiet air. On the slope the blossoms of the wine-wooded manzanita filled the air with springtime odors, while the leaves, wise with experience, were already beginning their vertical twist against the coming aridity of summer. In the open spaces on the slope, beyond the farthest shadow-reach of the manzanita, poised the mariposa lilies, like so many flights of jewelled moths suddenly arrested and on the verge of trembling into flight again. Here and there that woods harlequin, the madrone,[2] permitting itself to be caught in the act of changing its pea-green trunk to madder-red, breathed its fragrance into the air from great clusters of waxen bells. Creamy white were these bells, shaped like lilies-of-the-valley, with the sweetness of perfume that is of the springtime.

There was not a sigh of wind. The air was drowsy with its weight of perfume. It was a sweetness that would have been cloying had the air been heavy and humid. But the air was sharp and thin. It was as starlight transmuted into atmosphere, shot through and warmed by sunshine, and flower-drenched with sweetness.

[1] *minarets,* peaks resembling the slender towers attached to Mohammedan mosques

[2] *madrone,* an evergreen shrub of western North America

An occasional butterfly drifted in and out through the patches of light and shade. And from all about rose the low and sleepy hum of mountain bees—feasting Sybarites [3] that jostled one another good-naturedly at the board, nor found time for rough discourtesy. So quietly did the little stream drip and ripple its way through the canyon that it spoke only in faint and occasional gurgles. The voice of the stream was as a drowsy whisper, ever interrupted by dozings and silences, ever lifted again in the awakenings.

The motion of all things was a drifting in the heart of the canyon. Sunshine and butterflies drifted in and out among the trees. The hum of the bees and the whisper of the stream were a drifting of sound. And the drifting sound and drifting color seemed to weave together in the making of a delicate and intangible fabric which was the spirit of the place. It was a spirit of peace that was not of death, but of smooth-pulsing life, of quietude that was not silence, of movement that was not action, of repose that was quick with existence without being violent with struggle and travail. The spirit of the place was the spirit of the peace of the living, somnolent with the easement and content of prosperity, and undisturbed by rumors of far wars.

The red-coated, many-antlered buck acknowledged the lordship of the spirit of the place and dozed knee-deep in the cool, shaded pool. There seemed no flies to vex him and he was languid with rest. Sometimes his ears moved when the stream awoke and whispered; but they moved lazily, with foreknowledge that it was merely the stream grown garrulous at discovery that it had slept.

But there came a time when the buck's ears lifted and tensed with swift eagerness for sound. His head was turned down the canyon. His sensitive, quivering nostrils scented the air. His eyes could not pierce the green screen through which the stream rippled away, but to his ears came the voice of a man. It was a steady, monotonous, singsong voice. Once the buck heard the harsh clash of metal upon rock. At the sound he snorted with a sudden start that jerked him through the air from water to meadow, and his feet sank into the young velvet, while he pricked his ears and again scented the air. Then he stole across the tiny meadow, pausing once and again to listen, and faded away out of the canyon like a wraith, soft-footed and without sound.

The clash of steel-shod soles against the rocks began to be heard, and the man's voice grew louder. It was raised in a sort of a chant and became distinct with nearness, so that the words could be heard:

"Tu'n around an' tu'n yo' face
  Untoe them sweet hills of grace
    (D' pow'rs of sin yo' am scornin'!).
  Look about an' look aroun'
  Fling yo' sin-pack on d' groun'
    (Yo' will meet wid d' Lord in d'
      mornin'!)."

A sound of scrambling accompanied the song, and the spirit of the place fled away on the heels of the red-coated buck. The green screen was burst asunder, and a man peered out at the meadow and the pool and the sloping side-hill. He was a deliberate sort of man. He took in the scene with one embracing glance, then ran his eyes over the details to verify the general impression. Then, and not until then, did he open his mouth in vivid and solemn approval:

"Smoke of life an' snakes of purgatory! Will you just look at that! Wood an' water an' grass an' a side-hill! A pocket-hunter's [4] delight an' a cayuse's [5] paradise! Cool green for tired eyes! Pink pills for pale people ain't in it. A secret pasture for prospectors and a resting-place for tired burros. It's just boofull!"

He was a sandy-complexioned man in whose face geniality and humor seemed

---

[3] *Sybarites,* devotees of pleasure and soft-living

[4] *pocket-hunter,* one who hunts for small deposits of gold

[5] *cayuse,* an Indian pony

the salient characteristics. It was a mobile face, quick-changing to inward mood and thought. Thinking was in him a visible process. Ideas chased across his face like wind-flaws across the surface of a lake. His hair, sparse and unkempt of growth, was as indeterminate and colorless as his complexion. It would seem that all the color of his frame had gone into his eyes, for they were startlingly blue. Also, they were laughing and merry eyes, within them much of the naiveté and wonder of the child; and yet, in an unassertive way, they contained much of calm self-reliance and strength of purpose founded upon self-experience and experience of the world.

From out the screen of vines and creepers, he flung ahead of him a miner's pick and shovel and gold-pan. Then he crawled out himself into the open. He was clad in faded overalls and black cotton shirt, with hobnailed brogans on his feet, and on his head a hat whose shapelessness and stains advertised the rough usage of wind and rain and sun and camp-smoke. He stood erect, seeing wide-eyed the secrecy of the scene and sensuously inhaling the warm, sweet breath of the canyon-garden through nostrils that dilated and quivered with delight. His eyes narrowed to laughing slits of blue, his face wreathed itself in joy, and his mouth curled in a smile as he cried aloud:

"Jumping dandelions and happy hollyhocks, but that smells good to me! Talk about your attar o' roses an' cologne factories! They ain't in it!"

He had the habit of soliloquy. His quick-changing facial expressions might tell every thought and mood, but the tongue, perforce, ran hard after, repeating, like a second Boswell.[6]

The man lay down on the lip of the pool and drank long and deep of its water. "Tastes good to me," he murmured, lifting his head and gazing across the pool at the

side-hill, while he wiped his mouth with the back of his hand. The side-hill attracted his attention. Still lying on his stomach, he studied the hill formation long and carefully. It was a practised eye that traveled up the slope to the crumbling canyon-wall and back and down again to the edge of the pool. He scrambled to his feet and favored the side-hill with a second survey.

"Looks good to me," he concluded, picking up his pick and shovel and gold-pan.

He crossed the stream below the pool, stepping agilely from stone to stone. Where the side-hill touched the water he dug up a shovelful of dirt and put it into the gold-pan. He squatted down, holding the pan in his two hands, and partly immersed it in the stream. Then he imparted to the pan a deft circular motion that sent the water sluicing in and out through the dirt and gravel. The larger and the lighter particles worked to the surface, and these, by a skilful dipping movement of the pan, he spilled out and over the edge. Occasionally, to expedite matters, he rested the pan and with his fingers raked out the large pebbles and pieces of rock.

The contents of the pan diminished rapidly until only fine dirt and the smallest bits of gravel remained. At this stage he began to work very deliberately and carefully. It was fine washing, and he washed fine and finer, with a keen scrutiny and delicate and fastidious touch. At last the pan seemed empty of everything but water; but with a quick semi-circular flirt that sent the water flying over the shallow rim into the stream, he disclosed a layer of black sand on the bottom of the pan. So thin was this layer that it was like a streak of paint. He examined it closely. In the midst of it was a tiny golden speck. He dribbled a little water in over the depressed edge of the pan. With a quick flirt he sent the water sluicing across the bottom, turning the grains of black sand over and over. A second tiny golden speck rewarded his effort.

[6] *Boswell,* James Boswell, the famed biographer of Dr. Samuel Johnson. He kept complete records of almost all Dr. Johnson said or did.

The washing had now become very fine —fine beyond all need of ordinary placer-mining. He worked the black sand, a small portion at a time, up the shallow rim of the pan. Each small portion he examined sharply, so that his eyes saw every grain of it before he allowed it to slide over the edge and away. Jealously, bit by bit, he let the black sand slip away. A golden speck, no larger than a pin-point, appeared on the rim and by his manipulation of the water it returned to the bottom of the pan. And in such fashion another speck was disclosed, and another. Great was his care of them. Like a shepherd he herded his flock of golden specks so that not one should be lost. At last, of the pan of dirt nothing remained but his golden herd. He counted it, and then, after all his labor, sent it flying out of the pan with one final swirl of water.

But his blue eyes were shining with desire as he rose to his feet. "Seven," he muttered aloud, asserting the sum of the specks for which he had toiled so hard and which he had so wantonly thrown away. "Seven," he repeated, with the emphasis of one trying to impress a number on his memory.

He stood still a long while, surveying the hillside. In his eyes was a curiosity, new-aroused and burning. There was an exultance about his bearing and a keenness like that of a hunting animal catching the fresh scent of game.

He moved down the stream a few steps and took a second handful of dirt.

Again came the careful washing, the jealous herding of the golden specks, and the wantonness with which he sent them flying into the stream. His golden herds diminished. "Four, five," he muttered and repeated, "five."

He could not forbear another survey of the hill before filling the pan farther down the stream. His golden herds diminished. "Four, three, two, two, one," was his memory tabulation as he moved down the stream. When but one speck of gold rewarded his washing, he stopped and built a fire of dry twigs. Into this he thrust the gold-pan and burned it till it was blue-black. He held up the pan and examined it critically. Then he nodded approbation. Against such a color-background he could defy the tiniest yellow speck to elude him.

Still moving down the stream, he panned again. A single speck was his reward. A third pan contained no gold at all. Not satisfied with this, he panned three times again, taking his shovels of

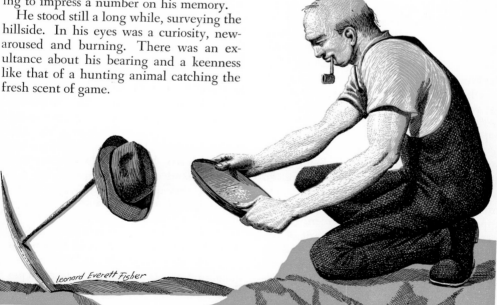

Leonard Everett Fisher

dirt within a foot of one another. Each pan proved empty of gold, and the fact, instead of discouraging him, seemed to give him satisfaction. His elation increased with each barren washing, until he arose, exclaiming jubilantly:

"If it ain't the real thing, may God knock off my head with sour apples!"

Returning to where he had started operations, he began to pan up the stream. At first his golden herds increased—increased prodigiously. "Fourteen, eighteen, twenty-one, twenty-six," ran his memory tabulation. Just above the pool he struck his richest pan—thirty-five colors.

"Almost enough to save," he remarked regretfully as he allowed the water to sweep them away.

The sun climbed to the top of the sky. The man worked on. Pan by pan, he went up the stream, the tally of results steadily decreasing.

"It's just booful, the way it peters out," he exulted when a shovelful of dirt contained no more than a single speck of gold.

And when no specks at all were found in several pans, he straightened up and favored the hillside with a confident glance.

"Ah, ha! Mr. Pocket!" he cried out, as though to an auditor hidden somewhere above him beneath the surface of the slope. "Ah, ha! Mr. Pocket! I'm a-comin', I'm a-comin', an' I'm shorely gwine to get yer! You heah me, Mr. Pocket? I'm gwine to get yer as shore as punkins ain't cauliflowers!"

He turned and flung a measuring glance at the sun poised above him in the azure of the cloudless sky. Then he went down the canyon, following the line of shovel-holes he had made in filling the pans. He crossed the stream below the pool and disappeared through the green screen. There was little opportunity for the spirit of the place to return with its quietude and repose, for the man's voice, raised in ragtime song, still dominated the canyon with possession.

After a time, with a greater clashing of steel-shod feet on rock, he returned. The green screen was tremendously agitated. It surged back and forth in the throes of a struggle. There was a loud grating and clanging of metal. The man's voice leaped to a higher pitch and was sharp with imperativeness. A large body plunged and panted. There was a snapping and ripping and rending, and amid a shower of falling leaves a horse burst through the screen. On its back was a pack, and from this trailed broken vines and torn creepers. The animal gazed with astonished eyes at the scene into which it had been precipitated, then dropped its head to the grass and began contentedly to graze. A second horse scrambled into view, slipping once on the mossy rocks and regaining equilibrium when its hoofs sank into the yielding surface of the meadow. It was riderless, though on its back was a high-horned Mexican saddle, scarred and discolored by long usage.

The man brought up the rear. He threw off pack and saddle, with an eye to camp location, and gave the animals their freedom to graze. He unpacked his food and got out frying-pan and coffee-pot. He gathered an armful of dry wood, and with a few stones made a place for his fire.

"My!" he said, "but I've got an appetite. I could scoff iron-filings an' horseshoe nails an' thank you kindly, ma'am, for a second helpin'."

He straightened up, and while he reached for matches in the pocket of his overalls, his eyes traveled across the pool to the side-hill. His fingers had clutched the match-box, but they relaxed their hold and the hand came out empty. The man wavered perceptibly. He looked at his preparations for cooking and he looked at the hill.

"Guess I'll take another whack at her," he concluded, starting to cross the stream.

"They ain't no sense in it, I know," he mumbled apologetically. "But keepin' grub back an hour ain't goin' to hurt none, I reckon."

A few feet back from his first line of test-pans he started a second line. The sun dropped down the western sky, the shadows lengthened, but the man worked on. He began a third line of test-pans. He was cross-cutting the hillside, line by line, as he ascended. The center of each line produced the richest pans, while the ends came where no colors showed in the pan. And as he ascended the hillside the lines grew perceptibly shorter. The regularity with which their length diminished served to indicate that somewhere up the slope the last line would be so short as to have scarcely length at all, and that beyond could come only a point. The design was growing into an inverted "V." The converging sides of this "V" marked the boundaries of the gold-bearing dirt.

The apex of the "V" was evidently the man's goal. Often he ran his eye along the converging sides and on up the hill, trying to divine the apex, the point where the gold-bearing dirt must cease. Here resided "Mr. Pocket"—for so the man familiarly addressed the imaginary point above him on the slope, crying out:

"Come down out o' that, Mr. Pocket! Be right smart an' agreeable an' come down!"

"All right," he would add later, in a voice resigned to determination. "All right, Mr. Pocket. It's plain to me I got to come right up an' snatch you out bald-headed. An' I'll do it! I'll do it!" he would threaten still later.

Each pan he carried down to the water to wash, and as he went higher up the hill the pans grew richer, until he began to save the gold in an empty baking-powder can which he carried carelessly in his hip-pocket. So engrossed was he in his toil that he did not notice the long twilight of oncoming night. It was not until he tried vainly to see the gold colors in the bottom of the pan that he realized the passage of time. He straightened up abruptly. An expression of whimsical wonderment and awe overspread his face as he drawled:

"Gosh darn my buttons! if I didn't plumb forget dinner!"

He stumbled across the stream in the darkness and lighted his long-delayed fire. Flap-jacks and bacon and warmed-over beans constituted his supper. Then he smoked a pipe by the smouldering coals, listening to the night noises and watching the moonlight stream through the canyon. After that he unrolled his bed, took off his heavy shoes, and pulled the blankets up to his chin. His face showed white in the moonlight, like the face of a corpse. But it was a corpse that knew its resurrection, for the man rose suddenly on one elbow and gazed across at his hillside.

"Good night, Mr. Pocket," he called sleepily. "Good night."

He slept through the early gray of morning until the direct rays of the sun smote his closed eyelids, when he awoke with a start and looked about him until he had established the continuity of his existence and identified his present self with the days previously lived.

To dress, he had merely to buckle on his shoes. He glanced at his fireplace and at his hillside, wavered, but fought down the temptation and started the fire.

"Keep yer shirt on, Bill; keep yer shirt on," he admonished himself. "What's the good of rushin'? No use in gettin' all het up an' sweaty. Mr. Pocket'll wait for you. He ain't a-runnin' away before you can get your breakfast. Now, what you want, Bill, is something fresh in yer bill o' fare. So it's up to you to go an' get it."

He cut a short pole at the water's edge and drew from one of his pockets a bit of line and a draggled fly that had once been a royal coachman.

"Mebbe they'll bite in the early morning," he muttered, as he made his first cast into the pool. And a moment later he was gleefully crying: "What'd I tell you, eh? What'd I tell you?"

He had no reel, nor any inclination to waste time, and by main strength, and swiftly, he drew out of the water a flashing ten-inch trout. Three more, caught in rapid succession, furnished his breakfast. When he came to the stepping-stones on his way to his hillside, he was struck by a sudden thought, and paused.

"I'd just better take a hike down-stream a ways," he said. "There's no tellin' who may be snoopin' around."

But he crossed over on the stones, and with a "I really oughter take that hike," the need of the precaution passed out of his mind and he fell to work.

At nightfall he straightened up. The small of his back was stiff from stooping toil and as he put his hand behind him to soothe the protesting muscles, he said:

"Now what d'ye think of that? I clean forgot my dinner again! If I don't watch out, I'll sure be degeneratin' into a two-meal-a-day crank."

"Pockets is the hangedest things I ever see for makin' a man absent-minded," he communed that night, as he crawled into his blankets. Nor did he forget to call up the hillside, "Good night, Mr. Pocket! Good night!"

Rising with the sun, and snatching a hasty breakfast, he was early at work. A fever seemed to be growing in him, nor did the increasing richness of the test-pans allay this fever. There was a flush in his cheek other than that made by the heat of the sun, and he was oblivious to fatigue and the passage of time. When he filled a pan with dirt, he ran down the hill to wash it; nor could he forbear running up the hill again, panting and stumbling profanely, to refill the pan.

He was now a hundred yards from the water, and the inverted "V" was assuming definite proportions. The width of the pay-dirt steadily decreased, and the man extended in his mind's eye the sides of the "V" to their meeting place far up the hill. This was his goal, the apex of the "V," and he panned many times to locate it.

"Just about two yards above that manzanita bush an' a yard to the right," he finally concluded.

Then the temptation seized him. "As plain as the nose on your face," he said, as he abandoned his laborious cross-cutting and climbed to the indicated apex. He filled a pan and carried it down the hill to wash. It contained no trace of gold. He dug deep, and he dug shallow, filling and washing a dozen pans, and was unrewarded even by the tiniest golden speck. He was enraged at having yielded to the temptation, and berated himself blasphemously and pridelessly. Then he went down the hill and took up the cross-cutting.

"Slow an' certain, Bill; slow an' certain," he crooned. "Shortcuts to fortune ain't in your line, an' it's about time you know it. Get wise, Bill; get wise. Slow an' certain's the only hand you can play; so go to it, an' keep to it, too."

As the cross-cuts decreased, showing that the sides of the "V" were converging, the depth of the "V" increased. The gold-trace was dipping into the hill. It was only at thirty inches beneath the surface that he could get colors in his pan. The dirt he found at twenty-five inches from the surface, and at thirty-five inches yielded barren pans. At the base of the "V," by the water's edge, he had found the gold colors at the grass roots. The higher he went up the hill, the deeper the gold dipped. To dig a hole three feet deep in order to get one test-pan was a task of no mean magnitude; while between the man and the apex intervened an untold number of such holes to be dug. "An' there's no tellin' how much deeper it'll pitch," he sighed, in a moment's pause, while his fingers soothed his aching back.

Feverish with desire, with aching back and stiffening muscles, with pick and shovel gouging and mauling the soft brown earth, the man toiled up the hill. Before him was the smooth slope, spangled with flowers and made sweet with their breath. Behind him was devastation. It looked like some terrible eruption breaking out on the smooth skin of the hill. His slow progress was like that of a slug, befouling beauty with a monstrous trail.

Though the dipping gold-trace increased the man's work, he found consolation in the increasing richness of the pans. Twenty cents, thirty cents, fifty cents, sixty cents, were the values of the gold found in the pans, and at nightfall he washed his banner pan, which gave him a dollar's worth of gold-dust from a shovelful of dirt.

"I'll just bet it's my luck to have some inquisitive one come buttin' in here on my pasture," he mumbled sleepily that night as he pulled the blankets up to his chin.

Suddenly he sat upright. "Bill!" he called sharply. "Now listen to me, Bill; d'ye hear! It's up to you to-morrow mornin' to mosey round an' see what you can see. Understand? To-morrow morning, an' don't you forget it!"

He yawned and glanced across at his side-hill. "Good night, Mr. Pocket," he called.

In the morning he stole a march on the sun, for he had finished breakfast when its first rays caught him, and he was climbing the wall of the canyon where it crumbled away and gave footing. From the outlook at the top he found himself in the midst of loneliness. As far as he could see, chain after chain of mountains heaved themselves into his vision. To the east his eyes, leaping the miles between range and range and between many ranges, brought up at last against the white-peaked Sierras—the main crest, where the backbone of the Western world reared itself against the sky. To the north and south he could see more distinctly the cross-systems that broke through the main trend of the sea of mountains. To the west the ranges fell away, one behind the other, diminishing and fading into the gentle foothills that, in turn, descended into the great valley which he could not see.

And in all that mighty sweep of earth he saw no sign of man nor of the handiwork of man—save only the torn bosom of the hillside at his feet. The man looked long and carefully. Once, far down his own canyon, he thought he saw in the air a faint hint of smoke. He looked again and decided that it was the purple haze of the hills made dark by a convolution of the canyon wall at its back.

"Hey, you, Mr. Pocket!" He called down into the canyon. "Stand out from under! I'm a-comin', Mr. Pocket! I'm a-comin'!"

The heavy brogans on the man's feet made him appear clumsy-footed, but he swung down from the giddy height as lightly and airily as a mountain goat. A rock, turning under his foot on the edge of the precipice, did not disconcert him. He seemed to know the precise time required for the turn to culminate in disaster, and in the meantime he utilized the false footing itself for the momentary earth-contact necessary to carry him on into safety. Where the earth sloped so steeply that it was impossible to stand for a second upright, the man did not hesitate. His foot impressed the impossible surface for but a fraction of the fatal second and gave him the bound that carried him onward. Again, where even the fraction of a second's footing was out of the question, he would swing his body past by a moment's handgrip on a jutting knob of rock, a crevice, or a precariously rooted shrub. At last, with a wild leap and yell, he exchanged the face of the wall for an earthslide and finished the descent in the midst of several tons of sliding earth and gravel.

His first pan of the morning washed out over two dollars in coarse gold. It was from the center of the "V." To either side the diminution in the values of the pans were swift. His lines of cross-cutting holes were growing very short. The converging sides of the inverted "V" were only a few yards apart. Their meeting-point was only a few yards above him. But the pay-streak was dipping deeper and deeper into the earth. By early afternoon he was sinking the test-holes five feet before the pans could show the gold-trace.

For that matter, the gold-trace had become something more than a trace; it was a placer mine, in itself, and the man resolved to come back after he had found the pocket and work over the ground. But the increasing richness of the pans began to worry him. By late afternoon the worth of the pans had grown to three and four dollars. The man scratched his head perplexedly and looked a few feet up the hill at the manzanita bush that marked approximately the apex of the "V." He nodded his head and said oracularly:

"It's one o' two things, Bill: one o' two things. Either Mr. Pocket's spilled himself all out an' down the hill, or else Mr. Pocket's so rich you maybe won't be able to carry him all away with you. And that'd be an awful shame, wouldn't it, now?" He chuckled at contemplation of so pleasant a dilemma.

Nightfall found him by the edge of the stream, his eyes wrestling with the gathering darkness over the washing of a five-dollar pan.

"Wisht I had an electric light to go on working," he said.

He found sleep difficult that night. Many times he composed himself and closed his eyes for slumber to overtake him; but his blood pounded with too strong desire, and as many times his eyes opened he murmured wearily, "Wisht it was sun-up."

Sleep came to him in the end, but his eyes were open with the first paling of the stars, and the gray of dawn caught him with breakfast finished and climbing the hillside in the direction of the secret abiding-place of Mr. Pocket.

The first cross-cut the man made, there was space for only three holes, so narrow had become the pay-streak and so close was he to the fountainhead of the golden stream he had been following for four days.

"Be ca'm, Bill; be ca'm," he admonished

himself, as he broke ground for the final hole where the sides of the "V" had at last come together in a point.

"I've got the almighty cinch on you, Mr. Pocket, an' you can't lose me," he said many times as he sank the hole deeper and deeper.

Four feet, five feet, six feet, he dug his way down into the earth. The digging grew harder. His pick grated on broken rock. He examined the rock. "Rotten quartz," was his conclusion as, with the shovel, he cleared the bottom of the hole of loose dirt. He attacked the crumbling quartz with the pick, bursting the disintegrating rock asunder with every stroke.

He thrust his shovel into the loose mass. His eye caught a gleam of yellow. He dropped the shovel and squatted suddenly on his heels. As a farmer rubs the clinging earth from fresh-dug potatoes, so the man, a piece of rotten quartz held in both hands, rubbed the dirt away.

"Sufferin' Sardanopolis!" he cried. "Lumps an' chunks of it! Lumps an' chunks of it!"

It was only half rock he held in his hand. The other half was virgin gold. He dropped it into his pan and examined another piece. Little yellow was to be seen, but with his strong fingers he crumbled the rotten quartz away till both hands were filled with glowing yellow. He rubbed the dirt away from fragment after fragment, tossing them into the gold-pan. It was a treasure-hole. So much had the quartz rotted away that there was less of it than there was of gold. Now and again he found a piece to which no rock clung—a piece that was all gold. A chunk, where the pick had laid open the heart of the gold, glittered like a handful of yellow jewels, and he cocked his head at it and slowly turned it around and over to observe the rich play of the light upon it.

"Talk about yer Too Much Gold diggin's!" the man snorted contemptuously. "Why, this diggin' 'd make it look like thirty cents. This diggin' is All Gold. An' right here an' now I name this yere canyon 'All Gold Canyon,' b' gosh!"

Still squatting on his heels, he continued examining the fragments and tossing them into the pan. Suddenly there came to him a premonition of danger. It seemed a shadow had fallen upon him. But there was no shadow. His heart had given a great jump up into his throat and was choking him. Then his blood slowly chilled and he felt the sweat of his shirt cold against his flesh.

He did not spring up nor look around. He did not move. He was considering the nature of the premonition he had received, trying to locate the source of the mysterious force that had warned him, striving to sense the imperative presence of the unseen thing that threatened him. There is an aura of things hostile, made manifest by messengers too refined for the senses to know; and this aura he felt, but knew not how he felt it. His was the feeling as when a cloud passes over the sun. It seemed that between him and life had passed something dark and smothering and menacing; a gloom, as it were, that swallowed up life and made for death—his death.

Every force of his being impelled him to spring up and confront the unseen danger, but his soul dominated the panic, and he remained squatting on his heels, in his hands a chunk of gold. He did not dare to look around, but he knew by now that there was something behind him and above him. He made believe to be interested in the gold in his hand. He examined it critically, turned it over and over, and rubbed the dirt from it. And all the time he knew that something behind him was looking at the gold over his shoulder.

Still feigning interest in the chunk of gold in his hand, he listened intently and he heard the breathing of the thing behind him. His eyes searched the ground in front of him for a weapon, but they saw only the uprooted gold worthless to him now in his extremity. There was his pick, a handy

weapon on occasion; but this was not such an occasion. The man realized his predicament. He was in a narrow hole that was seven feet deep. His head did not come to the surface of the ground. He was in a trap.

He remained squatting on his heels. He was quite cool and collected; but his mind, considering every factor, showed him only his helplessness. He continued rubbing the dirt from the quartz fragments and throwing the gold into the pan. There was nothing else for him to do. Yet he knew that he would have to rise up sooner or later, and face the danger that breathed at his back. The minutes passed, and with the passage of each minute he knew that by so much he was nearer the time when he must stand up, or else—and his wet shirt went cold against his flesh again at the thought—or else he might receive death as he stooped there over his treasure.

Still he squatted on his heels, rubbing dirt from gold and debating in just what manner he should rise up. He might rise up with a rush and claw his way out of the hole to meet whatever threatened on the even footing above the ground. Or he might rise up slowly and carelessly, and feign casually to discover the thing that breathed at his back. His instinct and every fighting fibre of his body favored the mad, clawing rush to the surface. His intellect, and the craft thereof, favored the slow and cautious meeting with the thing that menaced and which he could not see. And while he debated, a loud, crashing noise burst on his ear. At the same instant he received a stunning blow on the left side of the back, and from the point of impact felt a rush of flame through his flesh. He sprang up in the air, but halfway to his feet collapsed. His body crumpled in like a leaf withered in sudden heat, and he came down, his chest across his pan of gold, his face in the dirt and rock, his legs tangled and twisted because of the restricted space at the bottom of the hole. His legs twitched convulsively several times. His body was shaken as with a mighty ague. There was a slow expansion of the lungs, accompanied by a deep sigh. Then the air was slowly, very slowly, exhaled, and his body as slowly flattened itself down into inertness.

Above, revolver in hand, a man was peering down over the edge of the hole. He peered for a long time at the prone and motionless body beneath him. After a while the stranger sat down on the edge of the hole so that he could see into it, and rested the revolver on his knee. Reaching his hand into a pocket, he drew out a wisp of brown paper. Into this he dropped a few crumbs of tobacco. The combination became a cigarette, brown and squat, with the ends turned in. Not once did he take his eyes from the body at the bottom of the hole. He lighted the cigarette and drew its smoke into his lungs with a caressing intake of the breath. He smoked slowly. Once the cigarette went out and he relighted it. And all the while he studied the body beneath him.

In the end he tossed the cigarette stub away and rose to his feet. He moved to the edge of the hole. Spanning it, a hand resting on each edge, and with the revolver still in the right hand, he muscled his body down into the hole. While his feet were yet a yard from the bottom he released his hands and dropped down.

At the instant his feet struck bottom he saw the pocket-miner's arm leap out, and his own legs knew a swift, jerking grip that overthrew him. In the nature of the jump his revolver-hand was above his head. Swiftly as the grip had flashed about his legs, just as swiftly he brought the revolver down. He was still in the air, his fall in process of completion, when he pulled the trigger. The explosion was deafening in the confined space. The smoke filled the hole so that he could see nothing. He struck the bottom on his back, and like a cat's the pocket-miner's body was on top of him. Even as the miner's body passed on top, the stranger crooked in his right arm to fire; and even in that instant the miner,

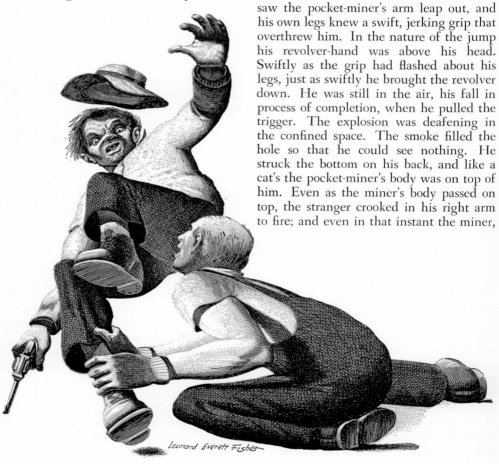

Leonard Everett Fisher

with a quick thrust of elbow, struck his wrist. The muzzle was thrown up and the bullet thudded into the dirt of the side of the hole.

The next instant the stranger felt the miner's hand grip his wrist. The struggle was now for the revolver. Each man strove to turn it against the other's body. The smoke in the hole was clearing. The stranger, lying on his back, was beginning to see dimly. But suddenly he was blinded by a handful of dirt deliberately flung into his eyes by his antagonist. In that moment of shock his grip on the revolver was broken. In the next moment he felt a smashing darkness descend upon his brain, and in the midst of the darkness even the darkness ceased.

But the pocket-miner fired again and again, until the revolver was empty. Then he tossed it from him and, breathing heavily, sat down on the dead man's legs.

The miner was sobbing and struggling for breath. "Measly skunk!" he panted; "a-campin' on my trail an' lettin' me do the work, an' then shootin' me in the back!"

He was half crying from anger and exhaustion. He peered at the face of the dead man. It was sprinkled with loose dirt and gravel, and it was difficult to distinguish the features.

"Never laid eyes on him before," the miner concluded his scrutiny. "Just a common an' ordinary thief, hang him! An' he shot me in the back! He shot me in the back!"

He opened his shirt and felt himself, front and back, on his left side.

"Went clean through, and no harm done!" he cried jubilantly. "I'll bet he aimed all right all right; but he drew the gun over when he pulled the trigger—the cur! But I fixed 'm! Oh, I fixed 'm!"

His fingers were investigating the bullet-hole in his side, and a shade of regret passed over his face. "It's goin' to be stiffer'n the devil," he said. "An' it's up to me to get mended an' get out o' here."

He crawled out of the hole and went down the hill to his camp. Half an hour later he returned, leading his pack-horse. His open shirt disclosed the rude bandages with which he had dressed his wound. He was slow and awkward with his left-hand movements, but that did not prevent his using the arm.

The bight of the pack-rope under the dead man's shoulders enabled him to heave the body out of the hole. Then he set to work gathering up his gold. He worked steadily for several hours, pausing often to rest his stiffening shoulder and to exclaim:

"He shot me in the back, the measly skunk! He shot me in the back!"

When his treasure was quite cleaned up and wrapped securely into a number of blanket-covered parcels, he made an estimate of its value.

"Four hundred pounds, or I'm a Hottentot," [7] he concluded. "Say two hundred in quartz an' dirt—that leaves two hundred pounds of gold. Bill! Wake up! Two hundred pounds of gold! Forty thousand dollars! An' it's yourn—all yourn!"

He scratched his head delightedly and his fingers blundered into an unfamiliar groove. They quested along it for several inches. It was a crease through his scalp where the second bullet had ploughed.

He walked angrily over to the dead man.

"You would, would you?" he bullied. "You would, eh? Well, I fixed you good an' plenty, an' I'll give you decent burial, too. That's more'n you'd have done for me."

He dragged the body to the edge of the hole and toppled it in. It struck the bottom with a dull crash, on its side, the face twisted up to the light. The miner peered down at it.

"An' you shot me in the back!" he said accusingly.

With pick and shovel he filled the hole. Then he loaded the gold on his horse. It was too great a load for the animal, and when he had gained his camp he trans-

[7] *Hottentot,* a South African native

ferred part of it to his saddle-horse. Even so, he was compelled to abandon a portion of his outfit—pick and shovel and gold-pan, extra food and cooking utensils, and divers odds and ends.

The sun was at the zenith when the man forced the horses at the screen of vines and creepers. To climb the huge boulders the animals were compelled to uprear and struggle blindly through the tangled mass of vegetation. Once the saddle-horse fell heavily and the man removed the pack to get the animal on its feet. After it started on its way again the man thrust his head out from among the leaves and peered up at the hillside.

"The measly skunk!" he said, and disappeared.

There was a ripping and tearing of vines and boughs. The trees surged back and forth, marking the passage of the animals through the midst of them. There was a clashing of steel-shod hoofs on stone, and now and again a sharp cry of command.

Then the voice of the man was raised in song:

"Tu'n around an' tu'n yo' face
  Untoe them sweet hills of grace
    (D' pow'rs of sin yo' am scornin'!).
  Look about an' look aroun'
  Fling yo' sin-pack on d' groun'
    (Yo' will meet wid d' Lord in d' mornin'!)."

The song grew fainter and fainter, and through the silence crept back the spirit of the place. The stream once more drowsed and whispered; the hum of the mountain bees rose sleepily. Down through the perfume-weighted air fluttered the snowy fluffs of the cottonwoods. The butterflies drifted in and out among the trees, and over all blazed the quiet sunshine. Only remained the hoofmarks in the meadow and the torn hillside to mark the boisterous trail of the life that had broken the peace of the place and passed on.

The man who wrote this story

JACK LONDON   1876–1916

Few authors have ever had as great a popular success as Jack London. During his writing years, dozens of novels, stories, and articles flowed from his pen. By 1913 he could claim that he was the best-known and the highest paid author in the world.

London simply told for his readers the story of his life and experiences. And his life had been an interesting one. He had been an oyster pirate before he reached sixteen. He had been a deep-water sailor, a tramp, and a prospector in Alaska during the Klondike Gold Rush. As a correspondent during the Russo-Japanese War, he had learned of war at first hand. These experiences provided the materials for many of his stories.

Because he was so popular, London was forced to write swiftly in order to keep up with the demand. Some of his writing, therefore, is far inferior to his best work. But for such great stories as *The Call of the Wild* and *The Sea Wolf*, Jack London is still remembered as one of America's best adventure writers.

Let's consider . . .

1. London summarized his description of the heart of the canyon with these words: "The spirit of the place was the spirit of the peace of living." What details in the first part of the story created this impression?

2. What made "the spirit of the place" flee on the heels of the buck? Look again at the description of the intruder and at what he said and did. Condense into not more than five sentences those essential

characteristics of his appearance and personality which a movie director would need to know if he were choosing an actor for this part.

3. Explain the way the miner discovered "Mr. Pocket." How do you explain his intense excitement—"the fever" that grew in him?

4. Why did he have to warn himself about "shortcuts to fortune"?

5. What persistent worry hounded him while he worked? How did he put his mind at rest?

6. Describe his elation at finding the treasure hole and his opposite reaction to the premonition of danger.

7. What plan did the miner devise for outwitting his assailant? How did he arrive at this plan? Why did he pretend he didn't know of the danger that threatened?

8. Describe the struggle between the miner and the stranger. Why did the miner continue to fire even after there was no need? Why did he give the stranger a decent burial?

9. How did Jack London create suspense in this story?

10. How did London let you know what his character was thinking? Did you find this method natural?

11. If a story is to have **unity,** it must give the effect of being a harmonious whole. Explain why the ending of "All Gold Canyon" gave unity to the story.

The writer's craft . . .

1. Like most modern readers, you either enjoy long descriptive passages of the **locale** (the setting) of a story or you dislike them intensely. Few readers are neutral in their attitude. Explain your feelings about such passages in "All Gold Canyon." Be honest and be fair. Consider the importance of these passages to the story.

2. In this story, there was considerable **atmosphere:** the mood or feeling created by (1) the events, (2) the place, and (3) the situation. Which one of these three do you think contributed most to your feelings about the canyon and to the atmosphere of the story? Explain why. Point out instances in the story in which the other two also contributed to the atmosphere.

3. One critic has said that Jack London was noted for his **anti-sentimentalism:** his direct, unemotional way of presenting people and situations. Do you think this story is lacking in emotional appeal? Where in the story might the author have built up the sentiment more and so made a greater appeal to your sympathies?

4. If you think London remained impersonal in his handling of characters and situations, what was there about his writing which held your interest?

5. Part of the pleasure of this story was its vivid style: a style distinguished by its sharp images. Note in the first sentence the way London speaks of the "great heart" of the canyon and the walls that "swerved back." The grass of the meadow was "spangled with flowers"; the snow-capped peaks of the Sierra were "towered minarets of white." He also used images in his description of the miner: "Ideas chased themselves across his face like wind-flaws across the surface of a lake."

List six images from this selection which you especially liked and which illustrate London's vivid style. Read them aloud in class and compare your choices.

6. Was Jack London a realistic writer or a romantic writer? Explain. Consider both his choice of material and the way he treated it.

Ararat

ZENNA HENDERSON

A hundred years ago man dreamed of traveling to distant lands. Today he dreams of penetrating outer space and, in imagination, creates new worlds inhabited by living creatures. What are these creatures like? Will they prove to be friends or enemies? What would happen if some of them landed on the planet Earth?

Science fiction writers have found an almost unlimited source of material in the known facts and imagined fancies which surround man's dreams about outer space. From this material have come stories as fantastic and bizarre as any Poe or Hawthorne ever created. From it have also come stories of human tenderness and hope.

We've had trouble with teachers in Cougar Canyon. It's just an Accommodation school anyway, isolated and so unhandy to anything. There's really nothing to hold a teacher. But the way The People bring forth their young, in quantities and with regularity, even our small Group can usually muster the nine necessary for the County School Superintendent to arrange for the schooling for the year.

Of course I'm past school age, Canyon school age, and have been for years, but if the tally came up one short in the Fall, I'd go back for a post-graduate course again. But now I'm working on a college level because Father finished me off for my high school diploma two summers ago. He's promised me that if I do well this year I'll get to go Outside next year and get my training and degree so I can be the teacher and we won't have to go Outside for one any more. Most of the kids would just as soon skip school as not, but the Old Ones don't hold with ignorance and the Old Ones have the last say around here.

Father is the head of the school board. That's how I get in on lots of school things the other kids don't. This summer when he wrote to the County Seat that we'd have more than our nine again this fall and would they find a teacher for us, he got back a letter saying they had exhausted their supply of teachers who hadn't heard of Cougar Canyon and we'd have to dig up our own teacher this year.

Well, it's understandable, I suppose, that we might get such a reputation. There are apt to be shocks in the Canyon for Outsiders—unintentional as most of them are.

We haven't done so badly the last few years, though. The Old Ones say we're getting adjusted—though some of the nonconformists say that The Crossing thinned our blood. It might be either or both, but the fact remains that the last two teachers managed to last until just before the year ended.

Anyway, Father wrote to a Teachers Agency on the coast and after several letters each way, he finally found a teacher.

404

He told us about it at the supper table.

"She's rather young," he said, reaching for a toothpick and tipping his chair back on its hind legs.

Mother gave Jethro another helping of pie and picked up her own fork again. "Youth is no crime," she said, "and it'll be a pleasant change for the children."

"Yes, though it seems a shame." Father prodded at a back tooth and Mother frowned at him. I wasn't sure if it was for picking his teeth or for what he said. I knew he meant it seemed a shame to get a place like Cougar Canyon so early in a career. It isn't that we're mean or cruel, you understand. It's only that they're Outsiders and we sometimes forget—especially the kids.

"She doesn't *have* to come," said Mother. "She could say no."

"Well, now—" Father tipped his chair forward. "Jethro, no more pie. You go on out and help 'Kiah bring in the wood. Karen, you and Lizbeth get started on the dishes. Hop to it, kids."

And we hopped, too. Kids do to fathers in the Canyon, though I understand they don't always Outside. It annoyed me because I knew Father wanted us out of the way so he could talk adult talk to Mother, so I told Lizbeth I'd clear the table and then worked as slowly as I could, and as quietly, listening hard.

"She couldn't get any other job," said Father. "The agency told me they had placed her twice in the last two years and she didn't finish the year either place."

"Well," said Mother, pinching in her mouth and frowning. "If she's that bad, why on earth did you hire her for the Canyon?"

"We have a choice?" laughed Father. Then he sobered. "No, it wasn't for incompetency. She was a good teacher. The way she tells it, they just fired her out of a clear sky. She asked for recommendations and one place wrote, 'Miss Carmody is a very competent teacher but we dare not recommend her for a teaching position.'"

"'Dare not'?" asked Mother.

"'Dare not,'" said Father. "The Agency assured me that they had investigated thoroughly and couldn't find any valid reasons for the dismissals, but she can't seem to find another job anywhere on the coast. She wrote me that she wanted to try another state."

"Do you suppose she's disfigured or deformed?" suggested Mother.

"Not from the neck up!" laughed Father. He took an envelope from his pocket. "Here's her application picture."

By this time I'd got the table cleared and I leaned over Father's shoulder.

"Gee!" I said. Father looked back at me, raising one eyebrow. I knew then that he had known all along that I was listening.

I flushed but stood my ground, knowing I was being granted admission to adult affairs, if only by the back door.

The girl in the picture was lovely. She couldn't have been many years older than I and she was twice as pretty. She had short dark hair curled all over her head and apparently that poreless creamy skin that seems to have an inner light of itself. She had a tentative look about her as though her dark eyebrows were horizontal question marks. There was a droop to the corners of her mouth—not much, just enough to make you wonder why . . . and want to comfort her.

"She'll stir the Canyon for sure," said Father.

"I don't know," Mother frowned thoughtfully. "What will the Old Ones say to a marriageable Outsider in the Canyon?"

"Adonday Veeah!" muttered Father. "That never occurred to me. None of our other teachers were ever of an age to worry about."

"What *would* happen?" I asked. "I mean if one of The Group married an Outsider?"

"Impossible," said Father, so like the Old Ones that I could see why his name was approved in Meeting last Spring.

"Why, there's even our Jemmy," worried Mother. "Already he's saying he'll have to start trying to find another Group. None of the girls here please him. Supposing this Outsider—how old is she?"

Father unfolded the application. "Twenty-three," he said, "Just three years out of college."

"Jemmy's twenty-four," said Mother, pinching her mouth together. "Father, I'm afraid you'll have to cancel the contract. If anything happened—Well, you waited over-long to become an Old One to my way of thinking and it'd be a shame to have something go wrong your first year."

"I can't cancel the contract. She's on her way here. School starts next Monday." Father ruffled his hair forward as he does when he's disturbed. "We're probably making a something of a nothing," he said hopefully.

"Well, I only hope we don't have any trouble with this Outsider."

"Or she with us," grinned Father. "Where are my cigarettes?"

"On the book case," said Mother, getting up and folding the table cloth together to hold the crumbs.

Father snapped his fingers and the cigarettes drifted in from the front room.

Mother went on out to the kitchen. The table cloth shook itself over the waste basket and then followed her.

Father drove to Kerry Canyon Sunday night to pick up our new teacher. She was supposed to have arrived Saturday afternoon, but she didn't make bus connections at the County Seat. The road ends at Kerry Canyon. I mean for Outsiders. There's not much of the look of a well-traveled road very far out our way from Kerry Canyon, which is just as well. Tourists leave us alone. Of course we don't have much trouble getting our cars to and fro but that's why everything dead-ends at Kerry Canyon and we have to do all our own fetching and carrying—I mean the road being in the condition it is.

All the kids at our house wanted to stay up to see the new teacher, so Mother let them, but by 7:30 the youngest ones began to drop off and by 9 there was only Jethro and 'Kiah, Lizbeth and Jemmy and me. Father should have been home long before and Mother was restless and uneasy. I knew if he didn't arrive soon, she would head for her room and the cedar box under the bed. But at 9:15 we heard the car coughing and sneezing up the draw. Mother's wide relieved smile was reflected on all our faces.

"Of course!" she cried. "I forgot. He has an Outsider in the car. He had to use the *road* and it's terrible across Jackass Flat."

I felt Miss Carmody before she came in the door. I was tingling all over from anticipation already, but all at once I felt her, so plainly that I knew with a feeling of fear and pride that I was of my Grandmother, that soon I would be bearing the burden and blessing of her Gift: the Gift that develops into free access to any mind —one of The People or Outsider—willing or not. And besides the access, the ability to counsel and help, to straighten tangled minds and snarled emotions.

And then Miss Carmody stood in the doorway, blinking a little against the light, muffled to the chin against the brisk fall air. A bright scarf hid her hair but her skin *was* that luminous matt-cream it had looked. She was smiling a little, but scared, too. I shut my eyes and . . . I went in— just like that. It was the first time I had ever sorted anybody. She was all fluttery with tiredness and strangeness and there was a question deep inside her that had the wornness of repetition, but I couldn't catch what it was. And under the uncertainty there was a sweetness and dearness and such a bewildered sorrow that I felt my eyes dampen. Then I looked at her again (sorting takes such a little time) as Father introduced her. I heard a gasp beside me and suddenly I went into Jemmy's mind with a stunning rush.

Jemmy and I have been close all our lives and we don't always need words to talk with one another, but this was the first time I had ever gone in like this and I knew he didn't know what had happened. I felt embarrassed and ashamed to know his emotion so starkly. I closed him out as quickly as possible, but not before I knew that now Jemmy would never hunt for another Group; Old Ones or no Old Ones, he had found his love.

All this took less time than it takes to say "How do you do?" and shake hands. Mother descended with cries and drew Miss Carmody and Father out to the kitchen for coffee and Jemmy swatted Jethro and made him carry the luggage instead of snapping it to Miss Carmody's room. After all, we didn't want to lose our teacher before she even saw the schoolhouse.

I waited until everyone was bedded down. Miss Carmody in her cold, cold bed, the rest of us of course with our sheets set for warmth—how I pity Outsiders! Then I went to Mother.

She met me in the dark hall and we clung together as she comforted me.

"Oh Mother," I whispered. "I sorted Miss Carmody tonight. I'm afraid."

Mother held me tight again. "I wondered," she said. "It's a great responsibility. You have to be so wise and clear-thinking. Your Grandmother carried the Gift with graciousness and honor. You are of her. You can do it."

"But Mother! To be an Old One!"

Mother laughed. "You have years of training ahead of you before you'll be an Old One. Counselor to the soul is a weighty job."

"Do I have to tell?" I pleaded. "I don't want anyone to know yet. I don't want to be set apart."

"I'll tell the Oldest," she said, "No one else need know." She hugged me again and I went back, comforted, to bed.

I lay in the darkness and let my mind clear, not even knowing how I knew how to. Like the gentle reachings of quiet fingers I felt the family about me. I felt warm

and comfortable as though I were cupped in the hollow palm of a loving hand. Some day I would belong to the Group as I now belonged to the family. Belong to others? With an odd feeling of panic, I shut the family out. I wanted to be alone—to belong just to me and no one else. I didn't *want* the Gift.

I slept after a while.

Miss Carmody left for the schoolhouse an hour before we did. She wanted to get things started a little before school time, her late arrival making it kind of rough on her. 'Kiah, Jethro, Lizbeth and I walked down the lane to the Armisters' to pick up their three kids. The sky was so blue you could taste it, a winey, fallish taste of harvest fields and falling leaves. We were all feeling full of bubbly enthusiasm for the beginning of school. We were light-hearted and light-footed, too, as we kicked along through the cottonwood leaves paving the lane with gold. In fact Jethro felt too light-footed and the third time I hauled him down and made him walk on the ground, I cuffed him good. He was still sniffling when we got to Arminsters'.

"She's pretty!" called Lizbeth before the kids got out to the gate, all agog and eager for news of the new teacher.

"She's young," added 'Kiah, elbowing himself ahead of Lizbeth.

"She's littler'n me," sniffled Jethro and we all laughed because he's five-six already even if he isn't twelve yet.

Debra and Rachel Armister linked arms with Lizbeth and scuffled down the lane, heads together, absorbing the details of teacher's hair, dress, nail polish, luggage and night clothes, though goodness knows how Lizbeth knew anything about that.

Jethro and 'Kiah annexed Jeddy and they climbed up on the rail fence that parallels the lane and walked the top rail. Jethro took a tentative step or two above the rail, caught my eye and stepped back in a hurry. He knows as well as any child in the Canyon that a kid his age has no business lifting along a public road.

We detoured at the Mesa Road to pick up the Kroginold boys. More than once Father has sighed over the Kroginolds.

You see, when The Crossing was made, The People got separated in that last wild moment when air was screaming past and the heat was building up so alarmingly. The members of our Group left their ship just seconds before it crashed so devastatingly into the box canyon behind Old Baldy and literally splashed and drove itself into the canyon walls, starting a fire that stripped the hills bare for miles. After The People gathered themselves together from the Life Slips and founded Cougar Canyon, they found that the alloy the ship was made of was a metal much wanted here. Our Group has lived on mining the box canyon ever since, though there's something complicated about marketing the stuff. It has to be shipped out of the coun-

try and shipped in again because everyone knows that it doesn't occur in this region.

Anyway, our Group at Cougar Canyon is probably the largest of The People, but we are reasonably sure that at least one Group and maybe two survived along with us. Grandmother in her time sensed two Groups but could never locate them exactly and, since our object is to go unnoticed in this new life, no real effort has ever been made to find them. Father can remember just a little of The Crossing, but some of the Old Ones are blind and crippled from the heat and the terrible effort they put forth to save the others from burning up like falling stars.

But getting back, Father often said that of all The People who could have made up our Group, we had to get the Kroginolds. They're rebels and were even before The Crossing. It's their kids that have been so rough on our teachers. The rest of us usually behave fairly decently and remember that we have to be careful around Outsiders.

Derek and Jake Kroginold were wrestling in a pile of leaves by the front gate when we got there. They didn't even hear us coming, so I leaned over and whacked the nearest rear-end and they turned in a flurry of leaves and grinned up at me for all the world like pictures of Pan in the mythology book at home.

"What kinda old bat we got this time?" asked Derek as he scrabbled in the leaves for his lunch box.

"She's not an old bat," I retorted, madder than need be because Derek annoys me so. "She's young and beautiful."

"Yeh, I'll bet!" Jake emptied the leaves from his cap onto the trio of squealing girls.

"She is so!" retorted 'Kiah. "The nicest teacher we ever had."

"She won't teach me nothing!" yelled Derek, lifting to the top of the cottonwood tree at the turn-off.

"Well, if she won't, I will," I muttered and, reaching for a handful of sun, I platted the twishers so quickly that Derek fell like a rock. He yelled like a catamount, thinking he'd get killed for sure, but I stopped him about a foot from the ground and then let go. Well, the stopping and the thump to the ground pretty well jarred the wind out of him, but he yelled:

"I'll tell the Old Ones! You ain't supposed to platt twishers—!"

"Tell the Old Ones," I snapped, kicking on down the leafy road. "I'll be there and tell them why. And then, old smarty pants, what will be your excuse for lifting?"

And then I was ashamed. I was showing off as bad as a Kroginold—but they make me so mad!

Our last stop before school was at the Clarinades'. My heart always squeezed when I thought of the Clarinade twins. They just started school this year—two years behind the average Canyon kid. Mrs. Kroginold used to say that the two of them, Susie and Jerry, divided one brain between them before they were born. That's unkind and untrue—thoroughly a Kroginold remark—but it is true that by Canyon standards the twins were retarded. They lacked so many of the attributes of The People. Father said it might be a delayed effect of The Crossing that they would grow out of, or it might be advance notice of what our children will be like here—what is ahead for The People. It makes me shiver, wondering.

Susie and Jerry were waiting, clinging to one another's hand as they always were. They were shy and withdrawn, but both were radiant because of starting school. Jerry, who did almost all the talking for the two of them, answered our greetings with a shy "Hello."

Then Susie surprised us all by exclaiming, "We're going to school!"

"Isn't it wonderful?" I replied, gathering her cold little hand into mine. "And you're going to have the prettiest teacher we ever had."

But Susie had retired into blushing confusion and didn't say another word all the way to school.

I was worried about Jake and Derek. They were walking apart from us, whispering, looking over at us and laughing. They were cooking up some kind of mischief for Miss Carmody. And more than anything I wanted her to stay. I found right then that there *would* be years ahead of me before I became an Old One. I tried to go in to Derek and Jake to find out what was cooking, but try as I might I couldn't get past the sibilance of their snickers and the hard, flat brightness of their eyes.

We were turning off the road into the school yard when Jemmy, who should have been up at the mine long since, suddenly stepped out of the bushes in front of us, his hands behind him. He glared at Jake and Derek and then at the rest of the children.

"You kids mind your manners when you get to school," he snapped, scowling. "And you Kroginolds—just try anything funny and I'll lift you to Old Baldy and platt the twishers on you. This is one teacher we're going to keep."

Susie and Jerry clung together in speechless terror. The Kroginolds turned red and pushed out belligerent jaws. The rest of us just stared at a Jemmy who never raised his voice and never pushed his weight around.

"I mean it, Jake and Derek. You try getting out of line and the Old Ones will find a few answers they've been looking for—especially about the belfry in Kerry Canyon."

The Kroginolds exchanged looks of dismay and the girls sucked in breaths of astonishment. One of the most rigorously enforced rules of The Group concerns showing off outside the community. If Derek and Jake *had* been involved in ringing that bell all night last Fourth of July . . . well!

"Now you kids, scoot!" Jemmy jerked his head toward the schoolhouse and the terrified twins scudded down the leaf-strewn path like a pair of bright leaves themselves, followed by the rest of the children with the Kroginolds looking sullenly back over their shoulders and muttering.

Jemmy ducked his head and scowled. "It's time they got civilized anyway. There's no sense to our losing teachers all the time."

"No," I said noncommittally.

"There's no point in scaring her to death," Jemmy was intent on the leaves he was kicking with one foot.

"No," I agreed, suppressing my smile.

Then Jemmy smiled ruefully in amusement at himself. "I should waste words with you," he said. "Here." He took his hands from behind him and thrust a bouquet of burning bright autumn leaves into my arms. "They're from you to her," he said. "Something pretty for the first day."

"Oh, Jemmy!" I cried through the scarlet and crimson and gold. "They're beautiful. You've been up on Baldy this morning."

"That's right," he said. "But she won't know where they came from." And he was gone.

I hurried to catch up with the children before they got to the door. Suddenly overcome with shyness, they were milling around the porch steps, each trying to hide behind the others.

"Oh, for goodness' sakes!" I whispered to our kids. "You ate breakfast with her this morning. She won't bite. Go on in."

But I found myself shouldered to the front and leading the subdued group into the school room. While I was giving the bouquet of leaves to Miss Carmody, the others with the ease of established habit slid into their usual seats, leaving only the twins, stricken and white, standing alone.

Miss Carmody, dropping the leaves on her desk, knelt quickly beside them, pried a hand of each gently free from their frenzy clutching and held them in hers.

"I'm so glad you came to school," she said in her warm, rich voice. "I need a first grade to make the school work out

right and I have a seat that must have been built on purpose for twins."

And she led them over to the side of the room, close enough to the old pot-bellied stove for Outside comfort later and near enough to the window to see out. There, in dusted glory, stood one of the old double desks that The Group must have inherited from some ghost town out in the hills. There were two wooden boxes for footstools for small dangling feet and, spouting like a flame from the old ink well hole, a spray of vivid red leaves—matchmates to those Jemmy had given me.

The twins slid into the desk, never loosing hands, and stared up at Miss Carmody, wide-eyed. She smiled back at them and, leaning forward, poked her finger tip into the deep dimple in each round chin.

"Buried smiles," she said, and the two scared faces lighted up briefly with wavery smiles. Then Miss Carmody turned to the rest of us.

I never did hear her introductory words. I was too busy mulling over the spray of leaves, and how she came to know the identical routine, words and all, that the twins' mother used to make them smile, and how on earth she knew about the old desks in the shed. But by the time we rose to salute the flag and sing our morning song, I had it figured out. Father must have briefed her on the way home last night. The twins were an ever present concern of the whole Group and we were all especially anxious to have their first year a successful one. Also, Father knew the smile routine and where the old desks were stored. As for the spray of leaves, well, some did grow this low on the mountain and frost is tricky at leaf-turning time.

So school was launched and went along smoothly. Miss Carmody was a good teacher and even the Kroginolds found their studies interesting.

They hadn't tried any tricks since Jemmy threatened them. That is, except that silly deal with the chalk. Miss Carmody was explaining something on the board and was groping sideways for the chalk to add to the lesson. Jake was deliberately lifting the chalk every time she almost had it. I was just ready to do something about it when Miss Carmody snapped her fingers with annoyance and grasped the chalk firmly. Jake caught my eye about then and shrank about six inches in girth and height. I didn't tell Jemmy, but Jake's fear that I might kept him straight for a long time.

The twins were really blossoming. They laughed and played with the rest of the kids and Jerry even went off occasionally with the other boys at noontime, coming back as disheveled and wet as the others after a dam-building session in the creek.

Miss Carmody fitted so well into the community and was so well-liked by us kids that it began to look like we'd finally keep a teacher all year. Already she had withstood some of the shocks that had sent our other teachers screaming. For instance. . . .

The first time Susie got a robin redbreast sticker on her bookmark for reading a whole page—six lines—perfectly, she lifted all the way back to her seat, literally walking about four inches in the air. I held my breath until she sat down and was caressing the glossy sticker with one finger, then I sneaked a cautious look at Miss Carmody. She was sitting very erect, her hands clutching both ends of her desk as though in the act of rising, a look of incredulous surprise on her face. Then she relaxed, shook her head and smiled, and busied herself with some papers.

I let my breath out cautiously. The last teacher but two went into hysterics when one of the girls absent-mindedly lifted back to her seat because her sore foot hurt. I had hoped Miss Carmody was tougher—and apparently she was.

The same week, one noon hour, Jethro came pelting up to the schoolhouse where Valancy—that's her first name and I call her by it when we are alone, after all she's only four years older than I—was helping

me with that gruesome Tests and Measurements I was taking by extension from Teachers' College.

"Hey, Karen!" he yelled through the window. "Can you come out a minute?"

"Why?" I yelled back, annoyed at the interruption just when I was trying to figure what was normal about a normal grade curve.

"There's need," yelled Jethro.

I put down my book. "I'm sorry, Valancy. I'll go see what's eating him."

"Should I come too?" she asked. "If something's wrong—"

"It's probably just some silly thing," I said, edging out fast. When one of The People says "There's need," that means Group business.

"Adonday Veeah!" I muttered at Jethro as we rattled down the steep rocky path to the creek. "What are you trying to do? Get us all in trouble? What's the matter?"

"Look," said Jethro, and there were the boys standing around and alarmed but proud Jerry and above their heads, poised in the air over a half-built rock dam, was a huge boulder.

"Who lifted that?" I gasped.

"I did," volunteered Jerry, blushing crimson.

I turned on Jethro. "Well, why didn't you platt the twishers on it? You didn't have to come running—"

"On *that?*" Jethro squeaked. "You know very well we're not allowed to *lift* anything that big let alone platt it. Besides," shamefaced, "I can't remember that dern girl stuff."

"Oh, Jethro! You're so stupid sometimes!" I turned to Jerry. "How on earth did you ever lift anything that big?"

He squirmed. "I watched Daddy at the mine once."

"Does he let you lift at home?" I asked severely.

"I don't know." Jerry squashed mud with one shoe, hanging his head. "I never lifted anything before."

"Well, you know better. You kids aren't

matter of a few inches and a few seconds so gravity manages the return. But Jerry and Susie never had. They were finally beginning to catch up. Maybe it *was* just The Crossing that slowed them down— and maybe only the Clarinades. In my delight, *I* forgot and lifted to the school porch without benefit of the steps. But Valancy was putting up pictures on the high, old-fashioned moulding just below the ceiling, so no harm was done. She was flushed from her efforts and asked me to bring the step stool so she could finish them. I brought it and steadied it for her—and then nearly let her fall as I stared. How had she hung those first four pictures before I got there?

The weather was unnaturally dry all Fall. We didn't mind it much because rain with an Outsider around is awfully messy. We have to let ourselves get wet. But when November came and went and Christmas was almost upon us, and there was practically no rain and no snow at all, we all began to get worried. The creek dropped to a trickle and then to scattered puddles and then went dry. Finally the Old Ones had to spend an evening at the Group Reservoir doing something about our dwindling water supply. They wanted to get rid of Valancy for the evening, just in case, so Jemmy volunteered to take her to Kerry to the show. I was still awake when they got home long after midnight. Since I began to develop the Gift, I have long periods of restlessness when it seems I have no apartness but am of every person in the Group. The training I should start soon will help me shut out the others except when I want them. The only thing is that we don't know who is to train me. Since Grandmother died there has been no Sorter in our Group and because of The Crossing we have no books or records to help.

allowed to lift anything an Outsider your age can't handle alone. And not even that if you can't platt it afterwards."

"I know it," Jerry was still torn between embarrassment and pride.

"Well, remember it," I said. And taking a handful of sun, I platted the twishers and set the boulder back on the hillside where it belonged.

Platting does come easier to the girls— sunshine platting, that is. Of course only the Old Ones do the sun-and-rain one and only the very Oldest of them all would dare the moonlight-and-dark, that can move mountains. But that was still no excuse for Jethro to forget and run the risk of having Valancy see what she mustn't see.

It wasn't until I was almost back to the schoolhouse that it dawned on me. Jerry had lifted! Kids his age usually lift play stuff almost from the time they walk. That doesn't need platting because it's just a

Anyway, I was awake and leaning on my window sill in the darkness. They stopped on the porch—Jemmy is bunking at the mine during his stint there. I didn't have to guess or use a Gift to read the pantomime before me. I closed my eyes and my mind as their shadows merged. Under their strong emotion, I could have had free access to their minds, but I had been watching them all Fall. I knew in a special way what passed between them, and I knew that Valancy often went to bed in tears and that Jemmy spent too many lonely hours on the Crag that juts out over the canyon from high on Old Baldy, as though he were trying to make his heart as inaccessible to Outsiders as the Crag is. I knew what he felt, but oddly enough I had never been able to sort Valancy since that first night. There was something very un-Outsiderish and also very un-Groupish about her mind and I couldn't figure what.

I heard the front door open and close and Valancy's light steps fading down the hall and then I felt Jemmy calling me outside. I put my coat on over my robe and shivered down the hall. He was waiting by the porch steps, his face still and unhappy in the faint moonlight.

"She won't have me," he said flatly.

"Oh, Jemmy!" I cried. "You asked her—"

"Yes," he said. "She said no."

"I'm so sorry." I huddled down on the top step to cover my cold ankles. "But Jemmy—"

"Yes, I know!" He retorted savagely. "She's an Outsider. I have no business even to want her. Well, if she'd have me, I wouldn't hesitate a minute. This Purity-of-the-Group deal is—"

". . . is fine and right," I said softly, "as long as it doesn't touch you personally? But think for a minute, Jemmy. Would you be able to live a life as an Outsider? Just think of the million and one restraints that you would have to impose on yourself —and for the rest of your life, too, or lose her after all. Maybe it's better to accept No now than to try to build something and ruin it completely later. And if there

should be children . . ." I paused. "*Could* there be children, Jemmy?"

I heard him draw a sharp breath.

"We don't know," I went on. "We haven't had the occasion to find out. Do you want Valancy to be part of the first experiment?"

Jemmy slapped his hat viciously down on his thigh, then he laughed.

"You have the Gift," he said, though I had never told him. "Have you any idea, sister mine, how little you will be liked when you become an Old One?"

"Grandmother was well-liked," I answered placidly. Then I cried, "Don't *you* set me apart, darn you, Jemmy. Isn't it enough to know that among a different people, *I* am different? Don't *you* desert me now!" I was almost in tears.

Jemmy dropped to the step beside me and thumped my shoulder in his old way. "Pull up your socks, Karen. We have to do what we have to do. I was just taking my mad out on you. What a world." He sighed heavily.

I huddled deeper in my coat, cold of soul.

"But the other one is gone," I whispered. "The Home."

And we sat there sharing the poignant sorrow that is a constant undercurrent among The People, even those of us who never actually saw The Home. Father says it's because of a sort of racial memory.

"But she didn't say no because she doesn't love me," Jemmy went on at last. "She does love me. She told me so."

"Then why not?" Sister-wise I couldn't imagine anyone turning Jemmy down.

Jemmy laughed—a short, unhappy laugh. "Because she is different."

"*She's* different?"

"That's what she said, as though it was pulled out of her. 'I can't marry,' she said. 'I'm different!' That's pretty good, isn't it, coming from an Outsider!"

"She doesn't know we're The People," I said. "She must feel that she is different from everyone. I wonder why?"

"I don't know. There's something about her, though. A kind of shield or wall that keeps us apart. I've never met anything like it in an Outsider or in one of The People either. Sometimes it's like meshing with one of us and then *bang!* I smash the daylights out of me against that stone wall."

"Yes, I know," I said. "I've felt it, too."

We listened to the silent past-midnight world and then Jemmy stood.

"Well, g'night, Karen. Be seeing you."

I stood up, too. "Good night, Jemmy." I watched him start off in the late moonlight. He turned at the gate, his face hidden in the shadows.

"But I'm not giving up," he said quietly. "Valancy is my love."

The next day was hushed and warm—unnaturally so for December in our hills. There was a kind of ominous stillness among the trees, and, threading thinly against the milky sky, the thin smokes of little brush fires pointed out the dryness of the whole country. If you looked closely you could see piling behind Old Baldy an odd bank of clouds, so nearly the color of the sky that it was hardly discernible, but puffy and summer-thunderheady.

All of us were restless in school, the kids reacting to the weather, Valancy pale and unhappy after last night. I was bruising my mind against the blank wall in hers, trying to find some way I could help her.

Finally the thousand and one little annoyances were climaxed by Jerry and Susie scuffling until Susie was pushed out of the desk onto an open box of wet water colors that Debra for heaven only knows what reason had left on the floor by her desk. Susie shrieked and Debra sputtered and Jerry started a high silly giggle of embarrassment and delight. Valancy, without looking, reached for something to rap for order with and knocked down the old cracked vase full of drooping wildflowers and three-day-old water. The vase broke and flooded her desk with the foul-smelling deluge, ruining the monthly report she

had almost ready to send in to the County School Superintendent.

For a stricken moment there wasn't a sound in the room, then Valancy burst into half-hysterical laughter and the whole room rocked with her. We all rallied around doing what we could to clean up Susie and Valancy's desk and then Valancy declared a holiday and decided that it would be the perfect time to go up-canyon to the slopes of Baldy and gather what greenery we could find to decorate our school room for the holidays.

We all take our lunches to school, so we gathered them up and took along a square tarp the boys had brought to help build the dam in the creek. Now that the creek was dry, they couldn't use it and it'd come in handy to sit on at lunch time and would serve to carry our greenery home in, too, stretcher-fashion.

Released from the school room, we were all loud and jubilant and I nearly kinked my neck trying to keep all the kids in sight at once to nip in the bud any thoughtless lifting or other Group activity. The kids were all so wild, they might forget.

We went on up-canyon past the kids' dam and climbed the bare, dry waterfalls that stair-step up to the Mesa. On the Mesa, we spread the tarp and pooled our lunches to make it more picnicky. A sudden hush from across the tarp caught my attention. Debra, Rachel and Lizbeth were staring horrified at Susie's lunch. She was calmly dumping out a half dozen *koomatka* beside her sandwiches.

Koomatka are almost the only plants that lasted through The Crossing. I think four *koomatka* survived in someone's personal effects. They were planted and cared for as tenderly as babies and now every household in the Group has a *koomatka* plant growing in some quiet spot out of casual sight. Their fruit is eaten not so much for nourishment as Earth knows nourishment, but as a last remembrance of all other similar delights that died with The Home. We always save *koomatka* for special occasions. Susie must have sneaked some out when her mother wasn't looking. And there they were—across the table from an Outsider!

Before I could snap them to me or say anything, Valancy turned, too, and caught sight of the softly glowing bluey-green pile. Her eyes widened and one hand went out. She started to say something and then she dropped her eyes quickly and drew her hand back. She clasped her hands tightly together and the girls, eyes intent on her, scrambled the *koomatka* back into the sack and Lizbeth silently comforted Susie who had just realized what she had done. She was on the verge of tears at having betrayed The People to an Outsider.

Just then 'Kiah and Derek rolled across the picnic table fighting over a cupcake. By the time we salvaged our lunch from under them and they had scraped the last of the chocolate frosting off their T-shirts, the *koomatka* incident seemed closed. And yet, as we lay back resting a little to settle our stomachs, staring up at the smothery low-hanging clouds that had grown from the milky morning sky, I suddenly found myself trying to decide about Valancy's look when she saw the fruit. Surely it couldn't have been recognition!

At the end of our brief siesta, we carefully buried the remains of our lunch—the hill was much too dry to think of burning it—and started on again. After a while, the slope got steeper and the stubborn tangle of manzanita tore at our clothes and scratched our legs and grabbed at the rolled-up tarp until we all looked longingly at the free air above it. If Valancy hadn't been with us we could have lifted over the worst and saved all this trouble. But we blew and panted for a while and then struggled on.

After an hour or so, we worked out onto a rocky knoll that leaned against the slope of Baldy and made a tiny island in the sea of manzanita. We all stretched out gratefully on the crumbling granite outcropping, listening to our heart-beats slowing.

Then Jethro sat up and sniffed. Valancy and I alerted. A sudden puff of wind from the little side canyon brought the acrid pungency of burning brush to us. Jethro scrambled along the narrow ridge to the slope of Baldy and worked his way around out of sight into the canyon. He came scrambling back, half lifting, half running.

"Awful!" he panted. "It's awful! The whole canyon ahead is on fire and it's coming this way fast!"

Valancy gathered us together with a glance.

"Why didn't we see the smoke?" she asked tensely. "There wasn't any smoke when we left the schoolhouse."

"Can't see this slope from school," he said. "Fire could burn over a dozen slopes and we'd hardly see the smoke. This side of Baldy is a rim fencing in an awful mess of canyons."

"What'll we do?" quavered Lizbeth, hugging Susie to her.

Another gust of wind and smoke set us all to coughing and through my streaming tears, I saw a long lapping tongue of fire reach around the canyon wall.

Valancy and I looked at each other. I couldn't sort her mind, but mine was a panic, beating itself against the fire and then against the terrible tangle of manzanita all around us. Bruising against the possibility of lifting out of danger, then against the fact that none of the kids was capable of sustained progressive self-lifting for more than a minute or so and how could we leave Valancy? I hid my face in my hands to shut out the acres and acres of tinder-dry manzanita that would blaze like a torch at the first touch of fire. If only it would rain! You can't *set* fire to wet manzanita, but after these long months of drought—!

I heard the younger children scream and looked up to see Valancy staring at me with an intensity that frightened me even as I saw fire standing bright and terrible behind her at the mouth of the canyon.

Leonard Everett Fisher

Jake, yelling hoarsely, broke from the group and lifted a yard or two over the manzanita before he tangled his feet and fell helpless into the ugly, angled branches.

"Get under the tarp!" Valancy's voice was a whip-lash. "All of you get under the tarp!"

"It won't do any good," bellowed 'Kiah. "It'll burn like paper!"

"Get——under——the——tarp!" Valancy's spaced, icy words drove us to unfolding the tarp and spreading it to creep under. I lifted (hoping even at this awful moment that Valancy wouldn't see me) over to Jake and yanked him back to his feet. I couldn't lift with him so I pushed and prodded and half-carried him back through the heavy surge of black smoke to the tarp and shoved him under. Valancy was standing, back to the fire, so changed and alien that I shut my eyes against her and started to crawl in with the other kids.

And then she began to speak. The rolling, terrible thunder of her voice shook my bones and I swallowed a scream. A surge of fear swept through our huddled group and shoved me back out from under the tarp.

Till I die, I'll never forget Valancy standing there tense and taller than life against the rolling convulsive clouds of smoke, both her hands outstretched, fingers wide apart as the measured terror of her voice went on and on in words that plague me because I should have known them and didn't. As I watched, I felt an icy cold gather, a paralyzing, unearthly cold that froze the tears on my tensely up-turned face.

And then lightning leaped from finger to finger of her lifted hands. And lightning answered in the clouds above her. With a toss of her hands she threw the cold, the lightning, the sullen shifting smoke upward, and the roar of the racing fire was drowned in a hissing roar of down-drenching rain.

I knelt there in the deluge, looking for an eternal second into her drained, despairing, hopeless eyes before I caught her just in time to keep her head from banging on the granite as she pitched forward, inert.

Then as I sat there cradling her head in my lap, shaking with cold and fear, with the terrified wailing of the kids behind me, I heard Father shout and saw him and Jemmy and Darcy Clarinade in the old pick-up, lifting over the steaming streaming manzanita, over the trackless mountainside through the rain to us. Father lowered the truck until one of the wheels brushed a branch and spun lazily, then the three of them lifted all of us up to the dear familiarity of that beat-up old jalopy.

Jemmy received Valancy's limp body into his arms and crouched in back, huddling her in his arms, for the moment hostile to the whole world that had brought his love to such a pass.

We kids clung to Father in an ecstasy of relief. He hugged us all tight to him, then he raised my face.

"Why did it rain?" he asked sternly, every inch an Old One while the cold downpour dripped off the ends of my hair and he stood dry inside his Shield.

"I don't know," I sobbed, blinking my streaming eyes against his sternness. "Valancy did it . . . with lightning . . . it was cold . . . she talked. . . ." Then I broke down completely, plumping down on the rough floor boards and, in spite of my age, howling right along with the other kids.

It was a silent, solemn group that gathered in the schoolhouse that evening. I sat at my desk with my hands folded stiffly in front of me, half scared of my own People. This was the first official meeting of the Old Ones I'd ever attended. They all sat in desks, too, except the Oldest who sat in Valancy's chair. Valancy sat stony-faced in the twin's desk, but her nervous fingers shredded one kleenex after another as she waited.

The Oldest rapped the side of the desk with his cane and turned his sightless eyes from one to another of us.

"We're all here," he said, "to inquire—"

"Oh, stop it!" Valancy jumped up from her seat. "Can't you fire me without all this rigmarole? I'm used to it. Just say go and I'll go!" She stood trembling.

"Sit down, Miss Carmody," said the Oldest. And Valancy sat down meekly.

"Where were you born?" asked the Oldest quietly.

"What does it matter?" flared Valancy. Then resignedly, "It's in my application. Vista Mar, California."

"And your parents?"

"I don't know."

There was a stir in the room.

"Why not?"

"Oh, this is so unnecessary!" cried Valancy. "But if you *have* to know, both my parents were foundlings. They were found wandering in the streets after a big explosion and fire in Vista Mar. An old couple who lost everything in the fire took them in. When they grew up, they married. I was born. They died. Can I go now?"

A murmur swept the room.

"Why did you leave your other jobs?" asked Father.

Before Valancy could answer, the door was flung open and Jemmy stalked defiantly in.

"Go!" said the Oldest.

"Please," said Jemmy, deflating suddenly. "Let me stay. It concerns me too."

The Oldest fingered his cane and then nodded. Jemmy half-smiled with relief and sat down in a back seat.

"Go on," said the Oldest One to Valancy.

"All right then," said Valancy. "I lost my first job because I—well—I guess you'd call it levitated—to fix a broken blind in my room. It was stuck and I just . . . went up . . . in the air until I unstuck it. The principal saw me. He couldn't believe it and it scared him so he fired me." She paused expectantly.

The Old Ones looked at one another and my silly, confused mind began to add up columns that only my lack of common sense had kept from giving totals long ago.

"And the other one?" The Oldest

leaned his cheek on his doubled-up hand as he bent forward.

Valancy was taken aback and she flushed in confusion.

"Well," she said hesitantly, "I called my books to me—I mean they were on my desk. . . ."

"We know what you mean," said The Oldest.

"You know!" Valancy looked dazed.

The Oldest stood up.

"Valancy Carmody, open your mind!"

Valancy stared at him and then burst into tears.

"I can't, I can't," she sobbed. "It's been too long. I can't let anyone in. I'm different. I'm alone. Can't you understand? They all died. I'm alien!"

"You are alien no longer," said the Oldest. "You are home now, Valancy." He motioned to me. "Karen, go in to her."

So I did. At first the wall was still there; then with a soundless cry, half anguish and half joy, the wall went down and I was with Valancy. I saw all the secrets that had cankered in her since her parents died—the parents who were of The People.

They had been reared by the old couple who were not only of The People but had been The Oldest of the whole Crossing.

I tasted with her the hidden frightening things—the need for living as an Outsider, the terrible need for concealing all her differences and suppressing all the extra Gifts of The People, the ever present fear of betraying herself and the awful lostness that came when she thought she was the last of The People.

And then suddenly *she* came in to *me* and my mind was flooded with a far greater presence than I had ever before experienced.

My eyes flew open and I saw all of the Old Ones staring at Valancy. Even the Oldest had his face turned to her, wonder written as widely on his scarred face as on the others.

He bowed his head and made The Sign. "The lost persuasions and designs," he murmured. "She has them all."

And then I knew that Valancy, Valancy who had wrapped herself so tightly against the world to which any thoughtless act might betray her that she had lived with us all this time without our knowing about her or she about us, was one of us. Not only one of us but such a one as had not been since Grandmother died—and even beyond that. My incoherent thoughts cleared to one.

Now I would have someone to train me. Now I could become a sorter—but only second to her.

I turned to share my wonder with Jemmy. He was looking at Valancy as The People must have looked at The Home in the last hour. Then he turned to the door.

Before I could draw a breath, Valancy was gone from me and from the Old Ones and Jemmy was turning to her outstretched hands.

Then I bolted for the outdoors and rushed like one possessed down the lane, lifting and running until I staggered up our porch steps and collapsed against Mother, who had heard me coming.

"Oh, Mother!" I cried. "She's one of us! She's Jemmy's love! She's wonderful!" And I burst into noisy sobs in the warm comfort of Mother's arms.

So now I don't have to go Outside to become a teacher. We have a permanent one. But I'm going anyway. I want to be as much like Valancy as I can and she has her degree. Besides I can use the discipline of living Outside for a year.

I have so much to learn and so much training to go through, but Valancy will always be there with me. I won't be set apart alone because of The Gift.

Maybe I shouldn't mention it, but one reason I want to hurry my training is that we're going to try to locate the other People. None of the boys here please me.

The woman who wrote this story

ZENNA HENDERSON   1917–

In her entire life, Miss Henderson has been out of her home state of Arizona only six weeks and has never been further east than Nebraska. After receiving two degrees from Arizona State Teacher's College, she taught for a year at a Japanese Relocation Camp during World War II. For security reasons the government had moved many west-coast Japanese people to these special camps in states away from the coastline.

In 1949, Miss Henderson sold her first story. She had written poetry before, but she discovered she had a knack for writing good stories of "fantasy and science fiction." Although Miss Henderson is something of a beginner in this field, her short stories have appeared in three anthologies and have been reprinted in England, Italy, and France.

Let's consider . . .

1. Keep in mind that this is science fiction and fantastic. (Not so many years ago splitting the atom seemed fantastic.) Before you start your discussion, be sure you understand the following terms: *The People, Group, Outsider, Old Ones, The Crossing, The Oldest, The Gift, lift, platt twishers,* and *sort.* You are not *told* what these terms mean, but you can guess from the context.

2. When were you first aware that there was something "different" about Karen's father and mother? In what ways were they different?

3. What first made you curious about the teacher, even before she arrived?

4. Why did Mother worry about an Outsider coming to the Canyon? What difficulties did she fear? About what members of the family was she concerned?

5. When Karen "sorted" Miss Carmody and Jemmy the first night, what did she learn about each of them?

6. The People realized that their ways might shock Outsiders. Therefore, they insisted that their children control their behavior when an Outsider was around. What kinds of actions were forbidden?

7. Why did Jemmy wait outside the school that first morning?

8. Why was Karen puzzled by (1) the old desks, (2) the red leaves in the ink well, and (3) what Miss Carmody said to the twins? What explanation finally satisfied her?

9. Jemmy fell in love with Valancy at first sight. Why was she afraid to let herself care for him? How did Jemmy describe her "difference"?

10. In spite of the fact that The People had powers which set them apart, the author made them seem as natural in some ways as people you know. Point out traits of character, physical growth, and ways of speaking which made them seem natural.

11. Valancy was the most successful of all the teachers who had ever come to Cougar Canyon. What incident, then, precipitated the holiday and picnic?

12. How did the author use this trip to the Mesa to bring the story to a dramatic climax?

13. What was the climax: Valancy's putting out of the fire, or the discovery that she was one of the Group? Give evidence from the story to support your answer. Remember that the climax is the highest point of interest in the story and often the turning point of the action. All preceding events have built toward it. What follows "ties up" the loose ends.

14. Why was Valancy impatient with all the "rigmarole" of the Old Ones?

15. What did Karen learn about Valancy when she went into her mind?

16. A well-constructed short story should end as soon as possible after the climax is reached. How did this story end? Why was Karen so happy about the way things turned out?

The writer's craft . . .

Science fiction is the name given to imaginative writing about outer space. Some writers of science fiction give free rein to their imaginations with the result that their stories are pure fancy without any basis in fact. Other writers of science fiction, because of their scientific backgrounds, limit themselves to what might be possible in the not-too-distant future. In either case, if science fiction stories are to be well told, they must offer more than the author's ideas about life in outer space.

1. A good science fiction story must somehow convince the reader—at least during the reading—that what happens is **plausible:** not only possible but highly probable because it has the appearance of truth. How can a writer make his fantastic tale seem believable? He must establish certain premises, and then work out a logical story in terms of these premises. For example, in "Ararat" Zenna Henderson established the premise that The People could lift. It followed logically, then, that if they wished to keep their identity secret, there could be no lifting in the presence of Outsiders. Give examples of other premises which Miss Henderson established.

2. Science fiction must also have characters that are somehow believable. Even though they may differ from the human beings you know, they must have sufficient depth to make you interested in what happens to them.

Explain why you found Valancy and the other characters in "Ararat" believable or unbelievable. Discuss your reasons for being interested in them.

3. Suspense is often an important quality in a short story since it keeps the reader uncertain of the outcome. How important is suspense in science fiction? Was there suspense in "Ararat"? If so, at what points in the story did the author create suspense? How did she create it?

4. You might enjoy writing a science fiction story of your own. Remember, however, that merely giving your story a fantastic setting or plot will not in itself make your story interesting. The action must be logically developed in terms of the premises you establish, and the characters must have sufficient depth to interest your readers.

Knowing words . . .

Even in comic books, advertisements, and magazine stories you will find passing references to people, things, places, or events in history, mythology, or literature. Such references are called **allusions.** They serve a very useful purpose by suggesting in a word or phrase what might take many words to explain fully.

For example, Zenna Henderson made an allusion to the Greek god Pan in her description of Derek and Jake. Pan was the Greek god of pastures and woods, of flocks and wild life. He was the patron of shepherds and hunters. In pictures and statues, he is represented as half man, half goat. His human face is given an impish appearance by a pair of pointed goat's ears. By her mythological allusion, Miss Henderson suggested an impish quality in the faces of the two boys.

Other mythological characters often mentioned in literary allusions are Hercules, Minerva, Venus, Mercury, and Jupiter. Choose one of these characters and find out about him or her in library reference books. Tell the class what this character represents and illustrate with an allusion of your own. For example, you might write this sentence as your allusion to the god Mercury: "He traveled with the swiftness of Mercury."

The Gift

JOHN STEINBECK

Growing up is never easy, as young Jody discovered when he faced one aspect of reality he had never known before. In this story, John Steinbeck reveals his sensitive understanding of human beings and his belief in their essential goodness.

At daybreak Billy Buck emerged from the bunkhouse and stood for a moment on the porch looking up at the sky. He was a broad, bandy-legged little man with a walrus mustache, with square hands, puffed and muscled on the palms. His eyes were a contemplative, watery grey and the hair which protruded from under his Stetson hat was spiky and weathered. Billy was still stuffing his shirt into his blue jeans as he stood on the porch. He unbuckled his belt and tightened it again. The belt showed, by the worn shiny places opposite each hole, the gradual increase of Billy's middle over a period of years. When he had seen to the weather, Billy cleared each nostril by holding its mate closed with his forefinger and blowing fiercely. Then he walked down to the barn, rubbing his hands together. He curried and brushed two saddle horses in the stalls, talking quietly to them all the time; and he had hardly finished when the iron triangle started ringing at the ranch house. Billy stuck the brush and currycomb together and laid them on the rail, and went up to breakfast. His action had been so deliberate and yet so wasteless of time that he came to the house while Mrs. Tiflin was still ringing the triangle. She nodded her grey head to him and withdrew into the kitchen. Billy Buck sat down on the steps, because he was a cow-hand, and it wouldn't be fitting that he should go first into the dining-room. He heard Mr. Tiflin in the house, stamping his feet into his boots.

The high jangling note of the triangle put the boy Jody in motion. He was only a little boy, ten years old, with hair like dusty yellow grass and with shy polite grey eyes, and with a mouth that worked when he thought. The triangle picked him up out of sleep. It didn't occur to him to disobey the harsh note. He never had: no one he knew ever had. He brushed the tangled hair out of his eyes and skinned his nightgown off. In a moment he was dressed—blue chambray shirt and overalls. It was late in the summer, so of course there were no shoes to bother with. In the kitchen he waited until his mother got from in front of the sink and went back to the stove. Then he washed himself and brushed back his wet hair with his fingers. His mother turned sharply on him as he left the sink. Jody looked shyly away.

"I've got to cut your hair before long," his mother said. "Breakfast's on the table. Go on in, so Billy can come."

Jody sat at the long table which was

covered with white oilcloth washed through to the fabric in some places. The fried eggs lay in rows on their platter. Jody took three eggs on his plate and followed with three thick slices of crisp bacon. He carefully scraped a spot of blood from one of the egg yolks.

Billy Buck clumped in. "That won't hurt you," Billy explained.

Jody's tall stern father came in then and Jody knew from the noise on the floor that he was wearing boots, but he looked under the table anyway, to make sure. His father turned off the oil lamp over the table, for plenty of morning light now came through the windows.

Jody did not ask where his father and Billy Buck were riding that day, but he wished he might go along. His father was a disciplinarian. Jody obeyed him in everything without questions of any kind. Now, Carl Tiflin sat down and reached for the egg platter.

"Got the cows ready to go, Billy?" he asked.

"In the lower corral," Billy said. "I could just as well take them in alone."

"Sure you could. But a man needs company. Besides your throat gets pretty dry." Carl Tiflin was jovial this morning.

Jody's mother put her head in the door. "What time do you think to be back, Carl?"

"I can't tell. I've got to see some men in Salinas.[1] Might be gone till dark."

The eggs and coffee and big biscuits disappeared rapidly. Jody followed the two men out of the house. He watched them mount their horses and drive six old milk cows out of the corral and start over the hill toward Salinas. They were going to sell the old cows to the butcher.

When they had disappeared over the crown of the ridge Jody walked up the hill in back of the house. The dogs trotted around the house corner hunching their shoulders and grinning horribly with pleasure. Jody patted their heads—Doubletree

Mutt with the big thick tail and yellow eyes, and Smasher, the shepherd, who had killed a coyote and lost an ear in doing it. Smasher's one good ear stood up higher than a collie's ear should. Billy Buck said that always happened. After the frenzied greeting the dogs lowered their noses to the ground in a businesslike way and went ahead, looking back now and then to make sure that the boy was coming. They walked up through the chicken yard and saw the quail eating with the chickens. Smasher chased the chickens a little to keep in practice in case there should ever be sheep to herd. Jody continued on through the large vegetable patch where the green corn was higher than his head. The cow-pumpkins were green and small yet. He went on to the sagebrush line where the cold spring ran out of its pipe and fell into a round wooden tub. He leaned over and drank close to the green mossy wood where the water tasted best. Then he turned and looked back on the ranch, on the low, whitewashed house girded with red geraniums, and on the long bunkhouse by the cypress tree where Billy Buck lived alone. Jody could see the great black kettle under the cypress tree. That was where the pigs were scalded.[2] The sun was coming over the ridge, now, glaring on the whitewash of the houses and barns, making the wet grass blaze softly. Behind him, in the tall sagebrush, the birds were scampering on the ground, making a great noise among the dry leaves; the squirrels piped shrilly on the side-hills. Jody looked along at the farm buildings. He felt an uncertainty in the air, a feeling of change and of loss and of the gain of new and unfamiliar things. Over the hillside two big black buzzards sailed low to the ground and their shadows slipped smoothly and quickly ahead of them. Some animal had died in the vicinity. Jody knew it. It might be a cow or it might be the remains of a rabbit. The buzzards overlooked nothing. Jody

---

[1] *Salinas,* a city in central California

[2] *scalded,* dipped in boiling water in order to loosen the pig's bristles

hated them as all decent things hate them, but they could not be hurt because they made away with carrion.

After a while the boy sauntered down hill again. The dogs had long ago given him up and gone into the brush to do things in their own way. Back through the vegetable garden he went, and he paused for a moment to smash a green muskmelon with his heel, but he was not happy about it. It was a bad thing to do, he knew perfectly well. He kicked dirt over the ruined melon to conceal it.

Back at the house his mother bent over his rough hands, inspecting his fingers and nails. It did little good to start him clean to school for too many things could happen on the way. She sighed over the black cracks on his fingers, and then gave him his books and his lunch and started him on the mile walk to school. She noticed that his mouth was working a good deal this morning.

Jody started his journey. He filled his pockets with little pieces of white quartz that lay in the road, and every so often he took a shot at a bird or at some rabbit that had stayed sunning itself in the road too long. At the crossroads over the bridge he met two friends and the three of them walked to school together, making ridiculous strides and being rather silly. School had just opened two weeks before. There was still a spirit of revolt among the pupils.

It was four o'clock in the afternoon when Jody topped the hill and looked down on the ranch again. He looked for the saddle horses, but the corral was empty. His father was not back yet. He went slowly, then, toward the afternoon chores. At the ranch house, he found his mother sitting on the porch, mending socks.

"There's two doughnuts in the kitchen for you," she said. Jody slid to the kitchen, and returned with half of one of the doughnuts already eaten and his mouth full. His mother asked him what he had learned in school that day, but she didn't listen to his doughnut-muffled answer. She interrupted, "Jody, tonight see you fill the wood-box clear full. Last night you crossed the sticks and it wasn't only about half full. Lay the sticks flat tonight. And Jody, some of the hens are hiding eggs, or else the dogs are eating them. Look about in the grass and see if you can find any nests."

Jody, still eating, went out and did his chores. He saw the quail come down to eat with the chickens when he threw out the grain. For some reason his father was proud to have them come. He never allowed any shooting near the house for fear the quail might go away.

When the wood-box was full, Jody took his twenty-two rifle up to the cold spring at the brush line. He drank again and then aimed the gun at all manner of things, at rocks, at birds on the wing, at the big black pig kettle under the cypress tree, but he didn't shoot for he had no cartridges and wouldn't have until he was twelve. If his father had seen him aim the rifle in the direction of the house he would have put the cartridges off another year. Jody remembered this and did not point the rifle down the hill again. Two years was enough to wait for cartridges. Nearly all of his father's presents were given with reservations which hampered their value somewhat. It was good discipline.

The supper waited until dark for his father to return. At last he came in with Billy Buck.

After supper, Jody sat by the fireplace and his shy polite eyes sought the room corners, and he waited for his father to tell what it was he contained, for Jody knew he had news of some sort. But he was disappointed. His father pointed a stern finger at him.

"You'd better go to bed, Jody. I'm going to need you in the morning."

That wasn't so bad. Jody liked to do the things he had to do as long as they weren't routine things. He looked at the floor and his mouth worked out a question before he spoke it. "What are we going to do in the morning, kill a pig?" he asked softly.

"Never you mind. You better get to bed."

When the door was closed behind him, Jody heard his father and Billy Buck chuckling and he knew it was a joke of some kind. And later, when he lay in bed, trying to make words out of the murmurs in the other room, he heard his father protest, "But, Ruth, I didn't give much for him."

Jody heard the hoot-owls hunting mice down by the barn, and he heard a fruit tree limb tap-tapping against the house. A cow was lowing when he went to sleep.

When the triangle sounded in the morning, Jody dressed more quickly even than usual. In the kitchen, while he washed his face and combed back his hair, his mother addressed him irritably. "Don't you go out until you get a good breakfast in you."

He went into the dining-room and sat at the long white table. He took a steaming hotcake from the platter, arranged two fried eggs on it, covered them with another hotcake and squashed the whole thing with his fork.

His father and Billy Buck came in. Jody knew from the sound on the floor that both of them were wearing flatheeled shoes, but he peered under the table to make sure. His father turned off the oil lamp, for the day had arrived, and he looked stern and disciplinary, but Billy Buck didn't look at Jody at all. He avoided the shy questioning eyes of the boy and soaked a whole piece of toast in his coffee.

Carl Tiflin said crossly, "You come with us after breakfast!"

Jody had trouble with his food then, for he felt a kind of doom in the air. After Billy had tilted his saucer and drained the coffee which had slopped into it, and had wiped his hands on his jeans, the two men stood up from the table and went out into the morning light together, and Jody re-

spectfully followed a little behind them. He tried to keep his mind from running ahead, tried to keep it absolutely motionless.

His mother called, "Carl! Don't you let it keep him from school."

They marched past the cypress, where a singletree hung from a limb to butcher the pigs on, and past the black iron kettle, so it was not a pig killing. The sun shone over the hill and threw long, dark shadows of the trees and buildings. They crossed a stubble-field to shortcut to the barn. Jody's father unhooked the door and they went in. They had been walking toward the sun on the way down. The barn was black as night in contrast and warm from the hay and from the beasts. Jody's father moved over toward the one box stall. "Come here!" he ordered. Jody could begin to see things now. He looked into the box stall and then stepped back quickly.

A red pony colt was looking at him out of the stall. Its tense ears were forward and a light of disobedience was in its eyes. Its coat was rough and thick as an airedale's fur and its mane was long and tangled. Jody's throat collapsed in on itself and cut his breath short.

"He needs a good currying," his father said, "and if I ever hear of you not feeding him or leaving his stall dirty, I'll sell him off in a minute."

Jody couldn't bear to look at the pony's eyes any more. He gazed down at his hands for a moment, and he asked very shyly, "Mine?" No one answered him. He put his hand out toward the pony. Its grey nose came close, sniffing loudly, and then the lips drew back and the strong teeth closed on Jody's fingers. The pony shook its head up and down and seemed to laugh with amusement. Jody regarded his bruised fingers. "Well," he said with pride—"Well, I guess he can bite all right." The two men laughed, somewhat in relief. Carl Tiflin went out of the barn and walked up a sidehill to be by himself, for he was embarrassed, but Billy Buck stayed.

It was easier to talk to Billy Buck. Jody asked again—"Mine?"

Billy became professional in tone. "Sure! That is, if you look out for him and break him right. I'll show you how. He's just a colt. You can't ride him for some time."

Jody put out his bruised hand again, and this time the red pony let his nose be rubbed. "I ought to have a carrot," Jody said. "Where'd we get him, Billy?"

"Bought him at a sheriff's auction," Billy explained. "A show went broke in Salinas and had debts. The sheriff was selling off their stuff."

The pony stretched out his nose and shook the forelock from his wild eyes. Jody stroked the nose a little. He said softly, "There isn't a—saddle?"

Billy Buck laughed. "I'd forgot. Come along."

In the harness room he lifted down a little saddle of red morocco leather. "It's just a show saddle," Billy Buck said disparagingly. "It isn't practical for the brush, but it was cheap at the sale."

Jody couldn't trust himself to look at the saddle either, and he couldn't speak at all. He brushed the shining red leather with his fingertips, and after a long time he said,

"It'll look pretty on him though." He thought of the grandest and prettiest things he knew. "If he hasn't a name already, I think I'll call him Gabilan Mountains," he said.

Billy Buck knew how he felt. "It's a pretty long name. Why don't you just call him Gabilan? That means hawk. That would be a fine name for him." Billy felt glad. "If you will collect tail hair, I might be able to make a hair rope for you sometime. You could use it for a hackamore." [3]

Jody wanted to go back to the box stall. "Could I lead him to school, do you think —to show the kids?"

But Billy shook his head. "He's not even halter-broke yet. We had a time getting him here. Had to almost drag him. You better be starting for school though."

"I'll bring the kids to see him here this afternoon," Jody said.

Six boys came over the hill half an hour early that afternoon, running hard, their heads down, their forearms working, their breath whistling. They swept by the house and cut across the stubble-field to the barn. And then they stood self-consciously before

---

[3] *hackamore,* a rope or halter used to break in horses

the pony, and then they looked at Jody with eyes in which there was a new admiration and a new respect. Before today Jody had been a boy, dressed in overalls and a blue shirt—quieter than most, even suspected of being a little cowardly. And now he was different. Out of a thousand centuries they drew the ancient admiration of the footman for the horseman. They knew instinctively that a man on a horse is spiritually as well as physically bigger than a man on foot. They knew that Jody had been miraculously lifted out of equality with them, and had been placed over them. Gabilan put his head out of the stall and sniffed them.

"Why'n't you ride him?" the boys cried. "Why'n't you braid his tail with ribbons like in the fair?" "When you going to ride him?"

Jody's courage was up. He too felt the superiority of the horseman. "He's not old enough. Nobody can ride him for a long time. I'm going to train him on the long halter. Billy Buck is going to show me how."

"Well, can't we even lead him around a little?"

"He isn't even halter-broke," Jody said. He wanted to be completely alone when he took the pony out for the first time. "Come and see the saddle."

They were speechless at the red morocco saddle, completely shocked out of comment. "It isn't much use in the brush," Jody explained. "It'll look pretty on him though. Maybe I'll ride bareback when I go into the brush."

"How you going to rope a cow without a saddle horn?"

"Maybe I'll get another saddle for every day. My father might want me to help him with the stock." He let them feel the red saddle, and showed them the brass chain throat-latch on the bridle and the big brass buttons at each temple where the headstall and brow band crossed. The whole thing was too wonderful. They had to go away after a little while, and each boy, in his mind, searched among his possessions for a bribe worthy of offering in return for a ride on the red pony when the time should come.

Jody was glad when they had gone. He took brush and currycomb from the wall, took down the barrier of the box stall and stepped cautiously in. The pony's eyes glittered, and he edged around into kicking position. But Jody touched him on the shoulder and rubbed his high arched neck as he had always seen Billy Buck do, and he crooned, "So-o-o Boy," in a deep voice. The pony gradually relaxed his tenseness. Jody curried and brushed until a pile of dead hair lay in the stall and until the pony's coat had taken on a deep red shine. Each time he finished he thought it might have been done better. He braided the mane into a dozen little pigtails, and he braided the forelock, and then he undid them and brushed the hair out straight again.

Jody did not hear his mother enter the barn. She was angry when she came, but when she looked in at the pony and at Jody working over him, she felt a curious pride rise up in her. "Have you forgot the woodbox?" she asked gently. "It's not far off from dark and there's not a stick of wood in the house, and the chickens aren't fed."

Jody quickly put up his tools. "I forgot, ma'am."

"Well, after this do your chores first. Then you won't forget. I expect you'll forget lots of things now if I don't keep an eye on you."

"Can I have carrots from the garden for him, ma'am?"

She had to think about that. "Oh—I guess so, if you only take the big tough ones."

"Carrots keep the coat good," he said, and again she felt the curious rush of pride.

Jody never waited for the triangle to get him out of bed after the coming of the pony. It became his habit to creep out of bed even before his mother was awake, to slip into his clothes and to go quietly down to the barn to see Gabilan. In the grey quiet mornings when the land and the brush and the houses and the trees were silver-grey and black like a photograph negative, he stole toward the barn, past the sleeping stones and the sleeping cypress tree. The turkeys, roosting in the tree out of coyotes' reach, clicked drowsily. The fields glowed with a grey frost-like light and in the dew the tracks of rabbits and of field mice stood out sharply. The good dogs came stiffly out of their little houses, hackles up and deep growls in their throats. Then they caught Jody's scent, and their stiff tails rose up and waved a greeting—Doubletree Mutt with the big thick tail, and Smasher, the incipient shepherd—then went lazily back to their warm beds.

It was a strange time and a mysterious journey, to Jody—an extension of a dream. When he first had the pony he liked to torture himself during the trip by thinking Galiban would not be in his stall, and worse, would never have been there. And he had other delicious little self-induced pains. He thought how the rats had gnawed ragged holes in the red saddle, and how the mice had nibbled Gabilan's tail until it was stringy and thin. He usually ran the last little way to the barn. He unlatched the rusty hasp of the barn door and stepped in, and no matter how quietly he opened the door, Gabilan was always looking at him over the barrier of the box stall and Gabilan whinnied softly and stamped his front foot, and his eyes had big sparks of red fire in them like oakwood embers.

Sometimes, if the work horses were to be used that day, Jody found Billy Buck in the barn harnessing and currying. Billy stood with him and looked long at Gabilan and he told Jody a great many things about horses. He explained that they were terribly afraid for their feet, so that one must make a practice of lifting the legs and patting the hooves and ankles to remove their terror. He told Jody how horses love conversation. He must talk to the pony all the time, and tell him the reason for everything. Billy wasn't sure a horse could understand everything that was said to him, but it was impossible to say how much was understood. A horse never kicked up a fuss if someone he liked explained things to him. Billy could give examples, too. He had known, for instance, a horse nearly dead beat with fatigue to perk up when told it was only a little farther to his destination. And he had known a horse paralyzed with fright to come out of it when his rider told him what it was that was frightening him. While he talked in the mornings, Billy Buck cut twenty or thirty straws into neat three-inch lengths and stuck them into his hatband. Then during the whole day, if he wanted to pick his teeth or merely to chew on something, he had only to reach up for one of them.

Jody listened carefully, for he knew and the whole country knew that Billy Buck was a fine hand with horses. Billy's own horse was a stringy cayuse with a hammer head, but he nearly always won the first prizes at the stock trials. Billy could rope a steer, take a double half-hitch about the horn with his riata, and dismount, and his horse would play the steer as an angler plays a fish, keeping a tight rope until the steer was down or beaten.

Every morning, after Jody had curried and brushed the pony, he let down the barrier of the stall, and Gabilan thrust past him and raced down the barn and into the corral. Around and around he galloped, and sometimes he jumped forward and landed on stiff legs. He stood quivering, stiff ears forward, eyes rolling so that the whites showed, pretending to be frightened. At last he walked snorting to the water-trough and buried his nose in the water up to the nostrils. Jody was proud then, for he knew that was the way to judge a horse. Poor horses only touched their lips to the water, but a fine spirited beast put his whole nose and mouth under, and only left room to breathe.

Then Jody stood and watched the pony, and he saw things he had never noticed about any other horse, the sleek sliding flank muscles and the cords of the buttocks, which flexed like a closing fist, and the shine the sun put on the red coat. Having seen horses all his life, Jody had never looked at them very closely before. But now he noticed the moving ears which gave expression and even inflection of expression to the face. The pony talked with his ears. You could tell exactly how he felt about everything by the way his ears pointed. Sometimes they were stiff and upright and sometimes lax and sagging. They went back when he was angry or fearful, and forward when he was anxious and curious and pleased; and their exact position indicated which emotion he had.

Billy Buck kept his word. In the early fall the training began. First there was the halter-breaking, and that was the hardest because it was the first thing. Jody held a carrot and coaxed and promised and pulled on the rope. The pony set his feet like a burro when he felt the strain. But before long he learned. Jody walked all over the ranch leading him. Gradually he took to dropping the rope until the pony followed him unled wherever he went.

And then came the training on the long halter. That was slower work. Jody stood in the middle of a circle, holding the long halter. He clucked with his tongue and the pony started to walk in a big circle, held in by the long rope. He clucked

again to make the pony trot, and again to make him gallop. Around and around Gabilan went thundering and enjoying it immensely. Then he called, "Whoa," and the pony stopped. It was not long until Gabilan was perfect at it. But in many ways he was a bad pony. He bit Jody in the pants and stomped on Jody's feet. Now and then his ears went back and he aimed a tremendous kick at the boy. Every time he did one of these bad things, Gabilan settled back and seemed to laugh to himself.

Billy Buck worked at the hair rope in the evenings before the fireplace. Jody collected tail hair in a bag, and he sat and watched Billy slowly constructing the rope, twisting a few hairs to make a string and rolling two strings together for a cord, and then braiding a number of cords to make the rope. Billy rolled the finished rope on the floor under his foot to make it round and hard.

The long halter work rapidly approached perfection. Jody's father, watching the pony stop and start and trot and gallop, was a little bothered by it.

"He's getting to be almost a trick pony," he complained. "I don't like trick horses. It takes all the—dignity out of a horse to make him do tricks. Why, a trick horse is kind of like an actor—no dignity, no character of his own." And his father said, "I guess you better be getting him used to the saddle pretty soon."

Jody rushed for the harness-room. For some time he had been riding the saddle on a sawhorse. He changed the stirrup length over and over, and could never get it just right. Sometimes, mounted on the sawhorse in the harness-room, with collars and hames and tugs hung all about him, Jody rode out beyond the room. He carried his rifle across the pommel. He saw the fields go flying by, and he heard the beat of the galloping hoofs.

It was a ticklish job, saddling the pony the first time. Gabilan hunched and reared and threw the saddle off before the cinch could be tightened. It had to be replaced again and again until at last the pony let it stay. And the cinching was difficult, too. Day by day Jody tightened the girth a little more until at last the pony didn't mind the saddle at all.

Then there was the bridle. Billy explained how to use a stick of licorice for a bit until Gabilan was used to having something in his mouth. Billy explained, "Of course we could force-break him to everything, but he wouldn't be as good a horse if we did. He'd always be a little bit afraid, and he wouldn't mind because he wanted to."

The first time the pony wore the bridle he whipped his head about and worked his tongue against the bit until the blood oozed from the corners of his mouth. He tried to rub the headstall off on the manger. His ears pivoted about and his eyes turned red with fear and with general rambunctiousness. Jody rejoiced, for he knew that only a mean-souled horse does not resent training.

And Jody trembled when he thought of the time when he would first sit in the saddle. The pony would probably throw him off. There was no disgrace in that. The disgrace would come if he did not get right up and mount again. Sometimes he dreamed that he lay in the dirt and cried and couldn't make himself mount again. The shame of the dream lasted until the middle of the day.

Gabilan was growing fast. Already he had lost the long-leggedness of the colt; his mane was getting longer and blacker. Under the constant currying and brushing his coat lay as smooth and gleaming as orange-red lacquer. Jody oiled the hoofs and kept them carefully trimmed so they would not crack.

The hair rope was nearly finished. Jody's father gave him an old pair of spurs and bent in the side bars and cut down the strap and took up the chainlets until they fitted. And then one day Carl Tiflin said:

"The pony's growing faster than I thought. I guess you can ride him by

Thanksgiving. Think you can stick on?"

"I don't know," Jody said shyly. Thanksgiving was only three weeks off. He hoped it wouldn't rain, for rain would spot the red saddle.

Gabilan knew and liked Jody by now. He nickered when Jody came across the stubble-field, and in the pasture he came running when his master whistled for him. There was always a carrot for him every time.

Billy Buck gave him riding instructions over and over. "Now when you get up there, just grab tight with your knees and keep your hands away from the saddle, and if you get throwed, don't let that stop you. No matter how good a man is, there's always some horse can pitch him. You just climb up again before he gets to feeling smart about it. Pretty soon, he won't throw you no more, and pretty soon he can't throw you no more. That's the way to do it."

"I hope it don't rain before," Jody said.

"Why not? Don't want to get throwed in the mud?"

That was partly it, and also he was afraid that in the flurry of bucking Gabilan might slip and fall on him and break his leg or his hip. He had seen that happen to men before, had seen how they writhed on the ground like squashed bugs, and he was afraid of it.

He practiced on the sawhorse how he would hold the reins in his left hand and a hat in his right hand. If he kept his hands thus busy, he couldn't grab the horn if he felt himself going off. He didn't like to think of what would happen if he did grab the horn. Perhaps his father and Billy Buck would never speak to him again, they would be so ashamed. The news would get about and his mother would be ashamed too. And in the school yard—it was too awful to contemplate.

He began putting his weight in a stirrup when Gabilan was saddled, but he didn't throw his leg over the pony's back. That was forbidden until Thanksgiving.

Every afternoon he put the red saddle on the pony and cinched it tight. The pony was learning already to fill his stomach out unnaturally large while the cinching was going on, and then to let it down when the straps were fixed. Sometimes Jody led him up to the brush line and let him drink from the round green tub, and sometimes he led him up through the stubble-field to the hilltop from which it was possible to see the white town of Salinas and the geometric fields of the great valley, and the oak trees clipped by the sheep. Now and then they broke through the brush and came to little cleared circles so hedged in that the world was gone and only the sky and the circle of brush were left from the old life. Gabilan liked these trips and showed it by keeping his head very high and by quivering his nostrils with interest. When the two came back from an expedition they smelled of the sweet sage they had forced through.

Time dragged on toward Thanksgiving, but winter came fast. The clouds swept down and hung all day over the land and brushed the hilltops, and the winds blew shrilly at night. All day the dry oak leaves drifted down from the trees until they covered the ground, and yet the trees were unchanged.

Jody had wished it might not rain before Thanksgiving, but it did. The brown earth turned dark and the trees glistened. The cut ends of the stubble turned black with mildew; the haystacks grayed from exposure to the damp, and on the roofs the moss, which had been all summer as gray as lizards, turned a brilliant yellow-green. During the week of rain, Jody kept the pony in the box stall out of the dampness, except for a little time after school when he took him out for exercise and to drink at the water-trough in the upper corral. Not once did Gabilan get wet.

The wet weather continued until little new grass appeared. Jody walked to school dressed in a slicker and short rubber boots.

At length one morning the sun came out brightly. Jody, at his work in the box stall, said to Billy Buck, "Maybe I'll leave Gabilan in the corral when I go to school today."

"Be good for him to be out in the sun," Billy assured him. "No animal likes to be cooped up too long. Your father and me are going back on the hill to clean the leaves out of the spring." Billy nodded and picked his teeth with one of his little straws.

"If the rain comes, though—" Jody suggested.

"Not likely to rain today. She's rained herself out." Billy pulled up his sleeves and snapped his arm bands. "If it comes on to rain—why a little rain don't hurt a horse."

"Well, if it does come on to rain, you put him in, will you, Billy? I'm scared he might get cold so I couldn't ride him when the time comes."

"Oh sure! I'll watch out for him if we get back in time. But it won't rain today."

And so Jody, when he went to school, left Gabilan standing out in the corral.

Billy Buck wasn't wrong about many things. He couldn't be. But he was wrong about the weather that day, for a little after noon the clouds pushed over the hills and began to pour down. Jody heard it start on the schoolhouse roof. He considered holding up one finger for permission to go to the outhouse and, once outside, running for home to put the pony in. Punishment would be prompt both at school and at home. He gave it up and took ease from Billy's assurance that rain couldn't hurt a horse. When school was finally out, he hurried home through the dark rain. The banks at the sides of the road spouted little jets of muddy water. The rain slanted and swirled under a cold and gusty wind. Jody dog-trotted home, slopping through the gravelly mud of the road.

From the top of the ridge he could see Gabilan standing miserably in the corral. The red coat was almost black, and

streaked with water. He stood head down with his rump to the rain and wind. Jody arrived running and threw open the barn door and led the wet pony in by his forelock. Then he found a gunny sack and rubbed the soaked hair and rubbed the legs and ankles. Gabilan stood patiently, but he trembled in gusts like the wind.

When he had dried the pony as well as he could, Jody went up to the house and brought hot water down to the barn and soaked the grain in it. Gabilan was not very hungry. He nibbled at the hot mash, but he was not very much interested in it, and he still shivered now and then. A little steam rose from his damp back.

It was almost dark when Billy Buck and Carl Tiflin came home. "When the rain started we put up at Ben Herche's place, and the rain never let up all afternoon," Carl Tiflin explained. Jody looked reproachfully at Billy Buck and Billy felt guilty.

"You said it wouldn't rain," Jody accused him.

Billy looked away. "It's hard to tell, this time of year," he said, but his excuse was lame. He had no right to be fallible, and he knew it.

"The pony got wet, got soaked through."

"Did you dry him off?"

"I rubbed him with a sack and I gave him hot grain."

Billy nodded in agreement.

"Do you think he'll take cold, Billy?"

"A little rain never hurt anything," Billy assured him.

Jody's father joined the conversation then and lectured the boy a little. "A horse," he said, "isn't any lap-dog kind of thing." Carl Tiflin hated weakness and sickness, and he held a violent contempt for helplessness.

Jody's mother put a platter of steaks on the table and boiled potatoes and boiled squash, which clouded the room with their steam. They sat down to eat, Carl Tiflin still grumbling about weakness put into animals and men by too much coddling.

Billy Buck felt bad about his mistake. "Did you blanket him?" he asked.

"No. I couldn't find any blanket. I laid some sacks over his back."

"We'll go down and cover him up after we eat, then." Billy felt better about it then. When Jody's father had gone in to the fire and his mother was washing dishes, Billy found and lighted a lantern. He and Jody walked through the mud to the barn. The barn was dark and warm and sweet. The horses still munched their evening hay. "You hold the lantern!" Billy ordered. And he felt the pony's legs and tested the heat of the flanks. He put his cheek against the pony's grey muzzle and then he rolled up the eyelids to look at the eyeballs and he lifted the lips to see the gums, and he put his fingers inside the ears. "He don't seem so chipper," Billy said. "I'll give him a rub-down."

Then Billy found a sack and rubbed the pony's legs violently and he rubbed the chest and the withers. Gabilan was strangely spiritless. He submitted patiently to the rubbing. At last Billy brought an old cotton comforter from the saddle-room, and threw it over the pony's back and tied it at neck and chest with string.

"Now he'll be all right in the morning," Billy said.

Jody's mother looked up when he got back to the house. "You're late up from bed," she said. She held his chin in her hard hand and brushed the tangled hair out of his eyes and she said, "Don't worry about the pony. He'll be all right. Billy's as good as any horse doctor in the country."

Jody hadn't known she could see his worry. He pulled gently away from her and knelt down in front of the fireplace until it burned his stomach. He scorched himself through and then went in to bed, but it was a hard thing to go to sleep. He awakened after what seemed a long time. The room was dark but there was a greyness in the window like that which precedes the dawn. He got up and found his overalls and searched for the legs, and then the clock in the other room struck two. He laid his clothes down and got back into bed. It was broad daylight when he awakened again. For the first time he had slept through the ringing of the triangle. He leaped up, flung on his clothes and went out of the door still buttoning his shirt. His mother looked after him for a moment and then went quietly back to her work. Her eyes were brooding and kind. Now and then her mouth smiled a little but without changing her eyes at all.

Jody ran on toward the barn. Halfway there he heard the sound he dreaded, the hollow rasping cough of a horse. He broke into a sprint then. In the barn he found Billy Buck with the pony. Billy was rubbing its legs with his strong thick hands. He looked up and smiled gaily. "He just took a little cold," Billy said. "We'll have him out of it in a couple of days."

Jody looked at the pony's face. The eyes were half closed and the lids thick and dry. In the eye corners a crust of hard mucus stuck. Gabilan's ears hung loosely sideways and his head was low. Jody put out his hand, but the pony did not move close to it. He coughed again and his whole body constricted with the effort. A little stream of thin fluid ran from his nostrils.

Jody looked back at Billy Buck. "He's awful sick, Billy."

"Just a little cold, like I said," Billy insisted. "You go get some breakfast and then go back to school. I'll take care of him."

"But you might have to do something else. You might leave him."

"No, I won't. I won't leave him at all. Tomorrow's Saturday. Then you can stay with him all day." Billy had failed again, and he felt badly about it. He had to cure the pony now.

Jody walked up to the house and took his place listlessly at the table. The eggs and bacon were cold and greasy, but he didn't notice it. He ate his usual amount. He didn't even ask to stay home from school. His mother pushed his hair back when she took his plate. "Billy'll take care of the pony," she assured him.

He moped through the whole day at school. He couldn't answer any questions nor read any words. He couldn't even tell anyone the pony was sick, for that might make him sicker. And when school was finally out he started home in dread. He walked slowly and let the other boys leave him. He wished he might continue walking and never arrive at the ranch.

Billy was in the barn, as he had promised, and the pony was worse. His eyes were almost closed now, and his breath whistled shrilly past an obstruction in his nose. A film covered that part of the eyes that was visible at all. It was doubtful whether the pony could see any more. Now and then he snorted, to clear his nose, and by the action seemed to plug it tighter. Jody looked dispiritedly at the pony's coat. The hair lay rough and unkempt and seemed to have lost all of its old luster. Billy stood quietly beside the stall. Jody hated to ask, but he had to know.

"Billy, is he—is he going to get well?"

Billy put his fingers between the bars under the pony's jaw and felt about. "Feel here," he said and he guided Jody's fingers to a large lump under the jaw. "When that gets bigger, I'll open it up and then he'll get better."

Jody looked quickly away, for he had heard about that lump. "What is the matter with him?"

Billy didn't want to answer, but he had to. He couldn't be wrong three times. "Strangles," he said shortly, "but don't you worry about that. I'll pull him out of it. I've seen them get well when they were worse than Gabilan is. I'm going to steam him now. You can help."

"Yes," Jody said miserably. He followed Billy into the grain room and watched him make the steaming bag ready. It was a long canvas nose bag with straps to go over a horse's ears. Billy filled it one-third full of bran and then he added a couple of

handfuls of dried hops. On top of the dry substance he poured a little carbolic acid and a little turpentine. "I'll be mixing it all up while you run to the house for a kettle of boiling water," Billy said.

When Jody came back with the steaming kettle, Billy buckled the straps over Gabilan's head and fitted the bag tightly around his nose. Then through a little hole in the side of the bag he poured the boiling water on the mixture. The pony started away as a cloud of strong steam rose up, but then the soothing fumes crept through his nose and into his lungs, and the sharp steam began to clear out the nasal passages. He breathed loudly. His legs trembled in an ague, and his eyes closed against the biting cloud. Billy poured in more water and kept the steam rising for fifteen minutes. At last he set down the kettle and took the bag from Gabilan's nose. The pony looked better. He breathed freely, and his eyes were open wider than they had been.

"See how good it makes him feel," Billy said. "Now we'll wrap him up in the blanket again. Maybe he'll be nearly well by morning."

"I'll stay with him tonight," Jody suggested.

"No. Don't you do it. I'll bring my blankets down here and put them in the hay. You can stay tomorrow and steam him if he needs it."

The evening was falling when they went to the house for their supper. Jody didn't even realize that some one else had fed the chickens and filled the wood-box. He walked up past the house to the dark brush line and took a drink of water from the tub. The spring water was so cold that it stung his mouth and drove a shiver through him. The sky above the hills was still light. He saw a hawk flying so high that it caught the sun on its breast and shone like a spark. Two blackbirds were driving him down the sky, glittering as they attacked their enemy. In the west, the clouds were moving in to rain again.

Jody's father didn't speak at all while the family ate supper, but after Billy Buck had taken his blankets and gone to sleep in the barn, Carl Tiflin built a high fire in the fireplace and told stories. He told about the wild man, who ran naked through the country and had a tail and ears like a horse, and he told about the rabbit-cats of Moro Cojo that hopped into the trees for birds. He revived the famous Maxwell brothers who found a vein of gold and hid the traces of it so carefully that they could never find it again.

Jody sat with his chin in his hands; his mouth worked nervously, and his father gradually became aware that he wasn't listening very carefully. "Isn't that funny?" he asked.

Jody laughed politely and said, "Yes, sir." His father was angry and hurt, then. He didn't tell any more stories. After a while, Jody took a lantern and went down to the barn. Billy Buck was asleep in the hay, and, except that his breath rasped a little in his lungs, the pony seemed to be much better. Jody stayed a little while, running his fingers over the rough red coat, and then he took up the lantern and went back to the house. When he was in bed, his mother came into the room.

"Have you enough covers on? It's getting winter."

"Yes, ma'am."

"Well, get some rest tonight." She hesitated to go out, stood uncertainly. "The pony will be all right," she said.

Jody was tired. He went to sleep quickly and didn't awaken until dawn. The triangle sounded, and Billy Buck came up from the barn before Jody could get out of the house.

"How is he?" Jody demanded.

Billy always wolfed his breakfast. "Pretty good. I'm going to open that lump this morning. Then he'll be better maybe."

After breakfast, Billy got out his best knife, one with a needle point. He whetted the shining blade a long time on a little carborundum stone. He tried the point and the blade again and again on his calloused thumb-ball, and at last he tried it on his upper lip.

On the way to the barn, Jody noticed how the young grass was up and how the stubble was melting day by day into the new green crop of volunteer. It was a cold sunny morning.

As soon as he saw the pony, Jody knew he was worse. His eyes were closed and sealed shut with dried mucus. His head hung so low that his nose almost touched the straw of his bed. There was a little groan in each breath, a deep-seated, patient groan.

Billy lifted the weak head and made a quick slash with the knife. Jody saw the yellow pus run out. He held up the head while Billy swabbed out the wound with weak carbolic acid salve.

"Now he'll feel better," Billy assured him. "That yellow poison is what makes him sick."

Jody looked unbelieving at Billy Buck. "He's awful sick."

Billy thought a long time what to say. He nearly tossed off a careless assurance, but he saved himself in time. "Yes, he's pretty sick," he said at last. "I've seen worse ones get well. If he doesn't get pneumonia, we'll pull him through. You stay with him. If he gets worse, you can come and get me."

For a long time after Billy went away, Jody stood beside the pony, stroking him behind the ears. The pony didn't flip his head the way he had done when he was well. The groaning in his breathing was becoming more hollow.

Doubletree Mutt looked into the barn, his big tail waving provocatively, and Jody was so incensed at his health that he found a hard block clod on the floor and deliberately threw it. Doubletree Mutt went yelping away to nurse a bruised paw.

In the middle of the morning, Billy Buck came back and made another steam bag. Jody watched to see whether the pony improved this time as he had before. His breathing eased a little, but he did not raise his head.

The Saturday dragged on. Late in the afternoon Jody went to the house and brought his bedding down and made up a place to sleep in the hay. He didn't ask permission. He knew from the way his mother looked at him that she would let him do almost anything. That night he left a lantern burning on a wire over the box stall. Billy had told him to rub the pony's legs every little while.

At nine o'clock the wind sprang up and howled around the barn. And in spite of his worry, Jody grew sleepy. He got into his blankets and went to sleep, but the breathy groans of the pony sounded in his dreams. And in his sleep he heard a crashing noise which went on and on until it awakened him. The wind was rushing through the barn. He sprang up and looked down the lane of stalls. The barn door had blown open, and the pony was gone.

He caught the lantern and ran outside into the gale, and he saw Gabilan weakly shambling away into the darkness, head down, legs working slowly and mechanically. When Jody ran up and caught him by the forelock, he allowed himself to be led back and put into his stall. His groans were louder, and a fierce whistling came from his nose. Jody didn't sleep any more then. The hissing of the pony's breath grew louder and sharper.

He was glad when Billy Buck came in at dawn. Billy looked for a time at the pony as though he had never seen him before. He felt the ears and flanks. "Jody," he said, "I've got to do something you won't want to see. You run up to the house for a while."

Jody grabbed him fiercely by the forearm. "You're not going to shoot him?"

Billy patted his hand. "No. I'm going to open a little hole in his windpipe so he can breathe. His nose is filled up. When he gets well, we'll put a little brass button in the hole for him to breathe through."

Jody couldn't have gone away if he had wanted to. It was awful to see the red hide cut. But infinitely more terrible to know it was being cut and not to see it. "I'll stay right here," he said bitterly. "You sure you got to?"

"Yes. I'm sure. If you stay, you can hold his head. If it doesn't make you sick, that is."

The fine knife came out again and was whetted again just as carefully as it had been for the first time. Jody held the pony's head up and the throat taut, while Billy felt up and down for the right place. Jody sobbed once as the bright knife point disappeared into the throat. The pony plunged weakly away and then stood still, trembling violently. The blood ran thickly out and up the knife and across Billy's hand and into his shirtsleeve. The sure square hand sawed out a round hole in the flesh, and the breath came bursting out of the hole, throwing a fine spray of blood. With the rush of oxygen, the pony took a sudden strength. He lashed out with his hind feet and tried to rear, but Jody held his head down while Billy mopped the new wound with carbolic salve. It was a good job. The blood stopped flowing and the air puffed out the hole and sucked it in regularly with a little bubbling noise.

The rain brought in by the night wind began to fall on the barn roof. Then the triangle rang for breakfast. "You go up and eat while I wait," Billy said. "We've got to keep this hole from plugging up."

Jody walked slowly out of the barn. He was too dispirited to tell Billy how the barn door had blown open and let the pony out. He emerged into the wet gray morning and sloshed up to the house, taking a perverse pleasure in splashing through all the puddles. His mother fed him and put dry clothes on. She didn't question him. She seemed to know he couldn't answer questions. But when he was ready to go back to the barn she brought him a pan of steaming meal. "Give him this," she said.

But Jody did not take the pan. He said, "He won't eat anything," and ran out of the house. At the barn, Billy showed him how to fix a ball of cotton on a stick, with which to swab out the breathing hole when it became clogged with mucus.

Jody's father walked into the barn and stood with them in front of the stall. At length he turned to the boy. "Hadn't you better come with me? I'm going to drive over the hill." Jody shook his head. "You better come on, out of this," the father insisted.

Billy turned on him angrily. "Let him alone. It's his pony, isn't it?"

Carl Tiflin walked away without saying another word. His feelings were badly hurt.

All morning Jody kept the wound open and the air passing in and out freely. At noon the pony lay wearily down on his side and stretched his nose out.

Billy came back. "If you're going to stay with him tonight, you better take a little nap," he said. Jody went absently out of the barn. The sky had cleared to a hard thin blue. Everywhere the birds were busy with worms that had come to the damp surface of the ground.

Jody walked to the brush line and sat on the edge of the mossy tub. He looked down at the house and at the old bunk-house and at the dark cypress tree. The place was familiar, but curiously changed. It wasn't itself any more, but a frame for things that were happening. A cold wind blew out of the east now, signifying that the rain was over for a little while. At his feet Jody could see the little arms of new weeds spreading out over the ground. In the mud about the spring were thousands of quail tracks.

Doubletree Mutt came sideways and embarrassed up through the vegetable patch, and Jody, remembering how he had thrown the clod, put his arm about the dog's neck and kissed him on his wide black nose. Doubletree Mutt sat still, as though he knew some solemn thing was happening. His big tail slapped the ground gravely. Jody pulled a swollen tick out of Mutt's neck and popped it dead between his thumb-nails. It was a nasty thing. He washed his hands in the cold spring water.

Except for the steady swish of the wind, the farm was very quiet. Jody knew his mother wouldn't mind if he didn't go in to eat his lunch. After a little while he went slowly back to the barn. Mutt crept into his own little house and whined softly to himself for a long time.

Billy Buck stood up from the box and surrendered the cotton swab. The pony still lay on his side and the wound in his throat bellowed in and out. When Jody saw how dry and dead the hair looked, he knew at last that there was no hope for the pony. He had seen the dead hair before on dogs and on cows, and it was a sure sign. He sat heavily on the box and let down the barrier of the box stall. For a long time he kept his eyes on the moving wound, and at last he dozed, and the afternoon passed quickly. Just before dark his mother brought a deep dish of stew and left it for him and went away. Jody ate a little of it, and when it was dark, he set the lantern on the floor by the pony's head so he could watch the wound and keep it open. And he dozed again until the night

chill awakened him. The wind was blowing fiercely, bringing the north cold with
it. Jody brought a blanket from his bed in
the hay and wrapped himself in it. Gabilan's breathing was quiet at last; the hole
in his throat moved gently. The owls flew
through the hayloft, shrieking and looking
for mice. Jody put his hands down on his
head and slept. In his sleep he was aware
that the wind had increased. He heard it
slamming about the barn.

It was daylight when he awakened. The
barn door had swung open. The pony was
gone. He sprang up and ran out into the
morning light.

The pony's tracks were plain enough,
dragging through the frostlike dew on the
young grass, tired tracks with little lines
between them where the hoofs had
dragged. They headed for the brush line
halfway up the ridge. Jody broke into a run
and followed them. The sun shone on the
sharp white quartz that stuck through the
ground here and there. As he followed
the plain trail, a shadow fell across in front
of him. He looked up and saw a high circle of black buzzards, and the slowly revolving circle dropped lower and lower.
The solemn birds soon disappeared over
the ridge. Jody ran faster then, forced on
by panic and rage. The trail entered the
brush at last and followed a winding route
among the tall sage bushes.

At the top of the ridge Jody was winded.
He paused, puffing noisily. The blood
pounded in his ears. Then he saw what
he was looking for. Below, in one of the
little clearings in the brush, lay the red
pony. In the distance, Jody could see the
legs moving slowly and convulsively. And
in a circle around him stood the buzzards,
waiting for the moment of death they
knew so well.

Jody leaned forward and plunged down
the hill. The wet ground muffled his steps
and the brush hid him. When he arrived,
it was all over. The first buzzard sat on
the pony's head and its beak had just risen
dripping with dark eye fluid. Jody plunged

into the circle like a cat. The black
brotherhood arose in a cloud, but the big
one on the pony's head was too late. As
it hopped along to take off, Jody caught its
wing tip and pulled it down. It was nearly
as big as he was. The free wing crashed
into his face with the force of a club, but
he hung on. The claws fastened on his leg
and the wing elbows battered his head on
either side. Jody groped blindly with his
free hand. His fingers found the neck of
the struggling bird. The red eyes looked
into his face, calm and fearless and fierce;

the naked head turned from side to side. Then the beak opened and vomited a stream of putrefied fluid. Jody brought up his knee and fell on the great bird. He held the neck to the ground with one hand while his other found a piece of sharp white quartz. The first blow broke the beak sideways and black blood spurted from the twisted, leathery mouth corners. He struck again but missed. The red fearless eyes still looked at him, impersonal and unafraid and detached. He struck again and again, until the buzzard lay dead, until its head was a red pulp. He was still beating the dead bird when Billy Buck pulled

him off and held him tightly to calm his shaking.

Carl Tiflin wiped the blood from the boy's face with a red bandana. Jody was limp and quiet now. His father moved the buzzard with his toe. "Jody," he explained, "the buzzard didn't kill the pony. Don't you know that?"

"I know it," Jody said wearily.

It was Billy Buck who was angry. He had lifted Jody in his arms, and had turned to carry him home. But he turned back on Carl Tiflin. "Course he knows it," Billy said furiously. "Can't you see how he'd feel about it?"

The man who wrote this story

JOHN STEINBECK 1902–

Like William Saroyan, Steinbeck uses his home state of California as the background for most of his stories. Unlike Saroyan, however, Steinbeck does not write about his own life. He prefers to write about people he has known, and these are the workers, the fruit pickers and farm hands, of his Salinas Valley.

During the depression years of the 1930's many small farmers lost all they had. Jobs were scarce, and homeless people were on the roads looking for food and work. Some of Steinbeck's best novels tell with great tenderness of the pain and suffering of these poor wanderers. In each of these novels, Steinbeck expresses his faith in the simple, primitive man.

"The Gift" illustrated another aspect of Steinbeck's skill and understanding. In this story he portrayed with feeling and sharpness a boy's realization of the indifferent cruelty of nature.

The Long Valley, a collection of short stories, and *The Red Pony,* from which "The Gift" was taken, are popular with young people. *The Grapes of Wrath,* a novel, was awarded the Pulitzer Prize.

Let's consider . . .

1. Your first interest, of course, was in Jody and the pony. That interest, however, would have been much less if John Steinbeck had not made the place where they lived so real and the details of the story so natural. He began by picturing Billy Buck, the character next in importance to Jody. What was your first impression of Billy? What details of that first picture made him especially real? Note even his table manners.

2. Jody was only ten years old. What kind of little boy did he appear to be before his father gave him the pony?

3. Jody's father and mother were rather quiet folk with little to say. You knew them rather by what they did and what they did not do. Give a short character sketch of each one. Show what Jody meant to his mother and to his father, in what different ways they showed their concern for him.

4. There seemed to be little hubbub on the ranch. Why was this so? Apart from Jody and the pony, what feature of ranch life impressed you most?

5. "Jody's throat collapsed in on itself . . ." All he could say when he first saw the pony was, "Mine?" Describe his feel-

ings, the surprise beforehand, and the part played by his father and Billy.

6. Why do you think he was so overjoyed to have a pony of his own?

7. What good advice did Billy give Jody about the way to treat his prize?

8. Getting acquainted with Gabilan, taking care of him, and waiting for the time when he could be broken to halter and saddle—all of these were a great experience for Jody. They took a long time. Steinbeck was deliberate in telling about them. Why weren't you impatient with the slow pace? If there were any spots where you wished he had hurried along, point them out and explain why you were impatient. What part of this experience do you think Jody enjoyed most? Tell what made it enjoyable.

9. Thanksgiving was going to be the great day. Jody could then ride Gabilan for the first time. What disappointment preceded the long-awaited day? In what way did it foreshadow the end?

10. In what way did chance play a part in the pony's catching cold and becoming fatally ill? How was Jody responsible? How was Billy Buck to blame? What was Mr. Tiflin's attitude?

11. "He's awful sick, Billy," was Jody's verdict as he looked at Gabilan the morning after the drenching. Describe the signs that made Jody sure.

12. Perhaps you have *never* cared for a sick animal; perhaps you have always had a pet to look after. In either case, you would appreciate Billy's and Jody's loving care of Gabilan. Which examples of such care will you remember longest? How did Jody show that he was only a little boy? When did he seem most mature?

13. Early in the story Jody encountered two big black buzzards and "hated them as all decent things hate them." How did they make *you* feel then? Under what circumstances did Jody meet the buzzards again? Do you condemn or approve his treatment of "the big one on the pony's head"? Explain.

14. Billy Buck was furious with Jody's father and said, "Course he knows it; can't you see how he'd feel about it?" What did he mean?

15. In what ways was the ending satisfying to you? Could you change it without becoming sentimental? Were Billy, Jody's father, and Jody consistent characters? Discuss.

The writer's craft . . .

Like all short stories, "The Gift" had a setting, a plot, a mood, a theme, a style, and believable characters. Each of these contributed to the total impression which the story made on you, the reader.

1. John Steinbeck selected a western ranch as the setting. Why was this setting an essential background for the story he had to tell?

2. Jody was the leading character. How did the setting help to shape his character and personality?

3. You came to know Jody as a person by

   a. His speech
   b. His physical appearance
   c. His feelings
   d. His actions
   e. His effect on others

List each of these on a separate sheet of paper. After each item jot down one or two incidents from the story in which the author revealed this information about Jody.

4. Explain how the plot of this story grew out of the setting and the characters. For example, you could show that because Jody lived on a ranch (the setting) he was able to receive a pony as a gift. Because Jody was an impressionable boy (the character) his affection for the pony contributed to the tragic climax. Show as many of these relationships as you can.

5. You will recall that the theme is the underlying idea of the story. Write the theme of "The Gift." Do you think that

Steinbeck was trying to teach a lesson? Discuss.

6. The **climax** is the point of highest interest. What point in "The Gift" would you name as the climax?

7. Arrange the following short-story elements in their order of importance in this story: mood, plot, characters, setting, theme. Give your reasons for choosing this particular order.

8. Romantic writers often portray life as better than it really is. Would you call Steinbeck a romantic writer or a realistic writer? List several characteristics of his writing which justify your opinion. Be sure that you consider the ending of the story.

9. Write a description of the total effect which "The Gift" made on you.

Knowing words . . .

One of the best ways in which to increase the size of your vocabulary is to widen your range of interests. Throughout "The Gift" John Steinbeck used terms associated with horses and riding. Perhaps before you read this story, you knew very little about these terms. With a little more attention to them now, you will remember them and so read other stories about horses with more understanding and interest.

In each of the following sentences one or more of these terms are printed in italics. First try to find the meaning of each term from the context of the sentence. Then check that meaning with a dictionary or the glossary at the end of the book. Be able to use each term in a sentence of your own.

1. "How you going to rope a cow without a *saddle horn?*"

2. He let them feel the red saddle, and showed them the brass chain *throat-latch* on the *bridle* and the big brass buttons at each temple where the *headstall* and *brow band* crossed.

3. He took brush and *currycomb* from the wall.

4. He braided the mane into a dozen little pigtails, and he braided the *forelock,* and then he undid them and brushed the hair out straight again.

5. Billy's own horse was a stringy *cayuse* with a hammer head.

6. He changed the *stirrup* length over and over, and could never get it just right.

7. Sometimes, mounted on the sawhorse in the harness-room, with *collars* and *hames* and *tugs* hung all about him Jody rode out beyond the room.

8. He carried his rifle across the *pommel.*

9. The first time the pony wore the bridle he whipped his head about and worked his tongue against the *bit* until the blood oozed from the corners of his mouth.

10. Jody's father gave him an old pair of *spurs* and bent in the *side bars* and cut down the strap and took up the *chainlets* until they fitted.

NOW THINK BACK

1. If you were going to discuss airplanes and flying intelligently, you would need to know the terms which apply to the structure of the machine and the way it is handled. In the same way, when you discuss the short story, you need to know certain terms which apply to its structure and development. You have been introduced to most of these terms already. If you aren't sure of one of the following terms, look it up in a dictionary. Discuss all of these terms in class until you are sure you know what they mean.

plot	theme	plausibility
character	conflict	style
setting	suspense	realistic
mood	irony	romantic

2. Select six of the terms from the list in Exercise 1. Write these terms on your paper, spacing them several lines apart. For each term, choose a different story from this part which you think illustrates the use of the technique, structural element, or classification described by that term. For example, if you listed the term *character,* you would choose a story in which the structural element of *character* was important and then explain why. Here is one way you might list and explain the term *character.*

> 1. *character:* In "The Gift" the story was built around the character Jody. Because he was such an impressionable young boy, the events in the story led to a tragic ending.

3. Humor contributed to your enjoyment of three of the stories in this part: "The Legend of Sleepy Hollow," "The Cop and the Anthem," and "Ararat." Tell whether the humor was brought out through the author's portrayal of the characters themselves. Was the humor of the kind which would make you laugh, or was it of the kind which just made you smile?

4. On radio and television, comedians are usually consciously funny, even though they may give the impression that they are not trying to be funny at all. Select several of the most popular of these professional comedians and discuss the ways in which they succeed in being humorous. Do they depend upon comic situations, or upon their ability to portray the kind of person whom their audience would consider funny? What kinds of situations and characters are nearly always humorous?

5. Washington Irving, Jack London, and John Steinbeck made effective use of American localities as settings for their stories. Which story did you enjoy reading the most? Account for your preference. Consider the way the background was worked into each of these stories.

6. "A Day's Pleasure" may be classified as a realistic story; "The Birthmark," as a romantic story; "The Gift" has features of both the realistic and the romantic. Illustrate briefly, but specifically, the truth of this last statement.

7. Which story in this part do you feel had the finest balance of plot, character, and setting in creating "the single effect" which the author intended? Consider the part each of these structural elements played in the story you selected.

8. Certain stories are memorable largely because of (1) the mood they create, (2) the suspense they sustain, or (3) the lesson in human behavior they teach. Select one story which you will remember for *each* of these reasons. Also explain what mood was created, how the suspense was achieved, and what lesson was taught.

9. Which of these stories did you enjoy the most? Which did you enjoy the least? Account honestly for your likes and dislikes.

Things to do . . .

1. Arrange the following authors chronologically, beginning your list with the earliest:

Hamlin Garland, Edgar Allan Poe, John Steinbeck, Washington Irving, O. Henry, Jack London, Zenna Henderson, Nathaniel Hawthorne.

2. Make a study of the men and women characters who have interested you particularly in this part. As a whole, which kind of characters do you think the authors have portrayed more skillfully? In order to decide carefully, list the important characters from this part under the following headings:

Realistic	Understanding	Pathetic
Romantic	Down-to-Earth	Dull
Too-good	Improbable	Fantastic

Supply other headings if you wish. Some characters could appear under more than one heading.

3. Assume that you had met Brom Bones, Georgiana, Katrina Van Tassel, Jemmy *or* Valancy at a party. Assume also that you were in the habit of keeping a diary. Write several paragraphs in diary form reporting your impression of one of these characters: his or her appearance, personality, and potentiality as a friend. You might even invent bits of conversation which you might have had with this person in order to make your diary entry more interesting.

4. Write a paper of about 350 words telling which you prefer to read and why: novels or short stories. Make your reasons clear by definite references to both types of literature. Include the titles of several stories and several novels you enjoyed.

5. Assume that you are about to write a short story. Describe a setting with which you are thoroughly familiar and which will have a direct bearing on the plot of your story and an indirect effect on at least one character. Indicate how this setting affects the plot and the character of your short story.

More to read . . .

Golden Tales of Our America by MAY LAMBERTON BECKER.
Dodd, Mead & Company, 1929.
Tales Before Midnight edited by STEPHEN VINCENT BENÉT.
Rinehart & Co., Inc., 1939.
Time To Be Young: Great Stories of the Growing Years edited by WHIT. BURNETT.
J. B. Lippincott Company, 1945.
Stories of School and College Life edited by ROBERT J. CADIGAN.
Appleton-Century-Crofts, Inc., 1942.
Modern American Short Stories edited by THOMAS R. COOK.
Charles Scribner's Sons, 1939.
A Humble Romance and Other Stories by MARY E. WILKINS FREEMAN
Harper & Brothers, 1937.
Main-travelled Roads by HAMLIN GARLAND.
Harper & Brothers, 1909.
Americans All: Stories of American Life edited by BENJAMIN A. HEYDRICK.
Harcourt, Brace and Company, 1941.
The Sketch Book by WASHINGTON IRVING.
The Macmillan Company.
Round Up: The Stories of Ring W. Lardner by RING W. LARDNER.
Charles Scribner's Sons, 1929.
American Short Stories edited by FRED LEWIS PATTEE.
Dodd, Mead & Company, 1925.
Best Stories of O. Henry selected by VAN H. CARTMELL and BENNETT CERF.
Garden City Books, 1954.
An American Family Album: Stories of American Life edited by FRANCES SPENCER.
Harper & Brothers, 1946.

OUR DAILY BREAD

Man's earliest attempt at earning his daily bread was largely a search for food. Today it is more a matter of his finding the kind of work that suits him best and permits him to make a good life for himself and his family.

When you read about Americans at work, you are reading the story of your country. Through literature you may learn of the thousands of different jobs which Americans perform and thus appreciate the complexity of modern life. You discover, too, that different regions offer different opportunities for earning a living. You also gain a deeper understanding of your nation's past by looking back at the work men used to do and at a pattern of living that is no longer a part of the American scene.

In many ways, America is the product of the willing hands and hearts of its people. American literature reflects the pride which Americans have always taken in a job well done.

OUR DAILY BREAD

The Riverman

STEWART EDWARD WHITE

For Jimmy Powers and the other loggers, their work was more than a way
to earn a living. It was a chance to show their skill and "long experience
with the ways of saw logs." Once a year, at the Fourth of July celebration,
they used these same skills and experiences to determine the champion.

I first met him one Fourth of July afternoon in the middle eighties. The sawdust
streets and high board walks of the lumber town were filled to the brim with people. The permanent population, dressed in
the stiffness of its Sunday best, escorted
gingham wives or sweethearts; a dozen outsiders like myself tried not to be too conspicuous in a city smartness; but the great
multitude was composed of the men of the
woods. I sat, chair-tilted by the hotel,
watching them pass. Their heavy woolen
shirts crossed by the broad suspenders, the
red of their sashes or leather shine of their
belts, their short kersey [1] trousers "stagged"
off to leave a gap between the knee and the
heavily spiked "cork boots"—all these were
distinctive enough of their class, but most
interesting to me were the eyes that peered
from beneath their little round hats rak-
ishly askew. They were all subtly alike,
those eyes. Some were black, some were
brown, or gray, or blue, but all were steady
and unabashed, all looked straight at you
with a strange, humorous blending of aggression and respect for your own business,
and all without exception wrinkled at the
corners with a suggestion of dry humor.
In my half-conscious scrutiny I probably
stared harder than I knew, for all at once

a laughing pair of the blue eyes suddenly
met mine full, and an ironical voice
drawled,

"Say, bub, you look as interested as a
man killing snakes. Am I your long-lost
friend?"

The tone of the voice matched accurately the attitude of the man, and that
was quite noncommittal. He stood cheerfully ready to meet the emergency. If I
sought trouble, it was here to my hand; or
if I needed help, he was willing to offer it.

"I guess you are," I replied, "if you can
tell me what all this outfit's headed for."

He thrust back his hat and ran his hand
through a mop of closely cropped light
curls.

"Birling match," [2] he exclaimed briefly.
"Come on."

I joined him, and together we followed
the crowd to the river, where we roosted
like cormorants on adjacent piles overlooking a patch of clear water among the filled
booms.

"Drive's just over," my new friend informed me. "Rear come down last night.
Fourther July celebration. This little town
will scratch fer th' tall timber along about

[1] *kersey*, coarse woolen cloth

[2] *birling match*, a contest in which two persons
cause a floating log to revolve by treading on it.
Each tries to make his opponent lose balance.

445

pond. And the man, his arms folded, his knees just bent in the graceful nervous attitude of the circus rider, stood upright like a statue of bronze.

A roar approved this feat.

"That's Dickey Darrell," said my informant, "Roaring Dick. Watch him."

The man on the log was small, with clean, beautiful haunches and shoulders, but with hanging baboon arms. Perhaps his most striking feature was a mop of reddish brown hair that overshadowed a little triangular white face accented by two reddish brown quadrilaterals that served as eyebrows and a pair of inscrutable chipmunk eyes.

For a moment he poised erect in the great calm of the public performer. Then slowly he began to revolve the log under his feet. The lofty gaze, the folded arms, the straight supple waist budged not by a hair's breadth; only the feet stepped forward, at first deliberately, then faster and faster, until the rolling log threw a blue spray a foot into the air. Then suddenly *slap! slap!* the heavy caulks stamped a reversal. The log came instantaneously to rest, quivering exactly like some animal that had been spurred through its paces.

"Magnificent!" I cried.

"That's nothing!" my companion repressed me; "anybody can birl a log. Watch this."

Roaring Dick for the first time unfolded his arms. With some appearance of caution he balanced his unstable footing into absolute immobility. Then he turned a somersault.

This was the real thing. My friend uttered a wild yell of applause which was lost in a general roar.

A long pike pole shot out, bit the end of the timber, and towed it to the boom pile. Another man stepped on the log with Darrell. They stood facing each other, bent-kneed, alert. Suddenly with one accord they commenced to birl the log from left to right. The pace grew hot. Like squirrels treading a cage their feet twinkled.

midnight when the boys goes in to take her apart."

A half-dozen men with peavies [3] rolled a white pine log of about a foot and a half diameter into the clear water, where it lay rocking back and forth, three or four feet from the boom piles. Suddenly a man ran the length of the boom, leaped easily into the air, and landed with both feet square on one end of the floating log. That end disappeared in an ankle-deep swirl of white foam, the other rose suddenly, the whole timber, projected forward by the shock, drove headlong to the middle of the little

[3] *peavies,* stout poles with a hook and spike at the end

Then it became apparent that Darrell's opponent was gradually being forced from the top of the log. He could not keep up. Little by little, still moving desperately, he dropped back to the slant, then at last to the edge, and so off into the river with a mighty splash.

"Clean birled!" commented my friend.

One after another a half-dozen rivermen tackled the imperturbable Dick, but none of them possessed the agility to stay on top in the pace he set them. One boy of eighteen seemed for a moment to hold his own, and managed at least to keep out of the water even when Darrell had apparently reached his maximum speed. But that expert merely threw his entire weight into two reversing stamps of his feet, and the young fellow dove forward as abruptly as though he had been shied over a horse's head.

The crowd was by now getting uproarious and impatient of volunteer effort to humble Darrell's challenge. It wanted the best and at once. It began, with increasing insistence, to shout a name.

"Jimmy Powers!" it vociferated, "Jimmy Powers."

And then by shamefaced bashfulness, by profane protest, by muttered and comprehensive curses I knew that my companion on the other pile was indicated.

A dozen men near at hand began to shout. "Here he is!" they cried. "Come on, Jimmy." "Don't be a high banker." "Hang his hide on the fence."

Jimmy, still red and swearing, suffered himself to be pulled from his elevation and disappeared in the throng. A moment later I caught his head and shoulders pushing toward the boom piles, and so in a moment he stepped warily aboard to face his antagonist.

This was evidently no question to be determined by the simplicity of force or the simplicity of a child's trick. The two men stood half-crouched, face to face, watching each other narrowly, but making no move. To me they seemed like two wrestlers sparring for an opening. Slowly the log revolved one way; then slowly the other. It was a mere courtesy of salute. All at once Dick birled three rapid strokes from left to right as though about to roll the log, leaped into the air and landed square with both feet on the other slant of the timber. Jimmy Powers felt the jar, and acknowledged it by the spasmodic jerk with which he counter-balanced Darrell's weight. But he was not thrown.

As though this daring and hazardous maneuver had opened the combat, both men sprang to life. Sometimes the log rolled one way, sometimes the other, sometimes it jerked from side to side like a crazy thing, but always with the rapidity of light, always in a smother of spray and foam. The decided *spat, spat* of the reversing blows from the caulked boots sounded like picket firing. I could not make out the different leads, feints, parries, and counters of this strange method of boxing, nor could I distinguish to whose initiative the various evolutions of that log could be ascribed. But I retain still a vivid mental picture of two men nearly motionless above the waist, nearly vibrant below it, dominating the insane gyrations of a stick of pine.

The crowd was appreciative and partisan —for Jimmy Powers. It howled wildly, and rose thereby to ever higher excitement. Then it forgot its manners utterly and groaned when it made out that a sudden splash represented its favorite, while the indomitable Darrell still trod the quarterdeck as champion birler for the year.

I must confess I was as sorry as anybody. I climbed down from my cormorant roost, and picked my way between the alleys of aromatic piled lumber in order to avoid the press, and cursed the little gods heartily for undue partiality in the wrong direction. In this manner I happened on Jimmy Powers himself seated dripping on a board and examining his bared foot.

"I'm sorry," said I behind him. "How did he do it?"

He whirled, and I could see that his

laughing, boyish face had become suddenly grim and stern and that his eyes were shot with blood.

"Oh, it's you, is it?" he growled disparagingly. "Well, that's how he did it."

He held out his foot. Across the instep and at the base of the toes ran two rows of tiny round punctures from which the blood was oozing. I looked very inquiring.

"He corked me!" Jimmy Powers explained. "Jammed his spikes into me! Stepped on my foot and tripped me, the—" Jimmy Powers certainly could swear.

"Why didn't you make a kick?" I cried.

"That isn't how I do it," he muttered, pulling on his heavy woolen sock.

"But, no," I insisted, my indignation mounting. "It's an outrage! That crowd was with you. All you had to do was to *say* something—"

He cut me short. "And give myself away as a fool—sure Mike. I ought to know Dickey Darrell by this time, and I ought to be big enough to take care of myself." He stamped his foot into his driver's shoe and took me by the arm, his good humor apparently restored. "No, don't you lose any hair, bub; I'll get even with Roaring Dick."

That night, having by the advice of the proprietor moved my bureau and trunk against the bedroom door, I lay wide awake listening to the taking of the town apart. At each especially vicious crash I wondered if that might be Jimmy Powers getting even with Roaring Dick.

The following year, but earlier in the season, I again visited my little lumber town. In striking contrast to the life of that other midsummer day were the deserted streets. The landlord knew me, and after I had washed and eaten approached me with a suggestion.

"You got all day in front of you," said he; "why don't you take a horse and buggy and make a visit to the big jam? Everybody's up there more or less."

In response to my inquiry he replied: "They've jammed at the upper bend, jammed bad. The crew's been picking at

her for near a week now, and last night Darrell was down to see about some more dynamite. It's worth seein'. The breast of her is near thirty foot high, and lots of water in the river."

"Darrell?" said I, catching at the name.

"Yes. He's rear boss this year. Do you think you'd like to take a look at her?"

"I think I should," I assented.

The horse and I jogged slowly along a deep sand road, through wastes of pine stumps and belts of hardwood beautiful with the early spring, until finally we arrived at a clearing in which stood two huge tents, a mammoth kettle slung over a fire of logs, and drying racks about the timbers of another fire. A fat cook in the inevitable battered derby hat, two bare-armed cookees, and a chore "boy" of seventy-odd summers were the only human beings in sight. One of the cookees agreed to keep an eye on my horse. I picked my way down a well-worn trail toward the regular *clank, clank, clink* of the peavies.

I emerged finally on a plateau elevated some fifty or sixty feet above the river. A half-dozen spectators were already gathered. Among them I could not but notice a tall, spare, broad-shouldered young fellow dressed in a quiet business suit, somewhat wrinkled, whose square, strong, clean-cut face and muscular hands were tanned by the weather to a dark umber-brown. In another moment I looked down on the jam.

The breast, as my landlord had told me, rose sheer from the water to the height of at least twenty-five feet, bristling and formidable. Back of it pressed a volume of logs packed closely in an apparently inextricable tangle as far as the eye could reach. A man near informed me that the tail was a good three miles up stream. From beneath this wonderful *chevaux-de-frise* [4] foamed the current of the river, irresistible to any force less mighty than the statics of such a mass.

A crew of forty or fifty men were at

[4] *chevaux-de-frise,* a military obstacle of timber with projecting spikes, like the logs in the jam

work. They clamped their peavies to the reluctant timbers, heaved, pushed, slid, and rolled them one by one into the current, where they were caught and borne away. They had been doing this for a week. As yet their efforts had made but slight impression on the bulk of the jam, but some time, with patience, they would reach the key-logs. Then the tangle would melt like sugar in the freshet, and these imperturbable workers would have to escape suddenly over the plunging logs to shore.

My eye ranged over the men, and finally rested on Dickey Darrell. He was standing on the slanting end of an upheaved log dominating the scene. His little triangular face with the accents of the quadrilateral eyebrows was pale with the blaze of his energy, and his chipmunk eyes seemed to flame with a dynamic vehemence that caused those on whom their glance fell to jump as though they had been touched with a hot poker. I had heard more of Dickey Darrell since my last visit, and was glad of the chance to observe Morrison & Daly's best "driver" at work.

The jam seemed on the very edge of breaking. After half an hour's strained expectation it seemed still on the very edge of breaking. So I sat down on a stump. Then for the first time I noticed another acquaintance, handling his peavy near the very person of the rear boss.

"Hullo," said I to myself, "that's funny. I wonder if Jimmy Powers got even; and if so, why he is working so amicably and so near Roaring Dick."

At noon the men came ashore for dinner. I paid a quarter into the cook's private exchequer and so was fed. After the meal I approached my acquaintance of the year before.

"Hello, Powers," I greeted him, "I suppose you don't remember me?"

"Sure," he responded heartily. "Ain't you a little early this year?"

"No," I disclaimed, "this is a better sight than a birling match."

I offered him a cigar, which he immediately substituted for his corncob pipe. We sat at the root of a tree.

"It'll be a great sight when that jam pulls," said I.

"You bet," he replied, "but she's a teaser. Even old Tim Shearer would have a picnic to make out just where the key-logs are. We've started her three times, but she's plugged tight every trip. Likely to pull almost any time."

We discussed various topics. Finally I ventured:

"I see your old friend Darrell is rear boss."

"Yes," said Jimmy Powers, dryly.

"By the way, did you fellows ever square up on the birling match?"

"No," said Jimmy Powers; then after an instant, "Not yet."

I glanced at him to recognize the square set to the jaw that had impressed me so formidably the year before. And again his face relaxed almost quizzically as he caught sight of mine.

"Bub," said he, getting to his feet, "those little marks are on my foot yet. And just you tie into one idea: Dickey Darrell's got it coming." His face darkened with a swift anger, and in its very deliberation I glimpsed the flare of an undying hatred.

About three o'clock that afternoon Jimmy's prediction was fulfilled. Without the slightest warning the jam "pulled." Usually certain premonitory *cracks,* certain sinkings down, groanings forward, grumblings, shruggings, and sullen, reluctant shiftings of the logs give opportunity for the men to assure their safety. This jam, after inexplicably hanging fire for a week, as inexplicably started like a sprinter almost into its full gait. The first few tiers toppled smash into the current, raising a waterspout like that made by a dynamite explosion; the mass behind plunged forward blindly, rising and falling as the integral logs were up-ended, turned over, thrust one side, or forced bodily into the air by the mighty power playing jackstraws with them.

The rivermen, though caught unaware, reached either bank. They held their peavies across their bodies as balancing-poles, and zig-zagged ashore with a calmness and lack of haste that were in reality only an indication of the keenness with which they fore-estimated each chance. Long experience with the ways of saw logs brought them out. They knew the correlation of these many forces just as the expert billiard-player knows instinctively the various angles of incidence and reflection between his cue-ball and its mark. Consequently they avoided the centers of eruption, paused on the spots steadied for the moment, dodged moving logs, trod those not yet under way, and so arrived on solid ground. The jam itself started with every indication of meaning business, gained momentum for a hundred feet, and then plugged to a standstill. The "break" was abortive.

Now we all had leisure to notice two things. First, the movement had not been of the whole jam, as we had at first supposed, but only of a block or section of it twenty rods or so in extent. Thus between the part that had moved and the greater bulk that had not stirred lay a hundred feet of open water in which floated a number of loose logs. The second fact was, that Dickey Darrell had fallen into that open stretch of water and was in the act of swimming toward one of the floating logs. That much we were given just time to appreciate thoroughly. Then the other section of the jam rumbled and began to break. Roaring Dick was caught between two gigantic millstones moving to crush him out of sight.

An active figure darted down the tail of the first section, out over the floating logs, seized Darrell by the coat-collar, and so burdened began desperately to scale the very face of the breaking jam.

Never was a more magnificent rescue.

The logs were rolling, falling, diving against the laden man. He climbed as over a treadmill, a treadmill whose speed was constantly increasing. And when he finally gained the top, it was as the gap closed splinteringly beneath him and the man he had saved.

It is not in the woodsman to be demonstrative at any time, but here was work demanding attention. Without a pause for breath or congratulation they turned to the necessity of the moment. The jam, the whole jam, was moving at last. Jimmy Powers ran ashore for his peavy. Roaring Dick, like a demon incarnate, threw himself into the work. Forty men attacked the jam at a dozen places, encouraging the movement, twisting aside the timbers that threatened to lock anew, directing pigmy-like the titanic forces into the channel of their efficiency. Roaring like wild cattle the logs swept by, at first slowly, then with the railroad rush of the curbed freshet. Men were everywhere, taking chances, like cowboys before the stampeded herd. And so, out of sight around the lower bend swept the front of the jam in a swirl of glory, the rivermen riding the great boom back of the creature they subdued, until at last, with a slackening current, the logs floated by, free, cannoning with hollow sound one against the other. A half-dozen watchers, leaning statuesquely on the shafts of their peavies, watched the ordered ranks pass by.

One by one the spectators departed. At last only myself and the brown-faced young man remained. He sat on a stump, staring with sightless eyes into vacancy. I did not disturb his thoughts.

The sun dipped. A cool breeze of evening sucked up the river. Over near the cook-camp a big fire commenced to crackle by the drying frames. At dusk the rivermen straggled in from the down-river trail.

The brown-faced young man arose and went to meet them. I saw him return in close conversation with Jimmy Powers. Be-fore they reached us he had turned away with a gesture of farewell.

Jimmy Powers stood looking after him long after his form had disappeared, and indeed even after the sound of his wheels had died toward town. As I approached, the riverman turned to me a face from which the reckless, contained self-reliance of the woodsworker had faded. It was wide-eyed with an almost awe-stricken wonder and adoration.

"Do you know who that is?" he asked me in a hushed voice. "That's Thorpe, Harry Thorpe. And do you know what he said to me just now, *me*? He told me he wanted me to work in Camp One next winter, Thorpe's One. And he told me I was the first man he ever hired straight into One."

His breath caught with something like a sob.

I had heard of the man and of his methods. I knew he had made it a practice of recruiting for his prize camp only from the employees of his other camps, that, as Jimmy said, he never "hired straight into One." I had heard, too, of his reputation among his own and other woodsmen. But this was the first time I had ever come into personal contact with his influence. It impressed me the more in that I had come to know Jimmy Powers and his kind.

"You deserve it, every bit," said I. "I'm not going to call you a hero, because that would make you tired. What you did this afternoon showed nerve. It was a brave act. But it was a better act because you rescued your enemy, because you forgot everything but your common humanity when danger—"

I broke off. Jimmy was again looking at me with his ironically quizzical grin.

"Bub," said he, "if you're going to hang any stars of Bethlehem on my Christmas tree, just call a halt right here. I didn't rescue that scalawag because I had any Christian sentiments, nary bit. I was just naturally savin' him for the birling match next Fourther July."

The man who wrote this story

STEWART EDWARD WHITE   1873–1946

The life of Stewart Edward White was as exciting as any of his novels. His boyhood was spent in a Michigan lumber camp and on a ranch in California. He did not start school until he was sixteen, although he had been tutored for many years. Still he was able to graduate from high school when he was eighteen, and had already published his first writings: a series of articles about the bird life he observed near his home.

After completing college, Mr. White joined the gold rush to the Black Hills of South Dakota. He found no gold, however, and went to New York to study law. On the side he took a course in short-story writing, and his first stories were so successful that he gave up his law studies and turned to writing. He finished two novels about his adventures in South Dakota, but they did not attract much attention. His third novel, *The Blazed Trail,* written in a cabin in the Hudson Bay area, brought him his first fame.

White wrote an amazing number of stories and novels, including *Simba* and *Daniel Boone.* He wrote easily and rarely found it necessary to change his work. And he could write in almost any place; in fact he wrote one novel while on a yacht off the coast of British Columbia, and another while in a grass hut in Central Africa where he was recovering from wounds inflicted by a leopard.

Let's consider . . .

1. How did the narrator of this story happen to meet Jimmy Powers and see the birling match?

2. Birling is an exciting sport requiring great skill. Describe the match. Explain the methods Roaring Dick used to dislodge his opponents.

3. Why did the crowd demand that Jimmy Powers compete? How was he defeated? How did he feel about his defeat?

4. In the narrator's second visit to the lumber country he saw the loggers at work. Describe what had happened. Why weren't the loggers able to break the jam?

5. You will recall that the *dramatic* in a story or play often involves the reader's feelings because it presents the unusual or unexpected. Describe the rescue as dramatically as you can.

6. Jimmy Powers was "awe-stricken" at his reward. Explain why his way of telling about it was characteristic of him.

7. Throughout the story Dickey Darrell was an important character, yet no mention is made of him at the end of the story. Explain why.

8. Many of your sports depend for success upon clever team work. Birling requires individual skill. In your opinion, which type of sport is more exciting? Explain.

9. Mention several sports with which you are familiar that require individual skill rather than team work. In which sport do you think there is a greater opportunity for unfair play? Why do you think some players take advantage of the opportunity?

The writer's craft . . .

A. When an author creates a leading character, he must be prepared to make him sufficiently interesting to warrant the reader's attention. The leading character does not necessarily have to be a hero nor even a sympathetic person. However, he must provide through his actions an insight into human behavior.

In "The Riverman" Stewart Edward White did not begin his story with the leading character. Instead, he began with a description of the people in the logging town. He dwelt in detail on their dress and attitude. He even described their eyes: "Some were black, some were brown, or gray or blue, but all were steady and unabashed, all looked straight at you with a strange, humorous blending of aggression and respect for your own business, and all without exception wrinkled at the corners with a suggestion of dry humor."

1. How did this general description of the loggers prepare you for the entrance of the leading character, Jimmy Powers?

2. In his first brief conversation with White, Jimmy Powers revealed something of his character. What aspects of it came out at once? What particular traits were not apparent until later?

3. How did the first birling match provide further clues to Powers' character?

4. When White returned to the logging town the second time, you were probably looking forward to his meeting with Powers. List the main incidents in this second part which revealed additional qualities in Powers' character. Explain what each told you about him.

5. Why was Jimmy Powers a suitable person to serve as a leading character? Could Dickey Darrell also have served as a leading character, but of a different type? Discuss.

B. The ending of a short story is always important because it is the last impression which the author leaves with you. Stewart Edward White ended "The Riverman" with Jimmy Powers' remark: "Bub, if you're going to hang any stars of Bethlehem on my Christmas tree, just call a halt right here. I didn't rescue that scalawag because I had any Christian sentiments,

nary bit. I was just naturally savin' him for the birling match next Fourther July."

1. Explain why this remark was in keeping with Powers' character as the author had developed it throughout the story.

2. Why did Powers' remark make an effective ending? Discuss. What impression did it leave with you?

3. Try your hand at writing another ending to this story, beginning with the loggers' return from breaking the jam. Be sure it is consistent with the personalities of the characters as the author had developed them in the story.

Knowing words . . .

Logging, like most lines of work, has its own vocabulary. In each of the following sentences taken from "The Riverman," a term familiar to loggers is printed in italics. When you are sure that you understand the meaning of these words, use each one in a sentence of your own.

1. I joined him, and together we followed the crowd to the river, where we roosted like cormorants on adjacent *piles* overlooking a patch of clear water among the filled *booms*.

2. A half-dozen men with *peavies* rolled a white pine log of about a foot and a half diameter into the clear water.

3. The decided spat, spat of the reversing blows from the *caulked boots* sounded like picket firing.

4. "I was just naturally savin' him for the *birling match* next Fourther July."

A Daring Deed

MARK TWAIN

In describing river boat pilots, Mark Twain wrote, "Your true pilot cares nothing about anything on earth but the river, and his pride in his occupation surpasses the pride of kings."

The pilot-house was full of pilots, going down to "look at the river." What is called the "upper river" (the two hundred miles between St. Louis and Cairo, where the Ohio comes in) was low; and the Mississippi changes its channel so constantly that the pilots used to always find it necessary to run down to Cairo to take a fresh look, when their boats were to lie in port a week; that is, when the water was at a low stage. A deal of this "looking at the river" was done by poor fellows who seldom had a berth,[1] and whose only hope of getting one lay in their being always freshly posted and therefore ready to drop into the shoes of some reputable pilot, for a single trip, on account of such pilot's sudden illness, or some other necessity. And a good many of them constantly ran up and down inspecting the river, not because they ever really hoped to get a berth, but because (they being guests of the boat) it was cheaper to "look at the river" than stay ashore and pay board. In time these fellows grew dainty in their tastes, and only infested boats that had an established reputation for setting good tables. All visiting pilots were useful, for they were always ready and willing, winter or summer, night or day, to go out in the yawl and help buoy the channel or assist the boat's pilots in any

way they could. They were likewise welcomed because all pilots are tireless talkers, when gathered together, and as they talk only about the river they are always understood and are always interesting. Your true pilot cares nothing about anything on earth but the river, and his pride in his occupation surpasses the pride of kings.

We had a fine company of these river inspectors along this trip. There were eight or ten, and there was abundance of room for them in our great pilot-house. Two or three of them wore polished silk hats, elaborate shirtfronts, diamond breast-pins, kid gloves, and patent-leather boots. They were choice in their English, and bore themselves with a dignity proper to men of solid means and prodigious reputation as pilots. The others were more or less loosely clad, and wore upon their heads tall felt cones that were suggestive of the days of the Commonwealth.[2]

I was a cipher in this august company, and felt subdued, not to say torpid. I was not even of sufficient consequence to assist at the wheel when it was necessary to put the tiller hard down in a hurry; the guest that stood nearest did that when occasion required—and this was pretty much all the time, because of the crookedness of the

[1] berth, job on board a ship

[2] Commonwealth, name given to the English government from 1649 to 1653

454

channel and the scant water. I stood in a corner; and the talk I listened to took the hope all out of me. One visitor said to another:

"Jim, how did you run Plum Point, coming up?"

"It was in the night, there, and I ran it the way one of the boys on the *Diana* told me; started out about fifty yards above the wood-pile on the false point, and held on the cabin under Plum Point till I raised the reef—quarter less twain—then straightened up for the middle bar till I got well abreast the old one-limbed cottonwood in the bend, then got my stern on the cottonwood, and head on the low place above the point, and came through a-booming—nine and a half."

"Pretty square crossing, an't it?"

"Yes, but the upper bar's working down fast."

Another pilot spoke up and said:

"I had better water than that, and ran it lower down; started out from the false point—mark twain—raised the second reef abreast the big snag in the bend, and had quarter less twain."

One of the gorgeous ones remarked:

"I don't want to find fault with your leadsmen,[3] but that's a good deal of water for Plum Point, it seems to me."

There was an approving nod all around as this quiet snub dropped on the boaster and "settled" him. And so they went on talk-talk-talking. Meantime, the thing that was running in my mind was, "Now, if my ears hear aright, I have not only to get the names of all the towns and islands and bends, and so on, by heart, but I must even get up a warm personal acquaintanceship

---

[3] *leadsmen,* men who measure the depth of the water by means of a weighted line, or leadline

with every old snag and one-limbed cotton-wood and obscure wood-pile that ornaments the banks of this river for twelve hundred miles; and more than that, I must actually know where these things are in the dark, unless these guests are gifted with eyes that can pierce through two miles of solid blackness. I wish the piloting business was in Jericho and I had never thought of it."

At dusk Mr. Bixby tapped the big bell three times (the signal to land), and the captain emerged from his drawing-room in the forward end of the "texas," and looked up inquiringly. Mr. Bixby said:

"We will lay up here all night, captain."

"Very well, sir."

That was all. The boat came to shore and was tied up for the night. It seemed to me a fine thing that the pilot could do as he pleased, without asking so grand a captain's permission. I took my supper and went immediately to bed, discouraged by my day's observations and experiences. My late voyage's note-booking was but a confusion of meaningless names. It had tangled me all up in a knot every time I had looked at it in the daytime. I now hoped for respite in sleep; but no, it reveled all through my head till sunrise again, a frantic and tireless nightmare.

Next morning I felt pretty rusty and low-spirited. We went booming along, taking a good many chances, for we were anxious to "get out of the river" (as getting out to Cairo was called) before night should overtake us. But Mr. Bixby's partner, the other pilot, presently grounded the boat, and we lost so much time getting her off that it was plain the darkness would overtake us a good long way above the mouth. This was a great misfortune, especially to certain of our visiting pilots, whose boats would have to wait for their return, no matter how long that might be. It sobered the pilot-house talk a good deal. Coming up-stream, pilots did not mind low water or any kind of darkness; nothing stopped them but fog. But down-stream

work was different; a boat was too nearly helpless, with a stiff current pushing behind her; so it was not customary to run down-stream at night in low water.

There seemed to be one small hope, however: if we could get through the intricate and dangerous Hat Island crossing before night, we could venture the rest, for we would have plainer sailing and better water. But it would be insanity to attempt Hat Island at night. So there was a deal of looking at watches all the rest of the day, and constant ciphering upon the speed we were making; Hat Island was the eternal subject, sometimes hope was high and sometimes we were delayed in a bad crossing, and down it went again. For hours all hands lay under the burden of this suppressed excitement; it was even communicated to me, and I got to feeling so solicitous about Hat Island, and under such an awful pressure of responsibility, that I wished I might have five minutes on shore to draw a good, full, relieving breath, and start over again. We were standing no regular watches. Each of our pilots ran such portions of the river as he had run when coming up-stream, because of his greater familiarity with it; but both remained in the pilot-house constantly.

An hour before sunset Mr. Bixby took the wheel, and Mr. W. stepped aside. For the next thirty minutes every man held his watch in his hand and was restless, silent, and uneasy. At last somebody said, with a doomful sigh:

"Well, yonder's Hat Island—and we can't make it."

All the watches closed with a snap, everybody sighed and muttered something about its being "too bad, too bad—ah, if we could *only* have got here half an hour sooner!" and the place was thick with the atmosphere of disappointment. Some started to go out, but loitered, hearing no bell-tap to land. The sun dipped behind the horizon, the boat went on. Inquiring looks passed from one guest to another; and one who had his hand on the door-knob and had turned it, waited, then presently took away his hand and let the knob turn back again. We bore steadily down the bend. More looks were exchanged, and nods of surprised admiration—but no words. Insensibly the men drew together behind Mr. Bixby, as the sky darkened and one or two dim stars came out. The dead silence and sense of waiting became oppressive. Mr. Bixby pulled the cord, and two deep, mellow notes from the big bell floated off on the night. Then a pause, and one more note was struck. The watchman's voice followed, from the hurricane deck:

"Labboard lead, there! Stabboard lead!"

The cries of the leadsmen began to rise out of the distance, and were gruffly repeated by the word-passers on the hurricane-deck.

"M-a-r-k three! [4] M-a-r-k three! Quarter-less-three! Half twain! Quarter twain! M-a-r-k twain! Quarter-less—"

Mr. Bixby pulled two bell-ropes, and was answered by faint jinglings far below in the engine-room, and our speed slackened. The steam began to whistle through the gauge-cocks. The cries of the leadsmen went on—and it is a weird sound, always, in the night. Every pilot in the lot was watching now, with fixed eyes, and talking under his breath. Nobody was calm and easy but Mr. Bixby. He would put his wheel down and stand on a spoke, and as the steamer swung into her (to me) utterly invisible marks—for we seemed to be in the midst of a wide and gloomy sea—he would meet and fasten her there. Out of the murmur of half-audible talk, one caught a coherent sentence now and then —such as:

"There; she's over the first reef all right!"

After a pause, another subdued voice:

"Her stern's coming down just *exactly* right, by *George!*"

[4] *M-a-r-k three,* mark: an indication of the water's depth as measured on a line dropped into the water. "Mark three" would be third marker on the line. "Mark twain" would be the second.

"Now she's in the marks; over she goes!"

Somebody else muttered:

"Oh, it was done beautiful—*beautiful!*"

Now the engines were stopped altogether, and we drifted with the current. Not that I could see the boat drift, for I could not, the stars being all gone by this time. This drifting was the dismalest work; it held one's heart still. Presently I discovered a blacker gloom than that which surrounded us. It was the head of the island. We were closing right down upon it. We entered its deeper shadow, and so imminent seemed the peril that I was likely to suffocate; and I had the strongest impulse to do *something,* anything, to save the vessel. But still Mr. Bixby stood by his wheel, silent, intent as a cat, and all the pilots stood shoulder to shoulder at his back.

"She'll not make it!" somebody whispered.

The water grew shoaler and shoaler, by the leadsman's cries, till it was down to:

"Eight-and-a-half! E-i-g-h-t feet! E-i-g-h-t feet! Seven-and—"

Mr. Bixby said warningly through his speaking-tube to the engineer:

"Stand by, now!"

"Ay, ay, sir!"

"Seven-and-a-half! Seven feet! *Six-and—*"

We touched bottom! Instantly Mr. Bixby set a lot of bells ringing, shouted through the tube, "*Now,* let her have it— every ounce you've got!" then to his partner, "Put her hard down! snatch her! snatch her!" The boat rasped and ground her way through the sand, hung upon the apex of disaster a single tremendous instant, and then over she went! And such a shout as went up at Mr. Bixby's back never loosened the roof of a pilot-house before!

There was no more trouble after that. Mr. Bixby was a hero that night; and it was some little time, too, before his exploit ceased to be talked about by river-men.

Fully to realize the marvelous precision

required in laying the great steamer in her marks in that murky waste of water, one should know that not only must she pick her intricate way through snags and blind reefs, and then shave the head of the island so closely as to brush the overhanging foliage with her stern, but at one place she must pass almost within arm's reach of a sunken and invisible wreck that would snatch the hull timbers from under her if she should strike it, and destroy a quarter of a million dollars' worth of steamboat and cargo in five minutes, and maybe a hundred and fifty human lives into the bargain.

The last remark I heard that night was a compliment to Mr. Bixby, uttered in soliloquy and with unction by one of our guests. He said:

"By the Shadow of Death, but he's a lightning pilot!"

Continued Perplexities

I promptly put such a strain on my memory that by and by even the shoal water and the countless crossing-marks began to stay with me. But the result was just the same. I never could more than get one knotty thing learned before another presented itself. Now I had often seen pilots gazing at the water and pretending to read it as if it were a book; but it was a book that told me nothing. A time came at last, however, when Mr. Bixby seemed to think me far enough advanced to bear a lesson on water-reading. So he began:

"Do you see that long, slanting line on the face of the water? Now, that's a reef. Moreover, it's a bluff reef. There is a solid sand-bar under it that is nearly as straight up and down as the side of a house. There is plenty of water close up to it, but mighty little on top of it. If you were to hit it you would knock the boat's brains out. Do you see where the line fringes out at the upper end and begins to fade away?"

"Yes, sir."

"Well, that is a low place; that is the head of the reef. You can climb over there, and not hurt anything. Cross over, now, and follow along close under the reef—easy water there—not much current."

I followed the reef along till I approached the fringed end. Then Mr. Bixby said:

"Now get ready. Wait till I give the word. She won't want to mount the reef; a boat hates shoal water. Stand by—wait —*wait*—keep her well in hand. *Now* cramp her down! Snatch her! snatch her!"

He seized the other side of the wheel and helped to spin it around until it was hard down, and then we held it so. The boat resisted, and refused to answer for a while, and next she came surging to starboard, mounted the reef, and sent a long, angry ridge of water foaming away from her bows.

"Now watch her; watch her like a cat, or she'll get away from you. When she fights strong and the tiller slips a little, in a jerky, greasy sort of way, let up on her a trifle; it is the way she tells you at night that the water is too shoal; but keep edging her up, on the bar now; there is a bar under every point, because the water that comes down around it forms an eddy and allows the sediment to sink. Do you see those fine lines on the face of the water that branch out like the ribs of a fan? Well, those are little reefs; you want to just miss the ends of them, but run them pretty close. Now look out—look out! Don't you crowd that slick, greasy-looking place; there ain't nine feet there; she won't stand it. She begins to smell it; look sharp, I tell you! Oh, blazes, there you go! Stop the starboard wheel! Quick! Ship up to back! Set her back!"

The engine bells jingled and the engines answered promptly, shooting white columns of steam far aloft out of the 'scape-pipes, but it was too late. The boat had "smelt" the bar in good earnest; the foamy ridges that radiated from her bows suddenly disappeared, a great dead swell came rolling forward, and swept ahead of her, she careened far over to larboard, and went tearing away toward the shore as if she were about scared to death. We were a good mile from where we ought to have been when we finally got the upper hand of her again.

During the afternoon watch the next day, Mr. Bixby asked me if I knew how to run the next few miles. I said:

"Go inside the first snag above the point, outside the next one, start out from the lower end of Higgins's woodyard, make a square crossing, and—"

"That's all right. I'll be back before you close up on the next point."

But he wasn't. He was still below when I rounded it and entered upon a piece of the river which I had some misgivings about. I did not know that he was hiding behind a chimney to see how I would perform. I went gaily along, getting prouder and prouder, for he had never left the boat in my sole charge such a length of time before. I even got to "setting" her and letting the wheel go entirely, while I vaingloriously turned my back and inspected the stern marks and hummed a tune, a sort of easy indifference which I had prodigiously admired in Bixby and other great pilots. Once I inspected rather long, and when I faced to the front again my heart flew into my mouth so suddenly that if I hadn't clapped my teeth together I should have lost it. One of those frightful bluff reefs was stretching its deadly length right across our bows! My head was gone in a moment; I did not know which end I stood on; I gasped and could not get my breath; I spun the wheel down with such rapidity that it wove itself together like a spider's web; the boat answered and turned square away from the reef, but the reef followed her! I fled, but still it followed, still it kept —right across my bows! I never looked to see where I was going, I only fled. The awful crash was imminent. Why didn't that villain come? If I committed the crime of ringing a bell I might get thrown over-

board. But better that than kill the boat. So in blind desperation, I started such a rattling "shivaree" down below as never had astounded an engineer in this world before, I fancy. Amidst the frenzy of the bells the engines began to back and fill in a curious way, and my reason forsook its throne—we were about to crash into the woods on the other side of the river. Just then Mr. Bixby stepped calmly into view on the hurricane-deck. My soul went out to him in gratitude. My distress vanished; I would have felt safe on the brink of Niagara with Mr. Bixby on the hurricane-deck. He blandly and sweetly took his toothpick out of his mouth between his fingers, as if it were a cigar—we were just in the act of climbing an overhanging big tree, and the passengers were scudding astern like rats—and lifted up these commands to me ever so gently:

"Stop the starboard! Stop the larboard! Set her back on both!"

The boat hesitated, halted, pressed her nose among the boughs a critical instant, then reluctantly began to back away.

"Stop the larboard! Come ahead on it! Stop the starboard! Come ahead on it! Point her for the bar!"

I sailed away as serenely as a summer's morning. Mr. Bixby came in and said, with mock simplicity:

"When you have a hail, my boy, you ought to tap the big bell three times before you land, so that the engineers can get ready."

I blushed under the sarcasm, and said I hadn't had any hail.

"Ah! Then it was for wood, I suppose. The officer of the watch will tell you when he wants to wood up."

I went on consuming, and said I wasn't after wood.

"Indeed? Why, what could you want over here in the bend, then? Did you ever know of a boat following a bend up-stream at this stage of the river?"

"No, sir—and I wasn't trying to follow it. I was getting away from a bluff reef."

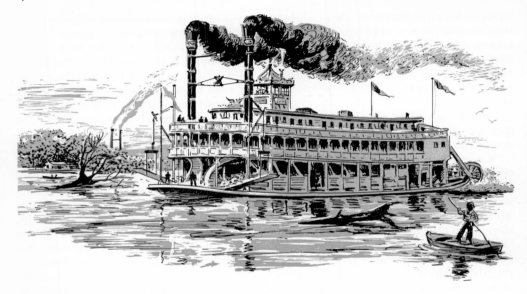

"No, it wasn't a bluff reef; there isn't one within three miles of where you were."

"But I saw it. It was as bluff as that one yonder."

"Just about. Run over it!"

"Do you give it as an order?"

"Yes. Run over it!"

"If I don't, I wish I may die."

"All right; I am taking the responsibility."

I was just as anxious to kill the boat, now, as I had been to save it before. I impressed my orders upon my memory, to be used at the inquest, and made a straight break for the reef. As it disappeared under our bows I held my breath; but we slid over it like oil.

"Now, don't you see the difference? It wasn't anything but a *wind* reef. The wind does that."

"So I see. But it is exactly like a bluff reef. How am I ever going to tell them apart."

"I can't tell you. It is an instinct. By and by you will just naturally *know* one from the other, but you never will be able to explain why or how you know them apart."

It turned out to be true. The face of the water, in time, became a wonderful book —a book that was a dead language to the uneducated passenger, but which told its mind to me without reserve, delivering its most cherished secrets as clearly as if it uttered them with a voice. And it was not a book to be read once and thrown aside, for it had a new story to tell every day. Throughout the long twelve hundred miles there was never a page that was void of interest, never one that you could leave unread without loss, never one that you would want to skip, thinking you could find higher enjoyment in some other thing. There never was so wonderful a book written by man; never one whose interest was so absorbing, so unflagging, so sparklingly renewed with every reperusal. The passenger who could not read it was charmed with a peculiar sort of faint dimple on its surface (on the rare occasions when he did not overlook it altogether); but to the pilot that was an *italicized* passage; indeed, it was more than that, it was a legend of the largest capitals, with a string of shouting exclamation-points at the end of it, for it meant that a wreck or a rock was buried there that could tear the life out of the strongest vessel that ever floated. It is the faintest and simplest expression the water ever makes, and the most hideous to a pilot's eye. In truth, the passenger who could not read this book saw nothing but all manner of pretty pictures in it, painted by the sun and shaded by the clouds, whereas to the trained eye these were not pictures at all, but the grimmest and most dead-earnest of reading-matter.

Now when I had mastered the language of this water, and had come to know every trifling feature that bordered the great river as familiarly as I knew the letters of the alphabet, I had made a valuable acquisition. But I had lost something, too. I had lost something which could never be restored to me while I lived. All the grace, the beauty, the poetry, had gone out of the majestic river! I still kept in mind a certain wonderful sunset which I witnessed when steamboating was new to me. A broad expanse of the river was turned to blood; in the middle distance the red hue brightened into gold, through which a solitary log came floating, black and conspicuous; in one place a long, slanting mark lay sparkling upon the water; in another the surface was broken by boiling, tumbling rings, that were as many-tinted as an opal; where the ruddy flush was faintest, was a smooth spot that was covered with graceful circles and radiating lines, ever so delicately traced; the shore on our left was densely wooded, and the somber shadow that fell from this forest was broken in one place by a long, ruffled trail that shone like silver; and high above the forest wall a clean-stemmed dead tree waved a single leafy bough that glowed like a flame in the unobstructed splendor that was flowing from the sun. There were graceful curves, reflected images, woody heights, soft distances; and over the whole scene, far and near, the dissolving lights drifted steadily, enriching it every passing moment with new marvels of coloring.

I stood like one bewitched. I drank it in, in a speechless rapture. The world was new to me, and I had never seen anything like this at home. But as I have said, a day came when I began to cease from noting the glories and the charms which the moon and the sun and the twilight wrought upon the river's face; another day came when I ceased altogether to note them. Then, if that sunset scene had been repeated, I should have looked upon it without rapture, and should have commented upon it, inwardly, after this fashion: "This sun means that we are going to have wind to-morrow; that floating log means that the river is rising, small thanks to it; that slanting mark on the water refers to a bluff reef which is going to kill somebody's steamboat one of these nights, if it keeps on stretching out like that; those tumbling 'boils' show a dissolving bar and a changing channel there; the lines and circles in the slick water over yonder are a warning that that troublesome place is shoaling up dangerously; that silver streak in the shadow of the forest is the 'break' from a new snag, and he has located himself in the very best place he could have found to fish for steamboats; that tall dead tree, with a single living branch, is not going to last long, and then how is a body ever going to get through this blind place at night without the friendly old landmark?"

No, the romance and beauty were all gone from the river. All the value any feature of it had for me now was the amount of usefulness it could furnish toward compassing the safe piloting of a steamboat. Since those days, I have pitied doctors from my heart. What does the lovely flush in a beauty's cheek mean to a doctor but a "break" that ripples above some deadly disease? Are not all her visible charms sown thick with what are to him the signs and symbols of hidden decay? Does he ever see her beauty at all, or doesn't he simply view her professionally, and comment upon her unwholesome condition all to himself? And doesn't he sometimes wonder whether he has gained most or lost most by learning his trade?

The man who wrote this selection

MARK TWAIN (Samuel L. Clemens)
1835–1910

The central fact in the life and writing of Mark Twain is the Mississippi River. It is a vital part of his most characteristic books, *Huckleberry Finn, Life on the Mississippi,* and *Tom Sawyer.* Even when the subject matter of his other books was quite removed from the River or the country around it, his writing still reflected the artistry of the frontier story which he had heard or read as a young man.

Samuel L. Clemens worked at a dozen or more jobs. As a newspaperman he learned *how* to tell stories. As a steamboat pilot, he collected his materials for the stories he wanted to tell. He was most proud of being a steamboat pilot and for many years was the only man to hold a pilot's license on both the Mississippi and Ohio Rivers. Later, he took his pen name, Mark Twain, from an expression used by steamboatmen to call out the depth of the channel.

During his newspaper days, Mark Twain developed a prose style that is seldom excelled. Other writers have used his standard for good writing as a model: "clearness of statement, directness, felicity of expression, photographic ability in setting forth an incident—style—good style— no barnacles on it in the way of unnecessary, retarding words."

"A Daring Deed" was originally one of the series of seven reminiscences prepared for *The Atlantic Monthly.* It eventually became one of the chapters in *Life on the Mississippi.*

Let's consider . . .

1. It was the ambition of every boy brought up along the Mississippi to become a river pilot. From the picture the author gave of the "august company" in the pilot-house, explain the fascination of the river pilot's life.

2. In seventeen months Mark Twain learned every snag and sandbar along the 1200 miles of river and became a master pilot. What did you learn from Twain's method of studying the river that would prove useful in your own studies?

3. The other pilots were very complimentary when Mr. Bixby accomplished the daring feat of passing Hat Island at night. Without being technical, give your impression of that deed.

4. Mr. Bixby taught Mark Twain well. What was there to praise in his method of teaching?

5. After the young pilot had mastered "the language of this water," he felt that "all the grace, the beauty, the poetry had gone out of the majestic river." Why was this so? Do you think that the fascination of a job is likely to disappear when you have mastered it? Discuss.

6. One sunset remained in his memory undimmed. Try to describe it.

The writer's craft . . .

1. You recall that regional writers weave authentic background materials so completely into the fabric of their writing that the reader feels he *knows* the particular locality in which the story takes place. Give several reasons why you could call "A Daring Deed" regional writing.

2. As you were reading "A Daring Deed," you probably felt that Mark Twain knew the Mississippi thoroughly. He created this impression by means of concrete detail, not only about the River itself but about the handling of a river boat as well. Select specific concrete details which indicate his firsthand knowledge of both of these. (Be sure to consider his use of technical river boat terms.)

3. Write a composition in which you describe a particular field of work with which you are extremely familiar. By

using concrete details, you will not only make your composition more interesting; you will also convince the reader that you know your subject.

Knowing words . . .

The face of the Mississippi that became "a wonderful book" to Mark Twain was a "dead language" to the passengers on the river boats. Some of the navigating terms were probably a "dead language" to you, but you could still appreciate the "daring deed." Now you can lay in a store of these simple terms for fuller understanding and for future reading: *larboard, starboard, leadsman* (lĕd), *yawl, buoy, tiller, grounded,* and M-A-R-K T-W-A-I-N.

If you are not sure of the meaning of each of the above terms, check them in the glossary at the back of the book. Then explain their meanings as they were used in this story.

Down the Mississippi

EMBARKATION

Dull masses of dense green,
The forests range their sombre platforms;
Between them silently, like a spirit,
The river finds its own mysterious path.

Loosely the river sways out, backward, forward,
Always fretting the outer side;
Shunning the invisible focus of each crescent,
Seeking to spread into shining loops over fields.

Like an enormous serpent, dilating, uncoiling,
Displaying a broad scaly back of earth-smeared gold;
Swaying out sinuously between the dull motionless forests,
As molten metal might glide down the lip of a vase of dark bronze;

It goes, while the steamboat drifting out upon it,
Seems now to be floating not only outwards but upwards;
In the flight of a petal detached and gradually moving skyward
Above the pink explosion of the calyx of the dawn.

John Gould Fletcher

A Farm

ROBERT P. TRISTRAM COFFIN

A farm is more than hives of bees
Or cows all feeding towards the breeze,
A farm is more than fields of stubble
And helping small lambs over trouble,
Weaning calves upon your fingers,
Mending carts while Winter lingers.

A farm is a mysterious place
Where you come out face to face
With yourself at lonely labor,
A farm is making a good neighbor
Out of rain or wind or snow
And guiding life along the flow
Of the soil beside a plow,
Saving Summer in a mow.
A farm is where boys grow to men
When they are barefoot still and ten,
And men stay boys enough to see
Brothers in butterflies and the tree.

A farm is something like a wife,
Labor that adds up to life,
A farm is something you can trust
To build you children out of dust.

The man who wrote this poem

ROBERT P. TRISTRAM COFFIN
1892–1955

Robert Peter Tristram Coffin wrote equally well in a variety of forms, and his published works include poetry, literary criticism, history, and fiction. Although his life was devoted to teaching, he wrote more than forty books. One volume of poems, *Strange Holiness,* was awarded the Pulitzer Prize in 1936.

While Dr. Coffin was still an undergraduate at Bowdoin College, he had the honor of being chosen as a Rhodes Scholar to study at Oxford, a famous English university. During his life he was awarded seven degrees, two of them from Oxford. He also received honorary degrees from Bowdoin College and the University of Maine.

Dr. Coffin was born and raised in the college town of Brunswick, Maine. When he had completed his formal education, he returned to live in Brunswick where he held the esteemed position of Pierce Professor of English Literature at Bowdoin College.

The poet's art . . .

1. In the first part of the poem, Robert P. Tristram Coffin listed some of the common sights and activities to be found on a farm. What are they? What other similar details might he have chosen? From what you know of farm work, are the poet's details representative?

2. In the second part of the poem, the poet described how a farm affects the people who live on it. What qualities did he think were developed by farm life?

3. Explain the meaning of these lines:

"Saving Summer in a mow."

"And men stay boys enough to see
Brothers in butterflies and the tree."

4. The last four lines of the poem summarize the poet's feeling. Express his thought in your own words.

5. Some of the poems you have read thus far were written in rhymed **stanzas:** groups of lines which follow a pattern which is usually repeated as a unit. The pattern of this poem is the **rhymed couplet:** a pair of lines with end rhyme. A poet chooses a rhyme pattern which suits his theme. Try to explain why this pattern was appropriate for this poem.

6. Coffin also chose a simple meter for this poem. You will recall **meter** is the rhythm of poetry. It is determined by the stresses or accents which fall naturally on certain syllables when words are arranged in a particular order. Notice the light and heavy stresses in these lines:

Ă fárm ĭs móre thăn híves ŏf beés

Ŏr cóws ăll feédĭng tówards thĕ breéze,

The stressed syllables indicate the number of feet in the line. When there are four feet in a line (as in this poem) the line is called **tetrameter.** The verse pattern in this poem is called **iambic tetrameter** because each foot is made up of one unaccented and one accented syllable.

Pick out two other couplets from the poem. Copy them on paper and mark the light and heavy stresses. Explain how these lines illustrate the iambic tetrameter pattern. Notice that individual lines may begin with a heavy stress or end with a light one. These are variations which keep the rhythm from being monotonous.

Stubb Kills a Whale

HERMAN MELVILLE

Two centuries ago whale oil was the nation's chief source of fuel and light, and many sailors were employed on vessels that went in search of whales. Life on these ships was both dangerous and exciting. "Stubb Kills a Whale" is taken from the book *Moby Dick,* a magnificent account of a whaling voyage.

The next day was exceedingly still and and sultry, and with nothing special to engage them, the Pequod's [1] crew could hardly resist the spell of sleep induced by such a vacant sea. For this part of the Indian Ocean through which we then were voyaging is not what whalemen call a lively ground; that is, it affords fewer glimpses of porpoises, dolphins, flying-fish, and other vivacious denizens of more stirring waters, than those off the Rio de la Plata, or the in-shore ground off Peru.

It was my turn to stand at the foremast-head; [2] and with my shoulders leaning against the slackened royal shrouds, to and fro I idly swayed in what seemed an enchanted air. No resolution could withstand it; in that dreamy mood losing all consciousness, at last my soul went out of my body; though my body still continued to sway as a pendulum will, long after the power which first moved it is withdrawn.

Ere forgetfulness altogether came over me, I had noticed that the seamen at the main and mizzen mast-heads [3] were already drowsy. So that at last all three of us lifelessly swung from the spars, and for every swing that we made there was a nod from below from the slumbering helmsman. The waves, too, nodded their indolent crests; and across the wide trance of the sea, east nodded to west, and the sun over all.

Suddenly bubbles seemed bursting beneath my closed eyes; like vices my hands grasped the shrouds; some invisible, gracious agency preserved me; with a shock I came back to life. And lo! close under our lee, [4] not forty fathoms off, a gigantic Sperm Whale lay rolling in the water like the capsized hull of a frigate, his broad, glossy back, of an Ethiopian hue, glistening in the sun's rays like a mirror. But lazily undulating in the trough of the sea, and ever and anon tranquilly spouting his vapory jet, the whale looked like a portly burgher [5] smoking his pipe of a warm afternoon. But

---

[1] *Pequod,* name of the whaling ship on which the action of this story occurs
[2] *foremast-head,* highest point of the mast (the vertical pole which supports the sail) which is nearest the ship's bow
[3] *main and mizzen mast-heads,* highest points of the second and third masts
[4] *lee,* side away from the wind
[5] *burgher,* villager

that pipe, poor whale, was thy last. As if struck by some enchanter's wand, the sleepy ship and every sleeper in it all at once started into wakefulness; and more than a score of voices from all parts of the vessel, simultaneously with the three notes from aloft, shouted forth the accustomed cry, as the great fish slowly and regularly spouted the sparkling brine into the air.

"Clear away the boats! Luff!" cried Ahab. And obeying his own order, he dashed the helm down before the helmsman could handle the spokes.

The sudden exclamations of the crew must have alarmed the whale; and ere the boats were down, majestically turning, he swam away to the leeward, but with such a steady tranquillity, and making so few ripples as he swam, that thinking after all he might not as yet be alarmed, Ahab gave orders that not an oar should be used, and no man must speak but in whispers. So seated like Ontario Indians on the gunwales [6] of the boats, we swiftly but silently paddled along; the calm not admitting of the noiseless sails being set. Presently, as we thus glided in chase, the monster perpendicularly flitted his tail forty feet into the air, and then sank out of sight like a tower swallowed up.

"There go flukes!" [7] was the cry, an announcement immediately followed by Stubb's producing his match and igniting his pipe, for now a respite was granted. After the full interval of his sounding had elapsed, the whale rose again, and being now in advance of the smoker's boat, and much nearer to it than to any of the others, Stubb counted upon the honor of the capture. It was obvious, now, that the whale had at length become aware of his pursuers. All silence of cautiousness was therefore no longer of use. Paddles were dropped, and oars came loudly into play. And still puffing at his pipe, Stubb cheered on his crew to the assault.

Yes, a mighty change had come over the

fish. All alive to his jeopardy, he was going "head out"; that part obliquely projecting from the mad yeast which he brewed.*

"Start her, start her, my men! Don't hurry yourselves; take plenty of time—but start her; start her like thunder-claps, that's all," cried Stubb, spluttering out the smoke as he spoke. "Start her, now; give 'em the long and strong stroke, Tashtego. Start her, Tash, my boy—start her, all; but keep cool, keep cool—cucumbers is the word—easy, easy—only start her like grim death and grinning devils, and raise the buried dead perpendicular out of their graves, boys —that's all. Start her!"

"Woo-hoo! Wa-hee!" screamed the Gay-Header [8] in reply, raising some old war-whoop to the skies; as every oarsman in the strained boat involuntarily bounced forward with the one tremendous leading stroke which the eager Indian gave.

But his wild screams were answered by others quite as wild. "Kee-hee! Kee-hee!" yelled Daggoo, straining forwards and backwards on his seat, like a pacing tiger in his cage.

"Ka-la! Koo-loo!" howled Queequeg, as if smacking his lips over a mouthful of Grenadier's steak. And thus with oars and yells the keels cut the sea. Meanwhile, Stubb, retaining his place in the van, still encouraged his men to the onset, all the while puffing the smoke from his mouth. Like desperadoes they tugged and they strained, till the welcome cry was heard— "Stand up, Tashtego!—give it to him!"

---

* It will be seen in some other place of what a very light substance the entire interior of the sperm whale's enormous head consists. Though apparently the most massive, it is by far the most buoyant part about him. So that with ease he elevates it in the air, and invariably does so when going at his utmost speed. Besides, such is the breadth of the upper part of the front of his head, and such the tapering cut-water formation of the lower part, that by obliquely elevating his head, he thereby may be said to transform himself from a bluff-bowed sluggish galliot into a sharp-pointed New York pilot-boat. [*Author's note.*]

---

[6] *gunwales,* upper edges of the boat's side
[7] *flukes,* triangular tail of the whale
[8] *Gay-Header,* Tashtego

The harpoon was hurled. "Stern all!" The oarsmen backed water; the same moment something went hot and hissing along every one of their wrists. It was the magical line. An instant before, Stubb had swiftly caught two additional turns with it round the loggerhead,[9] whence, by reason of its increased rapid circlings, a hempen blue smoke now jetted up and mingled with the steady fumes from his pipe. As the line passed round and round the loggerhead; so also, just before reaching that point, it blisteringly passed through and through both of Stubb's hands, from which the hand-cloths, or squares of quilted canvas sometimes worn at these times, had accidentally dropped. It was like holding an enemy's sharp two-edged sword by the blade, and that enemy all the time striving to wrest it out of your clutch.

"Wet the line! wet the line!" cried Stubb to the tub oarsman (him seated by the tub) who, snatching off his hat, dashed sea-

water into it.* More turns were taken, so that the line began holding its place. The boat now flew through the boiling water like a shark all fins. Stubb and Tashtego here changed places—stem for stern—a staggering business truly in that rocking commotion.

From the vibrating line extending the entire length of the upper part of the boat, and from its now being more tight than a harpstring, you would have thought the craft had two keels—one cleaving the water, the other the air—as the boat churned on through both opposing elements at once. A continual cascade played at the bows; a ceaseless whirling eddy in her wake; and, at the slightest motion from within, even but of a little finger, the vibrating, cracking craft canted [10] over her spasmodic gunwale into the sea. Thus they rushed; each man with might and main clinging to his seat, to prevent being tossed to the foam; and

---

[9] *loggerhead,* rounded post in the stern of the whaleboat

* Partly to show the indispensableness of this act, it may here be stated, that, in the old Dutch fishery, a mop was used to dash the running line with water; in many other ships, a wooden piggin, or bailer, is set apart for that purpose. Your hat, however, is the most convenient. [*Author's note.*]

[10] *canted,* tilted

the tall form of Tashtego at the steering oar crouching almost double, in order to bring down his centre of gravity. Whole Atlantics and Pacifics seemed passed as they shot on their way, till at length the whale somewhat slackened his flight.

"Haul in—haul in!" cried Stubb to the bowsman! and, facing round towards the whale, all hands began pulling the boat up to him, while yet the boat was being towed on. Soon ranging up by his flank, Stubb, firmly planting his knee in the clumsy cleat, darted dart after dart into the flying fish; at the word of command, the boat alternately sterning [11] out of the way of the whale's horrible wallow, and then ranging up for another fling.

The red tide now poured from all sides of the monster like brooks down a hill. His tormented body rolled not in brine but in blood, which bubbled and seethed for furlongs behind in their wake. The slanting sun playing upon this crimson pond in the sea, sent back its reflection into every face, so that they all glowed to each other like red men. And all the while, jet after jet of white smoke was agonizingly shot from the spiracle [12] of the whale, and vehement puff after puff from the mouth of the excited headsman; as at every dart, hauling in upon his crooked lance (by the line attached to it), Stubb straightened it again and again, by a few rapid blows against the gunwale, then again and again sent it into the whale.

[11] *sterning,* backing
[12] *spiracle,* breathing hole

"Pull up—pull up!" he now cried to the bowsman, as the waning whale relaxed in his wrath. "Pull up!—close to!" and the boat ranged along the fish's flank. When reaching far over the bow, Stubb slowly churned his long sharp lance into the fish, and kept it there, carefully churning and churning, as if cautiously seeking to feel after some gold watch that the whale might have swallowed, and which he was fearful of breaking ere he could hook it out. But that gold watch he sought was the innermost life of the fish. And now it is struck; for, starting from his trance into that unspeakable thing called his "flurry," the monster horribly wallowed in his blood, overwrapped himself in impenetrable, mad, boiling spray, so that the imperilled craft, instantly dropping astern, had much ado blindly to struggle out from that phrensied twilight into the clear air of the day.

And now abating in his flurry, the whale once more rolled out into view! surging from side to side; spasmodically dilating and contracting his spouthole, with sharp, cracking, agonized respirations. At last, gush after gush of clotted red gore, as if it had been the purple lees of red wine, shot into the frighted air; and falling back again, ran dripping down his motionless flanks into the sea. His heart had burst!

"He's dead, Mr. Stubb," said Daggoo.

"Yes; both pipes smoked out!" and withdrawing his own from his mouth, Stubb scattered the dead ashes over the water; and, for a moment, stood thoughtfully eyeing the vast corpse he had made.

The man who wrote this selection

HERMAN MELVILLE 1819–1891

Moby Dick was an obscure and forgotten book for seventy years. Today it is considered by many critics as America's greatest novel, and its author, Herman Melville, one of the world's great writers.

When Melville was twenty-one he made the most important decision of his life: he sailed as a cabin boy on a whaling vessel bound for the South Seas. Three years and nine months later he returned to America and began to write about his experiences. In seven years he wrote seven books, including *Moby Dick*. He continued to write until the end of his life, but never again did he equal this masterpiece about the great whale.

His first two books, *Typee* (1846) and *Omoo* (1847), are simple narratives of his travels in the South Sea islands. *Mardi* (1849) is a confusing allegory. Its obscurity and pessimism lost Melville many readers. He returned to simple storytelling with *Redburn* (1849) and *White Jacket* (1850).

Melville was living near Pittsfield, Massachusetts, when Nathaniel Hawthorne moved nearby. The two writers became friends, and Hawthorne encouraged Melville to write *Moby Dick* (1851). The book is more than a story of the search for the giant whale: it is the story of Man's struggle to understand himself and of his desire to explore the Unknown. It is an allegory of good and evil written in powerful prose.

Pierre (1852) was the last book of Melville's most productive period. In the forty years of his life after this period, he wrote three novels, two books of poetry and several stories. "Benito Cereno," a story, and *Billy Budd,* a short novel, are among his best-known works of this period. A dramatic version of *Billy Budd* was produced successfully several years ago.

Let's consider . . .

1. The *Pequod* was sailing "a vacant sea." Why was the sea so called, and what effect did it have on the crew?

2. The narrator (his name was Ishmael) came back to life "with a shock." Describe the sperm whale as he first appeared to Ishmael and the crew. What activities began immediately? Who gave the orders to "clear away the boats"?

3. *Moby Dick,* the book from which this selection was taken, has been called a "complete textbook of the whaling industry." Check carefully and then report on the early "antics" of the whale when he first sensed he was being pursued.

4. Patience and caution were essential in the boats. Point out the activities before and after the first harpooning which you consider most difficult and most necessary for success. Who directed the steps in the onset?

5. What part was played by "the magical line"? As it passed through Stubb's hands, "it was like holding an enemy's two-edged sword by the blade." Why was this so?

6. Why was the whale an extremely dangerous opponent? (Some whales have been known to be one hundred feet long. Try to find out how much sperm whales might weigh.)

7. As the blood of the whale poured over the water it was called "the red tide" and the "crimson pond." Find other graphic terms applied to it.

8. Stubb smoked a pipe all through the battle. What impression did you get from that fact?

The writer's craft . . .

A chapter taken from the middle of a full length book often seems incomplete and hard to understand. The reader does not know the identity of the characters, nor does he understand the action in the plot. However, even though "Stubb Kills a Whale" is a chapter from *Moby Dick,* it has a completeness and a unity which enables it to stand by itself. The way Herman Melville constructed the chapter with its definite beginning, middle, and end, as well as its effective shift from one mood to another, helped to make the chapter a self-contained unit.

1. Look again at the beginning. What mood did Melville achieve in these opening paragraphs? You will recall that mood refers to the emotional tone of a piece of writing.

2. How did the mood change in the middle of the chapter? In what way did the dialogue help to create this new mood?

(Notice the words which Melville used to describe the way the men spoke.)

3. After the battle with the whale was over, Melville closed the chapter on a quiet note. How did this ending serve to give a sense of completeness to this chapter?

Knowing words . . .

In describing the last few moments of the whale's battle for life, Melville managed to capture the scene's frenzied turmoil. The following sentences picture the height of the battle. Explain the meaning of each of the italicized words. Then rewrite the sentences, using synonyms of your own choosing in place of the words in italics. Sometimes you may need to use a phrase to capture the meaning of a word.

1. And now it struck; for, starting from his *trance* into that unspeakable thing called his "flurry," the monster horribly *wallowed* in his blood, overwrapped himself in *impenetrable*, mad, boiling spray, so that the imperilled craft, instantly dropping astern, had much *ado* blindly to struggle out from that *phrensied* twilight into the clear air of the day.

2. And now *abating* in his flurry, the whale once more rolled out into view! surging from side to side; *spasmodically dilating and contracting* his spouthole, with sharp, cracking, agonized *respirations*.

The Master Mariner

My grandsire sailed three years from home,
    And slew unmoved the sounding whale:
Here on the windless beach I roam
    And watch far out the hardy sail.

The lions of the surf that cry
    Upon this lion-colored shore
On reefs of midnight met his eye:
    He knew their fangs as I their roar.

My grandsire sailed uncharted seas,
    And toll of all their leagues he took:
I scan the shallow bays at ease,
    And tell their colors in a book.

The anchor-chains his music made
    And wind in shrouds and running-gear:
The thrush at dawn beguiles my glade,
    And once, 'tis said, I woke to hear.

My grandsire in his ample fist
    The long harpoon upheld to men:
Behold obedient to my wrist
    A gray gull's-feather for my pen!

Upon my grandsire's leathern cheek
    Five zones their bitter bronze had set:
Some day their hazards I will seek,
    I promise me at times. Not yet.

    I think my grandsire now would turn
        A mild but speculative eye
    On me, my pen and its concern,
        Then gaze again to sea—and sigh.
                                George Sterling

Songs of Work

The simple, earthy songs of workers form a body of folk music that has proved timeless in its appeal. Like folk dancing, these songs have their origins in the common people.

Work songs fall into two main groups: songs which are sung or chanted while working, and songs about work which are sung after the day's labor is finished. The first group provides a cadence or rhythm which sets a pace for the job being done; the second group provides a means of relaxation for the workers while they sing of their joys and sorrows. "Songs of Work" will give you a deeper understanding of the lives and feelings of the American workers.

The Erie Canal

I've got a mule, her name is Sal,
Fifteen years on the Erie Canal.
She's a good old worker and a good old pal,
Fifteen years on the Erie Canal.
Low bridge, everybody down,
Low bridge, we're coming to a town.
And you'll always know your neighbor,
Always know your pal,
If you've ever navigated on the Erie Canal.

Now git up, Sal, we've passed that lock,
Fifteen years on the Erie Canal.
We'll get to Rome 'bout six o'clock,
Fifteen years on the Erie Canal.
Just one more trip and back we'll go,
Through the rain and the storm and the sleet and the snow,
And ev'ry inch of the way we know
From Albany to Buffalo.

The Cowboy's Dream

Last night as I lay on the prairie,
And looked at the stars in the sky,
I wondered if ever a cowboy
Would drift to that sweet by and by.

Roll on, roll on;
Roll on, little dogies, roll on, roll on,
Roll on, roll on;
Roll on, little dogies, roll on.

The road to that bright, happy region
Is a dim, narrow trail, so they say;
But the broad one that leads to perdition
Is posted and blazed all the way.

They say there will be a great roundup,
And cowboys, like dogies, will stand,
To be marked by the Riders of Judgment,
Who are posted and know every brand.

I know there's many a stray cowboy
Who'll be lost at the great, final sale,
When he might have gone in the green pastures
Had he known of the dim, narrow trail.

I wonder if ever a cowboy
Stood ready for that Judgment Day,
And could say to the Boss of the Riders,
"I'm ready, come drive me away."

For they, like the cows that are locoed,
Stampede at the sight of a hand,
Are dragged with a rope to the roundup,
Or get marked with some crooked man's brand.

And I'm scared that I'll be a stray yearling—
A maverick, unbranded on high—
And get cut in the bunch with the "rusties"
When the Boss of the Riders goes by.

For they tell of another big owner
Who's ne'er overstocked, so they say,
But who always makes room for the sinner
Who drifts from the straight, narrow way.

They say he will never forget you,
That he knows every action and look;
So, for safety, you'd better get branded,
Have your name in the great Tally Book.

The Sheepherder

LEW SARETT

Loping along the day's patrol,
I came on a herder in Jackson's Hole;
Furtive of manner, blazing of eye,
He never looked up when I rode by;
But counting his fingers, fiercely intent,
Around and around his herd he went:

> One sheep, two sheep, three sheep, four . . .
> Twenty and thirty . . . forty more;
> Strayed—nine ewes; killed—ten rams;
> Seven and seventy lost little lambs.

He was the only soul I could see
On the lonely range for company—
Save one lean wolf and a prairie-dog,
And a myriad of ants at the foot of a log;
So I sat the herder down on a clod—
But his eyes went counting the ants in the sod:

> One sheep, two sheep, three sheep, four . . .
> Fifty and sixty . . . seventy more;
> There's not in this flock a good bell-wether!
> Then how can a herder hold it together!

Seeking to cheer him in his plight,
I flung my blankets down for the night;
But he wouldn't talk as he sat by the fire—
Coralling sheep was his sole desire;
With fingers that pointed near and far,
Mumbling, he herded star by star:

> One sheep, two sheep, three—as before!
> Eighty and ninety . . . a thousand more!
> My lost little lambs—one thousand seven!—
> Are wandering over the hills of Heaven.

The Jam on Gerry's Rock

A MODERN BALLAD

Come all ye true-born shanty-boys, wherever you may be,
Come sit ye on the deacon seat and listen unto me.
I'll sing the jam on Gerry's Rock and a hero you should know,
The bravest of all shanty-boys, the foreman, Young Munro.

'Twas on a Sunday morning, ere daylight did appear.
The logs were piling mountain high: we could not keep them clear.
"Cheer up! Cheer up, my rivermen, relieve your hearts of woe!
We'll break the jam on Gerry's Rock!" cried our foreman, Young Munro.

Now some of them were willing, while others hid from sight.
To break a jam on Sunday they did not think it right.
Till six of our brave shanty-boys did volunteer to go
And break the jam on Gerry's Rock with our foreman, Young Munro.

They had not picked off many logs till Munro to them did say,
"I must send you back up the drive, my boys, for the jam will soon give way!"
Alone he freed the key-log then, and when the jam did go
It carried away on the boiling-flood our foreman, Young Munro.

Now when the boys up at the camp the news they came to hear,
In search of his dead body down the river they did steer;
And there they found to their surprise, their sorrow, grief and woe,
All bruised and mangled on the beach, lay the corpse of Young Munro.

They picked him up most tenderly, smoothed down his raven hair,
There was one among the watchers whose cries did rend the air,
The fairest lass of Saginaw let tears of anguish flow;
But her moans and cries could not awake her true love, Young Munro.

John Henry

Well, every Monday mornin',
When the bluebirds begin to sing,
You can hear those hammers a mile or more,
You can hear John Henry's hammer ring, O Lordy!
Hear John Henry's hammer ring.

John Henry told his old lady,
"Will you fix my supper soon?
Got ninety miles o' track I've got to line,
Got to line it by the light of the moon, O Lordy!
Line it by the light o' the moon."

John Henry had a little baby,
He could hold him out in his hand;
Well, the last word I heard that po' child say,
"My daddy is a steel-drivin' man, O Lordy!
Daddy is a steel-drivin' man."

John Henry told his old captain,
Said, "A man ain't nothin' but a man;
Before I let your steel gang down
I will die with the hammer in my hand, O Lordy!
Die with the hammer in my hand."

John Henry told his captain,
"Next time you go to town
Uh-jes' bring me back a ten-pound maul
For to beat your steel-drivin' down, O Lordy!
Beat your steel-drivin' down."

John Henry had a old lady,
And her name was Polly Ann.
John Henry tuck sick and he had to go to bed;
Pauline drove steel like a man, O Lordy!
'Line drove steel like a man.

John Henry had a old lady,
And the dress she wo' was red.
Well, she started up the track and she never looked back,
"Goin' where my man fell dead, O Lordy!
Where my man fell dead."

Well, they taken John Henry to Washington,
And they buried him in the sand.

There is peoples from the East, there's peoples from the West
Come to see such a steel-drivin' man, O Lordy!
See such a steel-drivin' man.

Well, some said-uh he's from England,
And some say he's from Spain;
But-uh I say he's nothin' but a Lou's'ana man,
Just a leader of the steel-drivin' gang, O Lordy,
Leader of the steel-drivin' gang.

The poet's art . . .

These five songs of work will help you to understand what is sometimes called **oral literature,** a type very close to the hearts of workers because it is a spontaneous expression of their feelings. This oral literature has not the studied polish of loftier poetry. The themes are simple, the words are homely, and the emotions are direct, without pretense. The rhythms are in keeping with the pace of the work or are suitable for a tale of work well done and bravely.

1. Which of the five songs do you consider good accompaniments to work? How would the rhythm help the work and the workers?

2. Which songs can be called ballads? A **ballad** tells a story, usually keeping alive the memory of a gallant hero and his daring deeds. Which deed did you find most *dramatic?* Why?

3. Which song was pathetic because of the worker's reaction to the monotony of his job? Why did you feel sorry for him?

4. Which of the songs had a half-serious tone and a rhythm not quite in harmony with the anxiety of the mood? The rhythm was more in keeping with what the worker did than with what he felt. What do you imagine he was doing?

5. How were boats propelled on the Erie Canal? What did the rhythm of the song suggest? What did Sal's owner like about his job? What simple satisfaction did he find in it?

6. In "The Cowboy's Dream," the similes and metaphors conveyed a somewhat serious meaning. "Great roundup" was one; "stray yearling" was another. Find several more comparisons between the cowboys and the animals they cared for. What was the "great, final sale"? Who was the "Boss of the Riders"? Why is this figurative language so appropriate in a cowboy song?

7. How did the repetition of "one sheep, two sheep, three sheep, four . . ." in "The Sheepherder" reflect the tediousness of the job? Point out evidence in the poem of the effect of the job on the worker.

8. Tell the story of Young Munro briefly in your own words. What makes the story in rhythmic form more impressive?

Compare Young Munro with Jimmy Powers in "The Riverman." What qualities did they have in common? How were they different?

Notice that the ballad concentrates on one dramatic incident, excluding all other complications. The pathos frequently found in ballads is accentuated in the last lines. What was the pathos in this poem?

9. John Henry was the hero of a cycle of American ballads and tall tales. When he was not working on Mississippi river boats, he was a railroad steel driller. In this poem, what attributes did he have that might make him a fit comrade of Paul Bunyan? What in the poem showed that he had been a legendary character? How was his memory preserved?

Point of No Return

PAUL OSBORN
Based on the Novel by John P. Marquand

How can a man be sure he is gaining more than he is losing if he tries to move up in the world? Like many other people, Charles Gray had to find the answer to that question for himself. The position of vice-president of the bank was open, but he had to be sure he could walk upright to it like a man.

THE CAST

EVELYN GRAY	2ND TELLER	JESSICA LOVELL
NANCY GRAY	MISS MARBLE	LAURENCE LOVELL
BILL GRAY	MISS DINGLE	JOHN GRAY
CHARLES GRAY	ROGER BLAKESLEY	ESTHER GRAY
JOE	ANTHONY BURTON	TAILOR
1ST TELLER	MALCOLM BRYANT	MRS. BURTON
1ST CLERK	CONDUCTOR	MAID
2ND CLERK	JACKIE MASON	

ACT ONE

TIME: *The present.*

SCENE ONE: *The living-room of Charles and Nancy Gray in Sycamore Park, Connecticut.*

SCENE TWO: *The Stuyvesant Bank, New York City.*

SCENE THREE: *Same as Scene One.*

ACT TWO

On the way to Clyde.
Clyde, Massachusetts, 1929.
On the way back from Clyde.

ACT THREE

Same as Act One, Scene One.

ACT ONE

SCENE ONE

The living room of NANCY *and* CHARLES GRAY. *It is a typical suburban-style room, rather conventional. On a wall there is a painting of a three-masted ship in full sail. A card table is set up with breakfast things.*

As the curtain rises, EVELYN GRAY, *age eleven, is just sitting in a chair at right. She has her head buried in a geography book.*

NANCY'S VOICE (*Calling, offstage*): Bill —Evelyn—(NANCY GRAY *enters hurriedly from left. She is carrying a bowl of cereal.*)

NANCY (*Calling*): Evie! (*She looks up and sees* EVELYN.) Oh! I didn't know you were down, Evie. Good morning.

EVELYN: Good morning.

NANCY: Well, can't you look up at me to say good morning, darling?

EVELYN (*Looking up*): Good morn— (*She stops as she notices the card table.*) What are we eating in here for?

NANCY: Change. Variation. Besides the man is coming to wax the dining-room floor. (*She calls:*) Bill!

BILL'S VOICE (*Offstage*): Coming!

EVELYN: Where's Mary?

NANCY: She went to spend the night with her sister in Brooklyn. She won't be back until tomorrow afternoon.—Bill!

BILL: Here I am. (BILL *enters. He is thirteen. He starts to cross the stage, obviously on the way to the dining room. He does not look up, intent on working his yo-yo. He carries a magazine.*)

NANCY: Now hurry, darling, and get at your breakfast. The car will be here and you won't be finished. (*As* BILL *continues through the room, not looking up:*) Bill!

BILL (*Looking up and around*): What are we eating in here for?

NANCY: Change. Variation. Besides the man's coming to wax the dining-room floor.

BILL: Where's Mary?

NANCY: She went to spend the night with her sister in Brooklyn. She won't be

back until tomorrow afternoon. Is your father up yet?

BILL: He's in the bathroom. (*To* EVELYN:) Will you pass the sugar?

EVELYN: Please.

BILL: I don't have to say please to you.

EVELYN: You do, too! Doesn't he, Mother?

NANCY: All right, say please, Bill. It won't hurt you.

BILL: Will you please, kindly, and with alacrity, please pass the sugar, please. (*As* EVELYN *smiles:*) And don't look cute while you're doing it.

EVELYN: Mother!

NANCY: All right, now stop it, both of you! Evelyn, pass him the sugar and get on with your cereal.

BILL: Is Dad really going away tomorrow?

NANCY (*With a slightly mocking air*): He's going to Massachusetts—dear old Clyde, Massachusetts—the scene of his childhood.

BILL: Why is it?

NANCY: Because he was *born* there, darling. Born and brought up.

BILL: Why is he going back?

NANCY: Oh, just business of some kind. Now get on with your breakfast.

EVELYN (*Who has looked it up in her book*): "Massachusetts—Area—seven-nine-zero-seven square miles. Population—four-three-one-six-seven-two-one. Capital—Boston." It doesn't say anything about Clyde.

NANCY: Oh, it wouldn't, darling. Clyde is just a very *little* town—outside of Boston. Very pretty—very old—*very* very New England.

BILL: How long will Dad be gone?

NANCY: Oh, a long, long time. A whole day or two. We'll just have to struggle along without him. We probably won't even recognize him when he comes back. He'll have to get to know you children all over again, of course . . .

EVELYN: What are you talking about? You said he'd only be away for a day or two.

BILL: Oh, turn off your motor. Don't you know when Mother's being funny?

NANCY: Oh, I'm a funny woman.

(CHARLES GRAY *enters, newspaper in hand.*)

CHARLES: Good morning, everybody.

NANCY: Good morning, darling. (*They kiss.*)

CHARLES: What are we eating in here for?

NANCY: Change. Variation. Besides the man's coming to wax the dining-room floor.

CHARLES: Oh. 'Morning, Evie.

EVELYN: 'Morning, Dad.

CHARLES: 'Morning, son.

BILL: 'Morning, Dad.

CHARLES (*Sitting*): Where's Mary?

NANCY: She went to spend the night with her sister in Brooklyn. She won't be back until tomorrow afternoon.

CHARLES: Are you sure she's *coming* back?

NANCY: Oh, yes. She's left everything in her room.

CHARLES: Thank heavens. (*He passes his hand over his forehead.*)

NANCY: Headache?

CHARLES: A little.

NANCY: I'm sorry, darling.

CHARLES: It's just that we stayed out so late.

NANCY: Now, darling, who was it wanted to go to the Cliffords'? They had us in January and we had them and everything was square and now . . .

CHARLES: . . . we'll have to have them again. I know. Round and round.

NANCY: That's the way it is. How would you like your eggs?

CHARLES: Oh, boiled, for a change, I guess.

NANCY: Three minutes?

CHARLES: I never know what that means exactly.

NANCY: It means you let the eggs boil for three minutes.

CHARLES: I know *that!* I just mean what does it do to the egg? I don't like them too

hard so you have to dig for them—but I don't like them so soft that all that sticky, watery stuff gets all over you.

BILL: Albumen.

CHARLES: What?

BILL: That's the name for the white of an egg.

CHARLES: Oh. (*To* NANCY:) Well, just see that the albumen knows its place.

NANCY: I'd better make it four. (*She goes.* CHARLES *thinks a moment.*)

CHARLES: Bill—how do you pronounce f-o-l-k?

BILL: Folk.

CHARLES: How do you pronounce j-o-k-e?

BILL: Joke.

CHARLES: How do you pronounce the white of an egg?

BILL: Yolk.

CHARLES: Thought you just said it was albumen. (*He laughs.*)

EVELYN: "The llama and the alpaca have never been raised successfully anywhere except by the Indians on the high slopes of the Andes."

CHARLES: Really? That's a handy piece of information to have, Evelyn. What are you studying?

EVELYN: My geography.

CHARLES: Your geography! Five minutes before you have to leave? Is that the way you do your homework?

EVELYN: Um-hum. Some of it.

CHARLES: I assure you, Evelyn, you'll never get anything accomplished in little snatches like that. (*To* BILL:) Bill, you see that book sticking out there? Bring it to me. (BILL *does so.*) You see this book?

EVELYN: Yes.

CHARLES: This is Boswell's *Life of Johnson.* I have intended reading it all my life. My father loved it. In fact, this was his own copy. Some time ago I decided to spend thirty minutes a day reading it. On the train to town. Do you know how much I remember of it?

EVELYN: How much?

CHARLES: "Parnassus has its flowers of

transient fragrance, as well as its oaks of towering height, and its laurels of eternal verdure."

EVELYN: What does that mean?

CHARLES: I have no idea. Yet that's all I remember. Thirty minutes' reading a day will not materially improve your cultural deficiencies.

EVELYN: What does *that* mean?

CHARLES: It means you can't learn any geography by reading it five minutes before your school bus comes for you.

EVELYN: It's not the school bus. It's the school car. Why do you call it a bus?

CHARLES: Because it ought to be a bus. You kids ought to be going to a public school.

BILL (*Closing his magazine*): If we did get a boat, where would we keep it?

CHARLES: What?

BILL (*Alarmed—shouting*): The boat! The boat!

CHARLES: Now don't shout!

BILL: Yesterday you said it was about time you taught me to sail.

CHARLES: Oh, did I?

BILL (*Excited*): You haven't forgotten? You said since we live right here near the water we should have an eighteen-foot knockabout or something . . . You haven't forgotten?

CHARLES: No, no, of course not. Well, we'll think about it.

BILL: I don't see how you could forget a thing like that! You said . . .

CHARLES: Yes, yes, I remember, Bill. Don't shout! Put your magazine away and finish your breakfast. As a matter of fact, my father was always talking about getting me a boat, but he never did.

BILL: It's not hereditary, is it?

CHARLES: No, no, it isn't. (*The car horn is heard.*) Now there's your bus— your *car*, I mean. (*The children begin to gulp their food.* CHARLES *gazes at them a moment in dismay, then calls:*) Nancy!

NANCY (*Rushing in*): All right, children, come on. Last time we kept them waiting.

EVELYN: 'Bye, Dad.

CHARLES: 'Bye, Evie.

BILL: We'll talk about the boat some more tonight, eh, Dad?

CHARLES: All right, Bill.

NANCY: Come *on*, Bill!

(NANCY *and the children go off in a scramble. We hear their voices offstage.* CHARLES *sighs his relief and looks at his paper. In a moment,* NANCY *returns.*)

You know, we're awfully smart, getting up this twenty minutes earlier. Now we don't have to rush any more and we've time to eat for a minute before we have to go to the station and . . . (*She sits by* CHARLES.) That suit looks nice. The cleaners did a good job on it.

CHARLES: A little too much benzine for my taste.

NANCY: That'll wear off by the time you get to the bank. Oh, you've forgotten your handkerchief, though.

CHARLES: Never mind the handkerchief. I'm not running for any office.

NANCY: Oh, yes, you are, darling! And don't you keep forgetting it! You're right in there polishing apples.

CHARLES: All right, Nancy.

NANCY: What's the matter? You are in there polishing apples, aren't you?

CHARLES: I suppose I am, darn it. I suppose I've spent most of my life polishing one apple or another. If you have to earn a living, life is a series of apples. But I don't like to be reminded of it.

NANCY: Sorry. Oh, by the way, don't forget to put two hundred dollars in the housekeeping account. It's down to twenty and I'm going to draw on it again today.

CHARLES: Down to twenty? How'd it get down there?

NANCY: It just sank and sank.

CHARLES: We have the most eccentric sinking fund. . . . All right, Nancy.

(*A moment's pause.*)

NANCY: Charley, I've been thinking. If you're going to Clyde tomorrow, you'll be back by Thursday, won't you?

CHARLES: Thursday or Friday morning.

NANCY: How about asking the Burtons for dinner Friday night?

CHARLES: Nancy! You know we can't ask the Burtons!

NANCY: I don't see why not.

CHARLES: Because it would be too obvious.

NANCY: The Blakesleys are going to ask them. Molly told me.

CHARLES: If the Blakesleys want to creep to Anthony Burton, let them. I'm darned if I will.

NANCY: Well, if Burton gives that job to Roger Blakesley rather than to you . . .

CHARLES: Oh, Roger's a good man. Don't underestimate Roger.

NANCY: You'd never for a minute be worried about Roger Blakesley if you hadn't taken time out to go to the war—when Roger used that time to dig himself in solid—because you're twice the man that Roger Blakesley is.

CHARLES: You think so?

NANCY: You know you are, darling. Charley, why don't you ask Burton today how it stands? Tell him you can't sleep . . . Oh, I heard you tossing around last night. Tell him that if Roger Blakesley is going to get the job—well, at least you want to *know*. You might even tell him how they're making bets in the washroom as to whether you or Roger—all the clerks standing around in there . . .

CHARLES: I don't want to tell him that. It's embarrassing.

NANCY: Burton's the president of the bank. He doesn't know everything that goes on. He hates anything that makes the bank look undignified. After all, he's the one who is always saying banking is an "art."

CHARLES: Just how do you think I should open my remarks?

NANCY: You could say, "Look, Tony, everybody knows that you're considering either Blakesley or me for this vice-president vacancy. Now I've been around here long enough. Of course, I was out during the war and Roger wasn't . . ."

CHARLES: Nancy! That's the most unscrupulous . . .

NANCY: Yes—yes—all right—you don't have to mention that Roger wasn't. He knows that anyway.

CHARLES: Look, Nancy, I'm not going to mention anything. Have you any conception of what would happen if I said all that to Tony?

NANCY: Well, you'd know where you stood.

CHARLES: I certainly would.

NANCY: Well, maybe I got carried away a little?

CHARLES: You got carried away a lot.

NANCY: All right. But if you want to be an assistant vice-president all your life and sit at that desk that's not even on the carpet . . .

CHARLES: I don't. I'd like to be a big *vice*-president and sit at one of those big desks right up there solidly *on* the carpet, but I'm darned if I'm going to creep to it.

NANCY: And it would be "creeping" if you ask the Burtons here for dinner Friday?

CHARLES: It would. It most decidedly would.

NANCY: Okay, darling. Okay.

CHARLES: Okay. (*They sit a moment in silence.* CHARLES *looks up at her, sorry.*) Nancy, is it going to break your heart if I don't get the job? Because I may not get it, you know.

NANCY: I know. But we can hope. In fact, I had a dream last night. I dreamed today was the day.

CHARLES: What day?

NANCY: *The* day! About the job!

CHARLES: Well, did you dream I got it or did Roger Blakesley get it?

NANCY: You got it, silly. It was a dream, not a nightmare.

CHARLES: I hope you're right, Nance.

NANCY: You walked into the bank—it didn't seem any different from any other day—but after a few minutes Tony Burton came in and he called you over to his desk and he said, "Sit down, Charley. Now about this vice-president vacancy—it's yours."

CHARLES: What did I say?

NANCY: Oh, good heavens, I don't remember!

CHARLES: That's important! I took it, didn't I?

NANCY: Oh, you took it. You took it.

CHARLES: That's good.—Well, keep dreaming, Nance.

(*A moment's pause.*)

NANCY: Will you be taking the five-thirty home?

CHARLES: Yes, I suppose so.

NANCY: If you don't—call me.

CHARLES: I'll make it.

NANCY: We're going to the club for the dinner dance.

CHARLES: Oh, that's right. I'd forgotten.

NANCY: I thought maybe you had. (*Pause.*) Why is it you're going to Clyde exactly?

CHARLES: I don't know the details yet.

Some securities Tony wants me to look into. I once told him I was born and brought up in Clyde and he never forgets anything.

NANCY: I suppose you'll come back all—funny.

(CHARLES *looks at her, sharply.*)

CHARLES: What do you mean by that?

NANCY: You always act funny even when you only *think* about Clyde.

CHARLES: *I* don't act funny. It's just that you always get edgy if I even speak about it. I don't see why either.

NANCY: You know perfectly well why. Clyde's full of queer, ingrown people—you said so yourself.

CHARLES: Well?

NANCY: And *you* always get queer and ingrown whenever you speak about it.

CHARLES: Nonsense.

(*A moment's pause.*)

NANCY: I suppose you'll run into a lot of people you used to know.

CHARLES: I doubt it. I'll be too busy. Besides, after twenty years I probably wouldn't recognize them anyway.

NANCY: Of course you would. Jackie—. What's his name? The boy who lived next door to you?

CHARLES: Jackie Mason.

NANCY: Jackie Mason. Then that Lovell girl—the one you wanted to marry?

(*A slight pause.*)

CHARLES: I won't be seeing Jessica Lovell.

NANCY: Oh, you can if you want to!

CHARLES: I know I can if I want to but I don't want to.

(*Pause. Suddenly* NANCY *shudders.*)

NANCY: I'd hate to go back to the place where I was brought up! All those memories. People you have nothing in common with any more. I bet you'll feel the same way. Don't let it get you down, will you, darling?

CHARLES: As a matter of fact, I'm rather looking forward to it. Good heavens, I haven't been back to Clyde since I left there—a good twenty years ago.

NANCY: You won't like it.

CHARLES: I don't know. I'd sort of like to see our old house on Spruce Street again. I'm curious to see whether I'd feel the same way I did when my father was alive and we were all living there. (*He pauses a moment.*) I still can't help but feel my father was a highly intelligent man. He must have known what the odds were against him.

NANCY: That never stops anyone when he gets caught by it.

CHARLES: I was just thinking about him this morning. I suppose one of the reasons I got started working in a bank was because he was so erratic. He scared me. I wanted something solid and secure. (*He looks at his watch, suddenly.*) Oh, good heavens, now I've got to dash!

NANCY: Kiss me now so you won't have to at the station. (*They kiss.* CHARLES *hurries out for his coat, hat and brief case.*) And Charley—I don't want to sound picky —but if you should get to thinking about it and decide to say anything to Mr. Burton about dinner Friday . . . (*Suddenly* CHARLES *laughs.*) What's so funny?

CHARLES: The little woman kissing her husband good-bye. Everything depends on this moment. Get the job or Junior can't go to boarding school. And what about the next payment on the house? Good-bye, darling, don't come back without being the vice-president of the trust company. (*Again he laughs.*)

NANCY: Don't say that!

CHARLES: Why not?

NANCY: Because maybe you're right.

CHARLES: Now wait a minute.

NANCY: Because if you say that—if you *mean* it—maybe it *isn't* much, but it's all we have. Maybe it isn't much, but then maybe we *aren't* much. And if you feel that way, there won't be *anything* any more. (*She turns away to the sofa, near tears.*)

CHARLES: Nancy . . .

NANCY: If that's the way you feel . . .

CHARLES: Nancy, I'm not talking about

you. I'm talking about the whole set-up.

NANCY: It's the set-up we're in.

CHARLES: I know it is, darn it.

NANCY: And I'm part of the set-up!

CHARLES: I'm talking about the whole picture. It's so darned . . . Look, Nancy, I've just *got* to go! I'll miss the train. I've only got . . . (NANCY *hurries out without answering.*) Nancy—. (*He turns and picks up his brief case.*) Darn! (*As he starts out after her:*) Nancy!

(*In the darkness we hear*):

CHARLES' VOICE: Hello. Hello, Operator. For Heaven's sake let's get together on this. I'm calling Sycamore Park, Connecticut, 827.

(*The lights go up on a telephone booth at left.* CHARLES *is at the phone. The lights go up on a telephone booth at right.* NANCY *enters as the phone rings. She picks it up.*)

NANCY: Hello.

CHARLES: Hello—Nancy?

NANCY: Charley? What's the matter? Where are you?

CHARLES: Grand Central. I just got in.

NANCY (*Mystified*): What's the matter? What's happened?

CHARLES: Nothing—nothing—I just thought I'd—er—call.

NANCY: Oh.

CHARLES: No reason.

NANCY (*Quietly*): I see.

(*Slight pause.*)

CHARLES (*At a loss*): Er—get home all right?

NANCY: Fine.

CHARLES: Good. Well, I guess that's all. I just wanted to be sure you . . .

NANCY: Charley?

CHARLES: What?

NANCY: Why did you call?

CHARLES: Oh, darn it all, Nancy, I hate to start off the day this way. The way we did.

NANCY (*Soberly*): Me, too.

CHARLES: I didn't mean to be . . .

NANCY: Neither did I.

CHARLES: I got to thinking on the way down . . .

NANCY: So did I. On the way home . . .

CHARLES: And—(*He hesitates.*)—look, I guess I can ask the Burtons to dinner if . . .

NANCY: Don't, darling, if it makes you feel lousy.

CHARLES: Well, it's just that . . .

NANCY: I know. Let's skip the Burtons.

CHARLES (*With a sigh of relief*): All right, fine. (*Slight pause.*) What are you going to do all day?

NANCY: Oh, I'll find something.

CHARLES: Don't be too bored.

NANCY: Bored? Whatever made you think I was bored?

CHARLES: Well, out there all alone all day—nothing much to do . . .

NANCY: Nothing much to do! I'm running a home, Charley!

CHARLES (*Hurriedly*): Oh, sure, sure —I know—and it's a big job, too.

NANCY: Thanks. It *does* keep me busy at odd moments through the day. And then I *do* have the children later—that helps. Charley, I was thinking—on the way home—about your going to Clyde tomorrow. It's certainly a nasty time for you

to have to be away—just when Tony's going to pass out that job any minute. Out of sight out of mind.

CHARLES: I know. I thought about that, too.

NANCY: Don't think Roger Blakesley won't make the most of it.

CHARLES: Well, there's nothing I can do about it.

NANCY: You might ask Burton if you could put off going for a week or so.

CHARLES: I *can't* ask him that, Nancy.

NANCY: No, I suppose not. I don't seem to be able to stop coaching from the sidelines, do I?

CHARLES: That's all right. That's natural.

NANCY: And maybe today is the day after all.

CHARLES: Maybe, Nance.

NANCY: I don't suppose there's any way you could call it to Burton's attention, though.

CHARLES (*Right back where he was*): No! No, there isn't.

NANCY (*Hurriedly*): No, no, of course not. All right, good-bye, darling.

CHARLES: Good-bye, Nancy.

(*They hang up.*)

BLACKOUT

Let's consider . . .

1. This play is based on John P. Marquand's novel, *Point of No Return.* Marquand specializes in novels which portray well-to-do, middle-class people. What were you told in this scene that identified the Grays as a typical well-to-do, middle-class family?

2. As Charles was about to start for the bank, Nancy noticed that he had no handkerchief in his coat pocket. When she mentioned it, Charles said, "Never mind the handkerchief. I'm not running for office." Nancy replied, "Oh, yes, you are. . . ." What did she mean?

3. How did Charles feel about "polishing apples"? Do you think Nancy felt the same way?

4. Why was Nancy so eager for Charles to win the promotion? How do you think Charles felt about it? Did he want it as badly as Nancy?

5. When Nancy told Charles about her dream, he asked, "What did I say? . . . That's important!" Why was it important?

6. Nancy thought she knew how Charles could get the promotion. What do you think about her views on getting ahead? Were they useful? Were they right?

7. How did Charles feel about taking

advantage of Roger's weaknesses? How different were Nancy's and Charles' views? Explain.

8. Nancy's suggestions were meant to be helpful, but there were certain things that Charles refused to do. What were they? Why did he refuse to do them?

9. Why was Nancy so interested in having the Burtons over for dinner? What did Charles think of the idea?

10. Just before Charles left for work, what did he say that upset Nancy? What did you learn about Nancy by her reaction

to Charles' joking? What did Charles' remarks show you about his values?

11. Why did Charles call Nancy from Grand Central Station? How do you think they felt toward each other?

12. Whenever Charles mentioned Clyde, the town where he was born, Nancy thought of it as a place "full of queer, ingrown people." Why did she feel this way about Clyde, although she had never seen the town? Why did she shudder when she thought of her husband returning to his home town?

ACT ONE

SCENE TWO

The Stuyvesant Bank. One of the tellers enters and meets JOE, *the doorman.*

JOE: Good morning, Mike.

TELLER: Good morning, Joe.

CLERK: Hey, Mike . . .

TELLER: Who do you want your money on today?

CLERK: Two on Blakesley.

TELLER (*Surprised*): Yesterday you were on Gray.

CLERK: Yeah, I know—but Mr. Burton had a long talk with Blakesley yesterday and Blakesley acted in pretty good spirits when he left.

TELLER (*He moves away and approaches another clerk.*): How about it?

SECOND CLERK: Two on Blakesley.

TELLER (*Worried*): What's the idea? Everybody's turning to Blakesley.

SECOND CLERK: Old man had a long private talk with him yesterday.

TELLER: Guess maybe I got the wrong hunch here.

SECOND TELLER (*Coming up*): Mike . . .

FIRST TELLER: Yeah?

SECOND TELLER: Five on Gray!

FIRST TELLER (*Brightening*): Yeah?

SECOND TELLER: Sure. It's a cinch.

SECOND CLERK: Like heck it is.

SECOND TELLER: Just because the old man had a little talk with Blakesley doesn't mean anything.

SECOND CLERK: Hey, watch it!

(*They look up quickly and see that* ROGER BLAKESLEY *has entered.*)

JOE: Good morning, Mr. Blakesley.

ROGER: Good morning, Joe. Mr. Burton not in yet?

JOE: Not yet, Mr. Blakesley.

(BLAKESLEY *goes to his desk. His secretary,* MISS MARBLE, *is there.*)

MISS MARBLE: Good morning, Mr. Blakesley.

ROGER: Good morning, Miss Marble. Where are those papers on that Catlin thing Mr. Burton wanted me to look into?

MISS MARBLE: Right here, sir. (*She hands him the papers and he studies them as* CHARLES *enters.*)

ROGER: Oh, good. Thank you.

JOE: Good morning, Mr. Gray.

CHARLES: How are you, Joe?

JOE: Fine, thanks.

CHARLES: Are you a grandfather yet?

JOE: Not yet, but any minute now.

CHARLES: Good. (*He starts toward his desk.*) 'Morning, Roger.

ROGER: Hi, Charley. Missed you on the train.

CHARLES: No, I just made it. I didn't bother to come up to the car.

ROGER: I was just wondering about that Catlin business Tony wants us to look into. What do you think about it?

CHARLES: I think we ought to stay out of it. (CHARLES' *phone rings.* MISS MARBLE *answers.*) But you and I ought to talk it over before we meet the attorneys. How about lunch?

ROGER: Boy, I just can't make it. I have a date with Tony at the University Club.

CHARLES: Oh. There's a lot more to banking than you think, isn't there?

ROGER: Banking is an art, isn't it?

MISS MARBLE: Mr. Gray . . .

CHARLES: Good morning, Miss Marble.

MISS MARBLE: It's Mrs. Whitaker.

CHARLES (*Into telephone*): This is Mr. Gray . . . Yes, I'll hold on.

MISS MARBLE: She's called twice already this morning.

CHARLES: Good morning, Mrs. Whitaker.—Oh, I feel fine, thanks. How do *you* feel?— Fine, fine— You have? Really? What kind is it?— A Pekingese!— Yes, I like dogs very much. What's its name?— Julie!— That's nice. Does she bite?— A hole in the rug, eh? That's terrible. Well, that's the trouble with having dogs in the city. Oh, yes, of course we have to excuse them a lot. After all, they're not human. (*He adds quickly:*) Oh, I know, I know. I'm sure she's nearly human.—Practically speaks, eh?—Tonight? Why, yes, we were —At six-thirty? Why, no, I'd love to come out to your house at six-thirty, Mrs. Whitaker— No, it won't be inconvenient at all —All right—I'll look forward to talking to you and Julie both. Yes, that's right—All right, six-thirty, Mrs. Whitaker. Good-bye.

CHARLES *hangs up as* MR. BURTON *enters.*)

BURTON: Good morning, Joe. That baby come yet?

JOE: Not yet. Expecting any minute.

BURTON: Good. (*He goes to* ROGER:) Good morning, Roger.

ROGER: Good morning, Mr. Burton.

BURTON: Did you look into that Catlin matter?

ROGER: Oh, yes, I did. In my opinion, I don't think we ought to have any part of it.

BURTON: That's very sound judgment, Roger. I feel the same way about it. (*He stops by* CHARLES' *desk.*) Good morning, Charles.

CHARLES: Good morning, Mr. Burton.

BURTON: Everything under control?

CHARLES: Mrs. Whitaker's been after me . . .

BURTON: Well, as long as she's after you and not me.

CHARLES: Oh, she's nice enough if you tell her what she wants to hear.

BURTON: You handle her very adroitly, Charles. By the way, did you get a chance to look over the Catlin papers?

CHARLES: Yes, I did.

BURTON: What do you think?

CHARLES: I think we ought to stay out of it.

BURTON: That's exactly what Roger and I feel. (CHARLES *smiles slightly.*) Well— (*He nods and smiles and goes on toward his desk. Before getting there he turns.*) Oh, I forgot, I'd like to see you, Charley. Would you come over? (CHARLES *sits a moment, wondering.* BURTON *goes into his office where his secretary is waiting:*) Good morning, Miss Dingle.

MISS DINGLE: Good morning, Mr. Burton.

(CHARLES *comes in and stands.*)

BURTON: Sit down, Charley. I wanted to—oh, we'd better have Roger here. Miss Marble, will you ask Mr. Blakesley to step over here, please?

MISS MARBLE: Yes, Mr. Burton.

(*She goes to* BLAKESLEY.)

BURTON: How are Nancy and the children?

CHARLES: They're wonderful. They keep me out of trouble.

BURTON: Nancy's a fine girl. We ought to see more of her.

CHARLES: Well—she was saying—we ought to—to—(*He can't bring himself to say it.*)—see more of you, too.

Vasiliu

BURTON: Yes, we ought.

(BLAKESLEY *comes in.*)

ROGER: Did you want me, Mr. Burton?

BURTON: Yes, sit down, Roger.

ROGER: New picture?

(*He picks a photograph up from* BURTON's *desk.*)

BURTON (*Pleased*): Yes—yes—my girls gave it to me.

ROGER: Say—look at that—pretty nice.

CHARLES (*Looking at it, lamely*): Yes, pretty nice.

BURTON: Yes—yes, they're nice girls. Babs is at Sarah Lawrence now.

BLAKESLEY (*Intensely interested*): Really!

CHARLES (*Not to be outdone*): You don't say!

BURTON: We miss her, of course, but then we telephone her every evening.

BLAKESLEY (*Reading*): "To America's most representative daddy, Gladys, Olivia, Babs." Intelligent-looking kids, Tony.

BURTON: Thank you. Well—let's get down to business. It's about your running up to Clyde, Charley. (*He picks up a sheaf of papers that he refers to now and then.*) We have a new depositor who has applied for a six months' loan of three hundred thousand dollars. His name is Godfrey W. Eaton.

ROGER: You know him, don't you, Charley?

CHARLES (*Thinking*): No, I'm afraid not.

ROGER: No? He's at the Seneca Club. I met him playing golf. Everybody at the club knows Godfrey Eaton.

BURTON: Yes—it was very astute of you, Roger. (*To* CHARLES:) Roger brought him in to us the other day.

CHARLES: I see.

BURTON: Miss Dingle, do you have that listing of Eaton's?

ROGER: Yes, I've seen quite a bit of Godfrey lately. I'm surprised you never ran into him, Charley.

CHARLES: As a matter of fact, there're quite a few people I haven't run into.

ROGER: You don't get around enough, feller. Why, I changed from the Oak Knoll Club to the Seneca just to meet some new people. But you can sweeten a lot of contacts that way, too.

BURTON (*Reading*): It seems Eaton is the head of a substantial tile manufacturing company. He comes from the Middle West—owns a number of small factories there. Part of the collateral is in government bonds and part in stocks.

CHARLES: He sounds pretty safe.

BURTON: Yes, he does. Although we've got to be careful these days.

CHARLES: Of course, it's none of my business, but I wonder why he didn't go to his own bank.

ROGER: Well, I guess that was my fault, Charley. I sort of talked him into it. I've been selling him on the personal service of small banks.

BURTON: He's also a director of the Pacific Investors Trust. But still, Charles has put his finger on something. No matter how persuasive you were, Roger, why should Eaton come around to us?

ROGER: Because he likes us. He told me he liked you, too, very much, Tony.

(*He laughs lightly.*) But then why shouldn't he? I like you too, Tony. That's why the Stuyvesant Bank is a great bank. Everybody likes Tony.

CHARLES: I'd love Tony if he'd lend me three hundred thousand dollars. That's the way it is. Love and money.

(*They all smile again, then* BURTON *becomes business-like.*)

BURTON: He's putting up enough. There's only one security I question. It's an unlisted company from Clyde, Massachusetts—the Nickerson Cordage Company—a block of five thousand shares at twenty dollars a share.

ROGER: I think you're right, Tony, that should be looked into.

BURTON: That's why I'm asking you to run up there, Charley, since you once lived there and know the background. Look things over. Talk to people. How are you planning to go? Take the midnight?

CHARLES: No. I thought I'd take a plane to Boston tomorrow morning—and then a train to Clyde—(*He breaks off suddenly.*) Tony, is there any rush about this?

(*ROGER looks at him quickly. A moment's pause.*)

BURTON: How do you mean, Charles?

CHARLES: I mean, is there any reason I should go tomorrow? Would a week or so from now make any difference?

ROGER (*Quickly*): Well, it's certainly not too good to keep a man like Godfrey Eaton waiting.

(CHARLES *turns and faces him. They eye each other.*)

CHARLES: Why not? I imagine to a man like Eaton a few days wouldn't matter.

ROGER: I sort of had the feeling—well, that this ought to be finalized right now. Don't you think so, Tony?

BURTON: Have you any especial objections to going tomorrow, Charles?

(*A moment's pause.* ROGER *watches him.* CHARLES *throws it off.*)

CHARLES: No. Of course not. It *would* be better now.

(ROGER *is obviously relieved.*)

BURTON: Stay as long as you like and see if you can get some figures. As a matter of fact, I envy you getting away for a while. You're looking a little tired, Charles.

ROGER (*Putting his hand on* CHARLES' *shoulder*): I noticed that myself. You are looking a little tired, feller.

CHARLES (*Laughing*): Wouldn't you like to come along with me, Roger? Why don't you all come?

BURTON (*Rising*): I wish I could, for one. But I'm the representative daddy. Well, I see we're open.

CHARLES: Roger . . .

(CHARLES *and* ROGER *cross to their desks.*)

BURTON: Miss Dingle!

(BURTON *turns back to his desk. Waiting for* CHARLES *is* MALCOLM BRYANT, *a man of about fifty-two, whom we have previously seen enter the bank.*)

MALCOLM: Well, if it isn't Charley Gray.

CHARLES (*Puzzled*): Good morning . . .

MALCOLM: Charley, don't you remember me?

CHARLES (*Groping*): Why, yes, of course—I—

MALCOLM: Come on, I could tell you anywhere, Charley. The child is father of the man.

CHARLES: I just can't . . . Was it in the war?

MALCOLM: Longer ago than that. Over twenty years. I'm Malcolm Bryant.

CHARLES (*Staring at him*): Good heavens—Malcolm Bryant. I should have known you right away. Sit down, Malcolm. Good heavens, isn't that odd—we were just talking about Clyde. How are you, Malcolm?

MALCOLM: I dropped in to cash a government check and the cashier asked me if I knew anyone in the bank who could identify me, and I came in here to look around and there was you.

CHARLES (*He takes the check, initials it, and hands it to* JOE): Joe, cash it, will you please?

(JOE *takes the check and goes out.*)

MALCOLM (*Looking around*): So here's where you've ended up! What are you, Charley, a vice-president?

CHARLES (*Uncomfortable*): Well, no, I'm an assistant vice-president at the moment.

MALCOLM: How's Jessica?

CHARLES: Jessica? Oh—I don't know. I haven't seen her for a long time.

MALCOLM: What? Didn't you marry Jessica Lovell?

CHARLES: No.

MALCOLM: You didn't? Why didn't you? What happened?

CHARLES: Well, it's a long story, Malcolm . . .

MALCOLM: But you and Jessica were head over heels in love with each other . . .

CHARLES (*Uncomfortable*): Look, Malcolm, this isn't really the time or place . . .

MALCOLM: Was it her father?

CHARLES: Partially her father . . . Lots of things happened that year in Clyde, you know, Malcolm.

MALCOLM: I'll never forget those few months I spent in Clyde. A ghost town. A vital sort of ghost town. You've seen my book on Clyde, haven't you?

CHARLES: No, I never saw it.

MALCOLM: You didn't? It's the best thing the foundation ever got out. Here, wait a minute . . . (*He bends down and opens his brief case.* CHARLES *looks around uncomfortably.* ROGER *is trying to hear what is going on.* MALCOLM *straightens up, a book in his hand.*) I'm off on a trip and I usually take three or four copies along. It has an outline of my methods of research. Here, have one.

CHARLES: Why, thanks, Malcolm.

MALCOLM: *Yankee Persepolis*—that's what I call Clyde—Persepolis.

CHARLES: Why Persepolis?

MALCOLM: Where the Persians worshipped memories. I stopped off in Persia in thirty-five on my way to India. I was going there to study some dog worshippers. (MISS MARBLE, *overhearing him, gives a start.*) Not for you, you wouldn't like it. (*He puts his hand on* CHARLES' *arm.*) Wonderful to see you, Charley. I wish I knew everything that has happened to you since I used to know you.

CHARLES: That's a pretty tall order. Anyway I don't see why you'd want to know.

MALCOLM: Because I'm an anthropologist. Besides, I always liked you, Charley. And I'm interested in people academically.

CHARLES: Yes, people always were rather like guinea pigs to you. But I don't mind.

MALCOLM: I know you don't. That's why I always liked you. You've got a tough mind, Charley. When did you leave Clyde?

CHARLES: Oh, shortly after my father died.

MALCOLM: Then what?

CHARLES: Well, I'd been working in Boston . . .

MALCOLM: I know. What'd you do then?

CHARLES: Well, I met a man who asked me to look him up in New York. I did. I got a job here in the Stuyvesant, and I did well enough to hold it through the depression. I married a girl who worked downtown in a law office.

MALCOLM: That's right. That's your pattern. Children?

CHARLES: Two. And we bought a house in the suburbs.

MALCOLM: I know—Greenwich.

CHARLES: No.

MALCOLM: No?

CHARLES: Sycamore Park. It's not far from Greenwich though. And as a matter of fact I'm still paying for it. And right now there's a vice-president vacancy and it rests between me and that guy sitting behind me trying to hear what we're saying and he's got a tough mind, too. There! Does that answer everything?

(MALCOLM *laughs and* CHARLES *smiles.*)

MALCOLM: Do you love your wife?

CHARLES: I thought you'd ask that, and the answer is yes. I love my wife. I love my home and my children.

MALCOLM: I thought you would. You're essentially a monogamous type.

(JOE *has approached the desk.* CHARLES *looks up with relief and takes the money.*)

JOE: Here you are, Mr. Gray.

CHARLES: Thanks, Joe. (*He hands the money to* MALCOLM:) Here is your wampum. You'd better count it.

MALCOLM (*Putting it down on* CHARLES' *desk*): It has less intrinsic value than shell money. It's symbolism. Well, I'd better get going. I'm on my way to New Guinea.

CHARLES: New Guinea?

MALCOLM: Yeah, for the Pacific Investigation Institute. They had to have an anthropologist. Walter Sykes was going— you know, Sykes at the Peabody who did that work on the Micronesians?

CHARLES: Well, I . . .

MALCOLM (*Surprised*): Don't know him?

CHARLES: I'm afraid not.

MALCOLM (*Surprised*): Really? I thought everyone knew him. Anyway, his kidneys gave out last week and so they went around to the Birch Foundation and the Birch found me.

CHARLES: You know, Malcolm . . . (*He looks around and drops his voice.*) I've never told this to anyone but—a year or two after you left Clyde I tried to look you up in New York.

MALCOLM: You did?

CHARLES (*Nodding*): But you weren't here. I was still sort of upset about everything at that time. I thought you might take me on one of those trips of yours. You'd offered to take me on that one to Afghanistan, you know.

MALCOLM: I'd have taken you. That would have been funny.

CHARLES: Yes, it would have been. Well, you get a lot of queer ideas when you're that age.

MALCOLM: Yes, sir, I'd have taken you. And if I had you wouldn't be sitting here in this—whatever it is. It takes a lot of guts to be your type these days. Well, got to get going to New Guinea. (*He holds out his hand.*) Good-bye, good luck, Charley. I'll look you up when I get back.

CHARLES: Good-bye, Malcolm. Give my love to the head man.

MALCOLM: Give mine to yours. So long. (*He starts out, notices* MR. BURTON, *and giving* CHARLES *a glance points at him surreptitiously.* CHARLES *grins and nods.* MALCOLM *turns and goes out of the bank.*)

(*Slowly* CHARLES *sits down. He is very thoughtful. He looks up and sees* ROGER *watching him.* ROGER *looks away quickly. Suddenly* CHARLES *begins to think of something. A thoughtful frown comes to his brow.* MISS MARBLE *approaches his desk.*)

MISS MARBLE: Ready for me, Mr. Gray? (CHARLES *comes to a decision.*)

CHARLES: Just a minute. (*He rises and goes to* BURTON'S *desk.* BURTON *looks up.*) Mr. Burton, could I speak to you for a moment?

BURTON: Yes, of course, Charley.

CHARLES: I was just wondering. Was it *your* idea that I go up to Clyde on this matter?

BURTON: Well, I see what you mean, Charley. Roger *did* bring in this Mr. Eaton. I suppose it's his responsibility— but he doesn't know Clyde and . . .

CHARLES: What I wondered is—was it *your* idea that I go?

BURTON: Well, no, Charley. Now that you mention it, Roger suggested it. You know Clyde—and he thought you were looking a little tired—and thought it wouldn't hurt any for you to get away from the bank for a day or two.

CHARLES: I see. Thank you. (*He starts to turn away, stops, and turns back.*) Er— one other thing—er—Nancy suggested asking you whether—whether you and Mrs. Burton would like to come and have dinner with us Friday night.

BURTON: Friday night? Why, yes, Charley, we'd like to very much.

CHARLES: Good. Nancy will call Mrs. Burton. (*He nods briskly and starts back to his desk,* ROGER'S *eyes following him.*)

BLACKOUT

(*In the darkness we hear the ringing of a telephone. The lights go up on a telephone, right.* BILL *is there, reading his magazine. He is also eating an apple. He answers the phone.*)

BILL: Hello?—Yes—Okay . . . Hello?

(*The lights go up on the telephone booth, left.* CHARLES *is at the phone. He is in a hurry.*)

CHARLES: Hello, Bill. Is your mother there?

BILL (*Looking at the magazine*): She's taking a bath. You're going to the club tonight.

CHARLES: I know. I want you to give her a message.

BILL: Anything you say.

CHARLES: Tell her I'm not going to be able to get home. I've got some business I've got to attend to and I'll have to go straight to the club.

BILL (*Indifferently*): Anything you say.

CHARLES: I may not be there until just time to take her home.

BILL (*Reading his magazine*): Um-huh.

CHARLES: Bill . . .

BILL: Um-huh.

CHARLES (*Sharply*): Bill!

BILL (*Coming alive*): What?

CHARLES: Are you listening to me?

BILL: Of course I am.

CHARLES: All right. Tell her I won't have time to dress—so the shock won't be too great.

BILL: Okay. Dad?

CHARLES: Yes, Bill?

BILL: Dad, you believe there's a God, don't you?

CHARLES (*Confused*): Why—yes—sure, Bill . . .

BILL: Then if there's a God there must be an after-life, too.

CHARLES: Yeah—I guess so, Bill—Now I've got to catch my . . .

BILL: Then if there's an after-life—well
—when someone dies—he doesn't just—go
into nothing, does he? I mean, he must be
somewhere.

CHARLES: I guess that's right, Bill. If
you're interested in the subject we'll discuss
it when . . .

BILL (*Dispirited*): Okay, Dad. Skip it.
(CHARLES *is torn betweeen running for
his train and the feeling that this may be
an important moment in* BILL's *life. He
hesitates.*)

CHARLES: Look, son, these are very important matters. I don't want to seem . . .
(*He hesitates.*) Was there something *especially* that's disturbing you, Bill?

BILL: Well, I was just thinking this
afternoon about your father—and I got to
feeling sorry for him.

CHARLES (*Puzzled*): My father?

BILL: Yeah—that is, if he died—and if
there *is* an after-life—I was thinking how
terrible he must be feeling right now.

CHARLES: Why?

BILL: Because he never gave you the
boat he promised you.

CHARLES (*Shouting*): Now, look, Bill!

BILL (*Grinning*): You don't want to get
yourself in that spot, Dad.

CHARLES: All right, cut it out! Now you
give your mother that message, see?

BILL (*Looking at the magazine*): And
Dad—I found a beauty in a magazine. A
second-hand Lightning, only eight hundred
and fifty dollars.

CHARLES: Bill!

BILL (*Swiftly*): I'll leave it propped up
on the table for you so you can see it when
you get home from the club tonight. Okay,
Dad?

CHARLES (*Wearily*): All right, Bill, all
right. You see you're in bed before we get
home, too.

BILL: Oh, sure. 'Bye, Dad.

CHARLES: 'Bye, Bill.

                                        BLACKOUT

Let's consider . . .

1. As the scene opened, what impression
did you get of Roger Blakesley? Do you
think he asked Charles' opinion of "the
Catlin business" on purpose?

2. What did Charles' telephone conversation with Mrs. Whitaker indicate about
his personality?

3. What did you learn about each of
these characters when they met in Burton's
office: Mr. Burton, Roger, and Charles?

4. Obviously Roger was trying hard to

get the vice-presidency. Do you think that
Roger planned to have Charles make the
trip to Clyde? What reason would he have
for getting Charles out of the way for a
while? What difference, if any, was there
between his methods and those suggested
by Nancy?

5. Malcolm Bryant served to give the
reader some new ideas about Charles' life
in the past. What other points did he
bring out about Charles' character?

6. What made Charles go back to Mr.
Burton to ask him over for dinner?

ACT ONE

SCENE THREE

The same as Scene One. That night.

*In the darkness, we see the flicker of a
portable television set and hear the sound
of a horror picture—with appropriate gruesome organ accompaniment.* BILL *and*

EVELYN, *in their night clothes, sit watching it. There is no other light in the room.*

FIRST MAN: Now you lay there quiet
and ain't nobody gonna hurt you.

SECOND MAN: Ah, give her the woiks,
Spikey. You gettin' chicken?

FIRST MAN: Who's gettin' chicken? Put
that ice pick away.

SECOND MAN: Look out, she's gettin' the gag loose.

FIRST MAN: You didn't tie it tight enough. If she screams now . . .

(*Suddenly there is a piercing woman's scream.*)

FIRST MAN: Stop, you goon. Put that hammer down.

(*There is a pounding on the door. Men's voices shout.*)

FIRST COP: Open up, there!

SECOND COP: Open in the name of the law!

(*Loud pounding, a scream, a pistol shot, a groan and—as the organ music swells, frighteningly, the headlights of an automobile can be seen through the window. Quickly BILL jumps into action, EVELYN doing the same. They switch off the television set and we hear them scrambling out of the room, lugging the set with them. After a moment, NANCY and CHARLES can be heard coming into the house.*)

NANCY (*Offstage*): Look out for the furniture.

CHARLES (*Offstage*): I thought they were going to wax the floor.

NANCY (*Entering*): Tomorrow, he says. (CHARLES *turns on the lights as he follows* NANCY *in.*) I thought I heard—I'll take a look. (NANCY *exits in the direction the children have gone.*)

(*The light that* CHARLES *has turned on reveals* BILL's *magazine propped up on the table, and on the chair beside it rests a large square of cardboard upon which* BILL *has printed in large letters the word "BOAT" and drawn an arrow pointing toward the magazine.* CHARLES *stops and grins when he sees it. He takes off his coat and throws it over the chair. He picks up the magazine, looks at the advertisement* BILL *has mentioned, and tears it out. As he puts it into his pocket he discovers the copy of* MALCOLM BRYANT's *book that is also there. He takes the book out, glances at it, and tosses it onto the table.* NANCY *enters.*)

NANCY: Sound asleep. They're really very good, Charles.

CHARLES (*Sitting*): Um-hum.

NANCY: Tired?

CHARLES: Uh-huh. Not sleepy, though.

NANCY: I suppose we ought to go right up. We've got to go the airport in the morning. Do you want a glass of milk first?

CHARLES: Before we go to the airport or before we go up?

NANCY: Before we go up, silly.

CHARLES: No. Oh, these parties. Did you have a good time, Nancy?

(NANCY *sits on the sofa by him.*)

NANCY: Well, yes, in a sort of long-term way.

CHARLES: What do you mean, long-term way?

NANCY (*Kicking off her shoes*): You know. It's what I've told you before. I like feeling we belong somewhere. It's what I've always wanted.

(*She leans back in his arms.*)

CHARLES: Well, so do I. I guess everyone does.

NANCY: It isn't the same for a man. He always belongs much more than a woman, up to a certain point. A woman just has to tag along. It's nice, when she likes tagging.

CHARLES: Well, I'm glad you like it—but I don't see why.

NANCY: I'll tell you why. Because I'm married to a very nice man. (*They kiss.*)

CHARLES: Sorry I was late tonight. I had to go out and wet-nurse the Whitakers. They want to buy a ranch in Arizona for a hundred thousand dollars but they haven't anything to sell that shows a loss. They're all upset about it.

NANCY: Poor things. Did you put that two hundred dollars in the housekeeping account?

CHARLES: Yes. What's that got to do with it?

NANCY: I just wondered.

CHARLES (*Casually*): Oh, by the way, the Burtons are coming to dinner Friday night. (NANCY *straightens up as though jerked by wires.*)

NANCY: Charley!

CHARLES (*Grinning*): Um-hum.

NANCY: Now start at the beginning and tell me everything. Exactly how did it happen? Don't leave anything out.

CHARLES (*Laughing*): Well, Tony and Roger and I were talking about this Clyde business. Roger was pressing it all sort of hard—and well, then another fellow came in to see me—Malcolm Bryant . . .

NANCY: Never mind about Malcolm Bryant.

CHARLES: Well, it was something he said got me thinking—something about knowing how to handle the head man. He's going to New Guinea and . . .

NANCY: Never mind about New *Guinea*.

CHARLES: Anyway, it suddenly occurred to me—why was *I* being sent to Clyde? It was Roger's deal. So I asked Tony whose idea it was for me to go . . .

NANCY (*Furious*): And it was Roger's!

CHARLES (*Nodding*): That's right.

NANCY: To get you out of the way for a couple of days right now at the crucial moment!

CHARLES: It kinda looked that way. Of course, Roger said he was worried about me. Thought I looked tired and a couple of days away from the bank . . .

NANCY: Well, of all the low-down, sneaky . . . You wait until I see Molly!

CHARLES (*Starting up*): Now don't you dare tell any of this to Molly!

NANCY: But it's contemptible! I'd like to have that Roger Blakesley and . . . What did you do?

CHARLES: Nothing. What was there to do?

NANCY: Didn't you tell Roger what you thought of him?

CHARLES: Now what would be the point of that?

NANCY: Well, I wish I'd been there! I'd have . . .

CHARLES: Oh, no, you wouldn't! You just think you would.

NANCY: Well, I loathe—I just utterly loathe Roger Blakesley now! And there he was smirking around the club tonight.

CHARLES: You know what he said to me?

NANCY: What?

CHARLES: "Charley, I hope we can all be friends no matter what happens."

NANCY: Oh, I hate him—and Molly, too! Incidentally, what were you talking to her about tonight?

CHARLES: You. She said you always look lovely in those simple little dresses you wear.

NANCY: Molly can go—peddle her papers, too! Well, go on. You asked Tony to come to dinner. How'd you do it? Tell me exactly what you said.

CHARLES (*Blankly*): I said will you come to dinner Friday night.

NANCY: And what did he say?

CHARLES: He said "Yes."

NANCY (*Irritated*): But how did he *act*? Was he pleased, was he excited?

CHARLES: He didn't fall off his chair or anything.

NANCY: Well, how did it come up?

CHARLES: I'd gone up to his desk to ask him why I was the one being sent to Clyde.

NANCY (*Impatiently*): Did he realize that *you* knew that Roger had suggested your going?

CHARLES: He must have. Why?

NANCY: Tony's no fool. If he realized that Roger was trying to put a fast one over—And I bet you anything he *did*! That's wonderful.

CHARLES (*Uncomfortably*): Look—I didn't mean to get in any dig at Roger . . .

NANCY (*Radiant*): Mean it or not, darling, you did! You got in a genuine, honest, nasty dig! You were just exactly as contemptible as Roger himself! Oh, I'm proud of you! Now, let's see, does Tony like duck, do you know?

CHARLES: How the heck should I know if Tony likes duck!

NANCY: Listen, Charley, when you talk to him next see if you can steer the conversation around toward food a little.

CHARLES: Look, Nancy! Tony Burton is going to eat what we give him and like it! Will you please stop planning the menu now?

(*There is a pause.* NANCY *is cuddled against him. Each thinks his own thoughts. After a moment.*)

NANCY: Charley?

CHARLES: What?

NANCY: What will you do if he takes Roger?

CHARLES: Let's not think about it now, Nance.

NANCY: But we *are* thinking about it! Both of us. What will you do?

CHARLES: If they don't like you well enough to move you up, it's time to get out.

NANCY (*Bursting out*): It's so unfair! After years of work you become specialized, you get used to the ways of just one organization, you really become too old to start again in a new one.

CHARLES: Hey, wait a minute. I'm not so old.

NANCY: You've seen plenty of men your age looking for a job. Oh, if we'd only done something about investing for ourselves instead of for other people.

CHARLES: You don't do much of that, you know, Nancy, when you're working for a bank.

NANCY: And Bill and Evelyn growing up so fast.

(*A moment's pause. Suddenly* NANCY *clutches him, burying her face against him, sobbing softly.*)

Oh, Charley, we didn't used to be afraid!

CHARLES: Don't, Nance, don't!

NANCY: Now it seems to me we're afraid of everything!

CHARLES: Maybe fear's what makes the world go round.

NANCY (*Looking up at him, trying to smile*): Not love? I used to hear it was love.

CHARLES: Everyone's afraid of something—afraid of living, dying . . . Maybe it's better than being afraid of losing money. That's the way it is with the boys downtown. Do you know what I wish?

NANCY: What?

CHARLES: I wish we weren't always being pushed around. I'd like for once in my life to be able to tell someone off.

NANCY: Darling, you have such expensive tastes. You'd better just tell me off, if you want to, and let it go at that.

CHARLES: All right. But it's not the same thing.

NANCY: Anyway I'm awfully glad we're afraid of the same thing. It's healthy to have things in common. I'm awfully glad we're in the same boat, darling. (*She reaches up and kisses him, then gets up.*) I'm going to get myself a glass of milk— and then I'm going up. Sure you won't have one?

CHARLES: All right. I will. Thanks.

(NANCY *goes out left.* CHARLES *rises slowly, stretches, and again notices the book given him by* MALCOLM BRYANT. *He picks it up and starts to read it. Suddenly we see that he gets very interested. He reads it intently.*)

Why, the . . . (*As he reads,* NANCY *comes in with two glasses of milk.*) Why, the—!

NANCY: What is it?

CHARLES: Remember I said a fellow came in to see me today? Malcolm Bryant? He's an anthropologist. He came to Clyde —oh, when I lived there—to make a social survey of some kind.

NANCY (*Handing him the glass of milk which he has put aside*): Don't you want your milk?

CHARLES (*Taking the milk and in a moment setting it aside again, untouched*): Everybody invited him to their houses— told him everything—in fact were pretty nice to him.

NANCY: What do you mean a social survey?

CHARLES: Well—it's a study he made of Clyde—calls it a typical New England town—and (*He turns to the front of the book and reads.*) he's written it all out—

hasn't even bothered to disguise it so you won't know who he's talking about. Listen to this:

"It will be well to define the very definite social strata of this town, as follows:

"There are three distinct social groups, the upper class, the middle class and the lower class—but each of these will be divided into thirds—so we have the upper-upper, the middle-upper, and the lower-upper; the same way with the middle class —the upper-middle, the middle-middle, and the lower-middle; and the same way with the lower class . . ."

NANCY (*Laughing*): "The upper-lower, the middle-lower and the lower-lower."

CHARLES: Now just get this. "Typical of a lower-upper family are the Henry Smiths—father, mother, son and daughter. (*He looks up at NANCY.*) The ancestral motif is as marked in this group as it is in the *upper*-upper. The same importance is attached to the preservation of the heirloom and the decoration of the grave. Thus on a wall in the Smith home, hanging over the patriarchal chair is a jealously guarded primitive oil painting of a three-masted sailing vessel captained by the Smiths' ancestor, Jacob Smith."

(*He looks at NANCY and they both regard the painting on the wall. NANCY lets out an explosion of laughter.*)

NANCY: Good heavens, it's you! The Smith family is your family, Charley!

CHARLES (*Angrily*): I know darn well it is! And I remember the exact time when Malcolm asked about that picture and I remember my mother's taking the pains to explain it to him.

NANCY: What else does he say about you? Let's see—what are you—a *middle-*upper?

CHARLES (*Grimly*): A *lower*-upper. "Like other lower-upper families, they dwell on a side street, yet are received on Mason Street." He says Mason Street— that's Johnson Street, of course.

NANCY: That's where Jessica Lovell lived, isn't it?

CHARLES: That's right. "Mr. Smith"— that's my father, of course—"is a member of the Sibley Club, but is not a member of the Fortnightly Reading Club. An intellectual man, whose financial status varies with the stock market, he is free to indulge his whims because he is not bound by the rigidity of the upper-upper class. Therefore, he is able to enjoy his position as captain of the Volunteer Fire Department, a pastime which seems to afford him great amusement." It did, too. "His wife, Mrs. Smith, was Miss Jones, a physician's daughter (middle-upper). She runs their house in a lower-upper manner—(CHARLES *winces*.)—with the aid of one maid (middle-lower) coming in daily from outside. The son Tom, a likable—" (*He begins to mumble something unintelligible.*) Ah, nuts! (*He stops, disgusted.*)

NANCY: Don't mumble! I didn't get that. What about the son Tom? That's you!

CHARLES: It's just too darn silly!

NANCY (*Grabbing the book*): It's fascinating. Let me have it.

CHARLES: Now, Nancy—Now cut it out, Nancy!

NANCY (*Getting the book*): "The son, Tom, a likable young graduate of Dartmouth." (*She laughs.*) My likable young graduate from Dartmouth.

CHARLES: All right, all right.

NANCY: "—is received by the upper-upper but is not a member of the committee for the Winter Assembly—" (*Sympathetically:*) Ohh!—"He is, however, in a position to move by marriage to middle-upper, or possibly even *upper*-upper status!"

CHARLES: Come on, Nancy. Give it to me.

(*NANCY has sobered down and seems suddenly very serious.*)

NANCY: No, I want to read it. "He is on friendly terms with the daughter of Mr. Johnson (upper-upper), though there is little prospect of more than friendship." (*NANCY pauses a moment.*) That would be Jessica Lovell.

CHARLES: Nancy, don't—

NANCY (*She doesn't look at* CHARLES): "An upper-upper-class family may be typified by the Johnsons, who live on Mason Street in one of those fine, Federalist houses. The drawing room was consciously built to house its greatest treasure, a magnificent wallpaper from France. They call it, with modest humor, 'The Wallpaper Room.' This is all a fitting frame for the ritual of Clyde's upper-upper class. Mr. Johnson, the father of the daughter that Tom (lower-upper) is on friendly terms with, is a widower, descendant of shipowners in the late eighteenth century. Judith, his lovely only daughter, is eminently suited to give the family ritual an added charm. It would be a matter of marked interest if Tom (lower-upper) should ever be able to bridge the gap between himself and—" (*She stops reading.*) She must have been very beautiful, Jessica Lovell. You did love her a lot, didn't you, Charley?

CHARLES: Yes, I did. But that was twenty years ago.

NANCY: I know.

CHARLES: As far as I'm concerned, Jessica Lovell could be dead.

NANCY: Oh, no. She's always been terribly alive for you.

CHARLES: That's nonsense, Nancy.

NANCY: She did something to you. I don't know what. But she hurt you.

CHARLES: Of course she did, at the time. But it wasn't only Jessica. There were a lot of other things too . . .

NANCY (*Suddenly*): Oh, Charley, when you go up there to Clyde tomorrow—why don't you try to find out—find out what happened to you—get Jessica Lovell and Clyde out of your system once and for all.

CHARLES: All right, Nancy. Let's skip it now.

NANCY (*With a sigh*): All right. (*She rises.*) Well, I'm going up. What are you going to do? Sit up and worry about the bank?

CHARLES: No, I'm not. But I'm still not sleepy. I think I'll read awhile. (*He picks up Yankee Persepolis.*)

NANCY: Because if you're going to worry we might as well do it together.

CHARLES: I'm pretty well worried out tonight, Nancy. I'll just read.

NANCY: Don't be too long, will you? I won't be able to sleep till you come up.

CHARLES: I won't.

NANCY (*She hesitates a moment, then goes back to* CHARLES): Charley, are you sorry you married me?

CHARLES: Nancy, don't be . . .

NANCY: Are you sorry we had the children?

CHARLES: Of course not.

NANCY: Are you sorry you didn't marry . . .

CHARLES: Listen, Nancy. I love you, I love the children, now stop it. (*Slight pause.*)

NANCY: I'm going to miss you while you're gone.

CHARLES: I'll miss you. (NANCY *picks up her shoes and starts out again.*) Oh, heck, wait a minute. I'll go up, too. I've got to get that plane in the morning. (*He picks up the book again.*) That so-and-so.

NANCY: Who?

CHARLES: Malcolm Bryant. He might at least have made me a *middle*-upper. (*He drops the book into the wastebasket and both of them go off.*)

CURTAIN

Let's consider . . .

1. When Charles asked Nancy whether she had enjoyed the party, she replied, "Well, yes, in a sort of long-term way." What reasons do you think she had for saying this?

2. When Nancy learned of Roger's tricks to get the vice-presidency, she became angry. What differences were there

between Nancy's reactions and Charles' reactions to Roger's trickery?

3. When Nancy learned that the Burtons were coming for dinner, she was delighted. What did she say that indicated she was planning the dinner to win over Mr. Burton? Why didn't Charles want to talk about the dinner?

4. Charles said, "Maybe fear's what makes the world go round." Would this statement apply to his own life? Would it apply to most people? What things do you believe help to make the "world go round"?

5. Malcolm Bryant had given Charles the book about Clyde. From the passages Charles read to Nancy, what did you learn about the town?

6. Jessica Lovell was mentioned a number of times during the act. As yet, you do not know exactly what she meant to Charles. Just from the references to her in the first act, what do you think she meant to him? You will learn more about her in the next act.

ACT TWO

[Throughout this act, there are a series of flashbacks to the Clyde of Charles' youth. The first occurs after Charles meets his old friend, Jackie Mason. When their conversation drifts around to Jessica, the scene fades to the Wallpaper Room of the Lovell's home twenty years before. This is the familiar flashback which is often used in movies and television plays.]

A day coach. It is an antiquated affair and it rocks and rumbles on the roadbed. It is rather chilly. It is late afternoon.

CHARLES GRAY *sits in one of the seats looking out of the window, rapt in sober, nostalgic contemplation of what he sees. He has on his hat and topcoat, the collar turned up.*

After a moment, the CONDUCTOR *comes by.*

CONDUCTOR: Tickets, please.

CHARLES (*Startled*): Oh—yes. (*He fumbles through his pockets and produces his ticket. As the* CONDUCTOR *tears it,* CHARLES *looks out of the window.*) Isn't that Whiting's Creek out there?

CONDUCTOR: Yes, sir. Whiting's Creek.

CHARLES: It seems to me there used to be a—sort of little waterfall near here.

CONDUCTOR: Waterfall? (*He is puzzled. Then—*) Yes. Yes, there used to be a waterfall around here somewhere. But that was years ago.

CHARLES: Ah.

CONDUCTOR: They changed the creek to run around another way for some reason and that cut off the waterfall. (JACKIE MASON, *a man of about* CHARLES' *age, has entered and taken the seat in front of* CHARLES. *The* CONDUCTOR *passes on to him.*) Tickets, please. Oh, yes, I got yours.

(*The* CONDUCTOR *goes off.* CHARLES *looks up casually, then looks back out the window, then suddenly turns again and looks at the back of the head before him. He frowns, and leaning forward peers over the shoulder of the man before him.* JACKIE, *feeling his stare, slowly turns around to face him.*)

CHARLES (*His face lighting up*): Jackie Mason!

(JACKIE *hesitates a bare moment, then starts scrambling to his feet.*)

JACKIE: Charley Gray!

CHARLES (*With a broad grin*): Jackie Mason! I knew it was you from the back of your head!

(*They shake hands excitedly.*)

JACKIE: Charley Gray! I can't believe it! Well, if it isn't Charley Gray!

CHARLES: I was just sitting there looking out at Whiting's Creek and I looked up and I recognized you from the back of your head!

(*They continue to pump each other's hands.*)

JACKIE: Well, what do you know! What are you doing here?

CHARLES: Just going to Clyde on business. Here, let's switch this around.

JACKIE: I've been in the smoker! Well, what do you know! (*They pull one seat around so that they can sit facing each other. They sit.*) Charley Gray! (*He slaps* CHARLES' *knee.*) You don't look a day older, Charley!

CHARLES: You're looking fine, too, Jackie. Over twenty years . . .

JACKIE: I was just saying to Mother the other day—it still seems funny not to be able to go out in the back yard and yell for Charley to come over. Mother had a letter from your mother awhile back. Told us all about you. Married. Two kids.

CHARLES: That's right.

JACKIE: President of the Stuyvesant Bank.

CHARLES: I'm not the president, Jackie. In fact, I'm trying hard, at the moment, to become one of the five vice-presidents.

JACKIE: You stick to it, Charley. You'll get there. You've got success written all over you.

CHARLES: Have I?

JACKIE: You sure have. Some difference! (*He laughs.*) Remember in high school you used to say you didn't give a darn about getting on? Working, making money, meeting the right people? (*He laughs again.*) Why, I remember you said once you wouldn't walk across the street to meet John D. Rockefeller.

CHARLES: Did I?

JACKIE: You sure did! Thought that was all nonsense. Oh, well, kid stuff! I guess you've met a lot of the right people now, all right.

CHARLES (*Depressed*): Yes, I suppose I have. (*Snapping out of it.*) Well, how about you, Jackie? What have you been doing? Still at Wright-Sherwin?

JACKIE: Still there. In the accounting department.

CHARLES: Good.

JACKIE: Oh, it's nothing much—not like you, Charley.

CHARLES: What do you do?

JACKIE (*Shyly*): Well, matter of fact, I've been made the head of it.

CHARLES: No kidding! Well, you've certainly got where you wanted to get, Jackie.

JACKIE: Oh, I haven't done anything except in a small-town way.

CHARLES: I think you've done a lot. Not married though?

JACKIE: No—no—

CHARLES: Well, don't give up, Jackie.

(*A moment's pause. They look at each other and smile.*)

JACKIE (*Slapping* CHARLES' *knee again*): Charley Gray!

CHARLES: That's me.

JACKIE: You don't look a day older, Charley.

CHARLES: You look fine, too, Jackie.

JACKIE: How long you going to be in Clyde?

CHARLES: Just a day or two.

JACKIE: Be taking this train back to Boston?

CHARLES: Yes.

JACKIE: Good. I'll see you. I've been having to go up to Boston all this week.

CHARLES: Oh, by the way, the reason I'm here is to find out about the Nickerson Cordage Company. What do you know about it?

JACKIE: Pretty sound, as far as I know.

CHARLES: I'm glad to hear it.

JACKIE: I can't get over it. It's a small world.

CHARLES: It sure is.

JACKIE: You know, I've been in New York a couple of times. Went past your bank once.

CHARLES: Why didn't you come in?

JACKIE: Well, I don't know. Didn't know for sure you'd be there. Pete Mac-Donald was with me. Boy, we sure had a time. We took New York apart.

CHARLES (*Grinning*): Yeah?

JACKIE: Yeah.

CHARLES: Well, that's the way it goes. (*Looking out the window.*) My heavens, it all looks familiar. That's Brainard's Crossing, isn't it?

JACKIE (*Glancing out*): Yup.

CHARLES: Won't be long before we're in the tunnel now.

JACKIE: Nope. (*A moment's pause.* JACKIE *stirs uneasily.*) Charley . . .

CHARLES: Yes?

JACKIE: I—well, I . . . (*He stops.*)

CHARLES: What's on your mind, Jackie?

JACKIE: Well—(*He clears his throat.*) It's about Jessica Lovell.

CHARLES: Oh, yes. I was going to ask you about her. How is Jessica?

JACKIE: Oh, she's very well. Very well and busy. She has the same interest in things, but then you know Jessica.

CHARLES: Well, I don't know her now. It's been a long time.

JACKIE: I don't want to bring up any painful memories.

CHARLES: Painful memories? (*He laughs.*) Don't call them that, Jackie! They're too old. I'm glad to hear she's well and happy. She never married though, did she?

JACKIE: No—no, she didn't, Charley.

CHARLES: Her father?

JACKIE: No, I don't think it was entirely that. (*Slight pause.*) I think she always hoped that . . . (*He points to* CHARLES.)

CHARLES: Oh, nonsense! She knew I'd married, didn't she?

JACKIE: Yes. Jessica's a wonderful girl. She always wanted you to be happy. She's always wanted to hear about you. You see, Jessica had to talk to someone and I suppose I was elected. Just because you and I were such close friends. She still talks about you a lot.

CHARLES: Oh, come now! Maybe for a year or two after I left . . .

JACKIE: I wish you never had left, Charley. Of course I suppose you had to—with your father and all—it was pretty awful, the whole darn thing.

CHARLES: Jackie, it's all been over for years.

JACKIE: But you know—there's something about women—I think that women stay in love longer than men—once they fall in love.—I think you ought to call on Jessica while you're here, Charley.

CHARLES: Oh, no, I couldn't, Jackie.— Here comes the tunnel.

BLACKOUT

(*In the darkness we hear*):

CONDUCTOR'S VOICE: Clyde! Clyde! Kindly leave no articles in the car. Clyde! Station Clyde!

JACKIE'S VOICE: I hope you'll see her, Charley. Of course none of it was your fault. Nobody blames you at all. Just remember how she used to be. Sort of sad, you know, although she didn't show it much. So lonely until you came along. She's told me everything. She'll know you're here, Charley.

(*The noise of the train fades out, but the voices continue.*)

CHARLES' VOICE: My heavens, Jackie— you talk as if . . . Don't you realize this has been all over and done with for years? Look—I don't want to even think about it any more. That darned wallpaper room— I'll never forget the first time I saw it—the first time she took me home with her. We had to sneak into the house so we wouldn't wake the old man—I bumped into the darned furniture . . .

(*The lights have come up on*):

(THE WALLPAPER ROOM, *and as we hear* CHARLES' VOICE *describing the scene we have seen* CHARLES *and* JESSICA *entering in the semi-darkness and* CHARLES *bumping into the furniture.* JESSICA *turns at the sound.*)

JESSICA (*In a whisper*): Did you bump yourself?

CHARLES: Ran into something very solid.

JESSICA: Stand still until I turn on the lights. We mustn't wake Father.

CHARLES: Don't you think it's too late for me to come in?

JESSICA: Of course if you don't want to . . .

CHARLES: I do want to, Jessica . . .

JESSICA: Well, then.

(*She turns on the lamp and suddenly the lights come up fully.* JESSICA LOVELL, *about twenty-one, straightens up and smiles at* CHARLES, *who is about twenty-four. He is rather stiff and embarrassed.*)

CHARLES: Good heavens!

JESSICA: We call this the "Wallpaper Room." I can't imagine why, can you?

CHARLES: Good heavens! That's certainly a lot of wallpaper.

JESSICA (*Laughing*): Oh, you get used to it. You know, it's really queer that you've never been in this house before.

CHARLES: There're a lot of houses in Clyde I've never been in.

JESSICA: I mean it's queer *now.* Would you like some cold root beer?

CHARLES: Not very much. Would you?

JESSICA: Not very much. (*They both laugh and sit.*) In fact, it's rather queer we've hardly seen each other before. Both of us living in Clyde all our lives.

CHARLES: You've been away so much.

JESSICA: Yes, that's right. I've been away so much. Ever since I was fourteen, Father's taken me to Maine for the summers. And then at school at Westover and then Vassar. Were you ever at Vassar, Charley?

CHARLES: No, I went to Dartmouth.

JESSICA: No, I mean—oh, you know what I mean . . . But now I'm really back in Clyde.

CHARLES: I'm glad.

JESSICA: Are you? Oh, I wish I'd gone to school here—with all those people you know so well—then I wouldn't feel so far away and I wouldn't have worn this darn dress tonight. Why didn't you tell me it wasn't right for the movies?

CHARLES: I thought you looked lovely.

JESSICA: I felt—awful. (*Pause.*) Jackie Mason seems like a nice boy.

CHARLES: He is. (*Pause.*)

JESSICA: Charley?

CHARLES: What?

JESSICA: Why are we so formal in here? Is it the room? We've suddenly become . . . (*She stops.*)

CHARLES: It must be the room, yes. You've suddenly become the mysterious and unattainable Jessica Lovell again.

JESSICA: I'm exactly the same Jessica Lovell I have been all along. No more mysterious and no more unattainable than before.

CHARLES: It must be me.

JESSICA: It must be. (*Suddenly he looks at her, their eyes meet.* JESSICA *senses something.*) Oh! (*Suddenly* CHARLES *takes her into his arms and kisses her. He lets her go.*) Your necktie's crooked, Charley. It's been such a late spring, hasn't it? You sure you wouldn't like some cold root beer? (*Suddenly* CHARLES *takes her into his arms again. This time her arms go around his neck and she returns his kiss warmly.*) Oh, darling, darling . . .

CHARLES: I love you, Jessica . . .

JESSICA: Oh, yes, yes, I love you so much, Charley . . .

CHARLES: I've wanted to tell you . . .

JESSICA: I know—it's been awful—why didn't you?

CHARLES: I was scared . . .

JESSICA: So was I—scared you would— scared you wouldn't . . . (*They kiss.*) Oh, darling, what are we going to do?

CHARLES: I don't know—but right at this moment I don't care.

JESSICA: Everybody's going to find out.

CHARLES: I suppose so.

(*They kiss.*)

JESSICA: When did you first know, Charley?

CHARLES: That day you twisted your ankle.

JESSICA: I thought that was when.

CHARLES: I wanted to say something then . . .

JESSICA: I know. I thought you were going to.

CHARLES: I was scared.

(*They kiss.*)

JESSICA: Oh, Charley, if we had only . . .

CHARLES: Only what?

JESSICA: Nothing.

CHARLES (*Thoughtfully*): If we had only—met somewhere else, you mean, instead of in Clyde?

JESSICA: No, Charles!

CHARLES: So people would think that I . . .

JESSICA (*Quickly*): Do you think I care what people think?

CHARLES: I suppose if I lived here on Johnson Street—everything would be all right.

JESSICA: Don't *say* that, Charley!

CHARLES: And your father—he won't like it at all, will he?

JESSICA: He won't mind so much—honestly he won't—if he gets to know about it—gradually—and not all at once. (*She sees* CHARLES *frown and goes on hurriedly.*) I mean—if he could just see something of you—for awhile—without knowing that . . .

CHARLES: That his daughter's in love with a boy from Spruce Street?

JESSICA: Charley! Nothing in the world matters but you! Nothing!

(*She clings to him.* CHARLEY *kisses her. After a moment we hear:*)

LOVELL'S VOICE (*Offstage*): Jessica! Is that you?

(JESSICA *starts away, nervously.*)

JESSICA: Oh! Yes, Father.

LOVELL: Ah, good! We'll be right in.

JESSICA (*Nervously*): I thought he would be in bed.

(MR. LOVELL *and* MALCOLM BRYANT, *now about thirty-four, enter.*)

LOVELL: And this is the wallpaper I was telling you about. (*To* JESSICA:) I didn't hear you come in. I saw the light and . . . (*He sees* CHARLES:) Oh! Well, well, I didn't know we had company.

JESSICA: You know Charles Gray, don't you, Father?

LOVELL: Of course I know Charles

Gray, Jessica—or *of* Charles Gray. Where on earth did you find him? Not that I'm not very glad that you *did* find him. (*He shakes hands with* CHARLES:) How do you do, Charles?

CHARLES: How do you do, sir?

LOVELL: Jessie, this is Mr. Malcolm Bryant. (*To* MALCOLM:) My daughter, Jessica.

JESSICA: How do you do?

MALCOLM: I've been wanting to meet you, Miss Lovell. I've seen you around town a couple of times.

LOVELL: Mr. Bryant has just returned from studying the head hunters in Borneo and now he is making a social survey of Clyde.

JESSICA: I imagine you'll find some remarkable specimens in Clyde. This is Mr. Gray, Mr. Bryant.

MALCOLM: I'm glad to meet you, Mr. Gray. Do you live here in Clyde?

CHARLES: Yes, I live here. On Spruce Street.

LOVELL: That was not a happy remark of mine when I asked where Jessica found you. I'm delighted to have a Gray in the house.

MALCOLM: I'm still trying to orient myself. It's a little hard to get the general structure here, but it's a wonderful town—a beautiful, static, organized community. Let's see, your first name is Charles, isn't it?

CHARLES: That's right.

MALCOLM: Why don't we get on a first-name basis? I'm Malcolm, you're Charley, you're Jessie. Now let me get this straight. You're a college man, aren't you, Charley?

CHARLES: How did you know?

MALCOLM: Because it's my business to know social groups. Look at Jessica. She has Smith written all over her.

JESSICA: Vassar, please.

MALCOLM: Same pattern. Is your father a college man, Charley?

LOVELL: Charles' father was at Harvard with me for a short time—until he left us after Freshman midyears. Let's see, you went to Dartmouth, if I remember, Charles.

CHARLES: Yes, that's right, sir.

MALCOLM: Now why was that?

CHARLES: My aunt put me through college. She preferred Dartmouth.

LOVELL: I was extremely sorry to hear about your Aunt Jane, Charles.

CHARLES: Thank you, sir.

MALCOLM: Why, what did she do?

CHARLES (*Flatly*): She died.

MALCOLM: Oh, I beg your pardon.

CHARLES: A few weeks ago.

LOVELL: Heart, wasn't it, Charles?

CHARLES: Yes, sir.

LOVELL: Yes, everyone has always known about the Grays. "The Gray Heart," we speak of. I'm very sorry. Well . . . (*He turns to* JESSICA:) Mr. Bryant is very anxious to see the rest of the house. (*He turns to* CHARLES:) So, Charles, in case I don't see you again I'll say good-bye. Give your father my regards. Turn out the lights when Charles goes, Jessica.

MALCOLM: Good-bye, Charley. I want to meet your father some time.

CHARLES: All right.

MALCOLM: It's a wonderful town! (*To* MR. LOVELL *as they go:*) It's a way of life that has just the continuity I'm looking for.

LOVELL: My great-grandfather . . .

(*Their voices fade out.*)

JESSICA: You know, Charley, I think he likes you.

CHARLES: I don't see why you think so.

JESSICA: Because he talked so much and . . .

(*She hesitates.*)

CHARLES: —and I didn't do anything wrong . . .

JESSICA: Oh, Charley, don't! Father's not like that at all.

CHARLES: Never mind, Jessica. Everything's going to be all right.

JESSICA: Oh, it's got to, Charley! It's got to! I—I feel so terribly lonely. It's awful —being an only child. Of course, I love Father—but—well, he's always wanted me

to be so perfect. I suppose that's because Mother died suddenly when I was only six —I never really belonged anywhere. I used to watch the children go along Johnson Street to school—I had a governess, of course. I played with them a little but I never really got to know them. And when I went away to school—Father always brought me home week-ends.—Oh, dear, I sound like Emily Dickinson, don't I?

CHARLES: No, Jessie.

JESSICA: It's just as though I'd been asleep, or almost asleep, until that day I met you. I don't know what happened then. I don't see why you liked me.

(*She looks at him earnestly.*)

CHARLES: I guess it was that red hat— and your hair. And you seemed to be looking for someone and there wasn't anybody there but me.

(*They kiss. We hear the voices of* MR. LOVELL *and* MALCOLM BRYANT, *returning.*)

LOVELL'S VOICE: Well, you see, my great-great-grandfather . . .

JESSICA: Oh, dear!

CHARLES: We've certainly got to break him of that habit.

LOVELL'S VOICE: . . . Ezra Lovell, built and improved the house on River Street before the Revolutionary War. He was in the coastal trade. (*They enter.*) Why, Charles, still here? Fine! Jessie, Mr. Bryant is leaving.

CHARLES: I'll be saying good night now, too.

MALCOLM: I'll walk along with you, if I may.

CHARLES: Certainly.

LOVELL (*Extending his hand*): Good night, Charles.

CHARLES: Good night, sir.

LOVELL: It was nice of you to entertain Jessica. I like to have her see young people. I'm afraid Jessica's altogether too inclined to stick to her home. Perhaps we'll see you some time again.

JESSICA (*Laughing*): Some time again? Charles has promised to take me to a movie again tomorrow night, haven't you, Charles?

CHARLES: Yes—yes . . .

LOVELL: Really, Jessica—two movies in a row . . .

JESSICA: Don't forget, Charles.

(*She looks at him archly.*)

CHARLES: I won't. Good night, Jessica.

JESSICA: Good night.

CHARLES: Good night, sir.

LOVELL: Good night, Charles.

MALCOLM: Good night, Mr. Lovell. Good night, Jessie.

LOVELL: Good night, Mr. Bryant.

(*The lights dim out. In the darkness we hear:*)

JESSICA: Oh, Father, isn't he very nice?

LOVELL: Yes, Jessica, but I wouldn't get too interested.

(*The lights come up on Johnson Street. *MALCOLM* and *CHARLES* come in.*)

MALCOLM: Of course he would have that attitude, Charley. Laurence Lovell is a typical dessicated stuffed shirt with an absurd approach to everything. Jessica is a perfect tribal type.

CHARLES: You seem to think you know a lot about people just by looking at them, don't you?

MALCOLM: That's my business. Look at this street! You couldn't find a row of houses equal to that anywhere in the world, Charley. And all the Johnson Street people inside of them doing precisely the same thing at the given moment. It's a wonderful town. Just how well do you know the Lovells, Charley?

CHARLES: What? Oh, not very well.

MALCOLM: You're not quite in the same group, are you?

CHARLES: No, why?

MALCOLM: Still it seemed to me you were great friends with Jessica.

CHARLES: Look, suppose you mind your own business.

MALCOLM: That's just the thing you *had* to say. I should have known it. Not sore, are you?

CHARLES: No, I guess not.

MALCOLM: You see, you interest me. Charley, you have the greatest happiness vouchsafed any human being.

CHARLES: How do you figure that out?

MALCOLM: Because you're an integrated, contented part of a group. You understand your taboos and rituals, you're working happily under an almost immobile system. But don't try to break out of your group, Charley . . .

CHARLES: Look, if I want to break out of my group I will.

MALCOLM: That's just the thing you *had* to say, Charley! Perfect! Not sore, are you?

CHARLES: Are you trying to tell me not to see Jessica Lovell?

MALCOLM: It's just this, Charley, the social tribal structure is the same all over the world. In general stay away from the chief class or the *alii,* as they call it in Polynesia—unless you happen to be in it. Don't try to marry the head man's daughter.

CHARLES: And just why not?

MALCOLM: You lose mobility. It isn't any fun. You get mixed up in new rituals you know nothing about—new taboos you aren't educated emotionally to follow. Now as it is, *you're* mobile. You can move either up or down. You see, we all fit into a pattern, Charley.

CHARLES: That's just what you *had* to say. Perfect.

MALCOLM: But Jessica—her pattern makes it impossible for her to move anywhere at all. She has to remain exactly where she is—because she's in the "upper-upper" stratum . . . (*He snaps his fingers.*) There! That's the way I want to classify Clyde. There will be the three classes: the upper, the middle and the lower. Then I'll subdivide each one of these into the upper-upper, the middle-upper . . .

CHARLES: Here's where I turn off.

MALCOLM: Oh, Spruce Street down that way? Want to see it. Meet your family. From what I hear your father's hard to classify.

CHARLES: Some other time.

MALCOLM: Why?

CHARLES: It's a little late.

MALCOLM: You don't let anybody get away with anything, do you, Charley? You've got a tough mind.

CHARLES: Thanks. And Malcolm, I think you'll be surprised at what a democratic place Clyde really is.

MALCOLM: You do? Well, I hope you never find out different, Charley. And you won't—unless you try to break out of your class.

CHARLES: What do you think you need to break . . .

MALCOLM: Well, in Borneo, you have to have more shrunken heads . . .

CHARLES: And in Clyde?

MALCOLM: That's tougher. Here you need wampum—but it can't be just any wampum—it's got to mellow—it's got to be old wampum that your grandfather made or stole or however he got it. Still, wampum mellows faster now than it used to. Times change.

CHARLES (To himself): Wampum.

MALCOLM: That's right. Good night, Charley. My, it's a wonderful town!

(MALCOLM goes off. The lights fade to a single spotlight on CHARLES. Church bells are heard ringing in the distance. The lights come up on the GRAYS' living room. JOHN GRAY is seated at his desk.)

JOHN GRAY: What's the matter, Charles? You look as though you were thinking.

CHARLES: Yes, I—was thinking of something I want to do.

(CHARLES turns and moves into the living room as JOHN GRAY looks in the direction of the bells.)

JOHN GRAY: That's the Baptist bell. Do you realize it's always behind the Congregationalist? Of course my experience is almost completely without validity, but I've found it's usually a great deal better to think of doing something than to do it. Now take this paper I'm writing for the confounded Sibley Club. It was much

better thinking about it than doing it. Do you know how many tugboats there used to be in Clyde in the year 1902?

CHARLES: No.

JOHN GRAY: Well, there's not the slightest reason you should. But actually there used to be four tugboats tied up between the Nickerson Cordage Company and the old coal packet in 1902. Their names were the *Lizzie K. Simpkins,* named, I think, after the wife of Captain Simpkins who ran her. . . . Am I boring you, Charles?

CHARLES: No—No . . .

JOHN GRAY: I suppose you have no interest in the river. When I was your age I was on it all the time in my catboat. I knew every rock in it.

CHARLES: I never had the chance. You were always going to buy me a boat and teach me to sail—but you never did.

JOHN GRAY: Why, that's true, I didn't. Why didn't you ask me more often?

CHARLES: I asked you and asked you, but you never got around to it. When we had the money you were too busy with that—and when we didn't . . .

JOHN GRAY: Well, well, that's very depressing. And I'm already rather depressed this evening—so perhaps you'd better go and let me finish this paper.

CHARLES: Father . . .

JOHN GRAY: Yes, Charles?

CHARLES: I want to make some money. (*Pause.*)

JOHN GRAY (*Regarding* CHARLES *carefully*): Why, Charley, how very interesting.

CHARLES: I was thinking of getting a job in Boston. I don't believe I'm going to get anywhere if I stay at Wright-Sherwin, not for years and years.

JOHN GRAY: You couldn't be thinking of a brokerage office or a bond house, could you?

CHARLES: As a matter of fact—I was just thinking if you knew someone—if you wouldn't mind speaking to someone . . .

JOHN GRAY: Why, of course, Charles. I'd be delighted. This pleases me very much. It's about time you realized you can't get anywhere without money. It's strange so few people ever see it clearly.

CHARLES: I don't mean that money's everything.

JOHN GRAY: Oh, dear. Oh, dear me, of course it isn't. Naturally money isn't everything—but it seems to me that sometimes it helps.

CHARLES: I don't want anything for nothing. If I make money, I want to earn it.

JOHN GRAY: Yes, yes, of course you do—and that's very estimable. But do you remember what Jonathan Swift said about ambition?

CHARLES: I'm afraid not, Father.

JOHN GRAY: Oh, I wish you cared more for the polite adornments of the mind, Charles. He said: "Ambition often puts men upon doing the meanest offices: so climbing is performed in the same posture with *creeping*." I've never liked creeping.

CHARLES: And it would be creeping to want to get ahead?

JOHN GRAY: I think I can safely say that no one enjoys the comforts and pleasures to be derived from having money more than I—and yet I've never been able to creep for them. It has always been all or nothing with me. (*As* CHARLES *starts to speak, he holds up his hand.*) Now, no lecture, please. I know you think *my* way of getting ahead was—unfortunate. But because of the handicaps of never having enough capital—I was unable to beat the system. The system is not fluid and it's very hard to beat.

CHARLES: What system?

JOHN GRAY: Why, the system under which we live. The order. There's always some sort of order. There's always the bundle of hay out ahead, for any donkey who wants to get on, and They make it look like a very pleasant bundle.

CHARLES: Who are They?

JOHN GRAY: They are the people who own the hay. They are the people who run the system. And They have to toss out a little hay now and then to make the system work. They'll tell you there's plenty of hay for anyone who can get it. But the main thing is They don't want you to get it. It might be some of Their hay. You can get so far by effort, Charles. You will find that you can obtain a little hay but if you reach for more you'll get a sharp rap on the muzzle.

CHARLES: It seems to me that you've had a lot more hay than most people—at different times.

JOHN GRAY: Before I tried to get more of it, you mean? Now don't be so hard on me. I'm not going to do it again. That's all over.

CHARLES: What are you going to do with the seventy-five thousand dollars Aunt Jane left you?

JOHN GRAY: How very blunt! I suppose I might ask you what you are going to do with the five thousand dollars Aunt Jane left you, but I won't.

CHARLES: I'm going to put it in government bonds. But are you going to play the market with yours? I don't like to talk this way . . .

JOHN GRAY: I know you don't. That's all right.

CHARLES: I don't care about myself—but what about Mother and Dorothea? Why don't you set up a trust fund for them?

JOHN GRAY: An excellent idea. I'll have to think about it. Let's leave it that way. You can watch me, and I'll think about it. (*He stirs uneasily.*) But however did we get switched onto me? We were talking about you. How did this idea of your getting a job in Boston ever get into your head?

CHARLES: Oh, it just came over me.

JOHN GRAY: It couldn't have anything to do with Jessica Lovell, could it?

CHARLES: How did you know?

JOHN GRAY: Oh, one pieces little things together—from here and there. I saw you together a few times—I met Jessica Lovell on the street and she seemed remarkably gracious to me—remarkably gracious!

CHARLES: Yes, it has something to do with Jessica Lovell.

JOHN GRAY: Are you in love with her?

CHARLES: Yes.

(Pause. JOHN GRAY leans back.)

JOHN GRAY: Well! Now, this really does me a lot of good. I wonder what Laurence Lovell will say. Did you see Laurence Lovell?

CHARLES: I met him tonight.

JOHN GRAY: I suppose you sat in the room with the wallpaper. Wasn't Laurence Lovell surprised to see you there?

CHARLES: He asked Jessica where on earth she found me.

JOHN GRAY: Oh, dear me.

CHARLES: But then he said it wasn't a happy remark.

JOHN GRAY: Oh, my. I never did like Laurence Lovell. You and I must certainly do something about this. We had better go up to Boston on Monday. (He puts his hand on CHARLES' shoulder.) You really amaze me, Charles. There is a great deal to be said for love after all, isn't there? From now on you will want to do all the right things, wear the right clothes, meet the right people—all because you are in love with Jessica Lovell. Your life is changing . . . But remember, Charles, beware of too much ambition. Don't dull yourself to the refinements of life. Don't—creep—to your goal.

CHARLES: I won't, Father.

JOHN GRAY: That's good to know. (The telephone rings and JOHN GRAY answers it:) Hello?

JESSICA'S VOICE: Mr. Gray, this is Jessica Lovell.

JOHN GRAY: Oh, good evening.

JESSICA'S VOICE: Is Charles there?

JOHN GRAY: Yes, he's right here, Jessica. Just hold on, please. (He holds the phone out to CHARLES:) It's Jessica, Charles. (As CHARLES takes the phone, JOHN GRAY leaves.)

CHARLES (Into the phone): Hello.

JESSICA'S VOICE: Oh, darling, I had to call you before I went to sleep. I didn't

have a chance to say good night to you properly.

CHARLES (Abruptly): Jessica, I'm going to get a job in Boston.

(A moment's pause.)

JESSICA'S VOICE: Why?

CHARLES: Because I love you. I want to make some money.

JESSICA'S VOICE (Worried): But if you go to Boston I won't see you.

CHARLES: Yes, you will. You can come down there to see me.

JESSICA'S VOICE (Suddenly excited): Oh, yes—yes, of course I can. I can come and stay with my aunt sometimes—we can have dinner—go to the theatre . . .

CHARLES: Even see each other in public without your father's knowing . . . (A sudden pause.) What did he say after I left?

JESSICA'S VOICE (Faintly): Not to—get too interested in you. (Suddenly frightened.) Oh, Charley, he will like you! Give him time! Oh, I wish he had sixteen children, all of them girls! Please don't be cross, darling.

CHARLES: I'm not—I won't be. I'm so anxious to get started, Jessica.

JESSICA'S VOICE: Oh, yes, so am I!

CHARLES: I'll see you tomorrow night.

JESSICA'S VOICE: Yes—yes—good night, darling.

CHARLES: Good night, Jessica.

(He hangs up. He thinks a moment and starts to pace around the room.)

Mr. Lovell—there's something I've been wanting to say to you—about—er—er . . .

(The lights fade to a single spotlight on him. Suddenly his face takes on a determined expression.)

Now I won't waste time beating around the bush. I'll come straight to the point. Jessica and I are in love and we want to get married. I naturally hope you're not going to have any objections but whether you like it or not . . .

(He stops, shaking his head, hopelessly.)

Mr. Lovell, I want to ask you for the hand of your daughter in marriage . . . Bah!

(He grimaces in disgust.)

Good evening, Mr. Lovell. Yes, it *is* a nice evening, isn't it? Yes, I did want to say something to you. You see, Jessica and I want to get married. *(He waits, anxiously. Suddenly his face lights up. He holds out his hand, shaking* Mr. Lovell's.*)* Why, thank you, sir.—You've been expecting it, eh?—That's very kind of you, sir. *(He laughs.)* Well, we told you just as soon as we . . . You see, sir, I wanted to make a little money before I . . . Oh, I know, money isn't everything, sir, but it seems to me sometimes it helps. And with a girl like Jessica . . . You see, my Aunt Jane left me five thousand dollars and . . . Yes, I did, I played the market. Oh, I was very careful and I'm out of it now for good. *(Modestly.)* Well, it wasn't really clever of me, sir. I don't like the market. But I pyramided and I made about a hundred thousand dollars.

BLACKOUT

(The lights come up on The Wallpaper Room. We see Jessica *and* Mr. Lovell *seated.* Charles *enters.)*

Lovell: Good evening, Charles. Jessica tells me you want to see me about something.

Charles: Yes, sir.

Lovell: Well, sit down. I hope nothing is wrong with your job in Boston?

Charles: No, sir. Everything's fine in Boston. I think I may even be in line for a promotion soon.

Lovell: Well, that's fine, Charles. Your father's all right?

Charles: Oh, yes. Father's feeling very good these days.

Lovell: I understand he's making a good deal in the market—on paper, that is.

Charles: Yes.

Lovell: Well, you two got back early tonight. Didn't you go to the movies?

Charles: No, sir, we didn't. Not tonight.

Jessica: We had dinner at the Shore Club.

Lovell: The Shore Club? You're not a member, are you, Charles?

Charles: No, sir. My father is.

Lovell: I didn't know that.

Charles: It's quite recent.

Lovell: But how did you get there? I told you I didn't want you driving the Dodge at night, Jessica, and Charles hasn't a car, have you, Charles?

Charles: No, sir, but my father let me take his.

Lovell: Oh, has your father a car? What kind is it?

Charles: A Cadillac.

Lovell: Really. *(He sighs.)* Well, perhaps you had better tell me what you wanted to say, Charles.

Charles: Mr. Lovell—I want to marry Jessica.

(A pause. Mr. Lovell *sits looking at him, stunned. There is a silence.)*

Lovell: Pour me a glass of water, would you, please, Jessica?

Charles: You must have known, sir, that Jessica and I . . .

Lovell: Yes, Charles. And I must apologize for my behavior. Believe me, this is no reflection on you at all.

Charles: I'm sorry you feel this way about it, sir, but I thought we ought to tell you.

Lovell: Of course you had to tell me, Charles, but—oddly enough—for some reason—it never occurred to me that things had gone this far.

Jessica: Father, we don't have to talk about it any more now if . . .

Lovell: Of course we do, Jessica. Now is just the time to talk about it. *(To* Charles:*)* Well, Charles, you say you want to marry Jessica.

Charles: Yes, sir.

Lovell: I take it that means you are in love with Jessica.

Charles *(Smiling)*: Yes, sir. And I *do* know how you feel, sir. Jessica is used to a lot more than I'll be able to give her at the start, but—we are young and we do love each other.

LOVELL: How long have you known Jessica, Charles?

CHARLES: Why—all my life—I suppose . . .

LOVELL: No, I mean—how long have you been in love with Jessica?

JESSICA: Since this spring.

LOVELL: That's not very long, is it?

CHARLES: It's long enough to know that . . .

LOVELL: How old are you, Charles?

CHARLES: Twenty-five, sir.

LOVELL: Well, from all I hear you've done very well in Boston and I respect you for it. But as you point out, you will not be able to give Jessica everything she has been used to. And Jessica could never be quite the same in any other setting.

JESSICA: But Father, I don't care . . .

LOVELL: You would care, Jessica. Believe me you would. (*Again he turns to* CHARLES:) How much are you earning in Boston? You don't mind my asking, do you?

CHARLES: No, sir. Sixty dollars a week.

LOVELL: Well, well, that's splendid. But, Charles! For a girl like Jessica . . .

JESSICA: But, Father, I tell you I don't care.

LOVELL: Jessica, you have no idea what this means. (*To* CHARLES:) I don't wish to seem mercenary, but speaking realistically, Charles, it's hardly the time to talk about marrying Jessica now, is it?

CHARLES: Mr. Lovell, I have thirty-five thousand dollars besides that in government bonds.

(*A sharp pause.*)

LOVELL: Really! Did your father give it to you?

CHARLES: No, sir.

LOVELL: Did you make it yourself on the market?

CHARLES: Yes, sir. My Aunt Jane left me five thousand dollars and I . . .

LOVELL: I can't say I like that . . .

CHARLES: I don't either. But I wanted to marry Jessica. I didn't see any other way I could do it. I was desperate. If you know how I felt about the market you would appreciate how desperate I was. And now that I do have the money, I see no reason . . .

LOVELL: You realize that money is one thing and stock-market money another.

CHARLES: I suppose so, but as long as you don't lose it, it's money.

LOVELL: Still it is not the same as inherited money.

CHARLES: Everyone has to start some time, doesn't he, sir? I suppose your family did once, Mr. Lovell. So unless you have some other reason, sir . . .

JESSICA: Father, we had to tell you, didn't we?

LOVELL: Jessica, please! In case neither of you knows it, marriage is a serious matter. When two people are infatuated . . .

CHARLES (*Quietly*): I don't think it's quite fair to call it that, sir.

LOVELL: Oh, yes, I realize that is a graceless word. But when two people are —well, first in love, let's say—it is quite impossible to know each other or to realize the complications of each other's backgrounds. Jessica is my only daughter and . . .

JESSICA: Oh, Father—Father . . .

(*A pause.* MR. LOVELL *seems suddenly tired.*)

LOVELL: Oh, very well. If things have gone this far, I suppose . . . Very well, you may be engaged, but I don't want any public announcement until we get to know each other better. I suppose you must tell your family, Charles, but no one else. I want no engagement teas, no rounds of calling or other jubilation until matters are more definitely resolved.

CHARLES: When do you think that would be, sir?

LOVELL (*Sharply*): We'll see, Charles.

CHARLES: What I want is to *marry* Jessica, sir. So the sooner we can announce the engagement . . .

LOVELL (*Sharper*): There will be no

announcement, Charles, until we are sure we are ready.

CHARLES: Then it isn't really an engagement at all, is it?

JESSICA: Oh, Charley, please . . . We can be engaged—secretly—it will be such fun.

(*A moment's pause.* CHARLES *looks at* MR. LOVELL.)

CHARLES: All right. Whatever you wish, sir.

LOVELL: That's—more reasonable, Charles. Well, I shall say good night.

CHARLES: I'm leaving now, sir.

LOVELL: Good night, Charles.

CHARLES: Good night, sir. And—thank you. (*He goes to* JESSICA:) Good night, Jessica.

JESSICA: Good night. (*He kisses her.* MR. LOVELL *stands a moment, can't take it. He turns abruptly and goes out.* JESSICA *sees him and starts after him, hurt.*) Father . . .

CHARLES: Jessica . . .

JESSICA: Oh, Charley, he's hurt . . .

CHARLES: Jessica, why can't you face it? It's going to hurt him *when*ever or *whom*ever you marry.

JESSICA: I just can't *bear* to see him hurt. Oh, Charley, if you could only just—well, just do what he says for a little while until . . . Just for now—until he gets more used to it.

(CHARLES *looks at her a moment.*)

CHARLES: All right, if that's the way you want it . . .

JESSICA: Oh, Charley . . .

(*She goes into his arms.*)

BLACKOUT

(*In the darkness the telephone is heard ringing, and after a moment the lights go up on the telephone at right.* NANCY *enters.*)

NANCY: Hello—Hello . . .

OPERATOR'S VOICE: Is this Sycamore Park 827?

NANCY (*Quickly worried*): Yes—yes—who's calling?

OPERATOR'S VOICE: I have a call for Mrs. Charles Gray.

NANCY: This is Mrs. Charles Gray. Who's calling, Operator?

OPERATOR'S VOICE: All right, sir, here's your party. Booth two, please, sir.

(*The lights go up on the telephone at left.* CHARLES *enters and picks up the phone. He is excited.*)

CHARLES: Hello—hello—Nancy?

NANCY (*Sharply, worried*): Charley—what's the matter?

CHARLES: Look, Nancy . . .

NANCY: Are you all right? What's happened?

CHARLES: Nothing—nothing . . .

NANCY: Charley, tell me. I can't bear it.

CHARLES: You were right, Nancy. She did do something to me way back there.

NANCY: What? Who? Who did what?

CHARLES: Jessica Lovell. That's where it all started. I haven't thought it all through yet, but that's where it all started . . .

NANCY: Oh, I thought . . . Charley, what's wrong with you?

CHARLES: Why? Did I sound excited?

NANCY: Yes . . .

CHARLES: Oh, I guess I was a little. Were you asleep?

NANCY: Yes . . .

CHARLES: I'm sorry, Nance . . .

NANCY: That's all right. I got a little confused. What did you say about Jessica Lovell? Have you seen her?

CHARLES: No, I haven't seen her.

NANCY: You can if you want to.

CHARLES: I know I can if I want to but . . . Skip it, Nancy. I'll tell you when I get home. How are you, Nance?

NANCY: Well, I've been bearing up pretty well until now. What have you been doing?

CHARLES: Oh, nothing much. I registered at the hotel and it was too late to see anyone so I've been wandering around the streets looking at the houses. Our old

---

house on Spruce Street looks a lot smaller than I remembered it. And it's been painted brown now. My father always had it white. (*He pauses a moment.*) There're too many ghosts up here, Nancy.

NANCY: I told you there would be. Well, stop thinking now and go to bed. When are you coming home?

CHARLES: Just as soon as I can. Tomorrow I hope.

NANCY: Wonderful. If you don't come until Friday be sure to get home early, though. The Burtons, remember.

CHARLES: I know. How are the children?

NANCY: Well, there's no perceptible change.

CHARLES: What's happened since I left?

NANCY: Well, Bill cut his lip. A baseball hit him. And that man to wax the dining-room floor . . .

CHARLES: Yes?

NANCY: He never came.

CHARLES: Well, never mind. How about the Buick?

NANCY: What do you want to know about the Buick?

CHARLES: I don't know. I was just suddenly feeling lonely for you and the Buick.

NANCY: That's a nice association of ideas. The Buick's fine. It's asleep. How lonely are you?

CHARLES: Very lonely. I wish you were here.

NANCY: I'm glad you do. Come home as soon as you can and don't worry any more tonight about anything.

OPERATOR'S VOICE: Your three minutes are up . . .

NANCY (*Hurriedly*): All right, all right, we're all through, Operator. Don't put any more money in, Charley. Good night, darling . . .

CHARLES: Good night, Nance . . .

NANCY: I love you . . .

BLACKOUT

(*The lights go up on the* GRAYS' *living room.* JOHN GRAY, *looking very opulent, is standing talking to his wife while a* TAILOR *measures him.*)

TAILOR (*Measuring his raised arm*): Thirty-four and a quarter . . .

(*He jots the measurement down.*)

JOHN GRAY: —and eventually we could have a house in Pinehurst or Sea Island or Aiken. Oh, I have several plans in mind for us.

TAILOR (*As he collects his materials from the couch*): Thank you very much, Mr. Gray.

JOHN GRAY: I hope you make your train all right.

TAILOR: They'll all be ready for a try-on in two weeks' time. Good night. Good night, Mrs. Gray.

ESTHER: Good night.

(*The* TAILOR *exits as* CHARLES *enters.*)

JOHN GRAY: Ah . . .

ESTHER: Hello, Charley. Did you have a pleasant evening?

CHARLES: Yes, thank you, Mother.

(*He hesitates a moment, uncomfortably.*)

JOHN GRAY (*Looking at him*): What's happened to you, Charles?

CHARLES: Well, I might as well tell you. I'm engaged to Jessica, but I'm only to tell you and you're to tell no one. It isn't to be announced yet.

JOHN GRAY: Well . . .

(*He reaches for his coat.*)

ESTHER (*Springing to her feet and kissing him*): Oh, darling, I'm so happy. Of course, we knew you were attentive to Jessica but . . .

JOHN GRAY (*When he has his coat on*): Congratulations, Charles. I'm extremely happy for you.

CHARLES: Thank you.

ESTHER: Oh, Charley, isn't it wonderful!

CHARLES: Yes, yes, quite wonderful, Mother.

ESTHER: Well, I just think it's too exciting for words.

JOHN GRAY: I like Jessica Lovell very much. Did you—er—talk to Laurence Lovell?

CHARLES: Yes.

JOHN GRAY: Oh, my! I wish I had been there.

ESTHER: What did he say when you told him, Charles?

CHARLES: I don't think he liked it very much. He asked for a glass of water.

JOHN GRAY: Oh, dear me, a glass of water.

CHARLES: He said there should be no jubilation.

JOHN GRAY: Oh, my!

CHARLES: I don't think he thought it was serious until we began to talk about money.

JOHN GRAY: Why did he think it was serious then? I can't quite see that the salary you make would cause too deep an impression on Laurence Lovell.

CHARLES (*Uncomfortably*): Well—I have a few government bonds.

JOHN GRAY (*Looking at him*): Well— How much?

CHARLES (*Reluctantly*):   Thirty-five thousand dollars.

(*A dead silence.* JOHN GRAY *sits up and looks at him, a small smile on his face.*)

ESTHER: Why, darling, how perfectly wonderful! Why didn't you ever tell us?

CHARLES: Well, no use discussing those things . . .

ESTHER: But I think it's perfectly—don't you, John?

JOHN GRAY (*Who has been watching* CHARLES): I do, indeed, Esther dear—it's perfectly. (*He looks at* CHARLES:) Charles?

CHARLES (*Guiltily*): Yes, sir?

JOHN GRAY: It can't be—no, no, I'm sure not but—it can't be that you have— (*He whispers.*)—played the market, Charles.

CHARLES: Well, I did for a little while.

JOHN GRAY: Oh, my!

CHARLES: I don't believe in it, you know.

JOHN GRAY: Naturally, naturally, I know you don't, Charles.

CHARLES: And I'm out of it for good.

JOHN GRAY: Of course. Well, well, I can only repeat: "The power of love is incalculable." But—(*He looks at* CHARLES.) from what you say, I have the feeling that Laurence Lovell was mildly insulting.

CHARLES: I told you he didn't like it.

JOHN GRAY: And that's one part of it *I* don't like. I think I'd better go and see Laurence Lovell tomorrow.

CHARLES: No, Father.

JOHN GRAY: Yes, I think I will. What reason did he give for not telling anyone about the engagement?

CHARLES: He wants to wait until we know each other better.

JOHN GRAY: And you—agreed?

CHARLES: What else could I do?

JOHN GRAY: Oh, nothing—nothing—I presume . . .

CHARLES: I suppose you'd say I compromised . . .

JOHN GRAY: Oh, no—no . . .

ESTHER: Well, of course he didn't. And I think it would be very nice if we asked Mr. Lovell here to dinner. Don't you, John?

JOHN GRAY: No, Esther, I don't think it's necessary to go that far.

ESTHER: Well, I must tell Dorothea. She's gone to bed.

CHARLES: I wish you wouldn't tell . . . We're not supposed to tell anyone . . .

ESTHER: You've got to tell your own sister, Charles.

CHARLES: I'm afraid she'll spread it all over town.

ESTHER: I'll tell her not to tell. Oh, I'm so happy for you, Charley. Engaged!

(*She goes out.*)

(CHARLES *stands there motionless.* JOHN GRAY *looks up at him.*)

JOHN GRAY: For one who has just made such an important step toward happiness, you are looking rather tired, Charles.

CHARLES: Yes, I am rather.

JOHN GRAY: I wouldn't work too hard. It doesn't pay. You can't beat the system that way.

CHARLES: You can't beat it your way either. I hope you're being careful.

JOHN GRAY: As careful as a banker, Charles. I'm as sound as Electric Bond and Share. Shall I tell you something? I always wonder why I am doing so well until I remember this is the first time I've had any real working capital. You see, I'm pretty well up in the system now. Just between you and me—don't tell the ladies, it will only make them nervous—as of to-day—October 6, 1929—there is in the kitty six hundred and fifty thousand dollars.

CHARLES (*Nervously*): I don't like being out at sea in a canoe with just one paddle. When will you have enough, Father?

JOHN GRAY: Now are you going to lecture me again, Charles?

CHARLES: I know you're making a lot of money on paper, but why don't you get some of it off paper? I really wish you would, Father. The market is completely wild this year. The price of common stock has already discounted all conceivable earnings in any future time that you can see. It may still go up but it's terribly dangerous. At least take some of it and set up a trust fund for Mother and Dorothea.

JOHN GRAY: You may make a good investment man some day. That's very sound judgment. I'm going to do it—very soon. Now stop worrying and listen to an idea I have. Your mother and sister need a change. I was thinking of taking them on a trip. The Riviera—Monte Carlo . . . Even though I don't gamble myself, I've always wanted to watch those improvidents at Monte Carlo. Then Egypt, up the Nile, through to India, Japan, China . . . (*He looks at* CHARLES, *suddenly:*) You're afraid of money, Charles.

CHARLES (*Sincerely*): Yes. I am.

JOHN GRAY: Well, I'm going to relieve your mind. I've been thinking over all you've said and I think you're right. You can carry a good thing too far, can't you? You know, I think I really ought to set a limit. I'm going to stop all this and cash in as soon as I've made a million.

BLACKOUT

(*A single light goes up on the* GRAYS' *living room.* JOHN GRAY *lies motionless, stretched out on the sofa, one leg and arm hanging down. On the floor is a newspaper, an empty glass and a pill bottle.* CHARLES *is kneeling, dazed. He places the limp arm upon the body, kisses the forehead, reaches for the bottle and rises. Slowly he places the bottle into his pocket. The lights fade and we hear slow bells tolling.*)

(*The lights go up on Johnson Street as the bells fade out.* MALCOLM BRYANT *enters, and in a moment* CHARLES *enters from the opposite side. He is very thought-ful, preoccupied.)*

MALCOLM: Hello, Charley.

CHARLES: Oh, hello, Malcolm.

MALCOLM: Can't tell you how sorry I am. I liked your father.

CHARLES: Yes—everybody always liked Father.

MALCOLM: What are you going to do, Charley?

CHARLES: Well, right at this moment I'm on my way to . . . Mr. Lovell sent for me.

MALCOLM: Sent for you? What do you mean "sent for you"? What's up, Charley?

CHARLES: I don't know. He wants to have a little talk with me. About wampum, maybe, or lack of it.

MALCOLM: When I was in Papua I lived in a nice clear tribe. There was a nice young fellow there—warrior class, not chief class . . . He fell in love with the Chief's third daughter. They made him produce six pigs and a canoe for the marriage rites. Then they made him wear the double nose ring and they tatooed the omoo bird insignia on him. You don't get those tatoos off when once they're on. Poor fella. He was out of his group. He was very unhappy. He began to lose weight right away. He wasn't mobile.

CHARLES: Okay, Malcolm. I get it.

MALCOLM: Look, Charley, I'm getting out tomorrow—my work's finished here—going to New York for a week—then I'm off to Afghanistan. Come along with me.

CHARLES: Before I get the omoo bird tatooed on me?

MALCOLM: You've been in Clyde long enough. Get some fresh air in your lungs.

CHARLES *(Amused)*: From Clyde to Afghanistan in one step, eh?

MALCOLM: Sure.

CHARLES: Good heavens, Malcolm, I've got a job in Boston.

MALCOLM: You'd have a job with me. There's nothing more for you to get out of Clyde—and there's nothing more for you to get out of Boston either . . .

CHARLES: I've just got to get my whole life out of it, is all. Look, Malcolm, I'm doing pretty well in Boston. Even with things as they are, I've still got my job and Jessica and I . . . *(He hesitates and holds out his hand.)* Well, so long, Malcolm.

MALCOLM: So long, Charley.. Hope we run into each other again sometime.

CHARLES: I hope so too. Keep mobile.

MALCOLM: Same to you, Charley. So long.

(He nods and starts off. CHARLES *continues on his way.)*

(The lights fade on Johnson Street and come up on the LOVELL's *Wallpaper Room as* CHARLES *enters.)*

LOVELL: Good evening, Charles. Thank you for coming over.

CHARLES: Good evening, sir. Is Jessica . . .

LOVELL: She's in the library. I haven't had the opportunity to tell you how sorry I am.

CHARLES: Thank you.

LOVELL: I have heard what you have done toward settling your father's affairs. I understand there was practically nothing left and you have put all your savings in trust for your mother and sister.

CHARLES: I prefer they don't know that —but think it's my father's estate.

LOVELL: Naturally. Now Charles, nothing I have to say reflects on you personally, believe me. But there has been a change, and an unavoidable one, in the whole situation, and I am not referring to its financial aspects. Now I don't say there's anything verging on real scandal, Charles, but we must all face the implications of your father's sudden death at this especial time . . .

CHARLES: My father died of heart failure brought on by the strain of these last few days.

LOVELL: I know, Charles. But there is a doubt in people's minds. There always will be. Now I've thought this over carefully. I've been over it thoroughly with Jessica.

CHARLES: I'd like to see Jessica, please.

LOVELL: Jessica and I have been most unhappy. Most unhappy, I assure you. But it's an impossible situation, Charles. The whole thing is too impossible. We must end it. I hope you understand this, Charles.

CHARLES: I do. You have never thought I was good enough—or that I had enough money for Jessica.

LOVELL: That is very blunt, Charles.

CHARLES: I'd like to see Jessica, sir.

LOVELL: Very well. (*He walks over and calls:*) Jessica, will you come in, please? (*He turns back into the room:*) It's only fair that she should tell you herself. Fair for both of us.

(JESSICA *enters. She has been crying.*)

JESSICA: Oh, Charley—Charley . . .

LOVELL: Don't cry, Jessica, dear.

JESSICA: Oh, Charley, I'm so ashamed. I'm not fit to marry anyone.

LOVELL: Just tell Charles and then it will be all over, Jessie.

JESSICA (*Sobbing*): Oh, Charley, I can't marry you with both of you feeling the way you do—He's given up everything for me—I have to do what he thinks is best—Can't you see I'm all he has?

LOVELL: There, Jessica, it's all over now.

JESSICA: It doesn't mean I don't love you. I do. I do.

CHARLES: Then that's all there is to it,

isn't it? Jessica, do you remember what you said one night? If I saw you getting away you wanted me to tell you?

JESSICA (*Sobbing*): Oh, Charley, don't —don't—I can't bear it any more . . . I can't—I can't—please don't make it harder . . .

CHARLES: You wanted me to tell you . . .

(JESSICA *turns away from him, sobbing. Slowly* CHARLES *straightens up. He is dazed. He turns and hurries from the room. The lights begin to fade.*)

JESSICA: Charley! Charley!

BLACKOUT

(*In the darkness we hear:*)

CONDUCTOR'S VOICE: Boston train! Train to Boston! Coaches in the rear! Smoking car ahead! Train for Boston! 'Board!

(*We hear the noise of the train pulling out of the station. The lights come up on the day coach,* CHARLES *sitting by one of the windows.* JACKIE MASON *and a* STRANGER *enter.* JACKIE *halts by* CHARLES.)

JACKIE (*To the* STRANGER): See you in the smoker. (*To* CHARLES:) Here you are. Been looking all through the train for you.

CHARLES: Oh, hello, Jackie.

JACKIE: Well, how'd things go? Find out all you wanted to know?

CHARLES (*Abruptly*): What?

JACKIE: About the Nickerson Cordage Company.

CHARLES: Oh! Yes, I did.

JACKIE: Good. Well, how did it seem coming back to the old place?

CHARLES: Sort of nice, Jackie.

JACKIE: Pretty little town.

CHARLES: Yes. It hadn't changed as much as I thought it would.

JACKIE: Nothing changes very much in Clyde.

CHARLES: I wandered around—saw some of the old landmarks . . .

(*A moment's pause.*)

JACKIE: I'm sorry you didn't get to see Jessica.

CHARLES: I just couldn't make it, Jackie.

JACKIE: She knew you were here. (*Slight pause.*) You see, there's something I was going to tell you—on the train yesterday but—I hope you'll understand, Charley.

CHARLES (*Looking at him*): Understand what?

JACKIE: Well, you see—I've been seeing a lot of Jessica. (*He laughs, deprecatingly.*) I guess Mr. Lovell thought I was pretty harmless, but things can't help changing and that's what I wanted to tell you. I want to tell you that Jessica and I are engaged and are going to be married in June.

(*A sudden pause.* CHARLES *looks at him, dumbfounded.*)

CHARLES: Well!

JACKIE: Yes. You see, for years we didn't do anything but talk about you—and then —one day—well, as I say, things change.

CHARLES: How did—Mr. Lovell take it?

JACKIE: Well, I was a little surprised. He didn't seem to mind. It's funny when I had my talk with him he kept calling me Charles. Of course his mind isn't what it used to be. But he's really a grand old gentleman—and we'll all be living there together.

CHARLES: You're going to live there— with them?

JACKIE: Oh, yes, of course. He couldn't live without Jessica. As a matter of fact, I don't know if she could without him. They're very devoted. Really touching to see something as fine as that in this day and age.

(CHARLES *suddenly draws a deep breath. A little shudder passes over him which he shakes off. He turns to* JACKIE.)

CHARLES (*Sincerely*): I think it's splendid, Jackie. I wish you and Jessica all the happiness in the world.

JACKIE: Thanks, Charley, thanks a lot. (*A moment's pause.*)

CHARLES: So you're going to be married in June?

JACKIE: That's right. Although this is all

confidential, Charley. We're not going to announce it right away.

(*A sudden pause.* CHARLES *stares at him.*)

CHARLES: You're not?

JACKIE: No—we're keeping it a secret for awhile.

CHARLES: Did Mr. Lovell ask for a glass of water?

JACKIE: Why, yes, as a matter of fact, he did.

CHARLES: Did he say anything about there being no—jubilation?

JACKIE: Why, yes, he used that very word. How did you know?

(CHARLES *leans forward, earnestly, sincerely.*)

CHARLES: Listen, Jackie! You and Jessica get married in June! Don't let anything stop you, will you?

JACKIE: No, Charley.

CHARLES: You won't mind living there on Johnson Street with them, will you?

JACKIE: No, I think it will be fine.

CHARLES: So do I. Don't let anything stop you.

JACKIE: No.

(CHARLES *suddenly becomes very happy.*)

CHARLES (*Elated*): Well, I think that's fine. Fine? I think it's wonderful! Listen, Jackie, we always used to stick together, didn't we?

JACKIE: We sure did, Charley.

CHARLES: Well, we're still sticking together. Look, Jackie, let's celebrate—you and me.

JACKIE: Okay.

CHARLES: When we get to Boston let's you and me take the town apart.

JACKIE: If you don't sound like the old Charley Gray.

CHARLES: I *am,* Jackie. (*He slaps him on the knee.*) It's good to see you, Jackie.

JACKIE: Wonderful to see you, Charley.

CHARLES: You haven't changed a bit.

JACKIE: You're the same old Charley Gray.

CHARLES (*Slapping his knee again*): Jackie Mason . . .

JACKIE: Charley Gray . . .

CURTAIN

Let's consider . . .

1. In the flashbacks what did you learn about the relationship between Jessica and Charles? From Mr. Lovell's attitude towards Charles, what did you anticipate would happen?

2. Malcolm thought that Charles had "the greatest happiness" because he was "an integrated, contented part of a group." What group did Malcolm mean?

3. When he was young, Charles thought of Clyde as a democratic town. Malcolm saw it in a different light. What did he recognize which Charles failed to see until he was older?

4. What sort of person was John Gray? In what ways was he different from his son?

5. In your opinion what was John Gray's philosophy of life? He said to Charles, ". . . climbing is performed in the same posture with creeping." What do you think he was trying to tell Charles? Had Malcolm tried to tell Charles the same thing? If so, what expression did *he* use?

6. After Charles made a large amount of money, he asked Mr. Lovell's permission to marry his daughter. How was Charles' request received? Explain Mr. Lovell's attitude toward Charles. Do you think he intended to let the marriage take place? Why did he ask that the engagement be kept a family secret? What did he mean when he said that "money is one thing and stock-market money another"?

7. Why couldn't Jessica marry Charles? What was there in her own character that prevented the marriage?

8. When Charles called Nancy from Clyde, he was extremely excited. What had he realized? What did he mean by "that's where it all started . . ."?

9. In what great financial catastrophe did John Gray lose his money?

10. On the train ride back to Boston Charles learned that Jackie was going to marry Jessica and that Mr. Lovell had said exactly the same things he had said twenty years before. Why did Charles feel elated?

ACT THREE

The same as Act One, Scene One. The GRAYS' *living room. Early evening.*

As the curtain rises, CHARLES *and* NANCY *are seated with* MR. *and* MRS. BURTON. *The women are in long dresses; the men are in dinner coats, the only difference being that* CHARLES *is wearing a soft shirt and* MR. BURTON *a stiff one.* CHARLES *is bored and restless.*

BURTON: You know, everything—*everything* fits into banking somewhere. Essentially, banking is only knowing how to use extraneous knowledge. It is the oldest and the most basically human business there is in the world. In fact, I don't even like to think of banking as a business or even as a profession. It may startle you a little to hear me say this, but I'm very sure I'm right—banking, for a good banker, is an art. Don't you agree with me, Charles?

CHARLES (*Uneasily*): Well, it depends on . . .

NANCY (*Quickly*): I see your point, Mr. Burton. It's very well taken.

MRS. BURTON: What were you going to say it depends on, Mr. Gray?

CHARLES: Well, I suppose it depends on your definition of art.

BURTON (*Looking at him, coolly*): You know, sometimes you have a very cryptic quality, Charley. I never seem to know lately whether you're laughing at me or not. Sometimes you're an enigma.

CHARLES (*Smiling*): Well, you're not exactly an open book yourself, Tony.

MRS. BURTON: It's a good thing for Tony to have someone an enigma. Every-body licks Tony's boots so. That's why he's so impossible when he comes home. (*To* NANCY:) Is Mr. Gray impossible when he comes home, my dear?

NANCY (*Glaring at* CHARLES): Impossible!

MRS. BURTON: I wonder what they do at the bank. Especially before nine and after three. I have a few vague ideas.

BURTON: Even if it isn't *exactly* an art, Charley, you must agree that all experiences of any kind can be used in banking. For example, you remember that Mrs. Burton and I took a little trip in 1933. You hadn't been with us long then. Things were pretty tense in 1933, so we decided to go away. We went to Bagdad.

CHARLES: Why Bagdad?

NANCY (*Quickly*): It must be a fascinating place!

BURTON: It was. You really should go there some time, Nancy.

NANCY: I'd like nothing better.

BURTON: The cruise ship stopped at Beirut and from there Mrs. Burton and I took the side trip. We went on a bus that was, incredibly enough, as comfortable as a Greyhound bus right here in America.

(*The telephone rings long and loud in the next room. Both* MR. *and* MRS. BURTON *jump up, excitedly. They speak simultaneously.*)

MRS. BURTON: That must be our call to Barbara . . .

BURTON: There's Barbara at last . . .

(*They both start out, then stop and look at* NANCY, *awkwardly.*)

MRS. BURTON: Oh, I beg your pardon . . .

BURTON: Sorry . . .

NANCY: No, no, go right ahead. It's always long distance when it rings like that.

MRS. BURTON: It's just that we tried an hour to get Barbara before we left home . . .

NANCY: Please! Go right ahead.

(MRS. BURTON *exits*.)

BURTON: We won't be a minute—at least *I* won't! When Mrs. Burton gets on the phone with her daughter . . .

NANCY: It's perfectly all right.

(MR. BURTON *exits*. NANCY *turns back into the room and faces* CHARLES. CHARLES *looks at her*.)

CHARLES: All right, don't say it!

NANCY: But why do you have to disagree with *everything* he says? "It depends on your definition of art." "You're not exactly an open book yourself, Tony." "Why Bagdad?" At least let the man open his mouth without . . . And you wore a soft shirt after all instead of the stiff one I laid out for you!

CHARLES: I'm not going to wear a stiff shirt just because Tony Burton does!

NANCY: Oh, I hate it when you act this way! It's all because you went up there to Clyde! You've acted differently ever since you came back.

CHARLES: Maybe I have. I had a lot of time to think. (*He turns away*.) Oh, it's all so darned contrived!

NANCY: What is?

CHARLES: All of it! So superficial! The bank president and the big job, and what will happen to Junior—will he get to Exeter—and whether a boiled shirt will help. The values of it are childish. It hasn't any values at all!

NANCY: But you want the job . . .

CHARLES: Nancy, don't be so tense. Maybe it isn't as important as all that. Anyway . . .

NANCY: Don't say it! I can't stand it if you say it!

CHARLES: What do you think I'm going to say?

NANCY: That we have each other! I *know* we have each other but I don't want to hear it! It's been in your mind ever since you came home. Tell me later but don't tell me now!

CHARLES: Nancy, I'm doing everything I can . . .

NANCY: You're not! You're acting licked already.

CHARLES: Maybe I don't give a darn.

NANCY: And now I suppose you're going to say I've always been pushing you.

CHARLES: I wish you'd stop telling me what I'm going to say.

NANCY (*Turning away, upset*): Oh, it's not fair, it's not fair!

(*Suddenly they hear the* BURTONS *offstage*. NANCY *turns quickly and recovers*.)

MRS. BURTON (*Offstage*): I think Miss Smith is the red-headed one. Barbara likes her.

CHARLES: What isn't?

BURTON (*Offstage*): I really think we're going to have some luck this time, Althea.

MRS. BURTON: Oh, I do hope so.

NANCY: Here they come. (*The* BURTONS *enter*. NANCY *goes to them with a smile*.)

NANCY: Well, I take it, it was Barbara.

MRS. BURTON: No, it wasn't. It was one of the teachers. Barbara had gone down to the village but they expect her back any minute. I told her to have Barbara call us here, if you're sure it's all right.

CHARLES: Oh, perfectly. Isn't it, Nancy?

NANCY: Of course—although it frightens me.

CHARLES: It does me, too.

MRS. BURTON: What does?

CHARLES: Why—the same thing that frightens Nancy.

NANCY (*Quickly*): To think of the time when Evelyn will have to go away to school.

CHARLES: Yes, that's it.

NANCY: I don't know what we'd do without her.

CHARLES: Certainly don't.

MRS. BURTON: I know, I felt the same way, too.

BURTON: Well, we spent the night in quite a nice French hotel in Damascus, where Mrs. Burton bought that rare rug we have now in the library. My, it was hot! Remember, Althea?

MRS. BURTON: Yes, it was hot.

BURTON: There was plenty of ice water, though. Then at dawn we started right across the desert and toward the next evening the bus stopped at a place called Rutba Wells, right out in the middle of nowhere. Fortunately, it was run by the British and so was sanitary. And then, in the cool of the evening we went right across the desert to Bagdad—and there it was at dawn . . .

MRS. BURTON (To NANCY): It really was romantic.

NANCY: It must have been.

BURTON: A city on a muddy river, spanned by a bridge of boats. The next morning we went to the museum to see the ancient treasures from—er . . .

MRS. BURTON: Ur.

BURTON: Ur—Ur. And we met a man there—and this is the most exciting part—and he showed us some mud bricks that were actually parts of an account book. When you got used to them, you could see how they balanced their figures; and on one brick, believe it or not, there was even an error in addition that had been preserved through the centuries. Now what do you think of that, Charley?

CHARLES: Well—I'd say that . . .

NANCY (Quickly): It's incredible.

BURTON: Yes, it was. Yes, that meant a great deal to me. Well . . . Nancy, my dear, I wish you wouldn't always surprise me so.

NANCY: What have I done now?

BURTON: It seems to me you are so much more beautiful every time I see you. Or do I just forget?

NANCY: It might be that you just forget, mightn't it?

BURTON: We've really got to do something about seeing each other more often. Why don't you come to work some morn-

ing instead of Charles? I'm getting pretty sick of seeing Charley around.

(NANCY catches her breath.)

CHARLES (Smiling): Perhaps I'd better start looking for a job somewhere else.

BURTON (After a moment, puzzled): You know, Charles, I wish there weren't so many words, or it may be because I'm getting old that they confuse me more than they used to. Somehow they keep having more shades of meaning. Now even with Charles and me it's difficult. I say a word and he says a word and we can look it up in the dictionary, but it doesn't mean the same thing to either of us and it would mean something a little different to you, Nancy, and it would be something a little different to Althea. I don't suppose this is a very new thought of mine, but it's a thought.

MRS. BURTON: I'm not even sure it's a thought. Tony, I haven't the faintest idea of what you're talking about.

BURTON: But Charley knows, don't you, Charley? We both may be worrying about the same thing but we worry about it in different ways.

CHARLES (Slowly): Yes, I think I know what you mean. If we are both worried about the same thing—naturally your worry approaches it from one angle—and mine from quite a different one.

(NANCY looks frightened.)

BURTON: Exactly. I wish we could all get together, we might do something with the world, but of course we never can get together. That's the exasperating part of it.

MRS. BURTON: Really, Tony. (To NANCY:) Have you the slightest idea of what he's getting at?

NANCY: I'm not sure.

BURTON: Perhaps I'm being cryptic now, but all I'm saying is that I wish we might all be friends. I really hope we can be, no matter what may happen in the future, and the future isn't as clear as it used to be. That's all I'm trying to say. I just want us all to be friends, no matter what happens.

(*A moment's pause.* NANCY *is stricken,* CHARLES *turns away for a moment, then back.* TONY *is looking at* CHARLES.)

CHARLES (*Casually*): Why, of course, we'll all be friends, Tony.

BURTON: Fine. That's fine!

(*Again the telephone rings loud and long. Again the* BURTONS *jump up but this time* MR. BURTON, *being nearer the door, gets a head start.*)

MRS. BURTON: Now that *must* be Barbara!

BURTON (*On his way out*): You don't mind?

NANCY: No, no, of course not.

(MR. BURTON *exits.*)

MRS. BURTON: We'll try to make it short. Of course, when Mr. Burton and Barbara get to talking . . .

(*She exits. A pause.* CHARLES *takes a deep breath.*)

CHARLES: Well, I guess that's that. I'm sorry, Nance. I had the feeling it was coming.

NANCY: Oh, I didn't! I thought sure you were going to get it!

(*She cries softly.*)

CHARLES: He's been too nice all evening. He was trying to give me something soft to fall on.

NANCY: Oh, Charley, what are we going to do?

CHARLES: I don't know. These things are always awkward. It's embarrassing for Tony, too. Perhaps I'd better resign. (NANCY *wilts;* CHARLES *sits, depressed.*) I think when Tony said that about always being friends—that's what he meant. I suppose he can get me in somewhere else. Although I'll probably never have as good a position as the one I have now.

NANCY (*With a sob*): Oh! After all these years!

CHARLES: We might as well face it. In a business way I've gone as far as I will go. (*He gives a wry smile.*) You know what really shocks me most?

NANCY: What?

CHARLES: I thought I had myself all

prepared for any bad news I might get— that I wouldn't think it was complete disaster if I got it—but now—(*He puts his hand to his stomach.*)—right here—in the pit of my stomach . . .

NANCY: Mine, too.

(*A moment's pause.* CHARLES *takes a deep breath.*)

CHARLES: Well, anyway, thank heavens, it's over. Stomach or no stomach—I feel as if I can take a deep breath again. There's nothing more to expect from Tony Burton. If I want to say "Why Bagdad?" to him, from now on, I can.

NANCY: You said it anyway.

CHARLES: Yes—but now I can say it without being afraid. Or, what's even more important, now I don't even *have* to say it. (*They sit a moment in silence.* CHARLES *is very thoughtful.*) We can sell this house and move into a smaller one. We won't starve—after all, I can make . . . (NANCY's *head sinks into her hands.*) We'll get enough to educate Bill and Evie. We'll never make the Hawthorn Hill Club now, of course—but who cares? I never really wanted to be in that club anyway.

NANCY: I did.

CHARLES: Bunch of stuffed shirts—(*He rises, restlessly, wanders toward the hall and looks out.*) They're sure giving Barbara a going over. (*He wanders back into the room and stands, thinking.*) You know that's true.

NANCY: What is?

CHARLES: I never *did* want to be in the Hawthorn Hill Club. That's not just sour grapes.

NANCY: You tried hard enough to get in.

CHARLES: Yes, I did, didn't I? I wonder why. Why did I do all that to get somewhere I didn't want to be? (*He thinks.*) Why have I done a *lot* of things I've done, right from the very start! Do you know there was a time when I wouldn't walk across the street to meet John D. Rockefeller.

NANCY: When was that?

CHARLES: I mean there was a time when I *said* that—when I *felt* it—and then—(*He pauses, thinking back.*)—then from Spruce Street to Wright-Sherwin to Johnson Street to Boston to New York to the Stuyvesant Bank—drive, drive, drive—"Yes, sir." "No, sir." "Polish your apple, sir." Why? What was I trying to do?

NANCY: What everyone tries to do. Get on.

CHARLES: No, that's not the whole answer.—Nancy, I haven't had the chance to talk to you since I got back—but remember what you said you wanted me to do? Get Jessica Lovell—Clyde—all of it out of my system?

NANCY: Yes.

CHARLES: Well, they're out, Nancy. Going back there—and now losing the job—

has certainly kicked them out once and for all. From the time I first kissed Jessica Lovell in that wallpaper room—that's where it all started. That's where I started to creep. I think all my life I've been the Spruce Street boy trying to creep up to Johnson Street.

NANCY: You married me. That didn't get you much farther.

CHARLES: That's what saved me, Nancy. That's what saved me. But it wasn't just Jessica Lovell. It was everything back there. Clyde—my father—and Mr. Lovell—

NANCY (*With a look to where the* BURTONS *went off*): Charley . . .

CHARLES: That's where it started. That's where the donkey forgot everything else and started following the bundle of hay. (*He stops.*) Well, to heck with the hay. We'll live. The main thing is I don't have to try to beat the system any more. We're out of it, Nancy. (*Pause.* NANCY *is watching him. He grins.*) You know, I feel good. I mean really good—I mean strong, independent—like being able to tell somebody off. I'm free, Nancy—I'm free to—to —I'm free to read Boswell's *Life of Johnson,* if I want to. Doesn't it make sense to you, Nancy?

NANCY: I don't see why you can't read Boswell—or not join the Hawthorn Hill Club . . .

CHARLES: No, no, Nancy—you don't understand—it's not just the Hawthorn Hill Club, it's a whole way of life! Why, if I told Tony I didn't want to join the Hawthorn Hill Club . . . Good night, I'd practically be telling him off. But as it is now—I'm free—inside. (*He kneels and looks at her.*) Don't you get it, Nance?

NANCY: I don't know.

CHARLES: I'm going to say now what you wouldn't let me say before. We *have* got each other—*and* the children—*and* we're alive—and I'm going to try to buy Bill that boat *anyway.* See, Nance? See?

NANCY: You can't make me feel *glad* we've lost the job, Charley—but—maybe it's not the world-crushing tragedy I thought it was. And anyway, you said one wonderfully sweet thing.

CHARLES: What was that?

NANCY: That—marrying me—saved you.

CHARLES: It *did,* Nance. It *did.*

NANCY: And—as you say—we *have* got each other—maybe more now than before. We darn well better.

CHARLES: Oh, Nancy, you're a funny one.

(*He bends down and kisses her.*)

BURTON (*Offstage*): You know, Althea, I think Barbara sounded rather English.

MRS. BURTON: Yes, she has a lovely telephone voice.

(NANCY and CHARLES *break off quickly.* CHARLES *takes her hand.*)

CHARLES: Now don't worry about the rest of the evening. We'll all get along swell now.

BURTON (*Offstage*): I'm not sure I like that.

(*The* BURTONS *enter.* NANCY *rises.*)

CHARLES: How's Barbara?

MRS. BURTON: She's fine. Oh, dear, I'm sorry—this has all been terribly rude . . .

BURTON: You see, we're so anxious about Barbara. She hasn't liked several schools she's been to lately—but I really think Sarah Lawrence is going to turn out all right.

CHARLES: Good!

BURTON: You know, it's really cozy here. I like it. (*He hesitates.*) Charley, there's something I want to ask you. I guess it's all right, here in the bosom of the family. What do you think of Roger Blakesley?

(*There is a sudden dead pause.* NANCY *looks up at him, quickly.* CHARLES *turns slowly.*)

CHARLES (*Casually*): Why Roger's okay.

BURTON: No, now, we're all alone here. You can speak frankly. The women won't say anything. Do you like him or don't you?

CHARLES (*After a moment*): I think Roger is conscientious, energetic, and well

trained, but I can't say I like him much. Why should I?

BURTON: I rather like him. He's been on my conscience lately. He's so anxious, so much on his toes. He's always in there trying.

CHARLES: I don't know what else you could expect. I've been trying pretty hard myself.

BURTON: Not in the same way, Charley. You're subtler. You're developed, you've matured. Of course, I'm out of touch with things, being where I am, but I've been getting an idea—and maybe I'm entirely wrong. You're in more of a position to know than I am. It seems to me that Blakesley has some idea that we're considering him for that vice-presidency vacancy. Do you know anything about this, Charles?

(NANCY *looks at* CHARLES.)

NANCY: What did Blakesley think you were considering him for?

BURTON: That vice-presidency vacancy. I hadn't given it much thought until the other day when we were talking about your going up to Clyde. But Roger said a few things—and I got to thinking back and—well, when anyone gets ideas like that it's a problem to know what to do with him later. (*He looks at* CHARLES, *suddenly.*) *You* never thought any of us were considering Blakesley, did you, Charles?

CHARLES: Why, yes, Tony, I did.

BURTON (*Astonished*): Good heavens! (*He looks at* NANCY:) You *did?*

NANCY: Now that you mention it, I think it did cross our minds.

BURTON: You amaze me! Roger is quite useful, but he's not the right material at all. Your name comes up before the directors on Monday. I've spoken to them, of course. There won't be any trouble.

CHARLES: Thanks, Tony—that's—that's fine . . .

BURTON: That's what I meant when I said before—now that we'll be working together more closely, I hope we'll all be friends.

CHARLES: Well, here we are.

BURTON: I can hardly believe you didn't realize this, Charley.

CHARLES: I guess when you have a job you really never know where you stand, do you?

BURTON (*Looking at him, keenly*): I have the curious feeling that you don't seem overly elated about this, Charley.

CHARLES (*Quickly*): I'm sorry. I didn't mean to give that impression. It's just that —I'm a little confused.

BURTON: There's nothing to be confused about. The job is yours. A week from Saturday there'll be a little dinner. You'll be called on to make a few remarks. And oh, yes, I've taken the liberty of putting your name up for membership in the Hawthorn Hill Club. So many of us are there. I hope you don't mind. (*A moment's pause.*) I don't think I understand your attitude. You want the job, don't you?

CHARLES: Tony, please don't think I'm ungrateful. It's what I've been working toward all my life, I suppose. But a few minutes ago Nancy and I thought we weren't going to get it—and—curiously enough—I never felt better. And now— suddenly—I feel—well, a little like that time at Dartmouth when I won the half-mile at Freshman track. A little dull—a little tired and a little curious why I ran so hard.

BURTON: We all run hard to win. None of us wants to come in second.

CHARLES: No, I suppose so. And I did run like the devil.

BURTON: You know, of course, Charley, that you're really obligated to take the job. You owe it to us. The bank has invested a lot of time in you. Besides, this is the natural step in your life—it's the logical outcome—you can't change a line of it.

CHARLES: No, that's probably true. And I don't want to change a line of it. It's just that—well, I suppose nothing you ever work hard for turns out exactly as you thought it would.

BURTON: We've all felt that. I know I have. Sometimes you half resent success.

But you can't turn back now, Charley. It's too late.

CHARLES: That's true, isn't it? Tony, don't think I don't want the job. It means a lot to us. And I'm glad you want me. It's just that—from here on in—I want to be myself. The rest of my life I want to walk straight up and down—this way—vertical. I don't want to creep any more—I don't want to ever polish another apple—I— Tony, I've got to tell you this. I don't want to join the Hawthorn Hill Club.

BURTON: Really? Why not?

CHARLES: I don't like it.

BURTON: I've always liked the Hawthorn Hill Club.

CHARLES: That's fair enough, Tony. I never have.

BURTON: Well—you certainly must know I wouldn't try to dictate your club to you, Charley. In fact, I've never felt I could dictate to you at all.

(*A moment's pause. The maid enters and nods to* NANCY, *who rises.*)

CHARLES: Well, I guess that means Junior can go to Exeter.

MRS. BURTON: Charles, I see you're reading Boswell's *Life of Johnson*. You know, Nancy, I tried to read it once. It's the dullest thing I ever got into.

NANCY: Oh, no! Don't tell him that!

MRS. BURTON: I wonder if anyone ever really read it through.

CHARLES: I doubt it. I very much doubt it. (NANCY *and* MR. BURTON *are offstage.* MRS. BURTON *is off and as* CHARLES *starts off:*)

NANCY'S VOICE: Charley, bring some cigarettes.

(*He turns back into the room.* NANCY *enters.*)

NANCY: Charley, never mind the cigarettes.

(*She goes to him and kisses him.*)

CHARLES: What's that for?

NANCY: That's for free.

(*They start off.*)

CURTAIN

The man who wrote this play

PAUL OSBORN   1901–

The author of *Point of No Return* is a successful playwright who has shown his skill at original work as well as dramatic adaptations of best-selling novels. Born in Evansville, Indiana, he earned the degrees of A.B. and M.A. at the University of Michigan. After further study at Yale, he was engaged as English Master at the University of Michigan. He was fortunate in receiving his early training in playwriting under Professor George Pierce Baker, in the well-known Workshop 47 at Harvard.

Among Mr. Osborn's original plays are *The Vinegar Tree* (1930), *On Borrowed Time* (1938), and *Morning's at Seven* (1939). His adaptations include *A Bell for Adano*, based on the novel by John Hersey.

Let's consider . . .

1. When the act opened, Nancy was eager to agree with whatever Mr. Burton said. What was Charles' attitude?

2. When the Burtons left to answer the phone, Nancy and Charles spoke about the promotion. How did each of them feel about it? What did Nancy say that led Charles to make an effort to please the Burtons?

3. The second time the Burtons left the room, the Grays thought the promotion had been decided in Roger's favor. Explain how Charles reacted and why. What was Nancy's reaction? Do you think Charles was serious when he said he felt better? Or was that just "sour grapes"?

4. Charles said he was feeling freer than at any time in the past twenty years. What did he believe had started in Jessica's Wallpaper Room? Why did he say that his marriage to Nancy had saved him? Did it really save him?

5. When Mr. Burton finally told Charles of his promotion, what effect did this have

on Charles? Do you think he was pleased? What were his reasons for accepting it?

6. Once assured of the job, Charles made a small "declaration of independence." Do you feel he was actually winning independence for himself? Or was he just trying to recover a little of the freedom he felt he had given up by accepting the job?

7. Mr. Burton said to Charles, "But you can't turn back now, Charley. It's too late." With this in mind, explain what you think the title, *Point of No Return,* means.

8. Do you consider the ending of the play a happy one? Was getting the promotion actually happy for Charles? What happened to Charles' independence?

9. Several times during the play Charles mentioned that he wanted to have the time and freedom to read Boswell's *Life of Johnson.* Why then, did he tell Mrs. Burton that he doubted if *anyone* ever read it all the way through?

The writer's craft . . .

Early in every drama there is a bit of action or dialogue, called the **initial incident.** It arouses your interest because it introduces a problem in which the leading characters are involved.

The initial incident in *Point of No Return* occurred in Act I, Scene I, when the Gray family was at breakfast. Nancy's remark, "How about asking the Burtons for dinner Friday night?" introduced the initial incident which, as it developed, led Nancy to say, "Well, if Burton gives that job to Roger Blakesley rather than to you—." This incident introduced you to the first problem: who would be promoted to the vice-presidency at the bank? It also indicated that a conflict existed between Charles and Roger because both men were candidates for the promotion. However, the promotion was really the minor problem in the play.

The minor problem served as a framework for the major problem: could Charles maintain his integrity and his freedom and still get ahead in the world? The conflict in this major problem was within Charles himself, between his values and his ambitions. It was foreshadowed in the initial incident when Nancy said that the Blakesleys were planning to invite the Burtons to dinner and Charles replied, "If the Blakesleys want to creep to Anthony Burton let them. I'm darned if I will." This remark revealed that Charles was determined to keep his integrity as a person, even at the risk of losing the promotion.

Thus the initial incident established the two problems in the play: the outer, minor problem of the promotion, and the inner, major problem of whether Charles could get ahead and still be the person he wanted to be.

The part of a play which precedes the initial incident is called the **exposition.** It familiarizes you with the setting, introduces some of the leading characters, sets the tone of the play, and fills in the background which the audience needs to know in order to understand the play. Explain in detail what you learned about each of these from the exposition in *Point of No Return.*

After the initial incident, there is a series of events, called the **rising action,** which leads to the climax. In *Point of No Return* these events were primarily concerned with Charles Gray's development as a person. Paul Osborn, the playwright, took you beyond the outer conflict of whether or not Charles would be promoted, and into the deeper conflict involving Charles' struggle within himself. To do this, Osborn used the **flashback:** a device which interrupts the course of action to introduce events which occurred at a previous time. The purpose of these flashbacks was to let you see the place, people, and events which Charles was remembering. These flashbacks also let you see why Charles gained a fuller understanding of himself

by reliving his experiences. Characters in plays come to life by means of action as well as dialogue. If Charles had merely talked about his early life in Clyde, the play would have lost much of its intensity and you would have missed knowing him as thoroughly as you do.

The **climax** of a play is the point where the rising action reaches its greatest intensity. Usually the climax is a turning point in the conflict. Where did the climax occur in *Point of No Return?* In which way was it a turning point in Charles' life?

The play had a strong theme, which was quite easy to see when you understood Charles and his problem. You recall that the theme is the unifying idea upon which the writer builds his action. Usually the theme is directly related to the conflict in which the leading characters are involved. In *Point of No Return* the theme was concerned with Charles' conflict between getting ahead in the world and maintaining his integrity and his right to act as a free person. In Act III he said several things to Nancy which indicated that he had gained a new insight into his character. Look again at the dialogue on page 536. Begin with Charles' remark: "I never did want to be in the Hawthorn Hill Club," and continue through Nancy's reply: "I don't see why you can't read Boswell . . ."

1. Explain in your own words what Charles discovered about himself.

2. How did the conflict created by the promotion help Charles to understand and resolve his inner conflict?

3. Think carefully about your answers to the first two questions. Also, recall the conversation between Charles and his father in Act II (p. 519). Then, in a carefully worded sentence, state the theme of the play.

4. If you agree with the theme of the play, how could it apply to you and your desire to get ahead in the world? Discuss.

NOW THINK BACK

1. This part presented many different ways in which Americans have earned their daily bread. List these ways. Which ones would be difficult, if not impossible, today?

2. Choose the one worker portrayed in this part who you feel was most devoted to his chosen occupation. Explain how he showed his devotion.

3. Certain lines of work can be followed only in definite regions of the country. Select four jobs mentioned in this part and explain why they were regional.

4. Suppose you had to earn your daily bread as one of the characters in this part earned his. Write a short paper describing the opportunities, the dangers, the excitement, and the personal satisfaction you would find in that kind of work.

5. In real life and in fiction, the work a person has to do is not always rewarding —either in money earned or in personal satisfaction. Sometimes it is the nature of the work; sometimes it is the worker himself—his suitability for the job or his attitude toward it. Prepare a panel discussion on the subject, "The Job and the Worker." In your discussion try to present some helpful answers to the following questions. Illustrate your opinions by referring to the selections in OUR DAILY BREAD.

　a. What should a person look for in a job in the way of security, opportunity for personal and professional growth, and pleasant surroundings?

　b. What attitude should a person take toward his job and the people with whom he works?

　c. What is expected of workers today that was not essential in many jobs a hundred years ago?

　d. What should a person do if he finds that getting ahead in a job requires him to lower his standards, either of work or of honesty?

6. Which kind of work described here do you consider the most dangerous? Compare it with one other hazardous occupation and point out the greater dangers.

7. Was any person portrayed in this part responsible for his lack of success in his work?

8. Which song of work do you recall most vividly? Why is it impressed on your memory?

Things to do . . .

1. Radio and television quiz programs are fun for the contestants and the audience. Arrange for such a class program to test what you have learned from this part. Select one student to act as master of ceremonies and a group of ten students to act as contestants. The day before the quiz program, each student should prepare at least one original question on any selection in this part. He should write his question on paper and turn it in to the Master of Ceremonies, who selects the twenty best questions to use on the program. Each contestant is asked two questions. If he can't answer or gives an incorrect answer, he must sit down. The Master of Ceremonies then calls for a volunteer from the class audience to replace that contestant.

The purpose of this quiz program is to give the contestants a chance to show what they know. Therefore, the questions should refer to important characters, situations, events, and problems presented in this unit. They may also require a contestant to give an opinion which he can support by referring to a selection.

2. Divide into four groups, each group responsible for securing accurate information on one of the following "professions" at the present time: banking, sports writing, farming, lumbering. Each group should investigate the demand for workers in one profession, the training required, the

pay, the living conditions, and the regional limitations and advantages. Then the class should set a day for the groups to make a full report. Groups can use a panel discussion, a quiz program, or a radio broadcast to present their information.

3. Select a school hero and the one feat by which you would like to have him or her remembered. As a group compose a ballad about this feat. Choose the best first line from among those offered. One student, acting as secretary, can write it on the board and add additional lines as the class contributes them. Improvements may be necessary. You will find that four-line stanzas are easiest to handle. Also plan your rhythm to get four beats in lines one and three, and three beats in lines two and four. The second and fourth lines should rhyme.

4. Which kinds of work seem to you most typically American? Check your answers to make sure the work was not carried on elsewhere before America was discovered.

More to read . . .

Song of the Lark by WILLA CATHER.
Houghton Mifflin Company, 1915.
Four Young Teachers by GENEVIEVE CHASE.
Dodd, Mead & Company, 1948.
Come and Get It by EDNA FERBER.
Doubleday & Company, Inc., 1935.
Farm Boy by D. W. GORSLINE.
The Viking Press, 1950.
Tall Timber by STEWART H. HOLBROOK.
The Macmillan Company, 1941.
Arrowsmith by SINCLAIR LEWIS.
Harcourt, Brace and Company, 1945.
Start of the Trail by LOUISE RICH.
J. B. Lippincott Company, 1949.
Stage Door by GEORGE S. KAUFMAN and EDNA FERBER.
Dramatists Play Service, Inc., 1938.

Showman by WILLIAM BRADY.
E. P. Dutton & Co., Inc., 1937.
Wide Neighbors by MARY BRECKINRIDGE.
Harper & Brothers, 1952.
Malabar Farm by LOUIS BROMFIELD.
Harper & Brothers, 1948.
A Goodly Fellowship by MARY ELLEN CHASE.
The Macmillan Company, 1939.
The Stars at Noon by JACQUELINE COCHRAN.
Little, Brown and Company, 1954.
I Wanted to be an Actress by KATHARINE CORNELL.
Random House, Inc., 1939.
Dance to the Piper by AGNES DE MILLE.
Little, Brown and Company, 1952.
Many a Good Crusade by VIRGINIA GILDERSLEEVE.
The Macmillan Company, 1954.
An American Doctor's Odyssey by VICTOR HEISER.
W. W. Norton & Company, Inc., 1936.
Harvey Firestone, Free Man of Enterprise by ALFRED LEIF.
McGraw-Hill Book Company, Inc., 1951.
Ford: The Times, the Man, the Company by ALLAN NEVINS with FRANK ERNEST HILL.
Charles Scribner's Sons, 1955.
Minding Our Own Business by CHARLOTTE PAUL.
Random House, Inc., 1955.
From Immigrant to Inventor by MICHAEL I. PUPIN.
Charles Scribner's Sons, 1923.
A Cowman's Wife by MARY KIDDER RAK.
Houghton Mifflin Company, 1934.
Walter Reed: Doctor in Uniform by L. N. WOOD.
Julian Messner, Inc., 1943.
American Women of Science by EDNA YOST.
Frederick A. Stokes Company, 1943.

A TIME TO ENJOY

Americans are a fun-loving people, as well as a hard-working people. Even the pioneers found time for songs and story-telling, for appreciating the beauty of the land, and for enjoying the companionship of friends.

Today Americans have more leisure than any other people in the world, and they are learning to use it for the richest kind of enjoyment. They know that leisure does not imply just sitting idly in the sun, hands and mind empty and unoccupied. They know, too, that leisure is not merely a vacant interlude between periods of work. It is an active process that leads to a happier, fuller life.

In A TIME TO ENJOY you will meet a variety of people. Some knew how to use their leisure for the richest kind of enjoyment. Some helped to provide enjoyment for others. A few took a good look at life to find out what enjoyment really is.

A TIME TO ENJOY

Two Tall Tales

MARK TWAIN

Like many humorists, Mark Twain gives you something to think about as he makes you laugh. Your enjoyment of these two tales will be heightened as you grasp the truth underlying his humor.

My Watch

My beautiful new watch had run eighteen months without losing or gaining, and without breaking any part of its machinery or stopping. I had come to believe it infallible in its judgments about the time of day, and to consider its constitution and its anatomy imperishable. But at last, one night, I let it run down. I grieved about it as if it were a recognized messenger and forerunner of calamity. But by and by I cheered up, set the watch by guess, and commanded my bodings and superstitions to depart. Next day I stepped into the chief jeweler's to set it by the exact time, and the head of the establishment took it out of my hand and proceeded to set if for me. Then he said, "She is four minutes slow—regulator wants pushing up." I tried to stop him—tried to make him understand that the watch kept perfect time. But no; all this human cabbage could see was that the watch was four minutes slow, and the regulator *must* be pushed up a little; and so, while I danced around him in anguish, and implored him to let the watch alone, he calmly and cruelly did the shameful deed. My watch began to gain. It gained faster and faster day by day. Within the week it sickened to a raging fever, and its pulse went up to a hundred and fifty in the shade. At the end of two months it had left all the timepieces of the town far in the rear, and was a fraction over thirteen days ahead of the almanac. It was away into November enjoying the snow, while the October leaves were still turning. It hurried up house rent, bills payable, and such things, in such a ruinous way that I could not abide it. I took it to the watchmaker to be regulated. He asked me if I had ever had it repaired. I said no, it had never needed any repairing. He looked a look of vicious happiness and eagerly pried the watch open, and then put a small dice-box into his eye and peered into its machinery. He said it wanted cleaning and oiling, besides regulating —come in a week. After being cleaned and oiled, and regulated, my watch slowed down to that degree that it ticked like a tolling bell. I began to be left by trains, I failed all appointments, I got to missing my dinner; my watch strung out three days' grace to four and let me go to protest; I gradually drifted back into yesterday, then day before, then into last week, and by and by the comprehension came upon me that all solitary and alone I was lingering along in week before last, and the world was out of sight. I seemed to detect

533

in myself a sort of sneaking fellow-feeling for the mummy in the museum, and a desire to swap news with him. I went to a watchmaker again. He took the watch all to pieces while I waited, and then said the barrel was "swelled." He said he could reduce it in three days. After this the watch *averaged* well, but nothing more. For half a day it would go like the very mischief, and keep up such a barking and wheezing and whooping and sneezing and snorting, that I could not hear myself think for the disturbance; and as long as it held out there was not a watch in the land that stood any chance against it. But the rest of the day it would keep on slowing down and fooling along until all the clocks it had left behind caught up again. So at last, at the end of twenty-four hours, it would trot up to the judges' stand all right and just in time. It would show a fair and square average, and no man could say it had done more or less than its duty. But a correct average is only a mild virtue in a watch, and I took this instrument to another watchmaker. He said the king-bolt was broken. I said I was glad it was nothing more serious. To tell the plain truth, I had no idea what the king-bolt was, but I did

not choose to appear ignorant to a stranger. He repaired the king-bolt, but what the watch gained in one way it lost in another. It would run awhile and then stop awhile, and then run awhile again, and so on, using its own discretion about the intervals. And every time it went off it kicked back like a musket. I padded my breast for a few days, but finally took the watch to another watchmaker. He picked it all to pieces, and turned the ruin over and over under his glass; and then he said there appeared to be something the matter with the hair-trigger. He fixed it, and gave it a fresh start. It did well now, except that always at ten minutes to ten the hands would shut together like a pair of scissors, and from that time forth they would travel together. The oldest man in the world could not make head or tail of the time of day by such a watch, and so I went again to have the thing repaired. This person said that the crystal had got bent, and that the mainspring was not straight. He also remarked that part of the works needed half-soling. He made these things all right, and then my timepiece performed unexceptionably, save that now and then, after working along quietly for nearly eight

hours, everything inside would let go all of a sudden and begin to buzz like a bee, and the hands would straightway begin to spin round and round so fast that their individuality was lost completely, and they simply seemed a delicate spider's web over the face of the watch. She would reel off the next twenty-four hours in six or seven minutes, and then stop with a bang. I went with a heavy heart to one more watchmaker, and looked on while he took her to pieces. Then I prepared to cross-question him rigidly, for this thing was getting serious. The watch had cost two hundred dollars originally, and I seemed to have paid out two or three thousand for repairs. While I waited and looked on I presently recognized in this watchmaker an old acquaintance—a steamboat engineer of other days, and not a good engineer, either. He examined all the parts carefully, just as the other watchmakers had done, and then delivered his verdict with the same confidence of manner.

He said:

"She makes too much steam—you want to hang the monkey-wrench on the safety-valve!"

I brained him on the spot, and had him buried at my own expense.

My uncle William (now deceased, alas!) used to say that a good horse was a good horse until it had run away once, and that a good watch was a good watch until the repairers got a chance at it. And he used to wonder what became of all the unsuccessful tinkers, and gunsmiths, and shoemakers, and engineers, and blacksmiths; but nobody could ever tell him.

How I Edited an Agricultural Paper

I did not take temporary editorship of an agricultural paper without misgivings. Neither would a landsman take command of a ship without misgivings. But I was in circumstances that made the salary an object. The regular editor of the paper was going off for a holiday, and I accepted the terms he offered, and took his place.

The sensation of being at work again was luxurious, and I wrought all the week with unflagging pleasure. We went to press, and I waited a day with some solicitude to see whether my effort was going to attract any notice. As I left the office, toward sundown, a group of men and boys at the foot of the stairs dispersed with one impulse, and gave me passageway, and I heard one or two of them say: "That's him!" I was naturally pleased by this incident.

The next morning I found a similar group at the foot of the stairs, and scattering couples and individuals standing here and there in the street and over the way, watching me with interest. The group separated and fell back as I approached, and I heard a man say, "Look at his eye!" I pretended not to observe the notice I was attracting, but secretly I was pleased with it, and was purposing to write an account of it to my aunt. I went up the short flight of stairs, and heard cheery voices and a ringing laugh as I drew near the door, which I opened, and caught a glimpse of two young rural-looking men, whose faces blanched and lengthened when they saw me, and then they both plunged through a window with a great crash. I was surprised.

In about half an hour an old gentleman, with a flowing beard and a fine but rather austere face, entered, and sat down at my invitation. He seemed to have something on his mind. He took off his hat and set it on the floor, and got out of it a red silk handkerchief and a copy of our paper.

He put the paper on his lap, and while he polished his spectacles with his handkerchief he said, "Are you the new editor?"

I said I was.

"Have you ever edited an agricultural paper before?"

"No," I said, "this is my first attempt."

"Very likely. Have you had any experience in agriculture practically?"

"No; I believe I have not."

"Some instinct told me so," said the old gentleman, putting on his spectacles, and looking over them at me with asperity, while he folded his paper into a convenient shape. "I wish to read you what must have made me have that instinct. It was this editorial. Listen, and see if it was you that wrote it:

"*Turnips should never be pulled, it injures them. It is much better to send a boy up and let him shake the tree.*'

"Now, what do you think of that?—for I really suppose you wrote it?"

"Think of it? Why, I think it is good. I think it is sense. I have no doubt that every year millions and millions of bushels of turnips are spoiled in this township alone by being pulled in a half-ripe condition, when, if they had sent a boy up to shake the tree—"

"Shake your grandmother! Turnips don't grow on trees!"

"Oh, they don't, don't they? Well, who said they did? The language was intended to be figurative, wholly figurative. Anybody that knows anything will know that I meant that the boy should shake the vine."

Then this person got up and tore his paper into small shreds, and stamped on

them, and broke several things with his cane, and said I did not know as much as a cow; and then went out and banged the door after him, and, in short, acted in such a way that I fancied he was displeased about something. But not knowing what the trouble was, I could not be any help to him.

Pretty soon after this a long, cadaverous creature, with lanky locks hanging down to his shoulders, and a week's stubble bristling from the hills and valleys of his face, darted within the door, and halted, motionless, with finger on lip, and head and body bent in listening attitude. No sound was heard. Still he listened. No sound. Then he turned the key in the door, and came elaborately tiptoeing toward me till he was within long reaching distance of me, when he stopped and, after scanning my face with intense interest for a while, drew a folded copy of our paper from his bosom, and said:

"There, you wrote that. Read it to me— quick! Relieve me. I suffer."

I read as follows; and as the sentences fell from my lips I could see the relief come, I could see the drawn muscles relax, and the anxiety go out of the face, and rest and peace steal over the features like the merciful moonlight over a desolate landscape:

The guano is a fine bird, but great care is necessary in rearing it. It should not be imported earlier than June or later than September. In the winter it should be kept in a warm place, where it can hatch out its young.

It is evident that we are to have a backward season for grain. Therefore it will be well for the farmer to begin setting out his corn-stalks and planting his buckwheat cakes in July instead of August.

Concerning the pumpkin. This berry is a favorite with the natives of the interior of New England, who prefer it to the gooseberry for the making of a fruit-cake, and who likewise give it the preference over the raspberry for feeding cows, as being more filling and fully as satisfying. The pumpkin is the only esculent of the orange family that will thrive in the North, except the gourd and one or two varieties of the squash. But the custom of planting it in the front yard with the shrubbery is fast going out of vogue, for it is now generally conceded that the pumpkin as a shade tree is a failure.

Now, as the warm weather approaches, and the ganders begin to spawn—

The excited listener sprang toward me to shake hands, and said:

"There, there—that will do. I know I am all right now, because you have read it just as I did, word for word. But, stranger, when I first read it this morning, I said to myself, I never, never believed it before, notwithstanding my friends kept me under watch so strict, but now I believe I *am* crazy; and with that I fetched a howl that you might have heard two miles, and started out to kill somebody—because, you know, I knew it would come to that sooner or later, and so I might as well begin. I read one of them paragraphs over again, so as to be certain, and then I burned my house down and started. I have crippled several people, and I have got one fellow up a tree, where I can get him if I want him. But I thought I would call in here as I passed along and make the thing perfectly certain; and now it *is* certain, and I tell you it is lucky for the chap that is in the tree. I should have killed him sure, as I went back. Good-by, sir, good-by; you have taken a great load off my mind. My reason has stood the strain of one of your agricultural articles, and I know that nothing can ever unseat it now. *Good*-by, sir."

I felt a little uncomfortable about the cripplings and arsons this person had been entertaining himself with, for I could not help feeling remotely accessory to them. But these thoughts were quickly banished, for the regular editor walked in! (I thought to myself, Now if you had gone to Egypt as I recommended you to, I might have had a chance to get my hand in; but you wouldn't do it, and here you are. I sort of expected you.)

The editor was looking sad and perplexed and dejected.

He surveyed the wreck which that old rioter and those two young farmers had made, and then said: "This is a sad business—a very sad business. There is the mucilage-bottle broken, and six panes of glass, and a spittoon, and two candlesticks. But that is not the worst. The reputation of the paper is injured—and permanently, I fear. True, there never was such a call for the paper before, and it never sold such a large edition or soared to such celebrity; —but does one want to be famed for luancy, and prosper upon the infirmities of his mind? My friend, as I am an honest man, the street out here is full of people, and others are roosting on the fences, waiting to get a glimpse of you, because they think you are crazy. And well they might after reading your editorials. They are a disgrace to journalism. Why, what put it into your head that you could edit a paper of this nature? You do not seem to know the first rudiments of agriculture. You speak of a furrow and a harrow as being the same thing; you talk of the moulting season for cows; and you recommend the domestication of the pole-cat on account of its playfulness and its excellence as a ratter! Your remark that clams will lie quiet if music be played to them was superfluous—entirely superfluous. Nothing disturbs clams. Clams *always* lie quiet. Clams care nothing whatever about music. Ah, heavens and earth, friend! If you had made the acquiring of ignorance the study of your life, you could not have graduated with higher honor than you could to-day. I never saw anything like it. Your observation that the horse-chestnut as an article of commerce is steadily gaining in

favor is simply calculated to destroy this journal. I want you to throw up your situation and go. I want no more holiday —I could not enjoy it if I had it. Certainly not with you in my chair. I would always stand in dread of what you might be going to recommend next. It makes me lose all patience every time I think of your discussing oyster-beds under the head of 'Landscape Gardening.' I want you to go. Nothing on earth could persuade me to take another holiday. Oh! why didn't you *tell* me you didn't know anything about agriculture?"

"*Tell* you, you corn-stalk, you cabbage, you son of a cauliflower? It's the first time I ever heard such an unfeeling remark. I tell you I have been in the editorial business going on fourteen years, and its the first time I ever heard of a man's having to know anything in order to edit a newspaper. You turnip! Who write the dramatic critiques for the second-rate papers? Why, a parcel of promoted shoemakers and apprentice apothecaries, who know just as much about good acting as I do about good farming and no more. Who review the books? People who never wrote one. Who do the heavy leaders on finance? Parties who have had the largest opportunities for knowing nothing about it. Who criticize the Indian campaigns? Gentlemen who do not know a war-whoop from a wigwam, and who never have had to run a foot-race with a tomahawk, or pluck arrows out of the several members of their families to build the evening camp-fire with. Who write the temperance appeals, and clamour about the flowing bowl? Folks who will never draw another sober breath till they do it in their grave. Who edit the agricultural papers, you—yam? Men, as a general thing, who fail in the poetry line, yellow-colored novel line, sensation-drama line, city-editor line, and finally fall back on agriculture as a temporary reprieve from the poorhouse. *You* try to tell *me* anything about the newspaper business! Sir, I have been through it from *Alpha* to *Omaha,* and I tell you that the less a man knows the bigger the noise he makes and the higher the salary he commands. Heaven knows if I had but been ignorant instead of cultivated, and impudent instead of diffident, I could have made a name for myself in this cold, selfish world. I take my leave, sir. Since I have been treated as you have treated me, I am perfectly willing to go. But I have done my duty. I have fulfilled my contract as far as I was permitted to do it. I said I could make your paper of interest to all classes—and I have. I said I could run your circulation up to twenty thousand copies, and if I had had two more weeks I'd have done it. And I'd have given you the best class of readers that ever an agricultural paper had—not a farmer in it, nor a solitary individual who could tell a watermelon-tree from a peach-vine to save his life. *You* are the loser by this rupture, not me, Pie-plant. *Adios.*"

I then left.

Let's consider . . .

1. From your own experience what aspects of Twain's dealing with repairmen and working on a newspaper would you say are true? Give specific examples of your own experiences to point up each idea that the author has stated.

2. Mention several of the mistakes that Mark Twain made while editing the agricultural paper.

3. While Mark Twain was editing the paper, the circulation rose. How did the editor react to this rise in circulation? What is your opinion of newspapers or magazines which prosper because of the sensational aspects of their stories?

4. Summarize Mark Twain's thoughts about the newspaper business.

5. Both "My Watch" and "How I Edited an Agricultural Paper" were humorous stories, yet each provided the reader with some thoughtful comments on society. In your own words describe the theme, or underlying idea, of each story. Explain why you agree or disagree with each theme.

The writer's craft . . .

Hyperbole is a literary device in which extreme exaggeration produces a desired effect. Although it is frequently used for serious purposes, Mark Twain employs it as one of the chief sources of humor in "My Watch" and "How I Edited an Agricultural Paper." For example, he uses hyperbole when describing the effects of his watch slowing down: "I gradually drifted back into yesterday, then the day before, then into last week, and by and by all solitary and alone I was lingering along in week before last, and the world was out of sight."

1. Find other examples of hyperbole in these two sketches.

2. Write your own humorous example of hyperbole.

3. Now write a sentence in which you use hyperbole to make a serious point.

Knowing words . . .

How familiar are you with agricultural terms? Below are some that Mark Twain used in his story "How I Edited an Agricultural Paper." When you are sure of the meaning, use each in a sentence of your own.

1. guano
2. esculent
3. gourd
4. gander
5. furrow
6. harrow

Sleeping Outdoors

FREDERICK LEWIS ALLEN

Mr. Jones, the host, was enthusiastic about outdoor sleeping. His guest appreciated the excitement of this summer sport, but he was rather doubtful of its pleasures.

The most overrated summer sport in the world is outdoor sleeping.

I speak on this subject with some feeling, as, in August last, I tested it on a week-end visit with my friend Jones at his little mosquito ranch in the White Mountains. I can now understand why sleeping under a roof, in a real bed, is insufferable to a man who has been camping all summer: what he misses is the keen excitement, the constant entertainment, the suspense, of a night in the woods. As soon as he lies down in a real bed he becomes so utterly bored that he promptly falls asleep, only to wake up in the morning and find that he has missed the whole night.

The moment I arrived at Jones' camp on Saturday afternoon, I realized that he was the victim of the outdoor-sleeping fad. He was so under its spell that he immediately took me out to show me my cot. It was a frail, anemic canvas thing that screamed and creaked protests whenever it was moved or sat upon. It stood on a roofless sleeping-porch. Over it was the branch of a tender tree and over that was the open sky.

"Here," said Jones expansively, "is where you're to sleep. This region is the most wonderful place for sleeping in all the world. I actually look forward to the nights; I tumble in eagerly at ten o'clock, and don't know another thing till morning."

"You never know very much," I meditated inwardly, picking a yellow caterpillar off my cot. "How about blankets and things?" It took a vast amount of imagination to think of blankets, for the thermometer showed several degrees of fever.

"Oh, I'll give you all you want, and lots of mosquito-netting, too," Jones said. "You can make your bed just as you like; that's half the fun of the thing."

"Ah, yes."

Way down in my heart I had a foreboding that it would be rather more than half the fun. "Wonderful!" I simulated. "I haven't slept outdoors for years."

"Good!" said Jones.

Through the long evening I kept a stout heart and a cheery face; I even joked callously about the coming night, just as men sometimes joke about death and insanity and the dentist. I ate a heavy dinner, for breakfast looked very, very far away. I was as merry as ever. No one should say that I had blanched with fear. At nine-forty, Jones yawned.

"Why, it's nearly ten," said Mrs. Jones. "I had no idea it was so late."

"I was just going to suggest turning in,"

540

Jones observed. "I'll get your blankets and netting, if you like."

I rose, and with a steady voice bade my hostess good-night. The time had come. Jones got the things, and we went out on the sleeping-porch, where he dumped them on my cot. The temperature had gone down a degree or two, but the air was still a long way from cool. The winds were still slumbering. A mosquito was meditatively volplaning about.

"Is there anything else you want?" said Jones as he left me in what, in reasonable circumstances, would have been my bedroom, but was now merely the world at large.

"Nothing," I said, with fortitude. "Good-night."

I went into the house and ten minutes later I emerged, attired in a neat, but gaudy pair of pajamas. A lamp lighted my labors. The game was on; the mosquitoes and I were alone.

I shall withhold the tedious details of bed-making. Suffice it to say that I followed the golden rule of the art: don't let the feet escape; sacrifice everything else. If a single toe projects, the blankets will be up and about your neck before you know it. Then I folded a spare blanket into a pillow. Next came the hanging of the mosquito-netting.

Here I confronted several possibilities. First, there is the Roman style, in which one hangs the netting on a hoop and then projects the face precisely under the hoop, keeping it there all night. This style is somewhat like sleeping with an inverted waste-basket on the face, and is based on the fallacious notion that insects bite only the head. Now I could show you—but never mind.

Then there is another style. You suspend the netting gracefully by one or two points from a branch or some such supposed fixture, and let it depend in elegant festoons to the floor, securing the corners by lamps, vases, pitchers, or shoes. This method adequately answers the question: "What shall we do with the wedding present Aunt Alice gave us?"

There is also the Perpendicular Gothic [1] style—four posts erected at the corners of the cot, with netting draped over them. This, I decided, required too much construction, and I swung back to the second style mentioned. Securing some string, after a short, dark and eventful journey in the house, I hitched the string to the netting, tied it to a branch, made a beautiful pyramidal tent, and squirmed inside with all the delicate deliberation of a jackstraw player. At last I was on the creaking cot, and my tent still stood!

The laws of physics tell us that breezes pass through netting. This merely goes to show that physics has a big future. I had distinctly felt a slight zephyr outside; but now, as I balanced on my shoulder-blades on a Spartan [2] blanket, I thought that the heat had become even more breathless: I felt that I was being suffocated.

Isn't there some wild animal that builds itself a house and then crawls in to die?

But I was not going to give up; I forced myself to draw a long sigh of relief, and said to myself: "Oh, what wonderful air! How I shall sleep!" Yes, how?

I humped about a few times—creaking as I have never creaked before—till I thought I was more comfortable, pulled up a blanket cautiously, kicked it off warmly, rolled back into my original position, moved down six inches so that my head just reached the pillow, thought about mosquitoes a while, moved up four inches, thought about pillows, and then suddenly, with a great start, realized that I wasn't asleep. The fact stood out in my brain in huge staring capitals: YOU ARE WIDE AWAKE; YOU ARE NOT EVEN SLEEPY. It was clear that my nerves needed soothing if I was to get any sleep at all.

---

[1] *Perpendicular Gothic,* an English architectural style (1380–1530)
[2] *Spartan,* suggestive of the severe life of the ancient Spartans

People recommend many ways of soothing the nerves, but at times they are all dis-
appointing. I thought of sheep jumping
over a fence until all the sheep in my head
had gone lame. I counted up to three hundred and seventy-four, which must be
pretty nearly the world's record, but I noted
no good results. At the end of an hour I
was wider awake than ever and considerably more uncomfortable.

About this time I began discovering laws
of physics.

I. When a man lies on his side on a cot,
his weight is evenly distributed between
his ear and his hip-bone.

II. For every dead mosquito in the hand
there are two live ones in the bush that will
be along presently.

III. The use of netting rests on the
theory that it offers an obstruction to mosquitoes. This was first proved false in
1066, but people still—

Well, to tell the truth, that's as far as I
got. I inadvertently fell asleep in the middle of law number three. Physics is the
loser. I blame only myself.

At dawn, which in summer occurs

shortly after bedtime and lasts for several
hours, I was awakened by the birds, which
were making a dreadful din above me in
the trees. I found that four mosquitoes
were perched on the netting about fourteen
inches from my face—great, hungry fel-

Vasiliu

lows, regular eagles. They stared at me till I could have hidden myself for embarrassment. Presently a friend of theirs, bloated with drink, sailed down and sat beside them, singing a triumphant bloodlust song in a harsh, drunken tenor. He was plainly a degenerate going the pace that kills.

They say that if you look a wild animal in the eye he will turn away uneasily. I tried this on Macbeth, the new arrival—I called him Macbeth because he murdered sleep—but he was unabashed. I even spoke to him sternly, told him to go home and take his friends away with him, asked him what sort of place this was for a chap with a family; I appealed to his better self.

Macbeth's only reply was to crawl insolently through a tear in the netting and come straight at me. His song of triumph rose in sharp crescendo till he struck my nose; then it ceased. I was just reaching to kill him, even at the risk of disfiguring myself for life, when suddenly and without warning the netting gave way completely and fell about my ears. Can you imagine a worse predicament than to be pinned under so much wreckage with a mosquito that you personally dislike?

Well, I climbed out, rearranged my tent (while Macbeth's friends got at my ankles), sneaked in under the edge again, lay down once more, and looked about warily for Macbeth. He was nowhere to be seen. I suspected some treachery, and on the off chance slapped the back of my neck quickly and with tremendous force, but with no corpse to show for it.

From that moment to this I have never seen Macbeth. It is all very sad. I almost wish now that I hadn't been so harsh with him.

After I had given him up for lost, I took count of the insect life about me, and discovered a delightful game, called Insides *versus* Outsides. At four A.M. the score stood as follows: Insides, three mosquitoes, one spider; Outsides, one ant, one daddy-long-legs, two mosquitoes. A vigorous campaign then began: The Insides trying to get out, the Outsides trying to get in.

At four-thirty A.M., owing largely to my efforts, the aspect of things was somewhat changed, the score standing: Insides, one mosquito; Outsides, one wasp, six mosquitoes, two unclassified. (Mind you, I'm no etymologist; I don't pretend to know these eight-legged, hairy lads by name.)

The list of dead and injured was simply appalling.

After a while I tired of this game, but the mosquitoes were all for keeping it up indefinitely. Then, once again, I shut my eyes in the hope that sleep would knit the "ravell'd sleave of care." [3] It seemed, however, that the elements were all against knitting. The sun at that moment came up through the trees and shone straight into my eyes.

This worried me not so much on my account as on Jones'; I hated the thought of his coming out with his wife at breakfast-time, and finding me dead of a sunstroke on his porch.

Then I remembered that people didn't die of sunstroke. They only fainted and lost their minds.

Shortly after this I must have fainted, for I woke up to find I had been unconscious for at least two hours!

The last thing I remembered, before the coma set in, was killing a spider on my stomach at five forty-five.

It was now eight o'clock. The sun had moved round and I could hear the kitchen pump going, and see the housemaid, indoors, hiding matches and sweeping the dust under the rugs.

I felt sleepy, but otherwise moderately well.

Presently Jones came out in his bathrobe, and asked me how I had slept. I told him that that was just what I'd been wondering myself, and he wanted to know whether the mosquitoes had been thick.

I said, "No, not too thick to get through

[3] *"ravell'd sleave of care,"* a line from Shakespeare's tragedy *Macbeth*

the netting," and we both laughed and joked about the night as though it were the funniest thing in the world.

That's the way in such crises, when the terrible strain is over.

I avoided another night's excitement by telegraphing myself to come home at once on the most urgent business.

Mr. and Mrs. Jones were awfully cordial, and laid emphasis on the fact that in the future my cot would always be waiting for me on the porch. I explained that my business would be very exacting for a few years, and I doubted if I would ever be able to get away again.

I still cling to the old-fashioned idea that night is the time for sleeping, and not for hunting and recreation.

The man who wrote this essay

FREDERICK LEWIS ALLEN 1890–1954

The story of Frederick Lewis Allen's life is a story in two parts. Part One is a success story—the rise of a young writer to the position of editor in the world of journalism. Part Two is the story of that editor's desire to record contemporary history in an interesting, readable manner.

When Mr. Allen had reached the top of his profession, he began to write informal histories of America: *Only Yesterday,* the story of the 1920's; *Since Yesterday,* the story of the 1930's, and *The Lords of Creation,* the story of the financial era of 1900–1935.

In order to reach the top, Mr. Allen had to start at the bottom. By the time he was thirty-three years old he had worked for three different magazines, the U. S. Government (during World War I), and his *alma mater* (Harvard) before joining *Harper's Magazine.* By the time he was fifty years old, he was editor of that publication.

"Sleeping Outdoors" is one of his many essays—both serious and humorous—that have appeared in *Harper's Magazine* and *Century Magazine.*

Let's consider . . .

1. The author of this essay struggled with a variety of problems during his uncomfortable night. Describe these problems and the schemes he invented for coping with them.

2. What "delightful game" did Mr. Allen discover that kept him occupied at four in the morning?

3. How did he explain his awakening from a coma at eight o'clock? What had caused this state of unconsciousness?

4. How did he avoid having to spend another night "Sleeping Outdoors"?

5. Have you ever been obliged to "suffer through" a so-called pleasure? If so, describe your experience briefly to the class, making your predicament as amusing as you can.

6. Perhaps you have never slept outdoors —willingly or unwillingly—and, therefore, have no violent feelings about this "summer sport." You probably do have other enthusiasms which some of your friends would be happy to challenge. Choose some amusement, sport, hobby, or activity, the merits of which are open to debate. Select three enthusiasts to present the advantages, and three opponents to present the disadvantages of this debatable "enjoyment." Since this mock debate should also be an enjoyment, you may "stretch the truth" a little, as Mr. Allen did in this essay. Let the class decide which side presented the most convincing—as well as amusing— argument.

7. Mr. Allen's humor is the kind everyone can enjoy without too much analysis. Note such remarks as "his little mosquito ranch in the White Mountains" and "the

thermometer showed several degrees of fever." Jot down all the remarks you consider particularly humorous and take turns sharing them with the class.

The writer's craft . . .

The writer of humorous essays must have more than a keen sense of humor. He must also be able to communicate that humor to his readers. This is not always easy. From your own experience you know how frequently your friends fail to see anything funny in an incident that seems very funny to you. The humor falls flat even though you can show your amusement through facial expressions and gestures. The humorous writer must rely solely on language and his ability to use it effectively.

1. Mr. Allen created part of the humorous effect through his use of **anticlimax:** a sudden shift from a serious or even lofty idea to a rather trivial one. For example, he wrote, "I even joked callously about the coming night, just as men sometimes joke about death and insanity and the dentist." Naming the dentist immediately after such serious matters as death and insanity provided a surprising and amusing anticlimax.

2. Mr. Allen also made use of the **incongruous:** the combination of two items which would not ordinarily go together. For example, one of his "laws of physics" was that for every dead mosquito in the hand there were two live ones in the bush. Ordinarily you would not associate science with a variation of the popular saying, "A bird in the hand is worth two in the bush." Find other examples of the incongruous.

3. Allen added a humorous touch to his essay by using **personification:** a figure of speech in which inanimate objects are given human qualities. In describing the cot he wrote, "It was a frail, anemic canvas thing that screamed and creaked protest whenever it was moved or sat upon." Why do you think he referred to the cot as being anemic? What other illustration of personification do you find in this sentence?

4. Allen also achieved humor through exaggeration and pseudoseriousness (pretended seriousness). Point out his use of each of these.

5. Try your hand at writing your own humorous essay. Select as your topic an activity which some people take seriously but which you think is ridiculous. Use as many of Frederick Lewis Allen's devices for achieving a humorous effect as you can.

takes talent

there are two
kinds of human
beings in the world
so my observation
has told me
namely and to wit
as follows
firstly
those who
even though they
were to reveal
the secret of the universe
to you would fail
to impress you
with any sense
of the importance
of the news
and secondly
those who could
communicate to you
that they had
just purchased
ten cents worth
of paper napkins
and make you
thrill and vibrate
with the intelligence
   archy
               Don Marquis

Happiness

WILLIAM LYON PHELPS

Informal essays often contain provocative comments about ideas or beliefs which most people accept without question. In this essay, Mr. Phelps questions several popular beliefs about happiness and suggests a way to grow happier as you grow older.

No matter what may be one's nationality, sex, age, philosophy, or religion, everyone wishes either to become or to remain happy. Hence definitions of happiness are interesting. One of the best was given in my senior year at college by President Timothy Dwight: "The happiest person is the person who thinks the most interesting thoughts."

This definition places happiness where it belongs—within and not without. The principle of happiness should be like the principle of virtue; it should not be dependent on things, but be part of personality. Suppose you went to a member of a state legislature and offered him five hundred dollars to vote for a certain bill. Suppose he kicked you out of his office. Does that prove that he is virtuous? No; it simply proves that you can't buy him for five hundred. Suppose you went to the same man a month later and offered him a million dollars—that is, instead of making him a present, you make him and his family independent for life, for the best thing about having money is that if you have it you don't have to think about it. Suppose now, after listening to this offer, he should hesitate. That would mean he was already damned. He is not only not virtuous, he knows nothing about virtue. Why? Because his virtue is dependent not on any interior standard but on the size of the temptation. If the temptation is slight, he can resist; if large, he weakens. Such virtue is like being brave when there is no danger, generous when you have nothing to give, cheerful when all is well, polite when you are courteously treated.

So far as it is possible—it is not always possible—happiness should be like virtue. It should be kept or lost, not by exterior circumstances but by an inner standard of life. Yet many people who read this article will lose their happiness before next Sunday, though I hope they recover it. But why lose it even for a season? There are people who carry their happiness as a foolish woman carries a purse of money in her hand while walking on a crowded thoroughfare. The first man who is quick with his fingers, nimble with his feet, and untrammelled by conscience can and will take the purse away and disappear with it. He will have separated the woman and her money. Now if one's happiness is like that, an exterior thing, dependent on an enemy's volition, on any one of a thousand accidents to which we are all exposed—the happiness can be lost.

If the happiest person is the person who thinks the most interesting thoughts, then the mind is more important than either of these tremendous blessings, wealth and health. I never indulge in slighting remarks about money, because if I did I

546

should be a hypocrite. Money is a blessing; I should be glad to distribute a large sum to every one of my readers, of course reserving the usual commission. But money is not the chief factor in happiness. If it were, then everybody who had money would be happy and everyone without it would be unhappy; but there are so many wealthy people who are unhappy and so many poor people who are cheerful, that money, however important or desirable, is not the determining cause. It would be folly to speak slightingly of health. No one realizes what a blessing health is until one has lost it; then one has to devote time and energy and money to recover it. Anyone who is careless of his health is a traitor; because one's usefulness to do good in the world is usually seriously lessened by poor health. Yet even health is not the *sine qua non*.[1] People without it think they would be perfectly happy if they were well. A man with a toothache imagines that everyone in the world without a toothache is happy; but it is not so. There are healthy people who are not happy; and there are invalids whose face, eyes, and conversation reveal an inner source of happiness that enables them to triumph over bodily ills. They have overcome the world, the flesh, and the devil.

I should be sorry to lose what money I have; but unfortunate as it might be, such a loss would not permanently destroy my happiness. I should be sorry to be run over by an automobile and lose my right leg; but such a loss would not permanently destroy my happiness. Why not? Because my happiness is centred neither in my purse nor my leg, but in my mind, my personality. The Irish dramatist St. John Ervine lost a leg in the war. I asked him which he would prefer—to have two sound and healthy legs again and not to be able to write novels and plays, or to be as he is now, with only one leg, but an accomplished man of letters. He did not hesitate. He said there was no comparison pos-

[1] *sine qua non*, the one essential [*Latin*]

sible; he would far rather be a one-legged writer than a two-legged something else. "And yet," he murmured thoughtfully, "I do miss that leg."

There is another important consideration. If the happiest person is the person who thinks the most interesting thoughts, then we grow happier as we grow older.

I know that such a statement runs counter to the generally expressed opinion. The majority of novels and poems and the common gossip of society assume that youth is the golden time of life.

When I was an undergraduate, a distinguished man addressed us; and he said emphatically: "Young gentlemen, make the most of these four years; for they are the happiest years you will ever know." The remark was given to us with that impressiveness that so often accompanies a falsehood. For it was a falsehood. My classmates and I have been out of college nearly forty years; most of us are happier now than then.

The belief that youth is the happiest time of life is founded on a fallacy—on a false definition of happiness. Many people think that to be free from physical pain and mental worry is perfection; knowing that as we grow older our physical pains and mental worries are apt to increase, they assume that youth is the happiest time of life. We are, of course, all animals; but we ought not to be merely animals. I suppose that in the case of animals youth is the happiest time of life; a puppy is happier than an old rheumatic hound; a young jackass braying in the pasture is presumably happier than an old donkey laboriously drawing a cart; but these are merely animals and lack man's greatest gift—the possibility of development.

Those who say that childhood is the happiest time are unconsciously postulating the animal definition: A child is happiest because he is healthy and has no worries; when he is cold, somebody covers him; when he is hungry, somebody feeds him; when he is sleepy, somebody puts him to bed. Yes, but when he is *not* sleepy, somebody puts him to bed. There is the shadow on the sunny years; there is the fly in the ointment.

Personally I had rather have a few worries and aches, and go to bed when I choose. A child is as dependent as a slave. If you would rather be a healthy, well-fed slave than an independent man, you will prefer childhood to maturity. A child is at the mercy of adults both physically and mentally. They are stronger than he and can force him to do whatever they wish; they are cleverer than he and can invariably outwit him.

There are some foolish people who say, "Well, I mean to grow old gracefully." It is impossible; it can't be done. Let us admit it because it is true; old people are not graceful. Grace belongs to youth and is its chief charm. The poet Browning hints that youth has beauty and grace because youth would be intolerable without it. Young people are decorative; that is why we like them. They are slender, agile, fair, and graceful, because nobody could stand them if they were otherwise. It would be horrible if boys and girls, knowing as little as they do, were also bald, grayheaded, fat, wrinkled, and double-chinned; then they would be unendurable. But nature has so arranged matters that young people are physically attractive until they acquire some brains and sense and are able to live by their wits; then they lose these superficial advantages. As responsibility grows, beauty and grace depart. The child sits on your knee and reaches for your watch. You smile, and say, "Nice baby, can't have de watch!" But when he is thirty and reaches for your watch, you put him in jail. More is expected of us, more is demanded of us as we grow older; nothing is more tragic therefore than a woman of mature years with the mind of a child. There is in civilized society no place for her.

It is also often said that as we grow older we lose our enthusiasms. This need not be true; it is never true with right-minded individuals. There is a fallacy lurking in such a statement. The fallacy is this: We confound the loss of the object that aroused the enthusiasm with the loss of enthusiasm —a very different thing. Things that excite children often fail to arouse mature men and women—which is not a sign that maturity has lost sensitiveness to excitement; it may have lost interest in childish things. When I was a child, the happiest day in the year was the Fourth of July. It was not illusory happiness; it was real; it was authentic bliss. Its cause? On the Fourth of July Mother allowed me to rise at midnight, go out on the street, and yell till daybreak. Think of it! I, who was usually forced to retire at eight, was out on a city street at three in the morning, shrieking and yelling! It was delirious joy. Now suppose you should tell me that tomorrow I may rise at midnight and yell till daybreak. I decline. Does that mean I have lost my happiness or my enthusiasm? No; it means that I don't care to rise at midnight. During the daytime of the glorious Fourth I used to shoot off firecrackers hour after hour with undiminished zeal. Every now and then I would see a very old man, about thirty-two, come along, and I would offer him an opportunity to share my delight. He always declined. "Poor fellow!" I reflected. "Life is over for him. He has lost his happiness." It never occurred to me that people over thirty had any fun. I supposed they had to go through the routine of life but had no pleasure in it.

The fact that a girl of three is enchanted by the gift of a doll, and the same girl at seventeen insulted by it, does not mean that the girl at seventeen has lost either her happiness or her enthusiasm; but that the enthusiasm, formerly aroused by dolls, is now stimulated by something else.

If the happiest person is the person who thinks the most interesting thoughts, we are bound to grow happier as we advance in years, because our minds have more and more interesting thoughts. A well-ordered life is like climbing a tower; the view halfway up is better than the view from the base, and it steadily becomes finer as the horizon expands.

Herein lies the real value of education. Advanced education may or may not make men and women more efficient; but it enriches personality, increases the wealth of the mind, and hence brings happiness. It is the finest insurance against old age, against the growth of physical disability, against the lack of animal delights. No matter how many there may be in our family, no matter how many friends we may have, we are in a certain sense forced to lead a lonely life, because we have all the days of our existence to live with ourselves. How essential it is then in youth to acquire some intellectual or artistic tastes, in order to furnish the mind, to be able to live inside a mind with attractive and interesting pictures on the walls. It is better to be an interesting personality than to be an efficient machine. The reason so many go to destruction by the alcoholic route is because they cannot endure themselves; the moment they are left alone with their empty minds they seek for a stimulant, for something to make them forget the waste places. Others rush off to the movies, run anywhere always seeking something to make them forget themselves.

Higher education, the cultivation of the mind, is more important for women than for men, because women are more often left alone. A large part of masculine activity is merely physical; men run around like dogs. But a woman, even in these emancipated days, is forced to be alone more than a man. Now take the instance of a girl who has been brought up happily in a large family, with plenty of neighbors and friends, whose bright days pass in happy activities and recreations; she is married to a suburbanite in New Jersey. Every morning he takes the 7:37 train to New York and does not return till the 6:48 in the evening. The young wife, rudely transplanted from a cheerful home, is placed in an empty house in a town where she knows no one, and is alone all day. Heaven help her if she has no mental interests, no ideas, no interesting thoughts. I have no desire to underestimate the worth of physical comfort or the charm of youth; but if happiness really and truly consisted in physical ease and freedom from care, then the happiest individual would not be either a man or a woman. It would be, I think, an American cow. American cows and American dogs are ladies and gentlemen of leisure; in Europe they hitch them up and make them draw loads. Take, therefore, an average day in the life of an American cow, and we shall see that it is not far from the commonly accepted ideal of human happiness. The cow rises in the morning, and with one flick of her tail her toilet [2] is completed for the whole day. There is a distinct advantage over humanity. It takes the average woman—and it ought to—about three quarters of an hour every single day to arrange her appearance. The cow does not have to brush her teeth; the cow does not have to bob her hair; the cow does not have to carry a compact; the cow does not have to select appropriate and expensive garments. One flick, and she is ready. And when she is ready, breakfast is ready.

She does not have to light the kitchen fire herself or to mourn because the cook has left without notice. The grass is her cereal breakfast and the dew thereupon is the cream. After eating for an hour or so, she gazes meditatively into the middle distance, querying first, whether that grass yonder is lusher and greener than this, and second, if it be so, whether peradventure it is worth the trouble to walk there and take it. Such an idea as that will occupy the mind of a cow for three hours.

After grazing, like Goethe,[3] without haste and without rest, she reaches by noon the edge of a stream. "Lo, here is water;

[2] *toilet*, process of dressing, bathing, arranging hair, *etc.*

[3] *Goethe*, Johann Wolfgang von Goethe, famous German poet (1749–1832). "Without haste and without rest" is a translation of a line from Goethe's poem of that title.

what hinders me from descending and slaking my thirst?" She descends about waist-deep into the cooling stream; and after external and internal refreshment she walks with dignity to a spreading tree, and sits calmly down in the shade. There and then she begins to chew the cud. Cows are never perturbed by introspection or by worry.

There are no agnostic [4] cows, no Fundamentalist [4] or Modernist [4] cows; cows do not worry about the income tax or the League of Nations; a cow does not lie awake at night wondering if her son is going to the devil in some distant city.

Cows have none of the thoughts that inflict upon humanity distress and torture. I have observed many cows, and there is in their beautiful eyes no perplexity; their serene faces betray no apprehension or

[4] *agnostic, Fundamentalist, Modernist,* different schools of religious philosophy

alarm; they are never even bored. They have found some happy *via media* [5] by which they escape from Schopenhauer's [6] dilemma, who insisted that man had only the vain choice between the suffering of unsatisfied desire and the languor of ennui.

Well, since the daily life of an American cow is exactly the existence held up to us as ideal—physical comfort with no pains and no worries—wouldn't you like to be a cow? Very few human beings would be willing to change into cows, which must mean only one thing: Life, with all its sorrows, cares, perplexities, and heartbreaks, is more interesting than bovine placidity, hence more desirable. The more interesting it is, the happier it is. And the happiest person is the person who thinks the most interesting thoughts.

[5] *via media,* middle way [*Latin*]
[6] *Schopenhauer,* a German philosopher (1788–1860)

The man who wrote this essay

WILLIAM LYON PHELPS   1865–1943

For more than a quarter of a century this distinguished professor of English was known to Yale University students as "Billy" Phelps. He was a scholarly and learned man, but he was friendly and informal with his students. These qualities of informality, friendliness, and scholarship characterized his essays, numerous articles, and books and kept his work alive. Books which he wrote forty years ago are still in wide use today.

William Lyon Phelps made good use of both new ideas and traditional ideas. In his own way, he was a pioneer, introducing the first contemporary literature courses into the program of an American university. He also wrote discussions of such classic authors as Shakespeare and Milton.

His essay "Happiness" demonstrates the qualities of the man who received many

academic honors, and who could number among his friends the great literary figures of his time.

Let's consider . . .

1. What was Timothy Dwight's definition of happiness? Where did it place happiness? According to his definition, who is the only custodian of *your* happiness?

2. In what ways is the principle of happiness like the principle of virtue?

3. Although Mr. Phelps did not indulge in slighting remarks about money, what evidence did he offer that wealth is not the determining factor in happiness?

4. Mr. Phelps said that health is important but not the one essential to happiness. Think carefully and consider whether or not he overlooked two factors in loss of health which might be responsible for great *un*happiness even though many invalids radiate happiness.

5. Mr. Phelps stated, "The belief that youth is the happiest time of life is founded on a fallacy." Why do people assume that young people and children are most likely to be happy? Do you think you are happier now than you will be at forty or sixty? Support your answer.

6. From what you know of modern children, do you agree that " a child is as dependent as a slave"? Give specific instances to support your opinion.

7. What did the author say about losing enthusiasms as we grow older? What do you think?

8. What did he call "the finest insurance against old age"? How was it insurance?

9. While Mr. Phelps was teaching at Yale, he said he did not try to pour facts into the undergraduate's mind. Rather, he tried to decorate the walls of the mind with beautiful pictures. From your reading of this essay, do you think he succeeded? Why?

10. In your opinion, why did Phelps include the example of the American cow? Did it add to, or detract from, this essay? What effect did it have on the tone of the essay? Defend your opinion after careful consideration.

11. William Lyon Phelps was a very popular lecturer and attracted large audiences. However, no matter how many people were present, he always made each one feel as if he were being addressed personally. How did the author make you feel he was addressing himself to *you* personally?

12. What is the most "interesting thought" you can take away from this essay?

The writer's craft . . .

Informal essays, such as "Happiness," are characterized by a style which is graceful, appropriate, and effective. **Style** is the distinctive manner in which an author uses language: his choice and arrangement of words. Style is always an individual matter. If an author believes that good writing must be **concise**—clear and direct—even at the expense of gracefulness, then his style will have this quality. If he believes that good writing must be **euphonious**—pleasing to the ear—his style will have this quality.

The purpose which a piece of writing serves will also influence its style. For example, if you are writing a casual note to a friend, your style will not be the same as for a formal report. Good style is always appropriate to the author's purpose, to his material, and to the audience for which he is writing.

Standards which are current at a particular time also influence an author's style. Styles in writing, like styles in fashion, change with the times. The standard for good style in the colonial period was quite different from the standard accepted by twentieth-century writers. In general, present standards of good style call for such qualities as clarity, sincerity, and grace.

1. You would probably agree that the words *warm* and *personal* describe William Lyon Phelps' style. Think of two or three other words which would also describe his style.

2. An author's style should be appropriate to his material. Explain why Phelps' style was, or was not, suited to his topic and the audience for which he was writing.

3. Explain the qualities of style which are most appropriate for the following kinds of writing:

a. A casual note to a good friend
b. A letter to the principal of your school
c. A short science report
d. A thank-you note to a friend's mother for a pleasant week end
e. A letter of application for work

4. Select one kind of writing from this list and prepare it in the accepted form. Be sure that your style is appropriate.

A Dozen Pleasures

Everyone finds enjoyment in what he does and in the people he knows. He also finds enjoyment in what he thinks and feels. Poets are especially aware of these quiet enjoyments and have a genius for interpreting them with imagination. As you read their poems, your eyes will be opened to many pleasures you have felt but could not put into words.

Hymn to the Night

HENRY WADSWORTH LONGFELLOW

I heard the trailing garments of the Night
    Sweep through her marble halls!
I saw her sable skirts all fringed with light
    From the celestial walls!

I felt her presence, by its spell of might,
    Stoop o'er me from above;
The calm, majestic presence of the Night,
    As of the one I love.

I heard the sounds of sorrow and delight,
    The manifold, soft chimes,
That fill the haunted chambers of the Night,
    Like some old poet's rhymes.

From the cool cisterns of the midnight air
    My spirit drank repose;
The fountain of perpetual peace flows there,—
    From those deep cisterns flows.

O holy Night! from thee I learn to bear
    What man has borne before!
Thou layest thy finger on the lips of Care,
    And they complain no more.

Peace! Peace! Orestes-like [1] I breathe this prayer!
    Descend with broad-winged flight,
The welcome, the thrice-prayed for, the most fair,
    The best-beloved Night!

[1] *Orestes-like,* like Orestes, a character in Greek legend who was besieged with great troubles

A Winter Walk

HENRY DAVID THOREAU

When Winter fringes every bough
    With his fantastic wreath,
And puts the seal of silence now
    Upon the leaves beneath;

When every stream in its pent-house
    Goes gurgling on its way,
And in his gallery the mouse
    Nibbleth the meadow hay;

Methinks the summer still is nigh,
    And lurketh underneath,
As that same meadowmouse doth lie
    Snug in the last year's heath.

And if perchance the Chickadee
    Lisp a faint note anon,
The snow is summer's canopy,
    Which she herself put on.

Fair blossoms deck the cheerful trees,
    And dazzling fruits depend,
The north wind sighs a summer breeze,
    The nipping frosts to fend,

Bringing glad tidings unto me,
    The while I stand all ear,
Of a serene eternity,
    Which need not winter fear.

Out on the silent pond straightway
    The restless ice doth crack,
And pond sprites merry gambols play
    Amid the deafening rack.

Eager I hasten to the vale,
    As if I heard brave news,
How nature held high festival,
    Which it were hard to lose.

I gambol with my neighbor ice,
    And sympathizing quake,
As each new crack darts in a trice
    Across the gladsome lake.

One with the cricket in the ground,
    And fagot on the hearth,
Resounds the rare domestic sound
    Along the forest path.

Fable

STEPHEN CRANE

In heaven
Some little blades of grass
Stood before God.
"What did you do?"
Then all save one of the little blades
Began eagerly to relate
The merits of their lives.
This one stayed a small way behind,
Ashamed.

Presently, God said,
"And what did *you* do?"
The little blade answered, "O my Lord,
Memory is bitter to me,
For if I did good deeds
I know not of them."
Then God, in all his splendor,
Arose from his throne.
"O best little blade of grass!" he said.

I'll Tell You How the Sun Rose

EMILY DICKINSON

I'll tell you how the sun rose,—
A ribbon at a time.
The steeples swam in amethyst,
The news like squirrels ran.

The hills untied their bonnets,
The bobolinks begun.
Then I said softly to myself,
"That must have been the sun!"

*   *   *

But how he set, I know not.
There seemed a purple stile
Which little yellow boys and girls
Were climbing all the while

Till when they reached the other side,
A dominie in gray
Put gently up the evening bars,
And led the flock away.

Blue Squills

SARA TEASDALE

How many million Aprils came
   Before I ever knew
How white a cherry bough could be,
   A bed of squills, how blue!

And many a dancing April
   When life is done with me,
Will lift the blue flame of the flower
   And the white flame of the tree.

Oh, burn me with your beauty, then,
   Oh, hurt me, tree and flower,
Lest in the end death try to take
   Even this glistening hour.

O shaken flowers, O shimmering trees,
   O sunlit white and blue,
Wound me, that I, through endless sleep,
   May bear the scar of you.

Music

AMY LOWELL

The neighbor sits in his window and plays the flute.
From my bed I can hear him,
And the round notes flutter and tap about the room,
And hit against each other,
Blurring to unexpected chords.
It is very beautiful,
With the little flute notes all about me,
In the darkness.

In the daytime,
The neighbor eats bread and onions with one hand

And copies music with the other.
He is fat and has a bald head,

So I do not look at him,
But run quickly past his window.
There is always the sky to look at,
Or the water in the well!

But when night comes and he plays his flute,
I think of him as a young man,
With gold seals hanging from his watch,
And a blue coat with silver buttons.

As I lie in my bed
The flute notes push against my ears and lips,
And I go to sleep, dreaming.

I Like Words

MARGARET CASKEY

I like words,—
Silvery words that tinkle
Across the page like delicate wind chimes;
Like the full-throated shouting of strong men;
Solemn words that bring a catch to my throat
Like kneeling before an altar.
I like pompous, frock-coated words
That puff out their waistcoats like fat politicians
Strutting importantly across the page;
Eager, impetuous words that come racing and tumbling over each other
To reach the end of the sentence;
Comfortable words that purr contently
Like a cat upon the hearth.
I like crisp, scintillant words
Like the flashing cut of a knife;
Artless, carefree words that sing like happy children;
Friendly, folksy words still with the look of homespun on them;
Words that can make a living, breathing thing
Out of a scrap of rag and pulp,
That can make an impassioned oration out of empty air.
I like words. The empty white of paper
Catches at my pen in an insistent plea to be peopled.
I like words.

Recuerdo

EDNA ST. VINCENT MILLAY

We were very tired, we were very merry—
We had gone back and forth all night on the ferry.
It was bare and bright, and smelled like a stable—
But we looked into a fire, we leaned across a table,
We lay on a hill-top underneath the moon;
And the whistles kept blowing, and the dawn came soon.

We were very tired, we were very merry—
We had gone back and forth all night on the ferry;
And you ate an apple, and I ate a pear,
From a dozen of each we had bought somewhere;
And the sky went wan, and the wind came cold,
And the sun rose dripping, a bucketful of gold.

We were very tired, we were very merry,
We had gone back and forth all night on the ferry.
We hailed, "Good-morrow, mother!" to a shawl-covered head,
And bought a morning paper, which neither of us read;
And she wept, "God bless you!" for the apples and pears,
And we gave her all our money but our subway fares.

Velvet Shoes

ELINOR WYLIE

Let us walk in the white snow
  In a soundless space;
With footsteps quiet and slow,
  At a tranquil pace,
  Under veils of white lace.

I shall go shod in silk,
  And you in wool,
White as a white cow's milk,
  More beautiful
  Than the breast of a gull.

We shall walk through the still town
  In a windless peace;
We shall step upon white down,
  Upon silver fleece,
  Upon softer than these.

We shall walk in velvet shoes:
  Wherever we go
Silence will fall like dews
  On white silence below.
  We shall walk in the snow.

My Lady Is Compared to a Young Tree

VACHEL LINDSAY

When I see a young tree
In its white beginning,
With white leaves
And white buds
Barely tipped with green,
In the April weather,
In the weeping sunshine—
Then I see my lady,
My democratic queen,
Standing free and equal
With the youngest woodland sapling
Swaying, singing in the wind,
Delicate and white:
Soul so near to blossom,
Fragile, strong as death;
A kiss from far-off Eden,
A flash of Judgment's trumpet—
April's breath.

Evening Ebb

ROBINSON JEFFERS

The ocean has not been so quiet for a long while; five night-herons
Fly shorelong voiceless in the hush of the air
Over the calm of an ebb that almost mirrors their wings.
The sun has gone down, and the water has gone down
From the weed-clad rock, but the distant cloud-wall rises. The ebb whispers.
Great cloud-shadows float in the opal water.
Through rifts in the screen of the world pale gold gleams, and the evening
Star suddenly glides like a flying torch.
As if we had not been meant to see her; rehearsing behind
The screen of the world for another audience.

Acquainted with the Night

ROBERT FROST

I have been one acquainted with the night.
I have walked out in rain—and back in rain.
I have outwalked the furthest city light.

I have looked down the saddest city lane.
I have passed by the watchman on his beat
And dropped my eyes, unwilling to explain.

I have stood still and stopped the sound of feet
When far away an interrupted cry
Came over houses from another street,

But not to call me back or say good-by;
And further still at an unearthly height,
One luminary clock against the sky

Proclaimed the time was neither wrong nor right.
I have been one acquainted with the night.

The men and women who wrote these poems

EMILY DICKINSON   1830–1886

Emily Dickinson was an extremely active and social young lady until the age of twenty-six. Then, unexpectedly, she became a recluse and never ventured outside her home in Amherst, Massachusetts. She concealed herself even from members of her family, and it was only after her death that they discovered she had written more than twelve hundred poems. Miss Dickinson's poems are outstanding for their brilliant imagery and compression of huge ideas into small poems. She is considered America's first great female poet.

MARGARET CASKEY   1921–

The author of "I Like Words" has had ample opportunity to use the many kinds of words she describes. At Texas Christian University, she majored in English and journalism. She has since written advertising for radio and television. She now writes for an advertising firm in Dallas. Miss Caskey's poems have won prizes in the annual contests sponsored by Texas Christian.

EDNA ST. VINCENT MILLAY   1892–1950

Miss Millay was born in Rockland, Maine, was educated at Vassar College, and later moved to New York. For a time she supported herself by writing short stories, acting with the Provincetown Players, and translating French poetry. In 1920 she moved to the Berkshire Mountains and devoted the rest of her life to writing poetry. Her poems exhibit her mastery of form and subject matter. In 1923 she was awarded the Pulitzer Prize for *The Harp-Weaver and Other Poems*.

ELINOR WYLIE   1885–1928

In the seven years before her death, Miss Wylie matured into a major poet. Before then her poems had little merit other than their creation of a mood. Her reputation as an important poet is based almost entirely on the poems written during the last year of her life, which are collected in *Angels and Earthly Creatures* (1929). These poems are characterized by intellectual versatility, spiritual strength, and close attention to form.

ROBINSON JEFFERS   1887–

Born into a wealthy Pittsburgh family, Robinson Jeffers was educated in Europe as well as in America. For several years he studied medicine, but his only real desire was to write poetry. An inheritance from an uncle enabled Jeffers to give up his studies and devote his time to writing. He settled on a deserted strip of beach in California and began to write poems in a stone tower he built to house his family. Almost all of his poems are notable for their concentration of nature; for Jeffers sees nature as supreme and man as a small, perhaps temporary, opponent of nature.

The poet's art . . .

1. *Hymn to the Night.* As Longfellow personified Night in the first four stanzas, he heard or felt her presence. How did he describe her? What "spell" did Night cast over the poet? Why did he reverence her?

2. *A Winter Walk.* In which month do you think Thoreau took his walk? What made him think of summer? Which stanza best revealed his enjoyment?

3. *Fable.* Only a poet would think of little blades of grass as standing before God, relating the "merits of their lives." What made one blade "the best little blade"? Why did Crane call this poem "Fable"?

4. *I'll Tell You How the Sun Rose.* This poem implied a comparison between sunrise and sunset. What metaphor did the poet use to describe the coming of the sun? Close your eyes and picture *her* view of the "purple stile." What happened, literally, when the "dominie in gray" appeared? Which of the two poetic images did you prefer: the sunrise or the sunset?

5. *Blue Squills.* Sara Teasdale loved beauty with a sensitivity few poets can claim. How did she convey her love for the beauty of the blue squills? Why did she ask the "blue flame of the flower and the white flame of the tree" to burn and wound her?

6. *Music.* Some people think of musical notes in colors. How did Amy Lowell think of the notes of the flute? Why did she avoid looking at the flutist in the daytime? How did he change in her imagination when night came and he played his flute?

7. *I Like Words.* Margaret Caskey helped you to feel the quality of words by means of metaphors and similes. She told you what words *do* and what they are *like*. Select the three comparisons which you enjoyed the most.

8. *Recuerdo.* Again you see that a poem can say much in a little space. Miss Millay said little about these young people except that they rode "back and forth all night on the ferry." How do you know they were young? In what way were they wise? In what way were they foolish? Read the poem aloud. What does the rhythm do for the poem and for your enjoyment of it? What is the effect of the repetition of the first two lines?

9. *Velvet Shoes.* Even if you have never seen snow, which lines gave you the best idea of "white snow in a soundless space"? Notice how the pattern of each stanza exquisitely suited the thought. Note also the five-line form. Why do you think the variation of the beat and the definite rhyme scheme helped to reproduce the silence which so impressed the poet?

10. *My Lady Is Compared to a Young Tree.* Describe the young tree as the poet saw it. How could the sunshine be weeping? Did it seem natural for the poet to be reminded of his lady as he looked upon the young tree? Which points of resemblance appealed most to your imagination? What did you like about this poem?

11. *Evening Ebb.* In the first line, Jeffers gave you not only the setting of the poem but also the mood. What did the long, flowing lines add to the mood? How would short lines have changed the mood? What were the seven things which Jeffers mentioned to illustrate his opening statement?

12. *Acquainted with the Night.* What experiences did the poet give as evidence that he was "acquainted with the night"? What was the mood that he shared with the night? Why did he feel that "the time was neither wrong nor right"? Note the interlaced rhymes which form the pattern called *terza rima.*

Pigeons and People

GEORGE M. COHAN

Adapted for Television by JOSEPH SCHRANK

Not everyone finds enjoyment in the same things. Mr. Parker liked being with pigeons. He thought they had more sense than the people he knew. His ideas might strike you as being a bit unusual, but that does not mean they are necessarily foolish. Thoreau must have been thinking of someone very much like Mr. Parker when he wrote, "If a man does not keep pace with his companions, perhaps it is because he hears a different drummer. Let him step to the music which he hears, however measured or far away."

Mr. Parker has amused a great many people, first on the stage, then on the television screen. His creator, George M. Cohan, knew how to make people laugh because he was a comedian as well as a playwright. When *Pigeons and People* appeared on Broadway, Mr. Cohan played the part of Mr. Parker. This play was a "natural" for television adaptation. All that was needed were two simple settings and a limited number of characters. In the hands of a skillful television script writer, the play lost none of its whimsical charm.

For Americans, a quiet evening of television is A TIME TO ENJOY, especially when it brings them a play like *Pigeons and People*. As you read this television script, you will certainly *enjoy* Mr. Parker, even though you are never quite certain who he is or why Mr. Heath thinks he needs a "fresh start in life." As far as Mr. Parker is concerned, "the world's all right," but too many people are afraid to be themselves.

CHARACTERS

HEATH, *a tall, handsome man of 35–40.*
PARKER, *a medium sized, whimsical man of indeterminate age.*
CHASE, *a good-looking lawyer about Heath's age.*
TOKEM, *a Japanese valet, about 25–30.*
GILROY, *a big, burly detective. Age 50.*
FRISBY, *a distinguished-looking doctor. Age 45.*
McGUIRE, *a typical policeman. Age 40.*
GILES, *a good-looking housekeeper. Age 35.*
ELINORE ⎫ *two pretty, vivacious girls of 25.*
WINNIE ⎭
MRS. DUNLAP, *a fine-looking woman of 40.*
TWELVE CALM PIGEONS, *assorted ages.*
A PIGEON *that coos on cue. Age 6.*

SETS

1. *A spot in Central Park.*
2. *Living room of Heath's apartment. A large open doorway leads to an entrance hall. The room contains a grand piano, phonograph and radio, telephone, and the usual furniture.*
3. *Entrance hall of Heath's apartment. Door to outside. Doors to other rooms of apartment.*

ACT ONE

(*A spot in Central Park. Dusk. The lighting and atmosphere are somewhat mysterious, unreal.* HEATH *is gazing fixedly, with a curious intentness at* PARKER, *who is seated on a bench, some pigeons on the walk in front of him.*)

PARKER (*To pigeons, softly*): Here now, you—yes, I'm talking to you—you with the big grey head and one black eye— Stop pushing those little fellows out of the way —there's plenty of room for all—you should know that—you should have more sense—remember you're a pigeon—not a person. (*Sound of pigeon cooing in reply.*) All right—I accept the apology. (HEATH *is*

still gazing intently at PARKER, *trying to make up his mind to talk to him. Finally he decides and starts walking slowly over.*)

HEATH (*As he arrives at the bench*): I beg your pardon—

PARKER (*Looking up*): What for?

HEATH (*A bit taken aback*): Why— nothing— I—

PARKER: Do you always go around begging people's pardon for nothing?

HEATH: No, I don't. I just wanted to speak to you. That's all.

PARKER: Why not? This bench is public property.

HEATH (*Sitting*): Thank you. I hesitated to interrupt your conversation with the pigeons. It's wonderful the way you

charm them—the way you talk to them. Do you suppose they really understand you?

PARKER: Sure they do, and I understand them. They're easier to understand than people. (HEATH *laughs.*) Well, they are.

HEATH: There's hardly been a day this last month that I haven't come into the park just to watch them flock around you. Haven't you ever noticed me standing there taking it all in?

PARKER: Sure! Many a time.

HEATH: But I never got up enough courage to talk to you until now.

PARKER: Are you sure it's courage—or just—recklessness?

HEATH (*With a smile*): Is it that dangerous to talk to you?

PARKER (*Slowly, looking at him*): It could be. Very dangerous—

(HEATH *sits down next to him, they start talking.*)

*

(*Entrance hall of* HEATH'S *apartment. The outside door is opened by* HEATH.)

HEATH (*To* PARKER): Here we are. Step right in.

PARKER: After you.

HEATH: Oh, all right. (*He enters, followed by* PARKER, *and closes the door.*) This way. (*He leads way into living room not noticing* PARKER *is not following. As* HEATH *gets to the living room, he notices* PARKER *is not with him. Calling:*) Come on in! (PARKER *appears in doorway.*) Come in! (PARKER *comes into room slowly, taking a good look around as he does so, at the same time watching* HEATH *out of the corner of his eye.*) Make yourself at home. Throw off your coat.

PARKER: No, thanks. I'll be running right along.

HEATH: Don't be silly. Make yourself comfortable. (TOKEM, *a Japanese servant, enters.*) Oh, hello, Tokem! (TOKEM *helps him off with coat.*) Anybody ring me up?

TOKEM: Yes, sir. Mr. Chase. He say

don't forget dinner appointment with ladies.

HEATH (*Looking at watch*): Oh, yes! Take the gentleman's coat and hat, Tokem.

TOKEM: Yes, sir.

PARKER: No, no, that's all right.

HEATH (*Studies* PARKER *for a moment, then speaks to* TOKEM, *still watching* PARKER): Tokem, this is Mr. Parker.

TOKEM (*Bows to* PARKER): How do, sir?

PARKER: Hello!

(TOKEM *exits with* HEATH's *hat and coat.*)

HEATH: He's a good boy. Very competent and faithful. Come on now; why don't you throw off your coat? Just for a few minutes.

PARKER (*After a slight pause*): Well, that's all I can stay is a few minutes.

HEATH (*As* PARKER *starts taking off his coat*): Give it to me!

PARKER (*Moving to piano*): No, that's all right. I'll put it right here. (*Puts coat and hat on piano.*)

HEATH (*After watching him*): Sit down! Relax! Don't stand on ceremony here. Just feel that you're at home. (*Lights cigarette.*) Do you realize we sat on that park bench talking for over two solid hours!

PARKER: I didn't intend telling the story of my life when I started, but—

HEATH (*Interrupting him*): I know you didn't. But once you did start, I made up my mind that I was going to hear it all.

PARKER (*Smiles*): To tell you the truth, I didn't think it'd be so easy to get anybody to believe it.

HEATH: I don't think I've ever been so interested in anything as I am in your story.

PARKER: You mean that?

HEATH: I do. I mean about running away from life, as you call it. You've just been disappointed, that's all.

PARKER: That's it, is it?

HEATH: Yes. If any man ever deserved a fresh start, you do. And I'm going to see that you get the chance. What do you think of that?

PARKER: I'm doing a lot of thinking.

HEATH: Now, as I told you in the park —I'm no professional philanthropist. I want you to understand that.

PARKER: All right. And remember what I told you. I'm no subject for charity. I don't want anything from anybody.

HEATH: Wait a minute. Let's not go into that again. Just try to forget your pride and come down to earth. The world's all right.

PARKER: You bet your life the world's all right, and the world was always all right with me.

HEATH: Yes, and so are the people in it!

PARKER: You think so? (*Chuckles.*)

HEATH: Now what?

PARKER: It's all right. You have your own way about that one. Go right ahead. I'm listening. (GILES *enters*).

GILES: Is everything all right, Mr. Heath?

HEATH: Yes, thanks very much, Miss Giles. (*Indicating* PARKER:) Oh, this gentleman is Mr. Parker, a friend of mine, Miss Giles. (*To* PARKER:) Miss Giles is my housekeeper.

GILES (*Smiling at* PARKER): How do you do?

PARKER (*Sizing her up*): How do you do?

HEATH (*To* GILES): I want Mr. Parker to be very comfortable while he's here, and receive every attention. You'll see to that, won't you, Miss Giles?

GILES: Yes, indeed, sir.

HEATH (*Studying the effect of this on* PARKER): And have the spare room put in order right away.

GILES: The spare room. Yes, sir.

HEATH: And, Miss Giles.

GILES: Yes, sir.

HEATH: On account of a little mixup by the railroad, Mr. Parker's baggage has gone astray. So lay out some clean linen, and anything else that he might need until his trunks arrive. You understand?

GILES: Yes, sir. I understand perfectly. Thank you, sir. (*Bows to* PARKER:) Mr.

Parker. (*Turns and when she reaches the doorway, looks back over her shoulder and smiles at* PARKER, *then exits.*)

PARKER: You mean to say you're inviting me to stay here, to occupy a room here?

HEATH: That's what I wish you'd do. And give me a chance to talk to you for a day or two. All you need is a little sound advice; just get your bearings and the world will look all different to you.

PARKER: No, no, I couldn't do that. I couldn't impose on a man to that extent.

HEATH: Nonsense! Don't you suppose it will be a real thrill when you come to me a few days from now and say, "It's all right, Heath, I've found myself, thanks to you." And incidentally, it'll be one of the few really decent things I've ever done in my life.

PARKER (*After a pause*): Suppose I lied to you in the park?

HEATH: About what?

PARKER: About everything. (HEATH *looks at him questioningly.*) Suppose everything I told you this afternoon was just a pack of lies.

HEATH: You mean it was all a fabrication?

PARKER: I said, suppose. How do you know but what I'm a crook of some kind?

HEATH (*Smiles*): No, no. You're no crook.

PARKER: I told you that Parker was a phoney name. I wouldn't admit what part of the country I came from. You couldn't even check up on me. Did you really believe that story I told you in the park?

HEATH: Yes, Parker, I really did. And what you've just said is proof conclusive that you're not a crook.

PARKER: How do you mean?

HEATH: No crook who was clever enough to invent a story such as you told me in the park, and succeeded in making a man believe it, would then turn deliberately around and warn that man to be on his guard in case that story turned out to be a lie. (*Chuckles:*) No, sir. No crook would do that.

PARKER: Now you see, that's where you're dead wrong, because a clever crook might do just that.

HEATH: For what reason?

PARKER: Well, to get the fellow figuring just as you're figuring it out now. That no crook would do such a thing. See what I mean?

HEATH: No, I don't.

PARKER: Oh, yes, you do. You see it. And remember—I warned you.

HEATH: Warned me?

PARKER: Um hum. I mean in case—in case anything should happen.

HEATH: In case what should happen?

PARKER (*Smiling*): Now, you see. You're not sure of me at all. You're just trying to make yourself think you are.

HEATH (*Rather disturbed at this*): Well, of course, if you keep on talking this way and saying these things, why—(PARKER *is at piano now getting his coat and hat.*) Here, what are you going to do?

PARKER: I'm going to get along.

HEATH (*Crossing to him*): Oh, no, you're not. Give me that coat.

PARKER: Now wait a minute, Mr. Heath. You're a fine man, a decent man, and I want you to know that this meeting with you today made me feel that—well, that maybe I've been a bit wrong about people. I've told you things that I wouldn't tell anybody else in the world. So before I break loose altogether I think I'd better get along. (*He has put so much sincerity into this that it affects* HEATH.)

HEATH: Parker, you needn't be afraid to tell me anything. I'll treat it with the strictest confidence. I give you my word of honor.

PARKER: Yeah?

HEATH: Absolutely.

PARKER (*After a pause*): Well, suppose I were to tell you I'm a fugitive from the law. Would you believe that?

HEATH (*Looks at his man intently for a moment*): No. No. I wouldn't believe that, Parker.

PARKER: But suppose you found out it

was true. What would you do then? Would you turn me in?

HEATH (*After a pause*): No.

PARKER: Not even if you discovered that I was wanted for a major crime?

HEATH (*Forces a smile, then breaks into a chuckle*): You're having a lot of fun with me, aren't you, Parker?

PARKER (*Pauses, then looks to make sure they are alone*): You couldn't very well afford to harbor a murderer, could you?

HEATH: A murderer?

PARKER: Now, remember, you gave me your word—you swore yourself to secrecy.

HEATH (*Moving to cabinet. PARKER follows him*): And the question I'm to answer is, that if I should discover this to be true, would I or would I not hand you over to the authorities. Is that the question?

PARKER: That's the question, yes.

HEATH: And you're wanted for—

PARKER: Murder.

HEATH (*Thoughtfully, as he casually turns to cabinet and opens it*): Murder. I see. (*Suddenly produces a revolver from the cabinet and points it at PARKER. Calmly:*) Throw up your hands, Parker. (*PARKER just looks at him.*) Come on, do as I tell you. Throw up your hands.

PARKER (*There is a long pause as he studies HEATH*): Why, you don't mean that, do you?

HEATH: You bet I do. (*PARKER looks at him again for several moments, then turns away. HEATH follows, still covering PARKER.*) Come on, Parker. This is no joke. (*Sternly:*) Stick 'em up! (*The outer doorbell rings at this point. HEATH raises his voice:*) Come on, stick 'em up! (*PARKER raises his hands, dropping his hat and coat on the floor, and watches HEATH intently.*)

(*TOKEM appears in doorway.*)

TOKEM (*In a frightened voice*): What's the matter, boss?

HEATH: It's all right, Tokem. Nothing to worry about. (*The outer doorbell rings again.*) See who that is, Tokem. If it's Mr. Chase, show him right in. (*TOKEM hurriedly exits.*) I'm going to get to the bottom of this, Parker.

CHASE (*Excitedly, offstage*): What? He's got what, Tokem? (*Enters with TOKEM.*) Hello, Joe!

HEATH (*Still covering PARKER and speaking over his shoulder*): Hello, Frank! I'm glad you're here.

CHASE: What is all this?

HEATH (*To TOKEM*): Tokem, pick up that hat and coat. (*TOKEM picks up PARKER's hat and coat and places them on piano, then exits. To CHASE:*) Frank, search this fellow, will you—see if he's got anything on him.

CHASE: Do you mean it?

HEATH: Please!

(*CHASE throws his overcoat and hat on the piano and comes down to PARKER, behind him. CHASE is wearing a dinner jacket.*)

CHASE (*As he frisks PARKER*): What is this? Amateur theatricals?

PARKER: Yes, it's very amateurish, if you ask me.

(*CHASE finishes frisking PARKER, looks at HEATH and shakes his head.*)

HEATH (*To CHASE*): Nothing there, eh?

CHASE: Nothing in the iron line. Who is he?

HEATH: I'm not sure right now whether he is just a disappointed, misguided, poor devil, or a criminal of the deepest dye. But he'll tell the real story now; or he'll tell it to the police authorities. (*To PARKER:*) You can suit yourself, Parker. It's all up to you.

PARKER: Then you don't believe the story I told you in the park, do you?

HEATH: That's where I met him. I brought him here.

CHASE: What for?

PARKER (*Picks this up quickly*): Yes; that's what I want to know—what for?

HEATH (*Crossing to PARKER*): You know darn well what for. It was out of the goodness of my heart. I wanted to help you.

PARKER: I didn't ask you to help me. I told you I wouldn't accept any help. Why don't you tell the man the truth?

CHASE (*To* HEATH): Say, what is all this?

PARKER (*To* CHASE): I'll tell you what it is. This man got into conversation with me and asked me who I was. I told him a story. He said he believed it. I said I didn't believe he believed it. He said, "I'll prove it. Come to my home and I'll show you." Well, I came here with him. He offered me food, clothing, shelter. Said he wouldn't be satisfied unless I stayed here two or three days. I started to go and he wouldn't let me. He insisted that I stay. Finally I asked him how he'd feel if I turned out to be a murderer, or something like that, and he whipped out a gun and made me throw up my hands. That's the point we'd reached when you walked in. And that's the whole thing in a nutshell. (*Turns away.*)

CHASE (*To* HEATH): Is that all true?

HEATH: Yes, it's true enough, but this fellow's painting the picture in a different—

PARKER (*Coming back*): Oh, no, there are no *buts, ifs* or *howevers* about it. You know it's true. How do I know there isn't a catch to this somewhere—this Good Samaritan stuff of yours. I want to know what kind of a frame-up this is.

HEATH (*Indignantly*): What kind of a frame-up it is?

PARKER: You don't expect to get away with it, do you? Suppose I turned out to be someone of importance. Now you give that a little thought. Suppose I were to tell you that I'm one of the most influential men in the country.

HEATH: You don't expect me to believe that, do you?

PARKER: I don't care what you believe. You started this thing, now let's go through with it. I can hardly wait to speak my little piece now. Go on; get your cops.

(HEATH *and* CHASE *look at each other and both shake their heads hopelessly.*)

CHASE (*To* HEATH): For the love of Jupiter! How'd you walk into this one?

HEATH (*Trying new tactics, he goes into a laugh, to* CHASE): Wait a second. Wait a second. (*Laughing, he goes to the cabinet, and puts the gun away, then returns to* PARKER, *still laughing.* PARKER *has watched him suspiciously.* CHASE *watches him with interest.*) It's all right, Parker. You win. You've had your little fun. Go ahead!

PARKER: Go? Go where? What's the idea?

HEATH: Nothing except you're free to go if you want to.

PARKER: No sir. Not now. Not a chance. I don't leave here now without an apology.

HEATH: Are you kidding?

PARKER: No, I don't kid. I want a complete apology.

HEATH (*Looks at* CHASE): All right, I'm sorry. I apologize. Are you satisfied now?

PARKER: You call that an apology, do you?

HEATH: Well—

PARKER: I want to know what you're apologizing for.

HEATH: I don't know myself—I'm darned if I do. (*With a hopeless look at* CHASE, *he turns away.*) You're too much for me. I don't get you at all.

PARKER (*Defiantly following him*): Is that so? Well, let me tell you something.

HEATH (*His blood is up now; turns on* PARKER): What!

CHASE: Here, wait a minute. Let me handle this, Joe. (*He comes between them. To* PARKER): What are you looking for—trouble?

PARKER: Well, I've had plenty of trouble all my life.

CHASE: Oh, you think you can fight, eh?

PARKER (*After sizing up* CHASE): I think so. Yes. Yes, I can fight. I've been in a couple of battles.

CHASE: You have, eh?

PARKER (*Snaps this up*): Yes, I have. (*Another pause.*) Suppose I were to tell you that I used to be lightweight champion?

CHASE: *You* were?

PARKER: I didn't say I was. I said suppose I told you that?

CHASE (*Half amused, half sore*): Oh, shut up! (*Turns away.*)

PARKER: Is that so? (*Goes to phone.*) I'll find out if there isn't some redress for a man in a case like this. (*In phone:*) Hello! Get me Police Headquarters, please.

(HEATH *and* CHASE *make a dash for him. There is a struggle as they try to get the phone out of his hand and all three are talking at once ad lib.*)

HEATH (*During the above*): What are you doing, give me that phone!

PARKER (*Fighting for phone*): No, sir, I'm going to find out—(*Etc.*)

CHASE: Give me that phone! What's the matter with you—(*Etc. The argument and tussle continues until* CHASE *finally gets the phone away from* PARKER. *In phone:*) Hello—hello— No, no, never mind— No, it was a mistake, let it go. (*He hangs up. To* PARKER:) Say! What sort of man are you?

PARKER: I'm man enough not to stand for the insults you've been swinging at me.

CHASE (*Threateningly*): I'll swing something worse at you if you don't get out of here!

PARKER: Is that so? (*Indicates* HEATH.) Well, I happen to be this gentleman's guest, not yours.

CHASE: Jumping Jupiter! (*To* HEATH:) What do you want to do with this fellow, Joe?

PARKER: That's a fine question! What do you want to do with me! (*Gets his hat and coat and puts coat on as he addresses* HEATH:) There I was sitting in the park happy as a fellow could be. You come along with your joke sympathy and your phoney promises and bring me here and mix me up with people again. You ought to be ashamed of yourself for what you've done to me. (*Turns and goes toward door.*)

HEATH: I'm awfully sorry you feel that way about it, Parker. Won't you shake hands before you go?

PARKER: Why?

HEATH: I don't want to part bad friends. I'll feel guilty if we do. Come on, just a farewell handshake. (PARKER *just looks at him. The outer doorbell rings.*)

PARKER (*Thinks it over for a while, then relents*): All right. (*Shakes* HEATH's hand.)

(TOKEM *shows* ELINORE PAYNE *and* WINNIE LLOYD *into the room.*)

ELINORE (*As she enters, to* HEATH): Well, for heaven's sake, aren't you dressed? I thought we were going out to dinner!

HEATH (*To* ELINORE): We are, don't worry. (*To* WINNIE:) How are you, Winnie?

WINNIE (*To* HEATH): Hello, Joe! (*To* CHASE:) Did you get the theatre tickets?

CHASE (*At* WINNIE's *side*): I did. Musical show.

WINNIE: Good.

HEATH: This is Mr. Parker, Miss Payne —Miss Lloyd.

(*The two girls have looked at* PARKER *with interest.*)

THE GIRLS (*To* PARKER): How do you do?

PARKER (*Who has been looking on with amusement, acknowledges this*): How do you do?

HEATH: Mr. Parker's an old friend of mine. He dropped in to say hello. He's just going along.

PARKER: I want you to know it isn't easy to break away from such delightful company, ladies.

ELINORE (*Being polite*): I'm sorry you have to rush, Mr. Parker.

PARKER (*Turning to her*): I beg your pardon?

ELINORE (*Repeats*): I'm sorry you have to rush.

PARKER: Oh, it isn't that. But I understand that you'd rather be by yourselves.

ELINORE: Oh, don't be foolish!

PARKER: I'd feel like I was butting in.

ELINORE (*Laughs this off*): Oh, nothing of the sort! (*To* HEATH:) Make him stay, Joe. (*Has removed her wrap and sits on the settee.*)

WINNIE: Yes, make him, Joe.

(PARKER *looks at* HEATH.)

HEATH (*To* PARKER): Want to stay a while?

PARKER: Do you want me to?

HEATH: Do you want to?

PARKER: Well, as long as the ladies insist. (*Turns to the girls. He sits, smiling at them.*) Well, this is a great pleasure, ladies!

ELINORE: The pleasure's all ours, I can assure you.

PARKER: Thank you.

(*Both girls are more or less at a loss in trying to figure the man. They also get the by-play between* HEATH *and* CHASE, *which consists of significant looks and high-signs as* PARKER *seats himself. There is a moment of embarrassment on the part of all four which* PARKER *highly enjoys.*)

ELINORE (*Breaking it*): You'd better hurry and dress, Joe.

HEATH (*Reluctant to leave, fearing what* PARKER *may be up to next*): All right— I'll hurry as fast as I can. (*He goes out.*)

PARKER (*Calls after him*): Yeah, hurry up. (*Laughs. To the girls:*) He's in a hurry. The whole world's in a hurry. We don't any of us know where we're going, but we're all in a hurry to get there, as the fellow says. Now I could understand pigeons being in a hurry, because they've got such a wonderful sense of direction. (*This to* CHASE:) But strange to say, they're never in a hurry. (*To* ELINORE:) They're never in a hurry.

ELINORE (*Trying to appear interested*): Pigeons?

PARKER: Pigeons, yes. (*Slight pause.*) How do you figure them out?

ELINORE (*Trying to trail along*): Well, I don't know as I've ever tried to figure them out.

PARKER: No? Well, I don't suppose you've got anything on them. I don't imagine they ever tried to figure you out, either.

So it's an even break all around, you see. (PARKER *chuckles,* ELINORE *forces a smile and turns to* WINNIE. WINNIE *forces a smile also.*) Well, no matter how you look at it, it's all very remarkable, isn't it?

ELINORE (*A bit baffled*): Well, yes. Yes, it is, in a way.

PARKER: What do you mean, in a way?

ELINORE (*Stumped*): I mean it's—it's remarkable.

PARKER: Well, that's what I just said.

ELINORE (*Still perplexed*): Yes, I know. (*There is another pause of embarrassment.*)

PARKER (*Has quite a little laugh to himself here before he speaks*): You know, that was awfully funny, what this fellow Heath told you ladies about me.

ELINORE: What do you mean?

PARKER: That I was an old friend of his. (*Laughs.*)

ELINORE: Well, aren't you and Mr. Heath old friends?

PARKER: No. I never met him in my life till this afternoon.

(*The outer doorbell rings.*)

PARKER (*Coming over to the girls*): Now I ask you ladies a fair question. Do I look like a highwayman, a bandit, a cutthroat, or anything like that? (*The girls stare at* PARKER, *not knowing what to say.*)

CHASE (*To the girls*): Don't pay any attention to him.

PARKER (*Indignantly turns to* CHASE): What do you mean—don't pay any attention to me?

CHASE: Well, I'm paying attention to you.

PARKER: You people asked me to stay here. I've stood just about enough of this!

CHASE (*Losing his temper*): Yes? Well, so have I, and just about one more speech like that and I'll pick you up and throw you right out!

(GILROY *stands in doorway with* McGUIRE, *a uniformed policeman at his side.* TOKEM *is hovering near them apprehensively. The others have not yet noticed the newcomers.*)

WINNIE (*Apprehensively*): Keep cool, Frank.

ELINORE: Yes, for goodness' sake!

PARKER: It's okay with me. Let him throw me out. (*To* CHASE:) Go ahead, throw me out. You throw me out and then we'll see what'll happen.

GILROY (*Coming into the room*): What's all the fuss, gentlemen? What appears to be the difficulty here? (*They all turn and look at* GILROY *in amazement.*)

CHASE (*Immediately to* GILROY): Who are you?

GILROY (*To* CHASE, *taking his tone*): Who are you?

CHASE: What do you want here?

GILROY: Now don't get sassy with me, son. That won't get you any place you'd care to go. (*Takes badge from pocket,* crosses to CHASE *and shows it to him.*) There's my authority and my name's Gilroy. (*The badge has the desired effect on* CHASE. GILROY *speaks to* TOKEM *who makes a move to leave the room:*) Hey there, where are you going?

TOKEM: I tell the boss.

GILROY: You stay where you are until I tell you to tell the boss.

TOKEM: Yes, sir.

GILROY: McGuire, keep watch in the hall.

McGUIRE: Yes, Sergeant. (*Exits.*)

GILROY (*To all*): You may as well all sit down—you're going to be here for a while. (*PARKER laughs quietly.* GILROY *turns and looks at him, puzzled.*)

END OF ACT ONE

Let's consider . . .

1. In Parker's first speech he gave you a clue to what he believed about life. Why did he scold the pigeon and remind it that it was "not a person"?

2. Why was Heath curious about Parker? Why did he laugh when Parker insisted that he and the pigeons understood each other? Was Parker so much different from most people who talk to their pets?

3. Why did Heath invite Parker to his apartment? Why did Parker say, "I'm no subject for charity"? Was Heath entirely unselfish in wanting to help Parker?

4. Parker never said he was a crook or a criminal; he merely suggested that he might be. Why? Was he testing Heath's sincerity? Or was he just having a little fun? Describe Heath's reaction.

5. How did Heath explain the situation to Chase? What was Chase's reaction? Why wouldn't Parker leave after Heath put the gun away? Why did Parker try to call the police? Was he really angry?

6. How did Heath explain Parker to his lady guests? Why didn't Chase want Parker to tell what had happened earlier?

7. Why do you think Gilroy and McGuire arrived on the scene?

ACT TWO

(HEATH's *living room.*)

GILROY: Who's been calling Police Headquarters from here?

ELINORE: Police Headquarters?

GILROY: We traced the call. They claimed a mistake and hung up. Do you women know anything about it?

PARKER (*Butting in*): No, they don't know anything about it. I'll speak for them.

GILROY (*Turns to* PARKER): You speak for yourself. And wait until you're spoken to! (*Looks him over.*) You don't look so good.

PARKER: I feel all right.

GILROY: I'm not inquiring about your health. (*Slight pause.*) I was speaking to these two women. (*Turns to girls again.*)

PARKER (*Correcting him*): Ladies! Ladies! Ladies!

GILROY (*Turning quickly to him, resenting the correction*): Say, what do you think you are, a school teacher?

PARKER: I'm not saying what I am.

GILROY: Well, we'll find out what you are and who you are.

CHASE: I sure wish you would!

GILROY (*Turns and looks at* CHASE): Say! (*Crosses to him.*) What was the reason for the argument you were having with this fellow when I walked in?

CHASE: He started a dozen arguments without any reason at all.

GILROY: Is that why you rang up Police Headquarters?

PARKER: He didn't ring up Police Headquarters. I rang up Police Headquarters.

GILROY (*Looks at* CHASE, *then crosses to* PARKER): Oh, you did, eh?

PARKER (*Pointing to* CHASE): Yes, and he grabbed the phone away from me.

GILROY (*Looks suspiciously at* CHASE): Is that right?

CHASE: Yes, because he had no reason for calling up Police Headquarters. Now listen, Gilroy—(*Starting to explain.*)

GILROY (*Interrupting*): Hold it a minute! Whose place is this? Who lives here?

CHASE: This apartment belongs to my friend Mr. Joseph Heath of the Consolidated Life Insurance Company. I am Franklyn Chase of Hall, Metcalf and Chase, attorneys.

GILROY (*Turning to* PARKER): And what's *your* name?

PARKER: You want to know my name? (*Laughs to himself, turns to the girls and laughs, then back to* GILROY:) Why, you can call me Parker if you like.

GILROY (*Wisely*): Oh, can I? (*Gives a dry chuckle:*) That's very nice of you.

PARKER: It's all right with me.

(GILES *enters. She stops short in surprise as she surveys the scene.*)

ELINORE: Hello, Giles!

GILES: Hello, Miss Lloyd! (*To* TOKEM:) Tokem, Mr. Heath wants you.

GILROY (*To* TOKEM): Wait a minute. (*To* GILES:) Who are you?

GILES: I'm Mr. Heath's housekeeper.

GILROY: Where's Mr. Heath?

GILES: In his room, dressing.

GILROY: Dressing? What's he doing undressed?

CHASE (*Jumps up and blurts at* GILROY): Now see here, Gilroy—

(PARKER *is enjoying all this.*)

GILROY (*Interrupting*): Sit down.

(CHASE *sits.* GILROY *looks the group over. As he looks at* PARKER *he sees that the latter is looking at his feet and laughing to himself.* GILROY *looks at his feet uncomfortably, then at* PARKER *again.* GILROY *lifts his right leg and looks at his heel, at which* PARKER *enjoys himself greatly. To* PARKER:) What's the idea? (*He turns to* GILES:) Come on, show me this boss of yours.

GILES: Very well, sir.

GILROY (*To* TOKEM): You come along too. (*To the others:*) And remember that policeman out there in the hall. That's what he's there for—to be remembered. So as we were, and as we are.

PARKER: And as we should be, eh?

GILROY: Yes, till I find out something about this telephone business. (*To* GILES *and* TOKEM:) Come on.

(GILES *and* TOKEM *exit,* GILROY *following.* PARKER *sits laughing at* GILROY. GILROY *turns and sees him, glares at him and then exits.* PARKER *continues to laugh quietly.*)

CHASE: You think this is funny, do you?

PARKER (*Chuckling*): I think it's very funny. That policeman out in the hall.

WINNIE: What is all this, Frank?

ELINORE: Yes, who is this man?

CHASE: Oh, he's some fellow Joe picked up in the park. (*Rises.*) He told some sort of cock and bull story.

PARKER (*Rising*): Cock and bull story, eh?

(ELINORE *and* WINNIE *rise.*)

CHASE (*Has continued the speech, ignoring* PARKER's *interruption*):—that got to his heart strings, and he brought him home. Tried to be nice to him and this is the result. He's been acting like a fool ever since.

PARKER: Is that so? (*To the girls:*) They've been throwing me out of the house for the last half hour and I'm still here. Now is there any sense to that? (*To* CHASE:) If you want to throw somebody out, why don't you throw that cop out? He's got no right here and I know it. No cop has got a right to force an entrance into anybody's home without a search warrant. (*All three marvel at his self-assurance and look at one another in amazement.*)

WINNIE: He may be right, Frank . . .

CHASE: Oh, he doesn't know what he's talking about.

PARKER: I don't, eh? Well, I'll prove it to you. (*He starts for the phone.*) I'll show you in about two minutes that I know what I'm talking about. (*In phone:*) Hello—get me Police Headquarters, please.

CHASE (*Rushes to him and tries to get the phone away from him as before*): Give me that phone. Give it to me, do you hear? (*There is an ad lib argument until* CHASE *gets the phone and hangs up the receiver.*) What do you want to do, get the whole department over here?

PARKER: Well, I wanted to prove to you that I'm right about this cop being here.

CHASE (*Chuckling*): It's a waste of time getting sore at you, I can see that.

PARKER (*To the girls*): Now, you see, that's the first sensible thing he's said. It's a waste of time getting sore at anybody. Nothing stands a man in such good stead as an even disposition. Without that you can't have a real appreciation of what's going on around you. And believe me, what's going on around you is always pretty interesting, even when you don't know what it's all about. (*To* WINNIE:) Am I right, little lady?

WINNIE (*Trying to make an intelligent answer*): Why, yes. Yes, I should say so.

PARKER: You should say so? I should say so. You should say so? I should say

you should say so. So say I. (*Takes off coat and puts coat and hat on piano bench.*)

TOKEM (*Enters hurriedly, speaking, from the doorway*): Mr. Chase, please. Boss wants to see you please.

CHASE: Right. (TOKEM *exits. To the girls:*) Excuse me, girls. (*Takes a few steps toward doorway, then turns to* PARKER:) Do me a favor, will you? Try to act human for a few minutes if it's possible.

PARKER: Act human? There's nobody any more human than I am, young fellow.

(CHASE *shakes his head and exits.* PARKER *stands looking after* CHASE, *chuckling, then turns to girls:*) Why don't we all sit down and get acquainted? (*The three sit on sofa,* PARKER *in the middle. With a change of mood he strikes a tender note:*) You know it's a long time since I sat between two beautiful girls like this. (*He takes* ELINORE'S *hand and looks at it, then goes through the same business with* WINNIE.)—Two beautiful hands. (*Becomes emotional for a moment:*) The gentle touch of a woman's hand. (*Sentimentally:*) Memories. (*Pause.*) Well, I guess that's about all life is made up of—just memories. (*Looks at* ELINORE.)

ELINORE (*In his mood*): It seems so, doesn't it?

PARKER (*Smiles sadly*): Yes. (*To* WINNIE:) What do you think?

WINNIE (*In the same mood*): I think so.

PARKER (*To* ELINORE): She thinks so too. (*A pause.*) Well, we're all thinking anyway, aren't we? (*Slight pause.*) I'm thinking things about you. You're thinking things about me. All three of us sitting here thinking things about each other. It's wonderful, isn't it? (*A pause.*) You know there was something I was going to say to you two girls, but I guess I'd better not.

ELINORE (*Interested*): Oh, go on, Mr. Parker, say it.

WINNIE (*Anxiously*): Yes, please do. What is it?

PARKER: Well, suppose I were to ask you two girls to kiss me?

ELINORE (*Indignantly*): To what?

WINNIE (*Indignantly*): To kiss you?

PARKER: Well, what are you hollering about? I didn't ask you to kiss me. I said *suppose* I asked you to kiss me. (*Rises and moves a few steps away, the two girls watching him in amazement. He sees radio on cabinet: directly he sees it his mood changes. Girls rise.*) Well, I guess the only thing to do when a fellow gets all muddled up is to turn on the radio. (*He turns it on and a dance tune comes over the air. He listens for a moment, smiles and then starts dancing about the room.*) There you are, that's life. That's what the boys and girls like, that's what they call having a good time. Tiring themselves all out. Getting out of breath—bumping into everybody, wearing out their shoes, and everything else. (*Still dancing, edges over to* WINNIE:) Come on, you want to have a good time? Come on and dance.

WINNIE: No, thanks.

PARKER (*Insisting*): Oh, come on.

ELINORE (*Smiling*): Go on, Winnie. Why not?

WINNIE (*To* ELINORE): No, I don't feel like it. You go ahead if you want to.

ELINORE (*Moving toward* PARKER *who is still dancing*): All right, I'll dance with you.

(PARKER *takes her in his arms and they start dancing around the room,* WINNIE *watching them and laughing. As* PARKER *and* ELINORE *dance,* HEATH *enters, wearing dinner jacket. He is followed by* CHASE, GILROY, GILES, *and* TOKEM. HEATH *angrily separates* PARKER *and* ELINORE. PARKER *continues to dance by himself until* HEATH *turns off radio.*)

PARKER (*As* HEATH *turns off the radio he stops dancing and strikes a pose*): Every man his own partner when he has to be.

HEATH: What's the idea of all this?

ELINORE: Mr. Parker asked me to dance with him.

PARKER: I didn't do anything of the kind. I asked the other young lady to dance with me and you took her place. I didn't want to dance with you. I wanted to dance with her. Why don't you tell the man the truth?

(*They all look at one another in consternation at the man's impossible attitude.*)

GILROY (*Coming to* PARKER): Say, what are you trying to pull around here? What kind of a punk are you?

PARKER: A punk?

GILROY: Yes, a punk. I've heard all about you. Now put on your coat and hat and come along with me.

PARKER: Where are you going?

GILROY: What's it to you where we're going? Come on.

PARKER: Sure, I'll go with you. I don't care. (*Moving to get hat and coat.*) I'd just as soon be one place as another. (*To* WINNIE:) I'll have a good time no matter where I am. (*The phone rings. All look toward phone as* HEATH *picks it up.*) I'll bet that's Police Headquarters. (*Picks up hat and coat.*)

HEATH (*In phone*): Hello?—Yes.—Who?—Gilroy?

PARKER: What'd I tell you? (*Puts on his coat.*)

GILROY (*Takes phone from* HEATH. *In phone*): Hello?—Yes. Yes, hello Cap. (*Surprise:*) Just a few minutes ago you say?—Wait awhile. (*To others:*) Anybody ring Police Headquarters again?

CHASE (*Indicating* PARKER): Yes, he did the minute you left the room.

PARKER: Yes, and he yanked the phone out of my hand again too. You tell him the whole of it.

GILROY (*With a look at* PARKER, *he speaks into phone again*): Hello!—Just a minute, Cap. (*To* PARKER:) What was the idea—was there something you wanted to say to Police Headquarters?

PARKER: Yes, there's something I'd like to say to Police Headquarters, and I'd have said it if he hadn't yanked the phone away.

GILROY (*In phone*): Hello!—Listen,

Cap—there's a new kind of guy here that's got something to say to you. Hang on. (*Turns to* PARKER, *handing the phone to him:*) Here you are. You're so anxious.

PARKER: All right. (*Takes phone from* GILROY:) Hello, who am I talking to please?—Well, I asked you first, can't you answer a civil question?—Well, I want some information— I want to know who this fellow is that's here— Well, is he all right? Is he from Headquarters? Is he a regular cop: That's all I want to know— Well, what are you hollering your head off for? I've got a right to get police information, haven't I? I'm a citizen, a tax-payer— Well, that's all I wanted to know. (*To the others:*) He's a cop. (*Listens in phone:*) Parker—Parker— (*Spells:*) P-A-R-K-E-R. (*Listens:*) Well, I know there's a lot of them. I can't dispute that— Well, that's the only name I can give you— Yes, first and last— Yes, Parker Parker, that'll do— Is that so? Well, how would you like to go

and take one for yourself?—Say, listen, you switch me on to the Commissioner. I want to talk to the Commissioner.

GILROY (*Quickly moving to* PARKER *before he has finished the preceding speech and now grabbing the phone out of his hand*): Give me that phone. (*With contempt:*) You want to talk to the Commiss— (*Breaks off and speaks into phone:*) Hello, Cap. Gilroy again. Just a nuisance case, no consequence— See you in about ten minutes, Cap— Right. (*Hangs up and turns to* PARKER:) So, you want to talk to the Commissioner, eh?

PARKER: Well, how do you know the Commissioner doesn't want to talk to me? How do you know he hasn't wanted to talk to me for some time? A couple of years, for all you know. Oh, maybe you do know that. Maybe you know who I am yourself. I saw the look of astonishment on your face the minute you walked in here— And I suppose you said to yourself, "There he is. I've got him at last. I've landed him at last." Now that's what you said to yourself the minute you saw me, didn't you? Come on now, didn't you?

GILROY (*Knowingly*): Sure I did.

PARKER: And I suppose now you're going to take credit for a big sensational arrest, eh? Well, let me tell you something, if I'm nailed, there's the man deserves the credit, right there. (*Indicates* HEATH. *Then to him:*) And I'll see that you get full credit for it too, Mr. Heath. (*To* GILROY:) And let me tell you something else. If you turn me in, don't be surprised if a couple of your best friends and pals go up with me.

(*Everyone shows great interest.*)

CHASE: Who is this man, Gilroy? Who is he?

GILROY: I don't know who he is. I don't know what he's talking about.

PARKER (*Laughing, addressing others*): There you are. First he admits he knows me. Now he denies he knows me. Now what do you make out of that, huh?

GILROY (*Turning to* HEATH): You say

you don't want to enter any complaint against him?

HEATH: No, I don't want to make any complaint.

PARKER: A complaint against who? Against me? Now I ask you what have I done? There I was sitting in the park, minding my own business—

CHASE: Well, go on back to the park and mind your own business.

PARKER (*moving up to* CHASE): All right, I'll do that. I'll go back to the park and mind my own business. And if any of you people ever see me in the park again, you mind *your* own business. (*Puts on his hat. As he starts to sing he marches in time to the music, out into hallway.*) Here I go right back to the park, I don't care if the park is dark. Here I go, etc. (*He re-enters immediately, in step with* McGuire, *who, his hand on* PARKER's *shoulder, marches him back to the very spot he'd left.*) Here I come right back from the park, etc.

(McGuire *releases him, laughing and enjoying the situation.*)

GILROY (*To* PARKER): I've got to hand it to you. You're a great audience for yourself. (PARKER, *still laughing, again looks at* GILROY's *feet, then at* McGuire's. GILROY *and* McGuire *look at their feet, then glare at* PARKER, *which amuses him more.*)

CHASE (*Impatiently*): See here, Gilroy, we've got a dinner date. We've got to get along.

GILROY: Go ahead. Keep your dinner date. You folks needn't wait here, I'll manage this.

(ELINORE *and* WINNIE *get their wraps from piano and start putting them on.* GILES *helps* ELINORE.)

GILROY (*To* McGuire): You can run along too, Mac. I won't need you.

McGuire: Right, Sarge.

HEATH (*To* CHASE): Go ahead with the girls, Frank. Be with you in a few minutes.

PARKER: Yes, go ahead to your food and entertainment, now that you've had all the fun you want with a poor devil like me.

CHASE: Oh, shut up. Come on, girls.

(WINNIE, ELINORE *and* CHASE *exit, followed by* GILES *and* TOKEM.)

PARKER: Food and entertainment. Food and entertainment. All they think about is food and entertainment. Get me there. Faster, faster. Get me there, get me to my food and entertainment. Well, thank Heaven they'll never get me into a mess like this again.

GILROY: Say, listen. I don't get your racket at all.

PARKER: You don't, eh?

GILROY: No, I don't. Now as I understand it, this fellow Heath was just trying to be nice to you.

PARKER: He was, eh?

GILROY: Well, didn't he bring you here to his home?

PARKER: Yes, he brought me here to his home, and now he's throwing me out. That's pretty rotten treatment, that is . . . pretty rotten . . . after all his fine promises. . . . (*He breaks down and starts to cry.* HEATH *and* GILROY *look at each other, astonished.*)

HEATH: Now look here, Parker, you've got to listen to me. I've never been so sorry about anything in my life as I am about this whole occurrence. (PARKER, *slowly getting over his cry, sits and leans back on the settee watching* HEATH.) I apologize, Parker. Now will you please shake hands and tell me once and for all that you accept my apology. (*He offers his hand but* PARKER *just sits and looks at him without replying.*)

PARKER (*Over his crying spell*): Will you admit one thing more?

HEATH: Anything. What is it?

PARKER: You admit that you didn't believe the story I told you in the park.

HEATH (*Impatiently*): But I did believe the story you told me in the park.

PARKER: But do you still believe it?

HEATH: Yes, yes, yes, I still believe it.

PARKER (*Rising and extending his hand*): All right then, let's shake hands.

(*They shake hands.* TOKEM *enters and starts straightening up the room.*)

HEATH: Thanks, Parker.

PARKER: And does the invitation to stay here still go?

(*They stop shaking hands.*)

HEATH: What do you mean?

PARKER: You know what I mean. You asked me to stay here for a few days, didn't you? Don't you want to go through with it?

HEATH: All right, all right, I'll go through with it.

PARKER: Then why don't you have the boy show me to my room? I'm tired out.

HEATH (*Calling to* TOKEM): Tokem!

TOKEM: Yes, boss.

HEATH (*In sheer desperation*): Show Mr. Parker to his room. (*During the speech* PARKER *takes off his coat again.*)

TOKEM: Yes, boss.

GILROY (*To* HEATH): See here, you can't take a chance like this.

HEATH (*Hurriedly, to* GILROY): I know what I'm doing, Gilroy.

PARKER: If I'm not welcome here I don't want to stay.

HEATH: But you are welcome— Make yourself at home, and get a good night's sleep.

PARKER: That's all I need—a good night's sleep.

(HEATH *and* GILROY *exit.*)

TOKEM (*Timidly, to* PARKER): I take coat and hat, please?

(PARKER *hands them to* TOKEM.)

TOKEM (*Goes to doorway, pauses and turns to* PARKER): You go to your room, please. This way, please. (PARKER *does not answer and he repeats:*) I say, you go to your room, please. This way, please.

PARKER (*Moves up to him*): I'll let you know when I want to go to my room.

TOKEM: Yes, sir.

PARKER: And I won't go to my room till I'm ready to go to my room.

TOKEM: Yes, sir.

(PARKER *moves over to the piano and starts to play chopsticks,* TOKEM *watching him intently.* GILES *enters, pauses in doorway and watches him.* GILES *looks at* TOKEM *and nods to him.* TOKEM *exits.* PARKER *rises, goes directly to* GILES, *indicating chair.*)

PARKER: Will you do me a favor, will you sit down here for just a second?

(GILES *sits and he gets chair, brings it over and sits facing her.*)

Now this is between us, and it's very important, by the way. Which one of these two girls that were here does Heath play around with?

GILES (*Puts it delicately*): Well, I believe he's very much interested in Miss Payne.

PARKER: And you are fond of Mr. Heath, aren't you?

GILES (*Sort of bewildered*): Why yes, of course.

PARKER: So why shouldn't you go to him and warn him about this girl—have a talk with him about this girl?

GILES (*A bit puzzled*): Are you referring to Miss Payne?

PARKER: Yes. You're not going to accept defeat at her hands as easily as all that. Go to the man— Tell him you love him. You do love him—don't you?

GILES (*Dead cold*): I certainly do not.

PARKER: Can I depend on that? That you don't love him.

GILES (*Emphatically*): Of course.

PARKER (*A change of mood*): Thank Heavens! (*Slight pause.*) Miss Giles, don't you see that this was just my way of finding out if I had the right to say precisely what I'm going to say to you now? Suppose I were to tell you that from the moment I set eyes on you something here, (*Indicates heart.*) some indescribable something, cried out, "There she is, that's what you've been waiting for all your life." Suppose I were to tell you that—

GILES (*Frightened now, jumps to her feet and calls out*): Tokem! Tokem!

PARKER (*Rising, following her*): What are you calling him for?

GILES: Tokem! Tokem!

END OF ACT TWO

Let's consider . . .

1. Gilroy tried hard, in his own blustering way, to understand what was going on in Heath's apartment. Why did Parker laugh at him?

2. What happened after Heath left the room to dress? Was Parker making fun of Winnie and Elinore? How do you account for Parker's shift from seeming to be angry at Heath and Chase to being quite amused by everything?

3. Why didn't Parker object to going to the police department? What did he say about the Police Commissioner that had Gilroy worried?

4. How did Parker get Heath to let him stay on at the apartment?

5. Was Parker still having his joke on the world when he talked to Giles about love?

ACT THREE

(*Hallway.* TOKEM *rushes out of his room and into living room.*)

TOKEM: You call, Miss Giles?

GILES (*Without taking her eyes from* PARKER): Show Mr. Parker to his room.

TOKEM: Yes, Miss Giles.

PARKER (*To* TOKEM): I'll go to my room when I get ready to go to my room. I already told you that. And by the by, don't go 'way, I want to talk to you. (*Goes to* GILES *with another complete change of attitude.*) Miss Giles, I congratulate you. You've been tried and found true. I had you tabbed for a superior sort of person. I congratulate you, Miss Giles, and I'll make my report to Mr. Heath that you're certainly deserving of his implicit confidence, and any other little consideration he cares to show. And perhaps an increase in wages, who can tell? (*With a wise and knowing smile:*) Who can tell?

GILES (*Has taken all this wholesale and with a note of surprise, smiles*): You mean you were merely trying me out?

PARKER (*Smiles*): Well, you can't blame me for trying, Miss Giles. You're a very attractive woman. (*Laughs.*)

GILES (*Apologetically*): Oh, Mr. Parker. I'm frightfully sorry I misunderstood.

PARKER (*Smiles*): I quite understand. And now if you'll just give me a moment with this boy. (*Indicates* TOKEM.)

GILES: Why, of course. (*Smiling and over-polite now:*) And if there's anything I can do, why—

PARKER: We'll take that up later, shall we?

GILES (*Smiling*): I'll be right handy in case you need me.

PARKER (*Taking her hands*): In case I need you you'll come in handy, Miss Giles. (*Kisses her hands:*) You little devil you.

(*They both laugh merrily and* GILES *exits.* TOKEM *has been watching and listening to all this with open mouth.* PARKER *shakes* TOKEM's *hand. The outer doorbell rings.*)

PARKER: Is that the front door?

TOKEM: Yes, sir. (*Turns and exits into hallway.* FRISBY *enters.* PARKER *turns and sees him.*)

PARKER: Well, right out of the clear. (*He bows to* FRISBY.)

FRISBY (*Bows*): How do you do?

PARKER: How do I do what? What have I done? What do you mean?

FRISBY (*Looks at* PARKER *wonderingly*): I'm Doctor Frisby from upstairs.

PARKER: Oh, you are, are you?

FRISBY (*Laughs, then turns and looks at* GILES): Are you Miss Giles?

GILES: Yes, sir.

FRISBY: I had a telephone call from Mr. Heath, from the outside. He asked me to look in a moment, speak to you and inquire about a Mr. Parker.

PARKER: I thought so.

GILES (*Indicates*): This is Mr. Parker, Doctor.

FRISBY (*Looking at* PARKER): Oh, indeed? Uh huh. (*Smiles:*) I want to talk to you.

PARKER: What about?

FRISBY: About yourself.

PARKER (*Laughs*): You know it's awfully funny—the world is so topsy turvy that directly a man acts natural these days, they send for a doctor to come in and look him over. Am I right, Doc?

FRISBY (*Chuckles and tries to play along with him*): Well, there's something in what you say at that.

PARKER: At that? Yes, and at this and otherwise and also. (FRISBY *laughs.*) Now you think I'm off my nut, don't you?

FRISBY: No, no, nothing like that. (*He waves to* GILES *and* TOKEM, *dismissing them. They exit. Turns to* PARKER *and indicates a chair:*) If you'll be so kind.

PARKER (*Going to chair*): You want me here?

(FRISBY *brings chair over and places it facing* PARKER'S *chair. They bow to each other,* FRISBY *indicates chair again, and* PARKER *sits.* FRISBY *sits facing him. There is a pause as* FRISBY *leans back in his chair studying* PARKER *intently, his head on one side in his best professional manner.* PARKER, *amused by all this, suddenly leans over and taps* FRISBY'S *knee for reflex action.* FRISBY *looks at him in amazement.* PARKER *then taps his own knee, the foot jumps up and* FRISBY *laughs heartily,* PARKER *joining in.* FRISBY *has his laugh, then, sitting up straight in his chair, he leans toward* PARKER; *he is the doctor again.*)

FRISBY: Now just follow me with your eyes. (*He puts up both hands and slowly waves them from left to right, then back to left.* PARKER *follows the hands with his eyes, still amused.* FRISBY *stops for a moment, putting his hands on his knees and studying* PARKER. *Then he raises his hands to repeat the performance. As he does so,* PARKER *claps his hands, then claps* FRISBY'S *hands, starting to play pattycake.* FRISBY *hurriedly stops him, again laughing—then is serious.*) Now what do you say if you and I have a nice quiet little talk?

PARKER: Heath told you I was a crackpot, didn't he?

FRISBY: Why should he say that?

PARKER: Because I act natural. Because I shoot straight away. Because I cannot conduct myself in direct contradiction to my nature. Because I won't trail along with this fool idea of taking the whole thing seriously.

FRISBY: Of taking what seriously?

PARKER: Life. As it's being lived today. Who is he? What's he got? How'd he get it? What day is it? What's the date? How's the weather? Stocks are up—stocks are down. God bless you, old pal. How are the folks? The whole thing's a fake. You know it's a fake as well as I do.

FRISBY (*Chuckles*): Well, all that may be true, but what are we going to do about it?

PARKER: Do about it? Why sidestep it. Laugh at it. Run away from it, the same as I'm doing.

FRISBY: Run away from what?

PARKER: Life. The whole silly mess. Live in your own world, Doc. Think your own thoughts and say them.

(*Doorbell rings.* GILES *goes to door in entrance hall and opens it, admitting* MRS. DUNLAP *who enters with suitcase and hat box.*)

GILES: Goodness, this is a surprise. Mrs. Dunlap.

DUNLAP: Didn't Mr. Heath tell you I was coming?

GILES: No.

DUNLAP: That's strange. I sent him a wire.

GILES (*Notices tray with mail on hall table. Picks up telegram*): Oh, dear! Here's your telegram. He hasn't opened his mail.

DUNLAP: Well, I thought it strange he didn't meet me at the station. He always does, you know.

GILES: He's been very distracted—by the house guest he brought home with him.

DUNLAP: A house guest? In the spare room? Where am *I* going to stay?

GILES: I'm sure I can fix it. (*Goes to living room door.*)

DUNLAP (*Following her*): Well, I should hope it would be fixed. A nice state of affairs, a sister turned out to make way for a guest. (TOKEM *enters hallway.*) Hello, Tokem!

TOKEM: Mrs. Dunlap. (*Picks up her bags and follows them into living room.* FRISBY *and* PARKER *rise as the ladies and* TOKEM *enter.*)

GILES: This is Dr. Frisby, from upstairs. Mrs. Dunlap. This is Mr. Parker. Mrs. Dunlap, Mr. Heath's sister. (*"How do you do's" are exchanged.* GILES *continues to* PARKER:) There's been a little mixup, I'm afraid. Mr. Heath didn't open Mrs. Dunlap's wire. She always occupies the guest room when she visits New York.

PARKER: Seems to be a little room trouble here. First it's my room; (*To* DUNLAP:) now it's your room. But it seems to me there ought to be room for all of us in this world.

DUNLAP: Are you a friend of my brother's?

PARKER: Who's your brother?

DUNLAP: Mr. Heath.

PARKER: Oh, yes, yes. I forgot. You're Mrs. Dunlap, Mr. Heath's sister. What'd you come for?

DUNLAP: I came all the way from Albany to see my brother.

PARKER: You came all the way from Albany just to see your brother. No, no—I won't stand for that. We know better than that, don't we, Doc? (*Turns back to* DUNLAP:) No, no— I know a little something about brothers and sisters, and I know plenty about Albany, by the way. (*With a knowing look at* FRISBY:) Albany, Doc. (*To* DUNLAP, *confidentially:*) Why, how are all the boys up in Albany?

DUNLAP: I don't know any boys in Albany.

PARKER: You must know the Albany boys.

DUNLAP: Who do you think you're talking to? I have a husband.

PARKER: Well, he's one of the boys, isn't he? Where is your husband?

DUNLAP (*Coldly*): He's in Albany.

PARKER: Oh, you left him up there, did you? (*Chuckles:*) Well, that's all right. It's an even break. The chances are he's out for a good time himself. It'll be a rest for you both. (*To* FRISBY:) Now, that's my idea of married life. (*To* DUNLAP *again:*) So you left the old boy up in Albany, did you? (*Puts this in rhyme, kid fashion, and does a little step as he sings it:*) You see you can't fool me. You left him up in Albany. (*Strikes a pose, then turns to* FRISBY:) It's a wonderful world, Doc.

DUNLAP: In the name of common sense, what sort of person are you?

PARKER: I am a perfectly nice person. (*To* FRISBY:) Aren't I a nice person, Doc?

FRISBY: Would you like to prove it?

PARKER: I'd be glad to prove that.

FRISBY: Then give up the room to the lady.

PARKER: The lady hasn't asked me to give up the room. However, just to show you that I'm a gallant, accommodating, considerate gentleman, I'll make the gesture myself. (*Points to bags. To* DUNLAP:) Is that your baggage?

DUNLAP (*Coldly*): It is.

PARKER (*To* TOKEM): Boy! Take the lady's luggage to the room. (*To* DUNLAP:) That's fair enough, isn't it? What could be fairer than that?

(TOKEM *picks up the bags.*)

DUNLAP (*In a grateful tone*): Well, of course, I hate to do this.

PARKER: You do? Then don't do it! (*To* TOKEM:) Boy! Leave the luggage where it is. (TOKEM *puts bags down. To* DUNLAP:) I guess that settles the room argument.

(DUNLAP *appeals to* GILES *with a look.*)

GILES: Listen here, Mr. Parker. Mrs. Dunlap has got to have that room.

PARKER: Mrs. Dunlap just said she didn't want the room.

GILES: Of course she wants the room. (*To* DUNLAP:) You do want the room, don't you, Mrs. Dunlap?

DUNLAP: Of course I want the room.

PARKER: You do? Then why'd you say you didn't?

GILES: She didn't say she didn't.

PARKER: My mistake. I apologize. A correction shall be made. (*To* TOKEM:) Boy! Take the lady's luggage to the room.

(TOKEM *picks up the bags and exits.*)

GILES (*Going to hallway*): Come along, Mrs. Dunlap.

(DUNLAP *follows* GILES *to doorway.*)

PARKER (*Following* DUNLAP): I offer the room. You refuse the room. You fight for the room. I give you the room, and now you go to the room without a thank you. Is that the way it's going to be? (*He suddenly makes a noise like a sea lion and grabs the collar of her coat.* DUNLAP, *with an exclamation of fright turns and runs off through hallway.* GILES *follows her.* PARKER *stands looking after her and laughing for a minute or two; then comes back to* FRISBY.) There you are. That's life.

FRISBY: What are you trying to do, make a fool out of life?

PARKER: Well, why should I permit life to make a fool out of me? That's what's the matter with life, Doc. It's had too much of its own way. Somebody's got to give it a battle. Why not I? Look, Doc. I'm satisfied that there isn't a problem of any kind that couldn't be settled in ten minutes, if we'd all quit stalling and trying to be so darned polite. And that takes in all problems, mind you, national, international, social, political, economic, and otherwise.

GILES (*Enters hurriedly; speaking from doorway*): Mrs. Dunlap, she's fainted! Come quickly, please. (*She exits.*)

FRISBY (*Following her*): She's fainted? (*He disappears into* DUNLAP's *room.*)

(*Front door opens, admitting* HEATH *and* CHASE.)

HEATH: You should have waited downstairs in the car with the girls. (*Goes to living room.*)

CHASE (*Following*): Don't worry about the girls. I told them to take the car and drive home. You've got enough to worry about in here. (CHASE *and* HEATH *come*

to a halt when they see PARKER.) Oh, so you're still here, are you?

PARKER (*To* HEATH): What was the idea of sending a doctor in to examine me?

HEATH: Where is the doctor?

PARKER: He's with your sister.

HEATH (*Surprised*): My sister? What's my sister doing here?

PARKER: I don't know. She didn't have to come here to faint. She could have fainted up in Albany, just as well.

HEATH: My sister—my sister—she fainted?

PARKER: That's what the housekeeper told the doctor.

HEATH: What the heck are you talking about?

PARKER: Your sister.

HEATH: Where is she?

PARKER (*Indicates*): She's in there.

(HEATH *hurries out.*)

CHASE (*To* PARKER): Well.

PARKER: I thought you were going to the theatre.

CHASE: Theatre? We haven't even dined. You've turned this man into a total wreck. I'd just like to take and kick the stuffing out of you.

PARKER (*Defiantly*): Yes? Well you wouldn't say that if you were out on the sidewalk.

CHASE: Do you want to go out on the sidewalk?

PARKER: Do *you* want to go out on the sidewalk?

CHASE: Yes, I'll go out on the sidewalk with you.

PARKER: Not with me, you won't. I'm too smart. I know what you're up to. (*Turns away.*)

(HEATH *enters, worried.*)

HEATH: What a mess.

CHASE: What is it? What's the matter?

HEATH (*To* PARKER): You frightened the life out of Lindy. (*To* CHASE:) Dr. Frisby's trying to quiet her.

CHASE (*Crossing to* PARKER): Now what have you been up to?

PARKER: I've been up to nothing up to now.

CHASE: You heard what he said, the woman's hysterical.

PARKER: So are you. So is he. So is everybody. Why blame me for a world condition?

(*Doorbell rings.*)

CHASE (*Threateningly to* PARKER): Say, let me tell you something, Napoleon.

PARKER (*Snaps at this*): Don't call me Napoleon. I won't stand for that. (GILROY *enters and pauses just inside the doorway.* PARKER *sees* GILROY:) Well, here's a charming little surprise.

GILROY: Oh—(PARKER, *knowing what he is going to say, chimes in with him and they speak the line together:*) So you're still here, are you?

PARKER (*To* GILROY, *laughing*): I knew you were going to say that. (*Points to* CHASE:) He said the same thing when he walked in. You all say the same thing—you all do the same thing. You're making a fool out of the Declaration of Independence.

CHASE: I wish you'd take this man in charge. (*Looks at* PARKER.)

GILROY: What's he been doing now?

CHASE: He frightened a woman—they had to send for a doctor.

PARKER: They didn't have to send for a doctor. The doctor was here. And if it hadn't been for me he wouldn't have been here.

GILROY (*To* PARKER): Shut your mouth.

PARKER: Well, why doesn't he tell the truth? I want to tell you something, I haven't heard anybody say anything straight since I walked into the house.

(FRISBY *enters.*)

HEATH: How is she, Doctor?

FRISBY: Fine now. But I'd advise against her having any further conversations with this gentleman. (*Looks at* PARKER.)

GILROY: Come on, Parker. No more nonsense. Come along.

PARKER: No, sir. I don't go to Police Headquarters until I know what the charge is.

GILROY (*Impatiently*): There's no charge. We're just going for a walk. You needn't worry about Police Headquarters.

PARKER: I'm not worried about anything. I've got a clean cut case. I'll prove it to you. Listen to this. (*Turns to others, as to an imaginary court:*) Your Honor, there I was sitting in the park minding my own business, this fellow comes along and—

GILROY (*Dead sore now, slaps his palm down on table, interrupting* PARKER): Now, listen. For the last time, are you going to go out of this house with me or not?

PARKER: No, sir. Not a chance. Not with you. If I go, I go alone. I want to be alone. I can't get along with people. That's why I hang out with pigeons. I told you that. (*Moving to center and making this general:*) I don't know how you put up with each other—on the level, I don't. Why, it's a madhouse, a monkey cage. You can't live in it and be yourself. Not if you have any convictions, or strength of character. (*Looks at* GILROY:) Now look. There's the Police Department. Organized to keep the peace. Where do they keep it? Where is it? (*Laughs, indicates* FRISBY:) And the big doctor—the great reliever of pain—the great diagnostician. (*To* FRISBY:) Diagnose my case, will you, Doc? (*To the others:*) The old Doc doesn't know right now whether I ought to be put in a strait-jacket or sent to the United States Senate. (*To* FRISBY:) Now do you, on the level? (*To the others:*) It's just a guessing contest with these boys, that's all. (*Laughs, indicates* CHASE.) And the lawyer. The great representative of justice. He wouldn't hesitate for a minute to take the meanest man in the world, defend him and try to make him look like a public benefactor. (*To* CHASE:) Now would you, on the level? (*Laughs. Slight pause. To* HEATH:) Well, I'm going. But when I go, you just let me go. And don't try to find out anything more about me at all. A pigeon's a pigeon, and the park's a park. And that's where you'll find me most any afternoon, in case you want to take another look. But

remember, from now on I don't want to be disturbed.

FRISBY: Well, for Heaven's sake, who are you?

PARKER (*Smiles, indicating* HEATH): I'm the fellow that told him the story in the park. (*To the others:*) And as far as I'm concerned that's the end of the story. (*Chuckles:*) Well, I'm going. And I'm going alone. (*A pause, looks from one to another:*) Well, don't I even get the usual goodbye?

ALL (*In unison*): Goodbye!

PARKER (*Laughs heartily*): There's another fool habit, you know, that hello and goodbye. (*Mimics:*) Hello, goodbye—hello, goodbye! (*Laughs again:*) Who is he? What's he got? How'd he get it? What day is it? What's the date? How's the weather? Stocks are down. Stocks are up. (*Starting for doorway:*) Down with the rich. Pity the poor. God save the King. (*As he exits:*) Merry Christmas, Happy New Year. It's a fake. The whole thing's a fake.

(*He is heard laughing until the outer door slams.*)

(*The others stand and stare at each other in amazement.*)

GILROY: What do you say, Heath? Shall I put a tail on him?

HEATH: What do you think?

GILROY (*Starting for doorway*): Sure, I'll get the answer, leave it to me.

CHASE (*Calling to* GILROY *as he goes*): Let us know, Gilroy.

(GILROY *exits.*)

HEATH (*To* FRISBY, *after a slight pause*): What's your opinion, Frisby?

FRISBY (*Shaking his head*): I don't know. But it's been a splendid joke, no matter who it was on. (*Smiles knowingly:*) Good evening!

ALL (*In unison as before*): Good evening!

FRISBY (*Chuckles, turns and starts for doorway*): Good morning, good afternoon, good evening, hello, goodbye! (*Exits, chuckling.*)

CHASE: Joe, how did you ever happen to pick Parker up, anyway?

HEATH: I told you. He interested me.

CHASE: He'd interest anybody.

HEATH: Then why do you ask me how I happened to pick him up?

CHASE (*With a chuckle*): You're talking like him now.

HEATH (*Laughs*): Oh, shut up.

CHASE (*Laughs, then seriously*): I wonder if Gilroy'll find out anything about him?

HEATH: I think it'd be twice as interesting if nobody ever found out who he was.

CHASE: You mean that?

HEATH: Yes, I do.

CHASE: Then why did you say that you'd like to know who he was?

HEATH: Now you're beginning to talk like him too. (*Chuckles.*)

CHASE (*Laughs*): Maybe he's a disease, huh?

HEATH (*Shakes his head*): Well, he's something.

CHASE: Yes, and he's somebody. That's a moral certainty.

*

(*A bench in the park. It is morning. PARKER is sitting on his bench. GILROY is standing watching PARKER feeding pigeons.*)

GILROY: It's completely unofficial. Just for my own curiosity—that's all. I'll keep it absolutely confidential. You don't *have*

to tell me who you are but I sure would appreciate it.

PARKER: You really want to know, eh?

GILROY: I'd appreciate it.

PARKER: Okay.

(*He takes a wallet out of his jacket, extracts a card and hands it to GILROY. GILROY looks at it, obviously startled, and looks up at PARKER who is watching him with a smile.*)

PARKER (*Taking the card back*): I'll take that back, if you don't mind.

GILROY (*With great respect*): Yes, sir. I'm sorry I didn't recognize you, sir.

PARKER: Why be sorry? We wouldn't have had as much fun if you had, would we!

GILROY: No, sir. And if there's anything I can do for you—

PARKER: Sure you can—you can go about your job of putting down crime—so a man can sit quietly in the park anytime he wants to—with his friends the pigeons.

GILROY: Yes sir. Thank you sir. (*He salutes and exits.*)

(*PARKER turns to the pigeons.*)

PARKER (*To the pigeons*): I tell you—you birds don't know how lucky you are —that you're pigeons and not people. How they can stand one another—people I mean —is something I'll never understand. (*A loud coo.*) What's that? (*The loud coo is repeated.*) That's what I think too.

END

The man who wrote this play

GEORGE M. COHAN   1878–1942

George M. Cohan's theatrical education began when he was eight years old. His father and mother were a song and dance team in vaudeville, and George joined them on stage as soon as he could carry a tune. At thirteen he starred in the title role of *Peck's Bad Boy.*

He learned "show business" from the inside out. One success followed another, and *The New York Times* reported: "Cohan wrote both words and music, sang his own songs and danced them, wrote his own plays, directed them, starred in them and produced them."

In all, Cohan wrote fifty plays, three of which were outstanding hits: *Forty-five Minutes from Broadway* (1906); *Song and Dance Man* (1923); and *I'd Rather Be*

Right (1937). He also played the role of Nat Miller in Eugene O'Neill's *Ah, Wilderness* (1933), and was awarded a special Congressional Medal for his World War I songs "Over There" and "It's A Grand Old Flag" (1936).

When Cohan died, *The New York Times* included this tribute in its full-page obituary: "At the height of his career he was unquestionably the first man in the American theatre."

Let's consider . . .

1. How did Parker explain his actions to Giles? Do you think she believed him?
2. Parker knew why Dr. Frisby had dropped in. He also explained why Heath thought he was a "crack-pot." What reasons did Parker give? What did he suggest as a way out of this "whole silly mess"?
3. Why didn't Heath know his sister was coming? How did her visit complicate matters still further? What did Parker say and do that made her have hysterics?
4. What did Parker say was the matter with life? What did he think people should *stop* doing?
5. Why did Heath and Chase come back? Why did Parker refuse to take the blame for upsetting everyone?
6. What did Parker mean by the remark, "You're making a fool of the Declaration of Independence"?
7. Before Parker left, he decided to say what he thought of all of them. What did he say about each of them? Do you agree with what he said?
8. As Parker left, he was still making fun of the way people carry on the "fake" in life. How did you know that Chase and Heath had been influenced by Parker, in spite of themselves?
9. What was Parker's last joke? Was it a joke on you as well as on Gilroy? Do you agree with Heath that "it'd be twice as interesting if nobody ever found out who he was"?

10. What is your own theory about Parker's identity? Did the author give you any clues? Discuss your answer with the rest of the class.
11. Every day you say and hear such expressions as "How do you do?" and "Fine, thank you." You accept them as part of being sociable, but Parker didn't. Why? List six or eight other expressions which Parker might also question. Would he be right in questioning them? Explain your answer.
12. Parker was obviously critical of people like Heath and his friends. Do you think his criticisms would also apply to people you know? Would they sometimes apply to you? Why or why not?
13. At one point Parker said to Dr. Frisby, "Live in your own world, Doc. Think your own thoughts and say them." What did he mean?
14. Parker felt that people should act naturally. He also believed that they should say what they mean and mean what they say. Do you agree that this is a good policy? What would happen if you always followed it?
15. Parker had his own theory about the way people ought to behave. Did he always follow this theory? If you don't think he did, be sure to defend your answer.
16. *Pigeons and People* was written as a comedy and contains many humorous lines and situations. However, it has a basically serious *theme*, or main idea, which is gradually revealed through the dialogue and action of the play. As clearly as you can, state the theme of the play.

The writer's craft . . .

A. Parker certainly kept things moving. In fact, the other characters were never sure what he would do or say next. He was the focal point around which all the action revolved. Even though by everyday standards the action was contrived and implausible, you accepted it in the play just as you accepted Parker's unusual personality. The entire tone of the play demanded a "willing suspension of disbelief."

For example, it was most unlikely that Heath, a wealthy man, would invite Parker, a park-bench acquaintance, to spend several days in his home merely because Parker had told him his life story. But from the moment Parker arrived at Heath's house, the stage was set for the action of the play and for any event—no matter how unlikely—which the playwright might use to create the action.

In a play which is more realistic in tone, characters do not wander in and out with little or no reason. However, in *Pigeons and People* Elinore and Winnie merely appeared and disappeared with practically no relationship to what had gone before or what followed. List other characters in the play who seemed to appear "out of the blue."

As each new character appeared, Parker added to the implausibility of the situation by his unexpected remarks. And just as a particular situation seemed to be resolving into some kind of satisfactory ending, Parker would say something that immediately complicated the matter further. When Heath told Parker that he was free to leave, Parker refused to go until Heath apologized. When Heath agreed, Parker demanded to know what he was apologizing for. Heath, of course, didn't have the slightest idea, and thus Chase entered into the conversation. Soon Chase and Parker were involved in a heated argument and so the action was continued. Find other situations in the play in which Parker kept the action moving by his remarks and sudden shifts in tactics.

Even the ending would have been unlikely in real life. However, in terms of the play you accepted it. Explain why the ending was in keeping with the tone of the entire play.

B. Whenever you see a movie, a stage play, or a television drama, you willingly accept many **dramatic conventions.** These conventions are the standard practices which the playwright must use and the audience accept if certain aspects of real life are to be presented. In themselves, these conventions often seem illogical, but they serve an important function. For example, the opening and closing of a curtain in the theater may indicate a passage of time. In television a picture fade-out may serve the same purpose.

Each medium has its own conventions. In the movies, for example, you accept the fact that the characters are mere shadows projected on a screen, that they are several times larger than life size, and that at one moment you can see an entire army and at the next moment the face of a single person. The theater has its own conventions, too. You accept the fact that although you can hear two actors whispering on the stage, all the other actors pretend not to hear. Most scenes in the theater take place inside a room, and yet you aren't disturbed by the fact that the fourth wall of the room (the one toward the audience) is missing so that you may see what is happening inside.

Television has its own dramatic conventions. One of the most obvious conventions is that the characters appear far smaller than life size. Another is that the play is usually interrupted for the sponsor's "commercials." A third is that relatively few characters appear on the screen at a given time.

1. Can you think of other dramatic conventions of television dramas? Which of these conventions did you find in *Pigeons and People?*

2. When you first began watching television, which conventions did you find hardest to accept? Can you explain why?

3. Which conventions seemed so "natural" that you accepted them immediately without question?

He Made His Country Laugh

BENNETT CERF

It is not difficult to understand why the American people took Will Rogers to their hearts. Not only could he make his countrymen laugh; he could even make them laugh at themselves.

On the evening of August 15, 1935, a shiny red seaplane swooped down on a shallow river in Alaska, some three hundred miles inside the Artic Circle. A handful of curious Eskimos ran to the river bank. "We're lost," the pilot called to them. "Which way to Point Barrow?" One of the Eskimos shouted, "Northeast—only fifteen miles away."

The seaplane took off, wavered uncertainly in the air for a few moments, then plunged nose first into the earth with a sickening thud. The two occupants, crushed to death in a flight that would have taken ten minutes, had covered, between them, over a million air miles in the preceding three years. The pilot was Wiley Post, holder of the round-the-world record. His passenger was Will Rogers, America's unofficial ambassador of good will to all the nations of the earth.

Will Rogers' portfolio consisted of his homespun wit and sound common sense. He put into pithy phrases the inchoate thoughts of his fellowmen. He never looked up to the mighty—or spoke down to the masses. "He called a spade a spade—and made the spade like it." He won immortality with his humor, and with a piece of rope brought a troubled world a little peace of mind. How desperately we need another Will Rogers today!

All his life, he signed hotel registers "Will Rogers, Claremore, Oklahoma," but he really was born at Oologah, a few miles north. "You might say," he explained, "that Oologah was a suburb of Claremore. When I was born in 1879, it had about ten houses to Claremore's fifteen." When his future wife, Betty, visited Oologah, she was bound to notice him, because he was the only boy in town. He went calling with a banjo, and warbled, "Hello My Baby, Hello My Honey, Hello My Ragtime Girl" —not good, but loud.

Will's father was one eighth Cherokee; his mother, one quarter. He was genuinely proud of his Indian blood. "My forefathers didn't come over on the *Mayflower*," he boasted, "but they were waiting on the beach." Rogers, Senior, was affectionately known as "Uncle Clem" throughout the Indian Territory; when Oklahoma applied for statehood in 1906, he was the oldest member of the Constitutional Assembly. On his son Will he lavished wealth and affection, and planned for him a splendid education. But the boy had different ideas. "In school," he wrote, "I got to know more about McGuffey's *Fourth Reader* than Mr. McGuffey." He preferred horses to books and confined his studies to branding irons and lassos. Disapproving neighbors never did get over clucking tongues at his delinquencies. One of them watched his featured turn in the Ziegfeld Follies and reported, "He's still acting the fool like he used to do at home." The shy, modest Will often signed his love letters to Betty, "Your ignorant Indian cowboy."

Rogers reached Broadway via the unlikely route of Argentina and South Africa. He sailed to Buenos Aires under the mistaken notion that what the natives there craved most was American cowboys. When his stake ran out, he joined a troupe called "Texas Jack's Wild West Circus" and toured South Africa and Australia under the billing "The Cherokee Kid—The Man Who Can Lasso the Tail Off a Blowfly." By the time he was finished, he could, too.

He made his New York debut at the old Madison Square Garden in April, 1905. He participated in the "Wild West Exhibition" in the National Horse Show. On the opening night, a steer broke loose and headed straight for the arena boxes. Will roped it in the nick of time. Those of the spectators who hadn't fainted cheered wildly. On the strength of the front-page stories, Will rode his favorite pony, Comanche, into the number-one vaudeville house of the day—Hammerstein's Victoria Roof.

His act was approved, and he never lacked engagements thereafter, but he really didn't become a headliner until he started talking—and that was an accident, too. He got his ropes tangled one day, and while straightening them out, he explained his difficulties to the audience. His Oklahoma drawl made people laugh, and Will looked up, startled. Then he realized they were laughing with him. He kept on talking, and he never stopped.

Will Rogers was a reporter at large in a large world. His wit was pointed and timely, but it never was mean. He went straight to the heart of a subject. Politicians and diplomats might becloud an issue with double-talk; Rogers would clear it up with a one-sentence quip. His field for most intensive comment was the American scene, and in that panorama the target most often hit was Congress. Once asked, "Is the field of humor crowded?" he replied, "Only when Congress is in session." Then

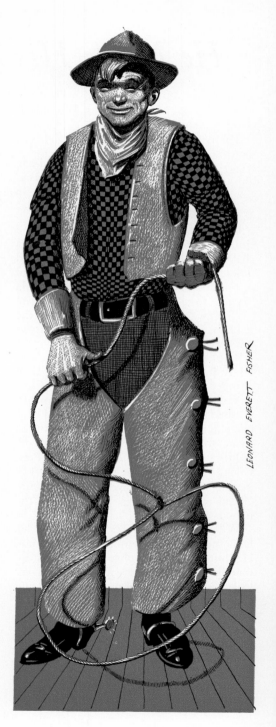

LEONARD EVERETT FISHER

he added, "There isn't much credit to being a comedian when you got the whole government working for you. All you have to do is report the facts, and I don't even have to exaggerate."

After a European tour, during which he visited Italy, Rogers remarked, "They told me there that Rome once had Senators. Now I know why it declined."

People in high places sought his company and invited him to speak at countless banquets. Even Chauncey Depew, after-dinner champion of his era, was forced to admit, "He's asked to more dinners than I am," but he added, "Of course, I don't have to bring a rope."

On being asked to dinner by a friend, Rogers replied, "No, thanks, I've already et." "You should say 'have eaten,'" his friend corrected. "Well," drawled Rogers, "I know a lot of fellers who say 'have eaten' who ain't et!"

Rogers would appear at a benefit performance in Texas, hop to England for a party at Buckingham Palace, and be back for a game of polo on Long Island in the course of a typical fortnight. Wherever he was, he typed his daily paragraph of comment on some highlight in the news. He was the guest of five Presidents at the White House, beginning with Wilson and ending with Roosevelt. At his first meeting with Coolidge, Rogers and Irvin S. Cobb were invited to the White House together. Both knowing the President's reputation for maintaining a sober face, Cobb bet Rogers that he could not make Coolidge smile. On being introduced, Rogers shook the President's hand and said, "I'm sorry —I didn't catch the name." He won the bet. Speaking once of a visit to Egypt, Rogers said, "It's quite a place, but I was the only tourist there who never went to see the sphinx. I've seen Cal Coolidge."

A legend has it that Will Rogers once walked up to the gate of Buckingham Palace and said to the guard, "I am Will Rogers, and I have come to see the king." The guard drew himself up haughtily, and

Rogers continued, "You tell him that when the Prince of Wales was out my way he told me to look up his old man sometime, so here I am." Rogers was admitted, had a long chat with the king, and stayed to lunch.

Lady Astor, born Nancy Langhorne in Greenwood, Virginia, U. S. A., once invited Rogers to her luxurious country estate in England. He looked over the establishment and commented, "Nancy, you certainly have out-married yourself."

From the home of the American Ambassador to France, he sent his niece a picture postal of the armless Venus de Milo, and wrote on the back, "See what'll happen to you if you don't stop biting your fingernails."

One reason he was liked, he figured, was that when people came to him for advice, he found out the advice they wanted and gave it to them. "This made them think they were happy and I was smart. It was as easy as that. I learned it from old Josh Billings.[1] There was a *real* humorist." He told the members of the New York Stock Exchange, "Country folks would appreciate you fellows more if you just sold them stocks that were going to go up. If they're not going up, don't let people buy them."

Radio had not yet blossomed into full flower in Will Rogers' day. Disk jockeys were unknown, and so were stars who drew ten thousand dollars a week. Nevertheless, Will did all right for himself on the air, although he never quite got used to a microphone. He did well in Hollywood, too. His biggest hits included *They Had To See Paris, State Fair, A Connecticut Yankee in King Arthur's Court*, and—his last—*Steamboat 'Round the Bend*. He took Hollywood in stride. "It's a comfortable kind of show business," he admitted. "Not much night work, and the only place you can act and at the same time sit down in front and clap for yourself." His favorite greeting for screen writers was, "Hi,

[1] *Josh Billings*, pen name of H. W. Shaw (1818-85), popular for his "horse sense" and humor

brother! Whatcha spoiling today?" He told an interviewer, "Shucks, I can't act. I just talk natural. And I'm sure different from the other movie stars: I still got the wife I started out with."

Political parties were fair game for Will Rogers; and he delighted, during election campaigns and national conventions, to take them to task. In 1932 he established the *Bunkless Party,* with himself as presidential nominee. His party platform was brief: "I want it understood first that my platform is made out of the planks carried in by the voters. And anybody with ten votes can have a plank. We are leaving room between the planks for any wisecracks we think we should insert. We will not only give the farmer relief—we'll cure him of being a farmer."

That same year he attended the Democratic National Convention. One of his reports said, "Oh, they was Democrats today, and we was proud of them. They fought, they split, and they adjourned in a dandy wave of dissension. That's the old Democratic spirit—one whole day wasted and nothing done. It's a sure sign things are getting back to normal."

Asked about his own political attachment, Rogers replied, "I'm not a member of any organized party—I'm a Democrat."

When illness prevented Rogers' reporting at his movie studio one morning, alarmed executives sent a titled specialist, who had just arrived in town amid appropriate fanfare, to examine him. The specialist looked him over carefullly and said, "You've been working too hard. What you need is relaxation and a good laugh or two. Take a few days off and go to see Will Rogers. He'll put you back in shape." "I hope you won't forget that," said Rogers, "when you're figuring out your bill." Mrs. Rogers relates that Will never wore glasses until Thomas Meighan observed him reading a newspaper at full arm's length. "You'll ruin your eyes that way," warned Meighan. "Here, try my glasses." Rogers did, and found them so satisfactory that he took them home. For the rest of his life, his glasses were ground to Meighan's prescription.

Will Rogers accepted criticism gracefully, but in general he could go his critics one better. At one period *The New York Times* was printing his comments on the national scene in brief letter form. Certain readers objected to the policies advocated by Rogers. The *Times* promptly ran an editorial stating that all remarks by Will Rogers were his own and were in no way to be construed as the policy of the newspaper, nor was the newspaper responsible for any statement of Mr. Rogers. Will's reply, printed soon after:

"Beverly Hills, Calif. Dec. 7.—I would like to state to the readers of *The New York Times* that I am in no way responsible for the editorial or political policy of this paper. I allow them free rein as to their opinion, so long as it is within the bounds of good subscription gathering. But I want it understood that their policy may be in direct contrast to mine. Their editorials may be put in purely for humor, or just to fill space. Every paper must have its various entertaining features, and their editorials are not always to be taken seriously and never to be construed as my policy. Yours, Will Rogers."

A few years before his death, Will Rogers wrote, "When I die, my epitaph, or whatever you call those signs on gravestones, is going to read: 'I joked about every prominent man of my time, but I hardly ever met a man I didn't like.' I am proud of that." He got the epitaph.

Sportsman, writer, actor, unofficial ambassador, philosopher, humorist, friend—more than a decade has passed since Will Rogers' death in 1935, and the American regard for him has, perhaps, entered into a new realm. To those who saw him, or heard him, or read his writings, he remains the chuckling spokesman of down-to-earth sanity, articulately epitomizing America's ability to laugh at herself; a unique figure in the opening third of the twentieth century. But he is becoming known as well to the young generation as a kind of legend typifying a better part of American culture —simple, good-humored, and essentially kindly skepticism, never malicious, never salacious, never cynical.

The Saturday Review of Literature wrote of him, "Somebody once gave him a license of free speech (or perhaps he took it without asking); but, at any rate, in the past few years he has probably turned over more heavy stones and thrown hot sunlight underneath than any man in the United States." His comments ranged all the way from "I never expected to see the day when the girls would get sunburned in the places they do now" to "The United States never lost a war or won a conference." They came from the mind of a man who loved his country, and his fellow men.

The man who wrote this selection

BENNETT A. CERF 1898–

Books are Bennett Cerf's business. For thirty years he has been publishing them, writing and talking about them, compiling them, and editing them. He is also a collector of rare books.

Mr. Cerf was born in New York City where he has spent most of his life. He was educated in the city public schools and at Columbia University. After he received his degree in 1920 he worked for a Wall Street brokerage house and for the *New York Herald Tribune* as a reporter.

By 1925, he felt he had gained enough experience in publishing to start a publishing house of his own. Two years later he founded another publishing house and is now president of both of them. One house reprints inexpensive editions of famous books; the other publishes standard and deluxe editions of both new books and classics.

Mr. Cerf has edited anthologies of plays, short stories, and jokes—almost a dozen volumes in all. He takes particular delight in re-telling a humorous story.

Let's consider . . .

1. Will Rogers "won immortality with his humor, and with a piece of rope brought a troubled world a little peace of mind"; yet the distinction he achieved came to him first by chance. What two incidents determined his career?

2. Why was his success as a humorist even more remarkable because of his background?

3. His *homespun wit* and *sound common sense* were his stock in trade. Explain each phrase by referring to one or two examples included in this selection.

4. Which examples of Will Rogers' wit did you enjoy the most? How were they characteristic of Rogers?

5. What was Rogers' attitude toward politics? Be sure you know how he used the word *Democrat*. Why do you think he often made Congress the target of his jibes?

6. Some humorists achieve their effect by long-drawn-out stories which keep the audience guessing. Will Rogers achieved his by brevity and understatement. Select two examples from this selection which illustrate these qualities.

7. Why do you think Rogers could "call a spade a spade and make the spade like it"?

8. Cerf said that Rogers "never looked up to the mighty—or spoke down to the masses." Select several anecdotes from this selection which illustrate the truth of Cerf's statement.

9. In what way did Will Rogers typify for the younger generation of this country "a better part of American culture"? Why did Cerf say that America desperately needs another Will Rogers?

The writer's craft . . .

In a full biography, the author tries to give a fairly complete story of a person's life. Obviously, he could hardly tell that story in a few pages. This selection about Will Rogers is not a true biography; it is more of a **biographical sketch.** Bennett Cerf chose to relate only those highlights in Will Rogers' life which would give the reader certain basic facts about the man and would communicate the "flavor" of his personality.

It is not always possible to classify a piece of writing as definitely one type or another. For example, you may find that an informal essay has many of the characteristics of a story, and a story about an historical figure may be largely biographical. Two of the major classifications in literature are *prose* and *poetry,* yet the prose of Thomas Wolfe, for example, has many of the characteristics of poetry: rhythm, imagery, and rich connotations. Passages which he wrote as prose have at times even been reprinted in the form of poetry.

Some readers like to analyze a piece of writing in order to determine its exact classification. Such a classification is not always possible because writers are creating an interpretation of human experience, not designing a literary package that meets the requirements of a particular type. An understanding of the general characteristics of different types of literature certainly will add to your appreciation and understanding of what you read. However, the real significance of any piece of literature—no matter what its type—lies in the meaning it has for you because it adds richness and enjoyment to your life.

Charity

In men whom men condemn as ill
I find so much of goodness still,
In men whom men pronounce divine
I find so much of sin and blot,
I do not dare to draw a line
Between the two, where God has not.

Joaquin Miller

The Hiltons' Holiday

SARAH ORNE JEWETT

In this story of quiet family happiness you will have an intimate view of a "vanished past" that might be quite forgotten if it were not kept alive in fiction.

I

There was a bright, full moon in the clear sky, and the sunset was still shining faintly in the west. Dark woods stood all about the old Hilton farmhouse, save down the hill, westward, where lay the shadowy fields which John Hilton, and his father before him, had cleared and tilled with much toil,—the small fields to which they had given the industry and even affection of their honest lives.

John Hilton was sitting on the doorstep of his house. As he moved his head in and out of the shadows, turning now and then to speak to his wife, who sat just within the doorway, one could see his good face, rough and somewhat unkept, as if he were indeed a creature of the shady woods and brown earth, instead of the noisy town. It was late in the long spring evening, and he had just come from the lower field as cheerful as a boy, proud of having finished the planting of his potatoes.

"I had to do my last row mostly by feelin'," he said to his wife. "I'm proper glad I pushed through, an' went back an' ended off after supper. 'T would have taken me a good part o' to-morrow mornin', an' broke my day."

"'Tain't no use for ye to work yourself all to pieces, John," answered the woman quickly. "I declare it does seem harder than ever that we couldn't have kep' our boy; he'd been comin' fourteen years old this fall, most a grown man, and he'd work right 'longside of ye now the whole time."

"It was hard to lose him; I do seem to miss little John," said the father sadly. "I expect there was reasons why 'twas best. I feel able an' smart to work; my father was a girt strong man, an' a monstrous worker afore me. 'Tain't that; but I was thinkin' by myself to-day what a sight o' company the boy would ha' been. You know, small's he was, how I could trust to leave him anywheres with the team, and how he'd beseech to go with me wherever I was goin'; always right in my tracks I used to tell 'em. Poor little John, for all he was so young he had a great deal o' judgment; he'd ha' made a likely man."

The mother sighed heavily as she sat within the shadow.

"But then there's the little girls, a sight o' help an' company," urged the father eagerly, as if it were wrong to dwell upon sorrow and loss. "Katy, she's most as good as a boy, except that she ain't very rugged. She's a real little farmer, she's helped me a sight this spring; an' you've got Susan Ellen, that makes a complete little housekeeper for ye as far as she's learnt. I don't see but we're better off than most folks, each on us having a workmate."

"That's so, John," acknowledged Mrs. Hilton wistfully, beginning to rock steadily in her straight, splint-bottomed chair. It was always a good sign when she rocked.

"Where be the little girls so late?" asked their father. " 'T is gettin' long past eight o'clock. I don't know when we've all set up so late, but it's so kind o' summer-like an' pleasant. Why, where be they gone?"

"I've told ye; only over to Becker's folks," answered the mother. "I don't see myself what keeps 'em so late; they beseeched me after supper till I let 'em go. They're all in a dazzle with the new teacher; she asked 'em to come over. They say she's unusual smart with 'rethmetic, but she has a kind of gorpen look to me. She's goin' to give Katy some pieces for her doll, but I told Katy she ought to be ashamed wantin' dolls' pieces, big as she's gettin' to be. I don't know's she ought, though, she ain't but nine this summer."

"Let her take her comfort," said the kind-hearted man. "Them things draws her to the teacher, an' makes them acquainted. Katy's shy with new folks, more so'n Susan Ellen, who's of the business kind. Katy's shy-feelin' and wishful."

"I don't know but she is," agreed the mother slowly. "Ain't it sing'lar how well acquainted you be with that one, an' I with Susan Ellen? 'T was always so from the first. I'm doubtful sometimes our Katy ain't one that'll be like to get married—anyways not about here. She lives right with herself, but Susan Ellen ain't nothin' when she's alone, she's always after company; all the boys is waitin' on her a'ready. I ain't afraid but she'll take her pick when the time comes. I expect to see Susan Ellen well settled,—she feels grown up now,—but Katy don't care one mite 'bout none o' them things. She wants to be rovin' out o' doors. I do believe she'd stand an' hark to a bird the whole forenoon."

"Perhaps she'll grow up to be a teacher," suggested John Hilton. "She takes to her book more'n the other one. I should like one of 'em to be a teacher same's my mother was. They're good girls as anybody's got."

"So they be," said the mother, with un-usual gentleness, and the creak of her rocking-chair was heard, regular as the ticking of a clock. The night breeze stirred in the great woods, and the sound of a brook that went falling down the hillside grew louder and louder. Now and then one could hear the plaintive chirp of a bird. The moon glittered with whiteness like a winter moon, and shone upon the low-roofed house until its small windowpanes gleamed like silver, and one could almost see the colors of a blooming bush of lilac that grew in a sheltered angle by the kitchen door. There was an incessant sound of frogs in the lowlands.

"Be you sound asleep, John?" asked the wife presently.

"I don't know but what I was a'most," said the tired man, starting a little. "I should laugh if I was to fall sound asleep right here on the step; 'tis the bright night, I expect, makes my eyes feel heavy, an' 'tis so peaceful. I was up an' dressed a little past four an' out to work. Well, well!" and he laughed sleepily and rubbed his eyes. "Where's the little girls? I'd better step along an' meet 'em."

"I wouldn't just yet; they'll get home all right, but 'tis late for 'em certain. I don't want 'em keepin' Mis' Becker's folks up neither. There, le' 's wait a few minutes," urged Mrs. Hilton.

"I've be'n a-thinkin' all day I'd like to give the child'n some kind of a treat," said the father, wide awake now. "I hurried up my work 'cause I had it so in mind. They don't have the opportunities some do, an' I want 'em to know the world, an' not stay right here on the farm like a couple o' bushes."

"They're a sight better off not to be so full o' notions as some is," protested the mother suspiciously.

"Certain," answered the farmer; "but they're good, bright child'n, an' commencin' to take a sight o' notice. I want 'em to have all we can give 'em. I want 'em to see how other folks does things."

"Why, so do I,"—here the rocking-chair

stopped ominously,—"but so long's they're contented—"

"Contented ain't all in this world; hopper-toads may have that quality an' spend all their time a-blinkin'. I don't know's bein' contented is all there is to look for in a child. Ambition's somethin' to me."

"Now you've got your mind on to some plot or other." (The rocking-chair began to move again.) "Why can't you talk right out?"

" 'T ain't nothin' special," answered the good man, a little ruffled; he was never prepared for his wife's mysterious powers of divination. "Well there, you do find things out the master! [1] I only thought perhaps I'd take 'em tomorrow, an' go off somewhere if 't was a good day. I've been promisin' for a good while I'd take 'em to Topham Corners; they've never been there since they was very small."

"I believe you want a good time yourself. You ain't never got over bein' a boy." Mrs. Hilton seemed much amused. "There, go if you want to an' take 'em; they've got their summer hats an' new dresses. I don't know o' nothin' that stands in the way. I should sense [2] it better if there was a circus or anythin' to go to. Why don't you wait an' let the girls pick 'em some strawberries or nice ros'berries, and then they could take an' sell 'em to the stores?"

John Hilton reflected deeply. "I should like to get me some good yellow-turnip seed to plant late. I ain't more'n satisfied with what I've been gettin' o' late years o' Ira Speed. An' I'm goin' to provide me with a good hoe; mine's gettin' wore out an' all shackly. I can't seem to fix it good."

"Them's excuses," observed Mrs. Hilton, with friendly tolerance. "You just cover up the hoe with somethin', if you get it— I would. Ira Speed's so jealous he'll remember it of you this twenty year, your goin' an' buyin' a new hoe o' anybody but him."

---

[1] *the master,* remarkably
[2] *sense,* understand

"I've always thought 't was a free country," said John Hilton soberly. "I don't want to vex Ira neither; he favors us all he can in trade. 'T is difficult for him to spare a cent, but he's as honest as daylight."

At this moment there was a sudden sound of young voices, and a pair of young figures came out from the shadow of the woods into the moonlighted open space. An old cock crowed loudly from his perch in the shed, as if he were a herald of royalty. The little girls were hand in hand, and a brisk young dog capered about them as they came.

"Wa'n't it dark gittin' home through the woods this time o' night?" asked the mother hastily, and not without reproach.

"I don't love to have you gone so late; mother an' me was timid about ye, and you've kep' Mis' Becker's folks up, I expect," said their father regretfully. "I don't want to have it said that my little girls ain't got good manners."

"The teacher had a party," chirped Susan Ellen, the elder of the two children. "Goin' home from school she asked the Grover boys, an' Mary an' Sarah Speed. An' Mis' Becker was real pleasant to us: she passed round some cake, an' handed us sap sugar on one of her best plates, an' we played games an' sung some pieces too. Mis' Becker thought we did real well. I can pick out most of a tune on the cabinet organ; teacher says she'll give me lessons."

"I want to know, dear!" exclaimed John Hilton.

"Yes, an' we played Copenhagen, an' took sides spellin', an' Katy beat everybody spellin' there was there."

Katy had not spoken; she was not so strong as her sister, and while Susan Ellen stood a step or two away addressing her eager little audience, Katy had seated herself close to her father on the doorstep. He put his arm around her shoulders, and drew her close to his side, where she stayed.

"Ain't you got nothin' to tell, daughter?" he asked, looking down fondly; and Katy gave a pleased little sigh for answer.

"Tell 'em what's goin' to be the last day o' school, and about our trimmin' the schoolhouse," she said; and Susan Ellen gave the programme in most spirited fashion.

"'Twill be a great time," said the mother, when she had finished. "I don't see why folks wants to go trapesin' off to strange places when such things is happenin' right about 'em." But the children did not observe her mysterious air. "Come, you must step yourselves right to bed!"

They all went into the dark warm house; the bright moon shone upon it steadily all night, and the lilac flowers were shaken by no breath of wind until the early dawn.

II

The Hiltons always waked early. So did their neighbors, the crows, and song-sparrows and robins, the light-footed foxes and squirrels in the woods. When John Hilton waked, before five o'clock, an hour later than usual because he had sat up so late, he opened the house door and came out into the yard, crossing the short green turf hurriedly as if the day were too far spent for any loitering. The magnitude of the plan for taking a whole day of pleasure confronted him seriously, but the weather was fair, and his wife, whose disapproval could not have been set aside, had accepted and even smiled upon the great project. It was inevitable now, that he and the children should go to Topham Corners. Mrs. Hilton had the pleasure of waking them, and telling the news.

In a few minutes they came frisking out to talk over the great plans. The cattle were already fed, and their father was milking. The only sign of high festivity was the wagon pulled out into the yard, with both seats put in as if it were Sunday; but Mr. Hilton still wore his everyday clothes, and Susan Ellen suffered instantly from disappointment.

"Ain't we goin', father?" she asked complainingly; but he nodded and smiled at her, even though the cow, impatient to get

to pasture, kept whisking her rough tail across his face. He held his head down and spoke cheerfully, in spite of this vexation.

"Yes, sister, we're goin' certain', an' goin' to have a great time too." Susan Ellen thought that he seemed like a boy at that delightful moment, and felt new sympathy and pleasure at once. "You go an' help mother about breakfast an' them things; we want to get off quick's we can. You coax mother now, both of ye, an' see if she won't go with us."

"She said she wouldn't be hired to," responded Susan Ellen. "She says it's goin' to be hot, an' she's laid out to go over an' see how her aunt Tamsen Brooks is this afternoon."

The father gave a little sigh; then he took heart again. The truth was that his wife made light of the contemplated pleasure, and, much as he usually valued her companionship and approval, he was sure that they should have a better time without her.

It was impossible, however, not to feel guilty of disloyalty at the thought. Even though she might be completely unconscious of his best ideals, he only loved her and the ideals the more, and bent his energies to satisfying her indefinite expectations. His wife still kept much of that youthful beauty which Susan Ellen seemed likely to reproduce.

An hour later the best wagon was ready, and the great expedition set forth. The little dog sat apart, and barked as if it fell entirely upon him to voice the general excitement. Both seats were in the wagon, but the empty place testified to Mrs. Hilton's unyielding disposition. She had wondered why one broad seat would not do, but John Hilton meekly suggested that the wagon looked better with both. The little girls sat on the back seat dressed alike in their Sunday hats of straw with blue ribbons, and their little plaid shawls pinned neatly about their small shoulders. They wore gray thread gloves, and sat very straight. Susan Ellen was half a head the taller, but otherwise, from behind, they looked much alike. As for their father, he was in his Sunday best,—a plain black coat, and a winter hat of felt, which was heavy and rusty-looking for that warm early summer day. He had it in mind to buy a new straw hat at Topham, so that this with the turnip seed and the hoe made three important reasons for going.

"Remember an' lay off your shawls when you get there, an' carry them over your arms," said the mother, clucking like an excited hen to her chickens. "They'll do to keep dust off your new dresses goin' an' comin'. An' when you eat your dinners don't get spots on you, an' don't point at folks as you ride by, an' stare, or they'll know you come from the country. An' John, you call into Cousin Ad'line Marlow's an' see how they all be, an' tell her I expect her over certain to stop awhile before hayin'. It always eases her phthisic [3] to git up here on the high land, an' I've got a new notion about doin' over her best-room carpet sence I see her that'll save rippin' one breadth. An' don't come home all wore out; an', John, don't you go an' buy me no kickshaws [4] to fetch home. I ain't a child, an' you ain't got no money to waste. I expect you'll go, like's not, an' buy you some kind of a foolish boy's hat; do look an' see if it's reasonable good straw, an' won't splinter all off round the edge. An' you mind, John—"

"Yes, yes, hold on!" cried John impatiently; then he cast a last affectionate, reassuring look at her face, flushed with the hurry and responsibility of starting them off in proper shape. "I wish you was goin' too," he said, smiling. "I do so!" Then the old horse started, and they went out at the bars, and began the careful long descent of the hill. The young dog, tethered to the lilac-bush, was frantic with piteous appeals; the little girls piped their eager good-bys again and again, and their father

turned many times to look back and wave his hand. As for their mother, she stood alone and watched them out of sight.

There was one place far out on the high-road where she could catch a last glimpse of the wagon, and she waited what seemed a very long time until it appeared and then was lost to sight again behind a low hill. "They're nothin' but a pack o' child'n together," she said aloud; and then felt lonelier than she expected. She even stooped and patted the unresigned little dog as she passed him, going into the house.

The occasion was so much more important than any one had foreseen that both the little girls were speechless. It seemed at first like going to church in new clothes, or to a funeral; they hardly knew how to behave at the beginning of a whole day of pleasure. They made grave bows at such persons of their acquaintance as happened to be straying in the road. Once or twice they stopped before a farmhouse, while their father talked an inconsiderately long time with some one about the crops and the weather, and even dwelt upon town business and the doings of the selectmen, which might be talked of at any time. The explanations that he gave of their excursion seemed quite unnecessary. It was made entirely clear that he had a little business to do at Topham Corners, and thought he had better give the little girls a ride; they had been very steady at school, and he had finished planting, and could take the day as well as not. Soon, however, they all felt as if such an excursion were an every-day affair, and Susan Ellen began to ask eager questions, while Katy silently sat apart enjoying herself as she never had done before. She liked to see the strange houses, and the children who belonged to them; it was delightful to find flowers that she knew growing all along the road, no matter how far she went from home. Each small homestead looked its best and pleasantest, and shared the exquisite beauty that early summer made,—shared the luxury of

---

[3] *phthisic*, a wasting disease of the lungs
[4] *kickshaws*, dainty trifles

greenness and floweriness that decked the rural world. There was an early peony or a late lilac in almost every dooryard.

It was seventeen miles to Topham. After a while they seemed very far from home, having left the hills far behind, and descended to a great level country with fewer tracts of woodland, and wider fields where the crops were much more forward. The houses were all painted, and the roads were smoother and wider. It had been so pleasant driving along that Katy dreaded going into the strange town when she first caught sight of it, though Susan Ellen kept asking with bold fretfulness if they were not almost there. They counted the steeples of four churches, and their father presently showed them the Topham Academy, where their grandmother once went to school, and told them that perhaps some day they would go there too. Katy's heart gave a strange leap; it was such a tremendous thing to think of, but instantly the suggestion was transformed for her into one of the certainties of life. She looked with solemn awe at the tall belfry, and the long rows of windows in the front of the academy, there where it stood high and white among the clustering trees. She hoped that they were going to drive by, but something forbade her taking the responsibility of saying so.

Soon the children found themselves among the crowded village houses. Their father turned to look at them with affectionate solicitude.

"Now sit up straight and appear pretty," he whispered to them. "We're among the best people now, an' I want folks to think well of you."

"I guess we're as good as they be," remarked Susan Ellen, looking at some innocent passers-by with dark suspicion, but Katy tried indeed to sit straight, and folded her hands prettily in her lap, and wished with all her heart to be pleasing for her father's sake. Just then an elderly woman saw the wagon and the sedate party it carried, and smiled so kindly that it seemed to Katy as if Topham Corners had welcomed and received them. She smiled back again as if this hospitable person were an old friend, and entirely forgot that the eyes of all Topham had been upon her.

"There, now we're coming to an elegant house that I want you to see; you'll never forget it," said John Hilton. "It's where Judge Masterson lives, the great lawyer; the handsomest house in the county, everybody says."

"Do you know him, father?" asked Susan Ellen.

"I do," answered John Hilton proudly. "Him and my mother went to school together in their young days, and were always called the two best scholars of their time. The judge called to see her once; he stopped to our house to see her when I was a boy. An' then, some years ago—you've heard me tell how I was on the jury, an' when he heard my name spoken he looked at me sharp, and asked if I wa'n't the son of Catharine Winn, an' spoke most beautiful of your grandmother, an' how well he remembered their young days together."

"I like to hear about that," said Katy.

"She had it pretty hard, I'm afraid, up on the old farm. She was keepin' school in our district when father married her—that's the main reason I backed 'em down when they wanted to tear the old schoolhouse all to pieces," confided John Hilton, turning eagerly. "They all say she lived longer up here on the hill than she could anywhere, but she never had her health. I wa'n't but a boy when she died. Father an' me lived alone afterward till the time your mother come; 't was a good while, too; I wa'n't married so young as some. 'T was lonesome, I tell you; father was plumb discouraged losin' of his wife, an' her long sickness an' all set him back, an' we'd work all day on the land an' never say a word. I s'pose 't is bein' so lonesome early in life that makes me so pleased to have some nice girls growin' up round me now."

There was a tone in her father's voice

that drew Katy's heart toward him with new affection. She dimly understood, but Susan Ellen was less interested. They had often heard this story before, but to one child it was always new and to the other old. Susan Ellen was apt to think it tiresome to hear about her grandmother, who, being dead, was hardly worth talking about.

"There's Judge Masterson's place," said their father in an every-day manner, as they turned a corner, and came into full view of the beautiful old white house standing behind its green trees and terraces and lawns. The children had never imagined anything so stately and fine, and even Susan Ellen exclaimed with pleasure. At that moment they saw an old gentleman, who carried himself with great dignity, coming slowly down the wide box-bordered path toward the gate.

"There he is now, there's the judge!"

whispered John Hilton excitedly, reining his horse quickly to the green roadside. "He's goin' down-town to his office; we can wait right here an' see him. I can't expect him to remember me; it's been a good many years. Now you are goin' to see the great Judge Masterson!"

There was a quiver of expectation in their hearts. The judge stopped at his gate, hesitating a moment before he lifted the latch, and glanced up the street at the country wagon with its two prim little girls on the back seat, and the eager man who drove. They seemed to be waiting for something; the old horse was nibbling at the fresh roadside grass. The judge was used to being looked at with interest, and responded now with a smile as he came out to the sidewalk, and unexpectedly turned their way. Then he suddenly lifted his hat with grave politeness, and came directly toward them.

"Good-morning, Mr. Hilton," he said. "I am very glad to see you, sir"; and Mr. Hilton, the little girls' own father, took off his hat with equal courtesy, and bent forward to shake hands.

Susan Ellen cowered and wished herself away, but little Katy sat straighter than ever, with joy in her father's pride and pleasure shining in her pale, flowerlike little face.

"There are your daughters, I am sure," said the old gentleman kindly, taking Susan Ellen's limp and reluctant hand; but when he looked at Katy, his face brightened. "How she recalls your mother," he said with great feeling. "I am glad to see this dear child. You must come to see me with your father, my dear," he added, still looking at her. "Bring both the little girls, and let them run about the old garden; the cherries are just getting ripe," said Judge Masterson hospitably. "Perhaps you will have time to stop this afternoon as you go home?"

"I should call it a great pleasure if you would come and see us again some time. You may be driving our way, sir," said John Hilton.

"Not very often in these days," answered the old judge. "I thank you for the kind invitation. I should like to see the fine view again from your hill westward. Can I serve you in any way while you are in town? Good-by, my little friends!"

Then they parted, but not before Katy, the shy Katy, whose hand the judge still held unconsciously while he spoke, had reached forward as he had said good-by, and lifted her face to kiss him. She could not have told why, except that she felt drawn to something in the serious, worn face. For the first time in her life the child had felt the charm of manners; perhaps she owned a kinship between that which made him what he was, and the spark of nobleness and purity in her own simple soul. She turned again and again to look back at him as they drove away.

"Now you have seen one of the first

gentlemen in the country," said their father. "It was worth comin' twice as far" —but he did not say any more, nor turn as usual to look in the children's faces.

In the chief business street of Topham a great many country wagons like the Hiltons' were fastened to the posts, and there seemed to our holiday-makers to be a great deal of noise and excitement.

"Now I've got to do my errands, and we can let the horse rest and feed," said John Hilton. "I'll slip his headstall right off, an' put on his halter. I'm goin' to buy him a real good treat o' oats. First we'll go an' buy me my straw hat; I feel as if this one looked a little past to wear in Topham. We'll buy the things we want, an' then we'll walk all along the street, so you can look in the windows an' see the han'some things, same's your mother likes to. What was it mother told you about your shawls?"

"To take 'em off an' carry 'em over our arms," piped Susan Ellen, without comment, but in the interest of alighting and finding themselves afoot upon the pavement the shawls were forgotten. The children stood at the doorway of a shop while their father went inside, and they tried to see what the Topham shapes of bonnets were like, as their mother had advised them; but everything was exciting and confusing, and they could arrive at no decision. When Mr. Hilton came out with a hat in his hand to be seen in a better light, Katy whispered that she wished he would buy a shiny one like Judge Masterson's; but her father only smiled and shook his head, and said that they were plain folks, he and Katy. There were dry-goods for sale in the same shop, and a young clerk who was measuring linen kindly pulled off some pretty labels with gilded edges and gay pictures, and gave them to the little girls, to their exceeding joy. He may have had small sisters at home, this friendly lad, for he took pains to find two pretty blue boxes besides, and was rewarded by their beaming gratitude.

It was a famous day; they even became

used to seeing so many people pass. The village was full of its morning activity, and Susan Ellen gained a new respect for her father, and an increased sense of her own consequence, because even in Topham several persons knew him and called him familiarly by name. The meeting with an old man who had once been a neighbor seemed to give Mr. Hilton the greatest pleasure. The old man called to them from a house doorway as they were passing, and they all went in. The children seated themselves wearily on the wooden step, but their father shook his old friend eagerly by the hand, and declared that he was delighted to see him so well and enjoying the fine weather.

"Oh, yes," said the old man, in a feeble, quavering voice, "I'm astonishin' well for my age. I don't complain, John, I don't complain."

They talked long together of people whom they had known in the past, and Katy, being a little tired, was glad to rest, and sat still with her hands folded, looking about the front yard. There were some kinds of flowers that she never had seen before.

"This is the one that looks like my mother," her father said, and touched Katy's shoulder to remind her to stand up and let herself be seen. "Judge Masterson saw the resemblance; we met him at his gate this morning."

"Yes, she certain does look like your mother, John," said the old man, looking pleasantly at Katy, who found that she liked him better than at first. "She does, certain; the best of young folks is, they remind us of the old ones. 'T is nateral to cling to life, folks say, but for me, I git impatient at times. Most everybody's gone now, an' I want to be goin'. 'T is somethin' before me, an' I want to have it over with. I want to be there 'long o' the rest o' the folks. I expect to last quite a while though; I may see ye couple o' times more, John."

John Hilton responded cheerfully, and

the children were urged to pick some flowers. The old man awed them with his impatience to be gone. There was such a townful of people about him, and he seemed as lonely as if he were the last survivor of a former world. Until that moment they had felt as if everything were just beginning.

"Now I want to buy somethin' pretty for your mother," said Mr. Hilton, as they went soberly away down the street, the children keeping fast hold of his hands. "By now the old horse will have eat his dinner and had a good rest, so pretty soon we can jog along home. I'm goin' to take you round by the academy, and the old North Meeting-house where Dr. Barstow used to preach. Can't you think o' somethin' that your mother'd want?" he asked suddenly, confronted by a man's difficulty of choice.

"She was talkin' about wantin' a new pepper-box, one day; the top o' the old one won't stay on," suggested Susan Ellen, with delightful readiness. "Can't we have some candy, father?"

"Yes, ma'am," said John Hilton, smiling and swinging her hand to and fro as they walked. "I feel as if some would be good myself. What's all this?" They were passing a photographer's doorway with its enticing array of portraits. "I do declare!" he exclaimed excitedly, "I'm goin' to have our pictures taken; 't will please your mother more'n a little."

This was, perhaps, the greatest triumph of the day, except the delightful meeting with the judge; they sat in a row, with the father in the middle, and there was no doubt as to the excellence of the likeness. The best hats had to be taken off because they cast a shadow, but they were not missed, as their owners had feared. Both Susan Ellen and Katy looked their brightest and best; their eager young faces would forever shine there; the joy of holiday was mirrored in the little picture. They did not know why their father was so pleased with it; they would not know until age had dowered them with the riches of association and remembrance.

Just at nightfall the Hiltons reached home again, tired out and happy. Katy had climbed over into the front seat beside her father, because that was always her place when they went to Church on Sundays. It was a cool evening, there was a fresh sea wind that brought a light mist with it, and the sky was fast growing cloudy. Somehow the children looked different; it seemed to their mother as if they had grown older and taller since they went away in the morning, and as if they belonged to the town now as much as to the country. The greatness of their day's experience had left her far behind; the day had been silent and lonely without them, and she had had their supper ready, and been watching anxiously, ever since five o'clock. As for the children themselves they had little to say at first—they had eaten their luncheon early on the way to Topham. Susan Ellen was childishly cross, but Katy was pathetic and wan. They could hardly wait to show the picture, and their mother was as much pleased as everybody had expected.

"There, what did make you wear your shawls?" she exclaimed a moment afterward, reproachfully. "You ain't been an' wore 'em all day long? I wanted folks to see how pretty your new dresses was, if I

did make 'em. Well, well! I wish more'n ever now I'd gone an' seen to ye!"

"An' here's the pepper-box!" said Katy, in a pleased, unconscious tone.

"That really is what I call beautiful," said Mrs. Hilton, after a long and doubtful look. "Our other one was only tin. I never did look so high as a chiny one with flowers, but I can get us another any time for every day. That's a proper hat, as good as you could have got, John. Where's your new hoe?" she asked as he came toward her from the barn, smiling with satisfaction.

"I declare to Moses if I didn't forget all about it," meekly acknowledged the leader of the great excursion. "That an' my yellow turnip seed, too; they went clean out o' my head, there was so many other things to think of. But 't ain't no sort o' matter; I can get a hoe just as well to Ira Speed's."

His wife could not help laughing. "You an' the little girls have had a great time. They was full o' wonder to me about everything, and I expect they'll talk about it for a week. I guess we was right about havin' 'em see somethin' more o' the world."

"Yes," answered John Hilton, with humility, "yes, we did have a beautiful day. I didn't expect so much. They looked as nice as anybody, and appeared so modest an' pretty. The little girls will remember

it perhaps by an' by. I guess they won't never forget this day they had 'long o' father."

It was evening again, the frogs were piping in the lower meadows, and in the woods, higher up the great hill, a little owl began to hoot. The sea air, salt and heavy, was blowing in over the country at the end of the hot bright day. A lamp was lighted in the house, the happy children were talking together, and supper was waiting. The father and mother lingered for a moment outside and looked down over the shadowy fields; then they went in, without speaking. The great day was over, and they shut the door.

The woman who wrote this story

SARAH ORNE JEWETT 1849–1909

Sarah Orne Jewett was born in the village of South Berwick, Maine. She traveled in Europe and spent much time in Boston, but South Berwick was her lifelong home and she always returned there to write.

This village and the people who lived in it became the subject matter of many of her stories. Many of the people she met while visiting patients with her doctor-father were recreated as story characters. Miss Jewett was a regionalist—a writer whose stories have their roots in a place and a way of life.

Her formal schooling was irregular. Her real education came from reading English and continental novelists in her father's library. These writers influenced Miss Jewett's own style when she began to write. Her first story appeared in *The Atlantic Monthly* magazine in 1869, when she was only twenty years old. At frequent intervals other stories and many sketches were published in the same magazine. From time to time they were collected in book form. Her best writing has been called "a miracle in pastel shades."

Let's consider . . .

1. What loss had the Hiltons suffered? Why were they reconciled to it? How did the opening conversation between husband and wife set the tone for the story and prepare you to meet the little girls?

2. Katy was evidently a Hilton and close to her father's side of the family; Susan Ellen favored her mother, but was —herself. What were some of the differences in the make-up of these two girls? Give instances to show how each resembled a particular parent.

3. John Hilton wanted his girls "to know the world, an' not stay right here on the farm like a couple o' bushes." What represented "the world" for him? Describe the little world into which he took his girls for a treat.

4. Mr. and Mrs. Hilton had different ways of looking at several things: their children's future, purchases for the farm, "kickshaws to fetch home," and "trapesin' off to strange places." Explain how the parents differed in their views of these matters.

5. Mr. Hilton thought Katy might be a teacher. What evidence is there in the story that she was interested in teaching? Do you think she would make a good teacher? Give your reasons.

6. Mrs. Hilton thought Susan Ellen would certainly get married and settle down. What do you think?

7. When the Hilton girls reached Topham Corners, what feature of the day's pleasure do you think impressed Katy most? Which impressed Susan Ellen? Which do you think you would have enjoyed?

8. Why do you think Mr. Hilton was rather glad his wife stayed at home?

9. John Hilton forgot his hoe and his seed. What did that indicate about him and about the holiday?

10. What was typical of the period and of Mrs. Hilton in her attitude toward the new pepper box?

11. What do you think the Hiltons' holiday did for them all? Why was it truly a "Time to Enjoy"?

The writer's craft . . .

You recall that style is a writer's distinctive manner of using language. In well-written prose, the content (*what* is being said) and the style (*how* it is said) are so completely blended that the final effect on the reader is a single impression. To change either content or style would automatically alter the final effect. For example, if a writer used breezy, lighthearted language to present a dignified spiritual message, the effect on the reader would not be serious; such writing would probably strike him as funny. The careful stylist will search long and hard to find the *right* word—the word that conveys the exact meaning and effect he intended. Thus, the style and content of his writing complement each other.

Sarah Orne Jewett's writing is a perfect illustration of the successful fusion of style and content. "The Hiltons' Holiday" is a quiet story. It has neither great suspense, nor fast-moving action. The setting, characters, plot, and style are fused to form a simple, tender narrative.

1. Suppose you had to find the "right word" to describe each character in this story. Look back over the story, especially at the statements of the characters. List your "right" words and discuss them in class.

2. Miss Jewett was especially careful to have the dialogue in her stories represent, as nearly as possible, the language which her characters would use. Notice the old-fashioned language in such expressions as "they beseeched me," or "so be they." Notice the words and expressions which were typical of rural people around 1890: "I'm proper glad," "I declare," or "call into" a cousin's house. And then notice the spelling of certain words to suggest the sound: "Wa'n't it dark gittin' home" or "your goin' an' buyin' a new hoe o' anybody but him." Find several other examples of each of these three characteristics of the dialogue in this story. Discuss your examples in class.

3. The writer of a good prose style is keenly aware of the sound and rhythm of language. If he uses these successfully, they not only fall pleasantly on the ear of his reader but also contribute to the total impression made by the piece of writing. Read the opening paragraph of "The Hiltons' Holiday" aloud. Notice especially the graceful rhythm of the language. How did this quality of the author's style create the tone and pace for the entire story? Select another paragraph in which the sounds of the language help create this quiet tone. Practice reading this paragraph softly to yourself and then read it aloud to the class.

Knowing words . . .

Rewrite each of the following sentences substituting one of the synonyms from the list for each italicized word.

greatness   tied
sorrowful   continual
          solemn

1. Now and then one could hear the *plaintive* chirp of a bird.

2. There was an *incessant* sound of frogs in the lowlands.

3. Just then an elderly woman saw the wagon and the *sedate* party it carried.

4. The *magnitude* of the plan for taking a whole day of pleasure confronted him seriously.

5. The young dog, *tethered* to the lilac-bush, was frantic with piteous appeals.

NOW THINK BACK

1. There are many ways to learn about people: from the way they live and dress, and from the way they earn a living. You can also learn about them from the way they spend their leisure time. What do Americans consider A TIME TO ENJOY? List all the enjoyable experiences mentioned in this part.

2. What difference did you find in this part between the pleasures described by poets and those described by prose writers? What reasons can you give to explain these differences?

3. Contrast the Hiltons' holiday with Frederick Lewis Allen's week-end visit. Consider the kind of enjoyments and experiences offered, the people involved, and their attitudes toward the experiences. Why did the Hiltons find so much enjoyment and Allen so little?

4. William Lyon Phelps believed that "the happiest person is the person who thinks the most interesting thoughts." In what ways were the ideas Phelps expressed in "Happiness" similar to the ideas expressed by Parker in *Pigeons and People?* In what ways were they different?

5. In your opinion, what radio or television entertainer comes nearest to being the Will Rogers of today? In what ways does he measure up to Rogers? In what ways does he fall short?

6. Margaret Caskey mentioned ten different *kinds* of words she liked. From four or five poems in this part, identify at least *one* word according to each of her classes. "Words that tinkle," "Solemn words," etc.

7. Consider all the different pleasures described in this part. Which one would you like to try? Tell what you would do and what kind of enjoyment you would get from doing it.

Things to do . . .

1. Imagine that a foreign boy or girl your own age had come to America for a year of travel and enjoyment. If you were asked to recommend various leisure-time activities or kinds of entertainment, which ones would you suggest? Which would your foreign guest enjoy as a participant? (You can assume that he or she would be willing to learn if the skill required were not too difficult.) Which would he or she enjoy as a spectator?

Choose one activity and one kind of entertainment you would like to recommend to this foreign boy or girl. Prepare a five-minute talk in which you explain (1) what the activity and the entertainment are, (2) why you think a foreign boy or girl would enjoy them, and (3) why many Americans enjoy them.

2. When people enjoy certain activities or entertainments, they sometimes overlook other equally enjoyable ways of spending their leisure time. Right now you may be limited in what you can do by a lack of funds or by the opportunities for enjoyment available in your community. However, you will soon be earning your own money and be free to travel.

In the Sunday editions of many large-city newspapers you will find a fairly complete coverage of most of the activities and entertainments which appeal to Americans. Don't overlook the sports section, the theater section, or the travel advertisements. Note, too, that gardening, stamp collecting, and bridge are popular leisure-time activities.

Make a list of all the different kinds of activities and entertainments which you can find in a Sunday newspaper. As you discuss your lists in class, you may be able to arrive at some general observations about what Americans like to do and why. Which do you think most Americans prefer to be: participants or spectators? Have leisure-time activities become too commercialized? Would Americans be happier if they returned to some of the simpler enjoyments of a hundred or two hundred years ago? These are just a few of the questions you might try to answer as you evaluate the idea of "enjoyment" as it is featured in a Sunday newspaper.

3. Prepare for a poetry-reading day. Read aloud one poem from this part or read one of your own choice. In your oral interpretation, try to convey the mood of the poem; for example, the silence of the snow which the poet captured so beautifully in "Velvet Shoes."

4. Perhaps your ideas about enjoyment may have been changed by reading A TIME TO ENJOY. Test yourself by comparing your present attitude and your past attitude toward one kind of entertainment you particularly enjoy: television, radio, travel, sports, reading, doing things with others. Explain what you find enjoyable and why. Also point out any changes in your attitude toward what is enjoyable that may be due to your reading of this part.

5. As young people become more mature, they develop certain standards by which to evaluate their leisure-time activities. They stop to consider whether the return in enjoyment is worth the cost in money, time, and energy. They also consider whether an experience will contribute to their growth as interesting and respected people. As a class, draw up a set of standards you could apply to many of your leisure-time activities.

More to read . . .

Showboat by EDNA FERBER.
  Grossett and Dunlap, Inc., 1928.
Opera Ballerina by MARIE-JEANNE.
  Dodd, Mead & Company, 1948.
Go Fight City Hall by ETHEL ROSENBERG.
  Simon and Schuster, Inc., 1949.
The Education of Hyman Kaplan by LEONARD Q. ROSS.
  Harcourt, Brace and Company, 1937.

The Year the Yankees Lost the Pennant by DOUGLAS WALLOP.
  W. W. Norton and Co., Inc., 1954.
New Guide to Better Photography by BERENICE ABBOTT.
  Crown Publishers, Inc., 1953.
Gertrude Lawrence as Mrs. A: An intimate biography of a great star by RICHARD STODDARD ALDRICH.
  Greystone Press, 1954.
Treadmill to Oblivion by FRED ALLEN.
  Little, Brown and Company, 1954.
Benchley Beside Himself by ROBERT C. BENCHLEY.
  Harper & Brothers, 1943.
Native American Humor 1800–1900 by WALTER BLAIR.
  American Book Company, 1937.
How to Ride your Hobby by ARCHIE FREDERICK COLLINS.
  Appleton-Century-Crofts, Inc., 1935.
Power Tennis by MAUREEN CONNOLLY.
  Barnes & Noble, Inc., 1954.
Out of the Blue by JOHN CROSBY.
  Simon and Schuster, Inc., 1952.
Hollywood Saga by WILLIAM DeMILLE.
  E. P. Dutton & Co., Inc., 1939.
Enjoyment of Laughter by MAX EASTMAN.
  Simon and Schuster, Inc., 1936.
Start Golf Young by DOUGLAS FORD.
  Sterling Publishing Co., Inc., 1955.
The Rise of the American Film by LEWIS JACOBS.
  Harcourt, Brace and Company, 1939.
Clown by EMMET KELLY.
  Prentice-Hall, Inc., 1954.
Film and Theatre by ALLARDYCE NICOLL.
  Thomas Y. Crowell Company, 1936.
American Humor by CONSTANCE ROURKE.
  Harcourt, Brace and Company, 1931.
Our Hearts Were Young and Gay by CORNELIA OTIS SKINNER and EMILY KIMBROUGH.
  Dodd, Mead & Company, 1942.
The Thurber Carnival by JAMES G. THURBER.
  Harper & Brothers, 1945.
Creative Hobbies by HARRY ZARCHY.
  Alfred A. Knopf, Inc., 1953.

AMERICANS AND THE WORLD

In terms of years, America is a comparatively young member of the world family of nations. In terms of power and influence, she has achieved a position of leadership.

By the middle of the nineteenth century, America was already making herself known. Washington Irving won recognition abroad among European writers. Edgar Allan Poe was "discovered" in France. Emerson lectured for several months to British audiences, and Hawthorne recorded his reactions to English life in a book entitled *Our Old Home*. Also during this period, peoples from both Europe and Asia were coming to America. Some, like Dickens and Thackeray—well-known English authors—came to lecture and returned to write essays and commentaries on American life. Others came to be a part of that life and what it offered in economic, political, and religious freedom. Through hard work, thrift, and ambition, these immigrants established homes and became a vital force in the role this country was to play in world affairs.

By the twentieth century, the world was growing "smaller." Modern inventions in transportation and communication broke down the barriers of time and distance. Two devastating world wars brought the peoples of many nations closer together in their common struggle for freedom. Americans began to travel to all parts of the world in the interest of science, industry, education, economic relief, rehabilitation, and social justice. Wherever they went, they took something of America with them and brought back a better understanding of other peoples.

AMERICANS AND THE WORLD

Home Founding

O. E. RÖLVAAG

The dream of actually owning a stretch of beautiful land filled the Norwegian immigrant Per Hansa with exaltation. With his family he crossed
the empty prairies and settled in the Dakota territory. Like immigrants
from the world over, he came to America to find a home.

I

On the side of a hill, which sloped gently
away toward the southeast and followed
with many windings a creek that wormed
its way across the prairie, stood Hans Olsa,
laying turf. He was building a sod house.
The walls had now risen breast-high; in its
half-finished condition, the structure resembled more a bulwark against some enemy than anything intended to be a human
habitation. And the great heaps of cut sod,
piled up in each corner, might well have
been the stores of ammunition for defence
of the stronghold.

For a man of his strength and massive
build, his motions were unusually quick
and agile; but he worked by fits and starts
today. At times he stopped altogether; in
these pauses he would straighten himself
up and draw his sleeve with a quick stroke
across his troubled face; with each stroke
the sleeve would come away damper; and

standing so, he would fix his gaze intently
on the prairie to the eastward. His eyes
had wandered so often now over the
stretch of land lying before them, that they
were familiar with every tussock and hollow. . . . No—nothing in sight yet! . . .
He would resume his task, as if to make
up for lost time, and work hard for a spell;
only to forget himself once more, pause involuntarily, and stand inert and abstracted,
gazing off into the distance.

Beyond the house a tent had been
pitched; a wagon was drawn up close beside it. On the ground outside of the tent
stood a stove, a couple of chairs, and a few
other rough articles of furniture. A stout,
healthy-looking woman, whose face radiated an air of simple wisdom and kindliness, was busy preparing the midday meal.
She sang to herself as she worked. A ten-
year-old girl, addressed by the woman as
Sofie, was helping her. Now and then the

girl would take up the tune and join in the singing.

Less than a quarter of a mile away, in a southeasterly direction, a finished sod house rose on the slope of the hill. Smoke was winding up from it at this moment. This house, which had been built the previous fall, belonged to Syvert Tönseten.

Some distance north from the place where Hans Olsa had located, two other sod houses were under construction; but a hillock lay between, so that he could not see them from where he stood. There the two Solum boys had driven down their stakes and had begun building. Tönseten's completed house, and the other three half-finished ones, marked the beginning of the settlement on Spring Creek.

The woman who had been bustling about preparing the meal, now called to her husband that dinner was ready—he must come at once! He answered her, straightened up for the hundredth time, wiping his hands on his trousers, and stood for a moment gazing off eastward. . . . No use to look—not a soul in sight yet! . . . He sighed heavily, and walked with slow steps toward the tent, his eyes on the ground.

It was light and airy inside the tent, but stifling hot, because of the unobstructed sunlight beating down upon it. Two beds were ranged along the wall, both of them homemade; a big emigrant chest stood at the head of each. Nails had been driven into the centre pole of the tent, on which hung clothing; higher up a crosspiece, securely fastened, was likewise hung with clothes. Two of the walls were lined with furniture; on these pieces the dishes were displayed, all neatly arranged.

A large basin of water stood on a chair just inside the tent door. Hans Olsa washed his face and hands; then he came out and sat down on the ground, where his wife had spread the table. It was so much cooler outside. The meal was all ready; both mother and daughter had been waiting for him.

"I suppose you haven't seen any signs of them yet?" his wife asked at last.

"No—nothing at all!"

"Can you imagine what has become of them?"

"The Lord forgive us—if I only knew!"

Her husband looked so anxious that she asked no more questions. Out of her kind heart rose a hopeful, "Don't worry, they'll get here all right!" . . . But in spite of the cheerfulness of the words, she could not give them that ring of buoyant confidence which she would have liked to show.

. . . "Of course!" said the girl with a laugh. "Store-Hans [1] and Ola have two good pairs of eyes. Leave it to them—they'll find us!"

The father gave her a stern glance; he didn't tell her in words to stop her foolish chatter—but she said no more. Without speaking once, he ate his dinner. As soon as he had finished, he tossed his spoon on the blanket, thanked them for the food, got up gloomily, and went back to the half-completed wall. There he sat down awhile, as if lost in thought . . . gazing eastward. His large, rugged features were drawn and furrowed with anxiety. . . . He sighed, and folded his big hands. "What can have become of Per Hansa?"

His wife was watching him closely as he sat there on the wall. By and by she told her daughter to finish washing the dishes, and started to go over where he was. When he saw her coming, he tried to begin working as if there were nothing on his mind.

"Hans," she said, quickly, when she had reached his side, "I think you ought to go out and look for them!"

He waited until he had got a strip of sod in place before he answered: "Easier said than done . . . when we haven't the faintest idea where to look . . . on such stretches of prairie!"

"Yes, I know; but it would make us all feel better, anyway . . . as if we were doing something."

---

[1] *Store-Hans,* **Big Hans**

Hans Olsa laid another strip of turf; then he stopped, let his hands fall to his sides, and began thinking aloud as he gazed off into the distance. . . .

"I know this much—you don't often find a smarter fellow than Per Hansa. . . . That's what makes it so queer! I don't suppose he's able to get much speed out of his oxen; but one thing I'm certain of—he has been hurrying as fast as he could. And we surely didn't come along very fast . . . but now it's the fifth day since we arrived here! If he made use of these bright moonlight nights, as he probably did, I begin to be afraid that he's gone on west of us somewhere, instead of being still to the eastward. . . . It's certainly no child's play to start looking for him!"

Hans Olsa slumped down on the wall, the picture of dejection. His wife quickly found a place beside him. Together they sat there in silence. The same fear that she felt him struggling with, a fear thrown into sharp relief by the things he had just been saying, had long since gripped her heart also.

"I feel so sorry for Beret, poor thing . . . and the children. You must remember, though, that he couldn't go very fast on account of her condition. . . . I think she is with child again!" She paused. "I dreamed about them last night . . . a bad dream. . . ."

Her husband glanced sidewise at her. "We musn't pay attention to such things. A bad dream is a good sign, anyway—that's what my mother always said. . . . But I suppose I'll never forgive myself for not waiting for him." He got up heavily and laid another strip of turf. "He's always been like that, Per Hansa; he never would take help from any man. But this time he's carried it a little too far!"

His wife made no answer. She was watching a short stout man with a reddish beard who had started up the slope from the direction of the house to the south of them. He had cheeks like two rosy apples, a quick step, and eyes that flitted all about;

he was noted among them for his glib tongue and the flood of his conversation. With hands stuck into the waistband of his trousers, and elbows out akimbo, the man looked half as broad again as he really was.

"Here comes Tönseten," said the woman. "Why don't you talk it over with him? I really think you ought to go out and look for them."

"Seen anything of them yet, Hans Olsa?" asked the man, without further greeting, as soon as he arrived. . . . "Well, well! this looks fine! Ha, ha! It's a warm house, you know, that's built by the aid of a woman's hand."

Hans Olsa wheeled on him. "You haven't caught sight of them yourself, Syvert, have you?"

"Caught sight of them? Why, man alive, that's just what I've come up here to tell you! I've had them in sight for over an hour now. Seems to me you ought to be able to see them easy enough—you who carry your eyes so high up in the air! . . . It won't be long before they arrive here, at the rate they're coming!"

"What's that you say?" the others burst out with one voice. . . . "Where are they?". . .

"I reckon Per Hansa must have got off his course a little. Maybe the oxen didn't steer well, or maybe he didn't figure the current right. . . . Look to the westward, neighbours! Look over there about west-northwest, and you'll see him plain enough. . . . No need to worry. That fellow never would drown in such shallow water as this! . . . I wonder, now, how far west he's really been?"

Hans Olsa and his wife faced around in the direction that Tönseten had indicated. Sure enough, out of the west a little caravan was crawling up toward them on the prairie.

"Can that be them? . . . I really believe it is!" said Hans Olsa in a half whisper, as if hardly daring yet to give vent to his joy.

"*Of course* it is!" cried his wife, excitedly . . . "Thank God!"

"Not the least doubt of it," Tönseten assured them. "You might as well go and put your coffeepot on the stove, Mother Sörrina! That Kjersti [2] of mine is coming over pretty soon; she'll probably have something good tucked under her apron. . . . In half an hour we'll have the lost sheep back in the fold!"

"Yes! Heavens and earth, Sörrina!" cried Hans Olsa, "fetch out the best you've got! . . . Per, Per, is it really you, old boy? . . . But why are you coming from the west, I'd like to know?"

Tönseten coughed, and gave the woman a sly wink.

"Look here, Mother Sörrina," he said with a twinkle in his eyes, "won't you be good enough, please, to take a peek at Hans Olsa's Sunday bottle? . . . Not that I want anything to drink, you understand—I should say not. But think of that poor woman out there, who has been suffering all this time without a drop! And I'd be willing to bet that Per Hansa wouldn't object to having his stomach warmed up a little, too!"

At that they burst out laughing, from mingled joy and relief; but Tönseten's laughter at his own joke was the loudest of all. . . . Work was resumed at once; Syvert began to carry the sods for Hans Olsa to lay up, while Mother Sörrina went off in a happy frame of mind, to make her preparations for the reception of the wanderers.

Before the half hour allotted by Tönseten had passed, the caravan came slowly crawling up the slope. Per Hansa still strode in the van,[3] with Store-Hans at his side; Ole walked abreast of the oxen, driving them with the goad. Beret and And-Ongen [4] sat in the wagon. Rosie came jogging along behind at her own gait; she gave a loud, prolonged "moo-o-o-o" as she discovered the other animals across the prairie.

Both families stood ready to receive them; Hans Olsa and Sörine, Tönseten and his Kjersti, all watching intently the movements of the approaching company; but the girl couldn't possess her patience any longer, and ran down to meet the new

---

[2] *Kjersti,* kyĕr'stĭ

[3] *van,* front

[4] *And-Ongen* (ănd-ôn'gĕn), "The Duckling," a pet name for Anna Marie

arrivals. She took Store-Hans by the hand and fell in beside him; the first question she asked was whether he hadn't been terribly scared at night? . . .

As the slope of the hill grew steeper, the oxen had to bend to the yoke.

"Hey, there, folks!" shouted Per Hansa, boisterously. "Don't be standing around loafing, now! It's only the middle of the afternoon. Haven't you got anything to do around here?"

"Coffee time, coffee time, Per Hansa . . . ha, ha, ha!" Tönseten was bubbling over with good spirits. "We thought we might as well wait a little while for you, you know."

. . . "You've found us at last!" said Hans Olsa, with a deep, happy chuckle. . . . He didn't seem able to let go of Per Hansa's hand.

"Found you? Why, devil take it, it's no trick to follow a course out here! You just have to keep on steering straight ahead. And you had marked the trail pretty well, all the way along. I found plenty of traces of you . . . I guess we stood a little too far to the westward, between Sioux Falls and here; that's how it happened. . . . So *this* is the place, is it? . . . The pastures of Goshen [5] in the land of Egypt—eh?"

"Just so, just so!" cried Tönseten, nodding and laughing. "Pastures of Goshen—right you are! That's exactly what we are going to call the place—*Goshen*—if only you haven't sailed in to mix things up for us!" . . .

Beret and the child had now got down from the wagon; the other two women hovered around her, drawing her toward the tent. But she hung back for a moment; she wanted to stop and look around.

. . . Was this the place? . . . *Here!* . . . Could it be possible? . . . She stole a glance at the others, at the half-completed hut, then turned to look more closely at the group standing around her; and suddenly it struck her that *here something was about*

[5] *Goshen,* the biblical land of plenty allotted to the Israelites in Egypt

to go wrong. . . . For several days she had sensed this same feeling; she could not seem to tear herself loose from the grip of it. . . . A great lump kept coming up in her throat; she swallowed hard to keep it back, and forced herself to look calm. Surely, surely, she musn't give way to her tears now, in the midst of all this joy. . . .

Then she followed the other two women into the tent; seeing a chair, she sank down in it, as if her strength had gone!

Sörine was patting her on the shoulder . . . "Come, get your things off, Beret. You ought to loosen up your clothes, you know. Just throw this dress of mine around you. . . . Here's the water to wash yourself in. Let down your hair, and take your time about it. . . . Don't mind Kjersti and me being around."

After they had bustled about for a little while the others left her. The moment they had gone she jumped up and crossed the tent, to look out of the door. . . . How will human beings be able to endure this place? she thought. Why, there isn't even a thing that one can *hide behind!* . . . Her sensitive, rather beautiful face was full of blank dismay; she turned away from the door and began to loosen her dress; then her eyes fell on the centre pole with its crosspiece, hung with clothes, and she stood a moment irresolute, gazing at it in startled fright. . . . It looked like the giants she had read about as a child; for a long while she was unable to banish the picture from her mind.

Outside the tent, Ole stood with his hand resting on one of the oxen. He was disgusted; the older people seemed to have clean forgotten his existence. They never would get done talking—when he, too, might have had a word to put in! . . .

"Hadn't we better unhitch the oxen, Dad?"

"Yes, yes—that's right, Ola. We might as well camp down here for the night, since we've run across some folks we used to know. . . . How about it, you fellows?" He turned to the other two. "I suppose there's a little more land left around here, isn't there, after you've got through?"

"*Land?* Per Hansa, what are you talking about? Take whatever you please, from here to the Pacific Ocean!" Tönseten's enthusiasm got so far away with him that he had to pull one of his hands out of his waistband and make a sweeping circle with it in the air.

"You must take a look around as soon as you can," Hans Olsa said, "and see if you find anything better that meets your fancy. In the meanwhile I've put down a stake for you on the quarter section that lies north of mine. We'll go over and have a look at it pretty soon. Sam Solum wanted it, but I told him he'd better leave it till you came. . . . You see, you would be next to the creek there; and then you and I would be the nearest neighbours, just as we've always planned. It makes no particular difference to Sam; he can take the quarter alongside his brother's."

Per Hansa drew a deep breath, as if filling himself with life's great goodness. . . . Here Hans Olsa had been worrying about him, and with kindly forethought had arranged everything to his advantage! . . . "Well, well, we'll have to settle all that later, Hans Olsa. For the present, I can only say that I'm deeply thankful to you! . . . Unhitch the beasts, there, Ola! . . . And now, if you folks have got anything handy, to either eat or drink, I'll accept it with pleasure."

. . . "Or *both,* Per Hansa!" put in Tönseten, excitedly.

"Yes, both, Syvert. I won't refuse!"

Soon they were all gathered around a white cloth which Mother Sörine had spread on the ground. On one side of it lay a whole leg of dried mutton; on the other a large heap of *flatbröd,*[6] with cheese, bread, and butter; in the centre of the cloth stood a large bowl of sweet milk, and from the direction of the stove the breeze wafted

to them a pleasant odour of fried bacon and strong coffee. Mother Sörine herself took charge of the ceremony, bringing the food and urging them all to sit down. The stocky figure of Per Hansa rocked back and forth in blissful delight as he squatted there with his legs crossed under him.

"Come, Sörrina, sit down!" he cried. "I guess we've fallen in with gentlefolks, by the looks of things around here . . . I suppose you think you're old Pharaoh [7] himself —eh, Hans Olsa?"

"Who do you call me, then?" inquired Tönseten.

"You, Syvert? Well, now, I really don't know what to say. Of course you'd like to be His Majesty's butler,[8] but you mustn't be encouraged—remember what happened to that poor fellow! . . . I think we'd better make you the baker [8]—it might be safer, all around. What's your idea, Hans Olsa?"

By this time they were all laughing together.

In the midst of the jollification came Sörine, carrying a plate with a large bottle and a dram glass on it. . . . "Here, take this off my hands, Hans Olsa—you will know what to do with it!"

Tönseten fairly bubbled over in his admiration for her:

"Oh, you sweet Sörrina-girl!—you're dearer to my heart than a hundred women! . . . What a blessing it must be, to have a wife like that!"

"Stop your foolishness!" said Kjersti, but her voice didn't sound too severe.

For a long while they continued to sit around the cloth, chatting, eating, and drinking, and thoroughly enjoying themselves. Hans Olsa seemed like a different man from the one who had eaten here at noon. His loud voice led the cheerful talk; his ponderous bulk was always the centre of the merriment; it seemed as if he would never tire of gazing into the bearded, roguish face of Per Hansa's.

---

[6] *flatbröd,* flat bread, a thin, dry Norwegian bread about three feet in diameter and made on the top of a special stove

[7] *Pharaoh,* a king of ancient Egypt

[8] *butler . . . baker,* references to the biblical story of Joseph

Once, as Per Hansa was slicing off a piece of mutton, he regarded the cut thoughtfully, and asked:

"I suppose you brought all your supplies through safe enough?"

"Oh, sure," answered Hans Olsa, innocently. "We had no trouble at all—didn't lose anything; that is, except for the leg that we left behind somewhere, east on the prairie. But that's hardly worth mentioning."

Per Hansa paused with the piece of meat halfway to his mouth, and looked at Sörine with an expression of deep concern:

"The devil you say! Did you lose one of your legs . . . ?"

Mother Sörine laughed heartily at him. "Oh no—not quite so bad as that. . . . But a leg of mutton might come in handy later on, I'll tell you; there aren't too many of them to be had around here."

Per Hansa chewed away on the meat and looked very serious. At last he said:

"That's always the way with folks who have more of the world's goods than they can take care. . . . But I'll promise you one thing, Sörrina: if I can get my old blunderbuss [9] to work, you're going to have your lost leg back again. . . . How about it, fellows? Have you seen any game that's fit to eat out here?"

II

They sat on until the first blue haze of evening began to spread eastward over the plain. The talk had now drifted to questions of a more serious nature, mostly concerned with how they should manage things out here; of their immediate prospects; of what the future might hold in store for them; of land and crops, and of the new kingdom which they were about to found. . . . No one put the thought into words, but they all felt it strongly; now they had gone back to the very beginning of things. . . .

[9] *blunderbuss,* an old-fashioned short musket

As the evening shadows deepened the conversation gradually died away into silence. A peculiar mood came drifting in with the dusk. It seemed to float on the evening breeze, to issue forth out of the heart of the untamed nature round about them; it lurked in the very vastness and endlessness surrounding them on every hand; it even seemed to rise like an impalpable mist out of the ground on which they sat.

This mood brought vague premonitions to them, difficult to interpret. . . . No telling what might happen out here . . . for almost anything *could* happen! . . .

They were so far from the world . . . cut off from the haunts of their fellow beings . . . so terribly far! . . .

The faces that gazed into one another were sober now, as silence claimed the little company; but lines of strength and determination on nearly every countenance told of an inward resolve to keep the mood of depression from gaining full control.

Per Hansa was the first to rouse himself and throw off the spell. He jumped up with nervous energy; a shiver passed over him, as if he were having a chill.

"What is it—are you cold?" asked his wife. She had instinctively sensed his mood as she looked at him—and loved him better for it. Until that moment, she had supposed that she herself was the only one who felt this peculiar influence.

"Such crazy talk!" he burst out. "I believe we've all lost our senses, every last one of us! Here we sit around celebrating in broad daylight, in the middle of summer, as if it was the Christmas holidays! . . . Come on, woman, let's go over to our new home!"

Everyone got up.

"You must do exactly as you please about it, Per Hansa," spoke up Hans Olsa with an apologetic air. "Don't feel that you must take this quarter if you don't like it. But as far as I can see, it's as good a piece of land as you could find anywhere around—every square foot of it plowland, except the hill over there. Plenty of water for both man and beast. . . . As for my part, if I can only sit here between you and Syvert, I certainly won't be kicking about my neighbours. . . . But I don't want you to feel that you have to take this quarter on my account, you understand. . . . If you do take it, though, we must get one of the Solum boys to go down to Sioux Falls with you the first thing to-morrow, so that you can file your claim. You'll have to do that in any case, you know, whichever quarter you take. . . . There's likely to be a lot of people moving into this region before the snow flies; we five oughtn't to part company or let anyone get in between us. . . . You've heard my best advice, anyway."

"Now, that's the talk!" Tönseten chimed in, briskly. "And considering the size of the head it comes from, it isn't half bad, either. You're right, Hans Olsa. Before the snow flies you're going to see such a multitude swarming around these parts, that the thundering place won't be fit to live in! Remember what I say, boys, in times to come—bear it in mind that those were Syvert's very words! . . . You've got to go straight to Sioux Falls to-morrow morning, Per Hansa, and no two ways about it! If one of the Solum boys can't go along to do the talking for you, why, I shall have to buckle down to the job myself."

Once more Per Hansa's heart filled with a deep sense of peace and contentment as he realized how matters were being smoothed out for him. They seemed to move of their own accord but he knew better. . . . Was he really to own it? Was it really to become his possession, this big stretch of fine land that spread here before him? Was he really to have his friends for neighbours, both to the north and to the south—folks who cared for him and wanted to help him out in every way? . . .

He was still chuckling with the rare pleasure of it as he asked, "You haven't discovered any signs of life since you came?"

"Devil, no!" Tönseten assured him.

"Neither Israelites [10] nor Canaanites! [10] I was the first one to find this place, you know. . . . But there's no telling how soon the drift will loosen, the way folks were talking back East last winter. And now the land office for this whole section of country has been moved to Sioux Falls, too. That means business; the government, you may be certain, has good reason for doing such a thing." Tönseten spoke with all the importance of a man who has inside knowledge.

Per Hansa looked at him, and a bantering tone came into his voice:

"I see it clearly. Syvert—it would never do to keep you around here as a mere baker! We'll have to promote you to a higher office, right away. . . . Now, boys, I'm going over to see this empire that you two have set aside for me. Ola, you hitch up the oxen again and bring the wagons along."

With these commands he walked rapidly away; the others had almost to run in order to keep up with him. Strong emotions surged through him as he strode on.

"It lies high," he observed after a while, when they had looked all the plowland over. . . . "There must be a fine view from the top of that hill."

They were bending their steps in this direction, and soon had reached the highest point. It seemed so spacious and beautiful to stand high above the prairie and look around, especially now, when the shades of evening were falling. . . . Suddenly Per Hansa began to step more cautiously; he sniffed the air like an animal; in a moment he stopped beside a small depression in the ground, and stood gazing at it intently for quite a while, then he said, quietly:

"There are people buried here. . . . That is a grave!"

"Oh no, Per Hansa! It can't be possible."

---

[10] *Israelites . . . Canaanites.* The Israelites were a nomadic Hebrew tribe in Palestine. The Canaanites lived in Canaan, the Promised Land where the Israelites eventually settled.

"No doubt about it," he said in the same subdued but positive tone.

Tönseten and Hans Olsa were so astonished that they could hardly credit the fact; they came over at once to where Per Hansa stood, and gazed down into the hollow.

Hans Olsa bent over and picked up a small stone that his eyes had lighted on; he turned it around in his hand several times. . . . "That's a queer-looking piece of stone! I almost believe people have shaped it for some use. . . . Here, see what you make of it, Syvert."

Tönseten's ruddy face grew sober and thoughtful as he examined the object.

"By thunder! It certainly looks as if the Indians had been here! . . . Now isn't that rotten luck?". . .

"I'm afraid so," said Per Hansa, with a vigorous nod. Then he added, sharply, "But we needn't shout the fact from the house-tops, you know! . . . It takes so very little to scare some folks around here."

He waited no longer but walked hastily down the hill; at the foot he called to Ole, telling him not to drive any farther; but first he turned to Hans Olsa to find out whether they were well across the line between the two quarters.

"No use in building farther away from you than is absolutely necessary," he said. "It's going to be lonesome for the womenfolks at times.". . .

. . . Awhile later, Tönseten was dragging his way homeward. For reasons that he wouldn't admit even to himself, he walked a good deal heavier now than when he had climbed the slope that afternoon.

Per Hansa returned with his other neighbour to the wagons, where Beret and the children were waiting. Again he inquired about the line between the two quarters; then asked Beret and Hans Olsa to help pick the best building place; his words, though few and soberly spoken, had in them an unmistakable ring of determination. . . . This vast stretch of beautiful land was to be *his*—and no ghost of a dead Indian would drive him away! . . . His heart began to expand with a mighty exaltation. An emotion he had never felt before filled him and made him walk erect. . . . "This kingdom is going to be *mine!*"

The man who wrote this selection

O. E. RÖLVAAG   1876–1931

The Homestead Act of 1862 provided that any man who would cultivate and care for 160 acres of land could have it free. Many oppressed European farmers came to America to "stake a claim" on this free land.

The Middle West attracted a large number of Norwegians. One of them, O. E. Rölvaag, saw the need for recording their pioneering story. He did so in novels written in his native language. These novels showed such a keen understanding and observation of all pioneers that some of them were translated into English.

While O. E. Rölvaag was writing his novels, he was teaching at St. Olaf College in Minnesota. He himself was graduated from there in 1905, after first working three years on his uncle's farm and attending Augustana College in South Dakota.

A critic has said of *Giants in the Earth,* his best known novel: "It is the fullest, finest, and most powerful novel that has been written about pioneer life in America." "Home Founding" is one of the central chapters of this novel.

Let's consider . . .

1. In this chapter from *Giants in the Earth* you met Hans Olsa, Syvert Tönseten, and Per Hansa. What traits distinguished each one?

2. Before Per Hansa arrived, his friends were anxious for his safety. What did this anxiety tell you about him and his friends?

3. There was great rejoicing when Per Hansa's caravan arrived. Describe its appearance. Why were his friends so happy?

4. What did the tent look like inside? Do you think Sörine was the type to make a successful pioneer wife? Explain.

5. Beret was different. What were her thoughts as the others chattered outside?

6. Hans Olsa had been thoughtful of Per Hansa while he awaited his coming. What had he done for him? What would Per Hansa have to do for himself?

7. How did the three men feel about their land? What hopes did they have for the settlement? On that first night, what misgivings crept into their hearts?

8. What meaning did the Indian grave have for these new settlers?

9. What characteristics did these Norwegians have which made you certain they would succeed in spite of hardships? What did you admire most in them?

The writer's craft . . .

Since no two languages are completely interchangeable, the task of translating from one language to another presents formidable problems. Most translators try to be faithful to the original author's intentions, but each translator must interpret that intention for himself. Thus variations and differences occur. However, this problem was partially solved in the translation of *Giants in the Earth* from Norwegian into English. The original author, O. E. Rölvaag, was on hand to help the translator. In his foreword to the book Rölvaag wrote, "The work of translating this novel has been a difficult task. The idiom of the characters offered serious problems. These settlers came from Nordland, Norway; and though the novel is written in one literary language of Norway, the speech of the characters themselves naturally had to be strongly colored by their native dialect;

otherwise their utterances would have sounded stilted and untrue. To get these people to reveal clearly and effectively their psychology in English speech seemed at times impossible; for the idioms of a dialect are well-nigh untranslatable."

The term **idiom** refers to the use of words in a way that is characteristic of a particular people, language, or region. All languages have idioms.

1. Discuss the meaning of the following idioms. Note that this meaning is quite different from the meaning of the separate words.

one foot in the grave	talking through your
fly into a rage	hat
a dime a dozen	get into a stew
stand your ground	watch your step
hot under the collar	

2. Make a class list of idioms as you hear them during the next few days. Don't confuse slang expressions with idioms. Slang is constantly changing and is usually used only by a small group. Idioms may have had their start as slang, but have been accepted as part of the spoken language.

Knowing words . . .

In describing Beret's actions Rölvaag wrote, "she stood for a moment irresolute." The word *irresolute* is formed by combining the root word *resolute,* meaning "firm" or "set in purpose," with the prefix *ir-,* a variation of the prefix *in-,* meaning "not." Thus *irresolute* means "not firm or set in purpose." Explain why Beret was irresolute.

In the following words, the prefix *ir-* is combined with root words beginning with the consonant *r.* If you do not know the meanings of the root words (without the prefix *ir-*) look them up in the dictionary. Then write a definition of each word as it appears with its prefix.

irregular	irrational
irresponsible	irresolute
irrelevant	irreligious

Talking Through My Hats

LILLY DACHÉ

Though Lilly Daché was but eighteen and could only write a few words of English, she was determined to come to America. After a few disheartening experiences in the new country, she thought that the whole venture might have been a mistake. However, she soon changed her mind and found herself saying, "This is the life. This is for me!"

At last it happened.

Somehow I was on my way to America. I did not quite know how. There had been tears and scenes and my mother had said no good would come of it. My father had said proper young ladies did not travel alone, especially across an entire ocean. My sister had said I would be an old maid.

I did not care. Always, it seemed, this itch had been inside of me. It was the same itch that made me order that bicycle cap, which so upset my mother and caused what you call the family crisis. But this was maybe ten years after that first hopeful start, when I was seven. Eleven years. For I was eighteen when I walked up the gangplank of the steamer at Boulogne, with all my hopes and fears churning inside of me, and a small case containing my most prized possessions clutched tightly in my hand.

I waved and waved to my sister standing on the dock and dabbing furtively at her eyes, and when the ship started I stood at the rail and watched the coast of France go farther and farther away, and I felt sad and happy all at once.

I did not have much money, for my good mother was still saving up for dowries for my other sisters. For me she had given up hope. What could you do, she said, with a daughter who had two left hands and red hair, and refused to stay at home and be a lady.

I was traveling second class, to save money, and it was a small, slow steamer. The trip took eleven days, I remember. And most of that time I sat in a deck chair and sewed, as all my training had taught me that it would be wicked to sit and do nothing for all that time. I had brought silks and laces and needles and thread along, and I stitched busily away making some dainty lingerie.

The people on board the ship were kind and jolly, and although I could speak no English, I made friends with many who spoke some French. I could read English and write it a little, and if people spoke slowly I could guess at what they said.

I enjoyed the meals aboard ship, for there were many things that we did not have so much at home. The oranges delighted me most. I formed a craving for the oranges, and some kind Red Cross people on board used to save their oranges from dessert and give them to me every day. This was wonderful, for in France we have few citrus fruits.

So I sat and sewed and ate my oranges and dreamed of America, the land of skyscrapers and automobiles and bright, shiny wonders. I had big hopes of this new land, even though I could not speak the language. I would soon learn English conversation, I told myself. I would do wonderful things and become rich and famous. I would go home to France someday and buy fur coats for all the family. And I would say to my mother:

"I earned these with my two left hands."

So the days slipped by, and it was at last the morning that we were to dock, and I stood at the rail with the other passengers and saw the Statue of Liberty all shadowy and mysterious in the fog, but with a special promise for me. There was a lump in my throat as I strained my eyes to see the skyline of New York.

When the ship docked, I moved slowly down the gangplank with the crowd, waving good-by to some of my shipboard acquaintances, and then as my feet touched solid earth I looked eagerly about me. This was it. This was finally America.

But somehow it did not seem like the New York of which I had dreamed so long. I looked for the skyscrapers. No skyscrapers. I looked for the fashionable crowds. No fashion. I said to the customs official, who was looking at my bags and who spoke some French:

"Where are the skyscrapers?"

He looked at me and grinned. He said:

"Girly, this is Hoboken!"

I was panicky. There must be some awful mistake. Perhaps I had taken the wrong ship, and landed in some strange land.

"Not New York?" I whispered.

"Not New York. The big town is across the river. Some of the ships dock on this side. It's O.K. The big town's only a ten-minute ferry ride away. You might see a skyscraper if you look over that way, but the fog's pretty thick this morning."

I had printed directions with me. I was to go to visit a cousin, who lived in a strange place called Burlington, New Jersey. I did not know where Burlington was, or how to get there. There was no one to meet me. My last letter must have been lost, I thought. My cousin must not have known when I was coming. I would have to find the way by myself.

First I showed the directions to the customs man, who was a jolly kind of person. It had my cousin's name and address on it. He called a porter and told him to carry my bags and put them and me safely aboard the correct train for Burlington.

The porter said it was yet an hour before my train would leave. I would have time to have breakfast if I liked, he said. He pointed across the street to a small place that was shaped like a railroad car with a big sign above it which said "EATS—JOE'S DINER." I should go there, he said, and then come back and he would take me to my train.

I was puzzled by that sign "EATS," but I went, because I was hungry. Inside was a long counter, and a smell of frying fat. I sat on a stool and a waitress asked me what I would have.

"Would you like some sweet potatoes, dearie?" she asked. "They're a specialty of the house."

She pointed to the words on the menu.

Sweet potatoes? I shook my head with emphasis. I did not eat sugar on potatoes.

Perhaps, I thought, this was a strange American custom. But just yet, I did not want to try it. I settled for ham and eggs, the national dish, which I still love.

Then I returned to the dock, found my bags and my porter, and was guided to the train for Burlington.

This was easy. Travel, I told myself, was really simple.

I settled myself in my seat on the train, with my bags and bundles around me. I tipped the porter and said:

"*Merci bien.*"[1]

Then I looked around.

It was not a pretty train. It needed to be scrubbed. The seats were dusty red plush and the windows were so dirty I could hardly see through them. But I was still

---

[1] *Merci bien,* Thank you [*French*]

full of excitement and happiness because at last I was here, and I did not start getting depressed right then.

It was later, after the train started and went rattling across flat, gray swamps that my bubbling-over feeling began to go flat, like champagne that has stood too long. I looked so eagerly out the dusty window, and all I could see was a gray, ugly land with bare factories here and there, and no trees or skyscrapers anywhere.

There must be some mistake, I thought uneasily. This couldn't be America—not the America I had heard about and pictured.

The people on the train did not look rich or fashionable, either. They did not laugh as much as French families would when they were going on a holiday trip. But perhaps this was not a holiday for these Americans. Perhaps they were just going home, or maybe to a funeral. So I said to myself.

After a while—it seemed a long time to me—the conductor called:

"Burlington!"

I gathered up my bags and packages and got off the train, and I thought:

"Now maybe it will be better. Perhaps I will see the skyscrapers now and all the fashionable people. Perhaps my cousin will be here to meet me and she will show me the real America."

But no.

No cousin, no skyscrapers. No fashionable people. Only four old men leaning against the station, which was painted a mud color, and the paint was peeling off. The station was in the middle of the street, which looked like the main street of the town, and the tracks went down the middle of this street, too. It was strange. Never had I seen a railroad as the chief attraction of a village before. The conductor called, "All aboard!" and swung back on the train steps, and the train rattled off down the street, and there I was, alone in a strange land with my bags, and not even one skyscraper in sight.

It was then that I thought perhaps my mother and my father and my sisters and my brother had all been right, and I was wrong. Perhaps I should never have come to America—if this was America, which I doubted.

I wanted to sit down in the middle of the dusty platform and scream. I felt the tears coming, and I shook my head to clear them away. I looked at the four old men, and they stared back, like four old owls, and nobody said one word.

I fished in my purse, to find the envelope with my cousin's name and address, dropping some of my packages. When I stooped to pick them up I knocked my so-beautiful Paris hat over one eye.

I could see, too, that my skirts, which were up to my knees, looked much too short, and my high-heeled French shoes looked somehow wicked. I do not know why. There is nothing really wicked about French heels. But from the way those four old men looked at me, I knew that was what they were thinking.

I went up to the nearest one and held out the envelope. I could not speak a word. My throat was too choked to make a sound. So I pointed to the envelope and looked a question.

The old man studied the envelope, lifted his hat and scratched his head. He said:

"This where you want to go, sister?"

I nodded, and he turned to the others and said loudly:

"Furriner, I reckon. Can't talk."

Then he shouted at me, as if I were deaf:

"Why'n't they meet you? They expectin' you?"

I could only shake my head, and that made the tears spill over.

"Now, now, don't cry, sister," the old man said, quick. "Reckon they didn't get your letter in time, maybe. It says here, High Street. That's it, right there. House is about two blocks down. Can't miss it. White house, with a brick walk and some geraniums in the windows."

I could not understand what he said, and this was becoming serious, so I broke out: *"Je ne parle pas l'Anglais."* [2]

"Oh, a Frenchie!" shouted the old man. "Can't speak English. Well, well, well, well, well."

He turned to the others and said:

"Had we better get Gus to take her, do you think? Wants to go to the Duval place, down the road. Can't understand English. A Frenchie."

After much gabble between the old men, I was stowed in an old and creaking car which was the town taxi, and was driven two blocks to the white house with geraniums.

My cousin opened the door, and since she had never seen me, she looked blank. I cried, in my native tongue:

"I am Lilly!"

Then she embraced me, and said she had not known when I was coming. The letter had not arrived. And she would never have known me, because she thought I was still a little girl. My mother had written that way. I was welcome, she said. I would love America.

But I was not so sure.

It was good to speak French again, and to talk of my mother and father, of mutual friends, and of Paris, and all of a sudden I knew that I was homesick. I, Lilly, who had dreamed and schemed for ten years to get to this wonderful new land—I was homesick.

I said to my cousin I was tired from the trip. I said I would like to go to bed, please. I said tomorrow I would talk more of the family and all the things at home. So I went to bed in a narrow gray room that frowned at me, and I cried myself to sleep.

But in the morning there was sun coming in my window, and a bird was singing in a tree outside, and I felt once more brave and cheerful. I went down to breakfast, and my cousin's husband, who was an American, already had gone to his work,

and we sat until noon over coffee and talked and talked.

I said it was difficult since I could not speak English, and she said I would soon learn, but until I did I could get along very well if, whenever anyone asked me a question, I just said "Yes."

But then I did not know what trouble a girl might invite by saying always only yes, and it seemed a wonderful and simple thing. My cousin said then that she had invited some of the ladies of the town in to meet me that same afternoon. She had called them while I was still sleeping. They were all very excited, she said, and were eager to meet her cousin from Paris. I was not to worry, she said, but just to answer "Yes" to everything.

This I had not expected. I said no, please. I said I could not talk to people yet. I said I was frightened. But my cousin was firm. I was to go up and change, she said, and just be calm, and remember to say yes.

I went to my room, and put on my best dress. It was black satin, with rows of fringe from the waist to the hem, and it came just to my knees. It was a good dress, and I had saved up for many weeks to buy it in Paris, but when I put it on I felt perhaps this was not a dress that would be fitting to Burlington, New Jersey. Still, it was the best I had, and so I wore it.

I had stage fright, I guess, and I stayed in my room until there had been several knocks at the door, and voices below, and my cousin called to me to come down.

Six or seven women were seated in stiff chairs around the parlor. The strange thing was that they all looked alike. Grim and gray and serious, with tight mouths and sober dresses that came to their ankles. My dress was much different.

My cousin introduced me to each in turn, and as I came in they stood up, and each one looked me carefully up and down, and even walked around me, to look at my back.

They looked at my black satin dress, and

----

[2] *Je ne parle pas l'Anglais,* I do not speak English [*French*]

my short-vamp, high-heeled shoes, and especially they looked at my short skirt. I felt
like the monkey in the zoo. My cheeks
burned, and I wanted to go through the
floor, but I could not, and so I had to stand,
while those gray women examined me, as
they would inspect a side-show freak, im-
personally, but determined not to miss one
small detail.

Then the talk, it started.

One woman said:

"Is that what they are wearing in Paris?"

I smiled and said:

"Yes."

"Much shorter than we are wearing
here."

"Yes."

"I hear you are a milliner. What are
the newest hats in Paris?"

"Yes."

"I mean, are they going to be bigger this
fall, or smaller? And with feathers or without?"

"Yes."

I could see this lady was growing angry,
but there was nothing I could do. Her
mouth set in a straighter line, and she said:

"Do you think I'm stupid, asking all
these questions?"

I smiled brightly, as best I could, and
replied:

"Yes."

My cousin fluttered to the rescue. She
explained that I did not understand English. She said that I knew only one word
—"Yes." But I could tell the ladies did not
believe her. I was not clear about what she
was saying, or what I had done, but I kept
a fixed smile, and said "Yes" to everything,
until at last the tea and cakes had been
served, and the ladies rose to go.

Then one of them chucked me playfully
under the chin and said:

"My dear, I guess you think we're just
a lot of horrid old frumps, don't you?"

And I said, smiling as sweetly as I could,
and shaking her hand:

"Yes!"

My cousin saw, too late, that the tea

party was a mistake. But she was a kind
woman, and she did not blame me. She
said only that I must work at learning English, and to help me she would have me go
to the market each day and buy the food.
Then, she said, I really would have to learn
the language.

The next morning she gave me a list,
with full instructions for reaching the grocery store, and started me on my way. But
I fooled her. I took my notebook along in
my purse, and when I got to the store I
handed the clerk the list, saying not one
word.

He was a young clerk, with eyes that
had a kind of twinkle, and he looked at me
and said:

"You new here?"

I only smiled.

"Where do you live?"

I smiled again, and handed him my notebook and pencil. He was puzzled, and
then he looked worried, and he wrote in
the book:

"Can't you talk?"

I wrote:

"I am French. I do not speak the English."

He smiled then, and there was a look of
relief on his face, and he wrote:

"Will you go to the movies with me tonight?"

I wrote: "Yes."

So it started, my real introduction to
America.

The young man, his name was Henry,
called for me at eight o'clock. We went to
the moving picture theater on the main
street, and I could not understand why
they showed two full pictures, and then
gave away sets of dishes at the end.

Whenever I asked a question about these
strange American customs, Henry thought
it was very funny, and laughed like crazy.
Afterward he took me to the drugstore, on
the other corner, where the windows were
full of fly specks and twisted crepe-paper
streamers, and he ordered two strange
dishes called banana split.

I looked at this funny mixture of ice cream and syrup and nuts and bananas and I could not eat it. Ice cream at eleven o'clock at night was wrong. At this hour I was hungry. I would have liked sausage and bread and cheese, as we had at home in France. Not ice cream. Not at eleven o'clock at night. But I tried to be polite, as my mother had told me, and I tried to eat the cold, sweet mess. But it was not a success. It did peculiar things to my stomach.

After that I went to the movies with Henry every Saturday night. And always afterward there was ice cream. And always I did not eat it, but slipped into the kitchen when I returned to my cousin's house and had bread and cheese and milk.

This was the America I first saw, and after several weeks I knew that this was not the thing for which I had prayed and schemed and wept for so many years in France. I wrote to my mother that things were not as I had thought, and perhaps it would be best for me to return to France.

I told my cousin that I must go to New York to find work, before I gave up and went back home. But she persuaded me to try Philadelphia first. It was a big city, she said, almost like New York, and she had friends there. She could help me to find a place.

So to Philadelphia I went, and through my cousin's connections was given a job designing in a store called Darlington's. I still could speak little English, but it did not seem to matter. They were kind to me, but Philadelphia depressed me, with its rows of houses all alike.

In France every house was different, even in the poorest villages, and there was an individuality about everything. Here the rows of drab houses, each with a front stoop exactly like the one next door, each with the same number of windows and the same grayish lace curtains, became a kind of nightmare to me. I did not see how people could tell which house to enter when they came home.

It was while I was in Philadelphia, too, that I saw the Mummers' Parade, which I was told was an annual event and a time of carnival and gaiety. I went with the crowds to watch, but I looked more at the crowds than at the parade. Carnivals and parades I had seen before, in France. But never had I seen so many thousands of people, all dressed alike. Many of the women I saw were dressed either in mustard color or in peacock blue, it seemed to me. The dresses were cut alike, and seemed to have come all from the same place. This was my first view of American mass production, and it terrified me. In France we made our own clothes, if we could not afford to have them made, and everyone looked different. Every French woman, no matter how poor, managed to have some individual touch about her costume. Here, it seemed to me, people and houses alike had been stamped out of some gigantic machine. It was a depressing thought.

It was wintertime now, and colder than I had ever known it to be in France. Though I had a black seal coat which my mother had bought me before I left, I seemed always to be shivering. One day I remember I was riding on a streetcar and got so cold I began to cry, from sheer misery. A lady who sat beside me asked me why I was crying. I sniffed and dabbed at my eyes and said:

"Oh, I came here to America expecting to find everything beautiful and gay, and now I do not like it at all. I am always cold, and I would not like to die of the cold. Besides I don't like the food. Especially I do not like this Philadelphia scrapple."

Having summed up all my woes, I felt better, and I added with decision:

"I intend to go back to France on the first ship that sails in the spring."

I did not know, you see, that ships sailed in the winter, or probably I would have gone and boarded one that very day. I had heard of the icebergs, and I supposed the boats could not go because of them. I myself was so cold that it seemed logical the ocean would be full of icebergs.

When things looked blackest, I received one day a letter from a friend I had known in France who had married an American. My mother had written to her, and she then wrote to me. I should come for a visit, the letter said. She lived in Buffalo, New York.

This came like a ray of light on a dark day. I told my boss I must be gone for a day. I borrowed enough money for the trip, and started out, to New York. Buffalo, I thought, must be a part of New York City. I would find out when I got there. And I would be back at work the next morning.

The train from Philadelphia was a better train than that first one on which I had ridden to Burlington. But not much better. The windows were still grimy and it still smelled of old smoke and stale lunches. Once more I looked through the windows of the day coach at the dreary flat lands and ugly factory buildings that stretched away in all directions.

I felt as dreary as the landscape, and I thought of all my high hopes of America. I began to think my parents were right when they said nobody in her right mind would want to leave *la belle France*.[3]

I wondered how they started, all these stories I had heard of a great, bustling new country, where everyone was busy and happy and the buildings reached to the sky. I think perhaps I wept a little, with my nose pressed against the glass, and I resolved that after the visit with my friend I would make plans to return as soon as possible to Paris, where at least people were gay.

In my purse was the letter. I took it out and read it again. Buffalo, New York, was where I should go, it said. I would ask a policeman.

Then the train plunged into a tunnel. People began putting on their coats and gathering up their bundles. As the train came up to daylight again there was a new feeling in the air. My spirits began to revive.

With the crowd, I walked along the cement platform, up stairways, out at last into the big, gray vault of Pennsylvania Station. The bustle and movement all around me acted like my father's good French wine on my spirits. Once more I felt brave, gay, adventurous.

I walked out to the street, and saw a policeman. My cousin had told me to ask directions of a policeman whenever I got lost.

I said to him, carefully selecting my few words of English: "Buffalo—which way?"

He was a young, handsome policeman, and he looked at me with interest.

"How's that again?" he asked.

"Buffalo," I repeated. *"S'il vous plaît."*[4]

I fished in my handbag and showed him the letter from my friend. I pointed to the address in the corner of the envelope.

"That place," I said, "is where I want to go."

The young policeman smiled, and pointed back to the station.

"You have to take a train, sister," he said. "Ask the ticket agent. You'll be there tomorrow morning."

"Tomorrow—but no! I have just today!" I cried. "Is this not New York?"

"This is New York City," he said carefully. "Buffalo, New York, is another town. It takes all night to get there."

I was almost in tears. This was just one more disappointment. It seemed nothing was as I had thought, here in this strange land of America. That New York was a state and also a city was something I had not been told.

I thanked the policeman sadly, and started walking slowly up the street. I was thinking only of my own misery, seeing nothing about me.

I thought of all the years I had dreamed of coming to this so-wonderful land. Of the tears and the arguments with my par-

[3] *la belle France,* beautiful France [*French*]

[4] *S'il vous plaît,* if you please [*French*]

ents. Of the time I had ordered the bicycle cap, when I was still a little girl, as the first step of my journey.

All these things I thought, and I felt most sorry for myself. I sniffed, and wiped my eyes. Aimlessly I started across the street, and all at once I heard the angry honking of automobile horns, the screech of brakes. A yellow taxicab screamed to a stop not an inch behind me. The driver leaned out of his window and shook his fist at me.

"Jaywalker!" he shouted. "Wake up!"

I woke up, in the middle of a wild jump for the curb. I woke up like a sleepwalker suddenly slapped in the face. I woke up with every sense tingling, and for the first time looked about me.

There was a wonderful roar all around. It filled the air and pounded in my ears. I looked up and saw a train thundering above me, on elevated tracks. I looked down, and felt the ground beneath my feet tremble, and heard the muffled roar of subway trains below. I looked to my right and saw cars speeding north. I looked to my left and saw cars rushing south. In the

middle of the street, trolley cars clanged and banged. On the sidewalks men and women, boys and girls made a lively, colorful, pushing throng.

"That'll teach you!" growled the taxi driver, as he ground the gears of his cab.

I smiled at him and waved, as I stood in a narrow island in the middle of the wide street, between the lanes of traffic. I could have kissed him, if he had waited.

I stood still, just where I was, and I looked up at the towering buildings all around me. Here, then, were the skyscrapers! At last! Great stores. Tall office buildings. And like a giant pulse, the roar

of traffic, above me, below me, to my right and my left.

I drew a deep, intoxicating breath of mingled gasoline fumes and the mixed perfumes of the crowds. There was the faint smell of rubber, the exciting smell of exhaust, the heady air of the city.

The street sign above my head said "Herald Square."

I felt the strong surge of life, like an electric charge. All at once I was fully awake, glad to be alive. I stood in wonder, savoring to the full the sights, the smells, the sounds.

This was no backwater, no Burlington. This was the full, rushing current of life. This was what I was looking for.

So I stood at the corner of 34th Street and Broadway, in the city of New York, and discovered America.

"This is life!" I said out loud. "This is for me!"

A few passers-by glanced at me with momentary curiosity, but they were too busy with their own affairs to take more than a passing interest. If I wanted to talk to myself, that was all right, in New York

City. If I wanted to wear a short black satin dress with fringe to the knees, that was all right, too. I did not look as strange as the Arab I saw walking with the crowds, in robes and turban. Or the Indian with his feather headdress that I met later in the day.

I walked with the crowds, up Broadway to Times Square, where I stood again and marveled at the hundreds of great electric signs, the many movie houses, the orange-juice stands, and the hawkers on the sidewalks. I stopped at one of the stands and had a hot dog. It was good, and I had another, with a glass of thin orange-flavored liquid.

I walked and walked, loving every sight, every sound, every smell. I went into a great five-and-ten-cent store, where stretching on every side were tables laden with imitations of everything the heart could desire. I bought pearl earrings for my cousin, for ten cents, and a bracelet to match for twenty-five.

Here no one stared at me, and when I stopped to ask directions in my halting, painful English, people were friendly and helpful.

I couldn't see enough. My feet hurt, and after a while my head ached, but I kept on. When it began to get dark, and lights went on in the office buildings, I remembered that I must get back to Philadelphia.

Bold now, after my day's adventures, I asked a policeman the way back to Pennsylvania Station. He explained carefully, pointing the direction I should take, and gave me a cheerful wink. I winked back, then turned and ran.

In the dusk, the city put on another dress. There were not so many crowds now, but there were many more lights, and I seemed to be walking through a twinkling fairyland. I looked up at the skyscrapers, with their rows of tiny lighted windows, reaching to the clouds, and my heart soared with them. I stopped to look in lighted shop windows, and spelled out the electric signs, all in beautiful colors—red, green, yellow, and blue.

As I walked the way the policeman had said, I felt something familiar in the roar above and below, and I looked up and saw the sign "Herald Square" once more. I was back at the place of my awakening, the place where I discovered America.

At night it was even more wonderful, with the blue flashes of the elevated trains from above, the lights of the cars below, the red and green traffic lights stretching as far as I could see. I stood there a minute, on the exact same spot where I had leaped that morning out of the way of the taxicab and its angry driver. Once more I listened to the roaring medley of sounds, held my hand on the pulse of the city. And my own pulse kept time.

So long as I live I will never forget that moment. For it was then that I knew my destiny, and knew that all my long years of hoping and planning were right, and meant to be. I knew that dreams could come true. In one of those flashes of knowing, I saw that my life would be here, in this great, rushing, roaring city, full of the sights and sounds and smells of life.

I knew that I would not go back to France, not now. Not until I had made my success, and that I was sure would come, too.

Then with light feet I turned my steps toward the great, brooding hulk of the Pennsylvania Station.

The prospect of Philadelphia, or of Burlington, did not depress me now.

I knew I was coming back.

The woman who wrote this autobiography

LILLY DACHÉ

In this selection from Miss Daché's autobiography, you learned about her early life. After she was settled in New York, she found a job in a small hat shop and, by saving most of her salary, was later able to buy the business from her employer. When customers came into the shop seeking hats, Miss Daché would convince them that they needed an original hat. As soon as the customer placed a deposit on a hat, Miss Daché would rush out, buy the material, and have the hat finished by the next day.

Within a short time, Miss Daché's business success made it necessary for her to move into a larger building and hire several employees. She is now recognized as one of the foremost hat designers in America.

Let's consider . . .

1. Miss Daché had to struggle to make her way as a successful hat designer. In many respects she is no different from other immigrants who have become an important part of America. Which of her early disappointments in this country would have discouraged you the most? Describe Lilly's feelings when she arrived in Hoboken.

2. Inexperienced as she was and ignorant of the English language, Lilly Daché encountered several helpful strangers. Who were they? How did they help her?

3. Describe the unfortunate party which Lilly's cousin gave for her the day after she arrived in Burlington, New Jersey. How might her cousin have been more helpful?

4. Lilly found Philadelphia not much more encouraging than Burlington. Why was Lilly depressed there?

5. Ignorance of geography can be responsible for mistakes which are amusing if *you* are not the one making them. What geographical knowledge of Buffalo and New York would have saved Lilly embarrassment? What good came of her mistake?

6. Lilly had almost despaired that her dream would ever be realized, when suddenly she knew "This is for me!" Where did the realization come to her? What did she see, and how did she feel?

7. What mistaken ideas did Miss Daché have about America, and particularly about New York, before she arrived in this country? If you know any Americans who have held equally unrealistic ideas about Europe, tell some of the experiences which opened their eyes to the truth.

The writer's craft . . .

1. As you were reading "Talking Through My Hats," you must have felt as though you were listening to Lilly Daché chat casually about her early experiences in America. Her gay, light-hearted style of writing flowed along as rapidly as a sparkling conversation. She not only presented her experiences concretely; she also added such personal touches as her awareness of new sights, sounds and smells, and her reactions to them. Find instances in which Miss Daché described her experiences in terms of her sense impressions.

2. There were other qualities which contributed to the personal tone of Miss Daché's style. Some of these were (1) short sentences, (2) a simple vocabulary, (3) repetition of the pronouns *I* and *my,* and (4) informal, everyday expressions such as anyone might use when talking to a friend.

If you enjoyed Miss Daché's style, you might try your hand at describing a similar experience in the same casual way. Think of an important "first" in your life. Write a description of it, using an informal, personal style. Give your composition a friendly, conversational tone.

Letter to an Intending Immigrant

ALISTAIR COOKE

One of the most popular radio programs in Britain is Alistair Cooke's weekly broadcast from America. He talks about anything which happens to interest him about this country, and the British people find his commentaries on American life completely absorbing. After you have read this "radio essay" you will understand why.

I was going downtown in the subway and was flattened up against the door reading the morning paper of a man breathing into my ear. If anybody in this train had had room to ram his elbow into my lungs, chances are I wouldn't have noticed it. That would have been just an occupational hazard of traveling in New York during the Christmas shopping season. But what I became aware of after a mile or so was a gentle nudge somewhere down there in the direction of my floating rib. This was such a friendly gesture that I tried to swivel my eyeballs in the direction it was coming from. I saw the upturned face of a man who might have been about five feet three or, then again, might have been a six-footer simply frozen at that altitude. He grinned and asked me if my name was Cooke. I said it was and he said his name was Schofield and he'd been in school with me in England twenty . . . well, several years ago. Before we lurched to a stop, his stop, he had time to tell me that he was working in a big department store downtown and had been over here for just about two years. I asked him if he was here for good. He gave a little laugh and said he certainly was. "I just upped and left," he said, and the train stopped and he vanished into the gasping school of New Yorkers peering at us through the aquarium windows.

This whole episode didn't last longer than thirty seconds, but it made me glad for him and set me contrasting his obvious good spirits with the fate and the faces of other English people I've run into in the past few years who also "upped and left." There was, for instance, an English girl who decided when the war was over that instead of having her children come back home to her from Canada, she would join them over here and start a new life in a new land. Her boy, it turned out, developed one of those boy soprano voices of remarkable purity. She began to fret—in the little Canadian town she'd settled in—and think back longingly to the church schools in England where this voice might be trained. Of course, she was homesick for more things than an English boys' choir. It was a useful and sensible excuse to give to friends on this side. She is back in London now, very contented in austerity, and her boy is proudly singing his head off.

I think also of a young man in his middle twenties who came here, hit on a good job, and quickly acquired the usual admirations: the bright tension of New York, the vigor and irony of its people, the autumn weather, the food, the women, the motor parkways, the theater. For a time he didn't seem to notice that this was costing him twice or more what these good things would have cost him at home if he'd been able to get them. He didn't need to notice, because he was a bachelor and such things as insurance and social security seemed like an old man's babble. This young and strapping Englishman was undoubtedly by now uprooted. His enthusiasm for many American customs was really a surprised contempt for his own previous ignorance of them. This is not a good basis for permanent admiration and he began to lose some of them, as he came to take them for granted. His job didn't pan out, and he found in the short and ruthless space of one month that New York is a bad town, and America a bad country maybe, to be poor in. With what he had left he went to Jamaica. Restlessness of course is a personal thing, but there was a conflict in it that I've noticed in other Britons who've sailed in here with shining eyes and left after a time in a mixed mood that is not pleasant to admit, for it is a mixture of disappointment and defeat. There is surely nothing to be ashamed of in disappointment. But many of these intending settlers can hardly fail to feel that American life is a far more severe challenge than they had figured on, and it has beaten them.

A century ago the whole adventure was, I think, materially harder on the people who made it, but psychologically not so tough. They knew before they ever left home that they were coming to a land with many less material comforts than Europe had to offer. They knew that the essential qualifications were physical hardihood, self-reliance, cheerfulness in the face of the adversity that was bound to come sometime, an indifference to social niceties, and a shrugging acceptance of dirt, bad luck, violence, and bankruptcy. The visitors who didn't prepare themselves for these hazards had nowhere to turn for sympathy. Their criticisms sounded niggling and effeminate. Thus in 1820, Washington Irving described such Englishmen: "They miss some of the snug conveniences and petty comforts which belonged to an old, highly-finished and over-populous state of society; where the ranks of useful labour are crowded, and many earn a painful and servile subsistence by studying the very caprices of appetite and self-indulgence. These minor comforts, however, are all-important in the estimation of narrow minds."

It sounds just like a British criticism of the traveling American today. Only the other day a young American film star (who was born on a small farm) caused a commotion in an "old, highly finished" hotel in Paris by demanding an air-conditioned room.

Nowadays an Englishman's complaints would not be likely to turn on such things. Now the material scales are weighted in America's favor. Today you can cross the three thousand miles of the American continent and never want for a private bathroom, a cement highway, a night baseball game, an airplane connection, a pair of nylon stockings, or a gallon of ice cream in six different flavors.

But the catch is that America is no more willing than it has ever been to give these things away for free. They are not in this country the luxuries that a secure upper class once exacted from a swarming and servile lower class. They are the minimum demands of comfort made by a population as fertile as its resources, in a country where comfort has accordingly turned into big business. A share of that comfort, a bigger share of satisfying and ingenious comfort than any other nation has ever known, can be bought by any worker with a steady wage. But the measure of that steady wage is the energy he can maintain. Visiting teams of British factory managers have remarked on the tenacity with which American workers compete through incentive schemes. You have only to lean out of any midtown window in New York, or in a score of other cities, to notice the furious concentration and energy of construction workers while they are on the job. At four-thirty they will quit like an exploding light bulb, but up to that moment they haul and hammer and drill and bulldoze with fearful zest.

A little time ago I left my office, as I usually do, about seven in the evening (not having the instinctive zest of the natives) and saw that the whole lobby of the skyscraper office-building—which spans something like the floorspace of Piccadilly Circus [1]—was covered with tarpaulin from which arose a network of ladders and scaffolding, a whole series of wooden platforms running about seven or eight feet from the ceiling. This scaffolding alone looked as if it might take a day or two to put up. But none of it was there at five o'clock when the offices of this building disgorged their three or four thousand employees. However, this was only the preparation for the job in hand. The job in hand was the painting of the whole of this great ceiling, which is about thirty feet from the ground. Sixteen men at various intervals were already up on the platforms and beginning to wave a kind of big flat brush, which from my angle looked about as wide as the tail of a whale. I had to come back that night to my office to catch the midnight news. There was not a man in sight, nor a paint brush, nor any tarpaulin or scaffolding. The night cleaners were already busy with their monster vacuum cleaners. And the ceiling was gleaming with its new paint.

This kind of shock greets the stranger wherever he goes. You have your house painted, or a wall knocked down, or new lighting sockets put in. And I should warn any incurable English perfectionist that half the time you will get a finished job something less than what would satisfy a first-rate craftsman. But this is neither their aim nor their interest. They do what they contract to do with remarkable speed and skill. Then they clean up your disordered home in a final cheerful burst and are on their way back to their wives, their shower-

bath, their steak and television sets. These men get paid better than any working-men have ever been paid, allowing for the exchange, the higher cost of living, and all that. The painters I just told you about were earning a hundred and thirty dollars a week—forty-six pounds ten [2]—which will take care of quite a lot of high cost of living. (I ought to add, though, that they pay just about the same, forty-six pounds ten, one week's wages, for the monthly rent of a small house.) If they work this way, they will keep their job. If they don't, they won't: that is the simple, brutal rule of life in America in prosperous times.

You can see how hard it is to start from scratch in this country, which already has a labor force of over sixty millions, and the fiercest kind of competition at all levels, from the laborer to the managing director. It sounds like a nightmare, and it may well be so to gentle, sensitive people who have no sympathy with the fight for life and merely want to earn enough money to give them leisure in their evenings, some fields to walk across, a little light and air. In the big cities of America these things too come at a high price. I sometimes feel that the house agents and real-estate men in all the big cities have measured every building and gauged exactly how many cubic inches of every little room are touched by sunlight for a few hours of the day. That room, once the real-estate agents discover its secret, will have its rent doubled. Several million middle-class families in the cities of England have a little back garden which they could reproduce in New York for a mere five thousand pounds.

It is hard for the romantic Englishman or woman to talk to Americans about these anxieties. Apart from seeming a chronic complainer, you will also tend to sound to Americans like a kind of immigrant they were long ago warned about. Washington Irving was on to this type too and wrote of them: ". . . they may have pictured Amer-

[1] *Piccadilly Circus,* a famous traffic circle in the heart of London

[2] *forty-six pounds ten,* forty-six pounds and ten shillings

ica to themselves an El Dorado,[3] where gold and silver abounded, and the natives were lacking in sagacity; and where they were to become strangely and suddenly rich in some unforeseen, but easy manner."

Well, that sort of character will be around for quite a time yet, but he grows increasingly peevish. It may be that present-day America, or rather, the movie and magazine myths about it, attract a semi-playboy type that is too soft to take the known risks of a hundred years ago. Unfortunately, the austerity and anxiety of Europe produce, too, many unassuming

---

[3] *El Dorado,* a legendary city of gold, hence any land of great wealth

and honest people who are looking for nothing more than a competence and a little peace and quiet. To the newcomer there is no easy guarantee of it. Sons of wealth can have it without any effort, for this country now has the biggest class of hereditary rich of any nation on earth. But for the newcomer there will be little concern about how he lived or what he was used to, or the kind of people he moved among. If he wants the same society in America, he must buy his way into it. Not what you seem to be, but what you prove you can do: that is still, for the stranger, the persistent pioneer requirement. You have been warned.

The man who wrote this essay

ALISTAIR COOKE 1908–

As you learned in this essay, Alistair Cooke serves as a kind of "interpreter" between England and the United States. He is well equipped to speak intelligently about both countries. Born in Manchester, England, Mr. Cooke went to college at Cambridge. Later he also attended both Harvard and Yale Universities in the United States and became an American citizen in 1941.

Mr. Cooke has held a number of positions as correspondent, commentator, and critic. He has served as special correspondent in American affairs for two London newspapers and *The Manchester Guardian.* He also served as a film critic and commentator—again on American affairs—with the British Broadcasting Corporation. Recently Mr. Cooke has been the Master of Ceremonies for the television program, *Omnibus.*

In addition to his many other occupations, Mr. Cooke has written several books. Two books of special interest to Americans are *One Man's America* and *A Commencement Address.*

Let's consider . . .

1. The episode which "set off" Alistair Cooke's "radio essay" took place in a crowded subway train. From the first paragraph pick out all the words and phrases which made you aware of the crushing crowd. How did this description set the tone of the whole essay?

2. The subway episode lasted no longer than thirty seconds. What happened? How did it "set off" Cooke's train of thought?

3. What was the purpose of this "letter"?

4. Cooke spoke of an English girl and of a young man in his early twenties, both immigrants. In what ways did they find American life "a far more severe challenge than they had figured on"?

5. Englishmen coming to America today face different kinds of adventures than their countrymen faced a century ago. What are some of these different adventures?

6. What did Cooke mean when he said, "Today the *material* scales are weighted in America's favor"?

7. According to Cooke, Englishmen (and other Europeans, too) find "the mini-

mum demands of comfort" made by all workers with a steady wage almost beyond their comprehension. What are some of these demands? Why are they so much more common in America than in England?

8. Cooke believed that the American worker has to pay part of the price for these comforts in the *energy* he must maintain on his job. This "fearful zest" is a source of wonder to visiting teams of British factory managers. What examples of this energy-on-the-job did Cooke give? Try to cite other examples you know which might astonish visiting foreigners who live at a slower pace than Americans.

9. Do you think Cooke was exaggerating when he compared the quality of the work with the prices paid for it in this country?

10. Why would it be extremely hard for an immigrant to start from scratch in the American labor market?

11. As Alistair Cooke viewed the whole picture facing an immigrant today, do you think his attitude toward America was favorable, skeptical, or neutral? Give reasons for your opinion.

The writer's craft . . .

A. Alistair Cooke has referred to his talks to the British people as "radio essays." He found that writing essays for listeners, rather than for readers, was an extremely challenging task. In his foreword to *One Man's America,* the book in which he published some of these talks, Mr. Cooke wrote: ". . . the essay form receives its most excruciating challenge over the radio. What you are trying to do is nothing less than write literature for blind men. Thoughtfulness must be entertaining. Any

meandering must be artful. Casualness must be calculated; if it is the real thing it is dreadful. Each sentence must distribute the elements of suspense. Ideally, everything that is said must flatter, excite, or tease the ear."

Select one of the characteristics which Mr. Cooke said the radio essay must contain and find an illustration of it in "Letter to an Intending Immigrant." Then read your illustration aloud. Ask the class to decide why it would "flatter, excite, or tease the ear."

B. Both Alistair Cooke and Lilly Daché wrote in styles which were personal and informal; yet their styles were not identical. Lilly Daché's style was extremely personal and chatty; Alistair Cooke's style was personal but more reserved. Each style was appropriate because it served the author's purpose.

Lilly Daché's purpose was merely to present her firsthand impressions of America. Alistair Cooke's purpose was to inform. He wanted intending immigrants—and his British radio audience—to understand certain aspects of life in the United States. To make his information about America more personal and graphic, he recounted some of his own experiences here, as well as the experiences of other Englishmen he knew about or had met. For example, he described his meeting with a young Englishman on a crowded subway. Then he contrasted the reaction of this young man to the American way of life with the reactions of other less-fortunate Englishmen.

1. Select several incidents in which Mr. Cooke used his personal experiences to illustrate some aspect of American life.

2. Write your own letter to an intending immigrant. Draw on your own experiences to illustrate your impressions of one or two aspects of life in your community.

You Can't Do That

JOHN P. MARQUAND

People from foreign countries are not the only ones who have migrated to another land. Americans, too, have felt the urge to discover what lies outside their native shores. They have ventured into every corner of the earth, and wherever they have set foot, they have left a definite impression of their country.

Since the year 1806 a cloak of red-and-yellow feathers has hung in the hallway of the March house on the Ridge, with a helmet made from the same plumage suspended above it. These two articles have always held the same position on the wall, except for such times as they have been put away in camphor to protect them from the moths. The cloak was brought there by John March and indicates very accurately the first venture of the March ships in the fur-and-sandalwood trade with China. It was hung there by John March when he returned as supercargo [1] on the brig *Polly*, Moses March, owner, and Elihu Griggs, master. A single glance at that cloak in the shady, spacious hallway of that square Federalist house is startling to anyone who is even remotely familiar with the curiosities of the South Seas.

It hangs there, an alien object, and yet, through association, somehow strangely suitable to a house like the old March house in a New England seaport town. Granted that its presence there is known to many scholars, familiarity cannot avert a shock of surprise at a sight of that vivid garment, for it is one of the most beautiful

objects ever conceived by the mind or executed by the hand of man. It is strange, too, to realize that if that cloak and the helmet above it were sold today, their price would probably equal the March profits in their precarious trade of another century. It is a long, fine cloak—and the Marches have always been careful of everything they have laid their hands on—one of the best of the hundred-and-some-odd feather garments which are known to be extant today, and there will never be another made. The o-o which supplied those yellow feathers, only one beneath each wing, a shy bird which once fluttered through the crimson-blossomed ohia and the tree-fern forests of the Hawaiian mountains, is virtually extinct, and the bird that wore the red plumage is in hardly a better case. He is vanishing from the face of this earth like the genial race whose ancestors collected and attached those feathers to their delicate base of fiber netting in a manner so admired by Captain Cook. Granted that the labor which went into the making of that garment is beyond all accurate calculation, the result was worth it. The reds and yellows are nearly as vivid as when the coat was new. They glisten there in the hallway, jewel-like, with a depth of luster and lacy velvet texture that is more vital than

---

[1] *supercargo*, a person on a merchant ship who has charge of the cargo, representing the shipowner in all transactions

inanimate. On an evening when the lights are lit, John March's cloak glows like flame and there is an element of awe in its splendor.

This is not odd, for it was intended to indicate greatness. The red lozenge pattern upon the yellow marks it as belonging not alone to one of the *alii* [2] but to a Hawaiian chief of a royal lineage that was very near to kingship. Its size and the amount of yellow is a sufficient indication of its former owner's greatness. If the shadow of a commoner were to touch the shadow of the man who wore it, that commoner would suffer death, for the man who wore it was sublimated in the complicated feudal ritual of his islands into a being more than human. The feather *kahili* [3] was carried behind him; an attendant bore his calabash [4] of koa wood to preserve his spittle, his nail parings, and his fallen hair, so that they might not fall into the hands of enemies whose kahunas, or witch doctors, might use them in fatal incantations. When the man who wore that cloak walked abroad, the populace assumed a prone position on pain of death. Some trace of the majesty of its first owner's presence still seems to linger about that feather cloak, incongruously, in a New England town.

The cloak was owned by the chieftain Kualai, as his name is spelled, probably incorrectly, in the March letter books and the log of the brig *Polly*, since there were no missionaries then to bring order to the Hawaiian phonetics—no missionaries, no mosquitoes, no red ants to kill the kou trees, no colds, and no disease. Kualai ruled his share of the Kona coast on what is now known as the Big Island, under the protection of the great king Kamehameha in the days when John March was young. In Kualai's youth he had been one of the king's best warriors; in the war exercises he could evade six spears thrown at him simultaneously from varying directions; and he

[2] *alii*, royalty [*Hawaiian*]
[3] *kahili*, a pole symbolizing authority [*Hawaiian*]
[4] *calabash*, a vessel

could trace his descent from one of the gods who had sailed with his attendants from the south.

Kualai gave his cloak and helmet to young John March when the *Polly* anchored in a bay on the Kona coast to exchange Yankee notions for sandalwood before proceeding to Canton. There is no doubt that John March valued the gift, for it is mentioned in his will. The clause reads:

"Item, the Feather Cloak that was given me by my friend Kualai on my first voyage to the Sandwich Islands, and the feather hat that goes with it, I leave to my daughter, Polly March, and I ask her to guard it carefully."

John March sailed other seas before he died and brought back other curious things, but there is every reason why the cloak should have had a value to him which was more than intrinsic; and his descendants have never sold that cloak because of the reason why it was given him, a reason that is closely connected with honor and integrity. John March was a shrewd trader, but he was an honest man.

In the New England harbor town which was the home port for the March ships, a voyage around the world was not an unusual matter when John March was young. As long as John March could remember, his town had been a port of travelers, although a part of it was cast in the narrow mold of puritanical tradition. When John March was young, no music was allowed in the white church with the rooster on its spire where merchants and clerks and shipwrights and returned mariners listened for three hours each Sunday to discourses on original sin. Not even the note of a pipe was allowed, to indicate the pitch for the singing of the psalms, because such a concession was considered an encouragement to the idolatrous errors of papacy. Yet in such surroundings of a Sunday one could see from the square box of the March pew a distinctly cosmopolitan congregation, for the world across the seas was closer to the town in those days than it has ever been since. Nearly every man and boy and most of the women in the pews and the Reverend Thomas himself, who thundered forth his nasal sermon while the sands ran from his hourglass on the pulpit, knew their geography as well as they knew the intricacies of their catechism. They could talk familiarly of the Baltic ports and of St. Eustatius and St. Kitts. There were plenty who knew the ivory factories and the slave pens on the Grain Coast and the anchorages along Fernando Po. There were plenty who had seen the sand upon the lead from soundings off Madagascar. The weather off Cape Horn was common talk. A restless, burning energy that made the town a lively place, except on Saturday nights and Sunday, had driven others to the factories at Canton. The townspeople were familiar with nearly every world port where money could be gained, for the town lived from shipping. One had to go, of necessity, a long way to make money then, what with European wars and privateers and orders in council and blockades. It was a time for gambling with lives and ships, a time of huge losses and huge gains, and no one could judge which until the ships came in.

It seemed hardly more than a piece of everyday business to John March when his father called him into the square parlor of the March house on the Ridge. It was an evening in April; a bright, fresh fire was burning in the parlor, and the candles were lighted on the mahogany table in the center of the room. Moses March and a man whom John March had never seen before were seated somewhat stiffly by the table with a punch bowl between them. When John March saw the punch, he knew that they were discussing important business, for his father, particularly in his later years, was abstemious with liquor. Moses March had not changed much since John March could remember him. His brown hair, done in a queue, was heavily streaked with gray, and the shrewd lines around his eyes and mouth were deeper and more pronounced. There was an added stoop to his lanky shoulders, but his eyes were as bright as ever and his voice was vibrant, without any quaver of age.

"John," said Moses March, nodding at his guest, "this here is Captain Griggs from Boston. Captain Griggs, he's been sailing for the Perkinses in the fur trade."

In many ways it seemed to John March that Captain Griggs was a younger replica of his father. The captain had the same bony facial contours and the same slouch to his shoulders. When he spoke he had the same flat voice, but his eyes were different—more mobile and less steady. The captain raised a hand before his tight-lipped mouth and coughed, then he rose from his chair with a creaking of his joints, a tall, somber man who might have been a deacon in a church. His eyes met John's and looked away toward some invisible object on the floor, then darted back and looked away again.

"Pleased to meet you," he said. . . . "I compliment you, Mr. March; he's handy looking, that's a fact."

"He's kind of peaked," said Moses March, "but John here's almighty quick at figures."

There was a silence. Captain Griggs ladled himself a fresh tumbler of punch, drank it at a gulp, and said, "He needs to be. It pays to be sharp, don't it, Mr. March?"

Moses March smiled in faint embarrassment. He had never been able to acquire a manner with his captains, nor to stop undue familiarity.

"Yes," he said, "I guess so . . . John, Captain Griggs is taking out the *Polly*. You're sailing with him, supercargo."

John March looked at Captain Griggs again. The captain was staring intently at a lemon peel in the bottom of his glass. The news was entirely unexpected.

"Where to, Father?" he asked.

"Where you haven't been, Son," said Moses March, "but you've heard the talk,

I guess. Up along the Northwest Coast for sea otter, trading with the savages, then to these new islands you've heard Enoch Mayo talk about, to put aboard sandalwood, then the whole cargo sold at Canton for tea. The *Polly,* she's sailing the end of the month. You'll start in working over the cargo tomorrow. Your mother, she'll get your things packed."

John March nodded without speaking, and he showed no emotion. It was not the first time that his father had surprised him, because it was one of his father's maxims never to talk about what he proposed to do until he was ready. His father was always reaching for something new; his mind was always working. Probably he had been pondering over the matter all winter, and now, as though he were speaking about arrangements for hauling firewood, he was making plans to send one of his vessels where a March ship had never gone before.

It was strange to think that while he sat there, a homely, uncouth man, his mind could reach around the world and back. His life had never seemed so plain or matter-of-fact. The order of the March house, each piece of furniture exactly in its place, had never seemed so perfect as when he spoke of that voyage. That literal order of the letter books and the columns in the ledger were all a part of the business. There was no expression of doubt, because they all knew by then that a ship could go wherever there was water.

Captain Griggs ladled himself another tumbler of punch and blew his nose on a long blue handkerchief which seemed to have imparted some of its own color to his nose. Not having been asked to sit down, John March stood examining his new captain, comparing him with other seafaring men whom he had met. The captain was evidently a heavy and competent drinker and no doubt a capable master, but behind his lantern jaws and his high, narrow forehead there were hidden convolutions of character beyond John March's grasp. He only knew that by the time the voyage

ended he would know the captain like a book. At the present time all John March could do was to stand staring at the pictures of his own imagination, striving to conjure up the sights which he and Captain Griggs would see. Captain Griggs was staring at him moodily across the brim of his glass.

"He'll do. He'll fill out," he said. "He'll be aft with the mate and me, of course. Does he know navigation, sir?"

"Yes," said Moses March; "he ain't a fool, but I hadn't aimed to make him a sailor. He'll handle this business ashore when I get through."

Captain Griggs nodded in a melancholy way. "I hope he ain't squeamish," he said. "He'll see some rough sights, like as not. We have a saying on the coast: 'You hang your conscience on the Horn.' "

"Yes," said Moses March, "I've heard it, but you, Captain, I'd like for you to keep your conscience on your ship."

"God bless you, sir," Captain Griggs said quickly, "no owner's ever complained of me. I'm always in my owner's interest. It's just dealing with these here savages, I mean. They've killed crews on the coast and they're murdering thieves on the islands." He rose stiffly. "You'll be satisfied, Mr. March. You'll be pleased as punch with me. There ain't no tricks in the trade that I don't know thereabouts. Four four-pounders and a bow chaser will be enough, and the grapeshot and plenty of small arms, and thanking you. I'll pick my own mate, and now I'll be under way, and I'll wish you a very good evening, and you, mister." He nodded to John March.

When the captain was gone, Moses March called to John March again.

"John," he said, "set down. You've been to the Baltic; you've been to the Indies; and I'd proposed keeping you ashore, but I want for you to learn this trade when it's still new." Moses March paused and rubbed his jaw. "I hear tell there's money in it, and we're going where there's money."

"Yes sir," said John March.

"It seems," his father continued, staring at the fire, "as how these savages put aboard furs, and these other savages put aboard sandalwood, for nothing more than notions and novelties in trading goods. Well, I got 'em for you; you and Griggs can get the rest. He'll try hard. He has his money and more than the usual prerequisites."

"Yes sir," said John March.

"And sandalwood and furs are worth a mint of money in Canton."

"Yes sir," said John March.

"You know about it, do you?"

"Yes sir," said John March; "I've heard 'em talking."

His father smiled. "That's right," he said, "listen to 'em talk, but keep your own mouth shut. Have you anything to say?"

John March thought a moment. He had a number of things to say, but he kept them to himself. "No," he said. "I can obey orders, I guess. You know what you're doing, I guess, Father."

Moses March stroked his chin slowly, and then he asked a sudden question: "How did you like Griggs?"

"He looks too sharp to me," John March said, "but I guess we'll get along."

"Yes," said Moses March, "he's sharp, but maybe that's all right. But mind you watch him, John. I'm sharp, but I guess I'm honest. Mind you watch him."

Even when he was three thousand miles away from town and farther than that by water, something of the town was always with him. The *Polly* was a part of the town because she had been built in the yards by the river, a good tight brig of two hundred and fifty tons. The crew was a part of the town, because most of the men before the mast had been born within its limits. The sense of the nearness of things he knew gave John March a certain peace when everything else was strange. The emptiness of the Pacific coast, the incredible size of its fir trees, the frowning menace of its mountains, would have oppressed him if it had not been for that sense of home. As it was, everyone stood together and behaved, in order to keep reputations intact when they got home.

John March was used to work. He was satisfactory to Captain Griggs, and he was treated well because he was the owner's son. Once they began bartering for furs off the Northwest Coast, there was no doubt that the captain knew his business, and John March admired in silence the way the captain worked. Martin Sprague, the mate, knew his business, too, in caring for the ship. The men were armed; there was a sharp lookout day and night. The fourpounders were loaded with grapeshot, and the matches were kept burning. Only a definite number of the painted dugout canoes of the Indians were allowed alongside, and only a certain number of savages were permitted on deck to trade. There were very few ships off the coast that year, so that the selection of pelts was particularly fine. Sea-otter pelts came aboard in great quantity in exchange for powder, shot, nails, muskets, beads, and blankets. It was a pretty sight to see the captain read faces and weigh the desire to sell. He seemed to have an intuitive sense of when to bargain and when to buy immediately.

"If there's any trade goods left after the islands," he said, "we'll stand back here again and use 'em up. It's a pity to see this fine fur wasting here. I wish we had six ships."

John March could feel the excitement as small goods turned suddenly into a valuable cargo. It was better than any figuring in the countinghouse to see the fur pelts come aboard and to estimate their probable value in a Chinese port.

"Yes, sir," said Captain Griggs, "it seems a pity to haul off and leave this. We ought to buy the villages out and to the devil with the islands and the wood."

They were in the cabin at the time, the captain and Sprague, the mate, a heavy muscular man, and John March, a thin blond boy.

"Mr. Sprague," said the captain, "pass the rum. What do you think, mister?

Shall we do all the trading here and simply water at the islands?"

Martin Sprague rubbed the palm of his left hand over the knuckles of his right. "I never seen trading so easy," he said. "Yes sir, I think I should."

Then John March spoke up; it was the first time on the voyage that he'd made a positive statement. "We can't," he said.

Captain Griggs set down his glass and scowled. "Young man," he said, "I'm surprised at you. You ought to know better. You do know better. You've behaved yourself fine up till now, my boy. You've done your duty, and more, and I shall be pleased to report favorably to your father if you continue, but there's two things for you to get inside your head. The first is, you were sent here to learn to trade. You don't know this business, and don't you forget it. The second is, I'm captain, and this brig goes where I tell it. I'm sorry to be obliged to tell you straight."

John March did not shift his position at the table. He knew that he was young and that he was green. He had interrupted solely from a conscientious sense inherited from his race. It had come over him that he was a representative of the March family and of the March cargo. Now that the eyes of the older men were upon him, he found himself stammering, because he was shy in those days, but his hesitation only made him the more determined to speak out.

"Captain," he said, "I understand what you say. This is your ship, of course, but you are under owner's orders, just as I am. A portion of these trade goods was allotted for furs and the rest for sandalwood. The owner's orders are to stop and trade at the Sandwich Islands. There may be more profit here, but we are to establish relations there. We may send out another ship."

Captain Griggs leaned half across the table. "Young man," he inquired, "are you insinuating I'm not looking after owner's interests? Because if you are, I will not tolerate it. I'm thinking of my owner all

the time, and a sight better than you are, maybe. We'll make for the islands tomorrow, and there's an end to that, but if there's any trade goods left when we're through there, why, then, with your kind permission, we'll come back here. I hope that satisfies you."

"Yes," said John March, "it does, and I ask your pardon, Captain."

Mr. Sprague rose. "I must be up with the watch," he said, "if you'll excuse me, sir. . . . Will you come with me, Mr. March?"

It was a fine night on deck, clear, with bright stars and a faint, quivering circle of the northern lights. The night was cool, without a breath of wind. The ship, with her own small lights, was like an insignificant fragment of a distant world anchored there in space. The mate took out his pipe and tinderbox.[5] There was a flash of spark as he expertly hit the flint against the steel, and then the tinder glowed.

"Johnny March," he said, "I've kind of got to like you. Now you listen to what I say. This kind of spark's all right, but not the kind that you were striking in the cabin. You leave the old man be. He's as good a master as there is, and he's honest with the owners, and that's all we have to care for. I've sailed with Griggs before. I don't need to tell you that a master's king aboard his ship, and you know it makes 'em queer. I've never seen a skipper yet who liked to be crossed. You better leave him be."

"Yes sir," said John March.

"And listen, Johnny," the mate said, "the islands are a fine place. You'll like the islands. The islands are like heaven, pretty near. The captain will take you ashore, of course, to make the bargain. You'll see plenty of funny sights, but keep your mouth shut, Johnny, except to say 'Yes sir' to the captain. We've got a long way yet to go."

"Yes sir," said John March.

---

[5] *tinderbox,* a box containing materials for making a fire

"That's right," said Sprague, "that's right. I like a tight-lipped boy."

It was said in the forecastle of the *Polly*, just as it was said aft, that Johnny March was taciturn. As a supercargo he had no fixed duties in working the ship, and few knew much about him except that he was March's son. They only saw him as a thin, brown-faced, gray-eyed boy with yellow hair who made no trouble or complaint. They did not know the impression which strange sights made upon him, because he was studiously silent on that voyage to the islands, hardly ever venturing a remark, only answering courteously when addressed. No one on the *Polly* knew—and perhaps it was just as well—that his thoughts were poetic, because there was no room for poetry on a Yankee trading brig.

The evening before they sighted land, he had a sense of the land's nearness. The banks of clouds off the port bow as the sun went down were pink and gold, and were more like land clouds than sea clouds. The *Polly* was moving in the steady breath of the trades, and the setting sun struck the bellying sails forward, making their colors soft and golden. The only sounds were the creaking of wood, the straining of ropes, and the splash of waves on the bow. He had seen many evenings like that one, but subtly this was different. There was a mystery in the warmth of the air, an intangible unreality in the cloud banks. Captain Griggs came and stood beside him, smelling strongly of rum.

"Mr. Sprague," he said, "you've got everything locked up, I hope. Tomorrow we'll be overrun by black thieves and their women. Clew up the courses and continue under topsails. Set a watch up in the crosstree and keep an eye out for breakers. We must not get in too close tonight. . . . And, Mr. March—"

"Yes sir," said John.

"You and I will go ashore."

"Yes sir," said Johnny March, and then he cleared his throat: "How will we speak to them, sir?"

"You'll soon learn, boy," said Captain Griggs. "You've got a lot to learn. These islands have kings, or chiefs, and the chiefs will have someone who can speak trading English. The sandalwood is up in the mountains. It will be the property of the king, or chief. We will agree to purchase so many piculs,[6] and he'll send his people to cut it. The chief will come aboard to to see our goods, and we will make a bargain for the cargo, payable when the wood is safe aboard, you understand. There's no need to make our crew work when the chief will make his people load it. The islanders are handy men on ships. We'll go to see the chief, and we'll make the chief a present. Break out that clock that strikes the hour, and two cutlasses. That will be enough, and maybe"—Captain Griggs paused and hesitated—"three yards of bright print calico; he ought to like it —paper's all they dress in."

"Yes sir," said Johnny March. "Did you say that they dressed in paper?"

The hard lines of the captain's face wrinkled into an indulgent smile.

"Young man," he said, "it's a fact they dress in paper, when they dress at all, which isn't often. The women, they pound it out of the bark of a tree. They have nothing else on the islands, or almost nothing. Time was when they'd sell a pig for three tenpenny nails. Will you come below for a glass of rum?"

"No, thank you, sir," said Johnny March. "I'll stay on deck—that is, if you don't mind."

The sun had dipped out of sight behind a bank of clouds, and then suddenly the light was gone. Without a prelude of dusk, the dark came over them like a warm black garment. It seemed only a second before that the sky had been red and gold. Then, in another second, the sky was a void of darkness, filled with the trade wind and with stars. He stood for a while listening

[6] *piculs*, Oriental units of weight

LEONARD EVERETT FISHER

to the wind singing through the ropes, and then he went below. It was still dark when John March was awakened by a long-drawn-out call and by Mr. Sprague's voice shouting, "Where away?" and he knew that they had come in sight of land. Once he was up on deck, the topsails were slatting sleepily, and off the starboard bow there was a glow in the sky like fire.

"We've hit it to a second, sir," the mate was saying to Captain Griggs. "Yonder's the volcano; we're in the lee of the mountains."

Captain Griggs was a shadow in the starlight. It was too dark to see his face, but his voice was satisfied. "A pretty piece of navigating," he said, "if I do say so, mister. There'll be an inshore breeze by dawn, and then we'll make the bay." He sniffed the air. "We can't be far from land," he said, "but there's no use heaving lead. It shelves off here as deep as hell. There'll be an inshore breeze with dawn."

"Is that a light yonder, sir?" asked Johnny March.

Near the horizon there was a twinkling, glimmering point.

"Your eyesight's good," the captain said.

"Yes, that will be a fire. We're close to land."

The dawn came as suddenly as the dark, in a swift rush of light, as though a hand had snatched away a veil, and John March saw the land. It was a solemn sight to see land which seemed to have risen out of nowhere. Off the bows of the *Polly* was a mountain, black and green, that rose in a gradual slope up into snow and clouds. The coast was dark from volcanic rock which made ugly black gashes between green forests. Close to the water's edge there was a fringe of palms and beeches between black lava headlands. The sea was smooth and calm and streaked with violet; the air was as soft as the air of spring at home and was subtly laden with the smells of land. All the colors were soft in a faint, early-morning haze. The black rocks merged into reds and purples. The greens of the upland forest blended subtly from shades of silver to emerald, and Captain Griggs was right—a soft breeze was filling the sails, moving the *Polly* gently along the coast.

"That's where the sandalwood comes from," Mr. Sprague was saying, "up yonder in the mountains. The coast here-abouts is the favorite place of the kings. Do you see the stone walls and the yellow thatch of the houses of the villages? The chiefs own straight from the tops of the mountains to the sea. How do you like it, son?"

The question made John March tongue-tied. "I think it's very handsome, sir," he said, "a very pleasant island."

The *Polly* was moving under topsails into a small bay. It opened out before them, a smooth amphitheater of water, sur-rounded by high cliffs. "Yonder's where the kings are buried," the mate said. "They scrape the flesh off their bones and tie them up in paper cloth and put them there in caves with their canoes."

At the head of the bay John March could see a beach fringed with tall palm trees, the leaves of which moved idly in the breeze, and he could see the thatch of houses beneath them. There was a dark crowd of people on the beach, pushing canoes into the water, log dugouts, bal-anced by an outrigger and manned by naked paddlers. Captain Griggs was wear-ing clean linen and a black broadcloth coat, although the day was hot.

"Mister," he said, "we'll anchor. Let go falls and clew up lower topsails and order the stern boat cleared."

By the time the anchor struck the water, the *Polly* was surrounded by canoes and the water was full of swimmers who were pulling themselves up the anchor chain, smiling and laughing; men and women as beautiful as statues, their straight dark hair glistening with the water. Captain Griggs stared at his visitors sourly from the quarter-deck.

"They've got the minds of children," he said. "The chief's man should be here. Look at those shameless hussies, will you? There's no decency on these islands. They don't care for decency; no, they don't care."

As Captain Griggs finished speaking, a native pushed his way through the crowd at the waist and walked aft; evidently a man of importance, because the crowd gave way respectfully. He wore a pair of sailor's castoff trousers, and his skin was lighter than the others'. His voice rose above the babel of strange words in English.

"Mr. Captain," he called out, "I am Kualai's man."

"Who's he?" asked Captain Griggs. "The chief?"

The other nodded, bobbing his head up and down, still smiling. "Yes," he said, "yes, yes. And he sends me because I speak English good. I've been a sailor on a Bos-ton boat. I speak English very good. Kualai sends me to say *aloha*. He is glad to see you. He asks you will you trade for wood?"

"Yes," said Captain Griggs, "we're here for wood. What's your name?"

"Moku," said the native. "Billy Adams Moku. Kualai ask what name."

The captain nodded condescendingly. "Captain Griggs," he said, "brig *Polly*. Moses March, owner. We're carrying very fine calicoes, ironware, tinware, lead and copper, and even a few muskets. Has your chief got wood?" Moku nodded. "The wood is coming down. Kualai, he will see you." He pointed to a laden canoe. "Kua-lai sends you food."

Captain Griggs looked at the canoe care-fully as it drew alongside. "Very good," he said. "When will he see me?"

"Now," said Moku. "He waits on the shore."

"Mister," the captain called, "have the stern boat lowered. Mr. March and I will go ashore, and, Mr. March, give that man a pocketknife and bring along the pres-ents."

The dark sand of the beach at the head of the bay seemed insecure under John March's feet, since he had been so long on the water. In the sunshine like a warm June day at home, every sight and sound was new. The crowd of natives standing on the beach drew back from them shyly and smiled, but their tongues kept chatter-ing busily; commenting, probably, on the way these strangers looked. The chief's man walked first, then Captain Griggs, nonchalant and cool, and then John March behind him. They walked along a path beneath a grove of coconut palms and beneath large broad-leafed trees such as he had never seen. They were threading their way through a settlement of houses made of dried grass, past small gardens enclosed between walls of black volcanic rock. His memory of that day always brought back living green against dark rock, and dark smiling faces and red hibiscus flowers. In his memory of the place a soft breeze was always blowing and there was always a strange dry rattle from the leaves of the coconut palms. There was a group of larger houses not far back from the beach which evidently belonged to men of importance. Natives were busying themselves about a fire in a pit; women and children were staring from open doorways. There was an open pavilion near the center of this group of buildings, and the chief's man led them toward it. Seated in a Cantonese armchair under the pavilion was one of the largest men that John March had ever seen. He was middle-aged, and so corpulent that the chair seemed to creak beneath his weight. A single look at his face was enough to indicate that he was the ruler, Kualai, of whom the man had spoken. The face was set in benign lines that could only have come upon it through suave and complete authority. It was all that was necessary to indicate his rank, but he also had the exterior show of office. He was wearing a yellow-and-red cloak of feathers, dazzlingly bright, which fell below his waist, and an attendant stood behind him holding a large stick which bore a tuft of colored feathers on the end. Moku stopped dead still at the entrance of the pavilion, and the great man rose from his chair and stepped slowly forward, gracefully, in spite of his heavy paunch. It was plain that he had seen other white men and knew something of their manners, because he smiled graciously and held out

L.E.FISHER

his right hand. At the same time he spoke melodiously in a language that was all vowels, so that his words sounded like rippling water.

"What's he saying?" asked Captain Griggs.

"Kualai," Moku translated, "he say he's, oh, very glad to see you."

"Well, I guess we're glad to see him too," said Captain Griggs as he shook hands. Then John March saw that Kualai was looking at him.

"He wants to know," said Moku, "who is the other man?"

"Tell him he's the son of the man who owns the vessel," said Captain Griggs.

"He wants to know," said Moku, "is he a chief's son?"

"Tell him yes," said Captain Griggs.

"He would like," said Moku, "to feel

his hair. He would like to know if it is real."

"Take off your hat," said Captain Griggs, "and let him feel your hair. Don't be afraid of him. He won't hurt you."

"All right," said Johnny March. He felt very much like a child as he walked toward Kualai, for the man, now that he was standing, must have been close to seven feet in height. His skin was glistening with coconut oil. He was stretching out his arm. He touched Johnny March's hair gently and then he pulled it softly. Johnny March looked at him and smiled, and Kualai smiled back.

"Break out the presents," said Captain Griggs, "bow to him and put 'em on the ground."

Kualai's face lighted up at the sight of the clock when John March held it toward him. It was evident that he had never seen such a mechanism—a battered ship's chronometer whose useful days were over. He touched it gingerly and imitated its sound.

"Tick-tick," he said, and John March nodded and repeated after him, "Tick-tick." That interchange of words always seemed to him ridiculous, but somehow there was an exchange of thought with the words that made them friends.

"He asks you to stay and eat," said Moku. "He will come on the ship tomorrow and see the goods, and he asks the young man to stay with him until the trade is over, to sleep inside his house."

Captain Griggs muttered something beneath his breath, and then he said, "March, you'd better stay."

"Yes, sir," said John March, "I'd be very glad to stay." He turned to Moku. "Tell him I'll be glad."

Then Moku spoke again: "Kualai says he will trade with the young man."

"All right," said Captain Griggs, "as long as I'm there too. And tell him"— Captain Grigg's eyes shifted toward the bay and back—"you tell him I want the wood measured on the beach and put

aboard by his people. Tell him my men are tired." And then he drew a bottle of rum from his pocket and added plaintively: "Ain't we had enough of this? Let's everybody have a drink, and bring on the dancing girls." Some half perceptible change in Captain Griggs's voice made John March turn to watch him. The Captain's face was bleak and impassive, but his eyes were shifting from point to point, from the chief to John March, then away to the matting on the ground, then to the houses of the settlement. John March knew him well enough by then to know that the captain was turning over in his mind some thought which he wished entirely to conceal.

"Ah," he said suddenly, "here comes some wood," and he nodded toward a path which led upward to the mountains.

A dozen men and women were staggering down the path in single file, each bearing a burden of long sticks, and John March knew from hearsay that these were the chief's people who had been sent to the upland forests where the sandalwood grew. The chief called out an order, which Moku ran to obey, and a few moments later a pile of the sandalwood lay on the matting before his chair, a heap of sticks which varied in size from a few inches to a foot in diameter. The bark had been stripped off, leaving a heavy wood of deep yellow which verged on orange. Captain Griggs ripped out his clasp knife, whittled at the sticks, and sniffed the shavings.

"It ain't bad," he said; "in fact, it's prime."

He was right that the wood was fine, since sandalwood was plentiful in the islands then, when the trade was new, and John March did not suspect that he would live to see the time when hardly a stick would be left standing on the entire island group. Captain Griggs stood there, staring at the pile of wood, apparently lost in thought.

"Tell him we'll pay him well for it," he said, and his voice was soft and almost kindly, "once he lands it on the deck."

But all the while John March was sure that Captain Griggs was concealing some other thought.

It took nearly two weeks to collect the wood and measure it, a space of time which moved in a peculiar series of days and nights, but it was strange to John March how soon the life there grew familiar. Though he could hardly understand a word which was spoken, though nearly every sight and sound in those two weeks was new, he became aware immediately of certain human values. Kualai, in his way, was a cultivated man of gentle breeding, who had developed his own taste for the arts, and qualities of understanding which were the same on that isolated island as they were elsewhere. He would sit for hours of an evening watching interpretive dances and listening to his minstrels sing of the exploits of his ancestors. He had a good eye for patterns in the tapa cloth, and a nice skill in various games of chance, which he played daily with his choice companions, but, above all, he had a sense of hospitality. He lost no occasion to make John March feel politely that he was a welcome guest. He took him fishing in his war canoe; he took him to the caves and the lava rocks; he took him to watch the young men perform feats of strength; he was even careful that John March's privacy should not be disturbed unduly. When he came aboard the *Polly,* he kept John March beside him. He was greatly pleased with the calico and nails and lead and copper in the trading cargo, but he went through the intricacies of the bargain in a detached way, like a gentleman. In those days trading was easy on the islands, before the chiefs were glutted with material possessions.

"He say he want you to be happy," Moku said the last time Kualai came aboard; "he want you to come again."

"Tell him we're happy," said Captain Griggs. "He understands when all the

wood's aboard that we'll give out the goods."

Moku nodded. "He understands," he said; "he knows you're good men."

Captain Griggs coughed slightly. "I shall want Mr. March back with me," he said, "tomorrow morning. . . . Mr. March, you come here; I want to speak with you in the cabin."

It occurred to John March, when they were in the cabin, that it was the first time since they had been on the islands that he and Captain Griggs had been alone. Captain Griggs rubbed his long hands together and poured himself a glass of rum.

"Young man," he said, "you've done fine. You've kept that old heathen happy, and that's all we needed—to keep him happy— and now we're all finished shipshape. We'll get the wood stowed tonight"—Captain Griggs smiled happily—"and tomorrow they can come and take off their goods, but I want you aboard first, understand?"

"Yes, sir," said John March, "but there's one thing I don't see. I don't see why you haven't put the goods ashore before this, sir."

Captain Griggs poured himself a second tumbler of rum.

"Young man," he said, "when you take a few more voyages you'll understand you can't trust natives. How do you know we'd get the wood if we put the goods ashore?"

"Because Kualai's honest," John March said.

Captain Griggs looked thoughtfully at the ceiling. "Maybe," he said, "and maybe not. Anyways, we've got the wood. You come aboard tomorrow." And Captain Griggs smiled genially, but even when he smiled, John March had a suspicion that something had been left unsaid, that there was some thought in the captain's mind of which he had not spoken.

Mr. Sprague came up to get him the next morning, carrying a bundle of small presents and perspiring in the heat of the early sun.

"Say good-by to the chief," he said. "The

captain's orders are to leave right now. You're to stay aboard until we sail. The quarter boat's waiting at the beach."

John March was sorry, now that it was time to go. He walked to Kualai and held out his hand. "Thank you very much," he said, and the interpreter, Moku, gave him back the chief's answer:

"He say for you to come back soon."

The canoes were gathering about the *Polly* already, by the time he reached the beach. He and Mr. Sprague sat in the stern sheets of the quarter boat while two men rowed, helped by a light breeze off-shore.

It was only when they were halfway out that John March was aware of something disturbing.

"Look," he said; "they're setting the lower topsails!"

"Yes," said Mr. Sprague shortly, "so they are. We've got a fair breeze, haven't we?"

"But it'll take a good six hours to put off those goods," said Johnny March.

Mr. Sprague put a heavy hand on his knee and smiled. "Don't you worry, boy," he said. "Captain Griggs will see about those goods."

They were beside the companion ladder by that time, and even John March was puzzled, but nothing more. He was not aware of Captain Grigg's idea until he was on the poop, then he saw the tarpaulins were off the guns and that men were beside them with matches, and then he saw that the decks were clear and that the sandalwood and the trade goods were all back in the hold. Captain Griggs grinned at him.

"Safe and sound," he said. "You've done very well, Mr. March; your father will be very pleased, I think. . . . Mister, you can man the capstan now."

John March found himself stammering: "But what about the goods, Captain? We haven't put the goods ashore."

"No, boy," said Captain Griggs, "we ain't going to. What's the use when we've got the wood aboard? Those goods are going to go for skins."

Even then John March did not entirely understand him. "But you can't do that," he said. "We owe the chief the goods."

"Listen, boy," said Captain Griggs, "this ain't like home. They're plenty of other chiefs, and plenty of other islands. Let 'em come and get the goods, and I'll blow 'em out of water. There ain't no law out here. Now you be quiet, boy."

For a moment John March found it impossible to speak. Now that the whole matter was completely clear, he knew that he should have suspected long ago what must have been in the back of the captain's mind. Captain Griggs proposed sheer robbery, but he would not have called it that. He would have called it a clever piece of business in a place where there was no law.

"You see," Captain Griggs was saying, "it isn't as though they were white people, Mr. March. More fools they, that's all."

Then John March found his voice. "Captain," he said, "this is a March ship. You don't leave until you've set those goods on shore. We don't do things that way, Captain. You can't—"

Captain Griggs turned toward him quickly.

"That'll be enough from you," he said. "Who says I can't? I'm trying to make a profit on this voyage. I can, and I will, and I'm taking full responsibility. If you don't like it, get below."

John March's tongue felt dry and parched as he tried to speak. Even in that short while a hundred things were happening. The fore-and-aft staysails and the lower topsail were set by then, and the call came from forward, "Hawser short!" A glance toward the beach was enough to show him that the islanders were aware of the captain's trick. Men were running toward the water. He could hear the beating of a drum. Men in canoes were gesticulating and shouting. Men with spears and clubs and slings were hurrying to the beach.

"Break out anchor, mister," shouted Captain Griggs, "and stand by them guns!

Forward there, pass out the small arms! By God, we'll show 'em!"

"Captain," said John March suddenly. He knew there was only one thing to do as he spoke. "If you go, you'll leave me here. I'm going back ashore."

Captain Griggs looked at him and laughed. "They'll kill you back ashore," he said. "Look at 'em on the beach."

John March spoke with difficulty. "You and I are different sorts of men," he said. "You can either set those goods ashore or I'm going."

"May I inquire," said Captain Griggs, "how're you going to go? Keep your mouth shut, boy!"

In the haste or getting under way, the quarter boat was still drifting alongside, and the captain must have perceived John March's intention from his glance.

He made a lunge at John March, but John March broke away, and then he went on the bulwarks.

"Get ahold of that fool!" shouted Captain Griggs. "Lay ahold of him!"

Two of the crew ran toward him, and he jumped, crashing into the quarter boat. "Get in there after him!" Captain Griggs was shouting. "Don't let him go!"

And then John March cut the painter [7] and the quarter boat was drifting from the side.

"You fool!" shouted Captain Griggs. "You hear my orders! Come back here or they'll kill you, March!"

Once the boat was drifting from the side, John March was amazed at himself. His anger and his lack of fear amazed him. He was standing amidships in the quarter boat, shouting back at Captain Griggs.

"I'd rather be killed ashore," he shouted, "than stay aboard with you!" Then he picked up the oars and began to row ashore, slowly, because the boat was heavy for a single man to handle.

"You hear me?" Captain Griggs was shouting. "Stay there and that will be the end of you."

John March saw that the anchor was aweigh and the *Polly* was standing slowly out to the open sea. His back was to the beach as he pulled toward it, but he heard the shouting and the beating of the drums. It must have been his anger at Captain Griggs that did not make him afraid, or an assurance within himself that he was right and Captain Griggs was wrong. A glance astern of the quarter boat as he strained at the oars showed him the *Polly* standing out to sea, but he did not look over his shoulder toward the beach. He did not look until the bottom of the quarter boat grated on the sand, then he shipped his oars carefully and stepped ashore. He found himself surrounded by shouting men who waved their spears and their fists in his face, but somehow they were not so real to him as the reality which lay inside himself. He only realized later that a single gesture of fear might have meant his death, but then he was so involved in his own preoccupation

[7] *painter,* a rope attached to the bow of a boat

and with the single desire which was in him that he walked calmly enough across the beach toward the palm trees and the thatched houses; the crowd in front of him gave way as he walked, and then followed on his heels. He was taking the path to Kualai's house, and the shouting around him died away as he drew near it.

Then he saw Kualai walking toward him in the feather cloak which he had worn the first day they had met, carrying a light throwing spear in his right hand. Kualai was shouting something to him—obviously a question which he could not understand —and Moku was standing near him.

"Tell Kualai," said John March, "that I come from honest people. Tell him that I have come here to stay until he is paid for his wood." He saw Kualai listening intently to his answer, and then Kualai raised his right arm and drove his spear into the earth.

"He says you are his son," Moku said. "He asks you: Will you please to shake his hand?"

The reaction from what he had done came over him when Kualai grasped his hand. He knew the harsh and accurate consequences of his action then, as the smells and sounds of that Polynesian village came over him like a wave. Captain Griggs had left him, and every vestige of home was gone. He was a stranger among savages, and he might be there forever, for anything he knew, yet even then he knew that he had done the only proper thing. Suddenly he found that he was homesick, because the chief was kind.

"Ask him if I can be alone," he said. "Tell him I want to be alone."

He was given a house of his own that night, next to where the chief slept. He was given a pile of woven mats for his bed and a piece of tapa cloth [8] to cover him. He was given baked pig and sweet potatoes and the gray paste made from the taro root, called poi, for his evening meal, and mullet from Kualai's fish pond. He was

[8] *tapa cloth,* made from the bark of a tree

as comfortable as he could have hoped to be that night. For a moment, when he was awakened early the next morning, he thought he was at home, until he saw the rafters and the thatch above him. Moku was standing near him in his ragged sailor breeches, and Kualai himself was bending his head, just entering the door.

"Wake up!" Moku was saying. "The ship is back!"

John March sat up on his bed of mats and rubbed his arm across his face. Although he spoke to Moku, his eyes were on Kualai.

"The ship?" he asked. "What ship?"

"Your ship," said Moku. "She come back, and now the captain, he unloads the goods."

John March stood up. He had no great capacity for showing emotion.

"Ask Kualai if he is satisfied," he said.

Moku nodded. "He says, 'Yes, very much,'" he said, and Kualai nodded back. "He asks for you to stay a long time—always."

"Thank him, please," said John March, "but tell him it's my ship. Tell him I must go to see that the goods are right."

"Kualai," Moku answered, "says he will go with you to the beach."

Mr. Sprague had landed in the longboat by the time they had reached the shore, and the beach was already covered with bolts of calico and small goods and ironware and lead and copper. Mr. Sprague nodded to John March formally as though nothing had happened. "The captain sends his compliments," he said, "and asks you to come aboard, so that he can resume the voyage." And Sprague grinned and added, "It's lucky for you, John March, that you're the owner's son."

John March looked at the goods upon the shore. "You can thank the captain for me for coming back," he answered. "You can tell him that I hope we both can forget what has happened, but the complete consignment is not landed yet. I'll stay here until the list is checked.

"You're an accurate man," said Sprague.

John March nodded. "I've been taught to be," he said, and he stayed there on the beach until every item was verified. Then he turned to Kualai and his interpreter.

"Tell the chief," he said, "that I believe that everything is right. Ask his pardon for the delay, but tell him our house will make any mistakes correct. Thank him, and tell him that I am going."

Moku spoke quickly in the musical language of the islands while Kualai stood, looking first at John March and then at the ship that brought him. After Kualai had listened, he stood silently for a moment. Then he smiled and spoke swiftly. He raised a hand and took off his feather helmet, and one of his men very carefully removed his feather cloak from his shoulders.

"He says there will always be wood for you," said Moku. "He asks you to take his coat."

The man who wrote this story

JOHN P. MARQUAND   1893–

John P. Marquand's novels are set in New England; the characters are New Englanders. This is the part of the country which Mr. Marquand knows best. He grew up in Rye, New York, spent every summer with his great aunt in Newburyport, Massachusetts, and attended Harvard University.

He completed his studies in three years and went to work as a reporter for the Boston *Transcript*. World War I interrupted his career, and he was sent to France with the AEF. After the war he worked on the New York *Tribune* until he could make a living by writing. The *Saturday Evening Post* published many of his short stories. The "Mr. Moto" series was popular among detective story readers.

Mr. Marquand's novels have one main theme: material success does not always assure happiness. He depicts his heroes reaching the pinnacle of success but finally discovering that their lives are empty and unimportant. This theme is suggested in Paul Osborn's adaptation of *Point of No Return*.

In 1937 Mr. Marquand was awarded the Pulitzer Prize for *The Late George Apley*. This early novel set the pattern for such later books as *H. M. Pulham, Esq., Point of No Return,* and *Sincerely, Willis Wayde*.

Let's consider . . .

1. What was your estimate of John on the morning he was summoned to his father's "square parlor"?

2. What did John March learn about Captain Griggs at their first meeting?

3. "I hear tell there's money in it, and we're going where there's money," Moses March told his son. For what port was the *Polly* bound? How was money to be made?

4. John's father told him to listen but to keep his own mouth shut. Under what circumstances did he first decide it was time to open his mouth? What did he say that made the Captain change his plans?

5. In what ways was Captain Griggs too sharp? What did he consider his sole obligation to the owner of the ship?

6. John and Kualai became friends at once. What characteristics did these two have in common, in spite of their differences in customs, language, and way of life?

7. When John, on orders from Griggs, was returning to the brig, he was aware of "something disturbing." What sharp trickery was the captain planning?

8. How did John thwart the captain's plans? What part did John's Puritan conscience play in his decision? Do you feel that Moses March would have taken the same action? Discuss.

9. John's reward was Kualai's cloak of red-and-yellow feathers. What did the cloak look like as it hung in the hallway?

10. This story did not begin at the beginning, but at a point long after the death of the leading characters. If you rearranged the story so that it would start at the beginning, with which paragraph would you start?

11. Why was Marquand's opening more effective? What did it tell you of the March family background that you needed to know in order to appreciate John March's role later on in the story?

12. In his novels, Mr. Marquand often satirizes upper-class New Englanders who lean heavily on their aristocratic and Puritan background. Do you think he was being satirical in this story? In what way did John March uphold a tradition of which Americans are proud?

The writer's craft . . .

John P. Marquand began "You Can't Do That" with a rather elaborate description of the feathered cloak which hung in the hallway of the March house. In great detail he pictured the cloak's color, design, and history. Then he explained how young John March had acquired this rare treasure and why he valued it even beyond its intrinsic worth. To John March and to his descendants, the cloak was a symbol because it stood for honor and integrity.

By introducing you to the cloak in this way, Marquand made you wonder why the cloak was so important. You may have guessed that it stood for an idea or belief—that it was a **symbol**—but you weren't given a complete explanation of its meaning until the very last line of the story. By referring again to the symbolism of the cloak at the end, Marquand gave his story a nice sense of unity.

Because a symbol always stands for something else, writers often find it a convenient device in story-telling. Like the cloak, symbols are usually concrete; therefore, they can be used to bring a complex or abstract idea into sharper focus than would otherwise be possible. For example, the spire of a church (a symbol) may bring to mind the idea of reverence for a Divine Being. Writers are not limited to the use of such material objects as a cloak, church spire, flag, or rainbow to symbolize an idea. Characters may also be used to symbolize an idea by standing for something other than themselves. For example, in "The Birthmark" Aylmer was not only a man of science; he was also a symbol of the power of intellect without soul.

Although the use of symbols in fiction often proves to be an effective device, it presents certain hazards. Characters who are created merely to symbolize an idea often fail to come alive as believable people. The writer may become so concerned with giving them symbolic meaning that he neglects to give them interesting personalities. A second danger in the use of symbols is that they may become so obscure that they are meaningless to the general reader. A private symbol—such as a ring, an open window, or a piece of music—may contain a world of meaning for the writer but have no meaning at all for the reader. However, in spite of the inherent dangers in the use of symbols, you will find ideas symbolized in much of the world's best fiction.

1. Look again at those passages in this story which deal with the feathered coat. How do you know the coat was a symbol for the natives as well as for John March? Explain what it symbolized for them.

2. Was any character a symbol of an idea or moral value in addition to being an interesting person?

3. You accept quite a number of inanimate and animate objects as symbols for ideas or beliefs. Try to explain the symbolic meaning of the following:

Statue of Liberty	a dove
a flag at half mast	a hooded skeleton
a wreath on a door	a heart with an arrow through it
clasped hands	
a lion	Uncle Sam
a snake	a pair of scales
a rainbow	a cross

A Worm's-Eye View

LOUIS L. SNYDER and RICHARD B. MORRIS

Three times in recent history Americans have left their homes to help freedom-loving people in other parts of the world to maintain their liberty. Among those who enlisted in this venture were the men and women of the press who, without actually fighting, made an invaluable contribution to the cause of liberty. The reports of war correspondents served not only to keep the people at home informed about events abroad; they also served to build a moral link between the battlefield and the home front. Some of these reports were more than mere news articles. They penetrated through the noise and confusion of war to reveal the dreams and heartaches of the common soldier. Americans are proud to accept such moving reports as a permanent part of their national literature.

A shy, gnomelike little fellow with an almost bald pate, Ernie Pyle was the idol of GI's on a dozen fronts. He deliberately avoided the command post in favor of the foxhole. He wrote only about what he personally witnessed and experienced. He lived with the men who fought and he accompanied them into battle. He reported what the GI's felt, what the war meant to them, and what they were dreaming about.

Pyle's dispatches were filled with homely details—the GI's home town, his address, the names of members of his family. He noted little acts of kindness and unselfishness, the sadness, loneliness, and ennui of men bored to distraction behind the lines, the raw courage of boys who, in battle, became men. To the people at home he made it clear that for the average infantryman the war extended just about a hundred yards to either side.

The little reporter, with his worm's-eye view of the war, didn't write about military strategy, because he felt that he knew nothing about it. He pictured tired, dirty soldiers who didn't want to die, and he wrote of heroism, anger, wine, cussing, flowers, and many, many graves. This was the human side of the war.

For all this the GI's loved the bald little reporter from Indiana. He was one of them.

Here is Ernie Pyle's description of the final push of the First Infantry Division in the North African campaign. Written in the front lines before Mateur [1] in early May, 1943, it shows the great reporter at his best.

---

[1] *Mateur,* a town in Tunisia

THEY ARE JUST GUYS FROM BROADWAY AND MAIN STREET

ERNIE PYLE

We're now with an infantry outfit that has battled ceaselessly for four days and nights.

This northern warfare has been in the mountains. You don't ride much any more. It is walking and climbing and crawling country. The mountains are big, but they are constant. They are largely treeless. They are easy to defend and bitter to take. But we are taking them.

The Germans lie on the back slope of every ridge, deeply dug into foxholes. In front of them the fields and pastures are hideous with thousands of hidden mines. The forward slopes are left open, untenanted, and if the Americans tried to scale those slopes they would be murdered wholesale in an inferno of machine-gun cross fire, plus mortars and grenades.

Consequently, we don't do it that way. We have fallen back to the old warfare of first pulverizing the enemy with artillery, then sweeping around the ends of the hill with infantry and taking them from the sides and behind.

I've written before how the big guns crack and roar almost constantly throughout the day and night. They lay a screen ahead of our troops. By magnificent shooting they drop shells on the back slopes. By means of shells timed to burst in the air a few feet from the ground, they get the Germans even in their foxholes. Our troops have found that the Germans dig foxholes down and then under, trying to get cover from the shell bursts that shower death from above.

Our artillery really has been sensational. For once we have enough of something and at the right time. Officers tell me they actually have more guns than they know what to do with.

All the guns in any one sector can be centered to shoot at one spot. And when we lay the whole business on a German hill the entire slope seems to erupt. It becomes an unbelievable caldron of fire and smoke and dirt. Afterward, veteran German soldiers say they have never been through anything like it.

Now to the infantry—I love the infantry because they are the underdogs. They are the mud-rain-frost-and-wind boys. They have no comforts, and they even learn to live without the necessities. And in the end they are the guys that wars can't be won without.

I wish you could have seen just one of the ineradicable pictures I have in my mind today. In this particular picture I am sitting among clumps of sword grass on a steep and rocky hillside that we had just taken. We are looking out over a vast rolling country to the rear.

A narrow path comes like a ribbon over a hill miles away, down a long slope, across a creek, up a slope, and over another hill.

All along the length of that ribbon there is a thin line of men. For four days and nights they have fought hard, eaten little, washed none, and slept hardly at all. Their nights have been violent with attack, fright, butchery, their days sleepless and miserable with the crash of artillery.

The men are walking. They are fifty feet apart, for dispersal. Their walk is slow, for they are dead weary, as you can tell even when looking at them from behind. Every line and sag of their bodies speaks their inhuman exhaustion.

On their shoulders and backs they carry heavy steel tripods, machine-gun barrels, leaden boxes of ammunition. Their feet seem to sink into the ground from the overload they are bearing.

They don't slouch. It is the terrible deliberation of each step that spells out their appalling tiredness. Their faces are black and unshaved. They are young men, but the grime and whiskers and exhaustion make them look middle-aged.

In their eyes as they pass is not hatred, not excitement, not despair, not the tonic of their victory. There is just the simple expression of being there as if they had been doing that forever, and nothing else.

The line moves on, but it never ends. All afternoon men keep coming round the hill and vanish eventually over the horizon. It is one long tired line of antlike men.

There is an agony in your heart and you feel almost ashamed to look at them. They are just guys from Broadway and Main Street, but maybe you wouldn't remember them. They are too far away now. They are too tired. Their world can never be known to you, but if you could see them just once, just for an instant, you would know that no matter how hard people work back home they are not keeping pace with these infantrymen in Tunisia.

After four days in battle, the famous infantry outfit I'm with sat on its newly won hill and took two days' rest, while companion units on each side of it leapfrogged ahead.

The men dig in on the back slope of the hill before any rest begins. Everybody digs in. It is an inviolate rule of the commanding officers, and nobody wants to disobey it. Every time you pause, even if you think you're dying of weariness, you dig yourself a hole before you sit down.

The startling thing to me about those rest periods is how quickly the human body can recuperate from critical exhaustion, how rapidly the human mind snaps back to the normal state of laughing, grousing, yarn spinning, and yearning for home.

Here is what happens when a unit stops to rest:

My unit stops just after daybreak on Hill 394. Foxholes are dug, outposts are placed, phone wires are strung on the ground, some patrol work goes on as usual. Then the men lie down and sleep till the blistering heat of the sun wakes them up.

After that you sit around in bunches, recounting things. You can't do much of anything. The day just easily kills itself.

That first evening is when life begins to seem like Christmas Eve. The mail comes up in jeeps just before dark. Then come the men's blanket rolls. At dark, hot food arrives—the first hot food in four days. This food is cooked in rolling kitchens several miles back and brought up by jeep, in big thermos containers, to the foot of the hill. Men carry the containers, slung on poles over their shoulders, up goat paths in the darkness to all parts of the mountain.

Hot food and hot coffee put life into a man, and then in a pathetic kind of contentment you lie down and you sleep. The all-night crash of the artillery behind you is completely unheard through your weariness.

There are no mosquitoes so far in the mountains, and very few fleas, but there are lots of ants.

Hot food arrives again in the morning before daylight. Your breakfast is at four A.M. Then begins a day of reassembling yourself.

Word is passed that mail will be collected that evening, so the boys sit on the ground and write letters. But writing is hard, for they can't tell in their letters what they have just been through.

The men put water in their steel helmets and wash and shave for the first time in days. A few men at a time are sent to a creek in the valley to take baths. The remainder sit in groups on the ground, talking, or individually in foxholes, cleaning their guns, reading, or just relaxing.

A two-month-old batch of copies of the magazine Yank arrives, and a two-week-old bunch of the Stars and Stripes. Others read detective magazines and comic books that have come up with their bedrolls.

At noon everybody opens cans of cold C ration. Cold coffee in five-gallon water cans is out in the sun to warm.

Soldiers cut each other's hair. It doesn't matter how it looks, for they aren't going anywhere fancy, anyhow. Some of them strip nearly naked and lie on their blankets for a sunbath. Their bodies are tanned, as though they had been wintering at Miami Beach. They wear the inner part of their helmets, for the noonday sun is dangerous.

Their knees are skinned from crawling over rocks. They find little unimportant injuries that they didn't know they had. Some take off their shoes and socks and look over their feet, which are violently purple with athlete's-foot ointment.

I sit around with them, and they get to telling stories, both funny and serious, about their battle. They are all disappointed when they learn I am not permitted to name the outfit they're in, for they are all proud of it and would like the folks at home to know what they've done.

"We always get it the toughest," they said. "This is the third big battle now since coming to Africa. The Jerry [2] is really afraid of us now. He knows what outfit we are, and he doesn't like us."

Thus they talk and boast and laugh and speak of fear. Evening draws down, and the chill sets in once more. Hot chow arrives just after dusk.

And then the word is passed around. Orders come by telephone.

There is no excitement, no grouching, no eagerness either. They had expected it.

Quietly men roll their packs, strap them on, lift their rifles, and fall into line.

There is not a sound as they move like wraiths in single file down tortuous goat paths, walking slowly, feeling the ground with their toes, stumbling, and hushfully cussing. They will walk all night and attack before dawn.

They move like ghosts. You don't hear or see them three feet away. Now and then a light flashes lividly from a blast of our big guns, and for just an instant you see a long slow line of dark-helmeted forms silhouetted in the flash.

Then darkness and silence consume them again, and somehow you are terribly moved.

---

[2] *Jerry*, the Germans [*Colloquial*]

"It may be that the war has changed me," Pyle wrote later, "along with the rest. It is hard for anyone to analyze himself. I find more and more that I wish to be alone. I believe that I have a new patience with humanity that I've never had before. When you've lived with the unnatural mass cruelty that mankind is capable of inflicting upon itself, you find yourself dispossessed of the faculty of blaming one poor man for the triviality of his faults. I don't see how any survivor of war can ever be cruel to anything, ever again."

Ernie Pyle hated the entire dirty business of war, but he felt his place to be with the men at the front. He was killed by a Jap machine-gun bullet on the island of Ie Shima.

Disconsolate GI's who loved the wistful little newsman placed this inscription on a simple monument at the spot where he was killed:

AT THIS SPOT
THE
77TH INFANTRY DIVISION
LOST A BUDDY
ERNIE PYLE
18 APRIL 1945

The men who edited this selection

LOUIS L. SNYDER   1907–
RICHARD B. MORRIS   1904–

Both Mr. Snyder and Mr. Morris are history professors. Louis Snyder teaches at the College of the City of New York, and Richard Morris teaches at Columbia University. They believed that newspaper stories were not only an excellent source of historical information; they were also an important type of literature—"literature written under pressure"—which is often overlooked. Acting on this belief, these distinguished historians gathered together many important and interesting news stories for publication in *A Treasury of Great Reporting*.

Let's consider . . .

1. "He deliberately avoided the command post in favor of the foxhole." Now that you have read this account, explain why Ernie Pyle was probably a greater reporter because he wrote from a foxhole.

2. Families of soldiers in that campaign watched eagerly for Pyle's reports in their newspapers. Why do you think they wished to read such poignant accounts of the hardships "their boys" were enduring?

3. Speaking of a long line of infantrymen making their way along a narrow path over a hill, Pyle said "there is an agony in your heart and you feel ashamed almost to look at them." Reread the account of that agonizing march. Which features of it moved you most?

4. Why did Ernie Pyle "love the infantry"?

5. The rapidity with which the boys "came back" in a rest period was startling even to Pyle, who knew them so well. Select two features of their rest period which amazed and attracted you. Describe what made you realize they were "just guys from Broadway and Main Street."

6. What do you consider the most pathetic part of Pyle's account? After thinking about the pathos of it, tell why you think Pyle said "their world can never be known to you."

7. Later Ernie Pyle wrote that perhaps the war had changed him. In what ways did he consider himself different?

8. The inscription on Ernie Pyle's simple monument has the word "buddy" in it. Why did he deserve that tribute from the infantrymen?

The writer's craft . . .

At the beginning of this selection, historians Snyder and Morris gave you a brief introduction to Ernie Pyle. They described his physical appearance and commented on his unique way of reporting. However, you learned far more about Ernie Pyle as a person from his own words.

Think of the experiences he reported in "A Worm's-Eye View." Recall that what he wrote always seemed to be the soldiers' story and not his own. Now write a brief character sketch of Ernie Pyle as you have come to know him through this selection.

Knowing words . . .

An infantryman would be familiar with each of the italicized words in the sentences below. When you are sure what they mean, use each of them in a sentence of your own. Discuss these words and your sentences in class. Since military terms occur so often in stories of the past fifteen years, you ought to be familiar with them.

1. The Germans lie on the back slope of every ridge, deeply dug into *foxholes*.

2. In front of them the fields and pastures are hideous with thousands of hidden *mines*.

3. If the Americans tried to scale those slopes they would be murdered wholesale in an inferno of machine-gun cross fire, plus *mortars* and *grenades*.

4. We have fallen back to the old warfare of first pulverizing the enemy with *artillery*.

5. They are fifty feet apart, for *dispersal*.

6. Hot *chow* arrives just after dusk.

"The Free Man . . ."

The free man willing to pay and struggle and die
    for the freedom for himself and others
Knowing how far to subject himself to discipline
    and obedience for the sake of an ordered society
    free from tyrants, exploiters and
    legalized frauds—
This free man is a rare bird and when you meet
    him take a good look at him and try
    to figure him out because
Some day when the United States of the Earth
    gets going and runs smooth and pretty there
    will be more of him than we have now.

From The People, Yes *by Carl Sandburg*

Sunday: New Guinea

KARL SHAPIRO

The bugle sounds the measured call to prayers,
The band starts bravely with a clarion hymn,
From every side, singly, in groups, in pairs,
Each to his kind of service comes to worship Him.

Our faces washed, our hearts in the right place,
We kneel or stand or listen from our tents;
Half-naked natives with their kind of grace
Move down the road with balanced staffs like mendicants.[1]

And over the hill the guns bang like a door
And planes repeat their mission in the heights.
The jungle outmaneuvers creeping war
And crawls within the circle of our sacred rites.

I long for our dishevelled Sundays home,
Breakfast, the comics, news of latest crimes,
Talk without reference, and palindromes,[2]
Sleep and the Philharmonic and the ponderous *Times*.

I long for lounging in the afternoons
Of clean intelligent warmth, my brother's mind,
Books and thin plates and flowers and shining spoons,
And your love's presence, snowy, beautiful, and kind.

[1] *mendicants,* friars who beg
[2] *palindromes,* a type of word puzzle

658

The man who wrote this poem

KARL JAY SHAPIRO 1913–

Karl Shapiro is the spokesman for his generation. He expresses in modern poetry the thoughts and emotions of his contemporaries. There is wide variety in his use of form and choice of subject matter. His approach is sometimes serious, sometimes satirical.

His first volume of poems was published during World War II when he was serving with the U. S. Army in the South Pacific. The critics were impressed with this volume, *Person, Place and Thing,* and Mr. Shapiro received seven different prizes and awards before the war ended. He was awarded the 1945 Pulitzer Prize for *V-Letter and Other Poems,* published while he was stationed in the South Pacific.

Mr. Shapiro is also an able critic. For a year he was Consultant in Poetry at the Library of Congress. In 1947 he returned to his native Baltimore to become Assistant Professor of Writing at Johns Hopkins University. He left this position in 1950 to edit *Poetry* magazine.

Poems, 1940–1953 is a collection of his best poetry; *Essay on Rime* is his definition of what poetry should be.

The poet's art . . .

1. The poet used contrast here to present a vivid war-time Sunday in New Guinea. Describe the call to worship and the answer as it was given in the first two stanzas.

2. Explain how the poet set up a contrast in stanza three. How did the last two lines take you back to the mood of the first two stanzas?

3. Nostalgia (a longing for things of home) possessed the poet. What common, natural features of a home Sunday did he long for in the place where all of them were impossible? Which ones did you find especially appealing?

4. A poem makes an impression when the words are just *right.* Consider the following italicized words. Explain why they convey exactly the impression intended:

> *dishevelled* Sundays
> *ponderous Times*
> clean, *intelligent* warmth
> *thin* plates
> *shining* spoons
> *snowy* (in the last line)

Why did each expression present a point of contrast between "Sunday: New Guinea," and "Sunday: U.S.A."?

Tuputala

ROBERT P. PARSONS

As men and women of the Armed Forces have traveled throughout the world, they have come to understand and appreciate ways of life quite different from their own. Even more important, they have made friends of the people with whom they lived. Captain Parsons tells you about his friend Tuputala, the best saxophone player in the Polynesian village of Mapusaga.

(1)

Like most Americans in Mapusaga, I became acquainted with Tuputala's saxophone before I met him. One evening during our early days at Mapusaga I was sitting in the old Mormon church, where we had our administrative office, when there came to my ears the sweetest saxophone notes I had ever heard. What interested me was that anyone who could play such pure notes should be playing so falteringly.

The fellow was playing Schubert's *Serenade,* but he would play a short phrase or two, then stop and repeat it, and then wait several moments before going on with the next phrase. I went out to investigate and found Tidwell (one of the fine vocalists of our hospital corpsmen) sitting on a cargo crate beside a large, light-brown Elysian [1] man. The Elysian was holding a saxophone and listening to Tidwell singing Schubert's *Serenade,* a phrase at a time. It was Tuputala, hearing the *Serenade* for the first time. In a few minutes Tidwell sang the whole piece through without a stop. Tuputala, sitting motionless and all ears, was allowing it to register on his infallible musical memory. Then he put his

lips to the sax and gave the lower hillside as flawless and sweet a rendition of the *Serenade* as anyone could want.

That was my introduction to Tuputala's saxophone, but I had to wait some weeks before I exchanged words with him. A few evenings later I went to my first Elysian dance, at a *fale* [2] in Faleniu. That was the first time I saw and heard the great Tuputala getting hot with a hot Elysian dance orchestra.

He was a musical clown as well as a musical artist. He could play almost any instrument—and whatever the instrument he started to play, he invariably pronounced it his favorite. He would have given his soul to own a saxophone, but he had never been able to save enough money to buy one. In fact, the only musical appliance he ever had a clear title to up to that time was a small piece of steel he used in producing steel guitar effects on an ordinary wooden guitar. He could get more fine melody from a three-dollar ukulele than many competent fiddlers can produce with a violin.

At dances he would beat time with his size fourteen bare foot, which went flap-flap on the floor so loudly you could almost

---

[1] *Elysian,* native to the Polynesian Islands

[2] *fale,* a large dwelling

consider it a part of the drum section. He also kept time with his head, and when he got into the hot and fast runs with his saxophone, his neck went through some alarming contortions. If the stringed instrument of a near-by player was the slightest shade off tune Tuputala would reach over with one swift movement, in the middle of a piece, and give the proper tuning key just a hair of a turn and go on as though nothing had happened. I don't think that was clowning. It was just that Tuputala could not endure a chord with a flaw in it, even a flaw too small for detection by ordinary ears.

(2)

One night in August, 1942, I was reading in my tent when a vague awareness came to me that something or someone was near the tent entrance. It might have been a moving shadow or it might have been a noise no louder than the moths made around the electric light above the table. I looked up from my book and there in front of the tent entrance stood Tuputala. How long he had been there I couldn't say. It might have been a half hour.

That is the Elysians' way of making a call. They just sneak up to your front door and stand there until you call them in. From their point of view there is a reason for this method. They can hear bare feet approaching at fifty yards, no matter how stealthy the approach. At twenty yards they know who it is, day or night, and at ten yards they know your mood and what you are thinking about. So before you are within twenty yards of their *fale* they can welcome you in.

If they don't notice you, it isn't because they don't know you are there—it means your presence is not desired. I have excellent hearing and vision, by the white man's standard, but the Elysians considered me, like all *palagi* (white people), practically deaf and blind.

I was speechless for a moment as I looked at Tuputala and he looked at me.

He said, "Oxcoose me, gentlemans Kaptin, you say I come in?"

"Sure," I said. "Come on in. You're Tuputala, aren't you?"

"Sure," he said, "dat's me." He sat down cross-legged on the floor in a corner of the tent. Then he wouldn't say anything for a few minutes. Just short non-informative answers to my questions that were partly social amenities and partly for the purpose of finding out the reason for his visit. But you can't hurry an Elysian in conversation. He has to go through the preliminaries, whether they take five minutes or a half hour.

If a high chief comes to call and only wants a bucket of garbage for his pigs, he will start by saying, "I call upon the mercy and love of God. It is so nice for us to meet this pleasant morning. All the round shells are in the bag and all the oranges are on the twig (meaning 'Well, here we are assembled together.') We are meeting, I hope, in the best of health, but not in disturbances."

Tuputala was embarrassed. It took him some time to come to the point, or points. At last he said, "Say, Kaptin, I got big trouble with Tuia." Then for half an hour he related how Tuia had induced him, three months earlier, to leave a good stevedoring job in Fagatoga and come to Mapusaga to play in one of Tuia's dance orchestras.

At that time a clever dance racketeer could operate different orchestras in different villages every night in the week and with fifty cents admission make a net profit of fifty dollars from each *fale* where one of his orchestras was furnishing the music. The musicians themselves received two dollars for the evening's work—if they could collect it from the orchestra owner.

The orchestra owners really owned the orchestras—bodies, souls, and instruments. They either owned all the instruments (as Tuia did) or had obtained exclusive orchestra rights in certain villages through arrangements with the high chiefs of those villages. There was no muscling in. You either had exclusive villages rights or you had nothing. It was tighter than a musicians' union in the States.

The proposition had looked very attractive to Tuputala because two dollars a day was considerable money for doing something that he had loved to do anyhow. It did not appear remarkable to Tuputala that he, acknowledged in every village as the number one saxophonist of the island, should not own a saxophone, or that he should be working for two dollars a day for a boss who was making so much money on Tuputala's playing that the boss could not even imagine what to do with it all.

The only thing worrying Tuputala was that he had never been able to collect one evening's pay in three months. That evening he had demanded a settlement. Harsh words had been exchanged. Tuputala had dared to talk back to Tuia and to tell Tuia what he thought of him because Tuputala was not, strictly speaking, a citizen of Mapusaga—and therefore not subject to the caprices of the chief.

Tuia had called Tuputala the equivalent of a base and uncouth yokel. He would pay Tuputala off and be rid of him and never again could Tuputala play in one of Tuia's orchestras or even touch one of Tuia's saxophones.

The "big trouble" about which Tuputala was now complaining to me had occurred in the pay-off. Tuia had shown him a lot of arithmetic, proving that he owed Tuputala exactly fifteen dollars. Tuputala thought it should be thirty dollars. The sums were so small because Tuputala's "board and room" were deducted from his salary. He had been occupying a mat in Tuia's *fale* and had moreover been eating four meals a day at the Tuia menage. Also Saki, Tuia's wife, had been washing Tuputala's lava-lavas[3] for him.

I asked Tuputala what he was going to live on, now that he was black-listed from Tuia's orchestra and had been thrown out

of Tuia's *fale* where he had been eating and using a sleeping mat. Tuputala was at a loss to understand my concern on this point. No Elysian has ever been known to worry about what the morrow will bring or fail to bring. He said that he would get his taro[4] "okay same like before" because he was now living with his "cushin" (cousin), Tavili, whose *fale* was only two *fales* down the hill from Tuia's.

I suggested that his cushin would expect some payment sooner or later for this, to which he replied, "No, dat is my *aiga* (family) and we don't pay no money to *aigas*." Maybe he would give his "cushin a presents sometimes like maybe can salmon or can peaches or pisoupo." (Pea soup was the first type of canned food to reach the islands. Thus, all canned food was likely to be called "pisoupo.") I asked him how long he could buy things like that with fifteen dollars. "Maybe long time," he said. "Tuia will give me de odda fifteen dolla when he hear you gentlemans Kaptin know about dis."

"How will Tuia hear about it?" I asked him.

"He maybe know about dat now," he said. And probably he was right, because nothing much was ever said or thought in Mapusaga that didn't spread to every *fale* in the village within a few minutes by some telepathy. Tuputala wanted to change the subject. He didn't want to be reminded that some day soon his money would be spent and his welcome at the home of his cushin might be worn out.

(3)

Tuputala made many visits to my tent after that. He wanted especially to talk about music and his musical ambitions. On the other island he had been a prize fighter, at ten dollars per infrequent fight, and since his early youth had made a bare living playing in dance orchestras or concert orchestras when not engaged in plantation labor. His only happiness had been

---
[3] *lava-lavas,* skirts made of printed cloth

[4] *taro,* starchy edible root of the taro plant

with music. He could be supremely happy if he could live by his music and not have to work as a stevedore or in taro patches.

All he really needed to make him happy, Tuputala said, was a saxophone. He wanted to make a down payment of twenty dollars with me, have me arrange for the shipment of a good secondhand sax from the States, and then pay a dollar or two at a time until the account was settled. I told him I would write to the States for a sax but that I should own it and he would play it. If he owned it, I told him, he would sell it at some period of want and then he would be unhappy again. The deal delighted him.

Tuputala talked about music. He said that all Elysians were pretty good natural musicians but that only rarely would one make the effort to study music seriously. That was why they didn't know the difference between a major and minor chord, or a major and minor key. He said they sang church music, popular American music, and their own folk songs all in minors just because they liked it that way, not because they knew what they were doing. He said, "De way dey sing 'De Sta Spangle Banna,' you American have hard time to know what it is dey sing." Tuputala was quite correct. You could scarcely recognize the music or words, but a chorus of Elysian school kids singing "De Sta Spangle Banna" was always so beautiful and soulful that it was a sure-fire tear-jerker for any American.

During the months we waited for the sax to arrive, Tuputala entertained me scores of times with guitar or ukulele. He could glance at a piece of sheet music, hum it to himself a moment while he flapped time with his bare foot, and then play it through flawlessly. He could listen to a new song on the radio, shut off the radio, and repeat it, usually better than the radio performance, without missing a word or a note. What awed me as much as his music was his ability to remember the words. Another of his stunts was to accompany popular music with my ukulele, which he did to

perfection, even when the number was one he had never heard before. He loved my radio. He loved the symphony concerts on the radio but said that only a rare Elysian could "know to like dat kind music." When he had daydreams he thought about going to Honolulu to study music seriously, like blind Joe Salonoa, the public school music teacher at Fagatoga.

Just a few nights after Tuputala's big quarrel with Tuia I borrowed Tuia's saxophone for Tuputala to play at one of our hospital crew dances. It broke Tuia's heart to do it and he said I was asking an impossible thing of him; that I was asking him to love an enemy who wanted to kill him. I reminded Tuia that he was an elder in the Mormon church—which upheld the Bible that advocated loving one's enemies, and that furthermore he didn't have to love Tuputala in order to let him play his saxophone at our dance.

Tuia said, "All right, I will lend the saxophone, not because I love Tuputala, but because it is your desire and because I love the Americans of this village."

When Tuputala came to see me the next day, I related how Tuia had wept in righteous protest before lending the saxophone. Tuputala's comment was: "But jus' only face his cries; sweet lips he got, but heart is mad want to kill."

(4)

The new saxophone arrived from Montgomery Ward ($75.00) a few days before Christmas. I sent word to Tuputala to come up and try it out. My new *fale* was perched high on the mountainside, difficult to reach without getting short of breath.

Tuputala came up the path in a full run. He stood in the doorway, panting. Sweat was streaming from his bare torso onto a freshly laundered lava-lava. He didn't wait to recover his breath; he even saw fit to dispense with the customary conversational preliminaries. His eyes were intent and his face was set in a smile of pleasant expectancy.

"You got it?" he asked, looking at me. Then his eyes shifted to the case in the corner of the room. "You got it!" he said.

"You unpack it and put it together," I said.

While assembling it, he doted over and fondled that saxophone like a mother dressing her first-born.

He put the mouthpiece to his lips and ran up and down a fast chromatic scale to test all the keys. "Oxcoose please, gentlemens," he said, "what you want de fust numba?"

" 'In the Mood,' " I said, knowing that to be his current favorite of the hot and fast section.

He made it moan and whine; he gave it rippling laughter, chortles, plaints, ineffably melodious sweetness, everything but actual words. He continued all evening, until we both had exhausted our memories of musical composition titles.

Three months later it was "necessary" for Tuputala to return to the island of his "auntie." When it comes time to make a journey to another island, there is no use talking about it—in Polynesia certainly no use talking against it; it is as natural an event as the migration of birds. Now he was torn between the migratory pull and a saxophone he didn't own but couldn't leave behind. There was only one solution.

He came to my *fale* on the evening before his departure, and stood on the porch so silently I didn't look up from my book until he said, "Hello, Kaptin, I come say *tofa* (farewell) to you."

I knew what he was leading up to; he had to take the sax with him. "But how can you do that? I have seventy-five bucks in that sax."

Grinning, he reached down under the waistband of his lava-lava and brought out a wallet. He walked over to the table and emptied its contents. We counted it—exactly seventy-five dollars.

"And where in the world did you get that?"

"My cushin," he said. "He want I look like a big man when I go my auntie's *fale*."

More months went by. I was missing Tuputala's visits and his recitals. Then I had occasion to be on the island of his auntie for a few days. I had no idea what village he might be staying in. No one seemed to know of him around the large village.

But on the last evening of our stay on the island we drove out to see Isaako, a native Mormon missionary, formerly of Mapusaga, who lived at the village of Nofo Alii (Home of Kings). We were sitting around the kerosene lamp, visiting with Isaako and his family, when I heard coming from a *fale* off in the bush some strains of uncommonly fine dance music. It sounded like a practice session of a small dance orchestra.

"I thought only one man in these islands could play a saxophone that well; a man named Tuputala," I said to Isaako.

"That *is* Tuputala," Isaako said. He told me about Tuputala's very wonderful saxophone. "Three hundred dollars it is worth," he said, "but some officers get it for him for only a hundred fifty."

The man who wrote this story

ROBERT P. PARSONS   1891–

During the summers of his childhood years, Mr. Parsons used to visit a lake in the backwoods of northern Michigan. The "intense admiration" which he developed for the lumberjack and the pioneer farmer influenced his own philosophy of life. He has never lost his faith in the "simple" life and in "primitive" people.

After graduation from high school, Mr. Parsons worked in Yellowstone Park and in the timber regions of Washington. He also spent some time with a road gang in Southern California.

When Mr. Parsons finished his studies at Harvard Medical School, he planned to become a specialist in the care of infants. But when World War I broke out, he joined the Navy "with the idea of getting out as soon as possible after the war's end. . . . It took 32 years."

During his service with the Navy, Dr. Parsons saw many countries, had many adventures, and wrote many books. He was shipwrecked in the Baltic, spent years in Haiti, edited the *Naval Medical Journal,* and was among the first Navy doctors to examine the survivors of the atomic blast in Nagasaki. His book *Mob 3,* which appeared in 1944, recounts his experiences in the South Pacific with Tuputala and other Polynesians whom he learned to know.

Now retired from service, Dr. Parsons states his formula for keeping young in this way: "Keep working, studying, learning; never relax curiosity; keep the mind open and busy."

Let's consider . . .

1. Edgar Allan Poe believed that a story "must attract instantly." Why did Parsons' introduction to "Tuputala" attract you instantly?

2. Contrast the formality of the Elysians with the informality of the American soldiers.

3. Tuputala was a natural musician. It seems strange, therefore, that he had never had an instrument of his own. Give as many reasons as you can why this was so.

4. What surprised you most about the village orchestras?

5. It was inevitable that, sooner or later, Tuia and Tuputala should quarrel bitterly. How did Tuputala explain their business arrangements to the "Kaptin"? Why do you think he sought the American?

6. Tuputala did not worry at all about what he was going to live on once he had

lost his job with the orchestra. Why not?

7. All this Elysian musician needed to make him happy was a saxophone. How did he get one? Aside from the seventy-five dollars he finally paid for it, what payment did he make to the "Kaptin"?

8. In many ways Tuputala and the other Elysians you met in this story were different from the Americans. Still, there were many points of resemblance. Which of these impressed you? Comment on them.

9. Why is the ending of this story effective?

The writer's craft . . .

A. Your memories of this story are probably all associated in some way with the colorful Elysian musician, Tuputala. It was his personality which provided the total single impression which the author wanted to create. The plot of the story (the planned sequence of events) was of so little consequence that it was almost nonexistent. Whenever action did occur, it served merely to illuminate some aspect of Tuputala's personality and so to contribute to the total single impression.

The author handled the setting of this story in much the same way that he handled the plot. If Tuputala had lived in a different part of the world, his entire way of life would have been different and so, of course, would he. Even the social customs of his village of Mapusaga helped to make Tuputala the kind of person he was.

Select one or two incidents from the plot and one or two aspects of the setting which illuminated Tuputala's character and contributed to the total single impression of the story.

B. Because the American captain told this story, you always saw Tuputala through his eyes.

1. In what ways did this point of view limit what you could learn about Tuputala?

2. In what ways did it increase your understanding of the musician?

3. Did the author add to the total single impression or detract from it by having the captain narrate the story?

Knowing words . . .

The prefix tele- signifies "far off" or "distant." Robert Parsons wrote ". . . nothing much was ever said or thought in Mapusaga that didn't spread to every fale in the village within a few minutes by some telepathy." The word telepathy means an unusual kind of thought transference from one person to another without any understandable means of communication.

List six words which begin with the prefix tele- and which signify "at a distance." Then use each word in a sentence of your own.

NOW THINK BACK

Below you will find seven statements which apply to the various selections in this part. Copy the numbers of these statements on your paper. After each number write the following information which relates to that statement:

The title of the appropriate selection
The nationality and/or part of the world involved
The contribution of that person to America, or America's contribution to him or her
The value which this selection had for you

1. Americans must pay in energy for the material comforts they demand.

2. He could hardly believe that he was to possess this big stretch of land and have his friends for neighbors, both to the north and to the south, friends who wanted to help him.

3. The GI's idolized him, and he immortalized the GI's.

4. A Puritan conscience operating far from New England made a friend for America.

5. "Absence makes the heart grow fonder."

6. War is not the sole interest of U. S. Army officers abroad.

7. Once she had discovered America, she knew that all the long years of hoping and planning were right, and meant to be.

Things to do . . .

1. If you had an opportunity to go to one of the foreign countries mentioned in this part, which one would you choose and what would you do there? Remember that your own country would be judged by your behavior and by the quality of your work. Prepare a three-minute talk in which you clearly identify *where* you would like to go, *what* you would like to do, and *how* you would act to create a friendly feeling toward America.

2. Which one of the foreigners mentioned in this part would you like to entertain in your home or have as a near neighbor? Imagine that he or she had just come to this country. What in your vicinity would you show your foreign friend in hopes of making him or her feel at home? What would you talk about? Prepare brief but specific notes for use in a class discussion. Select a chairman so that everyone will have a chance to contribute.

3. Assume that you are secretary of a student-faculty committee to plan assembly programs. Write a letter to one of the characters mentioned in this part or to one of the authors. Ask him or her to speak before the student body on a given date, or allow him a choice of two dates. Describe the occasion, especially if you want his talk to serve a particular purpose, such as awaken interest in good citizenship, world brotherhood, or choosing a career. Be sure to include those important details of (1) the time of the assembly program, (2) the time alloted for his talk, (3) the exact place where you will meet him, and (4) the fee you can afford to pay for his services. Explain briefly why you are particularly eager for him to address the school. Some speakers like you to suggest several topics within their range of experience and knowledge which the audience will enjoy and which would be especially suited to the occasion. Always allow the speaker to name his own topic if he prefers. Exchange letters for checking the content, style, and appropriate form. Consult a standard handbook for matters of form and punctuation.

4. Make a scrapbook of pictures illustrating life in each region of the world you have viewed in this part. (Use illustrated magazines and make this a class project.)

5. Secure booklets and maps from travel agencies or airlines so that you can trace a trip to the section of the world you found most inviting.

More to read . . .

My Uncle Jan by JOSEPH AUSLANDER and AUDREY WURDEMANN.
Longmans, Green & Co., Inc., 1948.
My Antonia by WILLA CATHER.
Houghton Mifflin Company, 1926.
Shake Hands with the Dragon by CARL GLICK.
McGraw-Hill Book Company, Inc., 1941.
Lost Island by JAMES NORMAN HALL.
Little, Brown and Company, 1944.
Singing Among Strangers by MABLE LEIGH.
J. B. Lippincott Company, 1954.
Hold Fast the Dream by ELIZABETH LOW.
Harcourt, Brace and Company, 1955.
My Name Is Aram by WILLIAM SAROYAN.
Harcourt, Brace and Company, 1940.
Americans One and All by HARRY SHAW and RUTH DAVIS.
Harper & Brothers, 1947.

* * *

The Eve of St. Mark by MAXWELL ANDERSON.
William Sloane Associates, 1942.

The American Way by GEORGE S. KAUFMAN and MOSS HART.
Random House, Inc., 1939.

* * *

My Turkish Adventure by PAMELA BURR.
W. W. Norton & Company, Inc., 1951.
Haiti: Highroad to Adventure by H. B. CAVE.
Henry Holt and Company, Inc., 1952.
Beyond the High Himalayas by WILLIAM O. DOUGLAS.
Doubleday & Company, Inc., 1952.
North from Malaya by WILLIAM O. DOUGLAS.
Doubleday & Company, Inc., 1953.
Hiroshima by JOHN HERSEY.
Alfred A. Knopf, Inc., 1946.
Far Far From Home by RUTH MCKENNEY.
Harper & Brothers, 1954.
Persian Adventure by A. S. MEHDEVI.
Alfred A. Knopf, Inc., 1953.
The Voice of Asia by JAMES A. MICHENER.
Random House, Inc., 1951.
The Making of an American by JACOB RIIS.
The Macmillan Company, 1928.
Syrian Yankee by SALOM RIZK.
Doubleday & Company, Inc., 1943.
A Penny from Heaven by MAX WINKLER.
Appleton-Century-Crofts, Inc., 1951.
Fifth Chinese Daughter by JADE SNOW WONG.
Harper & Brothers, 1950.

A TIME FOR ACTION

In 1906 all of San Francisco was destroyed by an earthquake and the fire which followed. In reporting that disaster, Jack London observed that in spite of the tremendous loss, the people remained calm. He wrote, "In all those terrible hours I saw not one woman who wept, not one man who was excited, not one person who was in the slightest degree panic stricken . . . Never in all San Francisco's history were her people so kind and courteous as on this night of terror."

If any nation is to endure, its citizens must be strong enough to meet each new crisis with courage. They must learn how to act in time of a national disaster which involves thousands of people; they must also learn how to act when the disaster is personal.

The people in A TIME FOR ACTION face different crises. Some of them see the need for action and meet the challenge successfully; others, for various reasons, are unable to act, or they act unwisely. But whether they succeed or fail, all are human beings living their lives the best way they know how.

A TIME FOR ACTION

Jack London Sees a City Die

LOUIS L. SNYDER and RICHARD B. MORRIS

Have you ever gone to a fire and stood as close to a burning building as the police would allow? Have you ever watched a forest fire licking its way along the underbrush toward dwellings in the distance? Recall the flaming heat, the crackling of the flames, and the frightful devastation. With these memories fresh in your mind, you may be able to appreciate the horror of the conflagration that raged through San Francisco.

Early in 1906 Jack London, a native San Franciscan, sailor, stoker, mill hand, janitor, and friend of the underdog, expressed a wish to work, crowbar in hand, shoulder to shoulder with intellectuals and workers, "to get a solid pry now and again" and set the whole edifice of society rocking. "Someday," he prophesied, "when we get a few more hands and crowbars to work, we'll topple it over, along with all its rotten life and unburied dead, its monstrous selfishness and sodden materialism."

The San Francisco earthquake, hard upon London's prediction, accomplished in a few moments more than all the crowbars London and his friends could have wielded in a generation. This master of swift and vivid action, one of the fabulously successful writers of modern times, happened to be near the scene and wrote a vivid firsthand account of the disaster. In a biography of her husband, Charmian London recounts the circumstances of the writing assignment. Jack was so deeply shaken by the catastrophe that he declared: "I'll never write about this for anybody. What use trying? One could only string big words together, and curse the futility of them." Soon came frantic wires from *Collier's Weekly*, asking for a 2500-word description of the earthquake and fire. The offer of twenty-five cents a word was too attractive for the narrator of the Klondike gold rush to ignore.

London dashed off the article. His wife snatched his scribbled sheets and swiftly typed them. The story was sent out over the wires, and, "just for luck," Jack mailed the manuscript simultaneously. Wild daily messages from *Collier's* followed for a week to come. "Why doesn't your story arrive?" "Must have your story immediately!" "Holding presses at enormous expense. What is the matter? Must have your story for May-fifth number."

The report arrived in time for the May 5 issue and was published under a banner title: THE STORY OF AN EYEWITNESS, BY JACK LONDON, COLLIER'S SPECIAL CORRESPONDENT. A blurb at the head told how the story was planned:

Upon receipt of the first news of the earthquake, Collier's *telegraphed to Mr. Jack London, who lives only forty miles from San Francisco, requesting him to go to the scene of disaster and write the story of what he saw. Mr. London started at once, and has sent the following dramatic description of the tragic events he witnessed in the burning city.*

671

The Story of an Eyewitness

BY JACK LONDON
Collier's Special Correspondent

The earthquake shook down in San Francisco hundreds of thousands of dollars' worth of walls and chimneys. But the conflagration that followed burned up hundreds of millions of dollars' worth of property. There is no estimating within hundreds of millions the actual damage wrought. Not in history has a modern imperial city been so completely destroyed. San Francisco is gone! Nothing remains of it but memories and a fringe of dwelling houses on its outskirts. Its industrial section is wiped out. Its social and residential section is wiped out. The factories and warehouses, the great stores and newspaper buildings, the hotels and the palaces of the nabobs, are all gone. Remains only the fringe of dwelling houses on the outskirts of what was once San Francisco.

Within an hour after the earthquake shock the smoke of San Francisco's burning was a lurid tower visible a hundred miles away. And for three days and nights this lurid tower swayed in the sky, reddening the sun, darkening the day, and filling the land with smoke.

On Wednesday morning at a quarter past five came the earthquake. A minute later the flames were leaping upward. In a dozen different quarters south of Market Street, in the working-class ghetto, and in the factories, fires started. There was no opposing the flames. There was no organization, no communication. All the cunning adjustments of a twentieth-century city had been smashed by the earthquake. The streets were humped into ridges and depressions and piled with debris of fallen walls. The steel rails were twisted into perpendicular and horizontal angles. The telephone and telegraph systems were disrupted. And the great water mains had burst. All the shrewd contrivances and safeguards of man had been thrown out of gear by thirty seconds' twitching of the earth crust.

By Wednesday afternoon, inside of twelve hours, half the heart of the city was gone. At the time I watched the vast conflagration from out on the bay. It was dead calm. Not a flicker of wind stirred. Yet from every side wind was pouring in upon the city. East, west, north, and south, strong winds were blowing upon the doomed city. The heated air rising made an enormous suck. Thus did the fire of itself build its own colossal chimney through the atmosphere. Day and night this dead calm continued, and yet, near to the flames, the wind was often half a gale, so mighty was the suck.

The edict which prevented chaos was the following proclamation by Mayor E. E. Schmitz:

"The Federal Troops, the members of the Regular Police Force, and all Special Police Officers have been authorized to KILL any and all persons found engaged in looting or in the commission of any other crime.

"I have directed all the Gas and Electric Lighting Companies not to turn on gas or electricity until I order them to do so; you may therefore expect the city to remain in darkness for an indefinite time.

"I request all citizens to remain at home from darkness until daylight of every night until order is restored.

"I warn all citizens of the danger of fire from damaged or destroyed chimneys, broken or leaking gas pipes or fixtures, or any like cause."

Wednesday night saw the destruction of the very heart of the city. Dynamite was lavishly used, and many of San Francisco's proudest structures were crumbled by man himself into ruins, but there was no withstanding the onrush of the flames. Time and again successful stands were made by the fire fighters, and every time the flames flanked around on either side, or came up from the rear, and turned to defeat the hard-won victory.

An enumeration of the buildings destroyed would be a directory of San Francisco. An enumeration of the buildings undestroyed would be a line and several addresses. An enumeration of the deeds of heroism would stock a library and bankrupt the Carnegie medal fund. An enumeration of the dead—will never be made. All vestiges of them were destroyed by the flames. The number of the victims of the earthquake will never be known. South of Market Street, where the loss of life was particularly heavy, was the first to catch fire.

Remarkable as it may seem, Wednesday night, while the whole city crashed and roared into ruin, was a quiet night. There were no crowds. There was no shouting and yelling. There was no hysteria, no disorder. I passed Wednesday night in the part of the advancing flames, and in all those terrible hours I saw not one woman who wept, not one man who was excited, not one person who was in the slightest degree panic-stricken.

Before the flames, throughout the night, fled tens of thousands of homeless ones. Some were wrapped in blankets. Others carried bundles of bedding and dear household treasures. Sometimes a whole family was harnessed to a carriage or delivery wagon that was weighted down with their possessions. Baby buggies, toy wagons, and gocarts were used as trucks, while every other person was dragging a trunk. Yet everybody was gracious. The most perfect courtesy obtained. Never in all San Francisco's history were her people so kind and courteous as on this night of terror.

All the night these tens of thousands fled before the flames. Many of them, the poor people from the labor ghetto, had fled all day as well. They had left their homes burdened with possessions. Now and again they lightened up, flinging out upon the street clothing and treasures they had dragged for miles.

They held on longest to their trunks, and over these trunks many a strong man broke his heart that night. The hills of San Francisco are steep, and up these hills, mile after mile, were the trunks dragged. Everywhere were trunks, with across them lying their exhausted owners, men and women. Before the march of the flames were flung picket lines of soldiers. And a block at a time, as the flames advanced, these pickets retreated. One of their tasks was to keep the trunk pullers moving. The exhausted creatures, stirred on by the menace of bayonets, would arise and struggle up the steep pavements, pausing from weakness every five or ten feet.

Often after surmounting a heartbreaking hill, they would find another wall of flame advancing upon them at right angles and be compelled to change anew the line of their retreat. In the end, completely played out, after toiling for a dozen hours like giants, thousands of them were compelled to abandon their trunks. Here the shopkeepers and soft members of the middle class were at a disadvantage. But the workingmen dug holes in vacant lots and back yards and buried their trunks.

At nine o'clock Wednesday evening I walked down through miles and miles of magnificent buildings and towering skyscrapers. Here was no fire. All was in perfect order. The police patrolled the streets. Every building had its watchman at the door. And yet it was doomed, all of it. There was no water. The dynamite was

674

giving out. And at right angles two different conflagrations were sweeping down upon it.

At one o'clock in the morning I walked down through the same section. Everything still stood intact. There was no fire. And yet there was a change. A rain of ashes was falling. The watchmen at the doors were gone. The police had been withdrawn. There were no firemen, no fire engines, no men fighting with dynamite. The district had been absolutely abandoned. I stood at the corner of Kearney and Market, in the very innermost heart of San Francisco. Kearney Street was deserted. Half a dozen blocks away it was burning on both sides. The street was a wall of flame. And against this wall of flame, silhouetted sharply, were two United States cavalrymen sitting their horses, calmly watching. That was all. Not another person was in sight. In the intact heart of the city two troopers sat their horses and watched.

Surrender was complete. There was no water. The sewers had long since been pumped dry. There was no dynamite. Another fire had broken out further uptown, and now from three sides conflagrations were sweeping down. The fourth side had been burned earlier in the day. In that direction stood the tottering walls of the Examiner Building, the burned-out Call Building, the smoldering ruins of the Grand Hotel, and the gutted, devastated, dynamited Palace Hotel.

The following will illustrate the sweep of the flames and the inability of men to calculate their spread. At eight o'clock Wednesday evening I passed through Union Square. It was packed with refugees. Thousands of them had gone to bed on the grass. Government tents had been set up, supper was being cooked, and the refugees were lining up for free meals.

At half-past one in the morning three sides of Union Square were in flames. The fourth side, where stood the great St. Francis Hotel, was still holding out. An hour later, ignited from top and sides, the St. Francis was flaming heavenward. Union Square, heaped high with mountains of

trunks, was deserted. Troops, refugees, and all had retreated.

It was at Union Square that I saw a man offering a thousand dollars for a team of horses. He was in charge of a truck piled high with trunks from some hotel. It had been hauled here into what was considered safety, and the horses had been taken out. The flames were on three sides of the square, and there were no horses.

Also, at this time, standing beside the truck, I urged a man to seek safety in flight. He was all but hemmed in by several conflagrations. He was an old man and he was on crutches. Said he: "Today is my birthday. Last night I was worth thirty thousand dollars. I bought five bottles of wine, some delicate fish, and other things for my birthday dinner. I have had no dinner, and all I own are these crutches."

I convinced him of his danger and started him limping on his way. An hour later, from a distance, I saw the truckload of trunks burning merrily in the middle of the street.

On Thursday morning, at a quarter past five, just twenty-four hours after the earthquake, I sat on the steps of a small residence of Nob Hill. With me sat Japanese, Italians, Chinese, and Negroes—a bit of

the cosmopolitan flotsam of the wreck of the city. All about were the palaces of the nabob pioneers of Forty-nine. To the east and south, at right angles, were advancing two mighty walls of flame.

I went inside with the owner of the house on the steps of which I sat. He was cool and cheerful and hospitable. "Yesterday morning," he said, "I was worth six hundred thousand dollars. This morning this house is all I have left. It will go in fifteen minutes." He pointed to a large cabinet. "That is my wife's collection of China. This rug upon which we stand is a present. It cost fifteen hundred dollars. Try that piano. Listen to its tone. There are few like it. There are no horses. The flames will be here in fifteen minutes."

Outside, the old Mark Hopkins residence, a palace, was just catching fire. The troops were falling back and driving refugees before them. From every side came the roaring of flames, the crashing of walls, and the detonations of dynamite.

I passed out of the house. Day was trying to dawn through the smoke pall. A sickly light was creeping over the face of things. Once only the sun broke through the smoke pall, blood-red, and showing quarter its usual size. The smoke pall itself, viewed from beneath, was a rose color that pulsed and fluttered with lavender shades. Then it turned to mauve and yellow and dun. There was no sun. And so dawned the second day on stricken San Francisco.

An hour later I was creeping past the shattered dome of the City Hall. Than it there was no better exhibit of the destructive force of the earthquake. Most of the stones had been shaken from the great dome, leaving standing the naked framework of steel. Market Street was piled high with the wreckage, and across the wreckage lay the overthrown pillars of the City Hall shattered into short crosswise sections.

This section of the city, with the exception of the Mint and the Post Office, was already a waste of smoking ruins. Here

and there through the smoke, creeping warily under the shadows of tottering walls, emerged occasional men and women. It was like the meeting of the handful of survivors after the day of the end of the world.

On Mission Street lay a dozen steers, in a neat row stretching across the street, just as they had been struck down by the flying ruins of the earthquake. The fire had passed through afterward and roasted them. The human dead had been carried away before the fire came. At another place on Mission Street I saw a milk wagon. A steel telegraph pole had smashed down sheer through the driver's seat and crushed the front wheels. The milk cans lay scattered around.

All day Thursday and all Thursday night, all day Friday and Friday night, the flames still raged.

Friday night saw the flames finally conquered, though not until Russian Hill and Telegraph Hill had been swept and three quarters of a mile of wharves and docks had been licked up.

The great stand of the fire fighters was made Thursday night on Van Ness Avenue. Had they failed here, the comparatively few remaining houses of the city would have been swept.

Here were the magnificent residences of the second generation of San Francisco nabobs, and these, in a solid zone, were dynamited down across the path of the fire. Here and there the flames leaped the zone, but these fires were beaten out, principally by the use of wet blankets and rugs.

San Francisco, at the present time, is like a crater of a volcano, around which are camped tens of thousands of refugees. At the Presidio alone are at least twenty thousand. All the surrounding cities and towns are jammed with the homeless ones, where they are being cared for by the relief committees. The refugees were carried free by the railroads to any point they wished to go, and it is estimated that over one hundred thousand people have left the peninsula on which San Francisco stood. The government has the situation in hand, and thanks to the immediate relief given by the whole United States, there is not the slightest possibility of a famine. The bankers and businessmen have already set about making preparations to rebuild San Francisco.

Let's consider . . .

1. Describe the astounding *speed* with which fires started and flames swept through the city.

2. Explain why the combination of earthquake and fire was so much more devastating than either of these catastrophes would have been if they had occurred separately.

3. An edict by the Mayor prevented chaos. What provisions in this edict do you think were the most important?

4. Why was dynamite used by the firefighters? What was the effect on the spread of the fire?

5. London described the first night of the fire as "a quiet night" although "the whole city crashed and roared into ruin." What incident reported about that night seemed most remarkable to you? What incident impressed you as most pathetic?

6. Throughout London's report, he continually contrasted the horrors of the advancing fire with the calm of those areas awaiting destruction. In this way he heightened the emotional tone of the entire report. What effect did he create by the use of such phrases as, "Here was no fire" and "two United States cavalrymen sitting their horses, calmly watching"?

7. The rapid demolition of Union Square was almost unbelievable. Describe the scene there as graphically as you can. Use comparisons to make your word-picture impressive.

8. Reread the paragraph on page 679, beginning "An enumeration of the buildings. . . ." London didn't expect his readers to comprehend the extent of the *general* destruction and loss of life. However, he did give them many examples of individual losses. Select two of these and show how complete the loss really was.

9. You have seen pictures of refugees fleeing from their homes in Europe and Asia. The San Francisco fire refugees were as pitiful as these war refugees. Select one section of the procession and one street scene. Explain why each was so rich in pathos.

10. In this report, Jack London, "a master of swift and vivid action," has written a masterpiece. Choose what you consider his most effective piece of description and read it to the class.

The writer's craft . . .

When Jack London's article, "The Story of an Eyewitness," first appeared in *Collier's* in 1906, many American authors were writing for magazines. Since colonial days, magazines have been a part of American life. Ben Franklin, with his usual foresight, was the first person to plan a magazine for the colonies. However, a competitor heard of Franklin's plans and published *The American Magazine* three days before Franklin's *General Magazine* came out. Actually the complete title of Franklin's publication was *General Magazine and Historical Chronicle for all the British Plantations in America*. For obvious reasons it was known as the *General Magazine*. Neither of these first two magazines had a very long life. *The American Magazine* ran for only three months; the *General Magazine,* for six. Other magazines appeared but did not long continue in publication for various reasons. There were no trains or trucks for distributing them; there were few post offices, and mail moved slowly. Besides, few Americans had the leisure time to devote to magazine reading. Nevertheless, new magazines continued to appear.

By 1825 the outlook for magazines had improved, and about one hundred were being published. Most of the space was devoted to essays and political articles; there was little fiction. *Godey's Lady's Book,* which appeared in 1830, introduced fashion notes and other items which appealed exclusively to women. This magazine had a large circulation and continued publication until 1898. Other important magazines which appeared around the middle of the nineteenth century were *Harper's Monthly* and *The Atlantic Monthly. Harper's* preferred to publish English authors, among them such popular writers as Charles Dickens and William Makepeace Thackeray. *The Atlantic Monthly,* under the guidance of its first editor, James Russell Lowell, showed a preference for American authors, accepting contributions primarily from established New England writers. Later editors welcomed contributions from writers all over the country. In the South such magazines as the *Southern Literary Messenger,* edited for two years by Edgar Allan Poe, and *The Southern Quarterly Review,* also came into circulation.

The increase in American magazines provided an opportunity for many writers to appear in print. A list of writers who contributed to early American magazines would include such distinguished names as Washington Irving, Ralph Waldo Emerson, Henry David Thoreau, Nathaniel Hawthorne, Henry Wadsworth Longfellow, Sidney Lanier, and many, many others.

Today, magazines play an increasingly important role in modern life. Like many of their predecessors, modern magazines aim both to inform and to entertain. Among the vast number now in circulation, there is a magazine that caters to nearly every interest and reading taste. The range of current magazines extends from those which specialize in news, like *Time* and *Newsweek,* to those devoted to special interests, like *Popular Mechanics* and *Theatre Arts Monthly.*

Your class might enjoy making a survey of the kinds of magazines which are available in your community. So that you will know what to look for, make a list on the blackboard of as many current magazines as you can which fall into the following categories. Add to this list as you discover additional magazines during your survey.

News magazines	Fashion
Picture magazines	Photography
Digests	Science
(book, magazine,	Hobbies
technical)	Travel
Magazines of general	Sports
interest	Farming
Literature	Others

After you have completed the list, divide the class into committees. Let each committee report on one particular category. Include in the report the following information:

1. The names of specific magazines that you read frequently or just occasionally.

2. The kinds of material to be found in these magazines: stories, essays, articles, pictures, cartoons, etc.

3. The particular reading audience for which these magazines are published. Support your conclusions with specific references to (a) the content, (b) the style in which it is written (scholarly, popular, technical), and (c) the kind and quality of illustrations.

4. The role that advertising plays in these magazines. Give the approximate percentage of space devoted to advertising as well as the kind: full page, full or partial column, spot advertisements, color or black and white. To what particular group of buyers is the advertising directed?

5. Include any other information about the magazines which you think the class would enjoy. Give each group of maga-

zines, and each individual magazine, a rating according to what it has to offer young people in useful and interesting information, and in value as worthwhile and enjoyable reading.

Knowing words . . .

Jack London referred to the *edict* of Mayor E. E. Schmitz which prevented chaos from developing after the earth-quake. An *edict* is a decree or command issued by someone in authority. It is also defined as an "authoritative proclamation."

These two words overlap in meaning but they also have a somewhat different meaning. A *proclamation* may be almost any kind of public announcement, whereas an *edict* nearly always implies a command. In a class discussion see how many proclamations and edicts you can recall. List them on the board and compare their different purposes.

A Psalm of Life

Tell me not, in mournful numbers,
   Life is but an empty dream! —
For the soul is dead that slumbers,
   And things are not what they seem.

Life is real! Life is earnest!
   And the grave is not its goal;
Dust thou art, to dust returnest,
   Was not spoken of the soul.

Not enjoyment, and not sorrow,
   Is our destined end or way;
But to act, that each to-morrow
   Find us farther than to-day.

Art is long, and Time is fleeting,
   And our hearts, though stout and brave,
Still, like muffled drums, are beating
   Funeral marches to the grave.

In the world's broad field of battle,
   In the bivouac of Life,
Be not like dumb, driven cattle!
   Be a hero in the strife!

Trust no Future, howe'er pleasant!
   Let the dead Past bury its dead!
Act, — act in the living Present!
   Heart within, and God o'erhead!

Lives of great men all remind us
   We can make our lives sublime,
And, departing, leave behind us
   Footprints on the sands of time;

Footprints, that perhaps another,
   Sailing o'er life's solemn main,
A forlorn and shipwrecked brother,
   Seeing, shall take heart again.

Let us, then, be up and doing,
   With a heart for any fate;
Still achieving, still pursuing,
   Learn to labor and to wait.

Henry Wadsworth Longfellow

Under the Lion's Paw

HAMLIN GARLAND

A basic American ideal is that each man is entitled to fair and just treatment. When life in America falls short of that ideal, there are always writers on hand to remind the nation that something is wrong.

I

It was the last of autumn and first day of winter coming together. All day long the ploughmen on their prairie farms had moved to and fro in their wide level fields through the falling snow, which melted as it fell, wetting them to the skin—all day, notwithstanding the frequent squalls of snow, the dripping, desolate clouds, and the muck of the furrows, black and tenacious as tar.

Under their dripping harness the horses swung to and fro silently, with that marvelous uncomplaining patience which marks the horse. All day the wild geese, honking wildly, as they sprawled sidewise down the wind, seemed to be fleeing from an enemy behind, and with neck outthrust and wings extended, sailed down the wind, soon lost to sight.

Yet the ploughman behind his plough, though the snow lay on his ragged greatcoat, and the cold clinging mud rose on his heavy boots, fettering him like gyves,[1] whistled in the very beard of the gale. As day passed, the snow, ceasing to melt, lay along the ploughed land, and lodged in the depth of the stubble, till on each slow round the last furrow stood out black and shining as jet between the ploughed land and the gray stubble.

When night began to fall, and the geese, flying low, began to alight invisibly in the near corn-field, Stephen Council was still at work "finishing a land." He rode on his sulky plough when going with the wind, but walked when facing it. Sitting bent and cold but cheery under his slouch hat, he talked encouragingly to his four-in-hand.

"Come round there, boys!— Round agin! We got t'finish this land. Come in there, Dan! *Stiddy, Kate,*—stiddy! None o' y'r tantrums, Kittie. It's purty tuff, but it got a be did. *Tchk! tchk!* Step along, Pete! Don't let Kate git y'r single-tree[2] on the wheel. *Once* more!"

They seemed to know what he meant, and that this was the last round, for they worked with greater vigor than before.

"Once more, boys, an' then, sez I, oats an' a nice warm stall, an' sleep f'r all."

By the time the last furrow was turned on the land it was too dark to see the house, and the snow was changing to rain again. The tired and hungry man could see the light from the kitchen shining through the leafless hedge, and he lifted a great shout, "Supper f'r a half a dozen!"

It was nearly eight o'clock by the time he had finished his chores and started for supper. He was picking his way carefully through the mud, when the tall form of a

---

[1] *fettering him like gyves,* restraining him as though he had chains on his legs

[2] *single-tree,* the swinging bar to which the harnessed horse is fastened

man loomed up before him with a premonitory cough.

"Waddy ye want?" was the rather startled question of the farmer.

"Well, ye see," began the stranger, in a deprecating tone, "we'd like t' git in f'r the night. We've tried every house f'r the last two miles, but they hadn't any room f'r us. My wife's jest about sick, 'n' the children are cold and hungry—"

"Oh, y' want 'o stay all night, eh?"

"Yes, sir; it 'ud be a great accom—"

"Waal, I don't make it a practice t' turn anybuddy way hungry, not on sech nights as this. Drive right in. We ain't got much, but sech as it is—"

But the stranger had disappeared. And soon his steaming, weary team, with drooping heads and swinging single-trees, moved past the well to the block beside the path. Council stood at the side of the "schooner"[3] and helped the children out —two little half-sleeping children—and then a small woman with a babe in her arms.

"There ye go!" he shouted jovially, to the children. "*Now* we're all right! Run right along to the house there, an' tell Mam' Council you wants sumpthin' t' eat. Right this way, Mis'—keep right off t' the right there. I'll go an' git a lantern. Come," he said to the dazed and silent group at his side.

"Mother," he shouted, as he neared the fragrant and warmly lighted kitchen, "here are some wayfarers an' folks who need sumpthin' t' eat an' a place t' snooze." He ended by pushing them all in.

Mrs. Council, a large, jolly, rather coarse-looking woman, took the children in her arms. "Come right in, you little rabbits. 'Most asleep, hey? Now here's a drink o' milk f'r each o' ye. I'll have s'm tea in a minute. Take off y'r things and set up t' the fire."

While she set the children to drinking milk, Council got out his lantern and went out to the barn to help the stranger about

his team, where his loud, hearty voice could be heard as it came and went between the haymow and the stalls.

The woman came to light as a small, timid, and discouraged-looking woman, but still pretty, in a thin and sorrowful way.

"Land sakes! An' you've travelled all the way from Clear Lake t'-day in this mud! Waal! waal! No wonder you're all tired out. Don't wait f'r the men, Mis'—" She hesitated, waiting for the name.

"Haskins."

"Mis' Haskins, set right up to the table an' take a good swig o' tea whilst I make y' s'm toast. It's green tea, an' it's good. I tell Council as I git older I don't seem to enjoy Young Hyson n'r Gunpowder.[4] I want the reel green tea, jest as it comes off'n the vines. Seems t' have more heart in it, some way. Don't s'pose it has. Council says it's all in m' eye."

Going on in this easy way, she soon had the children filled with bread and milk and the woman thoroughly at home, eating some toast and sweet-melon pickles, and sipping the tea.

"See the little rats!" she laughed at the children. "They're full as they can stick now, and they want to go to bed. Now, don't git up, Mis' Haskins; set right where you are an' let me look after 'em. I know all about young ones, though I'm all alone now. Jane went an' married last fall. But, as I tell Council, it's lucky we keep our health. Set right there, Mis' Haskins; I won't have you stir a finger."

It was an unmeasured pleasure to sit there in the warm, homely kitchen, the jovial chatter of the house-wife driving out and holding at bay the growl of the impotent, cheated wind.

The little woman's eyes filled with tears which fell down upon the sleeping baby in her arms. The world was not so desolate and cold and hopeless, after all.

"Now I hope Council won't stop out there and talk politics all night. He's the

---

[3] *"schooner,"* wagon

[4] *Young Hyson . . . Gunpowder,* varieties of China tea

greatest man to talk politics an' read the *Tribune*— How old is it?"

She broke off and peered down at the face of the babe.

"Two months 'n' five days," said the mother, with a mother's exactness.

"Ye don't say! I want o' know! The dear little pudzy-wudzy!" she went on, stirring it up in the neighborhood of the ribs with her fat forefinger.

"Pooty tough on 'oo to go gallivant'n' 'cross lots this way—"

"Yes, that's so; a man can't lift a mountain," said Council, entering the door. "Mother, this is Mr. Haskins, from Kansas. He's been eat up 'n' drove out by grasshoppers."

"Glad t' see yeh!— Pa, empty that washbasin 'n' give him a chance t' wash."

Haskins was a tall man, with a thin, gloomy face. His hair was a reddish brown, like his coat, and seemed equally faded by the wind and sun, and his sallow face, though hard and set, was pathetic somehow. You would have felt that he had suffered much by the line of his mouth showing under his thin, yellow mustache.

"Hain't Ike got home yet, Sairy?"

"Hain't see 'im."

"W-a-a-l, set right up, Mr. Haskins; wade right into what we've got; 'tain't much, but we manage to live on it—she gits fat on it," laughed Council, pointing his thumb at his wife.

After supper, while the women put the children to bed, Haskins and Council talked on, seated near the huge cooking-stove, the steam rising from their wet clothing. In the Western fashion Council told as much of his own life as he drew from his guest. He asked but few questions, but by and by the story of Haskins' struggles and defeat came out. The story was a terrible one, but he told it quietly, seated with his elbows on his knees, gazing most of the time at the hearth.

"I didn't like the looks of the country, anyhow," Haskins said, partly rising and glancing at his wife. "I was ust t' northern Ingyannie, where we have lots o' timber 'n' lots of rain 'n' I didn't like the looks o' that dry prairie. What galled me the worst was goin' s' far away acrosst so much fine land layin' all through here vacant."

"And the 'hoppers eat ye four years, hand runnin', did they?"

"Eat! They wiped us out. They chawed everything that was green. They jest set around waitin' f'r us to die t' eat us, too. I ust t' dream of 'em sittin' 'round on the bedpost, six feet long, workin' their jaws. They et the fork-handles. They got worse 'n' worse till they jest rolled on one another, piled up like snow in winter. Well, it ain't no use. If I was t' talk all winter I couldn't tell nawthin'. But all the while I couldn't help thinkin' of all that land back here that nobuddy was usin' that I ought o' had 'stead o' bein' out there in that cussed country."

"Waal, why didn't ye stop an' settle here?" asked Ike, who had come in and was eating his supper.

"Fer the simple reason that you fellers wantid ten 'r fifteen dollars an acre fer the bare land, and I hadn't no money for that kind o' thing."

"Yes, I do my own work," Mrs. Council was heard to say in the pause which followed. "I'm a gettin' purty heavy t' be on m' laigs all day, but we can't afford t' hire, so I keep rackin' around somehow, like a foundered horse. S' lame—I tell Council he can't tell how lame I am, f'r I'm jest as lame in one laig as t'other." And the good soul laughed at the joke on herself as she took a handful of flour and dusted the biscuit-board to keep the dough from sticking.

"Well, I hain't *never* been very strong," said Mrs. Haskins. "Our folks was Canadians an' small-boned, and then since my last child I hain't got up again fairly. I don't like t' complain. Tim has about all he can bear now—but they was days this week when I jest wanted to lay right down an' die."

"Waal, now, I'll tell ye," said Council,

from his side of the stove, silencing every-body with his good-natured roar, "I'd go down and *see* Butler, *anyway*, if I was you. I guess he'd let you have his place purty cheap; the farm's all run down. He's been anxious t'let t' somebuddy next year. It 'ud be a good chance fer you. Anyhow, you go to bed and sleep like a babe. I've got some ploughin' t' do, anyhow, an' we'll see if somethin' can't be done about your case. Ike, you go out an' see if the horses is all right, an' I'll show the folks t' bed."

When the tired husband and wife were lying under the generous quilts of the spare bed, Haskins listened a moment to the wind in the eaves, and then said, with a slow and solemn tone,

"There are people in this world who are good enough t' be angels, an' only haff t' die to *be* angels."

II

Jim Butler was one of those men called in the West "land poor." Early in the his-tory of Rock River he had come into the town and started in the grocery business in a small way, occupying a small building in a mean part of the town. At this period of his life he earned all he got, and was up early and late sorting beans, working over butter, and carting his goods to and from the station. But a change came over him at the end of the second year, when he sold a lot of land for four times what he paid for it. From that time forward he believed in land speculation as the surest way of getting rich. Every cent he could save or spare from his trade he put into land at forced sale, or mortgages on land, which were "just as good as the wheat," he was accustomed to say.

Farm after farm fell into his hands, until he was recognized as one of the leading landowners of the county. His mortgages were scattered all over Cedar County, and as they slowly but surely fell in he sought usually to retain the former owner as ten-ant.

He was not ready to foreclose; indeed, he

had the name of being one of the "easiest" men in the town. He let the debtor off again and again, extending the time when-ever possible.

"I don't want y'r land," he said. "All I'm after is the int'rest on my money—that's all. Now, if y' want o' stay on the farm, why, I'll give y' a good chance. I can't have the land layin' vacant." And in many cases the owner remained as tenant.

In the meantime he had sold his store; he couldn't spend time in it; he was mainly occupied now with sitting around town on rainy days smoking and "gassin' with the boys," or in riding to and from his farms. In fishing-time he fished a good deal. Doc Grimes, Ben Ashley, and Cal Cheatham were his cronies on these fishing excursions or hunting trips in the time of chickens or partridges. In winter they went to north-ern Wisconsin to shoot deer.

In spite of all these signs of easy life Butler persisted in saying he "hadn't enough money to pay taxes on his land," and was careful to convey the impression that he was poor in spite of his twenty farms. At one time he was said to be worth fifty thousand dollars, but land had been a little slow of sale of late, so that he was not worth so much.

A fine farm, known as the Higley place, had fallen into his hands in the usual way the previous year, and he had not been able to find a tenant for it. Poor Higley, after working himself nearly to death on it in the attempt to lift the mortgage, had gone off to Dakota, leaving the farm and his curse to Butler.

This was the farm which Council ad-vised Haskins to apply for; and the next day Council hitched up his team and drove down town to see Butler.

"You jest let *me* do the talkin'," he said. "We'll find him wearin' out his pants on some salt barrel somew'ers; and if he thought you *wanted* a place he'd sock it to you hot and heavy. You jest keep quiet; I'll fix 'im."

Butler was seated in Ben Ashley's store

telling fish yarns when Council sauntered in casually.

"Hello, But; lyin' agin, hey?"

"Hellow, Steve! how goes it?"

"Oh, so-so. Too dang much rain these days. I thought it was goin' t' freeze up f'r good last night. Tight squeak if I get m' ploughin' done. How's farmin' with *you* these days?"

"Bad. Ploughin' ain't half done."

"It 'ud be a religious idee f'r you t' go out an' take a hand y'rself."

"I don't haff to," said Butler, with a wink.

"Got anybody on the Higley place?"

"No. Know of anybody?"

"Waal, no: not eggsackly. I've got a relation back t' Michigan who's bent hot an' cold on the idee o' comin' West f'r some time. *Might* come if he could get a good lay-out. What do you talk on the farm?"

"Well, I d' know. I'll rent it on shares or I'll rent it money rent."

"Waal, how much money, say?"

"Well, say ten percent, on the price—two-fufty."

"Waal, that ain't bad. Wait on 'im till 'e thrashes?"

Haskins listened eagerly to this important question, but Council was cooly eating a dried apple which he had speared out of a barrel with his knife. Butler studied him carefully.

"Well, knocks me out of twenty-five dollars interest."

"My relation'll need all he's got t' git his crops in," said Council, in the safe, indifferent way.

"Well, all right; *say* wait," concluded Butler.

"All right; this is the man. Haskins, this is Mr. Butler—no relation to Ben—the hardest-working man in Cedar County."

On the way home Haskins said: "I ain't much better off. I'd like that farm; it's a good farm, but it's all run down, an' so 'm I. I could make a good farm of it if I had half a show. But I can't stock it n'r seed it."

"Waal, now, don't you worry," roared Council in his ear. "We'll pull y' through somehow till next harvest. He's agreed t' hire it ploughed, an' you can earn a hundred dollars ploughin' an' y' c'n git the seed o' me, an' pay me back when y' can."

Haskins was silent with emotion, but at last he said, "I ain't got nothin' t' live on."

"Now, don't you worry 'bout that. You jest make your headquarters at ol' Steve Council's. Mother'll take a pile o' comfort in havin' y'r wife an' children 'round. Y' see, Jane's married off lately, an' Ike's away a good 'eal, so we'll be darn glad t' have y' stop with us this winter. Nex' spring we'll see if y' can't git a start agin." And he chirruped to the team, which sprang forward with the rumbling, clattering wagon.

"Say, looky here, Council, you can't do this. I never saw—" shouted Haskins in his neighbor's ear.

Council moved about uneasily in his seat and stopped his stammering gratitude by saying: "Hold on, now; don't make such a fuss over a little thing. When I see a man down, an' things all on top of 'im, I jest like t' kick 'em off an' help 'im up. That's the kind of religion I got, an' it's about the *only* kind."

They rode the rest of the way home in silence. And when the red light of the lamp shone out into the darkness of the cold and windy night, and he thought of this refuge for his children and wife, Haskins could have put his arm around the neck of his burly companion and squeezed him like a lover. But he contented himself with saying, "Steve Council, you'll git y'r pay f'r this some day."

"Don't want any pay. My religion ain't run on such business principles."

The wind was growing colder, and the ground was covered with a white frost, as they turned into the gate of the Council farm, and the children came rushing out, shouting, "Papa's come." They hardly looked like the same children who had sat at the table the night before. Their torpidity, under the influence of sunshine and

Mother Council, had given way to a sort of spasmodic cheerfulness, as insects in winter revive when laid on the hearth.

III

Haskins worked like a fiend, and his wife, like the heroic woman that she was, bore also uncomplainingly the most terrible burdens. They rose early and toiled without intermission till the darkness fell on the plain, then tumbled into bed, every bone and muscle aching with fatigue, to rise with the sun next morning to the same round of the same ferocity of labor.

The eldest boy drove a team all through the spring, ploughing and seeding, milked the cows, and did chores innumerable, in most ways taking the place of a man.

An infinitely pathetic but common figure—this boy on the American farm, where there is no law against child labor. To see him in his coarse clothing, his huge boots, and his ragged cap, as he staggered with a pail of water from the well, or trudged in the cold and cheerless dawn into the frosty field behind his team, gave the city-bred visitor a sharp pang of sympathetic pain. Yet Haskins loved his boy, and would have saved him from this if he could, but he could not.

By June the first year the result of such Herculean toil began to show on the farm. The yard was cleaned up and sown to grass, the garden ploughed and planted, and the house mended.

Council had given them four of his cows.

"Take 'em an' run 'em on shares. I don't want 'o milk s' many. Ike's away s' much now, Sat'd'ys an' Sund'ys, I can't stand the bother anyhow."

Other men, seeing the confidence of Council in the newcomer, had sold him tools on time; and as he was really an able farmer, he soon had round him many evidences of his care and thrift. At the advice of Council he had taken the farm for three years, with the privilege of re-renting or buying at the end of the term.

"It's a good bargain, an' y' want 'o nail it," said Council. "If you have any kind ov a crop, you c'n pay y'r debts, an' keep seed an' bread."

The new hope which now sprang up in the heart of Haskins and his wife grew great almost as a pain by the time the wide field of wheat began to wave and rustle and swirl in the winds of July. Day after day he would snatch a few moments after supper to go and look at it.

"Have ye seen the wheat t'-day, Nettie?" he asked one night as he rose from supper.

"No, Tim, I ain't had time."

"Well, take time now. Le's go look at it."

She threw an old hat on her head—Tommy's hat—and looking almost pretty in her thin, sad way, went out with her husband to the hedge.

"Ain't it grand, Nettie? Just look at it."

It was grand. Level, russet here and there, heavy-headed, wide as a lake, and full of multitudinous whispers and gleams of wealth, it stretched away before the gazers like the fabled field of the cloth of gold.

"Oh, I think—I *hope* we'll have a good crop, Tim; and oh, how good the people have been to us!"

"Yes; I don't know where we'd be t'-day if it hadn't ben f'r Council and his wife."

"They're the best people in the world," said the little woman, with a great sob of gratitude.

"We'll be in the field on Monday, sure," said Haskins, gripping the rail on the fence as if already at the work of the harvest.

The harvest came, bounteous, glorious, but the winds came and blew it into tangles, and the rain matted it here and there close to the ground, increasing the work of gathering it threefold.

Oh, how they toiled in those glorious days! Clothing dripping with sweat, arms aching, filled with briers, fingers raw and bleeding, backs broken with the weight of heavy bundles, Haskins and his man toiled on. Tommy drove the harvester, while his father and a hired man bound on the machine. In this way they cut ten acres every day, and almost every night after supper, when the hand went to bed, Haskins returned to the field, shocking the bound grain [5] in the light of the moon. Many a night he worked till his anxious wife came out at ten o'clock to call him in to rest and lunch.

At the same time she cooked for the men, took care of the children, washed and ironed, milked the cows at night, made the butter, and sometimes fed the horses and watered them while her husband kept at the shocking.

No slave in the Roman galleys could have toiled so frightfully and lived, for this man thought himself a free man, and that he was working for his wife and babes.

When he sank into his bed with a deep groan of relief, too tired to change his grimy, dripping clothing, he felt that he was getting nearer and nearer to a home of his own, and pushing the wolf of want a little farther from his door.

There is no despair so deep as the despair of a homeless man or woman. To roam the roads of the country or the streets of the city, to feel there is no rood of ground on which the feet can rest, to halt weary and hungry outside lighted windows, and hear laughter and song within,—these are the hungers and rebellions that drive men to crime and women to shame.

It was the memory of his homelessness, and the fear of its coming again, that spurred Timothy Haskins and Nettie, his wife, to such ferocious labor during that first year.

IV

"M, yes; 'm, yes; first-rate," said Butler, as his eye took in the neat garden, the pig-pen, and the well-filled barnyard. "You're gitt'n' quite a stock around yeh. Done well, eh?"

---

[5] *shocking the bound grain,* placing the sheaves of grain on end in piles so that they support one another

Haskins was showing Butler around the place. He had not seen it for a year, having spent the year in Washington and Boston with Ashley, his brother-in-law, who had been elected to Congress.

"Yes, I've laid out a good deal of money durin' the last three years. I've paid out three hundred dollars f'r fencin'."

"Um-h'm! I see, I see," said Butler, while Haskins went on:

"The kitchen there cost two hundred; the barn ain't cost much in money, but I've put a lot o' time on it. I've dug a new well, and I—"

"Yes, yes, I see. You've done well. Stock worth a thousand dollars," said Butler, picking his teeth with a straw.

"About that," said Haskins, modestly. "We begin to feel 's if we was gitt'n' a home f'r ourselves; but we've worked hard. I tell you we begin to feel it, Mr. Butler, and we're goin' t' begin to ease up purty soon. We've been kind o' plannin' a trip back t' *her* folks after the fall ploughin's done."

"*Eggs-actly!*" said Butler, who was evidently thinking of something else. "I suppose you've kind o' calc'lated on stayin' here three years more?"

"Well, yes. Fact is, I think I c'n buy the farm this fall, if you'll give me a reasonable show."

"Um-m! What do you call a reasonable show?"

"Well, say a quarter down and three years' time."

Butler looked at the huge stacks of wheat, which filled the yard, over which the chickens were fluttering and crawling, catching grasshoppers, and out of which the crickets were singing innumerably. He smiled in a peculiar way as he said, "Oh, I won't be hard on yeh. But what did you expect to pay f'r the place?"

"Why, about what you offered it for before, two thousand five hundred, or *possibly* three thousand dollars," he added quickly as he saw the owner shake his head.

"This farm is worth five thousand and five hundred dollars," said Butler, in a careless and decided voice.

"*What!*" almost shrieked the astounded Haskins. "What's that? Five thousand? Why, that's double what you offered it for three years ago."

"Of course, and it's worth it. It was all run down then; now it's in good shape. You've laid out fifteen hundred dollars in improvements, according to your own story."

"But *you* had nothin' t' do about that. It's my work an' my money."

"You bet it was; but it's my land."

"But what's to pay me for all my—"

"Ain't you had the use of 'em?" replied Butler, smiling calmly into his face.

Haskins was like a man struck on the head with a sandbag; he couldn't think; he stammered as he tried to say: "But—I never'd git the use—You'd rob me! More'n that: you agreed—you promised that I could buy or rent at the end of three years at—"

"That's all right. But I didn't say I'd let you carry off the improvements, nor that I'd go on renting the farm at two-fifty. The land is doubled in value, it don't matter how; it don't enter into the question; an' now you can pay me five hundred dollars a year rent, or take it on your own terms at fifty-five hundred, or—git out."

He was turning away, when Haskins, the sweat pouring from his face, fronted him, saying again:

"But *you've* done nothing to make it so. You hain't added a cent. I put it all there myself, expectin' to buy. I worked an' sweat to improve it. I was workin' for myself an' babes—"

"Well, why didn't you buy when I offered to sell? What y' kickin' about?"

"I'm kickin' about payin' you twice f'r my own things—my own fences, my own kitchen, my own garden."

Butler laughed. "You're too green t' eat, young feller. *Your* improvements! The law will sing another tune."

"But I trusted your word."

"Never trust anybody, my friend. Besides, I didn't promise not to do this thing. Why, man, don't look at me like that. Don't take me for a thief. It's the law. The reg'lar thing. Everybody does it."

"I don't care if they do. It's stealin' jest the same. You take three thousand dollars of my money—the work o' my hands and my wife's." He broke down at this point. He was not a strong man mentally. He could face hardship, ceaseless toil, but he could not face the cold and sneering face of Butler.

"But I don't take it," said Butler, cooly. "All you've got to do is to go on jest as you've been a-doin', or give me a thousand dollars down, and a mortgage at ten percent on the rest."

Haskins sat down blindly on a bundle of oats near by, and with staring eyes and dropping head went over the situation. He was under the lion's paw. He felt a horrible numbness in his heart and limbs. He was hid in a mist, and there was no path out.

Butler walked about, looking at the huge stacks of grain, and pulling now and again a few handfuls out, shelling the heads in his hands and blowing the chaff away. He hummed a little tune as he did so. He had an accommodating air of waiting.

Haskins was in the midst of the terrible toil of the last year. He was walking again in the rain and the mud behind his plough; he felt the dust and dirt of the threshing. The ferocious husking-time, with its cutting wind and biting, clinging snows, lay hard upon him. Then he thought of his wife, how she had cheerfully cooked and baked, without holiday and without rest.

"Well, what do you think of it?" inquired the cool, mocking, insinuating voice of Butler.

"I think you're a thief and a liar!" shouted Haskins, leaping up. "A black-hearted houn'!" Butler's smile maddened him; with a sudden leap he caught a fork in his hands, and whirled it in the air.

"You'll never rob another man, damn ye!" he grated through his teeth, a look of pitiless ferocity in his accusing eyes.

Butler shrank and quivered, expecting the blow; stood, held hypnotized by the eyes of the man he had a moment before despised—a man transformed into an avenging demon. But in the deadly hush between the lift of the weapon and its fall there came a gush of faint, childish laughter and then across the range of his vision, far away and dim, he saw the sun-bright head of his baby girl, as, with the pretty, tottering run of a two-year-old, she moved across the grass of the door-yard. His hands relaxed; the fork fell to the ground; his head lowered.

"Make out y'r deed an' mor'gage, an' git off'n my land, an' don't ye never cross my line again; if y' do, I'll kill ye."

Butler backed away from the man in wild haste, and climbing into his buggy with trembling limbs drove off down the road, leaving Haskins seated dumbly on the sunny piles of sheaves, his head sunk into his hands.

Let's consider . . .

1. That first day at work "finishing a land," Stephen Council prepared you for his part of the story. What evidence did you find that he was industrious, provident, and kind?

2. When Mr. Council shouted to the kitchen "Supper f'r a half a dozen," he was referring to his own appetite. Actually this supper had to feed a half dozen hungry people. Where did they come from?

3. How were the strangers received by the farmer and his wife? What were the immediate needs of these strangers? In what specific ways did the Councils show their hospitality? Discuss the possibility of strangers' receiving the same treatment anywhere in America today.

4. What was your impression of the Haskins family on that first night of their arrival? What had driven them to such a plight?

5. "You jest let *me* do the talkin'" was Council's way of telling Haskins that the farm deal had to be handled shrewdly. What had made Butler "land poor"? What sort of person was he?

6. On what terms did Council secure the Higley farm for Haskins?

7. How did Haskins manage to stock and seed his farm? What else did Council do for the Haskins family?

8. Council insisted he didn't want pay for his kindness, and added, "My religion ain't run on such business principles." What did he mean?

9. What reasons did Butler give for raising the price on the farm when Haskins wanted to buy? What did Butler mean by the remark, "You're too green t' eat, young feller"?

10. What provoked Haskins to call Butler "a thief and a liar"? Was this accusation justified?

11. Butler's smile maddened Haskins. What happened? What prevented actual violence?

The writer's craft . . .

The ending of "Under the Lion's Paw" may have left you feeling rather disturbed. You sympathized with Mr. Haskins and did not want him to be treated unfairly. Yet, as the story ended, he had helplessly agreed to meet Mr. Butler's terms.

Why did Hamlin Garland use that ending? Why didn't he let Mr. Haskins find an unexpected solution to his difficulties, such as cleverly outwitting Mr. Butler? Or why didn't he have Mr. Butler undergo a sudden change of heart at the last minute and let Mr. Haskins have the farm according to the original agreement?

From the point of view of the reader, either of these solutions would have provided a "happy ending." From the point of view of the author, and his obligation to work out the problem in the story honestly and artistically, both endings would have been decidedly "unhappy."

You recall that a **realistic writer** like Hamlin Garland attempts to portray life truthfully without making it seem either better or worse than it really is. If he had "tacked on" a happy ending to "Under the Lion's Paw," he would have destroyed the illusion of reality so carefully created in the rest of the story. Mr. Haskins and Mr. Butler would have been acting "out of character"; they would not have been consistent.

You will also recall that when an author creates a **consistent character,** he gives him a definite and believable personality which, once established, sets a pattern for his behavior. If, at any point in the story, this character's behavior does not follow this pattern, the realistic quality of the story is lost. For example, Hamlin Garland did not depict Mr. Haskins as being particularly brilliant or clever. He was just an honest, sincere man who toiled long and hard for his family. Therefore, it would have been inconsistent for such a simple, straightforward person to outwit someone like Mr. Butler.

In your own words describe Butler's character. Why would it have been extremely improbable that Mr. Haskins could have outwitted him? Why would it have been inconsistent for Butler suddenly to act with kindness and generosity?

Whenever a character in a story acts in unexpected ways, check his behavior against the pattern set by the author. Look for clues which indicate that, given the right set of circumstances, this character *might* act in this way. Unless an author creates characters who are consistent with the personalities he has given them, his writing will fail to interpret human experience realistically.

Review the main events in the story. Did any of the characters act in an unexpected way? If so, did the circumstances justify their actions?

Knowing words . . .

You can often find a clue to the meaning of a new word if you will look carefully at the **context:** the sentence, or group of sentences, in which that word occurs. First figure out the meaning of each of the italicized words from the context. Then check that meaning with the definition in the glossary.

1. "Well, ye see," began the stranger, in a *deprecating* tone, "we'd like t' git in f'r the night."

2. They hardly looked like the same children who had sat at the table the night before. Their *torpidity,* under the influence of sunshine and Mother Council, had given way to a sort of *spasmodic* cheerfulness, as insects in winter revive when laid on the hearth.

3. He [Butler] hummed a little tune as he did so. He had an *accommodating* air of waiting.

I Have a Rendezvous with Death

I have a rendezvous with Death
At some disputed barricade,
When Spring comes round with rustling shade
And apple blossoms fill the air—
I have a rendezvous with Death
When Spring brings back blue days and fair.

It may be he shall take my hand
And lead me into his dark land
And close my eyes and quench my breath—
It may be I shall pass him still.
I have a rendezvous with Death
On some scarred slope of battered hill,
When Spring comes round again this year
And the first meadow-flowers appear.

God knows 'twere better to be deep
Pillowed in silk and scented down,
Where Love throbs out in blissful sleep,
Pulse nigh to pulse, and breath to breath,
Where hushed awakenings are dear. . . .
But I've a rendezvous with Death
At midnight in some flaming town,
When Spring trips north again this year,
And I to my pledged word am true,
I shall not fail that rendezvous.

Alan Seeger

In Flanders Fields

JOHN McCRAE

In Flanders fields the poppies blow
Between the crosses, row on row,
  That mark our place; and in the sky
  The larks, still bravely singing, fly
Scarce heard amid the guns below.

We are the Dead. Short days ago
We lived, felt dawn, saw sunset glow,
  Loved and were loved, and now we lie
  In Flanders fields.

Take up our quarrel with the foe:
To you from failing hands we throw
  The torch; be yours to hold it high.
  If ye break faith with us who die
We shall not sleep, though poppies grow
  In Flanders fields.

Vasiliu

The man who wrote this poem

JOHN McCRAE   1872–1918

Occasionally a poet becomes famous for a single poem. John McCrae's fame as a poet rests on his poem, "In Flanders Fields."

Mr. McCrae was a Canadian physician who enlisted in the Canadian Army to serve as a medical officer in France during World War I. He wrote "In Flanders Fields" during the second battle of Ypres. After the poem was published in an English magazine, it caught the public's attention and was widely reprinted. Because the author was speaking for American soldiers as well as Canadian soldiers, this poem has become a part of the literature of this country. "In Flanders Fields" is probably the best-known and most popular poem to come out of World War I.

McCrae died in France in 1918, shortly before the war ended.

The poet's art . . .

1. Explain why you think this poem had such wide appeal.

2. "In Flanders Fields" was written in a French poetic form called a rondeau. The **rondeau** contains fifteen lines, the ninth and fifteenth lines serving as a refrain and repeating the first half of the opening line. Now look again at the remaining thirteen lines. Only two sounds were used in the rhyme scheme: the long *o* sound and the long *i* sound. The poet established these sounds in the first stanza with the words *blow* and *sky*. All end words in this rondeau rhymed with these words. Using the letter *a* to represent one end sound, and the letter *b* to represent the other, write down the rhyme scheme of this rondeau.

3. In what way did the repetition of the refrain contribute to the emotional force of the poem? Which lines helped to build to the strong ending?

"Success Is Counted Sweetest..."

Success is counted sweetest
By those who ne'er succeed.
To comprehend a nectar
Requires sorest need.

Not one of all the purple host
Who took the flag to-day
Can tell the definition,
So clear, of victory,

As he, defeated, dying,
On whose forbidden ear
The distant strains of triumph
Break, agonized and clear.

Emily Dickinson

A Gray Sleeve

STEPHEN CRANE

When a nation is at war, the courage of its people may be tested in many ways as new crises arise. Since noon, rebel snipers had been pelting the Yankee infantry and halting its progress. Then the cavalry came to the rescue, led by a captain who thought he was equal to any crisis. He hadn't counted on his enemy being a terrified young girl who needed his help.

I

"It looks as if it might rain this afternoon," remarked the lieutenant of artillery.

"So it does," the infantry captain assented. He glanced casually at the sky. When his eyes had lowered to the green-shadowed landscape before him, he said fretfully: "I wish those fellows out yonder would quit pelting at us. They've been at it since noon."

At the edge of a grove of maples, across wide fields, there occasionally appeared little puffs of smoke of a dull hue in this gloom of sky which expressed an impending rain. The long wave of blue and steel in the field moved uneasily at the eternal barking of the far-away sharpshooters, and the men, leaning upon their rifles, stared at the grove of maples. Once a private turned to borrow some tobacco from a comrade in the rear rank, but, with his hand still stretched out, he continued to twist his head and glance at the distant trees. He was afraid the enemy would shoot him at a time when he was not looking.

Suddenly the artillery officer said, "See what's coming!"

Along the rear of the brigade of infantry a column of cavalry was sweeping at a hard gallop. A lieutenant, riding some yards to the right of the column, bawled furiously at the four troopers just at the rear of the colours. They had lost distance and made a little gap, but at the shouts of the lieutenant they urged their horses forward. The bugler, careering along behind the captain of the troop, fought and tugged like a wrestler to keep his frantic animal from bolting far ahead of the column.

On the springy turf the innumerable hoofs thundered in a swift storm of sound. In the brown faces of the troopers their eyes were set like bits of flashing steel.

The long line of the infantry regiments standing at ease underwent a sudden movement at the rush of the passing squadron. The foot soldiers turned their heads to gaze at the torrent of horses and men.

The yellow folds of the flag fluttered back in silken, shuddering waves as if it were a reluctant thing. Occasionally a giant spring of a charger would rear the firm and sturdy figure of a soldier suddenly head and shoulders above his comrades. Over the noise of the scudding hoofs could be heard the creaking of leather trappings, the jingle and clank of steel, and the tense, low-toned commands or appeals of the men to their horses. And the horses were mad with the headlong sweep of this movement. Powerful under-jaws bent back and straightened so that the bits were clamped as rigidly as vises upon the teeth, and glistening necks arched in desperate resistance to the hands at the bridles. Swinging their heads in rage at the granite laws of their lives, which compelled even their angers and their ardours to chosen directions and chosen faces, their flight was as a flight of harnessed demons.

The captain's bay kept its pace at the head of the squadron with the lithe bounds of a thoroughbred, and this horse was proud as a chief at the roaring trample of his fellows behind him. The captain's glance was calmly upon the grove of maples whence the sharpshooters of the enemy had been picking at the blue line. He seemed to be reflecting. He stolidly rose and fell with the plunges of his horse in all the indifference of a deacon's figure seated plumply in church. And it occurred to many of the watching infantry to wonder why this officer could remain imperturbable and reflective when his squadron was thundering and swarming behind him like the rushing of a flood.

The column swung in a sabre-curve toward a break in a fence, and dashed into a roadway. Once a little plank bridge was encountered, and the sound of the hoofs upon it was like the long roll of many drums. An old captain in the infantry turned to his first lieutenant and made a remark which was a compound of bitter disparagement of cavalry in general and soldierly admiration of this particular troop.

Suddenly the bugle sounded, and the column halted with a jolting upheaval amid sharp, brief cries. A moment later the men had tumbled from their horses, and, carbines in hand, were running in a swarm toward the grove of maples. In the road one of every four of the troopers was standing with braced legs, and pulling and hauling at the bridles of four frenzied horses.

The captain was running awkwardly in his boots. He held his sabre low so that the point often threatened to catch in the turf. His yellow hair ruffled out from under his faded cap. "Go in hard now!" he roared, in a voice of hoarse fury. His face was violently red.

The troopers threw themselves upon the grove like wolves upon a great animal. Along the whole front of woods there was the dry crackling of musketry, with bitter, swift flashes and smoke that writhed like stung phantoms. The troopers yelled shrilly and spanged bullets low into the foliage.

For a moment, when near the woods, the line almost halted. The men struggled and fought for a time like swimmers encountering a powerful current. Then with a supreme effort they went on again. They dashed madly at the grove, whose foliage from the high light of the field was as inscrutable as a wall.

Then suddenly each detail of the calm trees became apparent, and with a few more frantic leaps the men were in the cool gloom of the woods. There was a heavy odour as from burned paper. Wisps of gray smoke wound upward. The men halted and, grimy, perspiring, and puffing, they searched the recesses of the woods with eager, fierce glances. Figures could be seen flitting afar off. A dozen carbines rattled at them in an angry volley.

During this pause the captain strode along the line, his face lit with a broad smile of contentment. "When he sends this crowd to do anything, I guess he'll find we do it pretty sharp," he said to the grinning lieutenant.

"Say, they didn't stand that rush a minute, did they?" said the subaltern.[1] Both officers were profoundly dusty in their uniforms, and their faces were soiled like those of two urchins.

Out in the grass behind them were three tumbled and silent forms.

Presently the line moved forward again. The men went from tree to tree like hunters stalking game. Some at the left of the

---

[1] subaltern, a British military term meaning lieutenant

line fired occasionally, and those at the right gazed curiously in that direction. The men still breathed heavily from their scramble across the field.

Of a sudden a trooper halted and said: "Hello! there's a house!" Everyone paused. The men turned to look at their leader.

The captain stretched his neck and swung his head from side to side. "By George, it is a house!" he said.

Through the wealth of leaves there vaguely loomed the form of a large, white house. These troopers, brown-faced from many days of campaigning, each feature of them telling of their placid confidence and courage, were stopped abruptly by the appearance of this house. There was some subtle suggestion—some tale of an unknown thing—which watched them from they knew not what part of it.

A rail fence girded a wide lawn of tangled grass. Seven pines stood along a drive way which led from two distant posts of a vanished gate. The blue-clothed troopers moved forward until they stood at the fence peering over it.

The captain put one hand on the top rail and seemed to be about to climb the fence, when suddenly he hesitated, and said in a low voice, "Watson, what do you think of it?"

The lieutenant stared at the house. "Derned if I know!" he replied.

The captain pondered. It happened that the whole company had turned a gaze of profound awe and doubt upon this edifice which confronted them. The men were very silent.

At last the captain swore and said: "We are certainly a pack of fools. Derned old deserted house halting a company of Union cavalry, and making us gape like babies!"

"Yes, but there's something—something——" insisted the subaltern in a half stammer.

"Well, if there's 'something—something' in there, I'll get it out," said the captain. "Send Sharpe clean around to the other side with about twelve men, so we will

sure bag your 'something—something,' and I'll take a few of the boys and find out what's in the d——d old thing!"

He chose the nearest eight men for his "storming party," as the lieutenant called it. After he had waited some minutes for the others to get into position, he said "Come ahead" to his eight men, and climbed the fence.

The brighter light of the tangled lawn made him suddenly feel tremendously apparent, and he wondered if there could be some mystic thing in the house which was regarding this approach. His men trudged silently at his back. They stared at the windows and lost themselves in deep speculations as to the probability of there being, perhaps, eyes behind the blinds—malignant eyes, piercing eyes.

Suddenly a corporal in the party gave vent to a startled exclamation, and half threw his carbine into position. The captain turned quickly, and the corporal said: "I saw an arm move the blinds. An arm with a gray sleeve!"

"Don't be a fool, Jones, now!" said the captain sharply.

"I swear t'——" began the corporal, but the captain silenced him.

When they arrived at the front of the house, the troopers paused, while the captain went softly up the front steps. He stood before the large front door and studied it. Some crickets chirped in the long grass, and the nearest pine could be heard in its endless sighs. One of the privates moved uneasily, and his foot crunched the gravel. Suddenly the captain swore angrily and kicked the door with a loud crash. It flew open.

II

The bright lights of the day flashed into the old house when the captain angrily kicked open the door. He was aware of a wide hallway carpeted with matting and extending deep into the dwelling. There was also an old walnut hatrack and a little marble-topped table with a vase and two

books upon it. Farther back was a great, venerable fireplace containing dreary ashes.

But directly in front of the captain was a young girl. The flying open of the door had obviously been an utter astonishment to her, and she remained transfixed there in the middle of the floor, staring at the captain with wide eyes.

She was like a child caught at the time of a raid upon the cake. She wavered to and fro upon her feet, and held her hands behind her. There were two little points of terror in her eyes, as she gazed up at the young captain in dusty blue, with his reddish, bronze complexion, his yellow hair, his bright sabre held threateningly.

These two remained motionless and silent, simply staring at each other for some moments.

The captain felt his rage fade out of him and leave his mind limp. He had been violently angry, because this house had made him feel hesitant, wary. He did not like to be wary. He liked to feel con-

fident, sure. So he kicked the door open, and had been prepared to march in like a soldier of wrath.

But now he began, for one thing, to wonder if his uniform was so dusty and old in appearance. Moreover, he had a feeling that his face was covered with a compound of dust, grime, and perspiration. He took a step forward and said, "I didn't mean to frighten you." But his voice was coarse from his battle-howling. It seemed to him to have hempen fibres in it.

The girl's breath came in little, quick gasps, and she looked at him as she would have looked at a serpent.

"I didn't mean to frighten you," he said again.

The girl, still with her hands behind her, began to back away.

"Is there any one else in the house?" he went on, while slowly following her. "I don't wish to disturb you, but we had a fight with some rebel skirmishers in the woods, and I thought maybe some of them might have come in here. In fact, I was pretty sure of it. Are there any of them here?" The girl looked at him and said, "No!" He wondered why extreme agitation made the eyes of some women so limpid and bright.

"Who is here besides yourself?"

By this time his pursuit had driven her to the end of the hall, and she remained there with her back to the wall and her hands still behind her. When she answered this question, she did not look at him but down at the floor. She cleared her voice and then said, "There is no one here."

"No one?"

She lifted her eyes to him in that appeal that the human being must make even to falling trees, crashing boulders, the sea in a storm, and said, "No, no, there is no one here." He could plainly see her tremble.

Of a sudden he bethought him that she continually kept her hands behind her. As he recalled her air when first discovered, he remembered she appeared precisely as a child detected at one of the crimes of childhood. Moreover, she had always backed away from him. He thought now that she was concealing something which was an evidence of the presence of the enemy in the house.

"What are you holding behind you?" he said suddenly.

She gave a little quick moan, as if some grim hand had throttled her.

"What are you holding behind you?"

"Oh, nothing—please. I am not holding anything behind me; indeed I'm not."

"Very well. Hold your hands out in front of you, then."

"Oh, indeed, I'm not holding anything behind me. Indeed, I'm not."

"Well," he began. Then he paused, and remained for a moment dubious. Finally, he laughed. "Well, I shall have my men search the house, anyhow. I'm sorry to trouble you, but I feel sure that there is some one here whom we want." He turned to the corporal, who with the other men was gaping quietly in at the door, and said, "Jones, go through the house."

As for himself, he remained planted in front of the girl, for she evidently did not dare to move and allow him to see what she held so carefully behind her back. So she was his prisoner.

The men rummaged around on the ground floor of the house. Sometimes the captain called to them, "Try that closet," "Is there any cellar?" But they found no one, and at last they went trooping toward the stairs which led to the second floor.

But at this movement on the part of the men the girl uttered a cry—a cry of such fright and appeal that the men paused. "Oh, don't go up there! Please don't go up there!—ple—ease! There is no one there! Indeed—indeed there is not! Oh, ple—ease!"

"Go on, Jones," said the captain calmly.

The obedient corporal made a preliminary step, and the girl bounded toward the stairs with another cry.

As she passed him, the captain caught sight of that which she had concealed behind her back, and which she had forgotten in this supreme moment. It was a pistol.

She ran to the first step, and standing there, faced the men, one hand extended with perpendicular palm, and the other holding the pistol at her side. "Oh, please, don't go up there! Nobody is there—indeed, there is not! P-l-e-a-s-e!" Then suddenly she sank swiftly down upon the step, and, huddling forlornly, began to weep in the agony and with the convulsive tremors of an infant. The pistol fell from her fingers and rattled down to the floor.

The astonished troopers looked at their astonished captain. There was a short silence.

Finally the captain stooped and picked up the pistol. It was a heavy weapon of the army pattern. He ascertained that it was empty.

He leaned toward the shaking girl, and said gently, "Will you tell me what you were going to do with this pistol?"

He had to repeat the question a number of times, but at last a muffled voice said, "Nothing."

"Nothing!" He insisted quietly upon a further answer. At the tender tones of the captain's voice, the phlegmatic corporal turned and winked gravely at the man next to him.

"Won't you tell me?"

The girl shook her head.

"Please tell me!"

The silent privates were moving their feet uneasily and wondering how long they were to wait.

The captain said, "Please won't you tell me?"

Then this girl's voice began in stricken tones half coherent, and amid violent sobbing: "It was grandpa's. He—he—he said he was going to shoot anybody who came in here—he didn't care if there were thousands of 'em. And—and I know he would, and I was afraid they'd kill him. And so—and—so I stole away his pistol—and I was going to hide it when you—you—you kicked open the door."

The men straightened up and looked at each other. The girl began to weep again.

The captain mopped his brow. He peered down at the girl. He mopped his brow again. Suddenly he said, "Ah, don't cry like that."

He moved restlessly and looked down at his boots. He mopped his brow again.

Then he gripped the corporal by the arm and dragged him some yards back from the others. "Jones," he said, in an intensely earnest voice, "will you tell me what in the devil I am going to do?"

The corporal's countenance became illuminated with satisfaction at being thus requested to advise his superior officer. He adopted an air of great thought, and finally said: "Well, of course, the feller with the gray sleeve must be upstairs, and we must get past the girl and up there somehow. Suppose I take her by the arm and lead her——"

"What!" interrupted the captain from between his clinched teeth. As he turned away from the corporal, he said fiercely over his shoulder, "You touch that girl and I'll split your skull!"

III

The corporal looked after his captain with an expression of mingled amazement, grief, and philosophy. He seemed to be saying to himself that there unfortunately were times, after all, when one could not rely upon the most reliable of men. When he returned to the group he found the captain bending over the girl and saying, "Why is it that you don't want us to search upstairs?"

The girl's head was buried in her crossed arms. Locks of her hair had escaped from their fastenings and these fell upon her shoulder.

"Won't you tell me?"

The corporal here winked again at the man next to him.

"Because," the girl moaned—"because—there isn't anybody up there."

The captain at last said timidly, "Well, I'm afraid—I'm afraid we'll have to——"

The girl sprang to her feet again, and implored him with her hands. She looked deep into his eyes with her glance, which was at this time like that of the fawn when it says to the hunter, "Have mercy upon me!"

These two stood regarding each other. The captain's foot was on the bottom step, but he seemed to be shrinking. He wore an air of being deeply wretched and ashamed. There was a silence.

Suddenly the corporal said in a quick, low tone, "Look out, captain!"

All turned their eyes swiftly toward the head of the stairs. There had appeared there a youth in a gray uniform. He stood looking coolly down at them. No word was said by the troopers. The girl gave vent to a little wail of desolation, "O Harry!"

He began slowly to descend the stairs. His right arm was in a white sling, and there were some fresh blood stains upon the cloth. His face was rigid and deathly pale, but his eyes flashed like lights. The girl was again moaning in an utterly dreary fashion, as the youth came slowly down toward the silent men in blue.

Six steps from the bottom of the flight he halted and said, "I reckon it's me you're looking for."

The troopers had crowded forward a trifle and, posed in lithe, nervous attitudes, were watching him like cats. The captain remained unmoved. At the youth's question he merely nodded his head and said, "Yes."

The young man in gray looked down at the girl, and then, in the same even tone which now, however, seemed to vibrate with suppressed fury, he said, "And is that any reason why you should insult my sister?"

At this sentence, the girl intervened, desperately, between the young man in gray and the officer in blue. "Oh, don't, Harry, don't! He was good to me! He was good to me, Harry—indeed he was!"

The youth came on in his quiet, erect fashion until the girl could have touched either of the men with her hand, for the captain still remained with his foot upon the first step. She continually repeated: "O Harry! O Harry!"

The youth in gray manoeuvred to glare into the captain's face, first over one shoulder of the girl and then over the other. In a voice that rang like metal, he said: "You are armed and unwounded, while I have no weapons and am wounded; but——"

The captain had stepped back and sheathed his sabre. The eyes of these two men were gleaming fire, but otherwise the captain's countenance was imperturbable. He said: "You are mistaken. You have no reason to——"

"You lie!"

All save the captain and the youth in gray started in an electric movement. These two words crackled in the air like shattered glass. There was a breathless silence.

The captain cleared his throat. His look at the youth contained a quality of singular and terrible ferocity, but he said in his stolid tone, "I don't suppose you mean what you say now."

Upon his arm he had felt the pressure of some unconscious little fingers. The girl was leaning against the wall as if she no longer knew how to keep her balance, but those fingers—he held his arm very still. She murmured: "O Harry, don't! He was good to me—indeed he was!"

The corporal had come forward until he in a measure confronted the youth in gray, for he saw those fingers upon the captain's arm, and he knew that sometimes very strong men were not able to move hand nor foot under such conditions.

The youth had suddenly seemed to become weak. He breathed heavily and clung to the rail. He was glaring at the captain, and apparently summoning all his will power to combat his weakness. The corporal addressed him with profound straightforwardness, "Don't you be a derned fool!" The youth turned toward him so fiercely that the corporal threw up a knee and an elbow like a boy who expects to be cuffed.

The girl pleaded with the captain. "You won't hurt him, will you? He don't know what he's saying. He's wounded, you know. Please don't mind him!"

"I won't touch him," said the captain, with rather extraordinary earnestness; "don't you worry about him at all. I won't touch him!"

Then he looked at her, and the girl suddenly withdrew her fingers from his arm.

The corporal contemplated the top of the stairs, and remarked without surprise, "There's another of 'em coming!"

An old man was clambering down the stairs with much speed. He waved a cane wildly. "Get out of my house, you thieves! Get out! I won't have you cross my threshold! Get out!" He mumbled and wagged his head in an old man's fury. It was plainly his intention to assault them.

And so it occurred that a young girl became engaged in protecting a stalwart captain, fully armed, and with eight grim troopers at his back, from the attack of an old man with a walking-stick!

A blush passed over the temples and brow of the captain, and he looked particularly savage and weary. Despite the girl's efforts, he suddenly faced the old man.

"Look here," he said distinctly, "we came in because we had been fighting in the woods yonder, and we concluded that some of the enemy were in this house, especially when we saw a gray sleeve at the window. But this young man is wounded, and I have nothing to say to him. I will even take it for granted that there are no others like him upstairs. We will go away, leaving your d——d old house just as we found it! And we are no more thieves and rascals than you are!"

The old man simply roared: "I haven't got a cow nor a pig nor a chicken on the place! Your soldiers have stolen everything they could carry away. They have torn down half my fences for firewood. This afternoon some of your accursed bullets even broke my window panes!"

The girl had been faltering: "Grandpa! O Grandpa!"

The captain looked at the girl. She returned his glance from the shadow of the old man's shoulder. After studying her face a moment, he said, "Well, we will go now." He strode toward the door and his men clanked docilely after him.

At this time there was the sound of harsh cries and rushing footsteps from without. The door flew open, and a whirlwind composed of blue-coated troopers came in with a swoop. It was headed by the lieutenant. "Oh, here you are!" he cried, catching his breath. "We thought—— Oh, look at the girl!"

The captain said intensely, "Shut up, you fool!"

The men settled to a halt with a clash and a bang. There could be heard the dulled sound of many hoofs outside of the house.

"Did you order up the horses?" inquired the captain.

"Yes. We thought——"

"Well, then, let's get out of here," interrupted the captain morosely.

The men began to filter out into the open air. The youth in gray had been hanging dismally to the railing of the stairway. He now was climbing slowly up to the second floor. The old man was addressing himself directly to the serene corporal.

"Not a chicken on the place!" he cried.

"Well, I didn't take your chickens, did I?"

"No, maybe you didn't, but——"

The captain crossed the hall and stood before the girl in rather a culprit's fashion. "You are not angry at me, are you?" he asked timidly.

"No," she said. She hesitated a moment, and then suddenly held out her hand. "You were good to me—and I'm—much obliged."

The captain took her hand, and then he blushed, for he found himself unable to formulate a sentence that applied in anyway to the situation.

She did not seem to heed that hand for a time.

He loosened his grasp presently, for he was ashamed to hold it so long without saying anything clever. At last, with an air of charging an intrenched brigade, he contrived to say, "I would rather do anything than frighten or trouble you."

His brow was warmly perspiring. He had a sense of being hideous in his dusty uniform and with his grimy face.

She said, "Oh, I'm so glad it was you instead of somebody who might have—might
have hurt brother Harry and grandpa!"

He told her, "I wouldn't have hurt 'em
for anything!"

There was a little silence.

"Well, good-bye!" he said at last.

"Good-bye!"

He walked toward the door past the old
man, who was scolding at the vanishing
figure of the corporal. The captain looked
back. She had remained there watching
him.

At the bugle's order, the troopers standing beside their horses swung briskly into
the saddle. The lieutenant said to the first
sergeant:

"William, did they ever meet before?"

"Hanged if I know!"

"Well, say——"

The captain saw a curtain move at one
of the windows. He cantered from his position at the head of the column and steered
his horse between two flower beds.

"Well, good-bye!"

The squadron trampled slowly past.

"Good-bye!" They shook hands.

He evidently had something enormously
important to say to her, but it seems that
he could not manage it. He struggled he-
roically. The bay charger, with his great
mystically solemn eyes, looked around the
corner of his shoulder at the girl.

The captain studied a pine tree. The
girl inspected the grass beneath the window. The captain said hoarsely, "I don't
suppose—I don't suppose—I'll ever see you
again!"

She looked at him affrightedly and
shrank back from the window. He seemed
to have woefully expected a reception of
this kind for his question. He gave her instantly a glance of appeal.

She said, "Why, no, I don't suppose we
will."

"Never?"

"Why, no, 'tain't possible. You—you
are a—Yankee!"

"Oh, I know it, but——" Eventually he
continued, "Well, some day, you know,
when there's no more fighting, we
might——" He observed that she had
again withdrawn suddenly into the shadow, so he said, "Well, good-bye!"

When he held her fingers she bowed her
head, and he saw a pink blush steal over
the curves of her cheek and neck.

"Am I never going to see you again?"

She made no reply.

"Never?" he repeated.

After a long time, he bent over to hear a
faint reply: "Sometimes—when there are
no troops in the neighborhood—grandpa
don't mind if I—walk over as far as that
old oak tree yonder—in the afternoons."

It appeared that the captain's grip was
very strong, for she uttered an exclamation
and looked at her fingers as if she expected
to find them mere fragments. He rode
away.

The bay horse leaped a flower bed. They
were almost to the drive, when the girl uttered a panic-stricken cry.

The captain wheeled his horse violently and upon his return journey went straight through a flower bed.

The girl had clasped her hands. She beseeched him wildly with her eyes. "Oh, please, don't believe it! I never walk to the old oak tree. Indeed, I don't! I never—never—never walk there."

The bridle drooped on the bay charger's neck. The captain's figure seemed limp.

With an expression of profound dejection and gloom he stared off at where the leaden sky met the dark green line of the woods. The long-impending rain began to fall with a mournful patter, drop and drop. There was a silence.

At last a low voice said, "Well—I might—sometimes I might—perhaps—but only once in a great while—I might walk to the old tree—in the afternoons."

The man who wrote this story

STEPHEN CRANE   1871–1900

Near the end of the nineteenth century, Stephen Crane was one of the most talented young writers in America. He had shown a marvelous skill with words while he was still a schoolboy. He wrote articles for newspapers before he was out of his teens and had completed his first novel, *Maggie,* soon after his twenty-first birthday. The readers of his time found this book unacceptable because its language was too bold and too blunt. Long after Crane's death, the novel finally won recognition.

Crane crowded his brief life with action as well as with creative work. He reported the Spanish-American War and was a correspondent in Greece. By the time he was twenty-four, he had written a novel that has frequently been called a classic description of war, *The Red Badge of Courage.* It was so true to life that veterans of the War Between the States wrote to ask Crane if he had not fought with them at Antietam and Chickamauga—though Crane had been born six years after the war ended.

Crane aimed at complete honesty of treatment, yet a note of irony colors his work. His brilliant and colorful style, and some of the vividness and realness he brought into his writing, became a valuable inheritance to such American authors as Willa Cather and Ernest Hemingway.

Let's consider . . .

1. Describe the way in which the cavalry troop made the rebels retreat from the maple grove.

2. What unexpected sight did the cavalry find in the grove? How did the men react? What did the corporal see? What made the captain so angry?

3. Describe the meeting of the captain and the girl. Why did the captain suddenly become so conscious of his appearance? How did the girl react to his questions? Why did she back away from the captain?

4. What did the girl do when Jones started for the stairs? How did she explain the pistol? How did the girl's tears affect the captain and his men?

5. Why did the girl utter "a little wail of desolation" when she saw Harry at the head of the stairs?

6. Why do you think Harry gave himself up? What was his attitude toward his enemies? Why did the girl defend the captain?

7. How did the girl become involved in "protecting a stalwart captain" from attack by "an old man with a walking-stick"?

8. Why was the old man so angry at the soldiers? What had they done?

9. What kind of man was the captain? What might have happened to Harry and the old man if the captain had been different?

10. The captain and the girl found it

very hard to speak to each other. What was the barrier between them? Why did the captain expect the answers she gave when they talked at the window?

11. Why do you think the girl suggested a possible meeting and then was frightened at what she had done?

12. In your opinion, was this a story of human understanding or a story of romantic love? Support your answer by referring to specific lines or incidents in the story.

The writer's craft . . .

This story contained several romantic elements which offered the reader an escape from life's everyday, commonplace routines. They took him into a world which existed primarily in the writer's imagination. As in most romantic stories, the emphasis was on action rather than on interpretation. He was more concerned with telling a good story than with offering an analysis of human behavior.

1. The main characters were the captain, portrayed as a "chivalrous soldier," and the young girl, portrayed as a "maiden in distress." They fell in love at first sight, but Stephen Crane provided little in the way of reasons or motive for the actions of the characters. Were you able to accept this situation as adequately motivated—therefore plausible—or did it seem too invented? Explain.

2. In the characterization of the brother, what motives were given to explain his conduct? Were his actions believable? In

what way did he make it possible for the captain and the girl to act in a way that was noble and self-sacrificing?

3. What purpose did the grandfather serve in the story? Was he believable as a character? Discuss.

4. In spite of the fact that the characterizations were rather superficial, most readers would enjoy this story. What qualities did it have which made your reading of it enjoyable?

Knowing words . . .

The corporal in "A Gray Sleeve" was described as being *phlegmatic*. The word *phlegmatic* is derived from *phlegm,* a term used by medieval physiologists to describe one of the four cardinal humors which were believed to determine a person's physical and mental constitution. These humors were body fluids, and the one which predominated was responsible for a person's temperament. Phlegm was the fluid which caused sluggishness; hence, a phlegmatic person was sluggish and apathetic.

Words derived from the other three cardinal humors are *bilious, choleric,* and *sanguine.* Look up these words in the dictionary and then explain their meanings in the following sentences.

1. The delay put him into such a *bilious* mood that he annoyed everyone.

2. The boy dreaded the *choleric* outbursts of his stern father.

3. Nothing short of disaster could discourage a person of such a *sanguine* nature.

High Water

JOHN HERSEY

As you read this account of personal heroism, try to discover those qualities
of style that give the writing its dramatic force.

Winsted, Conn., Aug 27—(INS)—In a disaster, human beings discover what they and their fellows are made of. This is the story of how a handful of men in Winsted, Conn., made that discovery the night of the flood caused by Hurricane Diane.

These events took place mostly on the flat roofs of two one-story buildings at the lower end of the dangerous mile that someone in this typical American town of 11,000 persons later dubbed Hurricane Rapids.

It was about five-thirty in the morning. The hook-and-ladder engine of Winsted Volunteer Fire Company No. 3 was backed up on the high ground in front of the Church of St. Joseph and the Shrine of Our Lady of Fatima on Oak Street.

It was beginning to get light. The foreman of No. 3, Scott Weed, decided it was time to try to save the man and woman who had been signaling with a flashlight and calling for help all night from the second floor of the tenement block on the river side of the corner of Chestnut and Main, next to the Hotel Clifton.

These were Joe Cornelio and his sister, Maria, who had arrived from Italy only two weeks before.

Scott Weed was a stocky, ruddy, auburn-haired man of 43, married, with four children. He had been a volunteer fireman

for more than a decade. By day he worked as a foreman making adding machines in the Gilbert Clock Works, downriver.

Since early the previous evening, Weed and his men had been out, along with the local police and civil defense volunteers, alerting people to leave their houses.

One of the policemen was an ungainly, placid fellow named Farris Resha, 32, married, two children, who worked a night shift as a policeman and doubled by day as a machinist for the Underwood Corporation.

In the night, Weed, Resha, and the others had combed the tenement blocks over the stores along the river side of Main Street, breaking down doors if necessary to get people out of bed and out of their homes, to high land. In the torrential rain, they had cleared the street of all but a handful.

About midnight, the water had begun to overflow the river and run down the street. The civil defense sirens had gone off at 1:15 to warn people. Electric power had failed soon after and the city had gone black.

In two hours the river in the street had risen two feet and was rushing downtown at 20 miles an hour.

The rescuers had begun to go into the water, here and there hip-deep, using ropes, to get out whomever they could. But they had not been able to get to the Cornelios, for even when shallow the water there had been too swift to cross.

At about 3:30 the water in Main Street had begun to rise in great surges. Highland Lake above the city had begun to overflow and bridges upstream were giving way.

As it grew lighter, the men on the high-and-dry fire truck were aghast at what they saw up Main Street.

Whole buildings had begun to give way up, and boards and beams and refrigerators and clothes and funiture were coursing down what had now become rapids eight feet deep.

The pavement had been undermined several feet down. Slabs of concrete sidewalk ten feet square had been lifted and spun over and flung into the street.

Winsted Motors, at the top of the street, had been washed away and brand new Buicks were tumbling three quarters of a mile downstream like toys in a gutter. The roof of Winsted Motors had lodged itself halfway down the street, in front of the Town Hall.

The debris from the fallen houses was striking the tenement block where the Cornelios were stranded as the flood waters, deflected by St. Joseph's Hill, struggled back across an open lot to the river's proper bed.

Weed and his firemen decided it was time to try to get the Cornelios out.

They drove the engine down the ramp from the church to the edge of the water lapping against the hill.

Weed, together with Leo McMahon, 42, married, three children, employee of a printing office in Canaan and George Simmons, 31, married, two children, chemical worker in N. J. Keratene Company of Winsted, removed a 12-foot section of a hooked ladder from the truck. They carried it to the porch of a house near the highground corner of Chestnut and Main and got it across to the flat roof

of the one-story building on the corner, De Martino's grocery and liquor shop.

They went back then and got another ladder section and carried it up and bridged the gap to the next flat roof, over Ray's Washeteria and the Keystone TV Service.

Now they were on a wide platform, facing the Cornelios across the current, some 80 feet away, on the river side of the intersection.

Some of the men ran for ropes. They borrowed one from the truck of a man who puts up storm windows. They scavenged ropes from homes.

By this time the firemen on the roof had been joined by others, including Resha.

Soon the men returned to the roofs at Chestnut and Main with the ropes. But how were they to get a rope across 80 feet of turbulent water?

Resha suggested heaving a line across with a weight on it.

The men shouted to the Cornelios to leave their windows, then threw stones to break the glass to give as much opening as possible for a rope-end to enter.

They tried tying a stone to a rope and throwing it. It fell far, far short, again and again. The men tried for 45 minutes to get a rope over that way and failed.

Then a man named Dewey Plank, who loved to fish, ran home and got his spinner rod and ran back and climbed onto the roofs.

The cast looked impossible. The cloudburst was still falling. The wind was strong. There was a maze of telephone and light wires just above and in front of the Cornelios' windows. Plank had little room for backwhip because of the high house behind the flat roofs.

Plank flicked the rod and fed out line. He cast once. He was very short. He cast again. It went farther. After half a dozen casts his lure caught on a telephone pole near the Cornelios' windows. With a broom, Joseph Cornelio drew in the line.

Meanwhile, Resha and Weed had been tearing down television antennas from the roofs and had been ripping out long aerial lead wires. They fastened these together and tied them to the fish line and shouted to the Cornelios to pull.

Soon they had a wire across the river. It was easy then for the Cornelios to pull a rope over.

By noon, however, so much heavy debris was floating down the river from collapsed buildings up Main Street that Resha and a state policeman who had joined the group, Sidney Toomey, forbade a crossing.

The men shouted to the Cornelios to tie themselves to the rope.

During all this, the men on the roofs had been hearing shouts for help from their right, from a short dead-end street with the same name as the marooned pair across the way—Cornelio Avenue.

The street was lined with very small two-family houses, each with a front porch and a balcony upstairs. All the occupants were upstairs. The water was almost up to the balconies.

There were other people clinging to the roof of a tenement block on Main Street across Cornelio Avenue from the flat roofs.

Some of the men ran to the fire truck for an extension ladder, which they brought back, opened, and lashed.

An occupant of the first house up Cornelio Avenue, Norman Phillips, threw a long extension cord across to the flat roofs. Weed and McMahon tied the wire to the ladder and Phillips pulled it across.

In his raincoat and boots, Weed crawled across to Phillips' house on the horizontal ladder, dragging another ladder section behind him.

Weed dropped that ladder against the railing of Phillips' porch. By these ladders, Weed and another fireman, Ted Johnson, led two families to safety: the Angelo Garafalos and their children, the Michael Kreets and their two children.

Repeatedly during these rescues, the men on the flat roofs turned to the Cornelios across the way and waved and shouted to them, clasped their hands in boxers' victory salutes, and made the sign of the cross.

Now a boat appeared. No one knew where it came from. It was a light skiff about eight feet long, suitable for two or three passengers. Resha made it fast behind the roofs, while Weed and McMahon, moving the ladders to the near side of Cornelio Avenue, took out a family of five, the Bascettas; a widow, Alice Fairhart, and another family of four, the Cordanos.

Those who were rescued were terrified of crossing the ladders over the boiling water. The men called to them: "Be calm, take it easy."

Last to come from the near side of Cornelio Avenue were a young couple, Mr. and Mrs. Orin White. Mrs. White was expecting a baby any day. She worked her way alone across one of the horizontal ladders. Weed called to encourage her as she came: "Hurray! You're doing fine!"

Next, Dannie Smith, 25, who had worked at Winsted Motors, climbed along the fronts of the buildings on the near side of Cornelio Avenue and threw a rope across to the last house on the far side.

Along this rope Ted Johnson pulled the boat, and took from the balconies on the far side of Cornelio Avenue in several trips five Venezianos, including a 16-month-old baby, an elderly couple named Latino, their white cat with yellow ears, Skippy, and two cans of cat food, and two women, Josephine Lazzaro and Provinzina Amica, who had been praying all night.

All were now out of Cornelio Avenue. The men turned their attention back to Joseph and Maria Cornelio across the way.

The water was now ten feet deep in the gutted street and moving faster than before.

Then all the men on the roof, the rescued people and a crowd of 200 who had
gathered to watch on the slope by St.
Joseph's Church, saw a terrible thing: The
Clifton Hotel, a four-story wooden building just upstreet, raised up, turned slowly
around and moved back off Main Street
into the main bed of the river and floated
half a mile downstream. As it went the
two lower floors were gradually eaten
away. The upper stories settled, stayed
upright, kept moving.

Earlier in the night, before the water
had come up, a man named Sinclair Meggi-
son, who was staying in the Clifton, had
alerted all the other occupants of the hotel
and had sent them out. For some reason
he had said he thought he would spend
the night right there.

Three days later his body was found in
a room in the remainder of the hotel which
had planted itself upright, but only two
stories high, on Community Field, once
the site of town ball games.

Not long after the Clifton floated off,
most of Garibaldi Hall, a brick clubhouse

near the downstream corner of Chestnut
and Main, collapsed.

Huge sections of wooden buildings that
had fallen farther up Main Street now began to bombard the block the Cornelios
were in. Bit by bit the building crumbled,
until the upstream half was ripped and
bashed away. Its parts went out into the
river.

It appeared that soon the whole tenement block would be gone. It was urgent
to save the Cornelios.

The two officers asked for volunteers to
go over in the boat.

Three men offered to go: Joe Horte,
33, married, two children, truckdriver for
Negri Construction Company; Steve Jackson, 35, married, three children, laborer
for Nickerson Construction; George Newman, 29, married, three children, repairman
in Marshall's Garage.

The light skiff was made as secure as
possible. Two lines were tied to the bow,
two to the stern, and men held these from
the roofs upstream and down. Ropes were
lashed to the three men. A checkline was
made fast to the seat of the boat.

The men began to pull themselves across on the main rope to the Cornelios' window. Those on the roofs watched for big timbers or other floating hazards coming down Main Street. They pulled back on the checkline when the boat was threatened.

The three reached the other side. Jackson pulled himself up to the window on the main rope, cutting his feet badly as he did so. He put a leather mackinaw on Maria Cornelio and tied a line under her arms and let her down to the boat. He let her brother down the same way. He shinnied down the main rope.

The five started back in the three-man boat in the rough water.

Halfway across, Maria panicked, grabbed the main rope, and stood up. The boat capsized. All five fell into the river.

All had been lashed to the boat.

Jackson, Newman, Horte, and Joseph Cornelio clung to it, but Maria threw her arms over her head and her rope slipped off.

As she floated away Horte grabbed her and his rope broke and the pair were borne swiftly away from the boat. They were driven close to a slanting telephone pole and Horte caught it with one arm.

Maria fought, broke away, screamed, and drowned.

Horte could only hold the pole for a few seconds in the violent current.

In those seconds the state policeman, Toomey, though not an expert swimmer, let himself down a fallen telephone wire from the flat roofs and into the water. Seeing that he was soon in trouble, Johnson went after him, down the same wire. It took Resha, McMahon, Simmons, and Weed to rescue them both with ropes.

Horte let go.

Dannie Smith dived into the current without a rope, going after Horte.

Both men disappeared around a still-slanting inner wall of Garibaldi Hall, beneath a mural of Romulus and Remus being suckled by the wolf of Rome.

The men on the roofs got the boat, with Jackson, Newman, and Cornelio, as far as the awning of de Martino's store, which was awash. They hoisted the three up. Cornelio wanted to go after his sister. The men restrained him by force.

Then, Horte appeared, walking between two buildings on higher ground down to the left. And Smith appeared from a door just beyond Garibaldi Hall. Both had managed to catch themselves on debris at the bank.

It was afternoon. The rain had stopped. All the rescuers went to the Resha family's restaurant and had their first food and drink in 18 hours.

Gradually the water receded. In two days Main Street was a wild, dry arroyo ten feet deep strewn with battered cars and slabs of sidewalk and crushed lumber. Eighty per cent of the houses and stores on Main Street were condemned.

Four days after the flood Mrs. White had a baby son by Caesarian section.

Scotty Weed worked around town pumping cellars and clearing debris.

Officer Resha was asked to return to his day job at Underwood, but he did not go.

"It wouldn't be right to leave these people."

The man who wrote this selection

JOHN HERSEY 1914–

Because John Hersey was born in Tientsin, China, where his American parents were living, he is probably the only American writer who learned to speak Chinese before English. He left China in 1924, and when reaching college age studied at Yale College and Cambridge University.

In addition to working as a journalist for *Time, Life,* and *The New Yorker,* he at one time was a private secretary to Sinclair Lewis. During World War II he became one of America's outstanding war correspondents, and was commended by the Secretary of the Navy for heroic action under fire at Guadalcanal. In 1945 he was awarded the Pulitzer Prize for fiction. Some of his best known books are *A Bell for Adano, The Wall,* and *The War Lover.* One of the most powerful is *Hiroshima,* an account of the effects of the Atomic Bomb on six Japanese survivors.

Let's consider . . .

1. Cite examples of the physical devastation caused by the flood.

2. Why was it urgent that the Cornelio family be rescued?

3. Which incident in the rescue was most dramatic?

4. In his opening sentence John Hersey wrote: "In a disaster, human beings discover what they and their fellows are made of." What discovery do you think the people of Winsted made? Explain how reading Hersey's account might provide the people of Winsted with a better understanding of their discoveries.

5. Although John Hersey never judges the people or gives his opinion outright, by use of concrete incidents he develops his point of view. In your own words describe that point of view.

The writer's craft . . .

John Hersey wrote "High Water" in a sparse, journalistic style.

1. In what ways did these brief paragraphs add to the effectiveness of his account? In what ways did they detract?

2. List other characteristics of Hersey's journalistic style. Note such elements as vocabulary, length of sentences, and use of verbs.

3. Why is this style not appropriate to all kinds of writing?

4. Even though Hersey did not provide many details, he was able to build and sustain interest by focusing attention on the rescue of the Cornelio family. Explain why this narrative thread added to your interest in the story.

5. Compare Hersey's story with an account of a current event reported in your favorite newspaper. How does Hersey's account differ? In what ways is it similar?

6. Using a journalistic style, write an account of an exciting event in which you were involved or witnessed. Add human interest to your story by focusing attention on a single person or a small group of people.

Knowing words . . .

Each of the following sentences has one word in italics. When you are sure of the meaning of the italicized word, use it in a sentence of your own.

1. One of the policemen was an ungainly, *placid* fellow named Farris Resha.

2. Boards and beams and refrigerators and clothes and furniture were *coursing* down what had now become rapids eight feet deep.

3. The *debris* from the fallen houses was striking the tenement block.

4. They *scavenged* ropes from homes.

5. In two days Main Street was a wild, dry *arroyo* ten feet deep.

The Trip to Bountiful

A Television Play by HORTON FOOTE

By means of a trip back to her home in Bountiful, an old woman seeks to re-gain her sense of dignity and worth. By sharing her trip, you will discover the values and satisfactions which give meaning to her life.

Originally prepared for the Goodyear Television Playhouse production, starring Lillian Gish, the play was the first dramatic TV play to be included in the permanent film collection of the Museum of Modern Art.

CAST

Mrs. Watts	Ludie Watts
Jessie Mae Watts	Bus Driver
Ticket Man (railroad station)	Attendant
Thelma	Ticket Man (second bus station)
Ticket Man (bus station)	Sheriff

ACT ONE

The living room of a small apartment in Houston. It is furnished in the most ordinary manner. Sitting in a chair by a window is an old woman, Mrs. Watts. She is tall and thin and holds herself very straight. The hands in her lap are gnarled and twisted, but there is the feeling of great strength about them. She is constantly opening and closing the hands, nervously, as if to test their power. Putting on make-up in a corner of the room is Jessie Mae Watts, Mrs. Watts's daughter-in-law. Jessie Mae is in her early forties. An obviously vain woman, she is also hard and self-centered and domineering. Mrs. Watts hums to herself snatches of a hymn from time to time.

JESSIE MAE: Mother Watts, look out that window and tell me what time it is by the drug store clock.

(Mrs. Watts does so.)

MRS. WATTS: Three forty-five, Jessie Mae.

JESSIE MAE: Oh, I better get a move on. I want you to remind Ludie tonight to get our clock fixed.

MRS. WATTS: Yes, ma'am.

(Jessie Mae hurries into the bedroom. Mrs. Watts continues rocking and singing her hymn, her hands nervously working back and forth. Jessie Mae hurries in carrying a hat.)

JESSIE MAE: Mother Watts. Please stop that hymn singing. You want me to jump right out of my skin? You know what hymns do to my nerves. *(Mrs. Watts doesn't answer but stops. She rocks in silence.)* And don't pout. I can't stand pouting.

MRS. WATTS: I didn't mean to pout, Jessie Mae. I only meant to be silent.

(A pause. Jessie Mae gives her make-up one last going over.)

JESSIE MAE: Skip in the kitchen and get me a Coke. I'll drink it while I'm putting my hat on.

MRS. WATTS: All right.

(She goes and comes back with a Coke. She hands it to Jessie Mae. Jessie Mae takes the Coke and begins to drink it while putting on her hat.)

JESSIE MAE: Did your old-age pension check come today?

MRS. WATTS: No, ma'am. You asked me that twice before and I told you it hadn't.

JESSIE MAE: Well, it should be here. Today's the day.

MRS. WATTS: It didn't arrive.

JESSIE MAE: All right. *(She takes a swig from her Coke.)* That movie magazine I got last night is running a contest. First prize is a free trip to Hollywood. I'd enter it if I thought I could win. But I wouldn't win. I don't have that kind of luck. I'm gonna make Ludie take me to Hollywood one of these days. I want to visit Hollywood as bad as you want to visit Bountiful. *(Mrs. Watts is singing again.)* Mother Watts, I asked you not to sing. I'm nervous. *(Mrs. Watts stops. Jessie Mae has her hat on now.)* I'm ready. I'm gonna be home at seven. You get supper started. *(She starts out the door. She stops.)* And I want you to promise me you won't put a foot out of this house and start that Bountiful business again. You'll kill Ludie if he has to chase all over Houston again looking for you. And I'm warning you. The next time I'm calling the police. I don't care what Ludie says.

(She goes out slamming the door. Mrs. Watts sits quiet for a moment. Suddenly she jumps up. She screams.)

MRS. WATTS: And what about me? What about me? Sitting here cooped up in these two rooms. Me. A woman that was active all her young life, working the land. . . .

(Mrs. Watts stands for a moment. . . . Then she runs to the window and looks out. She thinks Jessie Mae has gone. She puts her hand in her dress and brings out a check. She runs to the desk and endorses

the back of it . . . She hears someone at the door. She pushes the check back inside her dress. Jessie Mae comes inside.)

JESSIE MAE: I forgot my movie magazine. I've read all the ones at the beauty parlor. (*She picks up a magazine and starts out the door. She pauses.*) Just in case you're trying to put something over on me with that pension check, I've told Mr. Reynolds at the grocery store he's never to cash anything for you.

(*She goes out. Mrs. Watts runs to the door and stands listening. Then she runs to the window and looks out. Again she is satisfied Jessie Mae is gone and runs to the bedroom and comes back with a suitcase. She starts to pack it.*)

Dissolve to: A ticket booth in a railroad station. There are several people in line waiting for tickets. Mrs. Watts comes running in. She keeps nervously looking back to see if she is being followed. She is humming the hymn softly to herself. She gets behind the line. A man finishes buying his ticket. She steps up to the window.

MRS. WATTS: I want a ticket to Bountiful, please.

TICKET MAN: Where?

MRS. WATTS: Bountiful.

TICKET MAN: Just a minute, let me look it up. (*He steps away from the window and begins looking the town up in a book.*) What's it near?

MRS. WATTS: Between Harrison and Cotton.

(*He looks through the book again.*)

TICKET MAN: Here's Harrison. But I don't see no Bountiful.

MRS. WATTS: Oh. Does the train stop at Harrison?

TICKET MAN: No. You take a train to Richmond. And from there you'd have to take a bus to Harrison.

MRS. WATTS: I see. What time does the train leave?

TICKET MAN: Six o'clock tomorrow morning.

MRS. WATTS: Six o'clock? I have to leave before that.

TICKET MAN: Then you better try taking a bus. There might be one leaving earlier.

MRS. WATTS: Yes, sir. (*She hurries out.*)

Dissolve to: The ticket window at the bus station. A young girl is buying a ticket there. She is very pretty.

TICKET MAN: Yes?

THELMA: I want a ticket to Old Gulf.

TICKET MAN: Yes, ma'am. (*He reaches for a ticket.*) Here you are. Change buses at Harrison.

THELMA: I know. How much please?

TICKET MAN: Four eighty.

THELMA: Yes, sir.

(*She gives him four eighty and steps out of line. A man steps up to the window.*)

MAN: Ticket to Leighton.

TICKET MAN: Leighton? Yes, indeed. (*He gets a ticket.*) Be seven sixty, please.

(*Mrs. Watts has come in with her bag. She is standing behind the man. She looks around the bus station nervously. She is humming snatches of her hymn. The man moves away. Two people have come behind Mrs. Watts. She is oblivious to the fact that the next turn is hers.*)

TICKET MAN: (*Calling*) Lady. (*She is so busy watching the door to the bus station she doesn't hear him.*) Lady . . .

MRS. WATTS: Oh, yes. Excuse me. I'd like a ticket to Bountiful, please.

TICKET MAN: Where?

MRS. WATTS: Bountiful.

TICKET MAN: What's it near?

MRS. WATTS: It's between Harrison and Cotton.

TICKET MAN: Just a minute. (*He looks in a book.*) I can sell you a ticket to Harrison or Cotton. But there's no Bountiful . . .

MRS. WATTS: Oh, yes, there is. It's between . . .

TICKET MAN: I'm sorry, lady. You say

there is, but the book says there isn't. And the book don't lie . . .

MRS. WATTS: But . . . I . . .

TICKET MAN: Make up your mind, lady. Cotton or Harrison. There are others waiting.

MRS. WATTS: Well . . . Let me see . . . How much is a ticket to Harrison?

TICKET MAN: Three fifty.

MRS. WATTS: Cotton?

TICKET MAN: Four twenty.

MRS. WATTS: Oh, I see, thank you. I'll have the one to Harrison, please.

TICKET MAN: All right. That'll be three fifty, please.

MRS. WATTS: Yes, sir. (*She reaches in her bag and takes out a check.*) Can you cash a pension check? You see I decided to come at the last minute and I didn't have time to stop by the grocery store.

TICKET MAN: I'm sorry. I can't cash any checks.

MRS. WATTS: It's perfectly good.

TICKET MAN: I'm sorry, it's against the rules to cash checks.

MRS. WATTS: Oh, is that so? I understand. How much was that again?

TICKET MAN: Three fifty.

MRS. WATTS: Oh, yes. I've got it all here in nickels and dimes and quarters. (*She takes out a handkerchief from her purse and puts it on the counter. She unties it and begins to take out coins. She talks as she counts.*) Here, I think this is three fifty.

TICKET MAN: Thank you.

MRS. WATTS: That's quite all right. I'm sorry to have taken up so much of your time. (*She picks up her bag and starts away.*)

TICKET MAN: Here, lady. Don't forget your ticket.

MRS. WATTS: Oh, my heavens. Yes, I'd forget my head if it wasn't on my neck. (*She takes the ticket.*) Thank you.

(*She starts away. The others step up into line to get their tickets. Mrs. Watts crosses to a row of benches where the girl we saw earlier is seated. There is an empty seat next to her. Mrs. Watts stops in front of the empty seat.*)

MRS. WATTS: Good evening.

THELMA: Good evening.

MRS. WATTS: Is this seat taken?

THELMA: No, ma'am.

MRS. WATTS: Are you expecting anyone?

THELMA: No, ma'am.

MRS. WATTS: May I sit here then?

THELMA: Yes'm. Are you going on a trip?

MRS. WATTS: Yes, I am. I'm trying to get to a town nobody ever heard of around here.

THELMA: What town is that?

MRS. WATTS: Bountiful.

THELMA: Oh.

MRS. WATTS: Did you ever hear of it?

THELMA: No.

MRS. WATTS: You see? Nobody has. Well, it's not much of a town now, I guess. I haven't seen it myself in thirty years. But it used to be quite prosperous. All they have left is a post office and a filling station and a general store. At least they did when I left.

THELMA: Do your people live there?

MRS. WATTS: No. My people are all dead except my son and his wife, Jessie Mae. They live here in the city. I'm hurrying to get to see Bountiful once before I die. I had a sinking spell this morning. I had to climb up on the bed and rest for an hour. It was my heart.

THELMA: Do you have a bad heart?

MRS. WATTS: Well, it's not what you call a good one. Doctor says it would last as long as I needed it if I could cut worrying out. But seems I can't do that lately. (*She suddenly jumps up out of her seat.*) Excuse me. Would you watch my suitcase?

THELMA: Certainly.

(*Mrs. Watts hurries off in the direction of the door. Thelma picks up her book and reads. Mrs. Watts comes hurrying back. She sits on the edge of the seat looking in the direction of the door.)*

THELMA: Lady, is there anything wrong?

MRS. WATTS: No, honey. I'm a little nervous, that's all. *(She jumps up again. Thelma watches her go. When she gets out of sight, Thelma again starts to read her book. Mrs. Watts comes running in and grabs her suitcase. In her confusion she drops a small white handkerchief. Neither she nor Thelma sees it.)* Say a prayer for me, honey. Good luck.

THELMA: Good luck to you.

(She is gone. A man comes in. He is Ludie Watts. He is in his early forties. He looks shabby and beaten. His face was once sensitive, but is now covered with bitterness and defeat. He stands in front of Thelma. She has gone back to reading her book. Jessie Mae comes in.)

LUDIE: You want to sit down, Jessie Mae?

JESSIE MAE: Yes. Go and get yourself a Coke if you want to. I'll wait.

LUDIE: All right. Want me to buy you a movie magazine?

JESSIE MAE: Yes. *(Ludie goes off to get her a movie magazine. Jessie Mae takes out a cigarette. Jessie Mae searches for a match. She can't find one. She turns to Thelma.)* Excuse me. Do you have a match?

THELMA: Yes, I do. *(She reaches in her coat and gets one. She hands it to Jessie Mae.)*

JESSIE MAE: Thank you. I hope you're lucky enough not to have to fool with any in-laws. I've got a mother-in-law about to drive me crazy. Once a month we have to spend the evening in the depot to try and keep her from getting on a train to go back to her home town. Oh, she's so stubborn. I could just wring her neck. Her son spoils her, that's the whole trouble. She's

just spoiled rotten. Do you live with your in-laws?

THELMA: No.

JESSIE MAE: Well, you're lucky. They're all stubborn. My husband is as stubborn as she is. We should be over at the depot right now instead of sitting here. She always tries to take the train. But no. We wait at the depot for five minutes and because she isn't there, right then, he drags me over here. I'm just worn out. I've had my fourth Coca-cola to keep my spirits up. People ask me why I don't have any children. Why? I say. I've got Ludie and Mother Watts. That's all the children I need. Of course, I can tell when she's gonna sneak out. Something said to me when I went to the beauty parlor this afternoon . . . She'll be gone when you get back. And she was. *(Ludie comes back in. He has a movie magazine in his hand.)* What did you bring me? *(He shows it to her.)* Oh, I've seen that one.

LUDIE: Have you seen Mama?

JESSIE MAE: No, you goose. Do you think I'd be sitting here so calm if I had? Personally, I think we're wasting our time here in the first place. She always tries to go by train.

LUDIE: But she can't go by train, Jessie Mae. How many times do I have to explain that to you? There hasn't been a train to Bountiful in twenty-five years.

JESSIE MAE: She doesn't know that.

LUDIE: She does by now.

JESSIE MAE: But we've always found her there. Remember that. *(A pause.)* Ludie, I know she's there. I know it. I'm never wrong about these things.

LUDIE: All right. Have it your way. Let's go.

JESSIE MAE: Well, now we're here, might as well inquire from someone if they've seen her wandering around.

LUDIE: I thought you said she wouldn't come here.

JESSIE MAE: I said I didn't think she would come here. I don't know what the crazy thing will do. I think we ought to turn it over to the police. That would scare her once and for all.

LUDIE: Well, we're not going to call any police.

JESSIE MAE: It's for her own good. She's crazy.

LUDIE: Why do you talk like that? You know Mama isn't crazy.

JESSIE MAE: Then why does she keep running off from a perfectly good home to try and get to some old swamp? Don't you call that crazy? I mean, she doesn't have to turn her hand. Hardly. We only have a bedroom and a living room and a kitchen. We're all certainly very light eaters, so cooking three meals a day isn't killing her.

LUDIE: Well, let's don't stand here arguing about it. People are looking at us. Do you want to go to the depot or not?

JESSIE MAE: It's your mother. I don't care what you do. Only you better do something. Let me tell you that. She's gonna clonk out some place. She'll get to Bountiful and die from the excitement and then we'll have all kinds of expenses bringing her body back here. Do you know what a thing like that could cost? Do you realize she had a sinking spell this morning?

LUDIE: I know you've told me a hundred times. What can I do about it?

JESSIE MAE: Call the police. It's their job to find missing persons.

LUDIE: I'm not going to call the police.

JESSIE MAE: Then I think I will. That'll settle it once and for all.

LUDIE: You're not calling any police. It would kill her.

JESSIE MAE: Well, this is killing me. I'm going to call the police. I'm tired of it, Ludie. I'm just tired of it.

(*She goes marching off. He sits down dejectly in the seat. Thelma has been watching all this time . . . She has tried not to be seen, but it should be apparent to the audience that she has heard all that has gone on. Ludie looks helpless and desperate. He mops his face with his handkerchief. He sees the movie magazine in his hand. He turns to Thelma.*)

LUDIE: Would you like this? I never read them, and my wife has seen it.

THELMA: Thank you.

(*She takes it and puts it in her lap. Ludie looks on the floor and sees a handkerchief that has been dropped by Mrs. Watts. He picks it up. He looks at Thelma and is about to question her. Thelma averts her eyes. He runs to the ticket window. There is a new man on duty.*)

LUDIE: Excuse me. Did an old lady come here and buy a ticket to Bountiful?

TICKET MAN: Sorry. I just came here for the night.

LUDIE: Where is the man that was on duty?

TICKET MAN: He's gone home.

LUDIE: Oh. (*Ludie sees Thelma again and goes back to her.*) Excuse me. But I found a handkerchief there that belongs, I think, to my mother. She's run off from home. She has a heart condition and it might be serious for her to be all alone. I don't think she has much money, and I'd like to find her. Do you remember having seen her?

THELMA: Well . . . I . . .

LUDIE: She's in her sixties and she'd be on her way to a town called Bountiful . . .

THELMA: Yes, I did see her. She was here talking to me. She left suddenly.

LUDIE: Did she say that she had a ticket on the bus?

THELMA: I believe so.

LUDIE: Thank you so much. (*Jessie Mae comes in.*) I was right. She was here. This lady says so. She says she has bought herself a ticket . . .

JESSIE MAE: Well, we're not going to wait. I've turned it over to the police.

LUDIE: Jessie Mae.

JESSIE MAE: Well, I have. It's the best thing, Ludie—I explained the whole thing to them. They said we should just go home. That she will never leave. She's just trying to get our attention. And once we show her we don't care if she goes or not, she'll come home of her own accord. The police say such things are quite common in young people and old people.

LUDIE: Now look, Jessie Mae . . .

JESSIE MAE: And that's just what we're going to do.

LUDIE: Jessie Mae.

JESSIE MAE: Come on, Ludie. (*She starts off.*) Come on, I say.

LUDIE: All right. (*He wearily follows Jessie Mae.*)

Dissolve back to the waiting room. Thelma is still there. A man has now taken Mrs. Watt's chair. An announcer calls stations . . . "Harrison. Cotton. Old Gulf . . . " Thelma gathers her things together.

Dissolve to: The inside of a bus. People are getting themselves settled for the ride. Thelma comes in, gives her ticket to the bus man and gets into a seat. Everyone is settled down. Then Mrs. Watts comes hurrying in . . . She seats herself next to Thelma.

THELMA: Hello.

(*Mrs. Watts jumps up from her seat. Then she recognizes Thelma.*)

MRS. WATTS: Oh. It's you. How do you do. Well, I made it. It's a small world. I didn't know you'd be on the same bus. Where do you go, honey?

THELMA: Harrison.

MRS. WATTS: Harrison!

THELMA: Yes. I change buses there.

MRS. WATTS: So do I go there. Isn't that nice?

(*She settles herself down in the seat as the bus driver says, "All aboard," and is closing the bus door and starting the motor.*)

Dissolve to: The bus station. Ludie comes running in. He goes to an attendant.

LUDIE: Has the bus for Harrison left?

ATTENDANT: Just pulled out.

LUDIE: Did you see an old lady get on there?

ATTENDANT: Have on a black hat? In her sixties?

LUDIE: Yes.

ATTENDANT: Yes, I did.

LUDIE: Oh. (*Jessie Mae comes in.*) Well, she's gone.

JESSIE MAE: I don't understand that. The police said . . .

LUDIE: The police! The police! I knew if she wasn't home when we got there, she wouldn't be coming home.

JESSIE MAE: Let me go phone the police and report it. They'll stop the bus and get her off.

LUDIE: You won't do any such thing. I'll get me a ticket and go after her.

JESSIE MAE: And not be here for work tomorrow and lose this job?

LUDIE: I'll get us back in time for work.

JESSIE MAE: Don't be a fool. I'm calling the police.

LUDIE: You're not.

JESSIE MAE: I am.

LUDIE: You're not.

JESSIE MAE: I am. (*They are screaming at each other.*)

Dissolve to: The inside of the bus. It is on its way. We dolly in for a close-up of Mrs. Watts's face. She seems serene and content. She is humming softly . . . "There's not a friend like the lowly Jesus" as there is music for the curtain.

ACT TWO

The inside of the bus. Thelma and Mrs. Watts are looking out the window. It is later that night.

MRS. WATTS: The bus is nice to ride, isn't it?

THELMA: Yes. It is.

MRS. WATTS: I'm sorry I couldn't take a train though.

THELMA: I tried to go by train but you couldn't get connections tonight.

MRS. WATTS: I know. When I was a girl I used to take excursions from Bountiful to Houston or Galveston. For the day, you know. Leave at five in the morning and return at ten that night. The whole town would be down to see you get off the train. I have such fond memories of those trips. (*A pause.*) Excuse me for getting personal, but what's a pretty girl like you doing traveling alone?

THELMA: My husband had just been sent overseas. I'm going to stay with my family.

MRS. WATTS: Oh, I'm sorry to hear that. Just say the ninety-first Psalm over and over to yourself. It will be a bower of strength and protection for him. (*She begins to recite:*) "He that dwelleth in the secret place of the most high shall abide under the shadow of the Almighty. I will say of the Lord he is my refuge and my fortress: My God; in Him will I trust. Surely He shall deliver thee from the snare of the fowler and the noisome pestilence. He shall cover thee with His feathers and under his wing shalt thou trust: His truth shall be thy shield and buckler." (*Thelma begins to cry.*) Oh, I'm sorry, I'm sorry, honey.

THELMA: That's all right. I'm just lonesome for him.

MRS. WATTS: Keep him under the Lord's wing, honey, and he'll be safe.

THELMA: Yes, ma'am. (*She dries her eyes.*) I'm sorry. I don't know what gets into me.

MRS. WATTS: Nobody needs be ashamed of crying. I guess we've all dampened our pillows sometime or other. I have, Lord knows.

THELMA: If I could only learn not to worry.

MRS. WATTS: I know. I guess we all ask that. Jessie Mae, my daughter-in-law, don't worry. What for? She says. Well, like I tell her that's certainly a fine attitude if you can cultivate it. Trouble is I can't any longer.

THELMA: It is hard.

MRS. WATTS: I didn't use to worry. I was so carefree as a girl. Had lots to worry me, too. Everybody was poor in Bountiful. But we got along. I said to Papa once after our third crop failure in a row, whoever gave this place the name of Bountiful. His papa did, he said. He said in those days it was a land of plenty. You just had to drop seeds in the ground and the crops would spring up. Cotton and corn and sugar cane. I still think it's the prettiest place I know of. Jessie Mae, my daughter-in-law, says it's the ugliest. But she just says that I know to get my goat. She only saw it once. And then on a rainy day, at that. She says it's nothing but a swamp. That may be, I said, but it's a mighty pretty swamp, to me. And then Sonny, that's my boy Ludie, I call him Sonny, he said not to answer her back. He said it only caused arguments. And nobody ever won an argument with Jessie Mae, and I guess that's right.

(*A pause. They look out the window.*)

THELMA: Mrs. Watts . . .

MRS. WATTS: Yes?

THELMA: I think I ought to tell you this . . . I . . . I don't want you to think I'm interfering in your business . . . but . . . well . . . you see your son and your daughter-in-law came in just after you left.

MRS. WATTS: I know. I saw them coming. That's why I left so fast.

THELMA: Your son seemed very concerned.

MRS. WATTS: Bless his heart.

THELMA: He found a handkerchief that you had dropped.

MRS. WATTS: Oh, mercy, that's right, I did.

THELMA: He asked me if I had seen you. I felt I had to say yes. I wouldn't have said anything if he hadn't asked me . . .

MRS. WATTS: Oh, that's all right. I would have done exactly the same thing in your place. Did you talk to Jessie Mae?

THELMA: Yes.

MRS. WATTS: Isn't she a sight? I bet she told you I was crazy . . .

THELMA: Well . . .

MRS. WATTS: Oh, don't be afraid of hurting my feelings. Everybody's crazy according to Jessie Mae that don't want to sit in the beauty parlor all day and read movie magazines. She tells me I'm crazy about a million times a day. That's the only time Ludie will talk back to her. He gets real mad when she calls me crazy. I think Ludie knows how I feel about getting back to Bountiful. I bet he'd like to be along right now. Once when I was talking about something we did back there in the old days, he just broke out crying. He was so overcome he had to leave the room.

(*A pause. Mrs. Watts starts to hum and sing "There's not a friend like the lowly Jesus."*)

THELMA: That's a pretty hymn. What's the name of it?

MRS. WATTS: "There's not a friend like the lowly Jesus." Do you like hymns?

THELMA: Yes, I do.

MRS. WATTS: So do I. Jessie Mae says they've gone out of style, but I don't agree. I always sing one walking down the street or riding the streetcar. Keeps my spirits up. What's your favorite hymn?

THELMA: Oh, I don't know.

MRS. WATTS: The one I was singing is mine. I bet I sing it a hundred times a day. When Jessie Mae isn't home. Hymns make Jessie Mae nervous. (*A pause.*) Did Ludie mention my heart condition?

THELMA: Yes, he did.

MRS. WATTS: Poor Ludie. He worries about it so. I hated to leave him. Well, I guess he'll forgive me in time. He's just gotten himself a job. Thank the Lord. He's been out of work for two years. He had a good living as an accountant and then his nerves gave out on him. So many people are nervous today. He wasn't nervous back in Bountiful. Neither was I. The breeze from the Gulf would always quiet your nerves . . . You could sit on our front gallery and smell the ocean blowing in around you. (*A pause.*) I regret the day we left. But, I thought it was the best thing at the time . . . There were only three families there then. Farming was so hard to make a living by, and I had to see to our farm myself; our house was old and there was no money to fix it, nor send Ludie to school. So I sold off the land and gave him an education. Callie said I could always come back and visit her. She meant it, too. That's who I'm going to stay with now. Callie. I got a card from her every Christmas except the last five. I wrote her last week and told her to expect me. Told her not to answer though on account of Jessie Mae opens all my mail. I didn't want her to know I was going. She'd try to stop it. Jessie Mae hates me. I don't know why, but she hates me. (*A pause.*) Hate me or not, I gotta get back and smell that salt air and work that dirt. I'm gonna spend the whole first month of my visit working in Callie's garden. I haven't had my hands in dirt in twenty years. My hands need the feel of dirt. (*A pause.*) Do you like to work the ground?

THELMA: I never have.

MRS. WATTS: Try it sometimes. It'll do wonders for you. I bet I'll live to be a hundred once I can get outside again. It was being cooped up in those two rooms that was killing me. I used to work the land like a man. Had to when Papa died. I got two little babies buried there. Renee Sue and Douglas. Diphtheria got Renee Sue. I never knew what carried Douglas away. He was just weak from the start. I know Callie's kept their graves weeded. Oh, if my heart just holds out until I get there. (*A pause.*) Where do you go from Harrison?

THELMA: Old Gulf. My family have just moved there from Louisiana. I'll stay with them until my husband comes home again.

MRS. WATTS: That's nice.

THELMA: It'll be funny living at home again.

MRS. WATTS: How long have you been married?

THELMA: Three years. My husband was anxious for me to go. He said he'd worry about my being alone.

MRS. WATTS: What's your husband's name?

THELMA: Robert.

MRS. WATTS: That's a nice name.

THELMA: I think so. But I guess any name he had I would think was nice. I love my husband very much. Lots of girls I know think I'm silly about him. But I can't help it.

MRS. WATTS: I wasn't in love with my husband. (*A pause.*) Do you believe we are punished for what we do wrong? I sometimes think that's why I've had all my trouble. I've talked to many a preacher about it, all but one said they didn't think so. But I can't see any other reason. Of course, I didn't lie to my husband. I told him I didn't love him, that I admired him, which I did, but I didn't love him. That I'd never love anybody but Ray John Murray as long as I lived and I didn't, and I couldn't help it. Even after my husband died and I had to move back with Papa and Mama I used to sit on the front gallery every morning and every evening just to nod hello to Ray John Murray as he went by the house to work at the post office. He went a block out of his way to pass the house. He never loved nobody but me.

THELMA: Why didn't you marry him?

MRS. WATTS: His papa and my papa didn't speak. My papa forced me to write a letter saying I never wanted to see him again and he got drunk and married out of spite. I felt sorry for his wife. She knew he never loved her. (*A pause.*) I don't think about those things much any more. But they're all part of Bountiful and I guess that's why I'm starting to think of them again. You're lucky to be married to the man you love, honey.

THELMA: Yes, I know I am.

MRS. WATTS: Awfully lucky. (*A pause.*) Did you see that star fall over there?

THELMA: No.

MRS. WATTS: It was the prettiest thing I ever saw. You can make a wish on a falling star, honey.

THELMA: I know. It's too bad I didn't see it.

MRS. WATTS: You take my wish.

THELMA: Oh, no.

MRS. WATTS: Go on. I've gotten mine already. I'm on my way to Bountiful.

THELMA: Thank you. (*A pause.*)

MRS. WATTS: Did you make your wish?

THELMA: Yes. I did.

(*Mrs. Watts closes her eyes. Thelma puts her coat over Mrs. Watts. She leans her head back against the seat and closes her eyes as we fade out.*)

Fade in: The interior of the bus. Two hours later. It has stopped. Thelma is shaking Mrs. Watts.

THELMA: Mrs. Watts. Mrs. Watts.

(*Mrs. Watts opens her eyes.*)

MRS. WATTS: Yes?

THELMA: We're here. It's Harrison.

MRS. WATTS: Oh, yes. Thank you, honey.

THELMA: I'll take our suitcases and meet you inside the bus station.

MRS. WATTS: Oh, yes. That's very kind of you.

(*Thelma takes the suitcases down and goes out of the bus. Mrs. Watts slowly gets out of her seat and is straightening her hat.*)

Dissolve to: The inside of the bus station. A man is lying against the inside of the ticket window half asleep. He wakes himself and sees the bus has come in. He comes out of the ticket office and goes half-way to the front door, as Thelma comes in with the two bags.

TICKET MAN: Want any help with those bags?

THELMA: No, thank you. (*He goes back inside the office. Thelma takes the bags and puts them down beside a bench. She goes over to the ticket window.*) Excuse me.

TICKET MAN: Yes?

THELMA: Is the bus to Old Gulf going to be on time?

TICKET MAN: Always is.

THELMA: Thank you.

(*She goes back to a seat near her suitcase. The man closes his eyes. Mrs. Watts comes in.*)

MRS. WATTS: What time is it, honey?

THELMA: Two o'clock.

MRS. WATTS: Two o'clock. I bet Callie will be surprised to see me walk in at two o'clock in the morning.

THELMA: Did you tell her you were coming today?

MRS. WATTS: No, I couldn't. Because I didn't know. I had to wait until Jessie Mae went to the beauty parlor which wasn't until this afternoon.

THELMA: My bus is leaving in half an hour.

Mrs. Watts: Oh, I see. I guess I'd better be finding out how I'm going to get on out to Bountiful.

Thelma: You sit down. I'll ask the man.

Mrs. Watts: Thank you.

(*She sits on the bench. Thelma goes over to the ticket man.*)

Thelma: Excuse me again.

(*The ticket man opens his eyes.*)

Ticket Man: Yes?

Thelma: My friend here wants to know how she can get to Bountiful.

Ticket Man: Bountiful?

Thelma: Yes.

Ticket Man: What's she going there for?

(*Mrs. Watts comes up to the window.*)

Mrs. Watts: I'm going to visit a girlhood friend.

Ticket Man: I don't know who that's gonna be. The last person in Bountiful was Callie Davis. She died day before yesterday. That is they found her day before yesterday. She lived all alone so they don't know exactly when she died.

Mrs. Watts: Callie Davis?

Ticket Man: Yes, ma'am. They had the funeral this morning. Was she the one you were going to visit?

Mrs. Watts: Yes, sir. She was the one. She was my friend. My girlhood friend. (*A pause.*) I guess I better sit down and think. (*She goes over to the bench.*)

Thelma: Is there a hotel here?

Ticket Man: Yes'm. The Riverview. It's a nice hotel. You can get meals there, too.

Thelma: How far is it?

Ticket Man: About five blocks.

Thelma: Is there a taxi around?

Ticket Man: No, ma'am. Not this time of night.

Thelma: Thank you. (*She goes over to Mrs. Watts at the bench.*) What'll you do now, Mrs. Watts?

Mrs. Watts: I'm thinking, honey. I'm thinking. It's come as quite a blow.

Thelma: I'm sorry. I'm sorry.

Mrs. Watts: I know. I know. (*A pause.*) It's come to me what to do. I'll go on. That much has come to me. To go on. I feel my strength and my purpose strong within me. I'll go on to Bountiful. I'll walk those twelve miles if I have to.

Thelma: But if there's no one out there what would you do at this time of night?

Mrs. Watts: I guess that's right.

Thelma: I think you should wait until morning.

Mrs. Watts: Yes. I guess I should. Then I can hire someone to drive me out. You know what I'll do. I'll stay at my own house, or what's left of it. Put me in a garden. I'll get along fine with the help of my government checks.

Thelma: Mrs. Watts, the man says there's a hotel not too far away. I think you'd better let me take you there.

Mrs. Watts: Oh, no, thank you. I wouldn't want to waste my money on a hotel. They're high as a cat's back, you know. I'll just sleep right here on this bench. Put my coat under my head, hold my purse under my arm. (*She puts the coat down on the bench like a pillow. She begins to look around for her purse.*) Have you seen my purse, honey?

Thelma: Why, no.

(*They begin to look around for it.*)

Mrs. Watts: Oh, my Lord. I remember now. I left my purse on the bus. Has it gone?

(*Thelma turns to the door and looks out.*)

Thelma: Yes, it has. You're sure you left it there?

Mrs. Watts: Yes. I am. I remember now. I didn't have it when I got off that bus. I kept thinking something was missing, but then I decided it was my suitcase that you had brought in for me. What am I gonna do, honey? All I have in the world is in that purse.

THELMA: I'll get the ticket man to call ahead. He can get someone to look on the bus in the next town.

MRS. WATTS: Thank you.

(*Thelma goes back to the ticket window. The man is drowsing.*)

THELMA: Excuse me again.

TICKET MAN: Yeah?

THELMA: This lady left her purse on the bus.

TICKET MAN: All right. I'll call ahead. How can you identify it?

MRS. WATTS: It's a plain black purse.

TICKET MAN: How much money?

MRS. WATTS: Thirty-five cents and a pension check.

TICKET MAN: Who was the check made out to?

MRS. WATTS: To me, Mrs. Carrie Watts.

TICKET MAN: All right. I'll call up about it.

MRS. WATTS: Oh, thank you. You're most kind.

THELMA: How long will it take to get it back?

TICKET MAN: Depends. If I can get ahead of the bus at Don Tarl, I can get them to send it back on the Victoria bus and it should be here in a couple of hours.

(*He goes. Thelma and Mrs. Watts go back to the bench.*)

MRS. WATTS: I don't know what I would have done without you.

THELMA: Try not to worry about the purse.

MRS. WATTS: I won't. I'm too tired to worry. Be time enough to start worrying when I wake up in the morning.

THELMA: Why don't you go on to sleep if you can.

MRS. WATTS: Oh, I thought I'd stay up and see you off.

THELMA: No. You go on to sleep.

MRS. WATTS: I couldn't go right off to sleep now. I'm too wound up. You know I don't go on a trip every day of my life.

(*Ticket man comes back to the window.*)

TICKET MAN: You're lucky. Bus hadn't gotten to Don Tarl yet. If they can find the purse it'll be here around five.

MRS. WATTS: Thank you. Thank you so much.

THELMA: Make you feel better?

MRS. WATTS: Yes. It does. Of course, everything has seemed to work out today. Why is it some days everything works out, and some days nothing works out. What I mean is, I've been trying to get on that bus for Bountiful for over five years. Usually Jessie Mae and Ludie find me before I even get inside the station good. Today, I got inside both the railroad station and the bus station. Bought a ticket, seen Ludie and Jessie Mae before they saw me. Hid out until they were gone. Met a nice friend like you. Lost my purse, and now I'm having it found for me. I guess the good Lord is just with me today. (*A pause.*) I wonder why the Lord isn't with us every day? It would be so nice if He was. Well, maybe then we wouldn't appreciate so much the days when He's on our side. Or maybe He's always on our side and we don't know it. Maybe I had to wait twenty years cooped up with Jessie Mae in a city before I could appreciate getting back here. (*A pause. Thelma rests her head back on the bench. Mrs. Watts rests her head back. She is humming "There's not a friend like the lowly Jesus."*) It's so nice being able to sing a hymn when you want. I'm a happy woman, young lady—a very happy woman.

(*Ticket man goes to the door and looks out.*)

TICKET MAN: You better get outside, Miss. Bus is coming up the road. It won't wait unless it sees we have a passenger.

THELMA: All right. (*She gets her bag.*) Good-by, Mrs. Watts.

MRS. WATTS: Good-by, honey. Good luck to you. And thank you for everything.

THELMA: That's all right. Good luck to you.

MRS. WATTS: Thank you.

(*Thelma goes out. The ticket man fol-*

lows her out. We can hear a bus pulling up. Mrs. Watts goes to the door. She stands waving. The bus is heard pulling out. The ticket man comes back in.)

TICKET MAN: Are you gonna stay here all night?

MRS. WATTS: I have to. Everything I have is in that purse and we can't go any place without money.

TICKET MAN: I guess that's right. *(He goes back inside the ticket window.)* Well, good night. See you in the morning.

MRS. WATTS: Good night.

(He puts his head on the window ledge and dozes off. Mrs. Watts sits on the bench. She rests her head back on the ledge. She is singing the hymn softly to herself as we fade out.)

Fade in: The ticket office an hour later. We dolly in to the ticket man. He is sound asleep and snoring slightly. The door opens. A man comes in. He is the Sheriff. He stands by the door for a moment looking around the bus station. He sees Mrs. Watts lying on the bench asleep. He goes over to her and looks down. He stands for a moment watching her sleep. He looks over at the ticket window and sees the man is asleep. The Sheriff goes over to the ticket man. He shakes him.

TICKET MAN: Yeah? *(He opens his eyes. He sees the Sheriff.)* Oh, hello, Sheriff.

SHERIFF: How long has that old woman been here?

TICKET MAN: About two hours.

SHERIFF: Did she get off the bus from Houston?

TICKET MAN: Yes, sir. I know her name. It's Watts. She left her purse on the bus and I had to call up to Don Tarl about it.

SHERIFF: Have you got her purse?

TICKET MAN: No. It hasn't come yet.

SHERIFF: She's the one, all right. I've had a call from the Houston police to hold her until her son can come for her.

TICKET MAN: She said she used to live in Bountiful.

SHERIFF: Yeah. I believe I remember some Wattses a long time ago over that way. I think that old ramshackly house about to fall into the Brazos River belonged to them.

TICKET MAN: That right? They must have been before my time. She claimed she was going to visit a Callie Davis. I told her she was dead. What do the police want her for?

SHERIFF: Police don't. It's her son. He wants to take her back home. Claims she's not responsible. Did she act crazy to you?

TICKET MAN: Not that I noticed. Is she crazy?

SHERIFF: They say so. Harmless, but hipped on running away from Houston to get back here. *(He starts over to her. He stands looking at her for a moment. He comes back to the ticket man.)* Poor old thing. She's sleeping so sound, I don't have the heart to wake her up. I tell you what. I'll leave her here. You keep your eye on her. I'll come on back about daylight and take her over. Her son is coming in his car. He should be here around seven-thirty. I'll go let them know in Houston she's here. If she gives you any trouble you just call me. But I don't think she will.

TICKET MAN: All right. I guess she can't go very far without her purse, and I'm gonna have that.

SHERIFF: I'll be back around six. If she isn't up by then, I'll wake her.

TICKET MAN: All right.

(The Sheriff goes out.)

Dissolve to: Bus station. Daybreak is just beginning. Mrs. Watts is waking up. She sits up on the bench. She goes over to the door and looks outside. She looks around the waiting room. She sees the ticket man asleep. She goes over to him and shakes him by the sleeve.

MRS. WATTS: Excuse me, sir. *(He doesn't hear her. She shakes his sleeve again.)* I said excuse me, sir. *(He opens his eyes. He lifts his head up.*)

TICKET MAN: Yes?

MRS. WATTS: Did my purse arrive?

TICKET MAN: Yes, ma'am. (*He reaches under the window to a ledge and gets it for her.*)

MRS. WATTS: Thank you so much. I wonder if you would cash a check for me?

TICKET MAN: I'm sorry. I can't.

MRS. WATTS: It's a government check and I have identification.

TICKET MAN: I'm sorry. I can't.

MRS. WATTS: Do you know where I could get a check cashed?

TICKET MAN: Why?

MRS. WATTS: I need money to get me started in Bountiful. I want to hire someone to drive me out there and look at my house and get a few groceries. Try to find a cot to sleep on . . .

TICKET MAN: I'm sorry, lady. You're not going to Bountiful.

MRS. WATTS: Oh, yes I am. You see . . .

TICKET MAN: I'm sorry, lady. You're not going any place right now. I have to hold you here for the Sheriff.

MRS. WATTS: The Sheriff?

TICKET MAN: Yes, ma'am.

(*A pause.*)

MRS. WATTS: (*Almost afraid he isn't*) You're joking with me. Don't joke with me. I've come too far . . .

TICKET MAN: I'm sorry. That's how it is.

MRS. WATTS: What has the Sheriff got to do with me?

TICKET MAN: He came in here last night while you were asleep and said I was to keep you here until your son arrived in his car this morning . . .

MRS. WATTS: I don't believe you. I don't believe you . . .

TICKET MAN: It's the truth. He'll be in here in a little while and you can ask him yourself. (*A pause.*)

MRS. WATTS: Then you're not joking?

TICKET MAN: No.

MRS. WATTS: All right. But I'm going, do you understand? You'll see. This is a free country. And I'll tell him that. No sheriff or king or president will keep me from going back to Bountiful.

TICKET MAN: All right. You tell him that. (*A pause. He turns away.*)

(*She goes back to the bench. She is suddenly very nervous.*)

MRS. WATTS: What time is my son expected?

TICKET MAN: Sheriff says around seven-thirty.

MRS. WATTS: What time is it now?

TICKET MAN: Around six. (*He looks up at the clock.*) Five of six. To be exact.

MRS. WATTS: Where can I get a driver?

TICKET MAN: Ma'am?

MRS. WATTS: If you can get me a driver, I can make it to Bountiful and back before seven-thirty.

TICKET MAN: Look, lady . . .

MRS. WATTS: That's all I want. That's all I ask. Just to see it. To stand on the porch of my own house, once more. Walk under the trees. I swear, I would come back then meek as a lamb . . .

TICKET MAN: Lady . . .

MRS. WATTS: Last night, I thought I had to stay. I thought I'd die if I couldn't stay. But I'll settle for less now. Much, much less. An hour. A half-hour. Fifteen minutes.

TICKET MAN: Lady, it ain't up to me. I told you the Sheriff . . .

MRS. WATTS: (*Screaming*) Then get me the Sheriff . . .

TICKET MAN: Look, lady . . .

MRS. WATTS: Get me the Sheriff. The time is going. They'll have me locked in those two rooms again soon. The time is going . . . The time is . . .

(*She begins to cry. She goes to the bench crying. The Sheriff comes in. She doesn't hear him. He looks as the ticket man. The ticket man shakes his head as much as to say: "Pitiful." The Sheriff goes over to her.)*

SHERIFF: Mrs. Watts?

MRS. WATTS: Yes sir. (*She looks up.*) Are you the Sheriff?

SHERIFF: Yes, ma'am.

MRS. WATTS: I understand my son will be here at seven-thirty to take me back to Houston . . .

SHERIFF: Yes, ma'am.

MRS. WATTS: Then listen to me, sir. I've waited a long time. Just to get to Bountiful. Twenty years I've been walking the streets of the city, lost and grieving. And as I've grown older and my time approaches to die, I've made one promise to myself, to see my home again . . .

SHERIFF: Lady . . . I . . .

MRS. WATTS: I'm not asking that I not go back. I'm willing to go back. Only let me travel these twelve miles first. I have money. I can pay . . .

SHERIFF: I think that's between you and your son.

MRS. WATTS: Ludie? Why, he has to do whatever Jessie Mae tells him to. I know why she wants me back. It's for my government check. She takes it from me to buy herself Cokes and movie magazines.

SHERIFF: I don't know nothing about that. That's between you and your son.

MRS. WATTS: Won't you let me go?

SHERIFF: Not unless your son takes you.

MRS. WATTS: All right. Then I've lost. I've come all this way only to lose. (*A pause. She sinks wearily down on the bench. After a moment she begins to talk. She speaks half to herself.*) I kept thinking back there day and night in those two rooms. I kept thinking . . . And it may mean nothing at all, but it did occur to me . . . That if I could just set foot there for a minute, even . . . or a second . . . I might get some understanding of why . . . (*She turns to the Sheriff. She begins to talk directly to him.*) Why my life has

grown so petty and so meaningless. Why I've turned into a hateful, quarrelsome, old woman. And before I die I'd like to recover some of the dignity . . . the peace I used to know. For I'm going to die. Do you hear me? I'm going to die. Jessie Mae knows that. She's willful and it's her will I die in those two rooms. Well, she shan't have her way. It's my will to die in Bountiful . . .

(*She sobs and starts to run out of the bus station. The Sheriff starts after her. But she doesn't get far. She stops herself. She seems suddenly very weak and is about to fall. He goes to her and takes her arm.*)

MRS. WATTS: I beg you . . . Let me go those twelve miles . . . (*A pause. For a moment her strength seems to come back.*) Understand me. Suffering I don't mind. Suffering I understand. I never protested once. Though my heart was broken when those babies died. I could stand seeing the man I loved go through life with another woman. But this twenty years of bickering. Endless, petty bickering . . . (*She again is overcome with weakness. She stands gasping for breath. They help her back to the bench.*) It's made me just like Jessie Mae sees me. It's ugly. I won't be that way. I want to go home . . . I want to go home. I want to go . . . (*She is unable to speak any more. She is on the verge of collapse. The Sheriff helps her over to the bench and settles her there.*)

SHERIFF: (*To the ticket man*) Roy! Call a doctor.

MRS. WATTS: (*Struggling with her last bit of strength.*) No. No doctor. Bountiful . . . Bountiful . . .

She is whispering the words. They grow indistinct. Music for the curtain.

ACT THREE

The front porch of an old ramshackle two-story house. The house hasn't been painted for years. The roof of the lower porch is sagging, the steps and the flooring are rotting away. There is no glass in the windows, no door in the doorway. The Sheriff and Mrs. Watts come in walking very slowly. They stop every few minutes while she looks around.

SHERIFF: Feeling better?

MRS. WATTS: Yes. I am. Much better.

SHERIFF: I hope I've done the right thing bringing you here. Well, I don't see what harm it can do. As long as you mind the doctor and don't get over-excited.

MRS. WATTS: I'm home. I'm home. I'm home . . . Thank you. I thank you. I thank you.

SHERIFF: You better sit down and rest now.

MRS. WATTS: Yes sir.

(He takes her to the steps. She sits.)

SHERIFF: I'll go on back to my car. Call me if you need anything. I'll stay until your son arrives.

MRS. WATTS: Thank you. You have been very kind. You say the store burned fifteen years ago?

SHERIFF: What was left of it. You see with the good roads we have now in the county, these little towns and their country stores are all disappearing. The farmers ride into Cotton or Harrison to trade . . .

MRS. WATTS: But what's happened to the farms? For the last five miles I've seen nothing but woods . . .

SHERIFF: I know. The land around Bountiful just played out. People like you got discouraged and moved away, sold off the land for what they could get. H. T. Mavis bought most of it up . . . He let it go back into timber. He keeps a few head of cattle out here. That's all . . .

MRS. WATTS: Callie Davis kept her farm going.

SHERIFF: Yes. She did. She learned how to treat her land right and it began paying off for her towards the end. I've heard she was out riding her tractor the day before she died. Lonely death she had.

All by herself in that big old house.

MRS. WATTS: There are worse things. *(A pause.)*

SHERIFF: Well, I'll go on back to the car now. You call me if you need anything.

MRS. WATTS: Thank you.

(He goes. Mrs. Watts is sitting on the steps looking out into the yard. There is great peace in her face.)

Dissolve to: The house and yard an hour later. The Sheriff comes up on the gallery. It is empty. He calls.

SHERIFF: *(Calling)* Mrs. Watts. Mrs. Watts . . .

(She comes to the door . . . She stands just outside of it.)

MRS. WATTS: Yes sir?

SHERIFF: Your son and daughter-in-law are out on the road in their car. They said they had to hurry back. I told them I'd bring you.

MRS. WATTS: Won't you ask them to please come in for a minute?

SHERIFF: All right. *(He comes up to the gallery.)* I have to be going on back to town now. Good-by, Mrs. Watts. *(He holds his hand out. She takes it.)*

MRS. WATTS: Good-by and thank you. You'll never know what this has meant to me.

SHERIFF: Glad I could oblige. *(Ludie comes up.)* I was just coming to tell you your mother wanted you to come in for a few minutes.

LUDIE: Thank you.

SHERIFF: I've got to get on back to town.

LUDIE: All right, Sheriff. Thank you.

SHERIFF: That's all right. Have a nice trip back.

LUDIE: Thank you.

(The Sheriff goes. Ludie goes up on the porch.)

LUDIE: Hello, Mama.

MRS. WATTS: Hello, son.

LUDIE: How do you feel?

MRS. WATTS: I'm feeling better, Ludie.

LUDIE: I'm sorry I had to have the Sheriff stop you that way, Mama, but I was worried.

MRS. WATTS: I know, son. Callie Davis died.

LUDIE: Is that so? When?

MRS. WATTS: They don't know. They found her dead. She'd been seen riding a tractor the day before they found her. Buried her yesterday. (*A pause.*) Sheriff took me by our burial ground. Callie had kept it free of weeds. Even planted a few rose bushes. Least I reckon it was Callie. I don't know of anyone else who would have taken the trouble. That was nice, wasn't it?

LUDIE: Yes. It was.

MRS. WATTS: The old house has gotten run down, hasn't it?

LUDIE: Yes, it has.

MRS. WATTS: I don't think it'll last through the next Gulf storm.

LUDIE: It doesn't look like it could. (*Car horn is heard in the distance, loud and impatient.*) That's Jessie Mae. We have to start back now, Mama. Jessie Mae is nervous that I might lose my job.

MRS. WATTS: Did you ask for the day off?

LUDIE: No. I only asked for the morning off. I said I'd be there by one.

MRS. WATTS: What time is it now?

LUDIE: Eight o'clock. We were a little late getting here.

MRS. WATTS: We can drive it in three hours.

LUDIE: I know, but we might run into some traffic. Besides I borrowed Billy Davidson's car and I promised to get it back to him by twelve.

MRS. WATTS: All right. (*She starts up from the gallery. She cries.*) Ludie. Ludie. What's happened to us? Why have we come to this?

LUDIE: I don't know, Mama.

MRS. WATTS: To have stayed and fought the land would have been better than this.

LUDIE: Yes'm.

MRS. WATTS: It's strange how much I had forgotten, Ludie. Pretty soon it'll all be gone. Five . . . years . . . ten . . . our house . . . You . . . Me . . .

LUDIE: Yes'm.

MRS. WATTS: But the river will be here. The fields. The woods. The smell of the Gulf. That's what I always took my strength from, Ludie. Not from houses, not from people. (*A pause.*) It's so quiet. It's so eternally quiet. I had forgotten the peace. The quiet. And it's given me strength once more, Ludie. To go on and bear what I have to bear. Do you hear me, Ludie? I've found my dignity and my strength.

LUDIE: I'm glad, Mama.

MRS. WATTS: And I'll never fight with Jessie Mae again—or complain. (*She points into the distance.*) Do you remember how my papa always had that field over there planted in cotton?

LUDIE: Yes, ma'am.

MRS. WATTS: See, it's all woods now. But I expect some day people will come again and cut down the trees and plant the cotton and maybe even wear out the land again and then their children will sell it and go to the cities and then the trees will come up again . . .

LUDIE: I guess.

(*A pause.*)

MRS. WATTS: I'm ready, Ludie.

LUDIE: All right, Mama.

(*He reaches his arm up to help her down the steps. Jessie Mae comes in.*)

JESSIE MAE: Ludie, are you coming or not?

LUDIE: We were just starting, Jessie Mae.

MRS. WATTS: Hello, Jessie Mae.

JESSIE MAE: I'm not speaking to you. I guess you're proud of the time you gave us. Dragging us all this way this time of morning. If Ludie loses his job over this, I hope you're happy.

LUDIE: I'm not going to lose my job, Jessie Mae.

JESSIE MAE: Well, you could.

LUDIE: All right, Jessie Mae.

JESSIE MAE: And she should realize that. She's selfish. That's her trouble. Always has been. Just purdee selfish . . . Where's your purse?

MRS. WATTS: Are you talking to me, Jessie Mae?

JESSIE MAE: Who else would I be talking to? Since when did Ludie start walking around with a pocketbook under his arm?

(*Mrs. Watts is looking around.*)

MRS. WATTS: Oh, I guess I left it inside.

JESSIE MAE: Where?

MRS. WATTS: I'll get it.

JESSIE MAE: No. Let me. You'll take all day. Where did you leave it?

MRS. WATTS: In one of the rooms downstairs.

JESSIE MAE: Wait and I'll get it. (*They start to go on.*) You all wait right there on that porch. I don't want to be left alone in this spooky old house. No telling what's running around in there.

MRS. WATTS: There's nothing in there.

JESSIE MAE: There might be rats or snakes or something.

LUDIE: I'll go.

JESSIE MAE: No. I'll go. Just stay here so if I holler you can come.

(*Jessie Mae goes into the house . . . Ludie helps his mother down the steps. By the time they have reached the bottom step, Jessie Mae comes out of the house with the purse.*)

JESSIE MAE: Here's your purse. Where's that money for that government check?

MRS. WATTS: I haven't cashed it.

JESSIE MAE: Where is it?

MRS. WATTS: It's right inside the purse.

(*Jessie Mae begins to search the purse.*)

JESSIE MAE: No. It isn't.

MRS. WATTS: Here. Give the purse to me. (*Jessie Mae hands her the purse. Mrs. Watts rummages around the purse. She suddenly begins to laugh.*)

JESSIE MAE: What's the matter with you? (*Mrs. Watts continues laughing.*)

MRS. WATTS: Oh, my Lord. What a good joke on me.

JESSIE MAE: Well, what's so funny?

MRS. WATTS: I just remembered. I left this purse on the bus last night and the ticket man had to phone ahead and get them to take it off the bus and send it back to me. I asked him to do it for that check. I certainly didn't put them to all that trouble for a dollar ninety-eight pocketbook. And do you know the check wasn't in that purse all that time?

JESSIE MAE: Where is it?

MRS. WATTS: Right here. (*She reaches into her bosom.*) Been there since yesterday afternoon. I forgot I never put it in that purse at all.

JESSIE MAE: Give it to me. (*She reaches to grab it out of Mrs. Watt's hands. Mrs. Watts pulls her hand back.*)

MRS. WATTS: Where's your manners?

JESSIE MAE: I'm too aggravated to have manners. Give it to me.

MRS. WATTS: All right. (*She takes the check and she tears it into little pieces. She throws them on the ground.*) Here's your check.

JESSIE MAE: You spiteful old thing.

LUDIE: Jessie Mae . . .

JESSIE MAE: That's what she is. Just spiteful and spoiled . . .

LUDIE: Go on to the car. I want to have a talk with Mama. We're gonna stop this wrangling once and for all else I'm walking out on you both.

JESSIE MAE: Well, you better hurry, or else I won't be here to walk out on. She's not coming into my house again. Not as long as I'm there. Now both of you talk that over. (*She goes out.*)

MRS. WATTS: I'm sorry, Ludie. I shouldn't have fought with her. I know. I know. I swore to myself I wouldn't ever again. I just don't know what got into me. (*A pause.*) I can get the check back for you.

LUDIE: It's not the check, Mama. You know that. It's not the check. (*He starts to cry.*)

MRS. WATTS: Don't son.

LUDIE: I don't mean to. But you and Jessie Mae make it so hard for me. Always pulling me this way and that. I try to please both of you . . . I . . . And it's killing me, Mama. It's killing me.

MRS. WATTS: I know. I know. Jessie Mae is right. We shouldn't live together. She brings out the worst in me and I reckon I bring out the worst in her.

LUDIE: But we have to live together, Mama.

MRS. WATTS: I know. I know. (*A pause.*) You go tell Jessie Mae I'm sorry. I won't fight any more. I've found my dignity and my strength. I'd lost it there for a minute, but I won't lose it again.

LUDIE: (*Wearily*) All right, Mama. Come on, let's go.

MRS. WATTS: No. You run ahead first and tell her I apologize. Ask her to let me come. That's the nice way to do it.

LUDIE: All right, Mama.

(*He goes. Mrs. Watts rests her body against the pillars of the porch. She goes down the steps and stoops in the earth by the steps. She scoops up a handful and looks at it, letting it run through her fingers back to the ground. Ludie comes back in.*)

LUDIE: Jessie Mae says all is forgiven.

MRS. WATTS: All right, son.

LUDIE: So come on and let's try and have a pleasant ride home.

MRS. WATTS: All right, son. (*They start*

away. She breaks out crying.)

LUDIE: Now, Mama. Please . . .

MRS. WATTS: All right, son. All right. I'm sorry. I won't cry ever again. (*She wipes her eyes. She starts out.*) I've had my trip. That's more than enough to keep me happy the rest of my life. (*She takes Ludie by the arm. They start out. She turns.*) Good-by, Bountiful. Good-by.

She takes one last look at the house. She waves one last farewell. She and Ludie go out. Music for curtain.

The man who wrote this play

HORTON FOOTE 1916–

Commenting on the problems of writing for television, Horton Foote has said, "It's a demanding medium, an exhausting one, but ultimately a very rewarding one." He speaks with authority since he is one of America's leading television dramatists. His standing in the foremost rank of television writers was acknowledged by the Museum of Modern Art in New York City when it selected "The Trip to Bountiful" as the first dramatic television play to be included in its film library. Horton Foote has also written a full length stage version of the play, which was successfully produced on Broadway.

Many of his plays are set in Texas, the state where he was born and still maintains a home. In addition to writing, Horton Foote has taught acting and other theatre arts at the American Theatre Wing, Bard College, and the University of Kansas City.

Let's consider . . .

1. What were Mrs. Watts' reasons for taking the trip back to Bountiful?

2. What personal satisfactions do you think she hoped to gain by working with her hands in the soil? Why didn't work in the city apartment provide these same satisfactions?

3. Why did Mrs. Watts like to sing hymns? Explain how her enjoyment of hymn singing helped you to understand her character.

4. What did Jessie Mae's concern for the government check reveal about her? What other incidents helped you to understand the kind of person she was?

5. Ludie Watts was caught in the struggle between his wife and mother. Do you think that he understood the sense of loss which his mother was experiencing? Explain.

6. Thelma and Mrs. Watts were both women without real homes. Point out similarities and differences in their situations.

7. How does Thelma reveal that some

young people seem to have found the values which were important to Mrs. Watts?

8. When Mrs. Watts learned that her friend Callie Davis, the last person living in Bountiful, had recently died, she said, "I guess I better sit down and think." What thoughts do you suppose passed through her mind? How does the death of Callie Davis make you realize the importance of Mrs. Watts' trip?

9. There is always a conflict between the younger and older generations. Describe the issues in this conflict as they are developed in the play. Do you think that Horton Foote has presented a valid case for both sides? Explain.

10. What overtones does the word *bountiful* suggest to you? Explain how naming the town *Bountiful* added to your understanding of the play.

11. At the end of the play, Mrs. Watts says, "Good-by, Bountiful, good-by." Explain (1) the literal meaning of these words and (2) the symbolic meaning.

The writer's craft . . .

The plot of this play is relatively simple. Mrs. Watts' trip to Bountiful serves as the thread that holds together what little action there is. No particularly dramatic events occur, but instead, the action moves almost casually from one rather quiet incident to another.

The character of Mrs. Watts is the focal point to the play, and by means of her characterization Horton Foote develops his theme.

1. Describe what you learn about Mrs. Watts through the play's *exposition*: the background information from which the play developed. Refer to specific passages.

2. What did you learn about her through the action of the play? Refer to specific passages.

3. Select several lines of dialogue that provide insight into Mrs. Watts' character. Explain what these lines tell you about her values.

4. The various characters in the play all illuminate some aspect of Mrs. Watts' character. Select three characters and describe how each helps you to understand Mrs. Watts more fully.

5. Describe your point of view towards Mrs. Watts and her pilgrimage to Bountiful.

6. After answering the above questions, you should be able to discuss what Horton Foote is saying about human experience. Write a paragraph in which you discuss the underlying ideas and values which give the play its unity and focus.

NOW THINK BACK

1. In A TIME FOR ACTION various people faced the same problem: they had to make a decision—as wisely as possible—and act on it. Some of them could have left the decision and action to others; some could have waited, hoping that in the course of events, any action on their part would be unnecessary. But they didn't.

Think about each of the characters listed below. Then prepare a chart in which you tell what important action was performed and the reason which prompted the action. Follow the example worked out for you on Henry Armstrong in "The Thousand-Dollar Bill." You will need to allow several lines for each character.

> Mr. Council
> Mr. Haskins
> Mr. Butler
> The cavalry captain
> The girl

Character	Selection	Action	Reason for the Action
Mrs. Watts	"The Trip to Bountiful"	Disobeyed her son and his wife and traveled to her old home of Bountiful.	She felt seeing her old home that she loved so dearly would help her to be content during her last years.

2. Whether you are aware of it or not, you often form an opinion of a person by what he does. For example, when you see a student crowd ahead in a line, you automatically put him down as inconsiderate and self-centered. From the selections in this part, select four characters whom you feel you could judge by their actions. Then write your opinion of each of these people in the form of a character reference—such as a banker would require if he were considering loaning money to that person, or an employer would need if he were planning to offer him a job.

3. Which of the crises presented in this part would you have found most difficult to meet? Do you think you would have acted in the same way as the person in the selection? Would you have acted for the same reasons? Think about these questions and be prepared to discuss your ideas.

4. Of all the poems presented in this part, which one do you think has the most meaning for modern readers? Explain why.

5. Think back to some disaster you have witnessed or read about. In what way were the actions of the people similar to the actions of the San Franciscans at the time of the earthquake and fire? How were their actions different?

6. After reading "High Water" what qualities of character and intellect do you think we should develop so that we will be able to face emergencies?

Things to do . . .

1. Magazines and newspapers regularly print feature stories about acts of daring, courage, and kindness. Sometimes the action led to outstanding personal success; sometimes it was performed with no thought of personal gain. Prepare a three-minute oral report on some action which

you believe is worthy of attention. Ask your librarian to suggest likely magazines or biographies in which to find materials for your report. Or you might tell about some person you know or you have heard about at home.

2. If you have not read John Hersey's *Hiroshima,* get a copy of it from the library and compare the way the Japanese people reacted to the destruction of that city and the way the American people reacted to the San Francisco disaster in 1906. What are some of the similarities in their reactions? What are the main differences?

3. If this nation is to endure and remain great, what are some of the challenges Americans must face today with the courage and initiative of their ancestors? From the challenges suggested, you might choose several of the most significant for further study and for a panel discussion.

More to read . . .

Double Play Rookie by JOSEPH ARCHIBALD.
 Macrae Smith Company, Publishers, 1955.
Run Silent, Run Deep by EDWARD LATIMER BEACH.
 Henry Holt and Company, Inc., 1955.
O Pioneers by WILLA CATHER.
 Houghton Mifflin Company, 1913.
Away All Boats by KENNETH DODSON.
 Little, Brown and Company, 1954.
Thunder Road by WILLIAM C. GAULT.
 E. P. Dutton & Co., Inc., 1952.
The Old Man and the Sea by ERNEST HEMINGWAY.
 Charles Scribner's Sons, 1952.
Pray For A Brave Heart by HELEN MAC-INNES.
 Harcourt, Brace and Company, 1955.

Red Planet by ROBERT A. HEINLEIN.
 Charles Scribner's Sons, 1949.
Let the Hurricane Roar by ROSE WILDER LANE.
 Longmans, Green & Co., Inc., 1933.
The Bridges at Toko-ri by JAMES MICHENER.
 Random House, Inc., 1953.
Uncle Tom's Cabin by HARRIET BEECHER STOWE.
 Coward-McCann, Inc., 1929.
The Raiders by WILLIAM E. WILSON.
 Rinehart & Co., Inc., 1955.

*   *   *

The Silver Cord by SIDNEY HOWARD.
 Charles Scribner's Sons, 1927.
"Beyond the Horizon" by EUGENE O'NEILL.
 In *Modern American Dramas* edited by HARLAN HATCHER.
 Harcourt, Brace and Company, 1941.
The Caine Mutiny Court-Martial by HERMAN WOUK.
 Doubleday and Company, Inc., 1954.

*   *   *

American Karakoram Expedition, 1953, K2, The Savage Mountain.
 American Alpine Club, 1954.
Men Under the Sea by COMMANDER EDWARD ELLSBERG.
 Dodd, Mead & Company, 1951.
Pilot by TONY LEVIER as told to JOHN GUENTHER.
 Harper & Brothers, 1954.
The Guideposts Anthology edited by NORMAN VINCENT PEALE.
 Prentice-Hall, Inc., 1953.
Seven Who Came Through by EDDIE RICKENBACKER.
 Doubleday & Company, 1948.

GLOSSARY

The purpose of this glossary is to provide a simple definition or synonym for each word, based on the meaning of that word in the context of a selection or in a vocabulary exercise. For a fuller definition or for other meanings of a word, students should consult a standard dictionary.

The system of indicating pronunciation is used by permission of the publishers of *Webster's New International Dictionary,* Second Edition, copyright, 1934, 1939, 1945, 1950, 1953, 1954, by G. & C. Merriam Co.

āle, chȧotic, câre, ădd, ȧccount, ärm, ȧsk, sofȧ; ēve, hĕre, ĕvent, ĕnd, silĕnt, makĕr; īce, ĭll, charĭty; ōld, ȯbey, ȯrb, ŏdd, sŏft, cŏnnect; fo͞od, fo͝ot; out, oil; cūbe, ûnite, ûrn, ŭp, circŭs; menü: chair, go; sing; then, thin; natᵾre, verdᵾre; ᴋ = ch in German ich; boɴ (French bon); yet; zh = z in azure.

A

abating (ȧ·bāt'ĭng). Reducing intensity; slowing.

abdicate (ăb'dĭ·kāt). To relinquish formally and voluntarily an office or high position.

abortive (ȧ·bôr'tĭv). Unsuccessful.

abracadabra (ăb'rȧ·kȧ·dăb'rȧ). Mysterious or meaningless words; a nonsense jingle.

abstemious (ăb·stē'mĭ·ŭs). Moderate in use of food and drink.

abstracted (ăb·străk'tĕd). Deep in thought.

abstruse (ăb·stro͞os'). Obscure.

acerbity (ȧ·sûr'bĭ·tĭ). Sourness of taste.

acquiesce (ăk'wĭ·ĕs'). To accept an event or action as being inevitable.

acquisitive (ă·kwĭz'ĭ·tĭv). Having a desire to acquire for oneself; grasping.

acrid (ăk'rĭd). Sharp or bitter tasting.

adamant (ăd'ȧ·mănt). An imaginary stone of impenetrable hardness.

adjunct (ăj'ŭngkt). Something added to, but not a part of, the original.

admonished (ȧd·mŏn'ĭsht). Cautioned, warned.

ado (ȧ·do͞o'). Confused action, great effort, turmoil.

adversary (ăd'vĕr·sĕr'ĭ). Enemy, opponent.

advert (ăd·vûrt'). Refer to; call attention to.

affinity (ă·fĭn'ĭ·tĭ). An attraction for someone or something.

agility (ȧ·jĭl'ĭ·tĭ). Nimbleness.

ague (ā'gū). A fit of shaking.

akimbo (ȧ·kĭm'bō). With the hand on hip and elbow bent outward.

alacrity (ȧ·lăk'rĭ·tĭ). Cheerful briskness.

aliment (ăl'ĭ·mĕnt). Nourishment.

aloofness (ȧ·lo͞of'nĕs). A reserved, withdrawn attitude.

ambiguities (ăm'bĭ·gū'ĭ·tĭz). Statements or actions which are not clear in meaning.

amidships (ȧ·mĭd'shĭps). The area on a ship that is mid-way between the bow and the stern.

amity (ăm'ĭ·tĭ). Friendship, goodwill.

anaconda (ăn'ȧ·kŏn'dȧ). Any large snake of the boa family that crushes its prey.

Anglophile (ăng'glȯ·fīl). A person who admires England and everything pertaining to that country.

antediluvian (ăn'tē·dĭ·lū'vĭ·ăn). Pertaining to the period before the Flood described in the Bible; everything which is very ancient or primitive.

antenna (ăn·tĕn'ȧ). A device which sends out or receives electromagnetic waves.

anthropology (ăn'thrȯ·pŏl'ȯ·jĭ). The science of man, which includes a study of man's cultural and social habits.

apex (ā'pĕks). Point.

apprising (ă·prīz'ĭng). Informing.

approbation (ăp'rȯ·bā'shŭn). General approval.

arbitrary (är'bĭ·trĕr'ĭ). Despotic, absolute.

arboreal (är·bō'rĕ·ăl). Pertaining to trees.

734

aridity (ă·rĭd'ĭ·tĭ). Dryness.
articulately (är·tĭk'ŭ·lăt·lĭ). Distinctly, intelligibly.
artillery (är·tĭl'ĕr·ĭ). Mounted guns.
asceticism (ă·sĕt'ĭ·sĭz'm). The practice of self-denial as a means of attaining a higher spiritual life.
ascribe (ăs·krīb'). Attribute; assign.
asperity (ăs·pĕr'ĭ·tĭ). Roughness; sharpness of temper.
astute (ăs·tūt'). Having keen intelligence.
attribute (ăt'rĭ·būt). Quality inherent in a person or thing.
audacity (ô·dăs'ĭ·tĭ). Bold assurance; reckless boldness.
avail (á·vāl'). Purpose.

B

bait (bāt). A portion.
bark (bärk). Canoe.
base (bās). Lowly; inferior in quality.
bas-relief (bä'rĕ·lēf'). Sculpture in which the figures project from a solid background. *French.*
bay (bā). A reddish-brown color—as a *bay horse,* or reddish-brown horse.
bedlam (bĕd'lăm). Any place or scene of wild uproar and confusion.
benefactor (bĕn'ĕ·făk·tĕr). One who does something for the good of another.
beneficial (bĕn'ĕ·fĭsh'ăl). Helpful.
beneficiary (bĕn'ĕ·fĭsh'ĭ·ĕr'ĭ). Person who receives benefits; anyone who is designated to receive funds or property according to the terms of a will or trust.
benefit (bĕn'ĕ·fĭt). An action for the good of someone else.
benign (bē·nīn'). Kind; having a gentle manner.
bereft (bē·rĕft'). Deprived of.
betty-lamp (bĕt'ĭ·lămp'). An old-fashioned oil lamp.
bevy (bĕv'ĭ). A flock.
bibliophile (bĭb'lĭ·ŏ·fīl). A lover of books.
birling match (bĕr'lĭng măch'). A contest between two loggers on a floating log, in which the object is to see which can force the other to lose his balance and fall into the water.
bit (bĭt). That part of a bridle consisting of a steel bar which is inserted into the horse's mouth.

blooded (blŭd'ĕd). Of pure blood or approved breed.
blurb (blûrb). Short description or advertisement written to increase sales.
boles (bōlz). Trunks (tree).
booms (bōōmz). Lines of connected floating logs which keep other logs within an enclosed area.
bow chaser (bou'chās'ĕr). A gun placed on a boat in a position which enables it to fire ahead at a vessel being chased.
breastworks (brĕst'wûrks). Breast-high defensive works which can be quickly erected.
bridle (brī'd'l). That part of a harness consisting of a headstall, bit and reins, used to control the horse's movements.
brig (brĭg). A two-masted, square-rigged vessel.
brindle (brĭn'd'l). Streaked or spotted.
brogans (brō'gănz). Stout, heavy shoes.
brow band (brou' bănd'). A leather strap which runs across a horse's head.
browse (brouz). Tender shoots or twigs of a tree.
bubble octant (bŭb''l ŏk'tănt). Instrument used in navigation.
buckboards (bŭk'bōrdz'). Four-wheeled horse-carriages with the seat, which usually has springs, raised above a flat, springless platform.
bulbous (bŭl'bŭs). Bulging.
buoy (bōō'ĭ). A distinctly marked floating object, moored to the bottom, which serves as a guide in navigation.
burgher (bûr'gĕr). Citizen.
burnished (bûr'nĭsht). Polished.

C

cairn (kârn). A pile of stones which serves as a monument.
candid (kăn'dĭd). Outspoken, frank, sincere.
candor (kăn'dĕr). Impartial frankness, plain truth.
cant (kănt). 1. Insincere talk. 2. A conspicuous angle.
capacious (ká·pā'shŭs). Capable of holding a great deal; spacious.
caprices (ká·prē'sĕz). Whims.
capricious (ká·prĭsh'ŭs). Acting according to whims; given to abrupt changes.

carbines (kär′bīnz). Rifles.

carmine (kär′mĭn). A crimson-red color.

carpet-bag (kär′pĕt · băg′). A traveling bag made of carpeting.

carrion (kăr′ĭ · ŭn). The flesh of dead animals.

cauldron (kôl′drŭn). A very large pot.

caulked boots (kôkt bōōts). Boots which have a projection in the sole to prevent slipping, such as spiked football shoes.

caustically (kôs′tĭk · lĭ). In a bitterly sarcastic manner.

cavalier (kăv′á · lẽr′). A gallant knight; gentleman.

cavilers (kăv′ĭl · ẽrz). Those who raise frivolous objections.

cayuse (kī′ūs). An Indian pony.

celestial bearings (sĕ · lĕs′chăl bâr′ĭngz). A term used in navigation to denote given locations by observing the positions of the heavenly bodies.

centrifugal force (sĕn · trĭf′ŭ · găl fōrs′). The force which impels a rotating body to move outward.

chainlets (chān′lĕts). Small chains which are part of a horse's harness.

chanticleer (chăn′tĭ · klẽr). A rooster—taken from the name of the rooster in "Reynard the Fox."

chirographical (kī · rŏ · grăf′ĭ · kăl). Pertaining to handwriting.

choleric (kŏl′ẽr · ĭk). Irascible, ill-tempered.

chores (chōrz). Odd jobs, tasks.

chow (chou). Food. *Slang.*

chronometer (krŏ · nŏm′ĕ · tẽr). An instrument on a ship or airplane which measures exact time and is used for navigating purposes.

cipher (sī′fẽr). Someone of no importance or influence.

ciphering (sī′fẽr · ĭng). Calculating.

cisterns (sĭs′tẽrnz). Tanks which hold liquids.

clairvoyant (klâr · voi′ănt). Having supernatural powers; a person who has the ability to perceive objects or people not discernible by ordinary sense perception.

clandestine (klăn · dĕs′tĭn). Secret; furtive. Usually implying a crafty or evil intent.

clarion (klăr′ĭ · ŭn). A trumpet-like sound.

claybank (klā′băngk′). A medium reddish brown color.

cleaving (klēv′ĭng). Cutting.

clew up (klōō ŭp). To haul up to a mast by means of lines (a sail).

clout (klout). A stupid person.

cognizant (kŏg′nĭ · zănt). Aware.

collateral (kŏ · lăt′ẽr · ăl). Valuables pledged for a loan.

collating (kŏ · lāt′ĭng). A gathering together of materials for the purpose of noting points of agreement or disagreement or for examining and verifying the arrangement.

colloquial (kŏ · lō′kwĭ · ăl). Of expressions, acceptable in informal speech and writing.

colloquy (kŏl′ŏ · kwĭ). Discussion, conversation.

communiqué (kŏ · mū′nĭ · kā). Official message or bulletin. *French.*

complacent (kŏm · plā′sĕnt). Satisfied; content.

compliance (kŏm · plī′ăns). Agreement.

composite (kŏm · pŏz′ĭt). Composed of several parts.

con (kŏn). To study carefully; examine.

congenial (kŏn · jēn′yăl). Most agreeable or satisfying; suitable.

consecrate (kŏn′sĕ · krāt). To make holy or sacred.

construed (kŏn · strōōd′). Understood; implied.

consummate (kŏn · sŭm′ĭt). Excellent; perfect.

contiguity (kŏn′tĭ · gū′ĭ · tĭ). Proximity; nearness.

convolution (kŏn · vŏ · lū′shŭn). A winding or turning; twisting.

cordon (kôr′dŏn). A protective line or circle of persons.

cormorant (kôr′mŏ · rănt). A variety of large, long-necked water bird.

corporeal (kôr · pō′rĕ · ăl). Material; physical; bodily.

cosmopolitan (kŏz′mŏ · pŏl′ĭ · tăn). Pertaining to the whole world rather than a particular vicinity; worldly.

cosmos (kŏz′mŏs). The universe.

Cracker (krăk′ẽr). Typical of the backwoods inhabitants of Florida and Georgia. *Colloquial.*

creased (krēst). Grazed (with a bullet).

creosote (krē′ŏ · sōt). An oily liquid made from the distillation of tar, and used as a wood preservative.

crib (krĭb). A rack which holds an animal's food.

crypt (krĭpt). An underground chamber or vault; a burial chamber beneath the main floor of a church.

cryptic (krĭp'tĭk). Hidden; mysterious.

cryptogram (krĭp'tō · grăm). A message written in code.

cryptographer (krĭp · tŏg'rá · fēr). A person who writes or understands coded messages.

cryptonym (krĭp'tō · nĭm). A secret name.

culinary (kū'lĭ · nĕr'ĭ). Pertaining to food and cooking.

cullottes (kŭ · lŏts'). An article of women's sportswear—a divided skirt that comes just below the knee and fits loosely about the legs.

curried (kûr'ĭd). Cleaned and dressed with a currycomb. (Said of the hair of a horse.)

currycomb (kûr'ĭ · kōm'). A large comb with sharp metal teeth used for combing and cleaning the hair of a horse.

cutlasses (kŭt'lás · ĕz). Heavy curved swords.

cynical (sĭn'ĭ · kál). Distrustful, bitter, pessimistic.

D

dawplucker (dô'plŭk · ēr). A worthless person.

debility (dē · bĭl'ĭ · tĭ). Weakness.

decamp (dē · kămp'). To break up camp.

declaimed (dē · klāmd'). Said; proclaimed.

decontrol (dē'kŏn · trōl'). To drop restrictions.

deforest (dē · fŏr'ĕst). To destroy trees and other growth in a region.

deform (dē · fôrm'). To spoil a shape.

déjeuner (dā'zhŭ'nā'). Lunch. *French.*

deliberately (dē · lĭb'ēr · ĭt · lĭ). Unhurriedly; carefully.

delineate (dē · lĭn'ē · āt). To describe; represent.

demeanor (dē · mēn'ēr). Manner; behavior; bearing.

democrats (dĕm'ō · krăts). Light, uncovered wagons with seats.

demoralization (dē · mŏr · ăl · ĭ · zā'shŭn). Loss of such qualities as courage, vitality, etc.; spiritual or mental deterioration.

denizens (dĕn'ĭ · zĕnz). Citizens; inhabitants.

denominated (dē · nŏm'ĭ · ná · tĕd). Gave the name; called.

deponent (dē · pō'nĕnt). One who gives evidence.

deport (dē · pōrt'). To force out of a country.

depository (dē · pŏz'ĭ · tō'rĭ). A place in which valuables or goods are kept.

detonated (dĕt'ō · nā · tĕd). Exploded.

detriment (dĕt'rĭ · mĕnt). Damage, hurt.

diabolical (dī'á · bŏl'ĭ · kál). Devilish, fiendish.

didoes (dī'dōz). Tricks, capers.

dilated (dī'lā · tĕd). Expanded.

disclaimed (dĭs · klāmd'). Denied.

discommoded (dĭs · kŏ · mō'dĕd). Inconvenienced.

disconsolate (dĭs · kŏn'sō · lĭt). Without cheer; dejected.

dismembered (dĭs · mĕm'bērd). Separated the limbs from the body; cut into parts.

disparagement (dĭs · păr'ĭj · mĕnt). An expression of low opinion.

dispersal (dĭs · pûr'sál). The act of scattering —as marching soldiers scattering or *dispersing* when enemy planes attack.

dissemble (dĭ · sĕm'b'l). To conceal one's true feelings or motives; to pretend.

dissimulation (dĭ · sĭm'ū · lā'shŭn). An act of pretense.

divers (dī'vērz). Various; several.

divertissement (dē · vĕr'tēs · mäN'). An entertainment. *French.*

divination (dĭv'ĭ · nā'shŭn). Power of foreseeing.

dogies (dō'gĭz). Motherless calves.

domiciliated (dŏm · ĭ · sĭl'ĭ · ā · tĕd). Resided.

dominie (dŏm'ĭ · nĭ). Schoolmaster.

dowered (dou'ērd). Endowed, given.

E

ecstatically (ĕk · stá'tĭk · lĭ). With great joy.

edifice (ĕd'ĭ · fĭs). Structure.

effaced (ĕ · fāst'). Destroyed; changed.

effeminate (ĕ · fĕm'ĭ · nĭt). Unmanly; weak.

efflorescence (ĕf · lŏ · rĕs'ĕns). Openness and warmth.

elevators (ĕl'ē · vā'tērz). Tall buildings where grain is elevated and stored.

efficacy (ĕf'ĭ · ká · sĭ). Effectiveness.

eloquent (ĕl'ō · kwĕnt). Pertaining to language that is powerful yet graceful.

emancipated (ê · măn'sǐ · pā'tĕd). Released from bondage or restraint.

embargo (ĕm · bär'gō). Prohibition; hindrance.

endeavors (ĕn · dĕv'ẽrz). Efforts; exertions.

enigma (ê · nĭg'mà). A puzzle; a person who tends to be obscure and difficult to understand.

ennui (än'wē; *French* äN'nwē'). Boredom. *French.*

ensign (ĕn'sīn). Flag, pennant.

enumerating (ê · nū'mēr · ā · tǐng). Listing.

ephemeral (ê · fĕm'ẽr · ăl). Having a brief existence, short-lived.

epicurean (ĕp · ǐ · kû · rē'ăn). Pertaining to the enjoyment of fine food.

epitomizing (ê · pǐt'ô · mīz · ǐng). Summarizing.

epochal (ĕp'ŏk · ăl). In the distant past.

equivocation (ê · kwǐv'ô · kā'shǔn). The use of ambiguous expressions, usually with an intent to deceive.

ergo (ûr'gō). Therefore. *Latin.*

erratic (ê · răt'ǐk). Different from the usual; eccentric.

erstwhile (ûrst'hwīl'). Former; formerly.

erudition (ĕr · ōō · dǐsh'ǔn). Learning.

evanescent (ĕv · à · nĕs'ĕnt). Barely perceptible.

evasive (ê · vā'sǐv). Tending to be elusive or shifty, not direct.

evinces (ê · vǐn'sĕz). Clearly reveals.

evitable (ĕv'ǐ · tà · b'l). Avoidable.

exchequer (ĕks · chĕk'ẽr). Treasury.

execrated (ĕk'sĕ · krā · tĕd). Detested, abhorred.

exemplification (ĕg · zĕm'plǐ · fǐ · kā'shǔn). Example, illustration.

expended (ĕks · pĕn'dĕd). Spent.

extant (ĕks'tănt). In existence.

extolled (ĕks · tōld'). Praised.

F

factitious (făk · tǐsh'ǔs). Artificial.

fain (fān). Willingly.

fairway (fâr'wā'). The unobstructed area of a golf course, not including tees, putting greens, and hazards.

fallacious (fă · lā'shǔs). Incorrect; misleading.

falls (fôlz). The tackle used in lowering and hoisting a ship's boat.

fatiguing (fà · tē'gǐng). Tiring.

feign (fān). To act in a deceptive manner; pretend.

feints (fānts). Deceptive actions which are not carried through; feigned motions.

felspare (fĕl'spär). (British spelling for *feldspar*). Minerals which constitute the largest ingredient of igneous rocks.

fissures (fĭsh'ẽrz). Deep narrow openings.

flats (flăts). Marshes.

flirt (flûrt). A sudden, deft motion; a brisk movement.

Floridiana (flŏr · ĭd'ĭ · ăn'à). A term applied to such things as documents, facts, art, craftsmanship, etc., which relate to the history or geography of Florida.

foolscap (fōōlz'kăp'). A kind of writing paper.

ford (fōrd). A place in a stream or river which is shallow enough to be crossed by wading.

forecastle (fōk's'l). The forward section of a merchant ship, usually used for crews quarters.

forelock (fōr'lŏk'). A long lock of hair which grows from a horse's forehead.

fortissimo (fôr · tĭs'ǐ · mō). Loudness.

fourpounder (fōr'poun'dẽr). A gun throwing a four-pound projectile.

foxholes (fŏks'hōlz'). Individual pits in a battle area for protection against enemy fire.

franchise (frăn'chīz). A privilege which provides immunity from restrictions.

freshet (frĕsh'ĕt). A stream or brook.

frigate (frĭg'ǐt). A light ship propelled by sails and oars.

furlong (fûr'lŏng). 220 yards—one eighth of a mile.

G

gambols (găm'bǔlz). Capers, frolics.

general-merchandise (jĕn'ẽr · ăl · mûr'chăn-dīz). A wide variety of articles for sale.

genius (jēn'yǔs). A spirit.

gentility (jĕn · tǐl'ǐ · tǐ). Good breeding; fine manners; refinement.

ghetto (gĕt'ō). Originally, a separated area of a city in which Jews were forced to live; now, quarters which are restricted to a particular group.

gigs (gǐgz). Small one-horse carriages having two wheels.

gimlets (gǐm'lĕts). Small tools used for boring holes.

girders (gûr'dẽrz). Heavy supports for the framework and foundation of a structure.

girdled (gûr'd'ld). Cut away the bark (of a tree).

gorget (gôr'jĕt). A specially colored patch on the throat.

granary (grăn'a·rĭ). A storehouse where grain is kept after it has been threshed or husked.

grenades (grĕ·nādz'). Small explosive shells.

grisly (grĭz'lĭ). Formidable; grim.

grist-mill (grĭst'mĭl'). A mill for grinding grain.

grounded (groun'dĕd). Struck bottom.

guerrillas (gĕ·rĭl'az). Soldiers who are not part of a regular army but wage independent warfare by means of surprise attacks.

gunwale (gŭn'ĕl). The side of a boat.

H

habitual (ha·bĭt'ū̠·ăl). According to habit.

habituated (ha·bĭt'ū̠·ā'tĕd). Accustomed or hardened to anything.

hackles (hăk''lz). Ridges.

hallow (hăl'ō). To make holy or sacred.

hallucination (ha·lū'sĭ·nā'shŭn). The experience of believing imagined thoughts or things to be true; a lack of distinction between the real and the imaginary.

halter-broke (hôl'tẽr·brōk). Of a horse, accustomed to wearing a *halter,* a headstrap and noose used for leading and tying.

hames (hāmz). Two curved leather straps in a harness to which the traces are attached.

hamstringed (hăm'strĭngd'). Disabled, crippled.

harbinger (här'bĭn·jẽr). Anything that foretells; herald.

harebell (hâr'bĕl'). An herb with blue flowers, often called *bluebell.*

harrow (hăr'ō). A farm implement with discs or teeth which pulverize the soil.

hay rake (hā' rāk'). A farm implement used for raking hay.

headstall (hĕd'stôl'). That part of a bridle which encircles the horse's head.

hempen (hĕmp'ĕn). Made of hemp; pertaining to rope.

hexagonal (hĕks·ăg'ô·năl). Six-sided.

hibernatorial (hī·bẽr·nă·tō'rĭ·ăl). Pertaining to winter.

hippogriff (hĭp'ô·grĭf). A legendary creature having the head and wings of an eagle and the body of a horse.

hirelings (hīr'lĭngz). Paid employees.

hoary (hōr'ĭ). White.

horse tank (hôrs' tăngk'). A tank where horses drink water; a watering trough.

hypocrisy (hĭ·pŏk'rĭ·sĭ). Professing to believe what one does not; feigned virtue.

I

ignominiously (ĭg'nô·mĭn'ĭ·ŭs·lĭ). In a degrading or humiliating manner.

imbibes (ĭm·bībz'). Absorbs.

immedicable (ĭm·mĕd'ĭ·ka·b'l). Incurable.

impel (ĭm·pĕl'). To force; cause.

impenetrable (ĭm·pĕn'ê·tra·b'l). That which cannot be pierced or passed through.

imperturbable (ĭm'pẽr·tûr'ba·b'l). Having a calm manner.

imprecation (ĭm·prĕ·kā'shŭn). A curse.

impunity (ĭm·pū'nĭ·tĭ). Without punishment.

inauspicious (ĭn·ôs·pĭsh'ŭs). Ill-omened.

incantations (ĭn·kăn·tā'shŭns). The speaking or chanting of words or sounds believed to have magic powers.

incarnate (ĭn·kär'năt). Appearing in human form; embodied in a person, as a demon *incarnate;* personified.

incentive (ĭn·sĕn'tĭv). A force which stimulates action.

incessant (ĭn·sĕs'ănt). Unceasing.

inchoate (ĭn·kō'ĭt). Undeveloped.

incorrigible (ĭn·kŏr'ĭ·jĭ·b'l). Unruly; unmanageable.

indictment (ĭn·dīt'mĕnt). A formal accusation.

indolent (ĭn'dô·lĕnt). Avoiding exertion; lazy.

ineludible (ĭn'ê·lūd'ĭ·b'l). Inescapable.

ineradicable (ĭn'ê·răd'ĭ·ka·b'l). Incapable of being erased.

inert (ĭn·ûrt'). Motionless.

inestimable (ĭn·ĕs'tĭ·ma·b'l). Incapable of being estimated; priceless; invaluable.

inexorably (ĭn·ĕk'sô·ra·blĭ). Relentlessly; stubbornly.

infractions (ĭn·frăk'shŭns). Violations.

ingeniously (ĭn·jēn′yŭs·lĭ). Cleverly, adroitly.

inimical (ĭn·ĭm′ĭ·kăl). Antagonistic, adverse.

inquest (ĭn′kwĕst). An inquiry held before a jury or some other official group; the findings of such a group.

inscrutable (ĭn·skroo′tȧ·b'l). Incomprehensible.

insolvency (ĭn·sŏl′vĕn·sĭ). Lack of funds; bankruptcy.

intractable (ĭn·trăk′tȧ·b'l). Wild, unruly.

inveterate (ĭn·vĕt′ẽr·ĭt). Firmly established, confirmed (of a habit).

irascibility (ĭ·răs′ĭ·bĭl′ĭ·tĭ). Characterized by sudden fits of temper, petulance, or stubbornness.

itinerant (ī·tĭn′ẽr·ănt). One who travels from place to place; not permanent.

J

jackstraws (jăk′strôz′). A game in which the players try to select single straws or thin sticks of wood from a heap without disturbing the other pieces.

japanned (jȧ·pănd′). Lacquered.

jettison (jĕt′ĭ·sŭn). To cast overboard.

jocose (jŏ·kōs′). Sportively humorous.

joists (joists). Small beams which serve as supports.

jurisdiction (joor′ĭs·dĭk′shŭn). Legal power; authority.

K

keep (kēp). Main tower of a medieval castle, used as a prison.

kilocycle (kĭl′ŏ·sī′k'l). A technical term which means one thousand cycles per second.

kneading (nēd′ĭng). Manipulating any substance by pressing and stretching it.

knight-errant (nīt′ ẽr′ănt). A wandering knight in search of adventure.

knolls (nōlz). Small hills.

kolache (kŏ′lăch·ĕ). Buns.

L

labyrinth (lăb′ĭ·rĭnth). An intricate, involved state; a confusing entanglement; a winding path with many dead-end offshoots.

larboard (lär′bōrd). That side of a ship which is on a person's left when he is standing on board and facing the *bow* or forward end; port.

laud (lôd). To praise.

leads (lēdz). Forward motions.

lee (lē). A sheltered place; the side that is away from the wind.

leonine (lē′ŏ·nīn). Lionlike.

lethargic (lĕ·thär′jĭk). Having chronic drowsiness and indifference; apathetic.

levee (lĕv′ē). An embankment which prevents a river from overflowing; a dock or pier.

levitated (lĕv′ĭ·tā·tĕd). Rose and floated in the air.

librettos (lĭ·brĕt′ōz). The words of operas or lengthy choral compositions.

locoed (lō′kōd). Crazed by eating locoweed.

loggerhead (lŏg′ẽr·hĕd′). A rounded post in the stern of a whaleboat, around which the line may be turned.

loquacious (lŏ·kwā′shŭs). Very talkative.

lowering (lō′ẽr·ĭng). Gloomy, threatening.

lozenge (lŏz′ĕnj). A diamond shape.

lustreless (lŭs′tẽr·lĕs). Without brilliance; dull.

lyceum (lī·sē′ŭm). An association which provides educational services.

M

maculate (măk′ŭ·lāt). Spotted.

madroños (mȧ·drō′ñyōz). A variey of evergreen shrub which bears a red berry.

magnanimity (măg′nȧ·nĭm′ĭ·tĭ). Nobleness of spirit; a sense of honor and generosity.

magnitude (măg′nĭ·tūd). Vastness.

makebate (māk′bāt′). One who excites quarrels. *Archaic.*

malingering (mȧ·lĭng′gẽr·ĭng). Pretending to be unable to do one's job; shirking.

mallards (măl′ẽrdz). Wild ducks.

malpractice (măl′prăk′tĭs). Physician's treatment injurious to the patient.

manifestations (măn·ĭ·fĕs·tā′shŭnz). Demonstrations.

manifold (măn′ĭ·fōld). Varied.

manticore (măn′tĭ·kōr). A legendary creature with the head of a man, the body of a lion, and the tail of a dragon.

marked (märkt). Noticed; singled out.

marts (märts). Markets.

mattocks (măt′*ŭ*ks). Tools used for digging.

mauls (môlz). Heavy hammers; heavy mallets.

maverick (măv′ẽr · ĭk). An unbranded animal; a motherless calf.

mean (mēn). Of little importance.

menial (mē′nĭ · ăl). Lowly.

metatarsal (mĕt · *a* · tär′s*a*l). Pertaining to a part of the human foot.

mien (mēn). Appearance; manner.

milch-cow (mĭlch′kou). Milk-producing cow.

minions (mĭn′y*ŭ*nz). Agents; servants.

miscreant (mĭs′krẽ · ănt). Villain, evil person.

misprize (mĭs · prīz′). To undervalue.

moiety (moi′ĕ · tĭ). Measure or portion.

monogamous (m*o* · nŏg′*a* · m*ŭ*s). Pertaining to the practice of having a single marriage during one's lifetime.

monopolies (m*o* · nŏp′*o* · lĭz). Exclusive control or ownership in particular areas.

monteiro cap (môn · tā′r*o* · kăp). Hunting cap.

morosely (m*o* · rōs′lĭ). Gloomily.

mortars (môr′tẽrz). Small cannons.

motif (m*o* · tēf′). A dominant idea or theme.

mudlarked (mŭd′lärkt). Run aground in mud.

multitudinous (mŭl · tĭ · tū′dĭ · n*ŭ*s). A great many.

munificent (mũ · nĭf′*ĭ* · sĕnt). Lavish, generous.

N

naivete (nä · ēv′tā′). Childlike simplicity; an artless quality.

navigators (năv′*ĭ* · gā′tẽrz). Those who direct or steer a plane or ship on its course.

negotiating (nĕ · gō′shĭ · ā · tĭng). Clearing; passing. *Colloquial.*

nicety (nī′sĕ · tĭ). 1. A fine point. 2. Exactness.

niggardly (nĭg′ẽrd · lĭ). Extremely stingy.

niggling (nĭg′lĭng). Unimportant, weak.

nostrum (nŏs′tr*ŭ*m). A medicine.

noxious (nŏk′sh*ŭ*s). Poisonous.

O

ohia (ō · hē′*a*). A type of timber tree. *Hawaiian.*

omnipresent (ŏm′nĭ · prĕz′ĕnt). Ever-present.

onerous (ŏn′ẽr · *ŭ*s). Burdensome.

option (ŏp′sh*ŭ*n). A choice; privilege.

oracles (ŏr′*a* · k′lz). People or things who communicate divine or highly authoritative statements.

oscillated (ŏs′ĭ · lā · tĕd). Changed frequently back and forth; fluctuated.

ostensibly (ŏs · tĕn′s*ĭ* · blĭ). Apparently. (Often the word carries a suggestion of pretense.)

P

pacifism (păs′ĭ · fĭz′m). The belief that all war should be abolished and that disputes should be settled by means of arbitration.

pacifist (păs′ĭ · fĭst). A person who believes in peace and the abolition of war.

pacify (păs′ĭ · fī). To calm or quiet.

pandered (păn′dẽrd). Spoken of in flattering terms.

panoply (păn′*o* · plĭ). A complete, and usually magnificent, covering for protection in warfare.

paradox (păr′*a* · dŏks). A statement which seems contradictory but may be true.

parley (pär′lĭ). To talk; confer.

paroxysm (păr′ŏk · sĭz′m). A fit.

parries (păr′ĭz). Defensive movements which serve to ward off blows.

pate (pāt). The crown of a person's head.

pater-familias (pā′tẽr · f*a* · mĭl′ĭ · *ă*s). The head of a family.

paternal (p*a* · tûr′n*a*l). Fatherly; pertaining to the father.

patriarchy (pā′trĭ · är′kĭ). A society in which the father is the head of the family.

patrimony (păt′rĭ · mō′nĭ). An estate inherited from one's father.

patriotism (pā′trĭ · *ŭ*t · ĭz′m). Faith in one's country.

peavies (pē′vĭz). Poles with a sharp spike and hook at the end, used by lumbermen in handling logs.

pedagogue (pĕd′*a* · gŏg). A schoolmaster, teacher.

pendent (pĕn′dĕnt). Hanging.

penury (pĕn′û · rĭ). Poverty.

peradventure (pûr'ăd·vĕn'tûr). Perhaps.
perambulations (pē·ăm'bŭ·la'shŭnz). Walks.
peremptory (pĕr·ĕmp'tŏ·rĭ). Arrogant, dictatorial.
perfidy (pûr'fĭ·dĭ). Breach of faith; treachery.
pertinacious (pûr·tĭ·nā'shŭs). Persistent, tenacious.
philharmonic (fĭl'(h)är·mŏn'ĭk). Pertaining to a love of music.
philology (fĭ·lŏl'ŏ·jĭ). Love of language and literature; the study of language.
philosophy (fĭ·lŏs'ŏ·fĭ). Love of knowledge and wisdom; the study of reality.
phlebitis (flĕ·bī'tĭs). A disease in which the veins are inflamed.
phlegm (flĕm). Calmness.
phrensied (frĕn'zĭd). (A variation of *frenzied*.) Frantic, wild.
phthisic (tĭz'ĭk). A wasting disease of the lungs.
physiological (fĭz'ĭ·ŏ·lŏj'ĭ·kăl). Pertaining to the functions of organs and other specific parts of living organisms.
piles (pīlz). Heavy poles driven into the bed of a river to form a wall or to serve as supports.
pious (pī'ŭs). Holy; religious.
piqued (pēkt). Took pride in oneself for something.
pithy (pĭth'ĭ). Pungent, forcible.
plaintive (plān'tĭv). Sad.
plashy (plăsh'ĭ). Splashing.
pliability (plī'à·bĭl'ĭ·tĭ). Flexibility.
plied (plīd). Worked at.
plowed (ploud). Tilled, furrowed.
politicaster (pŏ·lĭt'ĭ·kăs'tĕr). Petty politician.
polytone (pŏl'ĭ·tōn). An utterance or sound of varied tones.
pommel (pŭm'ĕl). A knob on the front of a saddle.
portent (pōr'tĕnt). An omen or forewarning.
portfolio (pōrt·fō'lĭ·ō). The qualifications of an ambassador for a specific job.
potent (pō'tĕnt). Powerful.
potentates (pō'tĕn·tāts). Rulers with great power.
potential (pŏ·tĕn'shăl). Within one's power; possible, but not yet realized.
potentialities (pō·tĕn'shĭ·ăl'ĭ·tĭz). The capacity for possible attainments.
preceptor (prĕ·sĕp'tĕr). A teacher.

precipitously (prĕ·sĭp'ĭ·tŭs·lĭ). Steeply.
premonitory (prĕ·mŏn'ĭ·tō'rĭ). A warning.
primal (prī'măl). First, original.
prodigiously (prŏ·dĭj'ŭs·lĭ). Pertaining to a huge increase in bulk; tremendously.
propensity (prŏ·pĕn'sĭ·tĭ). Disposition toward; inclination.
psalmody (săl'mŏ·dĭ). The singing of psalms.
purslane (pûrs'lān). A leafy weed used as an herb.

Q

quaff (kwȧf). To drink.
quaffer (kwȧf'ēr). One who is drinking.
quartz (kwôrts). A common solid mineral found in many rocks.
querulous (kwĕr'ŭ·lŭs). Habitually complaining.
query (kwĕr'ĭ). An inquiry; a question.

R

rancorous (răng'kēr·ŭs). Characterized by hatred or ill will, as a *rancorous* person.
rapacious (rȧ·pā'shŭs). Excessively greedy.
rapport (ră·pōrt', *French* rȧ·pôr'). A good relationship; mutual understanding.
ratiocination (răsh'ĭ·ŏs·ĭ·nā'shŭn). The act of reasoning; deducing by logical means.
reave (rēv). Seize. *Archaic.*
recondite (rĕk'ŭn·dīt). Obscure, but profound, research and knowledge.
redoubtable (rĕ·dout'à·b'l). Something or someone to be feared.
redress (rĕ·drĕs'). To set right; to remedy abuses.
renegade (rĕn'ĕ·gād). An outcast or traitor.
rent (rĕnt). A rip or tear.
reperusal (rē'pĕ·rōōz'ăl). A re-reading.
reprieve (rĕ·prēv'). A temporary escape.
resignation (rĕz'ĭg·nā'shŭn). Meekly accepting whatever occurs; submission.
resilience (rĕ·zĭl'ĭ·ĕns). Elasticity, ability to recover quickly, bounce.
respirations (rĕs'pĭ·rā'shŭnz). The acts of inhaling and exhaling air; breathing.
reticence (rĕt'ĭ·sĕns). Tendency to be silent and reserved; shyness.

reticule (rĕt'ĭ·kūl). A small handbag.

riata (rē·ä'tȧ). Lariat.

ricocheted (rĭk'ŏ·shād'). Rebounded.

Rockyfords (rŏk'ĭ·fôrdz'). A variety of muskmelon.

rod (rŏd). A linear measurement equal to five and one-half yards.

roiled (roild). Disturbed; confused.

rood (rōōd). A square measure usually equal to forty square rods.

ruckus (rŭk'ŭs). Turmoil; uproar.

ruminating (rōō'mĭ·nāt·ĭng). Chewing the cud.

russet (rŭs'ĕt). Reddish-brown color.

rusties (rŭs'tĭz). Defective cattle cut out of a roundup.

S

saddle-horn (săd'l·hôrn'). A knob on the front of a saddle; pommel.

saffron (săf'rŭn). An orange-yellow color.

sagacity (sȧ·găs'ĭ·tĭ). Mental acuteness; shrewd judgment.

salacious (sȧ·lā'shŭs). Risqué, indecent.

salient (sā'lĭ·ĕnt). Prominent.

sandspurs (sănd'spûrz'). Common bur grass.

sanguine (săng'gwĭn). Cheerful and optimistic.

sardonic (sär·dŏn'ĭk). Having a quality of bitterness and scorn.

sated (sā'tĕd). Filled to capacity.

savants (sȧ·vänts'). Scholars.

scantlings (skănt'lĭngz). Small cross-beams.

schisms (sĭz'mz). Divisions; differences.

scintillant (sĭn'tĭ·lănt). Sparkling brilliantly.

scions (sī'ŭnz). Descendants; offsprings; offshoots.

scourings (skour'ĭngz). Rides taken in search of something.

scurrilous (skûr'ĭ·lŭs). Using coarse and abusive language.

scrapple (skrăp''l). A food, often associated with the city of Philadelphia, consisting of boiled scraps of meat, herbs, and flour.

self-indulgence (sĕlf·ĭn·dŭl'jĕns). The practice of being lavish with oneself; gratifying one's desires and appetites.

sententious (sĕn·tĕn'shŭs). Pithy (saying or axioms).

sentimental (sĕn·tĭ·mĕn'tăl). Having a quality of tenderness.

sequestered (sē·kwĕs'tērd). Set apart from others; secluded.

seraphim (sĕr'ȧ·fĭm). A member of the highest order of angels.

servile (sûr'vĭl). Slavish, menial.

sextant (sĕks'tănt). A navigational instrument which measures angular distances and determines latitude and longitude.

shades (shādz). Ghosts, spirits.

sheathed (shēthd). Covered, encased.

shied (shīd). Thrown.

shoal (shōl). A place where the water is shallow because of rocks or sand bars.

shod (shŏd). Past tense of *shoe*—as in *shoeing* a horse.

sibilence (sĭb'ĭ·lăns). A hissing sound.

side bars (sīd' bärz'). The side sections of a saddle.

singular (sĭng'gů·lēr). 1. Extraordinary. 2. Consisting of one unit.

skepticism (skĕp'tĭ·sĭz'm). A tendency to question and doubt.

slough-hatted (slou'hă·tĕd). Wearing a hat covered with mud.

sluicing (slōō'sĭng). Flowing swiftly, as water through a floodgate.

somnolent (sŏm'nŏ·lĕnt). Pertaining to sleep; drowsy.

soporific (sō'pŏ·rĭf'ĭk). Sleep-producing; characterized by sleepiness.

spasmodically (spăz·mŏd'ĭ·kăl·lĭ). Intermittently; involuntarily.

spavins (spăv'ĭnz). Diseased ankle joints (of horses).

spend (spĕnd). To employ; to use.

spherule (sfĕr'ōol). A tiny sphere.

spiracle (spī'rȧ·k'l). Breathing hole.

spurs (spûrz). Sharp metal pieces attached to a rider's heels, used to goad a horse.

stabilizer (stā'bĭ·līz·ēr). Any device which enables an airplane to remain at a constant level.

staggers (stăg'ērz). A nervous disease of horses causing reeling and sudden falling.

stalwart (stôl'wērt). Stout, strong.

stance (stăns). Posture.

stanchion (stăn'shŭn). A pair of vertical bars used to secure cattle.

starboard (stär'bōrd). That side of a ship which is on a person's right when he is standing on board and facing the *bow* or forward end.

statics (stăt'ĭks). Pressure exerted by a motionless mass.

sterning (stûrn'ĭng). Backing.

Stetson (stĕt'sĕn). The name of a manufacturer of men's hats; the name given to large hats such as those worn by cowboys and ranchers.

stipulation (stĭp·ŭ·lā'shŭn). Condition; agreement.

stirrup (stĭr'ŭp). A leather, metal, or wooden loop which hangs from a saddle and supports the rider's foot.

stock (stŏk). Farm animals, livestock.

strata (strā'tá). (Plural of *stratum*). Levels, divisions.

stripling (strĭp'lĭng). A youth.

stupefaction (stū·pĕ·făk'shŭn). A state of being insensible, being devoid of thought and feeling.

suavity (swăv'ĭ·tĭ). A polished, worldly manner; smoothness; urbanity.

sublimated (sŭb'lĭ·mā·tĕd). Elevated.

subsistance (sŭb·sĭs'tĕns). Livelihood.

substance (sŭb'stăns). Material things.

substantial (sŭb·stăn'shăl). Respected (as *substantial* people); solid; well-to-do.

substantially (sŭb·stăn'shăl·ĭ). For the most part; essentially.

succor (sŭk'ēr). To aid, to comfort.

supernal (sŭ·pûr'năl). Ethereal; heavenly.

supernumerary (sū'pēr·nū'mēr·ĕr·ĭ). An amount which exceeds the usual; extra.

supersonic (sū'pēr·sŏn'ĭk). Faster than the speed of sound.

sustain (sŭs·tān'). To support.

switchel (swĭch'ĕl). A beverage made of water, ginger, molasses or vinegar, and sometimes rum.

syllogism (sĭl'ŏ·jĭz'm). Argument, reasoning.

T

taciturn (tăs'ĭ·tûrn). Not talkative, reticent.

tarp (tärp). (An abbreviated form of *tarpaulin*). A piece of waterproof canvas.

teal (tēl). A fresh-water duck.

tedium (tē'dĭ·ŭm). Boredom; weariness.

tee (tē). A small mound of earth from which a golfer begins play on a particular hole.

tenacity (tĕ·năs'ĭ·tĭ). Tendency to persevere.

tenure (tĕn'ûr). The period of time an official holds office.

terrain (tĕ·rān'). An area of land.

tethered (tĕth'ērd). Tied.

throat-latch (thrōt'lăch). A strap passing under the neck of a horse which aids in holding the bridle in place.

thwarted (thwôr'tĕd). Blocked.

tiller (tĭl'ēr). A bar used to control the rudder of a boat.

tongue (tŭng). A bar projecting from the front of a wagon, and extending between the animals drawing it.

torpid (tôr'pĭd). Dull.

traces (trā'sĕz). Two straps, attached to a harness, used to fasten a horse to a wagon.

tractable (trăk'tá·b'l). Easily handled, docile.

trammels (trăm'ĕlz). Pothooks which hang in an open fireplace.

trance (trăns). A motionless, dream-like state, seeming to be half conscious.

transfixed (trăns·fĭkst'). Made incapable of motion.

tranquil (trăng'kwĭl). Quiet, undisturbed.

transient (trăn'shĕnt). Temporary, passing, not permanent.

transpierced (trăns·pērst'). Pierced through; penetrated.

treacle (trē'k'l). Molasses.

tributary (trĭb'ů·tĕr'ĭ). A stream which flows into a larger body of water.

truculent (trŭk'ů·lĕnt). Aggressively cruel.

tugs (tŭgz). The traces of a harness.

tussock (tŭs'ŭk). A patch of grass, tuft.

twain (twān). Two.

U

uncomeliness (ŭn·kŭm'lĭ·nĕs). Unattractiveness.

undulations (ŭn·dů·lā'shŭnz). Wavelike falling and rising actions.

unhallowed (ŭn·hăl'ōd). Unholy.

unicorn (ū'nĭ·kôrn). A legendary animal with the body of a horse and a single long horn protruding from its forehead.

untenanted (ŭn·tĕn'ăn·tĕd). Unoccupied.

unwarrantable (ŭn·wŏr'ăn·tá·b'l). Without sanction of law; unauthorized.

usurpations (ū'zēr·pā'shŭnz). Illegal seizures.

V

vacuously (văk′ū · ŭs · lĭ). Emptily, vacantly.

vagary (và · gâr′ĭ). A capricious or fantastic act.

vaingloriously (vān′glō′rĭ · ŭs · lĭ). With boastful pride.

varlet (vär′lĕt). Knave, rogue.

venerable (vĕn′ẽr · à · b'l). Ancient.

verdure (vûr′dụr). A green growth of vegetation; greenness.

vestige (vĕs′tĭj). Trace.

vial (vī′ăl). A small glass container used for holding liquids.

vicariously (vī · kâr′ĭ · ŭs · lĭ). Through another's experiences.

victuals (vĭt′'lz). Food.

virulent (vĭr′ū · lĕnt). Poisonous.

visage (vĭz′ĭj). The appearance of a human face; countenance.

volplaning (vŏl′plān′ĭng). Gliding; usually used of an airplane.

volunteer (vŏl′ŭn · tēr′). Weeds or other growth from self-sown seed.

votive (vō′tĭv). Pertaining to the act of dedicating.

vouchsafed (vouch · sāft′). Bestowed.

vulgarian (vŭl · gâr′ĭ · ăn). A vulgar person.

W

wadding (wŏd′ĭng). Soft padding, usually of cotton.

wallowed (wŏl′ōd). Rolled about in liquid.

wantonly (wŏn′tẓn · lĭ). Unfeelingly.

withal (wĭth · ôl′). Thus; because of this.

woof-thread (wo͞of′thrĕd′). The horizontal thread in a loom, which crosses the vertical thread, or the *warp*.

Y

yawl (yôl). A ship's small rowboat.

yearling (yẽr′lĭng). An animal that is one year old.

yeoman (yō′măn). An independent farmer.

LITERARY TYPES

SHORT STORY

NOVEL

POETRY

• Supplementary reading

BIOGRAPHY AND AUTOBIOGRAPHY

ESSAY AND ARTICLE

INDEX